Sociology

Sociology

SEVENTH EDITION

Craig Calhoun

University of North Carolina at Chapel Hill

Donald Light

Rutgers University

Suzanne Keller

Princeton University

The McGraw-Hill Companies, Inc.

New York   St. Louis   San Francisco   Auckland   Bogotá
Caracas   Lisbon   London   Madrid   Mexico City   Milan   Montreal
New Delhi   San Juan   Singapore   Sydney   Tokyo   Toronto

McGraw-Hill

A Division of The **McGraw·Hill** Companies

Sociology

This book is printed on acid-free paper.
Text and photo credits appear on pages 625–628, and on this page by reference.

1 2 3 4 5 6 7 8 9 0 VNH VNH 9 0 9 8 7 6

ISBN 0-07-038069-4

This book was printed in Palatino by York Graphic Services, Inc.
The editors were Jill S. Gordon and Roberta Meyer;
the production supervisor was Annette Mayeksi.
The cover was designed by Karen K. Quigley;
The photo editor was Barbara Salz.
The drawings were done by Fine Line Illustrations.
Project supervision was done by The Total Book.
Von Hoffmann Press, Inc. was printer and binder.

Front and back cover art: Pablo Picasso, *The Bathers*, 1956. Stuttgart,
Staatsgalerie Stuttgart, (detail). © 1997 Estate of Pablo Picasso/
Artists Rights Society (ARS) NY.

Library of Congress Cataloging–in–Publication Data

Calhoun, Craig J., (date)
  Sociology / Craig Calhoun, Donald Light, Suzanne Keller.—7th ed.
    p.   cm.
  Includes bibliographical references and index.
  ISBN 0-07-038069-4
  1. Sociology.   2. United States—Social conditions.   I. Light,
Donald, (date).   II. Keller, Suzanne Infeld, (date).
III. Title.
HM51.C282   1997
301--dc20   96-11433

International Edition

When ordering this title, use ISBN 0-07-114108-1

Craig Calhoun is Professor of Sociology and History and Director of the University Center for International Studies at the University of North Carolina, Chapel Hill. Professor Calhoun founded UNC's Program in Social Theory and Cross-Cultural Studies and has served as Dean of the Graduate School and as one of UNC's "Bicentennial Speakers." He has also taught in China, England, Eritrea, Norway, and the Sudan and conducted research in these and several other countries.

A preacher's son, Professor Calhoun grew up in several communities in Kentucky, Illinois, Indiana, and California; learning about each new home was his first training in sociology. After studying at the University of Southern California and Columbia University, he won a scholarship to England and received his doctorate from Oxford University. He has taught in Chapel Hill since 1977.

Professor Calhoun's most recent books include *Neither Gods Nor Emperors: Students and the Struggle for Democracy in China* (California, 1995), which was awarded the American Sociological Association's Political Sociology Section Award for Distinguished Contribution to Scholarship, and *Critical Social Theory: Culture, History and the Challenge of Difference* (Blackwell, 1995). He is also the author or editor of several other books, including most recently *Habermas and the Public Sphere* (MIT, 1992), *Bourdieu: Critical Perspectives* (with M. Postone and E. LiPuma; Chicago, 1993), and *Social Theory and the Politics of Identity* (Blackwell, 1994). His articles have appeared in a wide range of scholarly journals, including the *American Journal of Sociology, Comparative Studies in Society and History, International Sociology, Sociological Methods and Research,* and *Theory and Society.* His work has been translated for publication in a half dozen languages.

Professor Calhoun is the editor of the American Sociological Association's journal, *Sociological Theory,* and has been elected chair of the ASA's sections on Comparative Historical Sociology and Sociological Theory. He is currently engaged in comparative historical research on nationalism and ethnicity, democracy and public life, and the social impact of global changes in communications and transport technologies.

Teaching is a central part of Professor Calhoun's work. In addition to teaching a wide range of sociology classes, he taught repeatedly in UNITAS, an experiment in multicultural living and learning for which he was the founding professor, and which he still serves as Faculty Advisor. In 1988, UNC undergraduates elected him to their honor society, the Order of the Golden Fleece.

Donald Light is Professor of Sociology at Rutgers University and Professor of Social and Behavioral Medicine in the Department of Psychiatry at the University of Medicine and Dentistry of New Jersey. Born and raised in Massachusetts, Professor Light went to college at Stanford and completed his graduate work in sociology at the University of Chicago and Brandeis University. Along the way, he helped to implement President Kennedy's Equal Employment Opportunity Program for minority workers and became increasingly interested in the field of education and health. He is now conducting research on the sociological changes taking place in the American health-care system.

Professor Light's first appointment was to the faculty of Princeton University, where he taught the introductory course in sociology as well as courses in education, deviance, and professions. It was there he met and became friends with Suzanne Keller and subsequently developed the first edition of this text. He has published a well-known study of medical training entitled *Becoming Psychiatrists: The Professional Transformation of Self* (Norton, 1980). He has edited and authored several volumes on health-care systems. Professor Light is the author of numerous articles, which have appeared in *The American Journal of Sociology, The Journal of Health and Social Behavior, The Administrative Science Quarterly, Daedalus,* and *The New England Journal of Medicine.*

Suzanne Keller is Professor of Sociology at Princeton University, where she has served as Chairperson of the Department of Sociology. She was born in Vienna, came to the United States as a child, but has spent a good part of her professional life in Europe. She received a Ph.D. in sociology from Columbia University in 1953. In 1957, she became an Assistant

v

Professor at Brandeis University, where she taught courses in social theory, stratification, and the sociology of religion. A Fulbright Lectureship in 1963 at the Doxiadis Center of Ekistics in Athens marked the beginning of her interest in architecture and community planning. At the completion of her Fulbright in 1965, Professor Keller joined the Center, where she remained until 1967. That year she came to Princeton University as a Visiting Professor, and in 1968 she was the first woman to be appointed to a tenured professorship there. She has held several elective offices in the American Sociological Association, including that of Vice-President, and most recently as President of the Eastern Sociological Society.

At Princeton, Suzanne Keller teaches courses on contemporary elites, comparative family systems, theories of humanity, and social psychiatry. The author of numerous articles and several books, Professor Keller helped launch the program in Women's Studies at Princeton. She is currently completing a book on the creation of community and embarking on a study of contemporary elites. A consultant to many universities, corporations, and government agencies, both here and abroad, Professor Keller has received a number of fellowships and honors, including a Guggenheim Award, honorary degrees, and, most recently, a Rockefeller Foundation grant for her work on community. She currently chairs the board of the DBH Foundation, for the advancement of humane and safe living environments.

CONTENTS IN BRIEF

CONTENTS

marked

BOXES

PREFACE

One of the great pleasures of sociology is that it is always new. This is partly because sociologists make new discoveries about patterns of social life and partly because sociologists develop new theories or ways of looking at social life. But crucially, it is also because social life itself changes.

MAKING SENSE OF SOCIAL CHANGE

Since society is the product of human action, it never stands still. Even maintaining tradition and keeping things stable requires effort. Most social change is small. Changes in individuals' lives—like new jobs or new children—do not necessarily change the whole of society. But behind these individual changes are bigger ones: the whole job market changes, the population grows larger. Occasionally, there are even bigger changes, like the transition from older industrial technology to new computer-driven communications and automation that changes job markets forever. New technology and changing cultural values have also changed the natural process of having children, as the opening example of this book shows.

This book has been revised to take account both of improvements in sociological knowledge and of changes in the social world itself. We have used the latest data available and explained the findings of the latest scientific research. We have given examples from contemporary social debates and public issues to illustrate how sociology brings us new insights. At the same time, we have also summarized the many sociological research findings that have stood the test of time, remaining consistent even as other features of society change. We have also presented the classical theoretical perspectives that shape all of sociological thought. In this edition as before, we focus especially on five key sociological concepts—function, structure, power, action, and culture—that have been central to sociology since it was founded and that continue to orient sociological research and theory.

Working on each new edition of this textbook takes us back to the joys of our own first encounters with sociology. What attracted us then still seems most important: the ability to connect the huge global trends and issues that shape the contemporary world with the immediate concerns of our daily lives. Sociology is unique in its capacity to improve our understanding on many different levels or scales of analysis from the personal through the institutional or organizational to the global. It helps us bring different dimensions of knowledge—economic, political, cultural—together in a sense of the rich fullness of social life.

LINKING GLOBAL AND LOCAL LEVELS

Because so many important international changes are taking place, and they have such basic implications for our lives, we have paid special attention in this edition to global trends and cross-cultural comparisons. This is apparent throughout the text. It is especially evident in the series of boxes headed "Global Issues/Local Consequences." The "local" in this case often means "Americans" but not always. In these boxes we ask how global forces affect people's everyday lives in various settings—as for example how the people who live in tropical rainforests are affected when the global economy brings economic incentives for increased lumber production.

SOCIAL DEBATES AND PUBLIC CHOICES

One of the reasons why sociology is important is that it allows us to understand the choices open to us, as individuals and as citizens. Precisely because the social world is the product of human action, we can have a voice in changing it. To highlight how sociology—and especially the five key concepts—helps us to understand public issues and choices better, we have introduced a series of boxes focusing on today's key "Social Debates." Whether the issue is how to improve schools or why abortion has become a political controversy, sociology's key concepts lead us to a deeper understanding of what lies behind social debates and what is at stake in them.

METHODS OF SOCIOLOGICAL RESEARCH

Sociology is not just a matter of perspectives and concepts, however. It is also a matter of scientific research. Throughout the book we bring the latest and best of this research to bear on explaining different parts of social life. One whole chapter focuses, as always, on research methods. But beyond this, we have added a series of boxes which brings out the methods sociologists used in conducting important recent research projects. These appear where the topic of the research—from sexual behavior to street gangs—is being discussed. But the boxes deal with the crucial question of *how* we gather information and test it to be sure it is accurate. They describe surveys and experiments, in-depth participant observation and cross-cultural comparisons, showing how researchers faced the challenges of going beyond common sense and surface observations to deeper and better information about important issues.

VISUAL SOCIOLOGY

A textbook like this is not just a summary of theory and research; it is an attempt to make sociology come alive with good examples and clear explanations. We do this first and foremost in our writing. But some of the biggest advances presenting sociological knowledge have come through improved visual techniques. A generation ago, most quantitative information was presented in the form of tables. Now, partly with the aid of computer graphics, we are able to present such information in much clearer, more easily understandable—and attractive—ways. Instead of just numbers, you will find many different kinds of graphics throughout this book, but these are not just colorful illustrations. Maps, pie charts, bar graphs and other pictures are ways of presenting sociological information visually. Usually, they allow you to compare information about different groups of people or different aspects of social life—like the differences in average income between men and women, or blacks and whites.

The same goes for photographs and even works of art. These are not just pretty pictures chosen for their attraction as decorations. They too are sources of sociological information. They are accompanied by captions that help you to see more of what the picture "says," but you should also work to develop the skill of "reading" visual information. We have combined new photographs in brilliant color with older, often black and white, photographs and art work that show earlier social conditions.

SUPPLEMENTARY PACKAGE

A textbook does not stand alone. It is usually only part of a class in which the most important component is the teaching of an experienced sociologist. To help both teachers and students, we have also prepared a comprehensive package of teaching and learning aids to complement this text and enrich classroom teaching.

Study Guide. Theodore C. Wagenaar (Miami University of Ohio) has revised this excellent, low-priced study guide for students. This guide contains learning objectives, chapter summaries, a clarification of key concepts, multiple-choice review questions with answers, critical thinking questions, and exercises designed to apply each chapter's content.

Instructor's Manual. The instructor's manual is again written by Theodore C. Wagenaar, Bradford Simcock, and Rodney Coates (all of Miami University of Ohio) and provides a wealth of information that will be of value in the classroom. The instructor's manual features teaching suggestions, print resources, and video resources.

Test Bank. A print test bank containing approximately 2,200 multiple-choice and 550 true/false test items has been significantly revised by William Snizek (Virginia Polytechnic Institute and State University). The new test bank reflects numerous changes within the seventh edition.

Computerized Test Banks. The print test bank items are also available on discs for IBM, both in DOS and Windows formats, and Macintosh personal computers.

Transparencies. A comprehensive set of 80 four-color, high-quality acetate overhead transparencies for classroom use is available for the seventh edition.

Primis Customized Readers. An array of first-rate selections, consisting in some cases of classic articles from the sociological literature and in others of interesting and provocative articles written for The

McGraw-Hill Companies by leading sociologists, is available for use with the seventh edition. These pieces are part of The McGraw-Hill Companies' Primis, a customized electronic database that allows instructors to select only those pieces they want to use in their classrooms. For additional information, see your McGraw-Hill sales representative.

Videotapes and Software Programs. The McGraw-Hill Companies offers a variety of videotapes and software programs suitable for classroom use in conjunction with the seventh edition of *Sociology.* For details, see your McGraw-Hill sales representative.

Videodisc—Points of Departure. A 60-minute videodisc based on various issues in the news from the NBC news network. Organized into 10 six-minute segments on topics such as culture, social inequality, and religion, students can learn to view the national news with a sociological perspective.

Webliography You can visit The McGraw-Hill Companies College Division home page on the World Wide Web at *http://www.mhcollege.com* and discover a comprehensive listing of selected reference sites in sociology, and particularly, the seventh edition of *Sociology.*

ACKNOWLEDGMENTS

It is a basic sociological lesson that the accomplishments of individuals usually depend on the support and cooperation of other people. This is certainly true of the preparation of this book. The three authors have all learned from each other as well as shared the labor of researching and writing. We have also benefited from the work of many others.

At McGraw-Hill, a number of different people played crucial roles at one stage or another. A book, after all, calls for printers and proofreaders, designers and warehouse clerks as well as authors. Most importantly, perhaps, we have been helped by the work of remarkable editors who have sought to improve the clarity of our writing, to help us make sociology come alive, and to make sure we didn't forget anything. We are deeply indebted to Ann Levine,

Mary Marshall, and especially Roberta Meyer (who not only performed a brilliant service as developmental editor, but worked tirelessly despite personal pressures). All have worked on previous editions as well, and are important reasons for the success of this book. So are Phil Butcher and Jill Gordon, the publisher and sociology editor at McGraw-Hill. We would also like to thank the talented editing, design, photo research, and production staff at The McGraw-Hill Companies—Kate Scheinman, Karen Quigley, Nancy Dyer, Barbara Salz, Annette Mayeski, Amy Smeltzley, and Joel Bernstein—for their determined efforts.

Two gifted teachers of sociology have often provided us with advice and feedback on our work. We are grateful to Ted Wagenaar of Miami University and Tom Gieryn of Indiana University. We have also been aided by a number of sociology teachers who reviewed the previous edition to help us see how it could serve their students better. These include Charles Case, Augusta College; Dana Dunn, University of Texas at Arlington; John V. A. Ehle, Jr., Northern Virginia Community College; Barrance V. Johnston, Indiana University Northwest; Ruby C. Lewis, Dekalb College; Kenneth E. Miller, Drake University; Kim D. Schopmeyer, Henry Ford Community College; and Avtar Singh, East Carolina University.

Perhaps the greatest help has come from our students. Among us, we have taught introductory sociology to many thousands of students over the years, and from them have learned a great deal about how to present sociological ideas and information. Some of these students have played an additional role as research assistants during the present revision of this text. Steve Pfaff, Mark Regnerus and Matt Titolo have all been a great help in updating statistics and tracking down information and research studies. We offer them our thanks, and to all our students, we dedicate this book.

Craig Calhoun
Donald Light
Suzanne Keller

PART 1

The Science of Society

CHAPTER 1

The Sociological Perspective

W hat could be more natural than the birth of a child?

Wilma and Willem Stuart, a Dutch couple in their thirties, were overjoyed: Wilma had given birth to healthy twin boys, Teun and Koen. At first the Stuarts did not pay much attention to the twins' different appearances. But as the months passed, the contrast became more obvious: Teun was blond and fair-skinned like his parents; Koen had dusky skin and fuzzy brown hair. When the Stuarts took the babies out in their twin stroller they became objects of curiosity. "What? Are those twins? How is that possible?" people asked. "He is called Koen? Such a Dutch name for such an exotic child!" Finally one neighbor confronted Wilma with what everyone believed: "Go on, tell your secret. Did you have two men at the same time?" (*New York Times*, June 28, 1995). For Wilma, the different-colored twins were like a scarlet letter *A* proclaiming infidelity.

In fact, the "secret" was that after five years of trying unsuccessfully to have a baby, the Stuarts had gone to a fertility clinic that specializes in *in vitro* fertilization, or IVF. (IVF is a procedure in which the woman's eggs are extracted from her ovary and mixed with the man's sperm in a petri dish. After a few days of incubation to ensure that fertilization has occurred, the resulting embryos are implanted in the woman's uterus.) When the stares and whispers started, the Stuarts consulted their doctor. DNA tests showed that Koen had a different father. Further investigation revealed that the clinic had performed several *in vitro* procedures the day Willem and Wilma had gone in to provide sperm and eggs; apparently a technician had broken the rules and used the same pipette for two procedures. Half of Koen's genes came from a man from the Caribbean island of Aruba who also had gone to the clinic with his wife. The Stuarts had wanted to protect their children from being stigmatized as "test-tube babies." Worn down by social disapproval in their village and afraid that Koen's Aruban father might claim him, the couple (using pseudonyms) went public. Overnight, social ostracism turned to smiles and congratulations, and the Stuart family was accepted again. Still, Wilma and Willem worry about their brown baby's future in a predominantly white society. This is only one of many cases where technology and social change make birth more than just "natural."

Throughout Asia, the ratio of girls to boys is increasing. Normally, about 106 boys are born for every 100 girls. Because male babies are less likely to survive infancy than female babies are, by early childhood the numbers of girls and boys are usually about even. But in India, for example, the overall sex ratio in 1991 was 929 females for every 1,000 males (Balakrishan, 1994). This pattern is not due to chance.

The preference for sons over daughters has been part of many Asian cultures for centuries. In much of India, the general attitude is, "Bringing up a girl is like watering a neighbor's plant" (Kusum, 1993). A daughter is a financial burden. Custom dictates that her parents present her future husband with a substantial dowry; once she is married, she is absorbed into her husband's family. In contrast, sons carry on the family name and, since they inherit the family land or business, keep accumulated wealth within the family. In the absence of social security plans and nursing homes, sons (and their wives) care for their parents in old age.

In the past, parents could only hope and pray for sons. But new technology has made the birth of sons a matter of choice, not just a wish. Amniocentesis and related procedures enable a woman to learn the sex of her unborn child and decide whether to carry the baby to term or abort. A study of women's centers in Bombay found that of 8,000 abortions preceded by amniocentesis, 7,999 of the fetuses were female (World Health Organization, 1992). When the Indian government outlawed the use of amniocentesis for sex-selective abortions, a black market in ultrasound quickly filled the gap (Balakrishan, 1994). Billboards proclaimed, "Better 500 rupees now [for ultrasound and abortion of females] than 50,000 rupees later [for a dowry]"; minivans equipped with ultrasound machines cruised the countryside, selling "choice" to families who lived far from modern medical facilities.

In China, the traditional preference for sons is complicated by the government's "one-child policy." In order to slow population growth, in 1979 the Chinese government instituted one of the strictest national birth control policies ever adopted (Cooney and Li, 1994; Yi et al., 1993). Couples must limit their families to one child only. As in India, the government of China has banned the use of technology for sex selection. Because the technology is widely available, however, couples can easily bribe doctors to tell them

Where are the girls? Although China's one-child policy doesn't dictate the child's sex, Asian cultures traditionally favor male children. Now, reproductive technologies have meshed with culture, enabling couples to satisfy their government and their wishes for a boy as well. In the process, girl babies are often sacrificed through abortion.

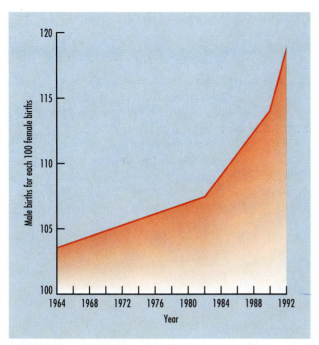

FIGURE 1.1 / *The Chosen Sex*

A cultural preference for boys combined with the government's strict one-child-per-family policy has skewed the ratio of boys to girls in China.

Source: Chinese Census and unpublished data, cited in *The New York Times,* July 21, 1993, p. A1.

the sex of a fetus. As a result, the sex ratio at birth in China has become increasingly skewed (Yi et al., 1993) (see Figure 1.1).

Reproductive technology, like all technologies, increases the capacity of human beings to control natural processes. Reproductive technology was originally designed to help couples who could not conceive children to become parents and to help couples who carry a genetic disorder (such as Tay-Sachs disease or sickle-cell anemia) and older women (who have a higher risk of giving birth to a baby with Down's syndrome) to know whether their babies will be healthy. This new reproductive technology has brought joy to thousands of couples. But new technologies can have unanticipated social consequences (Merton, 1968a). In Asia, prenatal tests are used to select sons over daughters, while in the West, high-tech reproduction raises new questions about identity. A family today might consist of a husband and wife who are both infertile and a child born with the help of an egg donor, a sperm donor, a surrogate

mother who carries the baby (conceived either by the husband and wife via IVF or artificial insemination with the husband's sperm) to term—and perhaps a nanny to help care for the baby (Orenstein, 1995). Who, then, are the child's "true" parents?

To understand the full impact of new technology and other phenomena, we have to look beyond the technology itself—and beyond the individuals who use this technology—to the social forces that shape human behavior. New reproductive technologies did not simply appear out of nowhere. Rather, they are part of an ongoing trend to medicalize childbirth and, more generally, to use science and technology to control nature. Postponement of parenthood and the desire for small families in the United States and other Western countries have also played a part, as have potentially high profits for fertility clinics (at least in the United States). In Asia, the strong traditional preference for sons in some cultures and the exercise of power by the Chinese government have fostered reproductive technology as well. To understand why couples decide to use reproductive technology and the consequences of these decisions, we must understand the social forces that influence their actions. Such understanding requires *sociological imagination.*

We begin this chapter with an overview of sociology. What does the sociological perspective add to our understanding of new technologies, world events, and our own lives? This section introduces five key sociological concepts that you will encounter throughout this book: social structure, social actions, functional integration, power, and culture. Next we look at sociology as a science and describe how sociologists use scientific methods to conduct research into social facts. Finally, we trace the origins of sociology and introduce the classical sociological theories that provide the basic framework for contemporary theory and research.

SOCIOLOGICAL IMAGINATION

Sociology is the study of the ways in which human life is socially organized. Sociologists use scientific research methods and theories to study social life in a wide variety of settings. They seek to understand intimate relationships, such as parenthood or friendship, vast global networks, and everything in between. Sociologists are interested in all the many ways people relate to one another. The other social sciences each focus on one dimension of social life: economics on the dynamics of markets and the exchange of goods; political science on government and power relations; anthropology on issues of ecology and cultural difference; psychology on relationships among biology, human development, and individual mental characteristics. Sociology includes all these dimensions. Sociologists are especially interested in the ways different aspects of social life influence each other—for example, how religious values may influence family decisions about birth technologies and how these decisions in turn affect the market for medical services, the number of children who will need school in the future, and so forth.

Sociology offers not only information but also a distinctive way of looking at the world and our place in it. Often we try to explain the things that happen to us by analyzing the motives of the people who were directly involved. Sociologists encourage us to look beyond individual psychology to the many recurring patterns in people's attitudes and actions and how these patterns vary across time, cultures, and social groups. For example, sociologists do not ask simply, "What motivates individuals to use ultrasound or in vitro fertilization?" They also ask, "What social conditions led to the development of reproductive technologies? What groups have promoted (or attempted to limit) the use of these technologies? Who has access to assisted reproduction?" Sociologists do not ignore individuals. Rather, they show that to understand the actions of individuals— and our own experiences—we have to understand the social context in which they take place. For example, the Chinese preference for boys is shaped by its relationship to a system of inheriting property and family names through men and a belief in ancestor worship. Both of these social characteristics cause the Chinese to feel a need for male descendants.

In the United States, access to medical assistance is determined in large part by ability to pay, and treating infertility is big business. In 1995 some 3 million Americans turned to fertility clinics (Begley, 1995). Couples spend at least $10,000 and sometimes as much as $100,000 in the quest to have a baby of their own. Some health insurance policies cover part of the cost of in vitro fertilization, but many do not; moreover, many women do not have private health insurance. This means that the "miracle" of new reproductive technology is available only to the relatively well off.

Birth technologies have social consequences. In the celebrated case of "Baby M," an upper middle class couple paid Mary Beth Whitehead to be a surrogate mother for them. After giving birth, Whitehead sued to keep the baby. She lost, but the case led many states to outlaw the practice of surrogate motherhood.

Many aspects of our private lives are shaped by forces beyond individual control—even the circumstances of our birth: how old our parents are; how many siblings we have, if any; how many other people of our age or generation will be competing for spaces in day care and later for jobs; and indeed, whether we will be born at all. Grasping this point is a critical part of what the great American sociologist C. Wright Mills called "sociological imagination." Sociological imagination means looking at our experiences in light of what is happening in the social world. It also means looking at broader social patterns that are not apparent through personal experience alone. People who have direct experience with reproductive technology, for example, see only one part of the puzzle. To grasp the whole picture requires systematic scientific study of attitudes and behavior patterns in different times and places, under different social circumstances and in different social classes, as well as the intended and unintended consequences of social actions.

Through the sociological imagination we come to see that we are more than just actors involved in our own personal dramas. We are caught up in larger social patterns acted out on a broader social stage. As Mills (1959/1970, pp. 3, 9) wrote:

> Nowadays [people] often feel that their private lives are a series of traps. They sense that within their everyday worlds, they cannot quite overcome their troubles, and in this feeling, they are often quite correct.
>
> In these terms, consider unemployment. When, in a city of 100,000, only one man is unemployed, that is his personal trouble, and for its relief we properly look to the character of the man, his skills, and his immediate opportunities. But when…[many thousands] are unemployed, that is a social issue, and we may not hope to find its solution within the range of opportunities open to any one individual. The very structure of opportunities has collapsed. Both the correct statement of the problem and the range of possible solutions require us to consider the economic and political institutions of the society, and not merely the personal situation and character of a scattering of individuals.
>
> Consider war. The personal problem of war, when it occurs, may be how to survive it or how to die in it with honor; how to make money out of it; how to climb into the higher safety of the military apparatus; or how to contribute to the war's termination…. But the structural issues of war have to do with its social causes; with what types of men it throws up into command; with its effects upon economic and political, family, and religious institutions; with the unorganized irresponsibility of a world of nation-states.

Sociological imagination helps us make sense of both personal experience and public issues.

We like to think that we make important personal decisions—such as whether to have children—for ourselves, independently. In fact, our personal choices are shaped by social forces. Changing birth rates illustrate this point. In the first part of this century, birth rates in the United States declined slowly but steadily. After World War II, however, the combination of an expanding economy, government support

for home owners and the growth of suburbs, pressure on women to leave the work force to make room for veterans, and other forces led to a huge baby boom. In the 1960s and 1970s, birth rates dropped again as singlehood, childlessness, and divorce became more common and more accepted. In the 1980s *this* trend reversed somewhat as the baby boom generation began having children and women who had postponed motherhood sought to catch up. Now, in the 1990s, many young women, alarmed by the much-publicized fertility problems of the previous generation, feel pressured to have babies early. These changes are the cumulative result of millions of individual decisions, but they are also responses to the political and economic climate of the times (Lasker and Borg, 1994).

Key Concepts

Sociology, like other sciences, uses concepts to help organize its views of social phenomena and to call attention to specific features and issues. Many concepts and terms borrowed from sociology are used in ordinary conversation—for example, *peer group* and *inner city*—but they have more precise definitions when used in the context of sociology. Here we introduce five key concepts that sociologists use to grasp the most important dimensions of social life.

Structure

Social structure is the pattern of relationships, positions, and numbers of people that provides the "skeleton" of social organization for a population, whether a small group or a whole society. *Relationships* exist whenever people enter into relatively stable, continuing patterns of interaction and/or mutual dependence—for example, marriage or employment at the interpersonal level, or institutions like the education and health-care systems on a larger scale and more abstract level. *Positions* (sometimes referred to as *statuses*) are recognized places in the network of social relationships—such as mother, president, or priest—that usually carry expectations for behavior (commonly called *roles*). The *numbers* of people within different categories (such as members of a sorority or the population of a nation, unwed mothers or women in the paid labor force) and especially the relative size of these categories (such as the percentage of a population over age sixty-five or the ratio of officers to enlisted men in an army) have social structural consequences.

It is important to distinguish between social structure and individuals, or "personnel." The structure of a university, for example, is relatively stable while personnel change continuously. Each spring a senior class graduates, to be replaced by an entering freshman class the next fall. The individuals in English 101 and Chemistry 404, on the soccer team and the campus newspaper staff, change. So may the specific people who occupy the positions of president, dean, department chair, and football coach. Some faculty become full professors and others switch universities. Despite these ongoing changes in personnel, the basic structure—the relationships between the administration, the faculty, and the student body, between professors and students, between upper and lower classmen, and so on—changes only slowly if at all. Structure shapes the possibilities open to people, but people also affect structure. For example, if enrollment declines, some professors may be laid off or offered only part-time positions. When the number of women going to college increased, so did the demand for women's dormitories, women's studies courses, and women's sports programs.

Social structure is an important source of stability in social life, but structural factors can also produce and shape change. The development of a strong family-planning program in China, culminating in the one-child policy, was a response to runaway population growth. Not only is China's population huge, but most of the growth is relatively recent, the result of better nutrition and health care under the Communist government. This means that a large proportion of China's population is young and entering the childbearing years, so that even if the number of children per couple goes down, many new babies will be born. Thus there was a *structural* reason (a huge population including a high percentage of people of childbearing age) to expect the population to grow rapidly. If population growth is not slowed in that country, all possible gains from economic development and improved agricultural activity will be "eaten" by a growing population instead of raising the overall standard of living. As part of its family-planning program, China invested in technologies to monitor pregnancy.

As we saw, China responded with aggressive population control policies. One unintended consequence of these policies was to provide Chinese couples with the means (ultrasound and abortion) to act on their traditional preference for sons over daughters. The resulting gender imbalance has major structural implications. When the birth ratio tilts toward boys, twenty years later there will be a shortage of women for men to marry. This means not only that some men will be disappointed in their search for a bride but also that there will be pressure for adult men to marry younger women (which may undercut attempts to improve the status of women through advanced education). Ultimately, there may be fewer daughters and daughters-in-law to care for people in their old age and hence more pressure on the government to support the elderly. If the government continues to encourage women to get higher education and move into traditionally male occupations, the shortage of women for traditionally female occupations and social roles will be even greater.

Fertility patterns are also reshaping social structure in Western countries. Birth rates are falling as couples decide to have fewer children (partly with the assistance of birth control technology). Our new family structure, in which one- and two-child families are the norm, has greatly changed the experience of family life, the demand for schools, the ease with which women can enter professional careers, and many other aspects of life in North America and Europe. Couples who plan smaller families also tend to wait longer to have children. About a quarter of first-time births in the United States today are to women between the ages of thirty and forty (Maranto, 1995). This means that twenty years from now about a quarter of the freshman class at colleges and universities will have parents who are at or near retirement age (creating pressures for older parents to remain in the work force and for the government to increase support for young people who pursue higher education).

Action

Action refers to behavior that is chosen rather than merely instinctual or reflexive. Action is social both because it affects other people and because it depends on conditions created by other people. Indeed,

While fewer children are available for adoption in the United States, the Chinese one-child social policy and the culture's preference for boys have combined to make Chinese girls available for adoption by Americans.

the very process of becoming a human being and an individual is social: We learn language, values, and in general how to do things primarily by means of social relationships.

Social actions may be taken not just by individuals but also by groups or complex organizations such as corporations or governments. As individuals we may act to change aspects of ourselves, for example practicing basketball daily in order to become a better player or joining Alcoholics Anonymous to try to stop the destructive effects of addiction on the body and on relationships. Both as individuals and in groups and organizations we may act to try to change society—to reduce racial conflict, reform the health-care system, save national forests, or stage a revolution. Some of the most important social actions create new relationships, as when marriage partners say "I do" or the founders of a new country or a new organization create a constitution to bring it into being and to give it social structure. These actions, in turn, create new conditions for action. After getting married, a man and woman may feel increasing internal and external pressure to have a baby; after the birth of a baby they may unconsciously slip into more sex-stereotyped roles, despite their intention to share parental responsibilities equally.

Often we take aspects of our social environment for granted, as if they had always been there or as if they had just appeared, magically and anonymously; we ignore the role of social action. The creation of new reproductive technology, for example, was not the inevitable product of a scientific conveyor belt that operates on its own momentum. Rather, it was "the result of a series of specific decisions made by particular groups of people in particular places at particular times for their own purposes" (Wajcman, 1994). The same resources might have been devoted to researching the *causes* of infertility and finding *preventive* treatment or to expanding adoption services to bring would-be parents and needy, abandoned children together.

China's one-child family policies and the use of sex-selective abortion by Indian families are clearly examples of social action. However, even private decisions made by individuals are social. Suppose a single, thirty-seven-year-old Atlanta woman becomes a mother by means of artificial insemination. How is her action "social"? First, it is social because it depends on current social conditions. Although the technology existed twenty-five years ago (and no doubt was desired by some "spinsters" of the day), at that time most physicians would have refused to help a single woman become pregnant. In addition, married or single, a woman well past thirty has a relatively high risk of carrying a baby with Down's syndrome. Now, however, single motherhood has lost most of its stigma, and modern prenatal tests can detect genetic problems during pregnancy. Second, her action is social because it affects others: the baby, the father (even an anonymous donor, if the child later wants to meet him), and society more generally.

Amniocentesis and related technologies have made it possible to detect some birth defects and genetic abnormalities *in utero*. Genetic tests can also predict a couple's chances of transmitting defective genes to their children. Parents who carry the gene for Tay-Sachs, a disease which causes slow, painful death during a baby's first years, have a one in four risk of transmitting this disease to their baby. In the past, they had to choose either the risk of pain and suffering or foregoing parenthood. Now they can learn in advance if they carry the gene for Tay-Sachs. If both parents carry the gene, they may choose to adopt a child rather than bring a child with Tay-Sachs into the world. These choices, in turn, are only possible because of other decisions to invest in developing the technology, because doctors are willing to perform the procedures, and so on.

Culture

Culture is the more or less integrated pattern of thinking, understanding, evaluating, and communicating that makes up a people's way of life. Many of the traits we think of as defining us as human—language, morals, technology, and skills—are elements of our culture that we learn through social relationships, beginning with our families, and through participation in cultural institutions, like schools and religious institutions. Our culture provides us with shared resources for thinking and acting, the most notable of which is language. Our culture also provides us with criteria for judging the significance of actions. One current issue is whether abortion should be legal and available to every American woman. We each make individual judgments about this issue (and countless others), but whether we decide the "right to life" of a fetus outweighs a "woman's right to choose" or vice versa, it is our shared culture that enables us to make sense out of these two ideas and

to debate them. Our culture places a positive value on life, in general, and also on choice, or freedom. Abortion is an issue on which different cultural values clash.

Cultural values lead people in many Asian societies to prefer sons over daughters. Less obviously, Asian cultures tend to put a higher value on the group (especially the family) than on the individual, and a higher value on social order and harmony than on personal freedom. Many Chinese feel that it is right and proper for the government to require couples to sacrifice their desire for more children for the greater good of society as a whole. But as in the case of abortion in the United States, in China the values of family and social order may work at cross-purposes: in acting on one value (the good of society) couples automatically violate another (the importance of large families).

Culture establishes ideals that shape our individual dreams and desires. In the West, childless marriages are more accepted today than in the past, but they still are not considered ideal. From the time we are little, we hear the phrase "when you grow up" followed by "and become a mother/father" so often that they begin to sound like the same thing (Lasker and Borg, 1994). Our ideals for women focus on motherhood, and our ideals for men, on fatherhood. Culture, amplified by social pressure, often makes childless couples in their mid-thirties feel unfulfilled. As more and more of their friends have children, they are left out (or feel left out) of social occasions. In general, our culture views people without children as selfish and strange. Not only couples, but childless single women, whether lesbian or heterosexual, feel abnormal. If having no children is seen as selfish, having just one child—denying him or her siblings— is only a little better. Despite evidence to the contrary, "only" children are stereotyped as being spoiled and maladjusted. Moreover, as a culture we prefer "natural" births to adoption, even when the natural births depend on high-tech medical interventions.

In addition, culture makes new technologies possible by providing a socially organized store of information on which doctors, inventors, government planners, and ordinary people alike can draw. American culture is deeply shaped by technology. We devote a great deal of energy to advancing technology, and the remarkable achievements of science and technology over the last 200 years have transformed our ideas of what is possible. We are far less likely than our ancestors were to believe in fixed limits imposed by nature or God and are much more likely to believe that there must be solutions to all our problems, if only we had the technology. We regard nature as a set of resources available to be exploited or manipulated, not as something sacred or powerful that we should be reluctant to change. This applies even to human nature, as the use of new birth-related technologies testifies.

Power

Power is the capacity of any one social actor to determine the course of events or the structure of social organization. Power may be exercised against the will of other social actors to cause them to do things they would prefer not to do, or it may be exercised by *shaping* the will of others to cause them to want to do (or to avoid) certain things. Exercising power in the first way mentioned, a police officer may use power to stop a criminal from stealing a car, or a carjacker may use the power of a gun to force a car owner to a drive to a deserted place where there are no police or other witnesses. Exercising power to shape the will of others, a manufacturer may use advertising to induce consumers to buy its products, including products they did not know they wanted or needed. The U.S. government uses its power to grant tax exemptions for mortgage interest in order to shape the structure of American society by making home ownership easier, thus supporting the middle class and people's commitment to their communities and to society as a whole. Note that power may be exercised by individuals, such as officials and outlaws, or by much larger social actors, such as corporations and governments.

The Chinese government is obviously using its power when it issues directives limiting families to one child and puts new technology to use to eliminate "inferior" births. Only an authoritarian government such as China's is in a good position to impose such an extreme and controversial policy. Other countries with comparable population problems but weaker governments—India, Indonesia, Nigeria—have had much more difficulty establishing effective family planning.

The idea of a government using its power to control reproduction is abhorrent to most Americans. But the practice is not as "foreign" as we think. In the 1930s, many American scientists endorsed eugenics—attempts to improve the quality of a population through selective reproduction. More than thirty states passed compulsory sterilization laws designed to purge society of "misfits"—alcoholics, drug addicts, epileptics, the mentally ill, criminals, and especially the mentally retarded, whose problems were thought to be hereditary. Eugenics was promoted as a scientific solution to a social (and economic) problem; in the words of one official, allowing misfits to procreate freely was a "public extravagance" (Larson, 1995, p. 120). The "science" was shaped, however, more by popular prejudices than by actual ability to predict. Abraham Lincoln's parents—one mentally disturbed, the other an alcoholic—would have been considered unfit to bear children! Nevertheless, involuntary sterilization statutes remained on the books in some states into the 1970s and 1980s. (Today, some people fear that advances in biogenetics may lead to new proposals for eugenics policies.)

Money provides a form of power. Fertility clinics in the United States are in large part commercial enterprises: those who can pay command services, while those who cannot are usually shut out. In Canada and most European countries, fertility services are available to most people through publicly funded national health-care systems. In these societies, broad groups have used their political power to demand that tax dollars be spent on providing health care for the entire population, rather than relying heavily on private insurance and private payments as is the norm in the United States. Even in the United States, people who pay for expensive fertility services are drawing on the federal government's support of research on fertility problems. Thus, this issue involves still other forms of power—the power of the government to tax citizens and to make decisions about how tax revenues will be spent and the power of the well-off (and the well-organized) to pressure the government to spend "the people's" money in ways that benefit these groups.

Sociologists also study the power of whole social systems, as distinct from the power of individuals, groups, or organizations. American society has more power than does Ethiopian society, for example. This does not mean just that America has the military might to defeat Ethiopia in battle or the economic muscle to push Ethiopia around. Rather, the levels of technological, economic, and social development in these societies shape people's lives. Americans may experience unemployment and poverty, but they seldom die of starvation. Ethiopia, in contrast, is subject to frequent and severe famines, attributable not only to climate but also to relatively primitive technology, low-level economic development, and social disorganization. Modern industrial society encourages people to think in terms of schedules, time clocks, and deadlines. These time pressures are coming increasingly to agricultural societies like Ethiopia, as they develop cities, offices, and modern industry. People must respond even if such a scheduled life does not always appear attractive. In both Ethiopia and the United States, our personal identities are intertwined more closely with our national identity than with our separate ethnic identities. We pay taxes and accept the obligation of military service—most of the time—because we believe that our survival as individuals and our way of life are tied to the survival of our country. Nationalism involves the power to mobilize these patriotic feelings. This power does not reside in any one social actor (though individuals and groups may call upon patriotic feelings), but in society as a whole.

Function

Births do not take place in isolation from the rest of society. The numbers of children born—male or female, healthy or handicapped—have an impact on schools, labor markets, marriage patterns, care for the elderly, and more. Different aspects of social structure and social organization tend to be functionally related to one another. What happens in one part of society affects and is shaped by what happens in others. For example, if new medical technologies are developed to keep premature babies alive, then insurance premiums have to go up to pay for this expensive technology.

Early sociologists often explained functional relationships by means of the "organic analogy." In an organism such as the human body, the heart, lungs, liver, brain, and other organs are structurally differentiated but functionally related. The lungs depend on the heart to pump blood; all other organs depend on the lungs to put oxygen into the blood; the brain directs many bodily operations through the nervous system, but also depends on the heart and lungs for oxygenated blood; and so on. If the heart is not

pumping regularly, or the lungs are not supplying enough oxygen, or parts of the brain are damaged, the entire system—the whole organism—is affected. Societies are not as tightly integrated as biological organisms, but their different parts also depend on each other in order to work as a system. Thus the new birth technologies can only exist because medical schools train doctors, researchers develop the technology, economies generate the wealth to pay for them, and so on.

The term function refers to the contribution any social relationship, position, organization, value, or other aspect of society makes to a larger social system. In a **functionally integrated** system, each of the parts is influenced by and dependent on its relationship to the others. Thus the function of schools is to produce students who are able to perform jobs needed by employers and to participate in public life as citizens of their country. We cannot fully understand schools by studying them in isolation; we need to look at their relationship to other parts of society. On another level, schools themselves are functionally organized: teachers of different subjects, administrators, students, custodians, and even material objects like blackboards and books all have different functions to perform. Functional integration is a matter of degree—that is, the parts of a group or a society may work more or less harmoniously with one another and may do a better or worse job of maintaining one another.

Sometimes one part of a social system operates in ways that undermine the effective workings of the system as a whole, in which case it is "dysfunctional." For example, some argue that the new reproductive technologies are dysfunctional, first because they drain resources from other, more pressing needs (such as health care, adequate nutrition, and education in child care and development for poor pregnant women), and second, because they lead would-be parents to use fertility treatments instead of adopting children, which leaves orphans and abandoned children without families to love and nurture them.

We may see the individual results of reproductive technology as good, perhaps even miraculous in enabling couples with fertility problems to have children, or as dangerous, morally questionable meddling with nature or divine will. This is a matter of personal judgment. But to *understand* this new tech-

To function properly for society as a whole, the parts within schools need to be smoothly coordinated, or functionally integrated. Here, students at a city high school meet with administrators to plan their programs.

nology—why it was developed, how it affects individuals and whole societies, who is helped (or hurt) most by it, and where it might lead—we need to consider all the dimensions described in the preceding pages. Depending on the topic they are studying and their theoretical perspective, sociologists might put more emphasis on one key concept—structure, action, culture, power, or function—than the others. But all five are important to thinking sociologically.

SOCIOLOGY AS SCIENCE

In everyday life, our understanding of the world is practical. We can walk without understanding the physiology of muscles; we can have a conversation without studying discourse theory. In other words, we can take many things in our everyday life for granted and act as if we understand them, even if we cannot fully explain them. Practical, everyday understanding enables us to do a great deal, but it is limited. The goal of any science is to enlarge our understanding of the world, that is, to go beyond practical knowledge and personal experience by means of the scientific method (Bourdieu, Chamboredon, and Passeron, 1991).

The Scientific Method

Science is a relatively new way of gathering and organizing information about the world. What we mean by **science** today is a systematic way of observing nature, interpreting what we see objectively, searching for relationships of cause and effect, and bringing systematic order to our understanding through theory. In the seventeenth century, this approach—pioneered by such physical scientists as Galileo, Copernicus, and Newton—grew into a "scientific revolution" that affected all branches of knowledge. All of the sciences we recognize today—from physics and biology to economics and sociology—have their roots in the scientific revolution.

The scientific revolution rested on two basic ideas, both of which remain crucial to science today. The first is **empirical observation.** The scientific method is based on evidence, not supposition or hearsay. Empirical information is information that can be acquired or verified through our five senses (sight, sound, smell, touch, and taste) or through extensions of our senses (like radio telescopes that "observe" waves we cannot see with our eyes). The second basic idea is **logical analysis.** We understand something, the scientific view holds, only when we can make rational sense of it, when we can present our understanding in logical form. Logic and empirical observation work hand in hand in science. We cannot comprehend cause and effect by observation alone; all we can see is that two things seem to happen together—like rain falling and flowers growing. To establish causation, we must also understand the logical steps that connect the two. (Rain does not cause flowering directly, but it provides one necessary condition for seeds to root and plants to flourish, if seeds are present in earth with sufficient nutrients and so on.)

The scientific method, based on empirical observation and logical analysis, seeks verifiable knowledge as distinct from mere opinion. Science does not accept something as true on the basis of authority (whether God's, the pope's, or the king's), or tradition (because people have always believed it to be so), or consensus (everyone believes it to be true). Scientific knowledge does not necessarily contradict authority, tradition, or consensus, but it may do so. In one of the most famous examples, Galileo challenged the prevailing view that the sun revolved around the earth, backing his conclusion with empirical observations and logical analysis. At first, people dismissed Galileo outright. He was contradicting what their parents and grandparents, and perhaps their mythology, believed (tradition); more important, he was challenging Church teachings (authority). Besides, everyone could see that the sun comes up in the east, crosses the sky, and goes down in the west (consensus). Yet in this case, science eventually prevailed.

The scientific method is enormously powerful. It has enabled a tremendous increase in knowledge during the modern era, knowledge that has led to great advances in technology. As powerful as science is, however, it does not produce "perfect" knowledge. First, scientific knowledge is incomplete: many phenomena have not been studied adequately and new research may cast doubt on what seemed settled. Second, some questions cannot be answered through scientific research (for example, whether or not God exists). Moreover, different people—including different scientists—start from different cultural vantage points, have different ways of looking at things, use different concepts and languages to describe things, and arrive at different insights. Working together, scientists can improve knowledge and technology and succeed in practical tasks like building bridges and launching spacecraft, but they can never totally eliminate the effects of different perspectives and arrive at one "truth."

As a science, sociology faces a special challenge. When sociologists use the scientific method of observation, they do not observe a "nature" that is external to human beings and more or less fixed in relation to them, but rather a world that is partly made by human beings, and one from which scientists can never be totally detached. The social world does not stand still, but constantly changes. Language, for example, exists only because people use it; but in the course of using it, people introduce small changes almost every time they speak. The social world is part of us and we are part of it. Social science observations are not simply interpretations of nature but are, at least in part, interpretations of people who are themselves interpreting and making their worlds (Giddens, 1984).

Empirical Observation

Empirical observation sounds straightforward: just "look and see." In fact, it is far more complicated. Sociologists must turn their observations into **data**: information that is specifically useful for answering sociological questions. This involves three main steps. The first is *abstraction*. The sociologist must pick out which features of the observed phenomenon are significant. What is significant depends on the question being asked. For example, when studying China's official policy on reproductive technology, the sex of the child is irrelevant because parents are only allowed to choose abortion in the case of likely birth defects, hereditary disease, and other problems. However, when studying how this technology is actually used (and how the policy is abused by parents eager to have sons), the sex of children becomes highly significant.

The second step in converting mere observation into data is *interpretation*. This is also important in the study of physical nature, as when meteorologists have to interpret and classify their observations of cloud patterns. Interpretation is an even bigger issue when one is studying social life because we have to make sense out of people's actions (Taylor, 1985b, 1995). Prenatal diagnostic tests, originally designed for women considered at high risk for bearing babies with birth defects or hereditary disorders, are now almost routine in Western countries, especially for women over age 30 (Browner and Press, 1995). Why? The obvious answer is that women want to make sure their babies are healthy (and if not, consider abortion) and that doctors perform these tests to gain necessary information about the health of the mother and fetus. However, a survey of pregnant women might reveal that they take the tests primarily because the obstetrician recommends them and he or she presumably knows best. A survey of obstetricians might reveal that they recommend prenatal tests primarily to guard against lawsuits by parents whose babies suffer from birth defects. Mere observation does not reveal motives or meanings.

The third step in turning observations into data is recording them in such a way that *replication* is possible. Replication means repeating the same study in another setting, with other subjects, to determine if the results are the same. There is always a possibility that the subjects of a single study are not representative of the population that they were chosen to represent, or that the researcher's methods were flawed. The presentation or publication of scientific findings must contain a precise account of the conditions under which the observations were made, including the way the researcher abstracted what was significant from other observations and how he or she interpreted the action observed. (Research methods are discussed in Chapter 2 and in specific studies presented in a series of Research boxes running through the book.)

Logical Analysis

Just as empirical observation is more complex than it might first appear, so is logical analysis. When we look at family life or religious institutions or any other aspect of social life, we see many different issues and phenomena bundled together. The first step in logical analysis is to decide which issue or issues we will focus on. *Units of analysis* are differentiated parts of a larger, more complex whole. Suppose a sociologist wants to study social groups and selects the members of a church. The first and most obvious units of analysis are individual members. A second unit of analysis is the relationships among those individuals: knowing which of them are friends, which are families, which work for the same companies, and so forth creates a new picture of the group. A third unit of analysis is the culture church members share, including their religious beliefs, their knowledge of the church's (or denomination's) history, and their understanding of church rituals and procedures. Still another unit of analysis

is the formal organization of the church—its structure of committees and responsibilities, the relationship between the minister and church members, whether the minister answers to a bishop, and so on. Each of these units of analysis is logically distinct from the others, and a complete picture of the church requires information about all of them.

Identifying relationships among the units of analysis, whether individuals, personal relationships, cultural beliefs, or organization structures, is the next step in logical analysis. A major task for the sociologist is figuring out which of the many things that exist at the same time in any social setting has the strongest influence on the others. For example, which has the strongest influence on such decisions as selecting a minister or choosing a deacon or elder—the members' beliefs (culture) or the way they are organized (structure)? This question relates to cause and effect. Sociologists are also interested in functional relationships among different units or between a whole and its parts. In a church choir, for example, a choir leader and singers with different voices (sopranos, altos, tenors, basses) all work together to create a common product—a musical performance that can only happen through social collaboration. Their different roles are thus functionally related; none precisely causes the other (not even the leader who conducts), but all depend on the others.

The third step in logical analysis is organizing knowledge as theory. A **theory** is an orderly, logical attempt to spell out relationships and explain how they work. Scientific theory is grounded in conditions and facts obtained through empirical observation. Why are the facts this way, the theorist asks, and not another way? For example, why do some Christian churches choose their ministers by elections, while others have priests sent by a bishop? In this case the answer depends partly on history (when and how different denominations came into being), partly on different beliefs (especially about the extent to which individuals achieve religious insight through prayer and Bible study or must learn religion from higher authorities), partly on different church structures (hierarchical versus egalitarian). Theoretical understanding of this issue depends on gathering all the partial explanations together and relating them to one another. For example, the practice of electing a minister may derive from the rise of more individualistic thinking (including the belief that individuals may have a direct relationship to God, an idea which grew during the Protestant

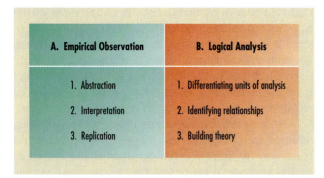

A. Empirical Observation	B. Logical Analysis
1. Abstraction	1. Differentiating units of analysis
2. Interpretation	2. Identifying relationships
3. Replication	3. Building theory

FIGURE 1.2 / The Scientific Method

Reformation) and also from more democratic thinking (including the idea that people should choose their leaders for themselves).

Ideally, theories are expressed with enough precision that they can be tested by returning to empirical observation and gathering more information. Such precision and testing are relatively easy for small, highly specific theories—for example, a theory that says that personal relationships among church members have more influence on voting for a new minister than do differences in religious beliefs. It is much more difficult to provide precision and testing for broader, larger-scale theories—for example, a theory that says that in all areas of social life, social structure is more important than individual choice. However, such broad theories—for example Karl Marx's theory that history is shaped mainly by class struggle or Adam Smith's theory that individual choices work for the common good (both discussed below)—provide guidelines for developing more specific theories that can be tested more directly.

Figure 1.2 provides an overview of the scientific method.

Social Facts

All sciences depend on both empirical observation and logical analysis. Different sciences face special issues, however, and so develop different approaches. For example, chemistry is heavily shaped by the use of controlled experiments to test theories. Tests of this kind generally are not possible in sociology. Sociologists gather as much data as possible on the ongoing processes of social life and also learn from unusual events—like revolutions or natural disas-

ters—in which certain kinds of social patterns are thrown into relief.

Just as different sciences use different approaches to gather data, so do they focus on different kinds of facts. **Social facts** are enduring properties of social life that shape or constrain the actions individuals can take. Because they are properties of social life, they cannot be located in the isolated individual but instead appear as external even though individuals participate in them (Durkheim, 1895/1982).

The economy is a good example of a social fact. No one person designed or created our economy, and no one person or group controls it. Individuals may change the economy by introducing new products or technologies or by creating new organizations and production strategies. Some people (government decision makers, heads of major corporations) exercise a powerful influence over economic trends; others (the homeless) exist on the fringes. But we all play a part in the economy to some extent. Indeed, it exists only as a result of many people and groups all *interacting* with one another. And the status of the economy—whether boom or recession—in turn affects individuals in the form of high or low interest rates, layoffs, and so on.

Some other social facts are *rates* of social phenomena, that is, the percentage of cases found in a population each year (or other time period). A crime rate is a social fact. So is a marriage rate, a birth rate, or a rate of infection from AIDS. These emerge only by considering many individual cases taken together. They affect people who have not committed crimes, married, been born, or contracted AIDS in any given year. Overall rates reveal social patterns that would not be apparent from analyzing separate cases. For example, the rapid growth of fertility clinics suggests that Americans are experiencing an epidemic of infertility. In fact, the fertility *rate* has not changed, but because the baby boom generation is much larger than the generations before it, the *number* of people experiencing fertility problems has increased.

As a shared means of communication, language is a social fact. To explain the emergence and spread of new words, phrases, and meanings, sociologists look for the social forces that may cause new words to be accepted. They study whether the new words are associated with prestigious public figures, whether they were repeated on MTV or in the movies, whether they are adopted first by one group in society and then spread to others, and so on.

Although social facts are relatively stable and enduring, they are never completely fixed. For this reason, sociology is not exactly like the physical sciences. Social life can never be fully described by a series of scientific laws that apply to all people, in all places, at all times. The relationship between mass and gravity does not change significantly from one part of the world to another, and so a brick will fall as fast in China as in Kansas. But the relationship between occupation and income, for example, does vary. In China, taxi drivers often earn more than doctors; this is not true in Kansas. In addition, human beings can change their world and the way they live. As a result, sociologists are always confronted with new phenomena to describe and explain.

THE ORIGINS OF SOCIOLOGY

Sociology was born in the late eighteenth and early nineteenth centuries, a period of sweeping social change in Western societies and around the globe. The social world that Europeans had known for centuries was disappearing, and the "modern era" had begun.

Sociology and the Modern Era

Three factors played a crucial role in bringing about what we now call the modern era. The first was *the rise of urban, capitalist, industrial society*. Until the eighteenth century, most Europeans lived in small, semi-autonomous agricultural villages where their families had lived for generations. The family was the heart of village life, providing and caring for its own (Laslett, 1973). These villages were part of larger countries whose rulers—usually kings—had begun to build empires. But except in times of war, affairs of state had little impact on the average man and woman. Travel was rare (there were no railroads or even stagecoaches) and "news" was mostly local gossip (there were no newspapers or regular postal deliveries). Everyone attended the same church (except in the rare Jewish enclave). The vast majority of people were farmers. Most did not own the land they worked. Rather, they rented from a landlord (often a member of the aristocracy) under agreements dating back centuries. This social order was thought to be ordained by God and was seldom questioned. A few people were born to rule, while the great majority were born to toil. Fathers had authority over their families, landlords over their tenants, and monarchs over all their subjects. People knew their duty and their place. Little changed from one generation to the next.

Likewise, the social order of premodern cities was stable. A well-established hierarchy governed social interaction. Masters were above journeymen, who were in turn above apprentices in craft guilds, just as dukes were above knights who were above serfs in the military and in the countryside. There even were rules about what kinds of clothing could be worn by people of different occupations and statuses. The church was the final authority on all matters, from birth to death (at least until the Protestant Reformation, which helped to usher in the modern era).

Life in these preindustrial villages and premodern cities was far from idyllic. Landlords exploited their tenants, often taxing them to the brink of starvation. Neighbors argued with neighbors, and family feuds sometimes spanned generations. Sanitation was poor, medical care primitive, and early death common. But however difficult, the boundaries and contours of social life were known.

The Industrial Revolution altered both the physical and the social landscape. In the nineteenth century, factories, coal mines, railroads, and telegraph lines destroyed the isolation that had sheltered traditional agricultural communities. Factory towns appeared almost overnight, and urban populations mushroomed. By 1850, more people in Great Britain lived in towns and cities than in the countryside. (The United States did not become predominantly urban until the twentieth century.)

Traditional social relationships were torn apart in the process. A new class of capitalist entrepreneurs, specializing in manufacturing and trade, was pushing aside the old landed aristocracy. Many people left (or were forced to leave) their villages to become wage laborers in factory towns, in the process losing their self-sufficient lifestyle. The Industrial Revolution created both new jobs and unemployment. Urban riots and squalor created an unsettling image of mass poverty and the threat of crime and rebellion within European societies.

A second crucial factor in the rise of the modern era was the discovery (or rediscovery) of *cultural differences*. Voyages to the "far corners" of the earth, the growth of long-distance trade, and the establishment

Residents of an English children's home in the 1870s. These boys were vagrants, crippled by industrial accidents and homeless because their families had fallen apart. They became wards of a charitable organization, which could address only a small portion of the immense social problems caused by industrial capitalism.

of colonial empires forced Europeans to confront the enormous range of different cultures in the world, each with its distinctive language, customs, beliefs, system of government, and ways of life. Increasing contact between Europeans and non-Europeans changed lives on both sides, most obviously through colonialism and slavery. Some of the effects were material, such as the growing wealth and power of seafaring, trading countries like Britain. Equally important, these contacts challenged prevailing notions of human nature. Most Europeans believed that their own culture was clearly superior, but scholars were perplexed by cultural diversity. Where had European civilization come from, and where was it headed? Scholars began to look at other countries and epochs, not just to learn about those people and places for their own sake but also to draw lessons for modern Western society and to learn about themselves (Calhoun, 1995).

The third factor in the birth of the modern era was *political and intellectual turmoil.* The American and French revolutions replaced old notions of duty, tradition, and submission to authority with new ideas of individual rights, equality, and freedom, thus threat-

ening monarchs everywhere. In a similar way, the Renaissance, the Protestant Reformation, the scientific revolution, and the Enlightenment challenged long-established beliefs about nature, religion, and human life. These cultural movements not only produced new diversity within Europe (such as different religious faiths within Christianity) but also caused dramatic growth in knowledge and cultural discussion. The invention of the printing press in the fifteenth century—first used by Johannes Gutenberg to print a Lutheran Bible—helped to spread these new ways of thinking and new debates.

Commonsense explanations of the world, based on past experience, no longer applied. Social philosophy, which dealt with what society *should* be like, could not explain what was currently happening in the real world. People needed factual information, put into perspective by systematically tested theories, to help them understand and adapt to the modern era (Nisbet and Perrin, 1977). And so a new discipline—sociology—came into being.

Rooted in a revolutionary era, sociology still grapples with the challenges that era raised: social change and the factors that keep society knitted together even amid change; diversity and questions about the similarities and differences among societies; and the tension between scientific explanations of social life on the one hand and tradition, common sense, and public opinion on the other.

Classical Sociological Theories

The theorists we think of as the founders of sociology did not see themselves as just launching a new intellectual discipline, but also as addressing pressing public problems. Auguste Comte (1798–1857), a philosopher born in the chaos that followed the French Revolution, sought a means to bring social change under control. Inspired by the physical sciences, Comte called for systematic analysis of the laws of social life that would lead to more rational forms of social action and eventually a better society. He called this new science "sociology," the first use of the word. Herbert Spencer (1820–1903) also took his cue from the physical sciences. Spencer saw the study of human societies as part of the more general study of evolution. He emphasized that in both biology and society, changes in structure and function go hand in hand. Evolutionary theory—before and after Darwin—had an enormous impact on early sociology. Indeed, Darwin borrowed a key phrase, "survival of the fittest," from Spencer. Adam Smith, author of the extremely influential book *The Wealth of Nations* (1776/1976), is remembered today as an economist. But there was no distinction between the disciplines of sociology and economics in Smith's day, and his writings were rich with sociological insights (discussed below).

Only in the mid- to late nineteenth century, as part of the general demand for more scientific knowledge and education, was sociology recognized as a separate academic discipline in European universities and did sociologists become specialists (rather than general social scientists). Americans began to play a prominent role in sociology around the turn of the century. In the twentieth century, sociology—as a specialized field of research and training—spread throughout the world.

In the following sections we will introduce the most important founders of sociology. They remain important because they inspired distinct traditions of theory and research, which continue today, and because sociologists (and other social scientists) still study their work for new insights.

Adam Smith, Jeremy Bentham, and Rational-Choice Theory

Adam Smith (1723–1790), one of sociology's ancestors, was interested in what holds society together. In Smith's view, the power and authority of a ruler were not the only or even the main source of social cohesion; societies were also functionally integrated by people's economic dependence on one another and by market forces. Smith (1776/1976) believed that people make choices (what to buy, what to manufacture, what career to enter) on the basis of very rational cost–benefit calculations. In doing so, they consider mainly the consequences to themselves, not how their actions will affect others. Yet in a free-market system, Smith maintained, economic choices motivated purely by self-interest ultimately lead to the efficient production of the goods consumers want and a corresponding rise in society's wealth. Thus competition works like an "invisible hand" to streamline production, maximize profits, and guide labor and investment into areas where demand is greatest.

The British philosopher Jeremy Bentham (1748–1832) expanded and revised Smith's views. Bentham (1789/1970) stressed that humans everywhere are motivated to act in ways that maximize pleasure and minimize pain. He disagreed with Smith's view that individual decisions, made on the basis of self-interest, automatically add up to the greatest good for society as a whole. To Bentham, the public good (defined as the greatest benefit at the lowest cost for the greatest number of people) could best be achieved by scientifically planned government action—what he called a "visible hand." Cooperation among social actors is not automatic, even when it would produce greater benefit for more people. If a government with the power to demand cooperation does not intervene, Bentham claimed, conflict among actors is likely to break out, with each trying to gain at the expense of the others.

The rational-choice theory that Smith and Bentham pioneered is still influential in sociology. Rational-choice theory stresses the role of individual decisions in shaping social facts (Coleman, 1990). This approach has been applied to how businesses make market decisions, how people decide to invest in more education, and even how young people choose whom to date and marry. (See the journal *Rationality and Society*.) Rational-choice theory is particularly important in public-policy analysis, where it helps to identify who will gain or lose from a new public program.

In many ways, however, rational-choice theory was part of the established view against which other sociological theorists rebelled. Challenging the idea that social patterns can be explained as the sum of individual actions, other sociological thinkers stressed the role of groups, social structure, culture, and historical change in creating the conditions for social action.

Marx on Class Conflict and the Structure of Capitalism

An economic historian, social theorist, and revolutionary, Karl Marx (1818–1883) is best known as the father of modern communism. In addition, Marx made enormous contributions to the fields of sociology and economics.

Marx (1867/1976) believed that the most significant social fact about the industrial societies of his time was their capitalist social structure. The means of production were privately owned and used to produce profits. Capitalism was extremely productive. It helped to create enormous new wealth and eventually spread throughout the world. But Marx showed it was also a system prone to crises, to recessions and depressions. While capitalists might dream of a purely economic society in which government played little role, in fact they needed state power to make the economic system work and to keep those who lost in the competitive struggle from rebelling.

A central theme of Marx's social theory was the division of society into opposing classes. These class-es were not simply different from one another; they had deeply contradictory interests, and the conflict between them (for example, between slaves and slave owners) shaped the nature of all social life. The two most important and contradictory classes in capitalist society were the **capitalists,** or **bourgeoisie,** who owned the land, factories, and machines, and the **proletariat,** or workers, who actually produced economic goods through their labor.

This structural division of society into opposing classes had strong implications for power relations. To Marx the interests of the capitalists and the proletariat were inherently contradictory. Capitalists were driven to maximize profits by exploiting workers and holding their wages down. Workers suffered and therefore were driven to overthrow the capitalist system, seize the means of production, and establish a classless society in which wealth would be distributed evenly. Of course, capitalists and the governments they supported would use all the power they could muster to stop workers from changing the social order. Workers, accordingly, would need the power that came from their numbers in order to resist, and they would probably have to engage in prolonged conflict with their oppressors in order to overthrow them. Revolution might or might not occur, but friction and struggle over social values and goals were inevitable. According to Marx, class conflict is built into a capitalist system.

Marx argued that social structure, rooted in economic production and class relations, shapes social action and even culture. Thus, the agricultural peasant economies of the Middle Ages gave rise to strong communities and religious faith, while the industrial capitalist economies of the modern era bred individualism and a more scientific outlook. Marx further held that class conflict is "the engine of history," the primary source of social change. There is room for social action in his view, but it is never free from the influence of previous actions and above all social structure. "Men make their own history," Marx wrote, "but they do not make it under circumstances chosen by themselves, rather under circumstances directly encountered, given, and transmitted from the past" (Marx, 1852/1979, p. 103).

One of Marx's central contributions to sociology was his emphasis on collective struggle as a form of social action. Because a small elite controls most of the wealth in society, most individuals have relatively little power by themselves. But workers would gain the power to change this social structure if they

In Karl Marx's view, capitalist society is dominated by those who control the means of production and reap profits from the labor of others. The deep division between social classes leads to struggles over social power and eventually to revolution.

joined together in unions and political parties. This approach called not just for action but for a change in culture. Workers had to break free of capitalism's idea that everyone should be considered only as an individual; they had to develop **class consciousness,** a sense of their shared interests and problems. Until class consciousness was developed, the capitalists would use their power to shape the workers' religious beliefs, leisure activities, and consumer preferences, fostering a "false consciousness" among the proletariat—that is, a misleading cultural orientation that would prevent workers from realizing that they were being exploited. Culture thus reinforced the power of elites in capitalism's class-divided social structure. Unless workers could change that structure, Marx argued, they could not gain power. Thus, he advocated revolution, to seize government and use its power to change social structure.

Many contemporary sociologists are influenced by Marx. Few are Marxists in the sense of accepting his entire doctrine and its politics, especially in view of the recent collapse of communism in Eastern Europe and the Soviet Union, but many follow Marx in focusing on the importance of capitalism as a social structure yielding unequal economic power. Many also agree with his emphasis on how people who are weak as individuals gain in power when they are socially organized.

Durkheim on Social Solidarity

Another early sociologist with enormous influence was the Frenchman Émile Durkheim (1858–1917). While Durkheim did not agree with Marx's strong emphasis on the economy as the basis of social structure and on the inevitability of class divisions, he did share Marx's concern for the forces that bind people together, or what he called **social solidarity** (Durkheim, 1893/1985).

For Durkheim, the key to social solidarity was functional integration. In Durkheim's view, there were two basic forms of social solidarity, mechanical solidarity and organic solidarity. **Mechanical solidarity** is based on strongly shared beliefs, values, and customs. This is what holds together small, simple, tribal societies and traditional agricultural villages, where everyone views the world in much the same way and engages in the same activities. Large, complex, modern societies, in contrast, are knit together by what Durkheim called **organic solidarity,** an

Émile Durkheim believed that shared social bonds hold modern society together. Mutual trust and interdependency create a "collective conscience," or sense of belonging, and help to make society as a whole greater than, and distinct from, the sum of its individual members.

interdependence that is based on a complex division of labor. In a modern society each person earns money from a specialized occupation and then uses that money to buy goods and services that thousands of others have specialized roles in producing. The social bonds this system creates are extremely strong. People are interconnected because differences in their skills and roles make them need each other to survive. Functional integration is greatest in modern societies that are based on organic solidarity.

Durkheim (1895/1982) argued that society forms a whole that is greater than the sum of its parts, and the study of society is at a different level from the study of individuals. To clarify these points, he used the analogy of a living organism described earlier in the chapter (hence the term *organic* solidarity). A whole person is more than the sum of the cells and organs that make up the body; there are characteristics of the interconnected living system that transcend its collection of parts. So it is with societies, yet we can profitably study the parts and how each is important to the functioning of the whole system. Durkheim emphasized the ways in which different social activities and institutions (like families, schools, and courts) fit together and support one another—even though no one plans the whole. The whole, in Durkheim's functionalist view, is held together through the interrelated workings of its parts.

Using the same functionalist reasoning, Durkheim argued that shared values and practices derived from culture also play a role in knitting society together (Durkheim, 1912/1965; Alexander, 1988). For example, religious services are occasions not only for worshiping God but also for affirming social bonds among members of the congregation and between the congregation and society as a whole. Religion and other elements of culture also function to provide people with a sense of rules and limits, with ideas about what they can reasonably expect. In times of rapid social change, such as the Industrial Revolution, these ideas are challenged. When reality deviates too far from expectations society suffers from **anomie**—a state in which breakdowns of social norms or rules make it difficult for people to maintain a clear sense of who they are, where their lives will take them, and what it all means.

Durkheim's main contribution to sociology was to define the broadly shared features of social life—culture, social structure, and especially functional integration—as social facts that must be studied on their own terms.

Weber on Rationalization and Status

Max Weber (1864–1920) was one of the most important German intellectuals of his day. Like the other early sociologists, Weber (1904/1958) believed that social facts must be analyzed using scientific methods. In contrast to Durkheim, Weber maintained that social facts are nothing more (or less) than the cumulative result of the social actions of individuals. Sociological explanations, he argued, must derive from an understanding of why individual people choose the actions they do. Where rational-choice theory stressed analysis of actors' "objective" interests, however, Weber stressed their subjective understanding and motivation. Sociologists must try to see actions from the point of view of the actor, looking beyond objective behavior to the subjective thoughts and feelings that shape particular actions. They must

Max Weber focused on the interplay of economic, political, and cultural factors in producing the distinctive social organization of the modern West. He stressed that for this type of organization, individuals had to adopt a more rational and less traditional orientation to social action.

interpret, not just observe. Weber called this approach *verstehen*, a German word that means empathetic understanding.

Like Marx and Durkheim, Weber wanted to understand the rapid social changes occurring in his time. He believed that the most significant trend in the modern era was an increasing *rationalization* of social action and social institutions—that is, a shift from traditional orientations (in which people accept the wisdom of the past as a guide to the future and strive to follow the ways of their ancestors) to more logical orientations (in which people assess the consequences of an act in deciding how to behave) (Weber, 1922/1968; see also Brubaker, 1984; Roth and Schluchter, 1979). The rise of science as the principal means of acquiring knowledge, the emergence of governments based on the rule of law, and the development of capitalism were all signs of this trend toward rationalization. For example, capitalism requires people to analyze markets, maximize the efficiency of production, calculate returns on investment, and create financial institutions to support economic expansion, all of which demand a logical, reasoned approach to the world. Rationalization, in turn, led to a dramatic increase in the power of formal organizations, from governments to giant corporations.

But Weber felt there was more to capitalism than rational calculation. Marx, he thought, had put too much emphasis on economic structure, ignoring the influence of culture on social action. More specifically, Weber saw capitalism as a product of cultural changes, particularly changes in religious beliefs and values. He maintained that the Protestant Reformation, which held individuals responsible for their own salvation and promoted the work ethic, laid the groundwork for capitalism (see Chapter 15). In Weber's view, people's cultural ideas play independent and important roles in shaping their actions and thus in determining the structure of society, including the economic system. Thus, economic changes sometimes *follow* cultural changes, not the other way around as Marx claimed.

Like Marx, Weber believed that power and conflict are fundamental elements of social life. But he argued that people's economic positions do not necessarily determine how the lines of the power struggle will be drawn. Often, he said, we care more about other social factors—such as race, religion, and personal tastes—in defining where people fit in the social hierarchy. These other social factors are the basis of **status groups.** Weber thought that status groups were at least as important as economic class in shaping political activity. In the United States, for instance, working-class whites might try to maintain their superior status over working-class blacks, even at the expense of joining together politically to improve their economic lot. Status-group differences generally work in favor of elites. When a person must go to the right schools, speak with the right accent, and have the right manners in order to be included at the top, many newly wealthy people will be barred from elite status, and elite groups will remain small and privileged.

Mead and Symbolic Interactionism

Many twentieth-century sociologists share Weber's belief in the importance of culture and social action. Whereas Weber was concerned mainly with broad generalizations about large-scale organization patterns, however, other sociologists have focused on the small-scale phenomena that make up everyday interaction. The goal of these other sociologists is to understand how individuals subjectively experience and understand their social worlds and how different people come to share a common definition of reality (Schutz and Luckmann, 1973).

The American school of sociology called **symbolic interactionism** centers around these concerns. Two founders of this school were George Herbert Mead (1863–1931) and W. I. Thomas (1863–1947), both of the University of Chicago. They began with the idea that much of human behavior is determined not only by the objective facts of a situation but also by how

Everyday human interactions were of major interest to George Herbert Mead. He viewed words, gestures, and expressions as symbols of what we think and feel; these symbols constitute the very foundations of social life.

people define that situation—that is, by the meanings they attribute to it. The most famous statement of this position comes from Thomas: "If men define situations as real, then they are real in their consequences" (Thomas and Thomas, 1928, p. 572). Suppose, for example, that you define American city streets as too dangerous to walk on at night. As a result, you never venture out after dark. In this case, an objective fact (the actual crime rate) is not determining your behavior as much as your understanding of the crime rate. That understanding is real for you because it keeps you home. Sometimes our definitions of situations become self-fulfilling prophecies (Merton, 1968a). If most people think it's too dangerous to go out after dark and so stay indoors, the absence of people on the streets can actually make the streets more dangerous because there are few people to observe or deter crimes.

Elaborating on the importance of our understandings of social situations, Mead reasoned that we learn what behavior and events mean through *interaction* with others. Through such interaction we come to learn our "places" in the social world and the roles we are expected to play in different situations. Even our sense of identity or self is shaped through social interaction, Mead (1934) asserted. By this he meant that we come to know ourselves largely by seeing how others react to us. But a person's thoughts and feelings are not directly accessible to others. Rather, we communicate by way of *symbols*—words, gestures, facial expressions, and other sounds and actions that have common, widely understood interpretations. Thus, much human behavior is shaped by symbolic interaction.

Symbolic interactionists focus on everyday behavior, such as what happens when you approach your instructor after class with a question. You first assess what the instructor is doing in order to determine how best to make your approach. If the instructor is talking to another student, you probably interpret this to mean that she is busy, and you remain silent. When you do speak, you monitor both your own words and actions and your instructor's responses. If the instructor smiles and leans slightly toward you, you probably assume she is being encouraging, so you continue confidently. If, however, she frequently glances out the window or at her watch as you speak, you probably read her actions as signs of impatience and may cut short what you have to say. In this way you exchange tentative cues and feedback as you fashion your social behavior. The result is the emergence of a shared understanding of what the situation means. Such shared understandings are essential to social life and of primary concern to interactionists (Blumer, 1969/1986). (We will examine this approach in greater depth in Chapter 3.)

W. E. B. Du Bois on Double Consciousness

In the United States, a key task for sociology was to come to terms with racial and cultural differences. One of the first African-Americans to receive a degree from Harvard University led the way. W. E. B. Du Bois (1868–1963) began his studies in Tennessee at Fisk University, a leading center of African-American higher education. A member of the black elite himself, while at Fisk Du Bois was exposed to the intense poverty of the rural South. At Harvard, he pursued his interest in philosophy, studying under William James. After graduating from Harvard, Du Bois began to move away from pure philosophy toward social science, seeking to develop a combination of theory and empirical methodology that would enable him to apply reliable, factual inquiries to major social problems (Zamir, 1995).

Du Bois held that the advancement of a large, historically subordinated population like African-Americans depended on education and on the leadership of a small elite, what he called "the talented tenth." This idea appealed to the emerging, upwardly mobile black middle class and contributed to the growth of integrationist organizations such as the NAACP (National Association for the Advancement of Colored People), in which Du Bois played a leading role. Du Bois's idea was also attacked (both during and after his lifetime) both by those who saw it as elitist and by those who favored a separatist solution to African-American problems or a return to Africa. An activist in black American struggles throughout his life, during the Great Depression of the 1930s Du Bois modified his earlier views and developed a more radical theory, influenced in part by Marxism. Du Bois also pioneered the study of the great sub-Saharan African civilizations that had been virtually ignored by European and American scholars, and he became more sympathetic to pan-Africanism, eventually moving to Ghana shortly before his death.

Three themes dominated Du Bois's sociological work. The first was the idea of "double consciousness" and the broader issue of the social construction of identity. Du Bois introduced this concept in *The Souls of Black Folk* (1903)—a book remarkable even for its title and the use of *Black* rather than *Negro,* which was the polite term at that time. **Double consciousness,** Du Bois wrote, is

> this sense of always looking at one's self through the eyes of others, of measuring one's soul by the tape of a world that looks back with amused contempt and pity. One ever feels his two-ness,—an American, a Negro; two souls, two thoughts, two unreconciled strivings; two warring ideas in one dark body, whose dogged strength alone keeps it from being torn asunder. (1903, p. 2)

Although Du Bois emphasized the specific double consciousness of being black and American, the concept could be applied to many other "outsider" situations (such as the experience of being a woman in a man's world) as well as to situations of consciousness split in more than two directions (such as the experience of African-American women, who may feel torn between their racial identities and their gender identities).

Du Bois linked double consciousness to the idea of a "veil" that obscured parts of a person's identity even from herself or himself, but he rejected the notion that double consciousness is something that could (or should) be overcome by choosing one side or the other. According to Du Bois, the inner tensions of double consciousness are reflections of outer or objective social conflict and therefore are important mechanisms for coping with social experience. The challenge for individuals is to find ways of integrat-

American sociologist and novelist W. E. B. DuBois helped to create the NAACP. During the 1930s he was influenced by the writings of Karl Marx, amd was, throughout his life, interested in the great sub-Saharan civilizations that had been largely ignored by European and white American scholars.

ing the two views of self into a stronger personal identity that changes the meaning of each. The challenge for society is to make creative use of differences, rather than seeing others in terms of fixed stereotypes or forcing everyone into the same cultural mold.

This notion led to Du Bois's second theme, collective struggle. Culture and social structure are not fixed and immutable, he argued. Though external and beyond the control of individuals, these aspects of society are subject to change through collective struggle. For example, the concept of race and the division of the human family into races on the basis of skin color is not a given, but rather is the result of social action and cultural influence (Du Bois, 1940). By extension, ideas about racial divisions can be changed through social action. Du Bois singled out three arenas for struggle—work, culture, and liberty—which correspond to the basic needs of individuals and to the basic requirements for a good life together in society. Striving to make a better society requires paying attention to all three and how they are interrelated, and thus it is both a spiritual and a material quest.

Third, Du Bois argued that both social and individual life are characterized by continual striving to reduce tensions and bring ideal possibilities into real existence. Whereas other sociologists saw struggle in terms of evolutionary ideas of the survival of the fittest, Du Bois maintained that human beings struggle not just to survive but to realize ideals. Different civilizations offer not only different designs for living but also different ideals and different strategies for realizing these ideals, whether in the form of technologies, patterns of social organization, or systems of religious beliefs. It is important to learn from one another and to be open to how different groups exercise creativity in their struggles. As Paul Gilroy has observed (1993), following Du Bois, the black cultures of the United States, the Caribbean, and Britain are both distinct and intertwined. African-American jazz influenced the development of reggae in Jamaica, and both influenced hip-hop, rap, and other musical currents in America and Britain. Musicians do not reflect just one, single culture but rather multiple and divergent influences; part of their creativity lies in knitting these together into a new whole.

Later sociologists have drawn on Du Bois's writings not only to better understand the impact of race on African-American life but also to gain insights into other issues. The idea of double consciousness, for example, and the broader issue of identity are important resources for making sense of cultural diversity and the many possible "doublings" that shape social and individual identities. In a world characterized by mass migration, the globalization of culture, and social movements based on differences in identity and lifestyle, this has become an increasingly important issue (Calhoun, 1994b).

Feminism and the Limits of Classical Theory

In the late eighteenth century, the Englishwoman Mary Wolstonecraft pointed out that theories of social and political rights were framed entirely from the male perspective. Answering Thomas Paine's famous appeal, *The Rights of Man,* written during the American Revolution, Wolstonecraft published *The Rights of Women.* Her work was cut short by early death—ironically, death in childbirth, a scourge on women that only became the object of medical attention very recently. (Her daughter, who survived, was Mary Shelley, the author of *Frankenstein, or the Modern Prometheus.*) During the nineteenth century, a number of women became involved in the social issues of the day. In America, the most important were Jane Addams and Charlotte Perkins Gilman. These women combined an active interest in social work with contributions to social theory. Addams was one of the founders of Hull House in Chicago, the first social work agency in this country; Gilman raised theoretical points about social issues, such as the impact on women's lives of a legal system in which they had no economic or political rights.

Despite the contributions of these and other pioneers, the voice of women was largely ignored by early sociologists (and other social scientists). Nor did male sociologists of the late nineteenth and early twentieth century pay much attention to women's lives or the ways in which gender shaped social relations, culture, and social action. The generic use of the word *man,* as though it included women as a subordinate category, was standard; researchers and theorists alike commonly wrote about social roles, such as citizen, economic actor, and cultural producer, as though they referred automatically and only to men (unless otherwise noted). None of the founding sociological theorists paid more than passing attention to the study of women's lives or the role of gender differences in society.

It was only in the 1960s and 1970s that the combination of the woman's movement and the growing number of female social scientists began to change this bias. When women (and to a much lesser extent men) called on social science to recognize the importance of gender in social life, however, they drew on the work of the founding theorists for conceptual tools. They examined the way that gender was shaped by social class, following Marx, and by race, following Du Bois. They examined the role women played in achieving the social solidarity that Durkheim emphasized—bearing primary responsibility not only for nurturing children but also for resolving conflicts within and between families and maintaining connections among family members as families were dispersed by the migrations and job changes characteristic of the modern era. Following Mead's lead, they examined the way gender shapes patterns of social interaction, discovering, for example, contrasting styles of male and female conversation (Tannen, 1994). Learning from Weber, they studied the impact of "rationalization" on gender roles. The twentieth-century emergence of professional specialists in fields from medicine to social work to embalming, and the growth of mass production and marketing of food, medicine, and clothing brought traditionally unpaid "women's work" into the commercial economy, at the same time making the work of "homemakers" less important. Now people could buy goods and services once provided at no cost by wives, mothers, and daughters.

Feminist theorists learned from the theories of the founding sociologists—and often disagreed with them. Such disagreement is not uncommon in science. Sociologists need the guidance and the analytic tools provided by those who have gone before, but they also need the courage to go beyond these teachers as they pursue their own studies.

Feminist sociologists are concerned with more than conducting the same sorts of research with women that have already been done with men. First and foremost, feminists call on sociology to recognize and take seriously the role of gender differences and gender relations in structuring virtually all aspects of social life. From personal identity and intimate relationships through education, work, and even the process of aging, not only are men's and women's lives different, but both are deeply shaped by the way cultures define genders. In Western societies, for example, women typically live longer than men (a fact influenced by male gender roles that contribute to higher rates of early deaths from war, crime, and heart attacks). The widespread view that women should define themselves in relationship to men (as wives or lovers) does not accommodate the fact that most will live the last ten years of their lives or more almost exclusively in the company of women.

Feminists have identified bias and distortions in the founding theories of sociology. As Dorothy Smith (1992) has shown, sociology was molded by men's special interest in those social settings where men are most prominent—the government, markets, religious hierarchies, corporations, and the like. Sociologists have paid much more attention to formal organizations, for example, than to family life. Traditionally, women have been locked out of public life; but at the same time, men knew little about the private world—for example, the suburban world middle-class men left behind when they went to their offices. This led to gaps in knowledge and biases in concepts. For example, economists used the word "work" to refer exclusively to paid employment, neglecting the economic value of housework, done primarily by women. According to Smith, doing sociology from women's standpoint will not just improve our understanding of women, or even of gender roles, but will also lead to a better understanding of personal relationships, which traditionally have been women's domain.

Just as sociology as a whole has grown and improved because of the contributions of feminist theory, so feminist theory benefits from advances in sociology. African-American sociologists, among others, have pointed to a bias in Smith's work (Collins, 1990). By focusing on the lives of middle-class, overwhelmingly white, suburban women like herself, Smith helped correct a gender bias in sociology but perpetuated a racial bias. The experiences of women of color—including their experience of being women—differ significantly from those of white women.

New viewpoints have led sociologists to challenge one of the basic assumptions of classical sociological theory—namely, that one can discover universal laws and principles of social behavior that will apply regardless of time period, cultural setting, and social actors. A more critical approach to sociology holds that one must always pay attention to the history of a theory, its cultural roots, and the social actors and actions that promoted (or suppressed) it. Advances in theory are not just the result of theorists changing their minds but also reflect changes in the social world a theory seeks to explain. Diverse voices are not a sign of indecision but a source of creativity.

Feminist sociology is perhaps the most important branch of critical social theory today.

In short, sociology continues to grow beyond its foundations. Theory continues to be revisited, revised, and rebuilt in light of greater knowledge and new issues. This keeps sociology a living science.

SUMMARY

1. Sociology is the study of human society and the many dimensions of social action and social relationships. C. Wright Mills coined the term sociological imagination to describe the ability of people to view their personal experiences in the context of what is happening in the world around them and to grasp broader patterns that are not accessible through personal experience alone.

2. Five key concepts have proved extremely useful in helping sociologists understand our complex, ever-changing social world. These concepts are social structure (relatively stable, enduring patterns of social relationships, of social positions, and of numbers of people); social action (conscious behavior that both influences and is influenced by the actions of others); culture (the shared ways of thinking, understanding, evaluating, and communicating that make up a people's way of life); power (the ability of a social actor to control the actions of others, either directly or indirectly); and function (the contribution a relationship, position, organization, or other social phenomenon makes to a larger social whole). In a functionally integrated system, what happens to one part of the system affects, and is affected by, the others.

3. Like all sciences, sociology rests on empirical observation (data that is collected with the aid of abstraction and interpretation and is subject to replication) and logical analysis (which entails identifying units of analysis, identifying relationships, and building theory).

4. Social facts are enduring properties of social life that shape or constrain the actions individuals can take. Social facts are not located in individuals but result from the interactions of individuals and groups.

5. Sociology emerged during the eighteenth and nineteenth centuries, a period of rapid social change. The "modern era" has its roots in the emergence of urban, capitalist, industrial society; the discovery of different (non-European) cultures: and political and intellectual turmoil. The views of the sociological thinkers of this period remain influential today.

6. Adam Smith was a founder of rational-choice theory, which holds that in making decisions people choose the course of action that is most advantageous to them. Jeremy Bentham expanded this concept. He maintained that government intervention is needed to help society function

smoothly and to allow as many people as possible to benefit from society's resources.

7. Karl Marx showed that the economic system of a society shapes all other aspects of social life and breeds persistent social conflict. According to Marx, power in a capitalist system is in the hands of the capitalists, who dominate the workers. The only way for workers to overcome their oppression is through planned social action and revolution.

8. Émile Durkheim focused on the social forces that bind a society together, a phenomenon he called social solidarity. Mechanical solidarity is based on a strong sharing of values, customs, and beliefs. Organic solidarity is interdependence that is based on a complex division of labor. Durkheim emphasized the functional relationships among different parts of society and warned of the dangers of anomie.

9. Max Weber is important for introducing into sociology an awareness of the subjective nature of social life, for balancing Marx's emphasis on economic forces with an equal stress on culture, and for balancing Durkheim's emphasis on functional integration with attention to power. To Weber, the most fundamental trend in the modern era is an increasing rationalization of social action and social institutions.

10. George Herbert Mead and the symbolic interactionists focused on everyday interaction rather than broader, large-scale social patterns. They maintained that people address and respond to others depending on how they interpret each other's cues, from which they develop a shared definition of the social situation.

11. W. E. B. Du Bois—novelist, activist, and sociologist—introduced the concept of double consciousness and the creation of identities, analyzed the role of collective struggle in social change, and emphasized human striving to achieve ideals.

12. Responding to long-standing neglect of the importance of gender, feminist sociologists have highlighted both the cultural processes that shape gender differences and their social consequences. Feminists not only conduct empirical research on women, but also develop new theories reshaping our understanding of social processes in general by focusing both on gender and on social activities and domains in which men have been less prominent than women.

REVIEW QUESTIONS

1. Define the five key concepts in sociology, and give an example of each.

2. What are the roles of logic and empirical observation in sociology?

3. Outline the origins of sociology and how it was shaped by the development of modern society.

4. Compare and contrast rational-choice theory and the perspectives of Marx, Durkheim, Weber, and Mead.

5. How do sociologists address issues of cultural or gender difference?

CRITICAL THINKING QUESTIONS

1. Use the sociological imagination to show the social side of some personal experience that you have had. Use at least one social fact in your response. Show how the sociological approach goes beyond common sense in accounting for your experience.

2. Select a major current event and apply the five key concepts to it.

3. Find a newspaper story about some social issue. How might common sense and sociology differ in explaining the issue?

4. How would the five key concepts each help explain some issue on your campus, such as sexual harassment, crime, increasing tuition rates, or academic dishonesty?

5. Show how neglect of either race or gender (or both) would distort understanding of an important social issue.

GLOSSARY

Anomie Disruption in the rules and understandings that guide and integrate social life and give individuals a sense of their place in it.

Bourgeoisie The social class in a capitalist industrialized society that owns and controls the means of production (the land, factories, machinery, and so forth).

Capitalists Members of the bourgeoisie. Capital is property that can be used to produce further wealth.

Class consciousness A sense of shared interests and problems among members of a social class.

Culture The shared, more or less integrated way of thinking, understanding, evaluating, and communicating that make up a people's way of life.

Data In science, information that is specifically relevant to the questions being asked.

Double consciousness A mismatch between one's image of oneself and the identity (or identities) ascribed to one by society.

Empirical observation The organization of sensory information into scientific data by processes of abstraction, interpretation, and replication.

Function The contribution a social relationship, position, organization, value, or other phenomenon makes to a larger social whole.

Functional integration The degree to which the different parts of a social system are so closely interrelated that what happens in one affects the others and is influenced by them in turn.

Logical analysis The development of theory by identifying distinct units of analysis and relationships among them.

Mechanical solidarity Solidarity that is based on common beliefs, values, and customs.

Organic solidarity Interdependence among a group of people that is based on an intricate division of labor.

Power The ability of a social actor to determine the shape of events or the structure of social organization.

Proletariat The members of a capitalist industrialized society who have no control over the means of production; the term refers primarily to the workers.

Science A systematic way of observing nature, interpreting what we see objectively, searching for relationships of cause and effect, and organizing knowledge through theory.

Social action Behavior that is intentional, not instinctive; depends on social conditions created by others; and affects other social actors.

Social facts Enduring properties of social life that shape or constrain the actions individuals can take.

Social solidarity The condition that results when underlying social forces bind people together.

Social structure Relatively stable, enduring patterns of social relationships, or social positions, and of numbers of people; patterns over which individuals have little control.

Sociological imagination A way of looking at our personal experiences in the context of what is happening in the world and perceiving broader social patterns that are not apparent through personal experience alone.

Sociology The study of human society, including both social action and the organization of social relationships.

Status groups Groups based on race, religion, personal tastes, and other noneconomic factors, which help establish a social hierarchy.

Symbolic interactionism An approach to human behavior as constructed in interaction and interpreted through culture, stressing the collective attribution of meaning to social life.

Theory A systematic attempt to explain how two or more phenomena are related.

Verstehen Weber's term for an empathetic understanding of what people are thinking and feeling.

CHAPTER 2

Methods of Sociological Research

An electrician found him lying in a pool of blood, a shotgun nearby: Kurt Cobain, age 27, leader of the rock band Nirvana, often described as the "crown prince of Generation X" (*Newsweek,* April 18, 1995). Nirvana's rocket ride to fame and fortune was apparently as unappreciated as it was unexpected. Cobain and other band members despised the slick, MTV-dominated rock establishment with its false idols, such as Madonna and Michael Jackson. The group's music was deliberately nasty and controversial, their tattered clothes and stringy hair deliberately grungy, yet their first major-label album sold nearly 10 million copies worldwide. With lyrics like "Oh, well, whatever, never mind," Cobain became the spokesman for nineties alienation.

A child of divorce, Cobain was sickly and unhappy, dabbling in drugs and dropping out of school. After Cobain's death, his father, to whom he had not spoken for eight years, said, "Everything I knew about Kurt, I've read in newspapers and magazines." Friends described Cobain as gentle and caring but also as self-destructive, frequently experiencing bouts of depression and engaging in drug abuse.

When news of Cobain's suicide hit the media, radio stations (especially in his home base, Seattle) were flooded with calls by distraught fans. One disc jockey began broadcasts by saying "Don't do it" and then frequently repeated the number of a suicide hotline.

We think of suicide as the most personal of all acts; as a decision individuals make for themselves, out of despair, anguish, or loss of interest in living. When a number of other young people took their own lives following Cobain's death, however, people were reminded that suicide is influenced by social factors—including famous examples. Suicide rates are generally higher in areas where radio stations broadcast

Durkheim classified suicide into four types according to the motivation for self-destruction. The death of Marilyn Monroe, which captured media attention around the world, is an example of egoistic suicide. The Japanese kamikaze pilots of World War II, some of whom are shown posing before their fatal mission, gave their lives in altruistic suicide. The panic of crowds on Wall Street during the 1929 stock market crash preceded widespread despair that led to cases of anomic suicide. Killing oneself in a seemingly hopeless situation, such as in prison, is an act of fatalistic suicide.

music emphasizing such problems as marital discord, alcohol abuse, and alienation from work (Stack and Gunlach, 1992). Moreover, the rate of suicide among teenagers is rising (see Figure 2.1). Suicide is the third-leading killer of fifteen- to twenty-four-year-olds (U.S. Department of Health and Human Services, 1995b).

Individual suicides can be the result of changes in employment prospects, family problems, disagreement with social values, and many other personal problems, but sociologists seek to understand suicide as a social *pattern.* They look not just at individual cases but at suicide *rates*—that is, at the proportions of suicides in different social groups. The insight that these rates could be explained as social facts led the great French sociologist Émile Durkheim to undertake one of the most important pieces of social research ever produced.

In Durkheim's day, as in our own, suicide was usually explained in individual terms: The victims were

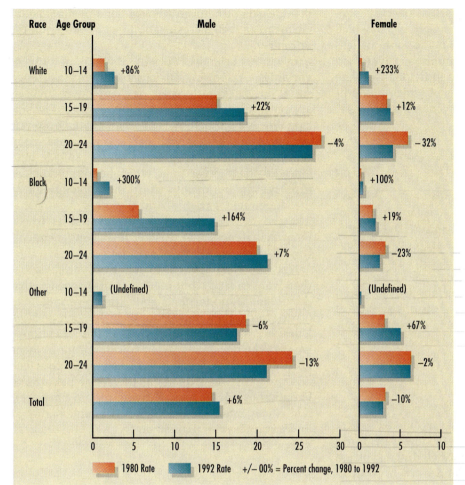

FIGURE 2.1 / Suicide Rates for Americans Ages Ten to Twenty-Four, 1980 and 1992

Psychological case studies may explain individual suicides, but they do not explain variations or changes in the *rates* of suicide among different social groups. Why is the rate of suicide climbing for ten- to nineteen-year-olds but not for most twenty- to twenty-four-year-olds? Why is the suicide rate for black youth—especially black males—rising faster than for white males and other youth?

Source: Adapted from U.S. Department of Health and Human Services, *Morbidity and Mortality Weekly Report,* April 2, 1995, p. 290.

assumed to be depressed, mentally ill, or stricken with some unbearable loss. But Durkheim knew that suicide was more common among some groups than others, and he suspected that this was due to social factors, not just to chance. He used systematic collection of data to help him test this suspicion, gathering information about the rates of suicide in different countries, in different seasons, and among people who belonged to different social categories and groups. He used government records that listed numbers of suicides and gave statistics about the victims: their age, sex, marital status, nationality, religion, and so forth.

Upon analyzing this information, Durkheim found that the usual explanations for suicide were inadequate. Suicide *rates* (not just numbers) varied between countries, between times of year, and between groups. If suicide were caused solely by personal

problems, why was there so much variation in its rates? He checked to see if it was simply because some groups had higher rates of mental illness, but the relationship between mental illness rates and suicide rates was not consistent. Some groups had high rates of mental illness but low rates of suicide; other groups showed high rates of both. Durkheim also noticed that women were more likely than men to be diagnosed as mentally ill but were less likely to commit suicide. Other unexpected information surfaced: Durkheim discovered that most people committed suicide during warmer, sunnier times of the year, not, as might be expected, during the cold, gloomy days of winter.

The facts and statistics that he collected led Durkheim to conclude that suicide, at least in part, depended on social circumstances. As he wrote in his classic study, *Suicide* (1897/1951, p. 145), suicide is based on "social causes and is itself a collective phe-nomenon." Characteristics of the *social group* in which people find themselves make suicide more or less likely; self-destruction is not simply a private act. Durkheim explained apparently individual, private acts in terms of collective causes of which the indi-vidual actors might not have been consciously aware.

SOCIOLOGY AND SCIENTIFIC RESEARCH

Durkheim's overriding goal was to establish sociolo-gy as a science. As we saw in Chapter 1, the scientif-ic method requires the systematic, empirical, and log-ical collection and analysis of data. In studying sui-cide, Durkheim was determined to show first, that the scientific method could be applied to social behavior and second, that the results of sociological research added a new dimension to our understand-ing of our world and ourselves.

The Research Process

Durkheim's research followed seven "model" steps: defining the problem, reviewing the literature, form-ing a hypothesis, choosing a research design, collect-ing data, analyzing the data, and drawing conclu-sions (see Figure 2.2). Each of these steps is crucial, but they do not always occur in precisely the model order.

Defining the Problem

The first step, defining the problem, is not as simple as one might think. What is suicide? A commonsense definition would be "deliberately ending one's own life." By this definition, jumping off a bridge or putting a bullet in one's head clearly qualify, but what about *not* taking necessary medication or *not* getting out of the way of a speeding truck? What about a soldier who sacrifices his own life to save his comrades in battle? Durkheim decided to count as *suicide* "all cases of death resulting directly or indi-rectly from a positive or negative act of the victim himself, which he knows will produce this result." By specifying both "doing" and "not doing," Durkheim broadened the commonsense definition of suicide to

include acts of heroism (the soldier's positive act of altruism) as well as resignation (*not* avoiding illness or injury).

Like other scientists, sociologists think in terms of **variables.** A sociological variable is any aspect of social life that can fluctuate or change over time, or appear in different amounts or frequencies. The sui-cide rate is a variable because it fluctuates from one period to another, as well as varying across social groups. Durkheim assumed that the suicide rate *depended* on other variables, which he sought to iden-tify. Thus, in Durkheim's study, the suicide rate was the **dependent variable,** and the other factors that influence it were the **independent variables** (those that fluctuate for other reasons, that is, independent-ly of changes in the rate of suicide).

Not only must researchers define the variables that they want to study, but they must also specify what they want to understand about those variables. In other words, they must state their research *problem*. Durkheim's problem—the focus of his attention—was not the question of what suicide meant to those killed themselves, nor how it made their families feel. His problem was explaining the social patterns of variation in suicide rates. Why do certain times, cer-tain places, and certain social groups have higher or lower suicide rates than others?

Reviewing the Literature

Sociologists decide what research questions to ask and where to look for answers largely on the basis of a review of the literature concerning the topic of interest to them. Durkheim, for instance, looked to see what was known about suicide. He found few existing studies regarding the causes of group differ-ences in suicide rates. This told him that his proposed research was not an unnecessary duplication of effort. It would fill a wide gap in human knowledge. Durkheim's review of the literature acquainted him with a number of existing theories. For instance, some people had claimed that suicide probably occurred most often in the bleak, cold months of winter. Looking at the data, Durkheim found this was *not* true. Durkheim also tested the theory that suicide is encouraged by the power of suggestion; that people decide to kill themselves because others put the idea of suicide into their minds. Durkheim's findings indicated that although suggestion may play a part, it probably is not a major cause of suicide.

FIGURE 2.2 / *Steps in the "Model" Research Process*

1. Defining the Problem Selecting a topic for research and defining key concepts	**5. Collecting the Data** Collecting the information that will test the hypothesis
2. Reviewing the Literature Familiarizing oneself with the existing theory and research on a topic	**6. Analyzing the Data** Working with and examining the data to shed light on the hypothesis
3. Forming a Hypothesis Defining the relationship between measurable variables so that they can be measured and the hypothesis tested	**7. Drawing Conclusions** Summarizing the outcome of the study, indicating its significance, relating the findings to existing theory and research, and identifying problems for future research
4. Choosing a Research Design Selecting a method for study: experiment, survey, field observation, or a historical approach	

In conducting research, all sociologists follow the same basic steps, though not necessarily in the same order.

Thus, Durkheim's research allowed him to both evaluate some old theories of suicide and explore the value of new ones.

Forming a Hypothesis

Durkheim's view of social life centered on the concept of *functional integration,* (see Chapter 1). He believed that some of the most important influences on people stemmed from how well integrated their social groups were—that is, on the social relationships and shared moral values of the group members. Well-integrated groups, Durkheim argued, were able to provide their members with effective social supports, a clear set of values, and a strong sense of self-identity. These ideas enabled Durkheim to form a hypothesis about suicide. A **hypothesis** is a tentative statement about how two or more variables affect, or are related to, each other. Durkheim's main hypothesis was that the more integrated people are into social groups, the less likely they are to commit suicide. The two variables involved in this hypothesis are (1) the degree of integration in a social group and (2) the rate of suicide. Durkheim proposed that the first of these variables is inversely related to the other: that is, the *lower* the level of social integration, the *higher* the rate of suicide.

Choosing a Research Design and Collecting Data

To test their hypotheses, researchers need facts, or **data:** statistics, interview results, and other pertinent information. The first step in gathering data is to decide how to observe and, if possible, measure the different variables to be studied. Some variables (such as the suicide rate) can be studied more or less directly. Others (such as degrees of alienation) can be studied only indirectly. An **indicator** is a "stand-in" measure: something that can be measured empirically in order to get information about an abstract variable that is difficult to measure directly. To measure social integration, Durkheim chose as indicators such factors as martial status and church membership. He reasoned that people who were married and active members of a church are more integrated into society than those who are single and have no church ties. The set of clearly measurable indicators gave Durkheim an **operational definition** of social integration.

The next step in gathering data is to choose a research design, that is, an actual plan for collecting the information that is needed. Some researchers conduct surveys and ask questions of many different people. Some investigators choose participant observation, living and working among the people being studied to learn firsthand how they think and behave. Some researchers conduct experiments; for example, they create an artificial situation in which they can observe how people respond to different stimuli. Still other researchers use historical records to gather data. For many problems, the best approach involves a combination of several research strategies: surveys plus observation plus document searches. We discuss all these specific data-gathering methods later in this chapter.

Whatever research design is used, the researchers' goal is to gather enough information to (1) develop a sound understanding of the problem and (2) test their hypothesis. Although this may sound simple and straightforward, it is often very difficult. Not only can a researcher encounter problems in collecting data, but a given set of data can often be interpreted in several different ways. Durkheim, for example, chose to rely on official government records that listed causes of death. This meant that he had to accept the interpretations that government officials, physicians, and family members gave of why a person died. Often, however, relatives are reluctant to admit that a death was suicide so official statistics probably underestimate the actual number of suicides.

Analyzing the Data and Drawing Conclusions

Once sociologists have collected their data, the next step is to analyze this information, often in the form of *statistics,* or data expressed in numbers. Analysis is the process of figuring out which parts go together to form a pattern or whole and how these pieces are related. To analyze statistics, sociologists use a number of measures (see the box "Basic Statistical Concepts"). However, analysis begins well before data are gathered. In defining the research problem, the sociologist decides what factors to study and how to measure them.

In analyzing his data, Durkheim looked for the social conditions under which suicide occurred more often and those under which it occurred less often. He found that Protestants committed suicide three times more often than Catholics, and Catholics more often than Jews. Single people committed suicide more often than married people, and married people with children least often of all. Durkheim reasoned that suicide rates are higher when people feel few or weak ties to a social group or community. He called this individualistic pattern **egoistic suicide.** The Jewish community was more tightly knit than the Catholic, the Catholic more tightly knit than the Protestant. Married people, especially those with children, had stronger social attachments than single people.

Common sense linked suicides to poverty, but Durkheim showed this to be false. Moreover, rapid economic improvement as well as decline was associated with more suicides. Any rapid change, Durkheim argued, may disrupt or undermine the social and cultural norms that give life meaning and give individuals a strong sense of identity, appropriate goals, and limits to their desires (see Chapter 1 on *anomie*). This loss of norms and meaning led to **anomic suicide.**

Durkheim also noted two other types of suicide. Very strong social groups could encourage **altruistic suicide,** as when a soldier chooses certain death to win a battle, save comrades, or avoid betraying his side if captured. This was in a sense the opposite of egoism. **Fatalistic suicide** occurred when people with terminal illnesses or other reasons to see their "real" lives as behind them and their futures as bleak chose to commit suicide.

The final step in the research process is to draw conclusions based on the results of analysis. An important task in drawing conclusions is to show how a particular piece of research sheds light on theoretical questions (for example, the relative importance of culture and structure in explaining suicide), or tests an existing theory (for example, that some suicides are the result of imitation), or suggests a new theory (for example, that suicide is a function of the level of social integration in a population). Durkheim's analysis confirmed his hypothesis that suicide rates rise when people's attachments to significant groups are weakened and fall when social ties are strengthened.

In science, conclusions are not regarded as final but are always open to question and reinvestigation. When research makes a significant contribution to sociological knowledge, it is usually published so that other sociologists can evaluate the conclusions independently.

Subsequent Research

No one research project ever exhausts an important topic. There is always room for work by subsequent researchers. These researchers may look at the subject from a different theoretical perspective. They may use better measures or different indicators of important variables. They may ask additional questions and gather additional data. Sociological knowledge grows through this process of continuing research in which many different investigators study closely related problems. Thus, Durkheim did not provide the last word on suicide. An American sociologist, David Phillips, has shown that the theory of social imitation—a theory Durkheim found in his review of the literature but believed his research refuted—seems to have more merit than Durkheim thought. This theory holds that suicide is encouraged by the power of suggestion—that people sometimes decide to commit suicide when they hear about others who have done so.

Basic Statistical Concepts

To analyze statistics derived from research projects and experiments, sociologists use a number of measures. The most basic of these measures are averages and correlations.

AVERAGES

Researchers distinguish three kinds of central tendencies, or averages, in the data that they collect. The **mode** is the figure that occurs most often in a set of data. For example, assume a researcher studies seven families and finds that their yearly incomes are as follows:

$ 31,000

$ 31,000

$ 40,000

$ 43,000

$ 47,000

$ 55,000

$205,000

In this group, the modal income is $31,000 per year. The mode provides no information about the range of the data; it is useful only for discerning which statistic appears most frequently.

The **mean,** commonly referred to as the "average," is found by adding all the figures in a set of data and then dividing the sum by the number of items. The mean income of seven families is $64,571.43 ($452,000 ÷ 7). The mean is useful because it reflects all the available data, but it can be misleading: The $205,000 income of one of the families obscures the fact that the other six families all have incomes of $55,000 a year or less. The mean is most helpful when the range of data does not include such extremes.

The **median** is the number that falls in the middle of a sequence of data. For the seven families here, the median income is $43,000. Unlike the mean, this measure does not allow extremes to mask the central tendency. Researchers often calculate both the mean and the median to present an accurate impression of their findings.

Sociologists may also want to find out to what extent a statistic varies from the mean (or another central point). Variation from the mean is measured by units of **standard deviation.** When taking this measurement, investigators calculate how far other recorded instances fall from the mean and then express whether each instance falls into the group closest to the mean, second closest to the mean, and so forth. In our example, the high level of variation could be expressed by noting, "Most of the families in the study are within one standard deviation of the mean."

CORRELATIONS

A **correlation,** as discussed later in the text, refers to a regular relationship between two variables. The strength of a correlation is usually expressed as a **correlation coefficient,** a decimal number between zero and one. When there is no correlation between variables (that is, the two have no relationship to each other), the correlation coefficient is zero. When the two variables are found together all the time, there is a perfect positive correlation, expressed as +1.0. When two variables are inversely related (that is, the presence of one is always associated with the absence of the other), there is a perfect negative correlation, expressed as −1.0. Usually, in the real world, researchers do not find perfect correlations. They usually find less extreme examples of association between variables.

The most common questions in data analysis concern whether two variables that are correlated have any *causal* connection to each other. It is always possible that a correlation is coincidental or the result of some third variable that is influencing the other two. Correlations therefore have to be checked for possible independent cause. This is one way of checking validity (sometimes called *statistical independence*).

To test this theory, Phillips (1974) selected a number of famous suicide cases, like that of Marilyn Monroe. He measured the amount of front-page press coverage that each of these suicides received. Then he compared the number of expected suicides (based on the previous year's pattern) during the following month with the actual number of suicides. He found a direct correlation between a highly publicized suicide and an increase in the suicide rate.

Phillips was not finished yet. He still had to test alternative hypotheses. Perhaps the publicity merely altered the timing of suicide, prompting people who were already set upon taking their own lives right away to go ahead with the act (Phillips and

Carstensen, 1986). If so, Phillips expected to find first a peak in suicides after the publicity and then an abnormal drop. But he found no such drop. Another hypothesis was that coroners might have become suggestible after so much publicity about suicide and classified more deaths as suicides and fewer homicides or accidents. If so, Phillips expected to find a proportionate decrease in the rates of other causes of death. He did not find that either. Maybe, then, the increase in suicides had to do with other conditions. If so, the suicides should not peak just after a front-page story, and the amount of publicity should not correlate with the increase in suicides. But the suicides did peak, and the variables did correlate. Finally, perhaps the increase was caused not by imitation but by grief. Phillips selected a sample of widely admired people whose suicides should have gen-erated an unusual amount of grief, but he found that the suicide rate was no more affected by the stories of these deaths than it was by the suicides of less well-known people. (The box "How to Read a Table" includes two tables from Phillips's research.)

Phillips kept up his systematic investigation of patterns of imitation. He found that the rates of fatal motor-vehicle accidents also rise after publicized suicides, suggesting that some single-car accidents may be disguised suicides (Phillips, 1986). Phillips found that teenagers are especially vulnerable to this social imitation. In the week following substantial TV coverage of a celebrity suicide, the suicide rate among teenagers leapt by over 22 percent on average (Phillips and Carstensen, 1988).

Phillips's findings about imitative suicide do not invalidate Durkheim's conclusion that suicide rates

How to Read a Table

Social scientists frequently use tables to display their research findings and to illustrate relationships between variables. Newspapers, magazines, and business reports also use this scientific mode of presenting information. Unless you know how to read tables, however, they can be more confusing than enlightening. What should one look for when interpreting a table? The following steps for interpreting Table 2.1 are general guidelines that can be applied to any table.

1. Tables present statistical information. The data can be read in rows (across from left to right) and columns (up and down). The words to the side or at the top label the rows and columns. The places where rows and columns meet are called "cells." Each cell contains a specific piece of information, which can be expressed as a word, a number, a percentage, or some other statistical measurement.

2. To read a table, you link rows and columns. In Table 2.1, the first column lists names of publicized suicides. Each of these names also starts a row, which continues to the right with these date of the suicide story, and statistics about suicides of other people after that story was publicized. You can read a table to find out new information: for example, how many more suicides took place after the death of Marilyn Monroe than would have been expected without her death? (Go down column one to the name, then go across to the last row on the right.)

3. You can look up individual pieces of information in a table, but the most important sociological use is to look for a pattern in the overall picture the data present. In Table 2.1 we see that famous suicides are followed by rises in suicide rates much more often than by declines.

4. Check where the data in the table come from. To assess the quality of the data, consider the source, which is usually printed in the headnotes and footnotes. The title of Table 2.1 says the stories were published on the front page of *The New York Times*. The small-type footnote gives the source of the data as (1) sociologist David Phillips's published article "The Influence of Suggestion on Suicide" and (2) suicide statistics published by the federal government. If the source had been a group with a vested interest in the subject depicted by the table, such as a suicide prevention agency, you might suspect bias.

5. You can draw conclusions from the data in a table and also ask questions for future research. For example, Table 2.1 suggests that suicide rates go up after well publicized suicides. To test this, we might gather information on the suicide rate after other famous suicides—for example, that of rock star Kurt Cobain, in 1994. We might also wonder whether the suicide rate would go up more the more the original famous suicide was reported in the press. To check this, David Phillips collected the data shown in Table 2.2. The answer was clearly "yes," the suicide rate went up much more the longer the original celebrity suicide stayed on page 1 of the newspaper.

TABLE 2.1

Rise in the Number of Suicides after Stories on the Front Page of The New York Times

Name of Publicized Suicide	Date of Suicide Story	Observed No. of Suicides in Month after Suicide Story	Expected No. of Suicides in Month after Suicide Story	Change in No. of Suicides after Suicide Story (Observed Minus Expected No. of Suicides)
Lockridge, author	March 8, 1948	1510	1521.5	−11.5
Landis, film star	July 6, 1948	1482	1457.5	+ 24.5
Brooks, financier	August 18, 1948	1250	1350.0	−100.0
Holt, betrayed husband	March 10, 1948	1583	1521.5	+ 61.5
Forrestal, ex-Secretary of Defense	May 22, 1949	1549	1493.5	+ 55.5
Baker, professor	April 26, 1950	1600	1493.5	+ 106.5
Lang, police witness	April 20, 1951	1423	1519.5	−96.5
Monroe, film star	August 6, 1962	1838	1640.5	+ 197.5
Graham, publisher, and Ward, implicated in Profumo affair	August 4, 1963	1801	1640.5	+ 160.5
Burros, Ku Klux Klan leader	November 1, 1965	1710	1652.0	+ 58.0
Morrison, war critic	November 3, 1965			

Source: From Phillips (1974, p. 344). Original source of suicide statistics: U.S. Department of Health, Education, and Welfare, Public Health Service (yearly volumes, 1947–1968).

TABLE 2.2

Rise in the Number of Suicides after Stories on the Front Page of the New York *Daily* News[*]

	NUMBER OF DAYS ON PAGE 1 OF THE NEWS[a]				
	0	1	2	3	4
Average rise in United States suicides after each suicide story	25.26	28.54	35.25	82.63	197.5

[a]*The suicide stories carried in The New York Times and listed in Table 2.1 fall into the following categories: 0 days—Lockridge, Baker, Lang, Graham, Morrison; 1 day—Landis, Brooks, Forrestal, Burros; 2 days—Holt; 3 days—Ward; 4 days—Monroe.*
[b]*Ward and Graham died on the same day, August 4, 1963. Half the rise in suicides in August 1963 has been credited to Ward and half to Graham. A similar procedure has been followed for Burros and Morrison, who died on November 1 and November 3, 1965.*
[*]*A less "high brow" paper, the News kept stories like this one on the front page much longer than the Times, thus allowing this measure of length of exposure.*
Source: From Phillips (1974, p. 345) with permission. Original source of suicide statistics: U.S. Department of Health, Education, and Welfare, Public Health Service (yearly volumes, 1947–1968).

Mourning a friend's death. After the suicide of a friend or celebrity, teenage suicides rise sharply, suggesting that young people are highly vulnerable to what has been called "copy cat suicide."

are related to degree of social integration. They simply show that Durkheim's theory does not tell the whole story. The theory that suicide is linked to imitation does not either, but considering the *combined* influence of social integration and imitation enables us to explain more of the variations in suicide rates than considering just one of these factors alone. In a single study, sociologists can assess the impacts of only a relatively small number of independent variables. Influences on human behavior are so numerous and complex that some things are inevitably overlooked. There may also be inaccuracies in data, as well as distortions due to chance. There is always room for more research, more efforts to refine our knowledge of the social world.

Frequently, the work of one researcher raises questions that others find intriguing and want to try to answer. Phillips's work, for example, suggests several new questions for future research: What other types of behavior does publicity trigger? Does it encourage prosocial as well as antisocial actions? Would government regulation of the publicity given to violence or the way it is reported minimize imitation? When other researchers try to answer such questions they build on Phillips's findings, and so sociological knowledge grows.

THE CHALLENGES OF SOCIOLOGICAL RESEARCH

Studying human social behavior presents a number of challenges, some common to all scientific research and some unique to the social sciences.

Validity and Reliability

Like other scientific studies, sociological research must be assessed in terms of both validity and reliability. **Validity** is the degree to which a study measures what it is attempting to measure—for example, the degree to which Durkheim actually measured social integration by using indicators like marriage rates. **Reliability** is the degree to which a study yields the same results when repeated by the original researcher or by other scientists. Lack of reliability usually indicates a problem in the research design. But reliability does not prove validity.

Subsequent studies of suicide rates have shown Durkheim's results to be reliable, but critics have questioned whether Durkheim's data were valid (Pescosolido and Mendelsohn, 1986). Might the data have been distorted? Perhaps Catholics appear to have fewer suicides than Protestants because they are more likely to disguise suicides. A good case could be made for the hypothesis that the better integrated a person is within society, the less likely it is that his or her death will be *classified* as a suicide. For example, officials in a close-knit community, respecting a family's wish to avoid embarrassment, might record the suicide as a death resulting from natural causes; or the officials might not suspect suicide because the person was deemed a leading citizen of the community.

Another challenge that researchers confront is specifying the relationship between variables. Sociologists are most interested in identifying cause-and-effect relationships, or relationships in which a change in one variable is caused by a change in another. In many cases, however, sociologists may not be able to determine a causal relationship between variables. They may only be able to show that two variables change together—are *correlated*—in some measurable way (see the box "Basic Statistical Concepts" presented earlier in the chapter). As mentioned previously, a correlation refers to a regular relationship between two variables. For example, if a high value of one variable (say, the divorce rate) is found together with a high value of another variable (say, the suicide rate), the two are said to be positively correlated.

The discovery of a correlation between variables, however, does not prove that they have a cause-and-effect relationship. Two variables may be correlated but have no causal link to one another. This is known as a **spurious correlation,** and it is a source of error in research. A crucial part of sociological analysis is distinguishing between meaningful correlations and spurious correlations. For example, someone might ask whether the relationship that Durkheim found between suicide rates and religious affiliation had a causal basis or if the connection was a spurious one. Perhaps both variables are the result of some third factor, such as differences in wealth or geographic region. Durkheim was aware that some third variable might explain his findings, and he tried to establish that this was not the case.

Theory and Research

Theory and research are inseparable in sociology. Theories are crucial in defining problems to be studied, formulating hypotheses, analyzing data, and drawing conclusions about them. Theories help to synthesize and bring order to research findings. At the same time, they are constantly revised in response to the knowledge that research provides. Without data derived from research, theories are simply unproven speculations and not part of science. Research can test propositions contained in a theory, and it can bring to light new empirical data that call for new or modified theories. In this way social theories are updated and refined.

Different theoretical perspectives can lead to research projects that complement each other by shedding light on different aspects of a problem. Thus, Durkheim's study of suicide (guided by an emphasis on functional integration) and Phillips's study of it (guided by a focus on the role of imitation in social action) each help us to understand variation in suicide rates. The most extensive possible knowledge about an aspect of social life often requires the use of several research methods and several theoretical approaches. For example, a sociologist might notice that Durkheim's research on suicide neglected questions about the meaning of suicide both to those who commit it and to the members of groups to which the victims belonged. Such a sociologist—perhaps a follower of George Herbert Mead and symbolic interactionism—could design a study to look closely at how each of a number of suicides occurred and what it meant to those involved. This would not replace Durkheim's approach, of course, for it would not tell us anything about suicide *rates*. But it could give us insights into how suicide is related to social integration and therefore complement Durkheim's work.

Ethical Issues

Sociologists are, almost by definition, "nosy." Although Durkheim's study of suicide was based on historical records, many sociological studies entail poking into other people's lives, in the here and now. For this reason sociologists have special ethical obligations to their subjects.

First, *sociologists must protect their subjects from harm.* Sociological research rarely exposes subjects to the risk of physical injury, but sociologists often ask subjects to reveal private information about themselves. Such information might not be known to the subjects' families, friends, or work associates, and it could embarrass the subjects, endanger their jobs and relationships, or even result in criminal liability.

In many cases the potential damage is subtle. Arlie Hochschild studied the division of labor in contemporary families and published the results in her book, *The Second Shift* (1989). Hochschild found that some couples described themselves as being equal partners, whereas in fact the wife did far more housework than the husband. However, the myth of equal partnership helped a couple to reconcile their different views of a "good marriage" (Hochschild, 1989). If a particular couple recognized themselves in the published study, they might be confronted with the fact that neither of them is as happy with their marriage as they tell each other, or even acknowledge to themselves. To minimize this possibility, Hochschild changed not only the names of the couples she studied but also other identifying traits such as their appearance and occupations.

One way to protect subjects is to conduct an *anonymous* survey. Questionnaires are delivered and collected in such a way that the researchers cannot identify a particular response with a particular respondent. Often, however, sociologists need to interview subjects face-to-face or to observe them in their homes, at work, or in a laboratory. In such cases, sociologists may offer *confidentiality,* that is, the researcher knows the identity of the subjects but promises not to reveal this information publicly. To guard confidentiality, the sociologist usually removes names and addresses from questionnaires, field notes, and other records; replaces these with identification numbers; and locks the master file linking names to numbers in a safe place. In most instances these precautions are sufficient. But the courts do not recognize sociological data as "privileged information"; unlike an attorney, a priest, or even (in some cases) a journalist, a sociologist may be ordered to turn over his or her records or to testify in court.

As a graduate student in sociology at Washington State University, Rik Scarce studied radical environmental and animal-rights activists who sometimes break the law to dramatize their cause (Monaghan, 1993a, 1993b, 1993c). When a group calling itself the Animal Liberation Front claimed responsibility for a raid on a university laboratory, in which 23 mink, mice, and coyotes were released and hydrochloric acid was poured on computers (causing an estimated $150,000 in damage), Scarce was subpoenaed to appear before a grand jury. Scarce acknowledged that he knew a prime suspect in the case quite well, but refused to answer any further questions. He argued that testifying about his sources not only would cause environmental activists to refuse to speak with him, curtailing his own research, but also would affect the sociological research effort as a whole.

Leaving the outside out. Sociologist and photographer Camilo José Vergara documents ghetto residents' escape from ugliness by creating soothing, warm environments inside their shabby buildings. Whatever personal information Vergara learns about the people whose homes he photographs remains confidential.

Sources would be less likely to trust other social scientists, and social scientists might shy away from controversial research that required confidentiality. The judge was not persuaded, and Scarce went to jail rather than violate his commitment to confidentiality.

As a second ethical obligation, *sociologists should never coerce or bribe people to participate in a study; participation in sociological research should be voluntary.* This requirement seems straightforward, but subtle influences may creep in. For example, residents of a nursing home are a "captive audience"; they may view the sociologist as a doctor or an administrator and feel obliged to cooperate. Students in an introductory sociology course may feel that their grade will suffer if they do not participate in their instructor's study. In some cases, however, reliance on volunteers can bias the results. People who agree to participate in a sex survey, for example, are a self-selected group who may be somewhat exhibitionist and therefore not representative of the general population.

Third, *researchers must be honest with subjects.* Ideally, sociologists obtain not just consent but *informed* consent from subjects. This point is particularly important when the people a researcher wants to study are illiterate, have low social status, or are unfamiliar with social research. In most cases, it is difficult or impossible to conceal a study. Participants in a laboratory experiment or respondents filling out a lengthy questionnaire know they are being studied. Sometimes, however, researchers make the difficult decision *not* to tell participants the actual purpose of the study in order to collect more accurate information. For example, a sociologist studying gender discrimination in the music industry might imply to subjects that he or she is studying management styles or marketing strategies. Field researchers, in particular, might not want to tell people all the ideas guiding their observations because this knowledge could alter the social processes they want to study. Thus, sociologists who study cults, gangs, or even corporations might keep the nature of their research projects secret. Deception must be justified in terms of compelling scientific or humanitarian concerns. A covert study of intravenous drug users, for example, designed to identify behavior patterns that increase the likelihood of contracting AIDS, might be justified.

Sociologists also have ethical obligations to their colleagues, to the scientific community, and to society as a whole. Ideally, sociologists make every effort to maintain *objectivity and integrity* in their research and their publications. This approach means not only reporting research findings accurately and truthfully but also spelling out the limitations of a study, publishing negative or anomalous findings as well as positive results, and acknowledging all sources of funding and all people (including students) who contributed to the study. When called on to offer professional judgments, whether in the courts, at public hearings, or for the media, sociologists should indicate the degree of their expertise and refrain from offering opinions that lack scientific credibility and could be misused.

Like medicine, law, and other professions, sociology strives to be self-policing. The American Sociology Association (ASA), the main association of professional sociologists, has drawn up a detailed Code of Ethics (1989) incorporating the principles listed above. The ASA's Committee on Professional Ethics is responsible for investigating complaints, mediating disputes, and, after due process, recommending action. In addition, most universities and colleges require that all major research projects be reviewed by committees charged with ensuring that research procedures do not violate the rights of human subjects.

RESEARCH STRATEGIES

Sociological research can be divided into two basic types: quantitative and qualitative. In **quantitative research,** sociologists count the instances of some social phenomenon and try to relate them to other social factors in statistical terms. Quantitative research employs a variety of statistical techniques to establish relationships between variables and to test for causal connections. (The box "Basic Statistical Concepts," presented earlier in the chapter, discusses some simple but important statistical measures.) David Phillips's work on the statistical relationship between highly publicized celebrity suicides and a rise in the general suicide rate is an example of quantitative research. So is Durkheim's work on suicide. Durkheim would undoubtedly have found computers and the many sophisticated statistical procedures available today enormously helpful in analyzing his data.

Of course, not all social phenomena can be counted or measured in quantitative ways. You can quantitatively measure the *rate* of suicide, for instance, but not the *meanings* that the act of suicide has for those who commit it. Thus, **qualitative research** is also important in sociology. In qualitative research, sociologists use verbal descriptions, firsthand observations, and sometimes pictures to interpret the meanings of social actions or to analyze patterns of social life in detail. A researcher who observes work groups to determine how leadership roles emerge or who interviews young children to discover the meaning they attach to their parents' divorce is doing qualitative research.

For both quantitative and qualitative research, there are many different methods of gathering data, from conducting surveys to making firsthand observations, from drawing on historical records to carrying out experiments. In the following sections we will examine the most important of these data-gathering methods and show how each is particularly well-suited to answering certain kinds of questions.

Surveys

Sociologists use surveys to measure public opinion, to test assumptions about behavior, and to predict how people will act. In a **survey,** sociologists collect data on a population by conducting interviews with a designated sample of respondents or by administering questionnaires to them or by doing both. Respondents may be asked to answer questionnaires by mail, over the phone, or in face-to-face interviews. Surveys are especially useful when sociologists want information from a large population about events that they cannot measure directly. For example, a survey on sexual behavior found that Americans are more conservative than stories in the media that emphasize promiscuity and alternative sex would lead one to believe (see Chapter 3). Surveys may also ask for socioeconomic facts (age, income, educational level, occupation, and the like). Because survey respondents may or may not answer questions truthfully, the results of surveys must be viewed as approximations.

Sociological surveys involve much more than simply asking people questions. If their results are to be reliable and valid, sociologists have to be systematic in choosing *whom* to question and *how* to ask the questions. The call-in polls on TV talk shows may generate publicity and even influence public leaders; but the people who watch these shows and take the time to call in are not necessarily representative of the entire American public. Careful sampling is the key

to accurate, scientific surveys. Although most surveys aim for quantitative data, interviews also yield qualitative data.

Choosing a Survey Sample

Most surveys are designed to collect information from a small number of people that can be used to make generalizations about the attitudes, behavior, or other characteristics of a much larger population. The **population** of any survey is simply the total number of people who share a characteristic that the sociologist is interested in studying. Say that a team of sociologists is interested in comparing attitudes toward abortion between younger (defined as aged twenty to thirty) and older (defined as aged fifty to sixty) American women. The survey population in this case would be all the women living in the United States between the ages of twenty and thirty and between the ages of fifty and sixty.

Because it is usually too costly and time-consuming to interview everyone in a population, sociologists canvass a **sample**—a limited subset of the population being studied. The sociologists studying abortion attitudes, for example, might choose a sample of American women from the two age groups. Usually a sample is designed to be as *representative* as possible. This means that relevant social characteristics—age, race, social class, and so forth—appear in the same proportions in the sample as they do in the larger population. The more representative the sample is, the more likely it is that the results will reflect the attitudes of the population as a whole.

Many people think that a large sample is more representative than a smaller one, but this is not always so. Perhaps the most famous counterexample was an attempt to predict the outcome of the 1936 presidential election. A popular magazine, *Literary Digest,* sent postcard ballots to 10 million Americans whose names had been collected from telephone directories and car registrations. From the 2 million postcards returned, the magazine predicted that Alfred Landon would beat Franklin D. Roosevelt by a landslide. Meanwhile, a young man named George Gallup sampled a mere 312,551 people and correctly predicted that Roosevelt would win. In this case, the smaller sample was more representative of the population at large. For one thing, in 1936, deep in the Great Depression, many voters did *not* have cars or telephones. These people—most of whom voted for Roosevelt—were excluded from the *Literary Digest* sample. Gallup used a **random sample,** in which everyone in the population of Americans of voting age had an equal chance of being selected.

Designing a representative sample is a real challenge. Campus newspapers and organizations frequently conduct surveys by handing out questionnaires at one or two locations. Such surveys are seldom representative. The first 100 students coming out of the sociology building, for example, may underrepresent science and arts students and overrepresent female students, who are more likely to take sociology than are male students. The sample would be more representative if the organization randomly chose 100 names from the complete roster of students at the school.

Constructing and Asking Survey Questions

The very wording and sequence of the questions that sociologists ask in interviews or on questionnaires affect the validity and reliability of the data that they get (Schuman and Presser, 1981).

WORDING The choice of words in survey questions can affect the results of the research. At first glance, for instance, it would seem that questions with the phrases "forbid speeches" and "allow speeches" would be logical opposites. But apparently the connotations of the words are different. In one poll some respondents were asked, "Do you think the United States should forbid public speeches against democracy?" Others were asked, "Do you think the United States should allow public speeches against democracy?" The responses did not dovetail: only 21.4 percent said that they would "forbid" the speeches, but 47.8 percent said that they would not "allow" the speeches (Schuman and Presser, 1981). In some cases researchers pretest a questionnaire to make sure that the wording and format do not bias the responses.

SEQUENCE The order in which sociologists ask questions can also affect the pattern of responses. Issues raised in earlier questions may influence how respondents think about later questions. Sometimes sociologists get different results just by reversing the order of two questions. For example, during the time when Americans were worried about communist threats, people were asked the following two questions: (a) "Do you think the United States should let newspaper reporters from communist countries come here and send back to their papers the news as they see it?" and (b) "Do you think a communist country like Russia should let American newspaper reporters come there and send back to America the news as they see it?" When people were asked question *a* first, 54.7 percent said yes to it. But when people were asked question *b* first, 74.6 percent said yes to question *a* (Schuman and Presser, 1981).

FORM OF RESPONSE On surveys, people can answer questions in one of two forms. In a *closed-response* question, respondents must choose from the set of answers provided by the researchers. In an *open-response* question, respondents answer in their own words. For example, sociologists might want to know what people most prefer in a job. They can ask this in a closed form: "Would you please look at this card and tell me which thing on this list you would most prefer in a job?" The card then lists five choices: high income, job security, short working hours, chances for advancement, and satisfying work that gives a feeling of accomplishment. Another type of closed-response question involves rating a given series of items or statements, for example, from 1 = "strongly agree" to 5 = "strongly disagree." The question can also be asked in an open form: "People look for different things in a job. What would you most prefer in a job?" When people were actually asked these questions, the answers differed with the form of presentation. For example, 17.2 percent of the respondents chose "chances for advancement" when they saw it among the responses, but only 1.8 percent volunteered this answer when they were asked the question in an open form. Sociologists have to be aware that the wording, sequence, and form of survey questions affect research results.

When survey researchers need more information than a short questionnaire allows, they may interview people by phone or in person. An **interview** is a conversation in which a researcher asks a series of questions or discusses a topic with another person. If they use open-response questions, interviewers can tell when to probe for more information and when to move to the next question. Good interviewers also know that the validity and reliability of interviews depend on the interaction between interviewer and respondent. They learn to tailor the tone or the pace of an interview to different kinds of respondents.

Experiments

The **experiment** offers scientists an extremely effective technique for establishing a cause-and-effect relationship. In experiments, social scientists can test a hypothesis—that one variable causally influences another variable—by exposing subjects to a specially designed situation that allows the researchers to control extraneous factors that may affect the variables. For instance, sociologists who wanted to study the effect of music on social interaction could use a closed room and hold the number of people, the lighting, the seating, the availability of refreshments, and so on constant (the same in every case). To test a hypothesis, researchers (1) systematically manipulate one variable and (2) observe the effect of the manipulation on the other variable. The factor that is systematically varied (in this experiment, music) is the independent variable; it is assumed to be the causal factor in the relationship being studied. The factor being studied (here, social interaction) is the dependent variable; it is the factor that is affected by the manipulation of the independent variable.

Experiments require a high level of control over all variables. Such control is extremely hard to achieve in researching sociologically interesting questions, but it can be approximated in *laboratory experiments* conducted with individuals and small groups. *Field experiments* are needed for larger populations; however, for both practical and ethical reasons, these are very difficult to conduct well and therefore are rare in sociology. Still, a look at each of these types of experiments is worthwhile.

Laboratory Experiments

In laboratory experiments, sociologists bring subjects into an artificial environment in which conditions can be carefully regulated. In an experiment that has become a classic, the social psychologist Philip Zimbardo (1972) constructed a "prison" in the basement of a building at Stanford University. Zimbardo was interested in the impact that the social roles of prisoner and guard had on behavior. Student volunteers were recruited through ads in a campus newspaper. The seventy who volunteered were carefully screened. Of these, the researchers chose twenty-four white, middle-class males with similar personality characteristics. Interviews and tests indicated that they were mature, intelligent, and emotionally stable—in Zimbardo's words, "the cream of the crop." The flip of a coin decided whether a student was assigned to the role of prisoner or guard.

To create a semirealistic atmosphere, the dozen student-prisoners were arrested without warning. They were taken by patrol car to an actual Palo Alto police station, where they were fingerprinted and "booked," and then they were transferred to the campus "jail." There, each student-prisoner was stripped, deloused, given a uniform and identification number, and marched to a cell. The student-guards had been told beforehand that they were responsible for maintaining law, order, and respect in the mock prison. They were asked to create their own rules and regulations and were warned to be alert for signs of a "prisoner rebellion."

Designed to run two weeks, the experiment was stopped after six days. Why? Because Zimbardo and his colleagues were frightened by what they observed. Some of the guards treated the prisoners like vermin, inventing creative ways to make them feel worthless. Other guards were tough but fair, and some were kind. But not once did a "good" guard interfere in an episode of abuse by a "bad" guard or complain to Zimbardo about what was happening.

Changes in the student-prisoners' behavior were equally alarming. One might expect that the students would have banded together to oppose harsh treatment. (After all, they had not committed any crime.) They did not. One student was put in "solitary confinement" (a small closet) for refusing to eat. His fellow prisoners at first protested. When a guard gave them the option of giving up their blankets for a night in exchange for releasing the prisoner, they caved in, choosing to keep their blankets and let the lone prisoner suffer. At a mock parole-board meeting, some begged to be released but none *demanded* to be let go. By the end of six days, the student-prisoners had been reduced to "servile, dehumanized robots."

The prison experiment vividly illustrated the degree to which the roles people play (the independent variable, controlled by the researchers) shape their attitudes and behavior (the dependent variable). All the students knew that they were participating in an experiment, in effect "playing a game" of prisoner and guard. Yet in less than a week, the experiment had become *too* real.

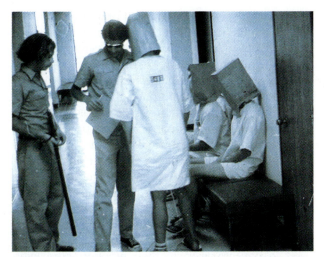

In the early 1970s Philip Zimbardo, a social psychologist, set up a mock prison in which student volunteers were assigned the roles of either prisoners or guards. The "guards" took their assigned roles very seriously, behaving aggressively and abusively toward the "prisoners," most of whom became passive and depressed. The methodology of Zimbardo's experiment revealed much about conformity to social roles, but it also raised ethical issues about treatment of human subjects. Stricter rules are now in place to guide researchers in designing their experiments.

Zimbardo's experiment also raised ethical issues about the treatment of subjects, as he was the first to admit. As noted above, stricter rules are now in place. Current guidelines require the researchers to explain the experiment or procedure to the subject; tell the subject only things that are true; warn the subject about any hazards; describe how the data are to be used; ensure the subject's confidentiality; and make certain that, before a subject gives consent, he or she is fully informed about the experiment.

Field Experiments

For ethical and practical reasons, most of the situations that interest sociologists cannot be re-created in a laboratory. However, it is much harder to conduct experiments and to establish a cause-and-effect relationship in the field (that is, in real-life settings).

The most famous field experiment of all time illustrates the difficulty. In the 1930s, researchers set out to study whether changes in working conditions, such as better lighting, would increase productivity of work groups at Western Electric's Hawthorne plant in Illinois (Roethlisberger and Dickson, 1939/1961). Mysteriously, every work group studied became more productive, no matter what aspect of the work environment was changed. Eventually, the researchers realized that the workers were simply responding to the attention they were receiving: Being studied by social scientists made them feel important and valued. This "Hawthorne effect" revealed the need for researchers to control for the effects of their own presence. The main way to do this is to compare two groups that are treated exactly the same in all respects except for the factor being studied. Thus, the *experimental group* might get brighter lighting while the *control group* does not, but both groups would get the same amount of extra attention.

Field experiments are sometimes conducted when policymakers want to find out what the impact of a particular policy will be by trying out the policy in one place and collecting data on its effects before implementing the policy on a large scale. The difficulties of large-scale experiments, however, minimize their usefulness in producing sociological data. Sometimes sociologists can study an event—like the introduction of a new policy in one state but not in others—as though it were an experiment. If they can measure enough of the relevant independent variables, sociologists can regard them as though they were controls over laboratory conditions. For example, changes in welfare policies have been studied as though they were experiments. Comparing states in which changes were made with a "control group" of states in which welfare policy remained the same, researchers have found that providing effective child-care programs increases the proportion of single mothers who are able to get jobs and stop depending on welfare (Harris, 1995).

Ethnography, Fieldwork, and Participant Observation

In experiments, sociologists attempt to influence or change people's behavior. In most field studies, however, sociologists try to observe unobtrusively. **Ethnographies** are studies in which researchers observe people in everyday settings, usually over a considerable period of time. The researchers' goal is to provide detailed descriptions and interpretations of social life as it happens—among, for example, children on playgrounds, homosexual men in bathhouses, or street gangs in urban neighborhoods. Systematic, mostly qualitative observation is a basic sociological research method. Ethnographic studies provide the kind of eyewitness accounts of social life that are not possible in experimental designs. This sort of research is often called *fieldwork* or *participant observation*.

The sociologist William Corsaro (1985), for example, studied children at play. For several months he watched and recorded how nursery school children played together. As often happens in fieldwork, he became such a familiar part of the social landscape that the children did not give his presence much thought. They saw him simply as a "big person" who acted more like them than other adults, and this perception gave him access to the children's culture. In conducting his participant observation, Corsaro had to solve some problems of method. How could he enter the children's world without upsetting or changing it? He had to remain unobtrusive but not so distant as to lose sight of how the children themselves understood their social world. Before he could even enter the playground, Corsaro had to negotiate with the "gatekeepers"—the school director, secretary, teachers, and parents. Once on the playground, Corsaro played with the children but did not affect the nature or the flow of their play episodes. (He con-

sidered play episodes the central unit of behavior in his study.) He never tried to start an activity or to substantially redirect one, and he never settled conflicts between the children.

Sociologists doing field studies are in close contact with their subjects, often around the clock. This may produce emotional reactions in the sociologists—and in their subjects (Kleinman and Copp, 1993). For example, the sociologists may become attached to their subjects and fail to note or be reluctant to report negative aspects of their behavior. The sociologists may feel an urge to take sides in quarrels within the group they are studying. They may become angry when their informants fail to live up to their expectations. Sociologists doing ethnographic fieldwork need to pay attention to their emotions and even learn from them (by asking themselves why they had a certain response and checking to see whether others had a similar or different reaction). Thus to some degree, the field-worker becomes one of the subjects of his or her own study.

Usually, as in Corsaro's study, field researchers openly identify themselves; however, when studying groups that are closed to, and suspicious of, outsiders, researchers might disguise their identities. In most cases this means that the sociologists simply observe the group in its everyday settings as its members go about their daily business, but the sociologists do not identify themselves or join group activities. For example, sociologists who had been researching sexual behavior went to homosexual bathhouses and passively watched the behavior of the men there (Weinberg and Williams, 1975). Because many of the gay men themselves stood around and watched, and because bathhouse patrons stayed emotionally and personally detached from one another despite their sexual encounters, the sociologists blended in. To maintain their cover, the researchers took their field notes in private areas of the bathhouse or after leaving. In interpreting what they saw, the researchers drew on several years' experience of studying sexual behavior. Clearly, they did not go to the bathhouses as voyeurs, but rather as scientists who approached the situation with a set of theoretical questions.

Keeping a sociological research mission secret may solve the problem of intrusion (that the sociologist's presence might alter the group's behavior), but it raises ethical questions about the subjects' right to privacy and the sociologist's responsibility to be honest.

Content Analysis

In some cases sociologists do not study people and groups directly but rather examine the products of social behavior. Sociologists often employ **content analysis** to uncover relevant information in historical and contemporary materials. Content analysis may be applied to almost any type of recorded communication—letters, diaries, autobiographies, memoirs, laws, novels, song lyrics, constitutions, newspapers, even paintings, all of which can reveal much about people's behavior. This research method provides a way to systematically organize and summarize both the *manifest* (or obvious, intended) content and the *latent* (underlying, perhaps unintended) content of communication. The computer, which allows researchers to analyze content from many perspectives, has proved a powerful research tool.

For example, suppose that a group of researchers decides to study the images of men and women in rock music videos. Because they cannot study every music video ever made, the investigators begin by collecting a representative sample of rock videos. Next, they list all the possible categories of content, such as song lyrics, clothing styles, gestures, and so forth. They then examine the sampled videos, noting as many specific items of content as possible. So far, the researchers have relied heavily on qualitative research—research that depends on interpretations. Once sufficient data have been collected, the researchers can move to statistically based—or quantitative—research methods; for example, they can count the frequency with which women appear in subordinate roles to men, and they can check to see whether these instances correlate with other variables. Two such studies found that music videos often portray women in subordinate roles, as sexual objects, or as targets of violence (Brown and Campbell, 1986; Sherman and Dominick, 1986).

Comparative and Historical Research

Sociologists cannot base generalizations and theories on a single group or population. For example, a survey of attitudes toward religion at one California college might not represent attitudes of all American college students or young adults, much less the attitudes of the American population as a whole. Likewise, sociologists need to look at data on other societies, not just their own; on other historical periods, not just current patterns; and on social change.

The primary goal of comparative research is to avoid overgeneralizing from the characteristics of one social group or social category of people, one society or time period. Comparative studies may employ any of the other research methods we have discussed. They may be qualitative or quantitative. They may use data gathered from surveys, experiments (though very seldom), participant observation, historical approaches, or content analysis. The crucial element is *comparison*—investigating similarities and differences (Ragin, 1987).

Comparative sociology usually takes the form of **cross-cultural research,** in which data from very different social settings are compared. Sociologists use data from different countries to investigate topics of general sociological interest such as nationalism, class structures, or welfare policies. Some comparative research projects are large-scale comparisons of many cases; others focus on a few cases or on one case only. Consider the topic of nationalism, the development of a strong national identity and political claims for territory and autonomy based on this identity. In studying this topic, Anthony Smith (1993) analyzed nearly a hundred cases from around the world. By contrast, Liah Greenfeld (1992) analyzed just five countries, getting a detailed look at each one. Still other researchers (e.g., Colley, 1992) look in detail at just one country, comparing different regions within that country and making only brief or implied comparisons to other countries. These different strategies can be applied to any empirical topic: fertility, economic development, crime, and so on. There is a trade-off between having a larger number of cases and being able to attend to variations in the social and cultural content of the variable being studied. The larger the number of cases, the more likely it is that the sociologist will use statistics to summarize his or her findings and to analyze the relationships among variables.

International comparative (or cross-cultural) research is growing rapidly in contemporary sociology. One reason for using such research is the great diversity of human cultures and forms of social organization. If we took the American kinship or religious or educational or political systems to be "natural" and failed to compare them with others in the world, we would have a very limited view of the range of human social organization.

Variety in education. As with all other aspects of social life, cultural values help to shape education. Cross-cultural research reveals that while Japanese children are learning the latest computer technology to prepare them for life and careers in the twenty-first century, Egyptian children focus on the ancient texts of Egyptian culture in classrooms far removed from the information age.

Another reason for using international or cross-cultural comparisons is that the people of the world are coming into closer relationship with one another. Increasingly, the economies of all countries are being drawn into a single global system. The media are becoming more international: soap operas made in Brazil are extremely popular in China; Hindi movies are shown throughout the Middle East; writers from Latin America and India are among the most popular in the United States; CNN is broadcast all over the world. Most important, people are tied together by the reality that armed conflict in one part of the world can threaten to spread beyond it. Comparative research enables sociologists to study these processes of **globalization.** Throughout this book, we will report on research that broadens our perspective by examining globalization or by describing social patterns in other societies.

Not all relevant comparisons involve contemporary cases, however. To understand long-term social change and very unusual events, sociologists rely on **historical studies.** For example, the rise of modern industrial organization is an extremely important topic for sociologists who study contemporary societies, but this rise took place over several centuries and can only be understood through historical methods. To this end, sociologists analyze both data collected by historians and other historical data that they gather themselves. Such data range from censuses, to police reports, to newspaper articles, to church and business records. The work of earlier sociologists may also provide an important source of data for historical comparisons.

In her classic study *States and Social Revolutions,* Theda Skocpol (1979) combined comparative and historical methods. Because revolutions do not occur very often, she had to focus on historical cases. Skocpol did not want to generalize from just one case and so chose three revolutions that took place in different cultural and historical settings. Through comparisons she sought to discover what these revolutions had in common and then what distinguished them from failed revolutions.

Skocpol began as any sociologist must: by defining the phenomenon to be studied—in this case, *social revolution.* She defined social revolution as "the rapid, basic transformation of a society's state and class structure accompanied and in part carried through by class-based revolts from below" (Skocpol, 1979, p. 33). Under this definition, a social revolution requires fundamental transformation of both *political* institutions (the state structure) and *economic* institutions (the class structure, or the distribution of wealth and property). A *coup d'état,* in which one totalitarian leader replaces another; a rebellion that disrupts everyday routines but does not result in fundamental change; or a "revolutionary" change such as industrialization, which does not alter the political structure, would not meet these stringent criteria.

Skocpol was not seeking to write historical narrative, a blow-by-blow account of events. Instead, she sought a general (or generalizable) causal theory of social revolution. To achieve this goal, Skocpol used a comparative methodology of analyzing the three revolutions for elements they had in common and elements unique to one or another example. In addition, Skocpol compared these three successful social revolutions with other historical situations where not-quite-revolutions failed to fundamentally alter both the political and economic structures in a society.

Skocpol identified certain elements that were present in each of the three successful cases—France, Russia, and China—but absent from cases where the revolutions failed: (1) the collapse of an autocratic (or dictatorial) monarchy resulting from the inability of the state's machinery to deal with international pressures and crises; (2) mass uprisings of peasants as an immediate or precipitating factor; (3) conflicts among elites to establish a new state structure on the ashes of the fallen ancient regime (inevitably becoming as centralized as what preceded it). These findings provided the basis for her theoretical argument that the success or failure of a social revolution is determined mainly by the structural problems in existing states, not by the ideology or actions of the revolutionaries.

Like all research projects, Skocpol's study of social revolutions is part of an ongoing effort that is never finished. The struggle to understand the social world requires many different methods, perspectives, and theories. It also requires that researchers—no matter how brilliant—*accept* that future research may challenge or modify their conclusions. One of Skocpol's students, Jack Goldstone (1991), used similar comparative-historical methods to conduct another study of social revolutions a dozen years after Skocpol's study. Goldstone added new variables and new cases, however, and found new results—such as the fact that rapid population growth often helped to produce the state crisis that led to revolution.

Science is always oriented toward new discoveries, not just settled truths. Remembering this is especially important for sociologists, because the social world they study is the product of human action. Not only can the social world be seen in different ways, but it can change.

SUMMARY

1. In his study of suicide, Émile Durkheim set an important precedent for examining an apparently private problem from a sociological point of view, thereby helping to establish sociology as a science.

2. Sociological research is grounded in the scientific method, which rests on the collection of empirical data to construct and to test theories.

3. All scientists follow the same basic research process. Ideally this entails seven steps: defining the problem in terms of specific variables; reviewing the literature; forming hypotheses, or tentative statements; choosing a research design; collecting data; analyzing the data; and drawing conclusions.

4. Sociological knowledge develops as research generates additional theories and more research. An example of continuing research is David Phillips's studies of imitation as a factor in suicide (a factor Durkheim did not find significant).

5. Sociologists face a number of challenges in doing research. First, they must make sure that their research is both valid and reliable. A study is valid when it measures what it is attempting to measure; it is reliable when repeated research produces the same findings.

6. Second, they must find dynamic ways to combine social theory and social research and so shed new light on social phenomenon.

7. Third, they must maintain ethical standards, including protecting subjects from harm; ensuring that participation is voluntary; being honest with subjects; and insofar as possible, being objective and candid in publishing or discussing their results.

8. There are two basic types of sociological research: quantitative research, which focuses on statistics, and qualitative research, which relies on verbal descriptions.

9. A survey is a systematic way of collecting data on a large population by questioning a designated sample of that population. A representative sample reflects the social characteristics of the population as a whole. In a random sample, everyone within a population has an equal chance of being selected. Survey responses can be affected by the wording of questions, the sequence in which they are asked, and the form of response that is permitted.

10. In experiments, which are relatively rare in sociology, the researcher puts subjects in a specially designed and controlled situation in order to isolate the impact of different variables. In laboratory experiments, sociologists carefully manipulate people under artificial conditions. In field experiments, researchers study the real-world impact of controlled alterations in the subjects' environments.

11. Ethnographies are studies in which researchers observe groups in their everyday settings, usually for long periods of time. The sociologists may or may not reveal their identity as researchers, and they may or may not participate in the group's activities.

12. Content analysis provides a way to systematically organize and summarize both the manifest and latent content of communication.

13. Comparative research enables sociologists to discover general patterns that are not tied to one social group or category or to one society or time. Such research may compare data from different countries and cultures, from different time periods, or both. International or cross-cultural studies are increasingly important because of globalization: peoples of the world are being drawn into closer relationship with one another. Historical studies are valuable for analyzing rare events and events that unfold over a long period of time.

14. Often sociologists use a combination of strategies—such as comparative-historical research—to investigate such major topics as social revolutions.

REVIEW QUESTIONS

1. Outline the steps in the research process.

2. Explain why it is important to clearly distinguish independent from dependent variables and why these variables must be clearly indicated in a hypothesis.

3. Define *validity* and *reliability*.

4. Compare random samples with nonrandom samples and explain why random samples are preferable.

5. Provide some advice for effective survey questions.

6. Suggest topics that would be best studied by each of the basic methods: survey, experiment, ethnography, historical study, content analysis, and comparative methods and cross-cultural studies.

CRITICAL THINKING QUESTIONS

1. Select a topic of interest. Briefly outline how you would complete a study of that topic following the steps of the research process. Explain why you made the choices you made.

2. Present a potential research project that could yield useful sociological knowledge but would raise serious ethical questions. How would you resolve those questions?

3. Explain why some people feel that establishing causality in the social sciences is more difficult than in other sciences.

4. Find a quantitative study in the newspaper or one of the newsweeklies. Describe the sampling method used by the study and discuss its strengths and weaknesses.

5. Some people argue that we should not "experiment" on people. Present your views about using the experimental method to do research.

GLOSSARY

Altruistic suicide Durkheim's term for suicide that results from extreme commitment to a group or community.

Anomic suicide Durkheim's term for suicide that results from a condition of social normlessness known as anomie.

Content analysis A research method that provides a way to systematically organize and summarize both the manifest and latent content of communication.

Correlation A regularly occurring relationship between two variables.

Correlation coefficient A decimal number between zero and one that is used to indicate the strength of a correlation.

Cross-cultural research Studies that describe social patterns in societies other than the researchers' own.

Data Facts, statistics, study results, and other pieces of observable information that are collected and used to construct theories.

Dependent variable In an experiment, the quality or factor that is affected by one or more independent variables.

Egoistic suicide Durkheim's term for suicide that results from social isolation and individualism.

Ethnographies Studies in which researchers observe people in their everyday settings, usually over an extended period of time.

Experiment A research method in which subjects are exposed to a specially designed situation that allows the researchers to control the factors that may affect the hypothetical cause-and-effect relationships among the variables they are studying. Experiments may be done in laboratories or field settings.

Fatalistic suicide The taking of one's own life to avoid what seems to be an inevitably bleak future if one goes on living.

Globalization The process by which the peoples of the world are being drawn into closer relationship with one another.

Historical studies Sociological research on past events, previous ways of life, or patterns of change over time.

Hypothesis A tentative statement that predicts how two or more variables affect, or are related to, one another.

Independent variable In an experiment, the quality or factor that affects one or more dependent variables.

Indicator Something that can be clearly measured as an approximation of some other, more complex variable.

Interview A conversation in which a researcher asks a series of questions or discusses a topic with another person.

Mean The average; obtained by adding all figures in a series of data and dividing the sum by the number of items.

Median The number that falls in the middle of a sequence of figures.

Methodology The procedures that guide research.

Mode The figure that occurs most often in a series of data.

Operational definition The set of clearly measurable indicators that will represent one of the variables in an analysis.

Population In a survey, the total number of people who share a characteristic that is being studied.

Qualitative research Research that depends primarily on verbal descriptions, firsthand observations, or pictures to study particular cases in depth.

Quantitative research Research that relies on statistical analyses of data.

Random sample In a survey, a method used to draw a sample in such a way that every member of the population being studied has an equal chance of being selected.

Reliability The degree to which a study yields the same results when repeated by the original or other researchers.

Sample A limited number of people selected from the population being studied who are representative of that population.

Secondary analysis Research that reanalyzes data drawn from previous research projects.

Spurious correlation A correlation between two variables that has no meaningful causal basis.

Standard deviation A statistical measurement of how far other recorded instances fall from the mean or another central point.

Survey A research method using questionnaires or interviews, or both, to learn how people think, feel, or act. Good surveys use random samples and pretested questions to ensure high reliability and validity.

Validity The degree to which a scientific study measures what it attempts to measure.

Variable Any factor that is capable of change.

PART 2

The Individual and Society

CHAPTER 3

The Structure of Social Interaction

Sex is everywhere. America flaunts sexuality in rock lyrics and videos, movies and TV shows, and ads for just about everything. Flip through magazines. Tune in the talk shows or the soaps. Take a walk through cyberspace. One cannot help but think that all across America, everyone is "doing it," night and day.

We may learn from our religion that sex is potentially sinful, permissible only in the context of marriage for the purpose of procreation. We may think of sex as a natural biological drive or instinct that, like hunger and thirst, must be satisfied. Or we may hold the Freudian view that sex is an unbridled horse, galloping out of control, which the ego constantly struggles to rein in. Too much control, in this view, spells repression.

Our personal experiences, however, are often quite different. Our culture may publicize sex, but for most people sex is an intimate, intensely private experience. Sex may be driven by hormones, but it does not come naturally. Adolescents' first sexual encounters involve a good deal of experimental fumbling. For adults, the best sex may be "comfy" rather than cataclysmic. But we rarely talk about sex, even—perhaps especially—with our partners.

To sociologists, sex is only one of many interesting, usually highly personal, but still socially structured forms of interaction. Social and cultural factors shape opportunities for sex, what we find arousing, who we approach, our expectations, what we actually do, and how we feel about it. Many aspects of sex that we take for granted as being "only natural" are in fact reflections of our culture and times. In seventeenth-century Europe, doctors considered female orgasm normal and common; women who had difficulty conceiving were advised to have orgasm more often. In the nineteenth century, however, female orgasm was declared unusual and possibly abnormal.

Doctors (all male) even debated whether there was such a thing. In the twentieth century, physicians "rediscovered" female orgasm but concluded that it was difficult to "achieve" and dispensed advice on improving technique (Laqueur, 1990).

Cultural knowledge about sex varies. Western physicians long maintained that masturbation caused warts, acne, hairy palms, blindness, and insanity, among other disorders; such assertions are now known to be false. People of different cultures have different tastes in sexual partners. While modern American culture idealizes thin women with almost boylike figures, West African men, like Europeans of earlier periods, prefer larger, more curvaceous women. All cultures condemn some sexual relationships and favor others. Older men dating younger women is acceptable in our culture, but older women dating younger men is less so. Depending on culture, extramarital sex may be punished severely, treated casually, or even institutionalized. The same is true of homosexuality.

A primary function of family and kinship systems is to regulate sexual activity, ensuring that children have parents to provide for them. Changes in patterns of sexual behavior—such as teenage pregnancy, premarital cohabitation, divorce, and remarriage—require adjustments in other areas: school programs for teen mothers, "palimony laws," dating services and "personal" columns, and recognition of stepfamilies.

Sex can be an instrument of power. Male violence against women with whom they have sex—whether strangers, prostitutes, lovers, or wives—is well-documented in many cultures and times. But power is not just a matter of physical force. To some degree, men in our society still are expected to initiate sex, and women are expected to resist or delay before "giving in." Some men feel they have a right to demand sex from their wives, whenever and however they choose. Even within egalitarian relationships, couples play power games, consciously or unconsciously using (or refusing) sex to assert dominance, to restore peace, or to get something they want.

Partner availability and choice depend on social structure. Imagine a diagram of your high school graduating class in which any two people who had ever kissed were connected by a line. We can predict where those lines go from other social factors. Football stars would be more likely to kiss (or more generally, to date) cheerleaders than members of the chess club. People tend to date members of their own race, though there are exceptions. Most lines would be between boy and girl, but not all. This diagram would describe a social network, the pattern of links among members of a population.

Of all the potential mates in a population, networks limit the people one actually meets. As a rule, they link people who are similar in age, education, race, social class, and other social characteristics. You may fall in love with a stranger across a crowded room, but the odds are high that the room will be crowded with people pretty much like you (Lewin, 1994).

Of course, sex is only one of many kinds of social interaction (and by no means the most common). We begin this chapter with a closer look at sex in America. Then we turn to basic patterns of interaction and relationships between friends, lovers, strangers, and even people who never meet face-to-face. After that we focus on interaction in the workplace, where impersonal and personal relationships intersect, and then we look at the structure of complex organizations, how organizations are changing, and the impact on people's lives. We close with explanations of the structure of social interaction.

THE SOCIAL ORGANIZATION OF SEXUALITY

Until recently, very little was known about Americans' sexual attitudes and behavior. Debates about family values have been informed—and misinformed—by anecdotal "evidence," pseudoscientific surveys and reports, and personal biases and impressions (Lewin, 1994). The National Health and Social Life Survey (NHSLS) of the early 1990s was the first nationwide, scientific study of what really happens in America's bedrooms (Laumann et al., 1994) (see the Research Methods box).

The NHSLS found considerable variety in frequency, number of partners, and sexual preferences and practices, but also found that relatively few Americans cheat on their partners or engage in exotic or "kinky" sexual practices. Moreover, married couples (and cohabitors) have sex more often than single people do and are more likely to find sex physically and emotionally satisfying.

To some degree, men and women are "ships passing in the night." Men think about sex and enjoy

Sex in America

When Alfred Kinsey began his pioneering sex surveys in the late 1930s, he believed (probably correctly) that most Americans would be reluctant to talk about their sex lives. So Kinsey relied on volunteers. Volunteers are a self-selected group who are likely to have more interest in the subject—and perhaps more varied experience—than the general public. They may answer questions honestly, but their answers will not be representative of the population as a whole. Furthermore, to cover a wide spectrum of sexual behavior, Kinsey sought out men in same-sex environments and homosexual networks. As a result, the Kinsey reports probably overestimated the amount of illicit sex and homosexuality in America. Nevertheless, the Kinsey reports went unchallenged for some forty years. Unwittingly, Kinsey was partly responsible for the assumption that Americans "played around" more than they admitted.

Until recently, most sex research—from Masters and Johnson's laboratory studies to mail-in surveys conducted by *Playboy, Redbook,* and other magazines—relied on volunteers. Then, in the 1980s, AIDS struck. Public health officials realized that they did not have sufficient scientific data to predict (or attempt to control) the spread of AIDS. Conservatives in government reluctantly conceded that AIDS-oriented research might be important, but they insisted on numerous restrictions. The National Institutes of Health (NIH) issued a request for research proposals that was so carefully worded it did not even use the word *sex.* Edward Laumann and his colleagues submitted several drafts of their proposal for a National Health and Social Life Survey (NHSLS). The NIH approved, but the Senate voted *not* to fund their survey.

Government rejection was a mixed blessing. The researchers were able to secure funding from private foundations. This meant that they did not have to restrict the survey to government-approved topics and questions, but it also meant a smaller-scale study. Originally the researchers had hoped to interview 20,000 people; loss of government funding forced them to scale down to 3,500. However, the size of a sample is not as important as how the sample is selected.

NHSLS researchers used the time-tested method called probability sampling. Working with the National Opinion Research Center (NORC), they used computers to select subjects at random. No survey is able to gain the cooperation of all of the people chosen, but the higher the response rate, the more likely the sample represents a true cross section. The NHSLS achieved an impressive response rate: Four out of five people contacted agreed to be interviewed.

The NHSLS researchers combined face-to-face interviews with a confidential written questionnaire to be filled out and sealed in a "privacy envelope" during the interview. Designing and administering questionnaires is an art. The way questions are worded, the order in which they are asked, and the interviewer's manner can all bias results. The NHSLS team wanted to avoid technical language, which many people do not understand, but they did not want to use slang terms, either, which tend to be demeaning. So, for example, they used the term *oral sex,* rather than the precise but unfamiliar terms *fellatio* and *cunnilingus.* They found that most people have difficulty describing sexual practices in their own words, and so posed questions that required only "yes," "no," "how many," or "how often" answers. As a partial check on respondents' giving "socially desirable" rather than honest answers, some questions were asked more than once, in different ways.

Most important, the NHSLS had to guarantee confidentiality. Information the respondents revealed about themselves could be used against them, for example, in divorce settlements. Moreover, in any large study many people are required to handle records, which raises the possibility of unintentional disclosure. For these reasons, interviewers recorded personal identification and interview responses on separate, distinctly colored forms. Office staff who handled one set of forms never saw the other, and the identifiers were later destroyed. This meant that the NHSLS researchers had to abandon plans for follow-up longitudinal research, but they were able to guarantee anonymity.

The NHSLS, like all surveys, has built-in limitations. Respondents may exaggerate, omit important facts, or give socially approved answers, especially on sensitive topics like sexuality. Surveys only measure what people *say* they do, not what they actually do. Respondents may not only lie to interviewers about how often they masturbate, for example, but they may also deceive themselves. Nevertheless, the NHSLS was an important first step in the systematic, scientific study of sexual behavior and attitudes in contemporary America.

pornography more than women do. Three-quarters of men say they always reach orgasm during intercourse, compared to one-quarter of women. No surprises there. But the NHSLS team was astounded by the following: One in five women said they had been forced to perform sexual acts against their will, usually by someone they knew well, often by someone they loved, including husbands. Yet less than 3 percent of men said that they had ever forced themselves on a woman. Some of this gender gap is undoubtedly due to underreporting by men, but the NHSLS researchers do not think this is the full story. Rather, they believe that men often fail to recognize how coercive women find their behavior. "Why didn't she say no?" some men ask. She did; but he did not listen, thought her resistance was token, or perhaps found her protests exciting—and assumed (wrongly) that she felt the same.

The NHSLS helped to resolve a long-standing debate about the prevalence of homosexuality. For years, the only authoritative source was the 1948 Kinsey report, which estimated that one in ten American men are homosexual. The NHSLS found the proportion was much lower: Only 2.8 percent of men and 1.4 percent of women identified themselves as gay, lesbian, or bisexual (Figure 3.1). Yet the 10 percent myth lingers. Why? Gay men, in particular, tend to live in New York, San Francisco, and other cities with large homosexual communities. As a result, homosexuals are *over*represented in urban populations and *under*represented (and/or secretive) in rural areas. This geographic pattern may explain why urban gay rights groups insist the 1-in-10 estimate is accurate (in some cities, especially some neighborhoods, it probably is), whereas religious conservatives (more likely to live in rural areas) believe homosexuality is even rarer than it is. It is also the case that many people who engage in some homosexual activities or relationships at some point in their lives do not consider themselves to be homosexuals.

The NHSLS team found that Americans have relatively few inhibitions about sex. The two topics respondents consistently avoided were family income and masturbation! Masturbation is still taboo in our society. Many people view masturbation as a sin, a lack of self-control, a symptom of psychological or social maladjustment, or appropriate only for certain people in special situations (adolescent boys or adults whose partners are away for a long time). Yet masturbation is common. A majority of men and a near-majority of women "admitted" that they masturbated on occasion—but most said they felt guilty afterward.

The pattern of answers was revealing. Popular wisdom holds that single people are more likely to masturbate than are people who are married or living with someone. Underlying this view is the unspoken assumption that each individual has a certain amount of "sex drive" that must be expressed; if a partner is not available, the individual is likely to "resort" to masturbation. In fact, the reverse is true: The more often people have sex with a partner, the more frequently they masturbate. "If you're having sex a lot, you're thinking about sex a lot" (Gagnon in *Time,* October 17, 1994, p. 68).

If sex were purely a matter of biological drive or individual psychology, masturbation and other activities would be distributed randomly. However, this is not the case. The better educated people are,

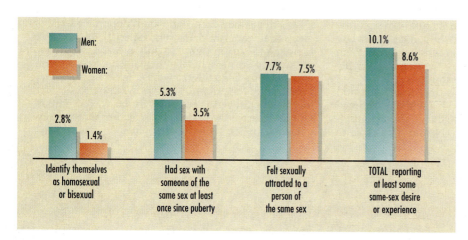

FIGURE 3.1 / Homosexuality—The 10% Myth

The NHSLS found the oft-cited one-in-ten figure for active or exclusive homosexuality to be a myth in terms of the population as a whole. However, the percentage of Americans who have experimented with homosexuality or fantasized about sex with a person of their own gender approaches one in ten.

Source: Edward Laumann et al., adapted from *Time,* October 17, 1994, pp. 62–66.

A highly successful clothing designer discovered how powerful—but complex—the links between sex and social structure can be. When he launched an advertising campaign built around young teenagers in sexually suggestive poses, the public saw exploitation instead of fashion. Within weeks, the ads were gone.

the more likely they are to masturbate. Contrary to stereotypes about bookish intellectuals, female graduate students are one of the least inhibited groups in the country. Women with conservative religious beliefs were the least likely to report masturbating; but they were the married women most likely to say they *always* experienced orgasm during sex with their husbands. Married Roman Catholics have sex more often than members of other religions (or no religion). Single Jewish males report the highest number of partners. Clearly social factors influence sex.

The social structuring of sex has important consequences for public policy. People do not choose sexual partners at random. The main victims of AIDS in the United States have been gay men and intravenous drug users, who tend to be socially and sexually isolated from the mainstream. Individuals who are monogamous and practice safe sex may be at high risk if their social networks include people who carry the disease (and if their partners are not 100 percent faithful). Individuals who have unprotected sex with numerous partners may be at low risk if their social networks include few people with AIDS. Still, no one is socially immune. Even though most people choose sex partners from within their own social network, some individuals venture outside, particularly when they engage in illicit behavior (such as extramarital affairs or bisexual activities). A one-night stand may introduce AIDS into a relatively safe network. The key point is that because the HIV virus is transmitted primarily through sexual contact and because sex is socially structured, the AIDS epidemic is a social problem that cannot be contained or stopped by focusing on individual behavior alone. Social patterns must be taken into account (see Chapter 14).

PRIMARY RELATIONSHIPS

A couple embrace on a street in Paris; at the same moment, a photographer snaps his shutter. The photo, which seems to capture the magic of Paris and the very essence of young love, is reprinted many times and becomes world-famous. Three people: two are lovers, one a stranger whom they do not even notice. Their private moment becomes his art.

For the couple, "the embrace" marks the beginning of a new life: they marry, raise children, share good times and bad, and come to know one another as well as they know themselves. For the photographer, "the embrace" launches a career that introduces him to a world of magazine editors, gallery owners, and collectors—people he knows superficially, if at all, but whose support enables him to pursue his craft. The couple and the world of photography represent two distinct types of groups, one rooted in the family and associated with the rural, village-based life of the preindustrial era, and the other a modern development linked to industrialization, urbanization, and the world of work.

The American sociologist Charles Horton Cooley (1905/1956) called the first type "primary groups" and the second type "secondary groups." **Primary groups** are distinguished by five main features:

1. Continuous face-to-face interaction

2. Strong personal identification with the group

3. Strong ties of affection among group members

4. Multifaceted relationships

5. A tendency to endure

Secondary groups, in contrast, are characterized by:

1. Limited face-to-face interaction

2. Modest or weak personal identification with the group

3. Weak ties of affection among group members

4. Limited, shallow relationships

5. A tendency to be fragile and short-lived

Primary and secondary groups are based on different kinds of relationships and different patterns of interaction. In primary groups (such as family or close friendship), people are intimately connected to one another; they know about many aspects of one another's lives; their interactions are emotionally charged; their identities are interwoven; and they see their relationship as ongoing, regardless of whether they live in the same area and meet frequently. Even if the lovers part, their romance will remain part of their individual life stories.

Secondary relationships, in contrast, are fleeting and superficial. People's knowledge of one another's lives is partial (for example, confined to work); their interactions are more formal and conventional (dominated by "small talk"); they usually are emotionally cool; if they move, change jobs, lose interest in a hobby, and so on, there is no expectation that they will keep in touch. The photographer will work with many magazine editors over his career, as he and they change jobs; only one or two will become personal friends.

Cooley emphasized two points. First, in modern societies the proportion of interaction that takes place in secondary relationships is increasing; hence, we cannot think of large-scale social organization simply as the family or the local community "writ large." Interactions and relationships are *qualitatively* different. Second, modern societies and secondary relationships depend heavily on norms of civility—the cultural rules that develop to regulate interaction among strangers in cities (as distinct from people in small villages, who know one another personally). An individual follows these norms—such as tipping waiters or waiting in lines—for the norm's own sake, not because he or she has a personal connection with the other people or expects to be rewarded. When norms for polite interaction with strangers and acquaintances are strong, modern society can flourish. When those norms are forgotten or ignored, civility suffers and the quality of life deteriorates.

Friends and Lovers

Friends and lovers are normally primary relationships. Individuals in all societies seem to seek—and perhaps need—both warm, enduring relationships that link them to social networks and groups, and intense, more individualistic, private relationships (Brain, 1976). However, the way people of different cultures define *friends* and *lovers* varies. In our society, friendship and love are matters of personal choice.

In other societies (such as the Bwanga, in central Africa), a man values his best friend more than his wife and brothers (Brain, 1976). The Bwanga consider kin unreliable and view marriage as a practical arrangement necessary for procreation. In contrast, friendship comes from the heart and lasts for life. Best friends exchange verbal endearments; hug, hold hands, and sleep side by side; give one another small presents; and rarely travel far without each other. In our culture Bwanga friends might be assumed to be lovers, but homosexuality is unknown. Many cultures officially recognize friendship with formal religious ceremonies that establish blood brothers or *compadrazgo* (god-siblings). These bonds are as important and binding as marriage. In modern Western societies, passion and lifelong commitment are "for lovers only."

Romantic Love

Romantic love is one of the defining features of our culture; some would say it is an obsession. What we experience as completely natural and as coming from deep inside, however, is molded by our culture. Modern, Western notions of romantic love date to the Middle Ages and the tradition of courtly love (Luhmann, 1986). Courtly love was based on a set of interlocking beliefs: Love is an uncontrollable emotion that strikes suddenly and irrevocably at first sight; the lovers are fated for one another, a destiny neither can escape; love leads to utter bliss, abject misery, or both; and love inspires and ennobles (Skolnick, 1978). Courtly love was *not*, however, part of marriage (Brain, 1976). To the contrary, the beloved was usually married to someone else, was forbidden, or was a distant, unobtainable fantasy. More often than not, the passion was never consummated. The lovers did not "live happily ever after" but rather were doomed to death, madness, or exile.

From the beginning, the ideology of romantic love glorified stories of star-crossed lovers, lovers whose relationship was forbidden. The most famous such lovers are Romeo and Juliet, children of two feuding families. Their story highlights the romantic notion of love as an overwhelming emotion that unites two individuals regardless of social and cultural rules. In sociological terms, it is a story of confrontation between personal passions and the social order.

The primary links between individuals and social structure are statuses and roles. **Statuses** are positions in the social order that define who we are in relation to others, and so play a key role in establishing social identity. The status of "parent," for example, defines certain rights and obligations in relation to children. Parents have an obligation to protect and provide for their children and the right to make decisions about their children's education, religion, and activities. At the same time, children have a right to protection and support by their parents and an obligation to respect and obey them. "Parent" is also a social identity that implies maturity and responsibility and tells others—a teacher, for example—who this individual is. All of us occupy many statuses at the same time; an individual's statuses taken together are called a **status set.** Thus a parent may be a husband to his wife, a boss to his employees, a buddy to his friends, and so on. As a person grows up and grows old, enters and graduates from schools, acquires and changes jobs, gets married or divorced, becomes more or less involved in his or her politics or sports, his or her status set changes.

Roles are cultural expectations regarding the behavior and attitudes of people who occupy a given position, as well as cultural guidelines for dealing with recurring situations. Parent is a social role. Most Americans expect parents to provide a home for their children and see that they are healthy, as well as to love them and take pride in their accomplishments (from the child's first steps, to college graduation). Customs such as setting bedtime hours, bandaging cuts, hugging, and giving birthday presents help parents achieve and express these goals. Of course, how actual parents play their role varies. Different ideas about child-rearing (based on ethnicity or religion); socioeconomic resources (income, marital status, education, community facilities); and role conflict (such as the overlapping demands on working parents) lead to different performances of the role of parent.

Some statuses dominate others. Returning to Romeo and Juliet: For each of them, the most important status—the **master status** that overshadows all the others—is that of unmarried child. As such, the normal role is to follow their parents' wishes and to get married—but specifically *not* to one of their family's archenemies (the Montagues or the Capulets). By refusing to play the roles that go with their statuses, Romeo and Juliet violate the social order.

One way of reading their story is as a cautionary tale: When people let their emotions get the better of them and fail to follow their prescribed roles, the social order fights back—and usually wins. But Shakespeare, writing several hundred years after the period in which the story was set, shifted the moral of the story slightly, encouraging audiences to sympathize with the doomed lovers and see their story as a tragedy. Today we go still further in the direction of seeing Romeo and Juliet as unjust victims of foolish families and an overly rigid social system. Our culture supports the priority of the individual over social obligations.

Especially in America, we emphasize the statuses that we choose for ourselves and achieve through individual effort. These **achieved statuses** are marks of success and individual accomplishment. (Examples of such statuses are college graduate, church deacon, home owner, and in some settings, gang leader.) **Ascribed statuses,** in contrast, are assigned by others, often on the basis of hereditary or biological factors such as race, sex, age, and nationality. Ascribed statuses are most likely to become master statuses. For example, teenagers (an ascribed status) are often viewed with suspicion, regardless of their individual characteristics. Husband and wife also tend to be master statuses. Because marriage is such an important social relationship, it highlights cultural differences in the value placed on ascribed versus achieved statuses.

Arranged Marriage

In Romeo and Juliet's day, parents had the right and obligation to select and approve a child's choice of marriage partner. Indeed, most cultures consider marriage and family—rearing children, inheritance, and carrying forward the family line—too important to be pinned on something as unpredictable and stormy as individual attraction. Marriages are arranged by families; finding a daughter- or son-in-law appropriate to the family's status is the family's top priority (although whether the two young people like each other may also be taken into account). Young people rely on their parents' wisdom. They expect love to develop *after* marriage, based on the statuses of husband and wife ascribed by their families and communities.

Followers of romantic love, in contrast, view marriage as an achieved status. Romantics spend years looking for the perfect mate and rely on extended courtship to "win" this ideal lover. (Ironically, the same ideology that encourages us to marry for love may be used by some, whose match is less-than-perfect, to justify extramarital affairs or divorce later.) We resent being told who is appropriate and who is not—as when our parents forbid us to date a certain boy or girl in high school or when friends insist on arranging a blind date. Our individualism draws us to stories like Romeo and Juliet, in which lovers defy their society and culture's rules and expectations.

Love and Marriage

The link between romantic love and marriage began in England as part of the general Protestant condemnation of the immorality, excesses, and "dangerous liaisons" of the aristocracy (Gay, 1995). Marrying for love appealed to the emerging British middle class. The image of two individuals pouring out their souls to one another merged with the spread of Protestantism and the rise of capitalism. Protestantism emphasized the importance of self-knowledge and cleansing the mind of evil thoughts, which became central themes in love letters of the day. At the same time, romantic love fostered the individual motivation, drive for personal achievement, and self-esteem needed in an expanding capitalist economy.

Nowhere did romantic love take deeper root than in America (Lystra, 1989). Judging by letters, the primary medium of communication at that time, nineteenth-century courtship was a process of self-disclosure and self-discovery, with lovers urging one another to express their "inner" self and "real" feelings. On one level, the function of these exchanges was to test a couple's compatibility before marriage. On another level, romance provided an emotional outlet for middle-class men, who were increasingly expected to exhibit a cool and calculating demeanor in their public lives. Only in romance could men "be themselves." Romance also functioned to bridge the widening gap between men's and women's worlds.

In early twentieth-century America, ideas about love—especially men in love—began to change (Stearns and Knapp, 1993). The "deromanticizing" of

Across cultures and centuries, romantic love has been denounced or encouraged. In nineteenth century America, men were supposed to be circumspect in their public lives, but they could share their feelings in letters to their beloved.

male love can be seen in *Esquire*, the first magazine designed specifically for men *as men* and the precursor of *Playboy*. Defining itself as an antidote to the "sweetness and light" of women's magazines, *Esquire* attacked modern women as irrational, frivolous, jealous, and nagging; published articles about war, adventure, and sports (men's private domains); and pictured women (along with cars and men's clothes) as consumer goods, not distant ideals, and love affairs as a leisure-time activity, almost a sport, rather than part of a search for a life-partner.

Esquire reflected changing male—female relationships. Nineteenth-century romance depended on mystery: Bachelors spent most of their time with other bachelors, pining for true love. Beginning in the early twentieth century, however, boys and girls saw each other every day in school; private, long-distance courtship was replaced by public dating, which involved boys posturing for other boys as well as the competitive pursuit of females. For males at least, love was "brought down to earth" (p. 790).

But to some extent the link between love and marriage was always a myth. While our culture encourages the belief that people should search for their "one and only" and that the match is largely a matter of psychological compatibility, sociology shows that our choices are not as free as we like to think.

Americans tend to marry at certain stages in life, especially in young adulthood when a first job seems secured. Our choice of a marriage partner depends in part on who we meet at this stage. We might have been equally compatible with someone we met as a teenager or in middle age; timing is critical.

Who we choose depends on whom we meet, which in turn depends on social structure and networks, as discussed above. People who go to college meet other college students and are more likely to marry within this category—which also means they are more likely to marry someone of the same social class (because who goes to college, and which college they go to, are shaped by social class).

Sociocultural similarity, in turn, fosters feelings of "compatibility." Opposites may attract, but such attractions are difficult to maintain. People from the same background are likely to have similar child-rearing values, political attitudes, and tastes. Similarity confirms our own beliefs and attitudes and makes us feel good about ourselves. Thus, although we are free to marry almost anyone, who we choose depends on sociocultural similarity, structural opportunity, and timing (Kalmijn, 1994).

"Falling in love" has always had a practical side. The ideology of romantic love does not exclude consideration of other qualities, but it is a question of priorities. In studies of partner preferences, love and mutual attraction receive top priority in all Western societies (except that French women put "dependable character" first) (Buss et al., 1990). Men rate good looks higher than women do, while women tend to put more emphasis on ambition and industriousness. Both sexes value emotional stability and maturity, a pleasing disposition, and education and intelligence.

Romantic love exacts a cost. Contrary to what we might expect, in societies where romance shapes expectations for marriage, divorce rates are much *higher* than in countries where marriages are arranged and personal attraction plays a minor role in the decision. In addition, close friendships outside of marriage—even same-sex friendships—are more likely to be seen as competing with marriage and to become a source of tension (rather than support) in societies that idealize romantic love.

Friendship

Like love, patterns of friendship depend on the cultural setting. What place friendship plays in a society, who becomes friends with whom, how cliques form, which friends last a lifetime, and what moral obligations go with friendship all vary. Among the Masai of East Africa, for example, friendship is ascribed. Males who go through initiation and other formalized stages of the life cycle together are expected to become comrades, and generally they do. Age-sets have names and are considered as important as kinship and clans; age-mates share everything (including even their wives' "sexual hospitality").

For the ancient Greeks, friendship was "achieved" or chosen, not ascribed. Aristotle and others idealized friendship as the most valuable and pure of relationships (Stern-Gillet, 1995). They ranked it far above marriage, which was seen as a utilitarian relationship, tied to the need to reproduce and maintain a home and constrained by statuses (head of household, wife and mother) and role obligations. Marriage was a necessity; friendship was an opportunity for true self-expression and genuine companionship. Greek ideals of friendship prevailed in Western societies well into the nineteenth century, at least in the upper and emerging middle classes.

With the rise of romantic love, however, friendship was downgraded somewhat. We still have and value friends, but we do not romanticize our relationships with them as we do with lovers—at least not as adults. Friendships among preadolescent girls, with their crushes, vows of undying devotion, confessions, and jealousies, are similar to romance and indeed serve as a rehearsal for more mature involvements (Simon, Eder, and Evans, 1992). But crushes seldom last a year, much less a lifetime.

Friends made in college or at work are more likely to endure than those from childhood, but they do not play the central role in most Americans' lives that friends do in other societies. Part of the reason is structural. Americans are highly mobile; for example, we are more likely than Europeans are to go away to college, rather than commute from our parents' homes, and to choose different colleges than our friends. As a result, childhood and high school friendships usually fade. Unlike Europeans, Americans often live in one community and commute to work in another, so that workplace friends are not also neighbors, which would reinforce ties.

In the United States, friendship occupies an ambiguous position as a "non-institutionalized institution" (Rawlins, 1992). Everyone recognizes the status of "friend," but individuals must negotiate for themselves what role they will play in one another's lives. This involves trade-offs—for example, between the desire to be independent and the desire to be able to depend on another (and be dependable), between the ideal of "friendship for friendship's sakes" and the reality of rewards and benefits, both tangible and intangible. Acquaintances may become casual friends, and casual friends, close friends—or the reverse—depending on personal inclination, stage in the life cycle, and social circumstances (such as one getting married or divorced, or moving).

In Australia, male friendships—bonds between "mates"—involve fewer ambiguities. Formed early in life, they last, not just because of individual liking but also because mateship is built into Australian society and culture (Brain, 1976). Given a choice between a better job at higher pay in another region and staying near their mates, Australian men choose the latter. Wives recognize that mates are important and will not be put aside after marriage. One reason that mateship coexists with marriage is that the relationships are based on different models. In the words of Australian anthropologist Robert Brain,

mateship began with the mutual regard and trust between men working together in the lonely bush, men whose isolation and need for cooperation called for mutual helpfulness. Cooperation was the first essential for survival . . . [and the] chief article of faith was that mates should "stick together." (1976, p. 68)

Mateship is shaped by the heroic ideals of loyalty and trust, not the romantic ideal of emotional intimacy. Mates may say little, but they know they can count on one another.

In the United States, conventional wisdom holds that women form stronger bonds than men do; that women talk, whereas men simply "hang out." Some sociologists (Cancian, 1986, 1987) hold that our concept of friendship has been "feminized." That is, the strength of a friendship is measured in terms of expressing feelings, a skill at which women tend to excel. Measured against the "feminine" standard of intimacy, male relationships have been characterized as immature and shallow.

Comparing patterns in Australia and the United States, the sociologist Barbara Bank (1995) found, as expected, that women in both countries put more emphasis on self-disclosure and expressions of affection than men do. However, American men value intimacy more than Australian men do, suggesting the difference is a product of culture as well as a reflection of gender. Bank holds that the "feminization" of friendship in America has been exaggerated. Male friendships in this country include elements of the loyalty, trust, and mutual assistance that define Australian mateship, as when men work together to fix a car. The aggressive elements of male friendships—teasing, competition, physical jostling, ritual put-downs—are often interpreted as a means of avoiding intimacy and hence a barrier to friendship. Bank disagrees: Expressing anger and disapproval to a friend suggests a high degree of comfort and trust.

Another sociologist, Karen Walker (1994), interviewed working-class and professional American couples. Men and women of both classes subscribed to the stereotype that women share feelings whereas men share activities—at least in the abstract. When asked about their own friends, however, a different picture emerged. Going to sports events with a buddy was symbolically important to men but relatively infrequent (once or twice a year). And while men denied that talking with friends was important, most reported that they did engage in conversations about such intimate matters as their wives' sexual preferences and fertility problems, as well as helping friends cope with their feelings after a divorce or when "coming out of the closet."

Again contrary to stereotypes, women enjoy shared activities—working out or shopping together, or going to concerts, clubs, or sports events with female friends. Professional women said they were friendly with many colleagues but did not like to burden others with their problems and thus discussed intimate matters only with their spouses (the classic "male" pattern). Many regretted that their everyday lives did not include female confidants. Working-class women are less likely to travel or to move and are more likely to work part-time or to stay home with small children and hence have more opportunities to talk among themselves. For the same reasons, their adult friends tend to be high school friends and neighbors. Structural factors also shape couples' joint social lives. Professional couples know more people but have few opportunities to develop strong, close, long-lasting networks of friends that play a central and stable social role in their lives. Less mobile, working-class men and women have fewer friends, but they know them longer and see them more often.

Friendship takes on special importance in later life (O'Connor, 1995). Young and middle-aged adults are involved in numerous relationships (with their spouses, children, other parents, co-workers, etc.), and to some extent, friendship is a leisure-time extra. Older people have fewer ready-made interactions, especially after retirement. As a result, friends are crucial to maintaining a sense of social connection (Johnson and Troll, 1994). Contrary to what their grown children may believe, older people have more fun with friends than with family (whose efforts to help may be seen as demeaning and intrusive).

The elderly face numerous obstacles to friendship, however. Those who remain in a suburban home or in a neighborhood where everyone they knew has left or died are isolated. Yet those who move—to a warmer climate, to a retirement community, or nearer to their children—have to start over. Most lose friends as the years pass. Making new friends can be daunting, especially for widowers whose wives ran their social lives. Poor health often limits older people's ability to entertain or visit friends. The elderly cope with these limitations in several ways (Johnson and Troll, 1994). Many expand their definition of *friend* to include acquaintances and caregivers, make fewer

demands for emotional intimacy and reciprocity (such as gift exchange), and keep in touch through letters, phone calls, and increasingly, e-mail.

SECONDARY AND INDIRECT RELATIONSHIPS

In contemporary society, friends and family are only a fraction of the people with whom we interact. Modern life requires that every day—whether we are at work, at play, or running errands—we deal with countless strangers, people with whom we are not familiar and with whom we have little or no social connection. The growth of urban society has not only increased the amount of interaction with strangers but also increased our dependence on one another. Americans, in particular, like to think of themselves as "free agents." Yet even as we become, more than ever, strangers to one another, we depend, more than ever, on one another to carry on our "individual" lives. "Interdependence is less a choice than a situation that confronts us in our modern circumstance" (Brown, 1995, p. 7). Interdependence is built into our society's division of labor, professional specialties, and organizations; our dealings with neighborhoods and the global marketplace; the communication and transportation systems on which we rely and the social services on which we depend. We are inextricably bound to the plumber who fixes our pipes, the neighborhood kids who shovel the snow, the principals of our children's schools, and countless others. We may chat, superficially, with bus drivers and shop clerks, but we do not have the time, energy, or inclination to become friends with all of the people we meet (though the possibility of expanding a face-to-face relationship always exists). "It is not our community ties but our interdependence that keeps us entangled" (Brown, 1995, p. 7).

Strangers

The German sociologist Georg Simmel (1950) was among the first to analyze the impact of strangers on social life. According to Simmel, the sheer number of people, events, and sounds that confront the individual in the city is overwhelming. Paying attention to everyone and everything is impossible. To cope

People in large cities would be overwhelmed if they stopped to pay attention to the hundreds of strangers they pass each day. For Georg Simmel, the urbanite's emotional shield developed as a means of survival.

with this mass assault on the senses, people develop a coat of armor, a shield of indifference. The reason urbanites may not strike up conversations in coffee shops or say hello to strangers on the street is not that they are coldhearted but rather that being able to "tune out" is an essential urban survival skill. A **stranger** is someone in the midst of a social group with whom he or she has no personal ties. More than simply being unknown, a stranger is an outsider. Thus a cousin who no one in the family has met before is not a stranger in the same sense as the people who occupy adjacent seats in a theater, even though you and they may chat.

Alfred Schutz, a phenomenological sociologist who worked in both the United States and Germany until the 1960s, also focused on the experience of being a stranger. Anticipating Albert Camus's famous novel *The Stranger,* Schutz held that being a stranger was more than a temporary experience of being in situations where one did not know people—it had become a defining feature of modern existence. Disconnected from other people, the individual is left to himself or herself to decide whether to act or to passively accept fate—and to face the bleak (existential) realization that, in the overall scheme of things, it probably does not matter (Schutz, 1967).

The experiences of (1) being a stranger much of the time and (2) constantly interacting with strangers sets us apart from people in earlier historical periods. A truly "modern" person is one who moves freely about in the world, interacting with many people he or she does not know, many of whom are very different in cultural background and social position. Contemporary research suggests that we have more benign or friendly interactions with strangers than Simmel imagined, and this in part offsets the alienation Schutz identified (Alexander, 1995; Seligman, 1993).

Though personally unknown and unconnected, strangers occupy a social status with culturally prescribed role expectations. Most of the people passing through an airport, for example, are strangers to one another and to airport employees. Some wear business suits and carry briefcases. They are treated specially by airline personnel (who assume they are frequent travelers) and are more likely to speak to one another than to mothers shepherding children or to longhaired young men carrying guitars. When business travelers do talk, they stick to a few topics: sports, business, movies, and TV. To delve into politics, personal life, or religion is bad form. Typically, they ask where each other is from, what line of business each is in, what company each works for, and perhaps where each went to college or business school. Given a possible connection, they probe to see if they have acquaintances in common ("Oh, you went to USC? Did you know Bill Martin?"). In short, we have cultural rules for dealing with strangers. We seek people who appear similar to ourselves; stick to safe subjects if we talk; and try to learn what statuses these strangers occupy and whether we are connected to them in any way.

Cooperation and Trust

You are alone in a strange city on a dark, deserted street. You need to withdraw cash from an automatic teller machine. As you insert your card your heart begins to pound. . . . The fear we experience in certain situations underscores the high degree of trust we feel most of the time. We give our credit card numbers to salespeople on the phone; send our children to school with bus drivers we have never met; hand our car keys to parking lot attendants and walk away. Usually our trust is well-placed.

We hear so much about crime in public places, we tend to overlook how often strangers cooperate. David Brown (1995) cites a line in a bank. When a number of people arrive at the same time, they form a line and wait their turn. We know from experience and observation that a line is expedient; it helps us cope with the problem of too many customers and too few tellers; and "it works for everyone . . . eventually" (Brown, 1995, p. 24).

Even in emergencies, where one might expect people to look out for themselves, cooperation usually prevails (Brown, 1995). When the World Trade Center in New York City was bombed in February 1993, the on-site police command center, set up for emergencies, was destroyed by the terrorist blast. Thousands of strangers coordinated their own evacuation. How? Interviews indicate that "perfect strangers" helped one another, drawing on emergency routines remembered from schooldays, airplane safety procedures they had never used, and images of coping with emergencies seen on TV. Their behavior was not random; shared norms made such apparently spontaneous coordination possible.

Most of our interactions with strangers are either emotionally neutral or friendly. Indeed, social life in modern societies requires a level of basic trust among people who are not involved in ongoing social relationships (Fukuyama, 1995). The nation's ghettoes illustrate what happens when basic trust breaks down. Family, friends, and near neighbors look out for one another, but *public* trust is missing. Store owners in-

stall bulletproof glass between themselves and their customers; people stay indoors much of the time; those who can, leave; those who cannot may tolerate the rules imposed by gangs as better than no rules at all. Ironically, the more people fear the streets and stay inside, the more unsafe streets become. Campaigns to "take back the streets" are organized efforts to end isolation and revive public life.

Conflict

Whenever people interact there is a potential for conflict. Ghetto residents may see police as hostile, not helpful; some parents support sex education, while others strongly oppose this; some residents of a co-op may want to make expensive renovations to increase the value of their apartments, while others may want to keep costs to a minimum.

Conflict is not necessarily bad, however. Conflict promotes innovation, creativity, and social change by challenging institutions and practices that may have outlived their usefulness. Because of conflict with the community, many police departments now have community liaison officers and special training for "difference (racial or ethnic) disputes" and family violence. Conflict may also promote unity and cooperation, as when neighbors unite to close down a crack house on their block or to prevent the location of a toxic waste dump in their backyard.

What is surprising about contemporary societies is not the amount of conflict but the level of voluntary politeness (Wuthnow, 1991). Most people apologize for bumping another passenger on a bus, for example. Most smokers obey the ban on smoking in public places. People in Iowa send money to victims of famine in Africa and flooding in Asia. Rescue teams from around the country volunteered to help after the bombing of the federal building in Oklahoma City in 1995. The tradition of the Good Samaritan has not disappeared.

Indirect Social Relations

"Strangers" usually refers to people with whom we interact face-to-face but with whom we do not have any personal, lasting relationship. Some of the most important strangers in our lives, however, are people we never meet. When we vote for a senator or a president, write to a newspaper columnist, make dona-

In modern societies, cooperation and communication can be quite spontaneous. At sporting events, thousands of fans often stand for "the wave."

tions to charity, board an airplane, we enter into relationships with people we will probably never meet in person. These are **indirect relationships** in which the parties are not involved with each other personally or face to face, but are linked indirectly by communications technology, bureaucracies, or other intermediaries (Calhoun, 1991). There is no expectation that we will get to know one another better and no clear obligation to look out for one another's welfare, but there is still a relationship (Brown, 1995). Throughout the modern era, more and more of social life has come to be organized on the basis of indirect relationships (Abu-Lughod, 1969; Calhoun, 1992).

In the movie *Roger and Me* a filmmaker documented the impact of a General Motors plant's closing on workers and neighborhoods in Detroit. He filmed laid-off employees receiving their last check; families being evicted from their homes; and auto

executives' wives playing golf as usual, oblivious to the changes taking place in their community. Over and over, the filmmaker attempted to interview Roger Smith, at the time the CEO (chief executive officer) of General Motors. The physical layout of the places Roger Smith frequents, plus a phalanx of security guards, keep the filmmaker at bay. He only glimpses the General Motors CEO from a distance at a stockholders meeting. Yet, as the movie's title indicates, the filmmaker—and more significantly, (former) GM employees—are involved in a relationship with Roger Smith that has serious consequences for their personal lives.

We usually think of power in personal terms, such as the power of a king over his subjects or a general over his troops. But in modern societies, the most dramatic forms of power are impersonal—the power of the market, for example, or of bureaucracies (Weber, 1922/1968; Habermas, 1988). Like Roger Smith, the CEO of a corporation is involved in indirect relationships with thousands of workers and consumers. When AT&T lays off thousands of employees, the CEO is doing what he thinks will make money for the corporation and for shareholders. Nonetheless, the CEO is taking social action, doing one thing rather than another, knowing that the action will affect an enormous number of people.

The same is true of a manufacturer that continues to sell a product it knows is dangerous. In the 1970s and early 1980s, A. H. Robbins continued to sell the Dalkon Shield even after it learned that this interuterine birth control device caused serious infections and sometimes infertility. More recently, Du Pont and other manufacturers have continued to sell breast implants despite charges that they are harmful. In each case, the corporate decision-makers took actions that affected thousands of strangers. Only after lawsuits required them to pay compensation did these corporations acknowledge that their actions involved a social relationship with consumers—and a social responsibility.

Our everyday experience with family, friends, coworkers, and even strangers does not prepare us for indirect relationships (Calhoun, 1992). We continue to think and act *as if* such relationships were direct and personal; we have trouble dealing with impersonal social forces and impersonal relationships.

Yet without indirect relationships, establishing large-scale social organizations such as modern governments, business corporations, and universities would be impossible. To understand the modern workplace and other social institutions, we need to understand how face-to-face interpersonal relationships coexist with impersonal, indirect relationships. Whether we work for General Motors, IBM, or the U.S. Army, our daily experiences consist of direct interaction with fellow workers, customers, clients, and others. But the purpose of our jobs, the structure of the organization as a whole, and the future of our careers depend in large part on the actions of people to whom we are related only indirectly.

INTERACTION AT WORK

Most adult Americans spend 35 to 45 hours a week or more on the job. They interact with numerous co-workers, managers, clients, suppliers, and others in the course of the workweek. For many, social contact is second only to their paycheck as a reason to work. They enjoy their jobs because they enjoy socializing.

Friendships often develop on the job. Slack time, work breaks, lunches, and commuting provide opportunities to talk and perhaps discover common ground unrelated to work (children of the same age, similar backgrounds, shared political, religious, or recreational interests). Millions of people who have no one to go home to—or no one at home to talk to—are intimate with at least one co-worker with whom they discuss personal worries, whose opinions they seek in making important decisions, and who they see socially outside the workplace (Marks, 1994).

Just as we find friends at work, so friends, family, and acquaintances help us find work. Beginning with the job interview, however, we are dependent on our ability to interact with strangers. How well we handle this social process can be as important as education, prior experiences, and references in determining whether we land the job. Job interviews are by definition unequal: The applicant is on trial, and the interviewer is the judge and jury. The job applicant is expected to be deferential; the interviewer is expected to limit herself or himself to job-related topics and not probe into the applicant's personal life or political and religious convictions. The verbal information they exchange is only part of the "test," however. All interactions with strangers involve quick judgments based on appearance, clothing, language, and mannerisms. Arriving late (however good one's excuse), dressing inappropriately, or behaving too casually can determine the outcome of a job interview before it begins.

Networks

Success on the job depends in part on understanding patterns of relationships, called **networks** because when the links among people are drawn on a chart, the resulting picture looks like a net or a web. At work, most people are involved in multiple, overlapping networks. The first is the group of co-workers who share the same factory floor or office space, or the members of an army platoon, who interact many times each day. Most co-workers are equals, but a few hold higher positions in the organization, and others, lower positions. The second network, represented by managers and supervisors, reflects the formal organizational hierarchy. For example, a soldier's links to the military hierarchy begin with a corporal, sergeant, and lieutenant and continue up to colonels and generals with whom the soldier seldom interacts. Third, most workers have a network of work friends that includes some (but not all) co-workers. The soldier's network of friends includes some people from his or her platoon and some from other platoons, but most at the same rank. In a corporation or a university, as in the military, becoming friends with someone much higher (or lower) in the hierarchy is rare.

Of course, not all workers interact primarily with fellow employees. Teachers spend much of their workday with students. Salespeople interact mainly with prospective customers; doctors and nurses, primarily with patients; lawyers, with clients, judges, and lawyers from other firms. They also are indirectly involved with the school board, the manufacturers whose goods they sell, the hospital board of directors, or the legislatures that pass laws. The structure of a complex organization is thus a mixture of the directly interpersonal and the impersonal.

Norms and the Negotiated Order

A key workplace skill is knowing what rules to apply to different interactions. It may be acceptable for a boss to pat an employee on the shoulder, for example, but not the reverse. It is acceptable for a salesperson to chat with one client about another client, but for a lawyer to do so would be a breach of trust. In short, workplace relationships are governed by norms.

The importance of shared norms stands out when co-workers, or workers and bosses, come from very

Americans in Tokyo: The Importance of Small Talk

With the globalization of trade, Japanese firms often need American workers to help adapt ads and products from one culture for the other. It is no longer unusual to find regular, full-time American employees in Japanese companies, and the number of Americans who study Japanese in the hope of working in Japan is growing. How well do the Americans adapt to the Japanese workplace? Do they fit in with their Japanese co-workers?

Laura Miller (1995) studied Japanese–American interaction at three firms in Tokyo. Too often, Miller maintains, cross-cultural studies produce lists of opposites: for example, Americans are verbal and Japanese are nonverbal; Americans are direct and Japanese indirect; Americans are competitive and Japanese cooperative. But all norms are situational: Japanese may speak little on meeting a stranger, but they are quite voluble in a Japanese coffee shop or public bath. To avoid such generalizations, Miller chose conversational analysis (see the discussion under Conversation Analysis, later in this chapter).

Miller found that misunderstandings were frequent. Knowledge of vocabulary and grammar is only part of language; to communicate effectively one must also know how phrases, pauses, and other conversational techniques are used. Americans and Japanese often began an interaction with different objectives and left with different conclusions. Nevertheless, complaining (a favorite workplace pastime), joking and teasing, conversing in a mixture of English and Japanese, mutual compliments—what we call "small talk"—bridged the gap. Through informal interaction, workers developed "a sense of themselves as fellow employees and colleagues rather than as either Japanese or American" (p. 154).

Miller recommends that individuals (and companies) approach cross-cultural interaction as an ethnographer might. A good ethnographer learns about another culture in part by examining the cultural assumptions and expectations *he* or *she* brings to a situation. The ethnographer is alert to his or her own negative character or ethnic evaluations ("he's too direct," "they are evasive"), which often are the main clue to underlying cultural differences. At this point the ethnographer/worker should stand back and ask, What cultural differences may be operating here? Above all, companies and co-workers should take the importance of small talk and frivolity in multicultural settings seriously.

---

different cultural backgrounds (see the *Global Issues/Local Consequences* box). However, even when people share similar cultural backgrounds, ground rules must be established. Only rarely do the formal rules of the organization or the titles people hold dictate precisely how individuals should act. Rather, patterns of interactions are based on a **negotiated order,** a collective definition of what the interaction means, what the players' positions are in relation to one another, and what behavior will be considered appropriate.

The first meetings of a college class illustrate negotiation. Some students may try to impress the teacher by showing off the knowledge they already have. Even if the teacher is impressed, other students may convey disapproval by groaning, not sitting next to the would-be teacher's pets, or challenging their comments. If the showing-off students still attempt to dominate discussion, the teacher may ask them to give others a chance; if they persist, the teacher may become annoyed, criticize their comments, and point-

edly ignore their raised hands. This, in turn, may embolden other students to exert more pressure of their own. In these ways, the teacher and other students negotiate an acceptable level of input from potentially domineering class members. Likewise, office or factory workers negotiate to reduce interruptions by a highly talkative co-worker, exert pressure on a worker who plays up to the boss, or "break in" a new co-worker or supervisor.

Groups within Organizations

Meetings play a crucial role in organizations, whether in a university, bank, hospital, TV station, or political group. As the sociologist Deirdre Boden writes, "Meetings are where organizations come together," where different coalitions with different agendas converge (1994, p. 81). Most actual business—setting goals, evaluating progress, collecting and circulating information, resolving misunderstandings—takes place outside meetings, through telephone calls, memoranda, reports, and the like. To a large degree meetings are ritual affairs that ratify the social structure of the organization, legitimate individual and institutional roles, and reaffirm solidarity and commitment to the organization. One of the main functions of meetings is to contain conflict through "ritualized combat." At university faculty meetings, for example, there are often clashes between those who defend the "classical values" enshrined in the "traditional curriculum" and those who want to "modernize" and introduce "cutting-edge" subjects. However much they may quarrel, by airing their differences in the context of a departmental meeting (rather than appealing to the Board of Trustees or to other "outsiders"), they affirm their commitment to the organization.

The social interaction in a meeting may be more important than the reason the meeting is called or the topic under discussion. The act of calling a meeting symbolizes power; likewise, who is invited is a measure of status. (Clerks and other lower-level functionaries generally are not present). "Who talks when, to whom, and for how long" are critical (Boden, 1994, p. 82). One basic distinction is between formal and informal meetings.

Formal meetings, whether regularly scheduled or specially convened, are typically announced in writing, follow a fixed agenda, have a designated chairperson, and include those people whose positions in the organization entitle them to be present. Typically the chairperson leads the discussion, selects speakers, determines when speakers' time is up, maintains order, and calls the meeting to a close, summing up. Decisions are rarely made during the meeting itself; but issues that require decisions may be raised, or decisions that have already been made may be announced. Formal meetings are "matters of record" in the form of minutes or official reports.

Informal meetings tend to be smaller and more task-oriented. Convened verbally, they typically have no designated chairperson, no fixed agenda, and no regular membership or required attendance. Who talks for how long is flexible. Such meetings are not officially recorded, though individuals may take notes and later write memos. Informal meetings often occur when a group within an organization wants to decide what position to take on an issue. These meetings often end with a division of labor as to who will seek further information or who will speak to members of other departments or to officials higher up in the organization.

As meetings illustrate, many of the most important workplace relationships involve interaction in groups. Georg Simmel (1902a, 1902b) was one of the first sociologists to recognize the complexity of group interaction and to analyze this systematically. He saw that the size of a group makes an enormous difference, both to its internal organization and external relations. This analysis starts with the contrast between a two-person group (or **dyad**) and a three-person group (a **triad**). Compared with other groups, a dyad is fragile. If one member leaves, the group ceases to exist. Also, there is no third party to mediate disputes. However, these qualities of a dyad increase the incentive for commitment and for partners to learn how to reconcile their differences. Three-person groups differ from dyads in several ways. If one person leaves, the group does not necessarily dissolve. A third party may threaten the relationship between the original two, or two may "gang up" on the third. On the other hand, coalitions may shift from one issue to the next, enhancing solidarity. As the number of members increases, the potential number of internal patterns of interaction and relationships increases exponentially (see Table 3.1).

In large groups, there is a limit on the amount and quality of communication among all members. Information is transmitted indirectly, through formal channels and the informal grapevine. Problem solving also changes with group size. A large group has a wider variety of skills and resources on which to draw, but the average contribution of individual members tends to be less than it would be in a small group. In short, as size increases, groups dynamics change.

TABLE 3.1

As Group Size Increases Arithmetically, the Number of Relationships Increases Geometrically

Size of Group	Number of Relationships
2	1
3	6
4	25
6	301
7	966

Source: A. Paul Hare, Handbook of Small Group Research (Free Press, Glencoe, Ill., 1976), p. 218.

At informal meetings, flexibility reigns. Group members may meet to plan their positions for a later, more formal meeting within an organization.

In a work setting, it is essential to keep groups focused on their tasks; this is the function of leadership. Even in workplaces, however, the "task group" is also an "emotional group" (Miller and Rice, 1967). While explicitly focused on doing work together, group members are also concerned about emotional issues: Are other employees getting ahead of them? Is the manager insulting them? Can they feel secure in their jobs? The social psychology of groups presents a major challenge to effective work organization. Group pressure can lead people to do things that they ordinarily would not do, or to remain silent when they doubt the wisdom of a decision. The psychologist Irving Janis (1982, 1989) coined the term **groupthink** to describe these situations. Especially in small, highly cohesive groups with a dynamic leader, members tend to be so intent on maintaining group solidarity that, consciously or unconsciously, they suppress their own doubts, dismiss contrary advice from knowledgeable outsiders, and collectively rationalize their decisions. Groupthink is loyalty gone awry. At the same time, people's strongest commitments to an organization are often based on their loyalty to a primary group of workplace friends and close associates. Group membership is a powerful motivator, for better or worse.

Leadership and Workplace Culture

Reflecting the dual nature of group life, leadership also has two dimensions, *instrumental* and *expressive* (Secord and Backman, 1974). **Instrumental leadership** focuses on explicit task management; **expressive leadership** focuses on maintaining group solidarity and good relations among members. Some leaders (and some organizations) combine these skills, while others arrange a division of labor.

When Apple Computer Corporation sets out to design a new product, for example, it appoints a manager, who then puts together a project team of engineers, designers, software specialists, and others (Garsten, 1994; Kidder, 1981; see also Moody, 1995). Some may have worked together on previous projects, but others will be strangers or know each other only by reputation. The manager is responsible for assigning initial tasks and for keeping the team on schedule (instrumental leadership). To maintain motivation, the manager also needs to build a sense of group solidarity (expressive leadership). He or she may buy everyone T-shirts with a group slogan, order in food when they work late (as is often the case), and encourage team members to develop different nontask identities, like the joker, the good listener, and the one who gives others neck rubs. The more pressure the group is under, the more important the emotional side of management: People push themselves because they do not want to let the group down. Balancing the emotional and instrumental aspects of group work and leadership are equally important in an army platoon or a surgical team.

Different organizations have different approaches, however. Apple Computer tries to foster company loyalty by creating an informal work environment, encouraging employees to dress and act in ways that express their individuality, and relying on emotionally intense but temporary project teams to get tasks done. IBM, in contrast, long required all its salesmen and executives to wear nearly identical blue suits and encouraged them to adopt similar lifestyles. Until recently, its management strategy was to encourage loyalty by maintaining a high level of stability within the company, not reassigning people very often. Both companies have been highly successful, and both have run into crises but in different ways. Apple developed its style in California, in the effort to create and sell a new kind of product, the personal computer, which was bought mainly by individuals. IBM developed its style in New York, in the effort to sell large, expensive, mainframe computers to businesses and bureaucracies. Thus the differences between the two companies reflected the context of their sales, as well as distinct managerial strategies and corporate styles. To see the impact of different workplace structures, we need to look at organizations as a whole.

COMPLEX ORGANIZATIONS: BUREAUCRACY AND ITS ALTERNATIVES

The word *bureaucracy* conjures up everything that people commonly do not like about large organizations: waiting in lines for hours, filling out endless forms, following rules that seem to have no purpose, being treated like a nine-digit number instead of a person. But like them or not, bureaucracies are a fact of modern society. We spend our lives moving from one bureaucracy to another. We are born in large hospitals, taught in formal educational systems, employed by multinational corporations, governed by state and federal agencies, and even buried by large mortuary firms.

Moreover, formal, bureaucratic organizations are not only nuisances. While rules and procedures can become too complex or rigid they can also be helpful. Bureaucracies enable people to accomplish tasks that they could not accomplish in an informal, loosely

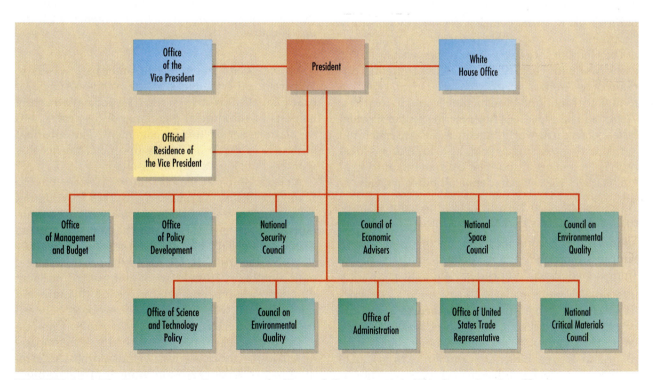

FIGURE 3.2 / The Bureaucratic Structure of a Formal Organization: The Organization Chart of the Executive Office of the President of the United States

As in any large organization, members of the executive branch of the U.S. government report to their superiors according to a formal plan. If, for example, you are a member of the Council of Economic Advisers, you report directly to the President, not to a member of the National Security Council.

Source: Office of the Federal Register, 1989, *Federal Register*, Washington, D.C., p. 86.

structured group (see Figure 3.2). When membership grows beyond ten or twelve people, face-to-face groups tend to break into subgroups that require more formal organization. This is true not only of work groups, but also of social clubs, such as fraternities and sororities. The task of keeping people organized generally grows more complex with scale. Thus, large organizations typically have more formal bureaucratic structures than do small ones. Yet even in large, complex institutions we find very different approaches to organization.

The Nature of Bureaucracy

Bureaucracies have existed in many societies and times, but they only became dominant in the modern era. Bureaucratic structure solved three main problems: how to organize a large number of people for a collective goal, how to coordinate diverse tasks, and how to manage political conflict (or power struggles). In the nineteenth century, as the size and complexity of Western government, markets, and municipalities grew, bureaucracies became increasingly common.

The German sociologist Max Weber, writing in the early twentieth century, was the first to define **bureaucracy.** Weber constructed an "ideal type," a model to highlight bureaucracy's major features. Weber's ideal type does not describe any individual bureaucracy; real-world bureaucracies are much too varied to fit into a single mold. Instead, Weber's ideal type is an analytical tool that calls attention to general features that help to define all bureaucracies:

1. Specialization: In bureaucracies, the main work of the organization is broken down into a clear-cut division of labor, and people are trained to specialize in performing each task.

2. Hierarchy of offices: Once an operation is divided into smaller, more manageable tasks, the various activities must be coordinated. If not, people in one department might design a bolt an eighth of an inch larger than the nut designed in another department (Blau and Meyer, 1987). The solution is to organize workers into a hierarchy, with each person responsible to the person directly above in the chain of command. Each position carries certain duties and privileges. The authority of those in higher positions resides in the offices they hold, not in the people themselves. Their authority is clearly defined and limited.

3. Rules: Activities and relationships in a bureaucracy are governed by explicit rules. In this way, people know exactly what is required of them. Rules make the workings of a bureaucracy orderly and predictable, even with changes in personnel.

4. Impersonality: Weber believed that emotions impede efficiency and therefore have no place in a bureaucracy. Personal detachment promotes rational decision making, he argued. Impersonality toward workers, suppliers, clients, and customers encourages fair treatment.

5. Rewards based on merit: Positions in a bureaucracy are awarded on the basis of technical qualifications (as measured by tests, educational degrees, and other standardized yardsticks), not on the basis of whom one knows, and promotions are based on performance. When supervisors give jobs and promotions to friends and relatives, the organization suffers. Not only will less competent people fill many positions, but individual effort and morale will diminish. If people are to give their best efforts to an organization, they need to know that their work will be properly rewarded.

No real-world bureaucracy conforms precisely to Weber's ideal type. None is completely formed, for example; all have two sides. The **formal structure** consists of the official positions, duties, rules, and regulations set by top management. The **informal structure** is made up of the unofficial norms that workers develop among themselves.

A classic study at the Hawthorne Western Electric plant (Roethlisberger and Dickson, 1939/1961) found that assembly-line workers routinely violated company regulations. For example, the company tried to maximize output by paying workers on a piece-rate basis, but the workers developed their own, informal definition of a fair day's work and exerted pressure on both "rate-busters" who exceeded this rate and on "chiselers" who fell short. The workers believed (perhaps correctly) that if they competed among themselves to earn more individually, the company might lower the piece rate or raise production requirements. Likewise, saleswomen at department stores develop their own standards and division of labor—in part to escape the monotonous, oppressive aspects of their job, in part to enhance their own sense of doing useful and satisfying work (Benson, 1986).

Bureaucracy may work where informal methods fail. The military has eliminated racial discrimination more fully than any other U.S. institution largely because it strictly follows the rules against bias.

The informal structure of an organization helps workers to solve problems not covered by regulations and to eliminate unpleasant or unnecessary labor. However, the informal structure may undermine the organization's goals, as at Western Electric where workers protected themselves by limiting their productivity. At the same time, strictly following the rules and procedures—without regard to the outcome—may also undermine organizational goals. *Ritualism,* as the sociologist Robert Merton called this (1968a), prevents people from recognizing and dealing with new conditions. But bureaucracy is not "all bad." In large part because of strict adherence to rules and regulations, the U.S. military has been more successful in eliminating racial discrimination than any institution in our society.

Formal organizations differ in *size*, ranging from the huge federal government with millions of employees to a small business with under 100 workers; in *complexity* (how many different kinds of jobs are required); in *centralization of control* (whether decision making is concentrated in a few hands or is dispersed); and in the *range of goals* (many or few).

Beyond Bureaucracy

The 1990s have brought a flood of organizational restructuring. American politics is dominated by debates over how to reform not only our health and welfare systems, but government generally. Everyone seems to agree that "government as usual" is not working, though there is little agreement about where to go from here. Nor is business proceeding as usual. Almost every week brings announcements of corporate mergers, takeovers, and downsizing. Has bureaucracy outlived its usefulness? What are some alternatives?

The Japanese Corporation

In 1989 and 1990, the huge Japanese Mitsubishi conglomerate made headlines when it purchased a controlling share of the stock in New York City's Rockefeller Center and, not long afterward, bought California's famous Pebble Beach golf course (Neff, 1990). The purchase of two national landmarks were only the tip of the iceberg: Mitsubishi's holdings in this country total at least $4 billion, and sales of Mitsubishi products (especially cars) in the United States were growing (Holstein, 1990).

Some of Mitsubishi's success is due to classic bureaucratic organization. For example, Mitsubishi has pulled together under one organizational umbrella a vast array of products and activities: Cars, oil, banks, food, computer chips, real estate, plastics, TVs, and chemicals all carry the Mitsubishi name. Mitsubishi is Japan's largest *keiretsu*, a group of large corporations in different industries that are all owned and controlled by the same parent company (Mishima, 1989; Wray, 1984).

But Mitsubishi has also thrived for decades on the basis of organizational strategies that do not fit Weber's bureaucratic ideal, strategies that helped to define an ideal type for large Japanese firms (Ouchi, 1981). The ideal type has helped to make Japan a global economic power (see Chapter 17), though in the mid 1990s many Japanese firms began to alter in efforts to cut costs. The defining features include:

1. *Lifetime employment:* In major Japanese corporations, workers are hired for life (until mandatory retirement at age fifty-five) and never face the risk of layoff or dismissal. If the need for labor in one division declines, workers are reassigned to divisions that are still growing.

2. *Emphasis on group achievement:* Workers are organized into teams of eight to ten people. Success is measured in terms of group accomplishments, not individual achievement. This allows individuals to exercise their unique talents and reduces inside competition.

3. *Promotion based on seniority:* In the typical American organization, promotions are based on individual performance; in Japan, promotions are largely determined by length of employment. Workers are hired as a group from high schools and colleges and generally move up the corporate ladder together as they age.

4. *Decentralized decision making:* Authority is more diffuse than in most U.S. corporations. Often top managers simply ratify plans made by subordinates. "Bottom-up" decision making boosts worker participation and morale and maximizes the chances that creative solutions to problems will be found.

5. *Holistic concern for employees:* Large Japanese corporations provide numerous personal services to their employees, including company-subsidized housing, mortgages, recreational facilities, vacations, and comprehensive health care.

In effect, large Japanese corporations function as an extended family in which loyalty and seniority take priority. The corporation–employee relationship is personalized—in opposition to some of the classic principles of bureaucracy. Not all Japanese workers are employed by large corporations, of course, and although smaller companies cannot offer features like lifetime employment they do tend to maintain a more personalistic style of organization than U.S. counterparts.

The Japanese model is under challenge, however. Big companies are "outsourcing" more of their tasks to small firms that offer employees few costly benefits and less job security. Economic pressure is increasing—along with pursuit of short-term profits.

Some younger Japanese employees welcome the change. They want more individual freedom than the old system offers. Others worry only that they will lose the good parts of this system if managers adopt more western approaches—not only conventional bureaucracy (already typical of Japanese government) but organizational structures in which loyalty plays less of a part and layoffs are more common.

Apple Computer: The Corporation as Campus

Apple Computer represents one of the most thorough and successful American attempts to create an alternative to bureaucracy (Garsten, 1994). Located in the silicon valley, Apple's headquarters—a spread-out collection of single-story stucco buildings with red tile roofs, a few glassy office complexes, a library, and a fitness center—looks more like a college campus than the headquarters of a major corporation. The architecture and layout are deliberate. Apple likes to think of itself as a place where people can learn and grow and where employees can seek self-fulfillment as well as a paycheck.

Like Mitsubishi, Apple works to build loyalty to the company as a whole as well as to specific work groups (or "teams") within the organization, to make work fun, and to provide support for employees in such nonwork areas as child care and further education. But Apple pursues these goals in distinctly American cultural terms. One of the first things a visitor notices is the number of people wearing bright-colored T-shirts with various slogans (and always, the Apple logo). Informality in dress and in personal interaction is not just allowed, it is required.

Employment at Apple begins with a week of orientation at "Apple University." New employees are

Dorm room or office? At Microsoft headquarters, individuality is king. Personal styles are reflected in employees' offices and clothing. The company hopes that its liberal policies will result in happier, more creative workers.

shown slides and videos that recount Apple's history and introduce the company's executives and products. Straightforward information and guest speakers are supplemented by videotaped, spontaneous comments by Apple employees: "Apple people are zany, they're a different breed" (p. 57). Periodically, lists of Apple values and goals are flashed on a screen, including such Zen-like slogans as "The journey is the reward." Recruits also participate in a simulated project in which ad hoc teams produce, say, a statue, which they try to "sell" to the whole group. At the end of orientation, each person receives a diploma, an ID badge, and a sweatshirt with a slogan.

To a large degree, Apple defines itself by what it is *not*. And what it is not, by implication and often explicit negative comparisons, is IBM. Apple sees the key to success as *change* and takes pride in its ability to transform products or reorganize in response to shifts in the economy, social habits, and customer interests. This is seen as a radical departure from "industrial-age" companies like IBM, where the emphasis is on *stability*, conformity, title, and rank (Sculley, 1987). According to Apple's corporate culture, stability leads to reaffirming past mistakes, or what insiders call "reinventing the wheel." To keep things moving and promote creativity, Apple engages in frequent reorganizations of people, functions, and products.

Some employees find in Apple a dream come true; others are disoriented by the lack of such familiar signposts as titles, departments, and clear career paths. Moreover, Apple's "antibureaucracy" contains several built-in problems. First, frequent reorganizations disrupt the loyalties that develop among coworkers, which can weaken commitment to the corporation (Howard, 1985). Second, the obligation to make work fun can have the opposite effect: "Fun" isn't fun when it's required. This policy undercuts workers' autonomy to negotiate their own relationships and informal routines. Finally, providing child care and other nonwork support makes executives feel entitled to make extra demands—such as late-night work sessions—in return. Apple's "carefree" atmosphere actually disguises high levels of stress.

Even innovative corporations depend on market success. As profit margins have been squeezed in the computer industry, economic pressures threaten Apple's distinctive style.

Burroughs Wellcome and Glaxo: Corporate Takeovers

Whatever style of internal organization a corporation has, it is also vulnerable to external pressures—including financial markets. A corporate takeover, thus, can transform an entire company overnight.

Since the 1980s, corporate mergers and takeovers have become increasingly common. Corporate takeovers may reap short-term profits for investors and top management, but takeovers nearly always mean that many workers are laid off or given early retirement (in part because the company needs to cut costs to pay off the debt the merger created). Between 1989 and 1995, an estimated 3 million workers were laid off, many of whom were highly skilled, well-paid professionals, middle managers, and technicians (Herbert, 1995). On the first business day of 1996, AT&T announced it would permanently lay off 40,000 employees, the largest single layoff in history.

Burroughs Wellcome, famous for the AIDS-fighting drug AZT, and Glaxo, known for its anti-ulcer drug Zantac, were two of the most respected and profitable corporations in the pharmaceutical industry. In March 1994 Glaxo acquired Burroughs Wellcome in a hostile takeover that created the largest pharmaceutical company in the world. In the process, $15 billion changed hands, two corporate cultures collided, and 5,000 lives were thrown into disarray (Yeoman, 1995). Before the takeover, the two London-based companies employed 62,000 people worldwide, including 5,000 in North Carolina's Research Triangle Park (RTP). The two companies had very different workplace cultures. Once owned by a nonprofit trust, Burroughs Wellcome resembled an academic think tank. The corporate philosophy was to hire good people and let them do what they did best. Scientists were not assigned specific tasks but rather were allowed to pursue their own research interests. When an idea looked promising, a scientist would select a team from different departments, do the basic research, then present a proposal to a committee. "It was the domain of the small scientific entrepreneur" (Yeoman, 1995, p. 12). Top managers knew researchers personally and spent much of their time visiting laboratories and "talking science." Burroughs Wellcome had a reputation for granting not only scientific freedom but also job security.

Glaxo had a more traditional bureaucratic structure. Top executives (whom the scientists rarely saw) would decide to target a particular disease, assign research tasks to different departments and groups, and manage the flow of information. Each scientist had a specific job to do, after which his or her research was passed to another department. Glaxo had a reputation for hiring top talent and paying top salaries but also for working employees hard and, when they ran out of ideas or steam, letting them

go. When Glaxo opened its research center in RTP, despite higher pay it was unable to lure scientists away from Burroughs Wellcome. So it tried another strategy: corporate takeover.

The impact of Glaxo's takeover on Burroughs Wellcome employees was similar to the impact of a natural disaster. Huge job cuts were announced. Given a choice between leaving voluntarily (with severance pay and continued health-care benefits) or remaining with no assurance of a permanent job, they were caught in a no-win situation. Many experienced symptoms of depression: backaches, headaches, trouble sleeping, loss of appetite, irritability, crying jags, and marital problems. Waves of denial, anger, and resignation—the classic stages of grief when a family member dies—swept through department after department. Burroughs Wellcome employees mourned not just the loss of their own jobs, or the elimination of a special corporate culture, but the rupture of an implicit social contract: "If I do a good job (especially if I have advanced training), and if my company is thriving (as Burroughs Wellcome was), my future work life is secure."

Similar reactions have been documented after factory and mine closings. But mass layoffs and "downsizing" are no longer isolated events, limited to a company in trouble or even a "dying industry." No one today can escape the anxiety that their company will be next. Long-term commitments between employers and employees are going the way of the unicorn, which, ironically, was the Burroughs Wellcome corporate logo.

EXPLAINING THE STRUCTURE OF SOCIAL INTERACTION

All of the founders of sociology sought to explain the interplay of social structure and social action (see Chapter 1). Most focused on large-scale social structures (whole societies or the economy) and sweeping social change (industrialization or the rise of capitalism). George Herbert Mead and Max Weber were also interested in the role that everyday behavior plays in preserving or changing social structure. Their work inspired a number of contemporary theories that deal specifically with social interaction. In recent years, these insights have spread throughout sociology (Fine, 1993). The idea that ultimately, social order depends on how social actors (whether individuals, large organizations, or social institutions) "confront, use, manipulate, and remake structure" (p. 69) is widely accepted.

Symbolic Interaction

George Herbert Mead's approach to social interaction rested on three basic premises (Mead, 1934; Blumer, 1969/1986). First, people act toward everything they encounter on the basis of what those people, activities, and situations mean to them. Second, we learn what things mean by observing how other people respond to them—that is, through social interaction. Third, as a result of ongoing interaction, sounds (or words), gestures, facial expressions, and body postures acquire symbolic meanings that are shared by people who belong to the same culture. For example, Americans tend to look directly at a speaker, an action that would be considered an insult or a threat in many cultures. We consider people who avoid eye contact to be "shifty." We also use our eyes to affirm status. When partners to interaction are unequal in power and prestige, the one who breaks eye contact first is signaling deference or submission (Ridgeway, Berger, and Smith, 1985). The lower-status person is also more likely to maintain eye contact when listening to the partner but to look down or away when speaking. In interaction between a man and a woman, the woman is most likely to break eye contact. When the woman is in a position of superior power (such as the traffic cop writing a ticket), however, the reverse is true. Mead believed that such symbolic communications are the building blocks of social order.

The same symbol can have different meanings, depending on the context. When you stare at someone who pushes in front of you in a supermarket line, your look expresses anger; when you stare at a member of the opposite sex in a bar, your look signals romantic interest. Interpreting symbolic messages depends on the ability to take the role of the other person. **Role-taking** means putting ourselves in the other person's place, imagining what that person thinks and feels, and anticipating what further actions he or she might take. We then decide what action of our own is likely to "go over" best or bring us closer to our goals.

Roles are not fixed and static. Social interaction may reinforce existing role relationships or introduce role change (Turner, 1990). Role change involves more than individual variations in interpretation; it means a change in social expectations. Role change is most likely when the abilities and interests of new social actors do not match role requirements—and when broader cultural and structural patterns allow or require change. For example, grandparents used to be distant, authoritative figures, responsible for upholding moral values and family heritage. On a visit to Grandma, children were expected to dress up and be on their best behavior. Cultural changes in lifestyle in the 1960s and 1970s often led to conflict between parents and grandparents over how to socialize children. In addition, more people become grandparents in their forties and fifties today, and elderly people in their sixties, seventies, and beyond lead more active lives. As a result, the role of grandparent has become more informal. Today's grandparents hope their grandchildren will see them as "fun people."

In the 1950s, the role of a CEO was that of industrial statesmen, responsible for maintaining "an equilibrium and working balance among the claims of the various directly interested groups . . . stockholders, employees, customers, and the public at large" (Frank Abrams, chairman of Standard Oil of New Jersey, 1951, in Reich, 1996). Critics argue that global competition, "electronic capitalism" (the ability to move money around in a matter of seconds), and other changes have contributed to the redefinition of the role of CEOs as agents for stockholders only, responsible for the bottom line but not for employees, consumers, or the community.

The Dramaturgical Approach

The idea of a social role comes, of course, from the theater and the roles that actors perform in plays. As Shakespeare wrote, "All the world's a stage." Sociologists who take the **dramaturgical approach** hold that much interaction follows familiar, predictable, cultural scripts, but how individuals interpret and play their roles, and hence the outcome of the "play," is never certain.

Consider the performance of the *maitre d'* of an elegant restaurant (Orwell, 1951). In the noisy confusion of the kitchen the *maitre d'* is the boss, responsible for seeing that food is prepared and presented perfectly. A demanding taskmaster for whom nothing is good enough, he rants and raves, struts and fumes. Then, like a performer who assumes a new character as he steps onto the stage, the *maitre d'* enters the dining room and his whole demeanor changes. Face serene, he glides across the floor, bows to the customers, ushers them to their table with elaborate courtesy, and makes them feel lucky to enjoy his attentions. The kitchen tyrant becomes the most refined host.

The American sociologist Erving Goffman (1959, 1974), a leader of the dramaturgical approach, saw social life as a series of improvisational plays or skits. Every social situation has a script, which outlines in general terms what is supposed to happen and what roles need to be played. However, in contrast to real theater, there is no director, so the actors (the participants) must negotiate among themselves who will play which role. They also must play their roles in ways that will elicit the desired responses from others, so that the play (the interaction) will have a "happy ending."

In an actual theater, actors strive to convince the audience that they are the characters they are playing. In much the same way, participants in social interaction work to convince the audience (other participants) that the roles they seek to play are genuine. Goffman coined the term **impression management** to describe people's efforts to control what others think about them. At a job interview, for example, the applicant attempts to sell himself or herself by acting poised, intelligent, friendly, and dynamic (and by "dressing for success").

Goffman's important insight is that impression management is not confined to such formal situations as a job interview but happens all the time. Our decisions about what we wear, where we live, what kind of car we buy, even whether we eat hamburgers or pasta are all aspects of impression management, "props" that support the identity we want to project.

One of the puzzles of social interaction is why others usually go along with our "act," even when they realize it is contrived. Goffman believed the answer is that each person's success at impression management depends on other people's playing complementary roles. You cannot present yourself successfully as a *maitre d'*, for example, if waiters and customers ignore you. To keep the show going, people act as if each other's performances were genuine. If someone blunders—for instance, if the *maitre d'* inadvertently burps as he greets a group of customers—the participants pretend not to notice (what Goffman called "studied nonobservance"). Diners do not stare at people at other tables or join in their conversations, but instead act as if they were the only diners in the room (a pattern Goffman called "civil inattention").

> Much of the activity during an encounter can be understood as an effort on everyone's part to get through the occasion and all the unanticipated and unintentional events that can cast participants in an undesirable light, without disrupting the relationships of participants. (Goffman, 1967, p. 41)

It is difficult to be on stage every minute—this is why social life has both "frontstage" and "backstage" regions. In a frontstage region, people are required to play their roles with all the skill they can muster. The dining room is frontstage for waiters. No matter how harried, annoyed, or exhausted they feel, waiters are expected to remain polite and helpful toward customers. In the kitchen, however, waiters are backstage. Here they can relax, joke about phony customers, and prepare themselves for their next performance. Virtually every role has a backstage to which a person can retreat. The doctors' lounge is backstage at a hospital, as is the teachers' room at a school. Backstage in their dorms students laugh about their professors, while backstage in their offices professors joke about their students. Computer networks can offer a "place" for backstage chat (Rasmussen, 1996).

Does this mean that most frontstage behavior is just an act—that the face people present to the world is merely a mask? Not necessarily. The more we play a role, the more genuine it feels, until eventually we are as convinced as our audience that we are the person we pretend to be. Recall your first days and weeks in college. At first you probably felt like an outsider and to some degree, an imposter, pretending you knew what you were doing. By Thanksgiving vacation, however, you had *become* a college student, in your own mind and in the eyes of others. So it is with all roles. The novice police officer wonders if people will accept his or her authority; the first-time mother worries about her competence until "something clicks" and, suddenly, she feels herself a mother.

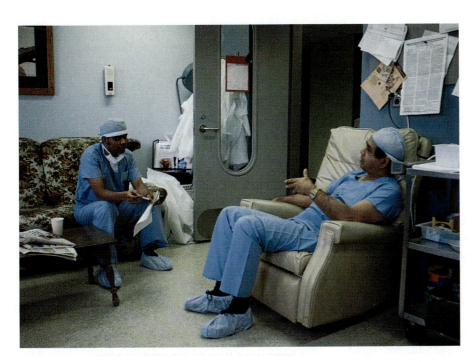

"Backstage," people can relax and prepare for their next appearance "on stage," in public or on-the-job interaction.

This transformation depends in large part on looking in the social mirror and seeing that other people accept one's role as genuine.

Ethnomethodology

Like Goffman, the sociologist Harold Garfinkel (1967) focused on the routines of everyday life, but where Goffman observed social interaction from a distance, somewhat like a critic watching a play, Garfinkel attempted to analyze it from the inside, as if he were a novice actor stepping onstage for the first time. This is not easy, for none of us is truly a novice at social interaction; we have all been interacting with others since the day we were born. As a result, we have grown so accustomed to our culture's scripts that we are not even aware they exist. For example, without thinking about it, most Americans walking on a busy sidewalk keep to the right (just as they do when driving in their cars) to avoid colliding with others. This shared understanding is just one of the millions of tacit, taken-for-granted bits of knowledge that provide order and structure to our social interactions. **Ethnomethodology** refers to the methods or ways in which people create order through everyday interactions.

Garfinkel invented a technique he called **breeching experiments:** To demonstrate the power of culture and everyday social understandings, he and his students intentionally violated norms and recorded people's responses. In one experiment, students acted as if they were guests when they visited their families. For as long as they could, they maintained a polite distance, talking about general topics, rather than personal ones; asking permission to use the bathroom or to get a glass of water; expressing gratitude to the "host" and "hostess" for their kind hospitality. The result?

> Family members demanded explanations: What's the matter? What's gotten into you? Did you get fired? Are you sick? What are you being superior about? Why are you mad? Are you out of your mind or just being stupid? (Garfinkel, 1967, pp. 47–48)

In attempting to restore normal relations, family members revealed some of their unstated assumptions about family interaction.

In other breeching experiments, Garfinkel's students attempted to bargain for items in a store (something Americans generally do not do); broke the rules of tic-tac-toe (erasing the opponent's first move); and closed in during a conversation until they were nose-to-nose with the unsuspecting subject. Each of these violations produced confusion and anxiety—in the students as well as in the "victim"—and often angry rebukes. These intense reactions confirmed the degree to which people depend on tacit, often unconscious, rules of interaction to structure their social encounters.

Conversation Analysis

The field of conversation analysis was pioneered by Harvey Sachs, who was a student of Erving Goffman and a colleague of Howard Garfinkel before his early death in a car crash. Like them, Sachs believed that one could learn as much by studying mundane, everyday behavior as by studying "big issues" and "massive institutions." Like them, he was interested in the way social order is *produced*.

Sachs developed the technique of recording casual conversations and analyzing them in minute detail. He studied casual phone calls between friends, informal conversations at work, calls to emergency public services, group therapy sessions, even radio talk shows. He was interested, not in the context or the content of these conversations, but in talk itself—how people decide who talks when, to whom, and for how long. This is basic not just to informal interaction but to the work of bureaucracies (Boden, 1995). Sachs found that all conversations have certain features in common: One person speaks at a time, transitions between speakers are frequent and rapid, and there are few gaps and overlaps. At the heart of conversation is the concept of *turn-taking*. Turns function like a revolving door, controlling the entry and exit of speakers into a conversation. Interruptions, very long turns, and even giving up a turn must all be justified.

Deborah Tannen (1990, 1994) has analyzed *miscommunication* between men and women in terms of the different ways the sexes use common conversational techniques. Men tend to view conversations as contests, in which there are winners and losers; their main goal is to protect themselves from being one-upped or put down. Women tend to see conversations as collaborations, the goal of which is reaffirming social bonds. As a result, men and women sometimes talk past one another. Consider the example in Figure 3.3. Zoe is hurt that Earl does not show concern about her health and that he then interrupts her. Earl is hurt that his romantic advances (bringing up the topic of love, touching her face) are

At a dinner party, Zoe feels a pain in her stomach and excuses herself to go to the bathroom. When she returns, Earl asks if she is alright and she tells him that she is having some medical tests. Rather than asking about the tests, he passes her some food.

> **Zoe (chewing):** With my luck it will be a gallbladder operation.
> **Earl:** So your sister's getting married? Tell me, really, what you think about love.
> **Zoe:** All right, I'll tell you what I think about love. Here is a love story. This friend of mine—
> **Earl (reaching over to touch her face):** You've got something on your chin.

FIGURE 3.3 / He/She Doesn't Understand

Source: Adapted from Deborah Tannen, "He/She Doesn't Understand," in *Gender and Discourse* (Oxford University Press, New York, 1994), pp. 76–77.

rebuffed. They might as well be speaking different languages! Many contemporary conversation analysts are interested not only in the structure of conversation but also in the functions, content, and interpretation of talk.

Social Exchange

Other sociological theorists emphasize the role exchange in social interaction. Exchange is guided by the norm of reciprocity (Gouldner, 1973). When someone does us a favor or gives us something, reciprocity requires that we repay the kindness, balancing the social ledger. The original giver then has an obligation to reciprocate to us. Thus exchange strengthens social bonds by creating new social obligations. Exchange is not limited to business transactions but is a basic element of all social interactions.

Rooted in the work of Georg Simmel (1950), exchange theory was revitalized by Peter M. Blau (1964) and George C. Homans (1974), who analyzed a wide range of social behaviors as processes of exchange. Both were interested in how actors gain or lose through interaction. Blau saw exchange in economic terms: In deciding whether to enter into interaction, as well as how to proceed, people weigh the costs and benefits of different social actions. Homans had a somewhat different approach. Adopting concepts from the school of psychology known as *behaviorism*, Homans held that people tend to repeat behavior for which they have been rewarded in the past and to avoid behavior for which they have been punished. Both Blau and Homans contributed to rational-choice theory, which suggests that in deciding how to act (and interact) people consciously calculate the potential costs and benefits, rewards and punishments. From this perspective, all social action is "premeditated."

Of course, power enables some people to profit more than others from an exchange—as in the workplace when a supervisor "requests" favors from subordinates. Exchange can also create power. Co-workers rely on one another for numerous acts of assistance (for example, covering the phone while they take a break or helping them master a new computer program). Usually this is a "fair exchange," but some workers—such as those with good computer skills—provide more favors than they need in return, and thus accumulate debts, which can be translated into power.

As Simmel (1955) showed, exchange networks create a web of affiliations that help to reduce conflict. In a university, for example, the sociology, psychology, economics, and other departments compete for students, new faculty positions, and other benefits. If the faculty of those departments also exchange favors—assistance with research, student recommendations, advice on dealing with administrative or teaching problems—their competition is likely to remain friendly. Thus, acts of exchange define networks; at the same time, positions in a network shape actual exchanges (Cook and Whitmeyer, 1992).

Exchange is not always "cold and calculating." Parents may sacrifice their own interests to promote their child's happiness and welfare, with no expectation of being rewarded in return (Emerson, 1976). Quite simply, helping makes them feel good.

The Sociology of Emotions

Sociologists have become increasingly interested in the powerful role emotions play in social life. Often we learn what someone else is feeling, not from what they say or do but from their facial expression (a wrinkled brow), their tone of voice (angry shouting), or body posture (slumped shoulders, a clenched fist). Each of these is a *symbolic gesture*. Our own emotions can betray us, as when our fear, anger, or love show even though we are trying to appear "cool." Some human emotions—joy, sadness, anger, fear—appear to be universal. Indeed, our expression of emotions may be rooted deep in our evolutionary past (which is why we find the facial expressions of apes and monkeys so humanlike).

Yet emotions, like all human behavior, are socially organized. Our ability to identify our emotions, to give them names, and to distinguish between different emotions is rooted in language and culture (Taylor, 1993). We can distinguish between anger and frustration, shame and guilt, because our culture makes these distinctions. Other cultures do not make the same discriminations or emphasize some emotions more than others. Largely because of our Judeo-Christian heritage, guilt—and its corollary, innocence—are prominent in Western cultures. Partly because of Confucian teachings, shame—and honor—play a more prominent role in Far Eastern cultures. The expression "saving face" is rooted in Confucian tradition. All cultures have rules about which emotions are appropriate in what situations (laughing during a funeral is usually taboo, though crying at weddings is acceptable) and who should and should not express certain emotions ("big boys don't cry").

Shame still plays a role in the West, of course. Indeed, the sociologists Thomas Scheff and Suzanne Retzinger (1991) see shame as the most basic of all human emotions. Shame ranges from mild embarrassment to extreme humiliation, but it is always social: It arises from the perception that others view us unfavorably. An insult, criticism, unrequited love, betrayal, or a snub leaves us feeling unworthy, unwanted, or excluded.

"In all social interaction, either the social bond is being built, maintained, or repaired, or it is being damaged" (Scheff and Retzinger, 1991, p. 64, italics deleted). The function of shame (and other emotions) is to alert us to information about the social environment, the state of social bonds, and perhaps a need to readjust. Emotions provide an important channel of communication and may convey more than words and deeds.

Shame can inhibit us from action or lead us to act in certain ways. Scheff and Retzinger (1991) studied quarrels between husbands and wives. Marital spats begin with signals of disrespect: directly or indirectly, one spouse puts down the other. If shame is ignored—if neither spouse acknowledges hurt feelings—the quarrel escalates. Anger can be seen as an attempt to ward off anticipated attacks and "save face." Anger leads to more put-downs, more anger, and so on. The couple may reach an impasse (the interpersonal equivalent of a "cold war") or one partner may "tune out" or storm out of the room, ending the interaction. If, however, the partners acknowledge hurt feelings and demonstrate respect, disputes usually can be resolved with minimal damage to the relationship. The same basic principles apply to disputes between neighbors or ethnic groups, political parties or nations.

While emotions are rooted in biology, psychology, and social relations, human beings can manage their emotions as their needs or the situation requires. Party guests usually summon up the gaiety owed their host, while mourners display the sadness proper for a funeral. "Each offers up feeling as a momentary contribution to the collective good" (Hochschild, 1983, p. 18). In countless interactions—between parents and children, husbands and wives, friends, lovers, and even strangers—people hide their anger, pretend gratitude, or suppress envy.

In some situations, emotions are totally manufactured because the specific job or social role requires people to express certain emotions in prescribed ways. A classic example, analyzed in depth by the sociologist Arlie Hochschild (1983), is the airline stewardess. Part of the job of "stewardess" is smiling and acting cheerful and confident no matter how she feels. Passengers may pester, insult, or sexually harass her; she may know that the pilot is experiencing trouble or that a passenger in Row F is going into labor. Whatever happens, she is expected to remain calm and to keep smiling. Likewise, employees of computer and other "new age" companies are required to appear happy, a bit zany, and totally involved in their work. In these settings, feelings are commercialized. The stewardess's smile is part of what customers "buy" when they purchase a plane ticket; Apple uses the image of the "zany" computer hacker to attract employees. As more and more people work in service industries, dealing with clients and customers in jobs that require manufactured emotions, more people turn to religion, self-help groups, and books and movies about spiritual quests to rediscover their authentic selves. But even this inner journey depends on social interaction (with a church, fellow seekers, an author or director) and social confirmation.

Interaction is one of the most creative aspects of social life, with its potential for "making a difference." At the same time, interaction depends on powerful structural and cultural patterns that make each of us somewhat predictable to others and in turn allow us to trust one another. These patterns provide the foundation for stable social life.

SUMMARY

1. Sociology shows that even the most intimate behavior—sex—is socially structured. Cultural norms, knowledge, and preferences shape our desires; social structure circumscribes our opportunities. Changing patterns of sexual behavior, in turn, influence social structure. Finally, sexual interaction both reflects and affects power. The results of a recent survey demonstrate that variations in sexual behavior are influenced by such social characteristics as education.

2. Social groups and relationships can be divided into three basic types: primary, secondary, and tertiary (or indirect). Primary relationships are intimate, personal, multifaceted, affectionate, and enduring. Classic primary relationships include friends and lovers, husbands and wives. How these relationships are defined varies cross-culturally.

3. Western notions of love are rooted in the tradition of courtly romance, that is, a tragic confrontation between individuals and the social order. Only in nineteenth-century England and especially America did romance become a prerequisite for marriage. In other societies and times, marriages have been arranged by families.

4. The ideologies behind arranged marriage and marrying for love highlight the importance of statuses (positions in the social structure) and roles (the behaviors and attitudes expected of people who occupy a given status). Some statuses are ascribed (assigned to people without effort on their part) and others are achieved (attained largely by personal effort). Often a master status dominates all others.

5. In some societies and times, friends have been closer, and more highly valued, than husband or wife. With the rise of romantic love in Western societies, the importance of friends declined. The importance of friends varies from society to society, with social class, and between males and females.

6. Secondary relationships are public, impersonal, limited, emotionally cool, and generally short-lived. Classic examples are salespeople and customers, professionals and clients.

7. One of the defining features of modern life is an increase in the amount (and importance) of interaction with strangers. Relations between strangers follow cultural guidelines and are usually cordial. Indeed, modern societies depend on norms of civility, politeness, and mutual trust.

8. In tertiary or indirect relationships, the parties may never meet, but they are connected through communications media or third parties (for example, a CEO on the one hand and employees and consumers on the other). Their actions may be motivated by broader social patterns (such as market forces); nevertheless, what each does affects the other. Impersonal, indirect relationships are essential to large-scale social organizations.

9. Interactions at work are shaped by overlapping networks, broad cultural norms adapted through negotiation, and group dynamics. The dual nature of group life requires both instrumental (task-oriented) and expressive (emotion-oriented) leadership, but these may be organized in different ways (for example, Apple versus IBM).

10. As the size of an organization and the complexity of its goals increase, so does the need for formal organization. According to Max Weber's "ideal type," a bureaucracy has five features: (1) a clear-cut division of labor with specialized tasks; (2) a hierarchy of offices with a chain of command; (3) explicit rules and regulations; (4) impersonality and emotional detachment to maximize rational decision making; and (5) rewards based on merit. No bureaucracy adheres strictly to Weber's ideal type, however; behavior is shaped as much by unofficial norms as by official rules and regulations.

11. Changing social conditions have led to change in organizational structure. One alternative to traditional bureaucracy is found in large Japanese corporations, which guarantee lifetime employment, emphasize group achievement, base promotions on seniority, diffuse decision making, and demonstrate holistic concern for employees. Another alternative is the "corporate campus model," which emphasizes flexibility, individuality, and informality, as opposed to the emphasis on stability, conformity, and formality in traditional bureaucracies. Corporate takeovers (which are increasingly common) may combine companies with different workplace cultures and almost always lead to layoffs, with serious social-psychological as well as economic consequences for employees.

12. Social order depends on how social actors (whether individuals, organizations, or institutions) adapt to, manipulate, and change social structure. Sociologists have developed six main approaches to explaining the structure of social interaction.

13. Symbolic interaction focuses on the symbolic aspects of social interactions and on how symbolic gestures and role-taking enable people to coordinate their behavior.

14. The dramaturgical approach sees social interaction as a kind of theatrical performance, with a frontstage and backstage area and numerous props. To some degree, we all engage in impression management.

15. Ethnomethodology looks at social interaction from the inside and uses breeching experiments to illustrate the importance of shared and often unconscious rules for interaction in different situations.

16. Conversation analysis examines how people use structure (especially turn-taking) both to coordinate talk and to achieve individual goals.

17. Social exchange theory views reciprocity as essential to human interaction. In deciding what action to take, people weigh the potential gains against costs and attempt to balance the social ledger.

18. The sociology of emotions sees the expression of feelings as a vital channel of communication that alerts us to the condition of social relationships but also as a medium that can be manipulated and even commercialized.

REVIEW QUESTIONS

1. Describe how even intimate relationships are shaped by participants' backgrounds, by culture, and by social structure.

2. Explain the distinctions between primary and secondary relationships and between direct and indirect relationships.

3. What is the sociological definition of a "stranger"? Why are interactions with strangers especially characteristic of modern society?

4. Describe the ideal type of bureaucracy and two alternative forms of corporate organization.

5. Summarize the six major approaches to explaining the structure of social interaction.

CRITICAL THINKING QUESTIONS

1. What is your ideal for a romantic partner? How do you think this is shaped by social structure and culture?

2. Describe a situation in which you were a stranger. How did this affect your actions and the way people treated you? What norms did you and the other(s) follow? Was the interaction cordial?

3. Are you affected more by direct or indirect relationships? Which areas of your life are more subject to influences from one or the other?

4. Use the idea of social networks to describe relationships in a place where you work, live, or enjoy leisure activities. How many of these relationships are limited to one social setting? How many involve other settings and activities?

5. What are the strengths and weaknesses of bureaucracy as a form of social organization? Can you imagine a modern society without bureaucracies? Which are most necessary? Least?

GLOSSARY

Achieved status A voluntary status a person attains largely through personal effort.

Ascribed status A status assigned to people by others.

Breeching experiments Harold Garfinkel's technique for exposing unconscious cultural assumptions by deliberately violating norms and recording people's responses.

Bureaucracy An organizational structure characterized by specialization and a clear division of labor, a hierarchy of offices, explicit rules, impersonality in decision making, and rewards based on merit.

Dramaturgical approach A sociological perspective in which social interaction is viewed as resembling a theatrical performance in which people "stage" their behavior in such a way as to elicit the responses they desire from others.

Dyad A two-person relationship or group.

Ethnomethodology A viewpoint on social interaction developed by Harold Garfinkel that focuses on the ways people make sense out of everyday interactions.

Expressive leadership Leadership for the purpose of maintaining good

spirits and relations among group members.

Formal structure The official positions, duties, rules, and regulations as set by the leaders of an organization.

Impression management Erving Goffman's term for the efforts people make to control how others see and respond to them.

Indirect relationships Relationships in which the parties do not interact directly but are linked indirectly by communications technology or third parties.

Informal structure The unofficial norms that develop among group members to solve problems not covered by regulations, to eliminate unpleasant or unnecessary labor, and to protect the members' interests.

Instrumental leadership Leadership for the purpose of directing group members to perform various tasks.

Groupthink The tendency of members of a group to lose the ability for critical, individual thought because of the value they place on solidarity with each other.

Master status One status that largely determines a person's social identity.

Negotiated order A shared definition of a situation arrived at by "testing out" actions and modifying them based on feedback from others.

Network The web of relationships among a set of people who are linked together, directly or indirectly, through their various communications and dealings.

Primary group An especially close-knit group characterized by the following five features: continuous face-to-face interaction, strong personal identity with the group, strong ties of affection among group members, multifaceted relationships, and a tendency for the group to be very enduring.

Role A set of behaviors, attitudes, obligations, and privileges expected of anyone who occupies a particular status.

Role-taking Imagining oneself in the role of another and thereby helping to understand the meanings that the other intends to convey.

Secondary group A nonintimate group characterized by limited face-to-face interaction; modest or weak personal identity with the group; weak ties of affection among group members; limited, shallow relationships; and a tendency to be short-lived.

Status A position in the social order that defines who we are in relation to others and plays a key role in establishing social identity.

Status set The full range of social positions occupied by any one person at a given time.

Stranger A person in the midst of a social group with whom he or she has no personal ties.

Symbolic gesture A gesture that has acquired symbolic meaning shared by people who belong to the same culture.

Triad A three-person relationship group.

CHAPTER 4

Culture

Ludwig van Beethoven is one of the two or three most famous musicians who ever lived. His symphonies are performed more than those of any other classical composer; his "Ode to Joy" has been made into both a hymn and a pop song. Busts of Beethoven—haughty, scowling, and disheveled—are familiar decorations and symbols of musical genius. When we say that someone "has culture," we mean, in part, that he or she recognizes and understands great music like that of Beethoven. We associate appreciation of symphonies and string quartets with elite status and "high culture," as opposed to popular culture. Even those of us who are not "cultured" in this sense recognize Beethoven's brooding profile and the opening bars of his fifth symphony. His image as well as his musical compositions are part of our cultural heritage. Whether or not we like Beethoven's music, whether or not we recognize his compositions, most of us accept our culture's judgment that Beethoven was a genius.

Beethoven's ability as a composer is uncontested. However, recognizing him as a genius means something more than acknowledging his talent and skill; it means seeing him as a special kind of person, as someone endowed from birth with extraordinary gifts that set him apart from others. Geniuses are not just original—they are original in a profound way that enables them to penetrate and transform their creative fields. A degree of eccentricity, and exemption from the ordinary rules of politeness and decorum, are part of the "genius package." Where do geniuses—and this whole idea of genius—come from?

Our culture teaches that geniuses are born, not made. Through intelligence and hard work, many people may be able to rise to the top of their field of endeavor. But geniuses have "something extra," something that cannot be taught or learned which

Why do geniuses always have messy hair? Part of our cultural image of genius is of someone who is too preoccupied with brilliant ideas to be concerned with such mundane things as neatness.

enables them to transform their creative field. Whatever the circumstances of their birth, they are destined for greatness.

In *Beethoven and the Social Construction of Genius* (DeNora, 1996), the sociologist Tia DeNora questions these assumptions. The very idea of genius is distinctive to modern Western culture. In the ancient world and in medieval Europe, artists were not distinguished from craftsmen. Indeed, most works of art were anonymous. The idea of genius developed in Europe in the late seventeenth and early eighteenth centuries as part of the growth of individualism, the belief in the distinctiveness and value of every individual (Pletsch, 1992). Before this the word *genius* referred to style or inspiration; by the nineteenth century it had come to refer to the person. (With a few exceptions, women have been excluded from this category.) Thus, being recognized as a "genius" depends not just on being brilliant but also on living and working in a culture that values originality and individual creators.

DeNora analyzes the social and historical contexts in which Beethoven rose to fame. In Beethoven's day, Vienna was the artistic and intellectual capital of Europe, with a large community of musicians, conductors, critics, and scholars, as well as aristocratic patrons and middle-class audiences. At that time instrumental music was beginning to move out of private salons into public concert halls. To restore music's lost luster, the aristocracy began to distinguish between *serious* music (intended to challenge and be difficult to play) and *amateur* or dilettante music (intended to entertain and be easy to learn). The elite's support for serious music was meant to set them apart from general audiences.

Beethoven was precisely what the musical aristocracy of Vienna needed. His emotionally complex and technically difficult compositions as well as his mercurial disposition helped to solidify this distinction. In lionizing Beethoven, the moody "serious" artist, the musical elite was serving its own interests as well.

DeNora's sociological analysis is not meant to debunk Beethoven's talent but rather to show that genius is a *social* creation. Beethoven was the right person and turn-of-the-century Vienna was the right time and place. Beethoven's "genius" depended on a highly integrated musical community, the backing of powerful aristocrats, endorsement by critics, eventual acceptance by a wider public, and a culture that valued individuality and innovation.

As we saw in Chapter 1, **culture** is the more or less integrated way of thinking, understanding, evaluating, and communicating that makes possible a shared way of life. Great music, literature, and paintings are only a small part of culture, which includes norms for appropriate behavior, values, knowledge, artifacts, language, and symbols that we use everyday.

Culture shapes our beliefs about what is important in life and our interpretations of what events mean. Modern Western culture, for example, recognizes certain types of music, writing, painting, and dancing as "art," but in other cultures the special category of objects and actions we call "the arts" does not exist. Music may be seen as a way of communicating with the spirits; storytelling as a means of passing on information to new generations; carving as a necessary part of producing an effective spear; and so on. Many of the "primitive" works of art that adorn our museums were originally created for religious purposes or for mundane, everyday purposes. Even within our own culture, people debate what is and is not art. Some view graffiti as art; others do not. Some think rap is brilliant; others consider it trash. But although we do not agree on specific examples, we all know what we mean by the word *art*.

The sociology of culture shows that our way of thinking and categorizing (such as distinguishing "art" from mundane objects and activities), our hopes and fears, our likes and dislikes, and our beliefs and habits are social creations, strongly influenced by the time and place in which we live. Virtually everything we say or do—from shaking hands to falling in love—is shaped by our culture and constructed with the resources our culture provides. We praise democracy, worship one God, and value competition in part because our culture teaches us to do so.

Even so, culture does not dictate thoughts and behavior—it leaves room for action. Culture is some-thing people develop, use, and modify as necessary. The sociologist Howard Becker (1986) captured this idea in describing culture as "shared understandings that people use to coordinate their activities." By creating and expressing the elements of our culture, by living them day to day, we are constantly communicating to each other an understanding of our social world. In the process, we also reshape culture, adapting it to meet new demands and situations. As a result, culture is constantly changing.

We begin this chapter by looking at the basic elements all cultures share: values, norms, symbols, language, and knowledge. In the second section we analyze the tension between cultural integration and cultural diversity, with special attention to the role language plays in maintaining cultural integrity, to the politics of identity, and to the postmodernist critique of cultural integration. In the third section we show that the production of culture is a social process. No longer dictated by elites, tastes and fashions are part of the search for identity in modern societies; but elites (and artists) still use cultural knowledge and appreciation as a form of capital. In the last section we look at the role of electronic media in accelerating the globalization of culture.

THE ELEMENTS OF CULTURE

The particular content of culture varies from place to place, but all human cultures have the same basic elements. These include values, norms, symbols, language, and knowledge. These are shared and help to make each of us who we are. At the same time, people use these elements of culture as a "tool kit" (Swidler, 1986), both to maintain and to change their way of life.

Values

Values are deeply held criteria for judging what is good or bad, desirable or undesirable, beautiful or ugly. They are the underlying, general, often unconscious and unexpressed standards by which we evaluate specific acts, objects, or events. The values people hold color their overall way of life, transcending any one particular situation. The statement "The Rocky Mountains are majestic; hiking there brings me closer to nature" is a specific judgment, based on the underlying value that "Nature is good and beautiful." Americans did not always think this way. Colonial Americans tended to view nature as dangerous, threatening, even evil, as something to be conquered and tamed. Thus values can change.

One enduring American value is competitive success: when we play, we play to win, not only in sports but also in politics, in business, in the classroom, and in our social lives. If there is no clear winner in a political election, for example, a runoff is held. Likewise, we have rules for overtime or "sudden death" in sports so that a winner can be decided. However, other cultures do not value success in competition. For example, Americans working in Southeast Asia were totally frustrated in their attempts to create "team spirit" among Laotians playing volleyball.

> To us, it's a game. I know when our teams compete, whether it's baseball or basketball—anything—we are serious, playing it because we like to win. With them, they aren't; they team up and have teams going, but they just don't give a hoot whether they win or not. (in Stewart and Bennett, 1991, p. 80)

Laotians value affiliation and group harmony rather than competition. In their culture the underlying goal of any social activity is to maintain good relations and save face.

Another American value is independence; we do not like to be "tied down." We join groups and organizations but prefer to do so as free agents, reserving the right to withdraw when the groups no longer serve our personal needs. If a job is not rewarding, or a marriage is unfulfilling, we move on, or at least know we have that option. Unlike most people in the world, we tend to see religion as a matter of personal choice. In many other societies children almost always follow their parents' religion as adults, and whole communities or even whole countries share the same religion.

People in other cultures also tend to remain in the community where they grew up, to consider relationships as more fixed, and to put less emphasis on the value of individual choice and more value on stable, dependable commitments. Arab cultures, for example, treat friendship as a lifelong, all-or-nothing commitment (Stewart and Bennett, 1991). They make a clear distinction between acquaintances and real friends. Individuals are expected to do anything for a friend, to spend any amount of money or travel any distance to help a friend in need. Americans use the term *friend* to describe everyone from a lifelong intimate to a casual acquaintance. Friendships may be close, but they are not binding. Faced with serious personal problems, many Americans will consult professionals (therapists, ministers, self-help groups) rather than "burden" their friends.

Sometimes cultural values are functionally integrated—for example, the values of competition, independence, and individual achievement reinforce one another. However, some cultural values may clash or compete, especially in complex, pluralistic societies like ours. For example, the tension between the values of individualism and community has always been a part of American culture (Bellah et al., 1985; Gans, 1988). The individual's right to "life, liberty, and the pursuit of happiness" is enshrined in our Declaration of Independence. We hold sacred the right to think for ourselves, judge for ourselves, make our own decisions, and live our lives as we see fit, free from unwanted entanglements and obligations. At the same time, however, we have a nostalgia for communities of the past in which families put down roots and stayed for generations, and everyone looked out for everyone else.

In their highly acclaimed book *Habits of the Heart* (1985), sociologist Robert Bellah and his colleagues concluded that although Americans do value community, individualism tends to win out when the two values conflict. The strong individualists they interviewed were not selfish; rather, they placed a high value on autonomy and self-knowledge and believed that to become your own person you must separate yourself from the values imposed both by the past and by your current social milieu. They also believed that, like themselves, other people should be free to have their own standards and live as they choose. Thus a high degree of individualism was associated with a high degree of tolerance. However, individualism has a cost: According to Bellah, individualists tended to feel lonely, isolated, and adrift.

Competing values do not necessarily lead to anguish; rather, they can help to define choices that people can then act on. Thus we must decide whether to leave home and make our own way in the world, aiming for greater individual achievement, or stay near our family and friends in the community where we were born. All modern people face such choices. Americans are somewhat more likely to pur-

this value in different ways—for example, living a bohemian lifestyle, seeking success as a stockbroker, taking camping and ecotourism vacations, or campaigning against big-government regulations.

Norms

A **norm** is a rule or guideline that says how people should behave in particular situations. Norms are narrower and more specific than values. For example, individualism and honesty are values; the rule that one student should not copy another student's homework is a norm derived from these values. Sometimes norms are made explicit, as in written laws or biblical commandments. More often, however, norms are unspoken customs that people implicitly know and follow. For example, when someone you don't particularly like asks you out on a date, you don't say, "I don't like you and never want to go out with you." Rather, you make an excuse such as "I'm busy that night" or "I'm seeing someone else." Norms operationalize values. They also help us to determine which values get the upper hand in a particular situation. In the example of the rejected date, consideration for another person's feelings overrides the value of honesty.

Norms are situational; that is, they apply to specific circumstances and settings. For this reason norms change more rapidly than values do. In the 1950s, smoking cigarettes was considered glamorous, sexy, and social. Norms held that a good hostess put out plenty of ashtrays before a party and that one should offer a cigarette to others before lighting up oneself. As evidence mounted that cigarette smoke (whether first- or secondhand) contributes to heart and lung disease, norms changed. Today, many Americans regard smoking as a dirty, dangerous addiction. Smokers now ask permission before lighting up in another person's home or car, or even in their own home or car when others are present. The underlying values—politeness and concern for health—haven't changed, but their application to the norms for smoking has.

Like values, norms vary from society to society. Behavior that is considered polite and appropriate in one society may be viewed as eccentric, embarrassing, or even disgraceful in another. At business meetings Americans generally "get down to business," setting aside social niceties until the task at hand is

When values conflict. Radical individualists, like this man in rural Idaho, separate themselves and their families from mainstream American society. They strongly oppose what they consider to be government intrusion in their lives.

sue individual achievement; America also serves as a magnet for people from other cultures who choose this path. But many Americans, perhaps the majority, put down roots wherever they choose to live. They are deeply committed to their immediate family and involved in a variety of social networks and informal groups (Gans, 1988).

Many of our current values date back to the time when the United States was a predominantly agrarian society. The ideal citizen was an independent, God-fearing, practical-minded, self-sufficient farmer, and life on the farm was considered natural and pure (Dalecki and Coughenour, 1992). Very few Americans today are farmers, and fewer still are independent. We still value autonomy but express

accomplished. In Latin American cultures, however, the distinction between work and play is not so sharply drawn (Stewart and Bennett, 1991). Business meetings are also social occasions, at which inquiries about one another's families and lengthy discussions of sports, restaurants, and politics are entirely appropriate. North Americans are often frustrated by Latin Americans' (apparent) unwillingness to take work seriously; Latin Americans, likewise, are puzzled by North Americans' seeming inability to enjoy themselves.

Norms also vary from group to group within a society. Hispanic-American men commonly greet one another with an embrace. So do Anglo-American women. But Anglo-American men more often shake hands or "play fight" (a slap on the back or a pretend punch). Among gay Americans, two men holding hands or kissing is acceptable. Among heterosexual Americans, such behavior by two men is taboo.

Much of the time, people follow the norms of their own culture more or less automatically. This is particularly true of unspoken norms that seem self-evident, such as answering a person who addresses you. We learn these norms from watching other people, from family stories, from our own past experiences, and from films, TV, and novels. This internalized sense of what is acceptable or unacceptable in different circumstances is very useful: If we had to stop and consider what to do at every encounter, social interaction would be virtually impossible (Bourdieu, 1990).

Although not as deep-seated as values, norms can be extremely powerful. The sociologist Harold Garfinkel (1967) demonstrated this power in an experiment. He asked students to address their parents formally, as "Mrs. (family name)" and "Mr. (family name)" instead of Mom and Dad when they went home for Thanksgiving vacation. This form of address did not violate the value of loving and respecting one's parents but only the norm of how to show this value in American society. Yet the parents were outraged. This is one set of norms that has not changed; try it with your own parents.

Norms vary in the importance that people assign to them and in the way people react to violations. **Folkways** are norms that are simply everyday habits and conventions. For example, we cover our mouths when we yawn and we shake hands when introduced because these are American folkways. People who violate folkways may be labeled eccentrics or slobs, but as a rule they are tolerated. In contrast, violations of mores provoke intense reactions. **Mores** are the norms people consider vital to their well-being and to their most cherished values. Examples are the prohibitions against incest, cannibalism, and sexual abuse of children. People who violate mores are considered unfit for society and may be ostracized, beaten, locked up, exiled, or even executed.

Some norms are formalized into **laws:** rules enacted by a political body and enforced by the power of the state. Laws may formalize folkways (as some traffic regulations do) or back up mores (as laws against murder and treason do). Political authorities may also attempt to introduce new norms by enacting laws that protect the civil rights of minorities or require people to recycle trash. In general, the laws that are most difficult to enforce are those that are not grounded in folkways or mores—for example, laws against gambling or drinking before age twenty-one.

Symbols

In addition to guidelines for behavior and judgments about what is "good" and "right," culture gives us notions about what things in our world mean. This is the primary function of **symbols**—objects, gestures, sounds, or images that represent something other than themselves. Geometrically, for example, a cross is merely two intersecting lines, but for Christians a cross symbolizes sacrifice, pain and suffering, faith, and the hope of salvation. Words, too, are symbols with meanings that people share. The word *green,* for instance, is just a unit of sound with no inherent meaning, but for English speakers this sound symbolizes a family of colors.

As these examples illustrate, symbols do not necessarily look like, sound like, or otherwise resemble what they stand for. Granted, symbols may sometimes derive their meaning partly from their inherent qualities (as in a lion's symbolizing a powerful empire, for instance). But the meaning given to symbols is frequently quite arbitrary, a matter of tradition and consensus. That is why, in different cultures, different symbols may represent the same concept. In some societies, for instance, black is the color of mourning, while in others white or red suggests grief. Nothing about these colors dictates their meaning. When meanings are arbitrarily assigned to symbols, those meanings can more easily be changed.

Even utilitarian objects may be layered with symbolic meaning. They are part of **material culture,** the

What's in a V? In England, the index and middle fingers held in a V with the palm facing inward is a rude insult. But during World War II, Winston Churchill turned this symbol around (palm facing outward) and made it stand for victory. Two decades later, students protesting the Vietnam War turned this same gesture into a peace symbol, and in 1989, pro-democracy demonstrators in China and Eastern Europe adopted the V for victory over government oppression.

physical objects made or used by human beings based on cultural know-how and understood by virtue of symbolic interpretation. We see cars, for example, as more than a means of transportation. Cars are a symbol of status, freedom, autonomy, mobility, and even patriotism and national standing (American-made versus Japanese cars). Americans, in particular, treat cars as a vehicle or medium for cultural expression, and advertisers know this. Ads for go-anywhere, 4-wheel-drive recreational vehicles are aimed at the young and adventuresome; ads for minivans emphasize convenience and safety features for family-oriented buyers; ads for luxury cars feature glamorous models in elegant settings. One reason advertising is so prominent in our culture is that it is so successful in using symbols to communicate these different kinds of messages (Schudson, 1984). Advertising is a primary means by which information about the social meaning of material objects gets distributed throughout our population. As such, "advertising is not just a business expenditure undertaken in the hope of moving some merchandise off the store shelves, but is rather an integral part of modern culture" (Leiss, Kline, and Shelly, 1986).

Individuals may add their own personal twists to the meaning of symbols. For example, to a middle-aged suburbanite, driving a jeep may be a way of holding onto youth; to a young inner-city male, a jeep may be a way of advertising his status. Interpretations may vary somewhat, but if people are to align their actions with the actions of those around them, they all must have reasonably similar understandings of the world. The collective creation and use of symbols is the very heart of social life. As Clifford Geertz has written:

> Undirected by…organized systems of significant symbols…man's behavior would be virtually ungovernable, a mere chaos of pointless acts and exploding emotions, his experience virtually shapeless. Culture, the accumulated totality of such [symbols], is not just an ornament of human existence but…an essential condition for it. (Geertz, 1973, p. 46)

Language

A **language** is a system of verbal and, in many cases, written symbols with rules about how those symbols can be combined to convey more complex meanings. It is impossible to overstate the importance of language (and writing, which augments the capacities of language) in the development, elaboration, and transmission of culture. Language enables people to store meanings and experiences and to pass this heritage on to new generations. Through language, we are able to learn about and from the experiences of others. In addition, language enables us to transcend the here and now, preserving the past and imagining the future. It also makes possible the formulation of complex plans and ideas. People could reason only on the most primitive level if they did not possess language.

Language has its own internal structure, its rules for combining speech sounds into words and words into meaningful phrases and sentences. The structure of language is an essential factor in conveying meaning. We cannot arbitrarily rearrange the sounds in a word or the words in a sentence and create a statement that another person is likely to comprehend. Languages have rules of grammar and syntax that must be followed if we want to be understood. Studying the internal structure of language is the primary concern of the discipline of linguistics.

Sociologists who study language are primarily interested in how people use language to coordinate their activities and to create and confirm social understandings (Bourdieu, 1991b; Levinson, 1983). One of the founders of sociology, Auguste Comte, wrote:

> Language forms a kind of wealth which all can make use of at once without causing any diminution of the store, and which thus admits a community of enjoyment; for all, freely participating in the general treasure, unconsciously aid in its preservation. (Comte, 1875–77, vol. 2, p. 213)

In other words, language is a resource that is available to everyone in society; everyone uses language to communicate; and communication in the same language helps to knit people together.

However, as the contemporary sociologist Pierre Bourdieu (1991b) has shown, language is also a source of social power. It not only knits people together, it differentiates among them. Language thus becomes a *social marker,* an indication of who people are, what groups they belong to, how educated they are, and their status in relation to ours. At a business meeting, for example, a person in authority usually conveys dominance by phrasing things in an assertive manner, while subordinate is likely to adopt a more tentative style of speaking. To a large extent a person's social identity is established and maintained through the patterns of language that he or she uses (Gumperz, 1982).

Language is also used to perform certain acts. When parents name a child, or a minister pronounces a couple husband and wife, they are *doing* something with words (Austin, 1965). When Auguste Comte coined the term *sociology,* he was using language to give an identity to the intellectual discipline he helped to found.

Knowledge

Knowledge is the body of facts, beliefs, and practical skills that people accumulate over time. It consists partly of procedural (or "how-to") information, such as how to drive a car or operate a computer. It also consists of information about places, people, and events (Where is the Rose Bowl? Who was our first president? What happens when milk is poured on Rice Krispies?). Often we have knowledge about things that we cannot verify for ourselves but that we accept as "truths." In our society, this includes knowledge that atomic energy can be harnessed and that germs cause disease. However, one person's "true" knowledge may be a source of skepticism to another person. Witness the debates over the biblical story of creation and evolutionary theories of human origin.

Modern society is accumulating knowledge at a fantastically rapid pace. This is partly due to the various branches of science, whose fundamental goal is to provide new knowledge. The amount of knowledge that science generates would be greatly limited, however, if it were not for modern methods of storing data. Books, microfilm, magnetic tapes, computer disks, and so forth can store vast quantities of information for long periods of time. Most recently, the merger of computers and telecommunications in the Internet has made it possible for people to exchange knowledge over great distances, often in a matter of minutes.

Control over knowledge is a critical source of social power in a modern "information society" such as ours (Bell, 1980; Giddens, 1990). While new technology has made rapid accumulation of knowledge possible, it has not created equal access to that knowledge. Many sociologists worry about a division of society into "knowledge-rich" and "knowledge-poor" classes.

A related concern is how to make sense of the enormous amount of information now available. For facts, statements, and numbers to become *knowledge,* as opposed to mere information, people need to be able to understand and use them. News editors, for example, sort through many new facts each day to make them manageable, giving priority to some (front-page or prime-time coverage), providing background information on others, and so on. This processing of information makes it easier to find and use, but it also gives power to those who determine what goes into the newspaper or on TV. It is important for us to be able to go beyond or behind the news—for example, by looking for more information on the Internet—and to have multiple sources that we can compare.

Not all knowledge takes the form of information that can be explained in words or formulas. Much *practical knowledge* is largely nonverbal. Knowing how to swim and how to shoot a hook shot in basketball are examples. A person does not need to know the physics and muscles involved in these activities. Even the best swimmers and basketball players have difficulty explaining to others how they perform so well; they "just do it." Practical knowledge is important in many areas of social life, from making judgments of taste, to making business deals, to making love (Bourdieu, 1990).

CULTURAL INTEGRATION AND DIVERSITY

"Max" has been in the United States eight years. Living with an uncle, he attended college, worked part-time, and earned a graduate degree in engineering. As Max approached thirty, his family in Bangladesh decided it was time for him to marry. Family members looked for a beautiful girl from a respectable family and found Sadya, a distant relative. Max and his parents met Sadya, liked her, and made a formal proposal of marriage, which her family accepted. The families negotiated the *kaaveem,* the amount the groom must pay as part of his religious obligations to his prospective bride, and set a wedding date. As the final step, "Mubin" (Max's original name) and Sadya fell in love.

A traditional wedding was held the next month in New York. On the wedding day, Sadya, wearing an intricately embroidered sari, much gold jewelry, and elaborate make-up sat in a back room. When Mubin

arrived, in a traditional silk tunic and pants, jeweled slippers, and turban, the bride's relatives blocked the entrance. With much laughter, they demanded that Mubin pay a high entrance fee, the bride being such a valuable asset; his relatives countered that the groom was such a "good catch" he should be admitted free. Eventually a token fee was paid, and Mubin was ushered into the main room and seated on a throne. Proper etiquette dictated that each guest visit the bridal room and praise Sadya's beauty and finery, while she sat silently, eyes downcast. Norms also dictated that the groom remain silent and solemn, while guests joked about his future married life. The marriage agreements were signed and Muslim prayers offered. The next day, Mubin's parents held a reception. The bride and groom posed for photographs, after which Mubin formally introduced his wife to each table of guests.

In a sense, Max/Mubin leads two lives. Fluent in English, educated in the United States, "Max" seems thoroughly Americanized to his classmates and co-workers. In his work life he is "Max" with an American accent. In his private family life, however, he is Mubin, who speaks the language, wears the clothes, eats the food, and practices the religion of his native Bangladesh.

Max/Mubin's story highlights a tension that has long existed in American society. On the one hand, there are social forces that encourage **assimilation,** the process by which newcomers to America, as well as other "outsiders," give up their culturally distinct beliefs, values, and customs and take on those of the dominant culture. On the other hand, there is a tendency to preserve cultural diversity, to keep one's own personal heritage alive, and to respect the right of others to do so. Max/Mubin's decision to pursue an American-style career, while leading a traditional Bengali life in his home, illustrates one solution to this problem. Increasingly, new immigrants to the United States are choosing this dual lifestyle.

The tension between assimilation and cultural diversity exists not just for those who must make individual choices about who they are and how they will act. A major question for our society today is, how much cultural diversity is "good" for the social order?

Cultural diversity refers to the presence of many different modes of understanding, different systems of values and tastes, different kinds of knowledge within the world as a whole, and within individual societies. While immigration, contacts with other cultures, and importation of cultural products are important sources of cultural diversity, such diversity does not necessarily come from the outside. The formation of new groups with new identities within a culture is equally important. The student counterculture of the 1960s was a source of cultural diversity, as is the gay subculture today. Cultural diversity is not simply a matter of preserving "old" ethnic identities but also of creating "new," nonethnic ones.

Cultural diversity is thus also a reflection of creativity, of the fact that human culture is made by human action and can also be changed. Americans seek out new ways to enjoy life, new forms of community, and new ways to distinguish themselves. Faced with enormous diversity, however, many ask whether there is a limit to the amount of diversity a society can incorporate.

Cultural integration refers to the degree to which a culture is a functionally integrated system, so that all the parts fit together well. On another level, the elements of culture are functionally integrated with *other* facets of society, such as social structure and power relations. When people have a highly integrated culture, there are few contradictions in the ways they think and act. Their religious, economic, and family lives are all of one piece. Simply by following established traditions, they can carry out the business of living with minimal inner conflict. Yet, as the anthropologist Ralph Linton (1947) stressed, a highly integrated culture is extremely vulnerable. The customs, beliefs, values, and technology are highly interdependent. Changes in one area invariably affect other areas, sometimes throwing the entire system out of balance. Cultural diversity may reduce functional integration, but it can also be a source of creativity and freedom of choice.

Degrees of Cultural Diversity

In general, the larger and more heterogeneous a society is, the higher is the level of cultural diversity. However, this is not always the case. Some large, complex societies, such as that of China, have remained closed to outside influences for much of their history, and they have developed ideologies that tend to prize cultural unity. Moreover, not all small societies have highly integrated cultures. Some, like Switzerland, have existed for hundreds of years with diverse languages, religions, and ethnic identities.

In many societies, however, one culture is dominant. The **dominant culture** is that of the group with the most social power and hence the capacity to impose its culture on others. As a rule, members of other groups must assimilate to the dominant culture to be regarded as full-fledged members of society. This has been the main pattern in the United States, although some immigrant groups (especially Northern Europeans) were more welcome and arrived with more resources than others (Southern and Eastern Europeans, Asians, Latin Americans). Over the years, many Native American children have been forced to assimilate while for a long time most African-American children were systematically *denied* assimilation.

As the last example illustrates, members of the dominant group may use their culture to maintain their power and privilege, denying cultural resources to minorities (Marger, 1991). The Roman Empire, for example, required political obedience from Jews, Franks, Egyptians, and other subject peoples, but it did not demand—or even offer—that they all become Romans, speak the same language, and hold the same values. In general, empires have been very tolerant of diversity; modern nation-states are often less tolerant (Calhoun, 1995). In many cases, minorities do not *want* to assimilate into the dominant culture. They value their separate beliefs, customs, and cultural identities and want to retain their group boundaries while enjoying free and equal participation in politics and the economy. Where free and equal participation is not available, they commonly seek independence as a separate nation.

Societies also differ in the extent to which they have one single and internally integrated dominant culture. The dominant culture in the United States has long been that of White Anglo-Saxon Protestants (or WASPs). But one of the distinctive features of American culture is that it has always been receptive to influences from other traditions. Whereas the English carried their "Englishness" with them to every corner of the once far-flung British Empire, the more permeable American culture not only has been shaped by English culture but also by the cultures of Latin America, Asia, Africa, the Caribbean, and Eastern Europe, transported via immigrants. Increasingly, American culture is influenced by books, movies, and television programs from around the world.

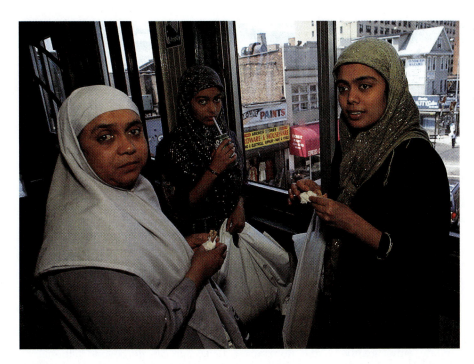

Holding the line on assimilation. Waiting for the subway in Brooklyn, New York, these Arab women wear traditional garments while snacking on Middle Eastern foods and American soda.

Yet the question of how open the United States should be to outside influences—and to outsiders—has never been resolved in favor of either cultural integration or cultural diversity. Should fundamentalist Christians, orthodox Jews, black Muslims, and the Amish be allowed to provide their own schools for their children? Should children who do not speak English at home be required to learn English and take other subjects in English at school? See Sociology and Public Debates box.

Linguistic Diversity

Language plays a key role in maintaining both cultural identity and cultural diversity. In many places today, people are multilingual, speaking a local language first and English, French, or Arabic as a second or third language. Multilingualism is not new. In the past, people who engaged in long-distance trade or lived in large empires needed to know two or more languages. Through most of its history, India was a collection of small states, each with its own culture and language; multilingualism was a practical necessity. In modern India, Hindi was declared the official language in an effort to promote national unity. But not all Indians speak Hindi. Furthermore, Hindi must compete with English, imposed by British

rulers when India was a colony and useful today for careers in the global economy.

A number of languages are spoken in Western Europe, which has a population only slightly larger than that of the United States. In addition to the national languages, some regions have a different dominant language, such as Basque, Catalan, Romanche, and Welsh. Most educated Europeans are multilingual, an asset that is growing in importance as the European community becomes more integrated. In order to get a job as a secretary at the European Community headquarters in Brussels, a person must be able to answer the phone and prepare a business letter in five languages and be fluent in at least two.

Language can be used as a political tool. Despite seventy years of Soviet domination that imposed Russian as the official language, many of the varied peoples of the former USSR continued to use their native languages, at least in private. During Soviet rule, language helped people to maintain their cultural identities; after the collapse of the Soviet government, language paved the way for new, independent nations. In Africa, the Amhara-speaking rulers of Ethiopia tried to make their language the national standard, but some linguistic groups fiercely resisted assimilation into Amhara culture. They responded *both* by becoming multilingual and by defending their native languages.

Should U.S. Schools Provide Multilingual Education?

America is, according to some Americans, becoming a "nation of strangers." The Census Bureau reports that in 1994, 8.7 percent of Americans were born in other countries; almost 32 million Americans speak a language other than English in their homes; and a full one-third of children attending urban public schools speak a foreign language first (Headden, 1995). How should our society, especially our schools, respond to growing linguistic diversity?

Should the family, the community, the schools, or the government have more power in determining what language people speak?

American schools have three basic choices. The first is to encourage children to assimilate, either gently (with special class and tutors) or forcibly (requiring all students to attend school taught in English and "sink or swim"). The second choice is bilingual education, part of a federal policy to help "children who are educationally disadvantaged because of their inability to speak English." In a typical bilingual program, students study "content" subjects (math, science, social studies) in their native language and take special classes in the English language until they are ready to take all classes in English. The third choice, sometimes overlooked, is multilingual education, in which both native English-speaking and non–English-speaking students take all subjects in two languages.

THE DEBATE

The debate over multilingual education tends toward two polar positions. On one side are those who argue that in order to become "full-fledged Americans," to participate in the country's public life as citizens and in the economy as workers, children need to become fluent in English. Accommodating "foreign" languages in schools, they argue, undercuts the incentive to learn English—and by extension, to become American. Indeed, some believe that our future as a nation depends on sharing a common language. On the other side are those who maintain that requiring children of diverse backgrounds to learn in English, and segregating them in special programs, demeans their native language and culture and may undermine self-esteem. Advocates of this position hold that our future as a nation depends on adapting to cultural and linguistic diversity in today's increasingly interconnected world.

ANALYSIS

Culture lies at the heart of this debate. Language is not simply one piece of culture but the primary medium through which cultures are maintained. Sharing a language enables us to participate in a culture. This works two ways. On the one hand, children who do not speak their native language typically lose touch with other aspects of their parents' culture. On the other hand, children who learn other languages have new opportunities to learn about other cultures, including their literature, art, history, and worldview.

Often language is used as a dividing line to mark who is or is not "one of us" and to support nationalist claims. However, sharing a language is not a necessary condition for nationhood. Switzerland has remained a well-integrated, prosperous, and highly stable nation for centuries, despite having three major and one minor recognized languages (French, German, Italian, and Romanche). Language can go beyond national boundaries, too. For example, most people in Latin America speak Spanish, but Latin America includes many different countries and cultures.

In the United States, we believe in self-determination, a form of social action that includes the right to elect our own government, to choose how to live, and to decide for ourselves what language to speak. But personal decisions about language have social consequences. Parents may encourage their children to speak English so that children will have better educational, occupational, and political opportunities, or they may discourage their children from learning English out of fear that the new language will pull the children away from their traditional culture and reduce the authority of the parents. This is not an easy choice: the futures of individuals, families, and communities are at stake. One college student explains the dilemma: "My parents don't know any English, and I can hardly speak Spanish anymore and that's painful to me" (in Headden, 1995, p. 40). But preserving immigrant languages and learning English is not an either/or choice. One goal of multilingual education is to provide enough experience with two languages to allow individuals to make a choice.

Social-structural factors fuel the debate over multilingual education. The United States is now home to people speaking some 300 native tongues. In the fall of 1995, Dade County school administrators counted 5,190 new students speaking fifty-two different languages (Headden, 1995). Providing bilingual education for all of these students is impossible. Equally significant is the concentration of non-native English speakers in certain communities and school districts. In Los

Angeles, for example, almost 43 percent of students speak Spanish as their first language (Headden, 1995). This concentration is, in turn, due to other structural factors, including industries that seek immigrant labor (such as agriculture in California) and proximity to Mexico. Most immigrants prefer to live among people who share their culture and speak their language, which means future immigrants are likely to go to areas where previous immigrants have settled. The structural concentration of Hispanics makes it easier for immigrants to speak only Spanish in their daily lives (to work with other Spanish speakers, shop at Spanish-language markets, and so on). As a result, children are likely to arrive at school knowing little English. Even within schools, the larger the proportion of students who speak a given language, the more likely students will use this language among themselves, making the transition to learning in English even more difficult.

Ultimately, decisions about multilingual education hinge on power. Should the family, the community, the schools, or the government have more power in determining what language people speak? English is the dominant language in the United States because English speakers have had the economic, political, and cultural power to require immigrants to assimilate—in some cases by force. Native American children were prohibited from speaking their own languages in schools run by the Bureau of Indian Affairs. In 1912,

the Louisiana Legislature banned the use of Cajun French in public schools (with the result that many Cajuns dropped out of school). As recently as 1971, it was illegal to speak Spanish in a public school building in Texas (Headden, 1995). Today there is a campaign to make English the nation's official language (for example, printing government forms in English only). Twenty-two states and numerous municipalities have already passed English-only laws, and a recent poll found that 73 percent of Americans agree with this goal (*U.S. News & World Report*, September 25, 1995). In a sense, schools are caught in the middle. (See Figure 4.1.)

The function of schools is to prepare children to become workers, citizens, and generally, to get along in society. What happens in schools (whether children learn English only or a second language as well) shapes opportunities for political participation, further education, and jobs, and even influences who students will meet and who they will marry. On the surface this seems to support the imperative that immigrants learn English. But given the multicultural character of America and the growing internationalization of the economy and culture, English-only speakers will be handicapped in the future. Put another way, monolingual education may be dysfunctional in a global economy. Ironically, while Americans debate multilingual education, millions of people in other countries are learning English as a second language.

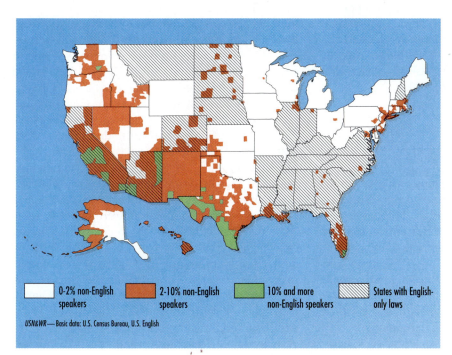

FIGURE 4.1 / *Only English Spoken Here?*

Most of the 6.7 million non-English-speaking people in the United States live in the Southwest, south Florida, and New York. So far, twenty-two states have enacted English-only laws. (Note: Demographic data as of 1990 census and laws as of August 1995)

Source: *U.S. News & World Report,* September 25, 1995, p. 41.

☐ 0-2% non-English speakers	☐ 2-10% non-English speakers	☐ 10% and more non-English speakers	☐ States with English-only laws

USN&WR — Basic data: U.S. Census Bureau, U.S. English

Multilingualism is one response to contacts with or conquest by other linguistic groups. Another is "creolisation," or the mixing of two or more languages to create a distinct dialect or even a new language (Hannerz, 1992). English is a product of creolisation. It is rooted in several regional Germanic languages that merged into Anglo-Saxon, or Old English, and in the French dialect of the Norman invaders led by William the Conqueror. Remnants of these different influences are still part of our language. For example, we have two words for many foods: an Old English word for the animal (*cow*) and a French word for the cooked food put on the table (*beef*, from the word *boeuf*). "Pidgin" languages are hybrids that have not become independent of their parent languages. Hawaiian pidgin mixes native Hawaiian and English, and even has some Asian influences (introduced by Asian laborers brought in by plantation owners).

The expression "mother tongue" indicates the attachment many people feel toward their first language. The world's people speak an estimated 2,000 different languages, but many of these languages are disappearing, especially those spoken by only small populations who lack political autonomy. At the same time, a small number of dominant languages— English, French, Spanish, Portuguese, Chinese, and Arabic—are being spoken by increasing numbers of peoples around the globe (see Figure 4.2). Migration, travel, and telecommunications have accelerated the pace of linguistic homogenization. Perhaps a quarter of the world's adult population speaks English today (Hauchler and Kennedy, 1994, p. 351).

Subcultures and the Politics of Identity

Subcultures are relatively stable groups within larger cultural fields. A **subculture** centers on a set of distinctive norms, values, knowledge, language, and symbols that members of a cultural minority share among themselves and use to distinguish themselves from the dominant culture (Fine, 1987; Fine and Kleinman, 1979). For a subculture to exist, people must identify with the subcultural group and have opportunities for communicating with one another, both face-to-face and through the mass media.

Immigrant groups are the model case of subcultures: Italian-Americans, Japanese-Americans, African-Americans. But not all ethnic groups become subcultures. The degree to which members of an ethnic group see themselves and are seen by others as culturally distinct depends, first, on how different their culture is from the dominant culture. Vietnamese immigrants generally have less in common with mainstream American culture than do immigrants from England. Second, the development of an ethnic subculture depends on the degree to which members of the group are structurally separated from the members and influences of the dominant culture. Korean immigrants, for example, tend to establish their own businesses, neighborhoods, and religious congregations, and so maintain a distance from mainstream culture.

Subcultures also form out of occupational groups, socioeconomic groups, age groups, and so on. Adolescents, for example, are active creators of a subculture revolving around music, dating, and the shared experience of being not quite adults and yet no longer children. Subcultures typically arise when people in similar circumstances find themselves isolated from the mainstream world. They may be isolated physically (such as inmates in prison, soldiers on a military base, poor people in a ghetto) or isolated by what they do and think, that is, by their shared worlds of meanings.

In the process of interacting with one another, members of subcultures not only identify with their own groups but also *de*identify with the dominant culture. For instance, from the point of view of homosexuals, the dominant culture in America (and the one from which they feel excluded) is a heterosexual culture. Similarly, from the point of view of atheists, the dominant culture is religious; from the point of view of African-Americans, the dominant culture is that of white people of Western European heritage; from the point of view of someone homeless and unemployed, the dominant culture is middle class.

Sometimes subcultures develop that are not just distinct from the dominant culture but that actively challenge that culture or try to change it. These are called **countercultures.** A good example is the student counterculture of the 1960s, whose members rejected the hard-work/success ethic, the materialistic focus, the deferred gratification, and the sexually restrictive morality of the "establishment." The student counterculture was loosely structured, with no clear leaders or set rules (though participants developed shared norms and values). Other countercul-

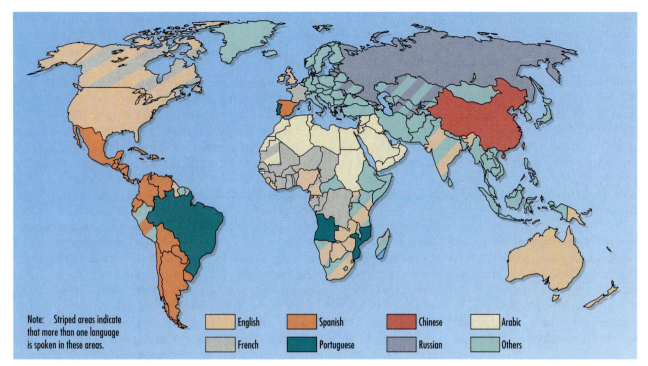

Note: Striped areas indicate that more than one language is spoken in these areas.

English   Spanish   Chinese   Arabic
French   Portuguese   Russian   Others

FIGURE 4.2 / A Comparative Look at Languages

The widespread use of a small number of dominant languages, spoken as a first, second, or even third language, is part of the globalization of culture. In many places, local or native languages are disappearing. However, in some areas (such as the former Soviet Union and the old Ethiopia) language has played a key role in the resistance to cultural and political assimilation and in the emergence of new nations.

Source: C. Moseley and R.E. Asher, eds., *Atlas of the World's Languages* (Routledge, London, 1994), pp. 223–224.

tures are tightly structured. The Hare Krishna, for example, maintain strong boundaries between their members and members of the dominant cultures, living apart and maintaining strict discipline.

Some countercultures operate in the open, advertising their differences; others maintain privacy and secrecy. Before the 1995 bombing of a federal office building in Oklahoma City, most Americans saw "hate groups" and the "radical right" as a bunch of extremists, not worth bothering about. The bombing led to the discovery of armed militias in many states, dedicated to resisting government control and taking the law into their own hands when necessary, and connected to one another by ideology, perhaps certain talk shows, and computer—in short, a counterculture, although the militia members may actually

see themselves as upholders of the "real" American values.

Today there is much debate over what identities are legitimate and which groups should be recognized as making positive cultural contributions. For example, are gays a legitimate subculture or a collection of deviant individuals? Are anti-choice activists who bomb abortion clinics a legitimate subculture or (again) a collection of deviant individuals? Are Haitian immigrants political refugees, fleeing terrorism and more recently anarchy in their homeland, or simply poor people seeking economic opportunity?

These and other related questions reflect the *politics of identity* (Calhoun, 1994b). Many groups today must struggle not just over material benefits but also over how others will see them and even how they will be allowed to see themselves. African-Americans, for example, have had to struggle to affirm the many contributions of black people to American and world culture. American history textbooks may mention blacks only in the context of slavery; courses in "world history" deal almost exclusively with Western history. At stake is an "African" identity that brings respect rather than the disrespect that stems from associations with slavery in the past and with poverty and other problems in the present. Likewise, women have had to fight for a place in history books and for recognition of their cultural contributions.

The politics of identity range from large-scale, or macro, issues, such as what groups deserve to be recognized as autonomous "nations" (Bosnians, Kurds, the indigenous tribes of the Amazon), to personal, or micro, issues, such as whether identifying oneself as a homosexual will cause one to lose a job or suffer harassment. These are not questions of right and wrong but rather of who receives cultural recognition.

Furthermore, people do not always fit neatly into one subculture or another. A person may be both gay and black; the child of a Jamaican mother and a Japanese father; or of Chinese heritage but born and raised in the United States. Depending on the situation, one or another identity may come to the fore. The choices people make about their identities also have political consequences. For example, should black women focus on their racial or gender identity? Some black activists argue that putting gender ahead of race is betrayal; others say the two can be combined in black feminist consciousness (Collins, 1991). On college campuses black women may be pressured to take sides or else lose friends.

Cross-Cultural Understanding

In contemporary American society and in the modern world generally, we are often called upon to interact with people and understand practices from other cultural backgrounds. Members of other subcultures are classmates; in multinational corporations we encounter managers and employees from different nations.

How do we deal with this? One response is **ethnocentrism:** viewing everything through the eyes of our own culture and its values. We all do this some of the time, but ethnocentrism, like egocentrism (being

self-centered), is self-limiting. If we assume that everyone has the same hopes, desires, and fears as we do, we will never understand their feelings and points of view.

The alternative, sometimes called **cultural relativism,** is to try to look at things in terms of their meanings in other cultures. This is the only way we can achieve real understanding. Cultural relativism requires that we be open-minded but not that we be morally neutral; understanding does not mean we have to approve of what we see. For example, we can understand that head-hunting among the highlanders of New Guinea does not have the same meaning that such behavior would have among the suburbanites of Wichita, Kansas, yet not approve of head-hunting. The distinction between understanding and approval is an important one. Ethnocentrism is most likely to occur when people confuse understanding with approval and refuse to try to understand beliefs and practices that they do not share.

Religion provides a familiar example of understanding without conversion. By learning the meaning of a religion's rituals, holidays, traditions, and customs we can gain a better understanding of that religion while still believing in and following our own religion (or none). For example, Jews do not practice baptism; any child born to a Jewish woman is considered a Jew. By studying the history and significance of this Christian custom, a Jew might learn that different Christian denominations disagree about the appropriate age for baptism (at birth or at maturity). This disagreement is rooted in differing interpretations of the part of the Bible that Judaism and Christianity share (the "Old Testament" to Christians, the "Torah" to Jews). There are also similarities in rituals and practice: the ceremony (*bar mitzvah* or *bat mitzvah*) held when a Jewish child reaches the age of maturity (thirteen) resembles the confirmation and first communion many Christian groups celebrate at about the same age. Thus by learning about similarities and differences a person of one faith can come to appreciate the beliefs and practices of another faith without placing a personal value on them.

Understanding more distant customs and beliefs is merely an extension of this mode of thinking. For example, to Westerners the Hindu ban on slaughtering cattle and eating meat may seem irrational, particularly in India where so many people go hungry. In fact, however, live cattle do more to support human life in India than they would if sliced into

(Above) In Zaire, Lesse girls prepare for a first menstruation ceremony. Secluded in a menstrual hut with other girls their age for a month, they receive instruction in sex, childbearing, and adult responsibilities from older women. At the conclusion of this time, the girls are presented to their community as "new women." (Right) At age thirteen, after years of study, a Jewish girl can celebrate her Bat Mitzvah. During the religious ceremony, she can hold and read from the Torah, the sacred texts of Jewish law.

steaks. Cattle consume food that is inedible for humans. Oxen pull plows; cows give milk; and cattle dung provides both fertilizer and fuel. In context, the "sacred cow" makes sense (Harris, 1975). The taboo against eating pork, shared by Jews and Muslims, and the (now largely abandoned) Catholic prohibition against eating meat on Fridays may have served practical functions of their own in the past. Today, however, the primary function of such customs is the affirmation of group identity itself.

Postmodernism

Cultural diversity is a fact of contemporary life. But what should be done about it? For some Americans it is a problem to be overcome by better communication and stronger enforcement of core cultural val-

ues. Others, including many members of minority groups (African-Americans, Hispanic Americans, Asian Americans, gay men, and lesbians), challenge the idea that they ought to conform to the core values of the dominant white, English-speaking, "straight" American culture. These contrasting views reflect a large debate over globalization of culture and whether this should produce a single "modern" culture or a greater appreciation of cultural diversity. Some advocates of diversity see the beginning of a new historical period—the postmodern era—in which the integrating forces that have shaped the last several hundred years will fade.

Postmodernists (Seidman, 1994; Lash, 1993; Lyotard, 1984) argue that "modern life" has been overly concerned with the pursuit of cultural integration. Modern culture, led by governments and other large bureaucracies, puts too much emphasis on trying to make everything fit together in a single, rational, consistent order. Modern culture also demands too high a level of conformity, idealizing cultural purity and integration at the expense of diversity and treating differences as problems to be overcome rather than as expressions of freedom and creativity. Modern culture tends to see only one route to progress, against which every cultural pattern can be judged as more or less advanced. In short, modern culture tends to be ethnocentric.

Postmodernists hold that there are many different ways of evaluating progress, not just one. They argue that the pursuit of order and cultural integration is dangerous in that it encourages dominant groups to suppress "disorderly" minorities (whether ethnic groups, political dissidents, or new schools of thought). Postmodernists welcome the new technologies that allow for widely different, often contradictory possibilities in contemporary culture. At the same time, however, they see these changes as undermining powerful, centralizing institutions such as the nation-state. In today's postmodern era, they argue, it is becoming harder for governments to exercise authority in the face of multinational corporations, mass migrations, the globalization of trade and media, and so on. It is also harder to rally political allegiance when people's cultural identities no longer spring from where they live (Pakistanis living in England or the United States often continue to call themselves Pakistani, for example). Inevitably, postmodernists say, the cultural patterns and social structures of the "modern" era will give way to new and more diverse ones. Not all sociologists agree with this prediction, but all recognize that the contemporary era is characterized by high levels of cultural change, diversity, and mobility.

How have these changes affected our own society and culture? Orlando Patterson (1994) identifies three distinct cultures in America today. One is *traditional*, the Main Street culture that clings to the belief that "America is for Americans." In the past, traditional America was both racist and xenophobic (or antiforeign). Although overt racism has declined, separatism has not. Traditional blacks as well as traditional whites choose to live "peacefully and separately" (p. 113).

The second America is *multicultural*. Miami and Los Angeles are no longer "American cities" in the traditional sense, but rather they are transnational cities. Many of their inhabitants are new immigrants from Latin America, the Caribbean, Asia, and Africa who maintain strong social, cultural, and economic ties to their homelands. Most are unskilled or semi-skilled laborers who came to this country in search of jobs and to fill economic niches that native-born Americans spurn. Unlike earlier immigrant groups, they tend to commute between their native countries and the United States and feel equally at home in both places. Thrown together by necessity, these communities coexist but do not mingle.

The third America is *ecumenical*, a "universal culture that emerged and continues to develop in the great cities and university towns of the nation" (p. 115). Grounded in the postindustrial or information economy, it draws people and ideas, art and technology, fashion and cuisine from everywhere (not just from traditional America and immigrant groups). Neither as insulated as traditional America nor as free-form as multicultural America, forward-looking rather than backward-looking, ecumenical culture selects and integrates values, beliefs, symbols, and norms that are not limited to one nationality, place, or way of life. This is not to say that ecumenical culture selects only the best. Patterson emphasizes that ecumenical culture is not utopia, but it is, he believes, the wave of the future, in which national borders and national identities will become increasingly irrelevant.

THE PRODUCTION OF CULTURE

We tend to think of culture as something preexisting, like the air we breathe. We learn, think, communicate, act, and interact in terms of our culture, relying on existing cultural patterns. But sometimes we modify these or create new ones. Culture is a product of social action.

Western culture emphasizes the role of creative individuals—geniuses like Beethoven—in cultural breakthroughs in the arts, in science, and in other endeavors. Sociology shows, however, that innovation is not simply a matter of individual creativity but a result of social action and institutional support. As Howard Becker demonstrated in *Art Worlds* (1984), production of even the most original art depends on a variety of other people and social supports: suppliers of paint and canvas, models, art dealers, art critics, gallery owners, museum directors, collectors, and admirers. In addition, other painters—past and present—provide the context for understanding a new artist's work. Thus creativity depends not just on individual genius but also on the social organization of an entire field of cultural production (Bourdieu, 1993).

Social structure and power relations influence both what is created and what is *available* to be seen or otherwise "consumed." Some groups—those making up a cultural elite—have more power than other groups to select what is exhibited in galleries, shown on television, or taught in schools. However, market forces and social movements also play important roles in this selection process. In the case of television, advertisers, who want to reach the broadest possible audiences, are more likely to back "popular culture" than "high culture." Advertisers must contend with groups like the conservative Christian Coalition, however, which monitor television for shows that are contrary to their moral views (for example, shows with too much sex or too positive a view of the gay lifestyle). These groups organize their members and supporters to threaten a boycott of advertisers who support such shows, and often advertisers back down.

Fashion and tastes illustrate the social production of culture. Both are related to social class. The elite may use fashion as a social marker, purchasing expensive clothes from exclusive fashion houses that are beyond the reach of lower classes. Sometimes members of the middle and working classes wait for high fashion to "trickle down" in the form of knock-off copies. Sometimes, however, lower classes resist elite domination and produce fashions of their own. The "grunge" style of dressing—ripped, baggy jeans and flannel shirts—originated among the young people of Seattle who sought alternative lifestyles. This fashion "trickled up" to the middle and upper classes, and now Ralph Lauren celebrates "grunge" in an entire line of clothes. Tastes also serve as social markers. Employers may base decisions about which of their employees are "executive material" not just on job performance but also on whether they display the right sort of taste and cultural knowledge to fit into elite society.

Fashion, in particular, reflects the search for identity in modern, Western societies (Davis, 1992). In other times and places, people dressed according to their position in society, which was fixed and unchanging. Today, however, people's social identities are in flux. Individuals actively (often self-consciously) seek to define and redefine their self-images. Because members of a society share many life conditions, they experience many of the same yearnings, confusions, and discontents. Fashion feeds on these collective identity instabilities.

Fred Davis identifies three recurring sources of identity ambivalence, three "cultural *fault lines*" (1992, p. 26): gender (Should women wear copies of men's suits, ties, and the like? Should men experiment more with colors and designs?); status (the tension between the Judeo-Christian emphasis on hard work and self-denial and the capitalist/consumer motto, "If you've got it, flaunt it"; in other words, understatement versus ostentation); and sex appeal (from the extremes of chaste, virginal styles to revealing, obviously erotic styles). Davis concludes that contemporary fashion is the product of a relatively

High fashion? In the 1960s, upper-class women would have sneered at this outfit, more hippie than high fashion, but in the 90s, Haight Ashbury has met the fashion runway. Nevertheless, don't expect to buy this ensemble without an upper-class income.

fluid social structure that leaves many questions about identity unanswered. Fashion does not resolve cultural tensions so much as it dramatizes them.

Over the past few decades, contemporary fashion has become increasingly eclectic and democratic due to such things as the growing affluence of the middle class in the 1960s, the advent of credit cards, and the invention of new technologies that make it possible to mass-produce acceptable, affordable copies of high fashion (Lipovetsky, 1994). The same blurring of class distinctions can be seen in taste. In a creative study of tastes in art, the sociologist David Halle (1993) found that while class differences are real, in contemporary America the similarities across classes are greater than the differences (see the Research Methods box).

Cultural Capital

Fashion is obviously a commercial enterprise, as is popular music. However, we like to think of the arts as belonging to a noncommercial realm; indeed, this is one of the connotations of the word *art*. We read poetry, go to museums, and listen to Brahms to cultivate our minds and to soothe our souls. But is that all? The French sociologist Pierre Bourdieu (1993) thinks we have other motives as well.

Bourdieu argues that one of the reasons people cultivate "artistic" tastes is to gain access to elite social circles—access that money cannot buy. Consciously or unconsciously, we try to accumulate **cultural capital:** cultural knowledge and appreciation that function as social and economic assets. Just as businesspeople accumulate economic capital—wealth—as a source of social power and a resource for social action, so people accumulate cultural capital. And just as families invest in houses, farms, and savings accounts, hoping to pass their wealth on to their children, they also invest in schools (either directly, by paying tuition at private schools, or indirectly, by paying more for a house in a good public school district), in encyclopedias and trips to museums, and in computers and educational software, all intended to give their children more cultural capital. This cultural capital is one of the most important ways in which families maintain their class positions across generations.

Expanding on the idea of cultural capital, Bourdieu suggests that contemporary societies include not one social elite, but several: Some elites are distinguished mainly by possessing wealth, others mainly by possessing political power, and still others (clergy, professors, painters, musicians, writers, and so on) mainly by possessing cultural capital. These elite circles sometimes overlap: Wealthy patrons of the opera meet conductors and performers at special receptions and benefits; musicians are invited to perform at the White House and are awarded honorary degrees by colleges and universities; and so on. These elites are able to coexist in part because they cultivate different tastes—jazz rather than opera, or old Volvos rather than new Mercedes—and so avoid competing on the terrain in which others claim superiority.

MASS MEDIA AND THE GLOBALIZATION OF CULTURE

Studies of the production of culture remind us that culture is never a static, "finished" product. Instead, it undergoes constant change as a result of decisions made by many different people who are both creators and consumers of culture.

Among the most important agents of cultural change are changes in the *mode* of communication. Today's electronic media are the latest step in a long line of cultural revolutions: the evolution of spoken language; the development of writing, which enabled people to store more information for longer periods than human memory allows; and the invention of the printing press, which made information and ideas available to a much wider audience. In this century the radio, the telephone, movies, then television, and most recently communications satellites, faxes, cellular phones, and computer networks joined this list of communication breakthroughs.

The electronic media have greatly extended the speed and distance over which people can "talk" to one another, as well as the size of the audiences involved in communications. The most recent innovation in communication is the fusion of computers and telecommunications. The Internet—the network of all networks—lies at the heart of a dramatic expansion in communication. People now use their computers to share information and views on such matters as cooking, bicycling, education, social movements, political campaigns, sex, humor, and business. Computer networking can be person-to-person (e-mail) or broadcast (bulletin boards and home pages), one-way (you call a home page to get information,

Inside Culture: A Study by David Halle

When we think about modern Western art, we tend to visualize galleries and museums as the setting for art. However, most of the paintings produced in the last 150 years were bought by private collectors for display in their homes, and only later were some of these modern paintings purchased by or donated to museums.

David Halle wanted to look at modern Western art in its proper context, the home. He was particularly interested in the relationship between tastes in art and social class. Halle selected four neighborhoods in and around New York City. Two were middle-class or upper-middle-class, one in the city and one in the suburbs; two were lower-middle-class or working-class, again one in the city and one in the suburbs.

Art usually refers to original works by recognized artists, but Halle was interested in the *content* of art in people's homes, not the artistic or financial value. As an operational definition, he broadened the term *art* to include all visual representations, then limited his study to paintings (including reproductions and original works by unknown artists), portraits (whether paintings or photographs), items from traditional or "primitive" cultures on display (rather than in practical use), and religious icons.

From each of the four study areas Halle chose a random sample of houses. To these addresses he sent a letter explaining the research with a *New York Times* review of one of his earlier projects. He visited the households a few days later, and nearly all agreed to participate. Halle and his assistant asked for a tour of the house and permission to sketch the floor plan and take photographs, then they interviewed the residents at some length.

Halle found that landscapes—especially tranquil landscapes, empty of people—were the most popular pictures on the walls of all social classes. Landscapes,

Halle surmised, "compensate" for the noisy, crowded reality of everyday life. Formal family portraits, once standard in upper-class homes, had all but disappeared, but Halle found informal family photographs, usually groups of framed pictures displayed on a table or shelf, in homes of all classes. Halle suggests that the popularity of family photographs reflects the tension between the desire for close, stable families and the instability of modern families: After divorces and remarriages, photos of ex-family members can easily be removed and replaced with photos of new family. Again, these themes crossed class boundaries.

"Tribal" or "primitive" art and religious icons followed different patterns. Tribal artifacts were displayed as art only in upper-class and upper-middle-class homes. In contrast, religious icons—statues and pictures of Jesus and Mary—where found almost exclusively in the living and dining rooms of working-class and lower-middle-class Catholic homes. Despite these surface differences, Halle holds that tribal art and religious art perform similar functions: they allow individuals to feel part of their community (whether liberal or traditional) and to contain or manage contradictions (supporting the principle of integration but not necessarily practicing integration at home; believing in the Catholic church but not practicing all of its teachings).

Halle confirmed the finding of other researchers, that people do use art to advertise (and to assess) social status. But by going into people's homes and looking at modern art in its natural context, Halle found that the similarities across classes outweigh the differences. The "general public" is more actively involved in defining tastes, more fluent in the symbolic language of art, than other research had indicated.

Source: Halle, David, 1993. *Inside Culture: Art and Class in the American Home.* University of Chicago Press.

---

such as a university catalog on-line) or two-way (you chat with others in a news group). With an estimated 100,000 new customers signing on *each month*, computer networks are growing exponentially (Piller, 1994). Eventually every person in the nation—indeed, on the planet—could by linked to everyone else via the "information superhighway."

Computer networks differ from other communication systems in several ways. They bypass political

boundaries, geographical barriers, and time zones. Messages fly over oceans, leap mountains, and cross national borders in a matter of minutes, even seconds. Networks are "open" 24 hours a day, seven days a week. Sender and receiver need not be available at the same time. No one is excluded because of physical disabilities, social obligations (child or elder care), "social handicaps" (physical appearance, shyness, a lisp), race, ethnicity, gender, or age. Networks create a social place where people with similar interests can exchange information without leaving home and or sharing a physical place. This anyplace, anytime communication enables "people to socialize, work, and learn based on who they are rather than where they are located" (Harasim, 1993, p. 22). Computer networks are *interactive*; they allow two-way communication to a far greater extent than broadcast media like TV (Rasmussen, 1996).

Global computer networks create the opportunity for—but do not guarantee—democratic communication. Networks may be used to promote freedom (allowing people to express their opinions anonymously, without fear of reprisal) or to intensify social control (the management of a corporation or a government agency may read people's e-mail. Networks may reduce the gap between the rich and the poor (by providing a common pool of information equally accessible to all) or widen the gap between the "info-rich" and the "info-poor" (by charging high fees for the "best" information). Networks may encourage political participation (by making it easier to vote and obtain a candidate's records) or encourage uninvolvement (by enabling people to mind their own business—to shop, view movies, do banking, and so on, without interacting with others face-to-face). Networks may support cultural diversity (through multiple channels that allow greater choice) or accelerate cultural homogenization (by creating a single, centralized market for goods and ideas).

Up until now, users have led the way in transforming data networks into social networks. But commercial interests and government regulators are hovering in the background, seeking opportunities for increased involvement and control. Who or what will determine the shape of tomorrow's networks remains an open question.

One of the most significant consequences of the growth of the mass media has been the *globalization* of culture. People watch Donald Duck cartoons in Indonesia; read French newspapers in Africa; dance to Michael Jackson records in Brazil; eat egg rolls, tacos, and couscous in Paris and New York; and listen to the British Broadcasting Corporation news on radios all over the world. Today few places on earth are untouched by outside cultural influences.

The globalization of culture is not entirely new. The great empires of the past and the spread of world religions introduced people of widely different cultures to common sets of laws, customs, beliefs, and

Santa Claus visits the Great Wall of China, just one example of the increasing spread of local customs and cultural symbols around the globe.

symbols. In the twentieth century, however, the process of globalization has become much more rapid. In the past, the two primary media of cultural diffusion were travel and literacy (Patterson, 1994). People learned about other cultures by traveling themselves, by reading travelogues, or by studying art, artifacts, and books produced by other cultures. Except for large-scale migrations (such as the importation of African slaves to the Americas), this exposure to other cultures was largely confined to elites. In the Asian and African societies colonized by Europeans, only a fraction of the population—native elites and urban workers—were exposed to Western influences.

The recent acceleration of cultural diffusion reflects not only the rise of mass communications but also the spread of mass literacy, the growth of global organizations such as the United Nations, and advances in long-distance transportation (Patterson, 1994). Large-scale immigration is another factor: In recent decades, thousands of Indians and Pakistanis have moved to Britain, West Africans to France, and Mexicans to the United States. Immigration does not just create subcultures; it also fosters the development of a new global culture.

The globalization of culture is not a one-way process, leading inevitably to Westernization or Americanization, what some call "cultural imperialism." Nor does globalization necessarily create a homogenized, watered-down, dull-gray culture. Small, traditional cultures may be overwhelmed, but globalization also allows for new and diverse combinations of formerly separate cultural traditions (Friedman, 1994). Further, non-Western audiences are not passive consumers of Western cultural products but actively reinterpret what they receive in terms of their own cultures and experiences (see the Global Issues/Local Consequences box). Today's global culture is truly that: globally produced and globally consumed (Robertson, 1993).

The development of the Jamaican musical form *reggae* illustrates cultural cross-fertilization (Patterson, 1994). Jamaica's rich musical tradition is based mainly on West African music, influenced by British popular melodies and lyrics. In the late 1950s, migrant laborers working in the United States began bringing home recordings of rhythm-and-blues and country music. Unable to afford imported records, much less record players, some young singers tried to imitate the music, but "the imitations were so bad that they were unwittingly original" (Patterson, 1994, p. 106). Local entrepreneurs who managed to acquire record players rented out their sound systems, along with their record collections and themselves as disk jockeys. To give a "live" quality to their shows, they "played" the turn table, slowing down or speeding up the records to produce new sounds, and added "voiceovers" with more Jamaican rhythms and cadences. Finally, the growing Ras Tafari cult, a back-to-Africa movement with religious overtones, provided ideological content.

Reggae grew rapidly in popularity, among tourists as well as working-class Jamaicans, due in part to the talent and showmanship of Bob Marley and other top singers. But the main push toward globalization came from working-class migrants who, in the late 1960s, began moving to Britain and the United States in increasing numbers. By the late 1970s, reggae caught the attention of African-American youth. Before long, young black Americans began creating their own versions of reggae, which became known as "rap." The music had gone full circle, from the crude imitations of African-American rhythm and blues; to Jamaica, where a new musical idiom developed; and then back to the United States.

The Jamaican-born sociologist Paul Gilroy, who now works in England, has described the cross-fertilization of black culture among Africa, North America, the Caribbean, and Europe as "the Black Atlantic" (Gilroy, 1993). The Black Atlantic is the result of the diaspora (breaking up and scattering) of West Africans to coastal regions of the northern hemisphere, where they were exposed to European (or white) cultures but still retained elements of their African heritage. It is, according to Gilroy, a culture that exists in the spaces between African, American, and European cultures, like a ship always crossing the Atlantic Ocean but never quite reaching shore. Even "local" cultural manifestations, such as reggae, blues, and jazz, reflect this multinational or "outer national" culture. As we saw in Chapter 1, the sociologist, W. E. B. Du Bois spoke of the "double consciousness" of being black and American (1903), but "doubling" of consciousness is an even broader phenomenon. The works of many important African-American writers, from Du Bois to Richard Wright, were inspired by their different experiences in Europe, which led to reexamination of their African-American identities.

The globalization of culture creates many opportunities for new hybridizations as well as creative diversity and "double consciousness." There are numerous examples of its creative benefits, from the novels of Isabelle Allende and Vikram Seth to the films of François Truffaut and Chen Kaige. But America's influence on the global culture does tend to be lopsided (Rieff, 1993).

Of all world powers, the United States has the shortest history and so is less tied to tradition in the way, say, Great Britain, France, China, and Japan are. At the same time, the United States has extensive experience in *producing* culture, especially popular culture that speaks to a diverse population. Our society is (or was) unique in its belief that newness, in and of itself, is positive. In a world on the move—both literally, in the form of mass migrations, and

GLOBAL ISSUES/LOCAL CONSEQUENCES

TV Comes to Amazonia

In June 1992, three television sets were turned on in the remote Amazonian town of Gurupá, Brazil (population 20,000) (Pace, 1993). For the first time in the community's 370-year history, residents were in visual and audio contact with the outside world. Located on a bluff above the lower Amazon River, surrounded by dense tropical rain forest, Gurupá is accessible only by boat (or private plane). The local economy is based on slash-and-burn agriculture, fishing, hunting, and collection of forest products. Ninety-five percent of the population ranks as poor, and most homes do not have electricity, indoor plumbing, or even outhouses. Slightly over 40 percent of the population is literate, and reading material is scarce. Before the 1950s, the only news of national and world events came via word of mouth from river merchants and other travelers. Battery-powered radios became available in the late 1950s, but not until the arrival of television did Gurupáns have regular exposure to Brazilian culture and world events.

What impact did TV have on patterns of social interaction and worldviews? The arrival of TV did *not* increase social isolation and passivity (the couch-potato syndrome); to the contrary, TV increased levels of social interaction. In the evenings, when news, soccer, and nightly *novelas* (Brazilian soap operas) were broadcast, the TV sets were turned toward windows that faced the street. Friends and relatives were invited inside; acquaintances and even strangers were welcome to congregate outside.

Patterns of social interaction did change, however. Before TV, the streets came alive between 7 and 10 p.m. as people took advantage of the cool night air to stroll along the town's main streets, sit in their doorways and watch the passing parade, and enjoy the music blasted from dance halls where young people congregated. After the arrival of TV, the promenades stopped and the streets were deserted most nights. Traditionally, males dominate the public sphere in Brazil, while females are limited to the domestic sphere. But women and children frequently joined the clusters of viewers outside homes with TVs. Parties, festivals, and even night school were rescheduled to accommodate the highly popular *novelas*.

In Western countries, increased TV viewing is associated with less reading and lower education levels. By contrast, in information-starved Gurupá, television increased an awareness of the outside world and kindled a desire for additional knowledge from books, magazines, and radio broadcasts.

In the West, TV viewing is thought to reinforce the status quo; in Gurupá, TV viewing increased class consciousness and possibly contributed to increasing class tensions as Gurupáns got their first glimpse of middle- and upper-class lifestyles in Rio de Janeiro and São Paulo. As a result, many residents began to question their own, much lower standard of living. Some blamed their community's poverty on individual laziness; others blamed their poor location and limited resources, corruption among the local elites, or capitalism in general, which was seen as rewarding greed and allowing wealth to be concentrated in the hands of a few. TV did not have much impact on political views, however. For decades the Brazilian government controlled the press and all political news, so even after the dictatorship ended (in 1985), most people remained skeptical.

Few deny that television has a strong impact on both behavior and cognition or understandings, but this example shows that television's impact is *mediated by culture*. Rather than producing the viewing patterns seen in the West, television in Gurupá increased social interaction, stimulated a desire for more knowledge, and heightened awareness of social inequality in this small Amazonian town.

Source: Richard Pace, "First-Time Televiewing in Amazonia: Television Acculturation in Gurupá, Brazil," *Ethnology*, 32, no. 2 (Spring 1993): 187–205.

psychologically, in terms of the collapse of old beliefs and certainties—American culture leads the way because Americans have already experienced and to some degree accommodated these new realities. To a high degree, the production of culture in America is commercialized—that is, it is designed to sell products, create needs and desires, and promote consumerism. Inevitably, though, Hollywood movies, TV serials, and popular music also "sell" American values such as democracy, freedom of speech, and individual choice. Moreover, the media present people in developing areas with images of different ways of life, images that may help them to prepare for and adapt to modernization. Whether people "buy" the entire package, from discos to democracy (Schell, 1989), is another matter.

SUMMARY

1. The term *culture* refers to a people's shared ways of thinking, understanding, evaluating, and communicating that make social life possible. We draw on culture to make sense out of our experiences and to coordinate our activities, and in the process we reshape culture to meet new demands and situations.

2. Values are deeply held standards that people use to evaluate themselves and other people, objects, and events. Americans value competition, achievement, and success. We prize individuality but at the same time long for community.

3. Norms are specific rules or guidelines for how to behave in particular situations. Norms operationalize values and help us to choose among competing values. Norms vary from society to society and also from group to group within a single society.

4. Symbols are objects, gestures, sounds, or images that represent something other than themselves. The meaning given symbols is often arbitrary, but the collective creation and use of symbols produce the shared understandings that are the heart of culture.

5. A language is a system of verbal (and, in many cases, written) symbols with rules about how those symbols can be put together to convey more complex meanings. Language is vital to the development, elaboration, and transmission of culture. Language can bind people together, but it also can be used as a social marker, indicating rank or status.

6. Knowledge is our stored body of facts, beliefs, and practical skills. Modern society is generating and storing knowledge at a very rapid rate, raising questions about who has access to which information and who should organize the flood of raw data.

7. An immigrant society, America has long struggled with the question of whether newcomers should be required to assimilate to mainstream culture or be allowed to maintain their cultural distinctiveness.

8. *Cultural integration* refers to the degree to which the parts of a culture form a consistent and interrelated whole. *Cultural diversity* refers to the presence of many different modes of understanding, systems of values and tastes, and kinds of knowledge in the world as a whole, and within individual societies. In many societies the group with the most social power forms a dominant culture.

9. Language, which may be used to maintain or to undermine distinct cultural identities, has played a key role in struggles for independence. Today, as in the past, many people are multilingual, but a small number of languages are becoming more and more dominant.

10. In large, complex societies such as that of the United States, there are many distinct subcultures. Some are variations on mainstream culture; others (called countercultures) oppose mainstream culture. The politics of identity consists of struggles to gain recognition and respect, whether as individuals, valued subcultures, or independent nations.

11. In today's world, almost everyone interacts with members of different cultures and subcultures. One response to cultural differences is ethnocentrism: judging everything in terms of one's own cultural values. To understand other people's customs and beliefs, however, one must view them in their own cultural context. This cultural relativism does *not* mean that one must approve or accept everything one encounters.

12. There is debate over how much cultural diversity a society can tolerate. Postmodernists argue that we are entering a new era in which the quest for order and for a common core of cultural values will be replaced by a new appreciation of diversity, individuality, and creativity. Powerful social institutions, such as the nation-state, will become increasingly irrelevant. Change is already evident in the emergence of three distinct cultures in America: traditional, multicultural, and ecumenical.

13. Sociology shows that the production of culture is a social process; cultural innovators always act within a social context. Fashion and taste, once dictated by cultural elites, have become increasingly democratic, in part as a result of the search for identity in modern societies.

14. Cultural knowledge and appreciation function as a form of capital, an investment that "pays off" in entrance to elite circles.

15. The electronic media—especially the fusion of computers and telecommunications in the Internet—have dramatically increased the speed and range of communication, raising new questions about freedom and control, equality and inequality, and political participation versus privitization.

16. The electronic media have also accelerated the globalization of culture, the process whereby the production of culture is influenced by people and cultures from around the world. So far, globalization has not led to "cultural imperialism" (one culture's obliterating others in its path) or to cultural homogenization. However, the global production of culture is drawn by commercial forces and promotes consumerism.

REVIEW QUESTIONS

1. Show how values and norms are closely linked. Use examples in your answer.

2. Distinguish among folkways, mores, and laws. Give examples of each.

3. List some forces that promote cultural integration and some forces that promote cultural diversity.

4. Describe what it means to be ethnocentric and what it means to be a cultural relativist.

5. Show how the media both reflect and affect culture.

6. Describe three ways in which culture is becoming more global.

CRITICAL THINKING QUESTIONS

1. How would you describe the "dominant" culture of the United States? How dominant is it? How much room is there for subcultures, counter-cultures, and alternative definitions of the mainstream?

2. Describe the symbols that are special to you and explain why they are special.

3. Present an argument that there is greater cultural integration or greater cultural diversity in the United States than in most other countries.

4. Develop the essential ingredients of a program to reduce ethnocentrism on your campus.

5. The media are an important agent of the globalization of culture. Do you think they introduce biases in the way we see and understand other cultures?

GLOSSARY

Assimilation   The process by which newcomers or members of a subculture give up their distinctive cultural patterns and take on those of the dominant culture of the society in which they live.

Counterculture   A group whose norms, attitudes, values, and lifestyle directly challenge or seek to change those of the dominant or mainstream culture.

Cultural capital   Elite or sophisticated cultural knowledge and tastes that function as social and economic assets.

Cultural diversity   The presence of many different modes of understanding, systems of values and tastes, and kinds of knowledge in the world as a whole, and within individual societies.

Cultural integration   The degree to which the parts of a culture form a consistent and interrelated whole.

Cultural relativism   The idea that any element of culture is understandable only in relation to the rest of its cultural context and to a particular time, place, and set of circumstances.

Culture   The learned norms, values, knowledge, artifacts, language, and symbols that are constantly communicated among people who share a common way of life.

Dominant culture   The group whose values, norms, traditions, and outlooks are imposed on the society as a whole.

Ethnocentrism   The tendency to view one's own cultural patterns as good and right and to judge other cultural patterns by those standards.

Folkways   Norms that are everyday habits and conventions.

Knowledge   The body of facts and beliefs people accumulate over time.

Language   A system of verbal (and usually also written) symbols with rules about how those symbols can be strung together to convey more complex meanings.

Laws   Norms that are enacted as formal rules by a political body and enforced by the power of the state.

Material culture   All the physical objects that people make and/or attach meaning to.

Mores   Norms that people consider vital to their well-being and to their most cherished values.

Norms   Specific guidelines for action that say how people should behave in particular situations.

Postmodernism   The theoretical position that the modern era has been dominated by the idea of historical progress, rationalism, and the pursuit of cultural integration and universalism; and that this modern era either is coming to an end or should be opposed.

Subculture   A set of distinctive norms, values, knowledge, artifacts, language, and symbols that a particular group in society uses to distinguish itself from the dominant culture.

Symbol   An object, gesture, sound, image, or design that represents something other than itself.

Values   General ideas that people share about what is good or bad, desirable or undesirable.

CHAPTER 5

Socialization and Identity Through the Life Course

In the winter of 1954, when Gregory Howard Williams was ten years old, family crisis and financial ruin forced his father to return to Muncie, Indiana, where he had grown up. Abandoned by their mother, Greg and his younger brother Mike accompanied their father on the long, bleak bus ride from Virginia. The three sat in the "white" area at the front of the bus. In this era of strict racial segregation, blacks were relegated to the back of the bus, symbolically out of the white passengers' sight.

"Boys," Tony Williams said to his sons a few hours outside of Muncie, "there's something I want to tell you." He leaned forward and spoke very softly so no one around them could hear. "Remember Miss Sallie who used to work for us in the tavern? Well, she's really my momma, so that means she's your grandma."

"But that can't be!" Greg whispered back in total disbelief. "She's colored!"

"That's right," Tony Williams continued. "She's colored. That makes you part colored too. Life is going to be different from now on. Muncie is full of the Ku Klux Klan. Once they know who you are and what you are, they'll do everything humanly possible to keep you 'in your place.' "

And so began Greg Williams's journey into American culture from an entirely new perspective. Born to a white mother and a very light-skinned mulatto father who for years had "passed" as white, Greg had grown up without an inkling of his black heritage. But in Muncie, where his father was considered a black man, Greg and his brother were considered black too. They soon learned that a different way of thinking and acting was required of them. No longer could they strike up friendships with white children, especially white girls. Even talking to a white girl could provoke severe reprisals. Greg and Mike had to learn to think of whites as a group apart from themselves, as people who generally disliked them and might even do them harm. Strict rules prescribed which parts of town the Williams boys could venture into. Although their maternal grandparents also lived in Muncie, on the other side of town, paying them a visit was out of the question. Two "colored boys" simply couldn't set foot in an all-white neighborhood, even if their own skin was white (Williams, 1995).

That the Williams boys had to relearn how to think and act in Muncie vividly illustrates that who we are and what we do does not just spring from inside us. It is partly a product of what our society tells us is appropriate and right. This process of learning the beliefs, norms, and values that are socially expected of us as members of a particular society or a particular social group is called **socialization**. Through socialization we come to learn the elements of a certain culture.

Through socialization we also come to accept that culture as a fundamental part of ourselves. This sense of self-identity fostered by socialization is depicted in the Williams boys' story. The first night that Greg met his black relatives in Muncie, his inner self kept crying out that he did not belong among them. But ten years later, when Greg was in college, his long-absent mother contacted him and suggested that her new white husband adopt the Williams boys. Doing so would have required them to deny their black heritage and forget about their years of being "colored." Without hesitation Greg refused, because being black was now part of his sense of self.

Although socialization is a process of learning cultural norms and values and making them part of one's self, it is not a matter of having a culture simply imposed on us. People have some freedom to interpret elements of culture as they adopt them. They can decide what roles they wish to play and how they will act them out in their own particular ways. Both Greg and Mike, for instance, were socialized into black culture and encouraged to "beat the system" of dominant white society. Greg went on to excel in school, go to college and law school, and become dean of the Ohio State University College of Law. Mike put his talents to work on the streets, excelling in the world of the small-time drug dealer, gambler, and hustler. That the two interpreted the same subcultural prescription in such different ways shows that socialization is not just a one-way process of social expectations impinging on people; it is also a

matter of people's giving meaning to those expectations and actively influencing what they, as individuals, become. In this way, socialization is also a matter of individual social action.

This chapter begins with a look at theories of socialization and the self. Here we explore how, through interactions with others in the process of growing up, people learn social expectations and ways of thinking that they incorporate into the self. We then turn to the topic of how socialization varies depending upon the social categories and groups to which a person belongs. Being male or female; black or white; rich, poor, or middle class makes a great deal of difference in what we learn to become. Our next section investigates three major factors involved in acquiring our self-identities: nature (or biological makeup), nurture (how we are socialized to conform to certain norms and values), and choice (our freedom of self-expression and individual action). The particular example on which we focus is the development of a person's sexual orientation and identity. From here we examine the major agents of childhood socialization: the groups and organizations that teach young people the elements of their culture. And finally, in our last section, we deal with the continuing process of socialization in adulthood, especially the way in which the norms and values of adults are aligned with the new social roles they come to play.

SOCIALIZATION AND THE SELF

Each of us possesses a sense of **self**—that is, a sense of having a distinct identity, of being set apart from other people and things. This sense may be stronger or weaker. A person's sense of self is not innate. Instead, we actively construct a sense of self through our interactions with others in the process of socialization as we learn to become members of particular groups. As the sociologist Charles Horton Cooley put it, "self and society are twinborn."

Cooley: The Looking-Glass Self

Based on observations of his own children, Cooley (1864–1929) developed the idea of the **looking-glass self**. We acquire our sense of self, he said, by seeing ourself reflected in other people's attitudes and behaviors toward us and by imagining what they think of us (Cooley, 1905/1956, 1964). In this way, other people serve as a kind of mirror (a looking glass) for viewing the self. The looking-glass self has three parts: what we think others see in us; how we imagine they judge what they see; and how we feel about those judgments.

Take the example of a teenage boy who thinks his classmates see him as a "brain" and who imagines that they judge braininess to be "nerdy." This reflected image may make him feel bad about himself because he sees himself as rejected by his peers. Of course, if the same boy imagines that being viewed as a brain makes his peers admire him, he could easily come to feel proud for standing out above the pack.

The looking-glass self is not a *direct* reflection of what other people see in us. Reading other people's opinions through their words and actions is not like reading descriptions in a book. The images of ourselves that we see in others are ones that we have interpreted and selected based on our own predispositions, expectations, and values (Franks and Gecas, 1992). What we see in the looking glass, in other words, is partly our own creation.

Even playing doctor with the family dog allows young children to imagine themselves in adult roles, experimenting with grown-up behavior, language, and feelings.

Mead: The Self as "I" and "Me"

George Herbert Mead (1863–1931), a contemporary of Cooley, traced the development of self-awareness to early childhood social interaction (Mead, 1934). The self, he argued, is composed of two parts: the "I" and the "me." The "I" is the self as *subject*, or initiator of thoughts and actions. The "me" is the self as *object*, as we imagine ourself from the perspective of other people. In social interaction, there is a continuous conversation between the "I" and the "me," as the "I" decides how to act while the "me" anticipates how others will respond.

Early childhood play helps to sharpen the "I/me" distinction. Young children spend much of their time role-playing. They make believe that they are doctors, police, and firefighters, or fantasy characters like Cinderella or Power Rangers. Often they take the roles of people important in their lives, what sociologists call **significant others** (Sullivan, 1953). Young children are especially fond of playing mothers caring for their babies, fathers lecturing children on their behavior, and teachers presenting a lesson to the class. This play allows them to see themselves from another person's perspective (as son or daughter from a parent's perspective or as student from a teacher's point of view).

As children mature, according to Mead, they learn how to take the role not just of specific others but also of the **generalized other**. Now they begin to think about what people in general will think about their actions. They learn, for example, to cover their mouths when coughing, not because a specific person told them to do so but because people in general suggest through their words and actions that this is a good idea. In this way, children come to assess themselves in light of cultural norms and values.

Freud: Sources of Conflict within the Self

Through interactions with others, according to Cooley and Mead, how we come to think of ourselves and our behavior is partly a matter of how other people think and what they expect of us. A third contemporary of Cooley and Mead, Sigmund Freud (1856–1939), shared this view, but added that socialization is inherently full of conflict—between inner needs and outer pressures, and also between forces within a person's psyche. These forces are: the **id**, a reservoir of innate biological drives aimed at obtaining physical pleasure; the **ego**, the choice-making, rational part of the self; and the **superego**, essentially a person's conscience, which embodies the moral standards of society. The ego's job, as Freud saw it, was to find safe and acceptable ways to satisfy the id without causing guilt or remorse to the superego (Freud, 1920/1953, 1923/1947). However, because the id and the superego are so diametrically opposed, this task is difficult. Pulled one way by biology, the other by society, we are, in Freud's view, perpetually prone to inner conflict.

Freud believed that two parts of the human psyche, the ego and the superego, are products of social interaction, particularly interaction between children and their parents. At birth, Freud argued, humans are irrational, amoral creatures, with nothing more to guide them than their pleasure-seeking impulses. It is not long, though, before a baby begins to learn that biological drives cannot always be gratified immediately. Food, for example, is not always available on demand. Through such discoveries the ego begins to develop. The ego consciously mediates between id impulses and the physical and social reality in which the child lives. The ego channels biological impulses toward courses of action that are safe and culturally approved.

The superego, too, develops in a social context—through a child's encounters with the demands of the larger culture, as conveyed initially by parents and other adults. Freud focused on cultural demands, such as toilet training, which curb the child's natural drives to obtain physical pleasure. Freud argued that a child's personality is shaped by how smoothly and completely the conflicts between id drives and cultural demands are resolved. With time, children learn that these demands are not just the preferences of their parents but also of the society and culture in which they live. Gradually, they internalize cultural norms and values and feel guilty when they violate them. At this point they have acquired a superego, a kind of internal watchdog over the self.

Piaget: The Cognitive Basis of Self

Psychologist Jean Piaget (1896–1980) emphasized the development of children's inherent cognitive or intellectual capacities. The ability to think—and thus to understand both oneself and one's environment—entails fundamental changes in thinking that occur in a series of stages as children grow older (Piaget, 1926/1955).

According to Piaget, children begin life unable to distinguish between themselves and others, or even between themselves and surrounding objects. Newborns, in other words, have no sense of self, no concept that they exist as separate persons. Gradually, however, through interactions with people and things, infants come to realize that the rest of the world is independent from them. An important part of this discovery is what Piaget called the **object permanence concept**, the realization that objects have a continuing existence apart from the baby's perception of them. A rattle, for example, does not cease to exist when it drops out of sight, nor does a mother when she leaves the room. With this important discovery, the child has made a first major step toward acquiring a notion of the self as a separate entity.

Another major advance in self-understanding comes toward the end of infancy, when the child develops the ability to engage in representational thought. **Representational thought** is the capacity to make one thing represent, or "stand for," another. Part of representational thought is the use of mental images to stand for real persons, objects, and actions. The ability to use mental images in this way allows toddlers to think about the self in ways they never could before. Not surprisingly, this is the age when the word me first comes into use.

Throughout much of childhood the sense of self is highly concrete in nature. During the school years, in Piaget's theory, a child's thinking is largely tied to the manipulation of tangible objects, even though those manipulations may be carried out in the child's head. This concrete mode of thinking is reflected in the self-concepts of school-age children. When asked to describe themselves, youngsters this age typically answer with a list of unquestioned "truths": "I'm a boy; I'm in the third grade; I'm good at playing soccer; I like to tell jokes; I'm the tallest kid in my class." It is not until adolescence, with the emergence of more abstract thinking, that young people begin to regularly view the self in a more reflective way. They start to form hypotheses about who they "really" are. In short, they develop a mature sense of personal identity.

A lasting contribution that Piaget made to the study of socialization and the emergence of a sense of self is his view of children as active participants in their own development. Just as Cooley saw people as active interpreters of their looking-glass selves, learning about the world in Piaget's view is not just a process of absorbing information. Rather, children actively interpret the experiences they have, giving meaning to them within the framework of their current level of understanding. This view of children as active participants in their own development is an important legacy of Piaget's work.

VARIATIONS IN SOCIALIZATION

Cooley, Mead, Freud, and Piaget pioneered important perspectives on the processes of socialization and human development, and their theories have guided researchers ever since. However, all four treated socialization as though it were basically the same for everyone. None (with the partial exception of Freud) gave much attention to how socialization varies for different people, depending upon the social groups and categories to which they belong. And yet, as our opening example of Gregory Howard Williams showed, these factors can greatly affect the beliefs, attitudes, and norms of behavior that people come to learn. In our society, being socialized as a black child is quite different from being socialized as a white child. Similarly, learning to be a female is different from learning to be a male, and learning to be the son of a welfare mother is different from learning to be a Rockefeller's son. Exactly what you learn about becoming a member of society depends upon your place in the social order.

Socialization and Gender Differences

When we hear that a friend has had a baby, our first question is likely to be, boy or girl? It is as though we need to identify the sex before we can form a mental picture of the baby. Language reinforces this: We need to know whether to say "him" or "her" because "it" does not sound very nice. To be spoken of as a human being, the baby needs a gender.

As soon as an infant's gender is known, the sociocultural world starts to socialize the child into male or female roles. Admiring grandparents will say "she" is pretty and "he" is handsome. When the baby becomes a toddler, "he" will get toy cars and "she" will get dolls. Even parents who want to raise their children without gender stereotypes find this impos-

sible, because friends, family, school, the media, and society as a whole pressure youngsters to conform. Although Mom and Dad may think that Barbie dolls promote an objectionable female stereotype, that will not stop their daughter from wanting one if her friends have them.

However, differences in socialization by gender run deeper than simply encouraging children to conform to gender stereotypes. In a probing look at how girls are socialized for the "mothering" role in our society (while men generally are not), Nancy Chodorow (1978, 1994) weaves a psychoanalytic explanation that builds on Freud's views. Chodorow argues that the reproduction of "mothering" in each new generation of women is due neither to biology nor to deliberate role training. Instead, women as mothers unintentionally create a mother-daughter relationship that fosters in girls a capacity for nurturance and a desire to take care of others. According to Chodorow, this is because girls never break away from their early sense of oneness with their mothers as completely as boys do. In Chodorow's view, boys' development entails identification with masculine role models, whose masculinity is defined essentially as rejection of all that is feminine. Girls' development, in contrast, does not involve this kind of psychological pulling away from the mother. As a result, girls come to define themselves more in relation to other people than boys do. This prepares them for their future role as the emotional center of the family and the caretaker of family members. Boys, in whom these same capacities are curtailed and repressed, are much better prepared for participation in the impersonal world of work.

As Chodorow built on Freud, another important researcher, Carol Gilligan, built on the work of psychologist Lawrence Kohlberg, who applied Piaget's concept of stages to moral development. Most advanced, he thought, are people who reason in terms of universal ethical principles—what is always right, regardless of context. But, Gilligan showed, this was a male model. It failed to recognize the more characteristically female approach of considering specific contexts, and how people are affected by and react to any individual's moral choices. According to Gilligan (1982, 1989), because men are socialized to be detached from other people, they tend to reason morally in terms of abstract concepts, such as equity and justice. Women, in contrast, are socialized to be connected to family and friends, so they tend to think about moral issues in terms of personal relationships and social obligations. According to Gilligan, this does not mean that women are inferior to men in their moral thinking; it simply means they have been taught to emphasize a different set of values. In addition, gender differences in moral reasoning are not absolute. Both men and women are *capable* of reasoning in terms of abstract principles *and* in terms of social obligations, but differences in socialization lead the two genders toward different moral styles.

Both Chodorow's work and Gilligan's work dramatically illustrate the importance of gender categories in socialization. From the very beginning, who we are and how we learn to think and act is very much a matter of whether we are male or female. This different socialization by gender affects more than just superficial qualities, such as style of clothing and manners of speech. Gender socialization influences some of our most fundamental ways of thinking and relating to other people. To be socialized is to become not just a member of society at large, but boys and girls, men and women, who think and act in ways "appropriate" to their gender.

Socialization and Social Class Differences

I used to dream about how I'd grow up and get married and live in one of those big, beautiful houses like they show in the magazines—you know, magazines like *House Beautiful*. God, all the hours I spent looking at those magazines, and dreaming about how I would live in one of those houses with all that beautiful furniture, and everything just right. . . . Life turns out a lot different in the end, doesn't it? (Thirty-six-year-old cannery worker, mother of three, married twenty years, quoted in Rubin, 1976, p. 43)

Although in every generation there is some movement up and down the social ladder, leaps from "rags to riches" are extremely rare. Most adults end up in the same social class into which they were born. Why does this happen? Why aren't dreams and hard work enough to win most working-class people the life they aspire to? Aspects of social structure, such as access to education and opportunities in the job market, play a big part. But socialization, too, tends to channel children from different social classes along the same paths as their parents. An important part of this socialization by social class involves the transmission of values.

That social-class positions are perpetuated by the values parents teach is suggested by the work of soci-

ologist Melvin Kohn, who has extensively studied this subject over many years. He and his co-workers have found very consistent differences in the values people hold for themselves and their children depending upon their social class (Kohn, 1959; Kohn and Schooler, 1983). Figure 5.1 shows some of the different values that working-class and middle-class parents stress. Working-class parents place more value on manners, neatness, good behavior in school, honesty, and obedience. Middle-class parents, in con-

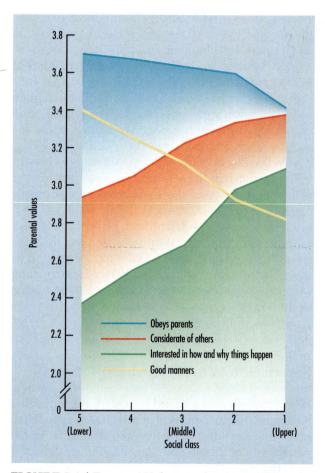

FIGURE 5.1 / Parents' Values and Social Class

In working-class families, parents strongly encourage their children to be well-mannered, neat, well-behaved, and obedient, all traits that are consistent with conformity. Middle-class parents emphasize considerateness toward others, curiosity, and self-control, traits that involve self-direction.

Source: Melvin L. Kohn and Carmi Schooler, *Work and Personality: An Inquiry into the Impact of Social Stratification* (Ablex, Norwood, N.J., 1983).

trast, place more value on consideration, interest in how and why things happen, responsibility, and self-control.

Comparing the items on these lists suggests a more basic, underlying difference between the two value systems. People in higher social classes are more likely to value traits that involve self-direction, while people in lower social classes are more likely to value traits that involve conformity to external authority. Valuing manners, for example, involves caring about whether children follow the rules of etiquette that society sets, whereas valuing responsibility involves caring about whether children are willing to be accountable for their own actions and choices. The first value stresses conformity to an *external* authority; the second value stresses the development of one's own *internal* controls.

Where do these different sets of values come from? Why do working-class parents want their children to follow established conventions and obey with no questions asked, while middle-class parents are more concerned about instilling self-direction and internalized standards? Kohn's research has shown that these class-based differences are directly related to the parents' experiences at work (Kohn, 1976, 1981; Kohn and Schooler, 1978). Work that provides opportunities for independent thought, initiative, and judgment—occupational *self*-direction—tends to foster middle-class values. Work that restricts these opportunities tends to encourage working-class values. Certain aspects of work are especially important in this regard (see Figure 5.2). When a person is not closely supervised, deals with data or people instead of with things, and has work that is complex enough to allow various approaches, he or she has the job-related independence conducive to valuing self-direction. Apparently, this same chain of influences operates in other countries besides the United States. Kohn found that in Japan, a non-Western capitalist state, as well as in socialist Poland, people in higher social classes placed more value on flexibility and occupational self-direction both for themselves and for their children (Kohn et al., 1986; Kohn et al., 1990).

One way to promote the value of self-direction to a greater extent in working-class children is to stress this value more in public schools. In this way, working-class children might have a better chance of acquiring the personal outlook needed to climb the occupational ladder. Such a program is certainly possible. The question is how much society wants to broaden the opportunities for working-class chil-

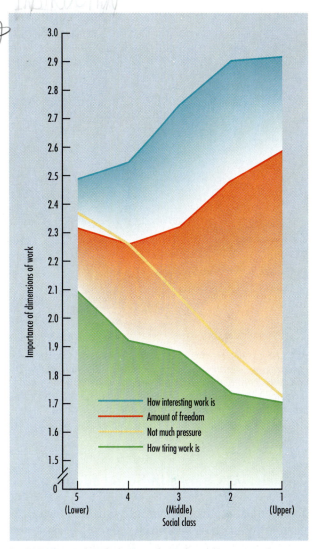

FIGURE 5.2 / What People Value about Work

Once in the workplace, what adults value about their jobs seems to reflect the lessons of childhood. Upper-class employees look primarily for work that is interesting and permits self-direction; lower-class employees are comparatively more interested in jobs with low pressure.

Source: Melvin L. Kohn and Carmi Schooler, *Work and Personality: An Inquiry into the Impact of Social Stratification* (Ablex, Norwood, N.J., 1983).

dren. We will return to this question in Chapter 12, which explores education. The point here is simply that socialization is not identical for everyone. Just as it varies depending upon a person's gender, so it also varies depending upon a person's position in the social hierarchy.

Not just a game. As this child works on a puzzle, with her encouraging parents watching, she develops the independence and confidence that come from trying, sometimes failing, and ultimately succeeding. In middle-class families, such traits are considered necessary for succeeding in the adult world.

Choice and Change in Social Identity

To say that socialization varies with such factors as gender, social class, and racial or ethnic background is not to say that members of a particular social group are all alike in their values, outlooks, and behaviors. In modern complex societies—especially those that place considerable value on personal freedom of choice—there are many different ways to be male, female, working-class, upper-class, Catholic, Baptist, black, or Hispanic. While there are cultural norms and social roles that people learn as members of these groups, they also have room for individual and collective choice regarding who they become.

Part of this choice involves people's freedom to select among roles to some extent. The roles we play are not always thrust upon us by others. We select many for ourselves, like choosing majors and career goals while in college. Throughout our lives we keep making such role choices regarding work, family, lifestyle, and interpersonal relationships. Earlier choices often tend to influence choices that follow.

This makes socialization and the construction of a personal identity best understood as a kind of narrative, or story, in which current adjustments and decisions both limit and create future options (Somers and Gibson, 1994).

Freedom to choose also entails the capacity to resist being socialized into roles we do not like. Girls can refuse to enter beauty pageants and insist on playing basketball or studying botany; boys can shun the football field and take up the violin. Working-class children can reject their parents' stress on obedience to authority and strive to set their own standards, while upper-class children can reject the tradition of socializing only with others in their class and instead choose to be with people from various classes. Even in Japan, a country known for its regimented socialization of children, the maverick still exists. For example, in a junior high in the small Japanese town of Omiya there is a young man who tries his hardest to find ways to stand out from the crowd (Kristof, 1995). This is difficult to do in a school system that stipulates everything from students' clothing to their deodorants and kinds of backpacks, but this young man, Kazuhiro, is both determined and ingenious. One ploy he has come up with is to drill a hole in the heels of his regulation sandals so that they make a *kakkoii* (cool) thumping sound as he walks down the hall. Kazuhiro boasts that he does no homework and is thinking of dying his hair blond. Among the student body at Omiya Junior High, where conformity is a drab way of life, Kazuhiro is greatly admired.

The humorous example of Kazuhiro has a more serious message. It suggests that people can act consciously to try to change the meaning of the roles they currently play and into which future generations will be socialized. Enough rebels in a highly regimented school can chip away at the rules they detest and instigate change in the educational system. We can see examples of this process in our own society. For instance, the meaning of being both black and female has changed greatly over the past several decades with the rise of the feminist and black consciousness movements (Collins, 1991). In these cases, both women and black Americans have deliberately tried to redefine their places in the social order—and have gradually succeeded. Individual and collective action has brought about significant social change.

This sort of change is possible because culture is not fixed. In American society, the identities that exist for people to be socialized into are never permanently settled. There is continuous (albeit usually gradual) change in the identities that are treated as culturally legitimate and which become the basis for social groups and movement. The belief that social identities—male, female, black, white, heterosexual, lesbian or gay—are constructed through social processes and are therefore changeable is called **constructionism**. The opposite view, that social identities are dictated by biology or enduring social forces and therefore are relatively fixed, is called **essentialism**. Essentialism implies that we can uncover the "essence" of what it means to be black, female, gay, and so forth, that people in these categories have a more or less stable set of characteristics that distinguish them from others. Because essentialism strongly downplays the role of individual action and choice, this view is much less congenial to most sociologists than constructionism is.

Whether you take an essentialist or a constructivist perspective on a social issue can matter a great deal. An essentialist view of the social category "Asians," for example, implies that all Asians are more or less the same in comparison with white or other Americans; however, this view minimizes the diversity of Asian identities (Indian, Korean, Chinese, Japanese, Vietnamese, Indonesian) and underestimates differences due to social class, gender, and so on. On the other hand, emphasizing constructionism can undercut efforts to claim a strong unity within a social category of people as the basis for their joint activism and pursuit of better treatment. This is one reason why many gay men and lesbians have argued that homosexuality is an essential characteristic, not simply a social construction and a choice. You will see the impact of essentialism and constructionism more clearly as we explore how a person's sexual orientation and identity develop as joint products of nature, nurture, and choice. In Sociology and Public Debates we discuss the controversy surrounding nature, nurture, and intelligence.

NATURE, NURTURE, AND CHOICE: THE CASE OF SEXUAL ORIENTATION AND IDENTITY

The term **sexual orientation** refers to a person's characteristic pattern in the choice of sexual partners (Reiter, 1989). Although most people think of sexual orientation as centering around the choice between opposite-sex or same-sex partners, this is not all that sexual orientation entails. People who are primarily drawn to one sex or the other can still be attracted to very different qualities in a mate. There are also people who never have sexual intercourse in their lives and have very few sexual urges, just as there are others who are driven to seek sex constantly. Some people think of sex as mainly a way to conceive children, while others consider it mainly a source of pleasure. These are differences in sexual orientation just as much as the choice of a same-sex or opposite-sex partner is. However, our discussion here will focus on the heterosexual/homosexual distinction because this is perhaps the most powerful and certainly the most controversial dimension of sexual orientation.

Heated debates have arisen over the relative contributions of nature (biological makeup), nurture (cultural learning), and personal choice in the development of a homosexual or heterosexual way of life. Recent evidence suggests the possibility of a biological predisposition for some men to be gay (LeVay, 1991; Hamer and Copeland, 1994). This view has appealed to gays and others interested in gay rights. If homosexuality is shown to be an inborn trait, perhaps people will stop condemning homosexuals as morally deviant, since they have no choice.

Whether biology's role in determining sexual orientation is large or small, cultural learning is clearly involved as well. At the very least, culture helps define the various sexual identities that are available for people to adopt. For example, prior to the Victorian era the boundaries between different kinds of sexual orientations were more fluid than they are today because the term *homosexual* had not yet come into use (Herdt, 1984; Kosofsky-Sedgwick, 1990). Although homosexual acts were recognized and often stigmatized, it was rare for people to be categorized by their sexual orientation. This changed with the introduction of a medical model of homosexuality. Now homosexuality came to be considered a pathological condition, a form of psychological "illness." People who before had enjoyed romantic same-sex friendships without a sense of wrongdoing now began to think of themselves as "one of those"—a deviant (Seidman, 1991).

With this new self-identity came a new sense of "we-ness," of being set apart from other people in a fundamental way. This sense of "we-ness" helped promote the growth of a homosexual subculture and community. That growth accelerated in the 1960s and

Nature, Nurture, and Intelligence

That the word intelligence describes something real and that it varies from person to person is as universal and ancient as any understanding about the state of being human. Literate cultures everywhere and throughout history have had words for saying that some people are smarter than others. . . . Gossip about who in the tribe is cleverer has probably been a topic of conversation around the fire since fires, and conversation, were invented. (Herrnstein and Murray, 1994)

With these words Richard J. Herrnstein and Charles Murray begin their book *The Bell Curve*, which has sparked enormous controversy. The book's title refers to the bell-shaped curve that results when the distribution of people's IQ scores is plotted on a graph. Most scores fall near the statistical average (which forms the high point of the bell), and there are declining numbers at each IQ level as you move toward the lowest and the highest scores (thus forming the bell's downward-sloping sides). There is nothing particularly controversial about Herrnstein and Murray's contention that intelligence varies from one individual to the next. What *is* controversial is the contention that these differences are largely genetic in origin and that a lower- or higher-than-average IQ score significantly affects a person's behavior and chances for success.

THE DEBATE

Herrnstein and Murray argue that IQ scores matter more than most people care to admit. A person's chances of getting a college degree, landing a high-status, high-paying job, and affording a comfortable lifestyle are all related to having a high IQ, they say. Conversely, they associate low IQ with a panoply of social ills: school failure, poverty, unemployment, poor job performance, welfare dependency, illegitimate children, neglectful parenting, and high crime rates. This is not to say that a high IQ is an automatic ticket to success and riches, nor that a low IQ destines a person to failure. But the statistical link between IQ and these outcomes exists, even when other variables are controlled. According to Herrnstein and Murray, IQ is the single best predictor of how a person will fare in life, better even than the social background from which that person comes.

> What *is* controversial is the contention that these differences are largely genetic in origin and that a lower- or higher-than-average IQ score significantly affects a person's behavior and chances for success.

Herrnstein and Murray go on to analyze where our society is heading in terms of IQ. They say that IQ is increasingly becoming the basis for social stratification—that is, for dividing society up into "levels" of people who have different amounts of resources (see Chapter 7). With growing equality of opportunity in American education and a growing number of jobs available for people of high intelligence, more and more of the smartest in our population are rising to the top, regardless of social class background. What is left at the bottom tends to be the low IQ people, who are more likely to suffer the devastating problems we mentioned before. This underclass includes a disproportional number of black Americans, because blacks on average have IQ scores roughly fifteen points lower than whites. Although Herrnstein and Murray say that the reason for this black/white IQ gap is still unknown, they suggest the possibility that heredity could be a significant factor. In their view, children's educational environments are becoming more equal in our society, through compensatory programs like Head Start, for example. As a result, they argue, less of the IQ differences between children can now be attributed to environment, so more must be attributed to genes. This is a matter of logic. As we equalize environments, what-

1970s, a time of liberal politics and civil rights movements, when homosexuals were increasingly becoming concentrated in major urban areas. A distinction was now made between being homosexual and being gay. The first referred simply to a person's sexual orientation and behavior, while the second described a personal identity and lifestyle that included norms of speech and dress, beliefs about self-fulfillment, and a set of sexual mores. Becoming gay involved being socialized into this identity and lifestyle; it was not just a matter of one's sexual inclinations. The gay press played a central role in conveying this new gay subculture to homosexuals. It helped pass on to the gay and lesbian population new models of thought

ever differences remain between people must be due more to heredity than they were before. In the end, we could have two largely hereditary social groups: a high-IQ elite versus a low-IQ underclass, each highly antagonistic toward the other.

Herrnstein and Murray's theory has been rejected by scientists from many fields (e.g., H. Gardner, 1995; Gould, 1995; Jacoby and Glauberman, 1995; Nisbett, 1995; Patterson, 1995; Sowell, 1995). Some critics doubt that we can even reliably measure human intelligence at all. Thinking, reasoning, and creating, they say, are complex processes that are hard to reduce to a single IQ score. What's more, and perhaps most significant, is that differences in IQ *between* groups (such as the average fifteen-point IQ difference between whites and blacks in our society) may *not* be due to genetic differences at all. The argument runs as follows: Just because heredity accounts for a large part of the variation in IQ among white middle-class Americans, who share similar environmental advantages, that does not mean that heredity also explains the differences *across* social classes or *between* racial and ethnic groups. If between-group IQ differences were caused by genes, how could we explain the fact that the average IQ scores for certain racial and ethnic groups have changed dramatically from one generation to the next as those groups move into the middle class? This finding suggests a greater role for socialization and other environmental influences in the development of racial and ethnic IQ differences. In fact, some critics point to a body of evidence Herrnstein and Murray ignored that suggests that heredity makes *no* contribution whatsoever to the average black/white gap in IQ (see Nisbett, 1995).

ANALYSIS

A sociological analysis can contribute greatly to sorting out the two sides of this debate. The key concept of **culture** plays a prominent role in it. Critics of Herrnstein and Murray argue that IQ tests are culturally biased. These tests, they say, favor those who come from white, middle-class culture—the same culture from which the test developers come. The classic example focuses on vocabulary test items. If a black teenager from a low-income family does not know the meaning of the word *regatta* on the vocabulary part of a cognitive test, is it due to low intelligence or simply to unfamiliarity with upper-middle-class sports? Herrnstein and Murray answer that there are very few questions with such blatant cultural bias on IQ tests and that the culturally loaded questions there are do not seem to be the cause of the black/white IQ gap. Instead, the black/white difference is *wider* on items that appear to be culturally neutral, such as measures of spatial and perceptual skills. These items, say the researchers, are good indicators of a person's "general intelligence."

Critics respond that this pattern is not unique to blacks, for it is also found among low-scoring groups of European ancestry. For instance, when European immigrants came to the United States, they tended to score below the national average on IQ tests, and lowest on the abstract questions. The same is true of Appalachian mountain children tested in the 1930s and of rural British children compared with those in cities and suburbs. "In short, groups outside the cultural mainstream of contemporary Western society tend to do their worst on abstract questions, whatever their race might be" (Sowell, 1995, p. 73). But, interestingly, as immigrant groups became integrated into the broader American culture, their test scores rose and eventually equaled or surpassed the national average. African-Americans, too, are closing the gap in IQ scores compared with whites. Over the past several decades, it has narrowed by an estimated four to eight IQ points (Nisbett, 1995). This is strong evidence for the link between culture and IQ: As educational and economic opportunities for black Americans have improved, so have their group's IQ scores.

The concept of **social structure** also informs *The Bell Curve* debate. Herrnstein and Murray argue that struc-

and behavior for everyday life and new conceptions of homosexuals as comprising an oppressed political minority (Seidman, 1991). The AIDs crisis that followed in the 1980s and 1990s helped to further strengthen the growth of a gay subculture and community with values and norms that new members could learn to adopt.

Still, there is always an element of choice. Only about half as many Americans consider themselves to be "homosexual" as report that they have engaged in homosexual acts (Laumann, et al., 1994). The act of "coming out," of declaring a homosexual orientation, is a deliberate decision to proclaim the legitimacy of one's sexual orientation and its central position in

Nature, Nurture, and Intelligence (continued)

tural changes in the labor market are largely what have made IQ increasingly important in our society. As modern technology and business have become far more complex, the numbers and kinds of jobs requiring high intelligence have grown. No longer is the number of very bright people much greater than the number of positions demanding intellectual talent. Many such jobs are now available, creating many opportunities for cognitively gifted people from lower social classes to rise in the social hierarchy. This trend has spawned the growth of the cognitive elite we mentioned earlier, an elite that initially has drawn people from all social backgrounds. But because differences in intelligence are strongly genetic in origin, Herrnstein and Murray say, social stratification is increasingly rooted in heredity. What's more, because people tend to marry others who are similar to themselves, including similar in intelligence, positions in the social hierarchy are likely to "run in families," passed on through genes from one generation to another.

Critics vigorously attack this aspect of Herrnstein and Murray's argument. They stress that the links between genes and IQ, and IQ and social class, are far too weak to draw the conclusion that genes determine a person's place in society and how well that person fares (H. Gardner, 1995). Herrnstein and Murray's own data show that IQ always explains less than 20 percent of the variance in the social outcomes they have studied, usually less than 10 percent, and often less than 5. And since they willingly admit that human differences in IQ are roughly 40 percent attributable to environment, the strength of genes in determining a person's niche in the world dwindles to very little (Gould, 1995). Clearly, an understanding of the American class structure is more likely to come from studies of social and economic factors than it is from studies of genetic differences and IQ.

Power, social action, and **functional integration** are likewise concepts that can clarify *The Bell Curve* controversy. Opponents of Herrnstein and Murray fear that members of the new cognitive elite who share Herrnstein and Murray's views will use the power that accrues from their money and prestige to change collective social actions aimed at improving opportunities for the disadvantaged. For instance, if elites assume that the underclass consists of people whose genetically based intelligence is too low to profit from remedial education programs, they may work to eliminate such programs, arguing that such programs cannot succeed. Herrnstein and Murray themselves suggest that we are probably close to reaching the limits of what education can do to raise the intelligence of children at the bottom of the IQ scale. They also have reservations about affirmative action both in education and employment. They argue that society loses when affirmative action results in a dramatic lowering of admissions or hiring standards, or leads to the rejection of highly qualified candidates in preference for much less able ones. Such outcomes, they say, undermine functional integration, in which people are matched to positions according to their abilities to fill them. Critics answer that the social benefits of affirmative action outweigh the costs. Since the 1960s, they point out, when antidiscrimination laws were first enacted, minority groups have made real progress in terms of higher wages and entry into higher-prestige jobs.

Americans will continue to debate for many years to come both the significance that IQ differences have for people and the extent to which these differences are genetic in origin. Scientific evidence regarding these issues, even when conclusively proven, will not settle the public controversy, because the debate is also about values. Regardless of the degree to which differences in IQ scores are hereditary, people who strongly value equality may reject Herrnstein and Murray's policy proposals in favor of policies that offer special help to people whose opportunities for advancement are limited by their position in society.

---

one's sense of self. In much the same way, becoming immersed in the gay or lesbian subculture, defining what one's sexual orientation means, and possibly becoming politicized about it also strongly entail individual choice.

The trend in the twentieth century has been to open up the range of choices in sexual orientation and identity. In the contemporary United States, the way that one man chooses to live his life as a homosexual can be very different from the way that other male homosexuals choose to live. Similarly, the way that one woman today defines what it means to be a lesbian can be quite different from the self-definitions of other lesbians. An expanding range of choice in sexual behavior and identity also exists for heterosexuals, many of whom have suffered in the past under rigid and restrictive definitions of male and female sexual roles. Perhaps the most dramatic change has been for women. For instance, until about 1980, a husband had a legal right to have sex with his wife whether she was willing or not (and still does in some states). A wife's refusal to have sex was grounds for divorce, and a husband could not be legally charged with rape if his wife was the victim. Today, in contrast, being a heterosexual married woman no longer means being the husband's sexual chattel.

When people with similar interpretations of their sexual identities join together on the basis of their shared beliefs and understandings, social movements and social change can result. A good example is how the meaning of lesbianism was reconstructed in the 1960s and 1970s and came to be widely shared by members of the feminist movement. As the American sociologist Steven Seidman writes in his book *Romantic Longings* (1991):

> For lesbians who "came out" in the midst of the women's movement, their sexual preference for women was frequently interpreted through the prism of feminism. To choose to bond primarily with women was viewed by many lesbians as a political act promoting sisterhood in the cause of all women's autonomy. . . . Lesbianism was seen as a political act of resistance to male dominance, . . . a choice to live for oneself and for other women. . . . This social and political concept of the lesbian signaled a dramatic change in the meaning of lesbianism. The lesbian stepped forward as an heroic figure, pioneering for all women an independent, women-centered life. (pp. 167–168)

In this case, freedom to choose a certain lifestyle and interpret what it means clearly led to new subcultural beliefs and values.

The role of choice, however, can also be overstated. Radical lesbians of the 1960s and 1970s were also a product of a certain historical period and culture. Different historical periods and cultures shape people's understandings of themselves and others differently. Thus, although there are elements of choice in all the various roles and identities we adopt, sociology teaches us that such choices are shaped by **culture**, **power relations**, and **social structure**. They are not made completely freely by autonomous individuals, because all of our thinking is also partly the product of external social forces.

Labeled by society as "other," gays and lesbians label themselves as "we." As members of a subculture, homosexual men and women can affirm their sexual identities while enjoying the ordinary activities of life.

AGENTS OF CHILDHOOD SOCIALIZATION

In a home in Shanghai, China, a little girl tells her mother that she *must* have a new jacket because her old one has a hole in the sleeve. Her grandfather overhears her and takes her aside. He shows her an ancient-looking jacket with numerous patches, all carefully sewn and resewn by his own hands. He wore this jacket with pride, he tells her, when he was a member of the People's Liberation Army and fought to overthrow the oppressive old regime. In that great era of social revolution all working people willingly made do with threadbare clothes. By the time the conversation ends, the little girl feels deeply ashamed of her self-centered demand (based on Kessen, 1975).

In a Japanese nursery school the teacher asks the children to paint a series of pictures that work together to tell a story. She places paints in the center of the table, where they might be spilled if there is grabbing, and deliberately provides fewer brushes than there are children. As the children work, they confer with one another about what part of the story they will paint next and eagerly await their turn with the paints and brushes (Lewis, 1989; Power, Kobayashi-Winata, and Kelley, 1992).

In a village in Italy a group of children are hotly debating whether scary things like ghosts and werewolves exist. Like their elders who sit in the village square vigorously debating politics and other important matters of the day, these children express their opinions with great emotion and vehemence, often shouting and poking their fingers at each others' chests. No one tells these youngsters to "stop arguing" and "be friends," as an American adult might. In Italy, having heated discussions is considered a natural part of friendship (Corsaro and Emiliani, 1992; Corsaro and Rizzo, 1988).

In an American home, two elementary school brothers are watching a children's TV game show. Three young contestants are answering geography questions, hoping to win a trip to wherever they wish in the United States. At the program's climactic ending the finalist races around the stage trying to locate capital cities on a giant floor map of Europe. Young viewers in the studio audience wildly cheer her on as she tries to complete the task in only 45 seconds.

Every society shapes its children in the image of its own culture. The Japanese encourage cooperation to complete group goals; the Italians cultivate skill at verbal negotiation and debate; Americans encourage children to compete with their peers for success. But cultures are not static, fixed for all time. They can change. For example, China has become much more consumer-oriented, less focused on self-sacrifice, as its culture has changed since the death of Communist leader Mao Zedong. Although the content of what is being learned is different in each of these examples, the *agents* of socialization—the groups and institutions instilling the cultural messages—are common to all four societies. Around the modern world, the family, the school, the peer group, and the mass media of communication are all deeply involved in teaching children the elements of their cultures. In the following sections we'll look at these four agents of socialization. Socialization is responsible for many different kinds of identities—for example, in terms of race, religion, class, nation, and gender. We will use gender as an example of how different agents of socialization influence children.

The Family

The family is the first social world children encounter. It introduces them to group life and intimate relationships, gives them their first experience of being treated as distinct individuals, and provides the mirror in which they begin to see themselves. The family is also children's first reference group, the first group whose norms and values they adopt as their own and refer to in evaluating behavior. However, a family is not an isolated group; it is part of a larger society. A family's values, attitudes, and lifestyles reflect the social class, religion, ethnic group, and region of the country of which it is a part. This means that children acquire selected versions of their society's culture depending on the background and experiences of their particular family.

Differences among families in the socialization of their children can be seen in the area of conveying gender roles. Some American families make a conscious effort to avoid all gender stereotypes in dealing with their children, while for others gender stereotypes take center stage. Most families, however, fall somewhere in the middle. They try to treat their sons and daughters similarly in many ways (Lytton and Romney, 1991), but despite these attempts some gender-role stereotypes creep in (Serbin, Powlishta, and Gulko, 1993; Paludi and Gullo, 1986; Rubin, Provenzano, and Luria, 1974). For instance, most parents tend to see their baby daughters as weak, soft, fine-featured, awkward, and delicate, while they see their baby sons as strong, firm, large-featured, well-coordinated, and hard. Parents also tend to be upset when a stranger mistakes their infant or toddler for a member of the opposite sex (McGuire, 1988). Fathers are particularly gender-conscious in relation to boys and tend to react more strongly to "inappropriate" behavior in a son than in a daughter, even when the child is only one year old (Snow, Jacklin, and Maccoby, 1983).

One way in which parents foster gender-typed behavior in their children is through the toys they buy and encourage their children to play with. This is particularly true in the gender socialization of boys. A Barbie doll is sold somewhere in the world every two seconds, and there are 2.5 Barbies for every household in America (Cunningham, 1993). But try to find parents who have bought a Barbie doll for their son! In fact, parents who spot their son happily dressing his sister's Barbie in a slinky evening dress might very well take the doll from him or strongly suggest that he play with something else.

This aversion to seeing children playing with gender "inappropriate" toys is nowhere near as strong for girls as it is for boys. "Boy toys," in general, are not viewed as being "masculine" as much as "girl toys" are viewed as being "feminine." Children of both sexes find many "boy toys" fun. In one study in which researchers observed parents and their preschoolers interacting in a room with lots of toys, both boys and girls spent less time playing with "female" toys (like a baby doll and a dollhouse) and more time playing with gender-neutral things (such as a puzzle or Play-Doh) or with "male" toys (like a ball and a gas station) (Idle, Wood, and Desmarais, 1993). Also, both parents—father *and* mother—more often offered "masculine" toys to their son *or* daughter than they did "feminine" ones. In this study, however, the toys considered masculine were fairly low on the scale of what most people would label "boyish." A ball, for example, is not as stereotypically masculine as, say, a GI Joe missile launcher or a Creepy Crawlers workshop. Most American parents do not buy such toys for their daughters, although a great many do for their sons.

Parents also channel their children in gender-stereotyped ways through the household chores they assign. In most homes girls are given "female" tasks, like helping with cooking and baby-sitting, while boys are given "male" chores, such as yardwork and small repairs (Baker, 1984). Higher-income parents are less likely to follow stereotypes in connection with household chore assignments, as are parents of an only-child daughter (Burns and Homel, 1989). In general, however, American girls are still being trained to

Girls don't only *like dolls. Both sexes can enjoy playing with toys that enhance their self-esteem and sense of mastery.*

do "women's work" around the home, while boys are apprentice handymen and lawn mowers.

At the same time that parents are encouraging sex-typed behaviors in their children, they may also be encouraging them to think about themselves in gender-stereotyped ways. For instance, many parents tend to attribute a girl's success in math to her diligent effort and a boy's success to his inborn talent (Yee and Eccles, 1988). In addition, many parents subtly communicate confidence in their son's future math success and doubt about their daughter's, even though the daughter is currently doing well. This tendency may explain why, from junior high school on, girls often have negative attitudes toward math and lower estimates of their own abilities, regardless of their actual performance.

Parents need not actually express gender-stereotyped ideas in order to encourage their children to adopt them. The models of behavior the parents provide are enough to affect children's thinking. For instance, children's thinking about sex roles is often more stereotyped and inflexible when the mother does not work outside the home and when her household duties are traditionally "feminine" (cleaning, shopping, cooking, and child care, but not "heavy" yardwork or fixing the car) (Levy, 1989). Even full-time working mothers may help encourage gender stereotypes if they choose (or have no choice but to accept) lower-status, traditionally "female" occupations for themselves (Serbin, Powlishta, and Gulko, 1993). Children's thinking is shaped not just by what their parents tell them but also by what they see their parents do (Parcel and Menaghan, 1994).

Schools

The preconception that school is a place for learning academic subjects tends to obscure the fact that considerable socialization takes place in school as well. While the official purpose of school is to teach young people intellectual and technical skills, school also teaches them cultural values and attitudes that prepare these young people for their roles as adults. This was illustrated in our earlier example of how the value of cooperation is instilled in Japanese classrooms. Japanese teachers are constantly providing opportunities for students to work together, just as adults in Japanese businesses work together cooperatively in close-knit groups.

Conformity to rules and regulations is another value taught in the schools of most modern societies. This lesson is part of what Talcott Parsons (1959) called "the hidden curriculum." Never explicitly taught, lessons in discipline and conformity are built into the structure of the classroom. Some of this hidden curriculum is a vestige from the nineteenth and early twentieth centuries, when public schools functioned as the agents for socializing rural and immigrant children to be good industrial workers. In that era, most factory jobs did require conformity and discipline, and so the schools, by training suitable workers, helped to functionally integrate society.

Conveying traditional gender roles can be part of the hidden curriculum too. In elementary schools, boys may be asked to wash blackboards or move tables, while girls are asked to pass out cookies (Richmond-Abbott, 1992). Even in nursery school, girls most often get attention and praise for being obedient and helpful, while boys more often get attention and reprimands for misbehavior. As they grow older, girls are more likely to be praised for their social skills and neatness and boys for the quality of their work (AAUW Educational Foundation, 1992). Teachers tend to think that boys contribute more ideas to a discussion or project, even when independent scorers find that both sexes participate equally (Ben Tsvi-Mayer, Hertz-Lazarowitz, and Safir, 1989; Dweck, Davidson, Nelson, and Enna, 1978; Evans, 1988).

Gender lessons are also built into the social structure of the typical school system. For instance, while 85 percent of elementary schoolteachers are women, 79 percent of principals are male (Baker, 1984); and while more mothers than fathers are active in the PTA and various school clubs, men tend to dominate school boards and councils (Evans, 1988). Repeatedly seeing men in positions of authority over women makes an impression on children. For example, a study of first-graders (Paradiso and Wall, 1986) revealed that those attending schools with female principals had less stereotyped views about gender roles than those in schools with male principals.

The continuing existence in schools of "boys' programs" and "girls' programs" tends to reinforce gender stereotypes as well. For instance, although home economics classes are now open to boys and shop classes to girls, the patterns of student choices cause these programs to remain largely segregated by gender. School sports programs are also segregated by gender, not so much by student choice as by administrative decree. Rather than integrate boys' and girls' sports teams, most schools have chosen to expand the number of sports available exclusively to girls. Of course, programs do not have to be officially segregated by gender in order to be thought of as being geared more to one sex than the other. The gender-stereotyped ideas of both students and teachers tend to make certain classes (such as math and science) largely the stronghold of boys, while others (like English and the arts) are widely considered a haven for girls.

The extent to which boys dominate discussions in math and science classes can be overwhelming to girls, making them feel intimidated and "dumb." In her inside look at eighth-grade students in their junior high classrooms, Peggy Orenstein (1994) summarizes her first impression of Mrs. Richter's math class this way:

> Occasionally, the girls shout out answers, but generally they are to the easiest, lowest-risk questions, such as the factors of four or six. And their stabs at public recognition depend on the boys' largesse: when the girls venture responses to more complex questions the boys quickly become territorial, shouting them down with their own answers. Nate and Kyle are particularly adept at overpowering Renee, who, I've been told by the teacher, is the brightest girl in the class. (On a subsequent visit, I will see her lay her head on the desk when Nate overwhelms her and mutter, "I hate this class.")
>
> Mrs. Richter doesn't say anything to condone the boys' aggressiveness, but she doesn't have to: they insist on—and receive—her attention even when she consciously tries to shift it elsewhere in order to make the class more equitable. . . .
>
> "What does three to the third power mean?" Mrs. Richter asks the class.
>
> "*I know!*" shouts Kyle.
>
> Instead of calling on Kyle who has already answered more than his share of questions, the teacher turns to Dawn. . . .
>
> Dawn hesitates and begins, "Well, you count the number of threes and . . ."
>
> "*But I know!*" interrupts Kyle. "*I know!*"
>
> Mrs. Richter deliberately ignores him, but Dawn is rattled: she never finishes her sentence, she just stops.
>
> "*I know! ME!*" Kyle shouts again, and then before Dawn recovers herself he blurts, "*It's three times three times three!*"
>
> At this point, Mrs. Richter gives in. She turn away from Dawn, who is staring blankly, and nods at Kyle.

> "Yes," she says. "Three times three times three. Does everyone get it?"
>
> "*YES!*" shouts Kyle; Dawn says nothing.

In these and many other ways, what goes on inside of schools helps convey to children the beliefs and values of the larger culture.

The Mass Media

Children are also socialized through the mass media, the forms of communication that reach large numbers of people: television, radio, movies, videos, compact disks and tapes, computer software, books, magazines, and newspapers. While all the mass media are important agents of socialization, the most influential for children is probably television. Television is found in almost every American home; it requires only minimal cognitive skills to comprehend; and its visual nature is very appealing to children (Signorielli, 1991). Overall, children in the United States (and other Western nations) spend more time watching television than they spend in school. That amounts to an average viewing time of more than 30 hours weekly (Winn, 1985). By the time a person reaches the age of sixty-five, nine full years have been devoted to TV watching (Dorr, 1986).

Parents and others are concerned about how television is socializing children. They are unhappy with the content of many shows—for one thing, with the violence they contain. Numerous studies suggest that watching television violence encourages aggression in children. One long-term study of teenagers found that a preference for violence on television was a more accurate predictor of aggressive behavior than socioeconomic background, family relationships, IQ, or any other single factor (Cater and Strickland, 1975). It is difficult to say which comes first, the aggressive behavior or the preference for violent shows, but a link between the two does exist.

Many people are also concerned about television's persistent portrayal of gender stereotypes (Furnham and Bitar, 1993). In an analysis of prime-time programs between 1969 and 1985, Nancy Signorielli (1989) found that while the number of female characters increased significantly over this fifteen-year period, and every season brought a few nontraditional female roles, males still outnumbered females by almost three to one. TV women were also less likely than men to be seen working outside the home, especially those who were married and had children. And if a female character did work she was apt to have a low-paying, low-prestige job (waitress, secretary, nurse). In appearance, prime-time TV women were generally young and attractive, while the male characters tended to be older, to work in higher-status occupations (e.g., physician, attorney), and to be in charge. Signorielli concluded that, with a few exceptions, gender-role images on TV remained stable, traditional, and conservative over the fifteen years she analyzed. The pattern has not changed much in the past few years. Although there has been a slight increase in the variety of jobs depicted for women on prime-time television, women in the workplace are still portrayed as being more focused on interpersonal matters (helping, caring, smoothing things over) than their male colleagues are and less involved in decision making, leadership, and political action (VandeBerg and Streckfuss, 1992).

These gender stereotypes are echoed in other mass media, including those geared exclusively to children. For instance, a classic study of prize-winning children's books found that nearly all presented highly stereotyped and unrealistic images of girls and boys, men and women (Weitzman and Eifler, 1972). The ratio of pictures of males to females was eleven to one; one-third of the books involved males only. When girls did appear, they were nearly always indoors, helping, watching, or loving the book's hero. When another team of researchers replicated this study, focusing on prize-winning books of the 1980s, they found the picture changed but not by much (J. A. Williams, Vernon, Williams, and Malecha, 1987). Male and female characters were now represented about equally; a third of the leading characters were female; and girls and women were more often pictured outdoors. However, only one female character worked outside the home, and she was a waitress. Although females were more visible, males still had more adventures, more responsibilities, and more fun.

As for magazines, advertisements especially exploit gender stereotypes (Masse and Rosenblum, 1988; Belknap and Leonard, 1991; Willis and Carlson, 1993). Men in magazine ads are usually portrayed as alone and aloof, independent and strong. Women are more often pictured as submissive, as seeking contact (through their gestures and glances), or as sexual props for male-oriented products like cars and razor

blades. Although the most recent studies of magazine ads suggest that their portrayal of men and women may be changing, that change is often in the direction of more "modern" but still unrealistic gender stereotypes. In one such study, for instance, women were found to be shown less often as homemakers who apparently depend on men, and more often as independent, self-centered individuals, "preoccupied with youthfulness and superficial appearance" (Busby and Leichty, 1993).

How does this barrage of gender stereotypes affect children? Probably the most widely studied topic is the influence of gender stereotypes seen on TV. Research has found that children who watch a lot of network television are more likely to describe males and females in stereotyped terms and to be more gender-typed themselves than are children who rarely watch TV or watch mainly educational programs (Fruch and McGhee, 1975; Kimball, 1986; Repetti, 1984; Rothschild, 1984; Signorielli and Lears, 1992). Of course, this relationship does not prove a cause-and-effect connection, but it suggests the possibility of one.

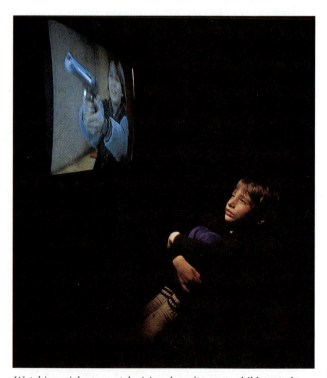

Watching violence on television doesn't cause children to be overly aggressive, but heavy television viewing is connected with stereotyped thinking about males and females.

Still, it is easy to exaggerate the impact of the mass media on gender socialization. Much of what people get *out* of TV, books, or magazines depends on what they bring *to* encounters with them. This was shown in a study of how teenagers interpreted the male and female characters in a Michael Jackson music video. In the video, Jackson becomes infatuated with a beautiful young woman and stalks her down a dark city street until eventually she opens her arms to him after encountering several other more threatening-looking men (Kalof, 1993). Female viewers tended to see the woman as either powerful and in control or frightened and vulnerable, while male viewers tended to see her as either playing hard-to-get or being submissive. These different interpretations largely depended upon the viewers' own personal experiences as young men and women, which in turn encouraged them to focus on different aspects of the characters' actions. Thus, the meaning that people give to the media's gender stereotypes is partly a product of what they already think and believe about the sexes.

Peers

Just as people actively construct their own interpretations of gender stereotypes seen in the mass media, so they also actively construct their own male or female selves. Children are not simply *taught* to become boys or girls; they make themselves into members of one gender or the other. They selectively appropriate information about being male or female from parents, schools, and the media, and then they creatively interpret and reproduce those ideas about gender in their own attitudes and behaviors, especially toward their peers (Corsaro, 1992). The result is the social construction of gender in each new generation.

Sociologist Barrie Thorne (1993) has studied this process by watching children with their peers in classrooms and on playgrounds. She presents evidence that gender identities and divisions between the genders are created by children in collaboration with each other as they go about their daily activities. Boys and girls routinely maintain gender boundaries, without any active encouragement from adults. In general, when given the choice, boys prefer to play with, sit next to, and even stand in line with other boys, while girls prefer to be with other girls. In part through these ritual separations, children sustain a gender dichotomy and teach each other what it means to be male or female.

Thorne gives many examples of how children who cross gender boundaries are quickly put back "in their place." Once Thorne observed a first-grade boy become increasingly curious about jumping rope, which is a "girls'" activity. When he volunteered to help swing the rope, the girls told him, "No way, you don't know how to swing it. You gotta be a girl." The boy walked away without challenging this widely accepted view. On another occasion, Thorne watched a popular boy look for a seat in the school lunchroom. As he approached a table with a mix of boys and girls, he said "Ooooh, too many girls!" The boys sitting there got up and followed him to another nearly empty table. Teasing is another common way to reestablish gender divisions (Eder, 1991). A boy who unthinkingly joined the end of a girls' line at the close of library period was sent scurrying over to the boys' line with an embarrassed look on his face when the other boys hooted, "Hey! Look at the new girl!" Thorne calls such behaviors "borderwork," because the children are actively maintaining the borders of their gender-segregated groups. Even the age-old game of boy-girl "chase" on the playground is a form of borderwork in Thorne's view, because the children are preserving, even accentuating, a division between the two sexes.

Many researchers have suggested that boys and girls choose to be apart because they have different styles of interaction that are not very compatible. According to this perspective, boys' play is more often marked by physical aggression, competition for status, and arguments over rules, while girls' play is more often characterized by intimacy, cooperation, and building connections (Moller, Hymel, and Rubin, 1992). However, Thorne is reluctant to agree that different styles of interaction play a major role in gender divisions. There is a great deal of variation in how members of each gender behave. The "typical boy" style and "typical girl" style that other researchers have described often come from a focus on children who stand out among their peers but are not really representative of everyone. In fact, there are far more behavioral differences among individual boys and individual girls than there are differences between the averages for the two genders. Thorne concludes that the question of why children create a gender divide may be less important than the issue of how this division currently affects gender socialization.

As a feminist, she hopes for social change in the direction of more cross-gender relationships based on mutual acceptance and friendship.

Gender roles, of course, are not the only things that young people teach one another. Peer groups also provide children with their first experience of equal-status relationships. Because adults compared with children are older, wiser, stronger, and "wealthier" (they control such important resources as the refrigerator and the TV remote control), adult-child relationships are asymmetrical, with the child always in the subordinate role. In contrast, children are, by definition, the social equals of their peers. This equal status makes peer groups ideal settings for learning norms of reciprocity, sharing, and equity. Anyone who has ever watched school-age children meticulously sharing a bottle of soda so that every glass gets *exactly* the same amount has witnessed this socialization occurring within young peer groups.

The peer group is also the ideal setting for children to learn about the meaning of friendship. By school age, children have developed a concept of friendship and the behaviors it entails, and they use this concept both as a guide for their own behavior and as a standard against which to assess the behavior of peers. This leads to more sharply defined role expectations. Children now feel they know what can be expected from friends and how they themselves should act in a friendship. Of course, children's concepts of "good" and "right" behavior from a friend do not always match those of adults. Children sometimes develop their own distinctive norms and values, their own peer outlooks on things. As a result, they are sometimes challenged to decide which norms or values to follow in which situations. This is a crucial skill for adulthood (Corsaro and Eder, 1990).

By early adolescence, being with friends has taken on major importance, and the issues of acceptance, popularity, and group solidarity are paramount. Adolescent boys tend to spend time with a group of male friends, while adolescent girls often gravitate to a single "best" girlfriend, to whom they disclose their problems, concerns, and fears. For both sexes, friends tend to be chosen from those of the same age, social class, race, and ethnic group (Dornbusch, 1989). In peer groups, adolescents develop a set of symbols—language, music, haircuts, clothing styles, and so on—to express the self. They use these collective symbolic actions to make sense of confusion, to form judgments and ways of thinking, and to guide their behavior (Willis, 1990).

In seeking to define themselves, adolescents often come into conflict with the power and expectations of their parents and other adults. Even when they do not join movements of active resistance (as in the youth culture of the 1960s), they tend to test the boundaries of what will be tolerated—for example, by experimenting with alcohol or illegal drugs. Adolescents are also likely to resist parental power in matters of taste, like fashion and music preferences,

Adolescence doesn't have to mean storm and strife. Many teenagers behave in ways that reflect their parents' values.

and there are often conflicts over whether parents will grant responsibilities, such as using the car or becoming sexually active, that adolescents believe they are ready to handle.

Nonetheless, adolescents often remain responsive to the preferences of their parents concerning future life goals and core values (Davies and Kandel, 1981; Krosnick and Judd, 1982). In fact, more often than not, peer values reinforce parental values rather than oppose them. In later adolescence, as peer-adult conflict begins to wane, adolescents usually choose a peer group that reflects values with which they feel comfortable, values that are often very similar to the ones they grew up with in the family. At this point, peer and family socialization may begin to parallel each other in more obvious ways. In general, however, peer and family socialization are never deeply at odds with one another regarding fundamental values. This is beneficial to society as a whole. The various agents of socialization need to be reasonably congruent in their teachings or society would suffer problems in its overall functional integration.

SOCIALIZATION IN ADULTHOOD

Although socialization is particularly important during childhood (when people first become members of human groups), the process of learning cultural norms and values goes on throughout life. As adults, we face a series of new roles into which we must be socialized. Becoming a husband or wife, a parent, a Cub Scout leader or a PTA member, a divorcée, a senior citizen, and even a terminally ill patient are all roles in which people must learn the attitudes and behaviors expected of them.

Desocialization and Resocialization

The lifelong nature of socialization is especially apparent in people who emigrate from one country to another and so must learn an entirely new culture. Mastering a new language, acquiring new customs, and learning new points of view can be an overwhelming, stressful task. Some immigrants liken it to a second childhood, in which basic skills and a sense of place in the world must all be acquired again from scratch (Portes and Rumbaut, 1990; Hein, 1994).

The Hmong refugees from Laos who came to the United States in the late 1970s are an example of an immigrant group that had trouble becoming socialized to a new way of life. In Laos, they had a traditional, homogeneous, nonliterate, agrarian society. Suddenly they had to adapt to a literate, highly technological, urban, and heterogeneous one. As one Hmong immigrant described the experience: "I feel like a thing which drops in the fire but won't burn and drops in the river but won't flow" (Portes and Rumbaut, 1990, p. 143).

Adding to the challenge was the fact that Hmong immigrant children attended American schools and so tended to learn American language and customs much faster than their parents. This disparity in the speed of acculturation between generations often contributed to stress in the home (Rick and Forward, 1992). Parents sometimes reported a loss of authority and respect, especially when they depended on their children to communicate for them in English with people outside the family. Many parents also worried that their children would no longer appreciate traditional Hmong culture.

Migrating to another country is not the only situation in which people are forced to learn an entirely new way of life. This process, called **resocialization**, also occurs in organizations known as total institutions. A **total institution** is a place where a large number of people are cut off from the broader society around them for a sizable period of time, during which they lead a totally regimented existence under the direction of a single authority (Goffman, 1961). Examples of total institutions are prisons, mental hospitals, and military boot camps (Davies, 1989).

In a total institution resocialization is typically preceded by the process of **desocialization**, in which people are stripped of their former values and self-conceptions. To aid in this process, they are also methodically stripped of clothes, adornments, and personal possessions that help them express their former identities. In exchange, they receive standard, nondescript, and often ill-fitting attire—for example, a drab uniform or hospital gown. Their hair may be shaved to further erase any vestiges of who they used to be. At the same time, newcomers to total institutions are deprived of the privacy and individual choice that normally helps to set them apart from others. They must undergo a debasing physical exam when admitted, after which they eat, sleep, and shower with the group. They are under constant supervision and surveillance. Every moment of every day is planned by others. These procedures destroy the newcomers' former sense of self and train them for deference to their superiors. In this way, total institutions foster psychological regression: They promote childlike feelings of helplessness and dependence to facilitate the institution's control over members' lives. At this point, members are ready to be resocialized to a new role, one that the total institution has designed for them.

Occupational Socialization

Although most of us will never enter a total institution, we must still be socialized into new roles throughout our adult lives. One role that the vast majority of us encounter is that of a worker and employee. Beginning with your first job after college, or even before, you, like millions of other Americans, must be socialized into an occupation.

A college education does not completely prepare young people for their first occupational roles. That is why large corporations frequently have training programs for the new college graduates they hire. Here the newcomers are taught the specific skills required of a manager, an accountant, an engineer, or whatever other career they have chosen. At the same time, they are indoctrinated into the "company way"; they learn the dress, demeanor, values, and beliefs expected of someone who holds their position in that particular firm.

Often people try to prepare themselves for socialization to a new work role. For example, new college graduates about to embark on their first "real" job in a large corporation mentally rehearse what the new experience might be like. If possible, they talk to other employees at that particular firm to get a feel for what working there involves. In subtle ways they may start to adopt new, more conservative values and behaviors in anticipation of those they believe the company will expect of them. All these changes are collectively called **anticipatory socialization**. Essentially, the graduates are starting to recast themselves in anticipation of the socialization they are about to undergo.

Anticipatory socialization is useful, but it is seldom enough when a life transition is major. In the case of adapting to a first corporate job, people almost never fully anticipate what they will encounter. In a classic study, Edgar Schein (1978) found that the transition entails four very difficult tasks. The first is coming to terms with the reality of a bureaucratic organization. New employees soon discover that others in the organization are often a roadblock to what they want to get done. Co-workers do not seem as bright, competent, or productive as they should be. Too often they appear to be illogical, irrational, and unmotivated. The new employee must learn to accept the human organization with all its weaknesses. "Selling," compromising, and "politicking" become essential skills.

The second task is learning to cope with resistance to change within the organization. New employees complain that their good ideas are undermined, side-

American workers—Japanese ways. At this Nissan factory in Tennessee, workers are instructed in the Japanese way of car making. Along with organization into teams, workers' habits and attitudes will have to conform to the Japanese way.

tracked, and sabotaged, or simply ignored. They discover that their recommendations, which seem so logical, are not implemented for one reason or another. The degree to which new employees learn to cope with resistance to change has important consequences for their future career paths.

The third task for new employees is resolving ambiguity related to their work. They find that some aspects of their jobs are poorly defined. They also have trouble getting the feedback needed to judge their own performance. Carving out a niche in the organization is a critical part of adapting to it.

Finally, new employees must learn how to get ahead in their organization. They must discover how to relate to their bosses, establishing a balance between overdependence and rebellion. At the same time, they must figure out the reward system. They must discover what is really expected of them, what is really rewarded in their organization, and how much they can trust what official statements say.

Since Schein conducted his research the process of becoming socialized into a large corporation has become even more complex. A growing number of today's largest corporations are multinationals— businesses that have operations and subsidiaries in many different countries. When a multinational builds a production facility in a foreign country, workers there must be socialized into a system that largely reflects the norms and values of the country where the company was founded and remains headquartered.

In Mazda's car plant in Detroit, for example, American workers must learn to adapt to a Japanese-style system in which production is organized around cooperative work teams of six to ten people.

The members of a team are jointly responsible for getting their assigned tasks done. Each member is expected to show dedication and commitment to the job that exceeds what is expected in the American system. Japanese managers expect people to continue working even when slightly ill, and they expect them to willingly take on extra work when a member of their team is absent. Absent workers must be genuinely ill, as verified by a doctor. Mazda does not grant its workers a standard number of "sick days," to be taken at a person's own discretion. American employees must also get used to the Japanese style of decision making, which is based on group consensus. All Mazda employees are expected to participate in decision-making meetings where both workers and managers collectively come to agreements about ways to improve production. At the same time, employees are expected to merge their own individual interests with those of the larger group (as they would in a family), and they are expected to make personal sacrifices for the good of the company. This is a new way of thinking for the many Americans who consider large corporations to be impersonal bureaucracies that are sometimes even the adversaries of workers (Fucini and Fucini, 1990).

Of course, not all Americans will go to work for a foreign-owned firm and be required to adjust to a whole new set of occupational norms and values; however, in other ways they will need to be socialized into the new roles they take on. Socialization does not end with childhood. The challenges of it continue in adult life whenever we join a new group or undergo a major life transition. Even dying is not without its elements of socialization. Socialization is a lifelong process for everyone.

SUMMARY

1. Socialization is the process of acquiring the beliefs, norms, and values that are socially expected of us as members of a particular society or a particular social group. It is one of the basic forces that shapes human social behavior. Another is a person's inherited biological potential. This potential establishes a range of behavioral possibilities on which environmental influences work. A third force shaping social behavior is a person's own freedom to make choices about who he or she will become.

2. Through their interactions with others during socialization people actively construct a sense of self. Sociologist

Charles Horton Cooley analyzed this process using the concept of a looking-glass self. We acquire our sense of self, he argued, by seeing ourselves reflected in other people's behaviors toward us and by imagining what they think we are like. Sociologist George Herbert Mead built on this perspective when he stressed that, through symbolic interaction with others, children learn both to anticipate what other people expect and to evaluate and adjust their own behavior accordingly. Another influential theory of socialization is that of Sigmund Freud. He saw socialization as a struggle between biologically based drives for pleasure and the rules of acceptable conduct society imposes on us.

Jean Piaget is a fourth theorist whose work has influenced ideas about how the sense of self develops. In his view, fundamental changes in children's thinking as they grow older provide the basis for the emergence of an increasingly mature sense of self.

3. Cooley, Mead, Freud, and Piaget pioneered important perspectives on the process of socialization, but all four treated socialization as though it were basically the same for everyone. This, however, is not the case. Exactly what you learn about becoming a member of society depends upon your place in the social order. Males and females, for instance, are socialized in different ways. They are prepared for different roles in society and different ways of thinking and acting. Members of different social classes also tend to be socialized differently. For example, lower-class children are taught to value obedience and conformity more than middle-class children are, which tends to prepare them for lower-status jobs that offer few opportunities for independent thought. This differential socialization by social class may help explain why lower social status is often perpetuated across generations.

4. Who we become is also a matter of individual social action. In modern complex societies—especially those that place considerable value on personal freedom of choice—there are many different ways to be male, female, working-class, upper-class, Catholic, Baptist, black, or Hispanic. While there are cultural norms and social roles that people learn as members of these groups, they also have room for individual and collective choice. Part of this choice involves people's freedom to select among roles to some extent, and to resist being socialized into roles they do not like. At the same time, people can act consciously to try to change the meaning of the roles they currently play and into which future generations will be socialized.

5. Heated debates have arisen over the relative contributions of nature (biological makeup), nurture (cultural learning), and personal choice in the development of a homosexual or heterosexual way of life. Recent evidence suggests the possibility of a biological predisposition for some men to be gay. This possibility has attracted great interest among gay men and lesbians because if homosexuality is proven to be innate, others may condemn it less. Whatever the role of biology in the development of sexual orientation and identity, cultural learning is clearly involved in it as well. At the very least, culture helps define the various sexual identities that are available for people to adopt. Still, there is always an element of choice in how particular people define and express their sexual identities. The very act of "coming out"—declaring a homosexual orientation—is something an individual chooses to do. In much the same way, becoming immersed in the gay or lesbian subculture, defining what one's sexual orientation means, and perhaps becoming politicized about it also strongly entail individual choice.

6. The family is a primary agent of childhood socialization. It introduces children to intimate relationships and group living, and it gives them a status in society. Cultural norms and values are also strongly instilled by children's peer groups. Norms and values related to fairness, sharing, and reciprocity are particularly suited to being learned in the egalitarian relationships that exist among peers. Although children's peer groups often develop their own norms and values, on important issues the norms and values of parents and children usually coincide. The mass media are also important agents of childhood socialization, as are schools. The official function of schools is to teach children academics, but the classroom conveys a great many values as well.

7. Socialization is certainly not confined to childhood. It continues throughout life and is especially important during major life transitions, such as getting married, having children, or retiring from work. When adults must internalize new norms and values very different from their old ones, the process is called resocialization. Often, resocialization is preceded by desocialization, the process whereby people are stripped of the values and self-conceptions held in the past in preparation for replacing these with new values and self-images. Extreme cases of desocialization occur in total institutions, organizations that deliberately close themselves off from the outside world and lead a highly insular life that is formally organized and tightly controlled. Examples are prisons, mental hospitals, and military boot camps. An important aspect of socialization in adulthood is teaching people the norms and values they need in their particular jobs. This is called occupational socialization.

REVIEW QUESTIONS

1. Compare Cooley's concept of the looking-glass self, Mead's ideas on role-taking, Freud's analysis of the internal dynamics of socialization, and Piaget's view of the cognitive basis for the development of a sense of self.

2. Describe some of the ways in which socialization varies by gender and by social class.

3. Discuss the contributions of nature, nurture, and choice to the development of some specific aspect of self-identity, such as sexual orientation and identity.

4. Briefly describe the role of each of the following in the socialization of children: family, schools, the mass media, and peers.

5. Explain why socialization is a lifelong process for everyone, and give two examples of socialization in adulthood.

CRITICAL THINKING QUESTIONS

1. Describe the relative importance of nature, nurture, and choice in your own socialization. Provide specific examples.

2. Give examples of socialization that you have experienced since beginning college.

3. Differentiate the roles of the following in your own socialization: your family, your peers, the mass media, and the schools you have attended. Identify the most important one and give reasons for your choice.

4. Present an argument pro or con regarding this issue:

Schools should become more like total institutions so that they can more effectively educate children.

5. Some people argue that we should more extensively regulate the socialization of young children, perhaps by having mandatory parenting classes or having children start preschool at a very early age. Present your ideas on this proposition, using some of the concepts from the chapter.

6. Which future occasion for socialization seems likely to affect you most deeply: entering your career, getting married, or retiring from your occupation. Why?

GLOSSARY

Anticipatory socialization The process of starting to adjust one's beliefs, norms, and values in anticipation of new socialization one is about to undergo.

Constructionism The belief that social identities—male, female, black, white, heterosexual, gay, and so forth—are constructed through social processes and are therefore changeable.

Desocialization The process of shedding one's self-image and values, usually followed by resocialization to a different set of values and a different view of the self.

Ego Sigmund Freud's term for the practical, reality-oriented part of the human psyche, which finds socially acceptable ways to satisfy biologically based pleasure-seeking drive.

Essentialism The view that social identities are dictated by biology or enduring social forces and therefore are relatively fixed. Essentialism implies that we can uncover the "essence" of what it means to be black, female, gay, and so forth—that people in these categories have a more

or less stable set of characteristics that distinguish them from others.

Generalized other An internalized general impression of what society as a whole expects of us.

Id Sigmund Freud's term for the reservoir of innate biological drives aimed at obtaining physical pleasure.

Looking-glass self Charles Horton Cooley's term to explain how others influence the way we see ourselves. We gain an image of ourselves by imagining what other people think about us.

Object permanence concept The realization, which emerges in infancy, that objects have a continuing existence apart from one's own perception of them.

Representational thought The capacity to make one thing represent, or "stand for," another. Part of representational thought is the use of mental images to stand for real persons, objects, and actions.

Resocialization The internalization of a new set of norms and values that are very different from those held in the past.

Self The sense of having a distinct identity that sets us apart from other people and objects.

Sexual orientation A person's basic approach to sexual relationships, including choice of partners and activities and the meanings attached to these.

Significant others People who are emotionally important in someone's life.

Socialization The process of acquiring the beliefs, norms, and values that are socially expected of us as members of a particular society or a particular social group.

Superego Sigmund Freud's term for conscience, the part of the human psyche that internalizes society's views of right and wrong.

Total institutions Organizations that deliberately close themselves off from the outside world and lead a highly insular life that is formally organized and tightly controlled. Examples are prisons, mental hospitals, and military boot camps.

CHAPTER 6

Deviance and Crime

Otis Chambers was graduating from Lee Senior High School in Marianna, Arkansas. To celebrate, Otis's brother Billy Joe, a self-made millionaire whose financial empire was based in Detroit, hired five white stretch limousines to transport family and friends to the graduation. When the entourage pulled into the school parking lot, the Chambers brothers were greeted like movie stars arriving at the Oscars. Cameras clicked, teenagers squealed, and small children pushed forward to grasp the crisp green bills Billy Joe was distributing casually, like autographs.

When Otis Chambers received his diploma, he was given an ovation befitting a football star or the class valedictorian. Otis was neither a distinguished athlete nor a distinguished student, but he had a glittering future. While most of his classmates would join the army, head to Memphis or Little Rock in search of work, or stay in Marianna to eke out a subsistence living, Otis had a job waiting in the family business: selling crack cocaine.

To residents of Marianna, Otis's older brother Billy Joe was living proof that a person could achieve almost anything if he wanted it badly enough and worked hard to get it. The son of sharecroppers who as a child picked cotton from dawn to dusk, he now wore $1,000 alligator shoes, drove fancy cars, and spent lavishly on his extended family. Against all odds, he had achieved the American Dream though he earned his wealth illegally, as a drug dealer.

News stories about the "crack epidemic" and the "drug culture" conjure up an image of an America in which easy money, disrupted and disorganized families, and lawlessness have replaced hard work, love of family, and respect for law and order. From this perspective, the Billy Joes of the world have nothing in common with the businessmen and women who commute from Connecticut to Wall Street or the "techies" who began fiddling with computers in a garage and later were able to challenge IBM. Drug dealers are a "breed apart"—or are they?

Billy Joe's life was actually a classic American "rags to riches" success story. Dropping out of school in eleventh grade, he traveled the well-worn path from the rural South to the urban, industrial North, as countless African-Americans had done before him. Had Billy Joe arrived in Detroit a decade earlier, he might have gone to work in the automotive industry, and settled down to raise a family. In the late 1970s, however, Detroit was a wasteland. Plants had closed, jobs and capital had dried up, and the middle and working classes (black and white) had fled to the suburbs. The best job Billy Joe could find was sweeping floors and washing windows in a shoe store. Caught between the poverty and prejudice of his native Arkansas and the poverty and hopelessness of the inner city, he was determined to escape.

Opportunity knocked in the form of crack, an inexpensive, highly addictive cocaine compound that first made its appearance in the late 1970s. Coincidentally, the Medellín drug cartel began looking for local U.S. distributors for this product around the time Billy Joe began looking for opportunity.

Billy Joe and his brothers approached the business as any entrepreneurs might. They identified a niche in the marketplace and learned how to buy wholesale, mass-produce, and market the new product. They taught themselves how to calculate risks, monitor cash flow, and assess profit margins. They instituted quality controls, employee rules and regulations, benefit plans, bonuses, and customer incentives. By the mid-1980s, when Otis graduated, the Chambers brothers were grossing $55 million a year (tax-free), more than any legal privately owned business in Detroit.

Hard work and huge profits notwithstanding, the Chambers brothers were criminals. "Like tobacco companies, they sold their product indiscriminantly and remorselessly, without regard for the tragic consequences" (Adler, 1995, p. 6). Crack kills babies, turns users into zombies, tears apart families, and wrecks neighborhoods. In effect, the Chambers brothers made their fortune selling "living death." Moreover, to maintain their market share they employed a security force that enforced discipline by cracking knees and heads, shooting people, and burning homes.

The brothers were responsible for their actions and were punished according to the rules of the American legal system. (One was killed in an auto accident, but the others are serving 25-year-to-life sentences.) Simply to write off Billy Joe and other underground entrepreneurs as criminals and deviants, however, ignores the social context that created their opportunities and limited their choices. The Chambers brothers are products of the same culture that reviles them. Far from rejecting mainstream American values, they embraced them. Trapped at the bottom of the economic heap in a society obsessed with wealth, caught between the culture of greed and the culture of need, they refused to give up. "The decade's cult of money, its tone of rising expectations, insisted that the dispossessed aspire to the goals of the dominant culture yet denied them the means to achieve those goals legally" (Adler, 1995, p. 5). Under the circumstances, the Chambers brothers made a rational career choice. What makes their story so chilling is not that they were so different from other Americans but that they were so similar, so wedded to the American Dream.

Deviance is any action that is perceived as violating some widely shared moral value or norm of a society's or group's culture. Deviance is not just a matter of what is atypical or uncommon. (Skydiving, for instance, is uncommon, but it is not deviant.) For behavior to be considered deviant, it must be seen as violating some socially defined standard. Because moral standards change over time and vary from one society or group to another, ideas of what is deviant vary and change.

In some cases cultural standards are codified into law and deviance constitutes criminal behavior. Not all violations of the law are considered deviant, however. For example, most people drive 5 to 10 mph above the speed limit on highways, and few see this as a moral failing. In other cases a particular deviant behavior may not be illegal, but it may be widely viewed as disreputable, unethical, immoral, peculiar, or "sick." It is not illegal for a professor to date an undergraduate in his or her class, but most people would consider this improper at best, and today many colleges and universities consider this grounds for dismissing the professor.

The public strongly disapproves of some acts of deviance (such as sexual abuse of children) while shrugging off others (such as buying pornographic magazines). People who commit serious acts of deviance are often given such negative labels as "nut," "slut," "crook," or "pervert." These labels enable us to think of deviants as being fundamentally different from ourselves. However, we view those whose deviant behaviors are considered minor as "normal" people who occasionally lapse. So-called minor acts of deviance are very common. How many people do you know who failed to return a library book, lifted pens and paper from the office where they work, ran a red light, told a lie, or cheated on their income taxes? Clearly, when we include such minor violations of norms, deviance is extremely widespread.

What distinguished the Chambers brothers from "normal" entrepreneurs was, first, that they sold cocaine, and second, that they used violence. But neither is unprecedented in our culture. President Franklin Delano Roosevelt's grandfather, Warren Delano, made the family fortune in large part by selling opium to the Chinese (Ward, 1985). In the 1880s and 1890s cocaine was hailed as a cure-all by physicians in Europe and America and was readily available in patent medicines, tonics, syrups, cigars, and cigarettes, and even Coca-Cola. Likewise, the use of force has long been part of our dollar-minded culture. Labor violence, pitting union members against strikebreakers and police around the turn of the century, cost hundreds of lives.

These examples from the past are not presented in an effort to excuse or condone the Chambers brothers, but rather to put their actions in perspective. A hero in a rural hometown may be "public enemy number one" in the city. The panacea of one period in history may be seen as poison in another period.

Public opinion has turned against cigarettes in recent years, yet the tobacco industry continues to peddle its highly addictive, potentially deadly product in the open.

In the first section of this chapter we look at the social construction of deviance. We show that who and what is labeled deviant depends on power relations in a society and that deviance can function both as a source of social stability and a catalyst for social change. We also look at ways of controlling deviance. Then we address the question of who becomes deviant—that is, who enters into a continuing pattern of deviance—looking at the roles of heredity and the environment, structural strain, deviant careers, and inadequate social control. Finally, we focus on crime, the criminal justice system, and different strategies for controlling crime.

THE SOCIAL CONSTRUCTION OF DEVIANCE

Deviance is a matter of *social definition*. It exists only in relation to the social norms that prevail in a particular place, time, group, and situation. Regardless of how heinous an act may actually be, no behavior is inherently deviant. Deviance is a property that people confer on some forms of behavior because of the norms they have established and consider "good" and "right."

If it is wrong to destroy other people's property, then is the fire bombing of an abortion clinic deviant? That depends on your views toward abortion. Those favoring choice condemn antiabortion violence of any kind, while abortion's foes might feel that destroying clinics saves lives.

TABLE 6.1
The Cultural Relativity of Deviance

Type of Act	PERCENTAGE WHO THINK ACT SHOULD BE PROHIBITED BY LAW[a]				
	India	Iran	Italy (Sardinia)	U.S.	Yugoslavia
Homosexuality in private between consenting adults	74	90	87	18	72
Public, nonviolent political protest	33	77	35	6	46
Failure to help another person in danger	45	56	80	28	77
Air pollution caused by a factory	99	98	96	96	92

[a]Percentages have been rounded off.

Source: Adapted from Graeme Newman, Comparative Deviance: Perception and Law in Six Cultures (Elsevier, New York, 1976), p. 116, table 4.

Social definitions of deviance vary widely among societies (see Table 6.1). They also vary within societies. In the United States, for example, groups differ on the question of abortion. Which is more deviant, performing abortions or performing violence against abortion clinics? Most people (whether for or against choice) condemn the assassination of physicians who perform abortions. But some groups feel strongly that abortion is a form of murder. Others feel equally strongly that abortion is a woman's right to choose and that the decision should be left to the individual. What is considered deviant also varies between different ethnic groups (to many Asians and Hispanics, for instance, failure to care at home for an elderly parent is considered the worst kind of deviance, but is more accepted among whites); between different social classes (in some urban ghettoes a young unmarried girl who gets pregnant is not likely to be considered deviant, but in most middle-class settings she is); between different occupational groups (dating a patient is considered deviant for a psychoanalyst but not for a dentist); between different geographic regions (in New York City it is deviant to greet strangers on the street, but in a small town in Georgia it is not); and between the two sexes (girls who regularly get into fistfights are considered much more deviant than boys who do the same). As mentioned previously, one group's "public enemy number one" may be another group's hero (see the Research Methods box).

Deviance varies not just from group to group but also from situation to situation. In our society (and most others) killing another human being is an act of deviance, *except* in self-defense or when the victim is a wartime enemy. Similarly, because norms change over time, so do definitions of deviance. Before the late 1960s, living together without being married was widely considered deviant—even grounds for expulsion from college. Today, in contrast, most Americans find cohabitation socially acceptable, especially if the couple is young, childless, and heterosexual.

Changes in definitions of deviance are an important part of social change. This change may be fast or slow, unorganized or organized. The growing number of men and women enrolling in college and graduate schools in the 1960s and 1970s, and therefore postponing marriage, for instance, had the unintentional effect of relaxing norms against premarital sex. Sometimes change requires organized collective action, such as the struggle of gay men and lesbians to end condemnation of their sexual preferences and lifestyles.

How such struggles are resolved can have serious consequences. For example, the gay rights movement led many communities to pass laws prohibiting discrimination against homosexuals in employment, housing, and public accommodations. In family matters, the gay movement had less success: only a few communities recognize homosexual marriages (though the number of such communities is slowly growing), and gay men and women may be denied custody of their children or the opportunity to adopt. When President Clinton attempted to fulfill a campaign pledge to admit gays to the military, he was obliged to compromise with a "don't ask, don't tell" policy. The highest-ranking female officer in the U.S. military was forced to resign because she acknowledged she was a lesbian.

Labeling and Power

Nearly everyone breaks the law occasionally or acts a little "odd" at times, but most people do not think of themselves as deviant, nor do others view them as deviant. According to **labeling theory**, derived from symbolic interactionism, being publicly branded as deviant has long-term consequences for a person's social identity (Blumer, 1969/1986; Lemert, 1951). Who gets labeled as deviant depends not just on what the person does but also on other social characteristics such as age, race or ethnicity, and social class.

The sociologist William Chambliss (1973) observed the labeling process at work in a Missouri high school. Chambliss identified two cliques at the school, "the Saints" and "the Roughnecks." The eight members of the Saints came from upper-middle-class families, were good students, and were active in school affairs. On weekends and on days when they cut classes, the Saints amused themselves with various forms of delinquency: heavy drinking, reckless driving, petty theft, vandalism, and games of "chicken." The people of the town considered them good boys who were sowing a few wild oats. The police did not arrest one Saint in the two years Chambliss observed them. The six Roughnecks, in contrast, came from lower-class families and were not good students. Most weekends they could be found hanging around the local drugstore, drinking alcohol from concealed bottles. They sometimes got into fights (usually among themselves) or engaged in petty theft, and they were frequently in trouble with the police. The townspeople considered them good-for-nothings. "Everybody agreed that the not-so-well-dressed, not-so-well-mannered, not-so-rich boys were heading for trouble" (Chambliss, 1973, p. 27). In addition, the police knew that the Saints' up-

per-middle-class parents would cause trouble if their sons were arrested, whereas the Roughnecks' parents lacked the power and influence to fight back.

With few exceptions, the members of both the Saints and the Roughnecks responded to differential labeling by meeting the community's expectations. Several members of the Roughnecks were arrested repeatedly, not only as teenagers but also as young adults. In contrast, the Saints left adolescence behind them, moving along upper-middle-class pathways, and remembered their teenage delinquency fondly as a youthful fling.

The selective application of deviant labels and formal sanctions raises important questions: *Whose* norms prevail in society as a whole? *Who* decides what behavior will be most widely labeled as deviant? *Who* decides which individuals or groups will be publicly or officially singled out as deviant?

In American society, both wealth and race help determine who holds the power to influence definitions of deviance. Actions that threaten or offend middle- and upper-class whites are most likely to be defined as deviant. Mood-altering drugs sold on the street (heroin, cocaine) are illegal, but mood-altering "medicines" acquired with a physician's prescription (tranquilizers, barbiturates) are not. Power also helps elites to avoid being labeled deviant themselves. For instance, savings-and-loan executives defrauded Americans of billions of dollars in the 1980s, but their wealth, connections, and respectable reputations protected them. Most were punished leniently, if at all.

Karl Marx held that a small ruling class of economic elites determines moral norms (and thus definitions of deviance) because these norms support the existing economic order. According to Marx, how severely society responds to the violation of its norms depends on how much the violation threatens established power relations. For example, drug addiction was not seen as a major social problem as long as it affected mainly the poor and ethnic minorities. However, once drug use and drug-related problems increased among middle-class whites, social action against drugs intensified (Ben-Yehuda, 1990). Moreover, the drug trade employed people who might otherwise have been part of a pool of cheap labor for conventional businesses. In cracking down on drugs, the elites were also attempting to stop this encroachment.

Thus, viewed from the Marxist and other power-oriented perspectives, the law and the criminal justice system reflect first and foremost the interests of

Islands in the Street: A Study of Urban Gangs by Martín Sánchez Jankowski

Gangs. The very word strikes fear into the hearts of middle- and upper-class Americans. To them, gangs are by definition lawless and deviant, perpetrators of often brutal acts of violence against rival gangs and others who get in their way. Yet in the neighborhoods where gangs operate they are a familiar feature of the social landscape.

The sociologist Martín Sánchez Jankowski was interested in why gangs persist, despite constant campaigns against them. Reviewing the literature, Sánchez Jankowski found that previous studies had focused on gangs in one neighborhood or city, or gangs belonging to a single ethnic group. To distinguish between characteristics that are unique to certain gangs and those common to all gangs, Sánchez Jankowski decided to conduct a comparative study as a participant observer.

In selecting a sample of gangs for study, Sánchez Jankowski had three main criteria. To control for the impact of different political and socioeconomic conditions, he wanted to study gangs in different cities. To determine what role (if any) ethnicity played in gangs, he needed to study gangs from different ethnic groups. Finally, he wanted to study gangs of varying size.

Sánchez Jankowski chose New York City, with its densely populated high-rise public housing projects, occupied primarily by Puerto Ricans, Dominicans, and African-Americans; Boston, with its row houses, occupied predominantly by working-class Irish; and Los Angeles, with its sprawling neighborhoods composed of single-family homes, often occupied by multiple Latino or Asian families. After identifying ethnic neighborhoods, Sánchez Jankowski contacted local officials to determine what gangs operated in each area and then selected a cross section of African-American, Latino, Asian, and white gangs.

At this point Sánchez Jankowski could not simply appear on a street corner and announce, "I am a professor and I want to study you" (1991, p. 9). He contacted community leaders, social workers, and clergy who worked with gangs to arrange for an introduction, but not an endorsement. He wanted to meet with gang members alone and negotiate on his own terms. At these initial meetings, most gang leaders found the idea of a book comparing gangs intriguing, but they were wary of the professor. Sánchez Jankowski found that his own identity and appearance worked both for and against him. The fact that he was not white (Jankowski is his adopted Polish father's name) made him more acceptable to Latino and African-American gangs but less acceptable to white and Asian gangs. Italian and Irish gangs in New York refused to participate, as did Asian gangs in Los Angeles. However, the four Irish gangs he contacted in Boston allowed him access because, not being Puerto Rican (a rival ethnic group), he was not perceived as a threat. He ended up obtaining consent from ten gangs in New York, ten in Los Angeles, and four in Boston.

The next step was to gain the trust and acceptance necessary for participant observation. To do so Sánchez Jankowski had to pass two tests. The first was a test of loyalty: Gang members engaged in illegal activities in his presence to see if he would inform on them. The second was a test of bravery or "heart": Gang members staged a fight with him to test his mettle and to learn

the governing class—those who have the power to control the legislatures, police, and courts. This perspective contrasts sharply with the ideal of justice being blind to differences in social power. How accurate is this description?

The sociologist Amitai Etzioni estimates that two-thirds of America's 500 largest corporations break the law, in varying degrees, during any ten-year period (in Gellerman, 1986). In one case that has taken decades to resolve, investigators described corporate crimes as a kind of murder. The Manville Corporation was one of the oldest and largest manufacturers of asbestos in America. Evidence that exposure to as-bestos dust causes debilitating, often fatal, lung disease began appearing in medical journals in the late 1920s. Executives at Manville knew about this information but did nothing to warn or protect workers and in fact suppressed incriminating research on the dangers of working with asbestos. This cover-up continued for forty years and resulted in numerous deaths but no criminal sanctions (Calhoun and Hiller, 1988). Apparently, the company's size and power acted as a shield. Often, then, the degree to which a given act is viewed as deviant depends not on the amount of harm it causes but on the power of those who have stepped across the line.

RESEARCH METHODS

whether he would be an asset or a liability if they were ambushed by a rival gang. He realized that among gang members it was acceptable to fight and lose but not acceptable to refuse to fight. Nonetheless, he was grateful that he had trained in karate and suffered only bruises in his fights.

Participant observation requires that the researcher both participate in group activities and observe the people he or she is studying. Alternating between gangs every month or so, Sánchez Jankowski slept where they slept, stayed with their families, traveled wherever they went, and in situations where he could not remain neutral, fought along with them (p. 13). After an initial period of suspicion, gang members seemed to forget (or to stop caring) that he was conducting research. Over and over he was told, "You don't look like a professor" or "You don't act like one." During observation periods he took notes and tape-recorded interviews and meetings; later he wrote daily and weekly summaries of what had occurred.

Sánchez Jankowski was also interested in the gangs' relationships with the communities in which they operated. Posing as a gang member, he observed how neighbors, business owners, and various officials interacted with gang members. Later he identified himself. He observed whether these people behaved differently after they learned he was not a gang member, and he requested formal interviews. Almost all nongang members agreed, with the stipulation that he protect their confidentiality.

Not surprisingly, Sánchez Jankowski encountered a number of ethical dilemmas. He observed illegal activ-ities countless times but kept his promise to remain neutral and not reveal the identity of individuals or the gang to authorities. If he had not guaranteed confidentiality, the gangs would not have cooperated; if he had not witnessed criminal activities, his picture of gangs would have been incomplete. As part of this agreement, he did not participate in any illegal activities himself (including taking drugs). Likewise, he guarded the confidentiality of officials, who candidly discussed the unstated rules and unofficial agreements that allowed them to work with gangs. In all, Sánchez Jankowski observed the twenty-four gangs over a period of ten years.

In a nutshell, Sánchez Jankowski found that the sharp contrast often drawn between "deviant" gang members and "normal" young adults was false. Far from being lazy, most gang members were energetic, enterprising, and eager to acquire the same things that most Americans want: money, possessions, power, and prestige. Boys joined gangs, not because of pathological tendencies or intimidation by older gang members, but because they wanted to get ahead. Gangs offered members business opportunities, entertainment, a place of refuge, and protective group identity, as well as physical protection. Most important, gang membership was a way of resisting (or postponing) the dead-end jobs, chronic poverty, and hopelessness they saw in their parents' lives.

Source: Martín Sánchez Jankowski, *Islands in the Street: Gangs and American Urban Society* (University of California Press, Berkeley, 1991).

The power of elites is not absolute, however. Especially in a pluralistic, democratic society, groups outside the governing class exert some influence on what is considered deviant. Beginning in the late 1960s, for example, consumer protection groups (such as Ralph Nader's Center for Science in the Public Interest) began effectively to lobby the federal government to protect consumers against dangerous products like asbestos and cancer-causing food additives. A current example is public pressure for tighter restrictions against cigarette smoking, despite intensive lobbying and extensive ad campaigns by the tobacco industry. Thus, it is possible for the public, with enough collective effort, to label the actions of powerful elites as deviant.

The Social Functions of Deviance

Deviance sometimes disrupts well-integrated social systems, but it can also serve positive social functions. Émile Durkheim (1895/1982), one of sociology's founders, was the first to analyze this seeming paradox. Durkheim argued that deviance is a natural part of social life—indeed, "an integral part of all

Smoking, from desirable to deviant. Despite conclusive scientific evidence that cigarette smoking causes cancer, tobacco executives—like those testifying at this Congressional hearing—continue to deny the facts. Nevertheless, the public's image of smoking has shifted from sophisticated, alluring behavior to a dirty, life-threatening addiction.

healthy societies" (1895/1982, p. 67). How can deviance be healthy for societies?

Durkheim's answer has two parts. First, in defining certain kinds of behavior as deviant, a group or community also defines what behavior is acceptable. The boundaries between acceptable and unacceptable are rarely hard and fast. Societies typically have a "permissive zone of variation" (in Durkheim's words) surrounding even strongly supported norms. Most norms are not expressed in highly specific ways. Rather, they are defined informally in the course of people's day-to-day activities. By testing the boundaries of permissiveness, deviants force other members of society to think about what they believe is normal and right.

Second, deviance tends to unite members of society in opposition to the deviant, thus reaffirming their social solidarity. When parents join to fight a pornography shop in their town or when citizens vote for a new, more honest politician, they unite against a deviant—the merchant who opened the pornography store, the unethical politician who accepted bribes. In this way members of a community can pour their collective energy into shoring up the social order.

Just as deviance may help people reaffirm norms that are threatened, it may also serve as a catalyst for social change. This was true of acts in defiance of racial segregation during the civil rights movement. In 1955, when Rosa Parks of Montgomery, Alabama, refused to move to the back of a bus where blacks were required to sit, she engaged in an individual act of defiance and deviance. But this time, attempts by whites to punish the deviant and force her compliance did not have the usual effect of reaffirming traditional norms. Instead, Mrs. Parks's action helped to launch a wider movement to bring social equality to African-Americans. (We discuss the civil rights movement in Chapter 20.)

Whether deviance reinforces existing norms or serves as a catalyst for new ones depends in part on the type of society. Simple, traditional societies tend to produce a high degree of consensus regarding acceptable behavior. Punishment of deviance usually leads to increased commitment to the status quo. Complex, modern societies, in contrast, tend to be heterogeneous, with many competing lifestyles and moral points of view. "In such societies, values, norms, and moral boundaries are not given; they are negotiated" (Ben-Yehuda, 1985, p. 15). As a result, deviance can often lead to a renegotiation of norms and to social change.

Social Control

Just as deviance is socially constructed, so are the measures employed to limit it. **Social control** refers to the efforts of a group or society to regulate the behavior of its members in conformity with established norms. Ideally people conform on their own because they have *internalized* the norms (absorbed them deeply into their way of thinking). But socialization is never perfect, and compliance with norms is not automatic. As a result, there must also be **sanctions,** or externally imposed constraints. Some of these are **informal sanctions:** unofficial, often casual pressures to conform. Positive informal sanctions involve rewards for conformity, such as a smile, a kiss, a word of approval. Negative informal sanctions involve informal penalties for *not* conforming, such as ridicule or ostracism.

Formal sanctions are official, institutionalized incentives to conform and penalties for deviance. Formal sanctions are especially needed in large, complex societies such as our own, where people hold competing ideas about appropriate behavior and the power of informal sanctions is diluted. The criminal justice system is the most important and visible institution of social control in modern societies, but it is not the only one. Businesses also exert social control: Employees who meet or exceed company goals are rewarded with raises and promotions, and employees who perform poorly or break company rules are penalized with demotions or dismissal. Schools use grades, awards, and graduation certificates to reward superior performance and good behavior and use detention, suspension, repeat courses, failure, and expulsion to punish poor performance and disruptive behavior. Informal social controls still play a role in modern societies, but formal sanctions are invoked when informal social controls fail or when informal sanctions encourage deviance (for example, classmates encourage cutting classes; teammates or co-workers support sexual harassment).

WHO BECOMES DEVIANT?

Deviant behavior always carries the risk of punishment, whether it be social disapproval or criminal sanctions. Why do some people regularly engage in deviant acts, while others do not? Can we predict with reasonable accuracy who will embark on a deviant career and who will not?

Heredity

Over the years, many people have tried to explain who becomes deviant in terms of individuals' inherent natures. In the nineteenth century, Cesare Lombroso, an Italian criminologist, examined the shape of criminals' skulls for evidence of shared, inherited traits. His investigation suggested that many criminals had high cheekbones, large jaws, and prominent brow ridges, similar to the facial characteristics of apes. To Lombroso, this confirmed that criminals were throwbacks to an earlier stage of evolution, "savages" among civilized people. Lombroso made one huge methodological error, however; he examined *only* the skulls of criminals, not a representative sample of the entire population. Some years later, when the British physician Charles Goring (1913) compared the skulls of criminals to those of ordinary citizens, he found no difference between the two, a finding that has consistently been replicated.

Other scientists of the time sought to identify the physical traits that demonstrated an aptitude for prostitution (Gilman, 1985). Photographs of known prostitutes indeed showed similar characteristics: dark hair, a strong jaw, a "hard" look. In fact, prosti-

Expelling deviants solidifies the group. Senator Alan Packwood became politically unacceptable to the Senate when several of his former female aides testified that he had sexually harassed them. Under pressure, Packwood ultimately resigned.

tutes in a given place and time looked alike because they belonged to an immigrant ethnic group whose poverty forced them into prostitution. Still other scientists, believing that Africans lived in unbridled promiscuity, examined African women to learn what made them so "oversexed." The image of the prostitute and the black woman gradually merged—as contrasted to the repressive ideal of proper—sexually pure—white womanhood.

These early researchers made five basic mistakes. First, they accepted their cultures' stereotypes and looked for evidence to prove those stereotypes correct. Second, they confused outward appearance (or phenotype) with underlying, inherited predispositions (genotype). Third, they did not use control groups (noncriminals, nonprostitutes). Fourth, they did not consider possible intervening variables (immigrant poverty). Fifth, they used small, nonrandom samples to generalize about entire social categories.

Today scientists recognize that human behavior is far too complex to explain in terms of biology alone. Even where biology plays a role (as in schizophrenia, bipolar disorder, depression, and other mental illnesses), environmental factors influence if, when, and how these biological traits will be expressed. Nevertheless, the idea that deviants are biologically different from other members of society lingers. In 1981, President Ronald Reagan asserted that crime is not a social problem, but "a problem of the human heart" and emphasized what he saw as the "permanent or absolute features of man's nature" (Kaminer, 1994).

Socialization

Other explanations of who becomes deviant focus on socialization. Psychodynamic theories trace deviant tendencies to early childhood. For instance, Sigmund Freud, the founder of psychoanalysis, argued that most people learn in the process of growing up how to inhibit or productively channel their innate drives toward pleasure and aggression. Some children, however, lack an appropriate adult with whom to identify, whose moral norms and values they can adopt as their own. Such children, according to Freud's theory, fail to develop a strong superego, the part of the psyche that serves as a conscience in guiding behavior. Freud believed that these people are especially prone to deviance.

Social-learning theorists maintain that children learn deviant behavior by observing and imitating others who behave deviantly, especially those they are close to (Bandura and Walters, 1959). Aggressive children often come from families in which the parents themselves tend to be psychologically disturbed, antisocial, and overly punitive or aggressive toward their children (Capaldi and Patterson, 1991; Bandura, 1986). The children lack models of self-control and may respond to punishment with increased aggression, contributing to a cycle of aggression and punishment. The key point is that deviant behavior is produced by the same processes of socialization as conforming behavior is.

A more social-structural view of learning is the theory of **differential association.** This theory holds that people who engage in deviant behavior tend to form social bonds with other deviants, who reinforce deviant norms and values (Gaylord and Galliher, 1988; Sutherland, 1949). Every social group transmits its own cultural norms and values to new members, a process that continues throughout life. Through differential association with deviants, people can be socialized to a drug subculture, a delinquent gang subculture, a politically corrupt subculture, or any number of other deviant lifestyles.

Howard Becker (1963) found that whether or not someone became a marijuana user depended on how much that person participated in the marijuana subculture. The more participation, the closer the social ties, the more likely that person would become a regular user. Experienced users had to teach initiates how to smoke marijuana, cultivate its effects, and enjoy them. In addition, initiates learned from users the "right" attitudes, including the belief that people who condemned marijuana were "squares." Such close association with experienced users was essential to acquiring a marijuana habit.

Adolescents are particularly open to learning the norms, attitudes, and values of any subculture to which they are exposed—including one involved in deviance. As Akers (1985, p. 148) put this, "The single best predictor of adolescent behavior, conforming or deviant, is the behavior of close friends." Both teenage drug use and teenage delinquency are primarily group behaviors. The reason is not just that peers strongly influence a teenager's behavior; a teenager tends to choose as friends others who accept what he or she already does. This pattern continues into adulthood. For instance, a gay man who "comes out" in a small town in Kansas may move to San Francisco to be with others who share his lifestyle. When sufficient numbers of people who reject some mainstream norms come together, a deviant subculture may be born.

Differential association can also help to explain why entire groups of people are prone to deviance. In other words, it can explain why the *rate* of deviance (number of deviant acts per unit of population) varies from group to group, neighborhood to neighborhood, or community to community. In one early study, for example, sociologists discovered that a high crime rate persisted in the same Chicago neighborhood for over twenty years as different ethnic groups came and went (Shaw, 1930). Obviously, ethnic cultural traditions could not explain the persistently high rate of crime. What the researchers found was that new arrivals to the neighborhood were constantly learning deviant norms of behavior from those who already lived there, especially in children's play groups and teenage gangs (Shaw and McKay, 1969). The newcomers then passed the deviant norms on to the next wave of immigrants, and so a deviant subculture was sustained and transmitted. Meanwhile, earlier immigrant groups moved out of the neighborhood into mainstream society. If groups that once encouraged deviance can later "go straight," however, socialization alone cannot explain who becomes deviant.

Modes of Adapting	Accepts Culturally Approved Goals	Accepts Culturally Approved Means
Conformist	Yes	Yes
Innovator	Yes	No
Ritualist	No	Yes
Retreatist	No	No
Rebel	No (creates new goals)	No (creates new means)

FIGURE 6.1 / Merton's Five Modes of Social Adaptation

Source: Adapted from Robert K. Merton, *Social Theory and Social Structure* (Free Press, New York, 1968), p. 194.

Structural Strain

Another perspective on why certain people or groups are more prone to deviance than others is Robert Merton's theory of **structural strain** (Merton, 1968a). In Merton's view, high rates of deviance are the result of a discrepancy between societal expectations and opportunities, between cultural goals and the means available for achieving them. Merton reasoned that to some degree all people internalize worthwhile goals in their culture. Everyone also internalizes the norms that govern proper and legitimate ways of working toward those goals. However, when legitimate opportunities are limited or nonexistent, people may seek alternative ways to achieve their goals or they may abandon the goals altogether. Merton's main point is that strains in social structure may invite deviance. "Some social structures," he wrote, "exert a definite pressure upon certain persons in the society to engage in nonconforming rather than conforming behavior" (Merton, 1968a, p. 132).

Merton's prime example was American society, which places tremendous emphasis on financial success. All children are taught that hard work brings prosperity. At the same time, however, legitimate opportunities to become wealthy are limited. The Chambers brothers, introduced at the beginning of this chapter, faced this dilemma. What can people do to resolve it? Merton identified five possibilities (see Figure 6.1):

1. **Conformity:** Continuing to seek culturally approved goals by culturally approved means, despite the discrepancy between expectations and opportunities. Black families who have stayed in the Arkansas delta for generations, barely eking out a living as sharecroppers, are an example.

2. **Innovation:** Pursuing culturally approved goals by culturally disapproved means (including illegal activities). The Chambers brothers seized an unlawful opportunity (selling crack) to achieve the widely shared goal of financial success.

3. **Ritualism:** Conforming so strictly to socially prescribed means of achieving goals that the larger goals are forgotten. The classic example is the bureaucrat who rigidly adheres to rules and regulations even when they lead to inefficiency and stifle creativity.

4. **Retreatism:** Abandoning both the goals and the means of achieving them that one's culture prescribes. Retreatists are dropouts from society—for example, the Chambers brothers' customers, poor people who had given up looking for work and respectability, whose dreams were reduced to their next pipe of crack.

5. **Rebellion:** Rejecting the approved goals and means of achieving them and embracing new, so-

cially disapproved ones instead. An example would be black separatists, who refuse to buy into the American dream (by legal or illegal means) and insist that blacks create their own society within America or in Africa, if necessary arming themselves against white power.

Merton's theory is partly a rational-choice model. Deviance, he claimed, is a rational option under certain social-structural conditions—namely, lack of legitimate channels to achieve culturally desirable goals. As long as the costs of deviance are not too high (the risk of getting caught and punished is relatively low, or social disapproval does not matter very much), it makes sense for some people to try deviant ways of getting what most people want. Merton's theory also has a social-psychological component. The absence of legitimate means produces frustration, Merton argued. This frustration, in turn, helps to fuel deviance as a way of getting back at the society that limits opportunities.

But why do some people who are thwarted in their efforts to succeed engage in deviant behavior, while others remain conformists? Newer versions of strain theory address this problem. Some suggest that the daily irritations and frustrations of life can push people predisposed to deviance over the line (Agnew, 1990). Others add that belonging to groups that support deviant activities can promote deviance (Cohen, 1965, 1966). Thus, structural strain, social stresses, and differential association all probably play a role in encouraging deviant behavior.

One of the most important implications of structural-strain theory is that we cannot explain deviance by looking only at deviants. We must look at the culture to see what goals and values it sets for people and what means it defines as acceptable. We must also look at the overall social structure to see what obstacles to success it creates and what incentives for deviance it provides. Last, we need to consider the functional integration of different parts of a society. A low level of functional integration fosters structural strains and different opinions as to what are acceptable or deviant means of acting.

Deviant Careers

Most teenagers who shoplift do not become professional thieves; most people who smoke pot do not become drug addicts; and most people who experi-

ment with unconventional sex do not join an alternative sexual subculture. In short, most people are deviant at one time or another, but relatively few enter into **deviant careers**—the progressive stages of integration into a deviant lifestyle plus identification with, and almost exclusive association with, a deviant subculture.

Why do some people progress from casual experimentation to sustained involvement? One obvious factor is how pleasant the initial experience is. If a teenage shoplifter gets away with the goods, or a first-time pot user gets high, that person is more likely to repeat the behavior. A second factor is whether initial experiences lead an individual to become involved with a group of people who encourage deviant behavior, such as using illicit drugs. A third factor is how close the deviant norms are to the norms of his or her family. For example, if parents blame their problems on another racial group (whether white or black) and regularly make disparaging remarks about minorities, their teenager is more likely to join a group of friends who decide to desecrate a synagogue, beat up a homosexual, or commit other hate crimes.

Early participation in deviant acts is an experiment, to see if there are rewards. If the experimental deviant is caught, his or her experiences with agents of social control may be painful: exposure, shame, humiliation, even arrest. Ironically, however, getting caught and being officially labeled deviant may encourage the very behavior it is designed to prevent. People who have been labeled "criminal," "crazy," or "queer" often find that they are excluded from respectable society. Deviant labels then tend to become self-fulfilling prophecies (Merton, 1968a). Shunned by the mainstream, the addict begins to associate almost exclusively with other addicts, the prostitute with other prostitutes, the delinquent with other delinquents. Gradually they learn techniques from more experienced offenders. Equally important, they learn rationalizations for deviant behavior. Drug dealers, for example, may see themselves as ordinary businessmen, supplying a market.

Thus, labeling helps to turn **primary deviance** (an initial violation of a social norm, about which no inferences are made regarding a person's character) into **secondary deviance** (violations that have become part of a person's lifestyle, social identity, and self-image). But labeling theory does not explain the initial entry into deviance. In most cases, no one forces a person to try drugs, steal cars, or sell his or her body for sex. The individual may not plan to embark on a deviant career, but he or she does decide to experiment with illicit behavior or give in to pressure to do so. This first step is not due just to individual difference or to individual moral weakness. The sociologist Travis Hirschi (1969) traces primary deviance to inadequate social control.

Inadequate Social Control

Very little crime is committed by young children because they are constantly under adult surveillance (Gottfredson and Hirschi, 1990). Not until adolescence are young people free enough from adult control to engage in criminal activity. (The younger age of some of today's delinquents may reflect earlier release from parental supervision.) Similarly, drug addicts tend to live in urban neighborhoods characterized by poverty, high crime rates, and large minority populations. According to Hirschi, the reason is not simply that drug use leads to crime or that minorities are more likely to use drugs and commit crimes. The crucial factor is that social control is reduced in these neighborhoods: The police presence is smaller and the distance from the disapproving eye of "straight" society is greater (Hirschi and Gottfredson, 1990) than in other environments.

Hirschi and his colleagues also focus on *self-control*—on perseverance, patience, sensitivity to others, and willingness to defer gratification. Hirschi maintains that inadequate parental control leads to inadequate self-control. If nobody consistently cares for the child, the child does not learn to care about others—or about herself or himself. Faulty or incomplete social learning makes deviance more likely. For example, in high-crime neighborhoods family structure tends to be weak. With many problems of their own, parents may fail to supervise the child's behavior, ignore symptoms of deviance, and be inconsistent in correcting "bad" behavior and praising "good" behavior.

Hirschi's views have drawn criticism, both for assuming that early experiences establish an irreversible pattern for adult life (Sampson and Laub, 1990) and for overlooking the possibility that the child's deviant behavior distances parents and is the *cause* rather than the consequence of inadequate parenting (Conklin, 1992).

The different theories of who becomes deviant described here do not so much compete as complement one another. John Hagan and Alberto Palloni (1990) found that some English families "specialized" in crime, generation after generation, from the nineteenth century on. Did members of these families inherit criminal tendencies? Possibly, but social struc-

Learning to steal. In this engraving from Charles Dickens's Oliver Twist, *Oliver runs down a London street clutching stolen food. Dickens's hero, hardly a thief by nature, stole as payment for his meager support. Dickens's writing helped to speed the development of child welfare services to save children from poverty—and society from the crimes they might commit.*

ture and socialization definitely played a large part. As members of the "criminal class," they were subject to structural strains that wealthier citizens escaped. Furthermore, as members of "crime families" they learned the techniques and rationales for committing crimes from their families; they were stigmatized by the labels applied to their parents; and perhaps they were not subject to as strong discipline, or taught the same rules, as children of more respectable families. In short, deviance is neither innate nor spontaneous but rather is the result of an ongoing process that involves individual action, social pressures, and social circumstances.

CRIME AND THE CRIMINAL JUSTICE SYSTEM

A **crime** is a violation of a norm that has been entered into law and is backed by the power and authority of the state to impose formal sanctions (fines, arrest, imprisonment). Crime and deviance overlap but they are not identical. Not every deviant act is illegal. Neither abusing alcohol nor being sexually promiscuous is a crime, yet most Americans would regard such behaviors as violations of their norms. In addition, all crimes are not considered to be equally deviant. Littering on a highway or betting in a football pool are crimes, but they are far less serious than armed robbery or murder. The norms that are most likely to be entered into criminal statutes are those that are seen as protecting people from significant harm and those whose supporters have enough power to pressure the state to enforce their ideas of right and wrong. Definitions of deviance are subjective, even when widely shared, but crimes are formally defined by explicit procedures of law.

What is or is not considered a crime varies, however. For centuries, blasphemy was a crime under English law. It is still punishable by death under Islamic law but is not a crime in the United States. Sexual relations between consenting adults of the same sex are illegal in many of the United States, but not in all other societies and times. A wife who commits adultery has been (and still is) punishable by death in some societies but not in the United States (Forer, 1994). Some illegal activities that used to be overlooked, such as dumping toxic wastes in unauthorized areas, now receive much more public attention. Entirely new crimes can spring up as society

changes. For example, the transformation of the U.S. economy from one based on manufacturing to one based on financial transactions, coupled with deregulation, created opportunities for new types of embezzlement. The entry of large numbers of women into the labor force, plus redefinitions of gender roles, made sexual harassment a crime. The general trend in modern societies has been to translate more and more norms into crimes and thus turn responsibility for social control over to the criminal justice system.

Types of Crime

The Federal Bureau of Investigation issues annual reports about two major categories of crime. The first (Type I crimes, or "Index Crimes") are crimes that cause serious harm to people or property: murder, rape, assault, burglary, theft, and arson. Type II crimes are less serious offenses: prostitution, drug abuse, illegal weapons possession, sex offenses, gambling, vandalism, and receiving stolen property.

Violent and Property (Type I) Crimes

A majority of Americans see crime as the biggest challenge facing this country (*Gallup Poll Monthly*, 1995). Many Americans believe we are in the midst of a tidal wave of **violent crime**—crimes like murder, assault, and rape that involve acts of physical violence against the victims. Yet official statistics collected by the Department of Justice and the FBI paint a different picture. Crime rates in the United States peaked in 1980, then began to level off and *decline* in the 1990s (see Figure 6.2). Why, then, are Americans so fearful?

Certainly, the news media contribute to public fears. TV docudramas, TV cop and crime shows, talk shows, and the news tend to overreport sensational crimes and *under*report "ordinary" crimes in which no one is hurt. Politicians are quick to jump on the crime bandwagon. Legislators vote for almost any bill that imposes tougher sentences, so as not to appear "soft on crime." But media hype and political grandstanding are only part of the explanation for the gap between public fears and official crime statistics.

First, one must distinguish between the number of crimes and the crime rate, usually measured as the number of crimes per 100,000 population. Crime rates

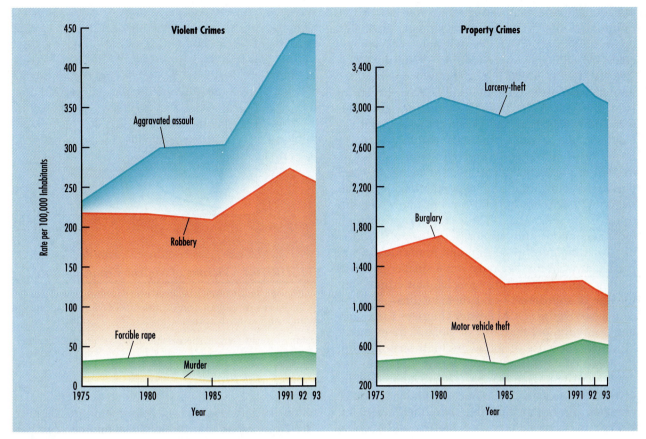

FIGURE 6.2 / Selected Crime Rates, 1975–1993

Source: *Uniform Crime Reports for the United States,* 1993, Federal Bureau of Investigation, (1995) Washington, D.C., p. 58, Table 1.

alert us to changes in the social patterns of crime. However, the public experiences crime not as a rate but as accumulating tragedies (Walinsky, 1995). In 1993, for example, the *rate* of violent crime in the Northeast declined by 8 percent. That means a precinct that suffered 100 murders in 1992 experienced "only" ninety-two murders in 1993. Statistically this may be good news, but to the public this means that ninety-two additional people were killed. And each murder claims not just one but many victims: family members, friends, neighbors, co-workers, and schoolmates whose shock, grief, anger, and fear linger long after a "case is closed" (if it is ever closed).

Second, FBI statistics are based on crimes *known* to the police. The National Crime Victimization Survey questions a representative sample of households about their own experience of crime during the preceding year. Its poll indicates that about half of all crimes are not reported to the police, either because the victims fear revenge or because they do not believe the criminal justice system will apprehend and punish the perpetrator. Other polls indicate the number of unreported crimes may be even greater.

Third, random violence—an unexpected attack by a nameless, faceless stranger—has increased (U.S. Department of Justice, 1994a). In the past, over half of murder victims knew their killer; beginning in 1990, this pattern reversed. Most homicides today are not crimes of passion, the result of jealously or simmering feuds between family members or neighbors. The FBI estimates that 53 percent of all murders now are "stranger murders": the murderer is neither related to nor acquainted with the victim. Moreover, police make arrests in fewer than three out of five murder cases. A man who kills a stranger during an urban holdup stands an even greater—80 percent— chance of getting away with murder (Walinsky, 1995).

Who are the killers? In 1993, two out of three known murderers were male (U.S. Department of Justice, 1994a). A third were between the ages of fifteen and twenty-four, and 10 percent were under age eighteen. Like athletes, criminals tend to peak early. In the 1960s and 1970s, crime rates were a direct reflection of population structure: The higher the proportion of young adults in the population, the higher the crime rate (Hirschi, 1993). In 1985, however, this trend reversed. Thus, while the proportion of teenagers and young adults in the population declined, crime rates in general and homicide rates in particular went up. Not only was a smaller group of young males committing more violent crimes, but the age of murderers—and their victims—also declined (see Figure 6.3). Males ages fourteen to twenty-four commit more than half of violent crimes today. Moreover, because of relatively high birth rates in the inner city, the number of poor teenagers in our population will soon climb—leading some sociologists to predict an "epidemic" of violent teenage crime beginning around the year 2000 (Walinsky, 1995).

Blacks are more likely to be the perpetrators—and the victims—of violent crime than any other group

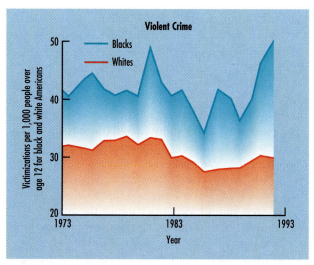

FIGURE 6.4 / *Victims of Violent Crime, by Race*

Although in absolute numbers more whites than blacks are victims of violent crimes, the *rate* of victimization is much higher for blacks.

Source: Anna J. Bray, "Who are the Victims of Crime?" *Investor's Business Daily* (January 12, 1994): 1, based on Bureau of Justice Statistics.

in our society (Figure 6.4). Nationwide, 26,239 murders were reported in 1993. Of this number, 29.2 percent of murderers were white and Hispanic, 39.5 percent were black, and 29.8 percent were of unknown race. Because blacks represent only about 12 percent of the population, the murder rate for blacks (44.7 per 100,000 population) was much higher than for whites and Hispanics (5.2 per 100,000 population).

Who are the victims? More than seven in ten murder victims in 1993 were male, almost half (48 percent) of whom were between the ages of eighteen and thirty-four. Fifty-one of every 100 murder victims were black, and forty-six were white. Most murders are committed by someone who is the same race and about the same age as the victim. However, the fact that murderers and victims come from the same social categories does not mean they are similar in other ways. Often the victims are innocent bystanders trapped by their race or poverty in high-crime neighborhoods, and frequently children.

Particularly alarming are the statistics on young black male victims. Although black males ages sixteen to twenty-four made up only 1 percent of the population age twelve and over in 1992, they experienced 5 percent of all violent crimes (U.S. Department of Justice, 1994a). At highest risk were black men

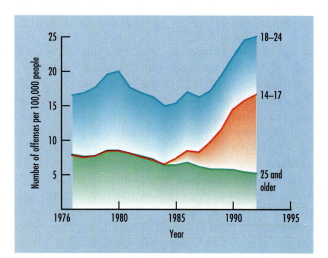

FIGURE 6.3 / *Murder by Age*

From the mid-1980s into the 1990s, the murder rates for teenagers and young adults increased sharply.

Source: *Newsweek*, August 15, 1994, p. 23.

ages sixteen to nineteen: Their rate of violent victimization was twice that of white males and three times that of white females the same ages. In two out of three violent crimes against black males, the assailant was armed, compared to less than one out of two for crimes against white males. The murder rate for black males ages twelve to twenty-four is 114.9 per 100,000, compared to 11.7 for white males the same age. The murder rate for black males age twenty-five and older is eight times that for the general population. At current rates, one in twenty black men will die from homicide.

The high rate of violent crime in the inner city is the result of a number of converging factors: large numbers of children born to single mothers, often teenagers themselves, and raised by the mother alone or by other relatives; high rates of unemployment; high levels of poverty, even among those who work (usually at unstable, low-wage jobs); constant exposure to violence on TV, on the streets, and even in schools; the easy availability of both guns and drugs; and general social disorganization. In predominantly black urban neighborhoods, police and emergency medical services tend to be slow to respond; community crime prevention activities (such as neighborhood watches) are rare; and bystanders are reluctant to intervene. As a result, arguments are more likely to lead to violence and perhaps murder (Peterson and Krivo, 1993).

Although violent crimes haunt the public, they are relatively rare, accounting for only a little over 10 percent of Type I (or "serious") crimes. People are much more likely to be the victims of property crimes such as burglary or theft (see Figure 6.2). Again, crime is not distributed evenly among the population. It affects the poor more than the rich: The victimization rate for households with family incomes of $10,000 or less is 30 percent higher than that for households with family incomes of $30,000 or more (Bray, 1994). Black Americans are three times more likely than whites to be robbed, are twice as likely to have a car stolen, and have a 50 percent higher rate of burglary.

Crimes without Victims

We think of crime as having an identifiable victim who suffers at the hands of another person. Some crimes, however, do not seem to have victims. **Victimless crimes** include prostitution, illegal sexual acts among consenting adults, illicit drug use, and

TABLE 6.2

Arrests for Crimes without Victims, 1993

Prostitution and commercialized vice	83,346
Drug abuse violations (all)	884,771
Illegal gambling	14,121
Drunkenness	558,833
Curfew, loitering (juvenile)	73,502
Runaways (juvenile)	136,785

Source: Federal Bureau of Investigation (1995), Uniform Crime Reports For the United States, 1993, p. 221. Washington, D.C.

gambling (see Table 6.2). In this type of crime, there is usually no complainant—that is, no one who feels he or she has been harmed. These acts are nevertheless designated as criminal because the community as a whole, or powerful groups within it, regard them as morally repugnant.

Supporters of criminalization argue that victimless crimes really do have victims. Compulsive gamblers rob their families of needed income; drunk drivers kill innocent motorists; prostitutes spread AIDS and other sexually transmitted diseases; drug users may resort to other crimes to support their habits. According to this view, society should control these kinds of behaviors because they *do* have harmful effects.

Opponents answer that the government should not try to legislate morality. Why should someone have the right to tell consenting adults what they can and cannot do if they are not hurting or bothering anyone else? From a more pragmatic standpoint, what is gained by denying large segments of the population goods and services they want? Such laws are not only difficult to enforce; they also create black markets and opportunities for organized crime.

Organized Crime

Organized crime is a self-perpetuating conspiracy that operates for profit or power and that seeks to obtain immunity from the law through fear and corruption (Abadinsky, 1981). Organized crime differs from other businesses in its heavy involvement in illegal activities and its almost routine use of bribery and violence. It specializes in providing illegal goods and services—selling illegal drugs, fencing stolen or illegal items (such as illegal handguns and stolen credit cards), and loan sharking (lending money at interest rates above the legal limit). Organized crime also provides legal goods and services by illegal means. In many U.S. cities, for instance, crime syndicates are able to monopolize garbage collection, vending machines, and taxi and limousine services by bribing public officials and threatening violence against potential competitors. In addition, they use legitimate companies to "launder" money earned through their illegal activities.

Crime syndicates often develop among immigrants who are not familiar enough with the mainstream culture to participate in its economy and who are suspicious of the police and other authorities who do not speak their language. As a result, organized crime has followed the pattern of "ethnic succession." The Irish crime syndicates in nineteenth-century America were followed by those of European Jews, and then, in the 1920s, by Italian crime families that gained power during Prohibition. When alcohol was legalized again in the 1930s, the Italian syndicates had the capital, the experience, the personnel, and the overseas contacts to move into the heroin trade. Italians remain prominent in American organized crime, but the ethnic picture has become more complex. One factor is the source of drugs, like heroin. In the 1960s, most heroin came from opium grown in Turkey,

processed in Marseilles, France, or Corsica, and then sold in the United States. In the 1970s, groups with contacts in other opium-producing countries—Mexico, Colombia, Pakistan, Iran, and countries of Southeast Asia—began to move in. Today's crime syndicates have been described as "a United Nations of drug smugglers" (Kerr, 1987, p. 1). (The Global Issues/Local Consequences box describes the international drug trade in more detail.)

Organized crime is not confined to the United States (Geyer, 1995). In Russia, once the center of a police state, mobsters and racketeers operate in the open; the Mafia is reasserting its power in Italy; in Liberia, weakened by 5 years of civil war, gangs of young men, ghoulishly dressed in women's dresses and wigs, roam the countryside; and in India, Asaam and other states are run by convicted criminals and killers, and journalists routinely write about "the criminalization of politics." In the United States gangs have "gone into business," primarily drugs, and increasingly resemble crime syndicates.

White-Collar and Corporate Crimes

One man robs a gas station of $250 and is sent to prison for six months; another makes $2.5 million

Busting the Fulton Fish Market. New York City police raided the city's major wholesaler of fresh fish, long controlled by the Mafia.

The International Drug Trade

A young black man in Washington, D.C., works at a trade in which his chances of being killed are a hundred times greater than in other occupations. Of course, the income from this work is several times more than he could otherwise earn (*The Economist,* July 14, 1990). In the mountains of Thailand, a Hmong woman tends a field of poppies that will bear crops for ten or twelve years, four or five times longer than rice, providing additional income for her family. In Medellín, Colombia, a self-made billionaire diversifies his investments to include vast real estate holdings and cattle ranches (Lee, 1989).

These three people, from very different cultural backgrounds, are all part of what is probably the largest organized criminal activity in the world today: the international drug trade. Drug trafficking, in turn, is linked to serious social problems: an increase in the homeless, babies born addicted to cocaine, corruption of government officials, both in the United States and abroad. The drug trade also helps to perpetuate armed gangs that use violence. In addition, drug trafficking lures otherwise "respectable" people into criminal activities that offer huge payoffs. Bankers may get involved in money-laundering schemes; judges may accept bribes to throw out cases or impose lenient sentences; police, from the cop on the beat to station chiefs and even commissioners, may accept payoffs.

These are local consequences of a *global* illegal industry fueled by a constant and growing demand for drugs in the wealthy industrialized countries. Americans are major contributors to this process. Not only are an estimated 6 million Americans regular drug users (*The Economist,* July 21, 1990), but Americans also pay the most money for drugs and reap the greatest profits. Coca leaves (from which cocaine is made) cost $2.10 per kilogram in the Andes highlands; at street level in the United States the price per kilo of processed cocaine is $90,000. Most of that money stays in the hands of Americans.

There is a ready supply of drugs to meet the constant and growing demand. In the less developed countries of the world, selling coca leaves can mean the difference between a near-starvation level subsistence and a decent standard of living. Yet of the roughly $2 billion a year that returns to the cocaine-producing countries in Latin America, very little finds its way to the poor. It flows mainly to the drug lords, who often block economic programs that would give peasants a chance to earn money outside the drug trade.

Drug lords also manipulate the press, the police, and the courts through bribes and terrorism. Drug money often funds political campaigns, many times for the traffickers themselves. The drug lords are frequently allied with right-wing military groups eager to maintain the existing social order against left-wing guerrillas who seek to change it. In its long fight against communism in the Western Hemisphere, the United States has occasionally given military and financial support to these right-wing groups, despite their known drug connections. Thus, America's foreign policies at times thwart American efforts to combat drugs at home.

Some observers think the American government's efforts to reduce the drug trade should focus on the home front, not abroad (Scott and Marshall, 1991). Simply cracking down on dealers, however, is not enough, because there are always others willing to take their places. Long-term solutions probably lie in drug-treatment programs, drug education programs, and assistance to disadvantaged communities, so that a teenager in the inner city will not see a chance to make more money in the drug trade than in other lines of work. In short, although the drug trade is a global problem, the solution may lie in dealing with the consequences it has in our everyday lives.

through illegal stock trading and is required only to return the money (plus "interest" in the form of fines). Terrorists who plant a bomb in a diplomat's car are charged with conspiracy and criminal homicide. Ford Motor Company sold millions of Pintos with rear-mounted gas tanks that the company knew might explode if the car was hit from behind. For the 500 people who were burned to death, Ford had to pay millions in damages, but it was not found guilty of criminal charges. Clearly, our society's responses to white-collar and corporate crime are quite different from its treatment of "common criminals."

The term **white-collar crime** was first used by the sociologist Edwin Sutherland to refer to "a crime committed by a person of respectability and high status in the course of his occupation" (Sutherland, 1949, p. 9). Embezzling, padding expense accounts, stealing from an employer, and evading personal income taxes all fall into this category. So does the misuse of public funds by government officials (accepting bribes, padding payrolls, and the like). One difference between white-collar crime and "common" crime is that white-collar crime seldom involves force or violence. White-collar crime, however, is more costly in dollars and cents. For example, bank embezzlers on average steal nearly 8 times as much as bank robbers (Clinard and Yeager, 1980). Yet only half of bank embezzlers go to prison, compared to 90 percent of bank robbers (*Sourcebook of Criminal Justice Statistics*, 1994). When politicians talk about the need for more law and order, they usually mean more money for police to fight street crimes not for federal investigators to fight white-collar crimes.

In contrast to white-collar crimes, which are committed for personal gain, **corporate crimes** are committed on behalf of a formal organization. Their primary goal is to boost company profits (or avoid losses). Unlike other criminals corporations are not persons and cannot be jailed. Indeed, corporate crimes are often handled outside the court system by government regulatory agencies (the Securities and Exchange Commission, the Federal Trade Commission, the Environmental Protection Agency, and so forth). In most cases, sanctions take the form of fines that are small in relation to earnings. A standard $50,000 fine for price fixing does not mean much to a corporation that has revenues in excess of $1 billion a year (Ermann and Lundman, 1992). The complex structure of corporations may also encourage corporate crimes by shielding those involved in them. Usually, no one person in a large corporation has authority over a particular action; responsibility tends to be diffuse. This allows managers to go along with policies they might not otherwise approve of. At the same time, managers can establish norms and sanctions that make it hard for whistle-blowers to report corporate crime. As a result, corporate crime is quite widespread.

Controlling Crime

In the first half of 1995, murder, robbery, and burglary rates in New York City dropped to their lowest level in a quarter of a century (Krauss, 1995). The 648 murders, for example, were 312 less than during the first half of 1994. Reported robberies dropped 22 percent, burglaries 18 percent, and motor vehicle thefts 25 percent. New Yorkers were safer in 1995 than in 1970.

What accounts for the "miracle" of 1995? Not surprisingly, New York City Police Commissioner William J. Bratton credits the police. In January 1995, Bratton not only deployed more police on the street but also ordered officers to make more arrests for minor offenses, such as urinating in public or unlicensed street vending. These minor arrests allowed police to frisk offenders for illegal guns or drugs, to check records for outstanding warrants, and to pump offenders for information about the drug and gun trade while they were under arrest. In addition, Bratton directed captains of local police precincts to keep daily records of crimes on a neighborhood map, as a general might do in a war zone, and plan their attack on crime accordingly.

Bratton, of course, has a vested interest in crediting police for the drop in crimes in New York, but few criminologists think there is a single, easy explanation. Some cite demographics: Not only did the number of "crime-prone" sixteen- to twenty-five-year-olds in New York decline, but a higher percentage of young people were recent immigrants with strong family ties and a desire to avoid brushes with the law. Some cite drugs: Evidence suggests that heroin (a depressant or tranquilizer) has begun to replace crack (a stimulant) in New York City as the drug of choice. The purity of heroin for sale on the streets is higher, and the price lower, than in the past, making it easier to get high for longer periods on less money. In addition, heroin acts to slow down the system, resulting in less violent acts of crime. Others point to guns: No one knows how many guns are on the streets of New York, but the number may be declining. Of people arrested for the minor offense of jumping subway turnstiles without paying the fare, the number who were armed declined significantly between 1994 and 1995.

Still others credit the courts and prisons. As of July 1995, 55,000 felons (about half from New York City) were behind bars, double the number locked up a decade earlier. Another 3,000 individuals thought to be involved in the drug trade had been murdered on the streets. Only additional research will explain the mystery in New York. Here, we will examine the scientific evidence for and against various anticrime strategies, beginning with the debate about gun control (see the Sociology and Public Debates box).

Police as Agents of Control

Police are the front line of the criminal justice system. Their job is, first, to protect innocent people and prevent crimes from taking place, and second, when a crime has been committed, to collect evidence, to arrest and book suspects, and to provide evidence in criminal trials.

In the 1960s, there were an average of 3.3 police officers for every violent crime committed (Walinsky, 1995). Today that ratio is reversed: 3.47 violent crimes for every police officer. This means that today's police officers must deal with eleven times as many violent crimes as their 1960s predecessors. The 1994 crime bill included a provision to add 100,000 police officers nationally by the year 2000. Adam Walinsky (1995) calculates that to return to the ratio of the 1960s, we would have to hire about *five million* new police officers. Walinsky argues that more police would be worth the cost. Today's undermanned police forces spend most of their time arresting people for crimes that have already been committed, leaving little time for preventing crime by establishing law and order in public places.

Others suggest that the way police interact with the community is as important as the number of police on the street. Jerome Skolnick and David Bayley (1986) studied the police force in Santa Ana,
California, which began a series of reforms in the early 1970s to bring community and police together. These reforms included *civilianization* (using civilians from the community to help file reports); *community mobilization* (appointing block captains to serve as liaisons between the police and the community); and *substations* (combination police station/social service centers where residents can get information on how to handle personal and community problems). While the crime rate in Santa Ana did not fall dramatically (in part because more residents were willing to report crimes), neither did it rise as fast as in other cities. Today a number of police departments are using similar reforms. The trend is toward problem-oriented policing (targeting the causes of crime) in addition to the traditional incident-oriented policing (responding to criminal actions) (Siegel, 1990).

Some police departments have not been successful in mobilizing support for community policing among their ranks. And concerns over police brutality, especially against minority groups, are rising. This concern made headlines in March 1991, when an amateur photographer filmed Los Angeles patrol officers brutally beating motorist Rodney King, an African-American. The four officers tried for beating King were found innocent, a verdict that sparked riots in Los Angeles and demonstrations around the country (see Chapter 20). Many minority groups (especially

At the trial of Los Angeles police officers accused of beating Rodney King, a black man, this witness (right), the jury, and the rest of the country watched a videotape of the assault. After the overwhelmingly white jury voted to acquit, the black community of south central Los Angeles rioted in protest.

Gun Control: Will It Lower Murder Rates?

The United States is one of the most heavily armed nations in the world (McDowall and Lizotte, 1993). Half the households have at least one gun. All told, Americans own 65 to 70 million pistols, 125 to 130 million rifles and shotguns, and a million or more "assault" weapons (designed for military use). There are as many privately owned guns in the United States today as there are privately owned cars! Two-thirds of all murders and suicides are committed with firearms today; guns also account for about 1,500 accidental deaths each year (U.S. Department of Justice, 1994b).

THE DEBATE

Given these statistics, calls for gun control surface regularly—and are regularly met with strong opposition. Supporters of gun control emphasize the cost in human lives and maintain that effective firearm regulations would cause a dramatic decrease in deadly crimes. Their main argument is that most murderers do not set out with the intention to kill; rather, when disputes arise they use whatever weapon is handy. The more guns in circulation, the more likely arguments and robberies will lead to murder. Opponents of gun control maintain that the great majority of gun owners are responsible, law-abiding citizens; that criminals, not guns, commit murder; and that the right to bear arms is guaranteed in the Constitution.

ANALYSIS

The first problem any gun-control policy would confront is a structural one in the form of the number of guns already in private hands in our society. These weapons are distributed among both law-abiding citizens and criminal owners, although these lines may be crossed, as when a licensed gun owner shoots his or her spouse. Given such widespread distribution, controlling new sales would not solve the problem. Gun ownership is in part a legacy of America's frontier past, when people used guns to hunt and to defend isolated farms and cabins, but the structure of the American way of life has changed. Today we are an overwhelmingly urban society, in which old reasons for gun ownership no longer apply. Not surprisingly, the strongest support for unrestricted gun ownership comes from people who live in areas with structural conditions closer to those of the past (especially the rural West).

> "Is the legitimate happiness of 10 million gun owners worth the lives of 10,000 murder victims? One hundred murder victims? One murder victim?"

The gun-control debate is shaped by cultural understandings and values rooted in earlier structural conditions. The right to bear arms was enshrined in the Constitution as part of a clause dealing with the need for militias—in an era when there was no standing army and when there was no sheriff nearby. The values forged on the frontier lived on—including the strong individualism for which Americans are noted. Guns figure directly in American cultural self-images, especially through mythical images of the Wild West, known worldwide from cowboy movies. Today's gun-control debate is shaped not only by celluloid legends of the past, but also by current media images. Most people's ideas about guns, the dangers of contemporary life, the need for self-defense, and the possible risks of gun ownership are based on the way guns are presented on TV. News coverage of violence is one factor, but fictional TV probably has even more impact. Many of our TV shows (crime and police shows, mysteries and thrillers, even—indirectly—hospital stories) feature guns. But the picture is distorted. For example, on TV, people who shoot guns hit their targets more often—and shoot innocent bystanders or are shot by their own guns less often—than happens in real life.

In the past, when America's population was spread across "wide open spaces," private ownership of guns served obvious functions. Fewer people hunt today, and for most of these people hunting is a hobby, not a main source of food and income. Guns provided pro-

black males) report that police harassment and police brutality are common. The 1995 O. J. Simpson trial made this apparent when the prosecution's case was damaged by the revelation that Mark Fuhrman, a white police detective who helped investigate the case, made a habit of referring to blacks as "niggers"

and planting false evidence to help ensure convictions. At the same time, many minority residents complain that the police do little to protect their communities, as, for example, during the Los Angeles riots.

Defenders of police cite the dramatic increase in drug-related crime in the inner cities and the fact

SOCIOLOGY AND PUBLIC DEBATES

tection to people who herded cattle, panned for gold, or lived in cabins and trapped beaver; locks and alarms are more effective for people who work in offices and live in apartment buildings. Yet guns are still an integral part of our economy. Gun manufacturers and importers prosper in large part because of legitimate gun owners and collectors, hunters and marksmen, who trade with one another, sponsor conventions, subscribe to gun magazines, and the like. Of course, guns are also integrated into American criminal activities. For example, turf fights between gangs who wielded knives and bicycle chains have been replaced by shoot-outs with automatic weapons. This, in turn, means that people on the fringes of criminal activity (store owners, neighborhood residents, even police) have more incentive to use guns than they did in the past.

Owning or using a gun is clearly a social action. It is action because it is a choice, not an automatic behavior or condition of life. It is social because of the huge impact guns have on American society. In part because of our attachment to guns, the United States is the most murderous country in the industrial world, with a 1990 rate of 10.5 murders per 100,000 population (compared to 0.8 in the United Kingdom, 1.0 in Japan, and 1.2 in Germany) (Kurian, 1990). The gun-control debate focuses not just on individual use of guns but also on social actions the government takes in response to gun ownership. The general idea of registering guns and otherwise controlling access to guns—seen by some as just another government restriction—is much debated. Even more controversial are actions the government has taken when its agents believed that illegal gun sales or stockpiling were at issue, as in the shootings at Ruby Ridge and the attack on the Branch Davidians.

Finally, guns are tools of power. They are used by some—criminals and underworld kingpins—to exercise power over others against their will. They are used by others to give themselves a sense of security in the face of high crime rates. However, a significant part of the gun-control debate is about the appropriate *balance of power* between the government and citizens (citizens both as individuals and organized into groups). Should the government have a monopoly over all legitimate use of force or violence (in which case only police and federal agents would be authorized to use guns)? Should ordinary citizens be empowered to use guns in self-defense? Should they be allowed to form militias and other groups to protect their interests (even if their interests defy government regulations)?

David McDowall and Alan Lizotte (1993) suggest that the real debate is not over the effectiveness of gun-control laws but over the right of individuals to own guns versus the collective benefits of gun control. Sociology can tell us that effective gun control would reduce murders, but it cannot answer value questions. As McDowall and Lizotte ask, "Is the legitimate happiness of 10 million gun owners worth the lives of 10,000 murder victims? One hundred murder victims? One murder victim?" (1993, p. 320).

The Silent March. Trying to pressure Congress to enact tough gun-control laws, families displayed the shoes of thousands of innocent relatives who had been slain in the crossfire of shootouts.

that criminals are often better armed than the police. Police work has become extremely dangerous, and fear may lead some officers to act brutally or hastily. In response, some locales have added stress-reduction courses to police training programs and set up civilian complaint review boards, designed to help identify officers whose conduct is inappropriate or inflammatory. However, police forces remain tight-knit communities, and officers seldom inform against each other in misconduct cases.

In short, the benefits of increasing the number of police must not only be weighed against the cost in dollars but also be combined with an effort to reduce abuses of civilian rights.

The Courts

In 1993, just over half the cases of aggravated assault and rape and less than 25 percent of robberies and other crimes against property in the United States led to arrests (see Figure 6.5). Of those arrested, only about 40 percent served terms in jail or prison (U.S. Department of Justice, 1987). In effect, the criminal justice system is a funnel, with a great many reported crimes at one end, a relatively large number of arrests in the middle, and few convictions and still fewer imprisonments at the other end.

One reason that many felons are not prosecuted or convicted is that their victims refuse to testify against them, because either they have cooled off or they fear revenge. A second reason why many felons never go to prison is that their crimes are reduced to misdemeanors (less serious offenses) through **plea bargaining.** In this process the district attorney offers to reduce charges if the suspect will plead guilty and relinquish the right to a trial. Plea bargaining saves the state time, expense, and trouble, but it puts some serious offenders back on the streets quickly and may also pressure some innocent people to plead guilty.

At every stage of the criminal justice process, selective judgments come into play. And discrimination occurs, intentional or not. First, the police use their judgment in making arrests. Then public prosecutors use their judgment in offering plea bargains. After this, judges decide which people are a danger to the community and so should be denied bail and sent to prison if convicted.

Poor nonwhites are disproportionately likely to get funneled all the way through the criminal justice system. About a quarter of all African-American males between the ages of twenty and twenty-nine are in jail, on parole, or on probation (U.S. Department of Justice, 1995).

The Imprisoning Society

LOCK'EM UP AND THROW AWAY THE KEY declared the cover of the February 7, 1994, issue of *Time* magazine. This headline reflected the current national mood. The 1960s and 1970s had been a period of relative lenience toward criminals. Beginning in the 1980s, however, the pendulum began to swing the other way. The United States today has a higher rate of imprisonment than any other Western nation; we spend more on prisons than we do on education (Forer, 1994).

Mandatory-Minimum Sentences and "Three-Strikes" Laws

"Three strikes and you're out" is the philosophy behind a number of new state laws that impose stiff, mandatory sentences on repeat offenders. As

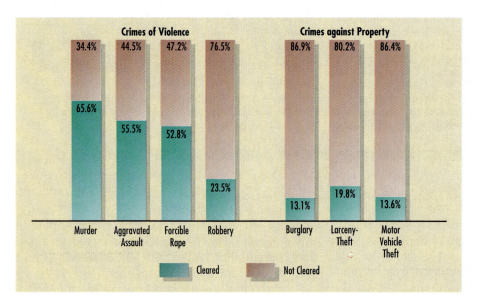

FIGURE 6.5 / Crimes Solved by Arrest, 1993

Source: Federal Bureau of Investigation (1995), *Uniform Crime Reports for the United States, 1993*, p. 208, Table 25. Washington, D. C.

of March 1995, thirteen states had adopted such laws and seven more had similar bills pending (Butterfield, 1995). Under the California law, one of the first, persons with a prior conviction for serious or violent felony receive twice the usual sentence when convicted for a second felony, and twenty-five years to life when convicted for a third felony. The goals of three-strikes laws are, first, to remove "career criminals" from the population and second, to prevent judges and juries from being too lenient.

Three-strikes laws are not a new idea (Kaminer, 1994). *Federal* mandatory minimum sentences date back to 1790 (see Table 6.3); almost every year, Congress adds new offenses to this list. In addition, the U.S. Sentencing Commission issues strict sentencing guidelines. Unlike those in most state courts, federal judges are not permitted to consider such mitigating factors as the defendant's family situation, community ties, employment history, or mental or emotional state.

Mandatory-minimum statutes get mixed reviews. In an analysis of the California law, the RAND corporation estimated that three strikes would reduce serious felonies by 22 to 34 percent, but at a high cost: an extra $4.5 to $6.5 billion a year (including the costs of new prisons and longer internment) (Greenwood et al., 1994). Unintended consequences may also have costs (Butterfield, 1995; Kaminer, 1994). For example, faced with life imprisonment, a criminal is more likely to attempt to shoot his or her way out of a confrontation with the police than to surrender. For the same reason, alleged second- and third-strike offenders refuse plea bargains and demand trials, resulting in a backlog of criminal cases.

Most mandatory-minimum sentences and three-strikes laws cast a wide net: Offenses that qualify as a third strike range from betting in an office pool, petty theft, and promoting prostitution to rape and homicide. No allowance is made for the circumstances under which the crime was committed, the motive, or the defendant's character (Kaminer, 1994). Should a woman who shoots a husband who has repeatedly beat her and her children receive the same punishment as a woman who shoots her husband for money? Mandatory-minimum sentences often violate the principle "Let the punishment fit the crime." As often as not, prosecutors refuse to prosecute and juries refuse to convict when they feel this principle is being violated.

Finally, mandatory-minimum sentences transfer judicial discretion from judges to prosecutors: in de-

TABLE 6.3

Federal Mandatory-Minimum Sentences
Congressional Enactment of Mandatory-Minimum Sentences Comprises a Brief Social History of Crime

1790
Life sentence for piracy; ten years for causing a ship to run aground with false lights

1888
Six months for bribery of a harbor master in Baltimore or New York

1913
Imprisonment or fine for commodities price-fixing

1934
Ten years for homicide or kidnapping committed during a bank robbery or larceny

1965
Life sentence for an attempt to murder the president or a member of the executive staff

1980s
Varying sentences for drug-related crimes (including selling drugs near a school; any involvement in a drug conspiracy; and possession of more than 5 grams of cocaine)

Source: Wendy Kaminer, "Federal Offense: Politics of Crime Control," The Atlantic Monthly, 273, no. 6 (June 1994): 102ff.

ciding how defendants will be charged, prosecutors in effect *pre*-decide how they will be sentenced. The Federal Judicial Center (Kaminer, 1994) found that only half of offenders who were potentially eligible for mandatory-minimum prison terms received them. Moreover, 68 percent of blacks were given the minimum sentence or more, compared to 57 percent of Hispanics and 54 percent of whites found guilty of equally severe crimes.

Overcrowded Prisons

Even before three-strikes laws, rates of imprisonment were climbing steadily (Figure 6.6). Between 1980 and 1992, the nation's inmate population grew at an average rate of 900 new prisoners each week, topping 1 million in the summer of 1994 (U.S. Department of Justice, 1995). During this period the percentage of minorities in the inmate population also increased. The rate of incarceration is 4,094 per

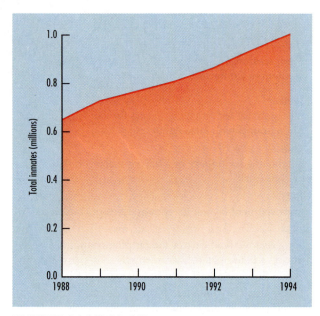

FIGURE 6.6 / Behind Bars

The number of people confined to prisons and jails climbed during the late 1980s and early 1990s, even though crime rates leveled off and dropped somewhat.

Source: Justice Department, in *The New York Times,* October 6, 1994, p. E3.

crimes as well as persuading convicted criminals not to commit additional crimes. There is little evidence that sending more criminals to prison and imposing longer sentences act as deterrents. In Pennsylvania, for example, reported crimes increased by 6 percent between 1985 and 1990, even though the prison population increased by 171 percent. Recidivism rates suggest that few prisoners are reformed: More than 68 percent of female and 80 percent of male state prisoners have been in prison before (Forer, 1994). "Incapacitation" means making it impossible for a person to commit other crimes. But locking up all of the 4 million convicted criminals in our society would be impossible. Moreover, there is no clear way to determine which criminals are dangerous. Most violent crimes are committed not by repeat violent offenders

100,000 adult black males in the population, compared to 502 per 100,000 adult white males. The number of female inmates increased by 227 percent. Even so, women accounted for less than 6 percent of sentenced prisoners in 1992. Drugs explain much of the growth in the prison population. In 1992, 22 percent of state prisoners and 60 percent of federal prisoners were drug offenders.

Prison systems have not been able to keep pace with the flood of inmates. By the 1980s, San Quentin, designed to hold 2,700 prisoners, had 3,900 inmates and growing security problems (Logan, 1985). The problem has gotten worse. In forty-one states the entire state prison system or one or more major institutions are under court order to reduce overcrowding or improve basic services. Estimates are that federal, state, and local governments will spend $30 billion dollars on corrections in 1995 (up from $4 billion in 1975) just to keep up with the growing number of inmates (Holmes, 1994).

Does imprisonment deter crime? incapacitate offenders? rehabilitate offenders? punish offenders as they deserve? (Forer, 1994). *Deterrence* means discouraging potential offenders from committing

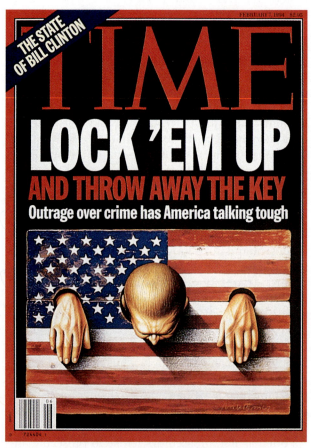

Tough mandatory prison sentences may be politically popular in some communities, but the laws have also had some unintended consequences. Faced with life in prison, for example, a criminal is more likely to shoot at police officers rather than surrender to them.

but by people with long histories of (nonviolent) crimes against property (Kaminer, 1994).

The question of whether imprisonment punishes offenders as they deserve is an ethical or moral problem, not a sociological one. But research does show that for young, first-time offenders, in particular, prison can be a brutalizing experience involving socialization to a subculture in which the only way to avoid becoming a victim is to victimize others. Prisons also may be schools for crime, in which "amateurs" learn new techniques and rationales for committing crimes from "professionals."

The Death Penalty

The United States is the only Western democracy that still imposes the death penalty. As of 1994, thirty-seven states and the federal government had statutes authorizing capital punishment (Costanzo and White, 1994). New York State imposed the death penalty in 1995.

Executions, however, are relatively rare. Each year there are about 22,000 homicides in the United States, 18,000 arrests, 300 death sentences, and fifty or sixty executions (usually eight years or more after the crime was committed) (Lewin, 1995). Moreover, the general trend has been to limit the number and types of crimes punishable by death (only first-degree murder under "special circumstances" in most states) and to make executions more "humane" (using painless lethal injections rather than the electric chair, for example) (Costanzo and White, 1994).

Public support for the death penalty is at an all-time high (Figure 6.7). No matter how the question is worded, about 70 percent of Americans say they favor the death penalty, and about 30 percent say they oppose it (Ellsworth and Gross, 1994). Neither group is swayed by practical considerations (Ellsworth and Gross, 1994). Supporters say they still favor the death penalty, even though there is no strong evidence that the death penalty acts as a deterrent. Likewise, opponents say they would not change their minds if new evidence showed that the death penalty was an effective deterrent and was cost-efficient (Sandys and McGarrell, 1995).

Why are death penalty statutes enacted but rarely used? Why does the majority of the public support the death penalty in principle but less often in specific cases? Why these seeming contradictions? Executions serve a symbolic and ceremonial function in our society; they are a public statement of our moral rejection of crime and murder (Gross, 1989). But mass killings by the state would invite outrage,

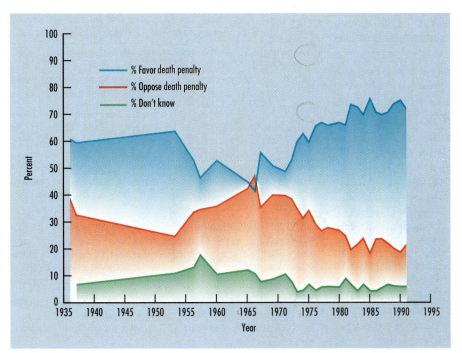

FIGURE 6.7 / *Changing Attitudes toward Capital Punishment*

Support for the death penalty declined in the 1960s, then climbed in the 1980s and 1990s. However, support for the principle of capital punishment does not necessarily translate into calls for the actual use of capital punishment.

Source: Phoebe C. Ellsworth and Samuel R. Gross, "Hardening of the Attitudes: Americans' Views of the Death Penalty," *Journal of Social Issues* 50, no. 2 (1994): 20.

at home and abroad, invoking comparisons to Hitler and Stalin. Occasional executions allow us to focus on one murderer and whatever he or she did to deserve death, and to collectively experience revenge.

Even in this era of budget cutting and belt tightening, the American public seems eager to punish offenders, at whatever cost. The reason is not simply vengeance. As Émile Durkheim (1893/1985) showed, punishment itself is satisfying. It serves a social function for law-abiding citizens. Punishing deviants and criminals reaffirms social solidarity and reinforces shared values. We punish, sociologists argue, not just to "correct" criminals but also to remind ourselves of the importance of the moral values of our community.

SUMMARY

1. Deviance is behavior that members of a group or society see as violating their norms. Some deviant acts elicit strong disapproval, while other, minor acts of deviance are considered lapses in an otherwise respectable lifestyle.

2. Deviance is a matter of social definition. What is or is not considered deviant varies from society to society, group to group, situation to situation, and it changes over time.

3. Whether people are labeled as deviant depends not only on what they do but on who they are. Deviant labels are most often applied to people and actions that threaten the vested interests of social elites.

4. Although deviance disrupts social systems, it also serves the positive functions of reminding people of the boundaries of respectability and enhancing social solidarity. In these ways, deviance may reaffirm existing norms; but it may also serve as a catalyst for change.

5. Social control refers to a group's or society's efforts to regulate behavior. Ideally people internalize norms; but society also uses sanctions (externally imposed constraints). Sanctions may be informal (such as gossip) or formal (jail sentences).

6. Early attempts to show that deviance was an expression of innate biological characteristics foundered. Today scientists place more emphasis on socialization, social learning, and social structure, summarized in the theory of differential association. One of the first truly sociological theories of deviance was Merton's theory of structural strain, the conflict between culturally induced desires and the structure of opportunity.

7. Virtually everyone commits deviant acts on occasion, but few embark on deviant careers. Primary deviance consists of initial violations of norms; secondary deviance is the long-term acceptance of the role of deviant. Labeling theory shows that social sanctions may backfire, turning primary into secondary deviance. Primary deviance may be explained in terms of faulty socialization leading to inadequate self-control.

8. A crime is a norm that has been entered into the law and is backed by the power and authority of the state. Not all deviant acts are crimes (and not all crimes are considered seriously deviant). The trend in modern societies has been toward codifying norms into law.

9. Polls show that Americans believe that violent and property crimes are rising, yet official statistics show the opposite. The media's emphasis on sensational crimes, the public's experience of crime, the high number of unreported crimes, and the increase in "stranger crimes" have all contributed to public fears. Most violent and property crimes are committed by young males, a high proportion of whom are black urban teenagers and young adults who prey on other African-Americans. The age at which young people commit crimes is declining, while the violence of their crimes is increasing.

10. So-called victimless crimes (prostitution, illicit drug use) raise questions about legislating morality. Organized crime provides illegal goods and services (such as drugs or prostitutes) or legal goods and services by illegal means, as well as a niche for immigrant groups not familiar with the culture. Although white-collar and corporate crimes probably cost society more than street crime, they rarely invoke stiff penalties, prison sentences, or deviant labels.

11. Widely recommended strategies for controlling crime include stiffer gun controls, putting more police on the street and improving police–community relations, and pressuring the courts to be tougher on criminals.

12. The trend in the United States has been to sentence more criminals to prison for longer periods. Three-strikes laws and other mandatory-minimum sentences may reduce crime, but they also have unintended consequences (such as clogging the courts). There is no strong evidence that imprisonment acts as a deterrent, reduces the number of potentially violent criminals in the population, or reforms convicts.

13. Polls show that support for the death penalty is at an all-time high in the United States. Closer examination indicates that while many support the death penalty in principle, most believe that mitigating circumstances should be taken into account. Despite new laws, executions are rare.

14. Whether or not imprisonment and the death penalty are effective in controlling crime, they function symbolically to reaffirm moral values.

REVIEW QUESTIONS

1. In what sense is deviance a matter of social definition?

2. How do labeling theorists explain deviance?

3. Summarize the theories explaining four major factors that may determine why some people become deviant while others do not: nature, social learning (including differential association), structural strain, and inadequate social control.

4. Explain how crime and deviance are both similar to and different from each other.

5. Briefly describe the types of crimes noted in the chapter.

CRITICAL THINKING QUESTIONS

1. You have been asked by the local city council to develop a plan for addressing deviance in the community. Develop a program of social control that incorporates aspects of the basic explanations of deviance. Indicate specifically which aspects of your plan reflect which explanation.

2. We saw that gang membership is considered normal in many communities where gangs flourish but is considered deviant in the rest of American society. What are some activities in which you engage that might be thought deviant by someone from another class, subculture, or country?

3. The chapter outlines several types of crime: violent crime, crime without victims, organized crime, and white-collar and corporate crime. Rank-order these from most to least serious and explain your ranking.

4. Discuss what changes you would make to the criminal justice funnel and why.

5. Prisons in America are too crowded. Given what you have learned in this chapter, suggest some other approaches to address the crime problem.

GLOSSARY

Conformity In Robert Merton's theory of structural strain, seeking culturally approved goals by culturally approved means.

Corporate crimes Illegal activities committed on behalf of a formal organization.

Crime A violation of a norm that has been entered into the law and is backed by the power and authority of the state.

Deviance Behavior that the members of a social group define as violating their norms.

Deviant career The gradual integration into a deviant lifestyle combined with an almost exclusive association with a deviant subculture.

Differential association The process by which people are socialized into the patterns of behavior that prevail in the group with which they associate the most. If these patterns of behavior are deviant, deviance is culturally transmitted.

Formal sanctions Official pressure to conform to social norms and values enforced by organizations such as police departments, courts, and prisons.

Informal sanctions Unofficial pressures to conform, including disapproval, ridicule, and ostracism on the one hand (negative sanctions) and approval and praise on the other (positive sanctions).

Innovation In Robert Merton's theory of structural strain, pursuing culturally approved goals by deviant means.

Internalization The process by which cultural standards become part of a person's personality structure.

Labeling theory The theory that people come to acquire a deviant social identity and pursue a deviant lifestyle because others have labeled them deviant and cut them off from the social mainstream.

Organized crime A self-perpetuating conspiracy that operates for profit and power and that seeks immunity from the law through fear or corruption. Organized crime specializes in providing illegal goods and services.

Plea bargaining The process in which a district attorney offers to reduce charges if a suspect will plead guilty and relinquish the right to a trial.

Primary deviance The initial violation of a social norm, about which no inferences are made regarding the motives or character of the person who committed the act.

Rebellion In Robert Merton's theory of structural strain, creating new goals and new means for pursuing them.

Retreatism In Robert Merton's theory of structural strain, abandoning culturally prescribed goals and means.

Ritualism In Robert Merton's theory of structural strain, adhering rigidly to norms while losing sight of underlying goals.

Sanctions Rewards for conforming to a social norm or penalties for violating it.

Secondary deviance A pattern by which people come to define themselves as deviants and undertake a deviant lifestyle as a reaction to their being labeled deviant by others.

Social control Society's efforts to regulate itself; the mechanisms by which social norms are upheld and by which their actual or potential violation is restrained.

Structural strain The discrepancy between societal expectations/cultural goals and the means available for achieving them.

Victimless crimes Crimes such as gambling and prostitution that often appear to lack victims (people who feel they have been harmed by them).

Violent crimes Crimes such as murder, assault, and rape that involve acts of physical violence against the victim.

White-collar crime Crimes committed by people in high status occupations in the course of their work.

PART 3

Difference
and Inequality

CHAPTER 7

Class and Stratification

Approached by water, downtown Manhattan appears as a mirage. Glittering towers of concrete, steel, and glass seem to rise directly from the water. The neo-Gothic spires of the Woolworth Building, the tallest skyscraper in the world when built in 1913, point to the mammoth boxes of the World Trade Center, built during the global expansion of commerce in the 1960s. Hidden among these architectural wonders is Wall Street, the financial heart of the United States, and, some would say, the world.

A 15- or 20-minute walk north lies Soho. Once a prosperous manufacturing district of factories and warehouses with elegant cast-iron fronts, Soho was all but abandoned when it was discovered in the 1950s and 1960s by artists who valued its spacious lofts and low rents. In the 1970s, major art galleries began opening branches downtown, followed by elegant shops and trendy restaurants. Soho became one of the most fashionable and expensive places to live, eat, and shop in Manhattan (forcing many artists to move out). Thus a center of production became a center of consumption, part of an international marketplace where elite global tastes were created.

Uptown, beyond the northern border of Central Park, lies another social world: Harlem. A sea of aging housing projects, run-down tenements (some condemned but still occupied), boarded-up and burnt-out buildings, and vacant lots, Harlem is home to many of the city's poor: largely Hispanics and African-Americans. Harlem's main streets are lined with small shops and storefront churches; numbers parlors and private (unlicensed) clubs; small *bodegas* selling soda, chips, cigarettes, canned food, and wilted vegetables; and liquor stores where the merchandise and cashiers sit behind bulletproof glass. But Harlem's mainstay is an underground economy of street peddlers offering new (and used) clothing, pirated tapes, inexpensive African statues and religious icons, incense, and fried food. Drugs are sold on street corners and smoked or injected in hallways and abandoned buildings. Malt liquor and pints of vodka or rum are drunk straight from the bottle, wrapped in brown paper bags; layaway plans take the place of credit cards; check-cashing stores serve as "banks"; and "exercise" means manual labor.

Between downtown (Wall Street and Soho) and uptown (Harlem) are Manhattan's main residential districts. The Upper East Side, known for the elegant prewar apartment buildings of Fifth and Park Avenues, the antique shops and designer boutiques of Madison Avenue, and "museum mile," is predominantly wealthy and WASP (white Anglo-Saxon Protestant). The Upper West Side, which begins with the Lincoln Center for the Performing Arts and stretches to Columbia University, prides itself on diversity. Tree-lined streets with townhouses called brownstones (most now converted to apartments and co-ops) mix with new high-rise buildings and old, low-rent "walk-ups" (five-story tenements). Ethnic restaurants, sidewalk cafés, and specialty stores have been joined by chain stores and other retailers catering to middle-class professionals, intellectuals, and performing artists.

The mostly white men and women who work on Wall Street, dine in Soho, and perhaps live on the Upper East Side studiously avoid Harlem, rarely venturing north of 96th Street (the last street with "good housing" on the east side). West-siders might work in Harlem, as doctors or social workers, but leave be-

Neighborhoods and power. In New York City, as in cities everywhere, the centers of power and money are separated from poorer neighborhoods. Here, lunchtime crowds enjoy the gleaming surroundings of the World Financial Center in downtown New York. Uptown, in Spanish Harlem, cheaper real estate and run-down buildings are the norm.

fore dark and head downtown for the theater or the ballet. Though a few buildings have been fixed up for middle-class African-Americans, most Harlemites have never seen Wall Street. From an "uptown" perspective, downtown is a white man's domain, the seat of financial markets and a market culture in which they do not participate (Zukin, 1991).

Like New York, the spatial layout of every city reflects the distribution of wealth, power, and prestige (Zukin, 1991). Some districts are the private preserve of the rich and powerful: the gleaming office buildings where they work, the well-kept buildings and clean streets of the neighborhoods where they live. Then there are the places the wealthy never go: the often-violent drug-ridden neighborhoods of the poor. Other areas are home to people who are neither rich nor poor and to small stores and businesses that provide a good living for their owners but lack the power of large corporations. Still others, like Soho, are centers of cultural power. The differences among these areas are not simply a matter of wealth but also a matter of taste—in art, food, entertainment, clothes.

In this chapter we look at one of the most significant features of the social landscape (reflected in most cityscapes): social inequality. In the first section we will show how inequalities are part of our society's social structure, maintained through power and expressed through culture. In the second section we look at social action and social mobility, or the possibility of changing one's position in society. Next we analyze the structural factors that contribute to poverty in the United States. In the last section we address the question of whether these inequalities are a necessary and inevitable consequence of some larger system, such as a capitalist economy, or whether they simply reflect the ability of some people to take advantage of others.

WEALTH, POWER, AND PRESTIGE: THE DIMENSIONS OF STRATIFICATION

The study of social stratification is the attempt to explain institutionalized patterns of social inequality. As the sociologist Gerhard Lenski (1966) put this, we want to know *who gets what, and why*. Part of the answer has to do with individual differences. In every society, individuals differ in their abilities, skills, strength, beauty, and ambition. These qualities may affect their standard of living, the respect they enjoy from others, and the influence they wield. A system

of social stratification, however, is based on more than differences among individuals.

Stratification refers to the division of a society into layers (or strata) of people who have unequal amounts of scarce but desirable resources, unequal life chances, and unequal social influence (Beteille, 1985). On each level, people occupy social statuses that give them access to different amounts of the three main dimensions of stratification: wealth (including income), power, and prestige. The status of banker is high on all three of these dimensions; that of homeless person is low on all three. Other statuses enjoy high scores on one dimension and low scores on the others. Most ministers in local churches, for example, have substantial prestige, or social esteem, in their communities, but their status generally does not bring them a great deal of power or wealth.

When we say that social stratification is institutionalized, we mean that inequalities are built into the social structure and may persist from generation to generation. A stratification system is considered **closed** to the extent that it is difficult or impossible to move up the social hierarchy. For example, under apartheid, the South African stratification system was largely closed for blacks. By contrast, the American system is relatively **open;** no positions are officially denied people because of their birth or other inherited characteristics (except that an immigrant cannot become president). American ideology holds that positions in the social hierarchy are mostly **achieved statuses** (see Chapter 3), that is, they are the results of individual effort and accomplishment. However, as we will show, there is still a class system: The population is divided along lines of wealth, prestige, and power, and the class position of a person's parents remains the best predictor of the class position that person will occupy.

Social stratification does not occur by chance or just as a result of individual differences in ability; it is a systematic arrangement that serves the interests of some people above the interests of others. No society has ever been found in which all members are perfectly equal, though the degree of inequality varies enormously (Lenski, Lenski, and Nolan, 1991; Sahlins, 1958). Among hunters and gatherers such as the San (or Bushmen) of Africa's Kalahari Desert, inequalities in wealth are virtually nonexistent; however, elders make most collective decisions, parents exercise authority over their children, and men enjoy power and privileges denied to women. Certain individuals may exercise more *influence* than others because of special qualities or skills, but they do not have power over others because of the roles they occupy or the possessions they control.

In larger societies, which have more accumulated wealth, whole groups are stratified into a stable hierarchy, and positions in this hierarchy are passed on from generation to generation by inheritance. The basis of such hierarchies varies widely (Smith, 1974, 1991). For example, spiritual status and other sources of cultural prestige may be valued more than material possessions. In India the prestige and power of Mahatma Gandhi were much greater than those of many wealthy businesspeople, even though he had few possessions, wore only a simple loincloth, and spent much of his life fasting. Indeed, the fact that he *chose* poverty contributed to his prestige and power. Furthermore, the caste system of traditional India emphasized spiritual status rather than material wealth. In other settings, sacrifices like Gandhi's might not be valued so much, and power may instead be based on physical strength, wealth, educational credentials, or democratic elections.

In modern industrial societies like the United States, wealth and income play an especially strong role in stratification. This emphasis on economic differences is reflected in the term *social class*. A **social class** is a group of people who occupy similar positions in the system of stratification because they occupy similar positions in the economy. Thus, when Americans speak of "the middle class," they mean people who are neither rich nor poor. Class position influences virtually every aspect of our lives, from the neighborhood in which we live, to our education, occupation, and income, to our choice of marriage partners, and even to the number of years we live.

No system of social stratification is ever so simple that everyone fits neatly into one layer or another. Status inconsistencies occur. For example, a "drug lord" may be extremely rich, but we would not consider him or her to be a member of the upper class. We recognize that power can come from control over a bureaucracy and not just from wealth. And we recognize that cultural factors, such as racism, may limit people's prestige and power independently of their wealth.

INEQUALITY AND SOCIAL MOBILITY

In the Declaration of Independence, the founders of the United States declared that "All men are created equal." A generation later the great French theorist Alexis de Tocqueville traveled around America and declared that the United States was a model for the organization of a more equal, democratic society and thus a blueprint for Europe's future. Of course, from the beginning there were exceptions. The phrase read "all *men* are created equal"; women were denied the vote and many economic privileges in American society until the twentieth century. Even more glaringly, the founders of the United States left intact the system of slavery that denied any rights at all to most African-Americans. Only after the Civil War was slavery abolished and formal equality granted to African-Americans, yet generations of struggle were still required to break down the barriers to full equality: unfair voter registration tests, job discrimination, segregated schools. Today African-Americans—and other minority groups—still suffer discrimination and a lower standard of living than does the white majority.

American culture values equality yet accepts a very unequal class structure as legitimate. Tension between the ideal and the reality is inevitable. Thus, Americans do not like rich people who think they are better than other people, but at the same time Americans do not think it wrong for the grandchildren of wealthy entrepreneurs to inherit fortunes that mean the grandchildren will never have to work. Although most Americans "believe in" the ideal of equality of opportunity, many resent government programs designed to increase the level of actual equality in American society.

The American Class Structure

Most Americans consider themselves part of the middle class, whether they are shop clerks, plumbers, engineers, or doctors. Middle class implies that they work for a living and do not depend on either welfare or inherited millions. This distinction among work, wealth, and welfare is catchy, but it obscures important differences. Is a lawyer who earns $200,000 a year really in the same class as a housekeeper who earns $12,000 a year, just because both work full-time for their living?

As this question indicates, there is no easy way to decide how many classes there are in American society. Sociologists commonly define classes by looking at people's wealth, income, and occupational characteristics.

Wealth refers to people's valuable property—to what they own, such as a house or stocks. Wealth represents "stored-up purchasing power" that can be drawn upon in times of need and passed from one generation to the next (Oliver and Shapiro, 1990). **Income,** on the other hand, refers to how much people receive from outside sources: The amount of money that flows into a household, regardless of how much flows out. There are two main sorts of income: Wages and salaries are returns on labor; interest, dividends, and rent are returns on property or capital.

Wealth is most important in distinguishing the very top members of the American class structure. These are people who inherit much of what they own. Their income comes mainly from investments, not from work, and this sets them apart from middle- and working-class Americans. The differences between middle- and working-class Americans have mainly to do with occupational characteristics—the kinds of jobs they hold, how much education their jobs require, how much the jobs pay, how much authority (that is, power) they have at work, and how much prestige they enjoy.

Prestige is the social esteem, respect, or approval that is awarded to people because they possess attributes that their society considers admirable (Goode, 1978). In the United States, occupation is a main source of prestige. Sociologists measure the prestige of occupations by asking representative samples of the population to rate the social standing of various jobs and then translating these rankings into prestige tallies ranging from zero (lowest) to 100 (highest). The results of such occupational surveys tend to remain fairly stable over time. As Table 7.1 shows, Americans rate most highly those jobs that confer power on an individual and require professional skills. However, high prestige does not always mean high income.

Considering all these factors, sociologist Harold Kerbo (1991, pp. 13–14) summarized the American class structure this way:

The **upper class** consists of families that own a great deal of property (including stock in major corporations and real estate) and enjoy the prestige and authority flowing from such ownership. These are the

TABLE 7.1

Prestige Ranking of Occupations in the United States

High Ranking Occupations	Score	Low Ranking Occupations	Score
Physician	86	Plumber	45
Lawyer	75	Bank teller	43
College/university professor	74	Brick mason	36
Physicist/astronomer	73	File clerk	36
Architect	73	Correctional institution officer	32
Aerospace engineer	72	Bus driver	32
Dentist	72	Retail salesperson	31
Psychologist	69	Truck driver	30
Clergy	69	Cashier	29
Pharmacist	68	Bellhop	27
Registered nurse	66	Taxi driver	28
Athlete	65	Garbage collector	28
Air traffic controller	65	Waitress	28
Elementary school		Bartender	25
teacher	64	Farm laborer	23
Airline pilot	61	Gas station attendant	21
Sociologist	61	Household servant	20
Financial manager	59	Car washer	19
Actor/director	58	News vendor	19

Source: Adapted from General Social Surveys, 1972–1993: Cumulative Codebook *(National Opinion Research Center, Chicago, 1993), pp. 937–945.*

old, established families such as the Rockefellers, the Du Ponts, the Mellons, and the Fords.

The **corporate class** is made up of people who have great bureaucratic authority in major corporations (and often government), usually not based on ownership of these corporations. These people include top corporate executives and corporate board members. There is some evidence that the upper class is shrinking in importance while the corporate class is growing in importance.

The **middle class** is composed of people who own relatively little property but whose occupations give them high-to-middle income, prestige, and authority. The middle class is subdivided into the *upper middle class* (lesser corporate managers, doctors, lawyers) and *lower middle class* (office workers, salespeople, and service workers).

The **working class** consists of people who own little or no property and whose occupations give them middle-to-low income and prestige and little or no authority. The working class is largely composed of manual workers (subdivided into skilled and unskilled) and low-end clerical workers.

The **lower class** includes individuals with no property who are often unemployed and have no authority and usually no prestige—that is, the poor.

The same basic class structure is found in nearly all economically advanced (industrial/postindustrial) societies.

Although relatively stable, the American class structure can and does change. Christopher Lasch (1995) saw the most revolutionary change in recent times as the emergence of a global elite whose livelihood derives from the manipulation of information and professional expertise. Members of this new elite have few ties to community, region, or country. Their fortunes are invested in global enterprises. They achieve further independence by sending their children to private schools, insuring themselves against medical emergencies through company plans, and hiring private security guards to protect them from violence. Members of an international culture of work and leisure, they have more in common with their counterparts in Brussels or Hong Kong than with other Americans.

The federal government does not collect data on classes as such. Rather, its data refer to the income

An American working-class home. While luxuries are few for a working-class family, life can still be comfortable. This couple owns two televisions, a VCR, a computer, and three vehicles.

and wealth of fixed percentages of the population—for example, the richest (or poorest) 1 percent, 5 percent, or 20 percent. Some differences of wealth and income are not due to class position so much as stage of life: People in their twenties typically have steady incomes but little accumulated wealth; conversely, retired people generally have accumulated assets (a home, cars, investments, and other property) but relatively small incomes. However, the difference between the wealth of a working teacher or plumber (who is still paying the mortgage on a house) and that of a retired one (who owns a house outright) is tiny by comparison to the difference between teachers and plumbers on the one hand and very rich people like the Rockefellers and Du Ponts on the other.

The Distribution of Wealth and Income

The distribution of wealth in the United States is extremely lopsided. Most Americans have very little wealth. Nearly two-thirds own their own home, but most owe a large part of its value to the bank that holds the mortgage. Only a little over 20 percent of Americans own stocks or bonds, and just 10.5 percent own any real estate besides their homes. Most households (73 percent) have some assets earning interest in a financial institution (for example, savings, checking accounts, and money market accounts), but the median value of these deposits is only about $3,600 (*Statistical Abstract*, 1994, p. 512). This means that most Americans live very close to the edge, financially. In an emergency (long-term unemployment or serious illness), they have very little to fall back on.

The rich—the 10 percent who own 70 percent of the nation's wealth—do not have such worries. The median net worth (all assets minus all debts) of the wealthiest 1 percent of the population is twenty-two times that for the remaining 99 percent of the population (Oliver and Shapiro, 1990). The disparity is even greater for capital assets (assets that can be used to generate income): the richest 1 percent of Americans have 237 times more productive wealth per person than do the other 99 percent. The wealthiest 0.05 percent of Americans (roughly 430,000 households) own 40 percent of all corporate stocks. In contrast, one-third of American households have zero or negative assets (that is, more debts than assets).

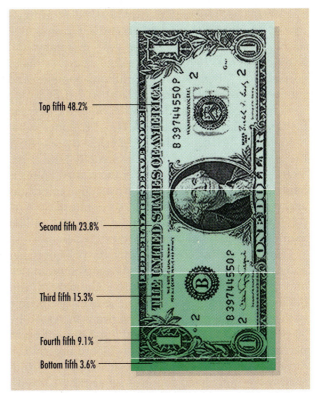

FIGURE 7.1 / *Distribution of Income in the United States, by Population Fifths*

Dividing the population into fifths illustrates the distribution of income (or wealth), but these population segments correspond only approximately to social class definitions.

Source: *Current Populations Report*, Series P-60, no. 188 (February, 1995).

Like the distribution of wealth, the distribution of income in the United States is very uneven. As shown in Figure 7.1, the bottom one-fifth of American families received 3.6 percent of the nation's total income in 1993, while the top one-fifth received 48.2 percent. The top 5 percent of households (including much of the corporate class) received 20 percent of all income—four times the share they would receive if income were distributed equally (Current Population Reports, 1995).

The Forbes Four Hundred, an annual profile of the 400 wealthiest Americans, includes two Fords, three Rockefellers, eight Gettys, and eleven Du Ponts, but four out of five members of this elite club are self-made members of the corporate class (*Forbes*, October

17, 1994). (See Figure 7.2.) In 1994, the country's twenty top-paid CEOs (chief executive officers) took home about $4.3 million per year in salary and bonuses (Byrne, 1995). The average salary of major corporation CEOs was $1.3 million; bonuses and profits on stock options bring the average CEO's pay to $2.8 million per year. This is 158 times the average factory worker's income ($24,411), 112 times what the average teacher earns ($35,291), sixty-six times the average engineer's income ($58,240), and nineteen times what the president of the United States is paid ($200,000). The 2.5 million wealthy Americans at the top end of the upper and corporate classes receive as much income as the more than 100 million members of the working and lower classes.

The 1980s was a decade in which the rich got richer and the poor got poorer, that is, the gap between rich and poor widened significantly (Greenstein and Barancik, 1990; Phillips, 1991). The average income of the wealthiest one-fifth of Americans increased by 30 percent and that of the wealthiest 1 percent by 75 percent (or $236,000 per person before taxes). The Reagan administration's tax cuts allowed the rich to earn more (and keep more of what they earned). People below the national average income lost ground, partly because of the elimination of many jobs (Figure 7.3). Middle-income families had to work more hours and/or send more household members into the workforce to maintain their 1980 standard of living.

This trend has continued (though more slowly) in the 1990s. During the recession of the early 1990s, the middle class was hit harder than at any other time since the Great Depression of the 1930s. In 1991, while the overall unemployment rate increased 15 percent, the unemployment rate for managers jumped 55 percent (Barnet, 1993). The situation was still worse for the working class; between 1989 and 1993, the United States lost 1.6 million manufacturing jobs (Barnet, 1993). Even with a dramatic increase in the number of two-income families, household income was stagnant. Many members of the working class experienced long bouts of unemployment and settled for low-wage jobs in the service sector.

Social Mobility

Social mobility refers to movement from one social position or level to another. It may take the form of a step up the social ladder, a climb to the top, or a step down. Rather than looking at individual

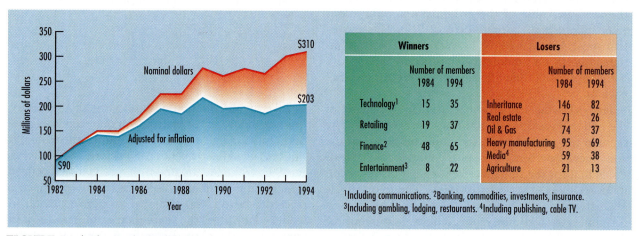

FIGURE 7.2 / The Rich Get Richer

The cutoff for admission to the Forbes Four Hundred was $310 million in 1994, more than double the price of admission a decade earlier ($150 million). Even after adjusting for inflation, the rich are getting richer. But *how* the rich acquire wealth is changing: "hard assets," such as real estate and oil and gas, are becoming less valuable, and ideas and innovations in entertainment, computers, and communications are becoming more valuable.

Source: *Forbes* 154, no. 9 (October 17, 1994): 101.

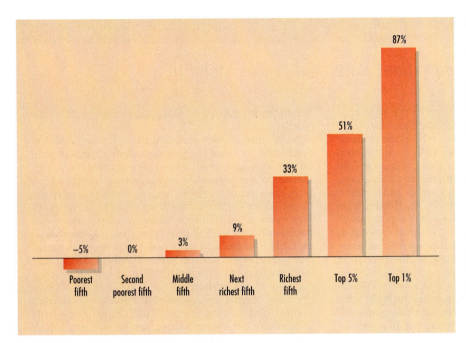

FIGURE 7.3 / *Average After-Tax Income Gains and Losses between 1980 and 1990, by Household Income Groups*

Note that the wealthiest Americans not only increased their earnings in the 1980s but also *kept* more of their earnings. Thus the average income of the wealthiest 1 percent increased by 75 percent, while after-tax income increased by 87 percent.

Source: *Congressional Budget Office,* in Melvin L. Oliver and Thomas M. Shapiro, "Wealth of a Nation: A Reassessment of Asset Inequality in America ...," *American Journal of Economics and Sociology* 49, no. 2 (1990): 129–151.

Americans who rose "from rags to riches," sociologists study *mobility rates*, general patterns of movement up or down the social scale. Research shows that most upward mobility takes the form of small steps up the occupational or economic ladder, not leaps from the bottom to the top. Thus, the child of a factory worker becomes a factory supervisor; the child of a teacher becomes a college professor. Because of the relative openness of the American stratification system, movement both up and down the social hierarchy is common (Blau and Duncan, 1967; Featherman and Hauser, 1978).

Sociologists also point out that social mobility in the United States often results from structural change, not individual success (Levy, 1987). **Structural mobility** refers to changes in the number and kinds of occupations available in a society, relative to the number of workers available to fill them. Structural mobility is not the result of individual talent, effort, or luck, but occurs because of external changes in opportunities. In some cases these changes may be cyclical, as when a periodic recession or depression causes large numbers of people to be temporarily unemployed or underemployed. In other cases, change is permanent and widespread, as when a new technology creates some new jobs but eliminates many others, or when an increase in international competition reduces sales of all kinds of domestic products.

Patterns of Social Mobility

Historically, the United States has been an upwardly mobile society. Over time, peasants became independent farmers, farmers became factory workers, blue-collar factory workers moved into white-collar office jobs, and so on. Large-scale immigration stimulated occupational advancement in this expanding economy. Contrary to popular belief, immigrants do not always take jobs away from natives but may actually help to create more and better jobs. For much of America's history, economic expansion created a shortage of industrial labor—a problem that immigrants helped to solve. Other immigrants became farmers, adding to America's agricultural wealth and expanding the market for the industrial goods produced in the cities. Finally, an influx of unskilled and semiskilled laborers during the late nineteenth and early twentieth centuries enabled experienced workers to move up the occupational ladder (see the Global Issues/Local Consequences box). For example, an artisan who once did all the work in the shop could hire assistants, expand operations, and become a manager.

The children of the Great Depression of the 1930s are "one of the few living examples of the [rags to riches] story (on a grand scale) that the United States has ever actually reproduced" (Newman, 1993,

GLOBAL ISSUES/LOCAL CONSEQUENCES

Immigration, Race, and Social Mobility

European immigrants who settled in the industrial cities of the northern United States after 1880 fared better, as a group, than did blacks who came to those same cities from the South. Traditionally, race has been considered the main reason for this difference. The European immigrants, despite differences in language, religion, and culture, "were after all *white* and a generation or two later it was possible for the descendants to shed as many of these markers as necessary" (Lieberson, 1980, p. xi). Blacks, by contrast, were permanently marked as different by their racial characteristics, which made them vulnerable to discrimination long after the European immigrants had blended in with the general population. An alternative explanation has maintained that the Europeans brought with them more cohesive family structures, a different work ethic, greater intelligence, and a more positive view of education as a means to advance in society.

In his classic book *A Piece of the Pie* (1980), Stanley Lieberson challenges both of these explanations. He cites data that suggest, for example, that blacks were at least as eager for education as European immigrants, and there was nothing inherent in their family structures that held them back. Blacks did suffer greater discrimination than European immigrants. Employers and labor unions generally preferred whites, despite linguistic and cultural differences. Racism did matter, but it was not the whole story. Other additional factors are needed to fully explain the differences between African-American migrants and European immigrants to the North.

Asian immigrants, Lieberson notes, were also distinguished by racial features and were victims of prejudice, and yet they have seen notable success. Lieberson's explanation involves two central ideas. First, the kind of work immigrants did was largely determined by the opportunities available in the place they came from. Those who left a desperately poor homeland were willing to accept work that was unacceptable to those who had had better work at home. Using mortality data—perhaps the only contemporary data available to measure quality of life—Lieberson suggests that conditions in the U.S. South (especially for black people) were worse than those in Southern, Central, and Eastern Europe. Thus, black immigrants to Northern cities were willing to settle for less, which would have put them at a disadvantage in earnings and mobility. It would also have earned them the hostility of white workers, who would have viewed them as competitors who could be exploited by employers to depress wages or break strikes.

Black migrants to the North thus started out in a disadvantaged position. To explain why they stayed behind over time, Lieberson offers his second central idea, the concept of *mobility niches*. He notes that different groups tended to concentrate in certain occupations: Italians became barbers; Irish became policemen and firemen; Swedes worked as carpenters; Greeks opened

p. 56). Born during one of the darkest periods in America's economic history, often forced to quit school to help support their families and then drafted to fight World War II, this generation spearheaded the exodus from the cramped ethnic neighborhoods of large cities to suburbia. Helped by the GI bill (which paid college tuition for veterans), government-insured low-interest home mortgages, and the booming postwar economy, this generation defined what we now think of as the middle class: a couple and their children living in a home of their own, one or two cars in the garage, family vacations, and the belief that their children would enjoy more rewarding work, and a higher standard of living, than they had. From their own experience, these postwar parents believed that sacrifice and hard work paid off.

They enjoyed a standard of living that was the envy of the world, and they were secure about their futures. The houses they bought in the 1950s for $10,000 to $15,000 were worth twenty times that much in the 1970s, providing a "nest egg" for retirement.

The children of postwar parents, the baby boomers, were children of plenty, raised in a culture of optimism. They saw the home, family, and comfortable lifestyle their parents had provided, not as a hard-won achievement but as "an expectation, a norm, an entitlement" (Newman, 1993, p. 2). Upward mobility was their birthright. When the U.S. economy slowed down and job opportunities dried up in the 1980s and 1990s, baby boomers were caught unprepared.

The main reason for the reversal in the long-term pattern of upward mobility was *deindustrialization*, a

restaurants; Russians traded in furs; and so on. Such occupations gave those groups a base from which to advance. But "niches" could absorb only small percentages of immigrant groups. In the case of each European group, immigration in large numbers continued for only a few years. U.S. government restric-

Learning a trade while still in high school, these German teenagers will have a smoother transition into the work force than their American peers. Young people who do not go on to college must make an abrupt shift from schoolwork to a job for which they have not been trained.

tions on immigration drastically curtailed the flow of immigrants from Europe and Asia during the 1920s and 1930s, but black migration from the South continued unabated. Newcomers who found themselves excluded from mobility niches worked to undercut earlier and more successful immigrants, at the same time reinforcing negative stereotypes in the minds of the dominant class. Also, the attitudes of whites changed as the demographic balance changed; that is, continuing black migration helped reduce the negative attitudes of whites toward other whites. In Lieberson's words, "The presence of blacks made it harder to discriminate against the new Europeans because the alternative was viewed even less favorably."

Thus, in Lieberson's analysis, while racism was present at the beginning, it was made more powerful by other changes. Race was not the most important factor in explaining the greater social mobility of European immigrants. Economic conflict was more important, and race was resorted to simply because it was the most obvious feature available to justify discrimination. In short, "differences between blacks and whites—real ones, imaginary ones, and those that are the product of earlier race relations—enter into the rhetoric of race and ethnic relations, but they are ultimately secondary to the conflict for society's goodies" (p. 382).

Source: Stanley Lieberson, *A Piece of the Pie: Black and White Immigrants Since 1880* (University of California Press, Berkeley, 1980).

cover term for the transformation of the American economy from one based on manufacturing to one based on service. Deindustrialization had a number of consequences. First, thousands of plants were closed, cut back, or moved to other regions and other countries. As a result, millions of blue-collar workers, who had became accustomed to unionized, high-paying jobs with full benefits, were stranded in the midwest and the northeastern "rust belt" cities. More than half of the estimated 11.5 million workers who lost their jobs between 1979 and 1984 and who found others jobs earn less than they did before (Snow and Anderson, 1993).

Second, while some jobs in the information sector of the service economy pay high wages to highly educated professionals, most new service jobs are at the low-wage end of the scale. For every doctor there are dozens of hospital orderlies; for every stockbroker, a fleet of clerical workers; for every successful restaurant owner, scores of poorly paid waiters, dishwashers, and the like (Newman, 1993). Bumped off the road to the middle class, many working-class men and women who once earned $12, $15, or $20 an hour making cars now struggle to get by on $4.50 an hour making hamburgers or $6.00 an hour cleaning offices. These low-end service jobs are also more likely to be temporary or part-time and to provide no benefits (health insurance, pension plans, paid vacations, etc.).

Third, white-collar workers were also hurt by economic shifts. In the late 1980s and early 1990s, tens of thousands of managers, professionals, and clerical workers—people who had educational credentials, years of work experience, and special expertise—were laid off in wave after wave of corporate downsizing (cutting overhead by cutting workers), takeovers, mergers, and bankruptcies. In some cases, full-time employees were laid off, then rehired as part-time or free-lance workers, without benefits. Today white-collar managers who suffer layoffs are likely to be unemployed for longer than blue-collar workers (Newman, 1993).

Children raised on the American dream are seeing that dream slip through their fingers as adults. Today's young adults are the first American generation to experience widespread downward mobility. "The 1990s are returning us to an earlier era in which birthright determined one's fortunes. Those who can afford the better things in life will have them from the beginning, and those who do not will find it much harder to lay hands on a middle-class identity" (Newman, 1993, p. 218). Not surprisingly, Americans now in their twenties are angry: at the huge national debt accumulated in the 1990s; at the student loans they took to pay for educations that are not paying off in terms of jobs and salaries; at the unaffordable cost of housing, health care, and other basics. In the next decade, as baby boomers begin to retire and to draw on Social Security and Medicare, generational politics are likely to heat up.

Who Gets Ahead?

Sociologists are interested not only in what proportion of the total population experiences upward or downward mobility but also in the factors that determine which sorts of people are most likely to experience such changes. In a classic study, Peter M. Blau and Otis Dudley Duncan (1967) addressed the question of how social origin affects a person's ultimate status and whether factors other than social origin are involved. The researchers developed a measure known as the *socioeconomic index* that allowed them to compare fathers' educational and occupational attainments with those of their sons. Blau and Duncan concluded that social origin affects ultimate social status primarily by influencing the level of education a person attains. Educational achievement, they believed, was the mechanism by which status is passed from one generation to another.

The Blau and Duncan model of status attainment was amplified by William H. Sewell and his colleagues (Hauser et al., 1982, 1983; Sewell and Hauser, 1976). They found that educational and occupational attainment are the outcome of two related processes: those that shape a person's status aspirations and those that convert the aspirations into a new status ranking. A family's class affects a child's later attainments through the personal influences that family members, teachers, and friends bring to bear on the child's status aspirations. The level of schooling the individual achieves then becomes the principal influence. Viewed in this way, occupational attainment is shaped by many links in a chain extending from birth across the life span: Parental status colors the adolescent's aspirations; aspirations contribute to the individual's educational attainment; educational attainment influences the person's first occupational placement; and the person's first job affects his or her later occupational opportunities.

The idea that status attainment is based on educational achievement rests on certain assumptions about society—most significantly, that individuals compete in relatively open educational and occupational systems. However, sociologists have uncovered the institutional, or structural, arrangements that circumscribe choices and actions at every stage (Kerckhoff, 1995). Education itself is stratified. Schools vary widely in kinds of educational resources they offer, say, from an inner-city school to a school in a wealthy suburb. Within schools, students are grouped according to "ability"; students in high-ability groups usually gain more than those in low-ability groups, widening the gap in achievement. As a rule, students from high-status families attend better schools, are rated as higher in ability, and so start out ahead.

In the United States, the transition from student to worker is relatively abrupt; once students graduate, they are on their own. Moreover, except at professional schools (law, medicine, business), education is not occupation-oriented. What counts is a diploma—ideally, a college or graduate degree from a prestigious school. In Germany, students are sorted into specific occupational categories in secondary school, usually take part in employer-sponsored work-study programs for several years after leaving full-time school, and take national exams that certify their competency in particular occupations. In Japan, many secondary schools have special relationships with prospective employers, receive lists of job openings, and list nominees from their schools (recommendations that are usually accepted). In the United

States, knowing people in high positions and going to the right schools counts more than actual achievement in school. Finally, the level at which a person enters the workforce in the United States and abroad does not necessarily predict level of attainment: the structure of opportunities varies in different companies, occupations, and industries.

To understand status attainment, then, one must take into account the structures of opportunity within which individual social action, in the form of occupational achievement, can occur. Whereas the opportunity structure of the 1950s and 1960s made it relatively easy for many (but not all) Americans to translate aspirations into education and education into jobs, the economic changes of the 1980s and 1990s have made such action more difficult. Likewise, the widening gap between inner-city and suburban schools, combined with the increasing division of the job market into separate low-skill, low-wage and high-skill, high-wage sectors intensifies stratification. Historically, a slide into poverty was a temporary crisis for many Americans (Duncan, 1984). Today, this slide more often appears to be permanent. The difference lies not in the skills and motivation of workers but in changes in the job market and the nature of work.

If rising from rags to riches is the American dream, falling into poverty is the American nightmare. Many Americans see poverty as a remote possibility, as a problem confined to a deviant minority, as something that happens only to "them" and never to "us" (Bane and Ellwood, 1989); but only a small proportion of Americans are, through inheritance, immune to downward mobility.

POVERTY IN THE UNITED STATES

Poverty is relative. Compared to people starving in Somalia, even many poor Americans are well off. While some unemployed workers may feel that getting just a minimum-wage job would help them to escape from poverty, a corporate executive who is laid off may feel poor if he cannot afford to send his children to a private college.

In order to develop a systematic picture of poverty in the United States, the government calculates an official *poverty line* based on the minimum amount of money that families of different sizes and compositions need to purchase a nutritionally adequate diet, assuming that they spend one-third of their income

TABLE 7.2	
Adjusted Poverty Threshold, by Family Size, 1993	
Number of Family Members	**Poverty Line**
1 person	$7,363
2 persons	9,414
3 persons	11,522
4 persons	14,763
5 persons	17,449
6 persons	19,718
7 persons	22,383

Source: Current Population Reports, 1995, Consumer Income, Series P60-188 (February), Table A-2.

for food (Table 7.2). This measure is adjusted each year for inflation. In 1993, the poverty line for a family of four was $14,763 per year, or a little over $1,200 a month. Above this level people may still feel poor, but only those below it are counted in official poverty statistics.

The use of the poverty line is controversial (Bane and Ellwood, 1989). Some critics argue that it is too high because it does not take into account such noncash or in-kind benefits as food stamps and school lunches, housing subsidies, and Medicaid. Other critics point out that the poverty line does not reflect regional differences in the cost of living: for example, it costs more to live in New York City than in rural Mississippi. Nor does the poverty line consider changing patterns of family expenses, such as the rising cost of housing or the cost of child care for the increasing number of families with working mothers (Bell, 1994; Ruggles, 1990). Moreover, the poverty line lumps together families and individuals who are chronically poor with those who have suffered a temporary setback, and it combines families and individuals who have almost nothing with those who are struggling but managing to get by. In spite of these limitations, the official poverty line is still the best and most widely used index.

In 1960, 39.5 million Americans—more than 20 percent of the country's population—were living in poverty. With John Kennedy's leadership and, after his death, Lyndon Johnson's War on Poverty, the number of poor Americans fell throughout the 1960s, hitting a low of 24.1 million (9.5 percent) in 1969.

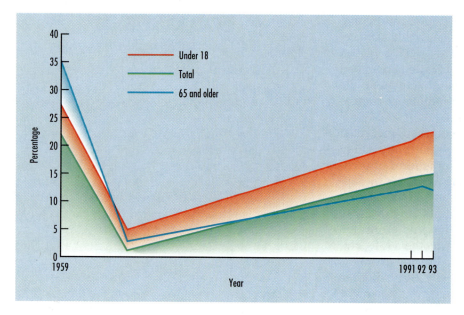

FIGURE 7.4 / Percentage of Americans Living Below the Poverty Line, 1959–1993

At greatest risk for poverty today are children below age 18; the proportion of elderly people living in poverty, after falling, has climbed again.

Source: *Statistical Abstract of the United States*, 1994, and U.S. Bureau of the Census, *Current Population Reports*, Series P-60, no. 188 (February).

Although the absolute numbers increased somewhat in the 1970s, the proportion stayed below 10 percent until 1980. During the Reagan and Bush presidencies in the 1980s, however, these improvements began to erode (Figure 7.4). In 1993, more than 39.3 million Americans—15.1 percent of the population—lived in poverty. Many live far below the poverty line. The annual income of the average poor family was $5,960 (or $1,671 per person) *below* what the government estimated a family needed for adequate nutrition in 1993 (Current Population Reports, 1995).

Who Are the Poor?

It is difficult to generalize about America's poor. Certainly the poor include unwed teenage mothers in inner-city ghettoes, but they are not the majority of poor people. Neither are the homeless. An accurate portrait of Americans living in poverty would include many people living in rural areas, many recently unemployed people with long histories of steady work, and many people who have suffered crises like divorce or death in the family. Although African-Americans and Hispanics are more likely to be poor, the majority of poor Americans (66.8 percent) are white (Current Population Reports, 1995). About half are either children under age sixteen or people over age sixty-five.

The Working Poor

Explanations of poverty in America tend to fall into three broad positions (Harris, 1993; Osterman, 1993). One camp holds that the poor are poor because they choose not to work; they lack motivation. A second argument is that the poor cannot work because of age, disability, the need to care for young children, or other reasons. The third major explanation for poverty is that there are not enough jobs to go around.

It seems reasonable to believe that people would not be poor if they worked, but while this may have been true in the past, a job no longer guarantees that a worker and his or her family will not be poor (Bane and Ellwood, 1989). The proportion of American workers with full-time, year-round jobs who did not earn enough to raise their families above the poverty level rose 50 percent between 1979 and 1992, to 18 percent of all workers (Lavelle, 1995).

Although there is no simple explanation for the growing number of working poor, two factors stand out. The first is the change in the occupational structure that occurred as America shifted from a manufacturing to a service economy, as discussed earlier. Displaced workers frequently experienced long periods of unemployment and ended up in jobs that paid significantly less than the ones they had lost, and new workers were unable to find the kinds of entry-level jobs that had been available a generation earlier.

Second, the value of the minimum wage set by the government declined steadily (see Figure 7.5). If the minimum wage were worth as much today as it was in 1968, adjusting for inflation, it would be $6.29 an hour in 1994 dollars—considerably more than the current $4.25 (Purdum, 1995). Contrary to popular stereotypes, the majority of minimum-wage workers are not teenagers but adults, many of whom support dependents and many of whom are among the working poor. A worker earning the minimum wage in a full-time, year-round job in 1994 fell $782 below the poverty line for a family of two, $2,890 below for a family of three, and $6,131 below for a family of four. Of course, not everyone earns this much: The federal minimum wage for waiters and others who receive tips is a mere $2.13 an hour.

In 1995, when President Clinton proposed to increase the regular minimum wage rate by 90 cents, to $5.15 per hour, conservatives argued that the increase would force companies to raise prices, causing inflation, and to lay off workers, increasing unemployment. In fact, studies of the last minimum-wage increase (also 90 cents), signed into law by President Bush in 1989, found no significant rise in unemployment. On the contrary, the increase in the minimum wage tended to pull *up* other workers' wages and generated new economic demand that kept other workers employed. Some restaurants (which employ about 40 percent of low-wage workers) may have raised their prices slightly, but there was no general increase in consumer prices (Novak, 1993).

Nonetheless, Clinton's proposed increase was defeated in Congress.

The working poor are especially common in rural America. The increasing dominance of large corporate farms not only has hurt small farmers but also has cut into income possibilities for whole communities that once depended on farmers. Many jobs, such as harvesting, are seasonal rather than year-round. Rural people often take work into their homes, addressing envelopes, embroidering jogging suits, or assembling stuffed toys to make enough money to get by. As Osha Gray Davidson writes, "Industrial homework is becoming to today's rural ghettos what sweatshops were to the immigrant tenements in the first half of this century: vehicles for the exploitation of a mostly female work force, characterized by low wages, unsafe working conditions, child labor, and little or no government regulation" (1990, p. 142). Such work enables people to stay on their farms, but seldom to escape poverty.

Welfare: Myths and Facts

Discussions of poverty inevitably lead to welfare; in the minds of many Americans, the two are almost synonymous. "Welfare" refers to Aid to Families with Dependent Children (AFDC), a program originally designed to give single mothers (most of whom, at the start, were widows) cash assistance so that they could stay home to care for their underage children.

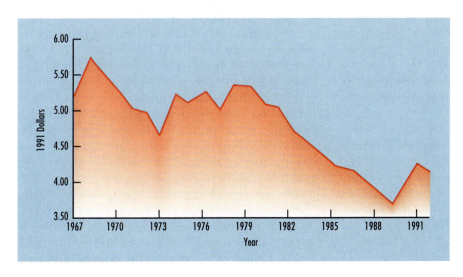

FIGURE 7.5 / *Value of the Minimum Wage in 1991 Dollars, 1967–1992*

One reason for the increase in working poor is that the value of the minimum wage has fallen.

Source: Economic Policy Institute, *The State of Working America,* Washington, D.C., April 1993.

For the working poor in the rural United States, money doesn't stretch far enough to buy a comfortable, well-maintained place to live. This run-down house is home to a Kentucky coal miner and his family.

At present, about 14 million people—two-thirds of them children—receive assistance from AFDC (Cushman, 1995). Today *welfare* has become a code word for an expensive, abused, and misguided social program that undermined the work ethic and the family and, by extension, threatens the country itself (Bray, 1992).

Many people assume that (1) most single mothers, and hence most welfare mothers, are African-American; (2) welfare mothers are lazy and uneducated, and do not work and do not *want* to work; (3) welfare functions as an incentive to bear children out of wedlock; and (4) welfare becomes a way of life, passed from one generation of single mothers to the next.

Looking at the data, sociologist Kathleen Harris (1996) finds that all of these assumptions are false. First, the majority of single mothers in the United States are white, and fewer than half of single mothers ever go on welfare. Of those receiving welfare benefits, the number of white and African-American mothers are about the same (House Ways and Means Committee; in Lavelle, 1995, p. 21).

Second, the majority of single mothers work while they are receiving welfare benefits, and most work

their way off welfare—though not out of poverty (Harris, 1993; Pavetti, 1992). Single mothers earn, on average, only a third as much as married fathers. One reason for this difference is that because of child-care responsibilities single mothers tend to work part-time for low hourly wages. However, even those who work full-time, year-round are disadvantaged. Many poor single mothers devote their young adult years to family responsibilities and child-rearing, rather than to school and work. When they do enter the work force they have less education, less work experience, and fewer job skills than other earners. As a result, they are only able to obtain low- or minimum-wage jobs that usually do not provide health-care benefits for their children. In addition, they usually have to pay for child care. In choosing work over welfare a young mother may place her children at risk because of reduced or absent health care and possibly unsafe or unhealthy child-care environments. Even so, most poor single mothers do work.

Welfare is often cited as a major reason for the breakup of families and the increase in single motherhood. Because only unmarried mothers with dependent children are eligible for benefits, critics argue, welfare discourages young couples from getting married or staying married and encourages poor women to have more children in order to receive higher benefits. The facts suggest otherwise (Harris, 1996). The real value of the welfare package (AFDC and food stamps) for a family of four dropped from $10,133 in 1970, to $8,374 in 1980, to $7,657 in 1992. Despite shrinking welfare benefits, the proportion of female-headed families more than doubled. If welfare were an incentive, states with highest benefits would have the highest rates of nonmarital childbearing. In fact, the reverse is true: States with the *lowest* benefits generally have the *highest* rates of nonmarital childbearing (National Center for Health Statistics, 1994).

Finally, welfare is seldom "a way of life," as some would claim. Seventy percent of AFDC recipients stay on welfare less than two years; only 7 percent stay on welfare more than eight years. Lifetime totals, which include women who get off welfare and then go back on, show that only 25 percent of recipients spend more than eight years on welfare (Ellwood and Bane, in Lavelle, 1995, p. 22; Pavetti, 1992). Even in families with mothers who stay on welfare for eight or more years, 80 percent of their daughters are self-supporting as adults; only 19 percent of these women became second-generation welfare mothers (Bray, 1992).

Proposals to reform welfare include requiring mothers who receive assistance to work or participate in job-training programs; putting a five-year lifetime limit on benefits; not increasing benefits to women who have another child while on welfare; requiring unwed teenage mothers to live at home and attend school; denying all cash payments (but not food stamps or Medicaid) to unwed teenage mothers; and cutting off welfare for legal as well as illegal immigrants. The underlying assumption is that the solution to welfare is work (and that welfare mothers are lazy and selfish). But the kind of work available is a crucial problem. Low- and minimum-wage jobs with no health-care benefits or child-care provisions force many women to choose between the stigma associated with welfare and the well-being of their children. They also prevent single mothers from getting additional education, which is the best way to stay out of poverty and off welfare in the long run (Harris, 1993). The problem is particularly acute for African-Americans, many of whom face the additional problems of life in inner-city ghettoes, where jobs (and good day-care facilities) are especially hard to come by.

The Ghetto Poor

Forty years ago, 63rd Street on the South Side of Chicago was known as the "Miracle Mile" (Wacquant, 1994). Nearly 800 businesses competed for space in an eighteen-by-four-block area. There were five banks and six hotels; large restaurants stayed open around the clock; the movie theaters, ballrooms, and taverns were never empty. Forty years ago, 63rd Street was the heart of a thriving black community. Today, fewer than 90 commercial establishments remain, mostly tiny eating places, beauty parlors and barber shops, and small clothing and liquor stores. Abandoned buildings, vacant lots littered with debris, boarded up storefront churches, and the charred remains of shops stretch as far as the eye can see. One of the few shopkeepers left from the old days describes 63rd Street today as "Berlin after the war" (p. 239).

Chicago's South Side is not unique (Duncan, 1987; Wilson, 1987; Wacquant, 1989; Wacquant and Wilson, 1989). In the black ghettoes of most major American cities, poverty is more severe, more widespread, and more persistent than it was thirty years ago, at the beginning of the civil rights movement; "the economic, social, and cultural distance between inner-city minorities and the rest of society has reached levels that are unprecedented in modern American history" (Wacquant, 1994, p. 233). Why is extreme poverty concentrated in inner-city, predominantly black neighborhoods? Why, more than a quarter of a century after the passage of antidiscrimination legislation, are 2.5 million African-Americans still trapped in poverty?

Popular explanations of the ghetto poor tend to assume that the problem lies in a "culture of poverty" that supports an array of vices and pathologies, including lack of education, chronic unemployment, teenage pregnancy and out-of-wedlock births, welfare dependency, gangs, drugs, and crime. Some commentators emphasize the breakdown of the African-American family; others see welfare as the culprit. The general impression is that this so-called underclass is made up of the undeserving poor, or the "dangerous class" that Karl Marx called the "lumpenproletariat."

William Julius Wilson (1980, 1987, 1991), a leading authority on the subject, takes issue with the view that ghetto residents do not value education, work, and family as much as other Americans do. Emphasizing social structure rather than culture or voluntary action, he argues that nonconforming and deviant behavior among the ghetto poor is the result, not the cause, of their living conditions and the restricted opportunities available to them.

In the past, manual labor, factory work, and government jobs provided a route out of poverty for African-Americans who had migrated to the city from the rural South and for those with a high school education or less. With deindustrialization, these jobs all but disappeared. Cities were particularly hard-hit because many surviving manufacturers, along with retail stores and warehouses, moved out. Most inner-city African-Americans cannot afford the cost of moving or commuting to the suburbs, where most entry-level blue-collar, clerical, and sales jobs are now located. Whereas the most common first job for their fathers a generation ago had been factory assembler or machine operator, the most common jobs reported by today's black male youths are janitor and waiter—if they work at all (Testa and Krogh, 1989). Nearly half of inner-city black youth aged sixteen to nineteen are out of school and unemployed.

A second factor in the rise of ghetto poverty, according to Wilson, was the migration of higher-income African-Americans out of the inner cities. As a result of legislation banning discrimination in housing, professional, middle-class, and working-class blacks were able to move to better neighborhoods within the city or to the suburbs. In the past, the presence of higher-income families in the ghettoes had provided a social buffer for poor families. In times of rising unemployment, better-off ghetto residents maintained such basic institutions as churches, schools, the black press, stores, banks, professional services, and recreational facilities. They also provided role models of stable, successful working families for children whose own families were worse off. Their departure led to greater social isolation of the most disadvantaged segments of the African-American community. Local institutions cut back services or closed their doors. Contact with people of different class and racial backgrounds became increasingly rare. Access to quality education and to job networks (the most common route to employment) was cut off. Because of unemployment, high mortality rates, and high rates of imprisonment, there is a shortage of marriageable men capable of supporting a family. These structural changes have led to unconventional family forms and to welfare dependency. The *communal ghetto* of the postwar era—a largely independent community with its own institutions, social hierarchies, and division of labor,

bound together by a collective identity—was replaced by the *hyperghetto*—composed of people too poor to leave, connected only by their struggle to survive and by pervasive hopelessness (Wacquant, 1994).

Wilson does not dismiss the impact of culture and socialization on ghetto poverty; rather, he holds that cultural maladies have structural origins. The combination of social isolation and widespread poverty creates a uniquely disadvantaged social environment that lacks the institutions, values, and role models necessary for success. In neighborhoods where many or most people are unemployed, men may *expect* not to work as adults, women may *expect* to bear children out of wedlock and spend long periods on welfare, and most people may *accept* these patterns as inevitable.

Douglas Massey and his colleagues (Massey, Gross, and Eggers, 1991) tested Wilson's hypothesis by measuring the impact of poverty rates, residential segregation, and residence in low-income public housing on individual outcomes, including male unemployment, teenage motherhood, and female-headed households. Comparing whites, Hispanics, and African-Americans, they found that life in poverty-stricken neighborhoods tends to promote male joblessness, teenage childbearing, and single motherhood; that the longer people have lived in these neighborhoods, the more likely they are to have these problems; and that racial segregation—in and of itself—further increases the odds that African-Americans will suffer these problems. Blacks who are equally poor but live in integrated communities are better off.

Loïc Wacquant maintains that today's black ghettoes were created, not by blind social forces, but through the exercise of power in deliberate attempts to segregate African-Americans. Housing is an example. On the one hand, the federal government subsidized the massive, mostly white middle-class exodus to the suburbs, not only with tax deductions, mortgage guarantees, and highway construction, but also by allowing or "overlooking" zoning laws and "racial steering" by sales and rental agents that ensured only whites would leave the city. On the other hand, the federal government allowed municipalities to prevent the spread of black neighborhoods by using urban renewal programs to raze low-income housing and make way for office buildings, theaters, hotels, and shopping malls, as well as the gentrification of old neighborhoods. At the same time, cities built high-rise public housing projects in already-poor black neighborhoods, thereby increasing the concentration of poverty. Cutbacks in social programs during the 1970s and 1980s completed the isolation of the inner city. Life for ghetto dwellers is often difficult and discouraging; yet to another disadvantaged population, ghetto residents may seem to be relatively well off (see the Sociology and Public Debates box).

EXPLAINING SOCIAL STRATIFICATION

Sociological explanations of stratification emphasize three themes. First, individual decisions and actions, alone, do not explain the unequal distribution of wealth, power, prestige, and life chances; rather, individual opportunities are shaped by a society's **class structure**—the relatively stable division of society into groups with sharply unequal resources and life chances. Second, while inequality may contribute to functional integration, it also reflects the **power** of elites to pursue their own goals at the expense of others. Third, inequality is not only a matter of "objective" levels of wealth and power but also of less tangible variables such as prestige and moral value.

Class Structure

Karl Marx (1867/1976) pioneered modern studies of class and stratification by showing that even though the modern "free-enterprise system" gave individuals opportunities that earlier economies had not, people's life chances were still largely determined by class position. Marx was concerned with a new division between rich and poor produced by early capitalism. He argued that this division was new in two senses. First, capitalism produced new sources of wealth: industrial production and large-scale trade. Merchants and factory owners grew spectacularly rich, seemingly overnight. Their wealth helped them gradually to replace the aristocrats of the old feudal era as the most influential class in society. Second, capitalism divided the rich from the poor in new ways. The old multilevel hierarchy (peasant, squire, knight, lord, king)—based equally on religious, political, and economic dimensions—was replaced by a two-level class structure based on private ownership of property. Capitalism divided society into owners of the means of production (capitalists) and people who could live only by selling their labor (workers). Many craft workers and small farmers who had been reasonably well-off and independent lost their traditional livelihoods and became landless laborers.

Marx argued that capitalists had to exploit workers in order to survive and make profits. He acknowledged that capitalist industry produced vast new wealth and created more opportunities for people to escape from poverty than previous economic systems had. But Marx argued that instead of allowing this new wealth to be distributed to benefit all members of a society, capitalism required that it be accumulated as capital investments that benefited the owners of the means of production at the expense of the workers. Through hard work and bright ideas, some small-business owners might join the capitalist class, but in the long run—as, for example, when the great-grandchildren of entrepreneurs have inherited their businesses—ownership of the means of production, rather than talent, hard work, or any other form of individual merit, explains wealth.

In the past, most studies of social class—and class consciousness—in the United States used the survey method to search for connections between people's class self-identification, attitudes, and political preferences and opinions. Contemporary sociologists have added subtleties and nuances to the concept of social class, as described by Marx and measured by survey research (Fantasia, 1995). Sharon Zukin (1991) has shown how the structure of inequality finds concrete expression in the spatial layout of cities (as in Manhattan, described at the beginning of this chapter). Residents of these different zones rarely interact with one another, and they experience different living conditions and develop distinct aesthetic values or tastes. Some sociologists have looked at class differences as cultural expressions of different social and economic experiences embodied in the evolution of distinctive rituals, customs, and traditions. Others have considered the mobilization of other identities (ethnicity, community, social movements, and the like) for class struggle. Many contemporary sociologists view social class more as a process than as a fixed position. How do upper-class women reconcile their prestige in the community with their subordinate position within their families? Do workers who sell symbols of upper-class status (flight attendants, personal trainers, etc.) become more aware of their subordinate status or identify with their clients? Do their interpretations lead them to action (or inaction)?

The Homeless

In the 1950s, the shantytowns and skid rows where the country's down-and-out once congregated virtually disappeared. Homelessness was no longer a problem. In the late 1970s and early 1980s, however, the number and visibility of homeless people suddenly began to climb. Today the homeless are a familiar feature of the urban landscape. Because they have no address, counting the homeless is problematic. Based on surveys of the number of adults sleeping in shelters and public places, it has been estimated that in a given month about 350,000 Americans are homeless (Jencks, 1994). But turnover is high. Every year some 1.2 million adults become homeless at least temporarily. About three-quarters of the homeless are male; about 60 percent are white and 40 percent are black; nearly all are unmarried; and most are relatively young (the mean age is thirty-seven) (Shlay and Rossi, 1992).

. . . .
Does society have an obligation to provide, at a bare minimum, shelter for all citizens?
. . . .

THE DEBATE

Where did the homeless come from, and why are they homeless? Does society have an obligation to provide, at a bare minimum, shelter for all citizens? People who answer yes to the latter question tend to believe that the homeless are victims of an economic system that values profits over people and that does not provide enough jobs to go around. They also point to a shaky social safety net, one that allows people who cannot function on their own (perhaps because of mental illness) or who experience a severe setback to fall through the holes. People who answer no to the question of society's responsibility tend to blame the homeless themselves for their situation and view them as just another group of "freeloaders."

ANALYSIS

Homelessness is in part a reflection of social structure, of social arrangements that narrow or expand life chances and opportunities. In the 1970s and 1980s, as the number of well-paid factory jobs shrank, more people were forced to take low-wage service jobs, and the competition for casual, unskilled, manual labor—the mainstay of marginal workers—increased. Not only were more people unemployed, they were unemployed for longer periods. This increase in poverty was exacerbated by cutbacks in government assistance.

At the same time, the supply of low-income housing was shrinking (Kozol, 1988). Some inner-city buildings were abandoned (or torched for insurance money); some were torn down to make way for urban renewal; and others were converted to middle- and upper-middle-class housing. Between 1973 and 1979, more than 900,000 housing units renting for $200 per month or less disappeared from the nation's housing market (Snow and Anderson, 1992). An estimated 1 million beds in single-room occupancy (SRO) hotels, which for centuries had provided the housing of last resort, were lost (Levitas, 1990). The government did little to slow the housing crunch; indeed, the Reagan administration cut funding for low-income housing by 75 percent (Lang, 1989; National Housing Task Force, 1988).

These structural factors set the stage for hopelessness. But not all chronically or desperately poor people become homeless. What makes some individuals more vulnerable than others?

To explain individual vulnerability, we must look at social action (and inaction). Many homeless people suffer from an "accumulation of troubles," problems which may or may not be the result of deliberate actions on their part: chronic unemployment plus mental illness, poor physical health, alcoholism, drug problems, criminal records, or some combination of these (Rossi, 1989). However, it is difficult to untangle cause and effect.

Other people's reactions to the homeless compound these problems. The homeless are treated as objects of curiosity, to be stared at and insulted, and objects of contamination, to be ignored and avoided. Occasional acts of goodwill may dull the pain, but the stigma of hopelessness is impossible to ignore; even in shelters and soup kitchens, volunteers maintain their distance. Our society's response to the homeless is essentially one of containment. Even people who claim sympathy for the homeless do not want "them" in "our" neighborhood—the NIMBY (*Not in My Back Yard*) phenomenon. Proposals to build new shelters or soup kitchens are met with strong local opposition. Agencies dedicated to helping the homeless no longer even try to find permanent housing and jobs, which are nonexistent, but instead settle into a familiar pattern of providing emergency, stop-gap assistance. Faced with a constant stream of desperate people, social workers may suffer "compassion fatigue." In the end, police are left with the assignment of limiting the mobility and reducing the public visibility of the homeless. One officer commented that his job is "to keep the homeless out of the face of other citizens" (Snow and Anderson, 1993).

People do not become homeless suddenly, once and for all; a "homeless career" develops in stages (Snow and Anderson, 1993). Progression from one stage to the next is not inevitable, but depends on the individual's actions and others' reactions to him or her. When individuals first hit the streets, they are frightened and disoriented. The *recently dislocated* do not know where to turn, whom to trust, or how they will survive. They tend to gravitate toward helping agencies such as the Salvation Army, to talk about their past identity and thus dissociate themselves from the homeless, and to take concrete steps to extricate themselves from their situation. A "homeless career" may end at this stage if the person finds a steady job, for example, or a room with a friend. *Straddlers* are in the second stage. They have learned how to get by and are less threatened by other homeless people. They still talk about getting off the street, but vague plans have replaced concrete actions. *Outsiders* have completed the break with conventional society. They are oriented toward surviving on the street (not leaving) and have adopted street identities. Such a person tends to see his or her past as having been lived by another person.

Averting their eyes as they walk past a woman sleeping on a steam vent or move to dodge a panhandler, many people behave as if the homeless were not there, as if they existed outside the boundaries of society. In some ways, however, the homeless are functionally integrated into the larger society. They provide the *raison d'etre* and primary clientele for the Salvation Army and similar organizations, social service agencies, shelters, church soup kitchens, drug and alcohol rehabilitation programs, and the like. To some degree, providing emergency services to the homeless has become an "industry" in itself.

To outsiders, the world of the homeless may seem chaotic, disorganized, meaningless; but street life has produced a culture or subculture with its own set of moral codes, patterns of social relationships, and identities (Snow and Anderson, 1993). Many homeless assert their belief that "what goes around, comes around" or "you reap what you sow," a norm of reciprocity that requires them to share what little they have, binding them together. The homeless also operate according a truce: "I mind my own business and expect others to mind theirs." Relationships on the street are characterized by quick and easy geniality on the one hand and distrust and impermanence on the other. Two men might declare themselves lifelong buddies soon after meeting, then go separate ways hours later. The tenuous nature of social ties among the homeless is largely a reflection of social circumstances. Because they rarely

Homeless families may form communities of their own, setting up shacks or tents on vacant lots.

stay in one place for very long and live their private lives in public places (whether the street or shelter dormitories), enduring relationships are out of reach.

To salvage self-esteem many homeless assert, "I'm down on my luck." The notion of luck exempts them from responsibility, while leaving open the possibility that their luck will change. Most homeless people engage in a good deal of storytelling, ranging from embellishments of the past to full-fledged fabrications (for example, a soon-to-be inherited fortune). Whatever the particular story line, the homeless do not passively accept the negative identity society assigns them. By unspoken rule, they never challenge one another's tall tales.

Finally, hopelessness reflects power relations. Corporations have the power to move plants, stores, and jobs out of the city or out of the country; real estate developers have the power to buy low-rent housing, evict tenants, and build new, more profitable structures; local governments have the power to pass laws prohibiting people from sleeping in parks, train stations, and other public places. The executives, urban developers, and mayors who make these decisions are not "bad people" who intend to make people homeless; rather, they have the power to pursue their profit objectives even when this means that others will suffer (directly or indirectly).

Although relatively powerless, homeless people do have choices. Thus, many use shelters only as a last resort, because they resent the loss of autonomy and individuality associated with shelters and also because they find shelters frightening, dangerous, and perhaps even more degrading than sleeping on the streets.

Functional Integration

Other sociologists, beginning with Herbert Spencer (1974) and Émile Durkheim (1893/1985), have argued that some degree of inequality contributes to functional integration. More recently, this view was developed by the American sociologists Kingsley Davis and Wilbert Moore (1945). Like Marx, Davis and Moore focused on the economic structure of society, but instead of emphasizing the formation of classes or the accumulation of inherited wealth, they stressed how opportunities to earn different levels of income motivate people.

Davis and Moore argued that some jobs are more important than others to the functional integration of complex societies. Since only a limited number of people have the talents—or are willing to invest in the education—needed to perform those jobs, it is necessary to pay them more than the average wages (or give them other extra rewards such as prestige, power, or pleasant working conditions) to motivate them. Thus, social inequality is functionally necessary. A society that failed to motivate people to perform important jobs would collapse.

There is little doubt that people can be motivated to choose certain jobs by pay or other rewards; for example, when computer scientists were in short supply in the 1980s, their pay and working conditions improved dramatically as companies competed to attract them. Critics have called other aspects of the Davis and Moore theory into question, however (see Kerbo, 1991, pp. 129–134). For example, are the best-paid jobs in American society really those that are functionally most important or those that require the most investment in education and training? We might agree that doctors are very important, need special talents, and must invest in a great deal of training, and perhaps that janitors are not very important, do not need special talents, and are easy to train. So doctors earn more than janitors. However, once we leave these extremes it is much less clear whether the theory holds. It takes more education and arguably more talent to be a schoolteacher than it does to be a financial manager, but teachers are paid much less than bankers. Are truck drivers really more important than nurses, or are they paid more because most are men?

In focusing on how motivation could be functional for society as a whole, Davis and Moore did not consider who benefited most from a particular structure of inequality. Nor did they consider the degree to which the belief that inequality is necessary makes it less likely that people will challenge the status quo.

Power

Marx held that the exercise of power in a capitalist society is a direct reflection of ownership of the means of production. Another founder of sociology, Max Weber, contended that there were other sources of power in modern societies and that power should be seen as a dimension of stratification in itself, not merely as a support for economic stratification.

In particular, Weber pointed to the power of those who run the bureaucracies that are so influential in modern societies. This consideration is especially important to the analysis of communist societies. Although Marx had thought of communism as the building of a classless society, in reality the power of the government bureaucracy became the basis for a new form of inequality under communism. In the Soviet Union, China, and other former or currently communist countries, senior bureaucrats gained access to more and better food and other goods through special shops. They had privileges denied ordinary citizens, from travel opportunities to summer houses and chauffeur-driven cars. Those who controlled essential resources (such as access to good jobs or scarce apartments) were able to demand bribes and favors from people who needed their help. The bureaucrats were even able to get special educational and job opportunities for their children and thus turn their individual good fortunes into inherited class privileges (Lenski, Lenski, and Nolan, 1991).

Even in capitalist societies like the United States, bureaucratic power can be an important basis for stratification. There are many examples of corruption, of course, like state highway commissioners who take kickbacks from construction companies. But even without corruption, high public or bureaucratic office can be a source of wealth. Members of Congress and state legislatures not only establish their own salaries but often receive free trips to exotic resorts and other favors from lobbying groups. Retired admirals and generals often become rich as consultants to corporations that seek their influence in selling products to the military.

Weber's point, however, was not just that bureaucratic power can be converted into economic income or wealth. Rather, he wanted to emphasize that power is an independent dimension of social stratification, not just a reflection of ownership of the means of production. In modern capitalist societies, most big businesses are run not by their owners but by professional managers (see Chapter 15). Millions of individuals, pension funds, and other corporations own stock in IBM, for example, but the company is a bureaucracy run by its chairman, president, and other top officials. These executives have connections to those in other corporations and to top government bureaucrats. By sharing their influence through such connections, they achieve a kind of class power (Domhoff, 1993).

Elections are another example. Each American citizen has the same power: one vote. This is democracy. However, when it comes to money for advertising, capacity to influence what is reported in newspapers or on TV, or resources to run a campaign, all Americans are not equal. This is the stratification of power. It is based not only on wealth but also on control of bureaucracies and other organizations. Antonio Gramsci (1971), one of Marx's followers, focused on cultural power. If the education system and the media teach us, first, to focus on getting rich rather than examining our social system, and second, that this system is natural and necessary, they are exerting power by convincing us to accept that system. Popular culture appears to be the "people's culture" (as opposed to elite culture), and often seems to rebel against "the system"; but most popular culture actually reflects and reinforces the inequality of a capitalist society, in which ideally anyone can get ahead though in reality few do (Grossberg, 1992).

Culture

Weber did not think that even wealth and power together could fully explain systems of stratification in modern societies. Cultural factors must also be considered, both as a source of stratification and as a dimension of inequality. For example, the lower value that many cultures place on "women's work" results in lower pay for certain occupations (nursing, for example) regardless of ownership of the means of production. Race and ethnicity are other cultural identities that can influence the workings of stratification systems. Weber used the term *status group* to describe groups of people whose prestige derives from cultural rather than economic or political factors.

Different societies attach prestige to different attributes. In traditional Indian society, as we indicated earlier, spiritual qualities are given special prestige; however, spiritual qualities are not all understood as individual accomplishments. In India's traditional **caste system,** one's spiritual status and position in the social hierarchy were determined at birth (Gould, 1971); everyone was a member of a caste, generally obligated to marry a member of the same caste and to observe strict rituals according to caste rank. High-caste Indians, especially Hindus, were charged with keeping a certain formal distance from members of lower-caste groups. A member of the highest caste, a Brahman, would feel defiled, "impure," or dirtied by physical contact with a Harijan, or "untouchable" (the lowest group, composed of street sweepers, scavengers, and swineherds). The prestige attached to caste and purity operated separately from, and overrode, wealth and power. Despite government attempts to abolish the caste system and end discrimination against lower-caste Indians, cultural position still affects how people are treated. Low-caste Hindus who achieve great economic or political success are still shunned by members of higher castes, while a poor but high-caste Brahman is still regarded by many as pure and holy. The caste system emphasizes ascribed status—rankings based on the social value placed on attributes beyond individuals' control. By contrast, though ascribed statuses like race and gender still matter in the U.S., most Americans prefer to emphasize achieved statuses—those that are the results of individual efforts and accomplishments.

To most Americans, spiritual purity is less likely to confer prestige. Instead, Americans emphasize other cultural and social factors, such as how people earn their money (their occupation), how they spend it (their mode of consumption), who they are (their ancestry), whom they know, and how successful or well-known they are. Being a neurosurgeon, earning several hundred thousand dollars a year, owning a large home, having an Anglo-Saxon surname, belonging to the "right" clubs, and having friends in positions of power are all sources of prestige in American society. As noted earlier, for most Americans, occupation is the main determinant of prestige. Americans value certain occupations for the honor they feel those occupations bring, not just for power or wealth.

Prestige is an important part of modern stratification systems (Bourdieu, 1984). Doctors, lawyers, and college professors consider their highly educated professions especially prestigious, and many would be disappointed if their children took jobs in business,

While they can't display it with their diplomas, graduates from prestigious universities like Stanford leave with "cultural capital," an unspoken edge in the business and social world that marks them as special. This privilege, of course, does not come without considerable hard work and a price tag of over $100,000.

even if that meant earning more money. Within the professions, individuals may be motivated more by the pursuit of prestige among their colleagues than by the pursuit of wealth. This is, indeed, one of the basic differences between professions and fields like business. Running a record store is not any more or less prestigious than running a clothing store, nor is managing a steel mill more or less prestigious than managing an automobile factory. We judge these businesses and those who run them mainly by the money they make. In contrast, we do not expect doctors to judge one another mainly by the money they make. If you ask someone who the best pediatrician in town is, you want that person to tell you which one takes the best care of children, not which one makes the most money. Doctors judge one another by the extent to which they keep informed about new techniques, follow accepted practices conscientiously, and put their patients' welfare above "merely financial" concerns. We think someone is a bad doctor if he or she refuses to treat someone in need, but we do not think a person is a bad grocer if that individual refuses to give vegetables to people with no money.

The French sociologist Pierre Bourdieu (1984) has shown that prestige is important not only to professionals but to people at all levels of the occupational hierarchy. Bourdieu suggests that class position depends not just on wealth or power but also on "cultural capital"—resources that benefit an individual because of the prestige they confer. A college degree,

for example, is not in itself a means of production or an instrument of power; however, it can be converted into wealth or power, as when it is used to get a good job or impress someone (Bourdieu, 1987). Sometimes cultural capital is effective where money is not. A Harvard graduate, for example, might be able to join certain elite clubs that would be closed to people without college educations, even if they were millionaires. At such clubs, individuals can meet with other members of the elite in business, law, or government.

Cultural capital is as unequally distributed as wealth or power. Most Americans do not have college degrees; still fewer have degrees from Harvard or other Ivy League colleges; and some elite college graduates can claim additional cultural distinctions—a year of study abroad, membership in the Phi Beta Kappa honorary society, or mastery of a foreign language.

Social Action

The example of cultural capital shows that class positions are shaped by social action. Choosing to study abroad, working hard enough to get into Phi Beta Kappa honorary society, and spending the time to learn a foreign language are all actions. The chances to participate in those actions are influenced by class background, but they are also matters of individual choice. Likewise, taking a general rather than a college-bound high school program or dropping out of high school are matters of individual choice. What is not a matter of choice is the general lowering of standards in urban public schools, which is the result of countless decisions by middle-class people to move to the suburbs, send their children to private schools, redraw school district boundaries, or reorganize school systems. This scenario is repeated in one city after another.

Each of the theorists we have discussed here—Marx, Weber, Davis, and Moore (and other functionalists)—emphasizes a different aspect of the relationship of social stratification to social action. Marx made two main points. First, he showed that class inequality is not mainly a result of individual action. Some new entrepreneurs may become business leaders and other business owners may go bankrupt, but this does not change *the system*. Moreover, capitalists do not exploit workers because they are bad people, Marx said, but because that is the only way they can make a profit and survive in a capitalist system. Their actions—like trying to keep wages as low as possible—are determined by their position in the class structure. In the same way, workers could not all hope to become capitalists—or even middle class—simply by working hard and saving money.

Marx held that the capitalist system requires that there be a large number of workers and only a small number of capitalists. So while a few workers might succeed in rising from rags to riches, not enough of them could become rich by their individual actions (or luck) to bring an end to poverty or inequality. The only way for workers to improve their situation, Marx thought, was for them to stop competing with one another and join together to overturn the capitalist system. Marx predicted that the inequality brought about by capitalism would be so extreme that workers would be led to choose revolution as a means of ending their exploitation (Marx and Engels, 1848/1976). This is what he meant by "class struggle." Instead of individual struggle to get ahead *within* capitalism, Marx called for struggle by the whole working class to *replace* the capitalist system with socialism.

While Marx was concerned with collective action to change the overall class structure, Weber was more concerned with individuals' efforts to change their own position, or that of their social group, within the class structure. These efforts inevitably required competition with other individuals and groups and therefore involved power and strategy. Weber discussed, for example, the ways in which some minority groups—especially religious minorities and groups of immigrants—form tight-knit communities and support one another's efforts to advance economically. Because they do not have much power as individuals, such groups need the strength that comes from coordinated social action (Parkin, 1976). Following Weber's lead, sociologists study the actions of subcultural groups like recent Asian immigrants to the United States. They point out that though these groups value the free-enterprise system, they do not approach it in a completely individualistic way; their action is socially organized and oriented toward family and community. Members of such groups lend one another money to set up small businesses, hire family members as employees, save large percentages of their income, and make sacrifices to send children to college (Light, 1993). Through all these actions they improve the class position of their families and their ethnic communities.

Looking at the problem of functional integration, Davis and Moore placed more stress on individual action. In their view, motivating a society's members to work was too important to be left to chance or individual whim. There had to be a socially organized way to make sure people got the necessary education and did the necessary work, and the structure of inequality filled the bill. According to this theory, the class structure guided individuals to act in ways that contributed to the overall functional integration of society.

Like generations of immigrants before them, recent newcomers to the United States often work long hours in family-owned businesses. For many, such commitment brings economic success.

Modern sociologists generally follow Marx in emphasizing economic structure as the most important factor in stratification. However, they follow Weber in that they believe that stratification is not based on wealth alone. Stratification of power and stratification of cultural values are also important and cannot be completely reduced to economic sources. While Marx stressed the ways in which structures of inequality produce conflict, a number of modern sociologists note that the same inequalities can be sources of motivation and important parts of functional integration.

SUMMARY

1. Stratification refers to the division of a society into layers (or strata) of people who have unequal amounts of scarce but desirable resources, which affects their life chances as well as their social standing. Some stratification systems (including the American class system) aspire to be open; some are closed (like the traditional caste system in India and South African apartheid). In practice most fall between these extremes.

2. Although Americans value equality, American society possesses a very unequal class structure. Most Americans think of themselves as middle class. Many sociologists define classes by looking at people's wealth (what they own), income (what they earn), and prestige (measured in terms of occupational characteristics). Sociologist Harold Kerbo divides American society into five classes: upper class, corporate class, middle class, working class, and lower class. Income and especially wealth are distributed very unequally in the United States.

3. The American dream of going from rags to riches is something of a myth. Although Americans as a group are upwardly mobile, most move up only a step or two, and some move downward. Though upward mobility has been more common historically, recent economic changes have produced an increase in downward mobility.

4. Despite the American belief in individual achievement, family status plays an important role in determining educational aspirations and attainment, but the structure of opportunity (beginning in schools) affects occupational status.

5. The level of poverty in the United States increased substantially in the 1980s and 1990s. Contrary to popular beliefs, most of the poor are white (though minorities have higher *rates* of poverty); most do not receive welfare payments; and most do not live in inner cities. Children are most likely to be poor, followed by single women heading their own households.

6. The fastest-growing group among the needy are the working poor—men and women whose wages do not enable them to provide adequate food, shelter, clothes, and other basics for themselves and their families.

7. Of the 14 million people who receive welfare, two-thirds are children; the numbers of white and black single mothers are roughly equal; most women work while on welfare; and most are on welfare less than two years. Also, the evidence suggests that welfare does not function as an incentive to bear more children out of wedlock.

8. The transformation of the communal ghetto to the hyperghetto has contributed to the chronic poverty of inner-city African-Americans. Wilson attributes the rise of ghetto poverty primarily to changes in the structure of urban economies (especially the loss of blue-collar and sales jobs that pay living wages and do not require higher education) and to the social isolation of the ghetto poor. However, racial discrimination and socialization to poverty may compound these problems.

9. Sociological explanations of poverty focus on social class structure, the power of elites, and the importance of intangibles (prestige and moral values) as well as tangibles (wealth and power).

10. Marx emphasized that societies are divided into classes based on people's positions in the economic structure (their relation to production). Davis and Moore highlighted the role of inequality in promoting functional integration. Weber held that stratification is multidimensional, reflecting wealth and income, power (the extent to which a person can compel others to act in a certain way), and cultural values and prestige. All of these factors—class structure, functional integration, power, and culture—create opportunities and obstacles for social action.

REVIEW QUESTIONS

1. What is social stratification? How is it institutionalized?

2. Contrast three basic approaches to social stratification: Marx's focus on structure, Weber's emphasis on power, and Davis and Moore's reliance on the concept of functional integration.

3. What is the role of prestige in social stratification?

4. How do differences of wealth and income produce the American class structure?

5. List some major predictors of social mobility.

6. Develop a profile of the poor in the United States.

7. How can the increase in the homeless population be explained?

CRITICAL THINKING QUESTIONS

1. Examine the effects of social stratification through the lenses of at least three of the five key concepts: social structure, social action, functional integration, power, and culture.

2. What consequences of social stratification do you see around you? Is Marx's perspective, Weber's perspective, or the functional integration perspective more useful to you in assessing stratification?

3. Is social mobility more desirable than having children enter the same class positions as their parents? What fac-

tors encourage or discourage mobility in the United States today?

4. Use concepts and theories presented in this chapter to develop a policy statement to Congress on how poverty can be effectively addressed in the United States.

5. Do you think it is possible for economic policies to benefit the rich, the middle class, and the poor at the same time, or must there always be a trade-off among the interests of these three groups?

GLOSSARY

Achieved statuses Statuses that are the results of individual efforts and accomplishments.

Ascribed statuses Statuses that are based on social valuations of factors beyond individuals' control, such as race, gender, or age.

Caste system A closed system of social inequality in which status is determined at birth, people are locked into their parents' social position, and differences of purity or prestige form the basis of hierarchy.

Class structure The relatively stable division of society into groups with sharply unequal resources and life chances—based in modern society, according to Karl Marx, on different positions in the capitalist system of property ownership and production.

Closed stratification system A social class system in which it is difficult or impossible to move up the social hierarchy. Also called a closed class system.

Corporate class The social class consisting of people who have a great deal of bureaucratic authority in major corporations (and in government), usually not based on ownership of those corporations.

Income What people earn during a particular time period, either from employment or investments.

Lower class The social class that includes people who do not own property, who frequently have no job, and who have no authority and usually no prestige.

Middle class The social class that comprises people who own relatively little property but whose occupations provide them with high-to-middle income, prestige, and authority. The middle class can be subdivided into the upper middle class and the lower middle class.

Open stratification system A stratification system in which there are few obstacles to social mobility, positions are awarded on the basis of merit, and rank is tied to individual achievement.

Prestige Social esteem, respect, or approval that is awarded to people because they possess attributes that their society considers admirable.

Social class People who occupy the same layer of a system of social stratification.

Social mobility The movement of people from one social position to another, either upward or downward.

Stratification The division of a society into layers of people who have unequal amounts of any given scarce reward or resource.

Structural mobility Changes in the number and kinds of occupations available in a society, relative to the number of workers available to fill them.

Upper class The social class that is made up of families who own large amounts of property, from which they derive a great deal of authority.

Wealth What people own and can draw on in times of need and can pass on to future generations.

Working class The social class that is composed of people who own little or no property, who sell their labor for a living, whose jobs give them middle-to-low income and prestige, and who have little or no authority.

CHAPTER 8

Race and Ethnicity

Seniors at the University of North Carolina (UNC) have a long-standing tradition of giving the university a class gift as they graduate. The class of 1987 commissioned a well-known sculptor to create a group of statues depicting student life for a space in front of the university's new library. In the fall of 1990, the statues were set in place. The outcry was immediate. The group of figures included two apparently African-American students—one balancing a book on her head and the other twirling a basketball on his fingertip. The single Asian-American student was primly dressed and carried a violin. Many students felt the statues reinforced racial and ethnic stereotypes. African-American students were portrayed as athletes (and thus not "serious" students) with roots in a "primitive" culture (represented by the black woman carrying a load on her head), while the Asian-American was a nerdish overachiever. The sculptor's attempt to capture the racial and ethnic diversity of today's university had backfired.

Tempers flared when someone knocked over one of the African-American statues and stole the basketball. The vandals were never caught. To this day no one knows whether they were racist whites who resented the inclusion of African-Americans in the group or African-American students protesting the stereotype of the black athlete. The chorus of complaints eventually led the chancellor to order the statues moved to a less prominent spot on campus.

Neither the administration, the faculty, nor the class of 1987 had anticipated such a strong reaction. The class of 1987 has specifically requested a multicultural image. When one asks a sculptor to represent different racial and ethnic groups in a limited space, the artist almost inevitably draws on cultural stereotypes. These stereotypes are not necessarily derogatory. Like other colleges and universities, UNC encourages coaches to seek star basketball players, many of whom are black. Universities need funds to operate; basketball makes money, and alumni, legislators, and others tend to give more to a school when its teams are winning. Sports scholarships often enable poor minority students, who might otherwise not be able to attend college, to do so. No one, black or white, protests a winning team. The school also seeks students who excel in math, science, and music, many of whom are Asian-American. No one protests admission on the basis of high grades and test scores. Furthermore, many black students are proud of their African roots, while many Asian-American students take pride in being more serious and proper than their rowdy classmates.

UNC is not alone. The statue incident is just one in a wave of racial and ethnic clashes that have hit American colleges and universities in the 1990s. Such episodes reflect the fact that America, ethnically diverse from its origin, has become a more multicultural society than ever. Racial and ethnic inequality has been one of our country's most difficult and enduring problems. At the same time, cultural differences are among our country's greatest strengths and sources of creativity. Questions about what it means to be "American," as well as questions about the causes of racial and ethnic inequality, remain unresolved.

We begin this chapter by looking at the sources of cultural diversity, emphasizing the role of immigration in the American experience. Then we will explore the different kinds of relations that exist between culturally distinct groups in a society, focusing on relations between dominant and minority groups that are matters of both power and social structure. Finally, we will profile four of the most prominent minority groups in this country: African-Americans, Hispanic-Americans, Native Americans, and Asian-Americans, examining in each case how members are—or aren't—functionally integrated into various aspects of American society and the consequences for socioeconomic inequality.

CULTURAL DIVERSITY

The Pledge of Allegiance asserts that the United States is "one nation, indivisible," but our country is also culturally diverse. People who call themselves "American" have cultural roots in just about every other country on earth and, in varying degrees, still identify with their ancestral heritages. As the incident at UNC illustrates, the ideal of cultural unity often clashes with the reality of cultural diversity.

A Nation of Immigrants

With the exception of Native Americans (American Indians), every American is one of 60 million immigrants or one of their descendants—immigrants who were pushed from their homelands by poverty and/or persecution and drawn to the United States as a "land of opportunity" (*Population Bulletin*, 1994). A few of us are descended from the colonists who established outposts on this continent in the seventeenth century; some, from an estimated 600,000 African slaves; and others from Spanish and French populations incorporated into the country as the United States expanded southward and westward.

Most of us are descendants of four main waves of immigration (*Population Bulletin*, 1994). The first wave (1790–1820) of immigrants, which began around the time the United States declared independence, consisted primarily of English Protestants, many seeking religious freedom. Immigrants making up the second wave (1820–1860) were mainly European peasants and artisans, displaced by the industrial revolution in Europe and drawn by the opening of the American West. This group of immigrants included roughly 5 million German, British, and Irish (mostly Roman Catholic), as well as Scandinavians. The third wave (1880–1914), which began after the Civil War in the United States and ended with World War I in Europe, included more than 20 million Southern and Eastern Europeans, many of whom were Eastern Orthodox or Jewish. By this time, the Industrial Revolution in this country was well under way. A majority of these immigrants settled in the major cities of the East Coast and found jobs in factories. Several hundred thousand Chinese, Japanese, and other Asians arrived during the same period to work on railroads and in West Coast cities. The fourth wave is still underway.

After 1914, immigration slowed to a trickle, in part because of the two World Wars and the Great Depression and in part because of restrictive U.S. immigration laws that established a quota system based on country of origin. Quotas were an attempt to maintain American cultural unity by admitting mostly people whom white Americans of European descent perceived to be like themselves—people who would readily be absorbed into mainstream American culture.

The 1965 Immigration Act abolished the national-origins quota system and established a preference system for people (1) with family members already in the United States or (2) with skills needed in the U.S. labor market. However, the new law did not totally eliminate cultural and racial bias. First, a system of regional quotas was established to admit roughly equal numbers of Europeans, Asians, Africans, and South Americans. On the surface, this policy seems evenhanded, but in fact it is skewed. For example, we admit as many immigrants from tiny Europe, with its relatively small population, as we do from heavily populated Asia.

Second, people who have close relatives in the United States are given preference over those who do not. Reuniting families is a worthy goal, but it favors groups who are already here, most of which are European. However, some non-Europeans (such as Indians and Pakistanis) have also benefited.

Third, the American government uses immigration as a tool in foreign policy. Refugees—individuals fleeing political persecution in their homelands—are given special treatment. However, decisions about who qualifies as a political refugee are selective. In the 1980s the United States admitted most Nicaraguans who claimed persecution at the hands of the communist Sandinista government (since over-

thrown) but was far less willing to grant refugee status to people from neighboring El Salvador, whose right-wing government was equally repressive. The crucial difference was that the government of El Salvador was an ally and the Nicaraguan government was an enemy. Before the communist regimes of Eastern Europe and the USSR collapsed, would-be immigrants from those countries were automatically considered refugees. The U.S. government did not grant the same privilege to people fleeing the Marxist regime in Ethiopia, even though they were far more likely to be imprisoned, tortured, or killed by their government than were Eastern Europeans.

Since the 1965 Immigration Act, immigration has increased dramatically (Figure 8.1). An estimated 10 million legal (and illegal) immigrants entered this country in the 1980s, exceeding the previous record of 9 million in the first decade of this century (Frey and Tilove, 1995). The newest immigrants differ from earlier groups in several ways. Eighty percent are either Latin American and Asian, with languages and traditions that differ from those of the European–American mainstream. They tend to be younger than the U.S. population as a whole and thus are more likely to have young children (now or in the near future). Finally, many are highly educated: More than half of the immigrants admitted under employment preferences in 1993 were managers and administrators or professional and technical specialists. For the first time, substantial numbers

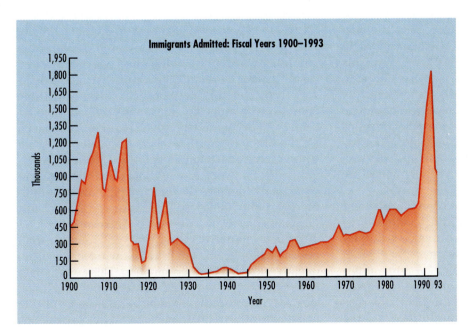

FIGURE 8.1 / *Immigration to the United States, 1900–1993*

In terms of numbers, immigration to the United States peaked in 1991 (in part because an amnesty program granted immigrant status to illegal aliens who were long-term residents). However, because the U.S. population as a whole has grown, the proportion of immigrants to native-born Americans was greater in the period 1905 to 1914 (11.1 immigrants admitted per thousand residents) than in the period 1984 to 1993 (3.8 immigrants per thousand residents).

Source: "Immigration to the United States: Journey to an Uncertain Destiny," *Population Bulletin* 49, no. 2, September (1994): 16.

Turn-of-the-century immigrants await entrance into the United States on Ellis Island, in the shadow of the Statue of Liberty. Successive waves of immigration have made the United States a diverse nation with a unique culture.

of immigrants are competing with middle-class Americans, not starting at the bottom.

The newest immigrants are changing the structure of the country. Three-quarters of them have settled in just six states (California, New York, Texas, Florida, New Jersey, and Illinois), and one-quarter live in eight metropolitan areas. This means that the impact of immigration, including increased demands on local school systems, medical services, and job markets, is much greater in some places than in others. High levels of immigration have precipitated a new form of "white flight" (see Chapter 12, Education). In the last half of the 1980s, for every ten immigrants who arrived in New York, Chicago, Los Angeles, Houston, and Boston, nine native-born residents departed. This time whites are not just abandoning the city for the suburbs; they are leaving whole regions for "whiter destinations," such as Tampa-St. Petersburg, Seattle, Phoenix, Atlanta, and Las Vegas, none of which attract many immigrants (Frey and Tilove, 1995, p. 44).

The combination of immigrant concentration and white dispersal is creating two distinct nations (Frey and Tilove, 1995). In some places America is rapidly changing and is both culturally and racially diverse. This America is represented by coastal ports of entry—from San Francisco to Houston in the West, from Boston to Washington and Miami in the East—plus Chicago in the Midwest. The "other" America is the rest of the country, in which the numbers and impact of immigrants are very small.

Racial and Ethnic Minorities in the United States

Most immigrant groups encountered discrimination in their early years in America. The second and third generations, however, tended to blend into the population at large and maintained their ethnic identity only loosely. Americans of German descent, for example, may take pride in their heritage, but most no longer speak German, live in primarily German-American communities, or suffer discrimination. Some groups, especially those who arrived more recently and encountered high levels of hostility (such as the Irish in northeastern cities and Poles in Chicago) have maintained stronger identities. A few groups remain very strongly identified with one another, partly because they have experienced continuing discrimination—especially African-Americans, Hispanic-Americans, and Asian-Americans.

The term **minority group** refers to groups or categories of people who are held in low esteem and frequently subjected to discrimination. This term derives from situations in which a majority of the population shares a common cultural identity and singles out for unequal treatment immigrants or subject populations who are considered "different." This label can be misleading, however. In some cases, the group whose rights and opportunities are restricted is a numerical majority. Thus, in South Africa under apartheid black Africans were treated as a minority group even though they made up 70 percent of the population. Women outnumber men by 52 to 48 percent in America but in many ways are treated as a minority. Women's values and demands are regarded as "special interests," while those of white men are regarded as "the public interest" (see Chapter 9). The most common criteria for singling out a category of people for minority-group status are race and ethnicity.

Defining Race and Ethnicity

One of the first things we notice about people (along with their sex) is their race (Omi and Winant, 1994). We see race as providing clues about *who* a person is. When we meet a person who is racially mixed or who belongs to an ethnic/racial category with which we are not familiar, we are momentarily caught off guard. Comments such as "Funny, you don't look Indian" or "You don't act black" betray underlying preconceptions about what Native Americans or African-Americans are supposed to be like.

The idea that the human family can be divided into distinct races dates to the nineteenth century and a series of pseudoscientific theories that used the language of Darwinian biology. According to this view, the races represented different branches of the human evolutionary tree; some (especially white Europeans) were naturally superior to others. Race was conceived as a fixed, objective, biological category, similar to species. Well into the twentieth century, scientists labored diligently to classify all humankind into distinct races, though they rarely agreed with one another on the number or characteristics of races and always stumbled on annoying "exceptions."

The problem of racial classification took on special importance in the United States, where democratic ideals coexisted uneasily with the institution of slavery (J. Marks, 1994). Many states had laws banning interracial marriage or miscegenation (some of which remained in force as late as the 1960s), but the fact that many white slave owners had mistresses and children of African descent was well-known. How could the courts decide who was black? The nation's answer was anyone with *any* known black African

ancestry (Davis, 1993). In the South this was known as the "one drop rule," meaning that one drop of black blood made a person black. This led to the biologically absurd conclusion that one black great-grandparent was enough to define a person as black, though seven white great-grandparents were not enough to define a person as white. Race was an all-or-nothing proposition: One could be black or white, but not somewhere in between.

Modern genetics has shown that the idea of distinct human races has no scientific meaning. The biological diversity *within* human groups is far greater than the difference between groups (J. Marks, 1994). Human beings come in a wide variety of sizes, colors, and shapes. There are fatter and thinner people in all groups, just as there are people with type O or type A blood. The differences between one population and the next lie in the *proportion* of people with certain traits or genes. Thus variations in the human species are a matter of gradations, not distinct groups with clear genetic boundaries. Race is a social, not a biological, category.

The idea of distinct races has been used as a political tool to limit the distribution of personal freedom, civil rights, education, housing, jobs, justice, and simple respect. For over 250 years, the United States was a "racial dictatorship" in which nonwhites were systematically excluded from politics and other social institutions (Omi and Winant, 1994). Despite change, this legacy remains etched into our social structure.

Race is also a social identity, recognized as significant by blacks as well as whites. In a sense, slavery created the category "black," or African-American, by treating Ashante and Ovimbundu, Yoruba and Bakongo as essentially the same. Over the years these groups mixed with one another (and with white Americans), "forging a new cultural style and new sense of identity out of their American experience and remnants of their African past and thus becoming a new people both physically and culturally" (Davis, 1993, p. 29). What began as an involuntary and derogatory identity over time became the basis for loyalty and pride, as well as political mobilization and cultural achievements.

Today, individuals may be considered disloyal if they do not put their African-American identity first. Black Americans who socialize with, date, or marry white Americans face as strong or stronger opposition than do white Americans who have cross-racial friends and lovers. This is one reason why white students often have difficulty understanding their black classmates (Blauner, 1991). White students tend to see the "race problem" as a product of color-consciousness, and the solution as color-blindness. Most view racial divisions as a piece of American history that America should (and to a large extent has) overcome. Nonwhite students more often see the "race problem" as a question of power that plays a central role not only in American history but in their own everyday experiences.

In sociological terms, then, **race** denotes a category of people who perceive themselves and are perceived by others as distinctive on the basis of certain biologically inherited traits. Race is a social and cultural category, the product of social actions that created political and economic inequality and established cultural categories. Although racial differences are not biologically significant, many people believe these differences are important and act on that belief.

An **ethnic group** consists of people who perceive themselves and are perceived by others as sharing a common history as well as distinctive cultural traits such as language, religion, family customs, and food preferences. Hispanics, for example, may be black, white, or any gradation in between. What unites Hispanics is their culture (which does not consider skin color significant). The term *ethnic group* is usually used to describe subgroups within a country. Polish-Americans, Navahos, French Canadians, and Ethiopian Jews are examples. The sociologist John Shelton Reed (1994) has argued that "Southern" is a U.S. ethnic group based on the cultural distinctions of southerners from Americans of other regions. The extent to which ethnic-group members actually share unique cultural traits is less important than the fact that they and others believe they are "different." Ethnicity, like race, is a social label.

Whether a group of people is regarded as a racial or ethnic group is largely subjective. In Germany and Eastern Europe, Jews were considered a separate race; during the Holocaust the "one drop rule" was used to determine who would be sent to death camps. In the United States today, Jews may see themselves and be seen by others as members of an ethnic group or as members of a religion. Anglo-Americans tend to see Hispanics and Native Americans as members of distinct races. Hispanics see themselves as members of a variety of different ethnic or national groups (Mexican, Cuban, Puerto Rican, Honduran); likewise, Native Americans see themselves as members of different nations (Sioux, Cherokee, Mohawk, Hopi).

Ethnicity is important to Americans (Waters, 1990). No matter how long their families have lived here, few people describe themselves as simply "American." The U.S. census form offers a choice of writing in a specific identity or checking "American" or "Don't Know"; in 1990 only 6 percent checked "American." For Americans of European descent, ethnic identity is flexible, voluntary, and largely symbolic. Whites may choose the identity of one or another parent or grandparent; claim different ethnicities in different situations (hence the saying, "Everyone is Irish on St. Patrick's Day"); or switch identities at different points in their lives. For African-Americans, Hispanic-Americans, Native Americans, and Asian-Americans, ethnic identity is not just a matter of personal choice. These ethnic labels are ascribed statuses (see Chapter 3) imposed by others, often on the basis of whether physical appearance deviates from white standards.

PATTERNS OF INTERGROUP RELATIONS

People of different cultures have come into contact throughout history—as a result of trade relations, migration, colonization, and military conquest. Sometimes they have defined their differences as racial, sometimes as ethnic, sometimes as matters of nationality or religion. Wherever such relationships involve large enough numbers of people that group as well as individual differences become significant, power becomes a crucial factor. When one group has vastly more power than the other, race and ethnicity may be used as a rationalization for colonizing, displacing, enslaving, or even exterminating the other. More subtly, one group may dictate the terms under which the other group must live, limiting their opportunities or requiring members of the subordinate group to give up their own culture to get ahead as individuals; but race and ethnicity may also provide the motivation for resistance, rebellion, and demands for mutual tolerance and respect.

Colonialism

Colonialism refers to the takeover and settlement of a territory by a foreign power, and subsequent political and social domination of the native population. European colonialism, which began in the fifteenth century, is history's prime example. At one time

Rudyard Kipling coined the phrase, "white man's burden" to describe the obligation of Europeans, especially the British, to rule and civilize peoples whom they considered culturally and racially beneath them.

Europeans ruled most of the southern hemisphere and perhaps half the world's population. Under colonialism, the foreign elite pursued lives of leisure while local people were forced to labor in fields and mines or as servants. Traditional political systems, patterns of land use, production methods, and other elements of local culture were exploited or banned to suit European goals. Small numbers of natives might be hired as soldiers or given enough European education to serve as clerks, but no more.

European colonialism contributed to modern notions about race by creating a situation in which officials needed to distinguish between Europeans (of whatever country or social class) and the native peoples they ruled (Todoroff, 1994). The resulting "color line" helped to rationalize the seizure of territories and treasure, and the exploitation, enslavement, and sometimes extermination of native peoples. Most European colonies won their independence in the decades following World War II. In a few "settler societies"—notably the United States, Australia, New Zealand, and South Africa—colonials seized control from the mother country and declared a new nation.

Displacement

In some cases the invading group does not stop at domination but seeks to displace the native population. Displacement is most likely in areas that are rich in natural resources and similar in geography and climate to the homeland of the invading group (Lieberson, 1961; Van den Berghe, 1978). Displacement may take the form of forced relocation, attrition (the native group gradually moves on or dies out), or expulsion. Displacements have occurred throughout history. In precolonial Africa, for example, warlike cattle herders from the north pushed smaller groups of hunters and gatherers off the plains of East Africa into less desirable areas, such as the Kalahari Desert.

The scale and frequency of displacement increased under European colonialism. The treatment of Native Americans is an example. Native Americans did not think of land as a commodity to be bought and sold and so did not see the arrival of Europeans as a threat. Then, as the numbers of white settlers increased, so did competition for land, and soon Native Americans were forced to relocate west of the Mississippi. But the flood of white settlers, with vastly superior weapons, continued (Spicer, 1980). To open the way for farmers and cattle ranchers, Europeans wiped out the buffalo, the Plains Indians' principal source of livelihood, then systematically attacked Native American villages and bands. Ultimately, the few remaining Native Americans were confined to inhospitable reservations. In much the same way, European settlers displaced and all but destroyed the native populations of Australia (aborigines) and New Zealand (Maoris).

Genocide

Genocide is the intentional, systematic attempt to destroy a national, racial, religious, or ethnic group. The term *genocide* was coined in 1944 by Raphael Lemkin to describe the Holocaust (the massacre of 6 million Jews in Nazi Germany), but there were ancient precedents. The destruction of the North African city of Carthage by Rome (after Hannibal's famous but unsuccessful attempt to conquer Rome) is an early example. The Romans not only demolished the city and its buildings but also sowed salt into the ground so that people could not live there anymore.

Genocide is most likely when a nation has suffered economic setbacks and/or military defeat (duPreez, 1994). To restore national self-esteem, leaders ask, "Who betrayed us?" The answer is likely to be a minority group that practices a religion that challenges the beliefs of the majority; that has links with outside enemies; and that is relatively prosperous. The goal of genocide is to "purify" the nation of the enemy within. The minority group becomes not simply a scapegoat but a sacrificial lamb.

Armenians were the first victims of modern genocide. Christian Armenians had been subjects of the Ottoman Empire, whose Muslim rulers tolerated cultural and religious diversity, for centuries. By 1900, however, the Ottoman Empire was crumbling and the Young Turks—ardent nationalists who were secular but suspicious of non-Turks—came to power. In 1915, after a disastrous defeat by Czarist Russia (blamed on alleged Christian Armenian traitors), the Turkish government ordered the deportation of the entire Armenian population. Those not killed immediately in their villages were driven through mountains and deserts without food or water; an estimated 1 million (more than half the Armenians in Turkey) perished.

The events leading up to the Holocaust were similar. According to Nazi ideology, Germany's defeat in World War I and subsequent economic collapse were the result of an international Jewish conspiracy. The Aryan race—the "master race"—had to be protected from Jewish contamination at all costs.

The Holocaust took place in two phases. In the first phase (1933–1940), long-standing prejudice was mobilized to isolate Jews by prohibiting intermarriage with Christians, stripping Jews of German citizenship, barring them from the professions, confiscating their property, forcing them to live in clearly defined ghettoes, and requiring that they wear an identifying Star of David sewn onto their sleeves. The long-term Nazi goal at this point was to deport Jews to some distant homeland.

In the second phase (1941–1945), the policy of forced emigration became one of annihilation. World War II not only made deportation impractical but also enabled extremists in the Nazi government to operate under the cover of emergency powers and wartime secrecy. In Germany, Austria, Poland, and Nazi-occupied Russia, Jews were rounded up, packed into airless cattle cars, and shipped to Buchenwald, Dachau, and other Nazi death camps. On arrival, some were immediately marched into "showers" that were combination gas chambers and crematoriums. Others were kept barely alive and forced to participate in their own destruction, for example by digging mass graves and shoveling in the bodies of fellow Jews. Still others were used in brutal medical experiments. Six million men, women, and children perished in the Holocaust. When the death camps were liberated in 1945, the survivors had been reduced to living skeletons, barely recognizable as human. Even today, visitors to Auschwitz and other death-camp sites see bone fragments and teeth in the deserted fields.

The Holocaust, writes Zygmunt Bauman,

> towers high above the past genocidal episodes in the same way as the modern industrial plant towers above the craftsman's cottage workshop, or the modern industrial farm, with its tractors, combines and pesticides, towers above the peasant farmstead with its horse, hoe and hand weeding. (1991, p. 89)

It was a distinctly modern form of evil. European Jews had been subjected to discrimination and periodic pogroms (attacks carried out by mobs) for centuries. But mob violence is usually short-lived. The only pogrom that occurred during the Holocaust was *Kristallnacht,* a night when German mobs (with government acquiescence) vandalized and set fire to Jewish homes, businesses, and houses of worship; perhaps a hundred Jews were killed. At this rate, the extermination of 6 million people would have taken 200 years (Sabini and Silver, 1980).

The Holocaust depended on such modern institutions as nationalism (the belief that belonging to a certain culture or ethnic group is the basis of all political rights); advanced technology (railroads, gas chambers); and bureaucratic organization. Bureaucracy substitutes technical efficiency for moral responsibility: High-level officials who dictate policy do not have to witness the consequences, nor do underlings have to understand their superiors' reasoning. Even in less extreme situations, bureaucracy tends to dehumanize social action. The Holocaust replaced the mob with the bureaucracy, collective rage with obedience to authority. The extermination of Jews took place out of sight; it did not depend on popular support but merely on the acquiescence of the German people—and also of Allied leaders, who knew but did not inform their publics of the death camps.

The Holocaust is not the only modern example of genocide. The massacre of Tutsis by Hutu in Rwanda and the campaign of "ethnic cleansing" against Bosnian Muslims in former Yugoslavia in the 1990s followed this pattern. One difference is that these atrocities took place in full view of the mass media.

Slavery

In some cases, powerful groups have economic motives for exploiting the labor of other peoples rather than getting rid of them (displacement or genocide). Indeed, in the early Nazi period, German rulers used Jews as forced laborers. **Slavery** is an institutionalized system of bondage in which the "master" owns and exercises complete control over the slaves, who are forced to perform involuntary labor. Slavery has occurred in many societies throughout history, including ancient Greece and Rome.

The slave trade that transported Africans to the Americas, however, was in some ways unique. In other times and places, slaves typically were captured in battle; in effect, they were prisoners of war. Europeans organized slavery as a business, buying Africans captured by rival tribes for "resale" in the New World. As the demand for slaves increased, Europeans paid Africans to conduct raids and kidnap other Africans for purely commercial purposes. Nearly half a million Africans were brought by force to America, where they were viewed as property and bought, sold, used, and abused at the will of the white majority. Many others were shipped to the Caribbean (where conditions, if anything, were worse), and smaller numbers to South America and to Europe.

The slave trade was driven by plantation economies centered on crops like sugar and cotton

Slavery has long existed in human socities. The word, in fact, originates from "Slav," referring to eastern Europeans and Russians whom the Vikings captured and forced into bondage in the ninth and tenth centuries. But Africans have probably suffered more from slavery than any single group in human history, partly because African slavery became part of the colonization of both North and South America.

that were most profitable when organized on a large scale, with high volumes of cheap but not necessarily skilled labor. In some settings slaves were treated relatively well as valued labor; in others, they were brutally abused. Slaves were not allowed to maintain cultural, village, or even family ties, out of fear that loyalty might lead to rebellion. Slavery was rationalized on the grounds that Africans were a "heathen," "backward," even "childlike" people, incapable of exercising the rights guaranteed to white men under the Constitution. A key feature of this system was the creation of a clear distinction—an uncrossable boundary—between slaves and the rest of the population. In other societies and times, slaves could earn their freedom through hard work and loyalty. In the United States, slavery was perpetual: Children born to slaves became slaves themselves. Visible physical differences and racist ideology aided in the institutionalization of slavery in the United States.

Segregation

After the Civil War, slavery was banned, but this did not reconcile white elites to the loss of cheap labor, or poorer whites to competition from free blacks. To defend their dominant status, whites instituted new boundaries and restrictions. Sharecropping created a cycle of borrowing and indebtedness that tied African-Americans to the lands they had worked as slaves. New "Jim Crow" laws were passed to prevent blacks from voting and bar them from public facilities. Social pressure was used to reward black leaders who called on others to cooperate and to prevent white liberals from encouraging blacks to demand civil rights. When these efforts failed, Southern whites resorted to violence (cross burnings, evictions, lynchings). This strategy of domination was designed to maintain the economic status quo by keeping blacks from mixing with whites.

Segregation is the enforced separation of racial or ethnic groups. It is a form of institutionalized discrimination, woven into the social structure. In a segregated society, only certain types of contact between the dominant group and racial or ethnic minorities are permitted. Typically, members of the subordinate group are not allowed to live in the same neighborhoods as those in the dominant group, attend the same schools, work in the same occupations, join the same clubs, or use the same public facilities (hotels, restaurants, washrooms, even water fountains). Segregationists particularly fear intermarriage. Segregation is largely a strategy for maintaining the "purity" of elites.

In the United States, segregation was rationalized on the grounds of "separate but equal" opportunities, as outlined by the Supreme Court in *Plessy v. Ferguson* (1896). Blacks had the same right to public education as whites, for example, but this did not mean blacks and whites had to attend the same schools. In practice, however, separate did not mean equal.

The South African system of *apartheid* was an even more extreme form of racial segregation, created in the early 1950s by Afrikaner nationalists—descendants of Dutch settlers who saw South Africa as *their* homeland and were violently opposed to any form of racial mixing. Under apartheid, every individual was assigned to a racial category at birth (as either white, black African, Indian, or "coloured," meaning mixed race); rights and opportunities were based on racial classification. Elections were for whites only. Blacks were considered citizens, not of South Africa, but of ten "homelands." Nonwhites were not permitted to purchase land in "white" areas or even enter these areas unless they worked there; work permits were granted on a temporary basis, and workers could not bring their families with them. At various times, groups of "redundant" workers were forcibly relocated to their assigned homelands and whole black townships were razed to make room for white development. Social contact between blacks and whites was strictly forbidden.

Resistance

Few, if any, peoples accept unequal treatment and abuse willingly and passively. When protesting or fighting back openly are too dangerous, members of minorities employ what James Scott (1985, 1987) has called "weapons of the weak." One strategy is to avoid confrontation and unpleasant interaction by "self-segregation." Even where laws do not force them to stay separate, members of the minority group may choose to isolate themselves. Self-segregation (as in the "Chinatowns" of U.S. cities) strengthens support networks and reinforces ethnic pride. Another strategy is covert resistance. For example, the minority may do as little work as possible—the source of the common myth that minorities are "lazy." They may also sabotage equipment in factories, pass secrets to enemies of the dominant group, or steal from elites.

Minorities are not always so weak that they must limit themselves to indirect and secret actions (Scott, 1987). In India, for example, Mahatma Gandhi developed the idea of nonviolent resistance to British colonial rule. Following the example of Jesus (whom Gandhi admired) as well as models from Indian culture, Gandhi and his followers would stage demonstrations and remain passive—go limp—when attacked by police. The goals of nonviolent resistance are (1) to disrupt existing patterns of social interaction with economic boycotts and work stoppages and with civil disobedience (deliberate mass violation of colonial law) and (2) to demoralize the police and make them look brutal in the eyes of the general

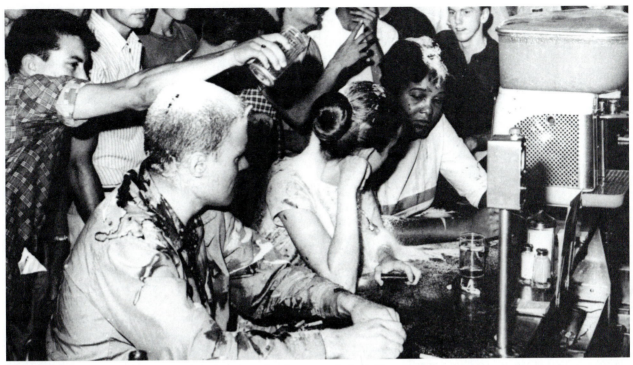

The civil rights movement used nonviolent demonstrations to expose the brutality and indignities of segregation. Here, jeering whites pour sugar, ketchup, and mustard on demonstrators holding a "sit in" at a segregated lunch counter in Jackson, Mississippi, 1963.

public. Thousands of Indian demonstrators were jailed, injured, and even killed, but India eventually won independence through nonviolent revolution.

Martin Luther King, Jr., urged similar tactics in the American civil rights movement of the 1950s and 1960s. The civil rights movement was sparked in part by the return of World War II veterans. In Europe, black and white soldiers had fought together to save the "free world"; Hitler's racist policies were universally condemned. Yet many black veterans came home to Southern communities where they were denied basic human rights. The 1954 Supreme Court decision in *Brown v. Board of Education,* which overturned the separate-but-equal doctrine and called for immediate integration of schools, raised black hopes; however, white Southern governors vowed to block school integration, and the federal government was reluctant to intervene. The combination of rising expectations and slow or no change in living conditions often leads to uprisings (Davies, 1974).

The civil rights movement was a true grassroots movement, which arose and spread spontaneously. Black churches, the one independent black institution allowed in the South, played a key role, provid-

ing leaders, communication networks, organization, and a "shared symbolic world" for expressing black hopes and containing black fears (Morris, 1984). Protestors confronted segregation directly but nonviolently with economic boycotts, sit-ins, mass demonstrations, and mass submission to arrest.

Nonviolent protest relies on the willingness of some members of dominant groups to recognize the suffering of the minority group and to acknowledge the justice of their cause. The civil rights movement succeeded in large part by prompting many whites to withdraw support from segregationist businesses and politicians. (See Chapter 20 for a more detailed analysis of the civil rights movement.)

The collapse of apartheid in South Africa was brought on in part by pressure from the world community in the form of economic boycotts and in part by the threat of violence and sabotage within South Africa. By recognizing black leaders and political parties, endorsing a constitution based on majority rule, and holding multiracial elections, white South Africans narrowly escaped armed rebellion.

Full-fledged revolt is most likely when the social minority group is a numerical majority. In Kenya and Rhodesia (now Zimbabwe), where black Africans greatly outnumbered British colonists, armed rebellion played a central role in the struggle for independence. The British had superior armies and weapons, but they eventually grew weary of the killing, the cost, and the absence of any prospect for peace on their terms. Most former colonies in Africa won independence through armed rebellion.

Prejudice and Discrimination

Eliminating formal restrictions on minority groups does not automatically mean that they will have equal access to education, jobs, and other opportunities or that they will be treated with respect. Discrimination can continue to operate informally long after legal segregation has been abolished; cultural prejudices do not disappear simply because the laws have changed.

Prejudice is a rigid opinion about a category of people, such as a racial or ethnic group, based on its members' real or imagined characteristics. (Prejudice can be positive or negative, but the term is most often applied to negative evaluations.) Prejudice is a *pre*judgment that persists in the face of contrary evidence. People are prejudiced when they are convinced that all members of a certain group have the same qualities; when they cannot see members of the group as individuals; and when they ignore evidence that would disprove their beliefs. Prejudice has a powerful effect on people's actions because it shapes their emotional responses as well as their thoughts.

Prejudices are not just individual attitudes; they are cultural norms. American children, for example, learn racial prejudices from their parents' conversation and behavior and from television, books, and other cultural sources. Often prejudices are maintained because people seldom come in contact with members of the scorned minority, except in unequal relationships (such as master and servant). Infrequent, unequal contact tends to perpetuate **stereotypes,** that is, fixed, simplified, distorted cultural generalizations about social groups and categories and their members.

Prejudice can lead us to make very different evaluations of the same behavior, depending on whether it is seen in members of our own group (in-group) or of another group against which we are prejudiced (out-group). In the words of sociologist Robert Merton:

Did Lincoln work far into the night? This testifies that he was industrious, resolute, perseverant, and eager to realize his capacities to the full. Do the out-group Jews or Japanese keep these same hours? This only bears witness to their sweatshop mentality, their ruthless undercutting of American standards, their unfair competitive practices. Is the in-group hero frugal, thrifty, and sparing? Then the out-group villain is stingy, miserly, and penny-pinching. All honor is due to the in-group Abe for his having been smart, shrewd, and intelligent and, by the same token, all contempt is owing to the out-group Abes for their being sharp, cunning, crafty, and too clever by far. (Merton, 1957, p. 428)

Discrimination refers to significant social decisions about, and actions toward, people based on their presumed racial or ethnic identities. Prejudice is a set of culturally supported opinions; discrimination is a series of social actions based on those opinions.

Prejudice and discrimination can function as part of self-fulfilling prophecies (Merton, 1968b; Myrdal, 1944). Because Afrikaners believed black Africans to be racially inferior, they denied them education, job opportunities, quality housing, and ordinary respect. As a result of prejudice and discrimination, many blacks in South Africa were uneducated, employed at menial jobs, ill-housed, and impoverished. This lower standard of living "confirmed" the belief that black Africans were inferior. Thus a false belief (racial inferiority) affected behavior in a way (lack of opportunity) that made the false belief seem true (see Figure 8.2).

The most extreme form of prejudice is called **racism:** the belief that members of certain racial or ethnic groups are *innately* superior or inferior. Racists believe that intelligence, industry, morality, and other important traits are biologically inherited and therefore unalterable. In the colonial period, racist ideology served as a rationalization for the conquest, subjugation, exploitation, and brutalization of the native populations by Europeans. Racist ideology also provided the excuse for both official segregation and unofficial discrimination in the United States. Finally, racist ideology promotes belief in sharp divisions and boundaries. One is either white or black, Aryan or other.

White Americans tend to think of racism as an individual phenomenon, as a set of hateful ideas and violent social actions expressed and practiced by a radical white supremacist fringe. African-Americans are more likely to view racism as part of our society's

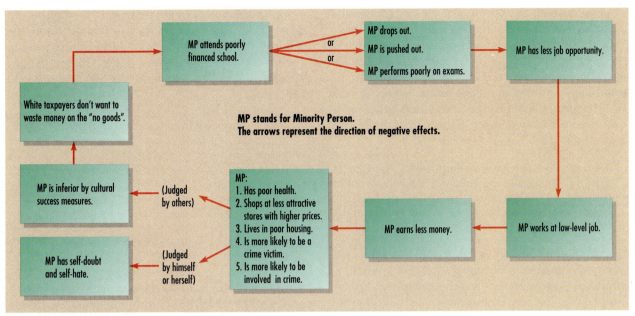

FIGURE 8.2 / *The Vicious Cycle of Prejudice and Discrimination*

Prejudice and discrimination function as a self-fulfilling prophecy, distorting how the dominant group views minorities and damaging minority self-esteem.

Source: From Richard T. Schaefer, *Racial and Ethnic Groups*, 4th ed. Copyright ©1990 by Richard T. Schaefer. Reprinted by permission of Little, Brown and Company.

social structure, so deeply ingrained in our traditions and practices that it may continue to operate in the absence of conscious prejudice or deliberate discrimination. Unintentional discrimination is often called **institutional racism.** For example, in hard times many employers (including the government) follow a "last hired, first fired" policy, laying off workers with the least seniority. This seemingly impartial practice discriminates against African-Americans who have not been able to build seniority because they were not offered jobs in the past.

Prejudice and stereotypes are not limited to elites. Subordinate groups have prejudices of their own, often against other subordinate groups or groups that have managed to overcome subordinate status. African-American prejudice against Jews is an example. Cornel West (1994) suggests that black anti-Semitism rests on three beliefs. First, blacks see Jews as benefiting from all the privileges accorded whites in our society and thus contributing, if only by complicity, to racial inequality. Second, many blacks have higher expectations of Jews than of other white ethnic groups. Given their common history of degradation and oppression, blacks and Jews should be "nat-

ural allies." When conservative Jews oppose affirmative action, for example, blacks feel doubly betrayed. Third, "black anti-Semitism is a form of underdog resentment and envy, directed at another underdog who has 'made it' in American society" (West, 1994, p. 112). One of the most upwardly mobile ethnic groups in America, Jews are highly visible in the upper levels of academia, journalism, the entertainment industry, and the professions. Rather than seeing Jewish mobility as the result of hard work, many blacks attribute this success to clannishness and favoritism among Jews. Some black leaders use stories of Jewish conspiracies as targets for black anger. At the same time, the media tend to overreport black anti-Semitism and underreport white anti-Semitism, diverting attention from institutionalized discrimination against blacks *and* Jews.

Assimilation

In an **integrated** (as opposed to segregated) society, interaction between different racial and ethnic groups is frequent and usually friendly (Blau and Schwartz,

1983). However, this does not necessarily mean that all groups are equal. Several patterns are possible.

In some societies members of different ethnic and racial groups mix freely, allow their various customs and values to blend, and intermarry, thus creating a totally new culture, an amalgamation. This is what the playwright Israel Zangwill had in mind when he described the United States at the turn of the century as a *melting pot*:

> There she lies, the great melting pot—listen! Can't you hear the roaring and bubbling? Ah, what a stirring and seething—Celt and Latin, Slav and Teuton, Greek and Syrian, Black and Yellow—Jew and Gentile. (1909, pp. 198–199)

In Zangwill's romantic play, a poor Jewish immigrant man marries a beautiful Christian woman, all animosities between their families disappear, and the couple lives happily ever after.

To what degree does the image of the melting pot apply to the United States? Certainly, the many influences that different groups have brought to this country have created a new and distinctively American culture, but racial, ethnic, and cultural differences have not simply melted away. Differences "melted" most among those people who (1) migrated earliest, (2) occupied more or less equal positions in the power structure, (3) had similar cultures to begin with, and (4) were most alike in physical traits labeled as racial (such as skin color). Thus, the differences between English, French, Irish, German, and Scandinavian ancestry do not figure prominently in American society today.

African-Americans are the most dramatic example of a group that has *not* blended in. European-Americans actively limited black Americans' access to the dominant culture; for example, it was illegal to teach slaves to read and write. At the same time they prevented slaves from maintaining their traditional cultures in this country, treating all African cultures as essentially alike and equally "heathen." Ironically, one of the best examples of a melting pot in the United States is the merging of different influences into a new and distinctive African-American culture. For example, blacks combined African rhythms and harmonies with adaptations of Christian hymns and folk music to create a uniquely American musical tradition—stretching from gospel, blues, and jazz to rock and roll and rap music. African-Americans have also made original contributions to technology, literature, and other arts.

Not all Americans have shared the melting-pot ideal. From the earliest days of this country, the Anglo-Saxon elite have expected newcomers to adopt their customs and values. John Quincy Adams expressed the sentiment in the early nineteenth century:

> To one thing they [immigrants to the United States] must make up their minds, or they will be disappointed in every expectation of happiness as Americans. They must cast off the European skin, never to resume it. They must look forward to their posterity rather than backward to their ancestors; they must be sure that whatever their own feelings may be, those of their children will cling to the prejudices of this country. (Quoted in Gordon, 1978, p. 187)

Thus, immigrants have been expected not only to embrace the dominant culture but also to surrender their cultural heritage. Calls to make English the official language of the United States are a contemporary version of assimilationism.

Assimilation describes the incorporation of a minority group into the culture and social life of the dominant group so that the minority eventually disappears as a separate, identifiable unit. Assimilation is asymmetrical. Whereas advocates of the "melting pot" hold that all groups will be equally changed into something new, proponents of assimilation hold that minorities must conform to the existing majority culture.

The sociologist Robert E. Park and his colleagues (1925) described assimilation in terms of stages. In the first stage, newcomers, who are not familiar with the dominant culture, struggle for a foothold. They can only manage to secure what others do not want—the poorest land, the most menial jobs, the worst housing. Typically, new immigrants gravitate to separate ethnic enclaves where they can feel more at home. In the second stage, they—or more likely their children and grandchildren—begin to learn the language and values of the dominant group. The struggle for survival becomes a struggle for respectability, better living conditions, and higher-paying, more prestigious jobs. This is an uphill battle, but gradually more members of the ethnic group achieve upward mobility, remnants of their traditional culture fade, and intergroup marriages occur. Assimilation is complete.

Not all groups have been "invited" to assimilate, as in the case of African-Americans, and not all groups have wanted to assimilate. Hispanic-, Asian-, and Native Americans, in particular, have actively worked to keep their cultural traditions alive. In recent years more Americans have begun to see cultural differences as a source of strength, to be preserved rather than "melted down" or absorbed.

Pluralism and Multiculturalism

Another pattern of intergroup relations is **pluralism,** in which different racial and ethnic groups within a society maintain their own cultural identities and social networks, yet participate in shared political and economic systems (Kuper and Smith, 1969). In plural societies, each group has its own language, religion, cuisine, and so on, and members interact socially (date, marry, form close friendships) primarily among themselves. Yet all are part of a functionally integrated society.

In thinking about plural societies, it is important to distinguish between *functional* integration and *social* integration. Groups in a plural society are functionally integrated in the sense that they depend on one another, but this does not mean that all are equal or that they treat one another with respect (social integration). In the era of apartheid, South Africa was a plural society in that its economy depended on contributions from blacks, whites, Asians, and coloureds,

even though these groups were strictly segregated and wealth and power were distributed very unequally. In Switzerland's plural society, by contrast, people of German, French, Italian, and Romansch heritage live in different regions and communities and preserve their distinct cultural ways, but no group dominates the others. Switzerland's ethnic groups are semiautonomous, members of a cultural "federation" in which separate and distinct groups coexist peacefully and equally.

Multiculturalism is a new term for placing a high value on social interaction among members of different ethnic groups; welcoming contributions of all groups to a larger, heterogeneous culture; and viewing cultural diversity as good and desirable. Ideally, new patterns of understanding and interaction depend not on conformity and sameness but rather on respect for differences. Education encourages members of each ethnic group to learn more about the others. People are free to make choices about cultural identities rather than being forced into categories chosen by others (Aronowitz, 1992; C. Taylor, 1995; Warner, 1992).

Multiculturalism is more than a prescription for better intergroup relations. It is also a recognition of the increasingly multicultural nature of social relations in a more international, globally integrated world (Lee, 1991). Multiculturalism has gained support in the United States, but it is not universally

American students get a taste of Indonesian culture. Multiculturalism holds that social and cultural interactions among peoples from different countries and ethnic groups are a source of strength and vitality.

applauded. Some opponents want to put more emphasis on assimilation to a single, more homogeneous American culture based on the English language. Other opponents of multiculturalism, including some black nationalists, advocate greater separation and autonomy for different ethnic and racial groups.

The Politics of Identity and Recognition

In ethnically and racially diverse societies, questions of personal and collective identity take on new meaning. The *politics of identity* is the struggle over what qualities will be attributed, socially and institutionally, to individuals, groups, and social categories, and which will be seen as legitimate or illegitimate, good or bad (Calhoun, 1995; Wiley, 1994). Identity is political in that it defines people's rights and duties and hence affects the quality of their lives. The struggle is not just about power and economic benefits, however, but also about self-respect and social legitimacy. The basic issue is whether people are recognized by others as they themselves would like to be seen.

In traditional societies, social identities are based on gender, age, parentage, and kin group. Individuals are born and remain in a certain station or status. Identities are rooted in cultural consensus (for example, about how men and women should behave), ceremony (initiation rites, marriage, and the like), and stable social networks. In contemporary societies, however, huge nation-states, mass migrations, wide ranges of personal choice, the mass media, and unstable and heterogeneous social networks all make identity problematic. People have to juggle different roles and reconcile conflicting expectations. Identity becomes a project or quest.

Debates over labels are part of the politics of identity. For example, Martin Luther King, Jr., referred to himself as *Negro* (from the Spanish for *black*, then considered more polite than saying "black" in English), a term Southerners pronounced as "Nigra" (or as the derogatory epithet "nigger"). In the later stages of the civil rights movement, Negro was replaced with *black* (as in "black pride" and "black power"). Today, however, many black Americans prefer the designation *African-American*, which shifts the emphasis from skin color to cultural heritage. In the past, white Americans used the term *colored* for people of African ancestry; today many blacks, or African-Americans, use the phrase "people of color"

to emphasize their identification with all nonwhite, non-European peoples who have been colonized or enslaved.

More than a matter of style or taste, the labels applied to a group signify who people are and hence how they should be treated. In most U.S. schools today, children learn not just about slavery but also about the cultural contributions of distinguished African-American scientists and artists. Their parents, however, were taught little about African-American culture in school; many encounter blacks only in low-level jobs and on the news and thus may associate black Americans with poverty, crime, unwed mothers, and welfare dependency. This negative image is one reason why blacks driving in wealthy white neighborhoods may be stopped and interrogated by police, simply because they are black.

The rise of Africentrism (sometimes spelled *Afrocentrism*) is an attempt to claim more respect (including self-respect) and legitimacy. *Africentrism* is the view that world history must be reinterpreted from an African-centered as opposed to a European-centered perspective and that much of European culture is derived from Egypt and other African sources (Early, 1995). In black communities today, Malcolm X, the black Muslim leader who advocated separatism and held that black history was the route to black pride, is sometimes more highly regarded than Martin Luther King, Jr., who advocated integration guided by Christian principles.

The American experience almost invariably alters identities. Immigrants from China may be surprised to find themselves classified as "Asian-Americans," along with Japanese, Korean, Vietnamese, and other immigrants who are in fact culturally distinct, speak different languages, and practice different religions. Likewise, the label "Hispanic" may be applied to people from very different cultural backgrounds. Muslim Bengalis and Pakistanis may be lumped together with the Hindu Indians they fled when India gained independence from the British empire (Espiritu, 1996). In some situations, such as on college campuses, pan-ethnic labels may be useful in establishing a group identity and group organizations and activities as a source of power and cultural self-defense (against American norms regarding dating, drinking, and the like). But in other settings, especially people's private and family lives, broad identities—such as "Asian-American"—are meaningless. Chinese are likely to marry other Chinese but not Japanese or Koreans; Indians marry other Indians but seldom Indonesians or Chinese; and so forth.

Indeed, members of each group are more likely to marry non-Asians than Asians of a different national or linguistic origin (Virk, 1995).

The politics of identity involves struggle *within* groups as well as between groups. Members of a group may disagree about how they want to present themselves and how they want to be seen. For example, some African-Americans are drawn to symbols of African ancestry, such as brightly colored Kinte cloth; others are not. The Nation of Islam (Black Muslims) promotes a strong, separatist identity which many African-Americans reject, and others enthusiastically support. Some welcome, and some resent, the increasing number of African and Caribbean immigrants.

These issues are complicated by multiple, overlapping identities. For example, some women of color see the women's movement as geared toward white, middle-class women and thus choose to put their black identity ahead of their female identity. Indeed, some see feminism as racial disloyalty, even defection. Others, such as the writer bell hooks (1993), hold that many images of black identity are biased in favor of black men; still others, such as the sociologist Patricia Hill Collins (1991), have argued for a specifically feminist understanding of black identity. Neither hooks nor Collins wants to choose between being black and being a feminist.

As the United States becomes more culturally and ethnically diverse, more and more people are experiencing what the sociologist W. E. B. DuBois (1903) called "double consciousness"—the sense of carrying two identities that were in potential tension, like black and American. He also pointed to the inner tension that can result from sensing that the image one has of oneself differs from the image reflected in the eyes, words, and behavior of others. DuBois held that the solution was not to choose one identity over the other but to combine the two in creative ways. (See Chapter 1.) This has become a major challenge, not just for individual Americans, but for our society as a whole.

MULTICULTURAL AMERICA

The racial and ethnic composition of the United States has changed more in the 1980s and 1990s than at any other time in the twentieth century (Figure 8.3).

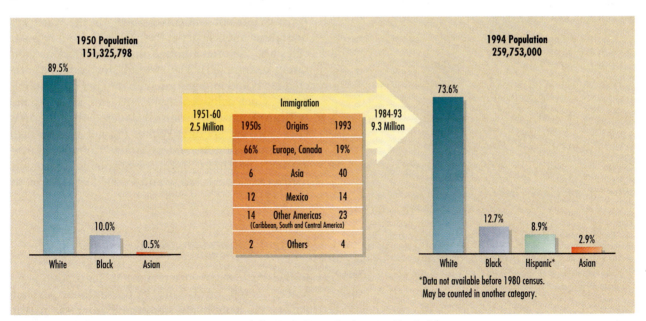

FIGURE 8.3 / *The Increasing Diversity of the U.S. Population, as Fueled by Immigration, 1950–1993*

The face of America is changing, but more noticeably in some places—such as coastal cities and college campuses—than in others.

Source: U.S. Bureau of the Census, U.S. Immigration and Naturalization Service, and the Urban Institute, in "Reinventing America," *Business Week*, Special Issue, 1992, and U.S. Bureau of the Census, *Statistical Abstract of the United States*, 1994.

Minority populations increased twice as fast as in preceding decades. Immigration was one reason; another was higher-than-average birth rates among minorities. Whites of European background are still the largest group in the country (see Figure 8.4), but one in four Americans today is of African, Asian, Hispanic, or Native American ancestry. Hispanics may soon be a numerical majority in New Mexico and California. By the year 2000, one-third of all school-age children will be members of non-European ethnic groups, and they will grow up to become a large proportion of the twenty-first-century workforce (*Report on Minorities in Higher Education*, 1988). Peaceful relations among racial and ethnic groups will be crucial for America's future.

Unfortunately, intergroup hostility seems to be increasing instead. These tensions arise because different ethnic groups have had very different ex-periences in the United States, have different opportunities and problems today, and often feel themselves to be in competition with one another.

African-Americans

Numbering 33 million, African-Americans are this country's largest racial minority. The history of Africans and their descendants in this country is unique. They are the only group whose ancestors were brought to this country by force and enslaved. Plucked from many different cultures, African slaves were thrown together indiscriminately and forbidden to maintain their native traditions. Thus, unlike voluntary immigrants, they were deprived of their culture (at least in part) and preexisting social networks.

Nevertheless, African-Americans developed a unique subculture, a framework for survival and struggle. The end of slavery marked the beginning of a long battle for equal rights. At the same time, black individuals and families strove to get ahead, often moving from the rural South to the urban North to do so. African-Americans have participated in every major event in American history—as soldiers in America's major wars, as pioneers in the westward migration, and as part of the great trek from farms to cities and factories (though their contributions were rarely recognized). The struggle for equality gathered focus and momentum with the civil rights movement, which achieved significant legal victories. But African-Americans soon discovered that the new laws were not enough. Whites did not give up their privileges willingly, and programs to promote integration sometimes produced hostile countermovements (see the Sociology and Public Debates box on page 224).

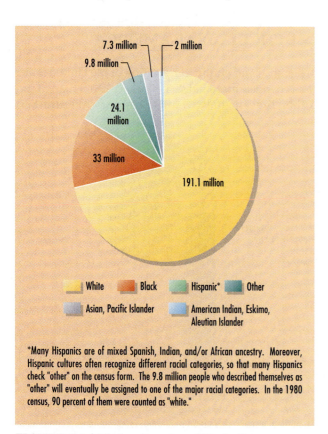

FIGURE 8.4 / Major American Ethnic Groups

Although cultural and racial diversity are increasing, the United States is still a predominantly white (European) society.

Source: U.S. Bureau of the Census, 1991. Preliminary release of 1990 census data.

*Many Hispanics are of mixed Spanish, Indian, and/or African ancestry. Moreover, Hispanic cultures often recognize different racial categories, so that many Hispanics check "other" on the census form. The 9.8 million people who described themselves as "other" will eventually be assigned to one of the major racial categories. In the 1980 census, 90 percent of them were counted as "white."

Current Political and Socioeconomic Status

In the thirty years since civil rights legislation guaranteed equal rights and opportunities, African-Americans have made significant progress. In politics, the number of black elected officials has climbed from a few hundred in the 1960s to more than 7,000 in the 1990s. African-Americans have been elected to every office in the country except president and vice president and have won important elections in which the majority of voters were white (such as the election for mayor of Detroit). Black voting rates are as high as or higher than rates for whites of similar socioeconomic standing. The main reasons seem to be strong community pressure to vote (mobilized through churches and informal social networks) and community solidarity (consensus encourages individuals to believe that their vote will count) (Ellison and London, 1992). Given high rates of defection from the two major political parties, black voters will be key to creating new Democratic (or perhaps Republican) coalitions, especially in the South.

African-Americans have also made significant gains in education, careers, and income (Roberts, 1995). The number of black lawyers and judges, scientists and engineers, real estate and stock brokers has increased sharply. Between 1970 and 1990, the proportion of black households with incomes over $50,000 grew by 57 percent (Hacker, 1992). Thus an increasing number of African-Americans have worked their way into the middle class. Like affluent whites, prosperous blacks tend to be well-educated, married, two-career suburban homeowners (Hacker, 1992).

Yet African-Americans still earn considerably less (on average) than white Americans, regardless of education (Tables 8.1 and 8.2). A "typical" black middle-class family might consist of a bus driver who earns $32,000 and his wife, who brings home $28,000 as a teacher or nurse. A white middle-class family is far more likely to be composed of a husband who earns $75,000 in a managerial position and a wife who works part-time or for supplemental income (Hacker,

TABLE 8.2

Education and Earnings of Black Men and Women

Education	EARNINGS PER $1,000 FOR WHITES	
	Men	Women
High school not finished	$786	$860
4 years of high school	$780	$916
1 to 3 years of college	$839	$918
Bachelor's degree	$764	$966
Master's degree	$870	$939

Source: Andrew Hacker, Two Nations: Black and White, Separate, Hostile, Unequal (Ballantine, New York, 1992), p. 101.

1992). White physicians and surgeons earn an average of $62,000 a year, compared to $40,000 for blacks (in 1990 dollars); white professors and college instructors in psychology earn an average of $32,687 versus $10,000 for blacks in comparable positions (Roberts, 1995). Moreover, a third of black lawyers and scientists work for government agencies. One out of five members of the armed forces is black (twice their proportion in the civilian economy), and the ratios for the postal service and urban agencies are similar. In a period of government budget cuts, this makes the black middle class particularly vulnerable.

While the black middle class has grown, so has the proportion of blacks living in poverty, widening the gap between middle-class and poor African-Americans. The poverty rate among blacks has remained about three times that of whites for more than two decades. In both good times and bad, the unemployment rate for blacks has been double that for whites. A greater proportion of blacks lack regular employment today than at any time since the Great Depression of the 1930s (Hacker, 1992; *Statistical Abstract*, 1995). Black children are four times as likely as white children to grow up in poverty—in part because they are more likely to be raised by a single mother. Moreover, African-Americans tend to be poorer than poor whites, to remain in poverty longer, and to live in high-poverty, high-crime neighborhoods (O'Hare et al., 1991). (See the discussion of ghetto poverty in Chapter 7.)

Residential segregation is a key reason for the socioeconomic gap between whites and blacks.

TABLE 8.1

Income and Earnings (Medians) for Black and White Men, Women, and Families*

	White	Black	Ratio†
Families	$38,909	$21,161	$544
All men	$21,645	$12,754	$589
All women	$11,036	$ 8,857	$803
Employed men	$31,012	$22,369	$721
Employed women	$21,659	$19,819	$915

*The listings for families, all men, and all women include all sources of income, from pensions and welfare payments to disability benefits and capital gains.
†Incomes of blacks per $1,000 for whites. Earnings for year-round full-time workers.
Source: Andrew Hacker, Two Nations: Black and White, Separate, Hostile, Unequal (Ballantine, New York, 1992), p. 100.

Affirmative Action

The term affirmative action first appeared in an order issued by President John Kennedy in 1961 requiring federal contractors to "take affirmative action to ensure that applicants are employed, and employees are treated during their employment, without regard to their race, creed, color, or national origin" (*CQ Researcher*, April 28, 1995). The goal of affirmative action was not only to stop discrimination but also to promote integration and to compensate minorities for past discrimination. This policy led to a range of programs to set goals and timetables for hiring minorities, to give minority applicants special preference in hiring or admissions, and to create "set asides" in which a percentage of government contracts are awarded to minority-owned firms. From the beginning, affirmative action has been controversial.

> **Supporters hold that affirmative action benefits not only minorities but society as a whole by increasing diversity on college campuses, by creating a multiethnic workforce more representative of the population as a whole, and by promoting interracial understanding by bringing members of different groups together in classrooms and in the workplace.**
> **Opponents of affirmative action argue that opportunities for higher education and jobs should be awarded solely on the basis of individual merit.**

THE DEBATE

Supporters hold that affirmative action has enabled minorities to go to college, enter new occupations, and start businesses. Although prejudice against minorities has declined, it has not disappeared; hence, affirmative action is still needed to ensure equal opportunity. Supporters hold that affirmative action benefits not only minorities but society as a whole by increasing diversity on college campuses, by creating a multiethnic workforce more representative of the population as a whole, and by promoting interracial understanding by bringing members of different groups together in classrooms and in the workplace.

Opponents of affirmative action argue that opportunities for higher education and jobs should be awarded solely on the basis of individual merit. In their view, affirmative action is a form of "reverse discrimination" that unfairly punishes white males. Moreover, it creates a double standard that tends to lower performance and morale. Far from promoting racial harmony, affirmative action creates a backlash of resentment among whites and perpetuates the idea that minorities and women are innately inferior and therefore need special help. Quoting Martin Luther King, who looked forward to the day when children would be judged "by the content of their character not the color of their skin," opponents of affirmative action hold that equal opportunity should be "color-blind."

ANALYSIS

Racial inequality has been part of our country's social structure from the beginning. The low socioeconomic level of blacks (as a group) today is the legacy of nearly four centuries of slavery and segregation. Only in the last thirty years have African-Americans enjoyed any degree of equal opportunity. Even in the absence of prejudice and discrimination, racial inequality would persist if institutions simply conducted "business as usual." For example, if college admissions were based on test scores alone, African-American children who grew up in poor families and attended substandard schools would have very few opportunities, regardless of their talent and abilities. In deciding whether to grant home mortgages and small business loans, "color-blind" banks might rely on statistical predictors—for example, using zip codes to "redline" risky neighborhoods. Homes and businesses in poor black neighborhoods would, again, be disqualified regardless of any particular applicant's financial promise. These policies and practices may be "color-blind," but the consequences are not.

Given the degree to which racial inequality is woven into our country's social structure, creating equal opportunity requires action. The federal government took the first step by pressuring companies and universities to actively recruit minorities. At the same time, blacks (and women) appealed to the Equal Employment Opportunity Commission and sued companies both for past discrimination (such as unequal pay) and continuing discrimination (for example, in hirings and promotions).

These actions, in turn, produced a *re*action, or backlash. In the 1990s, affirmative action became a "hot button" in the struggle between Republicans and Democrats, conservatives and liberals, to control the future direction of the American government. Polls show that public opposition to affirmative action is growing. Most of the opposition comes not, as one might think, from people who have had direct experience with affirmative action, but from those who have had none (M. Taylor, 1995). Indeed, the more contact whites have with blacks—in school, the workplace, their neighborhood—the more likely they are to defend affirmative action. Another source of opposition is a growing number of black professionals, managers, academics, and students who see affirmative action as stigmatizing successful blacks, who are assumed to have enjoyed special privileges because of their race, while doing little to help the most disadvantaged. For example, in *Reflections of an Affirmative Action Baby* (1991), Yale law professor Stephen Carter argues that the main impact of affirmative action has been to increase racial divisions and reinforce whites' stereotypes about blacks' (lower) abilities.

Much of the debate about affirmative action is rooted in our culture. We like to think of our society as a *meritocracy*, in which talent and hard work are rewarded and what counts is what you achieve, not who you are. At the same time we place a high value on *equality*, on the idea that everyone has an equal chance to use their talents to get ahead. Advocates of meritocracy tend to emphasize individual rights, whereas advocates of equality emphasize group outcomes.

But meritocracy and equality are ideals that are imperfectly realized in practice. On meeting someone for the first time, we inevitably notice that person's race, sex, age, attractiveness, clothing, and so on. Likewise, the notion of a pure meritocracy is commendable, but our society has always practiced "affirmative action" for certain groups. In considering applicants for the freshman class, colleges have long given special consideration to children of alumni, geographic diversity (North Dakota versus Boston), athletes, musicians, and others. How many white males feel "victimized" when their college or alma mater fields a winning football or basketball team? We hear no protests when veterans get special consideration for civil service jobs (whether they served in battle or at a desk). As a society and as individuals, we routinely grant preferential treatment; nevertheless, preferential treatment based on race tends to fan social tension and resentment.

Justice is not the only issue, however. Hiring and promotion policies are a functionally integrated part of the economy as a whole. Opponents see affirmative action as dysfunctional because it may lower standards for achievement in education and occupations and therefore may hurt the economy. Defenders argue that affirmative action is functional in granting opportunities to people whose contributions might have been ignored or suppressed, providing experience in diversity to students and workers who will be competing in a global marketplace, and potentially raising standards of living and achievement motivation in minority communities.

Power lies at the heart of the affirmative action debate. For 400 years, white Americans used their power to exploit black labor, assault black dignity, and deny black identity. The civil rights movement changed the distribution of power. This movement succeeded in part because blacks were united in their demand for equal rights, while whites were divided, with many sympathetic to the black struggle. In an almost complete reversal, the federal government used its power to integrate public schools and, later, to push for affirmative action. When first instituted, affirmative action met strong resistance but, along with civil rights legislation, achieved significant gains. In the expanding economy of the 1960s, affirmative action was easier to accept because there were more than enough jobs to go around. In the shrinking job market of the 1990s, however, people are worried about their own prospects and less willing to make room for minorities (and immigrants). As a result, the debate over affirmative action has heated up.

In the 1990s, affirmative action has been re-politicized as many groups—not only blacks and whites, but also professional associations, labor unions, and politicians of all stripes—seek to maintain or expand their positions. Additionally debating affirmative action offers the "political benefit" of diverting the public's attention from other powerful forces in the global marketplace and the U.S. economy that have stranded some workers and forced others to reduce their expectations.

Many white Americans see General Colin Powell's journey from Harlem to Head of the Joint Chiefs of Staff as proof that African-Americans enjoy equal opportunity in the United States today. Blacks are more likely to see General Powell as "the exception that proves the rule." Indeed, polls found that many African-Americans did not consider Powell, a light-skinned son of West Indian immigrants, "black."

Housing is the area in which there has been the *least* progress toward integration. The degree of residential segregation of African-Americans has remained virtually unchanged since 1970 (Massey and Denton, 1992). Nearly 30 percent—or 9 million blacks—live in almost complete racial isolation, primarily in inner cities. Moreover, racial isolation follows blacks to the suburbs (Massey and Eggers, 1990). For Hispanics and Asians, residential segregation declines as families move from immigrant to native status and from low to high socioeconomic levels. For African-Americans, segregation persists regardless of the length of time families live in metropolitan (versus rural) areas and regardless of income and education.

Residential segregation has far-reaching consequences: It affects the schools children attend, the friends they and their parents make, the job networks to which they have access, the health-care and other services available in an emergency, exposure to crime, and even the quality of the food and merchandise available for them to buy. Residential segregation may also contribute to ongoing (if often hidden) prejudice.

Polls indicate that most white Americans believe that Martin Luther King's dream of racial equality has been fulfilled (Wheeler, 1993). About three-quarters of whites believe that a black person has as good a chance as a white to be hired for any job today and that blacks overestimate the amount of discrimination in our society. Almost all whites say they support integration and equal opportunity, but many qualify this with comments about unfair advantages (under affirmative action), violence and illegitimacy in black communities, the lack of a work ethic, and black prejudice against whites (Bakanic, 1995). The general message seems to be, "I'm not prejudiced, but. . . ."

African-Americans have a different view (Wheeler, 1993). Most blacks (70 percent) do not feel that they have a fair chance of being hired for a job for which they are qualified, and many attribute racial inequality in jobs, income, and housing to discrimination. Doors may have opened, but not that much. In the words of a black Mississippian: "There's ways to get ahead. You've gotta go to school and work hard. If you're black, you've just gotta work harder and it takes a little longer, that's all" (Bakanic, 1995, p. 84). Others are not as optimistic: Half of blacks in one poll agreed that our nation is moving toward two societies, one black, one white—separate and unequal.

Hispanic-Americans

Hispanics, or Spanish-speaking Americans, are the second-largest minority in the United States. At least 22.8 million Hispanics are legal residents of the United States; others have immigrated without full legal documentation (U.S. Bureau of the Census, 1994a). Because immigration rates are high and because Hispanics now in this country tend to be young and to have large families, the Hispanic population is growing rapidly. If current growth rates continue, by the turn of the century Hispanics will pass African-Americans as the largest minority in the United States (*Statistical Abstract*, 1995).

The Diversity of Hispanic-Americans

"Hispanic" is an umbrella term for a diverse group of people with roots in different parts of Latin America who arrived in the United States at different times and for different reasons. Unlike European immigrants, who gradually gave up their native languages, most Hispanics continue to speak Spanish and to maintain other traditions (Nelson and Tienda,

1985). Whether by choice or not, most Hispanics have not been assimilated into mainstream America. Continuing immigration revitalizes Hispanic communities, protecting traditional values.

Mexican-Americans, or Chicanos, fall into two broad categories. Some are descendants of Spanish settlers who had lived in the Southwest long before the United States acquired this territory in the Mexican-American War of 1848. Robbed of their land, overwhelmed by waves of Anglo-Americans (especially after the discovery of gold in 1849), in effect they became colonial subjects (Almaguer, 1994).

The second group of Mexican-Americans is made up of more recent immigrants who began entering the United States early in this century as seasonal agricultural workers. Some came here legally under periodic agreements with the Mexican government; others came illegally, by swimming or wading the Rio Grande. Over the years agricultural interests in the Southwest became increasingly dependent on these migratory workers, and the smuggling of illegal workers became highly organized and professional (Rumbaut, 1991).

Driven by population growth, high unemployment, and severe poverty in Mexico and drawn by family connections and economic opportunity, legal and illegal Mexican immigrants continue to flow into this country. Increasingly, immigrants are bypassing the farms and ranches of the Southwest for urban jobs in the construction, light manufacturing, and service industries. In these positions, as on farms, Mexican nationals are particularly vulnerable to exploitation and abuse because they fear deportation. Continuing immigration also draws hostility from Anglo workers who see Mexican immigrants as a cheap reserve labor pool that drives down wages. One sign of backlash was Proposition 187, a 1994 referendum passed in California that denies schooling and other public services to illegal immigrants.

The United States acquired *Puerto Rico* in 1898 and governed it as a colony for fifty years. Puerto Ricans were granted American citizenship in 1917, and the island was declared a commonwealth in 1952. During the colonial period, a self-sufficient economy composed of small farmers was replaced with a plantation economy dominated by large landowners, followed later by a program of industrialization that could not absorb the island's growing population. After World War II, when the airlines introduced lower fares, as many as a third of Puerto Ricans left to seek work on the mainland, especially in New York City (Calderón, 1992). What makes the Puerto Rican situation unique is that immigration runs two ways: The island is part of the United States, so that entry and exit visas are not required; it is also close enough for immigrants to return home, periodically or permanently.

Most *Cuban-Americans* came to the United States as political refugees, fleeing Fidel Castro's communist dictatorship. Today Cubans are the largest ethnic

Hispanics maintain their cultural identity and pride with brightly colored, distinctly "Latin" murals and a traditional game of dominoes played on the street.

minority in Miami and have become a major force in that city's business and politics. They have proved to be one of the most politically organized Hispanic-American groups, focusing their efforts on persuading the U.S. government to isolate Castro's regime. Cubans are also among the most financially successful group of Hispanics. The first refugees had the skills and resources to establish an enclave economy in Miami, composed of Cuban-owned businesses, serving Cuban customers and clients, and employing less well-off Cuban workers.

Issues of Identity

By and large, different groups of Hispanic-Americans have remained distinct from one another as well as from the rest of the population. Most identify with their country of origin, not with Latin Americans as a whole. Indeed, the label and category "Hispanic" was created by the U.S. Census Bureau (Calderón, 1992). In the 1960s, activists sought to replace the term *Mexican-American*, which implied assimilation, with *Chicano*, which emphasized their Indian heritage. Today, many prefer the appellation "Latino" to "Hispanic," for similar reasons.

Hispanics face another "identity crisis," regarding racial classification (Massey and Denton, 1992). Many are of mixed racial origins. Their ancestors may include white Europeans, Amerindians, black Africans, and Asians. Patterns vary, depending on their country of origin. In Latin American cultures, race is viewed as a continuum running from white to Indian, with many variations in between. In the United States, however, one is either white or Indian, white or black. Terms for racially mixed identities are invariably pejorative (e.g., *half-breed*). As a result, Hispanics occupy an ambiguous position in the United States, lying somewhere between an ethnic and a racial minority. Some members of the same nationality may be treated as "white" (those of Spanish descent); others as "almost black" (those of Indian or African descent).

The identities Latinos or Hispanics choose for themselves vary from situation to situation and group to group (Massey and Denton, 1992). For Mexican-Americans, the probability of labeling oneself "white" and "American like everybody else" increases with age, education, income, and occupational status. However, even the most assimilated

individuals may emphasize their "Hispanic" identity when running for public office. At the neighborhood level, activists are more likely to use the label "Latino," and Mexican-Americans, Puerto Ricans, Dominicans, and others often cooperate on issues of collective concern, such as bilingual education (see Chapter 4).

Current Socioeconomic Status

Hispanics made modest social and economic gains in recent decades, but few Hispanics achieved equality with Anglo-Americans (U.S. Bureau of the Census, 1990b). In 1993, slightly more than half of Hispanics had completed high school (compared to more than 80 percent of non-Hispanic whites and African-Americans). Although the proportion of Hispanics in managerial positions and professional occupations has grown, Hispanics still tend to be employed in low-level jobs (as shown in Table 8.3). The median household income for Hispanics is about two-thirds that for non-Hispanic whites. On average, Hispanic males earned 63 cents for every dollar that non-Hispanic whites earned. (See Figure 8.5 for group differences.) Although both the unemployment and poverty rates for Hispanics have declined, the rates are still much higher than those for non-Hispanic whites. In 1993, 29 percent of Hispanics lived below the poverty line (compared with 9.6 percent of non-Hispanic whites) (U.S. Bureau of the Census, 1994a).

The main reasons usually given for high rates of poverty among Hispanics are low levels of education, recent entry into the labor force, poor English skills, and concentration in occupations that are vulnerable to recessions (Cattan, 1988). However, a recent study suggests that racist attitudes also play a part (Telles and Murguia, 1990). Hispanics vary in appearance from light to dark-skinned and from Anglo to Indian or Native American in facial features. The researchers found that the darkest and most Indian-looking Mexican-Americans earned significantly less than those who might "pass" as Anglos, regardless of education, occupation, and other variables. White Mexican-Americans are also more likely to live in the suburbs and to socialize with Anglos, while dark-skinned, Indian-looking Mexican-Americans are more likely to live in ethnic enclaves (Massey and Denton, 1992).

TABLE 8.3

Occupational Employment by Hispanic Origin and Sex, Annual Averages, 1993

	HISPANIC	NON-HISPANIC
Occupation	Percent Distribution, 1993	Percent Distribution, 1993
Men, 16 years and older	100.0	100.0
Managerial and professional specialty	11.6	27.9
Technical, sales, and administrative support	15.4	21.5
Service occupations	16.0	10.1
Precision production, craft, and repair	19.6	18.0
Operators, fabricators, and laborers	28.4	19.0
Farming, forestry, and fishing	8.9	3.7
Women, 16 years and older	100.0	100.0
Managerial and professional specialty	15.4	29.8
Technical, sales, and administrative support	40.9	42.9
Service occupations	24.6	17.5
Precision production, craft, and repair	2.5	1.8
Operators, fabricators, and laborers	14.8	7.4
Farming, forestry, and fishing	1.8	0.8

Source: U. S. Bureau of the Census Current Population Reports Series P20-475, "The Hispanic Population in the United States," March 1993, issued May 1994.

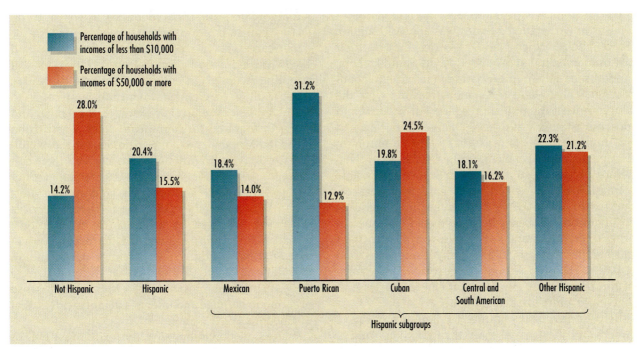

FIGURE 8.5 / Income Distribution for Hispanic Subgroups, 1992

Both wealth and poverty are distributed unevenly among Hispanic subgroups.

Source: U.S. Bureau of the Census, *Current Population Reports.* Population Characteristics, Series P-20, no. 475 (1994), pp. 16–17.

Native Americans

Native Americans play a central role in our national folklore; many geographic landmarks in the United States today bear Indian names, and they are the only ethnic group specifically recognized in the Constitution. Under the law, Indians are members of tribes that relate to the U.S. government as sovereign nations—though in practice, the government has rarely honored their sovereignty.

A Brief Social History

When Europeans "discovered" the New World, this continent was populated by diverse groups, ranging from the warlike Plains Indians to the fishermen of the Pacific Northwest, the trappers of the Northeast and Great Lakes regions, and the sedentary farmers in what are now the Carolinas, and from the great Inca Empire of Peru to the small tribes of hunter-gatherers in the Amazon. The two greatest Native American empires, the Inca of Peru and the Aztec of Mexico and Guatemala, were among the most advanced civilizations of their day.

Before contact with Europeans, the population of what is now the United States was about 10 million (Snipp, 1992). When Native Americans made their last military stand at Wounded Knee, South Dakota, in 1890, their total number had been reduced to about 300,000. There were three main reasons why the Native American population collapsed. The first and most devastating was disease. Native Americans had no immunity to diseases that were common in Europe (smallpox, cholera, typhus, influenza). Even before extensive contacts with Europeans, whole communities were wiped out by epidemics. The second reason was warfare, both with Euro-Americans and with other tribes, who were forced into one another's territories and sometimes recruited to fight one another. Perhaps 500,000 Native Americans died in battle. The third reason was genocide, in the form of forced marches into inhospitable territories and wholesale, premeditated slaughter.

Before Europeans came to America, Native American tribes shared more than 2 billion acres of land. By the turn of the century, those Native Americans who survived epidemics, warfare, and genocide were confined to reservations carved out of a total of about 90 million acres. Although legally defined as sovereign nations, reservations were admin-istered by the white-run Bureau of Indian Affairs (BIA). In return for yielding some of their sovereignty (for example, the right to an independent foreign policy), Indian tribes received schools, health care, and other services from the BIA, funded by the federal government; but the quality of social services was poor and the budgets low. Moreover, the BIA had the power to decide what Indians were allowed to do with their land and other resources, and it usu-ally did so in ways that benefited outsiders more than the tribes themselves (Yetman, 1992). Their sit-uation was best described as "internal colonization" (Snipp, 1992).

The general assumption was that Native Americans would eventually "disappear" as a dis-tinct racial or ethnic group. Hunting and fishing tribes were encouraged to become farmers; children were forcibly taken to boarding schools where they were forbidden to speak their native languages; a "termination" policy launched in the 1950s was de-signed to encourage Native Americans to relocate in selected urban areas, abolish the special status of Indian lands, and in effect put an end to the "Indian problem."

Against the odds, the Native American population has rebounded, and tribal identities, as well as a col-lective pan-Indian movement, are thriving. Native Americans who moved to cities in the 1950s and 1960s resisted assimilation (Snipp, 1992). Instead of adopting mainstream culture and lifestyles, Native Americans used elements of urban landscapes to maintain their heritage. For example, the danger and strength required for high-beam steel construction provided Mohawk men opportunities for the exhibi-tions of bravery traditionally expected by their cul-ture (Blumenfeld, 1965). Powwows (ceremonial coun-cil meetings) were held in gyms and auditoriums; urban Indian churches provided the social services that were provided by missions on reservations; Indian Centers and bars became the urban equiva-lent of tribal headquarters. Because urban Indian populations included members of different tribes, these institutions promoted pan-Indianism, a sense of common heritage and interests that overrides tribal distinctions.

Increasing slowly but steadily for the first half of this century, the Indian population grew fivefold be-tween 1950 and 1990, reaching more than 2 million (Eschbach, 1995). High birth rates and increased longevity account for some of this growth, but only some. As the stigma of being Native American faded, more Indians and individuals of mixed heritage openly identified themselves as Indians.

Beginning in the early 1970s, a number of Indian nations filed lawsuits demanding enforcement of broken treaties or restitution. The Sioux nation was awarded $122.5 million in compensation for the illegal seizure of the Black Hills; tribes living around Puget Sound won the right to 50 percent of the salmon harvest and are using the profits to build a fishing and aquaculture industry. The most controversial development initiative has been the growth of casinos on Indian reservations. Because of their special legal status, tribes are not subject to state laws restricting or banning gambling. Although highly profitable in some cases, these enterprises are controversial. Casinos provoke hostility in surrounding communities that disapprove not only of gambling generally but also of associated activities (such as prostitution). Often the casinos are run by outside operators, who take a large share of the profits, and

give relatively few jobs to Indians. Payments to tribal members, moreover, may encourage dependence rather than education, entrepreneurship, and independence. Furthermore, the casinos vest a great deal of power in decision makers—whether outsiders or chiefs turned CEOs. For most Native Americans, the rewards of these ventures are small.

Current Socioeconomic Status

Today's 2.23 million Native Americans are among the poorest minority groups in the country. By virtually every measure—education, income, employment, and health—Native Americans lag not only behind Americans as a whole but also behind other minority groups (Figure 8.6). Native Americans have unusually high rates of accidents, homicide, suicide, liver disease, influenza, pneumonia, and diabetes (all of which may be alcohol-related) and a life ex-

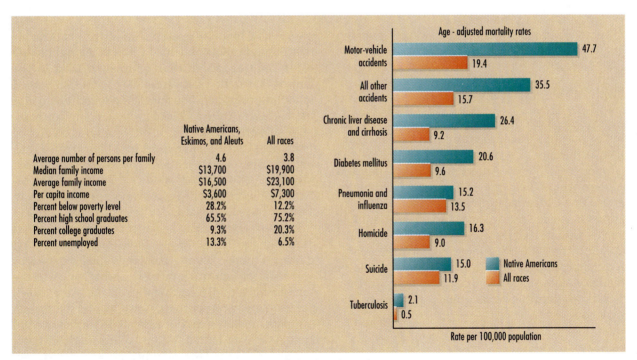

FIGURE 8.6 / Socioeconomic Characteristics of Native Americans

The poverty of many Native Americans translates into ill health, risky behavior, and shorter lives.

Sources: (Left) Data for American Indians in the thirty-three reservation states in 1980, from the U.S. Department of Health and Human Services, *Health Status of Minorities and Low-Income Groups*, 1991. (Right) U.S. Department of Health and Human Services, Indian Health Service, *Trends in Indian Health*, 1989, table 4.9, p. 39. Update: U.S. Bureau of the Census, *Statistical Abstract of the United States*, 1994.

The graduation ceremony at Oglala Laokota College in South Dakota includes a traditional Native American powwow.

pectancy ten years below the national average (Yetman, 1992).

Asian-Americans

Between 1965 (with the Immigration Act of 1965) and 1990, Asian immigration increased tenfold and continues at the rate of about a quarter million a year (Gardner, 1992). Asian-Americans are not only the fastest-growing ethnic category in the United States but also one of the most diverse. In the 1960s there were four major Asian-American groups in Los Angeles County (Chinese, Japanese, Korean, and Filipino); by the mid-1980s, there were at least twenty-five different groups (Espiritu and Ong, 1994). Today's 7 million Asian-Americans (including first and later generations) represent not quite 3 percent of the population.

A Brief Social History

Chinese began immigrating to the West Coast in the mid-eighteenth century. Their labor on the railroads earned them a reputation as hard workers. When the railroad was finished and unemployment began to rise, however, white workers turned on the Chinese. Lynchings, expulsions, and arson were not uncom-

mon. The Chinese Exclusion Act of 1882 halted further immigration and denied Chinese the right to become naturalized citizens or to own land in the United States. In most places they were also denied schooling, jobs, and housing. They withdrew to ethnic enclaves (called *Chinatowns*), keeping to themselves (Wong, 1982). Since the Immigration Act of 1965 more Chinese have come here than arrived during the first eighty years of Chinese immigration. More than two-thirds of today's 1.6 million Chinese-Americans are recent immigrants, primarily from Taiwan and Hong Kong.

Japanese immigrants began coming to the United States in the 1870s. These newcomers established groceries, flower shops, and other small businesses and took jobs as truck farmers and laborers in the lumber mills and fish canneries of the West Coast. Some became professionals. Anti-Oriental sentiments ran high, however, and in 1924 all immigration from East Asia was halted. After Japan attacked Pearl Harbor, the United States turned on its Japanese residents. On the West Coast more than 120,000 Japanese, including 70,000 who were American citizens, were rounded up and moved inland to guarded camps, or "relocation centers." While they were interned, whites seized their lands and took over their businesses. Only in 1988 did the U.S. Senate approve a bill to apologize officially for this violation of human and civil rights and pay a token $20,000 in reparations to every living Japanese-American who had been interned during the war.

In recent years Japanese immigration has slowed, largely because Japan's prosperous economy has offered people abundant opportunities at home. Most of today's 847,000 Japanese-Americans are second-, third-, and fourth-generation American citizens. They are among the most highly assimilated Asian immigrant groups.

The largest number of recent Asian immigrants come from the Philippines, followed by Korea, Vietnam, India, and China (Gardner, 1992). Compared to others immigrants, the new Asian-Americans have few cultural or historical ties to America.

Cultural Diversity

Asian-Americans differ from the other groups we have described in two important ways. Unlike Hispanic-Americans, who share the Spanish language and Roman Catholic religion, Asian-Americans do not have a common history or culture but rather come from different continents, speak many languages, and practice a wide range of religions, including Buddhism, Christianity, Hinduism, and Islam. Culturally speaking, Indians, Burmese, Taiwanese, and Samoan islanders have as little in common with one another as they do with native-born Americans.

Second, the newest Asian immigrants are also more economically polarized than other groups, with a highly visible and successful layer of professionals and a lower layer of semiskilled, low-paid laborers. Some have ties with global corporations and organizations and are part of a new worldwide "upper class." Others are refugees from wars they did not start and perhaps did not understand. Depending on their background and circumstances, in this country they may work as physicians or engineers, grocers or nurses, waiters or peddlers (see Table 8.4). Class divisions play a contradictory role, both dividing the Asian-American population and creating a class of professional social activists eager to promote pan-Asian unity (Espiritu and Ong, 1994).

Current Socioeconomic Status

For decades, Asian-Americans have been hailed as the "model minority." By almost every measure, Asian-Americans have equaled and often surpassed other groups of Americans (Winnick, 1990). The median Asian-American family income is higher than that of whites; Asian-American adults are overrepresented in the professions and other high-status occupations; and Asian-American students score higher on standardized tests (especially in math and science) than other American students and are twice as likely to obtain college degrees. But these statistics do not tell the full story.

For 150 years, Asians (or "Orientals") were stereotyped as the "yellow peril": sly, cunning, untrustworthy villains and—during World War II— as the "enemy within." The shift from the "yellow peril" to

TABLE 8.4

Ethnic Distribution of Selected Class and Nativity Groups, in Percent

	U.S.-BORN		FOREIGN-BORN	
Group	Managerial	Professional	Service	Operatives
Japanese	62	62	8	3
Chinese	21	25	30	34
Filipino	12	8	27	19
Korean	3	2	15	19
Vietnamese	0	0	10	17

Source: U.S. Bureau of the Census, Census of Population and Housing, 1990: PUMS A Sample [computer file] (U.S. Bureau of the Census, Washington, D.C.).

Four generations of a Chinese-American family celebrate at a restaurant in New York's Chinatown. For others, Chinatown is a tourist attraction; for many Chinese-Americans it is a "home away from home."

"model minority" began in the wake of the riots in the nation's black ghettoes in the 1960s, when the country was agonizing over racial turmoil (Chun, 1995). Suddenly the media noticed that many Chinese and Japanese Americans had quietly worked their way through school, moved to the suburbs, and joined the middle class. By implication, if Asians could overcome adversity, why couldn't "they" (blacks and Hispanics)?

The Asian success story seemed to validate the American dream: through hard work, self-discipline, and education, anyone can get ahead (Suzuki, 1995). However, there are other explanations. The model cultural values attributed to Asian-Americans—unobtrusiveness, docility, compliance—can be seen as a strategy for adapting to a hostile environment: Keep a low profile and do as you are told (Chun, 1995). The emphasis on education in Asian-American families is in part the result of limited opportunity. Early Asian immigrants were denied entry into craft and other unions and were rarely hired by white-owned businesses; schooling was one of the only avenues of social mobility open to them (Sue and Okazaki, 1995). Moreover, in school Asian-American students often were excluded from social and extracurricular activ-

ities, which encouraged them to be studious. The great expansion of the technical/bureaucratic sector of the economy after World War II created a demand for educated workers, especially in technical-scientific areas. Thus Asian-Americans benefited from structural mobility (changes in the occupation structure).

Moreover, Asian-American success has been exaggerated. The higher average *household* income of Asian-Americans is due largely to the fact that Asian families are large and children tend to live with their parents longer, so there are more workers to contribute to the family income. When one looks at *individual* incomes, Asian-American workers earn less than white workers with the same academic credentials. Although a high proportion of Asian-Americans work for high-tech, high-prestige companies, very few are promoted to managerial or administrative positions. And while some Asians are doing well, others live below the poverty line, working long hours for minimum wage (or less) in garment factories, restaurants, laundries, and private households.

Even positive stereotypes can be dangerous (Crystal, 1989). The belief that Asians can make it on their own has been used to justify their exclusion from minority programs, so that many are not getting help they need. Stereotypes about Asian success may fuel resentment among other American ethnic groups, as was evident in the hostility toward Koreans expressed by some blacks during the 1992 riot in Los Angeles (see Chapter 20). Finally, Asian-American success has depended on fitting in, which exacts such hidden costs as overconformity, over-control, pressure to achieve, conflict between generations, and a sense of lost identity (Chun, 1995). In some ways Asian-Americans are a model of the *costs* of assimilation—and the dangers of expecting all groups to seek the same forms of accomplishment, by the same routes, and with equal success.

SUMMARY

1. The United States is one of the most culturally diverse nations on earth. In recent years immigration to the United States has risen as a result of changes in immigration laws and in the international situation.

2. The term *minority group* refers to groups who are denied equal treatment in a society (whether or not they are in fact a numerical minority). Often minority groups are defined in terms of physical appearance (race) or cultural characteristics (ethnicity).

3. Race and ethnicity are social constructs. A race is a population that perceives itself and is perceived by others to have distinctive, inherited characteristics. Ethnicity is a social identification based on perceived cultural differences of a group. Although the notion of race has little biological significance and ethnicity is often flexible, both have been used as political tools and both affect social identity.

4. Ethnic politics come into play whenever cultural contact involves large enough numbers that people identify themselves, and are identified by others, in terms of group membership. Sometimes one group economically and politically subjugates another, as in colonialism. At other times, the more powerful group displaces, enslaves, or segregates the weaker group. In extreme cases, the powerful group may attempt to systematically annihilate the weaker group (genocide). Few people accept domination and abuse willingly. Resistance may take the form of self-segregation, covert actions, public protests, or armed rebellion.

5. Eliminating formal restrictions on minorities does not automatically lead to equality. Prejudice is a positive or negative attitude toward a group of people based on stereotypes regarding their real or imagined social characteristics. Not merely a personal opinion, prejudice is grounded in cultural norms and values. Discrimination is social action based on presumed differences between groups.

6. Intergroup relations do not inevitably lead to conflict. Patterns of accommodation include integration (mixing freely), assimilation (the absorption of minority groups into the mainstream culture and social life), pluralism (maintaining distinctive identities), and multiculturalism (maintaining *and* respecting cultural diversity).

7. In culturally and ethnically diverse societies, the issue of identity becomes politicized. The labels that are applied to (or chosen by) a group have serious consequences for their experiences and opportunities. Many people today have to come to terms with multiple identities or what DuBois called "double consciousness."

8. Because of both immigration rates and high birth rates among minorities in the United States today, the profile of America is changing. Intergroup harmony is more important than ever. But efforts to achieve racial and ethnic equality have been only partly successful.

9. African-Americans are the largest minority group in the country. They have made many gains since the 1960s, but they still lag behind whites in income, education, and other areas. The growth of a black middle class has been paralleled by an increase in ghetto poverty. Whatever their education and occupation, blacks earn significantly less than whites. Moreover, residential segregation (which affects education, aspirations, job networks, etc.) follows working- and middle-class African-Americans out of the cities, and limited interracial contacts contribute to ongoing prejudice.

10. Hispanic-Americans may surpass African-Americans as the country's largest minority group early in the twenty-first century. Hispanics share a language, a religion, and customs that may unite them on some issues; however, coming from many different Latin American societies, at different times, and under different circumstances, Mexicans, Cubans, and others have distinct identities. With some exceptions, Hispanics have less education, and higher unemployment and poverty rates, than other groups.

11. Native Americans are the poorest minority group in the United States. At one time, many people thought they would eventually become assimilated and "disappear" into the American mainstream. Instead, Native Americans maintained their traditions and, in terms of population, tribal rights, and economic enterprise, are enjoying a modest revival.

12. Asian-Americans are the fastest-growing category in the United States today and also the most diverse, in terms of both national origins and social class. Some Asian-Americans come from urban, educated, elite families in their land of origin and have prospered here; others are uprooted peasants who still struggle to find a foothold. Long vilified, in recent decades Asian-Americans have been viewed as a "model minority," a positive stereotype that exacts a cost in pressures to achieve, resentment by others, and identity confusion.

REVIEW QUESTIONS

1. What are the factors that contribute to the tension between the ideals of cultural unity and tolerance and the realities of cultural diversity?

2. What are the factors that contribute to the maintenance of cultural and racial biases?

3. How are minority groups different from racial and ethnic groups? Give an example of each.

4. How do the patterns of conflict and domination differ from each other?

5. How have acceptance and integration occurred?

6. Develop brief profiles of the minority groups discussed in the chapter: African-Americans, Hispanic-Americans, Native Americans, and Asian-Americans.

CRITICAL THINKING QUESTIONS

1. Examine immigration using at least three of the five key concepts (social structure, social action, functional integration, power, and culture).

2. Develop some policy suggestions for reducing both prejudice and discrimination.

3. The "melting pot" metaphor may not accurately reflect the relations among ethnic and racial groups in the United States. Construct another metaphor that you think would be more accurate and explain your rationale for it.

4. Use at least three of the five key concepts to analyze the situation of one of the minority groups profiled in the chapter.

5. Do you think that economic equality would end racial segregation in the United States? Why or why not?

6. In what ways has affirmative action encouraged functional integration of American society? In what ways has it discouraged it? What would be the consequences if it were cut back?

GLOSSARY

Affirmative action Special consideration and preferential treatment accorded to members of minority groups to remedy past discrimination.

Assimilation The incorporation of a minority group into the culture and social life of the dominant group so that the minority eventually disappears as a separate, identifiable unit.

Colonialism The economic takeover of one nation by another, more powerful nation, and the subsequent political and social domination of the native population.

Discrimination Exclusion or exploitation on the basis of group membership. While sometimes intentional, discrimination may also be institutional, that is, caused as a by-product of the regular operation of social institutions which affect groups unequally.

Ethnic group A category of people who perceive themselves and are perceived by others as possessing shared cultural traits.

Genocide The intentional, systematic attempt by a government to destroy a national, racial, religious, or ethnic group.

Institutional racism Racism that is so deeply ingrained in a society's traditions and practices that it continues to operate even in the absence of conscious prejudice or deliberate discrimination.

Integration The unimpeded interaction and contact between different racial and ethnic groups. This is sometimes termed "social" integration to distinguish it from functional integration.

Minority groups People who are singled out for unequal treatment in the society in which they live and who consider themselves to be victims of collective discrimination.

Multiculturalism An approach to life in a pluralistic society that calls for finding ways for people to understand and interact with one another that do not depend on their sameness but rather on respect for their differences. This view differs from other forms of pluralism in its emphasis on interaction and equality among groups.

Pluralism The coexistence of different racial or ethnic groups, each of which retains its own cultural identity and social networks while participating in the same economic and political systems.

Prejudice A categorical predisposition to like or dislike people for their real or imagined social characteristics.

Race A group of people who believe themselves to be and whom others believe to be genetically distinct.

Racism The doctrine that some races are inherently inferior and some are inherently superior.

Segregation The legal or customary restriction or prohibition of contact between groups according to such criteria as race, ethnicity, sex, and age.

Slavery An institutionalized system of bondage in which the "master" owns and exercises complete control over the slaves, who are forced to perform involuntary labor.

Stereotypes Fixed, simplified, and distorted generalizations about social groups and their members which are shared within a cultural context.

CHAPTER 9

Sex and Gender

Exposure to danger is not combat. Being shot at, even being killed, is not combat. Combat is finding . . . and killing or capturing the enemy. It's KILLING . . . And women CAN'T DO IT! Nor should they even be thought of as doing it. The requirements for strength and endurance render them UNABLE to do it. And I may be old-fashioned, but I think the very nature of women disqualifies them from doing it. Women give life. Sustain life. Nurture life. They don't TAKE it. (General Robert H. Barrow, quoted in *The New York Times*, July 21, 1991, p. E3)

Women have played a role in every U.S. military operation, beginning with the Revolutionary War. Today, more than one in ten American soldiers are women; 35,000 of them served in the Persian Gulf War of 1990–1991. Eleven were killed there—five in action—and two were taken prisoner. Yet women are still banned from one of the military's main activities: direct ground combat.

The official reason is that women are not as physically strong as men and are therefore less able to defend themselves. Women soldiers counter that they are already risking death or capture in noncombat units, including communications, transport, intelligence, and medical teams. Besides, today's advanced military technology requires brains as much as brawn, and hand-to-hand combat is increasingly rare. Some critics worry that women soldiers might become pregnant and leave their units short-handed, but more soldiers were taken out of service in the Persian Gulf because of sports injuries than because of pregnancies (*Newsweek*, August 5, 1991). Still others argue that the presence of women interferes with strong "male bonding" among soldiers. Yet a six-month experiment that mixed men and women on an aircraft carrier proved successful. The women performed as well as the men, and actually improved the atmosphere aboard ship. "We've become a little more civilized," acknowledged the skipper (*Time*, April 17, 1995, p. 37).

Many women suspect that the real issue in combat restrictions is **sexism**—the unequal treatment of men and women on grounds of sex or gender—and male antagonism toward women who enter military roles once reserved for men. Representative Pat Schroeder views combat prohibition as serving the self-interest of military men: "By pretending they were protecting women from harm, all they were really protecting them from was promotions" (in Quindlen, 1991, p. E19).

Combat restrictions are not the only obstacle women in the military face. A report of a Task Force on Women in the Military in 1988 found that sexual harassment of women is widespread in all the branches of military service, spanning ranks and work locations. Analyzing the data in the report, Firestone and Harris (1994) found that over 73 percent of the female respondents and 18 percent of the male respondents reported that they had been harassed (subjected to unwanted and uninvited sexual attention) within the last twelve months.

Since the report, the military has taken steps to identify and punish sexual harassment, especially after an incident in 1991 when a number of women (including naval officers) were assaulted by Navy aviators at their Tailhook convention in Las Vegas. A follow-up investigation uncovered widespread harassment and led to the resignation or reassignment of several admirals and the Secretary of the Navy.

Women have made some strides in military service in recent years. Since 1993, they have been allowed to fly combat missions in the Air Force. The Secretary of the Air Force is a woman. Since 1994, nearly 260,000 positions previously closed to women in military service have been opened up (Department of Defense memorandum, January 13, 1994). In 1995, for the first time, a woman was ranked number one in the graduating class of the U.S. Military Academy at West Point; she was head of her class in three programs—military, academic, and physical (*New York Times*, June 4, 1995). Day-care centers are now standard on military bases. One in six lieutenants is female. However, combat restrictions clearly limit career opportunities: Only one in thirty colonels is female and only three of 407 generals are women (Moskos, 1990). Getting to the top ranks usually depends on leading troops into battle. In sociological terms, the manifest *function* of banning women from combat may be to protect them, but a *latent function* is to restrict their military careers.

Gender is more than biology; it is a socially constructed set of distinctions and evaluations that reflects power and culture as well as social functions. Military service is an extreme case for the sociology of gender, but cultural ideas about male/female differences affect all of social life. Gender differences are among the most basic features of social structure, and they are maintained by power. All the key concepts are relevant to sex and gender, but these three will be most central to the following discussion.

THE SOCIAL CONSTRUCTION OF GENDER

In delivery rooms, babies are immediately classified as boys and girls. The term *sex* refers to biological differences related to reproduction. Far less obvious is *how* people should be male and female. Is that determined by our fixed biological identity or by social constructions of that identity? The term **gender** refers to nonbiological, culturally and socially produced distinctions between men and women and between masculinity and femininity (Laslett and Brenner, 1989; Oakley, 1972; Scott, 1986). The first time new parents dress their newborn boy in blue or their baby girl in pink, the sexual identity of the child is being socially constructed. Society establishes a set of cultural expectations for each gender, and children are taught to conform to what society expects. Sex differences, then, are the products of heredity and biology; gender differences result from socialization (see Chapter 5).

All societies use gender as an organizing principle, dividing the chores and rewards of social life into men's and women's roles. From clothing styles to careers, men and women are expected to be different. Historically, men and women have been viewed not only as different but also as unequal. In most times and places, the work, pastimes, traits, ideas, and even virtues ascribed to women have been viewed as less desirable and less worthy than those attributed to men. Thus, being rational (a supposedly masculine trait) is viewed as superior to being emotional (a feminine trait); being competitive (masculine) is more valuable than being caring (feminine); making money (traditionally a masculine role) is more important than rearing children (still primarily a

If boys and girls are innately different, why do parents go to so much trouble to dress them in gender-typed clothes? In diapers, this 6-month-old girl and her 7-month-old cousin would be indistinguishable.

feminine pursuit). Almost always, males have enjoyed far greater wealth, power, and prestige than have females, and this is still true in modern Western cultures, despite social change.

Gender inequality is virtually universal. Many people hold that the ultimate reason gender differences are so widespread is biology, which determines our fixed or "essential" identity.

Is Biology Destiny?

Despite biology's role in differentiating men and women, sociologists argue that it does not rigidly determine male and female behaviors.

Humans are extremely adaptive animals, capable of living in many ways in all kinds of environments. Compared with other species, we have few instincts or innate behavior patterns and a much greater capacity to learn and to change. As the evolutionary biologist Stephen Jay Gould (1984) warns, simplistic biological theories that stress the "naturalness" of gender inequality too often emphasize genetic limitations (which are few) rather than the range of potentialities (which are vast).

Both sides of the debate tend to assume that there are clear differences between men and women and then set out to find the reasons. But, in fact, the sexes are far more *similar* than different; we must not assume differences that cannot be demonstrated scientifically. Reviewing more than 2,000 books and articles on differences between the sexes, Maccoby and Jacklin (1974) concluded that, on average, males and females do not differ significantly in terms of sociability, suggestibility, self-esteem, achievement motivation, rote learning, analytical skills, and responses to auditory and visual stimulation.

Tests do show some differences: Males seem to be more aggressive than females and to perform better on visual-spatial tasks and in mathematics. Females tend to be more timid than males and to have superior verbal abilities (Jacklin, Maccoby, Doering, and King, 1984; see also Hyde, 1981; Sherman, 1978; Tavris and Wade, 1984). Experiments with the brain give credence to these findings (Shaywitz, et al., 1995; Witelson, 1992; Weintraub, 1991). Scientists have long known that men's and women's brains differ slightly. Women have smaller brains, but they have more neurons in the brain and a larger bridge between the two sides of the brain, which may help explain their better language skills and better intuition. Stimulations of the brain show that men have more activity in the part of the brain linked to action, especially aggression, while women's brains were more active in the region that controls complex expression of emotion.

Does this mean that biology rules in the brain? Not necessarily. Reliable sex differences have yet to be detected in the brains of male and female fetuses and newborns. Add to this the fact that once identified as male or female, boys and girls are treated differently. This means that a girl's developing nervous system is being sculpted differently from a boy's in daily social interactions. Although differences between boys and girls are small before puberty, at the onset of adolescence sexual maturation and cultural norms combine to produce noticeable differences. Adolescent girls often have crises of self-esteem and begin to lower their expectations for themselves (Gilligan, 1982). By high school, the division between male and female worlds is clear-cut (Richmond-Abbott, 1992). Biological factors may play a role in this process, but cultural influences are so pervasive that it is virtually impossible to isolate the effects of biology. As we saw in the public debates box in Chapter 5, nature and nurture seem to be inextricably intertwined.

Another reason to be cautious about drawing conclusions from biological differences is that for almost every behavior there is far greater variation *within* each sex than there is, on average, *between* the sexes (Bleier, 1984; Hyde, 1984; Thorne, 1993). A randomly selected woman may actually perform a "male" skill better than a man, and vice versa. As has been noted, there is also a tremendous amount of overlap in male and female behavior and skills, a point that gets lost in studies that group boys and girls, men and women. It does not always make sense, then, to judge a person's readiness to do a task on the basis of his or her sex; individual factors, such as training, character, and motivation, may be far more relevant.

Even for physiological differences, it is not clear that there are purely biological explanations. Male athletic champions can run faster and jump higher than their female counterparts; however, considering that American culture (and most others) provides much more encouragement, even pressure, for boys to participate in sports, it should not be surprising that they excel. In any case, the gap between male and female champions has steadily narrowed as girls and women have become much more active in sports over the last three decades (Doyle, 1985; Jordan, 1983).

Cultural context has a lot to do with determining a woman's physical ability. In agricultural societies, men think nothing of expecting women to work in the fields, and women grow relatively strong.

Culture also shapes how we perceive physical abilities. For instance, most people think nothing of seeing a woman carry a forty-pound child into a grocery store, yet when she checks out a ten-pound bag of groceries, she is "helped" to carry the bag to a car (Fenstermaker, West, and Zimmerman, 1991). Thus, cultural change, individual action, and cultural context all have an impact on the "raw material" that biology gives us.

To stress only biological features among all women is to take an "essentialist" position, arguing that the "essence" of femaleness can be found in certain reproductive organs or other physical features. To emphasize, by contrast, the variability of gender, the different ways of being female (or male), and the way culture and socialization shape gender identities is to take a "constructivist" view. Stressing the commonalities among women—starting from biology—can help to promote solidarity. It can also lead to inflexibility. Feminists have been divided on the issue of essentialism versus constructivism (Fuss, 1989; Butler, 1990). Most sociologists are at least partial constructivists (see Chapter 4 on socialization). But they recognize that being open to social construction does not mean that cultural categories or personal identities can change easily (Calhoun, 1994b). Indeed, some theorists warn that cultural constructions may make gender as fixed and determined as does the biology-as-destiny formulation. As Judith Butler (1990) notes, "In such a case, not biology, but culture, becomes destiny" (p. 8).

Cross-Cultural Comparisons

If gender characteristics were simply a matter of biology, then one would expect to find that gender roles do not vary much from one culture to another. But they do. What people consider masculine or feminine behavior is actually quite variable. Americans, for instance, think of men as being better suited to strenuous physical labor, but in many traditional societies, particularly in sub-Saharan Africa and in South America, women do most of the heavy work—carrying goods to market, hauling firewood, and constructing houses. Men hunt—and spend a lot of time talking. Similarly, while in the United States most doctors are men, in Russia most are women. In some cultures men are the main storytellers; in others, women are. In some societies agriculture is restricted to men, in others it is regarded as women's work, and in still others men and women work in the fields side by side. Whatever innate biological differences exist between the sexes, they allow for wide variation in actual social life.

The anthropologist Margaret Mead (1935/1963) was one of the first to study societies whose gender arrangements differ from our own. In three neighboring New Guinea tribes, she found evidence of aggression in women, passivity in men, and minimal differences in the roles of men and women. According to Mead the mild-mannered Arapesh expected both sexes to be gentle, cooperative, and maternal. In contrast, the neighboring Mundugumor believed both sexes were fierce, combative, and selfish. Both men and women there exhibited **machismo,** or compulsive masculinity. In the third tribe, the Tchambuli, ideals of masculinity and femininity were the opposite of ours. Women were the primary food providers for their families, shaved their heads, wore no ornaments, and dominated their men. The men were preoccupied with romance and beauty, spending their days primping and gossiping.

Mead took a relatively extreme position on the issue of social construction of gender. As she wrote, "Many, if not all, of the personality traits which we have called masculine or feminine are as lightly linked to sex as are the clothing, the manners, and the form of head-dress that a society at a given period assigns to either sex. . . . [T]he evidence is overwhelming in favor of the strength of social conditioning" (in Chafetz, 1970, p. 260). While no sociologist believes that biology completely determines gender roles, many believe that there is more cross-cultural consistency in male and female roles than Mead indicated. In hunting-and-gathering societies all over the world, for example, men are nearly always the hunters (Lenski, Lenski, and Nolan, 1991).

As mentioned previously, nearly every culture values the skills and traits that are considered masculine more highly than those considered feminine (Chafetz, 1984). Mead (1928/1968) noted that whatever the form the division of labor takes, the man's jobs are considered vitally important and the women's tasks are viewed as routine. For example, before the Industrial Revolution in England, spinning was seen as women's work and weaving as men's; weaving was better paid. When spinning machines were introduced, however, men claimed the right to operate them because they represented the high technology of the time and the operators were better paid than hand spinners or weavers. As weaving was devalued, more and more women became weavers (Pinchbeck, 1930; Thompson, 1968).

Cross-cultural comparisons, then, show a wide range of variation in what different cultures consider

The "weaker" sex? In our culture, we do not expect women—especially older women—to perform heavy physical labor. In rural villages in the Ukraine, however, farm work is considered women's work.

to be "male" or "female," "masculine" or "feminine." There is no one "essence" of maleness or femaleness (Fuss, 1989), but all societies do make distinctions between men and women. Historically, men were able to dominate women because they were physically stronger—a biological difference. The longer this domination went on, however, the more resources men could accumulate and thus the greater the inequality between men and women became. Male dominance became part of the social structure, supported by cultural norms and values as well as physical force, or power.

Gender Roles and Stereotypes

Many of our notions about masculinity and femininity date from the 1950s, an historically unusual period in our society. At that time a booming postwar economy and changing demographics combined to create a situation in which large portions of the U.S. population were able to live in their own homes, with the man as the sole provider and the woman as a full-time homemaker, devoted to raising her 2.4 children.

Even though more women are working today and new job opportunities are opening in formerly all-male fields, the social expectations and gender roles formed during the 1950s persist as society's ideal. **Gender roles** are the expected behaviors, attitudes, obligations, and privileges that a society assigns to each sex. Gender roles show up quite early, in children's play: Boys tend to dominate the aggressive activities in the playground while girls stand around or engage in more passive play, such as playing with dolls or jumping rope (Thorne, 1993). Gender roles are based on a set of gender stereotypes that have been challenged by both social scientists and the women's movement (Richmond-Abbott, 1992; Golombok and Fivush, 1994).

Gender stereotypes are oversimplified but strongly held and culturally reinforced ideas about the characteristics of males and females. They help maintain gender roles by shaping ideas about the tasks to which men and women are "naturally" suited. A 1990 Gallup Poll found that nearly six out of ten respondents believed that males and females have different personalities, interests, and abilities. Table 9.1 shows the different characteristics Americans assigned to the two sexes.

Gender roles and stereotypes reinforce each other. While stereotypes help to set up our expectations about the tasks men and women should perform, seeing people in traditional roles every day strengthens our belief that gender stereotypes are valid. For instance, we think that men are strong and forceful and therefore suited to police work; when we observe that most police officers are indeed male, we conclude that our stereotypes are right. Such reasoning is circular, of course. Because we do not routinely see men and women outside traditional gender roles, we have few opportunities to test our assumptions. Hence, we write off the policewoman or the father who stays at home as exceptions that prove the rule. As more women assume previously male roles (and vice versa), these stereotypes tend to weaken. However, they still retain the power to create major *role conflicts*—clashes between the demands associated with different roles—for both men and women.

Role conflicts may pose special problems for women who find themselves torn between the demands of motherhood and career. Even if a woman is able to manage both responsibilities, her employer and colleagues may see her as a bad bet for promotion. Fatherhood does not carry the same assumptions in the workplace or create such strong role conflict. Indeed, the more successful men are, the more likely they are to be married and have families; for women, the pattern is reversed (Ehrenreich and English, 1989). Women who decide not to become mothers tend also to be stigmatized (Fisher, 1991).

The high level of stress and frustration women experience from their role conflicts translates into feelings of distress. Overall, though, do women experience more distress than men do? Perhaps women appear to do so because they express their emotions more, or perhaps men simply express their distress in different ways, such as through anger. Mirowsky and Ross (1995) took these possibilities into account in a study of sex differences in distress, as measured by sadness, anxiety, malaise, and aches. They found that when emotional reserve and expressiveness are adjusted for, women actually experience anger more often than men, as well as the criteria for distress. They conclude that women genuinely do suffer distress more frequently than men—about 30 percent more often.

This is not to say that the male role in American society is free of stress. Fear of inadequacy and failure is the dark side of the pressure on men to achieve.

TABLE 9.1

How Different Do Men and Women Think the Sexes Are?

Question: Now I want to ask about some more specific characteristics of men and women. For each one I read, please tell me whether you think it is generally more true of men or more true of women.

Fifteen characteristics most often said to describe men				*Fifteen characteristics most often said to describe women*			
	OPINIONS OF				OPINIONS OF		
	Total	Men	Women		Total	Men	Women
1. Aggressive	64%	68%	61%	1. Emotional	81%	79%	83%
2. Strong	61	66	57	2. Talkative	73	73	74
3. Proud	59	62	55	3. Sensitive	72	74	71
4. Disorganized	56	55	57	4. Affectionate	66	69	64
5. Courageous	54	55	53	5. Patient	64	60	68
6. Confident	54	58	49	6. Romantic	60	59	61
7. Independent	50	58	43	7. Moody	58	63	52
8. Ambitious	48	51	44	8. Cautious	57	55	59
9. Selfish	47	49	44	9. Creative	54	48	60
10. Logical	45	53	37	10. Thrifty	52	51	53
11. Easy-going	44	48	40	11. Manipulative	51	54	48
12. Demanding	43	39	46	12. Honest	42	44	41
13. Possessive	42	38	45	13. Critical	42	43	41
14. Funny	40	47	34	14. Happy	39	38	39
15. Level-headed	39	46	34	15. Possessive	37	43	32

Source: Linda DeStefano and Diane Colasanto, "Unlike 1975, Today Most Americans Think Men Have It Better," The Gallup Poll Monthly, February 1990, p. 29.

Men are supposed to maintain an impression of strength and courage at all times. Gender stereotypes may prevent men from expressing warmth, tenderness, and sensitivity in their relationships both with wives and children and with friends of both sexes. Moreover, the emphasis men place on toughness and superiority can lead them to test and prove these attributes repeatedly by being physically aggressive, even violent. The male role also takes its toll in ill health. Men's life expectancy is eight years shorter than women's, and men suffer more heart attacks, stress-related illnesses, and alcoholism (see Chapter 14).

While members of both sexes complain about the constraints imposed by traditional gender roles, these roles tend to persist. Most men still choose predominantly male occupations; most women are in charge of child care and housework even if they work full-time outside the home. But, notes Patricia Hill Collins (1991), we are all shaped by multiple identities, including gender, race, class, religion, and sexual orientation—and even these standpoints provide var-

ied experiences. In short, even our differences have differences.

Gender Patterns in Values and Judgment

Not all gender differences are stereotypes; many real differences do exist, even if they are not innate. For example, many contemporary feminist scholars have stressed the value of the style of reasoning that women bring to moral and other decisions (Benhabib and Cornell, 1986; Gilligan, 1982). While men commonly try to narrow decisions down to a small number of clear and generalizable principles, women consider a wider range of contextual factors. Men are more likely to accept the limits within which an issue is initially posed, while women are more likely to consider other possibilities.

A well-known study illustrates these differences in moral reasoning. Kohlberg (1969) presented a series of dilemmas to his subjects and asked how they would resolve them. In one dilemma, a man cannot afford to buy a drug that will cure his dying wife. He can't borrow enough, nor will the druggist reduce the price or let him pay later. The man breaks into the store and steals the drug. Was he right or wrong, and why? Men tend to answer in terms of abstract ideas of justice and universal principles, and most find the husband was "wrong." Women tend to answer "right" more often, but they also ask for more contextual information and more details and sometimes propose solutions that are not included in the question (for example, society should have a program to provide the drug to those who are needy). Women's answers focus on concrete context, relationships, and the idea of caring, rather than on abstract ideals of equity and justice. Kohlberg initially treated the difference as a matter of better versus worse; he concluded that women did not reach as high a level of moral judgment as men did. However, Carol Gilligan importantly (1987) has argued that a moral orientation based on caring is no less valid than one based on justice; they are two ways of looking at the same picture, each proceeding from different ways of experiencing life.

Benhabib (1986) linked the contrast in moral perspectives to the sociological theory of George Herbert Mead. The justice orientation takes the standpoint of the "generalized other," which Mead saw as the most advanced. This means thinking not of any particular person but of people in general. The idea of the generalized other is important to matters like "human rights." But what about particular, concrete individuals? If we think only of the generalized other, Benhabib and Gilligan point out, we miss crucial features of sympathy and caring in social life. The caring orientation takes the standpoint of the "concrete other"—seeing the other person as an individual with a specific history and unique identity (emphasizing what makes us differ from one another). It works more in terms of needs and less in terms of rights. The moral principles leading from this standpoint are responsibility, bonding, and caring. As Gilligan and Benhabib suggest, the difference may be less a question of development than a matter of different but equally valuable styles of reasoning, with gender playing a prominent role in shaping who thinks each way.

Another study of values found substantial gender differences between male and female adolescents in the United States. Ann Beutel and Margaret Marini (1995) used data from questionnaires given to high school seniors from 1977 to 1991 to assess their value orientations on the measures of compassion, materialism, and importance attached to finding meaning in life. They found that females were consistently more likely to express concern and responsibility for the well-being of others, less likely to value materialism and competition, and more likely to think it very important to find purpose and meaning in life. These differences crossed class lines and held up even in the later years of the survey, when major changes were taking place in female occupational aspirations and young women were just as likely as young men to seek recognition in the job market.

It is clear that *some* differences between men and women are biological and that others are cultural. It is impossible to say precisely where the boundary lies, partly because biology and culture interact in every individual case; they are not completely separable (Haraway, 1992). It is also important to remember that just because a gender characteristic is culturally constructed does not mean that it is easy to change. It may be very deep-rooted in both culture and individual personalities.

Feminist Standpoint Theory

As we have just seen, women differ from men in their characteristic values and styles of judgment. They also have different real-life experiences from men: Women tend to be more central in the private sphere of the family and less so in the public sphere of work and politics, and they tend to be more vulnerable physically and economically. Given these differences, some feminist sociologists wonder what sociology might look like from a woman's standpoint (Smith, 1987; 1990).

Dorothy Smith, a Canadian sociologist, points out that the discipline of sociology has been built on the schemes, methods, and theories of the male social universe. Women have had to subordinate their own knowledge to these male ways of knowing and, in fact, to think of their world in the concepts and terms that men use to describe theirs. Women also end up being governed by these sociological assumptions, because sociologists are among those who establish the procedures by which we are ruled.

Smith would like to see women use their position as insiders in the private sphere and as facilitators and mediators in the traditionally male world of bureaucracies and markets to come up with new ways of knowing and new frames of sociological reference rooted in direct experience, not simply based on theorizing and socially constructed views of the world. As she says, "Women's direct experience places us a step back, where we can recognize the uneasiness that comes from sociology's claim to be about the world we live in, and, at the same time, its failure to account for or even describe the actual features we experience" (1990, p. 27). But Smith acknowledges that direct experience alone does not make one a sociologist; it is still necessary to look beyond that experience, to examine the social relations that shape our lives, to gain the conceptual knowledge that men have monopolized. Women have a head start in this task: Unlike men, they begin with a practical, commonsense knowledge of the world, to which they can add conceptual knowledge through the study of sociology. In theory, men could do the reverse, adding direct experience to their formal knowledge, but in practice they do not because they benefit from the existing power structure and division of labor.

Smith, then, attempts to ground feminist sociology in the concrete relationship of women's lives. In this she shares Gilligan's concern with the concrete and specific, as shown in women's style of moral reasoning. The feminist standpoint is rooted in the perspective provided by the specific conditions, practical activities, and social relations of women's lives—not simply of the personal life of the sociologist but also of the lives she studies.

PATTERNS OF GENDER INEQUALITY

Gender roles are far more open in the United States and other societies today than they were even a generation ago. Today's women enjoy a much greater degree of equality with men than their mothers or grandmothers did. Yet inequalities persist, affecting all of us, male and female.

Some of these inequalities are a legacy of years when females did not get as highly educated as males. For example, in 1993, 19 percent of women over the age of twenty-five were college graduates, compared with 25 percent of men (U.S. Bureau of the Census, 1995). This gap has closed for the youngest group of post-college adults (ages twenty-five to twenty-nine), and in 1993, 55 percent of all college students were female (up from 44 percent ten years earlier). Even so, parity in education does not translate into parity in the workplace: In 1992 a woman with a college degree earned an average of $30,394 per year, compared to $41,406 for a male college graduate (U.S. Department of Labor, 1994). Below,

we take a closer look at how men and women are treated differently in the workplace.

Gender Inequality in the Workplace

The women's movement into the paid labor force has been called "the basic social revolution of our time" (Hochschild, 1989, p. 249). The number of American women who work outside the home has been growing since the turn of the century, but in recent years the increase has been staggering (see Figure 9.1). The greatest change has occurred among white middle-class women; substantial numbers of black and other minority women, as well as working-class women, have always worked outside the home (Woody, 1989).

What has prompted the high rate of workforce participation among women today? Service jobs, traditionally filled by females, have expanded. At the same time, men's wages have been declining in real value, necessitating two salaries in the household. The high divorce rate has pushed many women into the job market, and some married women pursue a career as insurance against the economic effects of

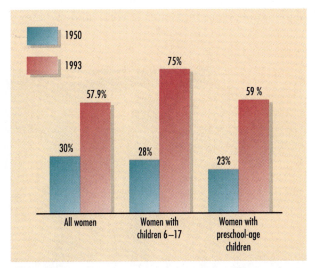

FIGURE 9.1 / Percentage of American Women in the Paid Labor Force, 1950 and 1993

In the decades since 1950, increasingly large percentages of women have joined the paid labor force. Most striking is the jump in the percentage of working mothers.

Source: U.S. Bureau of the Census, *Statistical Abstract of the United States*, 1994.

divorce. Finally, attitudes about working wives have changed. In 1993, the idea of a woman holding a job even if her husband could support her won an 86 percent approval rating, compared to only 22 percent in 1938 (*The Gallup Poll Monthly*, October 1993).

Labor force participation by women varies from country to country (Reskin and Padavic, 1994). In societies where sexes are strictly segregated, as in Muslim culture, women's participation in the formal labor force is lowest. In non-Muslim developing countries, men tend to monopolize the paid jobs (as they did earlier in Western societies). In fully developed countries, women approach the male rate of participation, especially in the Scandinavian countries. The smallest differences in participation rates are found in communist and socialist societies, where the ideological tradition holds that all able-bodied adults have an obligation to work. Gender differences in labor participation rates are significant because they help determine the relative economic positions of men and women, including a gender poverty gap (Casper, Garfinkel, and McLanahan, 1994). In 1991, women in the United States were 30 percent more likely to be poor than men.

For those women who do work, what does the workplace look like? For the most part, it is structured inequitably, both at home and abroad, in spite of changes in attitudes and opportunities in recent decades. The problems women face are occupational segregation of jobs into "men's work" and "women's work," pay gaps, blocked advancement, gender bias and harassment on the job, and the need to work a "second shift" at home. (It should be noted that a very small minority of men face some of the same problems.)

Occupational Segregation

The United States Census Bureau keeps track of how many men and how many women are employed in over 500 different occupations. Here is the picture drawn from the 1990 census (Reskin and Padavic, 1994):

■ Many women work in primarily female occupations (see Table 9.2).

■ Three out of five women work in clerical, sales, or service jobs; two-thirds of men work as managers, professionals, craft workers, or operators (Sorenson, 1994).

■ One-third of women work in just ten of the 503 occupations.

■ The most common occupations for women in 1990 were almost the same as those identified in 1940.

■ Only 11 percent of working women were employed in occupations that were at least 75 percent male.

Most working women are not "career women"; rather, they work in low paying occupations with little job security and few or no benefits, often serving men.

TABLE 9.2

Gender Segregation of the Workforce (Selected Occupations), 1994

Occupation	Total Employed (Thousands)	Percent Female
Secretary	3,397	98.9%
Receptionist	931	96.4
Bookkeeper	1,829	91.9
Bank teller	441	90.4
Computer operator	546	60.6
Computer programmer	549	29.3
Sales supervisor and proprietor	4,443	37.5
Sales worker	6,440	66.1
Registered nurse	1,956	93.8
Dental hygienist	97	100.0
Child-care worker	286	97.3
Cleaner or servant	500	95.8
Waiter or waitress	1,446	78.6
Sewing machine operator	619	86.0
Precision production occupation	3,921	23.9
Mechanic and repairer	4,419	4.5
Carpenter	1,265	1.0
Firefighter	210	2.1
Police and detective	968	15.6
Truck driver	2,815	4.5
Airplane pilot and navigator	104	2.6

Source: U.S. Bureau of Labor Statistics, Employment and Earnings, January 1995, Table II, pp. 175–180.

What we find is that, by and large, women are segregated into female jobs, which many people have labeled "women's work." A good measure of just how much occupational segregation exists is given by a statistical figure known as the *index of segregation*. If men and women were perfectly integrated across occupations, the index would equal 0; complete segregation in job occupations would yield an index of 100. In 1990 the index was 55, which means that 55 percent of all female workers would have to shift to mostly male occupations in order to drive the index down to 0 and perfectly integrate all occupations (Jacobsen, 1994).

The last several decades have seen a gradual decline in occupational segregation. The index dropped 11 points from 1970 to 1990, for example. Women have succeeded in moving into some traditionally male jobs, such as bank managers, bar-

tenders, insurance adjusters, and bus drivers. In many cases these breakthroughs occurred because the occupations had become less attractive to men and employers faced a shortage of male workers. In some situations, entire occupations have "tipped" toward females, as has occurred with bank tellers and telephone operators (Jacobsen, 1994; Reskin and Padavic, 1994). When that happens, the index of segregation is driven up a notch. Some women move back and forth between "male" and "female" jobs, but the trend is toward the latter; forays into male occupations tend to be sporadic and short-term (Rosenfeld and Spenner, 1992).

The main problem with occupational segregation is that it helps to create a gender gap in pay, for "women's work" is invariably paid less than "men's work" and is generally considered less desirable. Today women make approximately 70 percent of

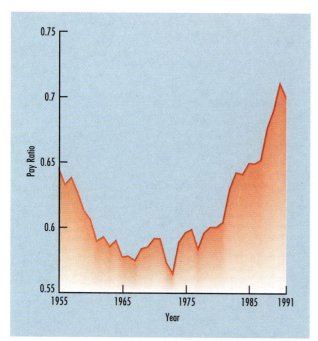

FIGURE 9.2 / Female-to-Male Pay Ratio, 1955–1991

Women's earnings have always lagged behind men's. Women's pay hit a low of around 55 percent of men's pay in the early 1970s; in the early 1990s it has hovered at 70 percent.

Source: Elaine Sorensen, *Comparable Worth: Is It a Worthy Policy?* (Princeton University Press, Princeton, 1994), p. 5.

what men earn (see Figure 9.2). For every $10,000 the average woman earned in 1991, the average man earned $14,306. The pay inequity generated by occupational segregation is thought to account for about 27 percent of the total pay gap between women and men (Sorensen, 1994).

Even when lower-status male jobs are compared with typical female ones, men earn more. Sewers and stitchers, for example, who are primarily female, earn a median income just over half that of carpet installers, primarily men. Even men working in traditionally female jobs are typically paid more than their female colleagues. Education does not eliminate this inequity. The average female college graduate earns less than a male worker with only a high school diploma. Minority women are doubly disadvantaged: On average, black female college graduates with full-time jobs earn no more than white male high school dropouts (Rhode, 1990).

Historically, black women have been the most segregated group in the labor force, largely confined to such low-status and low-paying occupations as domestic worker, factory worker, and field hand. In the 1970s, with the passage of antidiscrimination legislation, African-American women made significant gains. By 1985, black women earned almost 90 percent as much as white women. Their most significant gains were in government and public administration, transportation and communications, health, education, and social services. Not all benefited equally: In some cases black women just "moved over" into low-paying sales and office jobs, while white women "moved up." On the whole, however, the occupational status and incomes of black women improved. But these gains were offset by the sharp decline in employment opportunities and pay for black men, which left many African-American women as their family's sole earners. In 1993, 50 percent of households headed by black or Hispanic women had incomes below the poverty line (*Current Population Reports*, 1995).

Occupational segregation and wage discrimination are global phenomena (United Nations, 1991). Virtually everywhere in the world the workplace is segregated by sex, although countries differ in what occupations are considered primarily male or female. In India, for example, women hold most of the unskilled construction jobs while men predominate in clerical occupations. Still, in nearly every country women have a narrower range of occupations, and their work is valued less (Peterson and Runyan, 1993). Overall, the extent of occupational segregation in other countries is similar to that in the United States, but there are a few anomalies. Some "progressive" societies that emphasize egalitarianism (such as the Scandinavian countries) actually have *higher* levels of occupational segregation than do more "traditional" societies such as Japan, Italy, and Greece (Charles, 1992) (see the Research Methods box).

Comparable-Worth Issues

Sex differences in earnings are nothing new. Employers have always paid men more than women. Tax records from Paris for the year 1313 reveal that women's wealth was 65 percent of men's, just about what the pay gap is today (Reskin and Padavic, 1994). In nineteenth-century America women working in

Explaining Cross-National Patterns of Occupational Segregation

Maria Charles (1992) studied data from twenty-five industrialized countries to try to explain puzzling patterns of occupational segregation by sex. Why was the level of segregation highest in so-called progressive societies and relatively low in more traditional societies? Her research provided her with several explanations.

First, the traditional countries have fewer women in the formal labor force. Women outside the labor force fill traditional gender roles as housewives and mothers, but they are unpaid and therefore outside measurement. In more progressive societies, activities considered "women's work"—for example, child care and elder care—become paying jobs, and those jobs are filled by women, increasing gender segregation in the workforce. Second, in more modern societies, job titles put women's versions of the same job in different categories from men's. For example, a woman would be a "bookkeeper" and a man an "accountant." Third, the more modern countries tend to have large service and information sectors in their economies, providing many jobs in occupations where women are customarily concentrated.

To come to these conclusions, Charles had to make carefully controlled cross-national comparisons. The data had to be classified and measured in reasonably similar ways for each of the countries. She limited her sample to industrialized countries because nonindustrialized countries did not keep reliable records of the paid labor force. Charles was fortunate in having access to labor-market data for men and women in six occupational categories compiled by the International Labor Office (ILO). The ILO, an agency of the United Nations, keeps labor statistics from a number of countries in a standardized format.

After compiling her raw data, Charles devised an index to calculate an overall occupational sex segregation score for each country based on the six occupational categories. Because she wanted to *explain* the level of sex segregation in different countries—not just *describe* it—she had to be sure her dependent variable, the index of sex segregation, would capture all the different dimensions of sex segregation. She also had to make sure that the sex segregation measure did not get entangled with such other compositional effects as female labor force participation rates and the occupational structure.

Charles now had data showing the differences among the twenty-five countries in occupational segregation. Her next task was to account for the variation, which she accomplished by studying the impact of relevant social, economic, and cultural characteristics for each country, as taken from publicly available national and international sources. She focused, in particular, on the size of the service sector, the size of the employee class, female labor force participation, fertility, the extent of gender egalitarianism, the level of corporatism, labor force growth, and modernization (as measured by GDP). Then she used a sophisticated kind of statistical analysis to assess the effect of these independent variables on occupational segregation. Structures of opportunity—of available jobs—proved key.

---

manufacturing earned no more than 37 cents for every dollar a man earned. One woman in the 1860s found an effective way to solve this problem:

> I had no money and a woman's wages were not enough to keep me alive. I looked around and saw men getting more money, and more work, and more money for the same kind of work. I decided to become a man. It was simple. I just put on men's clothing and applied for a man's job. I got good money for those times, so I stuck to it. (Quoted in Reskin and Padavic, 1994, p. 102)

Today, women are seeking more practical solutions. One of these is the controversial policy of **comparable worth,** which calls for basing wages for a job category on the amount of skill, effort, responsibility, and risk the job entails, plus the amount of income the job produces, rather than other criteria. Statistics show clearly that jobs traditionally performed by women and/or minorities have been systematically devalued (Treiman and Hartmann, 1981; Wittig and Lowe, 1989). For example, a woman who provides full-time child care (arguably a highly responsible task) is typically paid less per hour than is a gas station attendant (Sorensen, 1994). Many women are leaving occupations vital to society, such as nursing and teaching, because the pay is low (Lewin and Tragos, 1987). Figure 9.3 shows the typical salaries

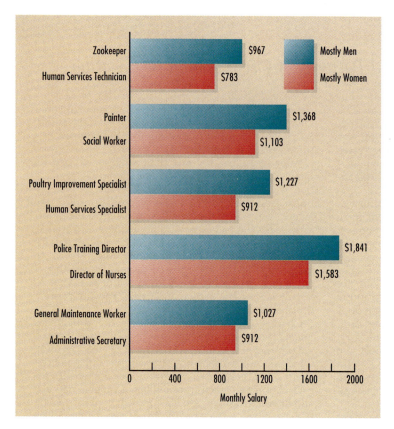

FIGURE 9.3 / Comparison of Monthly Salaries for Equally Valued Jobs Held Mostly by Men or by Women

Before instituting its pioneering comparable-worth program, the state of Minnesota compared the salaries of equally valued jobs held mostly by one sex or the other. Some of the results are shown here.

Source: Minnesota Department of Employee Relations, in Sara M. Evans and Barbara J. Nelson, "Comparable Worth: The Paradox of Technocratic Reform," *Feminist Studies* 15, no. 1 (1989): 174.

for pairs of jobs that have been judged to be of equal value by the state of Minnesota (which has led the way in exploring comparable-worth issues).

Advocates of comparable worth hold that it fulfills the spirit and the letter of antidiscrimination statutes passed by Congress that require equal pay for equal work. When wages for a job category dominated by women or minority males are lower than wages for a job filled predominantly by white males, and the two jobs are of comparable value to the employer, then discrimination is a strong possibility. The problem is, as Paula England (1992) points out, that comparable worth refers to a type of discrimination that is invisible to most judges, policymakers, employers, and even its victims:

> In our culture, it is easier to see that (1) women are discriminated against when they are not allowed into predominantly male jobs, than to see that (2) women are discriminated against when entire occupations are devalued and paid less because they are done by women and/or involve traditionally female skills. (p. 307)

Opponents of comparable worth maintain that employers are innocent of discrimination because they are merely paying market wages—the going market rate (Rhoads, 1993). According to this line of reasoning, if women want to get equal pay and higher salaries, then they should prepare themselves to go after the male-dominated jobs that pay more. Comparable-worth advocates counter that women should not have to change jobs to get a wage not affected by gender bias (England, 1992).

Another aspect of the comparable-worth debate is how to implement it. Establishing a comparable-worth policy requires job evaluations. Critics say that such evaluations are highly subjective and arbitrary. Proponents reply that evaluations are used in business all the time for all sorts of job classifications, so this would be nothing new (England, 1992). Critics warn that evaluations that result in lowering men's wages would alienate men, but advocates point out successful instances of implementation of comparable worth that raised women's wages while leaving men's earnings untouched.

Another argument against comparable pay is that it would be too costly, with estimates ranging from $2 billion to $150 billion per year for the U.S. workforce (Remick and Steinberg, 1984). However, studies of employers who have implemented comparable-pay policies here and abroad indicate that the cost has been greatly exaggerated. When phased in gradually, such reforms account for only 5 to 10 percent of the average American employer's payroll (Hartmann, 1987). In addition, there could be savings to the taxpayer because these policies help to raise women (and their families) out of poverty.

To date, comparable-worth programs have been implemented for the entire economy of Australia and the province of Ontario, the Canadian federal government as well as in seven provincial governments, twenty American state governments (to varying degrees), and a large number of local municipalities and private-sector businesses in the United States (Sorensen, 1994). Long-term results are not yet available for most programs. Minnesota, however, stands out as a success: The female-to-male pay ratio increased from 72 percent to close to 81 percent, and the wage penalty associated with female-dominated jobs declined from 21 percent to 3 percent. All this

was accomplished without penalizing male wages; men's pay, in fact, increased 3 percent, while women's increased 15 percent (Sorensen, 1994).

Blocked Advancement

Another dimension to gender inequality in the workplace is vertical segregation—the concentration of women at the bottom and men at the top of an organization. This happens because women get segregated into low-level jobs that are considered "female" but also because men get promoted faster. Many women who have the skills, motivation, and training to advance bump their heads against what has been called a *glass ceiling*—an invisible but impenetrable barrier to the upper levels of management (Blum and Smith, 1988; Hagan, 1990; Kanter, 1977; Lorber, 1994).

Female attorneys are an example. Ten years after graduation, women lawyers earn an average of $40,000 less than male peers, they are more likely to work in small firms, and even when they do work in large firms, they tend to be placed in less prestigious areas of the law and to receive fewer promotions. In

Women who have worked their way into management and corporate board rooms often remain on the outer edge. One "price of admission" to such jobs is dressing in feminine clothes that do not threaten their male colleagues.

the 1980s, female attorneys made up 25 percent of associates (lawyers working as nonpermanent employees) but only 6 percent of partners (permanent members) in U.S. law firms (American Bar Association, 1988). A 1995 report by the American Bar Association found that women are now actually losing ground, with the partnership rate for women falling even further behind that of men (*New York Times,* January 22, 1996).

A report released by the Federal Glass Ceiling Commission confirmed that "at the highest levels of business, there is indeed a barrier only rarely penetrated by women or persons of color" (quoted in *Newsweek,* March 27, 1995, p. 24). According to the study, women make up only about 5 percent of senior management in the largest 1,000 corporations. Still, that is up from 1.5 percent in the mid-1980s, and some people estimate the figure to be closer to 7 percent today. Moreover, the picture is rosier in middle management, where women fill more than 40 percent of the jobs (*New York Times,* March 16, 1995); the hope is that as these women advance in their careers, more and more of them will make it to the top. Meanwhile, more and more women are *starting* at the top by forming their own businesses. The number of female-owned sole proprietorships (small new businesses) is growing twice as fast as male-owned counterparts (Weeks, 1993).

Despite the progress they have made, women still face major hurdles (Lorber, 1994). People who advance in the workplace generally have a mentor, or role model, to provide them with advice; a sponsor in a senior position to recommend promotion; and networking connections, providing them with information about job opportunities. But where the workplace is dominated by men, these roles are generally filled by males. Women who think they would benefit from a same-sex mentor or sponsor are at a disadvantage.

Some women feel that they are being penalized in the workplace by taking what has been called the *Mommy track* (Lorber, 1994). Many corporations now try to make it easier for women to balance career and family responsibilities by offering flexible working hours and generous maternity leave. However, women who get on this track get off the fast track, and their commitment to work is often called into question. Because these women are unable (or unwilling) to put in fifteen-hour days at the office, they are overlooked for promotions; very few are

given the chance to prove they can be both mothers *and* corporate leaders. In these situations, many women simply opt out. Studies have found that within ten years of graduation from business school, 20 percent of women do not work at all outside of the home (*Newsweek,* March 27, 1995).

Many companies attempt to demonstrate their commitment to gender neutrality by hiring a few token women or putting a few in top-level jobs. But being a token takes its toll: Women in these roles report feeling extra pressure to perform, social isolation, and confinement to gender-specific roles (such as being required to take notes in a committee meeting) (Kanter, 1977). Kanter attributed these problems to the simple fact that the women were in a numerical minority (less than 15 percent of the whole group). Her solution is to increase the numbers of women, redressing the imbalance. Janice Yoder (1991) thinks the problems are not so much an effect of the small numbers of women as of their *increasing* numbers, which threatens the dominant status of the majority. She finds that women suffer from tokenism in direct proportion to the gender-inappropriateness of the job. The more skewed an occupation is in favor of men, generally the more prestigious and well-paid is that occupation, which makes the intrusion of women all the more unwelcome. Another factor working against token women in traditionally sex-segregated jobs is that they must not only show their competence on the job but also somehow "overcome" their gender (Mansfield, et al., 1991). This may lead some women to overcompensate by becoming "one of the boys" (Lorber, 1994).

Do token males in female-dominated occupations suffer the same consequences? It appears not. Because female-dominated occupations are generally less prestigious, having men infiltrate them may actually raise the status of the jobs. A study (Williams, 1992) of how men fared in the traditionally female professions of nursing, elementary school teaching, librarianship, and social work revealed that men received fair—and in some cases, preferential—treatment in hiring and promotion. Many men, in fact, found themselves on a "glass escalator," an invisible fast track that took them further up in their profession than they intended to go. Token males reported being accepted by their superiors (who were often male) and colleagues and fitting well into the workplace. The only discrimination they encountered came from outsiders, or clients, with negative stereotypes about men in particular positions. In some cases, positions of authority were blocked to the men because of affirmative action programs that reserved certain jobs for women.

Another study of male tokens focused on the nursing profession (Heikes, 1991). The male nurses reported feeling extra pressure to perform, as well as isolation from the dominant group, but the way they experienced these effects differed from how female tokens typically experience them. Males in our society are expected to excel, so the male nurses did not feel particularly burdened by performance pressures; indeed, they welcomed them. As for the isolation, it was often of their own making: they wanted to differentiate themselves from female nurses in order to improve their own status. Indeed, both physicians and patients tend to take male nurses more seriously than female nurses, asking them for technical or medical assistance rather than routine care. Supervisors criticize them less often, given them more freedom in planning their schedules, and are more likely to recommend they upgrade skills and move into higher-paying positions (Ott, 1989). Thus, sociocultural factors seemed to mitigate how males bore tokenism.

Gender Bias on the Job

The fact that men disproportionately hold the positions of power in the workplace sets the stage for gender bias. Men tend to be the ones who decide who gets hired for what jobs, and who performs well and deserves promotion. A number of laboratory studies have shown that the same résumé is given a lower rating and offered a lower starting salary when evaluators are told the applicant is a female rather than a male; that jobs labeled "feminine" are seen as requiring less effort and skill than identical jobs labeled "masculine"; and that successful performances by females are likely to be attributed to luck, while the same accomplishments by men are attributed to effort (Wittig and Lowe, 1989).

Both men and women tend to have negative attitudes toward female managers, as if they believed that women do not belong in positions of authority (Frank, 1988; Rosen and Jerdee, 1978; Statham, 1987). Female managers are caught in a double bind: If they conform to traditional definitions of femininity, they are seen as lacking necessary assertiveness; if they

conform to masculine models, they are seen as overly aggressive and difficult to work for (Rhode, 1990).

Gender bias can be especially strong when women choose to work in traditionally masculine occupations. Women police officers report that they are constantly being watched and tested by their male colleagues. They are expected to do such "female" chores as making coffee and tidying up, and they are subjected to coarse sexist remarks and rude jokes. Male officers do not want them as partners on patrol, and supervisors see them as suited only to desk jobs (Ott, 1989). One study of women in two traditionally male blue-collar occupations found that the women suffered more stress and got less satisfaction from their jobs than did school secretaries, who work in a predominantly female, and lower-paid, occupation (Mansfield et al., 1991).

The ugliest face of gender bias on the job is **sexual harassment**—the demand that someone respond to or tolerate unwanted sexual attention from a person with power over the victim. Sexual harassment can take the form of sexual jokes that make women feel uncomfortable, or it can be more serious, as when a woman's boss or co-worker makes a sexual advance—especially when the woman has clearly indicated such attention is unwelcome. Harassment is extremely serious when a woman's refusal of a sexual advance results in punitive treatment or denial of a promotion. Harassment has also been defined as *generalized* sexual talk or behavior that creates a hostile environment in the workplace. A key finding of a study of sexual harassment in the military was that the atmosphere of the work setting predicted the level of individual harassment (Firestone and Harris, 1994). That is, where sexual talk and behavior in the workplace created an intimidating environment, about 80 percent of the women reported encountering individual harassment. On the other hand, in a work setting free of overt sexual talk and behavior, only about 5 percent of women reported individual harassment.

Sexual harassment caught the nation's attention in 1991 during the Senate hearings on the appointment of Clarence Thomas to the Supreme Court. In the course of the hearings, Anita Hill, a law professor, accused Thomas of having sexually harassed her when she worked on his staff. He had persistently asked her for a date, she said, and made offensive sexual comments when she refused. Thomas denied

Sexual harassment on the job finally became a serious issue for Americans—one that needed to be brought into the open—as a result of Anita Hill's allegations during the confirmation hearings of Supreme Court nominee Clarence Thomas in 1991.

the accusations and was eventually confirmed as a Supreme Court justice. We may never know the full truth, but what scandalized many people was the fact that the Senate Judiciary Committee (all-male) initially ignored the charge of sexual harassment. Then, they refused to allow probes into Thomas's private life while tolerating a dissection of Hill's personal life. Finally, they did not allow expert testimony on sexual harassment that could have refuted criticisms of Hill's conduct (Fraser, 1992).

The Hill–Thomas episode is a good illustration of how the key sociological concepts help in analysis. Power lies in the hands of men, not only in the actual deeds of harassment but also in responding to accusations. In this context, it is not surprising that many women are reluctant to make the accusations in the first place. In any case, our culture effectively denies the seriousness of harassment, suggesting that "boys will be boys." The social structure of the Senate was (and is) extremely unbalanced in gender terms: Of 100 Senators, ninety-eight were male at the time of Thomas's confirmation. Functional integration does not serve women, because the procedures for responding to complaints are flawed; moreover, functional links between school and the workplace, and between one workplace and another, discourage women from speaking out if it means they will lose a valuable job recommendation or sponsor support.

Finally, the Thomas hearings made many women resolve to take action—to elect more women and to make their voices heard.

The "Second Shift"

Growing numbers of women work an eight-hour shift at their jobs, and then they put in another full shift at their home, cooking, cleaning, and caring for their children. From her own research and other time-use studies, sociologist Arlie Hochschild (1989) calculates that working women do fifteen more hours of work a week than their husbands do. This adds up to an extra month of twenty-four-hour days each year.

Women are the ones who keep track of doctor appointments, arrange for children's visits with friends, and call from work to check on the babysitter. Women do more of the daily jobs, like cooking and cleaning up, that lock them into fixed routines. Men take care of the car, the yard, and household repairs—nonroutine chores that are less frequent and often can be done when time permits. One study (Presser, 1994) found that among dual-earning couples women spent about nineteen more hours a week than men on routine chores, while men spent about six more hours a week than women on the nonroutine tasks (see Table 9.3). Men are more likely to do "fun" things with the children (such as trips to the zoo), while women more often perform such tasks as feeding and bathing. Just as there is a wage gap in the workplace, so there is a "leisure gap" at home. Husbands sleep longer and have more time to watch TV or pursue hobbies.

Hochschild suggests that women give in to their husbands on the "second shift" issue because they are locked into marriage in a way that men are not. For one thing, women earn less than men and so have more of an economic need for marriage. For another, marriage is less stable that it used to be, and divorce is more economically damaging to women than to men.

The "second shift" is also a matter of cultural expectations. In describing their future family life, students of both sexes tend to follow traditional gender roles (Machung, 1989). When asked whose job comes first, most say the husband's does. Both sexes agree that primary care of children is the wife's job. Although both sexes anticipate having careers, males

TABLE 9.3

Average Time Spent on Household Tasks by Working Husbands and Wives, 1987–1988

Household Task	MEAN HOURS PER WEEK	
	Husband	Wife
Female Tasks	6.7	25.7
Preparing meals	2.3	8.9
Washing dishes and cleaning up after meals	1.9	5.4
Cleaning house	1.7	7.2
Washing, ironing, and mending clothes	0.7	4.2
Male tasks	7.1	1.7
Outdoor tasks or other housework maintenance tasks (yard work, household repair, painting, etc.)	5.2	1.5
Automobile maintenance and repair	2.0	0.2
Neutral Tasks	3.8	5.9
Shopping for groceries and other household goods	1.3	2.7
Paying bills and keeping financial records	1.4	1.6
Driving household members to work, school, or other activities	1.2	1.6
Total	17.6	33.4
Number of respondents	2,388	2,388

Source: Harriet B. Presser, "Employment Schedules Among Dual-Earner Spouses and the Division of Household Labor by Gender," American Sociological Review 59 (June 1994), p. 354.

and females hold different attitudes toward work (Maines and Hardesty, 1987). Male students see their future in terms of a steady line of work and achievement. Most have clear ideas about where they want to go and how to get there. They expect to work for the rest of their lives and to be the main providers, even if their wives work. By comparison, women seem tentative and vague about their career goals. They want to work, but they see their career plans as depending on the needs of their husbands and children. They expect their careers to be interrupted or even halted at various times.

In general, the American workplace is not designed for people who want to make equal commitments to their family and their job. Some companies, as we have seen, make flexible arrangements so that career women can also stay on the "mommy track," but this choice tends to derail the career. Most companies still lag in providing any form of child-care assistance. Because caring for children is still seen as women's work, the burden of trying to balance work and children falls on women. Our culture still expects men to be only part-time parents, filling in for Mom now and then.

There are alternatives. In Sweden, the government provides public day care for all children. Parents of either sex who choose to stay home with a baby are guaranteed eighteen months' leave, continue to receive social security payments, and must be given their old jobs back at the end of the leave. The government requires employers to allow parents time off to care for a sick child and the option of part-time work when the child is a preschooler. Either parent may take advantage of these programs (Sorrentino, 1990). Even in Sweden, however, cultural forces come into play: Few men take advantage of paternity leave, and those who do often are ridiculed by their peers (Moen, 1989).

Our culture and society provide little help to working mothers. Juggling children and a career—plus a husband—requires exceptional energy, physical dexterity, managerial skill, and endless patience.

The Politics of Gender

Politics has long been regarded as a man's world (Epstein, 1988). Prevailing stereotypes have held that women lack the driving ambition, the lust for power, that is required for politics and that they are too "nice" to dirty their hands in struggles for power. Women were not even granted the right to vote in this country until 1920. Over the next half century, millions of women worked as volunteers for the major political parties and for particular candidates. However, hardly any women were nominated for political office themselves, nor were they admitted to the inner sanctums where the real business of party decision-making took place.

In the 1970s, as the modern women's movement gathered momentum, women's role in American politics began to change. The proportion of women who voted, traditionally low, came to equal and sometimes surpass the number of male voters. More and more women ran for elective office and won, reaching record high numbers in the 1990s (see Table 9.4). Most important, at every level of office the success rate of male and female candidates in recent elections was virtually identical; a candidate's sex did not seem to be a factor in deciding an election (*Information Please Almanac*, 1995, p. 41). Thus, it appears that one reason women are underrepresented in national and state offices today is not that they cannot win but that not enough women candidates run.

The upper echelons of politics are still largely closed to women. No women has been president of the United States or even run for that office; in 1995 only one woman was serving as a state governor. Underrepresentation of women among elected and appointed officials is worldwide. Of the 159 member states in the United Nations, as of 1990 only six were headed by women. Only 3.5 percent of all cabinet ministers were women, and ninety-three countries had no woman in a ministerial position (United Nations, 1991). Representation of women in parliamentary assemblies hovers around 10 percent, and rarely exceeds 25 percent. The business of governing, like other businesses, is gender-stratified. Large numbers of women work at low-level jobs in public

TABLE 9.4
Women in Elective Office, Selected Offices, 1975–1995

Elected Officeholders	PERCENT FEMALE			NUMBER OF WOMEN
	1975	**1981**	**1995**	**1995**
Members of U.S. Congress	4	3	10.3	55
Statewide elective officials	10	11	25.9	84
Members of state legislatures	8	12	20.6	1,536

Source: Center for the American Woman and Politics, Eagleton Institute of Politics, Rutgers University.

administration, political parties, trade unions, and other political organizations, but very few hold decision-making posts (Peterson and Runyan, 1993).

What prevents women from achieving these posts? Many factors have to do with structure. The horizontal and vertical segregation of women in the marketplace (described earlier) means that women have access to fewer resources, less status, and less experience exercising power than men do. The structure of education also comes into play, because, worldwide, men have more educational opportunity than do women, and education tends to be more highly valued than experience. The African country of Eritrea provides an example of this. When its new government came to power in 1992, it established educational standards for holding positions in government. This policy resulted in displacing women with

years of practical experience from governmental jobs, even those having to do with women's and children's welfare, in favor of men with formal degrees (often earned abroad) and no practical experience. Cultural factors also act to hold back political power from women. Most countries maintain the same gender stereotypes that have characterized the United States. In some societies, particularly the Muslim nations, religious beliefs confine women to the private sphere, and in every nation the domestic responsibilities women bear translate into less time for public service. At bottom, the issue of women's role in politics is a matter of power. Politics is almost defined by the exercise of power, and in most cultures, men have an advantage, gained from their training, expectations, resources, and experience.

SUMMARY

1. The debate over whether women soldiers should engage in combat highlights unresolved questions about the similarities and differences between men and women. Sociologists distinguish between sex (male or female biology) and gender (the set of conceptions that people have regarding masculine and feminine characteristics). Gender is a social construct; thus, we cannot assume that males and females are born with different abilities and temperaments.

2. Biology lays the foundation for all human behavior, creates physiological differences between the sexes, and determines what role a person may play in reproduction. But biology does not explain the belief that males and females

are opposites; indeed, research shows that the sexes are more alike than different. There is more variation within the sexes than there is between them.

3. Cross-cultural studies show that men and women are both capable of a wide range of activities and responsibilities; nevertheless, virtually all societies distinguish between men's and women's work and place a higher value on the former.

4. Gender roles are sets of cultural expectations about how a man or woman is supposed to think, feel, and behave. Gender roles are based on stereotypes about the differences between the sexes. Although social behavior is changing, gender stereotypes linger, creating role conflict for both women and men.

5. Some gender differences are real, and there is no good reason to eliminate them. Women, for example, have been found to bring a different style to moral reasoning than men do. The male orientation is toward justice and equity as applied to a "generalized other," while women base their moral attitudes on care, as applied to a "concrete other." Values also differ. Women have been found to be more compassionate, less concerned with materialism, and more concerned with finding meaning in life. The fact that women have different experiences from men has led some feminists to take another look at sociology from a feminist standpoint.

6. The number of women in the workforce has increased dramatically in recent decades, but a pattern of gender inequality on the job continues. Women still tend to be channeled into traditionally "feminine" occupations and to earn less than men even though they may perform comparable jobs. Current efforts to close this gap focus on the notion of comparable worth, basing wages on the amount of skill, effort, responsibility, and risk the job entails, plus the amount of income the job produces.

7. Another dimension to gender inequality in the workplace is the concentration of females in low-level jobs and males in high-level jobs. Women who wish to advance in an organization often hit a "glass ceiling"—an invisible and impenetrable barrier to management-level jobs. Token women in traditionally male occupations and upper-level positions experience extra pressures to perform, social isolation, and role stereotyping. Whether these consequences stem from the small numbers of women or from the fact that their numbers are increasing is not certain. Male tokens tend not to experience the same effects, or they experience them in positive ways.

8. Men's power in the workplace sets the stage for gender bias, which can be especially strong when women enter traditionally male occupations. The darkest aspect of gender bias is sexual harassment—the demand that someone respond to or tolerate unwanted sexual attention from a person with power over the victim.

9. Regardless of the type of paid work they do, most women work a second shift at home. Changes in attitudes toward men's and women's responsibilities for housework and child care have not kept pace with changes in women's work and married lives.

10. Women are playing a more active and visible role in American politics today than ever before. However, they are still excluded from the highest levels and from backstage areas of political decision-making. The same pattern is seen through much of the world.

REVIEW QUESTIONS

1. Why do sociologists use the term *gender* in their analysis of females and males?

2. Assess the arguments for the existence of biological differences between males and females.

3. Document the cross-cultural differences between females and males.

4. How do gender roles and stereotypes influence each other?

5. Review the state of gender stratification in the workplace.

CRITICAL THINKING QUESTIONS

1. To what extent are the issues of sex and gender affecting military life similar to or different from those in other institutions? What settings are most similar to the military? Which ones are most different? Why?

2. Essentialism and constructionism are based on contrasting views of the source and changeability of human identities—like gender. To what extent do you think "essential" common characteristics define gender? To what extent do you think it is culturally and socially constructed? Which features are more essential, which are more subject to construction?

3. How does thinking sociologically from the standpoint of women change what you see? Describe features of an important social institution that might be missed if sociologists were all men or looked only from the standpoint of men.

4. Do you think the media and public opinion today overestimate or underestimate the frequency and importance of sexual harassment? Why so?

5. Do you think that gender inequality can be eliminated from American society? What are the biggest obstacles?

GLOSSARY

Comparable worth The practice of basing wages for a job category on the amount of skill, effort, responsibility, and risk the job entails, to offset inequalities based on the sex or race of incumbents.

Gender All the socially constructed, nonbiological traits assigned to men and women.

Gender roles The distinct tasks and activities that society assigns to each sex and defines as masculine or feminine.

Gender stereotypes Oversimplified but strongly held ideas about the characteristics of males and females.

Machismo Compulsive masculinity, evidenced in posturing, boasting, and an exploitative attitude toward women.

Sexism The unequal treatment of men and women on grounds of sex or gender; usually refers to prejudice and discrimination against women.

Sexual harassment The demand that someone respond to or tolerate unwanted sexual advances from a person who has power over the victim.

CHAPTER 10

Generations and Aging

Today is Sydney Carton's forty-fifth birthday, but he is not celebrating, he is grieving—grieving over the loss of the dreams of his youth. When he graduated from college in 1972, Sydney was sure that he would have it made by the time he reached forty-five, but it is now clear that his life will never measure up to those high expectations. He and his wife Lucie have a three-year-old daughter, Kendall, and another baby on the way. Astronomical college tuitions loom in their future, beginning just fifteen years away. Lucie's widowed father, who has Alzheimer's disease, requires round-the-clock nurses, which Sydney and Lucie help pay for. Doctors tell them that the elderly man is in excellent physical condition and could live well into his eighties. Sydney and Lucie also have a large twenty-five-year mortgage on a house in an upscale suburb and sizable payments to make on the loans for their two cars. As if these financial pressures were not enough, the ax fell today at work. When Sydney got to the office he found his co-workers gathered around a bulletin board. Posted were the names of 300 people who had just been laid off in an effort to "restructure" the firm. A salary freeze had been put into effect for the remaining employees. Ten of those laid off were from Sydney's department, and two had one more year's experience than he. Management was obviously cutting highly paid people, and the ax had just missed Sydney. Next time he might not be so lucky (from Pollan and Levine, 1992, pp. 29–30).

The important sociological point to Sydney's story is that he is not alone. Around the country, many people of his generation, born in the thriving post–World War II years, are experiencing some of the very same problems (Graham, 1995). These problems stem partly from our society's **age structure.** A key aspect of social structure, this term refers to the numbers of people who are currently at each of the possible ages in a human life. Sydney was born into an exceedingly large generation, called the postwar baby boom. Between the years 1946 and 1964, some 76 million children were added to our population. The record-breaking size of this new generation has had social repercussions ever since, shaping all aspects of its members' lives, from their education to their wages and job opportunities to the family decisions they make.

Also influencing the lives of the baby boom generations are the particular historical and cultural periods in which they entered each part of the life course. By **life course** sociologists mean the sequence of stages in a life, from birth to death (Elder, 1987; O'Rand and Krecker, 1990). Just as a year is divided into seasons, so a human life can be divided into stages: infancy; childhood, adolescence; early, middle, and later adulthood; and old age. Being in the stage of adolescence in the rebellious 1960s had a very different impact on young people than being adolescents in the Great Depression of the 1930s. Similarly, being young adults during the cynical Watergate era was very different from experiencing young adulthood during the patriotic era of World War II. Who you are and what happens to you are partly products of the historical forces that impinge upon your generation at each point in its members' lives.

In this chapter we'll take a look at the baby boom generation, as well as at other generations in contemporary American society. We will point out exactly how a society's age structure affects people's lives and life chances and how historical events at each point in the life course shape people's opportunities. At the same time, we'll observe how each new generation helps to shape the society of which it is a part. We begin by comparing the baby boom generation with the generation that grew up during the Great Depression. From here we turn to three major concepts in the study of the human life course: age, aging, and life-course transitions. Each is a matter not only of biology but of culture. You will see the life course as a dynamic process that varies not only from stage to stage but from culture to culture as well. Then, in our next section, we explore four major stages of the life course—childhood, adolescence, adulthood, and old age—especially as they are experienced in the United States. Finally, we conclude with a look at the "graying" of our population—the

trend toward relatively larger numbers of older people, including a sizable number of very elderly. What this trend means for American society is an important issue for the twenty-first century.

GENERATIONAL DIFFERENCES IN LIFE CHANCES

Where a person goes to college is seemingly a matter of personal ability and effort. Getting accepted at Harvard is the reward for earning great high school grades, while receiving a string of college rejections is the result of being a poor student. This explanation is true but limited; it focuses only on the individual. It does not consider the larger social structures at work. One of these, of course, is inequality; not everyone can afford elite private schools. Another key structural factor is the generation into which a person is born. A young man in the generation that graduated from high school during World War II had a much better chance of being accepted at Harvard than a young man who applied in the late 1960s. The reason is simply numbers—how many people are competing for a limited number of slots. During the war years, not only was the total number of high school graduates smaller in this country than it was in the 1960s, but military service caused many young men to postpone a college education. As a result, there was less competition to get into elite schools, so gaining acceptance was easier.

The generation into which a person is born has many other important effects on life chances. The opportunities to be high-paid or low-paid, rich or poor, mobile or static on the social ladder are all affected by an individual's generation. This fact is clearly illustrated by comparing two generations: children of the Great Depression and the baby boomers.

Children of the Great Depression

In his book *Children of the Great Depression* (1974; see also 1978, 1987), sociologist Glen Elder focused on a sample of Americans born during a two-year period, 1920 to 1921. People born in the same year, or in a small number of consecutive years, are called a **birth cohort.** The birth cohort that Elder studied experienced the depths of the Great Depression of the 1930s as young adolescents. This historical accident affected their attitudes and behaviors, not only imme-

In the Great Depression, families suffered a great deal from economic deprivation; but many people who grew up during the 1930s remember their families drawing together in meaningful and pleasurable ways.

diately, but in their future lives as well. Cohort membership does not just influence people as children: "It affects them at every age, through the groups to which they belong, the others with whom they interact, and the social and cultural conditions to which they are exposed" (Riley, 1987).

As teenagers during the Great Depression, most of Elder's subjects experienced hard times in their families. Many of their parents had spells of unemployment and accompanying losses of income. However, it may have been the perceived loss of prestige that hurt these families most, a subjective feeling of "coming down in the world" that could not be measured in dollars alone. Many families tried to hide the hardships they were suffering from the outside world. One of Elder's subjects recalled that his parents spent

a considerable amount of money on new paint for the house but were very tight when it came to buying food. Why? Because everyone in the neighborhood could see the house's condition, but they could not see the food that went on the table.

As for the young adolescents on whom Elder focused, about 40 percent were expected to make significant contributions to family income through part-time jobs. As a result, many of them became acutely aware early in life of the cost of basic necessities like food, clothes, and housing. These early work experiences apparently instilled a strong sense of financial responsibility and conservativeness. Ideas like "money doesn't come easily" and "don't spend beyond your means" are, in general, heartily endorsed by people who experienced the Great Depression as working teenagers. Significantly, these adolescents did not usually respond with despair and resignation to the hardships they were suffering during the Depression; instead, they tended to react with positive responses, such as working harder.

In later years, the experiences of the Depression continued to affect Elder's subjects. Among men, Elder found a pattern of "vocational crystallization," in which they decided on a line of work early in life and then stuck with it. Especially for those who came from very deprived family backgrounds, there was an early narrowing of interest, vision, and desires, a zeroing in on *some* stable occupation. This may have been a reaction to the poverty they had experienced as adolescents. Most of Elder's male subjects, even those who had not experienced abject poverty, were very work-centered in their adult lives. They put great value on work achievements, although many also valued family life, children, and parenthood (Elder, Modell, and Parke, 1993).

Among the women Elder studied, there was a strong preference for pursuing traditional female roles, generally centered on family and household responsibilities. Especially for those from very deprived family backgrounds, there was a tendency to marry early and to give up working outside the home, at least when the first child was born. Perhaps, for these women, a focus on the family was an attempt to undo the "psychic disruptions" to their childhood families experienced during the Depression.

But these women's focus on the family was also made possible by a social structural factor: the size of the generation into which they were born (Easterlin, Schaeffer, and Macunovich, 1993). Theirs was a relatively small generation, so as the American economy rapidly expanded during World War II and after, it was easy for men of this age group to find work. A relatively small labor force was available for an ever-growing number of jobs. This favorable situation for workers put upward pressure on wages. A man's income alone could usually support an entire family quite comfortably. Most married women, therefore, did not need to work to make ends meet. This left them free to put their energies into producing and caring for a family. The children born to them started the mushrooming baby boom generation.

Interestingly, Elder found that people who experienced the Great Depression as teenagers were affected by it in dramatically different ways than those who experienced it as young children. Compared with those born in 1928 and 1929 (who were very young during the Depression), those born between 1920 and 1921 (who were teenagers at the time) were more self-directed and confident about their futures. Generally, they also achieved more in their adult lives than those who were born eight or nine years later. It appears that the Depression had more negative life consequences for those who went through it as very young children than for those who went through it as adolescents. Perhaps the older age cohort, having experienced the prosperous years of the 1920s in early and middle childhood, were more inclined to see the Great Depression as just a temporary setback, not the only way of life they knew. Perhaps, too, their experience of finding part-time jobs as teenagers to help their families survive gave them a sense of agency that the younger cohort lacked. In any case, their development was clearly shaped by exactly when in history they were born (Elder, Modell, and Parke, 1993).

The Baby Boomers

Remember the cartoon version of a python that swallows a pig? The snake's jaws open wide, then they snap shut, and the mouth bulges out. Slowly the bulge moves through the python's body, from head to middle to tail. This image of the pig-in-the-python is a useful analogy for the generation known as baby boomers (Jones, 1980).

From colonial times until now, the birth rate in the United States has steadily declined. On average, people have had fewer children. There was one huge exception to this trend. Starting in 1946, just nine months or so after the end of World War II, couples started having babies in unprecedented numbers. At first, sociologists thought that people were simply "making up for lost time" and having babies they could not have during the war. But the birth explosion continued for nearly two decades, and by 1964 (when the birth rate once again began to drop steadily), 76 million babies had been added to the American population. Since then, the size of this age cohort has expanded even more as immigration has pushed the generation's numbers to over 80 million—one-third the population of the entire United States.

Generations before and after the baby boom generation are much smaller in number. Because of this, baby boomers make a bulge in the American popu-

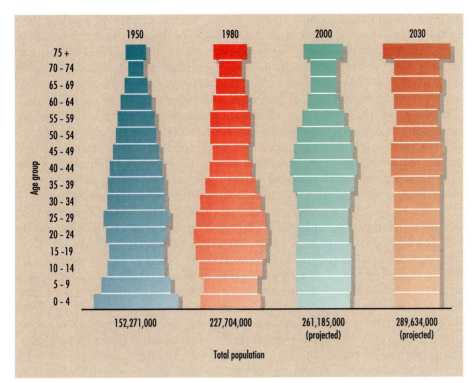

1950 — 152,271,000

1980 — 227,704,000

2000 — 261,185,000 (projected)

2030 — 289,634,000 (projected)

Age group: 75 +, 70 – 74, 65 – 69, 60 – 64, 55 – 59, 50 – 54, 45 – 49, 40 – 44, 35 – 39, 30 – 34, 25 – 29, 20 – 24, 15 – 19, 10 – 14, 5 – 9, 0 – 4

Total population

FIGURE 10.1 / U.S. Age Structure, 1950–2030

These charts clearly show the baby boom generation moving through its life course. In 1950, when the baby boom had just begun, an enlarged "base" appeared at the bottom of the U.S. age-structure chart. Then in 1980, when the boomers were adolescents and young adults, they formed a bulge in the chart's lower half. This bulge moves to the top half of the chart by the year 2000, when the boomers are middle-aged; by 2030, when the boomers are old, they will make the normal population pyramid look more like a rectangle.

Source: U.S. Bureau of the Census 1994. *Statistical Abstract of the United States.* Washington, D.C.: US GPO and Historical Statistics of the United States, Colonial Times to 1970.

lation structure (see Figure 10.1). As they age, they are like that pig passing through the python. The bulge slowly moves along from infancy, through childhood and adolescence, through the various stages of adulthood, and finally to old age. The leading edge of this slowly moving bulge has so far passed through five decades. Many baby boomers were children during the prosperous Eisenhower years and saw the launching of the first spacecraft *Sputnik* and the height of the cold war. For many, adolescence roughly began with John F. Kennedy's assassination and ended with the Vietnam war. Then came young adulthood during Nixon's Watergate era, and for many a comfortable status as young, urban professionals ("Yuppies"). Today, however, the "young" is starting to fade from the "Yup," a process that reached a milestone in 1996 when the first of the baby boomers turned fifty.

As we pointed out in discussing children of the Great Depression, an individual's life is shaped, in part, by the events occurring when that person reaches life's major way points (Riley, 1987). (One's experience is strongly influenced, too, by whether that person is male or female, rich or poor, American or Chinese, and so forth, and we address these issues in other chapters.) Consider how the baby boomers

were shaped by the things that happened to them when they were young. One is the development of suburbs. Baby boomers were the first generation of children to grow up mainly in suburbs, a fact perhaps related to our present mania for shopping malls and drive-through services. They also grew up in the prosperous years of a postwar economic boom. Their parents, for the most part, were highly optimistic about the future. New technology seemed to be making opportunities for advancement unlimited. Many baby boomers were encouraged to think of themselves as a special generation, heirs to the best of everything. But then, just as the oldest baby boomers were reaching young adulthood, the highly controversial Vietnam war arose. Not surprisingly, in this era when males could be drafted into the armed forces, baby boomers took the lead in antiwar protests. Thus, a whole series of historical events— the growth of suburbs, a long period of economic prosperity and expansion, the waging of a very unpopular war, to name just a few—occurred at specific points in the lives of baby boomers so as to make them in many ways different from any other generation.

Nevertheless, the baby boom generation is not just a passive product of the times it had lived through—

it has also helped to shape those times, sometimes quite dramatically. Because baby boomers outnumber the generations that preceded and followed them, they have caused social change at each stage of their development. In the late 1940s and early 1950s, baby boomers crowded maternity wards and nursery schools, making Dr. Spock and Dr. Seuss household names. Later in the 1950s and into the 1960s, they overloaded elementary schools. Then gradually, in the 1970s, elementary schools in the United States started emptying out as the last of the baby boomers left childhood behind and entered adolescence and young adulthood.

The baby boom generation has had an enormous impact on the marketplace as well. During the baby boomers' teenage years, for example, sales of acne medication and rock music skyrocketed. The demand for condominiums in the Sunbelt and other housing preferred by the elderly will likewise grow rapidly in the twenty-first century when the baby boomers retire.

At each stage in its history the sheer size of the baby boom generation has had an enormous impact on its members' life chances, especially their chances for social mobility (moving up or down the social hierarchy). According to Richard Easterlin (1987), being born into a huge generation can put a real damper on an individual's personal fortunes because the members of an exceedingly large generation must compete with one another for virtually everything. We mentioned this in our earlier example of getting into Harvard. It is certainly much easier to be accepted when competition is scarce (when there are relatively few high school graduates and most of those are away at war) than when society is brimming over with young people seeking higher education. The same principle applies to landing a job or getting a promotion. The more people competing for the same position, the slimmer any one individual's chances will be.

There is, however, a flaw in Easterlin's theory of how numbers and competition affect life chances. He underestimates the extent to which a large generation tends to create its own new opportunities. Thus, as the leading edge of the baby boom generation entered young adulthood, colleges and universities expanded to meet the burgeoning demand for higher education. And as this throng of college graduates then became working adults, their ever-growing buying power as consumers created the demand for more and more products that in turn expanded the econ-

omy and created the greater number of jobs that they needed. The members of the baby boom generation, in other words, are a force on the social landscape to which the rest of society has responded. At every stage of the life cycle, they have been the focus of media attention and social action—as suburban children, as protesting college students of the Woodstock generation, and as adults now hitting middle age. As a group, they have helped to change social structure in ways that have accommodated their large numbers and reduced competition among them.

The individual actions of baby boomers have also affected their life chances, often lessening downward pressures on their economic welfare (Bouvier and De Vita, 1991; Easterlin, Schaeffer, and Macunovich, 1993). For example, in comparison to members of their parents' generation, more baby boomers have decided to forgo marriage or have married at a later age. These decisions eliminate or at least postpone the responsibilities of family life, giving boomers more opportunity to accumulate financial resources. In addition, compared with their parents, many baby boomers have delayed the age at which they start to have children. Like the decision to delay marriage, this decision to delay childbearing helps give baby boomers time to establish themselves financially before taking on the added responsibilities of parenthood. A decision to have *fewer* children than their parents had is another choice that has helped to ease financial pressures on baby boomers. Whereas the three-child family was commonplace when the baby boomers were growing up, the two-child family is more the norm today. At the same time, many more mothers are working today than worked in their parents' generation, which again helps to make the baby boom couple better off economically. Taken together, these personal choices by baby boomers have given them more financial security than they otherwise might have had as the members of such a large generation.

But the economic picture for baby boomers is not entirely rosy, as the example of Sydney Carton at the beginning of the chapter suggests. Baby boom adults seem to have to work harder than their parents did to achieve the lifestyle they want. Many complain of a lack of leisure time and of work-related stress (Braus, 1995). Whereas many of their parents lived comfortably on the father's salary alone, most of the boomers feel that a family requires two incomes. This has been partly to pay for the spiraling house prices that struck in the 1980s as more and more baby

Running to stay in place? To achieve the lifestyle they enjoyed as children, many baby boomers delayed parenthood, depend on two incomes, have little leisure time, and report high levels of stress.

boomers competed for living space, the nonfamily child care needed when both husband and wife work, the high cost of college tuitions for the boomers' grown children, and the cost of helping to care for elderly parents, many of whom are now living much longer than in past generations (Bouvier and De Vita, 1991; U.S. Bureau of the Census, 1995a).

What's more, each consecutive birth year cohort in the baby boom generation seems to be having a more difficult time than its predecessors. This downward trend is particularly marked for people at the bottom of the income ladder who tend to be more "replaceable" in the labor market. The more recently these people were born in the baby boom era, the lesser their chances for upward mobility and the greater their likelihood of being poor (Browne, 1995).

Worst off of all are people born immediately *after* the baby boom was over. Contrary to Easterlin's theory, the members of this relatively small generation face the highest odds of sinking into poverty (Browne, 1995). This may be partly because they must compete for jobs with the many baby boomers who are still in the workforce. At the same time, economic trends affecting the demand for labor and America's occupational structure are at work as well. Upper-level jobs are no longer expanding at the rapid rate they did in the 1970s and early 1980s. Whereas executive, administrative, and managerial positions increased by

roughly 74 percent between 1972 and 1986, they are projected to increase by only 29 percent between 1986 and the year 2000 (Silvestri and Lukasiewicz, 1987). The result is blocked upward mobility for a sizable number of those in the generation that followed the baby boom (Krymkowski and Krauze, 1992). This blocked upward mobility is reflected in difficulties attaining a middle-class status. Whereas 60 percent of those born before 1959 had achieved a middle-class income by the age of 30, only 42 percent of those born in 1959 or later had reached this income level at this age (Duncan and Smeeding, quoted in Bradsher, 1995). Apparently, blocked upward mobility is a growing problem not just for those in the generation following the baby boom but also for those at the trailing edge of the baby boom itself.

Yet despite this downward trend in opportunities for social advancement, baby boomers, on average, are better off financially than their parents were at the same stage of life. Largely because so many mothers of young children are now working, and also because average family size is smaller, the average total income available to each member of a baby boom couple's household is about two-thirds higher than the average total income available to each member of a household when those baby boomers were children (Easterlin, Schaeffer, and Macunovich, 1993). The baby boomers also compare favorably with their parents in terms of their net worth—that is, the excess of their assets over their debts. Although a smaller proportion of them compared with their parents own their own homes, they still have more savings and accumulated wealth after what they owe to others has been taken into account (Easterlin, Schaeffer, and Macunovich, 1993). Thus, part of the problem for people like Sydney Carton may be an expectation that life has *unlimited* horizons and opportunities for advancement. These unrealistically high expectations are themselves a legacy of the baby boom generation.

Of course, to talk about *the* baby boom generation is an overgeneralization. Not everyone in this generation has unrealistic expectations and a sense of entitlement. Nor are all the members of the generation alike in other ways. In his book *Class of '66: Living in Suburban Middle America,* Paul Lyons (1994) documents how many baby boomers who came of age in the late 1960s did not get involved in antiwar or civil rights movements, did not smoke marijuana and experiment with other illegal drugs, and did not dress and act like hippies. For a large number of them, especially those who married and had families early, the radicalism and rebellion of the 1960s were things they observed from a distance, often with some distaste. Karl Mannheim, the first sociologist to show the power of generational influences, recognized that strong overall similarities could mask internal differences. He used the term **generation units** to refer to groups within the same generation that respond to their common historical experiences in markedly different ways and come to have distinctly different views from one another (Wolff, 1993). Differences in age, sex, social class, ethnic background, and so forth can help to form the bases of generation units. This concept is an important one to keep in mind because it counteracts the tendency to talk about generations as if they were monolithic.

AGE, AGING, AND LIFE-COURSE TRANSITIONS

To sociologists, **age** is not just the number of years since a person was born; it also involves a set of social definitions regarding what is required of and appropriate for people of different ages. These definitions differ from society to society, and they can change significantly with the passage of time. The term **aging,** too, has a sociological meaning different

from the everyday one. In everyday speech, *aging* usually refers to the process of growing older in the later stages of life, but sociologists use the term more broadly. To them, aging is the process of growing older that begins on the day we are born and continues until we die. To sociologists, what is important about aging is not just the chronological progress people make but also their transitions to new age-related statuses and roles.

Social Definitions of Age

All cultures include sets of norms regarding expected and appropriate behavior for people at each stage of the life course (Keith, 1990). These norms help to define what it means to be a certain age. As aspects of culture, age-related norms vary from one society to another. In the Chinese city of Hong Kong, for instance, youth is considered a time to be impulsive and free of responsibilities, while middle age is seen as a time to be burdened with work and family obligations and old age is a time to be cared for by others and to enjoy abundant leisure. Entirely different norms prevail in many other cultures. In the Irish town of Blessington, for example, youth is not viewed as a period of exemption from responsibilities but rather a time of starting to "get established" by finding a job, marrying, beginning to have children, and perhaps even buying a house. Similarly, in Blessington, old age is not considered a time of unlimited leisure but rather an age at which people who remain healthy have an obligation to share their knowledge and skills with others by getting involved in community affairs (Ikels et al., 1992). Clearly, what it means to be elderly, middle-aged, or young is not simply mandated by the calendar (Clausen, 1986). These stages of life are culturally constructed in particular social contexts.

As a cultural construct that carries with it certain expectations, age helps to channel people in and out of social roles and statuses (and the rights and responsibilities that go with them). In American society, late adolescence to early adulthood is considered the "right" age to finish formal schooling, leave home, and find a full-time job. Retiring and receiving a pension is considered "right" when people are in their sixties. Every human society establishes timetables that define "normal" age ranges for other major life events such as marrying, having children, and having grandchildren.

These timetables, of course, can change over time. For example, in a survey conducted in the late 1950s, 80 percent of the males and 90 percent of the females felt that the best ages for a man to marry were between twenty and twenty-five. By the late 1970s, however, only 42 percent of Americans felt that a man should marry this young. Similarly, in the late 1950s, the overwhelming majority of people believed that nineteen to twenty-four were the best ages for a woman to marry. Two decades later, this view had changed, especially among American women, only 36 percent of whom now preferred such a young age of marriage for a woman (Rosenfeld and Stark, 1987). Such changing norms often make it harder for people to decide whether or not their own lives are "on schedule" (Neugarten and Neugarten, 1987).

Just as age helps to usher people into statuses and roles, it also helps to organize the distribution of a society's valued resources—money, power, and prestige (O'Rand and Krecker, 1990). For instance, the aging baby boomers will have political clout well into the twenty-first century because they will have the power of numbers and of accumulated wealth. This does not mean that they will necessarily enjoy high prestige, however. In modern societies such as our own, where social and technological change occurs so rapidly, the elderly are often viewed as old-fashioned and their knowledge as obsolete. In contrast, in many preindustrial societies, although certainly not all (Foner, 1993), advanced age may be more prestigious, partly because the knowledge of the few remaining elders is considered much more useful.

The process of classifying people into social categories according to their age is known as **age grading.** Although age grading is widespread in our society, it has not always been so. The importance we now attach to age and age differences first emerged in the late nineteenth century and took firm hold only in the early decades of this century (Chudacoff, 1989). Before 1850, age grading was simply not as significant as it is today in regulating and organizing people's behavior and society's institutions.

Take education. Schools were not age-graded until the 1870s. Before that time, it was not uncommon to find teenagers in the same classes with very young children, or fourteen-year-olds sitting side-by-side with young adults in their twenties at universities such as Harvard and Yale. Students then did not enter and leave school at the precise ages that have, in the century and a half since, become routine. In 1804, the new president of the University of North Carolina

at Chapel Hill was only twenty-four years old—younger than some of his students! In that era, someone's age was an unreliable predictor of that person's progress and placement in the educational system. Today, in contrast, most students march through school in lockstep with others of the same age—though this strict age grading is gradually starting to change in colleges and universities.

Government involvement in many facets of social life has helped to standardize the life course on the basis of chronological age (Guillemard and Rein, 1993). State laws that require children to start school by the age of six result in classrooms filled at each grade level with youngsters who were born within a year of one another. These age cohorts then progress through the educational system together, graduating together from high school and college and starting careers together. Forty-some years later, at age sixty-five, they qualify together for Social Security benefits and retire from the workforce with others the same age.

Although our society is quite age-graded, other societies have age grading even stricter than in our own. The pastoral Masai of East Africa, for instance, recognize four age grades for males—boy, warrior, junior elder, and senior elder—and each grade is assigned very specific rights and duties. The boys, who are still under the authority of their parents, are responsible for herding their family's livestock. Warriors (called *morani*) range in age from fifteen to thirty and live as bachelors in separate villages under the supervision of a committee of elders. Junior elders (ages thirty to forty-five) are permitted to marry, own cattle, and establish their own homesteads, while senior elders (above age forty-five) are responsible for governing and conducting public affairs. In this society, a thirty-year-old, no matter how wise, will not be a political leader, and a forty-year old, no matter how strong, will not be a warrior. For Masai males, the allocation of roles is almost completely determined by age (Bernardi, 1955; Ole Saitoti and Beckwith, 1980; Spencer, 1988).

In most modern societies, in contrast, age is one of many characteristics used to allocate statuses, roles, and resources. In fact, American society has instituted laws that limit the extent to which age can be a determining factor in the distribution of rights and opportunities. It is illegal, in many contexts, to deny employment or housing to someone simply because that person is too old or too young. Still negative stereotyping based on age, called **ageism,** persists

(Butler, 1989). Older people are the usual victims of ageism in American society, where younger is defined as better and people spend fortunes seeking medical fountains of youth (face-lifts and cell therapies, for example). When a television newscaster is fired because of wrinkles or gray hair, ageism has led to outright **age discrimination:** the denial of rights, opportunities, and resources to someone exclusively because of that person's age (Levin and Levin, 1980).

Transitions: The Process of Aging

In one important respect, age is fundamentally different from other ascribed statuses, such as race and gender. Being black or white, male or female, is a lifelong status, except in rare cases. Age, in contrast, is a **transitional status** because people periodically move from one age category to another, that is, people undergo the process of aging.

As people age, they face different sets of expectations and responsibilities, enjoy different rights and opportunities, and possess different amounts of power and control. Consequently, transitions from one age status to another are societally important. They are often marked by **rites of passage,** which are public ceremonies—full of ritual symbolism—that record the transition being made.

In his classic 1908 analysis, French anthropologist Arnold van Gennep (1908/1961) graphically described the rite-of-passage ceremonies in which Masai boys and girls became adults. Traditionally, the ceremony for boys took place every four or five years and involved young adolescents between the ages of twelve and sixteen:

> The candidates . . . smear themselves with white clay and wander from kraal to kraal [living areas] for two or three months. Their heads are shaved, and an ox or sheep is killed. The morning after the slaughter each candidate cuts down a tree which the girls plant in front of his hut. The following morning the boys go out into the cold air and wash with cold water. [Circumcision is then performed, using primitive tools.] The operator cuts the foreskin; an ox hide containing the blood which has been shed is placed on each boy's bed. The boys remain shut up for four days. Then they come out and tease the girls and often dress as women. . . . They adorn their heads with small birds and ostrich feathers. When they are healed, their heads are shaved; when their hair grows back sufficiently to be combed, they are called *morani,* or warriors. (van Gennep, 1908/1961, pp. 85–86)

The ceremony for girls was more brutal and permanently damaging. Female "circumcision" was (and still is) genital mutilation, including excision of the clitoris. Upon healing, the woman was "married off."

The Masai ceremonies link coming of age to a level of physical suffering—especially for girls—that most present-day Americans would not accept. We should be aware how often engaging in violence, though less formalized—from fighting to football to gang shootings—marks coming of age for American boys. And we do have some complex and formal ceremonies as well. Consider the debutante ball, Texas-style, with $20,000 gowns, limousines, elaborate floral displays, and at least somewhat physically demanding rituals of its own:

> Instead of a simple curtsy, Texas debs sink slowly to the floor (this requires really good quadriceps) and touch their foreheads to the floor in front of their "dukes." They then look up at the "duke" (you don't want to dwell too much on the symbolism of this posture), and with his permission they slowly rise from the floor (which takes *great* quadriceps). (Ivins, 1990)

Like the Masai ceremony, though less brutally, the debutante ball affirms not only the importance of growing up but the social dominance of men. Celebrating and reaffirming the importance of certain life-course transitions is also an occasion for reinforcing power relations.

Debutante balls, religious confirmations, graduations, weddings, retirement dinners, and funerals are all examples of rites of passage in American society. Rites of passage are important both for the individual who moves to a new age status and for the society in which that person lives. These ceremonies typically use stories and symbols to explain the meaning of the age transition. In the process, both the individual and the society are reminded of the rights and responsibilities that go along with the new status. The importance of rites of passage can be seen in their persistence, even despite social changes that might tend to make them obsolete. For example, few people today would consider a thirteen-year-old mature enough to assume the many rights and responsibilities of adulthood. And yet, among Jews, a boy still symbolically becomes a man at age thirteen through the bar mitzvah ceremony. The persistence of this ritual through centuries of changing Jewish life signals the significance all cultures attach to their rites of passage.

Most cultures and religions include rites of passage. For Hispanics and Hispanic-Americans, a girl's quinceanera *(15th birthday party) marks her coming of age. In the past and in traditional villages today, the* quinceanera *means a girl is ready to be married.*

Although people today often worry about being "on time" for their passage to new life-course statuses (experiencing them when others their age do), in recent years there has been more variability in the ages at which people *actually* undergo certain of these transitions. For example, although our culture may still define twenty-one or twenty-two as the "appropriate" age to graduate from college, certain social changes—increasing divorce rates, increasing rates of female participation in the labor force, big swings in unemployment rates—are bringing older adults back to colleges and universities at nontraditional ages. If this trend continues, the American college graduation rite of passage will no longer be as age-graded as it has been in the recent past.

The age at which Americans undergo the transition to retirement is also becoming more variable. In recent years, throughout the Western world, a great many older wage-earners have been retiring from the workforce before the age at which they qualify for a public old-age pension; some retirees are as young as fifty-five. Thus, the age of retirement has become more flexible than in the recent past. It is now less standardized by chronological age alone and more dependent upon structural factors in the workplace that affect the availability of jobs, as well as a person's individual situation and life-course choices (Guillemard and Rein, 1993).

Here you can see that two aspects of social structure are being simultaneously affected. There is a declining average age at which retirement occurs in Western populations, and at the same time there is more variability in the age at which people make this transition (some people now make it at age fifty-five, while others wait until their seventies). The timing of this transition no longer tightly ranges just a few years to either side of age sixty-five. This same pattern can be seen in the timing of other major life transitions. For instance, the age of having a first child is generally rising in our society, but there is also a broadening range of ages during which this event occurs. A growing proportion of older women (many in their forties), are now having first children, while at the same time a growing number of women are having first children very early in the life course (as young teenagers). In short, there is increasing heterogeneity in the timing of transitions, making it harder to generalize about them (George, 1993).

THE STAGES OF LIFE

Modern Western cultures, such as our own, typically divide the life course into four major stages: childhood, adolescence, adulthood, and old age. These divisions are not universal, however. Some preindustrial cultures do not recognize a distinct stage of adolescence, and others do not make a sharp distinction between adulthood and old age, either. The !Kung of Africa's Kalahari Desert (Ikels et al., 1992), for example, have no sharp age grades. In !Kung society (the exclamation mark signals a "click" sound), all adults do the same work and have the same rights and obligations. Teenagers do not undergo an extended "pre-adult" period of training, nor do adults live any differently from each other depending upon their age. Older !Kung continue to live with their children throughout their entire lives, and no matter how elderly they become, they never retire from labor. Americans, in contrast, are much more accustomed to thinking of life in terms of a series of social milestones and phases. In the remainder of this chapter we will use the stages of childhood, adolescence, adulthood, and old age to organize our discussion, but bear in mind that these four stages are socially constructed concepts.

In his pathbreaking work *Childhood and Society* (1950), Erik Erikson proposed eight social-psychological challenges that people face as they pass through the life course (see Figure 10.2). According to Erikson, each challenge must be dealt with in some way, either positively or negatively, and how a person deals with a current challenge affects how well that person will cope with subsequent challenges. With its roots in Sigmund Freud's psychoanalytic theory, Erikson's theory is strongly psychological. It can, however, be extended in a sociological direction by asking, How do the challenges at each stage of life differ for people who live in different historical or cultural contexts, or who differ in terms of race, gender, or social class? Thus, Erikson's theory will give us a framework for looking more deeply at the variations in people's experiences at each stage of the life course. We will begin our discussion of each stage with a brief review of Erikson's theory, highlighting the challenges he described as crucial. Then we will consider sociological research on the actual life experiences of people—from our own society today, from the past, and from other cultures.

Stages	Developmental Tasks	Basic Strengths	Basic Antipathies
Infancy	Basic Trust vs. Basic Mistrust	Hope	Withdrawal
Early Childhood	Autonomy vs. Shame, Doubt	Will	Compulsion
Play Age	Initiative vs. Guilt	Purpose	Inhibition
School Age	Industry vs. Inferiority	Competence	Inertia
Adolescence	Identity vs. Identity Confusion	Fidelity	Repudiation
Young Adulthood	Intimacy vs. Isolation	Love	Exclusivity
Adulthood	Generativity vs. Stagnation	Care	Rejectivity
Old Age	Integrity vs. Despair	Wisdom	Disdain

FIGURE 10.2 / Erikson's Stages and Developmental Issues

Erik Erikson believed that in each stage of the life course people confront a major developmental issue that they must resolve in some way. A favorable resolution leads to positive feelings and social relationships, whereas an unfavorable one has the opposite outcomes. In this figure, the first column lists the stages of the life course in which each issue is confronted; the second column specifies what each issue entails; and the third and fourth columns tell the basic strengths and weaknesses that can result depending upon how the issues are resolved.

Source: Reproduced from *The Life Cycle Completed: A Review*, by Erik H. Erikson, by permission of W.W. Norton & Company, Inc. Copyright © 1982 by Rikan Enterprises, Ltd.

Childhood

In Erikson's theory, infants face the challenge of being totally dependent on others to provide for their basic needs. This sets the stage for the development of *basic trust versus mistrust*. Babies who receive loving, reliable care learn to trust other people and to see the world as secure, while those whose care is erratic come to view the world as unpredictable and acquire a basic mistrust of others. The second childhood challenge in Erikson's theory occurs during toddlerhood, when the child begins to strive for some independence from adults. The issue now is developing *autonomy versus shame and self-doubt*. Toddlers who are encouraged to be independent learn to master simple tasks and develop a healthy sense of self-sufficiency, while those whose autonomy is thwarted come to doubt their abilities and feel shame about the self. Around the age of four or five, further strivings for independence lead to the stage of *initiative versus guilt*. Now children increasingly initiate interactions with peers and try to take on more responsibilities, such as helping with household chores. If parents and others are supportive of these efforts, children develop feelings of self-worth, but if their initiatives meet with rejection or ridicule, feelings of guilt develop. Finally, when they reach school age, children struggle to acquire skills and information and to relate to a larger social circle. Depending upon their experiences, this challenge leads to the development of *industry versus inferiority*—that is, to an eager self-confidence in tackling new tasks or to a sense of being less able than others.

Child's play? According to Erik Erikson, the main psychosocial task for young children is developing initiative. Climbing, running, and jumping are not "just" play, but represent the child's efforts to test and prove his or her competence.

Erikson's theory assumes that childhood is a special period during which people face the important tasks of developing senses of security and competence. Children, in his view, must be given loving support and understanding to help them accomplish these goals. This perspective on childhood has not always prevailed, however. In fact, the idea of childhood as a distinct stage in the life course is a fairly recent cultural invention. During the Middle Ages, children of all social classes were encouraged to move quickly into their adult roles (Shorter, 1975). Very few of the special activities that we consider part of a happy childhood—songs, games, stories, abundant leisure—were available to children in this era. The idea that children should be cherished, nurtured, protected, and distanced from the sometimes harsh realities of adult life took hold in upper-class families by the eighteenth century; however, these luxuries were denied to children of the middle and working classes for another hundred years or more. Even at the turn of the twentieth century in the United States, 18.2 percent of all children aged ten to fifteen were employed in the workforce to help support their families, two-thirds of them in often harsh and exploitive industrial jobs (Fyfe, 1989).

Between the 1870s (when child labor in sweatshops was socially acceptable) and the 1930s (when such child labor had become immoral and illegal), the cultural meaning of childhood underwent a fundamental redefinition. Children went from being viewed as useful economic assets (valued for their labor and their wages) to being viewed as essentially useless—but priceless!—family members (Zelizer, 1985). This shift in the definition of childhood was made possible partly by the fact that new technologies were eliminating many of the very low-skilled jobs that children once filled. Also, especially during the prosperous 1920s, parents were often earning enough money that they could afford to let their children stay in school. These economic changes encouraged a new, more sentimental view of children. The new attitude had already developed in richer families; now it spread more widely. Children came to be given almost sacred value and were seen as deserving a highly protective world in which to grow.

Today, these sentimental ideals may be gradually fading, and the world in which children live may no longer be so protective (Neustadter, 1993). Many social observers warn of the erosion of childhood (Postman, 1982; Suransky, 1982; Winn, 1984). They

Industrialization led to brutal exploitation of children, which lasted for several generations in Europe and the United States. Not until the early twentieth century was child labor first regulated and then eliminated. This exploitation was not considered shameful because children were expected to contribute financially to their families.

point to the involvement of many children in behaviors that carry "adult" responsibilities—behaviors such as sexual activity, the use of alcohol and other drugs, and the witnessing of interpersonal violence. This trend may be partly due to the dissemination by television and other mass media of information that was once the exclusive domain of adults (Postman, 1982). Postman calls TV an "open admission technology," which means that any viewer of any age can watch whatever is shown—sex, violence, drug use, and other aspects of adult life.

Some observers are highly disturbed by this erosion of childhood. They fear that when children are rushed into adulthood they not only miss out on the simple pleasures of childhood but also are prepared poorly for later years. Others disagree, however, saying it is a mistake to shield children from the complexities of adulthood or to sugarcoat the tensions and challenges of modern life. They applaud portrayals in films, TV, and literature of children confronting difficult challenges, for they feel this helps prepare young people for the important life decisions they must inevitably face. They also believe that the "protected childhood" of maximum leisure and limited responsibilities simply does not fit well with the realities of modern family life. Increases in divorce and in households where both parents work

may well require children to mature more quickly than was common, say, during the 1950s.

No doubt this debate over the changing nature of contemporary childhood will continue unresolved for some time. One reason is that childhood experiences in the United States are so varied that it is hard to generalize about them. It may be impossible to prescribe one best method of raising children in light of the differences in cultural beliefs, economic circumstances, and family structure that make American society so heterogeneous.

Adolescence

Adolescence is an even more recent cultural invention than childhood is (Kett, 1977). It was not until the end of the nineteenth century that social commentators began to describe adolescence as a particularly vulnerable stage in development. Psychologist G. Stanley Hall (1905/1981) helped to pioneer recognition of adolescence as a time of storm and stress but also of possibility and promise. He argued that teenagers should be given a chance to experiment with and explore various roles available to them before they enter the adult world. This view is echoed in Erikson's theory. He described adolescents as facing the challenge of *identity versus role confusion*. *Identity* is an understanding of who one is and where one is going. Adolescents who are unable to develop a sense of identity experience confusion over who they are and what they will do with their lives.

New ideas about adolescence were partly a product of changing social conditions. As twentieth-century America became increasingly urban and industrialized and positions for unskilled laborers became increasingly scarce, education was no longer a luxury but rather a necessity. Instead of being rushed into adulthood, young people were urged to finish high school and even college. Later, during the Great Depression of the 1930s, staying in school was encouraged for another reason: It kept young people from crowding the shrinking market for full-time jobs. Thus, between 1900 and 1956, the proportion of Americans graduating from high school rose from 6.3 percent to 62.5 percent.

Adolescence as we know it today took shape in the 1940s and 1950s, when the segregation of young people in schools fostered the development of an "adolescent society," a teenage subculture with its own tastes and standards (Coleman, 1961). That subculture was in many ways the product of post–World War II affluence, which set the stage for a dizzying series of social changes and role redefinitions. For example, many teenagers now had access to cars, which meant that dating was no longer done under the watchful eyes of adults. This change in part accounts for the increase in teenage sexual activity.

There are signs that the age at which children become adolescents is slowly creeping downward. The "bobby-soxers" who swooned over Frank Sinatra in the 1940s were fifteen to eighteen years old; the "teenyboppers" who mobbed the Beatles in the 1960s were ages twelve to fourteen. The age at which teenagers begin dating and using cosmetics has dropped from fifteen or sixteen to only eleven or twelve (Neugarten and Neugarten, 1987).

The average age of first sexual experience is also moving downward (Gelman, 1990; Zeman, 1990). In 1988, 80 percent of adolescent girls and 86 percent of adolescent boys had experienced sex by age nineteen, and sizable proportions had been sexually initiated much earlier than that (25 percent of the girls and 33 percent of the boys by age fifteen) (Dorius, Heaton, and Steffen, 1993). Still, there is substantial variability in the age at which teenagers begin having sex. The age at which a particular teenager becomes sexually active depends, among other things, on his or her physical maturity, the parents' sexual precocity when they were adolescents, the intactness of the young person's family (girls in father-absent homes tend to have sex sooner), the degree of religious commitment, the family's socioeconomic background (girls living in poverty tend toward early sexual activity), the social integration of the community in which the young person lives, and the age at which friends and classmates begin having sex (Flannery, Rowe, and Gulley, 1993; Udry and Billy, 1987; DiBlasio and Benda, 1994).

Adulthood

Beginning in the 1960s, as the first baby boomers graduated from high school and began attending college in record-breaking numbers, a growing proportion of young people were remaining financially dependent on their parents into their early twenties. Today, an increasing number of those who have graduated from college are returning home for a time to live. Among men and women age eighteen to twenty-four, 68.3 percent live with parents or other relatives.

About 40 percent in this age group have returned to their parents' home after previously leaving the nest (Riche, 1990). Thus, adolescents today are facing contradictory messages: Many cultural signals tell them to grow up faster, but a lack of opportunities (the right job or mate, affordable housing) makes it difficult to assume complete adult independence as they move into their twenties. As a result, the adolescent years are being stretched out at both ends (Ianni, 1989). Young people are being pushed into adolescence earlier and staying there longer.

The length of the delay in taking on adult commitments varies from one individual to the next. In fact, there seems to be an increasing diversity in how and when adolescents make the transition to adulthood. One study that compared 1960 high school graduates with those who graduated in 1980 used three events to measure the achievement of adult status: completing one's education, getting married, and having a child (Buchmann, 1989). While 23.4 percent of the 1960 cohort had completed all three status changes within four years after high school graduation, only 11.0 percent of the 1980 cohort had done so. And over a third of the more recent cohort had not yet experienced any of the three changes even by the end of the 1980s. This increased variation in the timing and sequencing of events involved in becoming an adult is part of the general "destandardization" of life-course transitions we discussed previously.

Yet despite the increased variation in exactly when the transition to adulthood is completed, people in their twenties and thirties face many of the same tasks. Erik Erikson (1950, 1982) saw the central task as one of connecting to other people. He labeled the challenge of young adulthood *intimacy versus isolation.* Young adults must partially fuse their own identities with those of other people, forming deep friendships, falling in love and marrying, producing and raising children. The danger is that they will fail to commit themselves to others because they fear a loss of self, and thus they will feel isolated and lonely. Daniel Levinson (1978), a pioneer in the systematic study of the life course for men, added to this challenge the young adult task of carving out a niche in life (see Figure 10.3). Men in their twenties begin to make choices about marriage, occupation, and residence, choices that will define their place in the adult world. Around age thirty, these choices take on a new seriousness. They can no longer be thought of as experimentation; now they are "for real." The late thirties are a time of settling down and settling in—

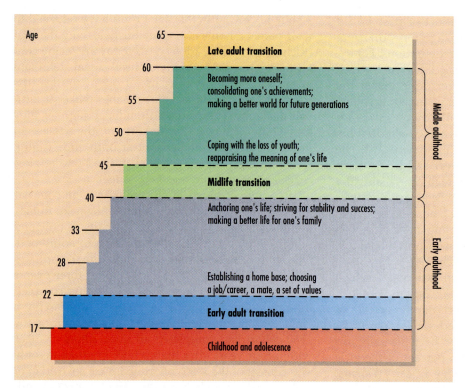

FIGURE 10.3 / Levinson's Stages and Transitions in Adulthood

Like Erikson, Levinson saw two distinct stages within adulthood: early adulthood and middle age. Each has both stable (or structure-building) periods, in which a person reviews and evaluates past choices and considers the future, and transition periods, in which one feels suspended between past and future and struggles to bridge the gap. Levinson argued that although the biological age at which a person enters a particular period may vary somewhat, most pass through the same stages in the same order.

Source: Adapted from Daniel J. Levinson et al., *The Seasons of a Man's Life* (Knopf: New York, 1978), p. 57.

anchoring roles more firmly and advancing in a chosen occupation.

The same kind of increasing commitment to roles and responsibilities has been found to occur among women in their twenties and thirties (Helson and Moore, 1987), but the phases of adulthood for women may not be as predictable as they are for men (Rosenfeld and Stark, 1987). This difference is primarily because the timing of childbearing can vary so much among women, and it affects decisions about work and career. A woman who has children in her twenties may not enter the workforce until her late thirties, and so she reaches the stage of career consolidation in her middle to late forties, which is ten to fifteen years behind the typical man. Another woman may concentrate on her career in young adulthood and postpone motherhood until her thirties or even forties. In American society today, knowing a woman's age alone tells you very little about her marital, parental, or occupational status. However, if you also know when she had children and how many she had, this is a very good predictor of her participation in the workforce and her occupational advancement (Hanson, 1983).

Regardless of how they map out their early adult years, both men and women eventually make a

midlife transition—that is, a movement from the self-perception of being young adult to the self-perception of being middle-aged. In Levinson's research this transition usually occurred between ages forty and forty-five, although others have found that particular life events can trigger it earlier or later (Vaillant, 1977). In any case, during the midlife transition, people must face the signs of advancing age and the finite nature of the life course they imply. For 70 to 80 percent of the men Levinson studied, the midlife transition—popularly called the "midlife crisis"—was psychologically wrenching. Suddenly, with a new sense of limited time before them, they began to question their marriages, families, and careers. "What have I done with my life? What do I really get from and give to my wife, children, friends, work, community—and self? What is it I truly want for myself and others?" (p. 60). For some, like Sydney Carton (the man profiled at the beginning of the chapter), the realization that their youthful dreams might never be realized was particularly agonizing.

But men who negotiated this transition well found middle adulthood to be the most creative time of their lives. They became more attached to others and more secure in themselves. For women, too, the middle years often bring greater self-confidence (Helson and Moore, 1987). This can be a time when people feel a heightened sense of making a worthwhile contribution to the world, both in what they produce at work and in their guidance of younger generations. Erik Erikson called this a sense of generativity. For women, regardless of their involvement in careers and affairs in the community, a sense of generativity especially derives from guiding younger generations within the family (Lowenthal, Thurnher, and Chiriboga, 1975). For men, contributions outside the family are often of equal importance. Not everyone achieves a sense of generativity, however. Erikson referred to the challenge as one of *generativity versus stagnation*. Those who resolve it successfully feel a growing sense of self-fulfillment, while those who do not are self-centered, stagnant, and bored.

Although Erikson conceived of his life-course stages as centered on universal challenges, in reality the quest for a sense of generativity and fulfillment is probably a luxury that occurs more often in societies where simple survival is not a constant struggle. The patterns of events in the life course vary from one society to another, just as they vary from one generation to the next. Generational change in adult roles is apparent in our own society. Marriage, parenthood, family, and work mean different things to middle-aged Americans today than they did to their parents or grandparents when they were in middle adulthood. Adults in their thirties and forties today divorce more frequently, change jobs more of-

ten, and have a greater propensity to move to new locations than their parents or grandparents did. These patterns are partly related to the value that a generation raised in rapid technological change places on variety and newness. Seeking the latest and the best is part of the baby boomer mind-set, but some of this propensity for change is also related to competition in such a large age group. Promotions within a single company, for instance, are often slow for baby boomers because competition for the few higher-level jobs is great. As a result, many baby boomers feel compelled to hopscotch from firm to firm in search of a higher rung on the career ladder. Such generational forces have changed important aspects of adulthood in our society. As we enter the first half of the twenty-first century, they may also begin changing what old age is like.

Old Age

The Abkhasians, a people living in the Caucasus Mountains in the former Soviet republic of Georgia, are famous for their longevity. Many maintain fully active and healthy lives well into their eighties and nineties, and an unusually large number of both men and women live to be over 100 (Benet, 1976; Garb, 1984). Biological factors are partly responsible. The Abkhasian genetic makeup apparently programs them for "late blooming" at each stage of the life

Young adulthood is a time for getting together with friends, looking for "Mr or Ms Right," and developing a capacity for intimacy—a willingness to allow people to know you as you are, to accept others for who they are, and to make commitments.

course; because of their genes they physically age more slowly than people elsewhere do. Diet and exercise may also make contributions. Abkhasians eat large amounts of healthy foods like fresh fruits and vegetables, cornmeal and other grains, cottage cheese and yogurt, and little saturated fat and refined sugar. They have no need for exercise gyms or jogging paths because the physical demands of farming and herding help keep them fit to a ripe old age. At the same time, the pace and pressures of life in the modern industrialized world are largely absent in this peasant society of simple farmers, where social change comes slowly. This undoubtedly reduces the Abkhasians' incidence of stress-related illnesses.

In addition, the Abkhasians probably stay active into old age because their culture *expects* them to do so. Older Abkhasians rarely complain about their physical ailments (according to one of their proverbs, "The ill-tempered don't live long"). The elderly here assume that they will keep on living their lives much as they always have done. They see nothing negative about growing older. In fact, they look forward to old age. This is partly because they rarely become detached from the ongoing life of the community; they remain integrated through close and supportive networks of family and friends. Old people are needed and valued among the Abkhasians and are an important part of Abkhasian society.

This social context is an excellent one for successfully dealing with the last of Erikson's eight life-course challenges: *integrity versus despair.* According to Erikson, elderly people can either accept themselves and their aged status and feel that their lives are integrated into coherent and satisfying wholes, or they can regret the past, feel helpless about the future, and fear death to the point of despair. For the Abkhasians, old age is such an accepted and valued part of the life course that disappointment and despair in it are relatively uncommon.

Although the American elderly will probably never have a status as honored as elderly Abkhasians, there is a strong likelihood that our view of old age will become increasingly positive as the baby boomers enter this stage of life. Between the years 2011 and 2029, this huge generation, some 80 million strong, will reach the important milestone of age sixty-five. Having this many elderly in our population is apt to change our attitudes in many ways. While wrinkles may not become chic in the twenty-first century, the glorification of youth in our culture may gradually diminish, to be replaced with a growing acceptance of old age and a more favorable image of its mean-

ing. The sheer size, power, and accumulated wealth of the baby boom generation will all work to change cultural perceptions of the aged (Rukeyser, 1995). Already the realities of life among America's elderly are far more positive than many younger people think.

Lifestyles and Personal Relationships

At age ninety-six, Ethel Nixon is always on the go. She lives in a retirement village in California but still does her own shopping and cleaning, and she regularly drives to visit her two sons, five grandchildren, and six great-grandchildren. When Mrs. Nixon appeared on the "Tonight Show," she became an overnight celebrity because she defies the stereotype that people her age are confined to nursing homes, dependent on their adult children, or neglected, abandoned, and alone.

Mrs. Nixon may be unusual in her vigor at nearly 100 years old, but her self-reliance is far from unique. A majority of the 3.6 million Americans aged eighty-five and older still maintain independent households, even though many are poor and most have no income other than Social Security. Only about 11 percent of those over eighty-five live with their children. Like so many other myths about the aged, the belief that they are a drain on their children's time and finances is generally false. One poll found that older Americans are four times more likely to give financial aid to their children than to receive such aid themselves, and other studies confirm that the giving of aid between generations is far from one-sided (Hogan, Eggebeen, and Clogg, 1993). Moreover, less than 1 percent of older people say that they would want to live with their children (Horn and Meer, 1987). Apparently, the shift to an "empty nest" is associated with a significant rise in marital happiness (White and Edwards, 1990). This does not mean that the elderly are necessarily cut off from their children. Many stay in close contact with sons and daughters, even across a sizable distance, and both sides can derive satisfaction from the relationship.

The trend toward the elderly's living alone will increase even further as the baby boom generation reaches retirement age (Macunovich, Easterlin, Schaeffer, and Crimmins, 1995). Because the baby boomers have fewer children than their parents did, their opportunities for moving in with grown children are fewer than those of the previous generation. Some see this as a potentially negative factor in baby boomers' future life satisfaction (Easterlin, Schaeffer, and Macunovich, 1993). However, given the independence that Americans in general value, this situation may be less negative than some anticipate. Aging baby boomers may miss having more children only in times of real personal need, such as disabling health problems. On the positive side, there is evidence that, in such times of need, grown children of the elderly, even if few in number, usually make the family adjustments needed to care for an aged parent (Silverstein, 1995). This is not to say that neglect of the elderly does not occur in our society. The stress of a heavy caregiving burden can erode affection between middle-aged adults and their elderly parents, giving rise to elder abuse (Olson, 1994). However, the problem is not as widespread as many people believe, affecting only an estimated 4 percent of the older population. Most of the care that frail and infirm elderly Americans receive is provided without compulsion or compensation by family members (Soldo and Freedman, 1994).

Another reason why an increased trend toward living alone may not be such a drawback for older Americans is that friends are such an important source of satisfaction and social support for them. Most elderly Americans spend a substantial amount of time cultivating friendships with peers. In one study, half the older people questioned reported having between eleven and forty friends on whom they could call for assistance in their daily lives (Quadagno, 1986). These relationships were reciprocal: Someone who had a car would drive friends to church or to the shopping mall; another would make a larger cake or pot of soup than she needed and share the surplus with her neighbors; still another would regularly read to a friend who had trouble with her eyes. Often the elderly see others their own age as more reliable sources of support and assistance than younger people are, even more so than their own children (FitzGerald, 1986).

With their increased connections to others their own age, most elderly Americans do not see themselves as lonely, not even those who are widowed, divorced, or never-married. In one study, 88 percent of those over sixty-five reported that loneliness was not a problem for them (Russell, 1989). Interestingly, loneliness may be less a matter of one's degree of separation from other people and more a matter of one's *expectations* for community. In very individualistic societies, such as our own, where people do not expect to be living in a large group, living alone does

not usually cause loneliness. Rather, it is in societies where expectations for community run high, yet the structures facilitating it are eroding, that feelings of loneliness are most common (Jylha and Jokela, 1990).

Many older Americans facilitate the task of connecting with other people by moving to retirement communities, where opportunities for social involvement abound (Johnson and Troll, 1994). People in retirement communities tend to maintain very active social lives, including active sex lives (McCarthy, 1989). The retirement community lifestyle seems to have some benefits. Most studies show that people in retirement communities enjoy better health and live longer than older people in other settings do (Quadagno, 1986).

The active involvement of residents in retirement communities generally exists regardless of their social-class backgrounds. For example, in a classic study of a newly constructed apartment complex for low-income elderly in California, Arlie Hochschild (1978) found that the forty-three people who lived there formed a genuine community of involved and caring friends. Within a few months of having a coffee machine installed in their communal recreation room, the residents of Merrill Court had organized a wide range of groups and activities: a service club, a

Friendship takes on renewed importance in old age—when a person's children are grown, he or she has retired, and perhaps lost his or, more likely, her spouse. With friends their own age, older people can admit frailties—and have fun—without feeling they are interrupting someone's busy schedule or burdening them with their problems.

bowling league, a morning workshop, Bible study classes, monthly birthday parties, potluck lunches and suppers, dances, card games, sight-seeing bus tours, and even a five-piece band (complete with washtub bass) that entertained the "old folks" at nearby nursing homes. Residents who were more reticent to join in were wheedled and cajoled by their neighbors, and those who had to stay at home because of poor health had their shopping, cooking, laundering, and socializing needs all taken care of by friends who would stop by to help out.

Although the interests and activities of residents in more well-to-do retirement communities often differ from those of the residents at Merrill Court, a high level of socializing and involvement is common to both. In Florida's Sun City, for example, home to many retired executives and professionals, the whirl of social activities centers heavily around golf, cultural events, artistic pursuits, and civic involvement. Residents took great pride in their busy schedules, and many were quick to remind author Frances FitzGerald of the community's advertising slogan: "The town too busy to retire" (FitzGerald, 1986). With the huge baby boom generation of healthy, active adults poised to start entering old age in another fifteen years, the retirement community model of social involvement will probably become even more widespread in the twenty-first century.

Widowhood and Gender Differences

Of the forty-three residents of Merrill Court when Hochschild studied it, thirty-five were widows. This unbalanced social structure reflects a simple fact about mortality: American women live seven to eight years longer, on average, than American men do. Our society, therefore, has nearly five times as many widowed women as widowed men. Also, because women tend to marry older men, they are likely to be widowed during a large portion of their old age. By their sixty-fifth birthday, about 25 percent of married women are widowed; half of the remaining ones will be widowed by age seventy-five. Only one man in five will lose his wife during the same time span (Clausen, 1986). Put another way, for people aged sixty-five or older, 75 percent of the men but only 40 percent of the women are living with their spouses (U.S. Bureau of the Census, 1990c).

The experience of widowhood is also different for men and women. In some ways, it is more difficult for men to adjust to, for they lose not only their wife but often a system of domestic support as well, one that they have always taken for granted. Men now in their sixties and seventies tend to be unfamiliar with cooking and household chores, so widowers may experience physical decline due to skipped meals and poor nutrition. Widowhood also clashes with men's self-definitions as independent and resourceful. They are not accustomed to asking for help, so they may get less assistance than they need from relatives and friends. At the same time, men often have less developed skills for forging social ties than women do because in marriage they have traditionally let the wife be the couple's "social director." Not surprisingly, then, among those over age sixty-five, rates of suicide are much higher for widowed men than for men who are still married.

This is not to say that adjustment to widowhood isn't difficult for women. They lose a lifetime partner who, during the retirement years, they have spent almost all of their time with. Many retired couples become single units, going everywhere together. Death of half of the unit can be devastating to the survivor. Widows may also lose their husband's pension, creating economic insecurity, especially if the woman has been a housewife all her life and does not receive a private pension of her own. These factors help explain why elderly American widows on average have less income than elderly divorced or never-married women do (Schwenk, 1992). It also explains why the poverty rate for widows age sixty-five and older is over four times the poverty rate for married men the same age (21 percent versus only 5 percent) (Holtz-Eakin and Smeeding 1994).

Despite the fact that many elderly widows would like to remarry, remarriage among the widowed elderly is predominantly a male prerogative. The reasons are both demographic and cultural. Among the roughly 10.5 million widowed Americans aged sixty-five and over in 1992, 82 percent were women and 18 percent were men (Saluter, 1992). This means that for every 100 widowed women in this age group there were only twenty-two widowed men. And because older men have the option of marrying younger women, their pool of eligible partners is even larger, making an elderly widowed woman's chances of remarriage even less. As a result, men aged sixty-five and older are eight times more likely to remarry than women this age are (Horn and Meer, 1987). Interestingly, social status affects remarriage rates in opposite ways for men and women. The more education a woman has and the higher her income, the less likely she is to remarry, while the reverse is true for men.

Work and Retirement

The proportion of men over age sixty-five who remain employed has dropped from about 67 percent in 1940, to 46 percent in 1950, to 26 percent in 1970, to about 16 percent today (the decline is much smaller for women in this age group because of their historically lower rates of full-time employment outside the home) (U.S. Bureau of the Census, 1987, 1995b). The declining proportion of elderly men who are working is due to several factors. Technological changes have eliminated some jobs once filled by older men. Also, these technological changes have sometimes rendered obsolete the skills and expertise possessed by older workers. Plant relocations and closings, in addition, often encourage older men to retire, for they are usually less willing than the young to move in order to find work. Then, too, there is a general trend for a growing percentage of elderly people to retire from the workforce as a country's economic development and wealth increase (Clark and Anker, 1993). The more prosperous people are, the more likely that they will be able to afford to give up working in old age.

In addition to giving older Americans an income to live on when they retire, various government retirement programs (like Social Security) and private pension plans have in effect defined sixty-five as the "official" age for leaving the workforce (it will be raised to sixty-seven in the year 2000). Some of these programs have traditionally provided economic incentives for retiring "on schedule" (Quinn and Burkhauser, 1994). Thus, despite the fact that laws have eliminated mandatory retirement ages, most people choose to retire at age sixty-five, and a growing number of men as well as women retire even before then (Morris and Bass, 1988; Quinn and Burkhauser, 1994). Many choose to leave their jobs as soon as they are able to support themselves through a retirement package—a combination of Social Security, private pension programs (which cover only about half of those people now working), and personal savings. With the life span still increasing for people in our society, most Americans today can expect to spend about a quarter of their lives retired.

The transition to retirement can be stressful, however, especially for men. Men approaching old age today are more fully engaged in the world of work and more likely to derive their core identity from their job than are women of the same generation. A job is a source of not only income and status for men but also pride and meaning. A job structures one's days, weeks, and years, offers social contact, and ideally provides opportunities for creativity and personal fulfillment. For some men, retirement creates a huge void in their lives.

Yet a majority of older Americans look forward to retirement (Clausen, 1986; Quadagno, 1986). Only 7 percent leave the workforce unwillingly (Russell, 1989). Evidently, after three or four decades of work, most jobs are simply not intrinsically interesting enough to keep people at them if they do not need the earnings. In her study of Sun City, Florida, Frances FitzGerald was struck by how many of the middle- and upper-middle-class men when interviewed had no regrets about leaving their jobs.

> Civil servants, corporate executives, schoolteachers, independent businessmen—indeed, many of the same people who talked with such pride about the professional success they had had—told me that they planned their retirement years in advance. A number said they would have retired earlier if they had been able to afford it. One man who had traveled all over the world for the Department of Agriculture . . . said that he had retired at fifty-five because he was "sick of working." Another man said that he had sold his chemical company "in order to get out of the rat race" and in order to fish and play golf. (FitzGerald, 1986, pp. 229–230)

Once the transition is made to retirement status, the reality often lives up to the expectation. Many retirees say that they enjoy their new situation. They report a sense of well-being as high as or higher than that of younger people who are working (Gove, Ortega, and Style, 1989). This may be because they can now lead less pressured lives and can structure their daily activities according to their own interests and preferred pace. Many chose to use their life-skills in volunteer work. According to a Harris Poll, only 11 percent of full-time retirees said they would consider taking a job and returning to the workforce (Russell, 1989). As one man in FitzGerald's study put it: "I miss the competitiveness of business, but I'd hate to go back to work. Pressure, pressure pressure—I don't want to get involved" (p. 230).

This general satisfaction with retirement varies, however, depending on socioeconomic conditions and on the characteristics of the job left behind. People from high-status occupations, although they tend to retire later, are more likely to report that they enjoy retirement than are people from low-status jobs, probably because high-status workers tend to be healthier and to have more money with which to enjoy themselves. But those who had the greatest power in their former occupations are more likely to experience high levels of stress during the transition to retirement.

There are also some elderly people who choose not to retire, at least not at the age at which retirement is generally expected. Many of these people continue working at least part-time, not only because they enjoy their work but also because they feel they need to save more money for a comfortable retirement (Kaye, Lord, and Sherrid, 1995). Working longer in order to enlarge a retirement nest egg may become a growing trend among the baby boom generation (*Congressional Quarterly*, 1993). Moreover, because of an increased demand for labor in the twenty-first century, as smaller age cohorts take over the task of running the American economy, more and more elderly boomers may be drawn out of their initial retirement and into a second phase of employment. Already almost a third of American retirees reenter the labor force at some point, even if only temporarily. Certainly older Americans who wish to work should have many opportunities to do so in the first half of the next century (Hayward, Hardy, and Liu, 1994).

Economic Circumstances

As a group, older people are economically much better off today than in the past, partly because of general economic prosperity and partly because of Social Security, Medicare, and private pension benefits. The proportion of men and women aged sixty-five and older living below the poverty line has fallen from 35 percent in 1959, to 25 percent in 1970, to 12 percent today. In 1970, the incidence of poverty among the elderly was double the national average; today it is actually below the average poverty rate of 14 percent for all age groups (Hess and Markson, 1991).

Some older people today are extremely well off, leading social critics to call them "greedy geezers" (Hess, 1990) who take advantage of federal assistance programs and reduced-rate services for seniors even though they do not really need them. These very wealthy seniors, however, are only one part of the total picture. Their economic asset can obscure the fact that the elderly are a highly diverse segment of the population (Holtz-Eakin and Smeeding, 1994). One study found that economic inequality among the elderly is greater than for any other age group. While the richest one-fifth of the elderly gets 46 percent of the elderly's total resources, the poorest one-fifth gets only 6 percent (Crystal and Shea, 1990). This is a key reason for proposals to restrict government old-age benefits—like Medicare—only to those with financial need.

The poorest of the elderly suffer severe economic hardship. Widows, members of minority groups, and the chronically ill tend to be the worst off financially (Golant and La Greca, 1994; Morgan, 1991). Poverty also increases with age. People eighty-five and older are twice as likely to live in poverty as those aged sixty-five to sixty-nine. These disadvantages tend to accumulate for certain people. For instance, about 64 percent of black women who live alone and who are age seventy-two or over live in poverty (U.S. Bureau of the Census, 1990b). Such statistics tell us something else important about poverty among the elderly: The same groups that are most likely to be poor early in life—racial and ethnic minorities, women who are heads of households—remain the ones who are most likely to be poor in old age (Pampel and Hardy, 1994). And since there is growing racial and ethnic diversity among the elderly (a doubling of the proportion of nonwhite elderly is projected between now and the year 2050), the incidence of poverty in this age group may start to creep upward again.

Medical expenses are a financial burden for many elderly people, even those who are not poor. Out-of-pocket health-care costs are eating up larger proportions of the income of older Americans. In the early 1960s, the elderly spent less than 6 percent of their income on health care; thirty years later the proportion had risen to 18 percent, and it is expected to climb even higher in the future (U.S. Congress, House of Representatives, 1990). While Medicare covers older people for hospital expenses and certain other medical costs, it does not cover nursing home costs or the cost of home care (Margolis, 1990). These additional health-care expenses can be sizable for seniors. They partly account for the fact that the elderly today are spending at a significantly higher rate and saving at a significantly lower one than their parents did at the same stage of the life course (Nasar, 1995).

AGE STRUCTURE: THE GRAYING OF AMERICA

Long-Term Trends

The age structure of our society is changing, as Figure 10.1 showed. The long-term trend is toward relatively fewer young people and relatively more old ones. This change—which is causing a "graying" of American society (Myers, 1990)—can be seen in two simple statistics. One is the *median age* of the population, the age that divides the population in half, so that 50 percent are older than the median and 50 percent are younger. The median age of Americans has increased throughout this century and promises to go even higher in the decades ahead. In 1900, the median age was 22.9 years; by 1950, it had risen to 30.2 years; and by 1995, it was 34.3 years. By the year 2020, the median age will be about 40 years, and by 2050, about 46 years! The same story is told if we look at the *proportion of Americans aged sixty-five or older.* That proportion has increased during this century and will continue rising during the next one. In 1900, a mere 4.1 percent of the population was aged sixty-five or older; by 1950, the percentage had risen to 8.1 percent; and by 1995, it was 12.8 percent. Looking ahead, in the year 2020, about 18 percent of the population will be sixty-five or older, and in 2050 that figure will rise to about 25 percent. As America moves into the next century, children, adolescents and young adults will become a diminishing proportion of our population.

There are two fundamental causes of this graying of American society. First of all, average life expectancy has increased substantially throughout this century. A white male born in 1900 could, on average, expect to live forty-seven years and a white female could expect to live forty-nine years. Today, men can expect to live to about seventy-two and women to almost eighty. Increasing life expectancy is due to improvements in the general standard of living (better nutrition and sanitation) and especially in medical care.

A second cause of the graying of our population is the aging of the baby boom generation. Although the median age in the United States has increased from 1900 to the present, there was one exception to this trend. In the decades during and just after the baby boom, the median age actually declined, from 30.2 years in 1950, to 29.4 years in 1960, to 27.9 years in 1970 (after which it began to move consistently up-

ward again). Interestingly, this short-term decline in the median age of the population occurred at the same time that the proportion of Americans aged sixty-five and older continued to increase! Such a pattern was possible because the large baby boom generation statistically overwhelmed the relatively smaller birth cohorts moving through their sixties and seventies. But now the baby boom bulge is moving toward its own "gray" years. Because birth cohorts of younger people have been consistently smaller than those of the baby boom generation, an increasingly rapid graying of the American population is inevitable during the next half century.

What differences in social life can Americans expect from a graying age structure? Inevitably, when the boomers begin to reach their sixties (not long after the start of the next century), there will be more retired people and fewer adults still working. Perhaps there will be labor shortages in the twenty-first century; perhaps society will not be able to produce enough goods and services to support an increasingly dependent elderly population; perhaps we will also see more elderly people working, a possibility we mentioned earlier. There will certainly be financial pressures on the whole society. As cost-conscious employers drastically cut back on their pension programs, many baby boomers may find it hard to achieve a comfortable retirement unless they greatly increase their current rate of saving (*Congressional Quarterly*, 1993). But since saving more is very difficult for many of today's boomers, a sizable proportion of them may be forced to supplement their retirement incomes with the paycheck from a job.

The possibility also exists that government programs designed to assist the elderly (like Medicare and Social Security) will not have enough money to survive when the baby boomers retire. As the boomers reach old age, these programs will take an ever-increasing chunk of the federal budget. However, the ratio of employed people to retired people will have fallen significantly, so fewer working Americans will be available to pay for the programs out of income tax dollars (Habib, 1990). A growing imbalance between workers and retirees is already visible. In 1945, each person receiving Social Security was supported by thirty-five workers, whereas in 1985, each Social Security recipient was supported by only *three* workers. This growing imbalance is sure to fuel the social debate over the size and form that government-sponsored benefits for the elderly should take in the future (see the Sociology and Public Debates box).

The Politics of Aging and Generational Conflict

American baby boomers today, now middle-aged, are paying an unprecedented portion of their earnings to support Social Security and Medicare for the elderly. Since 1960, the maximum annual FICA tax (most of which is spent on these programs) has risen by over 3000 percent—from a mere $300 a year to over $9,000. The baby boomers' acceptance of this tax is partly based on the assumption that today's young people will in turn help to support them when they reach retirement age; however, evidence is growing that this assumption may be incorrect. The younger generation may be unable to support the aged boomers to the same extent that the boomers have supported the current generation of elderly.

THE DEBATE

It is not that today's young adults are opposed to the concept of helping the aged; they may simply not be able to afford to give their elders much financial help. The problem is basically one of numbers. Given the huge baby boom generation and its anticipated longevity, there will be too many elderly boomers drawing on public funds and too few younger workers paying FICA taxes. The most optimistic estimates are that the members of the post-boom generation will have to pay nearly a quarter of their earnings to keep old-age benefits going for the elderly boomers. In the most pessimistic scenario, over 40 percent of wages will be drawn from working people's paychecks to support the retired boomers (Longman, 1987). This pessimistic forecast may be more realistic, if the younger generation continues to be downwardly mobile, with lower wages to tax. What's more, because of cutbacks in public spending for children in our society, an increasing number of young people may be growing up impoverished and poorly educated. Such children are not likely to become high wage earners, so their tax dollars will not go far in helping to support a large elderly population. As adults they may have trouble finding jobs and may even end up drawing on public funds rather than contributing to them.

The baby boomers reply that the issue is one of fairness. They have endured heavy tax hikes to give the current elderly some security, so they are entitled to the same rewards when they themselves grow old. Most boomers, after all, are not wealthy enough to forgo public assistance when they retire. Private pension plans are being cut back, and saving for retirement is increasingly difficult in today's economy (*Congressional Quarterly*, 1993). The costs of taxes, housing, and college tuitions for children are too high to make significant savings more than a distant dream for most. The baby boomers feel that continuation of old-age support is a right that they have earned. If others try to deprive them of it, they will band together to demand it, and the result could be political warfare between old and young.

> Baby boomers feel that old-age support is a right that they have earned. They will band together to demand it, and the result could be political warfare between old and young.

ANALYSIS

The major catalyst for this conflict between generations is our society's social structure. The baby boom generation is much larger than subsequent generations, and most of its members are expected to live well into their seventies and eighties. How can a relatively small number of young and middle-aged adults manage to pay pensions and medical expenses for all these senior citizens? The ratio of old to young is just too high. The number of people who are too old or too young to work relative to the number of working-age people is called the dependency ratio—the nonworkers are dependent on the workers to pay taxes and support social programs. America is experiencing a rising dependency ratio largely because of a growing number of elderly retired. According to one Census Bureau projection, by the year 2030, the ratio of Americans age sixty-five and over to Americans age twenty to sixty-four could be as high as 1 to 2.2 (Longman, 1987). This means that the social benefits going to each elderly person would be paid for out of the pockets of a little over just two working adults.

Culture also enters into this generational conflict. Our current cultural values support aiding the elderly out of public funds. This view has not always prevailed, however. In fact, during most of our history, support of the elderly has been considered a personal

SOCIOLOGY AND PUBLIC DEBATES

or family matter, not a societal one. That is why, in order to pass the Social Security Act in the 1930s, the Roosevelt administration had to present it to the American people as a kind of individualistic self-paid pension, in which the elderly would draw out money from the fund that they had paid into it when younger. This portrayal of the system was a fiction. According to one calculation made a decade ago, a married worker who retired at age sixty-five and had paid the maximum in FICA taxes would recover his or her contribution to Social Security in just a little under two years (Kollmann and Koitz, 1986). Lower-income workers who had paid less in taxes would recover their contributions in as little as one year. Thus, what you are paying in FICA taxes is not for your own retirement but for the support of those who are already retired. Misunderstanding of this fact persists even today, which is one reason why some people oppose having income limits placed on old-age benefits: They think that such a policy denies to wealthier seniors the benefits that they have paid for during their working lives.

The development of a cultural consensus that the elderly should get public help was encouraged by several factors. One was the high rate of poverty among the aged in the middle of this century, a rate that peaked near 30 percent in the mid-twentieth century and was becoming a national scandal (Holtz-Eakin and Smeeding, 1994). Support for public assistance for the elderly was also promoted by a more favorable view of retirement in this country. By the 1950s, Americans had started to see retirement not as an empty time of life to be dreaded but as a pleasant period with a chance to indulge interests beyond those at work (Longman, 1987). In order for this leisure to be enjoyed, however, the elderly required public funding. Some observers speculate that, as the graying of our society continues, the pendulum of cultural values may swing away from a more collectivist view of caring for the elderly to a more individualistic view that the elderly should care more for themselves. This is particularly likely if there is a growing perception of inequality between the generations, with the elderly seeming to get more than their fair share relative to the middle-aged and young (Bengtson, 1993).

How the conflict between the generations will turn out is clearly a matter of power. The baby boomers have the strength of numbers—they make up roughly a third of the population. They also have the power that comes with organization. The American Association of Retired Persons (AARP) is one of America's most powerful political organizations. It lobbies on behalf of the elderly, provides them with information, and helps to organize economic benefits like special discounts. Older people are also among our most politically active citizens. People over sixty-five are much more likely to vote than those under twenty-five, for example, and more likely to attend party meetings and make financial contributions to candidates.

Even though the baby boomers will command many votes and have much political influence in their old age, their power will be far from absolute. They must still win support from working-age Americans in order to have their desires for social programs met. One study found that this winning of support is more likely in a pluralistic democracy such as our own, where competing interest groups vie for influence rather than forming coalitions to share power. It is also more likely in a country that lacks a strong leftist political party and where parties are not based largely on social classes (Pampel, 1994). In such societies, including the United States, the elderly tend to win more in public funds than do the young.

Any program for the elderly that a society adopts is a form of collective social action, so this generational struggle is really a battle over which collective actions to take and how to fund them. Whatever the choices, they will have a better chance of working if they are functionally integrated with other aspects of society. For instance, programs that survive must be in sync with cultural values and perceptions. If the elderly are widely viewed as relatively privileged rather than needy, it will be hard to sustain public support for their financial aid (Bengtson, 1993). The system of paying for social programs must also fit the social order. Social Security and Medicare paid for from payroll taxes makes little sense when the national payroll is not large enough to support them. This matter of societal "fit" must be taken into account as the debate between old and young continues into the twenty-first century.

Source: Geoffrey Kollmann and David Koitz, "How Long Does It Take for New Retirees to Recover the Value of Their Social Security Taxes?" Congressional Research Service, 21 January 1986, report no. 86-10 EPW, Table 1, p. 11.

Adding to the economic crisis may be the spiraling costs of health care. If future increases in life expectancy are achieved by huge investments in high-tech medical treatments, there may be both a greatly expanded elderly population and a society in which a large proportion of its resources goes toward keeping elderly people alive (Callahan, 1987). The practice of medicine will be affected also. More physicians will become specialists in health problems and diseases that affect the elderly, for that is where the greatest demand will be. Other industries targeted to the senior market will also flourish—everything from retirement communities to nursing homes to convalescent aids. Conceivably, the baby boomers could even change our attitudes about death and dying. It might become easier, for instance, for people to choose the time they wish to die.

The Very Old

One of the same factors that is causing the graying of the American population—our increased longevity—is also causing a substantial rise in the proportion of very old people. In fact, the "oldest old" (those eighty-five and over) are the fastest growing age group of American elderly. Between 1960 and 1994, when the American population overall grew by 45 percent and those over sixty-five doubled their numbers, there was a 274 percent rate of growth for the oldest-old segment. In 1994, these very aged accounted for 10 percent of all elderly Americans. It is estimated that by 2050 they will comprise 24 percent of the elderly population and a full 5 percent of our population as a whole (U.S. Bureau of the Census, 1995a).

Many people worry about the caretaking needs of such a large number of very old people. They are concerned that as more and more Americans live to advanced ages we will have more instances of chronic, disabling illnesses such as severe arthritis and osteoporosis, Parkinson's disease, and Alzheimer's. Caring for an aged parent with one of these chronic conditions can be financially and emotionally draining on middle-aged sons and daughters who are fast approaching their own retirement years. Statistics show that with age comes an increased chance of being dependent on others. For instance, while only 1 percent of Americans aged sixty-five to seventy-four lived in a nursing home in 1990, nearly 25 percent of those eighty-five and older did

Madame Jeanne Calment, the Frenchwoman who celebrated her 120th birthday in 1995, may be the oldest person alive today. Living almost a century-and-a-quarter is extraordinary. But living until almost one hundred is becoming more common. People who survive into their nineties tend to have fewer ailments than people in their seventies, and remain hardy and healthy to the end.

so, and half of the oldest old who still lived at home needed some assistance to perform everyday activities such as bathing and preparing meals (U.S. Bureau of the Census, 1995a).

But these same statistics also reveal that a sizable segment of the eighty-five-and-over population—some 38 percent—live fully independent lives. Apparently, it is easy to be overly pessimistic about the vigor and resiliency of many of those who live to such advanced age. A rapidly growing population of oldest old does not necessarily mean exploding sales of wheelchairs, feeding tubes, and respirators. In fact, the *really* old—those in their nineties and over—may be better off healthwise in many respects than people twenty years younger (Angier, 1995). They tend to have fewer ailments than people in their seventies do, and when they die they tend to do so quickly, without the agonizing and costly lingering of many younger elderly. This is shown in Medicare statistics. The average annual Medicare payments for people who survive into their nineties is only a third that of people who die by age seventy.

Thus, there seems to be a kind of age "hump" that occurs in the nineties, and those who live past it, because of their physical robustness, are on a more gradually sloping trajectory of illness and disablement than many younger elderly people are. The oldest person alive whose age is clearly documented is a Frenchwoman who turned 120 in 1995. She is in remarkably good condition for someone this age. Far from being despondent about her advancing years, she says, "Aging actually suits me rather well. I had to wait 110 years to become famous, and I intend to enjoy my fame as long as possible" (quoted in Angier, 1995, p. 5). Every additional year that this oldest centenarian-plus survives both extends the possible limits of the human life span and attests to the physical vigor of some of the oldest old.

SUMMARY

1. The generation into which a person is born has many important effects on life chances. The opportunities to be high-paid or low-paid, rich or poor, mobile or static on the social ladder are all affected by an individual's generation. This fact is illustrated by comparing children of the Great Depression with children of the baby boom. Because children of the Great Depression formed a relatively small generation, they put upward pressure on wages during the rapid economic expansion after World War II. Many of the men of this generation were able to find good-paying jobs, comfortably support a wife and family, and buy a house in the suburbs. The baby boom generation, in contrast, because of its far larger size, has faced much more competition for jobs among its members. Wages for the boomers are such that, for many of those who are married, both husband and wife must work in order to make ends meet. Each consecutive birth cohort in the baby boom generation seems to be having a more difficult time than its predecessors.

2. Age is a characteristic that every society uses to move people into and out of statuses and roles, rights and obligations. The process of creating social categories based on age is known as age grading and varies from culture to culture and from one historical period to another. Points in the life course when old roles give way to new ones are known as transitions. Life-course transitions may be ambiguous, or they may be clearly marked for both individuals and society by symbolic rites of passage.

3. Erik Erikson conducted the most influential study of human development—a series of stages from birth to death, known as stages of the life course. For each of eight stages he identified a major developmental challenge that all people face and resolve either positively or negatively. In modern Western societies, such as our own, most people think in terms of four major life-course stages: childhood, adolescence, adulthood, and old age. People in certain other societies view the life course differently than we do.

4. Childhood as we know it is a fairly recent cultural invention. The idea that children should be nurtured and protected from the adult world dates only from the Renaissance, and it was not embraced among the middle and working classes until the late nineteenth century. Some observers believe that we are now returning to a time when children are being exposed to adult activities and responsibilities at a much younger age.

5. Adolescence is a time of questioning and experimentation, as teenagers forge their own identities, or sense of who they are. Adolescence as we know it took shape in the 1940s and 1950s, when the segregation of young people in schools fostered the development of a teenage subculture with its own tastes and standards.

6. Adulthood involves a series of changes and new challenges for people. The midlife transition, a "crisis" for many men and some women, is a time for reevaluating what has been accomplished so far and for deciding what can realistically be achieved in the years remaining.

7. Contemporary American society tends to be youth-centered, which creates many negative myths about growing old. Yet research indicates that older Americans usually do not lead lives of loneliness and despair. Most are self-reliant and socially active, despite the problem of widowhood, which is especially common among women. It is a myth, too, that the elderly are primarily poor and financially dependent on their children. In fact, the percentage of older people living below the poverty line has fallen dramatically in the last two decades. And despite the common assumption that many older people feel "lost" after leaving work, most express substantial satisfaction with their lives after retirement.

8. The age structure of our society is changing. The long-term trend is toward relatively fewer young people and relatively more old ones. This "graying" of American society is due to increased longevity, a declining birth rate, and the fact that the huge baby boom generation is starting to enter later middle age. The trend will continue in the decades ahead as the baby boomers grow old, a process that is bound to affect our society in many ways.

9. In addition to helping cause a graying of American society, increased longevity is also substantially increasing the number of very old Americans. In fact, the "oldest old" (those eighty-five and over) are the fastest growing age group in our society. Contrary to popular opinion, many of these very elderly remain quite independent and in relatively good health until the very end of their lives.

REVIEW QUESTIONS

1. Using examples, explain how the generation into which a person is born can have many effects on life chances.

2. Explain what sociologists mean by saying that age is a cultural construct.

3. Define aging in sociological terms and give examples of transitions to new age-related statuses and roles.

4. Describe childhood, adolescence, and adulthood as stages of the life course in American society.

5. List several myths about old age and refute them.

6. What social forces are causing a "graying" of American society, and what changes in social life can we expect as this process continues into the twenty-first century?

CRITICAL THINKING QUESTIONS

1. This chapter describes some of the unique experiences of people raised during the Great Depression and people born during the postwar baby boom. What unique experiences will sociologists some day use to categorize your generation?

2. How valid are Erikson's descriptions of the stages and challenges of the life course for people you have known, or for your own experiences so far?

3. Present your own views on the disappearance of child-

hood. Is it real? How much of a problem is it? Be sure to respond to the chapter's content in your answer.

4. In light of the chapter's discussion about old age, what do you foresee for your own old age? To which other groups will your experience be similar? From which will it differ?

5. You have been recently elected to Congress. Discuss what types of legislation you will promote to address the "graying" of American society.

GLOSSARY

Age Biologically, age is the number of years since a person was born. Sociologically, it also involves cultural definitions about what is required from and appropriate for people of different ages. These definitions vary from one society to another.

Age discrimination The denial of rights, opportunities, and services to someone exclusively because of that person's age.

Age grading The process of classifying people into social categories according to age.

Ageism A system of negative evaluations of people based upon their

age. Ageism is most commonly applied to the elderly.

Age structure The number of people in a society at each stage of the life course.

Aging The process of moving through the life course, from birth to death.

Birth cohort A category of people who were born in the same year or in a small number of consecutive years.

Generation units Groups within the same generation that respond to their common historical experiences in markedly different ways and come to have distinctly different views from one another.

Identity The sense of who one is and where one is going, involving a sense of continuity about one's past, present, and future.

Life course The socially defined sequence of stages in a human life, from birth to death.

Rites of passage Public ceremonies that celebrate and record the transition from one age status to another.

Transitional status A status that is not permanent, but changes over time. Age is a transitional status because people periodically move from one age category to another.

Social Institutions

The Family

For nine days in the fall of 1994 Americans held their collective breath as they waited to hear of the fate of two little boys kidnapped from their mother. On morning and evening news programs Susan Smith, the twenty-three-year-old mother, could be seen sobbing and clutching the hand of her ex-husband, David, as she pleaded for the safe return of Michael, age three, and Alex, age fourteen months. It was an ordeal that every parent could sympathize with. The image of a mother forcibly separated from her children, whose lives were at risk, intuitively appealed to our strong sense of family. As a nation, we were outraged at the action of the kidnapper.

Imagine, then, the outrage Americans felt when they learned that the mother had actually killed her own sons and then consistently lied about it, putting the blame on a phantom carjacker. Her action violated our strongest family values—the mother–child bond, the protection owed children by their parents, the family as a haven of safety, the preservation and continuation of the family. So violent was public reaction that prosecutors in Susan Smith's hometown of Union, South Carolina, sought the death penalty for her self-confessed crime.

At the trial that would determine her punishment, prosecutors painted her as conniving and manipulative, willing to drown her little boys in order to win the love of a man who had spurned her, a man who had told her he did not want to be a father to her children. The defense, however, painted a different picture. Here, they said, was a woman whose own family life was dysfunctional. Sexually abused since the age of fifteen by her stepfather, divorced from her husband, and rejected by her lover, she was a troubled woman whose disappointments and woes had pushed her over the edge of sanity. Friends testified on her behalf that she loved her children and was a perfect mother in spite of her unstable family history (*New York Times,* July 9, 1995, p. 8).

In the end Susan Smith escaped the death penalty. She is now serving a life term, without parole. But the Smith case is not closed in the national consciousness. We are left to ponder what forces could so rip apart family ties. This was a unique case, but daily the newspapers give reports of abused children and battered wives. Are these signs of a new crisis of the family, or has there always been a "dark side" in which powerful emotions turn to evil instead of good? How far does the reality of family life vary from the reassuring myths we hold about it? Family is perhaps our most deeply valued social institution, but it seems to be challenged by recent cultural changes and the loss of some of its traditional functions. Yet many Americans are working hard to keep family life strong, to minimize child abuse and spousal violence, to limit divorces or protect children's rights if divorce does occur, to make sure single fathers take responsibility for their children. We struggle to make sure that cases like Susan Smith's remain exceptional, but we recognize that violence, conflict, and abuse of power within families are too common.

In this chapter we first consider the functions and structure of family and how the structure can vary from culture to culture as well as within a society and over time. The traditional nuclear family, for example, is but one form found in our society today; we take a look at some alternative types. We then turn our attention to marriage and divorce, considering how we decide whom, when, and whether to marry, as well as what makes us divorce and what effects divorce has. Next we look at family violence, especially abuse of wives and children—a reflection of the power structure in the family. Finally, we take a look at the future of the family and the cultural wars looming on the horizon as differing views of family clash.

FAMILY FUNCTIONS AND STRUCTURE

A **family** is any group of people who are united by ties of marriage, ancestry, or adoption, especially those having the responsibility for rearing children. In some form the family is part of the social organization in all societies. Indeed, it is probably the most basic of all social institutions.

Functions of the Family

The family is considered so important because it responds to some of the most fundamental human needs, both individual and collective:

■ The *need for love and emotional security:* The family involves a set of "loving obligations" to share both material and emotional resources. Ideally, the family offers warmth, loyalty, concern, willingness to sacrifice for the good of others, and unconditional love (Dizard and Gadlin, 1990).

■ The *need to regulate sexual behavior:* All societies place limits on the sexual behavior of their members, including limits regarding who can have sexual relations with whom. Forbidding sex between family members related by close common descent (called the *incest taboo*) is a universal restriction.

■ The *need to produce new generations:* At the same time, the family fulfills the *need to socialize children.* Children are society's "raw recruits." They must be taught the elements of culture needed for competent participation in social life. The family is the primary arena for social learning.

■ The *need to protect the young and the disabled:* During infancy and early childhood, humans are dependent on their parents for food, clothing, shelter, and basic care. Even as adults, many people experience episodes of illness or disability during which they need help. The family sees its members through these times.

■ The *need to "place" people in the social order:* The structure of a society is an intricate web of social roles and statuses. People must somehow be placed within these statuses and motivated to play the appropriate roles. Even in the United States and other societies that stress equal opportunity and social mobility, people's ascribed statuses, including their national, ethnic, racial, religious, class, and community identities, derive largely from family membership.

Variations in Family Structure

The family functions just listed are common to all societies. The structural forms for fulfilling these functions, however, vary from one society to another. Most people think their way of organizing family life is not only morally right but natural. Only the basics of procreation are determined by biology, however; the rest varies from culture to culture. Male dominance is among the most widespread features of family life, but even its extent and form varies, as the following examples suggest.

■ To the Nayar of Kerala, India, it is natural for a woman's brother—rather than the children's biological father—to share in the raising of her children. During adolescence, a Nayar girl is encouraged to have several lovers. If she becomes pregnant, one or more of these lovers acknowledges paternity and pays the cost of delivery. Beyond this, however, none of the lovers has any obligations toward the girl or the child. The girl's kin are responsible for caring for her and the baby. Property and privileged status pass not from father to son but from mother's brother to nephew (Gough, 1978).

■ Among the Betsileo of Madagascar, a man is allowed to have several wives. Each wife is housed in the village adjoining one of the rice fields that the man owns. Wealthier men with more rice fields can support more wives. The first and most senior wife, called the *big wife,* lives in the village next to the best, most productive rice field. The husband lives mainly with this woman but visits the others as he oversees his other fields (Kottak, 1991).

■ In the foothills of the western Himalayas, brothers share a wife. The oldest brother arranges the marriage, and his brothers become co-husbands, with all of them living together in a single household. Any children the wife bears call all the brothers "father." The brothers are free as a group to marry additional women if they wish, in which case all the wives are shared by all the husbands (Berreman, 1975).

Social scientists have categorized such variations in family structure using a number of criteria, one of which is the number of partners involved in a marriage. Both culturally and legally, U.S. society advocates **monogamy,** marriage between one man and one woman. Other societies permit **polygamy,** marriage involving more than two partners at the same time. When a man has more than one wife at the same time (as in the case of the Betsileo, above), it is known as **polygyny.** Much less common is **polyandry,** in which a woman has more than one husband at the same time.

Among the Shiites of India, polygamy—marriage to more than one partner at a time—is acceptable. Here, a Shiite husband poses with his wives and children.

Another structural criterion is the degree of importance given to marital ties, as opposed to blood ties. When marital ties are paramount, a husband and wife and their immature children form a core unit, called the **nuclear family.** This arrangement is the traditional structure in the United States and in most other modern Western countries. It also exists in somewhat different forms in other societies, such as the Betsileo, in which a man may establish several nuclear families in separate villages. Of course, multiple marriages are not required for a person to belong to more than one nuclear family. In the United States, for example, most people are eventually members of two nuclear families. The first, called the **family of orientation,** consists of parents and siblings. The second, called the **family of procreation,** consists of one's spouse and children.

When family structure gives priority to blood ties, the arrangement is called an **extended family.** An extended family consists of blood relatives (beyond the nuclear family) who live together in a single household. Spouses of blood relatives are considered peripheral to the core family unit. A common form is the three-generation extended family, in which some of a couple's married adult children live with their parents, along with their own spouses and children. Although not a common arrangement among most cultures in the United States, the three-generation extended family is the preferred form of family organization in a number of other societies.

This kind of extended family can be subclassified by pattern of residence. Under a system of **patrilocal residence,** a newly married couple lives with or near the husband's family: married sons stay at home while married daughters move away. Under a system of **matrilocal residence,** in contrast, a son leaves his family to set up housekeeping with or near his wife's family. When a newly married couple establishes a new home of their own, as the case of the nuclear family, it is known as a **neolocal residence.**

Another criterion for categorizing family structure is rules of descent. In American society, we recognize children as descending from both their mother's and father's kin group, and they may inherit from both lines. This type of system is called **bilateral descent.** A survey of some 250 societies found 30 percent in this category (Murdock, 1949). Forty percent of the societies in this survey followed the rule of **patrilineal descent,** in which people are considered members of their father's kin group only, and about 20 percent of the societies surveyed practiced **matrilineal descent,** in which kinship is traced through the female line only. Not surprisingly, matrilineal descent is often found with matrilocal residence, and patrilineal descent with patrilocal residence.

A final set of criteria for categorizing family structure are norms regarding who wields authority in the home. Power may be vested more in males **(patriarchy)** or in females **(matriarchy),** or it may be divided relatively equally between the two **(egalitarian authority).** Throughout history the predominant pattern has been patriarchy, the system found among the ancient Greeks, Romans, and Hebrews, as well as in most other societies. Despite legends of Amazon women, complete matriarchy has not been the norm in any society. The authority of women, however, varies from family to family, depending upon personalities and the relationship between the spouses. As a general rule, egalitarian patterns are becoming more prevalent in modern societies.

There is, however, a great deal of variation in family structure *within* large, complex societies like the United States. Less than half the American families today are "intact" nuclear families. With the high divorce rate we are seeing more and more blended families consisting of stepparents, stepchildren, and stepsiblings. In addition, various ethnic groups differ in family structure. Asian and Hispanic Americans, for instance, have lower divorce rates than white or black Americans. African-American children today are more likely to grow up in single-parent households and to live in an extended family than are white children (Ruggles, 1994a). Compared to white single parents, black single parents are more likely to be never-married than divorced. African-American families are also more likely to be headed by women than are families of other groups. Families among recent immigrants and the lower class tend to be larger than families of longtime and middle-class Americans.

Family structure varies over time as well as between and within cultures. No family pattern is etched in stone. In India, family structure has changed over time to accommodate the increasing legal rights accorded women. Women have gained the right to initiate divorce, for example, and the ancient custom of urging widows to throw themselves on their husbands' funeral pyre has been banned—though in both cases there are those who struggle against the changes. The opposite has taken place in West Africa. Traditional matriarchal patterns there gave women more equality than they have since enjoyed under colonialism or after independence. This is partly because new laws that followed European models tended to give men control of family property.

Over time, families in Western Europe have declined in size and become less patriarchal and less likely to be extended groupings. Families in America have also undergone a long-term decline in the number of family members living together. A declining birth rate contributes to that, as well as the fact that fewer aging parents are living with their adult children (Ruggles, 1994b). Finally, the traditional nuclear family grouping has taken a blow over time: in 1950, 63 percent of Americans lived in a nuclear family household, yet in 1993 only 19 percent lived in such households, though others still consider themselves members even though they lived apart (see Figure 11.1). We now turn to a consideration of what has happened to this type of family structure.

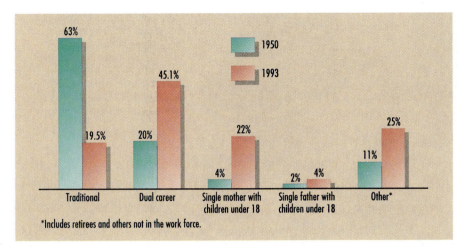

FIGURE 11.1 / American Family Structures, 1950 and 1993

Over a span of four decades the "traditional" family as a percentage of all family structures has dropped more than 40 percent—from 63 percent to 19.5 percent. The percentage of dual-career families has more than doubled in that time, and single-mother families have quintupled.

Source: U.S. Bureau of the Census, *Statistical Abstracts of the United States.* Washington, D.C.: US GPO, 1994.

THE NUCLEAR FAMILY

The Traditional Ideal

Beaver Cleaver comes home from school to his spick-and-span suburban home, where Mom provides him with milk and cookies and listens sympathetically to whatever minor complaints Beaver has about his life. Dad comes home from work and with his wise words magically provides solutions to any and all family problems. Welcome to the world of the nuclear family in the 1950s, as brought to us by countless reruns of TV sitcoms such as "Leave It to Beaver." Many Americans look nostalgically back on that lifestyle and contrast it to the "crises" we seem to face today: broken homes, soaring divorce rates, overworked families, gang violence, teen pregnancy, drug abuse, and so on. People wonder if there is any way to return to the "way things were."

But is this really the way things were? The TV sitcoms of the 1950s misrepresent a number of facts. First of all, the "traditional" family they portrayed was actually quite a new phenomenon in American society (Coontz, 1992). After World War II, more people got married at an earlier age than before. They also started having more babies, causing a baby boom. At the same time, cranking up the postwar economy produced many jobs in many different areas, leading to more mobility and the growth of suburbs around manufacturing sites. Wartime savings combined with a burst of prosperity allowed young families to buy their own homes and provide them with all sorts of modern conveniences. Extended family ties and roots in one locale lost favor. New values came into play: amusement, satisfaction in household roles, self-indulgence.

The 1950s sitcoms also gave a skewed picture of American social life. Most American families could not afford full participation in the consumerism represented by June Cleaver's washing machine and Hoover vacuum cleaner. At least one-quarter of Americans lived in poverty, and many families could not manage on Dad's salary alone (Coontz, 1992). The TV shows ignored such major factors as cultural diversity (the Hispanic gardener on "My Three Sons" was named Frank Smith), segregation, systematic violation of minority civil rights, low pay for "female" jobs, and the misery that lay beneath the facade of many "ideal" families. While there may have been fewer divorces in the 1950 than today, there were undoubtedly many more unhappily married people.

The point to remember as we consider the structure of the family today is that we should not be blinded to the flaws of the past and long for a "simpler" time. The traditional ideal was never the reality, nor is what we consider new today so very new. Pressures on the American family are of long standing. Americans themselves do not actually agree on what is the preferred form of family structure. A Gallup poll taken in 1993 asked if it is generally better for society if the man works and the woman is the homemaker: 26 percent strongly agreed and 37 percent strongly disagreed, with the rest evenly split between moderate agreement and moderate disagreement. An overwhelming majority approved of a

More ideal than real? While many Americans look longingly back at the perfect family life seen on television's Father Knows Best *(shown here) and* Leave It To Beaver, *these "fifties" families were less traditional—or typical—than we like to think.*

woman's holding a job, even if her husband is able to support her (*The Gallup Poll Monthly*, October 1993).

The Modern-Day Reality

Today's nontraditional families tend to be smaller, more inclusive, and more open to role variation than was yesterday's rigid ideal of a breadwinning husband, a stay-at-home wife, and their children. The types of families that we consider here are those in which both parents work outside the home, those in which grandparents play an active role, those in which parents and children of dissolved marriages are blended, and those with single parents.

Dual-Career Families

The full-time homemaker is becoming a rarity in the United States. Whereas in 1948 only 22 percent of married American women were employed outside the home, the proportion has now risen to 63 percent. Seventy-three percent of married women ages twenty-five to forty-four and 72 percent of mothers of school-age children work outside the home (U.S. Department of Labor, 1994).

When millions of married women took jobs outside the home during the 1960s and 1970s, most found only relatively low-paying, low-status jobs such as waitress, salesclerk, and bank teller. These jobs added to the family income, but they did not offer much opportunity for advancement. In most two-worker families, women's jobs took second place to men's. This was true not only of families in which men had high-status, high-paying careers (like law or business) but also of families in which men had blue-collar jobs; these, too, generally offered more pay, security, and rewards for seniority than did women's jobs. In recent years, however, **dual-career families** have become more common. These are families in which both husband and wife hold jobs that offer opportunities for advancement.

Dual-career families earn more than other families do, but they face their own particular challenges. For example, what happens when the wife or husband gets an offer for a promotion that involves transfer to another city? Child care and division of household chores can also become issues. Men today may be doing a little more around the house and women a little less, but the division is still lopsided. More employed women work a "second shift" at home after a full day at their jobs (Hochschild, 1989). One study found that employed mothers of children under the age of three put in up to 90 hours a week of combined work and child-care responsibilities (Scarr and Weinberg, 1986). Although both husbands and wives agree that unequal division of household labor is unfair, wives are more likely to cite it as a reason for marital troubles (Burris, 1991).

Dual-career families need child care for children too young to stay alone, and the arrangements parents make depend in large part on income (Frankel, 1991). Children from low-income families are most likely to be cared for by a relative or friend in a home setting, while children from higher-income families are more likely to be enrolled in organized group care (*Current Population Reports*, 1990b). More than half of preschool children in child care are looked after by nonfamily helpers in out-of-home facilities (APA Task Force on Day Care for Preschool Children, 1993). This trend is worldwide: 65 percent of four-year-olds in New York City, 80 percent in Beijing, and 95 percent in Tokyo are enrolled in preschool facilities (Tobin, Wu, and Davidson, 1989).

Some parents choose preschool to enrich their children's experience, not just for care. Evaluating the quality of day care depends on factors from cleanliness to the stimulation offered by activities to the attention provided by caretakers. But what about day care versus family care? Studies are inconclusive. High-quality day care can be helpful and is especially valuable to children without siblings and those whose home situations are problematic. Poor-quality day care can have harmful consequences for a child's social behavior, especially if that care starts at an early age and exceeds 20 hours per week (APA Task Force, 1993).

Even in the best of cases, day-care problems can arise. The caregiver may not show up; sickness may prevent the child from attending the day-care center; parents' and children's holiday and vacation schedules may not coincide. Generally it is the mother who stays home and misses work in these situations. As a result, her career is more likely than her husband's to be interrupted or stalled (Blau and Robins, 1989; Klerman and Leibowitz, 1990). Moreover, the fatigue, stress, and role conflict the mother experiences may adversely affect the quality of her interaction with her child (APA Task Force, 1993).

Multigenerational Families

The last century has witnessed a shift from extended family to nuclear family as the preferred living arrangement. Steven Ruggles (1994b) attributes this shift to a number of factors. First, education has become more important than inheritance in determining careers; as a result, fewer children are living in their parents' home in order to carry on a family business. Second, economic changes have brought about greater mobility. Americans think nothing of moving to another state to take a job, resulting in fewer ties to the parental base. Elderly Americans themselves are more prosperous than in generations past, so many of them can afford a retirement home in a sunny clime. Finally, a shift in values puts more emphasis on individualism and independence and less on family ties than in times past. For these various reasons, the trend is toward smaller households, whether these are nuclear families, just couples, or other variants. Despite media claims that "empty nests" are filling again as adult children return home, there is not much empirical evidence for this (White, 1994).

Grandparents may not be living with their grown children in an extended family, but they are not out of the picture. Far from it. Most family members enjoy closer, more affectionate ties with the older generations than was true when the grandparent lived in the middle of the family's daily stresses and turmoils (Cherlin, 1995). The amount of contact between grandparents and their offspring depends primarily on distance: the closer they live, the more contact. Another factor is age: younger grandparents are likely to be more involved with their grandchildren than are elderly ones. Grandparents also tend to be more important in the lives of their daughters than in the lives of their sons, especially if a daughter has been divorced (Aldous, 1995). Divorce of an adult child is fairly common in parents' experience, affecting about half of parents above age sixty (Spitze et al., 1994). Grandchildren help to keep parent–child relations close in these situations.

A companionate style of grandparenting, in which the grandparent and grandchild are pals, is increasing. In *The New American Grandparent* (1986), sociologists Andrew Cherlin and Frank Furstenberg report that about 50 percent of the grandparents they surveyed said that they had seen at least one of their grandchildren that day or the day before, and 70 percent had seen a grandchild within the past week. Unlike many parents today, grandparents typically have ample time to play with the children, read to them, help with their homework, or take them out. And, because older people are living longer, they stay close to their grandchildren longer. At the beginning of the century, a fifteen-year-old had a fifty-fifty chance of having two living grandparents; by the 1970s that chance had risen to nine out of ten (Cherlin, 1995).

In good health and with plenty of time to spare, many of today's grandparents enjoy close, active relationships with their grandchildren.

The longevity of aging parents and the often slow deterioration in their health may create pressures on their adult children, the so-called sandwich generation, caught between the needs of their own children and the needs of their parents. Conventional wisdom holds that the well-being of this beleaguered middle generation suffers from these responsibilities; however, a longitudinal study of multigenerational care has shown that taking on additional caregiving tasks has minimal effects on the adult children and that the troubles of the sandwich generation may be a myth (Loomis and Booth, 1995).

Unfortunately, not all older people are cherished members of their families. The abuse of elderly people by family members is on the rise in our society. A survey conducted by the U.S. Congress, House of Representatives, Select Committee on Aging (1990), found that at least 1.5 million elderly Americans, or one in twenty of the elderly population, are abused each year. Unreported cases make the actual number even higher. Elder abuse may take the form of physical assaults (including sexual abuse), neglect (withholding food, medical treatment, or personal care), financial abuse (theft or misuse of assets), or psychological abuse (such as threats of abandonment).

A study of abused and nonabused elderly people (Pillemer, 1986) found that it was not the stress of caring for physically impaired parents that brought about abuse, as is commonly believed. The critical difference between the two sets of families was that the abusers were dependent on the elders for housing, financial assistance, or other needs. The abusers responded with violence to their ongoing need for the aging parent, not to their parent's neediness. Two-thirds of the abusers in the study had mental or emotional problems or were alcoholics. There was no evidence that the abusers had been abused themselves, nor were they under chronic financial stress. The study suggests that the degree to which elderly Americans are at risk for abuse depends primarily on the characteristics of the caregivers.

Blended Families

Many divorced people remarry in this country, and about half of those who do are already parents (Bumpass, Sweet, and Martin, 1990). The result is the creation of **blended families,** also called stepfamilies. In 1992, over 11 percent of all American children were living with one biological parent and one stepparent (Cherlin and Furstenberg, 1994). Estimates are that a fourth of American children will live with a stepparent before reaching the age of sixteen (Miller and Moorman, 1989). By the year 2000, stepfamilies will very likely outnumber traditional nuclear families (Pill, 1990).

Blended families have brought about a new look at what kinship means (Cherlin and Furstenberg, 1994). Mere blood ties or the mere fact of marriage does not necessarily create a feeling of kinship. Building a relationship—seeing someone regularly, making connections, giving and receiving help—achieves kinship. This is not an easy task. In stepfamilies, kinship relations tend to be on a par with in-law relations; in fact, in France the word for *stepparent* (*beau-parent*) is the same as for *parent-in-law*.

The main reason kinship is so difficult to establish is that in a remarriage following a divorce, the stepparent is not moving into a vacant role. The stepchild still has a nonresident biological parent, so it's not immediately clear what the stepparent's role is to be (Schwebel, Fine, and Renner, 1991). Often stepparents have unrealistically high expectations of becoming an instant parent, entitled to all the love, acceptance, obedience, and respect that children owe a "real" parent. Research has shown that it can take years to make the adjustment (Cherlin and Furstenberg, 1994). The wise stepparent accepts the fact that he or she has only a limited license to parent and lets time take its course for the forging of bonds.

Several factors can ease the transition (Cherlin and Furstenberg, 1994). One is the age of the stepchildren. It is much easier for preschoolers to accept a stepparent as a "real" parent than for older children to do so. It is also easier if the stepchildren do not see their nonresident parent too often. But perhaps the most important factor is the quality of the relationship between the stepparent and the resident parent. If they can establish boundaries around themselves and work out a shared conception of how the family is to be managed, they are much more likely to create a successful stepfamily. Unfortunately, there are no generally accepted norms, no blueprints, for this endeavor.

Stepfathers have an easier time establishing relationships with their stepchildren than do stepmothers, who typically do not live with their stepchildren. "Stepfathers . . . often can fill a vacuum left by the departed biological father. Stepmothers, in contrast, must inhabit the space already occupied by the biological mother" (Cherlin and Furstenberg, 1994, p. 371).

As for the children, they often resent the intrusion of a stepparent into their lives and regard his or her efforts at closeness as phony. The remarriage also forces them to give up the fantasy that their biological parents will reconcile. Adolescents are particularly resentful of the addition of another person in their home at a time when they are trying to assert their independence. The stepparent and children may compete for the resident parent's attention and affection. Even when the relationship goes well, some children worry that they are betraying the nonresident parent. To further complicate matters, there are stepbrothers and stepsisters, stepgrandparents, and in-laws from previous marriages to contend with.

Single-Parent Families

Another increasingly common variation of the family is the single-parent family. These families are formed through divorce, separation, or death of a spouse or by having children while single. Between 1970 and 1993 there was more than a twofold increase in the proportion of American families with single parents (from roughly 13 percent of all families to 27 percent). Although two-thirds of single-parent families are white, the pattern is far more common among African-Americans. Sixty-four percent of African-American families with children include only one parent, compared with 23 percent of white families with children and 36 percent of Hispanic families with children (*Current Population Reports*, 1993a).

Birth outside of marriage is on the rise—from 4 percent of all births in 1950 to 30 percent in 1992 (National Center for Health Statistics, 1995b). Although the rates are significantly higher for blacks than for whites (68 percent as opposed to 23 percent), unwed parenthood is more strongly correlated with poverty than race (*Current Population Reports*, 1993a; Gringlas and Weinraub, 1995). In addition, like the TV character Murphy Brown, more middle-class white women are choosing this option; but while their numbers are rising rapidly, they remain a small fraction of single mothers. Rising rates of out-of-wedlock births reflect changes in culture; such births are much less stigmatized now than they were in the 1950s. This pattern has also contributed to changes in how social functions are met. Where fathers do not support their children (and mothers are

SOCIOLOGY AND PUBLIC DEBATES

Teenage Pregnancies: What Can Be Done?

The United States has the highest teenage pregnancy rate of any industrialized democratic nation, even though American teenagers are no more sexually active than those in Canada or Europe (Miller and Moore, 1990). Every year more than a million American teenagers become pregnant. In 1991, 530,000 teenagers gave birth; of these, 11,000 were *fourteen or younger* (*Statistical Abstracts,* 1994). The majority of teenage mothers do not get married (Coontz, 1992).

Some teenagers are at higher risk for unplanned parenthood than others. Sociologist Karen Pittman (1993) identifies four risk factors: being sexually active early, being African-American or Hispanic, living in a poor neighborhood with segregated schools, having low school achievement and aspirations. Robert Plotnick (1992) also finds that unfavorable attitudes toward school and low educational expectations increase the likelihood of teen pregnancy and childbearing. Overall, one in five poor young women with below-average skills becomes a mother, compared with fewer than one in twenty who are financially and academically better off (Pittman, 1993).

Teenage parents have become an object of intense social policy debate because they have so few options, tend to rely on state assistance, and raise children who are likely to be dysfunctional both in the home and in school.

THE DEBATE

The debate surrounding unwed teen parenthood centers not on whether one favors the phenomenon or not (most people do not) but on how to understand it and what, if anything, to do about it.

On one side are those who think that public policy encourages unwed teenagers to have children. The welfare program known as Aid to Families with Dependent Children (AFDC) has historically provided financial assistance to unmarried mothers on an escalating scale: the more children, the more benefits. Many politicians today believe that this program serves as a disincentive to marriage and an incentive to childbearing. They believe that the only way to break the cycle of pregnancy is take away the monetary incentives to give birth; they want to revamp the welfare system to reduce benefits, reward "responsible" behavior, institutionalize "family values," and promote work.

Others, however, argue that welfare policy actually has little or no effect on unwed motherhood; in fact, the states with the *lowest* AFDC benefits are generally the ones with the *highest* rates of nonmarital childbearing (Harris, 1996). Reducing welfare will only shove impoverished teenage mothers further into poverty and increase the health risks of their children. In the view of these social observers, it is not welfare policy that needs to be changed but rather educational policy. Children need to be taught sex education early, so that they are familiar with birth control techniques before they become sexually active. Those who are sexually active need access to birth control devices and advice.

Proposals for sex education or provision of birth control, however, offend many on the political and religious right. They believe that education in sexual techniques only encourages sexual activity, and they are also vehemently opposed to abortion as a means of birth control. Advocates of choice in abortion counter that the religious right disapproves of unmarried pregnant teenagers without offering them a way out of their dilemma.

ANALYSIS

Many sociological elements underlie the issue of teen pregnancy and single parenting. The fact that it is concentrated among African-Americans and the very poor indicates structural dimensions. Unemployment rates are highest among young black men in the inner-city communities. They are not in a position to marry and support the girls they get pregnant. Pregnancy may not seem objectionable to teenage girls who live in

relatively poor), the children's economic needs are likely to be met by government or charity. Both the children and their mothers are likely to become long-term welfare recipients unless new social institutions (like free day care) perform some functions formerly handled by families. Teenage single mothers are especially vulnerable to poverty and welfare dependence; accordingly, they are the object of much debate about social policy (see the Sociology and Public Debates box). It remains to be seen whether changes in welfare in the United States will help or hurt poor people who are not functionally integrated in society.

Comparing all types of mother-only households with two-parent families, Sara McLanahan and Karen

bleak economic circumstances and feel there are few options open to them. In other words, where structural poverty reigns, teenagers see little to lose in unwed parenthood.

They may even see something to gain. The cultural values of the white middle class cause that group to disapprove of teen childbearing, but lower-class teenage girls may regard a baby as a source of pride, a sign of womanhood. In their experience there may not be many realistic role models for choosing not to be pregnant and for staying in school. Culture shapes how different groups view the issue. Within the African-American subculture, for example, teenage childbearing is widely accepted; it does not meet with the moral objections found in much of the rest of American society. White Americans may look on high rates of teen pregnancy as a sign of crisis in the black community, but blacks may see such rates as the result of a family structure shaped by slavery, systematic discrimination, and economic dislocations over the last two hundred years.

> If a teenager has evidence that an education will lead the way out of poverty, that teenager will be less likely to drop out of school and raise a child with whatever help the state provides.

Functional relationships also play a part. Because unwed teenage mothers are concentrated in inner cities or rural areas that lack resources for economic opportunity, schooling, may seem irrelevant. It is hard to keep students in school when the link to eventual jobs seems tenuous, at best. Many teenage single mothers depend on their own mothers or other female relatives as well as on meager welfare benefits, knitting them in functional interdependence. In a larger sense, however, this interdependence is dysfunctional, since it is forced on them by conditions of urban blight and rural neglect and the pressures of poverty.

A teenage girl becomes a single teenage mother through a series of actions (and nonactions). First, of course, there is the sex act by which she becomes pregnant, which in many cases involves a decision not to use birth control. Then, there is the decision not to terminate the pregnancy. Finally, there is a decision not to get married. These actions are largely determined by the structural and cultural conditions outlined above.

Another factor underlying these actions has to do with power. For many teenage girls, especially those with little to hope for in their lives, the act of having a baby is a sign of power, of taking control of an aspect of their lives and affirming adult status. Girls may also hope that the child will give them power over the father, although this is not often the case. Boys have the upper hand in this power game because they find it easier to walk away. But boys, too, may view the birth of their child as a sign of power—showing their potency, their ability to sow their seed and leave their mark like a living graffiti signature. Power gets exercised by the state also: how much access is provided to family service agencies, how much welfare is provided, and how much child care, if any, is provided.

What does this analysis tell us can be done about the problem? First, it suggests that though education and availability of birth control may influence teen birth rates, there is a deeper issue. At bottom, the answer seems to lie in giving these youngsters some alternatives they would value—"something to lose" by becoming teenage parents. If a teenager has evidence that an education will lead the way out of poverty, that teenager will be less likely to drop out of school and raise a child with whatever help the state provides. Student loans and job-training programs are tangible means of giving hope; family planning services and improved access to birth control are more likely to reduce pregnancy than are programs that focus on changing attitudes or values (Plotnick, 1993).

Booth (1989) found significant differences in economic well-being, levels of stress, and parent–child relations. Almost one in two single-mother families lives below the poverty line, compared with one in ten two-parent families (see also Pittman, 1993). This difference can be explained by the fact that women earn less than men on average, yet they bear most of the economic cost of raising children when unmarried, separated, or divorced. Many women do not get child support, and of those that do, many get less than the full payment.

Single mothers report being less satisfied with their lives and more worried than do married mothers or women with no children (McLanahan and Booth,

1989). Divorced mothers, in particular, are more likely to be depressed than are married women and married or single men. This psychological vulnerability is probably related to high levels of stress. In many cases, single mothers are coping with a change in residence, a new job or an increase in working hours, and new social relationships, as well as worries about their finances and children.

Much has been written about the single-mother family in poor, black, inner-city ghettoes. These *matrifocal* (mother-focused) families are composed of a mother, her dependent children, one or more of her grown daughters and their children, and sometimes other relatives, such as a grandmother or an aunt. Here the mother is the center of the household, with help from other adult females. Some observers see the absence of intact nuclear families in the black lower class as evidence of family pathology (Edelman, 1987). Others, however, contend that matrifocal families are a positive adaptation to the absence of male providers. These males do not necessarily want to shirk their roles as fathers and husbands: generally unemployed or underpaid, they drift to the outskirts of family life to avoid facing their failure day in and day out (Taylor, Chatters, Tucker, and Lewis, 1990).

While most single parents are mothers (over 7 million in 1993), the number of single fathers with primary responsibility for their children is now considerable (1.32 million) (*Current Population Reports,* 1993a). One reason is that sex roles have relaxed, making child-rearing an acceptable activity for men. Also, many men consciously strive to be less like their own fathers, who were preoccupied with work and distant from their children. Finally, changes in the divorce laws have made the courts more likely to grant joint custody or even sole custody to the father.

One survey of single fathers found that the most difficult problem for them, as for single mothers, was balancing the demands of work and child care (Greif, 1985). Most of them found they had to choose between their work role and their parent role. The more children there were, the younger the children, and the less established the father was in his career, the greater were the problems. Most of the fathers cut back on the time spent at work; sixty-six of the 1,136 surveyed changed jobs, and forty-three were fired.

The number of children living in single-parent homes is huge (Bumpass and Sweet, 1989b). Over half of all children born between 1970 and 1984, and more than 80 percent of African-American young-sters, will spend time in a single-parent family. For most, this will not be a brief experience. Only 36 percent of children who are born to unwed mothers or whose parents separate will become part of a two-parent family within five years.

Growing up in a single-parent family, black or white and regardless of how adaptive, is associated with numerous problems. Compared with children in two-parent families, children of single parents are more likely to have lower educational goals and complete fewer years of school, to have lower earnings, to be poor in young adulthood, to marry and bear children at an early age, to get divorced, and to become involved in delinquency, alcohol abuse, and drugs (Pittman, 1993).

Identifying cause and effect is tricky. Many problems of single-parent families can be traced to their poverty rather than to their family structure. When researchers compare families that have similar standards of living, the differences between single-parent and two-parent families are far smaller (though they do not disappear entirely). Another question is whether the single family's problems can be attributed to the strains of getting divorced (or never marrying) or to preexisting conditions that explain why the parent never married or why the marriage broke up. Finally, is single parenthood a problem in and of itself, or do single parents just have more problems than married parents do? To study this issue, Marcy Gringlas and Marsha Weinraub (1995) compared a sample of mostly white, middle-class, middle-aged women who chose to be single mothers with a comparable group of married mothers to see what effect, if any, single parenting has on the child in a home without a history of marital discord or dissolution. They found no problems in preschoolers in single-mother homes, but they did find problems among preadolescents in such homes in their academic, behavioral, and social competence; the researchers related these problems to maternal stress and the lack of social supports for the single-parent family. Thus, Gringlas and Weinraub suggest reframing the question in single-parent studies from "Is one parent enough?" to "What must one parent alone have in order to be successful?"

Smaller Families

American families have been getting smaller. In 1960 the average family size was 3.67 persons; in 1993 that number was down to 3.16 (*Current Population Reports,* 1993a). In 1990 the number of childless married couples (both those who had never had children and those whose children had left home) outnumbered couples with children under age eighteen living at home, 27.8 million to 24.5 million (*Current Population Reports,* 1990).

One reason for the increase in families without children at home is today's longer life span. A couple who marry young and stay married can now expect almost fifty years of togetherness, as compared with only about thirty-five years for those who married in 1920. A much smaller proportion of married life now needs to be devoted to child-rearing.

Many women are marrying later in life and having correspondingly fewer children. For some, the cause is infertility, which becomes more of a problem as women get into their mid-thirties. For others, it is a matter of choice. Americans seem to prefer smaller families these days. In 1972, 41 percent of Americans thought two children the ideal number; by 1989, 55 percent thought so. Those favoring four or more children declined from 31 percent to 8 percent (Wood, 1990).

Many more women today are childless than in times past. While only about 10 percent of women born in 1940 have no children, more than 30 percent of those born since 1954 are expected to remain childless. Some factors that have contributed to this trend include the development of more effective contraceptives, the availability of abortion, the dual-career household, and changing attitudes toward family life. Women who decide to remain childless tend to be white, urban-dwelling, employed, financially secure, not devoutly religious, and highly educated. Education has a particularly important role in childbearing decisions. Women who complete college or graduate school not only postpone childbearing in those years but also delay it further to establish their careers. The longer childbearing is postponed, the less likely it is that a woman will bear children (Pebley and Bloom, 1982).

MARRIAGE AND DIVORCE

Marriage may be defined as a socially recognized union between two or more people that involves sexual and economic rights and duties. In providing the framework for raising a family, marriage serves a crucial function for society, but it also benefits individuals. It provides companionship, stabilizes relationships, and softens life's blows. Marriage is associated with lower levels of alcohol and cigarette consumption, higher earnings, and longer life span than is true for unmarried people (Lillard and Waite, 1995). Married men tend to experience these benefits immediately, while a married woman taps in as the marriage progresses and her financial well-being increases.

As we shall see, no society leaves the choice of marriage partner and the age at first marriage completely to personal preference. Likewise, divorce decisions are influenced by social forces.

Deciding Whom to Marry

Even in the United States, where most people feel we are free to marry whomever we wish, powerful social forces push us into marriage with an "appropriate" partner (Turner and Helms, 1988). Like members of all other societies, Americans have norms defining the range of acceptable mates from whom a person can choose. Some of these norms require that people marry *within* their own social group (tribe, nationality, religion, race, community, and so forth). These are called rules of **endogamy.** Other norms require that people marry *outside* a particular group to which they belong. These are called rules of **exogamy.** Often these rules operate as a circle within a circle. Rules of exogamy bar marriage within a small inner circle (such as one's own close relatives), while rules of endogamy establish an outer circle that defines how far afield people can go in search of a mate (not outside one's own race or social class, for instance).

Arranged Marriages

> Stupid and dangerous as it seems in retrospect, I went into my marriage at 25 without being in love. Three years later, I find myself relishing my relationship with this brilliant, prickly man. . . .

This is how Shoba Narayan describes her arranged marriage to a fellow Indian (*New York Times,* May 4, 1995, p. C1). Shoba, a graduate of an American college, had thought she had bought into the American system of individualism. She was determined to fall in love and marry someone who was not from India.

But she had tried love and found that it did not sustain a relationship. So when her parents offered to find a "suitable" match for her, she decided to give it a try. The first step was to match her horoscope with that of a potential husband within her religion, caste, and social class. Next, her parents met with his parents to verify their compatibility. The final step was up to the couple. After a brief courting period, Shoba agreed to the young man's proposal. The first two years were a "getting to know you" period, after which the young couple found themselves gradually falling in love.

Shoba's successful arranged marriage is not a fluke. Arranged marriages have a high success rate (or at least a high rate of lasting without divorce): 90 percent in Iran, 95 percent in India, and similar high percentages among Brooklyn's Hasidic Jews and Muslims in Turkey and Afghanistan (*New York Times,* May 4, 1995, p. C8). Societies find arranged marriages desirable for a number of reasons. In those places where newlyweds become part of an extended family, the family has a heavy stake in the type of spouse chosen. The person must share the family's ideas about what is good and proper, as well as pull his or her weight in the household. In such situations, intense emotional attachments can have a disruptive effect, imperiling customary family relationships and practices. Finally, in many of these societies a substantial amount of wealth is exchanged when a couple gets married (as a bride price or dowry), so both families have a strong interest in ensuring that the marriage lasts. Arranged marriages are most often found in societies where elders control land or other resources on which future generations depend for their livelihood. The elders have more power over young people than is the case in most Western societies, where people choose their own careers.

Still, marriage in the United States is not left entirely to free choice. Parents influence their children's choices in a variety of informal, sometimes invisible, ways: the neighborhoods they live in, the schools they choose, the religious community they join, their sense of "our kind" and "their kind," even what they eat and how they dress. All these factors help to determine the type of people their children will meet, choose as friends, and later date. Jewish-American parents, for example, do not arrange marriages for their children, but many make sure that their children meet other Jewish children and develop a strong sense of ethnic identity.

Marrying for Love

Within the informal constraints it imposes on mate selection, American society firmly believes romantic love is an important basis for marriage. In fact, American culture idealizes and exalts romance (Rougemont, 1939/1990; Luhmann, 1986). It is the main theme of our popular songs, movies, and TV shows. Entire industries—from bridal magazines to dating services and honeymoon hotels—are built on the notion of romance.

Our culture's commitment to romantic love has its advantages. Love helps weaken the ties to a young couple's families of orientation, making them more willing to move into their own independent world. There, they are free to love each other without creating tensions, jealousies, and competition among other household members. Since an independent living arrangement requires the married couple to depend heavily on each other, romantic love is a more reliable motivation for their mutual support than a sense of duty would be.

As a basis for marriage, however, romance does have its limitations. In some ways it conflicts with the daily demands of married life. Romance thrives on mystery, distance, and uncertainty, whereas daily married life is anything but mysterious. Marriage is a business partnership as much as a fairy-tale romance: it involves compromise, specialization and division of labor, financial arrangements, and communication. By exalting romance, our society may be undermining the very relationships it tries to promote: stable, enduring, child-producing marriages.

Deciding When and Whether to Marry

Just as societies have norms regarding whom a person should marry, so they also have norms regarding the appropriate age for first marriage. In parts of rural India, for example, an estimated 40,000 to 50,000 children, many under the age of seven, marry on the first and second days of the full moon cycle in May. Although child marriages are officially outlawed in India, the timing is considered auspicious in the Hindu religion, and many parents are willing to risk a fine or imprisonment to take advantage of it. In any case, child marriages are often mutually convenient for Indian families; the bride's parents do not have to support her very long, and the groom's par-

Marry first, love later. In cultures that practice arranged marriages, couples are paired by their parents. It is hoped that such unions will result in the harmonious and mutually beneficial joining of two families. Here, a Hindu bride and groom share their wedding feast.

ents gain a dowry and what amounts to an unpaid slave (*New York Times*, May 15, 1994). In the United States, by contrast, child marriage has never been the norm. The minimum legal age for marrying (set by each state) is usually sixteen with parental consent and eighteen without it.

Most Americans do not choose to marry at the minimum age, and have never done so. For example, many people imagine that Americans used to marry young, but in 1890 the median age at first marriage was twenty-six for men and twenty-two for women (*Current Population Reports,* 1993a). Median ages then dropped until the 1950s, when they hit an all-time low: twenty-two for men and twenty for women. From that time the ages have increased; in 1993, the average age for a man to marry was twenty-six and the average age for a woman, twenty-four, an all-time high. The gap in the ages of men and women has closed since the nineteenth century, in part because of the fact that the sexes are having more common life experiences, such as years of schooling and career paths.

In the United States, first-time marriages are going out of style. In 1988 almost half of all marriages were actually remarriages, 14 percent higher than in 1970 (DeWitt, 1992). About 40 percent of the remarriages

united two divorced persons; in about half the marriages, one of the couple was marrying for the first time; and in the remaining 11 percent one or both of the partners were widowed.

Of course, not everyone gets married at all. Some people never find a spouse, some do not even want a spouse, and some couples choose to live together in lieu of institutionalized marriage.

Staying Single

Despite the fact that singlehood was quite common in the eighteenth and nineteenth centuries, for both women and men, the idea gradually took hold in this century that a woman who remained a spinster was an object of pity. In 1957, at a time when marriage rates were climbing, 80 percent of Americans who responded to a survey believed that a woman who stayed unmarried must be "sick," "neurotic," or "immoral." Today, only a minority of Americans take such a negative view. In one survey, only a third of young adults agreed that "It is better to be married than to go through life single." A quarter disagreed, and the rest were uncertain (Bumpass, Sweet, and Cherlin, 1989).

Reflecting these changes in attitudes, singlehood among men and women under the age of thirty-five has risen sharply. Single adults in the United States now number about 72.6 million, of whom 42.3 million have never been married and 23.6 million live alone (*Current Population Reports*, 1993a). This increase can be attributed to a number of social and economic trends: the postponement of marriage, the rise in the divorce rate (about a fourth of adults living alone are separated or divorced), career breakthroughs for women and easing of credit discrimination against them (giving financial independence), and the growing independence of young people from their parents.

The proportion of African-American women who never marry is particularly high. It has increased from about 9 percent for those born in the late 1930s to 22 percent for those born in the early 1950s (compared with 4 percent and 7 percent of white women the same ages). Some of the reasons for this difference have to do with social structure. Because of the higher rates of early death and imprisonment for young African-American men, black women face a "marriage squeeze." In particular, black men in steady jobs are in short supply. Faced with the prospect of a husband who is less able to support her than her extended family is, a young black women may be more likely to decide to remain single. Other reasons are cultural. In general, African-Americans attach less stigma to bearing children out of wedlock than do many other ethnic groups. This makes the desire for children less of a motivation for marriage among blacks.

Of late, however, there is another group that does not view marriage as a necessary vehicle for childbearing and raising a family: older, college-educated working women. Between 1982 and 1992, the birth rate among never-married women who worked in a professional or managerial capacity almost tripled (Siegel, 1995). In a study of a sample of these women, Judith Siegel (1995) concluded that while some of them were unable to find a husband, others never looked very hard for "Mr. Right." They simply wanted a family, felt the time was right, and had the financial independence to follow through on their decision. It appears that many women today find barriers to marriage less significant than increased opportunities to raise a child outside of marriage.

For some people, then, singlehood is imposed by circumstances, while for others it is a deliberate, conscious choice. Those who choose it tend to value their independence over the advantages of married life. In any case, with the rise of a singles' subculture, being single today does not necessarily mean being alone.

Cohabitation

In 1993, 3.5 million households consisted of unmarried couples—over five times more than in 1960 (*Current Population Reports*, 1993a). This increase in **cohabitation** began among college students in the 1960s and early 1970s and then gradually spread to other segments. Today a cohabitor may be young or old; never-married or divorced, separated, or widowed; affluent or poor. Almost half the American population has cohabited at some time by their early thirties, and a majority of marriages since 1985 were preceded by cohabitation (Nock, 1995). But cohabitation is no longer just a stage on the way to marriage; increasingly, it is taking the place of marriage (or remarriage).

One reason for the increase in cohabitation is cultural: The norms governing sexual relationships have changed. Not so long ago, couples who were living together usually hid the fact from their families and landlords. However, the moral imperative to marry and the idea that marriage is a prerequisite for sexual relations or even parenthood have faded (Bumpass, 1990; Thornton, 1989).

Cohabitation may also have increased as a functional adaptation to the high divorce rate and the challenges facing married couples today. Many young people look at the number of failing marriages and decide to try living together before making a legal commitment; eight out of ten young people who say they expect to cohabit give this as their primary reason (Bumpass, 1990). For many cohabiting couples, then, living together is part of the courtship process, a prelude to marriage. However, only about 50 percent of these couples end up getting married, and they are less likely to stay married than are couples who married without first living together. Research suggests that their relationships fail because cohabitors are less committed to marriage to begin with and more likely to hold unconventional family values than are other couples (Booth and Johnson, 1988; Bumpass, 1990; Bumpass and Sweet, 1989a; Nock, 1995).

About 10 percent of cohabiting couples stay together without getting married. For these couples cohabitation is a long-term alternative to marriage, a way to achieve some of the functions of a family without participating in the institutions of society that sanctify and legalize marriage. The high risk of divorce and the complications of stepfamily life involved in remarriage probably contribute to this trend toward deinstitutionalization of marriage (Cherlin and Furstenberg, 1994). These unmarried couples often have children and may be indistinguishable from married parents except for the absence of formal institutional recognition. However, it is that difference which may account for the fact that cohabitors report lower levels of happiness, less commitment to their relationships, and more problems with their parents than do married individuals (Nock, 1995). Cohabitation does not yet have the institutional status of marriage, with its strong, consensual norms, formalized union, and enforced intimacy that intensifies commitment.

The increase in cohabitation has had structural *consequences* as well. Families have had to come up with new definitions of kin networks and lines of inheritance, and governments have had to devise new rules for welfare eligibility and entitlement to give married couples and cohabiting couples equivalent rights

(Ramsoy, 1994). One type of cohabiting couple, however, has not been treated equivalently: homosexuals. Most states and religious bodies withhold recognition of gays and lesbians, even though they often life together in stable relationships and may even raise children. At this point only a few countries and a handful of American municipalities permit homosexuals to register their partnerships and receive benefits.

Deciding to Divorce

Nine out of ten Americans get married at least once, but many of these couples do not live together happily ever after. Current trends suggest that close to two-thirds of new marriages will end in divorce (Martin and Bumpass, 1989). Nearly 32 percent of couples who divorce will do so before their fifth anniversary and about 63 percent before their tenth (National Center for Health Statistics, 1995a). Since the nineteenth century the proportion of marriages ended by death of a spouse has declined, while the proportion ended by divorce has increased, more or less steadily. Divorce rates climbed in the 1960s and 1970s, reached a peak in the early 1980s, and have

While they cannot legally marry, gay and lesbian couples can enjoy rituals that are similar to marriage ceremonies. Whether American society should officially recognize such unions remains a hotly debated issue.

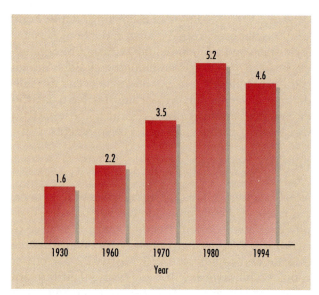

FIGURE 11.2 / Divorce Rate per 1,000 People in the United States, 1930–1994

Divorce rates climbed steeply from the 1930s to the 1980s, but they have declined slightly in the last decade.

Source: U.S. Department of Health and Human Services, National Center for Health Statistics. *Vital Statistics of the United States.*

dropped slightly since then (see Figure 11.2). Still, the U.S. divorce rate remains high compared with the rates in earlier eras and in other societies. Rates in Italy, Israel, and Japan are, for example, much lower (White, 1990).

Explaining the U.S. Divorce Rate

Americans often cite alcoholism and drug abuse, infidelity, physical and emotional abuse, disagreements about gender roles, financial problems, and sexual incompatibility as reasons for divorce. But these personal difficulties do not explain the whole increase in divorce *rates*. To understand that, we "need to examine change in the social institutions that structure individual experience" (White, 1990, p. 904).

One important change is in the law. It used to be that the sole grounds for divorce were adultery or cruelty, but now it is much easier to get a divorce. Recent "no-fault" divorce laws permit "irreconcilable differences" and "irremediable breakdown" of the marriage as grounds. All that is required is for one partner to want a divorce. Neither party is deemed guilty and neither is punished. How much

the legal changes are cause or effect in terms of the high divorce rate is difficult to say: increases in divorce pointed to the need for more liberal laws, which in turn eased the entire process (Furstenberg, 1994).

Gender-role changes have also had an effect. The entry of millions of women into the workforce has taken wives and mothers out of the home, reducing their traditional domestic roles and giving them the potential for financial independence. The mere fact that a woman has a job does not cause divorce, but a woman who can support herself is less likely to remain in a troubled marriage than is a dependent wife. Again, cause and effect are difficult to sort out (Bumpass, 1990). While women with independent incomes may feel freer to leave an unhappy marriage, a high divorce rate may prompt women to enter the job market in the first place to prepare themselves in the event of divorce.

Cultural factors are related to these gender-role changes. Values have shifted from a philosophy of self-sacrifice for the good of the family to an emphasis on self-fulfillment, autonomy, personal happiness, and personal growth (Cherlin, 1995). Marriage has become more couple-oriented and less child-oriented. If the principal reason for getting married today is to satisfy one's personal and psychological needs through love, then there is less social and cultural pressure to stay together "for the children's sake" when those needs are not met.

The trends feeding the high divorce rate seem clear, but what explanation is there for the *decline* in the divorce rate in the last decade or so? Frank Furstenberg (1994) attributes this drop to a pattern of postponed marriage (for schooling or economic reasons), a reduction in premarital pregnancy (resulting in fewer ill-considered marriages), an aging population (meaning that a larger proportion of married couples have passed through the high-risk years for divorce), and growing rates of cohabitation (many cohabiting couples in effect "divorce" before marrying, and some choose to stay together without ever marrying).

The result of most of these trends is that marriage has become deinstitutionalized. Instead of a lifetime obligation, supported by a web of formal laws and informal norms, marriage today is more a matter of personal preference, "a voluntary relationship that individuals can make or break at will" (Poponoe, 1990, p. 43).

Divorce rates do decline over the life course. Is that related to marital happiness or other factors?

Lynn White and Alan Booth (1991) take note of research that shows that marital happiness is greatest in the first few years of marriage and drops thereafter. They suggest that the longer a marriage lasts the more barriers there are to its dissolution (children, home ownership, shared social networks) and the fewer attractive alternatives there are (such as remarriage prospects). A couple's marital unhappiness must outweigh these obstacles in order for them to decide to divorce.

Who Gets Divorced?

Sociological research suggests that some marriages are more prone to divorce than others (Booth and White, 1980; Huber and Spitze, 1980; Leek and Pearson, 1991; White, 1990; Yoder and Nichols, 1980). The likelihood of divorce is highest when:

- The husband and wife live in an urban area.

- They both work, but their incomes are not high.

- They married early.

- They have not been married long.

- The wife has egalitarian attitudes about division of labor in the home and the husband does not.

- Neither husband nor wife has strong religious convictions.

- Both husband and wife are liberal in their attitudes.

- Both husband and wife are rather pessimistic about life.

- One or both have parents who are divorced.

African-American couples are 20 to 30 percent more likely to divorce than white couples (National Center for Health Statistics, 1995a). Marriages for black couples typically last a little longer than white marriages, but that may be because black couples separate for a longer time before divorcing. Conversely, Hispanics and Asians are less likely to divorce than other Americans.

Having children appears to have mixed effects on a marriage (Waite and Lillard, 1991). Marital stability tends to increase when the couple has one preschool-age child, but the odds of divorce tend to increase when the children are older or were born before the parents got married.

None of these factors alone, nor even all of them together, make divorce inevitable. As they accumulate, however, the statistical likelihood increases that the marriage will eventually be dissolved. No group is immune. For example, the Catholic church imposes strong sanctions against divorce, yet Catholics in this country are as likely to divorce as non-Catholics are (Bumpass, Martin, and Sweet, 1991).

The Impact of Divorce

Both men and women suffer when they divorce, but women are the biggest losers (Wallerstein and Kelly, 1980). Part of the reason has to do with social structure. As noted earlier, women tend to earn less income than men and usually retain custody of the children. Child support payments from the father are often significantly less than the cost of raising a child and typically are very difficult to collect. After a divorce, many women experience a dramatic decrease in their standard of living, while men usually see an improvement in theirs (Holden and Smock, 1991). Women are less likely than men to remarry (Cherlin and Furstenberg, 1994) and thus less likely to improve their economic situation through this avenue.

Culture also plays a part in the outcome of divorce. When a man is divorced, his primary role, defined in terms of employment, remains unchanged. In contrast, women have to develop new lives as single parents. They must enter the job market, often for the first time and often at the low-paying entry level where they may be supervised by much younger workers. At the same time they must juggle the responsibilities of home and work.

In a divorce, one or both of the parents want out of a marriage, but the children rarely want their parents to separate. That makes the breakup particularly traumatic for children. The first year or two after the divorce constitute a critical period during which many short-run problems show up: acting out, anger, depression, behavioral problems in school (Cherlin, 1995). Typically, in that time the custodial parent (generally the mother) is undergoing the stress of the marital split, needing to find employment, and often moving—to a new town, to a smaller house, into parents' home. Thus, at a time when parenting is diminished, the child must adjust to jarring transitions, including in some cases a new school and new set of friends.

Most children resume normal development after the initial crisis period, but some suffer long-term effects from a divorce. In their study of sixty middle-class families over a period of eighteen years, Judith Wallerstein and Joan Kelly found that as young adults the children of a divorce exhibited pervasive unhappiness and loneliness and reluctance to make a commitment to a partner (Wallerstein and Blakeslee, 1989). Another study has found that marital disruption increases the likelihood that male offspring will end up with a lower occupational status than their fathers (Biblarz and Raftery, 1993). Two factors seem to account for this disparity: the stresses and diminished income in the single-parent family and the loss of socialization by the father in the home. It has also been found that children in single-parent families are more than twice as likely to drop out of high school than are children in two-parent families (Cherlin, 1995). The chances of dropping out increase if the divorce results in a move, uprooting a support system that may have helped to offset the pains of a parental split.

More and more children are suffering the instability of *multiple* divorces. As families break up, reform, and break up again, these children often find themselves overwhelmed with new sets of stepparents, stepsisters and stepbrothers, and in-law relations that come and go. These revolving-door relationships only intensify the problems that crop up in the one-time divorce.

As demoralizing and disruptive as divorce is for children, it is well to keep in mind that the child who lives in an intact home that continually brews tension is probably not better off and may even suffer worse problems. Moreover, not all children of divorce experience the same problems or to the same extent. The long-term picture suggests that while children of a divorce do have a higher risk of encountering bad experiences later in life, most of them do not undergo such problems (Cherlin, 1995).

VIOLENCE IN THE FAMILY

From the time we are children we are taught that strangers are the source of danger and the family is the source of safety. In fact, the opposite is often true: Home is among the most violent of places, and our own family members are the people usually most dangerous to us (Gelles, 1983; Lincoln and Straus, 1985; Steinmetz and Straus, 1974).

Why is the family so prone to violence? One reason is that people make a large emotional investment in family relationships. As a result, petty disagreements can escalate into major conflicts. Another reason is the power differential within the family. A husband is usually larger and stronger than his wife; both parents are bigger and stronger than their young children. Physical aggression becomes a way to assert control in family relationships.

A third factor is cultural. Americans tend to approve of physical aggression—in sports and in movies and television programs, for example. Indeed, we are more accepting of violence in the family than in other social groups. Many Americans still believe it is normal for brothers to fight, understandable for a husband to lose his temper and hit his wife, and necessary for parents to physically punish their children. Fourth, the isolation of nuclear families makes violence in the home less visible and less subject to social control. At the same time the cultural value we place on a family's privacy makes outside authorities reluctant to intervene. Finally, family violence reflects entrenched cultural attitudes toward those who are its main victims—children and women. Predictably, attitudes vary across cultures and across time.

Child Abuse

Is spanking a child an abusive act? The Swedes think so; their government makes it a crime to spank or hit a child. However, a Gallup Poll taken in 1994 found that two-thirds of Americans agreed that a "good hard spanking" was sometimes necessary to discipline a child (*The Gallup Poll Monthly*, May 1994, p. 19). But even on this point Americans show some ambivalence: About the same percentage would report a parent who repeatedly spanked or slapped a child as an abuser. Support for spanking is found in all parts of the United States, but feelings are strongest in the South (Flynn, 1994).

While there may be room for debate about milder forms of punishment, most people agree about what constitutes the more serious forms of child abuse—physical acts that result in bruises, head injuries, burns, fractures, and the like. Although less obvious and dramatic, child neglect—failure to provide a child with adequate food, clothing, shelter, medical care, or supervision—is even more widespread (Green, 1991). The U.S. Department of Health and Human Services (1990) estimates that in 1989, at least 1,200 children and perhaps as many as 5,000 died because of abuse or neglect, and more than 160,000 were seriously harmed. About 2.4 million reports of suspected child maltreatment were filed that year, of which 918,000 had been confirmed by 1992—double the number of decade earlier.

It is not known if this dramatic increase is due to a real rise in the incidence of child abuse or to a greater willingness to report incidents. According to the 1994 Gallup Poll, one out of every seven Americans reported having been punched, kicked, choked, or even more seriously abused by a parent while growing up. Yet in a survey taken nine years earlier, only one out of every fifty parents admitted to such abuse of their children. In general, victim reports are more trustworthy than parental admissions, but even victim memories have been found to be suspect in some cases. Children reporting on abusive acts can be especially vulnerable to leading questions and to tailoring their stories to what they think the interviewer wants to hear.

According to the sociologists Richard Gelles and Murray Straus (1988; Gelles, 1995), the typical child abuser is a young single parent who was married for less than ten years (or not at all) and had a child before the age of eighteen. Often the person is plagued by money worries, has recently experienced other stresses (such as divorce or the death of a family member), and has few friends or relatives in the community. In many cases, abusive parents were victims of or witnesses to family violence when they were young.

While the abuse of young children is most likely to be reported, teenagers are also frequent victims, and their parents give similar reasons. They are demanding, cause stress, and do not listen to reason. Children who are disabled, suffer from learning problems, or are otherwise "different" are also at high risk of abuse (Ammerman, Lubetsky, and Drudy, 1991).

Children who are abused or severely neglected may experience a drop in intelligence and increased risk of depression and suicide (*New York Times,* February 18, 1991, p. 11). As young children, they tend to be hyperactive, easily distracted, and unpopular with their peers. As adolescents and adults, they

Beaten to death by her mother, Elisa Izquierdo's death was a brutal reminder of the high incidence of child abuse in the United States.

are more likely to abuse drugs or alcohol and to become involved in juvenile delinquency and violent crime.

Some sociologists maintain that child abuse can end only when the social conditions that bring it about are alleviated (Gelles, 1985, 1995). This would involve identifying families at risk for abuse and providing them with various forms of support and assistance (child-rearing classes, rent supplements, drug treatment, day care, parent support groups, and so forth). In general, researchers find that people use violence as a last resort, when they feel the need to compensate for a lack of such other resources as money, knowledge and respect (Wolfe, 1985). All fifty states now have laws requiring doctors and teachers to report child abuse and neglect to the police; also, public and private social services have been enlisted to help treat and prevent these problems (Straus and Gelles, 1986).

Spouse Abuse

Force or the threat of force between husband and wife is also common in America. Michael Johnson (1995) distinguishes between two types of spousal violence. One, which he labels "common couple violence," occurs sporadically in a family and grows out of conflicts that "get out of hand." Such incidents rarely escalate into serious violent acts, and they are just as likely to be initiated by women as by men.

The other type of violence is less common but far more serious. It involves the need for a husband to exert absolute control over his wife and to continually demonstrate that control, no matter how compliant she may be. Johnson calls this type of violence "patriarchal terrorism," because it is rooted in patriarchal traditions and results in systematically terrorizing wives. Typically, beatings occur once a week and escalate in seriousness over time.

According to a national survey, about 1.4 million wives, or thirty in 1,000, are assaulted by their husbands in any given year (Gelles and Straus, 1990). The typical wife beater is young, has been married for less than ten years, and is employed part-time or not at all. He feels a need to play the role of male provider and to dominate his wife and children, but he lacks the social and economic resources to do so without physical force.

A number of researchers have tied wife battering to *status inconsistency*—that is, a gap between the role a man thinks he ought to play in relation to others and the actual position in which he finds himself. Status inconsistency can occur at any social level. A man who has a college degree but drives cabs for a living may feel status inconsistency; so does a man whose wife earns more than he does or is more steadily employed. *Status ambiguity* has also been associated with wife beating: One study found that cohabiting men are more likely than husbands to beat their partners, perhaps because their role in the household is less clearly defined (Ellis, 1989).

Ultimately, the roots of wife abuse lie in our culture (Okun, 1986). The tradition of male superiority dictates that the husband should always be in charge. Indeed, Western culture has traditionally approved the use of violence by husbands to "keep their wives in line." For most of recorded history, a man who killed an unfaithful wife had the law on his side. Moreover, males are socialized in ways that reward them for acting tough. Finally, male folklore and pornography portray females as enjoying aggressive treatment by males.

Many battered wives stay with their husbands. Compared with women who move out or seek help, women who put up with abuse are more likely to be young, to have few job skills, to be unemployed, and to have small children (Gelles and Straus, 1988). Thus, they lack the social and economic resources, and sometimes the will to leave. Typically, an abusive husband alternates beatings with periods of kindness and contrition, allowing his wife to hope the problem has gone away (Walker, 1979). Battered wives are often ashamed to admit to anyone what is happening; many blame themselves. But few passively accept abuse. Most report that they fight back during an attack and seek help to stop the violence (Gelles and Straus, 1988; Gondolf and Fisher, 1991).

The tragedy of spousal violence became a national drama in 1995 when former football star O. J. Simpson was tried for the murder of his ex-wife Nicole. Simpson had a history of beating Nicole, who had repeatedly called the police for help. Prosecutors argued that this was evidence of the likelihood that he committed the murder, but they did not prove their case to the satisfaction of the jury. What was made clear during the trial was that there had been little legal restraint placed on Simpson after his earlier beatings of Nicole. Most experts agree that the most effective way to reduce wife abuse is to combine criminal sanctions for abusers with counseling and shelter for victims (Lerman and Cahn, 1991). Unfortunately, many communities lack the resources to implement this advice.

THE FUTURE OF THE AMERICAN FAMILY

Shifting gender roles, high divorce rates, economic dislocations, blended and reblended family groupings, longer life spans—all these phenomena occurring at the same time have placed the American family at a crossroads. Even though Americans are fairly tolerant of such unconventional arrangements and lifestyles as cohabitation, divorce, and childlessness, researchers find that we still place a high value on traditional notions of marriage, parenthood, and family life. In other words, we still look back with nostalgia on how things used to be. The problem is that, as Stephanie Coontz notes, "old family strategies and values no longer seem to fit the new rules of the game" (1992, p. 277). It is difficult to construct new forms to meet changing social conditions when we are still longing for the past.

What can be done? Coontz makes some suggestions: If we are to nourish the strengths of the step-family, we must outgrow prejudices and stereotypes about "broken families" and adopt new values, guidelines, and support systems to ease the adjustment. If working mothers are to manage their dual roles at work and the home, companies are going to have to institute such programs as job sharing, parental leave (for both child care and elder care), day-care options, and flexible hours. Husbands are going to have to cast off old notions of being exempt from household and child-care tasks and take on their fair share. The concept of the "private family" in which problems are swept under the rug must give way to a willingness to seek outside help and to rely on larger kin networks when trouble intrudes the family unit. Both individuals and policymakers need to recognize that marriage is not the only tie that binds; more and more couples are choosing cohabitation.

David Elkind (1994) characterizes the recent transformation of the family as the shift from the nuclear family, with its clear-cut divisions between public and private lives, home and the workplace, children and adults, to the "permeable family," which can take many forms and is more fluid, more flexible, more vulnerable to outside pressures, and more attuned to adults than to children. Elkind sees the need for a further transition to the "vital family,"'which nurtures and energizes both children and their parents. He describes four characteristics of the vital family:

■ *Committed love*, which goes beyond romantic love and consensual (contractual) love to establish a relationship based on resolution of differences, open communication, and mutual support.

■ *Authentic parenting*, which takes the place of unilateral parenting and shared parenting. It allows parents to "be themselves, rather than what they believe they should be" (p. 214). Either parent feels free, say, to take a year off from work to be with the baby; men are relaxed caregivers, not needing to "prove" themselves.

■ A sense of *community*. We do not just acknowledge the diversity of society; we attempt to integrate the

differences—sharing goals, aspirations, and responsibilities with other families.

■ *Interdependence*. Instead of seeing ourselves as dependent members of a family, or alternatively, as independent members, we recognize our interdependence.

Cultural Wars: Family Values, Child-Rearing, and Abortion

Much of the debate about the future of the family plays out in cultural wars being waged in the United States today. The main protagonists are the conservative (often Christian fundamentalist) and the liberal segments of society. James Davidson Hunter (1991) describes the two sides as representing an impulse to orthodoxy (relying on a fixed higher moral authority) and an impulse to progressivism (shaping views according to the prevailing assumptions of contemporary life).

According to Hunter, the cultural conflict is not over how well or how poorly the family is doing but over what constitutes the family itself. Conservatives want to preserve the idealized family, in which the man is dominant, motherhood and childhood are sanctified, and obligations are to the family, not to oneself. For example, they look on liberalization of divorce laws and the high divorce rate as willful abandonment of family obligations, as are attempts to take the mother out of the home. Progressives see the need to share authority in the home and allow more room for individual autonomy to family members. The idealized family is antithetical to this vision, and so progressives are willing to conceive of a variety of family types—single parents, cohabitating couples, homosexual unions, and so on.

These divergent views are flashpoints for a number of issues that touch on family values. For instance, are feminist calls for more equity in the home and workplace an attack on the family? That is how many conservatives view it. Are laws that prevent homosexuals from adopting children an attack on the family? That is how many progressives see it. Does public moralizing on the need for Christian values in the home constitute an infringement of church on the state? Does liberal rejection of that moralizing constitute a failure to address basic needs for discipline and guidance of the young? In what follows we look more closely at two "hot button" issues: child-rearing and abortion.

Child-Rearing

Child-rearing techniques are particularly fertile ground for disagreement (Bartkowski and Ellison, 1995). Conservative family experts believe it is a parent's duty to inculcate in the child a respect for authority and the need to submit to it, whether it is parental authority in the home or divine authority in life. Progressive family experts advocate more democratic values in parenting and attention to a child's psychosocial needs in order to nourish a "healthy" personality. They view the family as a dynamic unit that responds to changes in the social climate. Conservatives value Bible-based child training, firm parental leadership, and male dominance of the family. Progressives see the need for proactive, ungendered parental roles.

Conservatives tend to favor punishing children physically whenever they willfully defy parental authority. For them, corporal punishment indicates what deviation from biblical principles will provoke.

Progressives, on the other hand, oppose physical punishment; they advocate setting firm guidelines and using pragmatic disciplinary techniques such as time-outs, reasoning, and positive reinforcement.

The Abortion Debate

RANDALL TERRY (spokesman for the pro-life organization Operation Rescue): The bottom line is that killing children is not what America is all about. We are not here to destroy our offspring.

FAYE WATTLETON (president of Planned Parenthood): Well, we are not here to have the government use women's bodies as the instrument of the state, to force women into involuntary servitude. . . . [T]he fundamentals of personal privacy are really the cornerstones upon which our democracy is built. (Hunter, 1991, p. 49)

As this exchange indicates, the abortion controversy is rooted deeply in fundamental principles, even to the extent of defining what America stands for. Opposition to abortion has become the basis for a major social movement (see Chapter 20). As it re-

Openly disagreeing over America's policy toward abortion, both sides in this struggle hold radically different views about the role of women in modern American society.

lates to the family, this debate touches on reproduction rights, the limits of legitimate sexuality, the public and private role of women, questions of child raising, adoption, the definition of the family, even the origins of life itself.

The abortion controversy centers on questions of autonomy and obligation (Hunter, 1991). Pro-life adherents believe mothers have an obligation to the unborn as well as to the born. A mother's traditional duty has been the protection of her children—and who needs protection more than an entity that cannot defend herself or himself? Moreover, the conservatives maintain, abortion is a denial of a woman's most important and satisfying role in life: motherhood. Pro-choice activists point out that motherhood is only one role among many suitable and satisfying roles. Abortion allows a woman to escape the burden of carrying an unwanted pregnancy to term and raising an unplanned child. Enforced motherhood takes a woman's autonomy away by not allowing her reproductive rights and by enfringing on her rights in the workplace.

As the law currently stands, a woman in the early stages of pregnancy does have the right to terminate the pregnancy. But what the Supreme Court grants, it can take away. If the balance of the Court tips from pro-choice to pro-life—and it is teetering now—it is likely that the law will change. If that is the case, pro-choice forces will gear up, just as the pro-life forces did after *Roe v. Wade,* and we will see renewed battles on this issue.

The cultural conflict is intense and occasionally ugly, and it is consequential because a large part of it takes place in the political arena. It is important to note that the two political sides represent polarizing impulses in American society today (Hunter, 1991) and that most Americans actually occupy a vast middle ground: their opinions are not as rigid as those of the people who make the news. And polls show they are not giving up on the family, even if they are not returning to the nuclear family of the 1950s. A 1991 Gallup Poll found that 93 percent of baby boomers (then aged thirty-six to forty-seven) said that family life was "very important" to them, and 73 percent said they expected to have a "happier family life" than their parents had. The challenge for society is to accommodate the new family structures, especially to take them into account in deciding how schools and workplaces are to be run.

SUMMARY

1. The family is a key element of social organization, charged with providing love and emotional security and regulating sexual behavior, reproduction, socialization, protection, and social placement.

2. Family structure varies among cultures, within cultures, and over time. Two basic forms are the nuclear family, emphasizing marital bonds, and the extended family, emphasizing blood ties. Rules of descent, residence, number of partners, and authority also characterize variations in family form.

3. Although the traditional nuclear family is still valued in our society, fewer than half of American families now match this ideal. Some others approximate it; others are more different. Nontraditional families today include families in which grandparents have an active role, blended families, and single-parent families. People are also marrying later, delaying childbearing, and having smaller families.

4. Decisions involving marriage are both cultural and economic. Some societies routinely produce arranged marriages, others value marriages of love, and still others promote elements of both types of marriage. Societies also have norms about when to marry. Some people make the decision not to marry, choosing instead to remain single or cohabit with a partner.

5. Changes in divorce law, changing gender roles, and shifts in cultural values have contributed to the high divorce rate in the United States. Some marriages are more prone to divorce than others. The effects of divorce can create serious problems for many individuals, but particularly for women and children, who typically experience a decline in their standard of living after divorce.

6. Domestic violence causes serious and lasting problems in families. Typical victims are children of young, impoverished parents, and wives who lack economic resources and job skills. Husbands, too, can be on the receiving end of violence, but the acts are generally far less serious. Some of the roots of domestic violence are in the power structure, and some are cultural.

7. The American family is at a crossroads today, embarking on new forms even as many people look back with nostalgia on the idealized nuclear family. Both individuals and policymakers need to respond wisely to the changing social conditions. A cultural conflict between conservatives and progressives plays out in the midst of these changes.

REVIEW QUESTIONS

1. What functions are served by the family? Which one do you think is the most important, and why?

2. Provide some examples of how the family varies cross-culturally.

3. Explain the usefulness of such concepts as patrilocal, matrilocal, and neolocal residence; bilateral, patrilineal, and matrilineal descent; and patriarchy, matriarchy, and egalitarian authority patterns.

4. What are some of the sociological reasons behind the decisions whom and when to marry?

5. What are some sociological reasons for the current high divorce rate?

6. Compare the modern-day family with the traditional ideal.

7. Provide some basic data on alternatives to the nuclear family: singlehood, cohabitation, childless marriages, and single-parent families.

8. Provide some basic data on teenage pregnancy and family violence: How common are they? What groups are most affected?

CRITICAL THINKING QUESTIONS

1. Describe your own family of orientation, family of procreation (present or future), and extended family.

2. The chapter notes that matriarchy has not been the norm in any society. Explain why this is so, drawing on at least three of the five key concepts (social structure, social action, functional integration, power, and culture).

3. Extend the chapter's analysis of the future of the family by drawing on the five key concepts and other family-related issues raised in previous chapters.

4. Freedom to choose partners based on love has not brought more stable marriages. What are the advantages and disadvantages of arranged marriages and of individual choice of marriage partners?

5. How do the characteristics of modern American family life reflect American culture generally or reflect functional (or dysfunctional) responses to other social forces?

GLOSSARY

Bilateral descent The reckoning of descent through both the father's and mother's families.

Blended families Families formed by the marriage of two people one or both of whom also have children. Also called stepfamilies.

Cohabitation An arrangement in which a couple lives together without being formally married.

Dual-career family A family in which both husband and wife hold jobs that offer opportunities for professional advancement.

Egalitarian authority A pattern in which power within the family is vested equally in males and females.

Endogamy A rule that requires a person to marry someone from within

his or her own group—tribe, nationality, religion, race, community, or other social grouping.

Exogamy A rule that requires a person to marry someone from outside his or her own group.

Extended family A household consisting of married couples from different generations, their children, and other relatives; the core family consists of blood relatives, with spouses being functionally marginal and peripheral.

Family Any group of people who are united by ties of marriage, ancestry, or adoption, having the responsibility for rearing children.

Family of orientation A nuclear family consisting of oneself and one's father, mother, and siblings.

Family of procreation A nuclear family consisting of oneself and one's spouse and children.

Marriage A socially recognized union between two or more individuals that typically involves sexual and economic rights and duties.

Matriarchy A pattern in which power within the family is invested in females.

Matrilineal descent The reckoning of descent through the mother's family only.

Matrilocal residence An arrangement in which the married couple, upon marriage, sets up housekeeping with or near the wife's family.

Monogamy Marriage restricted to one husband and one wife.

Neolocal residence An arrangement in which the married couple, upon marriage, sets up a new residence.

Nuclear family Ideally a household consisting of husband, wife, and their immature children; blood relatives including adult children are functionally marginal and peripheral.

Patriarchy A pattern in which power within the family is vested in males.

Patrilineal descent The reckoning of descent through the father's family only.

Patrilocal residence An arrangement in which the married couple, upon marriage, sets up housekeeping with or near the husband's family.

Polyandry Marriage consisting of one wife and two or more husbands.

Polygamy A marriage arrangement consisting of a husband or wife and more than one spouse.

Polygyny Marriage consisting of one husband and two or more wives.

Education

Critics of American education have often drawn unflattering comparisons between American students and their Asian counterparts. Japanese students can quit school at age fifteen if they wish, for example, and yet almost none of them do. In America, by contrast, the high school dropout rate has long been a matter of national concern: About 20 percent of white students, 30 percent of blacks, and 50 percent of Hispanics fail to graduate from high school (U.S. Bureau of the Census, 1995b). The dropout rate only hints at the dramatic differences between American and Asian students. In Japan, Taiwan, and China, students spend more hours a day and more days a year in the classroom than Americans do. And after school, when American adolescents are hanging out, watching TV, or working at part-time jobs, Asians are more likely to be involved in extracurricular activities, lessons, and enrichment classes.

The common stereotype of Asian students, however, is of joyless, stressed-out grinds forced to learn large amounts of material by rote in classrooms dominated by lockstep routine. They may do well on exams, we think, but their experience of school must be a miserable one. This image is false. In fact, most Asian children *enjoy* school and are enthusiastic about learning (Stevenson, 1992). Why? In part because Asian cultures place an extremely high value on education and expect all students to be able to excel if they work hard enough.

In America, by contrast, although much lip service is paid to the importance of education, the message from the larger culture is that money, not learning, is the most important element in success (Barber, 1993). Americans also see achievement in school as being much more closely related to individual talent than do Asians, who regard achievement as the result of hard work. Other factors exert an influence, too; for example, in Asian countries a standard curriculum exists for each grade, and all students are expected to master it. This means that in Asia, educational goals are uniform and clear—a sharp contrast with the United States, where curricula vary enormously among local school systems and even within individual schools. It also means that Asian teachers at a given level work on the same material at the same time, so that they can consult with one another, sharing ideas and expertise. This helps them perform more effectively in the classroom and frees more of their time for individual work with students.

In this chapter we will consider schools as agents of education, crucial to the functional integration of modern society. To sociologists, **education** is a structured form of socialization in which a culture's knowledge, skills, and values are formally transmitted from one generation to the next. Learning takes place in many places besides schools, of course: People learn from the examples of their families and friends and in all kinds of settings. They continue to learn after they complete their formal educations and leave school. Learning is part of many social activities and institutions—as when new employees learn a company's rules and procedures, when new parents learn how to diaper their baby, and when retired people learn new hobbies. In this chapter, however, we focus on schools and those aspects of education that modern societies seek to foster through the organization of schooling. As we shall see, what schools teach includes both the explicit content of the curriculum—English, algebra, history, and other academic subjects—and an implicit curriculum of socialization—lessons in how to behave in groups, how to fit into a hierarchy, and other aspects of social behavior.

As the contrast between Asian and American students illustrates, education in a given society is closely tied to the values of the larger culture. The high value given to education in Asian cultures and the expectation that students will work hard in school clearly support Asian students' academic success. By contrast, American culture's emphasis on material success, together with a tendency to ascribe high performance in school to talent rather than effort, act to discourage determined study of academic subjects. In addition, we see that the power of school administrators in Asian countries to define a standard national curriculum has important effects on what goes on in the classroom.

We begin the chapter with a look at the functions that educational institutions serve in society—the

ways in which schools are connected to and support other parts of the social order. We then discuss how schools mirror the existing power structure and consider how resistance to schools may actually help maintain existing power relations. Then we consider the question of who gets how much and what kind of education in America. We then move on to look at efforts to reform the schools, particularly those designed to foster equal opportunity. Finally, we briefly discuss education as a profession.

THE SOCIAL FUNCTIONS OF SCHOOLS

In preindustrial societies, children are primarily educated by their elders and peers in the course of daily activities. Girls watch women garden, cook, clean house, and care for children. Boys watch men farm, fish, hunt, herd livestock, and make tools. Through these informal observations, children learn the skills they will need when they grow up. They also acquire the beliefs and values of their culture informally, often by listening to the stories and myths that the elders tell. In modern societies, by contrast, even though some learning takes place this way, there is too much to learn for all of education to be this loosely structured and informal. Instead, most of education is carried out in formal, specialized institutions, namely, schools.

Schools perform two basic functions, a manifest function and a latent function (Merton, 1968a). The **manifest function** of schools is to teach students specific subject matter, such as reading, writing, arithmetic, and other academic skills. The **latent function** of schools is to teach social skills and attitudes, such as self-discipline, cooperation with others, obedience to authority figures, and the importance of working hard to attain a goal.

Societies may differ in how manifest or latent a skill is in the curriculum: In Asian countries, for example, cooperation with others is more explicitly taught than it is in American schools. Schools themselves may also differ in how well they perform these functions. Schools may fail at teaching academic skills, as when students fail to master English or math, or they may fail at teaching latent skills, as when automatically passing poor students to the next grade teaches that success is not necessarily due to hard work. And as this example suggests, the two kinds of teaching are interrelated. A school in which students were not taught some rules of social behavior (to pay attention in class, not to talk impulsively) would probably do a poor job of teaching academic skills as well.

Both kinds of teaching, manifest and latent, play a vital role in fostering the functional integration of society and in maintaining its social structure. If children were not taught to read or write, they would have difficulty earning a living in our society, and ultimately our culture would fail to be passed on. Similarly, society depends on succeeding generations of young people leaving school ready to fit into the existing social and occupational structure.

When people evaluate schools, they usually focus on how well schools perform their manifest functions. How well do students do on standardized tests, for example, and how do they compare with students around the country or in other parts of the world? The latent functions of schools are less often evaluated. Parents, teachers, and others may agree that it is important for students to learn self-discipline, the value of hard work, and so on, but because these kinds of learning are rarely part of any formal curriculum or lesson plan, they are less often a focus of attention. Indeed, the school's latent role in socializing children has been called the **hidden curriculum** (Parsons, 1959; Jackson, 1968). The hidden curriculum can be seen as a set of unwritten rules of behavior that prepare children for the world outside the family—the world of large, formally structured organizations. From kindergarten on, children must learn to be quiet, wait, line up, control their impulses, be pleasant to others, and follow the teacher's instructions. Most Americans agree that the lessons of the hidden curriculum are necessary and desirable. Indeed, surveys often show that Americans consider a lack of discipline to be one of the biggest problems in schools today (Elam, 1990). Critics, on the other hand, point out that what the hidden curriculum teaches are the very qualities—docility, self-control, obedience, and the like—that people need if they are to function effectively in an office or a factory. In effect, the hidden curriculum is designed to mold students into good cogs in the modern industrial machine.

Through their manifest and latent functions, schools provide society with many services and benefits. Schools are called on to enable students to meet the demands of the workplace, to function as citizens, and to perform practical activities within their family lives. To meet each of these functional imperatives, schools perform a variety of tasks. How they perform various tasks depends not only on their tech-

nical proficiency and resources but also on the demands of powerful interest groups, among them parents, employers, legislators, religious organizations, and civic groups.

Among schools' many social functions are the following:

■ *Teaching skills.* Schools are called on to teach an enormous variety of skills. Some of these skills are general (English, geometry), some are practical (telling time, making change), and some are highly specific and job-related (welding, computer programming).

■ *Transmitting culture.* Schools pass on many kinds of knowledge about the culture in which students live. This knowledge is passed on both directly, as in lessons in American literature, history, and government, and indirectly, as in praise for individual achievement and success in competition with others. In the contemporary United States, schools are often called on not only to transmit the "mainstream" European cultural heritage but also to present elements of Asian, African, and other cultures.

■ *Encouraging cultural adaptation.* In addition to transmitting cultural patterns from the past, schools are expected to help students adapt to cultural innovation and even to help accomplish change. For example, schools have been called on to help improve race relations by adopting textbooks that present positive images of racial and ethnic minority groups.

■ *Instilling discipline.* Schools teach children to sit still, raise their hands when they have a question, ask permission before leaving their seats, and so on. As schooling progresses, the emphasis shifts from discipline imposed by the teacher to self-discipline maintained by students themselves. Self-discipline is especially important for middle-class jobs that require employees to be self-motivated and organize their own activities; it is less important for routine manual labor, as on assembly lines, where tighter controls are maintained on individual behavior. It has thus gained in importance over time as fewer members of the workforce now do manual labor, and it is emphasized more in schools in which students are believed to be destined for middle-class jobs.

■ *Encouraging group work.* In the family setting, children may not have much experience working with a group of peers on shared tasks. Because this skill is important to work and to other activities in adult life, schools are called on to provide children with the opportunity to learn to work effectively and cooperatively in groups.

■ *Promoting ethical behavior.* Although schools sometimes teach ethics in formal classes on the subject, they more often teach "right and wrong" in the form of rules students must follow. For example, students are taught not to cheat on exams, not to copy the work of other students, not to plagiarize, not to lie, not to use objectionable language, not to monopolize play equipment, not to take things that belong to others, not to damage school property, and a host of other moral lessons.

■ *Selecting talent and rewarding achievement.* Schools do more than teach—they use grades and other means to identify which students have the most ability and to provide them with credentials for going on to college or getting good jobs. As we saw earlier, Americans see achievement as more closely related to innate ability than to hard work, and so they emphasize selecting talent. Asian schools, which tend to assume that nearly everyone has similar abilities and that differences in achievement are related to effort, emphasize rewarding achievement. In both settings, schools are called on to evaluate students and to identify those who are best prepared for work or for the next higher level of education (see the Global Issues/Local Consequences box).

Sociologists have studied how the "hidden curriculum" of the schools—the training in obedience, discipline, and conformity—has prepared the great masses of American society for jobs in factories and bureaucracies in which conformity and the repetition of simple tasks are much more important than creativity and problem-solving ability.

GLOBAL ISSUES/LOCAL CONSEQUENCES

Asian Lessons for U.S. Schools

With more and more jobs requiring computer competency and other technical skills, American educators and politicians have become concerned about our ability to equip future workers with the skills they need. Education is a key to global economic competitiveness, and as manufactured goods from other countries—such as Japan, China, Taiwan, and Korea—find acceptance throughout the world, the educational performance of students in these countries is often cited as a reason.

Research has consistently demonstrated that students of several Asian and European countries do better at reading and math than American students of the same age (Stevenson, 1992; Resnick and Nolan, 1995) (see figure). We have noted in the text several possible reasons for this fact, among them the cultural expectation in these countries that all students have the ability to succeed in school if they work hard and the use of a national curriculum that all students are expected to master. American culture, as we have seen, stresses individual differences in ability, and the American public is unlikely at any time soon to change its educational system to one that includes a national curriculum. It may therefore prove difficult to take a "lesson" from other countries in how to improve our schools.

To achieve change, it may be necessary to arouse more concern among parents, students, and the public about America's educational deficit. Typically,

American parents think their children's academic performance is good or satisfactory. More than three times as many American mothers as Asian mothers said they were very satisfied with their child's work in school (Stevenson, 1995). Moreover, American students share this positive view of their achievement. More American students than Chinese students rated themselves as "among the best" in various skills (Stevenson, 1992).

What, then, can American schools learn from their more successful counterparts in Europe and Asia? At the very least, two things:

■ First, it is necessary to set clear, consistent high standards for student performance.
■ Second, exams should test what students have been asked to learn. Such exams can provide feedback to show how well or how poorly schools are doing with their goals. Most other countries give students a demanding exam at the end of compulsory schooling—around age sixteen—which gives educators and the country as a whole a useful indication of how the schools are doing.

We all—students, teachers, and the public—should expect and demand more from our educational system and not simply engage in wishful thinking about being "the best."

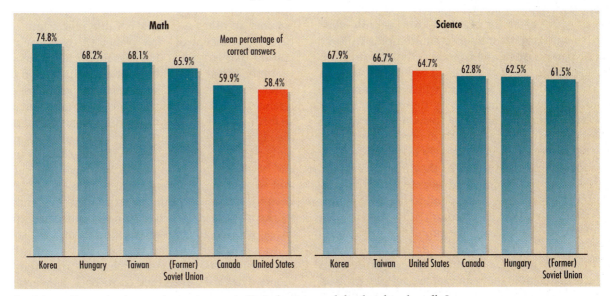

In Asian cultures, teachers and parents expect all students to work hard and to do well. In contrast, Americans believe that differences in ability (rather than hard work and high expectations) lead to high achievement.

POWER, STRUCTURE, AND RESISTANCE

The various social functions of education are not simply neutral goods, nor are the mechanisms schools use to accomplish these functions. Conflict surrounds the schools' larger goals and their procedures. Curriculum, standards, rules, testing procedures, class size and structure, and virtually every other aspect of schooling are matters of concern to parents and community groups. Tension also exists between the goals and desires of students and those of their schools: Students may resist homework or grading, for example, which schools see as necessary to their function of teaching skills and rewarding achievement. Finally, specific procedures in a given school system may operate to the disadvantage of students from certain class or ethnic backgrounds. Rewarding "ability," for example, discriminates against children from homes that have prepared them poorly for school.

School systems—like other institutions—are organized in ways that reflect the distribution of social power. School curricula, for example, are usually shaped by powerful cultural elites. All American school systems pursue basically similar goals, but these goals affect children of different classes and races differently. Most schools have the goal of teaching every child standard English, for example, but this goal is easier for children from middle-class English-speaking families to attain than for children whose parents speak nonstandard dialects or a foreign language.

Confronted with a school in which goals and procedures are established not by themselves but by powerful others, students may respond with various types of social action, conscious or unconscious. They may try to work within the system to get ahead, they may try to fight the system, or they may give up on the goals of the system and eventually drop out. These three responses correspond to the three different strategies Albert Hirschman (1970) showed that people have when they have problems in powerful organizations. They can demonstrate *loyalty* by trying to work within the existing rules and procedures of the organization; they can exercise *voice* by protesting or trying to change the system; or they can *exit*, either by withdrawing their emotional investment or by physically leaving. In this section we will examine the relation between power, class structure, and resistance to the established values and practices of school systems.

Power and Class Structure

Some sociologists have taken the position that schools are agencies by which those who hold power in capitalist societies perpetuate the existing social structures and social-class power relations. Schools do this partly by saturating students with the language, symbols, values, and concepts of capitalism and by excluding those of any other ideology (Apple, 1979, 1982). Capitalism is also bolstered by the fact that schools in many ways mirror the capitalist workplace, and therefore prepare people to fit into the capitalist economic system. Schools, it is argued, are authoritarian in structure, much like a bureaucratic corporation, and schools promote both submissiveness and diligence, characteristics desired by capitalist enterprise (Bowles and Gintis, 1976).

Sociologists who focus on the school's role in perpetuating the capitalist power structure believe that schools do not socialize everyone for the same social roles. Schools, they maintain, socialize students from different social backgrounds differently, in ways that are consistent with their future places in society. Schools, in other words, teach different "status cultures" (a concept of Max Weber's); they teach the culture that is typical of a certain social status. For example, topics brought up for class discussion may differ from class to class, reflecting social-class differences in leisure-time activities, entertainment, and so forth. The result of all such differences is that middle-class students will fit more easily into society's higher-status positions. They will know how to speak and act in these positions and will have that important (if intangible) asset, a middle-class "background." Less advantaged students, in contrast, marked by their speech, manners, and past experiences, will have been socialized to fit into the status culture of the blue-collar worker. Schools thus help some students get ahead much more than they do others. They may even hold some back, as when students whose native language is not English are presumed to be less intelligent because they have language difficulties.

The dilapidated condition of this South Bronx high school classroom symbolizes the low priority our society assigns to educating inner-city youth. One way students respond to this message is by resistance.

Resistance

Students from lower-class backgrounds or of a race or ethnic status different from that of teachers in a school may feel alienated from the curriculum and the middle-class "school culture" imposed by the educational powers that be. Such students may engage in **resistance,** or behavior that rejects school values and procedures. As we saw above, resistance may involve voice (acts of protest) or exit (mental and emotional withdrawal or actual dropping out). Resisting may produce positive change, as when students and parents join to protest oversized classes or limited course offerings. But more often it is counterproductive and may lead students to end up with worse life chances than if they had played by the rules and tried to succeed in school.

Students may turn to resistance when they feel the rules of school are stacked against them—which they may be. Resistance is a social process in which some students—usually but not always those who are doing less well academically—withdraw their mental and emotional investment from school activities and place it more in nonschool ones, whether gangs or jobs or video games or TV. At the same time, they are often part of a subculture that devalues success in school and dismisses those who succeed. What such

students are resisting is a system in which they find it hard to maintain their self-esteem, one that labels them as failures. Rebelling against the values and rules of the school, or ultimately dropping out, is a personal act of resistance.

In the long run, however, these individual acts of resistance actually support those in power by helping preserve the existing ethnic and class structure of society. For example, if black students decide to cut class and not to study hard because success in school is "white," this is resistance to an educational system in which the odds of success are greater for whites; but it is also a response that is likely to lead blacks to hold worse jobs and have lower incomes and fewer opportunities in life. If working-class students decide to drop out and take manual jobs in order to hang out with their peers who do not find their academic weakness a matter to criticize, they may feel better in the short run. In today's economy, however, such an act condemns them to higher chances of unemployment, lower wages, and fewer chances of upward mobility.

Both of these cases, and most others, are instances of "tacit resistance," that is, resistance that does not take the form of overt, organized protest. Sometimes, however, students do organize to protest against the biases of their school systems. Black students, for example, have demanded access to black publications and more attention to the achievements of blacks in school curricula. Other students have demanded more teachers of their own class, race, or ethnic background. Such explicit protests follow the general logic of collective action and social movements (see Chapter 20). Here our discussion will focus on tacit, less overtly organized, resistance.

The classic sociological account of tacit resistance in school is that of Paul Willis (1977), who studied a boys' comprehensive school (similar to a high school) in what he called Hammertown, a small industrial city in central England. The school, which contained both middle-class and working-class students, was— like most schools—an environment in which middle-class students did better and got more praise from teachers.

A number of working-class boys developed a culture of their own that reflected resistance to and rejection of the school culture. Willis, who spent a great deal of time talking to "the lads," as they called themselves, about their perceptions of school, concluded that their antischool culture was rooted in the "shop floor culture" of their fathers, who were mostly employed as metalworkers. Like their fathers, "the lads" valued physical strength, aggression, brawdy humor, and macho domination of women. In school, "the lads" broke rules, acted out in class, and generally defied the authority of teachers. They dismissed middle-class students as "earholes," the nickname referring to these students' tendency to listen quietly in class and do what they were told. As the nickname suggests, "the lads" saw these students as passive and weak compared with themselves. Their counterculture therefore allowed them to reject their devaluation by the school and to construct a positive image of themselves as tough, strong, sexy, and manly.

Unfortunately, however, the very behavior by which they asserted this positive image was behavior that would make it likely that they would fail in school, drop out, and end up manual workers (or unemployed) like their fathers. Thus, their perception that school was a middle-class institution that did not value them turned into something of a self-fulfilling prophecy (Merton, 1968a). Their school experience taught "the lads" to be working-class, even though in theory it was designed to open up the possibility of upward mobility based on merit.

Willis's analysis was extended to America and to issues of ethnicity as well as class by Douglas Foley's (1990) study of high school students in "North Town," Texas. Like Willis, Foley found an antischool culture among poorer students, especially Mexican-Americans. Feeling (with reason) that the schools were biased against them, Mexicano students developed a defiantly macho counterculture. As one Mexicano student put it:

> School is a place where you find out you are dumb and that the gringos are better than you are. They always get all the breaks. They never do anything wrong. The Mexicans are always the ones who get in trouble. After a while Mexican kids get so they don't care. They just give up. (Foley, 1990, p. 85)

Foley found that this perception was largely accurate. In his conversations with teachers and his observations of classroom sessions, he encountered many examples of teachers' bias against Mexicano students. As one teacher said:

> I don't mean to say anything bad or derogatory, but the Latin kids, some of them are about one step above an animal when it comes to learning. Some of these slow learners just don't have it upstairs. They seem to be more skilled and talented with their hands. . . . We need more vocational curriculum for the Latins. Too many of them will never be able to cut it in an academic curriculum. (p. 104)

In a classroom, Foley heard a teacher say to some Mexicano students, "What do some of you people think this class is, a welfare line?" On another day, the same teacher said, "Some of you kids are too slow to be in school. You need to be out in the fields doing something useful. . . . I've gotta get me some students in here to replace you brown deadbeats" (p. 106).

Feeling devalued by school, these students cut class, broke school dress and behavior rules, and generally resisted the demands of the school environment until they were of age to drop out. They looked forward to working full-time at jobs "real men" did, as opposed to schoolwork, which was considered boring and sissy (Foley, 1990). Therefore, like the English students Willis studied, many of Foley's Mexican-American students ended up taking social action that guaranteed their academic and occupational failure, with the result that the class structure that existed in "North Town" was reproduced for another generation. (See the Research Methods box.)

Using Ethnography to Understand the Culture of a School

Douglas E. Foley's book *Learning Capitalist Culture: Deep in the Heart of Tejas* (1990), cited in the text, is what he calls a work of "ethnographic realism." The book is based on extensive research. Foley did his original research over a period of sixteen months in 1973 and 1974. He also lived in the town he called "North Town" for six-week periods during the summers of 1977, 1985, 1986, and 1987, and he spent a number of weekends there as well. Altogether, his studies of "North Town" occupied him on and off for fourteen years.

To do his *ethnography*, or portrait of a culture, Foley employed the technique known as *participant observation*. Since his primary interest was the behavior of high school students, he began by getting permission from the school board to attend classes and other school activities for an entire school year. However, he did not just stand in the corner of the classroom taking notes. As a participant observer, he joined in school activities. He worked out with the basketball team. He went to all school sports events, including out-of-town games, sometimes riding on the bus with the players. He went to students' parties after the games. In school, he sat through classes, hung around in the halls, ate lunch with students, played Ping-Pong in the gym, and talked with teachers in their lounge. An accident—the breakdown of his van—proved especially useful; he and a number of students in the automotive shop rebuilt the engine together, which provided rich opportunities for informal talk and observation. To gain the students' acceptance, he wore casual clothes and took no notes at all during his first three months in school, writing up his experiences when he got home in the evenings. (Later he took notes, but discreetly.) Eventually he became a familiar presence in the school and was called "Doc" by the students. Some of them befriended him, asking for personal advice and borrowing his books. Although he was never accepted completely—especially by some teachers and school administrators, who feared that he had come to write an exposé of some sort—he was able to gather an enormous amount of information. As Foley writes:

The manner in which we talked with people was informal, open, and occasionally even confrontational. The more we became a part of the community and people's personal histories, the more we talked to people like friends and colleagues rather than interviewees. The more we talked to people with-

out tape recorders and notepads, the more they talked back in an outspoken way. We started out being rather passive participant observers, asking few questions, and we ended up actively involved in community events, people's lives, and animated conversations. This progression was particularly true of my relations with the youth. I certainly did not become a teenager again, but North Town youth were surprisingly open and frank about themselves and about their town and school. (p. 215)

When it came to presenting his material, Foley decided to adopt some of the techniques of the "new journalism"—as practiced by writers like Tom Wolfe and Norman Mailer, who differ from journalists of the past by not pretending to have objectivity and not excluding their own experiences from their narrative of events. Accordingly, Foley decided to tell his story in informal language and in a way that made his own experiences clear. He also decided to disclose some of his own personal history, for example, comparing his own high school experiences with those of his subjects.

To confirm his original research, Foley did follow-up studies of "North Town" over several years. These studies allowed him to check the accuracy of his original observations and to see whether the passage of time had changed things. In Foley's view, such a double check of his work was valuable in making sure that his original research was not too impressionistic.

Finally, Foley wrote his book, shaping his many findings into a coherent portrait of his subjects. Guided by what he knew from his studies of sociological theory and the work of other researchers (such as Paul Willis), he explained how the culture of the various groups within "North Town" high school developed and what implications this had for the students. He notes in his book:

This is. . .the story of how these youth learn a materialistic culture that is intensely competitive, individualistic, and unegalitarian. . . . This study shows how schools are sites for popular culture practices that stage or reproduce social inequality. The school is a cultural institution in which youth perform their future class roles. (p. xv)

This conclusion was supported by Foley's day-by-day participation in his subjects' lives over a period of years.

WHO GETS WHAT KIND OF EDUCATION?

Not everyone gets the same *amount* of education, and even when students are in school the same number of years, they do not get the same *kind* of education. Schools constantly engage in a process of sorting, in which students are differentiated by ability, achievement, goals, and other criteria and given different amounts and kinds of education as a result. Paradoxically, although education is considered a main means to upward mobility, overall it works largely to reproduce the existing social structure—as we saw in the Willis and Foley studies we just considered.

One concept touched on at the beginning of this chapter underlies much of the discussion that follows: Americans tend to believe that *differences in innate ability* are basic to success and failure in school. By contrast, other cultures (as those of Asia) see hard work as more fundamental. American schools are organized to reflect allegiance to the notion that some students are brighter and more talented than others and that these differences are crucial to academic success. As we shall see, this idea is important in determining which students get what kind of education.

Rising Educational Levels

The amount of education that the average American gets has increased dramatically throughout the twentieth century. Twice as many Americans are high school graduates today as were as recently as 1960, when only 41 percent had completed four years of high school (U.S. Bureau of the Census, 1994d, pp. 157–158). Today, more than 80 percent of young people finish high school. This development has changed the meaning of holding a high school diploma: Once it used to set a person apart as being well-educated, but now it is a minimum credential for even many low-level jobs.

The same process has affected college degrees. In 1890, only 3 percent of the population held a bachelor's degree. Today, this figure is over 20 percent of the population. More than a million Americans receive bachelor's degrees each year, and a B.A. or B.S. is required for most middle-class jobs. By comparison, at the beginning of the twentieth century even careers such as law and medicine did not require a college education. During the twentieth century, both of these professions and many others first began to require a bachelor's degree and then later to require a graduate degree. Higher and higher levels of edu-

Students graduate from Harvard Medical School. The percentage of Americans earning bachelor's—and higher—degrees has risen hand-in-hand with an increase in educational requirements for jobs and professions.

cation were also required for engineers, nurses, college professors, social workers, and librarians. The Ph.D. degree was introduced in the 1870s for students training for scientific or scholarly research. As late as 1920, only 615 Ph.D.s were awarded in the entire United States—but by the 1990s, more than 40,000 were being awarded each year.

There are two basic reasons for these changes. One is the explosion of scientific and technical knowledge during the second half of the twentieth century, which has meant that an aspiring professional has a much larger body of information and skills to master. Consider the technical and complex field of modern medicine, for example, compared with medicine in the early twentieth century, when few effective treatments were available and diagnosis was often a matter of guesswork. The other reason for the great increase in higher education is **credentialism,** the practice of requiring higher credentials for jobs that were associated with fewer credentials in the past. For example, it has become common for employers to require college degrees for secretaries, clerks, and sales representatives—jobs that seldom required a college education a few decades ago and that (unlike medicine) may not really require the mastery of a large body of new knowledge and skills.

What credentialism has meant for a large proportion of the population is that what once seemed to be success in school—a high school diploma—no longer guarantees a good job. Even students who work hard and earn decent grades may find themselves stuck at the bottom of the job ladder if they do not continue their studies past high school. Some sociologists have argued that it made sense for employers to add the diploma requirement, even for jobs that had long been done successfully by employees without diplomas. Entry-level jobs are now concentrated in service areas requiring more academic skills. Even jobs involving factory labor might now require a worker to use a computer. In addition, in a society in which people often move far from their birthplace, employers need an easy way to assess their prospective workers, who are usually strangers to them. A high school diploma indicates that a job applicant will be reasonably reliable and diligent in work habits. Thus, from the perspective of functional integration, the requirement of a high school diploma for most entry-level jobs fits the needs of a modern high-technology society with a mobile population.

Those who focus on power relations say that this cannot be the whole story. They point out that de-

manding more credentials is another way of perpetuating the social-class system, of ensuring that most people end up at the same job level as their parents (Collins, 1979). Thus, the steady rise in credential requirements in the job market—a tendency known as "creeping credentialism"—is part of a vicious cycle for the poor and for ethnic minorities. No matter how hard they try to better themselves by getting a better education than their parents, the jobs they want often remain beyond their reach.

These better jobs largely go to those with (at least) a college degree. In 1992, the average annual earnings of a college graduate were $32,629; of a high school graduate, $18,737. Over a worker's lifetime, the comparison is $1,421,000 versus $821,000, a difference of $600,000 (U.S. Bureau of the Census, 1994c) (see Figure 12.1). A degree from an elite school boosts earnings even more. In a study conducted in the 1970s, the 15 percent of students who attended the country's most elite private institutions could expect to earn 85 percent more on average than those who had not graduated from college (Coleman and Rainwater, 1978). More recent research shows that it is still a good investment to attend an elite private institution. The selection of certain majors (for example, business management, economics, and engineering) may also yield high incomes (Kominski, 1990) as will the achievement of a professional degree. In addition, workers with college degrees have

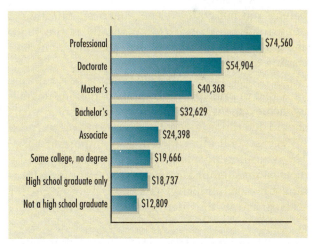

FIGURE 12.1 / Mean Annual Earnings for Persons Ages 18 and Over by Level of Education, 1992

Get your degree. As this chart shows, higher education and higher incomes go together.

Source: U.S. Bureau of the Census, 1994. *More Education Means Higher Earnings.*

also done better than those with less education at "holding their own" during periods of economic decline, such as 1979–1989, when U.S. men's average earnings fell (Acs and Danziger, 1993).

Variations in Educational Attainment

Rising average levels of education have affected the whole U.S. population. At lower levels of schooling, the gap between races and classes has nearly closed. Blacks are almost as likely as whites to graduate from high school today, for example; in 1960 they were only half as likely to do so. However, blacks are only half as likely as whites to graduate from college today (U.S. Bureau of the Census, 1995b).

In general, educational opportunities go disproportionately to those whose parents had educational opportunities before them (Hout, Raftery, and Bell, 1993). The children of educated middle- and upper-class parents both get more education and are more likely to get into better schools. The children of white Americans (more educated on average than black and Hispanic Americans) also get more education. For the most part, the gaps between the well-educated and the less educated only close when the educational system as a whole expands. With expansion, for example, there are more places in colleges than there are children of college graduates to fill them. This creates opportunities for children whose parents did not go to college. American educational opportunities expanded dramatically in the 1960s and early 1970s. Today, with federal budget cutbacks leading the way, they are contracting.

The American educational system is based on the view that in principle the combination of innate ability, achievement through work, and personal goals should determine how much education a person gets. In fact, several other factors play important roles. The education people get is largely determined by their parents' emphasis on and resources for education; by race, ethnicity, and class; by funding for schools; and by the internal policies of schools.

Parents and Cultural Capital

Children do better in school when their parents care about and are involved in their education. One reason widely cited for the success of Asian immigrant children in American schools, for example, is the in-

terest and concern their parents show in their children's school performance. Since many Asian immigrants are members of the working class, this shows that parental involvement is helpful to students of any class or economic status (Lewis, 1995). In America generally, however, middle- and upper-class children have the advantage over those of lower classes because their parents are typically more involved in their schooling. Moreover, their greater financial resources go hand in hand with a greater amount of what has been called **cultural capital** (Bourdieu, 1984; 1993). Cultural capital consists of advantages like early exposure to standard English, plenty of books and educational toys, help with homework, and opportunities to develop musical or artistic talent. Just as well-off parents have the financial capital to ensure that their children go to good

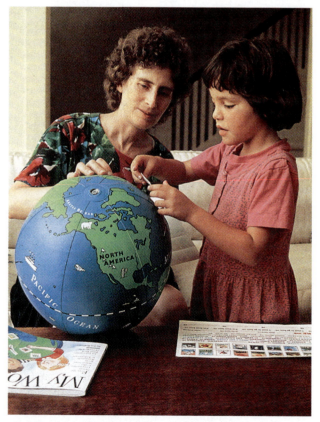

A major reason for class differences in educational achievement is parents' cultural capital. Because of their own backgrounds, middle- and upper-class parents feel comfortable with schooling; they see teachers as partners (not "experts") in their children's educations; they provide more out-of-school educational experiences; and they are actively involved in their children's learning.

schools, they also have the cultural capital to give them an advantage once they are in school.

The greater involvement of middle- and upper-class parents in their children's education has been confirmed by a great deal of sociological research (Bourdieu and Passeron, 1991). For example, Annette Lareau (1989) found that upper-middle-class parents read to their children regularly, buy them educational toys, volunteer to help in their classrooms, supervise their homework, and monitor their progress closely. When problems arise, these parents intervene. Most working-class parents, in contrast, do none of these things. In fact, they often know surprisingly little about how their children are doing in school. They assume that the teachers "know what they are doing" and simply hope for the best.

This class-related difference in parents' involvement in their children's school does not necessarily stem from working-class parents' indifference to education. However, a number of social forces conspire to keep them at arm's length from the classroom. One is a feeling of academic incompetence. Most working-class parents have only a high school education, and many are high school dropouts. They see themselves as unqualified to get involved in their children's education. Some even fear that efforts to do so may cause more harm than good. As one working-class mother told Lareau:

> You know, a lot of things that I might do with her here at home might frustrate her, or, you know, confuse her or something. They have a different arithmetic system now and they are doing all kinds of different stuff with the kids. So, rather than taking two or three hours to sit down and have them explain it to me and make sure I know what I'm talking about [laughs nervously] it is better just to leave it at school. (Lareau, 1989, p. 109)

Another factor that separates working-class parents from their children's education is the passivity caused by their lower social status compared with that of teachers and other school professionals. "Teachers intimidate me," said one mother with only a high school education. "They have always intimidated me. To me they are right up there [pointing to the sky] next to God and doctors" (Lareau, 1989, p. 112). In contrast, upper-middle-class parents see themselves as of equal or higher social status compared with that of teachers. As a result, they seldom hesitate to approach a teacher and ask for information, or even criticize and demand.

In upper-middle-class families there is also a connection between work and home that is absent in working-class families. Upper-middle-class parents "bring the office home," not only in the form of paperwork and computer disks but also in the form of colleagues and clients invited home for dinner. Such parents see education as their children's "work," which should also be a part of home life. Since they view themselves as teachers in the home environment, it is natural for them to intervene in other aspects of their children's education. This is not true of working-class parents, for whom a sharp line separates home and school, just as it does home and work.

The importance of family cultural capital to school performance is also shown in studies of children's progress over the summer vacation (Heyns, 1978). Typically, during the school year, children of different classes and races make progress at approximately the same speed. During the summer, however, children from families that do not have books and other sources of intellectual stimulation tend to fall behind those from advantaged families. When poorer children attend stimulating summer programs, however, they too make progress during the summer.

Most researchers agree that parental involvement in education helps a child succeed in school (Clark, 1983, 1990; Coleman, 1987a; Coleman and Hoffer, 1987; Epstein, 1986, 1987; Rich, 1986). Yet even efforts to involve working-class parents in their children's education, as valuable as these are, will not eradicate the differences in cultural capital that give well-off children a marked advantage in school.

Tracking and Testing

American schools are based on the ideal of equal educational opportunity, but they are organized along lines that assume very significant differences in individual ability. It has been argued by critics that equality of opportunity in school is undermined by the practice of **tracking**, which is grouping students according to their *perceived* abilities and interests. Tracking is usually done on the basis of scores on intelligence (IQ) tests rather than on measures of academic achievement (Mensh and Mensh, 1991). Students are typically assigned to upper, middle, or lower tracks very early in their school careers. Critics of the practice point out that affluent whites tend to be assigned to the highest track, while low-income whites, blacks, and Hispanics are placed in the lower

This young girl's score on a standardized test may determine whether she is assigned to an upper, middle, or lower track; what subjects she is offered and at what level; how teachers perceive her potential (as "college material" or not); and what opportunities are open to her.

tracks. Thus, lower-class students may be channeled into lower-status and lower-quality classes almost as soon as they enter school.

One major argument for tracking is that students learn better in homogeneous groups, where everyone has the same level of talent or the same learning problems. Yet research suggests that homogeneous groups are beneficial only to students at the very top of the performance hierarchy (Gamoran and Nystrand, 1990; Robinson, 1990). These fortunate few profit from more stimulating classroom environments, with better, more interested teachers, smaller classes, and sometimes more resources. But the gains to these students do not outweigh the damage done to the much larger number of youngsters assigned to unchallenging programs designed for those who have been labeled slow learners. As a result, tracking produces no *net* educational benefit (Glazer, 1990), yet it continues to be so widely practiced that virtually all American public school children experience some form of tracking at some point in their educations (National Education Association, 1990). Sociologists ask why.

One answer involves the key concept of power and power relationships. Middle- and upper-class parents of high-achieving students demand tracking because they believe it is the best way to provide stimulating classes and college preparatory instruction for their sons and daughters. Because these parents have disproportionate power in the educational system, teachers, principals, and school boards listen to them. To ignore these parents' wishes is to risk having them transfer their children to private schools, leaving the public schools largely to poor and minority youngsters. This not only would promote social-class segregation but also would deprive the public schools of support from middle-class parents who are most likely to have the ability to obtain more resources for those schools. Because of their high status in the community, upper-middle-class parents who prefer tracking often command deference from educational administrators. At the same time, educators wield their own power in support of tracking. Educators generally feel that homogeneous groups of students learn better and are easier to teach. They also find it enjoyable to teach advanced classes to the "top" students, and such positions are often used as rewards for the best and most senior teachers on the staff. The result of all these forces is that tracking persists, even though critics question its value (Slavin, 1990).

Tracking, of course, is not identical across the United States. In some schools, the upper track is very exclusive, including fewer students than the total number able to do the work required in it. In other schools, the upper track is much more inclusive, even open to average or below-average students who seem to have potential. How tracking systems operate makes a big difference. They work best—that is, create more opportunity and help more students—when there is mobility among tracks. In these systems, students shift fairly readily from track to track as their performance rises or falls, rather than getting permanently stuck. Such systems not only seem to produce higher achievement, but the gaps between tracks are smaller, so that lower-track students do not lag behind their upper-track peers so dramatically (Gamoran, 1992). Tracking also seems to work better when it is based on students' actual achievement—what they have learned—rather than on IQ scores.

Aptitude testing may initially determine whether students are assigned to a high or low track, and then later in students' school careers such testing may play an important role in determining which college students are admitted to or whether they go to college at all. While in many countries exams are required for college admission or placement, these exams usually test the students' mastery of a stan-

dard curriculum, one that is the same for every secondary school student. In the United States, however, we lack a standard curriculum or even national standards to measure school achievement. Instead of measures of what students have actually learned, we rely heavily on "aptitude" tests—the best known of which is the SAT (Scholastic Aptitude Test). The reliance on these tests not only reflects the lack of a standard curriculum but also the American belief in the significance of differing levels of ability. The SAT is supposed to measure academic potential and readiness for further study. Its critics, however, have noted that SAT scores vary directly with family income: the lower the income, the lower the average SAT score (see Figure 12.2). Blacks and some other ethnic minorities also score lower than whites, and women score lower than men (Manzo, 1994) (see Figure 12.3). Apparently, the SAT's "aptitude" is distributed in a way that mirrors the distribution of wealth and power in the larger society.

Educators have been troubled for about twenty-five years by a decline in SAT scores. Average scores peaked at around 940 in the late 1960s and early 1970s, fell to a low of 893 in 1982, and climbed grad-

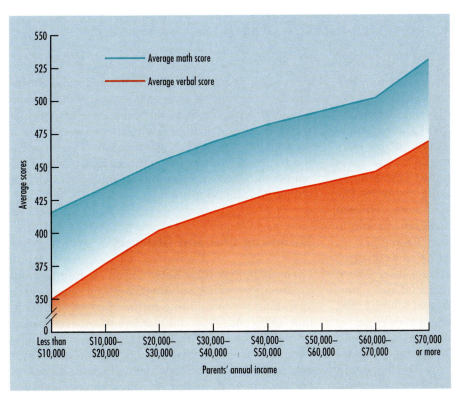

FIGURE 12.2 / Family Income and SAT Scores, 1994

What exactly do the SATs measure? If high scores go with high incomes, are wealthier students smarter than their poorer peers, or, as a group, is it simply their experiences and educations that are superior?

Source: *College-Bound Seniors National Report: 1994 Profile,* Educational Testing Service, 1995.

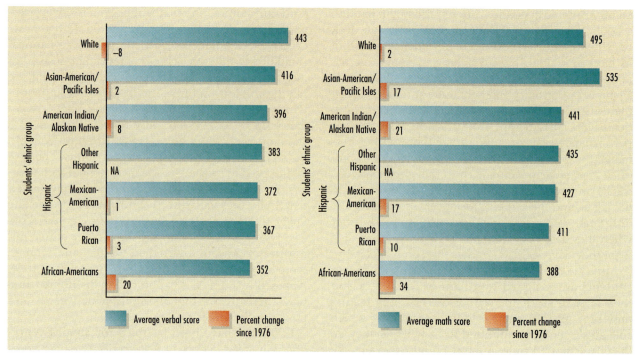

FIGURE 12.3 / *Race and SAT Scores, 1994, with Percentage of Change Since 1976*

What do radical differences in SAT scores really tell us? Minorities tend to have lower incomes and poorer schools than whites, so are we simply looking at another link between education, income, and SAT scores? Note that since the 1970s the scores of black students have risen significantly, perhaps as a result of greater educational and economic opportunities.

Source: Kathleen Kennedy Manzo, "SAT Scores Continue Recent Trends," *Black Issues in Higher Education* 11, no. 14 (September 8, 1994): 11.

ually back to about 902 in 1994. There are two possible reasons for the decline. One is that the pool of students taking the test grew as college opportunities expanded after 1960—and then shrank somewhat with the financial contractions of the early 1980s. (A larger pool of students would tend to lower scores, since students who would not ordinarily be aiming for college would be taking the test.) The other explanation is that the drop in scores reflected a decline in the quality of teaching and learning in American schools. The Educational Testing Service (ETS), which publishes the SAT, says that its research supports the former view. Accordingly, after 1994 it revised the scoring of the test so that students' scores are numerically higher: An old verbal score of 500, for example, would be a new score of 560. What the ETS hoped to accomplish with this change was to make an average numerical score correspond to average performance on the test, which it no longer did once the larger pool of test-takers brought the aver-

age down. The new scoring of the SAT caused controversy, and the debates that followed the change included renewed calls for some kind of national standards to determine what schools would teach and achievement tests to measure how well the specified subject matter had been learned. Actual attempts to devise such standards, however, have met strong political opposition.

Dropping Out and Illiteracy

Even unskilled jobs now require a high school diploma; yet millions of Americans quit school every year. Reasons for quitting include lack of identification with counselors and teachers who have low expectations for these students; teachers who are inexperienced, uninterested, or inept and therefore turn students off; lack of clearly defined goals and values that encourage students to stay in school; uninvolved parents; and a rigid school bureaucracy that seems to have senseless rules (D. Mann, 1986; Rendon and Mathews, 1989).

Studies also reveal that minority students from low-income families are more likely to drop out of high school than are others. Fewer blacks (about 30 percent) are dropping out today than in the past, but the black rate still exceeds that for whites (about 20 percent). The dropout rate for Hispanics—over 50 percent—is becoming a national scandal (U.S. Bureau of the Census, 1994d). Students from single-parent homes and large families and those from big cities and from the South are also more likely than others to drop out. The families of these children are less likely to have books or study aids at home or to foster learning. In short, it is socially, academically, and economically disadvantaged students who tend to drop out of school (Ekstrom, et al., 1986; Natriello, Pallas, and McDill, 1986).

As we saw earlier in our discussion of resistance to school, exit, or dropping out, is the ultimate act of school resistance. Many of the youths studied by Willis and Foley, who were members of an antischool culture, were only in school because they had not yet reached the age to drop out. A recent study of the families of dropouts provides a fuller picture of how antischool attitudes usually develop. Ted Okey and Philip Cusick (1995) studied twelve families of dropouts—all white Midwesterners. They found that students who dropped out had held negative attitudes toward school from their earliest years, even from kindergarten. They learned this view of school from their parents, who had learned it from *their* parents, because the families had a history of poor performance in school going back two generations. The dropouts' parents disparaged school and the promised benefits of education. They saw no connection between study and the world of work and no possibility of doing better occupationally or financially as a result of success in school. Their memories of school were overwhelmingly negative:

> I didn't get along with authority real well, didn't get along with the teachers, didn't get along with the principal, didn't enjoy the classes . . . got lost somewhere . . . and I had this constant aggravation from the counselor, from the principal, from teachers who thought I was a troublemaker. (p. 255)

As Okey and Cusick characterized the dropouts' parents:

They had entered school reluctantly, were unhappy there, were picked on by students, were bored by subjects, were disliked by teachers and disliked teachers in return. They reported low effort, motivation, and interest; and they were often in trouble. According to their own recollections, they skipped school, fought, learned little or nothing, refused to comply, and dropped or were pushed out. They were indifferent to learning and the rewards it promised. Furthermore, within the family, the younger generation—among them the dropouts—had heard their parents' stories about school; the way in which their parents were treated; the injustices; and their parents' opposition, resistance, and defiance. "School as an all-around bad experience" was part of the family history and lore, passed from generation to generation. (p. 256)

Such parents can be seen as burdening their children with "negative cultural capital" from the very beginning of their school careers. Typically, the negative behavior and conflict with school authorities begin early (Ensminger and Slusarcick, 1992).

Most dropouts have been on vocational or general nonacademic tracks. Many are somewhat older than their classmates because they have repeated a grade or two. Many come from families with problems—poverty, drug or alcohol use, a history of unemployment, time spent in prison, and other problems. Many also come from nonintact families. Family problems may affect school performance in several ways: Single parents or troubled parents may have less time and energy to invest in their children's education, and the frequent changes of residence associated with family breakup mean that children's schooling is often disrupted, as by moving from one school to another in midyear (Astone and McLanahan, 1991).

Sociologists have suggested many approaches to combating this complex and stubborn problem. Parents can be taught to take more interest in their children's education and to monitor their children's progress. Programs to identify potential dropouts at the first sign of discipline problems, poor grades, and poor attendance have often been proposed. So have programs that keep dissatisfied, restless, low-achieving teenagers in school, even with monetary incentives if need be (Ekstrom et al., 1986).

One reason why educators and the general public find the dropout rate to be of concern is that students with fewer years of schooling are less likely to have learned the basic skills that they need to function in society—perhaps the most basic of all being the ability to read and write, that is, literacy. Functional literacy requires more than the most minimal ability to read and write. It requires reading and writing well enough to perform everyday tasks, such as reading a map or the directions on a medicine bottle. Although the United States, as a nation of immigrants, has always had a sizable number of citizens who have trouble reading and writing (Graubard, 1990), the problem seems to be growing. The results of the National Adult Literacy Survey, published in 1993, set up five levels of literacy, from level one (lowest) to level five, and reported that more than 20 percent of American adults were functioning at the lowest level (Kirsch et al., 1993). This meant that they were either illiterate or had such limited skills that they could only do rudimentary tasks such as finding the time or place of a meeting on a form. Of the more than 40 million people in this group, nearly two-thirds had not finished high school. Another 25 percent of those surveyed, about 50 million more adults, were functioning only at literacy level two—they could read a map, fill out a simple form, and locate information in text (Kirsch et al., 1993). Since today's job market requires literacy for most jobs, it is not surprising that the large numbers of barely literate Americans are a cause for national concern. Schools are assumed to have failed in a fundamental way if they turn out a great many students who have difficulty reading.

The reasons for the schools' failure in teaching basic literacy are a matter for debate. David Hawkins (1990) argues that schools have taught the rudiments of reading and writing—such as letter and word recognition, spelling, and grammar—but they have done little to develop the *motivation* to read by supplying children with a rich assortment of interesting, appropriate books. When students are given only textbooks and worksheets, they do not develop an interest in reading that stays with them outside the classroom.

EDUCATIONAL REFORM

In the United States, schools have long been seen as instruments of social reform. They have been called on to assimilate immigrants, encourage moral values, and promote social mobility since the earliest days of this country. Indeed, free public education was pioneered by the United States as a means of preparing citizens to participate in a democratic so-

ciety. Schools have been the *objects* of reform as well. From the era of Noah Webster, who reformed American spelling, through campaigns to eliminate corporal punishment, professionalize teaching and increase teachers' pay, reduce rote memorization, teach sex education, end racial segregation, and introduce computer technology, reform movements have abounded. Such movements, whether they have focused on pedagogical techniques or the social organization of schools, have largely been the by-products of larger social movements (Berube, 1994). Efforts to end racial segregation in the schools, for example, were a part of a broad-based civil rights movement.

Today, there is widespread concern that American schools are not performing as well as they should be. Data showing that American students are lagging behind their peers in other countries have raised fears that American industry will fall behind in an increasingly competitive world economy. American schools are being criticized for more than failing to teach the basics, however; they are also being attacked for failing to teach discipline and for failing to provide opportunity to all students. At the same time, there is a *reaction* to some of the reforms of the past, such as affirmative action and curriculum revision. The turmoil over education suggests how important it is and how very much Americans expect of their schools. Because schooling affects children, education is always an issue that touches emotions connected with family and morality; and because education is expensive and is supported mainly by taxes, schools are attractive targets for those who want to cut government spending. Finally, the uncertainty about how children learn best, and about what is best for them to learn, leaves room for extensive and continuing debate.

In 1993, the Gallup Poll (Elam, Rose, and Gallup, 1993) reported that 47 percent of their respondents, when asked to "grade" their local public schools, gave them an A or B. Somewhat surprisingly, when asked to rate the nation's public schools, only 19 percent of the respondents gave them the same grade. However, when respondents were asked to rate the public school attended by their eldest child, the number giving As or Bs was 72 percent. What this means is that the more people know about the schools, the higher their rating of school quality. It suggests that the "crisis of confidence" in the public schools exists as something of a media phenomenon—something that everyone "knows" exists, but that exists in the abstract, somewhere else. And despite alleged public opposition to taxation, fully 90 percent of the survey respondents thought that "more should be done to improve the quality of the public schools in the poorer states and in the poorer communities," with 68 percent willing to pay more taxes to do so and 60 percent willing to pay more taxes to improve inner-city schools specifically (Elam, Rose, and Gallup, 1993).

Desegregation and Beyond: Race and Schools in America

Perhaps the single biggest reform effort ever undertaken in American education was the attempt to desegregate the public schools and to use them as a means to advance black Americans and promote broader racial integration. This effort began with the 1954 Supreme Court ruling *Brown v. Board of Education,* which declared that racially segregated schools were unconstitutional. The plaintiff in this case, a five-year-old black girl named Linda Brown, had to walk past an all-white school in her neighborhood in Topeka, Kansas, to get to the more-distant black school to which she was assigned. The Court ruled that such segregated education was inherently unequal. Before *Brown,* most public schools were segregated by law, and the schools provided for black Americans were greatly inferior to those provided for whites. Black schools commonly lacked indoor plumbing and running water; teachers were trained and paid less; textbooks were dated; and teaching tools like movies and slide projectors were absent.

As the civil rights movement began to organize after World War II, segregated and unequal education for black Americans became a focus of concern. In fact, from the days of the black educator Booker T. Washington (1856–1915) and the founding of black colleges—Fisk University (1866), Howard University (1867), Tougaloo College (1869), and Tuskegee Institute (1881)—there had been debates about whether blacks were better educated in separate schools or together with whites. But by the 1950s, concern was growing that black children were poorly served by segregated schools. Backed by white supporters, black Americans brought lawsuits to end this unequal treatment. The most famous was the suit that eventually became the landmark *Brown v. Board of Education.*

The process of desegregation sped up after the 1964 Civil Rights Act and the enactment in 1965 of a program of federal aid to public schools, enabling the federal government to require integration as a condition for receiving federal money (Taeuber, 1990). As a part of the 1964 Civil Rights Act, a team of sociologists led by James Coleman (1966) was asked to undertake a nationwide study of inequality in American public schools. Coleman found that while there were significant differences between predominantly black and predominantly white schools in expenditure per pupil, building age, library facilities, number of textbooks, teacher characteristics, and class size, these did not have a great impact on actual learning. It was mainly the child's social environment—especially the attitudes and behaviors of family members and peers—that seemed to set the stage for academic success or failure. Schools, in other words, were seldom able to compensate for a child's lack of opportunity to practice important cognitive skills (reading, writing, computation, listening and speaking, problem solving) outside the classroom (Clark, 1990).

The courts, interpreting Coleman's finding that socially advantaged children were more likely to do well in school, concluded that every child in a school district had a right to be in a school with a comparable distribution of "advantaged" and "disadvantaged" children. Since advantaged status was correlated with race, this interpretation provided a rationale for redistributing children throughout a school system—usually by busing (discussed below). This was a policy choice Coleman himself argued against for years. The Coleman Report did provide a strong rationale for **compensatory education,** enrichment programs that help students from disadvantaged backgrounds catch up with more privileged students.

A few years after the Coleman Report was published, Christopher Jencks and his colleagues took Coleman's diagnosis one step further in a book called *Inequality* (1972). Jencks too found that social inequality outside the classroom is the major determinant of inequality within it. But he argued that schools could not alter this fact: schools could not work miracles in society as a whole. Reforming the schools would not alter the differences in power and privilege that have always been part of the American social structure. Instead, Jencks argued that inequality should be attacked directly, with economic measures, not through school reform.

One remedy for inequities within school systems has been, as we have noted, to counteract the racial imbalance caused by discriminatory housing patterns by busing students to create roughly the same racial balance in each school in a district. In the late 1960s busing prompted a great reduction in public school segregation, especially in the South. Despite its effectiveness in achieving desegregation (and despite support of integration by a majority of the American people), busing has never been popular (Formisano, 1991). Opponents of busing worry about their children's safety, dislike the time children must spend riding the bus rather than doing homework or engaging in extracurricular activities, and regret the loss of neighborhood schools (Armor, 1989). Opposition to busing does not necessarily reflect underlying racism (some blacks oppose it); at times opposition to busing has resulted from interracial conflict that has erupted from integration itself (Olzak, Shanahan, and West, 1994).

When mandatory busing is instituted, some parents remove their children from public schools, either sending them to private school or moving to a predominantly white area not affected by busing. The departure of white families from neighborhoods undergoing busing and other forms of racial integration is known as **white flight;** this phenomenon not only undercuts desegregation but impoverishes the tax base of inner-city districts as middle-class whites flee. In some cities with mandatory busing, white flight has been substantial enough to cause great concern (Armor, 1989; Taeuber, 1990). In Norfolk, Virginia, for instance, the federal courts actually ordered a halt to busing in the lower elementary grades in an effort to halt white flight (Armor, 1991). However, especially in the South, white flight has even occurred in some towns where busing was never used to achieve integration. In such cases the goal of departing whites was simply to avoid integrated education. Simple racism may motivate most white flight, but it may be compounded by lower-middle-class and working-class whites' fear of downward mobility; integrated schools seem to threaten their children's education and their own social and economic position in a time of increasing competition for jobs (Mickelson and Ray, 1994).

Another remedy that has been applied in schools (and workplaces) in an attempt to make opportunity more nearly equal has been **affirmative action,** explicit effort to overcome the effects of discrimination by improving the competitive chances of minorities. In education, the big affirmative action issue is college and university admissions. Although affirmative action is often considered an attempt to make up for the wrongs of the past—in the case of African-Americans, slavery and a long history of discrimina-

The Supreme Court decision (Brown v. Board of Education) *declaring segregated schools unconstitutional met strong, often violent resistance in the South. Here, African-American students attending the newly integrated Central High School in Little Rock, Arkansas, 1957, leave school under the protection of federal guardsmen.*

tion—it is really aimed at resolving present-day inequities that stem from current patterns of discrimination. Moreover, criticisms of affirmative action that assert that blacks are now given "unfair" preferences, in college admissions, for example, neglect the fact that college admissions have always involved special preferences. Children of alumni, athletes, students with special abilities, and generally whites of well-off families have long been admitted to colleges before minorities (Reed, 1995).

Although affirmative action has aided black progress, blacks themselves are divided over whether it is a good idea. Some think that black students do better in all-black colleges where friction with whites does not exist and where black achievement is more readily recognized (Traub, 1994). Many whites (and some nonblack ethnic minorities, notably Asians) have become open opponents of affirmative action, led by conservative politicians. Despite fears that unqualified black students are taking places in college that "should" go to whites, segregation in colleges still persists, especially in the South (Applebome, 1995a). However, selective colleges do find it difficult to find enough African-Americans and Hispanic Americans with outstanding high school records to achieve substantial enrollments of these groups. Some of these colleges do lower or otherwise change admissions criteria for some minority students. To make up for this, they rely on some combination of supplementary programs and greater effort and determination on the part of students. Of course, some blacks and Hispanics are not in any sense educationally disadvantaged and would be admitted without affirmative action—and some critics argue that affirmative action casts unwarranted doubt on these students' achievement.

Financing, Choice, and Accountability

American public schools are primarily financed by taxes paid by local property owners, and in some school districts these taxes are substantial. Several proposals to reform school financing have been advanced in recent years, and although these have usually been presented as proposals to improve school quality or increase school choice, the desire to reduce local taxes is almost invariably involved. The "school choice" program most often advocated is a *voucher system.* Under this plan, each child in a given school district (or state) would be given a "voucher" worth a set dollar amount of schooling, and the child and his or her parents could choose between a public school or any private school, religious or secular. This plan has been supported by parents of children in religious schools, which for constitutional reasons are not allowed public funds. Voucher plans are also advocated by political conservatives, who like the idea of ending the "state monopoly" on education and assert that vouchers permit a "free market" in which the "consumer" can "buy" the education he or she chooses. Opponents of voucher systems note many problems: Vouchers rarely would cover the entire cost of private schooling; not enough private schools exist to serve students who might want them; transportation costs to a chosen private school might be prohibitive; private schools might largely be closed to very poor students, to minorities, and to those with limited English or with handicaps (Corwin and Dianda, 1993). Permitting vouchers, these critics argue, would increase stratification in schooling as the best and wealthiest students left public schools for private schools, leaving public schools to serve a needier population and with less money to do so (Astin, 1992).

Another proposal to reform school financing is *privatization,* which involves turning over the school functions to an outside organization or business. Generally, the appeal of privatization is efficiency—more or better education for less money. Although in some communities privatization has been tried with some degree of success, it has also failed to live up to its promises. In Chelsea, Massachusetts, the management of the troubled public schools was taken over by Boston University in 1989. So far, significant progress has been made in the Chelsea schools, with modest gains in attendance, test scores, the dropout rate, and the postsecondary education rate (*Education Digest,* 1993). The experience of the Baltimore public schools has been quite different, however. There, in 1992, the operation of nine public schools was turned over to a for-profit firm called Education Alternatives, Inc. (EAI). Although EAI claimed that it could operate the schools more efficiently and improve student performance, it did not do so. The schools EAI ran were cleaner and in better repair, but the students' academic performance as measured by test scores was lower; and EAI actually spent several million dollars *more* than the public school budget (Walsh, 1995).

The "business" of education: John T. Golle, head of Educational Alternatives Inc. (EAI), visits with first and second graders in Michigan. Attempts to privatize school systems have shown moderate success, at best. EAI executives blame lack of cooperation and financial mismanagement by local school officials; educators blame the corporation's emphasis on technology (such as computer labs) and profits over students and teachers.

Another aspect of school reform has been the demand that schools perform better and be *accountable* for their performance. The voucher plan is one way of trying to promote accountability: Parents who are unhappy with their child's schooling can move him or her to a private school. Allowing parents to "home school" their children also promotes accountability. The common thread is a focus on *results,* the output of an educational system. Critics who emphasize the importance of accountability argue that school systems are often too concerned about input: school facilities, class size, number of teachers and their salaries, expenditure per pupil, and the like. What really should matter, they insist, is what children have learned at the end of the school day or the school term or the school year.

The educational approach spawned by such demands is known as **outcome-based education** (OBE). The concept is that education should begin with an explicit set of goals for exactly what children should learn. All children should be expected to meet the goals, and they should advance in school only when the goals are met (Witmer, 1993). Although this sounds sensible enough in theory and has met with enough acceptance to be adopted in many states, outcome-based education has also been harshly criticized. An initial criticism was that OBE would hold back brighter students in a class, since a whole class

would keep working on a topic until all students mastered it. It has also been argued that teachers would "teach for the test," concentrating on cramming students with the "right answers" rather than really encouraging them to explore a subject. Even more criticisms erupted over questions of content: Just what were these goals that students were supposed to meet? Where OBE was actually implemented, it turned out that school authorities were not simply specifying the ability to do long division or to read well enough to understand a newspaper. Instead, they set objectives like requiring that students "demonstrate those behaviors that denote a positive social, emotional, and physical well-being" or that "each student shall gain knowledge and have exposure to different cultures and lifestyles" (Manno, 1995). With goals as vague as this, it is hard to understand how it could be determined whether students had met them. Furthermore, some of the goals, even though vague, caused controversy. Conservatives who advocated a "back to basics" curriculum were upset by goals that seemed to stress attitudes, dispositions, and sentiments (Manno, 1995). Although many educators continue to advocate clearer standards for what is to be taught, to be useful these standards must express measurable goals if accountability in education is ever to be a reality.

Education as a Profession

One problem that stands in the way of educational reform is the relatively low pay and low status of teachers in the United States. This stems historically from the fact that most elementary and secondary schoolteachers have been women. Teachers were often unmarried women who earned so little that they had to board with families in the towns where they worked. The pattern of low pay continued even as more married women entered teaching, for they were expected to be supported by their husbands.

Even though men as well as women teach school nowadays, teachers are still paid poorly, especially in relation to their years of schooling. This is a special problem in areas such as math and science, where those with enough training to teach can get jobs that pay far more in private industry. Low salaries mean that many of the best and the brightest young college graduates do not choose teaching; and as long as teachers' salaries are based on taxes, this is unlikely to change, given public resistance to tax increases.

Efforts to professionalize teaching have a long history. They have two goals—to improve the social and economic status of teachers and to improve teaching. So far, such efforts have had only mixed success. There are continuing efforts to impose minimum standards for classroom teachers and to improve evaluation procedures and promotion possibilities. For example, the title "master teacher"—with a higher salary attached—has been used to reward outstanding teachers, instead of rewarding them with a promotion out of teaching and into an administrative job. Efforts to improve teachers' preparation have often not had the desired effect, since they often have emphasized more courses in education rather than in the subject matter to be taught. An alternative suggestion (yet to be accepted) is that teachers first get a degree in their chosen subject and then take education courses in graduate school, leading to a master's degree in education. This would help put teachers' education more nearly on a level with the training for other professions. Some critics have argued that efforts to professionalize teaching are not really likely to benefit teachers or students as much as "teacher educators"—professors of education (Larabee, 1992). Efforts at professionalization rarely stress classroom creativity or knowledge of the sub-

There is no substitute for an imaginative, enthusiastic, committed teacher, who knows how to teach. Our society pays lip service to the importance of teachers, but fails to offer the salaries and support that would encourage "the best and the brightest" to become teachers.

ject to be taught; rather, they seem bent on creating a research-oriented "science" of pedagogy. Yet it is clear that good professional teachers are needed, and they need training in education as well as in the subject matter they teach. As the key ingredient in any educational system, they deserve support. At the present time, society demands much of teachers, pays lip service to their importance, and offers scanty rewards for their efforts.

SUMMARY

1. Education is a structured form of socialization in which a culture's knowledge, skills, and values are formally transmitted from one generation to the next. Schools perform two basic functions, a manifest function and a latent function. The manifest function is to teach specific subject matter, such as reading, writing, and arithmetic. The latent function is to teach social skills and attitudes, such as self-discipline and obedience to authority. Schools' latent functions have been called the hidden curriculum.

2. Schools are called on to perform many functions in society. Among these are teaching skills, transmitting culture, encouraging cultural adaptation, instilling discipline, encouraging group work, promoting ethical behavior, selecting talent, and rewarding achievement.

3. School systems, like other institutions, are organized in ways that reflect the distribution of power in society. Powerful cultural elites, for example, shape school curricula. Students from middle-class backgrounds have advantages in school compared with students from less advantaged backgrounds, since their culture and experiences are more "in sync" with school culture. Students from minority or non-English-speaking backgrounds may have difficulty in a school environment.

4. Students may engage in resistance, or behavior that rejects school values and procedures. Resistance is often counterproductive in that it results in school failure and ultimately in diminished life chances. Resistance to school among working-class students acts to preserve the class structure of society.

5. The amount of education that Americans get has increased dramatically throughout the twentieth century. More than a million Americans receive bachelor's degrees each year, and more jobs than ever now require a degree. Higher levels of education are being increasingly required for many types of jobs, a practice known as credentialism. The average annual earnings of a college graduate are nearly twice those of a high school graduate.

6. Educational opportunities go disproportionately to those whose parents had such opportunities before them. Children whose parents care about their education and who are well provided with cultural capital have an advantage in school.

7. Tracking is the practice of grouping students according to their perceived abilities and interests. Critics charge that tracks assigned to students reflect social class, and note that research has failed to demonstrate that most children learn better in homogeneous groups. Tracking systems work best when there is mobility among tracks and when it is based on students' actual achievements rather than on IQ scores.

8. About 20 percent of those who enter high school drop out before they graduate. Students who drop out usually have a history of problems in school from their early years and often are burdened with "negative cultural capital" from their families. Students with fewer years of schooling are more likely to lack basic literacy, the ability to read and write. Functional illiteracy seems to be a growing problem in the United States.

9. A number of efforts have been made to reform the schools. Perhaps the single biggest reform has been school desegregation, which began with the Supreme Court's *Brown* v. *Board of Education* decision (1954), declaring racially segregated schools unconstitutional. Before *Brown*, black schools were generally inferior to those for whites. One technique for achieving racial balance in schools has been busing. Opposition to busing has been considerable, and white flight from the public schools has made it harder to achieve integration in many areas. Affirmative action, which sometimes involves giving preferences in college admission to minority students, has aided black progress but continues to be controversial.

10. Other school reforms that have been advocated include privatization, or turning the management of a school system over to a private agency or company, and systems of school choice such as the use of vouchers. Privatization has met with mixed results. Voucher systems, which would permit tax moneys to go to private and religious schools, present a number of problems and have not been widely implemented.

11. The movement toward accountability in education has spawned an approach called outcome-based education. In this plan, children would be given a clear set of goals and would advance in school only when the goals were met. Controversy still surrounds this approach.

12. Efforts to professionalize teaching have a long history, but despite their importance in any educational system, American teachers still have relatively low status and low pay. Reforms in teacher education have been suggested as a way of improving this situation.

REVIEW QUESTIONS

1. What are the social functions of schools? Give some examples.

2. How does the educational system reflect the power structure in society? What are the causes and consequences of student resistance?

3. The level of education has risen in the United States as a whole; and at the same time, functional illiteracy has increased. Explain the apparent paradox.

4. How do cultural capital and tracking affect the distribution of higher education?

5. Describe efforts to achieve racial equality in educational opportunity, including successes and setbacks.

6. Discuss the pros and cons of current proposals for educational reform, including: vouchers, privatization, accountability, and professionalization.

CRITICAL THINKING QUESTIONS

1. Are educational institutions in the United States today more focused on preparing workers and others with the skills society needs, or with providing individual students with the opportunities to fulfill their potentials and desires? What are the virtues and pitfalls of each goal?

2. In what ways have you seen social class at work in shaping educational opportunities, the content of instruction, or the achievement of students?

3. The number of years Americans spend in school has increased dramatically. To what extent is this needed to meet new functional demands for education and to what extent is it due to credentialism?

4. On balance, are educational institutions today more of a force for social change or for conserving the existing culture by passing it on to the next generation?

5. What do you think are the most important goals for an educational system? What reforms do you think would best help American schools to meet these goals?

GLOSSARY

Affirmative action   Explicit effort to overcome the effects of discrimination by improving the competitive chances of minorities.

Compensatory education   Enrichment programs to help disadvantaged students compete on a more nearly equal basis with privileged students.

Credentialism   The requirement that a person hold a diploma or degree as a condition of employment.

Cultural capital   Advantages such as exposure to books, educational toys, and opportunities to develop special talents that help one succeed in school.

Education   The formal, systematic transmission of a culture's skills, knowledge, and values from one generation to the next.

Hidden curriculum   A set of unwritten rules of behavior taught in school that prepare children for academic and social success in the world outside school.

Latent function   The function of the schools in teaching social skills and attitudes.

Manifest function   The function of the schools in teaching academic skills, such as reading and writing.

Outcome-based education   Educational reform concept that would require explicit educational goals and evaluation of students to see if they meet them.

Resistance   Behavior that rejects school values and procedures.

Tracking   Grouping students in school according to their perceived abilities and interests.

White flight   The departure of white families from neighborhoods undergoing school desegregation (busing) and other forms of racial integration.

Religion

H e draws crowds by the millions; his support can prop up or topple governments; his word can influence national and international policy; he has written a best-seller; and across the world millions of children are named after him. He is Pope John Paul II, spiritual leader of the Roman Catholic faith and a major political influence in many Catholic-dominated nations. In 1994 it was John Paul's intervention that changed the cast of the report of the U.N. population conference held in Cairo. The first draft of the document endorsed access to abortion as a fundamental right of all women. Under the pope's direction, Vatican delegates to the conference lobbied and filibustered as they lined up Latin American allies as well as Islamic nations opposed to abortion. The result was inclusion of the statement that "in no case should abortion be promoted as a method of family planning" (*Time*, December 26, 1994/January 2, 1995).

In the United States, Ralph Reed, the director of the Christian Coalition, does not have the prestige or the enormous constituency that the pope enjoys, but he does have political power. The Christian Coalition is a grassroots organization anchored in the "religious right" and committed to what it calls a pro-family agenda: in particular, school prayer and opposition to abortion. Reed's group is credited with obtaining at least half the fifty-two-seat gain in the House of Representatives for the Republicans in 1994. In return for their support for the Contract with America, Reed and his followers expect congressional help with their right-wing causes. Republican candidates for the 1996 presidential race rarely made a step without consulting Reed, and they tailored their platforms to his agenda. The Christian Coalition has also been active at the local level, where it targets school boards. According to Reed, "The future of America is not [shaped] by who sits in the Oval Office

347

but by who sits in the principal's office" (*Time,* May 15, 1995, p. 31). The conservative Christians who form the Christian Coalition do not represent the center of American religion, but they have managed to position their organization at the center of American politics.

Religion's secular power can also be observed in other parts of the world today and in other religious traditions. In North Africa, the Middle East, India, and parts of the Far East, fundamentalist sects among Jews, Muslims, and Hindus are attempting (often with great success) to impose their beliefs on whole nations, through actual or virtual control of the government.

From these examples it is clear that religion plays a central role in all parts of the world today: It is not just a matter of purveying cultural values but also of exercising political power. At the same time, as students of sociology we should not lose sight of the fact that religion is only one social institution among many in the world. Millions of people remain unaffected or unimpressed by religious fervor and intervention in politics. One can still find a widespread apathy to religion as well as a substantial number of agnostics and atheists. It was not too long ago that slogans proclaiming "God is dead" seemed to herald the end of religion. Many people thought the scientific knowledge and rationalistic thinking of the modern era would simply eliminate religion. While this has not happened, religion has been *changed* by the new ways of thinking. Instead of a decline of religion we have seen what sociologist Stephen Warner (1993) calls a rise of "religious adaptability." That is, in response to challenges posed by religious diversity and nonreligious cultural forces, some religious leaders are articulating their beliefs more forcefully, actively recruiting members, and trying to use political means to advance their religious ends. These efforts are often being met by counterefforts on the part of other religious leaders and secular leaders who call for a strong separation of church and state. Thus, when we study the sociology of religion in the modern world, we also find ourselves studying the relationship between the religious and the secular.

DEFINING RELIGION

[Scientology] contains the secrets of the universe. [Actor John Travolta (in *Time,* May 6, 1991)]

Scientology is quite likely the most ruthless, the most classically terroristic, the most litigious and the most lucrative cult the country has ever seen. [Vicki Aznaran, former leader of Scientology (in *Time,* May 6, 1991)]

What *is* Scientology? The Church of Scientology was founded in the late 1950s by L. Ron Hubbard, a former science fiction writer (Wilson, 1990). The goal of the organization is to release individuals from the grip of painful emotional and physical experiences and to replace grief and apathy with enthusiasm and exhilaration. To achieve this goal, members must enroll in a series of courses, each rationally planned and measured (hence the name "*Scien*tology"). Only a small number of those who embark on this quest, which may cost thousands of dollars and take years to complete, will obtain harmony with the universe and mastery over their fate.

In a mere four decades, Scientology has grown from a handful of self-help groups to a multimillion-dollar organization that claims to have 700 centers in sixty-five countries and some 6.5 million followers (*Los Angeles Times,* June 24, 1990; *Time,* May 6, 1991), though these figures are disputed (*Encyclopaedia Britannica,* 1994). From its beginning, Scientology has been controversial. Many psychiatrists and sociologists dismiss it as bogus (Bainbridge and Stark, 1980). Journalists have exposed gaps and apparent lies in founder Hubbard's biography. Numerous lawsuits have charged the group with terrorizing its critics, brainwashing and exploiting its recruits, and defrauding its members of thousands of dollars. Eleven of its top leaders were imprisoned for burglarizing federal agencies that were investigating the organization.

So, is Scientology really a religion? The answer is of more than academic interest. It matters to parents who want the courts' help in "deprogramming" children whom the parents feel were "brainwashed" by the church. It matters to individuals who believe that Scientology damaged their emotional health, depleted their life savings, or broke up their families. It matters to companies and communities that became involved in business deals without knowing that their partners were connected to Scientology. It matters to members of the church who want public recognition and tax deductions for their contributions. And it matters to society as a whole.

Because of the constitutional separation of church and state, the U.S. government does not normally become involved in internal religious matters, but for tax purposes it must decide whether a group does or does not qualify as a religion. The Internal Revenue Service can deny tax-exempt status to any self-proclaimed religious organization that operates for other than religious purposes, that enriches individuals, that engages in partisan politics, and that commits crimes. It can also require that a church have a recognized creed or statement of beliefs and form of worship, a formal doctrine, a distinct ecclesiastical government, ordained ministers, established places of worship, and regular congregations and religious services (Podus, 1996). The IRS has been battling the Church of Scientology since the early 1960s. Initially it ruled that fees paid to the Church for counseling sessions, which Scientologists consider central to their religious practice, were payments for services and could not be tax-deductible. This ruling was upheld by the Supreme Court in 1989. Then, in 1993, the IRS reversed itself as part of an undisclosed settlement agreement with the Church of Scientology. The IRS's shifting position shows that the boundary between religious and commercial practices is a fine one, and where it is drawn is consequential for many segments of society (Podus, 1996). In other parts of the world, the government of Spain has expelled Scientology from the country, while the High Court of Australia has formally recognized it as a church (Wilson, 1990).

As this example shows, defining religion is exceedingly difficult. Must religion involve a belief in a supernatural being? If so, then Chinese Confucianism, which teaches proper ways to live in this world, would be disqualified. Must there be an idea of one supreme being or God? That would leave out religions such as Hinduism, which recognize many gods. Is the notion of "salvation" sufficient to identify a group as a religion? If so, EST and other therapy groups from the human-potential movement within psychology would have to be included. In fact, religion has never been defined in a way that satisfies everyone, because the various definitions have tended to favor some claims over others.

Sociological definitions of **religion** focus in varying degrees on three basic elements, all stressed by the most influential founder of the sociology of religion, Émile Durkheim (1912/1965). The first element is *beliefs*. As we saw in Chapter 4, beliefs are basic elements of *culture*. For many religious people belief in God or a supreme being is crucial. Second,

religion is not just a matter of what people believe but also of what they do, so many sociological definitions of religion focus on the presence of distinctive *social practices* that represent organized, highly patterned forms of social *action*. The most significant of these are rituals, such as ceremonies of worship. Religion also shapes social action by instructing believers to perform certain actions or refrain from others, such as do the Ten Commandments and the Golden Rule. Third, in defining religion, sociologists ask whether a group has created a *moral community*. Religions, they suggest, must draw people together in a social *structure* and organize relations in terms of moral commitment and standards of right or good behavior.

KEY CONCEPTS IN THE SOCIOLOGY OF RELIGION

First and foremost, religion is a matter of culture, but because it is such a pervasive and influential social institution, religion can also be viewed through the lens of each of the other key concepts: action, structure, function, and power. Indeed, religion cannot be fully understood unless seen through all of these dimensions.

Culture: Religious Beliefs and Symbols

In Chapter 4 we learned that beliefs and symbols are crucial elements of culture. At the heart of religion lies a system of sacred beliefs and symbols. Beliefs are cultural certainties that do not require empirical proof to be accepted as true or real. The Mbuti Pygmies of Africa believe that the forest in which they live is a supernatural being. They personify it as Mother and Father, Life-Giver, and occasionally Death-Giver. Their belief is an example of **animism**, or the idea that things in the world (a forest, a tree, an animal, a mountain, or a river, for instance) have active, animate spirits. In some religions people believe in ancestral spirits. An example is Shintoism, most of whose 38 million followers are Japanese.

More familiar to Westerners is the religious belief known as **theism**, which is the idea that powerful supernatural beings are involved with events and conditions on earth. *Monotheists*, such as the world's 1.8 billion Christians, 17 million Jews, and 950 million

Muslims (*Encyclopaedia Britannica*, 1992), believe in a single supernatural being, called God, Yahweh, or Allah. *Polytheists*, in contrast, believe in several deities. Today's 720 million Hindus, most of whom live in India, have a pantheon of many minor gods and five major ones, who are in turn reflections of a higher, more sacred principle of Brahman, or "Oneness."

In other religions, beliefs center on a supernatural force rather than a supernatural being. Polynesians, for example, believe in a force called *mana*, which can inhabit objects and people. A canoe that is able to withstand intense storms or a farmer whose crops flourish is said to possess mana. This kind of religious belief is most common in preindustrial countries.

Émile Durkheim was one of the first sociologists to propose explanations for the religious beliefs that people develop. Durkheim (1912/1965) identified the distinction between the *sacred* and the *profane* as an essential part of a religion. By *sacred* he meant that which is set apart from everyday experience and inspires awe and reverence. The profane, in contrast, is that which is mundane and ordinary. It is the community that bestows sacredness on things. Religion, in turn, functions to promote social unity and to create moral and intellectual consensus. So, according to Durkheim, a central element in the definition of religion is that it pertains to what the community has determined to be sacred.

Durkheim began by studying Australian aboriginal clans, which he believed were the simplest kind of human society and therefore should have elementary forms of religion. A central part of aboriginal religion is the **totem:** an object (usually an animal or plant) that symbolizes both the clan itself and that which the clan considers sacred. Durkheim was intrigued by this dual symbolism of the clan and the sacred. He argued that in worshipping a totem, the aborigines were essentially revering their own society or social group. Durkheim concluded that religious beliefs stem from people's experiences with the social forces that shape their lives. For instance, a belief in divine creation arises from the fact that we are products of a culture that seems outside us and is not of our own making. "We speak a language that we did not make," wrote Durkheim; "we use instruments we did not invent, we invoke rights that we did not found, a treasury of knowledge is transmitted to each generation that it did not gather itself" (Durkheim, 1912/1965, p. 212). By extension, we our-

selves are fashioned by external forces beyond our control, forces that deserve our awe and devotion. The same idea is embodied in the belief in a god who created the world.

Certain basic beliefs pervade religions in America today (*The Gallup Poll Monthly*, January 1995; February 1995). About 96 percent of Americans believe in God; 90 percent believe in a heaven, and 73 percent believe there is a hell. Two-thirds of Americans acknowledge the existence of the Devil, and 72 percent believe in angels. Those with postgraduate educations, liberal ideological leanings, and higher incomes tend to be the most skeptical of these phenomena. Older people are less likely to believe in a hell or the Devil than are younger people. Women are more likely than men to believe in angels (78 percent to 65 percent) and miracles (86 percent to 71 percent).

In addition to beliefs in deities, spirits, or supernatural forces, most religions incorporate moral principles. These beliefs about what is right and wrong, good and bad, proper and improper, are not just abstract ideas, but prescriptions for behavior. Adherents of the religion are expected to use these principles as guides in their daily lives (Gellner, 1972). In some nontheistic religions (those without ideas of a deity), the moral principles are paramount. Buddhists, for instance, are less concerned with revering the Buddha than with achieving the ethical and spiritual ideas that the Buddha set forth in his message of the "four noble truths." Other religions that focus on a striving toward moral goals are Confucianism and Taoism, both of which originated in China.

Virtually all religions are expressed through *symbols*, or things that stand for something other than themselves. Nothing is symbolic in and of itself. People agree among themselves about what the symbolic meanings are and assign those meanings to various words, actions, and objects. The Christian communion ceremony, for example, includes both symbolic acts (drinking wine and eating bread to commemorate the Last Supper) and symbolic objects (the wine and bread themselves, symbolizing the blood and body of Christ). Durkheim argued that the use of such religious symbols often involves what he called *collective representation*: communication from larger social bodies to individuals. Thus, the various symbols used in a Christian communion speak from all those who share the Christian faith (including past generations) to all those who are currently participating in the ceremony.

Social Action: Religious Practices and Experiences

The rituals and ceremonies of religion are a form of social action. Sociologists often refer to "ritual practices" or "religious practices" to indicate actions that are performed repeatedly in accord with rules or an understanding of deeper, shared meaning. These practices can satisfy personal religious needs, such as creating a link to God through prayer, but they also can establish a religious community, as when a Roman Catholic congregation gathers to celebrate Holy Communion.

Religion is also a form of social action whereby believers express their faith, communicate it to others, seek supernatural guidance or intervention, honor their deities, affirm their sacred beliefs, or simply produce religious experiences. Religious practices take many forms. They may be shared or solitary, compulsory or optional, rigidly structured or open to creative innovations. Music, dance, prayer, meditation, feasting, and fasting are just a few of the many activities carried out in the name of religion.

Some religious practices can be classified as **rituals,** or standardized sets of actions used in particular ceremonies or on other specific occasions. Rituals rely on symbols to convey their meaning and to reinforce that meaning for participants. The ritual cleansing with water in a Christian baptism or the ritual reading from the Torah in a Jewish bar mitzvah are solemn acts that convey deep spiritual meaning to participants and help to give them a sense of religious community (Douglas, 1970; Gluckman, 1962; Turner, 1970). Rituals can be secular, too, but they are accorded much less sanctity. For instance, the custom of requiring people to stand when a judge enters a courtroom is a ritual that lends respect and gravity to a court of law.

Religions also prescribe actions that are not rituals. These include moral instructions for living one's daily life, as well as prohibitions. Jews are told to eat only kosher foods. Christians are told to "do unto others as you would have them do unto you." Muslims are told that it is immoral to charge interest on a loan to other Muslims. Some versions of Christianity have encouraged their people to have large families to bring new souls into the world and expand the numbers of Christians. Others have encouraged celibacy in the belief that refraining from sex keeps one's thoughts closer to heavenly purity. As each of these examples shows, religions help to organize the social actions people take (or refrain from taking), as well as their beliefs.

People who claim to be followers of a particular religion do not necessarily observe all of that religion's rituals and other practices. Not all professed Christians go to church, for example, and not all who go to church take communion. While 60 percent of Americans say that religion is "very important" in their lives, only 30 percent report going to a religious service at least once a week (see Figure 13.1). When asked if they actually attended a church or a

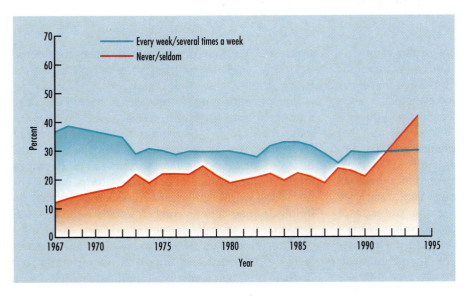

FIGURE 13.1 / Reports on Religious Service Attendance, 1967–1994

Over the past three decades the percentage of Americans who reported attending religious services at least once a week has declined from close to 40 percent to 30 percent, and the percentage who report attending "seldom" or "never" has increased from 11 to over 40 percent.

Source: Surveys by the National Opinion Research Center, in "America: Land of the Faithful," *The American Enterprise,* November–December 1990, p. 97; *Gallup Poll Monthly,* February 1995.

Determining Rates of Church Attendance

C. Kirk Hadaway and his colleagues (1993) suspected that rates of church attendance reported by respondents in polls and surveys were inflated. After all, everyone wants to look good. And if cultural norms hold that church attendance is desirable, it is understandable that a person might exaggerate how often he or she goes to church. This is not a matter of outright lying to the survey researcher, but more a reflection of wishful thinking and good intentions. But how were the researchers to arrive at the true data?

Hadaway et al. checked the church attendance of two different groups, the Protestant population of a county in Ohio and the Catholic population in selected dioceses (church administrative districts) in the United States. The researchers used two different methods of gathering data. In the case of the Protestant group they collected three types of data: (1) estimates of religious preferences based on telephone polls, (2) estimates of church attendance based on telephone polls, and (3) actual counts of church attendance for all Protestants in the county. Based on their telephone survey of 602 randomly selected county residents, they estimated that Protestants numbered about 66,565 persons and that close to 36 percent of them had attended church in the last seven days. The researchers then tracked down every Protestant church in the county and either obtained average attendance figures from the church organization or estimated attendance from the number of cars in the lot during a service. The results? An attendance total of 13,080, or 19.6 percent of Protestants in

the county—a little more than half the self-reported attendance of 36 percent.

They found similar discrepancies in reported and actual attendance among Catholics. In this case, the researchers used as their database dioceses representing a cross section of the country. Making use of a nationwide survey of religious affiliation completed in 1990, they estimated the adult population that is Catholic for each diocese. (They were able to do this because the survey data contained county codes, and dioceses usually consist of a set of counties.) The researchers then obtained attendance data from the dioceses, which conduct a count of all individuals attending a religious service on a given weekend in the fall. They compared this attendance count with the self-reported weekly attendance figures obtained from Gallup Polls. The results? Whereas 51 percent of Catholics *say* they attended church within the last week, the actually counted attendance is closer to 28 percent—again, about half of what was expected.

Catholics are much more likely to say they go to church than Protestants, and they are also more likely to actually go. However, for both groups the general findings hold true: Self-reports of church attendance are substantial exaggerations. This study shows that sociologists need to be careful about using people's reports on behavior that is normative. Researchers should attempt to supplement survey questionnaires by systematically checking self-reports against other data sources.

synagogue "in the last seven days," 38 percent responded in the affirmative (*The Gallup Poll Monthly*, February 1995). There is reason to believe that these self-reports overstate the case, however. Using a variety of data sources and ways of collecting data (see the Research Methods box), one study found that church attendance among Protestants and Catholics is roughly half that reported in polls (Hadaway, Marler, and Chaves, 1993). Moreover, denominations that surveys and polls indicate must be growing are actually declining; for example, the number of Americans claiming to be Episcopalians should have made the denomination increase by 13 percent between 1967 and 1990, whereas the membership in fact declined by 28 percent. The researchers attribute this gap in part to the desire of respondents to live

up to social norms (church attendance is considered desirable) and internalized rules ("I go to church every Sunday").

Regular attendance at religious services is greatest among Roman Catholics, followed by Protestants, and then Jews (*Emerging Trends*, November/ December 1987). In part, these differences reflect the different meanings that the various religious groups attach to attendance at services. Compared to the rest of the world, Americans come across as fairly religious in their actions and beliefs (see Table 13.1, but note that it uses self-reported data).

In addition to ritual actions, religion is characterized by powerful and important experiences that reaffirm members' faith (Stark and Bainbridge, 1985). Sometimes religious experiences involve intensified

TABLE 13.1

Cross-cultural Comparison by Percent of Religious Actions and Beliefs, 1981–1983

Country	Attend Church Monthly	Member of Religious Association	Feel Religious	Believe in God	Believe in Life After Death	Believe in the Devil
USA	59.4	53.7	81.3	95.6	70.5	65.9
Britain	22.9	20.9	53.0	72.5	46.5	30.3
France	16.5	3.8	48.3	59.0	35.0	16.1
Germany	33.9	11.9	53.5	68.2	36.0	16.1
Italy	48.1	5.7	80.2	82.2	46.4	28.2
Mexico	74.6	17.0	74.3	97.0	64.2	51.3
Norway	13.9	8.8	43.4	67.6	40.9	27.0

Source: Robert A. Campbell and James E. Curtis, "Religious Involvement Across Societies: Analyses for Alternative Measures in National Surveys," Journal for the Scientific Study of Religion 33, no. 3 (1994): p. 221.

awareness of a supernatural being or power. This may be accompanied by a sense of spiritual cleansing or purification. The so-called born-again experience associated with conversion to fundamentalist Christianity often takes this form (Tipton, 1982). Other religious experiences involve transcending the here and now in deep emotional experiences or ecstasies (Evens and Peacock, 1990). Certain Muslim groups, for instance, use violent whirling, dancing, and shouting to reach states of altered consciousness. In other religions drugs may be ritually used to achieve the same goal. Religious experiences also include the feeling of having attained personal contact with a deity. People may even report being given divine revelations. Closely related is a sense of oneness with other people (especially members of one's own religious group) or a strong identity with nature. Ritual provides occasions for religious experience to take place on a regular basis. Both rituals and the experiences they encourage are shaped by religious symbols and beliefs.

Social Structure: Religious Community

One of the most important features of religion is its creation of what Durkheim called **moral community.** This community is composed of people whose shared beliefs, symbols, practices, and experiences bind them together into a larger social whole. So important is community to the life of a religion that its absence is seen as a serious problem. Many contempo-

rary clergy, for example, are concerned that the spread of TV evangelism promotes religion without community. Religious broadcasts may create the illusion that viewers are in church, talking face-to-face with the minister, but in fact they are alone in their homes and are strangers to one another and to those in the televised church. They can connect and disconnect their religious attachments simply by turning their sets on and off.

Religious communities are not just groups of people who happen to share beliefs and engage in common rituals. They have an organized, and usually enduring, social structure. In the United States today, many religious groups, such as the United Methodist church, have formal organizations that give them a national structure. The Roman Catholic church, with its system of priests, bishops, and cardinals under a pope, has a fully international structure. The social structure of religious groups encompasses a variety of organizations, including central offices, seminaries for training religious leaders, publishers of prayer books and hymnals, distributors of items such as communion wafers and choir gowns, youth camps, and overseas missions. Religious groups also have a structure in terms of the relationships between members. People are more likely to marry within their religion. Prayer groups of Christians in business establish a network of links that promotes business as well as religion.

The scope of a religious community varies with the type of society involved. In a small tribe, religion encompasses everyone and affects every aspect of

Religion is universal, but beliefs and practices vary. At the core of Buddhism is the belief that cleansing oneself of worldly desires, and ultimately of selfhood, lead to Nirvana. In predominantly Buddhist societies such as Myanmar, formerly Burma (shown here), most young men enter monasteries for a year or more; some remain monks for life.

life. People might seek the guidance of ancestral spirits regarding how to handle family concerns, how to decide political matters, when to plant and harvest or hunt and fish, or how to cure an illness. The religious community and society are virtually one and the same (Calhoun, 1980; Evans-Pritchard, 1965; Fortes, 1969). In larger, more complex societies, religion is more compartmentalized. People may seek guidance on family matters from their minister, but they turn to a physician when a family member is ill or to a banker for advice on investments. Furthermore, larger societies often encompass a variety of religions, each with its own churches, schools, charities, and so forth.

Religion and Functional Integration

Even in large, complex societies, religions help achieve functional integration in both the religious community and society at large. Religious involvement helps knit society together in several ways. First, it encourages adherence to and sharing of moral standards. It helps to create meaningful social bonds among people in local religious communities. For example, in the United States, churches have often helped immigrants adapt to their new homeland (Greeley, 1972). Churches modeled after those in the immigrants' homelands provide a haven of traditional beliefs and customs that help ease the transition to a new way of life. Second, religions link local communities together through national and international organizations, as well as shared rituals. Finally, when respect for secular social institutions is made part of religious beliefs and practices, religions help to legitimate the established social order.

The extent to which religious institutions help to achieve functional integration varies from one society to another. In some societies, nearly everyone is a member of the same religion. For example, in both France and Ireland, Catholicism is predominant. In others, like the United States and India, there are many different religions. The extent of religious involvement also varies. The United States has one of the highest rates of attendance at religious services in the world (see Figure 13.1). In some societies, such as Iran and Great Britain, the government officially supports one religion. In others, including the United States, church and state are officially kept separate.

One way that religion legitimates the established social order is by sanctioning the prevailing social arrangements. Guy Swanson (1974) showed this in a study of fifty non-Western societies. Just as Durkheim had suggested, each society tended to reflect itself in its religion. For instance, in societies where elders occupied important positions, ancestors were worshiped; and in societies with large inequalities in wealth, religion tended to support a wide gap between rich and poor. In our own society, television evangelists who encourage people to fulfill their individual potential are endorsing American cultural values of ambition and individual opportunity.

Religious legitimation of the established social order also can be seen in what the sociologist Robert Bellah (1970) calls national, or civil, religion. **Civil religion** is essentially a sanctifying of the nation by associating its history, values, and institutions with

Nearly all religions revolve around rituals which are centered on symbols of the sacred. During the Polish struggle against communism in the 1980s, workers hung a portrait of Polish-born Pope John Paul II on a factory gate. Throughout the revolution, the Catholic faith provided a source of strength and a sense of community for workers in different industries and cities.

God's special favor. One study of civil religion among elementary school children found that 85 percent believed that America "has been placed on this earth for a special purpose," that it is God's chosen nation, and that its success is a reward for its goodness (Smidt, 1980). Most adults also feel that our country was created "under God" and that from God the government derives its ultimate legitimacy. The United States Constitution expressly forbids any ties between the state and particular religions, however, so civil religion involves a very general seeking of blessings from God. God's aid is invoked at the opening of Congress, at political party conventions, at swearing-in ceremonies, and in political speeches, including every presidential inaugural address but one (George Washington's second, which was only two paragraphs long).

Civil religion, then, creates links between the sacred and the secular. In so doing, it encourages willingness to care about and sacrifice for the public good (Bellah and Hammond, 1980; Coleman, 1983). Civil religion can come in both conservative and liberal forms and can stress both our freedom to choose and our obligations to one another (Wuthnow, 1988).

Sometimes the idea of religious community is used in more radical ways. For example, during the Middle Ages the Franciscan monks renounced all personal property in favor of a communal sharing of possessions. This lifestyle, intended as a message to the world about proper Christ-like behavior, created conflict with the church hierarchy. A similar process has occurred in modern times with the rise of liberation theology, a movement started by Latin American Catholic priests concerned about the gap between rich and poor. Uniting religious conviction with social activism and ministering especially to the poor and landless, these priests founded "base ecclesial communities," or settlements in which, like early Christians, they emphasized a common struggle against oppression (Gutierrez, 1973, 1983; Pena, 1994). Liberation theology had its heyday in the 1960s and 1970s, but its influence has waned in recent years for a number of reasons: a political turn to the right, a rise in popularity of evangelical Protestantism in Latin America, and conflicts with the nondemocratic institution of the Roman Catholic church, with its centralized hierarchy and top-down authority (Smith, 1994). The pope essentially instructed the priests to focus on spiritual concerns and get out of politics. Liberation theology could revive, however, if its leaders rethink basic ideas about politics and plans of action, playing the waiting game instead of trying instantly to transform the social and political landscape (Levine, 1995).

Power in Religious Communities

As the contrasting examples of civil religion and liberation theology show, religious faith may be the basis for involvement with power relations, either supporting them through civil religion or struggling to change them, as in liberation theology.

Although many religious groups emphasize equality (or at least community) among believers, they give greater power to some members than others. Generally, we can distinguish two roles in a religious group: the leadership role accorded to some members, such as priests, and the follower role characteristic of other members.

Priests have played a crucial role in defining modern religions and giving them their distinctive culture. As the sociologist Pierre Bourdieu (1991) notes, religious leaders have the power to mobilize religious communities and to divide the sacred from the profane. The history of many religions can be viewed as a struggle among various groups for the power to designate correct beliefs and practices, thereby dominating the organization. According to Bourdieu, every religious body represents the power of its current leaders as well as previous struggles over how to define that religion and organize religious life.

The establishment of an individual priest's power is often a critical factor in defining a religious community, because a local minister or rabbi can give a church or synagogue much of its distinctive identity. In many of the world's religions priests have had a near-monopoly on the interpretation of sacred texts because they were among the few members of the society who could read.

In addition, religious factions or different religions may compete with one another for authority. Each church carves out its own religious community, and different churches tend to be at odds over the kind of community the larger society should build and the share in that community each church should have. As religions develop national and international church bureaucracies, these organizations tend to become weapons in power struggles among believers over what the church should do. For example, should Christian churches accept homosexual members, even letting them preach? In 1992, the Southern Baptist Convention decided it would not and expelled two North Carolina congregations that disobeyed. As societies become larger and include members of different religions (as well as people who are nonreligious), occasions for competition and conflict multiply. For example, Jews and other non-Christians in the United States protest when Christians use their power to spend public money on religious symbols (such as Christmas decorations) or to promote religious practices (such as Christian prayers in the school).

TYPES OF RELIGIOUS INSTITUTIONS

Most religious communities organize themselves into some type of institution—some set of relatively stable roles, statuses, groups, and values. The forms that religious institutions take vary greatly, however, depending on such factors as their size, doctrines, membership, origins, and relations with the rest of society. On the basis of such factors, sociologists recognize *church*, *sect*, and *cult* as the three major forms of religious institutions.

Churches and Sects

The sociologist Ernst Troeltsch (1931) viewed religious institutions as typically falling into the categories of either churches or sects. Table 13.2 lists some of the characteristics of church and sect according to Troeltsch and his followers. Note that any given religious group need not conform 100 percent to one or the other list of features. These descriptions are merely *ideal* types, which serve as conceptual tools that can be used to measure reality and to make comparisons (see Chapter 1).

Troeltsch defined a **sect** as a small, exclusive, uncompromising fellowship of people seeking spiritual perfection. Members typically are voluntary converts, and their lives are largely controlled by the sect. Troeltsch found that a sect is usually characterized by asceticism; members adopt austere, disciplined lifestyles. Most sects are concerned strictly with their own religious doctrines. They see themselves as select groups that have been granted spe-

TABLE 13.2
Church and Sect

Characteristic	Church	Sect
Size	Large	Small
Relationship with other religious groups	Tolerant	Rejects; feels it has sole truth
Wealth	Extensive	Limited
Religious services	Limited congregational participation; formal; intellectual emphasis	Extensive congregational participation; spontaneous; emotional emphasis
Clergy	Specialized; professional	Unspecialized; little training; part-time
Doctrines	Liberal interpretation of Scriptures; emphasis upon this world	Literal interpretation of Scriptures; emphasis upon other world
Membership	By birth or ritual participation; social institution embracing all socially compatible	By conversion; moral community excluding unworthy
Social class of members	Mainly middle class	Mainly lower class
Relationship with secular world	Endorses prevailing culture and social organization	Renounces or opposes prevailing cultural standards; requires strict adherence to biblical standards

Source: Adapted from Liston Pope, Millhands and Preachers: A Study of Gastonia (Yale University Press, New Haven, Conn., 1942).

cial enlightenment. Often they discourage their members from extensive participation in worldly affairs because they consider the world outside the sect to be decadent, corrupt, and sinful.

As a sect grows, Troeltsch believed, it typically evolves into a **church**—a large, conservative, universalist religious institution. Its growth increasingly comes from those born into the group, not from conversion. A church is more tolerant of other religious groups than a sect is. Because it is large, a church tends to acquire a certain amount of social and political power, and often it retains that power by becoming associated with the government or the ruling class. A church thus accommodates itself to the claims of powerful groups and the dominant institutions, and it tends to support the society's status quo. The Church of England, the Catholic church in Spain, and the Muslim Shiites in Iran come close to this ideal type.

Although Troeltsch's descriptions offer many valuable insights about church and sect, some sociologists think that his models may lead to confusion over how to classify certain real-life religious institutions. Granted, there are both churches and sects with all the traits in Troeltsch's definitions—but there are also churches with some of the traits of sects, as well as sects with some of the traits of churches. For this reason, some sociologists prefer to classify religious institutions according to just one dimension: the institution's acceptance of or rejection of its social environment (Johnson, 1963; Stark and Bainbridge, 1985). At one end of this continuum is the church that is at one with its social environment; at the other end of the continuum is the sect that exists in a perpetual state of tension with the larger society. Most religious groups tend to fall somewhere in between these two extremes.

This model has the advantage of emphasizing the dynamics of an organization as it moves up or down the scale of tension with its environment. For example, as a sect gains stability and respectability, it begins to coexist more harmoniously with the surrounding society, thus moving closer to the church end of the continuum.

Cults

Stark and Bainbridge (1985) reserve the label *sect* for schismatic institutions formed when dissidents break away from an established church, claiming to be the authentic, cleansed version of the faith. The Puritans who broke with the Church of England and formed their own religious community are one example of a sect. In contrast, other religious institutions in tension with their environment are imported from other cultures or are formed when people create entirely new religious beliefs and practices. These institutions have no prior ties to established religious bodies in the same society. Stark and Bainbridge refer to these more innovative institutions as **cults.** In its early years Christianity was considered a cult. In fact, all the major religions of the world started as cults.

Stark and Bainbridge categorized cults into three types on the basis of how tightly they are organized. *Audience cults* have practically no formal organization. The members are actually consumers of cult doctrines delivered over the airwaves or in books, magazines, and newspaper columns. In *client cults*, the religious leaders offer specific services to those who follow them. Although the leaders are well-organized, the clients are not members of congregations. Scientology is often cited as an example of a client cult because it uses an organized network of paid staff members to teach cult doctrine to groups of clients.

Some client cults evolve into *cult movements* as they become larger and more tightly organized. If the growing movement is innovative and unusual, it may generate opposition in its social environment, and the label "cult" may be used pejoratively. This happened with the Reverend Sun Myung Moon's Unification church, an evangelical, messianic brand of Christianity whose early proponents (known as "Moonies") aggressively proselytized in the streets. In responding to opposition, cult leaders tend to tighten their organizational structures, make sharper distinctions between insiders and outsiders, and impose stronger demands of loyalty. Cults that permit their members to pursue normal lives and occupations typically arouse less opposition than do cults whose members abandon their normal activities and rupture ties to conventional institutions in order to become full-time followers.

The question of whether a religious group is a church, sect, or cult can become part of the competition for power and authority. As in the case of Scientology, one person's cult is another person's legitimate religion. Also, cults or sects that thrive tend to become more institutionalized and to take on the characteristics of churches. Ironically, this process can disillusion members, because it tends to make religion seem more "everyday" and less "sacred," weakening the religious experience.

RELIGIOUS INNOVATION

We tend to think of religions as relatively conservative forces that lend their support to the status quo. But religion is not always "conservative." **Religious innovation** takes place when groups create new religions or change existing ones to better meet people's needs. Take the Islam faith, for example. Its leaders innovated in important ways when they started using mass communication technology to spread messages to the faithful around the world. This international communication network produced change within Islam that the leaders may not have anticipated or intended: One such change was the increased capacity for "celebrity" leaders (such as Iran's Ayatollah Khomeini) to influence believers far away, superseding the influence of local religious leaders in the individual countries.

Some religious innovation results in a new religious movement or church. In the sixteenth century, for example, priests and other leaders who set out to reform the Roman Catholic church in many cases ended up forming new denominations as part of the Protestant Reformation. In what follows we look at some more recent results of religious innovation: the Mormon faith and the Unification Church.

The Founding of the Mormon Faith

The Church of Jesus Christ of Latter-day Saints, better known as Mormonism, was founded in upstate New York in 1830 by Joseph Smith, who was inspired, he said, by a series of sacred visions. The first took place while Smith was still a teenager. Confused by the many modern Christian sects that competed for followers, Smith decided to ask God which faith was right. He describes his experience alone in the woods where he went to seek divine guidance:

. . . immediately I was seized by some power which entirely overcame me, and had such astonishing influence over me as to bind my tongue so that I could not speak. Thick darkness gathered around me, and it seemed to me for a time as if I were doomed to sudden destruction. . . . Just at this moment of great alarm, I saw a pillar of light exactly over my head, above the brightness of the sun, which descended gradually until it fell upon me. (Quoted in Marty, 1985, p. 199)

Out of the light appeared two persons, suspended in the sky and dazzling Smith with their brightness. One identified the other as his "beloved Son" and instructed Smith to listen to what he had to say. Smith boldly asked which of all the sects was right. He was told that all were wrong, that all in fact were corrupt and abominations.

Some people advised Smith that the vision was the work of the devil, trying to weaken Christian faith, or was a hallucination, perhaps a sign of mental strain. However, Smith interpreted the event as a visitation from God, intending to express strong dissatisfaction with existing churches. Later, Smith claimed to have a second vision, in which a messenger from God revealed the whereabouts of a sacred text written on golden tablets. According to his account, Smith found the tablets, translated them, and published them as the Book of Mormon. Shortly thereafter he confirmed his two brothers and three other young men as the first followers of the Mormon faith. Thus the seeds of a new religion were sown.

Many new religions begin as a reaction against increasingly secularized religions, but most of them eventually dwindle and die out. Not Mormonism. It has enjoyed the highest growth rate of any new faith in American history (Stark, 1984). By 1840, only ten years after Smith and his five followers declared themselves the first Mormons, membership had reached about 30,000. Ten years later, membership had doubled, despite persecution from non-Mormons, a change in leadership, and a grueling migration across the Great Plains and Rocky Mountains to start a new community in Utah. By 1950 there were over 1 million Mormons, and by 1990, 7.5 million in 129 countries and territories. Mormonism has a strong missionary element, with an emphasis on conversions. Approximately 300,000 conversions and/or baptisms each year allow Mormons to expand both their membership and their geographic reach (Marty, 1991).

The Unification Church

Like Joseph Smith, Sun Myung Moon had a vision as a teenager in Korea that convinced him that he was a chosen individual. In Moon's revelation, Jesus appeared and said that he had been unable to complete his mission of perfecting humanity and that Moon was to finish the job. Over the next few decades Moon formulated his teachings, drawing on Korean variants of Confucianism, Buddhism, Taoism, and shamanism. His religion is also rooted in some of the unorthodox Christian beliefs that emerged from the encounter of Protestant missionaries with Korean culture (Chryssides, 1991). Unification church doctrine holds that Jesus opened the doors to Paradise, but his crucifixion prevented him from establishing a true family and opening the way to the Kingdom of Heaven. That task was to fall to a second messiah, who was to come in this century to a place like Korea, where there were many religions and strong political divisions in need of unification.

As the Lord of the Second Advent (or messiah), Sun Myung Moon needed to establish three blessings that God intended man to achieve: individual perfection, true family, and an ideal society under God's dominion. By virtue of being the messiah, Moon achieved individual perfection. By marrying, siring sinless children, and engrafting Unification church members into the holy family through their own marriages, the second blessing is accomplished. (This is the rationale behind the mass weddings of Unification adherents.) To achieve the ideal society, or Kingdom of Heaven, the forces of evil must be overthrown. Moon has long viewed communism as the satanic element on earth that must be eliminated. In a country torn into two parts (a communistic North Korea and a capitalistic South Korea) and suffused with myriad religious teachings, Moon's hybrid message of unification has had great appeal. In recent years Moon has exploited the collapse of communism in Russia and the rise of capitalism in China through high-level political contacts and economic investments (Clifford, 1990). These ventures into the political realm are not unlike the political involvement of the pope and of the Christian Coalition described in the chapter opening. They also reflect a tradition in Korea of intertwining religious and political themes. For instance, Confucianism was linked to the traditional imperial dynasty, and Korean Christians have been linked with anti-Japanese nationalism.

When the Unification church spread to other countries, the Korean roots of its teachings were not relevant to the host country. In those cases, innovation continued. In the United States, for example, the church adapted to Americans' emphasis on the individual by providing for more personal emotional expression (Parsons, 1989). Techniques of interaction, moral practices, and social habits in the religion draw from the secular culture of emotions in American society. At the same time the Unification church had to establish rigid boundaries with secular American society to protect the purity of its beliefs, a strategy that was not really necessary in its Korean context.

RELIGION AND SOCIAL CHANGE

In addition to innovating from within, religious institutions and beliefs respond to changes in the societies around them. The Protestant Reformation, for example, was only partly a response to internal disagreements within the Roman Catholic church. It was also a response to broader social changes: the rise of cities from feudal agricultural societies, the decline of feudal organization of power along military and religious lines, the development of a new middle class. In turn, the Reformation itself had an enormous impact on modern societies. It toppled kings, stirred feelings of nationalism when national identities came to be associated with particular religious beliefs, and unleashed wealth that had been concentrated in the monasteries. It was in the context of the Reformation that Gutenberg developed the printing press with movable type, making possible the first Christian Bible widely available to ordinary people in their everyday language. When people learned to read in order to study the Bible, they seldom stopped there: increasing literacy had its own political and social impact. Perhaps above all, the Protestant Reformation contributed to the coming of the modern era by changing people's ways of thinking rationally about their economic affairs.

The Religious Roots of Modernization

In *The Protestant Ethic and the Spirit of Capitalism* (1904/1958), Max Weber argued that some of the Protestant reforms laid the groundwork for modern capitalism by promoting new attitudes toward work and investment. He began with the observations that capitalism emerged in Christian-dominated Europe, not in Asia or Africa, and that Germany, which was largely Protestant, was more industrialized than the parts of Europe that remained largely Catholic. Weber also noticed that Protestants were more likely than Catholics to become industrial millionaires. He wondered what could explain these patterns. To find an answer, he examined Protestant beliefs, particularly those of John Calvin (1509–1564) and his followers.

At the heart of Calvinist doctrine is the concept of predestination, the belief that a person's fate after death, whether it be salvation or damnation, is determined at birth. Eternal life, according to Calvinists, is bestowed by God's grace, not by individual merit. Thus, Calvinists could not turn to a priest for intercession with God or obtain a promise of absolution from a church hierarchy. No human efforts, even by members of the clergy, could alter God's plan. Nor could mere humans hope to learn God's particular intentions for them. These beliefs left Calvinists with a profound uncertainty about their future and a deep sense of isolation. Many responded by trying to prove they had a place among God's chosen few by achieving success in life. This meant hard work, frugality, self-denial, and astute investment for future gain—in short, a kind of worldly asceticism. The Calvinist outlook is captured in such traditional sayings as "The devil finds work for idle hands" and "A penny saved is a penny earned." Weber called this outlook the *Protestant ethic.*

This ethic, according to Weber, fostered the spirit of capitalism because it consisted of ideas and attitudes that stimulated the growth of privately owned businesses. For one thing, it encouraged the owners of the means of production to reinvest their profits rather than spending them all on luxuries (as many earlier aristocrats had done). Calvinists were highly motivated to make this personal sacrifice, for they saw self-denial of material pleasures as the road to business success; and success, in their minds, was proof of God's favor.

Weber's theory that Protestant values laid the groundwork for capitalism and economic modernization has been much debated since he first proposed it (Marshall, 1982). Some critics have argued, for example, that the changes Weber described were not confined to Protestants, but affected some Catholics as well. Others argue that religious changes followed capitalist development rather than paving the way for it. All the same, Weber's theory is an excellent example of the interplay between religion and the secular world. As religious beliefs were changed in an effort to purify Christianity, those beliefs set in motion forces that had the potential to alter the economic system. Thus, Weber showed how religious reform and change in the secular spheres of society can go hand in hand.

Religious Responses to Secularization

An unintended by-product of the Protestant Reformation was the **secularization** of modern society: It became more concerned with worldly matters and less concerned with spiritual ones (Nord, 1995). Secularization occurred for several reasons:

■ As noted above, capitalism focused attention on matters of business. Even though the Calvinists were motivated by theological yearnings, the net effect was to drive a wedge between religious and nonreligious activity.

■ The Reformation gave rise to questioning and more rationalistic approaches to thought in general. The creation and growth of science, endorsing reason and systematic observation as supreme authorities in our knowledge of the world, accompanied modernization. As people have come to "believe in" science, to accept its rationalistic outlook, the capacity for faith in the supernatural may have gradually eroded.

■ Modern societies are much more heterogeneous than are traditional societies, not just in terms of racial and ethnic diversity but also in terms of religious diversity. With such a large number of religious beliefs to choose from, it is difficult to think of any one of them as embodying absolute truth, and so the traditional authority of religion may be eroded further.

■ The nature of modern life, with its complex machines and rapid pace, is not always compatible with spirituality. If the angels spoke to us at all times, observes sociologist Peter Berger (1979), the business of modern living would probably grind to a halt. A substantial degree of concern with secular matters is essential if modern societies are to keep running.

From the eighteenth century to the present day, many scientific or rationalistic thinkers have predicted that relentless secularization would eventually spell the end of religion. Marx thought that when socialism made society more scientifically planned and egalitarian, religion would no longer have a function to perform, because it existed largely to bind people to the old order and protect it from rebellion. Durkheim and Weber did not go quite so far, but both thought that secular views and interests would become so predominant that there would be little room left for spiritual concerns.

There is no simple answer to the question of whether societies are religious or secular. They are often both at once. Secularization involves the removal of more and more aspects of social life from the immediate control of religious institutions. The creation of public schools is an example of secularization, yet all the people in those schools may continue to believe in God and go to church regularly. Most religious leaders no longer claim to have authority over questions of physical science, as they did when they flatly contradicted Galileo's argument that the earth revolved around the sun. At the same time, however, religious leaders have not relinquished authority over moral questions.

One religious response to secularization, then, has been to work out a kind of division of labor between secular and religious authority—a division between church and state, between religion and science. Indeed, instead of looking at secularization as declining religion, it might be more accurate to view it as the declining scope of religious authority (Chaves, 1994). Many mainstream churches coexist well with largely secular societies and play important functional roles within them. And if a religious organization becomes too secularized in today's society it may be supplanted by a newer, more vigorous, and less worldly religion. Thus, there tends to be a constant balancing of secularization and intensification of religion (Beckford, 1989). Finally, just because people define many aspects of their social life in nonspiritual or nonreligious terms does not mean that they value the religious and spiritual parts of their lives any less. Churches today are less powerful than in the Middle Ages, but there was probably more religious apathy among the ordinary people in medieval times than there is in modern times. The decision today to adhere to a particular religion is increasingly a matter of personal choice rather than a question of socialization and ingrained habit (Demerath, 1995).

Fundamentalism

Not all religious institutions or leaders accept the kind of division of labor with secular institutions described above. Many emphasize both the priority of religion and the importance of a strict adherence to the original "basics" or "fundamentals" of whichever religion they profess. **Fundamentalism** is a type of religious movement that seeks to establish or reestablish a pure way of life grounded in religious teachings and principles that followers believe to be under siege. Among the "fundamentals" of such a movement are generally the following: a central doctrine or worldview that serves as the Truth; a Messenger, or one who embodies the Truth and first conveyed it; a select community of believers who draw clear distinctions with outsiders; a destiny, or certainty of a utopian future; and a strong sense of what is evil, both in the outside world and hidden among the faithful (Frykenberg, 1994). Fundamentalism arises from confrontations with others who do not share the beliefs, either because they are members of competing religions or because they are not religious. Fundamentalist movements are most likely to develop in modern, pluralistic, secular societies where cultural certainties and traditional communities have been supplanted or challenged. As one scholar put it:

> [They] seem to be a way of coping with the experience of chaos, the loss of identity, meaning and secure social structures created by the rapid introduction of modern social and political patterns, secularism, scientific culture and economic development. (Ruether, 1992)

In the last several decades, fundamentalism has had an impact in most parts of the world. Here we will focus on four recent episodes of fundamentalist revival: Islamic and Jewish fundamentalism in the Middle East, Hindu fundamentalism in India, and Christian fundamentalism in the United States.

Islamic Fundamentalism

When the Shah of Iran brought his country into the modern era with the help of oil revenues and American military backing, he seemed to be in total control. However, modernization benefited only a small number of Iranians, an elite group that adapted readily to Western ideas and lifestyles. The vast majority of Iranians were unemployed, dislocated, and hounded by a repressive secret police force. Many of them gathered in mosques, where they plotted the overthrow of the Shah and the return to a pure form of Islam, untouched by Western ways. To the astonishment of the world they succeeded in forcing the Shah to resign in favor of a fundamentalist regime led by the Ayatollah Ruhollah Khomeini (Abrahamian, 1985).

The revolution in Iran reverberated throughout the Muslim world. Today fundamentalist (or "true") Islamic movements are active and powerful in societies as diverse as Egypt, Algeria, Iraq, Nigeria, Central Asia, and the Gaza Strip and West Bank in Israel. These movements have in common a focus on religious morality, a return to basic Islamic teachings, renewed pride in being Muslim, and the need for political action to establish theocratic states. To understand the impact of these movements we must look back at the history of Islam.

Islam dates back to the seventh century A.D., when (followers believe) an angel of Allah, or God, revealed himself to an Arab trader named Mohammed. The religion that Mohammed founded shares many elements with Judaism, Christianity, and other earlier traditions. The main difference is the reliance on the Koran (or Qur'an), the Islamic holy book in which Mohammed recorded Allah's message. Muslims revere the Koran as the literal dictations of the thoughts of Allah, which are not subject to interpretation or even translation.

Islam, like Christianity, developed many local variations as it spread throughout the world. However, all Muslims share certain important traditions, including affirming that "there is no God but Allah and Mohammed is his last prophet"; praying at regular intervals during the day; contributing a portion of income to charity; daytime fasting during the month of Ramadan; and, if possible, making a pilgrimage (*Haj*) to the holy city of Mecca in Saudi Arabia at least once in a lifetime.

From the beginning, Islam was a messianic religion, oriented to converting others and spreading its message universally. The drive to expand and the duty to protect the religious community led to the tradition of the *jihad*, or holy war against those who threaten the community, and the belief that those who died fighting the infidel died a martyr. Up until World War I Muslims ruled most of the

The Shiite branch of Islam, brought to world attention by the overthrow of the Shah of Iran in 1979, rejects Western, secular influences. Shiites believe that to purify society, secular leaders and laws must be replaced with a religious state. Here, Shiite women in Teheran, wearing traditional dress, train to protect their faith.

Mediterranean world and the East almost as far as China, but Islam's glorious past has been overshadowed by recent humiliations as Arabs and other Muslims were conquered by European colonial powers, forced to accept the creation of Israel, and defeated several times by Israeli armies backed by the United States and other Western powers. Islamic fundamentalism can be seen as an attempt to "salvage that history" (Hunter, 1990, p. 60). Many zealous Muslims look forward to the day they will see Western culture submit to resurgent Islam (Shirley, 1995).

Other factors contributing to the rise of Islamic fundamentalism are the despair, poverty, and disillusionment that accompany failures of modernization; fragmentation of religious authority in Muslim societies; a perceived need to keep the faith pure; and the emergence of patrons (such as the governments of Iran and Saudi Arabia) for fundamentalist groups (Piscatori, 1994). But the Islamic fundamentalist movement is hardly monolithic. Rival fundamentalist groups compete for power in many countries, including Egypt, Algeria, Iraq, and areas of Palestinian influence. The Iranian variant reflects an early and deep split between branches of Islam

(Arjomand,1996). The upshot of this competition is that ideology gets sharpened and radicalized, pushing various fundamentalist groups to more and more extreme views and actions.

Perhaps the most significant division among Islamics can be seen in the differences between the Sunni and Shiite sects, a split that began with a struggle for succession to leadership in the seventh century. Most Arab leaders, including those in Iraq, Egypt, and Algeria, belong to the Sunni branch of Islam. They consider themselves—or at least present themselves—as devout Muslims, but they are committed to the separation of church (or mosque) and state. The Shiites, by contrast, have a long tradition of blending politics and religion. It was Shiites who plotted the overthrow of the Shah and created a theocracy in Iran. Fundamentalists of each denomination claim a unique understanding of the "true" fundamentals of the faith, and they are often in conflict with each other.

Islamic fundamentalists are at the center of world politics today. They have come to power or share power in other countries besides Iran—most notably Sudan. Sudan's brand of Islam was, historically, relatively moderate partly because it lacked the tradition of elite clergy, such as the "mullahs" who sought power in Iran. Sudanese Islamic fundamental-ism—partly a political tool of a government bent on uniting an ethnically diverse population (Viorst, 1995). Fundamentalists are threatening the secular governments in many other states. In Algeria, for ex-ample, secular elements may still be in control of the government and the military, but Muslim funda-mentalists dominate community life in the schools, hospitals, unions, mosques, and neighborhood stores (Shirley, 1995). Something similar is happening in Turkey, where the strongest political party is funda-mentalist; its skillful grassroots organization has firmly established the party at local levels. Slights to Turkey by other countries are perceived as religious bias. Responding to the threat of a veto of Turkey's membership in the European customs union, the Turkish prime minister warned: "If our European friends reject us on the grounds that we come from a different religion, then they will make themselves a Christian club, and there will be a confrontation in the world" (*New York Times*, March 2, 1995, p. A1).

Islamic fundamentalists have also taken on the whole Western notion of human rights. In 1989, Salman Rushdie's novel *The Satanic Verses* brought worldwide condemnation from Muslims because of one scene that they considered blasphemous to their religion. Iran's Ayatollah Khomeini issued an edict promising heaven to any Muslim who killed Rushdie or his publishers. Rushdie was forced into hiding, his Italian and Japanese translators were stabbed (one fatally), and a paperback edition was postponed be-cause no one wanted to risk publishing it.

Hindu Fundamentalism

Salman Rushdie has the distinction of raising the ire of fundamentalist elements in two major faiths. The publication in 1995 of Rushdie's *The Moor's Last Sigh* brought cries of outrage from a right-wing Hindu nationalist party because it included a very unflat-tering parody of its leader, Balasaheb K. Thackeray. Thackeray's power is such that he was able to get the book banned in Bombay and convince the national government in India to bar further imports of the novel altogether. Ironically, in 1989 Thackeray had vigorously opposed the banning of Rushdie's *Satanic Verses* in India (after it was banned in several Islamic countries), arguing that it was a free country and Muslims must learn to take their lumps along with

everyone else (*New York Times*, December 2, 1995, p. A4).

India has been particularly hard hit by the politics of religious fundamentalism. Many fundamentalists are found not only in its Hindu majority but also in the Islamic minority and even smaller Sikh minority. Hindu fundamentalism is closely allied with nation-alist aspirations to have a country that is both reli-giously oriented and "cleansed" of "alien" elements, especially Islamic ones. Hindu nationalists have found a forum at a time when separatist tendencies within India are in collision with a widespread long-ing for a national identity (Varshney, 1993).

Religious divisions have been a frequent cause for violence and bloodshed. The pacifist Hindu leader Mahatma Gandhi was assassinated by a Hindu reli-gious fanatic for allegedly being "pro-Muslim." Prime Minister Indira Gandhi was assassinated by her Sikh bodyguards, provoking interreligious riots throughout the country. Her two sons also were killed by religious fanatics. Thousands of other Indians have been killed in this ongoing violence.

Hinduism is an ancient religion that has given rise to innumerable independent and sometimes conflict-ing religious beliefs, practices, experiences, and or-ganizations (Klostermaier, 1989). Unlike many other religious traditions, Hinduism is not based on either an historical person or the authority of a book (Embree, 1994). The main Hindu texts offer sociopo-litical, ethical, and spiritual guidance, couched in narratives about the adventures of gods, kings, he-roes, and lesser mortals. Hindus do not worship a single God but recognize an enormous pantheon of deities. At the heart of Hindu religion is the concept of *dharma*, a code of conduct for people in various so-cial categories (or castes), situations, and stages of life. Hindus believe that every person, every living creature, every act, every aspect of life has its place in the cosmic order. If that order is violated, chaos re-sults (Madan, 1989; Mahmood, 1989).

Hindu fundamentalism is not new, but it is cur-rently experiencing a revival. The movement for Indian independence from Britain earlier this cen-tury gathered inspiration from the idea of a past golden age of Hinduism, the belief that first Muslim and then British invaders defiled this heritage, and the conviction that India had to restore the rules of *dharma* in order to regenerate itself. However, the great leaders of that movement—Gandhi, Nehru, and other members of the Congress party—all advocated the creation of a secular, democratic state in which

Religious fundamentalism has become a powerful political force, nowhere more than in India. Hindu nationalists view Islam as foreign, on a par with British colonialism. These demonstrators seek to tear down an almost 500-year-old Muslim mosque, which they believe is on the holy ground where the Hindu god Rama was born, and build a Hindu shrine.

members of different religions would live together in peace. In a much quoted statement, Gandhi declared, "I am a Hindu, a Sikh, a Muslim, and a Christian" (in Mahmood, 1989, p. 340).

Ironically, the very success of India's independence has contributed to the divisions and violence in India today (Malik and Vajpeyi, 1989). Under the protection of Indian laws, minorities are seeking a larger share of India's prosperity, and Hindus are resisting their advances. Today's Hindu fundamentalism takes many forms, including increased attendance at temples; the revival of religious symbols and rituals; organizations dedicated to "liberating" Hindu temples that had been converted to mosques by Muslim rulers; attempts to "reconvert" converted Muslims and Christians back to Hinduism; demonstrations against "affirmative action" programs for lower-caste Hindus; electoral victories for the Hindu nationalist party; and the resurgence of a paramilitary group (Rashtryia Swayamsevak Sangh, or RSS) that was widely held responsible for Gandhi's assassination. The RSS makes use of a disciplined youth corps to indoctrinate young Indians in the idea of a purely Hindu nation (Embree, 1994).

Hindu fundamentalists make much of the suffering Hindus have suffered at the hands of non-Hindus. Under the rule of the Arabs and the British, Hindus were long a persecuted majority in their own land. Today, in the Muslim states of Pakistan and Bangladesh Hindus are denied full rights under the law. In Sri Lanka Hindus are fighting for survival against the Buddhist majority. At the same time, many Hindus in India see the government as appeasing minorities—for example, by allowing Muslims to apply their own family laws (as in divorce cases). Even members of India's Westernized middle class appear to be responding to the call for Hindu nationalism (Embree, 1994; Malik and Vajpeyi, 1989).

Jewish Fundamentalism

The headlines were shocking: "Rabin Assassinated." But what was even more shocking was that Yitzhak Rabin, the respected prime minister of Israel, was killed in November 1995 not by an Arab, an enemy of the Jewish state, but by a fellow Jew, a member of a radical religious group on the right. What brought Jewish fundamentalism to this point?

There have long been elements of the Jewish religion that vowed to keep themselves from the secular world and live strictly within their traditions. For these Jews, known as *haredin,* resistance to modernization takes the form of resolutely refusing to assimilate to it. These Jews wear the traditional black coats of mourning for the Jewish exile from the Holy Land, they study only the Torah and Talmud (the holy texts and commentary), in their schools (yeshivas), and they adhere to the strictest rituals and customs. In the eyes of these ultra Orthodox Jews, the *state* of Israel does not exist because Jews should be governed by their religion. They do not speak Hebrew in their everyday lives because it is the language of the holy texts and must not be sullied by secular use. This brand of fundamentalist Jew is quiescent as opposed to activist. They see the Torah as the guide for how the world should be organized but do not view themselves as having to act to see that this order comes about (Heilman, 1994).

More recently, some ultra Orthodox Jews have become politically active. These fundamentalists also adhere to traditions and rituals, but they are willing to go on the offensive to defend their way of life—to take preemptive strikes before the world can change them (Kepel, 1994). These activists have built settlements in the occupied territories that Israel took from the Arabs after the 1973 war. For them, reclaiming their ancient homeland represents the fulfillment of biblical prophesies. Many of these fundamentalists perceive the greatest threats to their way of life coming not from those who are most unlike them but from Jews who have acculturated in the modern world and staked out a middle ground. Samuel Heilman (1994) describes the nature of this threat:

> The absolutely different represent an unthinkable evil, but those who occupy a moderate middle ground and make it seem that one can be a little bit secular without abandoning Orthodox Judaism represent the insidious and thinkable alternative to the fundamentalist way of life. Deviation from the central core values is first toward the middle ground and only from there toward the periphery. Hence the fundamentalist struggles are more vigorous against reforming Jews than Gentiles and, among Jews, most puissant against those who claim to define Orthodoxy in modern terms. To fundamentalists, compromises are the most threatening. (p. 183)

By participating in a peace process that was leading toward returning land to the Arabs, Prime Minister Rabin appeared to the fundamentalists to

Young Israelis mourn the assassination of Prime Minister Yitzhak Rabin, who was murdered not by an Arab, but by one of the haredin *(fundamentalist Jews) who believed that in seeking peace with Israel's Arab neighbors, Rabin was betraying his country and his faith.*

be compromising the future of the Jewish people and putting them in danger. In the months preceding the assassination, at political protests and religious meetings throughout Israel, angry fundamentalists called Rabin a traitor, a murderer, and a Nazi (*U.S. News and World Report*, November 20, 1995). Some extremist rabbis fueled the fires by citing an Orthodox law sanctioning the taking of Rabin's life. Rabin's killer apparently fell under the influence of these extremist elements while a student at a university whose teachers and students were steeped in religious nationalism. Following Rabin's death Israelis engaged in massive soul-searching. Extremist rhetoric died down for a while, and Rabin's successor, Shimon Peres, vowed to continue the struggle for peace. But, at the same time, the peace process was challenged by a new series of violent actions from fundamentalists among both Jews and Muslims.

Christian Fundamentalism

Like other religious traditions, Christianity has fundamentalist components, but these can vary depending on the culture. For instance, in some countries fundamentalism may be rooted in the Roman Catholic faith, as in Italy and many Latin American nations, while in others it is anchored in Protestant denominations. All the Christian fundamentalist movements have in common the desire to transform a chaotic, unstable, morally ambiguous society into a God-fearing, God-directed nation in which moral authority reigns supreme. In winning converts, fundamentalists believe they are not only saving souls but ultimately rescuing the nation. They believe that the world is divided between the forces of good and evil, that they know who the enemy is, and that they can accept no compromise. In most cases, the way to the future lies in restoring the traditions of the past (Ammerman, 1994)—and the means for doing so are found in politics, as we saw in the case of the Christian Coalition.

Christian fundamentalism has become an especially significant voice in American religion (Marsden, 1990). It was nurtured in this century by a mesh of social conditions and ideas: destabilizing external factors in society, such as increasing ethnic diversity, migration, and alienation, and unifying internal factors in the movement, including theological training, authoritarian leadership, strict norms, strong ideology and organization, and missionary

zeal (Wuthnow and Lawson, 1994). Over the last two decades American fundamentalism has undergone changes. Once identified mainly with rural and small-town lower-class, less well-educated Southerners, it has come to flourish in major metropolitan areas, in all areas of the country, and among the better-educated. Fundamentalists are linked together outside their church denominations by a range of organizations, including nondenominational seminaries for training ministers, specialized bookstores, and Christian schools.

Fundamentalists believe that the Bible is the ultimate authority on spiritual matters and that its historical and scientific assertions are literally true. This is known as the *doctrine of biblical inerrancy*. Most fundamentalists, for example, reject the theory of evolution in favor of the biblical story of divine creation. They also sense that trends in secular society are threatening them. Concern about protecting children from perceived evil influences is an important part of fundamentalism (Bartkowski and Ellison, 1995; Lienesch, 1993). One reason Christian fundamentalists have begun to take a more active role in political life is that they see trends such as acceptance of homosexuality, rising divorce rates, and single-parent families as threats to social values they hold dear. This is what links them to conservatives who are not part of a fundamentalist Christian movement and also what distinguishes them from many people in the upper middle class whose social values became more liberal in the 1960s and 1970s.

The increasing political activity of fundamentalist groups has given rise to what has been called *the new Christian right*. Many forces contributed to the politicalization of fundamentalists (Himmelstein, 1990; Wuthnow, 1983, 1988). One was the presidency of born-again Christian Jimmy Carter, which increased the public's recognition of evangelicals and gave them more legitimacy. A second impulse was the emergence of a broad conservative movement and a new set of social issues, including abortion rights, the Equal Rights Amendment and feminism generally, sexual liberation, gay and lesbian rights, drug abuse, prohibitions on school prayer, and pornography. Suddenly, important political issues seemed entwined with moral questions. President Ronald Reagan actively courted the new Christian right and sided with it on most issues. The third reason for the new political visibility of fundamentalists was that they had developed an extensive infrastructure—including huge "superchurches," broad communication networks, up-to-date methods of computerized fund-raising, targeted lobbying, and an electronic ministry—that enabled them to mobilize political conservatives and religious traditionalists who usually shied away from politics.

RELIGION IN THE UNITED STATES TODAY

Although highly visible and politically powerful today, Christian fundamentalism by no means represents the entire American religious scene. Unlike societies in which a single religion predominates, the United States is characterized by religious pluralism (see Figure 13.2). This means that Americans can choose among dozens of religions, from Roman Catholic to Rastafarian.

While most Americans claim a broad religious orientation, many choose no specific denomination like Presbyterian or Methodist. Some attend nondenominational Christian churches. Others practice a private form of religion that the sociologist Thomas Luckmann (1967) has called **invisible religion:** They think of religion as a subjective, personal experience, not as a group doctrine. Studies suggest that this outlook is widespread. For instance, in a survey of Christians in Minnesota, two-thirds said that people could "reject some church teachings and continue to have deep Christian faith" (Chittister and Marty, 1983, p. 79). These "unaffiliates" usually are not members of traditional churches and congregations. They

tend to keep their faith, worship, and spiritual life to themselves (Hart, 1987). This does not mean they lack religious beliefs. Almost half believe in life after death, and two-fifths believe in a literal interpretation of the Bible (Greeley, 1989). The existence of invisible religion helps explain why, although 96 percent of Americans say they believe in God, only about 30 percent say they attend religious services weekly (*The Gallup Poll Monthly*, February 1995). In terms of the three dimensions of religion introduced at the beginning of this chapter, these people emphasize belief more than practices or religious community. Some theologians are concerned about the pervasiveness of invisible religion because they fear it can undermine the sense of community that churches offer.

There is much talk about religious change in the United States. In the 1960s, many people asked "Is God dead?" in the wake of the publication of a best-selling book on that theme by theologian Harvey Cox. In the 1970s, the fundamentalist movement and evangelical movement became prominent. Nevertheless, we should not exaggerate the extent of religious change. Reviewing major studies of religion in the United States over the past quarter century, the sociologist Andrew M. Greeley (1989) found more stability than change. Today as in the past, Americans are more religious than their European counterparts (about a third of whom say they have no religion). Moreover, religious beliefs and practices have not changed very much since the eve of World War II (when data were first collected). A majority of Americans still hold traditional religious beliefs in God, the divinity of Jesus (if they are Christian), and

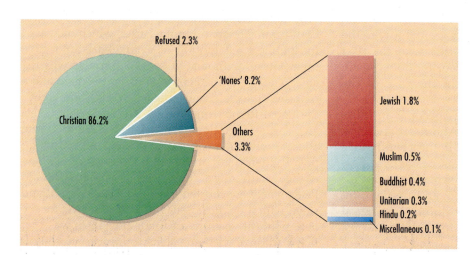

FIGURE 13.2 / *Religious Affiliations of the American People*

The overwhelming majority of Americans identify themselves as Christian, and most of them are affiliated with a Protestant church. A little over 8 percent of Americans do not affiliate with any particular religion.

Source: Barry A Kosmin and Seymour P. Lachman, "Religious Self-Identification," in Kenneth B. Bedell, ed., *Yearbook of American and Canadian Churches 1995* (Abingdon Press, Nashville, Tenn., 1995).

TABLE 13.3

Religious Beliefs

	Year	Percentage Answering Yes

A. Do you believe in the existence of God or a universal spirit?

	1944	97%
	1954	96
	1967	97
	1981	95
	1994	96

B. Do you believe that Jesus Christ ever actually lived [and] do you think He was God [not] just another leader like Mohammed or Buddha?

	1952	77
	1965	75
	1983	76

C. Do you believe there is a life after death?

	1944	76
	1952	77
	1965	75
	1975	76
	1985	74

D. Do you think there is a heaven where people who have led good lives are eternally rewarded?

	1952	72
	1965	68
	1980	71
	1994	90

E. Do you believe there is a hell?

	1952	58
	1965	54
	1980	53
	1994	73

Sources: Andrew M. Greeley, Religious Change in America (Harvard University Press, Cambridge, Mass., 1989), p. 14 , table 2.1; The Gallup Poll Monthly, January and February 1995.

with the broader society have changed significantly. Religious affiliation is a dynamic process. As one denomination loses followers, another gains in strength. As one sect disappears from the social landscape, a new one emerges and attracts adherents. One of today's major changes, suggests the sociologist Robert Wuthnow (1988), is an overall decline in denominationalism. There is much less competition among Protestant denominations like Baptists and Methodists; Protestant and Catholic leaders are more cooperative. The boundaries between denominations are more fluid, with people moving fairly readily from one denomination to another. But data on changes in church membership tell us little about changes taking place in how the people in each religious group feel and think. For this we must look more closely at events occurring in each of the major religions today.

Roman Catholics

Most Catholics I know well have a dense and complicated love for the official, institutional Church; through their love run antipathies and dissent (to say nothing of doubt) like a constant low-grade fever. (B. G. Harrison, 1994, p. 42)

The ambiguity in Barbara Harrison's rumination accurately reflects the state of the church today for many of the 26 percent of Americans who identify themselves as Roman Catholic (Kosmin and Lachman, 1995). The church has instituted far-reaching reforms in the last few decades to make the religion more accessible to ordinary people, yet it has been unyielding on certain teachings that many of its followers find difficult to adhere to.

The Second Vatican Council that met between 1962 and 1965 eliminated the Latin mass and meatless Fridays, allowed lay Catholics more of a part in the communion and permitted them to take on administrative and liturgical duties once reserved for priests, redefined non-Catholics as separated brothers and sisters (not "heretics"), and repudiated anti-Semitism. These reforms are the result of a power struggle between those who wanted to keep priestly power in the church hierarchy and those who wanted to give more voice to the laypeople (Ebaugh, 1991).

The impact of Vatican II was dramatic. Catholicism became more personalized, with individuals

the afterlife (see Table 13.3). Although fewer accept the literal truth of the Bible, more say they read the Bible daily and exhibit accurate knowledge of its contents. About the same percentage of Americans today say they attended religious services in the last seven days as was reported in 1939 (The Gallup Poll Monthly, February 1995).

Of course, religion in the United States is not completely static. Beliefs and rituals have been relatively stable, but the organization of religious communities, their patterns of social action, and their relations

deciding spiritual and moral issues for themselves. For example, more than four-fifths of young-adult Catholics reject their church's teachings on birth control, premarital sex, divorce, and remarriage; many also reject the doctrine of papal infallibility. Yet they remain solidly Catholic in their fundamental convictions about life, death, and God, and they say they intend to remain in the church, though on their own terms (Greeley, 1990). One homosexual put it this way: "Why should I leave? That would be fragmenting the community. . . . I would go to my cat before I would go to my cardinal for moral direction. I don't pay any attention to him or to the Pope. But I have no reason to leave the Church" (quoted in B. G. Harrison, 1994, p. 55). To many, "Catholic" has come to be an ethnic or cultural identity.

These challenges to priestly authority have provoked counterreactions among church officials

Easter Sunday at the San Fernando Cathedral in San Antonio, Texas. Despite disagreements with church teachings (for example, on birth control, divorce, and abortion), many Americans consider themselves devoutly Roman Catholic.

(Segers, 1990). On the one hand, some priests and higher officials have responded by attempting to meet their parishioners' call for a more liberal and activist church, for example, by endorsing such unconventional activities as support groups for divorced Catholics and for homosexuals. On the other hand, Catholic leaders (most notably in Rome) have attempted to slow the pace of change and insist on traditional values. Pope John Paul II has spoken out strongly against liberalizing and politicizing the church. A papal encyclical (pastoral letter to the church) in October 1993 listed contraception, artificial insemination, homosexual acts, masturbation, premarital sex, abortion, and adultery as "morally unacceptable" sins and declared that opposition to central teachings was punishable by purging from the church (B. G. Harrison, 1994). As a result of these struggles and recent social changes, American Catholics today face several issues: a shortage of priests, controversy over the role of nuns in the church, tension between Catholics who are comfortable with church teachings and Catholics who are not, and strains between the liberal parts of the Catholic church in the United States and the conservative Vatican leadership.

Despite these struggles, Roman Catholics are gaining on Protestants in numbers among American Christians, partly because of high rates of Hispanic immigration. At the same time there are increasingly fewer differences between Protestants and Catholics in their class, education level, income, and political attitudes. Both groups have grown more alike, and the more conservative members of both groups have found common cause in the campaign against abortion rights.

Protestants

For generations, the Methodist, Presbyterian, Episcopalian, and Congregational churches have been integral parts of nearly every American community. These mainline, established, predominantly white denominations are still relatively large and central to American life, but they are increasingly in crisis. Membership has declined by 20 to 40 percent since 1965; of the more than 40 percent of Americans born into mainline churches during this period, one in five left (Greeley, 1989). At the same time, the evangelical movement within the Protestant churches was attracting new members in record numbers. Membership in the fundamentalist, conservative Southern Baptist Convention rose 20 percent; in the Seventh-Day Adventists, 36 percent; and in the Assemblies of God, 62 percent.

Like the Catholic church, mainline Protestant churches play a large role in providing social services in their communities: counseling programs, meals-on-wheels, soup kitchens, homeless shelters, and the like. The more fundamentalist congregations focus their outreach on conversion and political lobbying and social welfare activities for their own members, such as birth counseling. Many conservative Christians, concerned about the performance and teachings of secular institutions, are active in movements like home-schooling (Hunter, 1991).

Evangelicals

Evangelical movements share three distinguishing beliefs: The Bible is the highest authority on the word of God; eternal salvation comes only through acceptance of Jesus Christ, who atoned for humanity's sins; and "the kindest thing one person can do for another is to tell him or her of this gospel promise of salvation" (Marsden, 1990, p. 23). Evangelicals are distinguished from other Protestants purely on theological lines. They stress telling others about the "good news" (gospel) of God's saving grace, and they are not necessarily politically conservative. Some American evangelicals are in fact left-wing activists for social justice, though more are conservative and fundamentalist at this time. Historically, evangelicals were significantly less educated and less affluent than most of the general population. Today, however, more and more evangelicals can be found in professional and managerial occupations in the so-called knowledge class, where they are remarkably resistant to the liberal ideology generally associated with that class (Schmalzbauer, 1993).

Televangelism

Televangelism—using TV technology to "sell" evangelical themes (usually in combination with on-air fund-raising for Christian causes)—is an especially American, mostly Protestant version of evangelical practice (Himmelstein, 1990). It got a huge boost in

the 1960s when the Federal Communications Commission (FCC) ruled that broadcasters could satisfy their public service requirement by selling airtime to religious organizations. The mainline denominations, leery of the place of television in religion and reluctant to ask for donations to cover the costs, backed away from broadcasting; the evangelical groups were not at all shy and soon dominated the airwaves (Hadden, 1993).

The influence of televangelists peaked in the 1980s. At that time three national networks broadcast religious programming full-time, 60 million people tuned in at least once a week, and annual income from the TV pulpit soared to $2 billion (Peck, 1993). Surveys found that the audience for religious TV was socially and religiously diverse (Wuthnow, 1990). Although most electronic ministries were headquartered in the South, only one out of three viewers

During the 1980s, evangelical Christiantity rose to renewed prominence in the United States, thanks partly to preachers like Robert Schuller (shown here) who used television. Taken from the word for several key books of the New Testament, "evangelism" refers to spreading the "good news" of Christ's promised salvation and seeking converts or renewals of faith.

lived there. Most were white evangelical Protestants, but one in five was black, about the same proportion was Roman Catholic, and a third belonged to mainline Protestant groups. Like regular TV viewers, they tended to be older and less educated than the average American, and many seemed to feel that they had been left behind. A majority of religious TV viewers said they were distressed by "the way standards have been changing in America" (p. 97).

Toward the end of the 1980s the viewing audience fell off sharply in the wake of a series of financial and sexual scandals that rocked several major ministries. Also contributing to the decline of televangelism were the growth in active participation within local churches and the rise of new means of communication, such as computer networks. Televangelism did not disappear altogether from the airwaves, however, and the recent growth in cable and local stations has set the stage for a revival (Hadden, 1993).

Jews

Jews have been part of the American religious scene since the nation's beginning. In general, Jews have had an easier time gaining acceptance in the United States than in European countries, where national identity is based on membership in a common ethnic group and a state church (Lipset, 1990). Although Jews make up less than 2 percent of the population, they have long been accepted as one of the three major religious groups in America, along with Protestants and Catholics. Jews have for the most part prospered in the United States, finding most social, economic, and political doors open to them at least since the 1960s (Eisenstadt, 1990). In recent years, however, incidents of anti-Semitism, such as vandalism of synagogues, have increased. Tensions are especially high between Jews and some African-American groups like Louis Farrakhan's Nation of Islam.

Like Christianity, American Judaism is divided into a number of denominations. Orthodox Judaism is the most traditional in its beliefs, ethnic loyalties, and religious practices (such as wearing skullcaps, or *yarmulkes*, keeping dietary laws, and strictly observing the Sabbath). Most members of Orthodox synagogues trace their ancestry to the urban ghettoes and villages of Eastern Europe, and many still speak Yiddish. Reform Judaism is the most liberal and assimilated branch. Its members tend to be middle or upper class and to trace their ancestry several generations to Germans who migrated before the rise of Hitler in the 1930s. Conservative Judaism falls between these two, providing a religious home for Eastern European Jews who are more assimilated to American culture and more likely to be highly educated professionals than are the Orthodox Jews but who tend to be more traditionally religious than the Reform Jews (Lipset, 1990). The boundaries between the groups are not rigid, however. Jews sometimes choose a synagogue because they like the rabbi or the "feeling" of the congregation—just the way many Christians choose a parish to join.

Despite religious and socioeconomic differences, all Jews share certain concerns (Glazer, 1990). One is the memory of the Holocaust, in which more than 6 million European Jews were slaughtered in Nazi death camps. Few Jews take for granted their survival as a people, and periodic flare-ups of anti-Semitism, here and abroad, keep this experience a living memory.

Closely related to the fear of another Holocaust is fear for Israel's survival. Even if they are not religious, most Jews feel a kinship with Israel, identify with Israeli defeats and victories, and support Israel through financial contributions and votes for pro-Israeli politicians in America. The 1992 election of a more moderate government in Israel and the progress of the Arab/Israeli peace talks brought rising hopes for peace and new optimism among American Jews, an optimism that was momentarily shattered by the assassination of Prime Minister Yitzhak Rabin late in 1995.

A third concern is for the survival of Jews and Judaism in America. In this context, *survival* refers not to physical safety but to cultural identity. Nine out of ten Jewish youths attend universities, where they are likely to adopt universalist values that discourage ethnic loyalty. Jewish intermarriage rates are approaching 50 percent, and birth rates are low. Because American Jews are a small minority in a predominantly Christian country, and because Judaism does not encourage conversion (even of spouses), there is concern that their distinctive heritage may disappear. However, in recent years there has been a revival of interest among American Jews in religious rituals, symbols, and activities of Jewish social groups.

Around the time Christians celebrate Easter, Jews celebrate Passover, when God told the Angel of Death to pass over the homes of Jews enslaved in Egypt, allowing them to escape to freedom. Although increasingly assimilated, more American Jews are observing their traditional holidays and rituals.

RELIGION AND CULTURE WARS

In Chapter 11 we saw how Americans were divided on certain family issues, based on a split between conservative and liberal elements in society. On the conservative side is a loose coalition of Christian fundamentalists, Orthodox Jews, and strict Catholics, united in the battle against their progressive counterparts for control of America's secular culture (Hunter, 1991). As one Orthodox rabbi explained it:

> "Quite frankly, it would be better if we did things separately, the way we've always done them. But we can have a greater impact sometimes if we work together. . . . We traditional Jews appreciate any positive efforts on the part of the Christian clergy and leaders to protect moral standards. (Hunter, 1991; p. 17)

Perhaps the loudest voices are raised in the intense debate over abortion. The conservatives oppose abortion based on their belief in the sanctity of life from the moment of conception and on the biblical command to "be fruitful and multiply." But religion not only shapes attitudes; it also provides the organization to mobilize protests at abortion clinics and to target political figures who are pro-choice. This is an area in which the new Christian right has been especially active.

Another divisive issue drawn along religious lines in America today is schooling (see the Sociology and Public Debates box). Religious conservatives object to many aspects of secularization in the public schools, including bans on school prayer, lack of equal access for Bible-reading groups and prayer clubs, what they regard as the immoral content of textbooks, the teaching of evolution, sex education, and the withholding of public funds for religious education. One response has been to take children out of the public schools and educate them at home; estimates suggest that the number of children schooled at home increased from about 15,000 in the early 1970s to around 700,000 in 1990, most of them in conservative Christian homes (Hunter, 1991), and it has probably more than doubled since 1990. At the same time there was tremendous growth in religiously affiliated schools, particularly in the Evangelical camp. As in the case of abortion, religious groups provide the organizational basis for getting sympathetic public officials elected and mounting protests in the schools. In Bedford, New York, for example, the Christian Coalition gathered 400 supporters at a

Does Religion Have a Place in America's Public Schools?

American public schools tend to be doggedly secular. Not only are prayers not allowed in the classrooms, but school curricula assiduously avoid mention of religious ideas or concepts or any religious explanations of modern phenomena. As Warren Nord (1995) notes: "The conventional wisdom among educators is that religion is irrelevant to virtually everything that is taken to be true and important." (p. 1) There are reasons for this: the restrictions outlined in the First Amendment, the secularization of civilization in general, the compartmentalization of religion in people's lives today, the lack of interest in religion that many intellectuals exhibit. And yet the vast majority of Americans profess to believe in God, and religious ideas structure the debate on many important public issues today. Should religion, then, be incorporated into the school curriculum?

Opponents argue that the First Amendment *removes* religion from public education. Proponents believe the First Amendment assures the government's *neutrality,* to religion, not its hostility.

THE DEBATE

Those who argue against religion having a place in public schools rely on the First Amendment of the United States Constitution, which states that the government can neither establish a religion nor prohibit the free exercise of religion. They interpret that to mean that public institutions should not be used for religious teaching, especially if that teaching promotes the views of one group over another. For example, presenting the Christian explanation for creation taken from the Bible may slight the views of other religious faiths. The same holds true for Bible readings or prayers in the classroom. Any government-approved prayer is likely to offend *someone*. In addition to being unconstitutional, the introduction of religion in the schools is just too controversial in a pluralistic nation that cannot agree on religious beliefs.

Those who argue that religion does have a place in the school range from fundamentalists, who would *subordinate* school curricula to religion, to those who feel that a knowledge of the world is not complete without some familiarity with religious thought. After all, religion is the source of many of our cultural influences, moral values, intellectual ideas, and artistic inspirations. To teach secular means of making sense of the world without any reference to religious explanations is to ignore some of our most powerful belief systems. As for the First Amendment, it is supposed to assure neutrality of government in religious matters, not hostility. Secular knowledge is often hostile to religion, so is it fair to exclude religion from the schools? Moreover, while the courts have not allowed the *practice* of religion in the public schools, they have not ruled against the *study* of religion. In any case, the government shows a religious face in other aspects of public life: coins with the slogan "In God We Trust," a pledge of allegiance that refers to "one nation, under God," a Congress that opens each day with a prayer.

ANALYSIS

We can understand this controversy better by examining it through the lens of the key concepts. First, the

meeting to denounce the school district for promoting occultism in the schools. Suspecting that many of these protestors were outsiders rounded up by the Coalition, the district superintendent scheduled a second meeting and required those attending to show identification as residents of the district. Of the 900 or so people who showed up, only five spoke in favor of the conservative agenda (*New York Times*, November 22, 1995, p. B5).

Other issues today that unite religious conservatives against religious and secular progressives are feminism, crime, homosexuality, AIDs—almost any social problem that has a moral dimension or violates biblical injunctions. Perhaps the most important are those that relate to family life. Hunter notes that in this century the differences among different faiths have become less salient than the differences between orthodox and progressive elements within each faith.

debate is clearly linked to culture. Schools are intended to impart culture to young people, yet they are committed not to impart one of the most influential aspects of that culture, religion. Certain cultural beliefs are partly responsible for this proposition. We value rationalism as the basis for obtaining knowledge; at the same time we tend to view rationalism as being opposed to religion in our culture. Cultural diversity also plays a part: We are fearful of stepping on people's toes in the way we present religious ideas.

Second, the controversy is an issue of power. The schools have power over the children in their charge, and through what they teach, over society. Ralph Reed of the Christian Coalition demonstrated an understanding of power when he targeted the principal's office as the focus of political action. Power also lies in the hands of publishers, who create the textbooks and decide what will and will not be included. The graduate schools of education that train teachers also help decide what should be in the curriculum. The courts exercise power every time they decide what is appropriate in teaching about religion. Behind all these purveyors of power lies the power of an idea: the notion of a sharp separation between the realm of personal belief and the realm of knowledge, and the consignment of religion to the former.

Social structure comes into play when we consider the school curriculum or the contents of textbooks. Books are written without discussions of religion; curricula are designed with no place for it; tests are prepared with no questions about it. In short, the whole structure of the educational system denies religion a place within that structure. It would be hard for an individual teacher to include it even if no one were to stand in the way.

The teacher who does try to introduce religion into the curriculum must take certain actions beforehand. He or she needs to learn more about religion as well as how to present the material without bias toward one belief system. Action is involved on the other end of the equation, too: If religious teaching amounts to indoctrination, this limits the freedom of choice (action) that students have about their own religious beliefs and also limits the freedom that parents have to influence their children's choices.

Addressing the problem of bias requires seeing how the issue is functionally integrated into the larger system. There is a functional relationship between the ways in which we think about personal conviction, including our religious views, and what we think we can fairly express in public institutions. If we believe that matters of conviction are intuitive and not rational, then we are likely to think that it would be difficult to teach them in a scholarly or unbiased manner. To change this point of view would require seeing religious ideas as objects of empirical knowledge, just as we see scientific ideas. However, the widespread distinction made between science and religion makes this possibility unlikely. Functional integration is also at work on the institutional level. Teachers find it difficult to teach religion because they have never been taught how to teach it nor have many of them been taught religion themselves—a reflection of the schools in which they have studied. Markets play a role as well. Publishers put in their books what educators want to see; books are more likely to lose a sale if they include something that some people strongly do not want than if they omit something that some others want. If the material is not in the book, it is a lot more difficult and riskier for a teacher to try to teach it.

While the progressives have accommodated themselves to secular society and secular solutions to social problems, the conservatives have increasingly distanced themselves. Hunter portrays these competing moral visions as engaged in cultural warfare, but some observers think he may overstate the case. After studying two Protestant seminaries, one liberal and one conservative, Carroll and Marler (1995) found that there was not a consensus about either vision within each school; they concluded that both sides were "less at war than at cross purposes," the main effect of which was "misunderstanding and tension within and between the two cultures which feed 'culture skirmishes'" (p. 19). Still, it does seem true that religious conservatives, unhappy with what they consider the radically secular presumptions of cultural and political elites in the latter part of this century, have retreated to religious groups that share their unhappiness and offer personal and political resolutions, such as day care, employment connections, schools, dating services, social activities, and, above all, political action.

SUMMARY

1. In defining religion, sociologists focus on three basic elements: beliefs, social practices, and moral community. Durkheim defined religion as a set of beliefs and practices pertaining to sacred things that unite people into a moral community.

2. Regardless of the specific characteristics of different religions, all have certain elements in common. These include religious beliefs and symbols, which are elements of culture; rituals and ceremonies, which are forms of social action; and religious community, a form of social structure. Religion may support or contest the existing social order, that is, contribute to functional integration or to schisms based on power conflicts.

3. Sociologists distinguish among three types of religious institutions: church, sect, and cult. A church is a large, conservative religious institution that tends to coexist harmoniously with the larger society. A sect, in contrast, is a small, uncompromising fellowship of people who seek spiritual perfection and tend to reject the larger society. Sects form when people break away from established churches and claim to have adopted a more authentic, purer version of their faith. A cult is like a sect in most respects except its origins. Cults are imported from other cultures or are formed when people create entirely new religious beliefs and practices.

4. Religion is not necessarily a conservative force in society. Religious innovation results in changes in an existing religion to better meet people's needs or in the creation of a new religion. Mormonism and the Unification church are the results of religious innovation.

5. Religions not only change from within; they also respond to changes in society. The Protestant Reformation, for example, was partly a response to broad social changes.

In turn, religious change can promote social change. Max Weber believed that the rise of modern capitalism had important roots in certain religious ideas of the Protestant Reformation. In particular, the Calvinist concept of predestination encouraged hard work, frugality, and astute investment in order to be successful in life and thus provide proof of God's favor.

6. Modernization has generally been accompanied by secularization, which entails a greater concern with worldly matters than with spiritual ones. But secularization has not spelled the end of religion. Many established churches have accommodated themselves to a secular world and have worked out a division of labor between secular and religious authority.

7. Another response to secularization has been the growth of fundamentalism, in which conservative religious groups reject secular concerns and seek to restore pure religious beliefs to preeminence in people's lives. Often they use political means to do so. Fundamentalist groups are found in most of the world's major religions, including Islam, Hinduism, Judaism, and Christianity.

8. Contrary to popular impressions, religious beliefs and practices in the United States have remained remarkably stable over the years. However, religious organizations have undergone significant restructuring. Since Vatican II, the Catholic laity have become more active in their church and also more independent in deciding moral and spiritual issues, despite Vatican injunctions. Mainline Protestant churches have lost members, while evangelical denominations have grown. For third- and fourth-generation American Jews, religion plays an important role in maintaining ethnic identity. At the same time, many more people have described religion as a personal or private matter.

REVIEW QUESTIONS

1. What are the three basic elements of religion?

2. What are the differences between churches, sects, and cults? Give an example of each.

3. How has religion helped to bring about social change?

4. What is meant by religious pluralism, and what are the implications?

5. Summarize the current trends in mainline American churches.

CRITICAL THINKING QUESTIONS

1. Using the five key concepts—social structure, social action, functional integration, power, and culture—describe how your own religion or some religion with which you are familiar works as a social institution.

2. The chapter analyzes how religion can bring about social change. Using what you have learned in this and other chapters, predict some social changes that religion may help to bring about.

3. The chapter notes that Americans are more religious than Europeans. Using what you know about the culture and social structure of American and European societies, develop some possible explanations for the difference.

4. Using what you have learned in this and other chapters, project trends in mainline American churches. Will funda-

mentalist congregations eventually become more mainstream? How would this change them? Will mainline churches continue to lose members?

5. How has reading this chapter affected your approach to or understanding of both your own religion and religiosity in general?

GLOSSARY

Animism   The idea that things in the world are imbued with active, animate spirits.

Church   According to Troeltsch, a large, conservative, universalist religious institution that makes few demands on its members and accommodates itself to the larger society.

Civil religion   Bellah's term for a sanctifying of the nation by associating its history, values, and institutions with God's special favor.

Cult   According to Stark and Bainbridge, a religious group that tends to exist in a state of tension with the surrounding culture and that has no prior ties to any established religious body in the larger society.

Evangelicals   Christians who feel a calling to emphasize the teachings of the Scriptures and to bear witness to God's influence on earth.

Fundamentalism   The view that religious teachings and principles have eroded in modern societies and a pure

way of life must be reestablished by returning to religious basics (or "fundamentals").

Invisible religion   The view that religion is a subjective, personal experience, not a matter of group doctrine.

Moral community   A group of people who share religious beliefs, symbols, and practices that bind them together into a social whole.

Religion   According to Durkheim, a set of beliefs and practices pertaining to sacred things that unite people into a moral community. According to Stark and Bainbridge, organizations primarily engaged in providing people with the hope of future rewards to compensate for things they greatly desire but have not obtained in life; this hope is based on a set of beliefs in supernatural forces, beings, or places.

Religious innovation   An effort to create new religions or to change existing ones to better meet people's needs.

Ritual   A standardized set of actions used in a particular ceremony or on some other specific occasion.

Sect   As defined by Troeltsch, a small, exclusive, uncompromising fellowship that makes heavy demands on its members and sets them apart from the larger society. As defined by Stark and Bainbridge, a religious group formed by breaking away from an established religious body.

Secularization   The process by which people and their social institutions become more concerned with worldly matters and less concerned with spiritual ones. Secularization is often associated with modernization.

Theism   The idea that powerful supernatural beings are involved with events and conditions on earth.

Totem   An object, plant, or animal that is worshiped as the mystical ancestor of a society or other special group.

CHAPTER 14

Health and Health Care

he Black Death—bubonic plague—devastated the population of Europe in the mid-fourteenth century. Spreading rapidly by physical contact with the sick and dying and by bacteria loosed in the air by their coughs and sneezes, this dread disease killed millions. In some cities, more than half the population died; it has been estimated that as much as a third of the population of Europe may have succumbed to the illness. The child's rhyming game ring-around-the-rosy is a distant reflection of the grim days of the plague: The dark ring around a red sore was a sign of the disease; the "pocket full of posies" were flowers for the dead—which also helped to disguise the smell of decaying corpses, since people died faster than they could be buried. "All fall down" meant the devastation of death itself.

In the Middle Ages, disease was a mystery. It would be centuries before it was known that plaque was caused by a bacterium carried by rats and fleas. At the time, plague was simply an inexplicable catastrophe to the human populations it ravaged. Eventually, medical science did begin to understand the nature of infectious disease. The discoveries of the late eighteenth and nineteenth century—that germs could cause disease, for example, and that vaccination could prevent it—began to make disease more understandable and less terrifying. Science began to "conquer" one disease after another—smallpox, rabies, tuberculosis, polio, measles. People began to believe that epidemics of infectious disease were a thing of the past.

Yet now, 600 years after the Black Death swept Europe, plagues are back. The most visible is **AIDS** (*a*quired *i*mmune *d*eficiency *s*yndrome), but it is only one of a number of epidemic infectious diseases to appear in recent years. Another is Ebola hemorrhagic fever, which took hundreds of lives in a sudden

Waves of the Black Death, or bubonic plague, ravaged Europe from the fourteenth through the seventeenth centuries, reducing Europe's population by more than 50 percent and creating social chaos and economic stagnation. In the late twentieth century, many believed that modern medicine had conquered most contagious diseases. But the AIDS epidemic, the return of tuberculosis, and new viruses such as Ebola show this declaration of scientific victory was premature.

outbreak in 1995. Tuberculosis, the disease that once confined thousands of people to years in sanitariums, had all but disappeared by the 1960s, thanks to successful drug treatment. Now it is back, killing 2.7 million people worldwide in 1993 alone (Platt, 1994). Why are infectious diseases returning? This question was brought home to many Americans by the best-selling book *The Hot Zone* (Preston, 1994) and the 1995 film *Outbreak* starring Dustin Hoffman.

But perhaps the question should be, "Why are we letting infectious diseases return?" For disease is more than a medical problem—it is also a social problem. Many diseases can be prevented by vaccination or treated with available medicines, and yet these preventive and treatment measures are not used. Vaccination programs, for example, have been defunded as our success in nearly wiping out some dis-

eases has lulled us into ignoring their continuing threat. Treatments may be unavailable to those who live far from a doctor or hospital, and treatments may not be sought by those who do not recognize their symptoms as serious or lack money or insurance to pay for care.

Perhaps the most important factor in the resurgence of infectious disease is the neglect of research into these diseases compared with the research effort into the chronic "diseases of civilization," particularly heart disease and cancer (Garrett, 1994). These diseases are the leading cause of death for most Americans, particularly the well-off, and they are the diseases that have attracted most of the research money. Cancer and heart disease are high-prestige specialties in medical research, and billions of dollars go to physicians and laboratories that study these diseases. By comparison, infectious disease is a low-status field, in part perhaps because of its association with poverty and poor living conditions. Research into infectious diseases often does not involve basic biochemical science but instead less glamorous study of how diseases are transmitted, what behaviors are involved, and which populations are at risk. Although these investigations are important to public health, the epidemiologists and public health specialists who conduct them must compete with established and prestigious research institutes for a declining amount of federal research money. Finally, people who have diseases clamor loudly for cures, while efforts at prevention are less dramatic and have fewer dedicated advocates.

Many small plagues arise each year. Most are stopped, die down at least temporarily, or are contained by quarantine. Whether one of them will eventually spread and devastate our society as the Black Death devastated medieval Europe is a sociological as well as a medical question. As the struggles over the federal government's funding of AIDS research and prevention efforts have shown, this is a matter of power. It is also a matter of social action because people can help stop disease by changing their behavior—for example, in the case of AIDS, by using condoms and avoiding risky sex and intravenous drug use. People can also organize and act to increase public awareness or pressure the government to take effective action. Whether they succeed is partly a matter of culture, not only because scientific knowledge is part of culture but because cultural values and prejudices shape the way people respond to infectious disease. For example, instead of orga-

As this poster illustrates, the control or containment of disease depends as much on social factors as on medical breakthroughs. These factors include: changes in social behavior (abstinence or, second best, protected sex); revision of cultural attitudes (a turn back of the "sexual revolution"); the distribution of power (the groups hurt most by AIDS and other epidemics tend to be poor and powerless); and social action (such as Hollywood mobilizing to raise support for AIDS research and education).

nizing to fight AIDS, many Americans dismissed the disease as a "gay problem" and fought against the prevention programs that might have slowed its spread. Finally, as we shall see throughout this chapter, the sociology of health is a matter of social structure. Disease affects the rich and the poor very differently. Well-off people rarely die in infancy, of childhood diseases, of untreated chronic illness, or of on-the-job accidents; they are more likely to suffer from the diseases of old age. Social structure is also involved in the way infectious diseases spread— more rapidly in packed cities, for example, and through networks of social relationships. In short, whether some future plague hits the United States is in part a sociological question.

In the first part of this chapter, we look at social patterns of disease. We see how modern society has helped spawn its own set of physical ailments and how they affect social groups differently. Then we shall consider the resurgence of infectious diseases, with AIDS as a prominent example, examining how social factors as well as microbes are involved in this alarming phenomenon. Next we turn to the health-care industry in the United States and the changes that have affected it recently. Finally, we address some problems of U.S. health care: unequal access to care, spiraling costs, and the health insurance crisis.

SOCIAL PATTERNS OF DISEASE

The Chronic Diseases of Modern Life

In 1900 the leading causes of death in the United States were pneumonia, influenza, and tuberculosis. Today these acute infectious diseases rarely kill; instead, most people die of chronic diseases such as heart disorders or cancer (see Figure 14.1). The primary reason for the change is that we now have antibiotics and other drugs that can cure most infectious diseases. In addition, standards of living and public health have greatly improved. More people today eat a healthier diet, drink comparatively clean water and uncontaminated milk, and live in environments relatively free of insects, rats, and other carriers of disease. These factors tend to protect people from *acute* infections so that they may live long enough to develop the *chronic* "diseases of civilization" (those associated with modern life in highly developed countries). For example, lack of exercise and a diet high in fats and salt have been linked to the development of heart and vascular disorders. Similarly, modern dietary patterns and long exposure to low-level carcinogens (cancer-causing substances) have been associated with certain malignan-

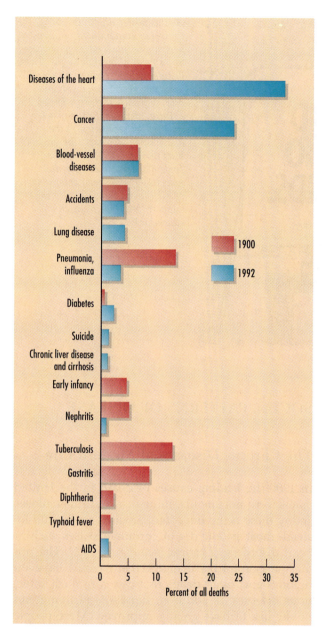

FIGURE 14.1 / Leading Causes of Death in the United States, 1900 and 1992

While medical advances since 1900 have drastically cut death rates from pneumonia and other infectious diseases, deaths from heart disease and cancer have risen sharply.

Sources: National Office of Vital Statistics, *Vital Statistics of the United States,* Vol. 1 (U.S. Government Printing Office, Washington, D.C., 1954), p. 170, and U.S. Bureau of the Census, *Mortality Statistics,* 1900–1904 (U.S. Government Printing Office, Washington, D.C., 1906); National Center for Health Statistics, *Vital Statistics of the United States, Monthly Vital Statistics Report,* June 12, 1991.

cies. Prosperity can thus have negative as well as positive physical consequences.

What would happen if these risks of modern life were greatly reduced or even eliminated? What if most people in the industrialized world quit smoking, ate a healthier diet, got regular exercise, and avoided carcinogens? Of course, everyone would still die eventually. But according to James F. Fries (1983) of the Stanford University School of Medicine, people would live longer, more active lives and would remain comparatively free of disease until their last few years. He calls this process a **compression of morbidity** (**morbidity** is the rate at which a disease occurs in a population). With a compression of morbidity, suffering from disease would be confined to the very end of life for most people.

How likely is it that a widespread compression of morbidity will occur in this country in your lifetime? The answer depends mainly on how much we are able to reduce the factors that give rise to chronic diseases. Some reductions people can undertake by themselves, such as giving up smoking, drinking less alcohol, eating a diet low in fats and salt, and getting more exercise. Reduction of environmental pollution, in contrast, is more a matter of collective effort. Emissions from smokestacks, cars, toxic waste dumps, and nuclear reactors have been implicated in many cancers and other diseases. The workplace, too, contains many health hazards, and certain occupations pose particular risk by exposing people to carcinogens. Controlling the environmental pollutants and toxins that cause work-related cancers requires that society adopt a "get-tough" policy with businesses that do not meet minimum safety standards. The compression of morbidity, in other words, depends very much on social policies.

Structural Inequality and Disease

Although people of all classes become ill, poverty is linked to ill health throughout the world. Poverty means exposure to many threats to health: inadequate or unhealthful food; poor, unsafe, and unsanitary housing; and more exposure to stress and violence that can cause injury and disease. Poverty also means lack of access to preventive health care such as prenatal care and prompt treatment of minor ailments before they become major. The frustrations of poverty may also foster self-destructive behavior such as alcoholism, smoking, drug abuse, and other forms of risk-taking that weaken the body's immune system and leave a person more vulnerable to disease and infection.

Inadequate diet alone can cause illness. Since one recent survey found that 5.5 million American children go hungry much of the time (Pear, 1991), this is not a minor concern. Although programs begun in the 1960s and 1970s to reduce hunger—for example, food stamps and school lunch programs—made headway in ensuring that most Americans had enough to eat (Brown, 1987), these programs began to be cut by the federal government in 1981. In addition, a surge of unemployment in the early 1980s left many people ineligible for assistance. The result was a huge increase in demand at soup kitchens and food pantries run by private charity. A rise in the infant mortality rate in several states and urban areas was subsequently linked to inadequate diets (Brown, 1987). In some poorer countries, hunger is an even more serious problem, with substantial numbers of people subject to malnutrition and starvation.

Given the relationship between poverty and disease, it is hardly surprising that unemployment exerts a detrimental effect on health. For many of the approximately 500 million people worldwide who have lost (or never had) a job, unemployment means having to do without many of life's necessities. In poor countries, medical care may not be easily accessible even for working people. For those with no income, it is simply unavailable. Moreover, many countries have no "safety net," such as welfare programs or disability benefits, for people who lose their jobs. When these countries suffer economic recession and unemployment rates rise sharply (as happened in the Latin American nations in the wake of their debt crisis in the mid-1980s), the impact on national health can be devastating (Musgrove, 1987).

The effects of unemployment on health extend beyond loss of income. Even in the United States, where workers' compensation and other programs offer some assistance and where many families have two wage earners, the experience of unemployment itself can still undermine health. One study (Brenner, 1987) stirred controversy by showing that the death rate from heart disease increases when unemployment rises. Unemployment has also been linked to anxiety, depression, and abuse of alcohol and tranquilizers (Kessler, House, and Turner, 1987). This is true even when preexisting conditions and behaviors that may have contributed to job loss are taken into account. Apparently, unemployment statistics can serve as barometers of health, and reductions in unemployment can yield health improvements.

Although Americans spend more on health care than do the people of any other country, the United States is not the world's healthiest nation. The high poverty rate is one major reason. Poverty also largely explains the higher rates of many diseases among black and Hispanic-Americans, since they are on average poorer than whites. Statistics such as **mortality rates,** or death rates, illustrate the problem. The overall infant mortality rate has been falling, but it is edging upward again in some areas, particularly where government aid for prenatal, maternal, and preventive health services has been cut. In the United States, the infant mortality rate is 7.9 per 1,000 among infants less than one year old, compared with Finland's 4.4, Japan's 4.4, and Sweden's 4.8 (*American Journal of Public Health,* 1995). It is much higher in places with a high concentration of poor people.

Average life expectancy tends to be highest in industrialized countries in which income is most equally distributed, such as Iceland, Norway, Sweden, Switzerland, the Netherlands, and Japan (Wilkinson, 1990). Not surprisingly, when most people in a country get adequate nutrition and health care, the population as a whole is healthier and lives longer. For the poor, in contrast, poverty and illness often go hand in hand. The poorer you are, the less healthy you are likely to be; and the less healthy you are, the more your income declines. Moreover, not only do the poor in the United States get the diseases of poverty, such as infections and illnesses related to poor diet, but they are also more likely to suffer from the so-called diseases of affluence—cancer and heart disease. The explanation of this paradox is that poor people's diets are fattier and saltier, poor people are exposed to more pollutants, and their lives are frequently more stressful.

The connection between poverty and poor health is worldwide. There is a strong correlation between per capita gross national product and such indices of health as infant mortality and life expectancy. In the more developed nations the infant mortality rate averages 10 per 1,000 infants; in the least developed countries it averages 69 per 1,000. Similarly, life expectancy at birth averages seventy-four years in the more developed countries, but only forty-nine in the least developed ones (Population Reference Bureau, 1994).

The patterns of disease in underdeveloped countries differ appreciably from those in developed countries. Infectious, parasitic, and respiratory diseases cause more than 40 percent of the deaths in underdeveloped countries but only about 10 percent of deaths in industrialized countries. The most widespread diseases in poorer regions are diarrheal, transmitted by human fecal contamination of food, water, and soil; only about a third of the people in underdeveloped countries have access to safe water. Parasitic diseases such as malaria and schistosomiasis also tend to be widespread in poorer countries, infecting a quarter of the world's population overall. Malaria, which is transmitted by mosquitoes, is the most prevalent disease worldwide—with around 300 to 500 million new cases every year—despite the fact that it can be prevented by routine administration of inexpensive drugs (Kondrachine and Trigg, 1995).

Schistosomiasis—caused by a snail-borne parasite—chronically infects some 200 million people. Both malaria and schistosomiasis are debilitating diseases that sap energy and strength.

Many underdeveloped countries spend much of their health budgets establishing medical schools and building hospital complexes. However, this approach addresses the health care of only 10 to 15 percent of the population, usually the elite. The resources are used mainly to cure chronic disease using increasingly expensive technology (intensive-care units, bypass surgery, life-support systems, whole-body scanners). The health needs of the population at large would be better served by campaigns to eliminate parasitic and infectious agents, hunger, and contaminated drinking water. Since most of these conditions can be dramatically reduced at relatively modest cost, the suffering they cause is largely preventable.

Currently, four-fifths of the world's population does not have access to *any* permanent form of health care. The public health services of the sixty-seven poorest countries, excluding China, spend less on health care than the richer countries spend on tranquilizers alone. Moreover, richer countries (chiefly, Australia, Canada, Germany, the United Kingdom, and the United States) are attracting physicians from the poorer ones. Although it costs eight times more to train a physician than to train a medical auxiliary, many poorer countries continue to emphasize training physicians. If the goal of good health is to be

achieved for the great masses of the world's population, existing health-care strategies will have to be dramatically transformed (Mahler, 1980, 1981).

Gender and Health

In America, as in most places around the world, the medical profession has historically been dominated by men. This may be one reason why medical research has shown a male bias. Not only has there been relative neglect of research on women's health problems, such as osteoporosis and breast cancer, but even those conditions that affect a substantial number of women as well as men, such as heart disease and alcoholism, have been studied primarily from a male perspective. For example, two large, wide-ranging, and important studies of cardiovascular disease involved thousands of male subjects but no women (Doyal, 1995). Most studies of AIDS have also been done solely on men, even though the disease is increasing substantially among women and its transmission and effects are different in the female reproductive system (Doyal, 1995).

Male bias within the medical profession may also be seen in approaches to women's medical treatment that are not sensitive to women's needs. Until comparatively recently, complete removal of a diseased breast or uterus was often recommended to women with little or no explanation of possible alternative treatments. And when a health issue involved both a man and a woman, such as birth control, it was commonly considered to be the woman's responsibility. Many women have also objected to their male doctors' treating their pregnancies as illnesses rather than as the normal events they are.

It is interesting that marriage, which is associated with positive health benefits for men, is associated with health problems for women (Doyal, 1995). In part this is because of the risks involved in childbearing, which has caused death and disability to many women throughout history and still does so frequently in less-developed countries. A woman who cannot bear children, on the other hand, may find her self-image and even her mental health impaired, especially if she lives in a culture that values women principally as mothers. In such cultures, a man may divorce a wife who fails to produce children, leaving her destitute. In India, such wives have been burned to death by their husbands, who pass the murders off as "kitchen accidents"—and the law looks the other way (Doyal, 1995). Other health threats to married women come from abuse by their husbands. In the United States, as many as one in five women have been abused by husbands or partners (Doyal, 1995).

Beginning in the late 1960s, the women's movement drew attention to the special health problems of women and their less-than-satisfactory treatment by the medical profession. One milestone in this effort was the publication of *Our Bodies, Ourselves* by the Boston Women's Health Collective, a popular book that aimed at both supplying health information to women and empowering them to take charge of their own health care. One sign that change is occurring within the medical profession itself is the rising number of women physicians. By the mid-1990s, 40 percent of new doctors were women, and this figure continues to rise (U.S. Bureau of the Census, 1994d, p. 191).

Dangerous Products

One of the ironies of the current age of greater freedom for women is that many women have chosen to use their new freedom to engage in an activity known to bring disease and death: smoking. Indeed, as increasing numbers of men have stopped smoking for health reasons, the rate of smoking among women has increased. Despite innumerable warnings from public health officials at all levels, substantial numbers of young women—and men—take up smoking every year. The health consequences are devastating. Smoking-related diseases, such as lung cancer, emphysema, and heart disease, kill an estimated 350,000 Americans a year and account for about 20 percent of the national death toll (American Medical Association, 1993; U.S. Bureau of the Census, 1994d).

One reason why people continue to take up smoking is that cigarettes are the most heavily advertised consumer product. Every year, tobacco companies spend over $4 billion on cigarette advertising and promotion in the United States alone (Centers for Disease Control, 1995). Therefore, smoking is maintained not only by the actions of individuals who choose to smoke but also by the actions of the tobacco companies, which pour enormous amounts of money into promoting a product known to be dangerous.

In recent years, critics of smoking have taken action themselves, in a variety of efforts to discourage smoking. Besides publicizing the health dangers

Doctors *endorsing a brand of cigarettes?! This 1947 ad, which appeared in a national news magazine, was typical for its day. Today we know that smoking is the single leading threat to public health, that second-hand smoke is a health hazard, and that nicotine is highly addictive. Yet tobacco continues to be grown and aggressively marketed—a reminder that social and economic power are intertwined with public health.*

associated with smoking, they have lobbied successfully for laws restricting smoking in public places and for tighter enforcement of laws against sales of tobacco to minors. Class-action lawsuits against tobacco companies have been launched, with the rationale that tobacco companies should be forced to pay damages to people injured by their dangerous products, just as manufacturers of defective automobiles, unsafe drugs, and other products have been required to do. (Thus far, tobacco companies have successfully fought such suits.)

Although tobacco companies have responded to criticism of their products in a variety of ways, such as launching "smokers' rights" campaigns, the rate of smoking in the United States continues to decline, particularly among men. Women, probably because of the notion that smoking helps them keep thin and because of pressure from the larger culture not to be overweight, are continuing to take up the habit in adolescence and early adulthood at a higher rate than men.

Cigarettes are by no means the only dangerous product to be marketed and used to the detriment of health. Many women in the United States and around the world used the Dalkon Shield intrauterine device for years until its hazards led to successful lawsuits against its manufacturers in the 1980s. Silicon breast implants, which thousands of women chose to have in the 1970s and 1980s, have similarly been blamed for a variety of health problems. In this case, corporations saw an opportunity to make profits by supplying a product that would exploit American culture's emphasis on physical attractiveness in females, and many women bought the product—only to feel later that their health had deteriorated as a result.

Infectious Diseases in the Age of AIDS

As major threats to public health, infectious diseases were once thought to be a thing of the past in the United States. Indeed, in 1967 the U.S. surgeon general declared that it was time for scientists to close the book on infectious disease and to focus instead on fighting chronic illnesses like heart disease and cancer (*CQ Researcher*, June 9, 1995). In recent years, however, frightening outbreaks of infectious disease have occurred in the United States and around the world.

Sometimes these have been familiar diseases, such as tuberculosis and plague, but at other times entirely new diseases have emerged. In 1976, for example, a new type of pneumonia was identified among 182 people who had attended an American Legion convention in Philadelphia. Subsequently known as "Legionnaires' disease," it was found to have been spread through the air-conditioning system in the convention hall. In 1979, the first cases of toxic shock syndrome were identified; these were ultimately linked to the use of superabsorbent tampons, which furnished a medium for the growth of toxin-producing staphylococcus bacteria. In 1981, the first cases of AIDS were reported in homosexual men. Other outbreaks of infectious disease in the United States have included Lyme disease, a multisymptom disorder spread by infected ticks; hantavirus, a severe flulike ailment spread by mice; and in 1993 a virulent form of *E. coli* infection that killed four children and sickened at least 500 people in the Pacific Northwest who ate tainted meat. Outside the United States there were horrific outbreaks of tropical fevers, such as the Ebola hemorrhagic fever (the subject of *The Hot Zone*) in central Africa, Lassa fever in West Africa, and Rift Valley fever in Egypt, as well as pneumonic plague in India and cholera and malaria in several countries.

What nearly all these disease outbreaks have in common is a relationship to some change or disruption in human social organization. Technological change helped to cause some of them: From the air-conditioning ducts that spread Legionnaires' disease to the artificial fibers in the tampons that offered a comfortable environment to toxic shock bacteria, the adoption of new products encouraged disease transmission. Changes in living conditions also spread disease: Housing construction in woodland areas has been tied to Lyme disease, and urbanization, warfare, migration, land clearance, and dam construction have affected tropical disease outbreaks.

Perhaps most significantly, the spread of AIDS throughout the world from its probable birthplace in Africa was made possible by modern transportation. AIDS first spread along a new highway that was built from Kinshasa, Zaire, across central Africa to Mombasa, Kenya. Truck drivers and the prostitutes they patronized spread the infection along the highway and from there throughout central Africa (Garrett, 1994). Air travel by persons infected with the AIDS virus probably spread it from Africa to Europe and the Americas. The fact that air travel is now a link in the spread of infectious disease is particularly ominous, since a single infected person could conceivably get on a plane anywhere in the world and start a new outbreak thousands of miles away within hours or days.

This fact and the striking increase in infectious disease outbreaks in recent years has led to calls for public health efforts worldwide to increase infectious disease surveillance efforts (*CQ Researcher*, June 9, 1995). Rapid identification of outbreaks is essential if the spread of infectious diseases is to be curbed. In addition, research on infectious disease, which had been rapidly defunded in the rosy optimism of the "conquest over disease" days, will need to be increased and reinvigorated if more epidemics are to be avoided. Prevention efforts, too, such as vaccinations, which have been neglected in the recent past, need to be reemphasized. Unfortunately, budget cuts in research and in crucial public health facilities such as the Centers for Disease Control and Prevention make it unlikely that the United States will lead any such effort.

Some commentators on recent disease epidemics who have noted their link to human activities have suggested that these diseases are best seen as a response to environmental change. Rapidly increasing human population is a factor in many outbreaks, and it has even been suggested that these diseases are "the Earth's revenge" against human destruction of the worldwide ecosystem (Preston, 1994). In this view, the emerging infections are a kind of immune response to overpopulation and consequent destruction of the natural world. Although this interpretation is controversial, there is no doubt that people's actions—not just germs and viruses—are very much involved in the new outbreaks of infectious disease and that people's actions must be involved in combating them.

AIDS

AIDS is caused by the human immunodeficiency virus (HIV), which destroys the body's ability to fight off infections and cancers. AIDS kills by allowing other diseases and infections to run rampant through a body unprotected by a healthy immune system. The virus is spread through contact with the blood, semen, vaginal secretions, or breast milk of an infected person. Thus, a person may become infected by having unprotected sexual intercourse with an infected partner, sharing a hypodermic needle with an infected person, getting a contaminated blood transfusion, or (in the case of babies) being in the womb of an infected mother.

Once in a new host's body, the virus may remain inactive for years. During this period, unless the infected person is tested for HIV, he or she may unknowingly transmit it to other people. No one knows how HIV is eventually activated, but once this happens the immune system is progressively weakened so that the person is vulnerable to the so-called *opportunistic infections* that ravage the body and eventually lead to death. The most common opportunistic infections include virulent and disfiguring forms of herpes, cryptococcus, salmonella, and yeast infections. Pneumonia, meningitis, a rare form of cancer known as Kaposi's sarcoma, and tuberculosis also occur frequently in people who have AIDS. In fact, tuberculosis, which had been almost eradicated in the United States, is once again becoming epidemic, largely because AIDS has given it an opportunity to develop and spread in densely populated urban areas. TB is also spreading because of poor monitoring of treated patients, lack of follow-up treatment—especially among the poor—and the advent of drug-resistant forms of the disease (Platt, 1994).

In the United States, an estimated 2 million people have tested positive for the HIV virus. About 45,000 new cases are reported annually. The United States has about one-tenth of the world's HIV carriers (Wulff, 1996). Of this number, about 50 percent will develop AIDS and die within ten years. At the twelve-year mark, only 34 percent will still be alive (Gorman, 1996). Because AIDS is a new disease, it is not yet known whether the remaining 15 percent of infected people who show no impairment after ten years of living with HIV will eventually succumb to it. The 1996 return of basketball star Magic Johnson to NBA competition 4 years after testing positive for HIV dramatizes the possibilities for longer, fuller lives despite the disease. Still, although new drugs and treatments for AIDS are being developed and doctors are now more successful in treating opportunistic infections, the long-term outlook remains bleak. So far, of those who have developed full-blown cases of AIDS—more than 300,000 people as of September 1993—not a single person has been known to recover.

The HIV virus can spread with alarming speed through a population. Among a sample of homosexual men in San Francisco who had a history of other sexually transmitted diseases, for example, the rate of infection rose from under 4 percent to over 75 percent in less than eight years (Winkelstein et al., 1987). What causes the AIDS virus to spread so quickly? The answer, according to the sociologist Peter Bearman (1992), lies in social structure. A high degree of interconnectedness among members of population segments that engage in risky behavior allows the virus to spread quickly in those segments. In the United States, the close networks among and risky behavior associated with two populations—gay men and intravenous drug users—have resulted in very high rates of HIV infection in those groups.

The impact of social-structural variables is apparent in the different social patterns that underlie the transmission of AIDS in other countries. For instance, the AIDS virus has spread rapidly in eastern and central Africa, the area where it first appeared. In Malawi, a third of the population is HIV-positive, and in some cities of Tanzania, 40 percent of adults are infected. In contrast to the United States, the AIDS virus in Africa is transmitted overwhelmingly by heterosexual intercourse. One study found that in eastern and central Africa in general, 80 percent of the HIV-positive adults had acquired the virus through heterosexual contact and another 10 percent through contaminated blood transfusions. That left only 10 percent for unprotected homosexual contact and sharing of contaminated needles, the most prevalent means of transmission in the United States (N'galy and Ryder, 1988).

How an infectious disease like AIDS is transmitted determines what sorts of actions are defined as risky for the disease. Sociologists study the transmission of disease in order to see how social factors contribute to it. Such research can be particularly helpful in determining how social action might be modified to reduce the risk and incidence of the disease. Bearman (1992) argues that to predict the spread of AIDS in the years ahead, we must focus on the fact that AIDS can spread from person to person, and from group to group, only through an exchange of contaminated body fluids. Bearman emphasizes that it is people's *actions*, not attributes like their gender, race, age, or sexual orientation, that determine who is most at risk of contracting AIDS:

> . . . if IV drug users didn't share dirty needles, they would not be at risk to AIDS. It is not the drug abuse that defines risk to HIV. In the same manner, men

who do not exchange fluids during sex are not at risk to HIV. It is not homosexuality, but the exchange of fluids during sex which defines risk behaviors. (Bearman, 1992)

AIDS is now spread from one group to another primarily through unprotected sexual intercourse. While gay men are a strongly bounded population, bisexual men who have sexual relations with both men and women can serve as bridges for the AIDS virus to move from the homosexual population into other populations. The more such bridges there are, the greater the rate of sexual mixing between groups and the faster the spread of the virus.

Among intravenous drug users there are even more bridges to other segments of the population. Female drug users, although they tend to have stable sexual relationships with men who also use drugs, frequently resort to prostitution to help support their drug habit. Heterosexual non-drug-using men who buy these sexual services are putting themselves at risk for infection with HIV. Similarly, heterosexual male intravenous drug users tend to have many non-drug-using partners, and these men rarely use condoms. Not surprisingly, 62 percent of the cases of heterosexually transmitted AIDS among women comes from unprotected sexual contact with a male drug user (National Research Council, 1990).

The threat of AIDS has changed the American social landscape. It has caused changes in sexual behavior, putting a damper on the "sexual revolution" of the 1960s and 1970s. This is most apparent among gay men, many of whom are now having sex with fewer partners and are avoiding risky behavior such as anal intercourse (which enables the AIDS virus to enter the bloodstream through small tears in the lining of the rectum) (Friedman, et al., 1987). There has also been an increase in the use of condoms and a decrease in the use of recreational drugs (which can impair judgment in assessing the risk of sexual behavior) (Siegel, et al., 1989).

While the most effective social action against AIDS is clearly activity aimed at decreasing the incidence of risky behaviors, many effective measures are opposed by people whose cultural values lead them to oppose programs and strategies for various "moral" reasons. For instance, programs that allow intravenous drug users to exchange used needles for sterile ones, or that give out bleaching kits to addicts with instructions on sterilizing needles, have been

Public health reflects cultural values. Our culture views the use of some drugs (heroin, cocaine) as deviant, but tolerates the use of other, equally dangerous and addictive drugs (nicotine, alcohol). Some Americans hold that intravenous drug users "deserve what they get," whether it be AIDS or other health problems. Others see drug addiction, like alcoholism, as a disease and drug users as deserving of treatment, not a "death sentence." Still others believe that slowing the spread of AIDS in all groups contributes to the public good and overrides other considerations.

criticized by groups can claim that these efforts condone illegal drug use and make it easier. Efforts to make condoms available and teach safer-sex guidelines to students in public schools face opposition from those who consider sexual abstinence to be the only appropriate form of safer sex for unmarried teens. These groups worry that any form of sex education will encourage sexual behavior among young people.

Since the beginning of the epidemic, people with AIDS and their advocates have claimed that the federal government's commitment of funds for research and prevention has never been proportionate to the impact and threat of the disease—and that this inadequate response is a reflection of widespread prejudice against homosexuals and intravenous drug users. Not until AIDS became perceived as a threat to the larger population, activists argue, did there seem to be much national concern about developing strategies for prevention and treatment.

The slow response to the AIDS crisis in the United States is one reason more than a million Americans are now HIV-positive. The alarming fact that this number is still growing has created uncertainty about whether the already overburdened health-care system can cope with the avalanche of new AIDS cases that is expected by the year 2000. People with AIDS require a considerable amount of care and treatment, much of which they are unable to pay for themselves. In 1990 alone, $8.5 billion was spent on Americans with AIDS, and as the epidemic progresses these costs will spiral higher (Makadon, et al., 1990). It is currently estimated that the lifetime cost of treating an AIDS patient is over $100,000 (Hellinger, 1993) (see the Sociology and Public Debates box).

From the beginning of the U.S. AIDS crisis, homosexual communities throughout the country have mobilized to take up some of the slack in AIDS treatment and prevention. In San Francisco, for example, a number of volunteer organizations have provided information, medical referrals, help with housing, financial assistance, counseling, home-attendant services, and hospice care (Arno, 1986). These efforts not only have been of immense help to people with AIDS but also have helped to minimize the burden on public institutions. (Patients who can live at home with help, for example, do not have to be hospitalized). Drug users and drug-treatment agencies have made some efforts to provide similar services for

How Should the Government Respond to AIDS?

Among those Americans who lack access to the health care they need are many patients with AIDS. From the beginning of the AIDS epidemic, some doctors, nurses, and other care providers have refused to treat AIDS patients out of fear of contracting the disease themselves. People with AIDS who can find a source of treatment may be bankrupted by the cost of their care. Nearly all insurers deny coverage to those with AIDS and many to those who are infected with HIV, the virus that causes AIDS. Even AIDS patients who do have insurance will typically lose it just as their illness becomes serious, because when illness forces them to leave their jobs, they lose their insurance coverage (Daniels, 1995).

> **People with AIDS . . . may be bankrupted by the cost of their care.**

THE DEBATE

The AIDS epidemic has raised a number of difficult questions for the government. It has helped fuel the demand for health-care reform, as care of AIDS patients is very expensive and (without insurance) falls largely to federal and state governments through Medicaid. In 1995, the care of AIDS patients is expected to cost more than $15 billion. Another quandary for the government at various levels has been how to encourage AIDS prevention. Public health measures such as safer-sex education and the distribution of condoms and free hypodermic needles have been proposed by health authorities but bitterly opposed by members of the public whose cultural values strongly disapprove of sex education, homosexuality, and drug use. This clash of cultures has stood in the way of AIDS prevention.

ANALYSIS

Helping to stop the spread of AIDS would mean using tax dollars to provide (a) safe-sex education, including homosexual relations, (b) access to clean needles for drug addicts, and (c) access to condoms for high school students. These moves were needed early on in order to keep the AIDS problem from reaching epidemic proportions. But they were opposed by many for whose cultural values the notions of sex education, homosexuality, and drug use were repugnant. This clash of cultures stood in the way of better prevention of AIDS (and still does).

Advocates for AIDS patients have mobilized to attract support for their cause and embarrass public officials into taking action (such as funding research and expediting the approval of new drugs). These groups had to organize themselves for collective action and to tackle AIDS issues as matters of politics, of power. The best-known advocacy group is known as ACT-UP. The members of this group have staged a number of flamboyant and theatrical public events to draw attention to AIDS issues and to put public officials on the spot. AIDS activists have also tried to mobilize support for those public officials who have urged scientific research on the disease, better prevention, and more funding for care of AIDS patients.

The spread of AIDS, as we have seen, was a matter of social structure. The disease has been passed mainly through sexual contact and sharing needles in drug use. This has set up a distinction between AIDS patients who contracted the disease by their own (socially stigmatized) actions and the much smaller number of "innocent victims" such as those who have contracted the disease through blood transfusions. This added to the burden of the former group and meant that "innocent victims" were particularly effective spokespeople (tennis star Arthur Ashe, for example), or "poster children" (Ryan White) for the need for AIDS treatment. The social-structural location of AIDS—its concentration in specific populations—made it easier for the larger public to ignore or minimize the problem and much harder for the affected groups. It made AIDS different from diseases that might affect a similarly large number of people without affecting a comparable percentage of any one social group. On the other hand, it made it much easier to mobilize those groups to do something about the disease.

Dealing with AIDS clashed with the functional integration of the health-care system. For most Americans who are not elderly or poor, most health care is paid for largely by private, for-profit insurance. Any HIV-positive person who has insurance but who for any reason must leave a job will never again be able to get insurance coverage, since any new employer's insurance can decline any employee with a "preexisting condition" such as HIV. In other health-care systems, loss of a job would not also mean loss of health care.

The United States already pays more for health care than any other country. Many citizens want to make cutting costs their first goal. But what responsibility should the government take for the care of AIDS victims? Part of the problem, as we have seen, is that if the government does not do enough to prevent AIDS, it pays the cost later in caring for victims.

people with AIDS, but their efforts have not been as effective as those of gay advocacy groups (Friedman et al., 1987).

Despite the slow response of government officials and the lack of funding for research, the life expectancy of people with AIDS has improved over the last few years. New drugs are currently in development, and others, such as AZT, have proved effective in slowing the pace of the disease's development in HIV-positive people. Such treatment breakthroughs, though, remain out of reach for many people who are HIV-positive or who have AIDS, because they are extremely expensive. AIDS patients who have medical insurance either lose it once they become too ill to work or exhaust their benefits.

Researchers are working on a vaccine that would keep HIV from developing into full-blown AIDS. Some experts believe that a vaccine will be developed within fifteen years—a short time from the scientific standpoint, but an eternity for people who are already sick.

THE HEALTH-CARE INDUSTRY

The health-care industry in the United States is huge and rapidly growing. This vast enterprise now employs more than 5 million people: doctors, nurses, technicians, therapists, pharmacists, and others who work in a variety of settings. In 1993 health-care expenses accounted for 14.6 percent of the country's gross domestic product, and this figure is expected to rise to 17.3 percent by 1998 (Steuerle, 1994). It has been estimated that by the year 2030, when the baby boom generation will be well into old age, 26 percent of GDP will be allotted to medical services, supplies, and equipment (Morganthau and Hager, 1992). This is why health-care reform was a top priority of the Clinton administration in 1993 and why the Republican congressional majority targeted Medicare and Medicaid for reductions in their 1995 budget plans. In exploring how the health-care industry developed its present size and form, we begin with a look at how so many personal and social problems came to be seen as requiring medical attention.

Medicalization: Redefining Illness

An important by-product of the growth of the health-care industry and the prestige of physicians, discussed in the next two sections, is an increase in the number of conditions that are thought to be of medical concern. In the not-too-distant past, birth and death usually occurred at home, with family members and friends at hand. Now most people are born and die in a hospital, surrounded by bright lights and expensive machines. People who were addicted to alcohol or drugs or gambling were once considered sinners. Our more secular society now considers such addictions illnesses. Conditions that used to be accepted as part of life—baldness, wrinkles, obesity, acne, small breasts, lack of interest in sex, anxiety, sleeplessness, infertility, aging, hyperactivity in children—are today deemed appropriate for medical intervention (Conrad, 1992; Zola, 1972). Even antisocial behavior is now often defined as a medical problem. Lawbreakers of all kinds, from shoplifters to mass murders, may be labeled "sick." This trend toward including personal problems in the realm of medicine has been called **medicalization.**

Medicalization has given doctors wide leeway to intervene in people's private lives. Doctors may now scrutinize patients' entire lifestyles—what they eat, whether they smoke, how much they drink and exercise, how many hours they spend at work, and what the various stresses in their lives are. A modern doctor's "prescription" might be to stop smoking, eat fewer fatty foods, or begin an exercise program. Going further, physicians may attempt to influence the habits of an entire society—promoting restrictions on smoking, for example.

Another sign of medicalization is the use of medical arguments to help advance causes not immediately or directly connected with the treatment of illness (Zola, 1972). For example, loud rock music is cited as being damaging to hearing and bad for children's mental health. Environmental pollution is condemned not only for being destructive to plants and animals but also for causing some forms of human cancer. One great exploiter of medical rhetoric has been the advertising industry, which touts the health benefits of everything from high-fiber cereals to low-fat cookies and "lite" beer.

Medicalization also involves a redefinition of social issues and a reassignment of blame. For example, to characterize homeless people as mentally ill is to obscure the fact that much homelessness is related to unemployment among unskilled workers and a lack of affordable housing (Snow, et al., 1986). Although considering some deviant behavior (such as alcoholism and drug abuse) as illness would seem to be compassionate, doing so raises questions of social control (Conrad, 1992). For instance, can a company's random drug testing violate the employees' rights if the stated goal is to protect their health? As medicalization reaches into more areas of people's lives, such questions are of growing concern.

Through social action, opponents of medicalization have attempted to recapture some aspects of human behavior from organized medicine (Fox, 1977). For instance, women's health groups have noted that women's natural life processes have been medicalized to an extent that grants the medical profession great control over women's lives (Conrad, 1992). Such groups have pressed for the demedicalization of the birth process, setting up birthing centers and clinics in which babies can be born in a homelike setting and mothers can be spared as much medical intervention as possible (often they are attended only by nurse-midwives). Similarly, patients' advocates have maintained that terminally ill people should be allowed to die without heroic intervention if they wish. Other attempts at demedicalization can be seen in self-help groups. People who have a problem in common—obesity, gambling, spouse abuse—have formed groups to help one another cope with their problem without turning to medical authorities. However, these efforts have made only minor inroads in reversing the medicalization trend. In general, American society now thinks of medical intervention as appropriate for a great many human activities.

The Status Elevation of Doctors

Doctors occupy a position of such esteem in the United States that it is hard to believe that they have not always done so. Yet through much of American history a doctor's social position and income were little better than that of a manual worker. In colonial America, for instance, anyone could become a doctor merely by calling himself or herself one. There were no medical schools or medical societies to license or regulate what was a free-for-all trade. Sometimes clergymen tried to provide medical care to their parishioners. Documents of the time record a doctor who sold "tea, sugar, olives, grapes, anchovies, raisins, and prunes" along with medicines, and also tell of a woman who "Acts here in the Double Capacity of a Doctoress and Coffee Woman" (quoted in Starr, 1982, p. 39).

Medicine became a full-time vocation in the United States (though still not an established profession) in the early years of the nineteenth century, when medical schools began to open around the country (Conrad and Schneider, 1980). This change did not mean that all doctors were educated in medical schools. Many still learned their trade through apprenticeship. Moreover, in addition to those who called themselves doctors, there were a variety of medical "specialists": abortionists, midwives, bonesetters, and cancer curers, for instance (Starr, 1982). One reason so many of these people found clients at this time was the primitive nature of medical science. Effective anesthesia was unknown, as was the crucial fact that microscopic agents—germs—cause many diseases. Even doctors who received medical school training used crude techniques and had little understanding of disease. In such circumstances, the efforts of trained physicians to distinguish themselves from ordinary people who concocted herbal remedies, or traveling peddlers who sold elixirs, had only modest success.

During the 1920s, scientific advances coupled with the rise of the American Medical Association (the AMA, the physicians' major professional organization) enabled doctors to acquire enough political and social power to prevail over other people who claimed to be healers (Burrow, 1971; Larson, 1977; Starr, 1982). The widespread acceptance of scientific medicine as superior to traditional attempts at curing put trained physicians in a position to assert that medical education was a prerequisite to becoming a legitimate doctor. In essence, medicine began to define itself as a true profession—one that, because of its expertise, deserved to dominate the care of sick people. New laws set licensing requirements for doctors and made medicine a legally defined monopoly (Conrad and Schneider, 1980; Freidson, 1970). The AMA also pressed for legislation that limited the kinds of drugs that could be sold to the public directly. Previously, preparations containing opium, cocaine, and other powerful drugs could be bought by anyone; now a doctor's prescription was needed to obtain these substances (Starr, 1982). At the same time, physicians secured the right to set their own fees; before the mid-nineteenth century, some states set limits on the amounts that doctors could charge. Such autonomy in setting fees and making other decisions about one's services is an important part of professional status. Soon after World War I, the medical profession as we know it had begun to appear, and subsequent decades have seen its prestige continue to rise.

One measure of physicians' dominance of the modern health-care system is that only they have the authority to diagnose illness, prescribe and evaluate treatments, and convey information to patients. Seriously ill people may not be fully informed about what is wrong with them, often because their doctors assume that they lack the expertise to understand medical information or are so upset by their condition that they will misinterpret any information given. As a result, many patients develop a childlike dependence on their doctors. In recent years, some patients have rejected this position, asserting that they have a right to know about their health status and to participate in their own medical care. However, the voice of the doctor is still supreme in most cases. The biggest challenge now comes not from patients but from insurance companies and other third parties who pay for medical services.

Doctors assume their position at the top of the health-care system after a long period of socialization into the practice of medicine. As medical students, interns, and residents, those who train to be doctors internalize the ideals of the profession. Some of these ideals involve dedication to caring for the sick. However, others involve maintaining the prestige of the profession (learning never to criticize another doctor in front of laypeople, for instance) and accepting the idea that the practice of medicine involves a high degree of autonomy. Since the work entailed is thought to be very complicated, it is often assumed that those who do it must be extraordinarily gifted. Accordingly, many young doctors go beyond professional pride to a sense of superiority or arrogance (Freidson, 1970).

High social status, combined with the power to control access to health care, have enabled physicians to demand some of the highest pay levels of any group in the United States. American doctors also earn far more than their colleagues in other countries, even in countries with excellent health care, such as those of Scandinavia. This has a good deal to do with how health care in the United States is organized as a business.

Health Care as a Business

Medical care was once a comparatively simple business. Services were provided by doctors who treated patients in their offices or made house calls, and the costs involved were fairly modest. The provision of medical care has changed drastically since these simple times. Now the doctor is usually a specialist, not a general practitioner, and his or her office is full of expensive equipment. More and more kinds of specialized tests and treatments must be done in high-tech clinics and in hospitals. Costs have gone up. People are often unable to pay for the treatment they need, and they must rely on private insurance or government assistance to pay their medical bills. The rising costs of such care have spurred a number of changes in the American health-care system. Essentially, those who pay the bills for care—insurers and the government—have begun to demand economic accountability from health-care providers (Goldsmith, 1984).

Signs of this fundamental change are everywhere (Burke and Jain, 1991). Insurance companies, for example, have started managed-care programs in which the company reviews a policyholder's hospital stay and treatment before it is undertaken and while it is under way. If the insurance company decides that a procedure is not essential, it may refuse to pay for it. Employers who pay for medical insurance are also entering into people's health-care choices. For instance, some are gathering data on the fees charged by different hospitals and doctors, identifying particularly expensive ones, and discouraging employees from using them. Others are requiring their employees to get a second opinion when a doctor tells them they need surgery. Still others are putting "service contracts" out for competitive bid—that is, they are offering a health-care provider the chance to "service" all their employees *if* it can do so at an attractive price (Leyerle, 1984; Light, 1988).

The federal government, too, is cutting back on its two major health-insurance programs, Medicare for the elderly and Medicaid for the poor. Eligibility requirements for Medicaid have been tightened substantially. Once offered to more than 70 percent of the country's poor, by 1983 this program was available to only 47 percent, and by 1990 to only 38 percent (*Consumer Reports,* 1990a; Davis and Rowland, 1983). Two-parent families, for example, are usually ineligible for Medicaid, and single adults are rarely covered unless they are elderly or disabled. Besides reducing the numbers of people eligible for Medicaid, recent cutbacks have limited benefits and the fees paid to physicians and hospitals (Kern and Windham, 1986). This means that many low-income people who are covered by Medicaid cannot always get the medical care they need. As a result, public hospitals that provide free care to the poor have been flooded with patients who are unable to pay. In 1995, various balance-the-budget measures debated in Congress threatened further deep cuts in Medicare and Medicaid.

Another belt-tightening measure is the prospective payment system (PPS), a new way of compensating hospitals for treating Medicare patients. Previously, a hospital submitted a bill for services rendered and Medicare paid it. Under the PPS, the hospital receives a fixed amount from Medicare for a given procedure (gall bladder removal, cataract surgery, appendectomy). Analyses suggest that PPS does indeed reduce Medicare expenditures (Russell and Manning, 1989). However, it also provides an incentive to discharge patients early, because hospitals are paid the same amount for a particular service whether they keep the patient for three days or ten. Under the old system of reimbursement, hospitals earned more money by providing more care. Under PPS, they earn more by providing *less* (Guterman and Dobson, 1986).

In response to PPS and the managed-care programs of private health-insurance providers, hospitals have changed some of their procedures. First, they have found various ways to reduce the number of days a patient stays in the hospital. They now do all the preliminary tests and paperwork before admission. Patients scheduled for some kinds of surgery are often admitted to the hospital early in the morning of the same day their surgery is scheduled. In addition, some hospitals are designating certain rooms as reduced-rate areas to accommodate patients who need further recuperation but require fewer services than other patients.

Cost concerns have also led to new forms of health-care delivery. One is the **health maintenance organization,** or **HMO,** a health-care organization that provides medical services to its subscribers for a fixed price each year. Since HMOs lose money if patients require many expensive treatments, they usually stress preventive care to keep people healthy. Another new and growing form of health-care delivery is the **preferred provider organization,** or **PPO.** A PPO is a group of doctors that offers specific services to specific groups of patients (such as all the employees of a company) at discount prices. The organization's clients get a price break, and doctors get a steady stream of patients. A PPO also allows considerable freedom: A patient can choose to go to a doctor outside the PPO (but must pay the difference in the fees). Similarly, doctors who see PPO patients are free to see non-PPO patients. PPOs come in many forms and sizes. They may be organized by doctors, by employers, by insurance companies, or by hospitals that want to expand their range of services.

Although many of these changes in health-care delivery were welcomed as good ideas, criticisms were also quick to follow. HMO members have sometimes found themselves denied needed treatments, prescription drugs, home health care, or nursing services (Spragins, 1995). HMOs have also been criticized for refusing to pay for their members' care in hospital emergency rooms, leaving some members with substantial bills to pay out of pocket (Pear, 1995). Hospitals now find themselves in a situation in which they must compete to market their services and attract paying patients. One way they have tried to remain financially afloat is to give up activities that lose money. Unfortunately, this has meant closing their doors to poor patients and cutting some services, such as trauma care, that are used disproportionately by the uninsured (Burns, 1990).

Increasingly, the provision of medical services is being taken over by for-profit corporations, and these corporations are being consolidated into even larger corporations—what some have called the "medical-industrial complex" (Light, 1986; Relman, 1990).

This corporatization has important consequences for health care. As one researcher has written:

> As health care becomes a profitable market for corporate investment, health services are treated as commodities—products that are bought and sold in the marketplace like automobiles, hats, iron, or oil. The deciding factor as to whether to provide a service or produce a particular piece of equipment is made according to whether that "product" will sell. The bottom line is marketability and whether the company providing the service will make a profit on its sale. (Levitt, 1986, p. 483)

Hospitals are not the only profit-making enterprises in the health-care field (Stoesz and Karger, 1991). In recent years, medical laboratories, kidney dialysis centers, CT scan units, ambulatory-care clinics, nursing homes, and many other enterprises have been organized as corporate ventures. Doctors, too, are becoming more entrepreneurial, incorporating themselves in group practices and investing in expensive medical equipment so that they can perform costly tests and procedures in their offices. And like hospitals, groups of doctors are establishing women's health centers, psychiatric centers, and other clinics.

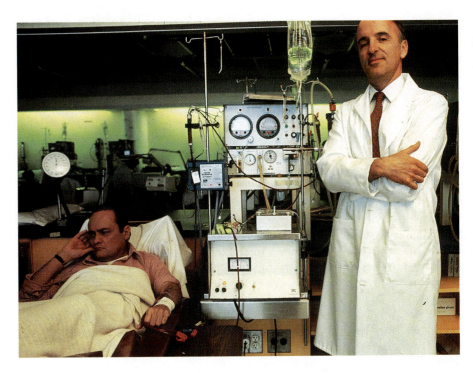

Expensive, high-tech medical procedures such as kidney dialysis (shown here) have raised new questions. Is health care a basic right or a business? Should health care be administered by the public or the private sector? Who should pay?

In the context of such extensive corporatization, the independent physician may find it increasingly hard to compete.

PROBLEMS OF THE U.S. HEALTH-CARE SYSTEM

The American health-care system has developed into what it is today as a result of the competing interests and demands of a number of groups. Patients have wanted top-quality care; doctors and other professionals have wanted to provide quality care while advancing their status and incomes; hospitals and other providers have wanted to use new medical technologies as they have become available; and both federal and state governments have been called on to pay for care. Health care has become extremely expensive in part because of the conflicting demands of these interested parties, hence the wave of calls for health reform in the 1990s.

Any realistic proposal for health-care reform should start with the recognition that health care in the United States is a functionally organized system (Marmor, 1994). All its parts are interrelated, and in many cases they depend on one another. Thus, changes in one will necessarily bring changes in others. For example, major hospitals, which are gener-

ally linked to universities, are not just providers of specialized, advanced care; they are both part of the training system for new doctors and major sources of care for uninsured people who turn up in their emergency rooms. Reducing their funding would affect the supply of new doctors and the treatment of people injured in car accidents, as well as advanced specialty programs for which university hospitals are known—cancer care, high-tech care for infants, and so on. Similarly, whether we pay for health care directly as consumers, via insurance, or through taxes affects both the kind of health care we get and how equally it will be available to the population. It even affects what kind of medical research will be done, because as we have seen, different segments of the population suffer from different illnesses, and research is driven not only by scientific interest and humanitarian goodwill but also by the availability of funding.

All countries face the need to ensure that their populations receive health care, but different countries take different approaches to meeting this need. Some, like Canada, have national health insurance systems. Others, like Britain, have government-operated national health systems. The United States lacks a well-coordinated, functionally integrated system, which is one reason why health-care costs have risen more rapidly in the United States than anywhere else. It is often said that health care in the United States is the best in the world, and indeed America is a leader in medical science and in the technological capabilities of its hospitals. It is the social organization of American health care that is the problem: Many citizens have no access to this excellent care or cannot afford it.

Three issues stand out as problems in the contemporary American health-care system: equality of access to health care, the total cost of health care to the country's taxpayers and consumers, and the implications of funding health care through private, for-profit insurance companies. All three are distinctively American issues, because no other major industrialized country lacks a program of health care for everyone, faces comparably high costs, or tries to finance health care largely on the basis of private insurance.

Unequal Access

The American system of health care has three tiers: one for the well-off and well-insured (the upper classes, the elderly through Medicare, and the middle class with "good" jobs at large companies), one

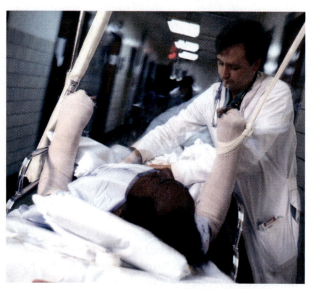

In many countries (particularly in Northern Europe), governments have tried to equalize the distribution of quality health care. In the United States, the gap between the rich and poor grows more acute in access to health care and even the experience of illness. Here a doctor examines a patient "parked" in the hallway outside a hospital emergency room.

for the poor who are eligible for government-funded Medicaid, and one for the 39.7 million citizens with no insurance and too little income to afford a serious illness (U.S. Bureau of the Census, 1994b). In short, access to the health-care system is highly unequal because it is based on the ability to pay.

An abundance of evidence shows that the uninsured are at a great disadvantage in the current health-care system. For instance, one study found that insured Americans receive 90 percent more hospital care than the uninsured do, and the reason is not that they experience 90 percent more serious illness (Davis and Rowland, 1983). When the uninsured get seriously ill for a long period of time, they are often forced to go begging for treatment, hoping that doctors and public hospitals will not turn them away. Many of the uninsured also forgo preventive health care (routine checkups and screenings). As a result, they tend not to detect health problems until they are well-advanced and more expensive treatment is needed, or even until it is too late to treat them at all.

Spiraling Costs

The ever-increasing cost of health care—nearly $1 trillion in 1994—makes the problem of unequal access even worse (Waid, 1995). In a sense, the health-care system is a victim of its own success. Its guiding philosophy—vigorous and even heroic efforts to cure disease—has led to an array of extremely expensive high-tech treatments, such as organ transplants and coronary bypass surgery. Once these procedures are available, the demand for them spreads quickly, for everyone understandably wants the best and the latest that medical science has to offer. As a result, lives are saved but medical costs rise spectacularly, to the point that private insurance companies and Medicare/Medicaid have begun to balk at paying the bills.

New medical technologies also add to the cost of health care by requiring highly trained workers to operate the new equipment and perform the new procedures. Ironically, the growing number of doctors in the United States boosts health-care costs as well. Young doctors, eager to attract patients, are quick to offer the new high-tech treatments. Older doctors must then do the same to stay competitive, so the nation's health-care bill rises ever higher.

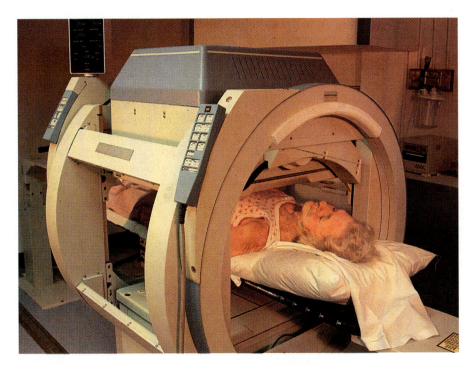

The United States has the most advanced—and the most expensive—health care in the world. New medical technologies, "defensive medicine" (to guard against malpractice suits), and the growing proportion of elderly people in our population all contribute to the skyrocketing costs of health care.

The skyrocketing cost of malpractice insurance adds to the dilemma, as more people are suing physicians for treatment that has gone wrong. In 1990, American doctors paid $4.5 billion in malpractice insurance premiums. This extra cost is paid by all insured doctors—good, bad, or mediocre—and it is inevitably passed on to patients. In response to the threat of being sued for malpractice, doctors are increasingly practicing what is called "defensive medicine." They give patients every conceivable diagnostic test and routinely call in consultants to protect themselves from patients' charges that they were not careful enough. The American Medical Association estimates that defensive medicine costs between $12 billion and $14 billion a year (Marshall, 1990).

Another factor is the aging of the American population: Older people, in general, use more medical services than younger ones. Between 1940 and 1990, the proportion of the population that is elderly nearly doubled, from about 7 to about 12 percent. This trend will continue as the baby boom generation ages. By 2030 an estimated 25 percent of Americans will be elderly, a fact that has ominous implications for the total cost of health care.

Finally, many of the millions of Americans who lack health insurance not only may not get the care they need but also place a financial burden on tax-payers, hospitals, and other patients. In 1988, unpaid hospital bills alone amounted to over $8 billion (*Consumer Reports*, 1990b). Hospitals and doctors who care for the uninsured typically raise the fees they charge insured patients in an effort to compensate for their losses. In New Jersey, for example, hospitals add onto each patient's bill a 13 percent surcharge to cover the cost of treating people who are unable to pay. As a result of such measures, medical charges rise, insurance premiums spiral, and adequate health care moves beyond the reach of more people.

The Health Insurance Crisis

The cycle of rising costs had led to a crisis of health insurance in the United States. The higher the cost of medical insurance rises (recently at rates between 10 percent and 25 percent a year), the greater the number of Americans who either do without insurance or buy reduced coverage. Particularly hard hit are the unemployed, the self-employed, and part-time workers, all of whom must pay the entire health insurance premium themselves. Also affected are people who work for small businesses, which often have enough trouble surviving without having to pay for employee medical insurance. Even large firms are feeling the health insurance pinch. Whereas in 1984, 37 percent of large American companies paid the entire health insurance premium for their employees, just four years later only 24 percent did (*Consumer Reports*, 1990b). Today, most American firms ask their workers to pay some of their health-care costs through out-of-pocket deductibles and premium co-payments. Of course, those who are earning relatively low wages may not be able to afford the co-payments, so they too give up their health insurance, expanding the pool of people who have no safeguard. As noted above, nearly 40 million Americans—about 15 percent of the population—lack health insurance of any kind. This figure is certain to rise in the mid 1990s as congressional cuts in Medicaid reduce the number of people covered.

Many people believe that they have good health insurance but fail to realize how vulnerable to disaster they are should serious illness strike. This vulnerability arises from the way in which insurance companies do business. In response to the skyrocketing costs of health care, insurance companies are refusing to issue policies to people with medical conditions that might prove expensive. If one of their policyholders falls seriously ill, they may raise the premium charged to that person by as much as 200 percent (*Consumer Reports*, 1990b). These tactics allow the insurance firm to offer more competitively priced premiums to their healthy clients, but the person who is seriously ill is left in a dilemma. He or she can neither do without insurance nor switch to another insurance company, because no other carrier wants to insure a person who is already sick. So that unlucky person is stuck with staggeringly high premiums, no matter how much money has already been paid for premiums. Even worse, the insurance firm may refuse to renew the policy, leaving the high-risk individual or his or her employer unable to purchase insurance at any cost.

Although in the past this problem has affected mainly individual or small-group buyers of insurance, that pattern is changing. Large-group purchasers of insurance are no longer always bastions of security. One woman in California who purchased insurance through a group of thousands of college alumni saw her premium rise to $16,000 a year after it was discovered that her eight-year-old daughter had been born with only one kidney, which did not function completely. According to one expert on health insurance, "No one in this country with private health insurance coverage who is in any kind of group plan is free from the kind of uncertainty that competition is producing" (Daniels, quoted in Kolata, 1992, p. A1). Problems of this sort will continue as long as most Americans rely on private insurance for health-care coverage.

SUMMARY

1. Although some striking outbreaks of infectious disease have begun to appear in recent years, most of the major causes of death in this country are chronic disorders (such as heart disease and cancer). The victories over the infectious diseases that once were major threats to the public health (such as influenza and pneumonia) have come about mainly because of the development of antibiotics and vaccines. Chronic conditions are said to be "diseases of civilizations" because they arise from factors associated with modern life (for example, a sedentary lifestyle, a diet high in salt and fats, exposure to low-level carcinogens). If these negative influences could be reduced, Americans would enjoy a compression of morbidity, meaning that disease would be confined to the last few years of life in most cases.

2. Poverty is linked to ill health around the world. Poverty entails increased exposure to a number of health threats, such as hunger and unsafe housing, and also lack of access to health care. The patterns of disease in underdeveloped countries differ significantly from those in developed countries; infectious, parasitic, and respiratory diseases cause nearly half the diseases in less developed countries. Four-fifths of the world's population has essentially no access to health care.

3. Bias against women in the male-dominated medical profession may be one reason why there has been relative neglect of women's health problems. Threats to women's health may come from childbearing and from abuse by husbands. The women's movement has sought to improve health care for women; one sign of progress is that more women are becoming physicians.

4. Some industries produce products that are dangerous to health, such as cigarettes. Although the health dangers of smoking have been publicized, people continue to take up the practice, in part because cigarettes are the most heavily advertised consumer product. Recent years have seen increasing efforts to restrict smoking.

5. In recent years, frightening outbreaks of infectious disease have occurred throughout the world. Sometimes these have been well-known diseases such as tuberculosis, but some diseases are new. These include Legionnaire's disease, toxic shock syndrome, Lyme disease, hantavirus, a new strain of *E. coli* infection, tropical fevers such as Ebola, and AIDS. These disease outbreaks have in common a relationship to some change or disruption in human social organization. Air travel is now a link in the spread of infectious disease, which is ominous since it means that disease can spread from place to place very quickly. Research on infectious diseases and their prevention needs to be pursued.

6. AIDS has brought a number of social consequences in its wake. These include changes in sexual behavior and attitudes, more openness in discussion of sexual matters, increased discrimination against homosexuals and other high-risk groups, and challenges to civil liberties.

7. The American health-care industry is enormous and still growing. Part of its expansion has involved the status elevation of doctors. A by-product of the medical profession's prestige has been the medicalization of American society. Many problems that were once the province of the clergy, the family, or the courts are now taken to doctors. At the same time, medical care has undergone a process of corporatization. Financial pressures on hospitals have caused some of them to decrease services that lose money, such as caring for the poor.

8. The American health-care system has three tiers: one for the well-off and well-insured, one for the poor who are eligible for Medicaid, and one for the roughly 40 million people who have no insurance. Thus, the health-care system offers first-class care to those who can pay and may offer no care at all to those who cannot.

9. Health-care costs have been rising sharply due to a number of factors: many high-tech treatments and highly trained medical workers, the ever-increasing costs of both malpractice insurance and the defensive medicine doctors practice to reduce the threat of malpractice suits, the fact that the American population is growing older and elderly people have more medical problems, and the millions of uninsured families who cannot pay their hospital bills and so increase the prices charged to insured patients.

10. Medical insurance has been growing ever more expensive, both to individuals and businesses. Even people who do have private insurance may lose it if they become ill and their rates rise dramatically or their policies are not renewed. Seriously ill people who lose insurance generally cannot find another insurer, since most policies do not apply to "preexisting conditions."

REVIEW QUESTIONS

1. What is the difference between disease, illness, and sickness? Give an example of each.

2. What is the relationship between poverty on the one hand and health and health care on the other?

3. Why has the incidence of hunger increased?

4. How did AIDS become an epidemic in the United States?

5. How has the social status of doctors increased over time?

6. What are some of the consequences, both positive and negative, of the high social status of doctors?

7. What are some ways of reducing the high cost of health care?

CRITICAL THINKING QUESTIONS

1. Develop some suggestions for social policies designed to reduce the effects of poverty on health and health care.

2. Choose a major health problem—such as hunger, smoking, or AIDS—and analyze it from the perspective of at least three of the five key concepts (social structure, social action, functional integration, power, and culture).

3. Develop some suggestions for social policies designed to reduce the incidence of hunger, smoking, or AIDS cases.

4. What is your opinion about a national health-care system for the United States? What kind of approach would cut costs? Improve the quality of care? Improve the distribution of care? Why?

5. How has health care been changed by processes of professionalization? Can you imagine an alternative?

GLOSSARY

AIDS Acquired immune deficiency syndrome, a fatal disease caused by the HIV virus and transmitted through contact with infected bodily fluids.

Compression of morbidity A hypothetical situation in which people live longer, more active lives and remain comparatively free of disease until their last few years.

Health maintenance organization (HMO) A health-care organization that provides medical services to its subscribers for a fixed yearly price.

Medicalization The trend toward including personal problems in the realm of medicine.

Morbidity The rate at which a disease occurs in a population.

Mortality rate The relative frequency of deaths among members of a population segment.

Preferred provider organization (PPO) A group of doctors offering specific services to groups of patients, such as the employees of a particular company, at discount rates.

PART 5

Social Change
and Globalization

CHAPTER 15

Work, Organizations, and the Economy

Rockefeller Center: a cluster of Art Deco buildings in midtown Manhattan, built in the 1930s when almost no one had much money, except people like the multimillionaire descendants of John D. Rockefeller. Dominating its plaza is a statue of Prometheus, Titan of Greek mythology and symbol of benevolent power and strength. The tourists who flock there in December—to gaze at the enormous Christmas tree, take in the show at Radio City, and watch the skaters gliding around the outdoor ice rink—seldom stop to think that someone *owns* this complex. To them, it is just there.

For this reason, many Americans had an unsettling surprise when they learned in 1989 that Mitsubishi Estate, probably the largest real estate development company in Japan, had purchased a controlling interest in Rockefeller Center. Suddenly, they were reminded that Rockefeller Center is not an American monument, like the Statue of Liberty; rather, it is part of an **economic system.** In functional terms, an economic system is the web of social institutions that fulfills our basic societal need for goods and services. A building complex like Rockefeller Center is an investment. The Rockefeller heirs created it to house businesses that need places to carry out their work. Consumers, in turn, buy the products of these businesses, contributing to their profits and to the rents collected by the owners of the buildings they use. Without the wheels of an economic system endlessly turning behind the scenes, there would be no Rockefeller Center—in fact, no New York City and no United States.

Increasingly in the twentieth century our economic system has reached beyond the web that connects producers and consumers in our own society. Modern American businesses operate on a worldwide scale, entwined in a global economy that stretches from New York to Paris, from Cairo to New Delhi, from Sydney to Tokyo and Hong Kong. The American economic system is the largest component of this global network, but it is no longer the unquestioned leader. The United States' share in the worldwide sale of many products has declined in the past few decades, while those of various Asian and Western European countries have grown. And older "rust belt" American industries, like steel and cars, are not the only ones that have lost out to international competition. American makers of high-technology products—from computers to medical equipment, from electronic instruments to telecommunication devices—are also struggling to survive against strong competitors from other nations.

The U.S. example illustrates that a country's position in the global economy is not fixed for all time. Dramatic changes can occur, even in just a few years. Another good example is Japan. In its boom years between 1986 and 1991, Japan was an astonishing international success story. Flourishing Japanese companies flooded world markets with their goods, and many Americans were coming to prefer these products over those made in the United States. Japanese economists estimated that the total value of the goods and services their country produced each year would surpass that of the United States by the year 2000, even though Japan has only half as many people. But these extremely optimistic projections never came to pass. With excessive Japanese borrowing and investment in new production facilities, the shimmering bubble of prosperity suddenly burst. Unbought goods began to pile up in Japanese warehouses, and more than 10,000 Japanese firms went bankrupt (*Asahi Shimbun*, 1994). On the world currency market, the value of the yen fell sharply. Mitsubishi even put Rockefeller Center on the market to raise cash.

This abrupt turn of fortunes illustrates how susceptible today's national economies are to the choices made by consumers and investors not only at home, but in other nations too. Every country increasingly depends for its economic well-being on the success of commercial ventures in a worldwide economic system. And increasingly every country's economic upswings and downturns are influenced in part by the volatility of international markets. The international value of a country's currency, products, and real estate can bounce from high to low and back at a very rapid pace. Consider foreign direct investment in the United States, the

money that people in other countries spend to acquire or establish businesses in America. It peaked at over $70 billion between 1988 and 1990, fell to less than $20 billion in the 1991–92 recession, and was back to over $50 billion by the start of 1995 (Fahim-Nader and Zeile, 1995). Such remarkable volatility in global economic trends can bring equal volatility in a country's domestic economic fortunes. The waves of expansion and contraction that national economies ride are now greatly influenced by a vast, interconnected sea of global business.

This chapter begins by examining the major form of economic organization in the world today: capitalism. We look at what capitalism is, how it developed, and the major alternative to it: socialism. We then turn to the organizations that conduct America's business, from giant corporations down to small family-owned stores. Finally, we look at work in the United States, one of the social activities that underlie our economic system. These various topics are so broad, and of such importance in sociology, that as we discuss them each of our five key sociological concepts—social structure, social action, functional integration, power, and culture—will come up repeatedly. If any one of these concepts is most important, however, it is functional integration, because markets constitute functionally integrated systems that work at least partially beyond the control of any individual actor (although individual economic actions can have considerable influence too). At the same time, corporations and other economic institutions are also wielders of power. Decisions made by those who run these institutions and control their vast resources can have far-reaching effects not only on individuals, but on entire nations and even on whole regions of the globe.

CAPITALISM: THE ECONOMIC SYSTEM OF MODERN SOCIETIES

Thousands of employees of NBC (the National Broadcasting Corporation) work in its Rockefeller Center headquarters. As they skim financial reports, produce TV shows, and enter computer data, they are engaging in some of the millions of different activities that make up American capitalism. Although capitalism is just one way of structuring an economic system—of patterning social relationships and positions to produce and distribute goods and services—it is the predominant form of economic organization in the world today. Capitalist ideology is so embedded in American culture that alternatives to it seem unnatural to us, counter to what we think of as basic human inclinations.

Defining Capitalism

Although the exact form a capitalist system takes can vary considerably, **capitalism** in general has four essential characteristics:

1. *Private ownership* of the means of production.

2. *Self-interest and the profit motive* as the major economic incentives.

3. *Competitive markets* for labor, raw materials, and products.

4. Repeated investment for the purpose of building and expanding productive facilities, called *capital accumulation*.

These four attributes constitute a pure model, or ideal type, of capitalism.

The first of these characteristics is probably the easiest to understand. In a pure capitalist system all the material means of production—from farmlands to oil refineries to factories producing ballpoint pens—are owned by private individuals or corporations rather than by the state. These means of production are forms of **capital,** or wealth that is invested to generate more wealth by producing goods and services. Capitalist ideology holds that private ownership of capital is an inalienable right. In a capitalist system, power acrues mainly to the owners of capital—the capitalists—not to the workers who contribute labor to the production process.

The second defining feature of capitalism concerns how people make economic choices. In a capitalist system, these decisions are based on self-interest. Consumers buy the goods and services they want (limited only by their ability to pay). Workers choose the jobs they wish to hold (constrained only by their individual backgrounds, training, and experience). Producers select the goods and services they wish to sell (restricted only by the availability of investment dollars and raw materials, the interests of consumers, and the ability to earn a profit). Although these may seem self-centered ways of making economic choices,

their cumulative results can be quite beneficial for society as a whole. This point was convincingly argued by Adam Smith, whose book *The Wealth of Nations* (1776/1976) helped to develop modern capitalist ideology (see Chapter 1). According to Smith, economic choices motivated purely by self-interest ultimately lead to the production of the goods and services consumers want and a corresponding rise in society's wealth. Thus, millions of individual choices motivated by self-interest together lead to the functional integration of the economy as a whole.

Of course, central to the self-interest of producers in a capitalist system is the motivation to maximize profits to increase their own wealth and prestige. How could this motive, which seems so selfish, possibly contribute to the good of the whole society? The answer is that, in trying to maximize profits, producers are constantly searching both for new products that meet consumers' wants and needs and for a new cost-reducing methods of manufacturing those products (lower costs mean both a larger volume of sales if the selling price can be reduced and a greater return on each item sold). As a result, from society's standpoint, resources are being used efficiently, and consumers are getting the goods and services they desire at a reasonable price. Everyone benefits, not just the entrepreneur.

But what is to prevent an enterprising capitalist from charging exorbitant prices to maximize profits? The safeguards against this are the competitive markets that exist in a capitalist economy. If one firm's products are overpriced, consumers will simply reject them in favor of similar products produced by other firms. The same competitive forces operate in the market for labor and other resources. If one firm tries to boost its profits by paying workers less than the going wage, its best employees will find work elsewhere, resulting in poorer-quality products and loss of sales. In the end, such a firm will probably be forced to increase its wages or be driven out of business. The result, again, is that society benefits. Products are priced fairly, workers are paid fairly, resources are used efficiently, and capitalists earn a "normal" profit. At least this is how the pure model of capitalism works. In reality, giant corporations may compete unfairly with smaller businesses or try to hold down the wages of workers who cannot easily find other jobs. At this point, however, we are concerned only with the workings of pure capitalism.

Another result of competitive markets in a capitalist system is that producers are motivated to invest part of what they earn in improving their businesses. As Max Weber put it, capitalism means "production for the pursuit of profit and *ever-renewed* profit" (1904/1958). Capitalists cannot sit back and let their existing companies give them a high income and a comfortable way of life. If they do, they are likely to fall behind their competitors and be driven out of business. So capitalists use some of their profits to make their products or manufacturing methods even better, thus keeping or even increasing their competitive edge. In *The Protestant Ethic and the Spirit of Capitalism,* Weber argued that changes in religious values associated with the Protestant Reformation encouraged this necessary ingredient of modern capitalism (see Chapter 1). Christians were urged, for example, to avoid conspicuous consumption and luxury goods, to wear simple clothing, to work diligently, and to seek ever-growing success for the greater glory of God.

The Development of Modern Capitalism

Although capitalism seems natural to us in modern Western nations, it has not always existed. Its features came together and began to dominate the economic landscape only in the late eighteenth and early nineteenth centuries. This is when Britain began its Industrial Revolution; Germany, France, and the United States followed soon after. Before this, agriculture had been the main source of wealth and the dominant occupation in every society.

The key to the Industrial Revolution was dramatically improved methods of production, occurring first in agriculture. With fewer people needed to produce food, more could live in cities and work in manufacturing jobs. Industrial productivity then improved as manufacturers began to use *specialization and division of labor*. No longer did a single craftsperson make a product from beginning to end. Instead, the manufacturing process was broken down into small steps, and each step was performed by a worker who specialized in doing that task as efficiently as possible. As labor was divided, tasks also became simpler. This meant both that less skilled workers could be hired and that machines could be developed to perform some of the work. Every investment in laborsaving machinery further increased productivity by enabling the same number of workers to produce even more goods. As a result, some workers lost their jobs, but society's total wealth increased.

The ability of industrial capitalism to expand the wealth of nations served as a moral justification for it. Before the rise of capitalism, the profit motive had been equated with personal greed; now it was seen as benefiting society as a whole. The social theorist Bernard de Mandeville summed up this new outlook by declaring that certain "private vices" can become "public goods." He meant that from the viewpoint of individual morality, it might in fact be selfish and greedy to seek wealth aggressively; but if in doing so you create more wealth, not just for yourself but for others, you are also serving the public good, even if unintentionally (Dumont, 1977; Hirschman, 1977).

Modern capitalism not only transformed the production of goods but also expanded their distribution enormously. Previously, most trade had been local because long-distance shipping was difficult and risky. Capitalism led to the integration of national markets as roads and railroads were built and to a great expansion and regularization of international trade. A market now extended as far as ships could travel. Raw materials were imported from faraway rural places to the increasingly industrialized nations of the West, and manufactured goods found buyers worldwide. As Karl Marx and Friedrich Engels wrote: "The need of a constantly expanding market for its products chases the bourgeoisie over the whole surface of the globe. It must nestle everywhere, settle everywhere, establish connexions everywhere" (Marx and Engels, 1848/1976, p. 451). The global reach of capitalism has continued to expand ever since the initial Industrial Revolution. It was, for example, one of the major factors behind the efforts of Europeans to colonize much of the rest of the world, especially in the nineteenth and twentieth centuries. In addition to foreign raw materials, capitalists needed ever-bigger markets for their products. Thus, after the British conquered India, they set out to eliminate the local textile industry there so that Indians would have to buy British cloth.

The Globalization of Capitalism

From the late 1940s through the 1960s, the United States was the unquestioned leader of the capitalist world, with the most goods sold abroad and the most international investments of any nation. Since the 1970s, however, the global market has changed. We opened this chapter with one dramatic example: the purchase of Rockefeller Center by a Japanese corporation. Such takeovers are signs of a new global economy in which the United States is no longer the clear leader and in which competition is intense. Not only Japan but several other Asian countries like Korea and Taiwan have become serious competitors. Many European countries have also become competitors, and Germany, especially, has rebuilt after the ravages of World War II to become a formidable economic power. One study of fifteen major industries showed that although the United States had the largest market share in all of them in 1970, by the late 1980s it had lost ground in every one but two (aerospace and paper products), and foreign competitors had actually outstripped the United States in five of the fifteen (banking, chemicals, electrical equipment and electronics, iron and steel, and nonferrous metals) (Franko, 1989).

Even in our own country foreign competition plays an important role. (See the Global Issues/Local Consequences box.) During the 1980s we not only failed to increase our share of sales abroad, but we also failed to stop the growing American preference for foreign products of many different kinds. By 1987, for example, we were importing more than 26 percent of our cars, 31 percent of our engineering and scientific instruments, and 60 percent of our radios and TVs (U.S. Bureau of the Census, 1990c). In 1993, the value of what we imported was over $139 billion more than the value of what we exported, a huge trade deficit (see Figure 15.1). At the same time, the relentless globalization of economic markets has led to new conceptions of "domestic" economies. It is increasingly difficult to speak of the U.S., British, French, or Japanese economy as though it were a separate unit with clear boundaries. As the current secretary of labor and former Harvard professor, Robert Reich, explains it:

When an American buys a Pontiac Le Mans from General Motors, he or she is engaging unwittingly in an international transaction. Of the $20,000 paid to

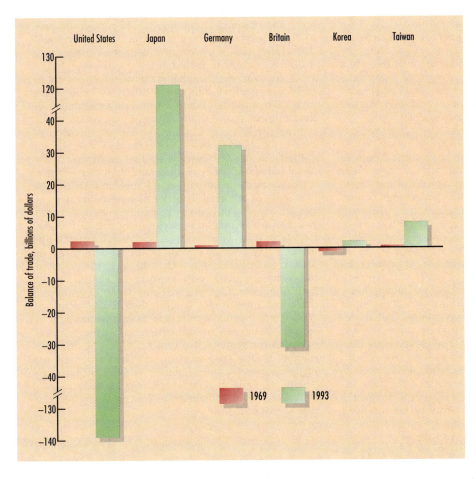

FIGURE 15.1 / The Changing Balance of International Trade, 1969–1993

America's balance of trade—the difference between the value of what we import and the value of what we export—has grown increasingly *out* of balance over the last twenty-five years as international trade has expanded. Whereas in 1969 the United States had a modest trade surplus, by 1993 it had a trade deficit of about $139 billion. This huge deficit occurred at the same time that Japan was enjoying a trade surplus of $121 billion, and Germany a trade surplus of $32 billion.

Source: World Bank, *World Development Report 1995*, 1995, table 13, pp. 186–187.

Competing in the New Global Economy

As America struggles to maintain a prominent place in the new global economic order, consequences for citizens of the United States abound. Loss of international sales by American-based firms means loss of jobs in the United States, which in turn means reduced national income and national wealth. According to Linda Stearns (1992), the international decline of U.S. manufacturing industries has hurt the vast majority of Americans, directly or indirectly. One way is through the drop in factory wages that has accompanied the loss of jobs. Between 1980 and 1989, as more than a million manufacturing jobs were eliminated from our economy, the average real hourly wage of American factory workers dropped by 8.5 percent. Today, factory workers in Japan, France, Italy, Germany, and Great Britain all earn more on average than their counterparts in the United States (*Economic Report of the President*, 1991).

Workers who lose jobs in manufacturing often seek new ones in the service sector. However, without a healthy manufacturing base on which to build, higher-paid service jobs (in communications, research and development, transportation, insurance, law, advertising, accounting, finance, and so forth) are not as abundant as they otherwise would be. What are available are a great many low-paying service jobs—retail salespeople and cashiers, waiters and waitresses, food counter and food preparation workers, janitors and cleaners, nurse's aides and hospital orderlies (Stearns, 1992).

Given this general decline in higher-paying jobs, it is no wonder that Americans have suffered a drop in their standard of living. This decline has occurred both in absolute terms and in comparison with citizens of other countries (Pomice, et al., 1992). In terms of per capita wealth, the United States currently ranks ninth, behind the four Scandinavian countries, as well as Germany, Iceland, Switzerland, and Japan (Organization of Economic Cooperation and Development, 1990). Clearly, there are great personal consequences to America's slipping competitive edge in the global economy.

To make matters worse, Americans are finding themselves increasingly vulnerable to investment decisions made by huge multinational corporations. Global corporations will set up business in one country when it suits them, only to quickly shift their capital elsewhere when doing so makes more financial sense. As a result, highly developed countries around the world, including the United States, now face some of the same investment instability that has long plagued Third World nations. The ability of huge multinational corporations to take advantage of opportunities in the price of labor and other resources reduces their commitment to specific locations and increases the chances that even good workers in thriving industries can lose their jobs.

In order to improve their position in the global economy and enhance job security for American workers, American firms must be willing to invest in domestic production. This means not only buying new machines and equipment, but also supporting public investment in education, job training, transportation, and other government spending programs that are needed for a healthy domestic economy. However, many business leaders have instead favored increases in military spending to maintain the stable international environment in which global trade and investment can flourish (Ferguson and Rogers, 1986). The consequence is a weakened domestic American economic base.

Some sociologists suggest that to boost investment at home the United States needs a national industrial policy, like those of its major competitors (Stearns, 1992). In countries like Germany and Japan, government and business see themselves as partners in promoting national economic interests. The government deliberately aids the growth of certain industries that it deems essential to the economy's well-being. In the 1950s, for example, the Japanese government set out to build a competitive computer industry by establishing protective tariffs and quotas, sponsoring research-and-development projects, and giving financial assistance to firms. By 1970, Japan's share of the global computer market exceeded 60 percent (Stearns, 1992).

Linda Stearns (1992) proposes that an American national industrial policy would entail three things. First, it would foster the development of new industries with high growth potential (robotics or biogenetics, for example). This it would do by providing a well-educated workforce, research-and-development assistance, and long-term loans at low interest. Second, a national industrial policy would encourage the modernization of older industries (like steel) that still have the potential to become internationally competitive. Here it would limit foreign imports to give firms a period of protection during which they could invest in new technologies. Third, a national industrial policy would help to ease the demise of uncompetitive industries with no potential for growth. It could, for example, offer job training to displaced workers and discourage declining firms from wasting money on additional capital investments. Only in these ways, Stearns believes, can the United States revitalize its economic strength in the new global economy.

GM, about $6,000 goes to South Korea for routine labor and assembly operations, $3,500 to Japan for advanced components (engines, transaxles, and electronics), $1,500 to West Germany for styling and design engineering, $800 to Taiwan, Singapore, and Japan for small components, $500 to Britain for advertising and marketing services, and about $100 to Ireland and Barbados for data processing. The rest—less than $8,000—goes to strategists in Detroit, lawyers and bankers in New York, lobbyists in Washington, insurance and health-care workers all over the country, and General Motors shareholders—most of whom live in the United States, but an increasing number of whom are foreign nationals. The proud owner of the Pontiac is not aware of having bought so much from overseas, of course. General Motors did all the trading, within its global web. (Reich, 1991, p. 113)

American corporations are no longer the "national champions" they once were. In the 1950s, the health of the large American corporations meant the health of the U.S. domestic economy. These companies primarily employed American workers, paid dividends to American stockholders, and made products for American consumers. Consequently, relatively little of their wealth "leaked out" abroad, making their fortunes linked to those of the country as a whole. "As steel goes, so goes the nation" was the motto of U.S. Steel, and it contained a great deal of truth. Today, however, with the increased globalization of production, we can no longer expect that thriving "American" companies necessarily mean a thriving domestic economy. Much of the money American firms now spend goes to citizens of other nations. For example, in 1990, 40 percent of IBM employees were foreign nationals, and this percentage was growing. Employees of Whirlpool, another large "American" business, are now mostly from other countries, as are employees of Seagate Technology, a California-based world leader in making hard-disk drives for computers. As Charles Exley, head of National Cash Register, has commented: "National Cash Register is not a U.S. corporation. It is a *world* corporation that happens to

For decades, the United States was the car-producing capital of the world. The automobile industry played a major role in the U.S. economy, and American cars were in demand everywhere. The dramatic increase in sales of Japanese cars in the United States in the 1970s foreshadowed the emergence of today's global economy. Responding to changing social and economic conditions, Japanese manufacturers produced the smaller, more fuel-efficient, better-engineered cars consumers wanted. Today most cars are produced by global corporations with offices, factories, and parts from many countries.

be headquartered in the United States" (quoted in Epstein, 1990–1991).

Another example of the new global corporation is Nestlé, a $36 billion business, the biggest food company in the world, which receives 98 percent of its sales outside its headquarters country of Switzerland. Nestlé is genuinely multinational, not only in terms of its global operations (it does business on five continents) but also in terms of its own corporate culture:

> As the 1990s began, its chief executive officer was German and five out of ten of its general managers were also not Swiss. An American was in charge of selling pet food in Japan. An Indian was running the coffee operation in Australia. A Scotsman was handling yogurt sales in France. In Nestlé's Asian-Pacific territory the top marketing managers represented ten different nationalities. So determined to adapt to local conditions is Nestlé that it even has a factory in the Ivory Coast to produce dehydrated yam flakes. (Barnet and Cavanagh, 1994a)

Such vast corporations that think of themselves as world-based will play a prominent role in the economic world of the twenty-first century. These huge companies will increasingly become cultures of their own, with their executives in a sense being citizens of the corporation.

Government Involvement in Capitalist Systems

Adam Smith never imagined that capitalism would someday operate on the vast global scale it does today. He also did not anticipate that national governments would intervene in economic activities to the extent that they now do. Smith had a basically functional view of economies. He thought that all the economic actions of individuals who are allowed to make choices based on their own self-interest would combine to produce the best overall integration of an economic system. Government, he believed, should adopt a *laissez-faire* policy, leaving businesses, workers, and consumers alone to make economic decisions as they please. In Smith's view, competition would provide the rewards and punishments needed to make the whole system work. Governments should only be called on to act as "enablers," providing producers and consumers with the goods and services they need (such as money, roads, and civil courts) to carry out their economic transactions.

Other economic thinkers have argued that governments must be more involved in economic systems because ideal integration of an economy will not come about naturally. For the most part, this view has prevailed. "Enabler" is only one of the roles that governments play in modern capitalist systems. Another role is that of "assister," offering help to various social groups, such as the poor, the unemployed, the disabled, and certain industries threatened by low-priced imports from abroad. More controversially, governments can assist one group in its economic struggle against another, as in helping businesses to break up labor unions (or labor unions to defend themselves). At the same time, governments are also "regulators" in modern capitalist systems. They protect businesses from unfair competition, consumers from potentially harmful products, minorities from unfair discrimination, and so forth. Governments are major "consumers" of goods and services, too. Government contracts provide long-term guaranteed business for corporations and make it possible for them to conduct extensive research and development. This research and development, in turn, results in new inventions that benefit society. Development of the modern computer industry, for example, including the vast array of personal computers and software, was supported largely by contracts from the military and other government agencies, such as the IRS (Burnham, 1983).

In the United States today, government plays a major and necessary role in the economy, both as regulator and as consumer. Without government agencies to keep the potential excesses of American free enterprise in check, business fraud, predatory pricing, unsafe products, and environmental pollution would be far more widespread than they are, possibly even threatening the very viability of the system. The role of government as a major consumer is also critical. Government spends billions of American tax dollars yearly to buy goods and services that American businesses produce. Especially important are government purchases of high-technology goods because they help to push innovation forward.

Socialism: An Alternative to Capitalism?

One alternative to capitalism is **socialism,** which comes in many forms but always puts social cooperation ahead of competition, and the needs of society ahead of the wishes of a wealthy social class. The most

President Franklin D. Roosevelt's "Back to Prosperity Program" was designed both to boost the economy and to relieve personal hardship. Tens of thousands of unemployed workers were given jobs on public works. These men were members of the Civilian Conservation Corps, assigned to a reforestation project in Luray, Virginia.

common approach to achieving socialism has been ownership or control of the means of production by society as a whole or by communities of workers.

The Socialist Critique of Capitalism

The concept of socialism was developed in the nineteenth century by critics of capitalism's excesses. Capitalism at the time of the Industrial Revolution was shocking to many people. Early coal-powered factories caused terrible air pollution. New technologies put thousands of craftsmen out of work. All the profits seemed to go to the factory owners, not to the workers who actually produced the goods. There were huge disparities in income between the wealthy capitalists and those who toiled on the shop floors (disparities that persist today). Owners tried to deny workers the right of free assembly because they feared it would lead (as it often did) to the formation of labor unions. Greed seemed to be winning out over morality and the collective good, as producers held down wages, increased the length of the workday, and overused the earth's nonrenewable resources, all to create greater profits. Critics began clamoring for a "moral economy" (Thompson, 1968). They wanted a system that would not just avoid cap-

italism's abuses (child labor, dangerous working conditions, long hours for very low pay) but would also save traditional community life, which capitalism seemed to be destroying. It was in this context that socialism arose.

Many of the early socialists were Christians whose religious beliefs condemned the seemingly unbridled greed of capitalism. Others were workers in skilled crafts who found themselves jobless due to the rise of factories. Still others were utopian thinkers trying to conceive of the best possible society. Among these early critics of capitalism, Karl Marx has been by far the most influential. Marx was not primarily a moral critic of capitalism, an advocate of traditional crafts, or a utopian thinker. He was a social scientist trying to develop empirically a theory that related economics to social organization.

As we saw in Chapters 1 and 7, Marx focused on the exploitation of the working class by the capitalist class. He argued that this abuse was an unavoidable structural consequence of capitalism, not just a moral failing of capitalists. Capitalist profits came mainly from paying workers less than the full value of the goods they produced. Raising workers' pay would greatly cut or eliminate profits, thereby reducing capitalists' motive to stay in business. Yet workers who were not paid much could not afford

A central point in the socialist critique of capitalism is the exploitation of workers. This photo, taken at the height of the Industrial Revolution in the United States (circa 1910), shows young boys working the night shift in a glass factory, with no protective equipment. Child labor and unsafe workplace conditions have been outlawed in the United States and other developed countries, but are still common in the less developed countries on the outer edges of the world capitalist system.

to buy the goods that capitalist industry produced in ever-greater quantities. When the demand for goods fell, each capitalist would naturally lay off workers, but this would only make things worse by reducing demand still further, since unemployed workers do not buy much. If capitalism did not collapse in the midst of one of these downward-spiraling crises, workers, in Marx's view, would eventually recognize their common interests and join together to overthrow the capitalist system.

Marx was right in some of his predictions, wrong in others. He correctly predicted the series of worsening crises that culminated in the Great Depression of the 1930s. He even predicted that capitalists would sometimes resort to war when faced with the crisis of overproduction and underconsumption that created depressions. What Marx did not predict was that capitalists would accept the government economic intervention that since the 1930s has prevented the recurrence of another Great Depression (although the milder economic downturns called recessions continue to plague capitalist economies around the world; Wallerstein, 1984). Marx was also wrong in thinking that workers in advanced capitalist societies would inevitably slide into such abject poverty that they would join together and revolt. In modern industrialized capitalist states over the last 200 years,

workers generally have become better off, even though they have not closed the gap between themselves and capitalists. But perhaps this rising standard of living for workers in industrialized nations has been achieved partly through capitalist exploitation of workers in underdeveloped countries (Roxborough, 1990). This may be why the socialist revolutions that have occurred in the world have not been in advanced capitalist countries but in poorer nations making the transition to capitalist development.

Experiments in Socialism

Socialists have not only criticized capitalism, they have also tried to change it. In the United States, their efforts have focused on reforms designed to bring more social responsibility to capitalism, reforms such as minimum-wage laws, unemployment insurance, and welfare benefits for the poor. In Western Europe, socialists have brought about even greater reforms, especially stronger protections for workers, more help for the disadvantaged, and free or low-cost health care. These countries have essentially kept the basic features of capitalism but have insisted that the system have even more of a social conscience than is typical in the United States. As a result, many Western European countries are often called *social democracies*. Elsewhere, for example in Russia, Eastern Europe, China, and Cuba, socialists have waged revolutions to try to replace capitalism from the ground up, doing away with private ownership, competitive markets, and the profit motive. In general, socialist reforms have been much more successful than revolutionary socialism has been. This fact is illustrated in the following discussions of socialist reform as it has been carried out in Western Europe versus socialist revolution as it occurred in the former Soviet Union. A third topic about socialism—how it has worked in Third World nations—we reserve for Chapter 17 on global inequality.

SOCIALIST REFORM. Most of the democratic states of Western Europe have economic systems that have incorporated socialist reforms. Here socialists of various kinds, both Marxist and non-Marxist, have joined forces with trade unions and other groups to compete for power through elections. The most successful democratic socialist parties have been those of Scandinavia, but socialists have also been in control for extended periods in Austria, Germany, France, Great Britain, and Spain, and they have shared power in Italy.

Western European socialism differs from the socialist economic system that Marx envisioned. For one thing, it does not involve public ownership of all the means of production. In Sweden, socialist governments have regulated industry but have not taken it over. In France, socialists have called for public ownership of only certain essential industries. Most Western European socialist systems have not involved extensive central planning of what to produce, how to produce it, and how to distribute it. Instead, there has been a great deal of competition among individuals and firms for goods and services, raw materials, and labor. Thus, the democratic socialist states of Western Europe have not overthrown capitalism; however, they *have* used government to limit capitalism's excesses and to protect the welfare of workers.

Some aspects of Western European socialism have worked better than others. Public takeover of essential industries (called *nationalization*) has had no more than mixed success. While some nationalized businesses have flourished, others have not. Nationalization has worked better for utilities and transport industries than for industrial producers. Problems are particularly common when the govern-

ment has taken over a nearly bankrupt firm to prevent its employees from losing their jobs. Democratic socialist efforts to provide for the welfare of private-sector workers have met with more consistent success. Such efforts have resulted in extensive unemployment benefits (thus cushioning the impact of recessions), national health-care systems, old-age pensions, and programs to help the poor. They have also brought about better working conditions, such as higher minimum wages and more stringent safety standards in the workplace. All these welfare provisions have not cost Western European countries their prosperity. For instance, Sweden (which has had a socialist government for most of the time since 1945) has long had a higher average standard of living than the United States. And recently, under socialist presidents, both Italy and France enjoyed higher rates of economic growth than the United States did (although socialism is certainly no guarantee of economic expansion). Finally, socialist reform movements in Western European nations have also substantially reduced the level of economic inequality in these countries (Inglehart, 1990).

SOCIALIST REVOLUTION. Socialist revolutions and the creation of communist states have occurred in various parts of the world in the twentieth century—from Russia and the "satellite" countries of Eastern Europe, to China, Cuba, Vietnam, and other Third World nations. But because the former Soviet Union had the first successful socialist revolution and what is so far the longest-lived communist regime, we will use it as our example in this section.

The Russian Revolution occurred in October 1917 when the Bolsheviks (Lenin's faction in Russian politics) seized power. Especially under Lenin's successor, Joseph Stalin, the Bolsheviks created a dictatorial central government dominated by members of the Communist party. This was not altogether inconsistent with Marx's concept of a dictatorship of the proletariat designed to eliminate the evils of capitalism and lead the way to true **communism,** in which the state would eventually wither away because it was no longer needed. The transitional stage before that was called socialism.

In keeping with socialist principles, all important means of production became publicly owned in the Soviet Union. Economic decisions, instead of being left to the workings of the market, were placed in the hands of a central planning board. Creating a series of annual and five-year plans, the central planners in Moscow determined which goods to produce and in what quantities, where and how to produce them, and how to distribute the output. Local ministries then set output quotas for Soviet factories and other enterprises, all of which were staffed by state-paid workers. In this way, the planners hoped to establish a system of production and distribution that was less wasteful and fairer than a capitalist one, and also less prone to capitalism's vicious cycles of overproduction and underconsumption.

From the beginning there were problems. Peasants resisted the collective farming of state-owned land, so the USSR had trouble consistently feeding its people. In industrial development, military output was given priority over consumer goods. Consumer products—from toilet paper to cars to TV sets—were of poor quality and in chronic short supply (Aslund, 1989). People had to spend hours every day tracking down necessities like soap and toothpaste. They formed long lines at the mere rumor that some desirable item was about to be delivered to a certain store, a big part of the reason worker absenteeism was so high in the Soviet Union (Shmelev and Popov, 1989).

In addition, the centrally planned Soviet economy became bogged down in bureaucracy and corruption, encouraged by the dictatorial control of a small governing class of Communist party members. Producers had no incentive to make desirable, high-quality products in cost-conscious ways. Soviet state-owned enterprises were not subject to the laws of supply and demand, as they would have been under capitalism. If their costs outstripped their revenues, the state subsidized them. All a Soviet manager had to do was meet production goals. The state was responsible for supplying raw materials, and the state purchased all the finished products, for delivery to state-run stores. The careers of managers depended more on pleasing higher-ups in the bureaucracy than on satisfying the people who bought their goods. Thus, there was little motivation to improve the quality of products or to design new ones not called for by the central planners. There was also little motivation to operate efficiently, which is why the Soviet system used two and a half to three times more resources than the American capitalist system to produce a given amount of output (Aganbegyan, 1988).

Another problem inherent in the Soviet centrally planned economy was the overwhelming job of coordinating producers and suppliers. Imagine being in charge of supplying all the businesses in the United States with each and every material they need in the right amounts at the right times. No wonder short-

Shortages of basic consumer goods contributed to the collapse of communism in the former Soviet Union. As shown here, shoppers had to wait hours in long lines to purchase a loaf of bread.

ages and late deliveries of raw materials were the norm in the Soviet Union. Producers were often forced to use inferior substitute materials—whatever it took to get the goods out. Ironically, then, although central planning was meant to create greater economic integration than capitalism could, the result was just the reverse: a dysfunctional production and distribution system in which the different parts of the economy were poorly integrated.

By the mid-1980s, the problems of the system had reached crisis proportions. Soviet Premier Mikhail Gorbachev launched a campaign for *perestroika*, a restructuring of the Soviet economy that would gradually introduce a number of capitalist reforms into the state-owned system (Zaslavskaya, 1990). But the reforms of *perestroika* were too little and too late. By 1988, the Soviet economy was in shambles and growing worse by the day. In 1991, an attempted coup by Communist party hard-liners provided a rallying point for popular discontent, and the communist regime was overthrown. The various republics of the old Soviet Union formed a Commonwealth of Independent States, all renouncing communism, and most calling for a change to capitalism. Other countries of the former Eastern European communist bloc also turned to capitalism as a remedy for their problems.

The Transition from Communism to Capitalism in Eastern Europe

The transition to capitalism has not occurred at the same pace in all the countries of Eastern Europe (Baylis, 1994). It has probably proceeded fastest and furthest in the Czech Republic, followed by Hungary and Poland, and slowest and least in countries like Albania and Bulgaria. Russia, by far the largest of the formerly communist states, falls more or less in the middle. In general, the countries most open to rapid and extensive transformations were those that had the most developed economies to begin with.

Even in countries where officials and citizens welcomed capitalist principles, these principles could not be implemented overnight. It is relatively easy to allow entrepreneurs to open privately owned bakeries and taxi services, but it is much harder to find private investors for such things as huge, technologically backward steelworks. When such investors have been found, they have usually insisted on laying off large numbers of workers in order to hold costs down. Such moves have created considerable public discontent.

Although former communists have come to power through open elections in several of the formerly communist states, this does not spell the return of communism. The successful ex-communists present themselves as social democrats, committed to a moderate form of capitalism. This stance appeals to many voters for whom the recent social and economic changes have been traumatic. Even successful transformations that have produced dynamic economies have been difficult for ordinary people because of the high unemployment and rising prices they often bring.

A rapid transition from communism to capitalism raises important problems of functional integration (Burawoy and Lukács, 1992; Kovács and Tardos, 1992). In the United States and other capitalist countries, a variety of social institutions are joined together to make capitalism work and to curb its potential excesses. We have laws regulating property, pension funds, and interest rates. We have financial markets where corporate stocks and bonds can be traded, as well as a government agency to make sure that the trading there is honest. We also have a vast banking network that enables businesses to obtain loans, and more government agencies to regulate banking practices. Modern corporations depend on these and other capitalist institutions, which in the West have developed gradually over hundreds of years. The Eastern Europeans are trying to develop them in a matter of decades or less. Predictably, there are problems.

Among these problems, the absence of regulatory institutions is high on the list in importance. Although businesspeople in America often complain about government regulation, a capitalist system depends on it. Without the Securities and Exchange Commission, for instance, fraud in financial markets would probably be widespread, and investors would not be willing to trust their money to them. This, in turn, would reduce the resources available to corporations. Similarly, our Occupational Safety and Health Administration ensures that capitalists do not try to cut costs in ways that endanger their workers, while the Environmental Protection Agency sees to it that American businesses do not make their profits at the price of a severely polluted and blighted world. The countries of Eastern Europe have none of these

One consequence of the rapid transition from communism to (unregulated) capitalism has been the emergence of the "New Russians," entrepreneurs whose sudden wealth (often acquired through black market activities) and conspicuous consumption set them apart from ordinary Russians.

regulatory institutions for private enterprise, yet without them it is very hard to create a viable capitalist system.

Another serious problem confronting Eastern European nations in their transition to capitalism is the rising crime rate that seems to be linked to new market freedoms. In Hungary between 1989 and 1990, crimes against property grew by 69 percent, and Poland showed a similar pattern. Contributing to these rapidly rising rates is the fact that the rules of the new social and economic systems are not yet clearly established, and officials often lack the capacity to enforce whatever new laws exist (Lotspeich, 1995). Most disturbing to many is the emergence of organized-crime networks that engage in such classic crime-syndicate activities as extorting "protection money" from businesses.

Crime has helped produce a new class of conspicuously consuming rich in Eastern Europe—people who buy very expensive, often imported products, even while their countrymen are struggling to make ends meet. For instance, a few hours after the first Eastern European Rolls-Royce showroom opened in Moscow, a "businessman" arrived with a suitcase full of money and purchased a $262,000 car. In other upscale Moscow stores there are plenty of cash-paying buyers for $5,000 fake fur coats, $6,000 Cartier watches, and diamond earrings with a price tag of $250,000 (Popowski et al., 1994). This ostentatious consumption by the Russian *nouveau riche* is a source of discontent in a country where nearly 80 percent of the people live at or below the poverty level.

Another reason for the discontent that many Eastern Europeans feel is the fact that their cultural norms are also rapidly changing. As we discussed in Chapter 1, Émile Durkheim (1893/1985, 1897/1951) argued that culture functions to provide people with a set of rules and limits, as well as ideas about what they can reasonably expect. In times of rapid social change, when these elements of culture are challenged, people may lose their social bearings and come to question who they are and where they should be going. This condition is known as anomie and is linked to rising crime and discontent. One study of how Eastern Europeans view their current situation found that many of their feelings do in fact conform to what Durkheim's theory of anomie predicts (Arts, Hermkens, and Van Wijck, 1995).

BUSINESS INSTITUTIONS IN THE UNITED STATES

In addition to analyzing the structural principles around which an economy is organized (public versus private ownership, competitive markets versus central planning), sociologists study the various institutions within which economic action takes place. These include trade unions, chambers of commerce, stock exchanges, government agencies, and many other sorts of organizations. The most important economic institutions in the United States are business enterprises, including giant corporations on the one hand and small businesses on the other.

Corporate America

When we speak of corporate America, we are referring mainly to large corporations, even though many smaller businesses are incorporated too. In corporate America, a few giant companies dominate most of the economy. Some operate mainly in one industry; they produce oil or steel or cars, for example. Most, however, are diversified; they are made up of many smaller companies producing and selling many kinds of goods and services. For instance, the giant corporation RJR/Nabisco is a leading tobacco company, cookie manufacturer, soft-drink producer, and real estate holding firm.

The distinguishing feature of a corporation is its institutional structure. A **corporation** (the word means "created body") is an organization created by law to have an existence, powers, and liabilities of its own. Corporations can own property, sue or be sued in a court of law, and enter into binding contracts, just as individuals can (Dan-Cohen, 1986). Ownership and management are generally separated in a corporation. The corporation is owned by its shareholders, the thousands or even millions of people and other corporations that have bought shares of its stock. These shareholders are seeking an investment that will earn them a profit; they are not seeking to run the corporation. If shareholders do not like the way "their" corporation is being run, they are much more likely to sell their stock than to try to change corporate policy. The operation of a corporation is in the hands of corporate managers, the hundreds or thousands of employees charged with supervising other employees.

Successful techniques of large-scale capitalization and internal management have enabled corporations to grow enormously. One of the largest industrial U.S. corporations, Ford Motor Company, made $5.3 billion in profits in 1994, selling nearly $130 billion worth of its products and holding $219 billion in assets (*Fortune*, April 15, 1995). Corporate growth may be based on inventing new products, improving production processes, or engaging in better marketing. It may also be achieved by buying other companies. In this way, corporations grow not only by fulfilling their function in the economy but also by exercising their power. The most dramatic example of this occurs with a hostile corporate takeover, in which the firm being taken over does not want the merger. In the 1980s and 1990s, waves of hostile takeovers shook the corporate world, such as the takeover of Nabisco (mainly a food products firm) by R. J. Reynolds Tobacco. The ensuing conflicts and power struggles became the basis for the book and movie "Barbarians at the Gate." Such large-scale mergers generally increase the power of general managers, lawyers, and financiers at the expense of those whose specialized skills lie in production processes.

The power of American corporations contrasts strikingly with that of ordinary citizens, creating what the sociologist James Coleman (1982, 1990) has called an "asymmetric society"—a society in which the power of a large corporation vastly outweighs that of the average person. A large corporation can muster resources far in excess of what the average person can even imagine. It can also accomplish undertakings vastly greater than any one individual can. And when an individual is pitted against a huge corporation, the corporation usually has a great advantage. This is the case with victims of occupational disease, like asbestosis or cancers caused by working with toxic substances. Giant corporations can drag out lawsuits over personal damages for years or even decades, knowing that the person suing will eventually die or run out of money and energy to continue fighting (Calhoun and Hiller, 1988). Although large groups of people working together can sometimes affect the decisions of powerful corporations (for example, see Jonas, 1992), it takes a concerted and persistent effort to sway these vast organizations, and often the influence exerted on them is relatively small (Hathaway, 1993).

Who Controls Corporations?

The characteristics of top managers who run corporations have changed over time. In the early years of capitalism, the managers were often the founders of the companies or the children of the founders (this pattern still exists in the newer corporations of South Korea and Japan). Many of these early managers were inventors or entrepreneurs with little formal education who started small and watched their business grow. Then founders began to be replaced by hired managers, usually employees from production in the case of manufacturing firms. These were people with hands-on experience of how the company made its products. Today, corporate executives are more likely to have marketing, law, or finance backgrounds, and most have earned an MBA (preferably from Harvard, Stanford, or one of the other elite business schools) or a comparable graduate degree. Top executives today hardly ever start on the shop floor. Even in heavy industry, they are more at home with computers than with production equipment.

Theoretically, top managers of corporations must answer to the company's board of directors, which in turn is responsible to stockholders. Most boards of directors consist of twelve to fifteen senior executives at the firm, prominent businesspeople from other companies, and public figures. The board is charged with protecting the stockholders' interests and, to some extent, the public's interests by overseeing the legalities of operations. But while a board's responsibility to owners exists in theory, in practice it is not always strongly exercised. Top management usually picks board members, and the board rarely challenges management unless a crisis occurs (Herman, 1981).

Some sociologists argue that top managers, board members, and major stockholders form a "capitalist elite" or "corporate class" (Mills, 1951; Domhoff, 1993). They say that members of this elite share similar backgrounds (most are white males educated at top business schools), have similar interests, behave in similar manners, and control corporate America by creating a series of **interlocking directorships:** networks of people who serve as directors of two or more corporations (Haunschild, 1993; Mintz and Schwartz, 1986). Figure 15.2 illustrates the interlocking directorships of General Motors and other large firms. According to Michael Useem (1980), one of the proponents of this view, these network ties create a feeling of solidarity and common purpose among owners and managers of different corporations. That purpose, Useem holds, is to maximize the rate of return on capital. He believes that the capitalist elite is largely successful at achieving its shared goals because of the power it collectively exerts over the economic system.

Other sociologists contend that the concept of interlocking elites can be overstated. Top executives of corporations are not always of one mind, they say.

Edward Herman (1981), who has extensively studied top corporate managers and those who sit on corporate boards of directors, has found that members of these two groups often have opposing interests that keep them from always supporting the same policies. For example, a bank may have a seat on the board of directors of a company for which it has arranged loans. The bank's representatives are likely to be primarily concerned with the company's financial security and thus opposed to risky moves that managers might support. There are times, then, when directors and managers disagree, which helps to limit the influence of interlocking elites. This view is echoed by Neil Fligstein (Fligstein, 1990, 1995; Fligstein and Brantley, 1992). He argues that power relations exercised over a firm by outsiders are much less important in determining the decisions of large corporations than power relations within the firm (between different divisions, for instance, or different levels in the corporate hierarchy). He also maintains that competition with other firms for markets is far more important than any power exercised by interlocking elites who span different corporations.

Yet regardless of how interlocked the leaders of modern corporations are, their power is still enormous. Even within their individual companies, corporate executives make decisions that can affect the welfare of thousands of people. They decide whether to use dangerous chemicals in their plants and how much to spend on safety procedures. They decide whether to rebuild factories in the Midwest or move production to the South or to South Korea. On these and other issues, middle- and lower-level managers can seldom challenge the wishes of top corporate heads, on whom their careers depend (Jackall, 1988). In all these ways, top corporate managers constitute an extremely powerful group, one that exercises power both inside and outside the corporation.

The Global Power of Multinationals

The influence of a large, powerful corporation often reaches far beyond the country in which that firm is headquartered. Many of America's largest businesses today are **multinational corporations,** firms with operations and subsidiaries in many countries. Critics charge that multinationals have grown too big, too rich, and too powerful. It is nearly impossible for many national governments to regulate them. The annual incomes of big oil companies, such as Exxon, and big auto producers, such as General Motors, ex-

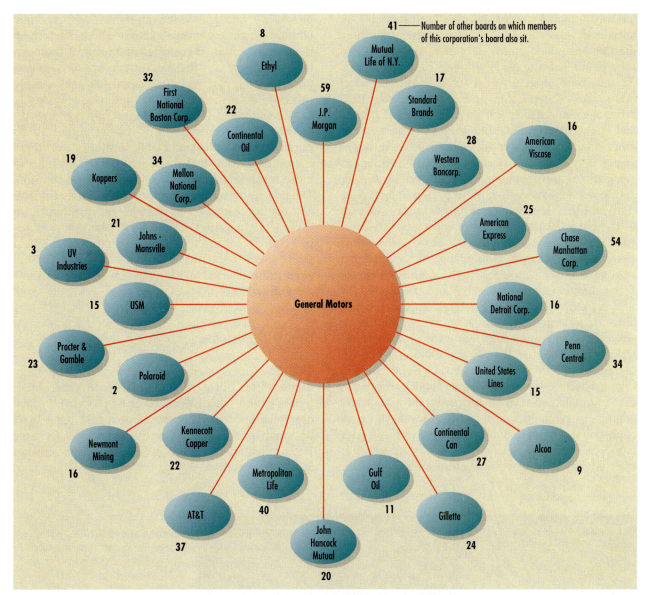

FIGURE 15.2 / *The Interlocking Directorships of General Motors with Other Firms*

The members of the board of directors of General Motors also sit on the boards of directors of many other U.S. corporations. In the year this study was conducted, GM board members were linked in this fashion to twenty-nine other firms. The board members of these other firms in turn sat on the boards of many other companies. Exactly how many others is shown by the number adjacent to each firm's oval.

Source: Beth Mintz and Michael Schwartz, "Interlocking Directorates and Interest Group Formation," *American Sociological Review* 46 (December 1981), fig. 3, p. 857.

ceed the gross national products of most of the nations in which they do business. Indeed, the financial resources of major multinational corporations are so large that these companies can often manipulate the economies of smaller nations. For example, if a multinational wants to avoid paying taxes in a country where tax rates are high, it can shift profits to low-tax-rate countries simply by judicious selling to its own divisions elsewhere.

Multinational corporations can also have a significant impact on the political and social institutions of the countries in which they operate, especially in developing nations. For instance, when multinationals become extensively established in a developing country, they often use their substantial influence to keep taxes and wages low and to foster other conditions that increase their profitability (Chase-Dunn, 1975). As a result, income distribution in the host country often becomes more unequal and economic development lags (Bornschier and Ballmer-Cao, 1979; Bornschier and Hoby, 1981). At their most blatant and aggressive, multinationals may use bribery and other illegal means to achieve their goals in developing nations. They may even try to topple unsympathetic governments. A highly publicized example was ITT's spending of $1 million to help overthrow Chile's socialist president Salvador Allende in the early 1970s. Because of the embarrassment such disclosures have caused, some multinationals now have policies to limit their involvement in a host country's politics (U.N. Commission on Transnational Corporations, 1978).

Many critics charge that such self-imposed restrictions are not enough. Today a new economic power structure is emerging—one that transcends the political power of nations (Barnet and Cavanagh, 1994a). Increasingly, GM, IBM, Pepsico, General Electric, Pfizer, Shell, Volkswagen, Exxon, and perhaps 100 other global corporations influence the prosperity, balance of payments, and political strength of the countries in which they operate. Each of these companies is wealthier than all but a handful of countries. Given the huge volume of business these companies do and the vast numbers of people they employ, governments are increasingly dependent on them to maintain the economic health of their nations. Imposing on these giant corporations restrictions that the corporations do not like may simply cause them to move their operations elsewhere, to the detriment of the host nation. This is a new dimension to the exercise of power by organizations pursuing economic gain. Public authority over them is eroding as they become larger, more powerful, and more multinational in their approach and location. The end result for ordinary people is a loss of power and control, because the political arena in which individuals can influence policy with their votes is losing clout compared with the economic sphere in which there are no public elections. This trend makes even more important the question of who controls corporations.

Small Businesses

The American economy is composed not just of large corporations but also of a great many small businesses (those with 100 or fewer employees). In fact, nearly half of the American labor force is employed by small businesses (U.S. Bureau of the Census, 1995b). Examples are the neighborhood dry cleaner and service station, the suburban construction com-

Alan's Bakery is one of the small, owner-operated businesses that are one of the fastest growing sectors of our economy and create more new jobs than do large corporations.

pany, most real estate agencies, and small-scale manufacturers of specialized products.

It is hard to generalize about the people who run small businesses except to say that they are different from the executives in the corporate elite. For one thing, managers of small businesses are also likely to be the owners of those businesses; for another, they are not usually graduates of Ivy League business schools. These small-business owner/managers come from a wide range of backgrounds. Many are women and members of ethnic minorities. Even if they get to be multimillionaires, they will not wind up in the same social circles (or even very often the same vacation spots) as the corporate elite.

Although small businesses differ greatly in the skills and resources of their owners and in their financial stability, they often share certain problems. Lack of capital is almost a defining feature of a small business, especially at the beginning. Banks are reluctant to lend money to unproven enterprises, so many entrepreneurs start by using their own savings, often supplemented by loans from family members. Another common problem is vulnerability to fluctuations in the marketplace (Markusen and Teitz, 1985). These may be seasonal, a result of the business cycle, tied to changes in the industry involved, or due to local changes in the business environment (as when a neighborhood declines and customers move out).

Despite these problems, hundreds of thousands of new small businesses are started each year. Owning one's own store, restaurant, or office seems to reflect the value Americans place on independence. Small-business people like being their own bosses. Since Americans also value hard work, they are often unconcerned about the many hours involved in running a small business. Small-business owners typically work for more than forty hours a week, and often entire families help out.

The many ethnic minority members who own small businesses are often recent immigrants. For example, a sample of restaurants in New York City revealed that 60 percent were immigrant-owned (Aldrich and Auster, 1986). One motivation for owning a small business is the desire to avoid the discrimination that minorities often experience in the larger economy, especially against those whose language and culture are outside the American mainstream. For some ethnic entrepreneurs, self-employment, with all its risks, is more attractive than a low-paying job working for someone else. This view, however, is not widely shared among native-born black Americans, for whom self-employment is generally considered a rather *un*promising means of upward mobility. Many African-Americans believe that starting a business involves even more hurdles of discrimination than working for others does (Tang, 1995). Among the minority-group members who favor starting a business, many come from countries with large numbers of self-employed people, so their cultural experience serves as a model for entrepreneurial ventures (Yuengert, 1995). Many, too, are attracted by the business opportunities in their neighborhoods, where the demand for ethnic services and products is often high. When an ethnic minority is characterized by extended families, the incentive to start a small business is often combined with the ability to do so, because family members can serve as a pool of much needed low-wage or even free labor.

Small businesses of all kinds are born in hope every year, but the mortality rate among them is very high. Over 50 percent fail within two years; 75 percent within five years; and 90 percent within ten years (Aldrich and Auster, 1986). Smallness and newness are definitely liabilities in the business world. One study of small businesses owned by Asian minority-group members found that those which were most successful tended to be run by people who were both well-educated and had the money to finance the venture well (Bates, 1994).

Small businesses are extremely important to the American economy. Although large companies account for a greater percentage of existing jobs, small companies generate many more new jobs (Birch, 1987). In fact, fully two-thirds of the new jobs created in the United States each year are with firms that employ twenty or fewer people. Jobs are central. After all, it is mainly through our work—and the income it generates—that most of us are integrated into the economic system.

WORK IN THE UNITED STATES

All I do now is get up in the morning, go there, and I don't be thinking about that. Like a machine, that's about the only way I can feel. (Will Robinson, bus driver, in Terkel, 1972, p. 201)

Work. It is how we spend most of the waking hours of our adult lives. It is what provides us not only with an income to live on but also with an important part of our sense of identity and purpose. Few things are more rewarding than meaningful, enjoyable work, and few things are more discouraging than work that is boring or stressful.

Work is clearly a form of social action, since it is oriented toward and coordinated with the actions of other people. As such, work is distinctly human, as Karl Marx (1867/1976) pointed out. Animals may build and produce things—birds make their nests, bees their honey—but they do not work. They do not devise a plan and self-consciously execute it, keeping the needs and actions of others in mind.

The Meaning of Work

The importance Americans place on work is revealed in the first question we often ask when meeting someone new: "What do you do?" By this we mean not what are your hobbies or how do you spend your leisure time, but what is your occupation, what *work* do you do? Work is one way of defining other people and ourselves. If the man sitting next to you on a plane says he is a prizefighter, you get a very different impression than if he says he is a psychiatrist. For most occupations—factory worker, nurse, physical education teacher, stockbroker, dairy farmer, scientist, hairdresser, auto mechanic, priest—we have certain expectations about the kind of people who fill them. At the same time, when we ourselves enter an occupation, we tend to mold our behavior to conform to what we think is appropriate for that particular social role.

Most Americans have favorable opinions about their work, particularly those in white-collar, professional, and technical occupations for which substantial training is required. Mathematicians, biologists, lawyers, and journalists are among the most satisfied. Between 80 and 90 percent of them report they would choose the same kind of work again. By comparison, only 24 percent of blue-collar workers say that they would choose the same occupation again (Tausky, 1984).

You might assume that job satisfaction is higher among professionals because their jobs bring relatively high pay and prestige. These rewards are important aspects of job satisfaction, but they are not the only reasons people express pleasure with their work. Others include the inherent interest of the work itself, the sense that one is doing something worthwhile and contributing to society, the sense that one

is supporting oneself and one's family and doing what is expected of an adult, the pleasure of developing competence at something and exercising a skill, and the enjoyment of being with coworkers.

Unfortunately, not all jobs offer these satisfactions. Many blue-collar factory jobs, for instance, are inherently boring, unchallenging, and socially isolating, as well as poorly paid and without prestige. It is not that manual work in general is inherently unsatisfying; craftspeople with high levels of skill, autonomy, and opportunity for creativity report high levels of satisfaction. The manual workers who are most likely to be discontented are those who do the same manual tasks all day long, who are pressed to do these tasks as quickly as possible, and who never have the sense of seeing a process from beginning to end. These people are likely to feel alienated from their work environment, even from society as a whole. To them, a job is just a means of earning a paycheck. This view of work is one reason that trade unions have focused so intently on increasing wages for blue-collar workers. When people are convinced that life's pleasures are all outside the workplace, having enough money to pursue outside interests becomes of paramount importance.

Even when people are not happy with their jobs, they nevertheless derive a large part of their identities from them. It seems to be important to people to believe that they are productively employed. For this reason, losing a job has more than just economic consequences. It hurts people psychologically. It also cuts them off from networks of workplace acquaintances who are very important social supports to many people. But although staying employed is a crucial concern to most Americans, our economy is not organized on the principle of providing meaningful work to as many people as possible. Instead, it is organized on the principle of capital accumulation. As a result, jobs are constantly being eliminated by new technology, corporate restructuring, and international competition. (We will look in more detail at the causes and consequences of unemployment later in this chapter.) Because of the growing possibility of becoming unemployed through no fault of their own, both blue-collar workers and high-level managers increasingly approach their jobs with a sense of anxiety. This anxiety pervades the whole meaning of their work.

Karl Marx believed that both worker dissatisfaction and unemployment were inherent in a capitalist system, where the organization and management of production are separate from the manual labor involved.

Blue-collar workers have no control over the production process, their work is not organized in any socially unifying way, and they labor for the enrichment of capitalist employers whose goal of maximizing profits tends to encourage worker exploitation. To Marx, it was inevitable that workers under capitalism would feel alienated, dehumanized, and unfulfilled because they are treated merely like cogs in the overall production process, not like skilled employees who are performing a meaningful and valued role.

Power in the Workplace

In most modern work settings, the coordination of labor is bound up with control, with managers seeking to maximize their power in relation to workers (Simpson, 1985). Control in the workplace is related to the size of an organization (Edwards, 1979). In small firms, control is direct and face-to-face and is usually exercised by the owner of the company and a few top managers. This kind of control—called *simple control*—can be both arbitrary and harsh. Workers question or disobey the managers' wishes at their own risk. As organizations grow and become more complex, simple control is impossible. There is a limit to the number of workers any one manager can supervise directly, and workers may become unionized and thus have some protection against arbitrary dismissal or discipline from management.

To deal with the demands of a large organization, managers have devised two new styles of control that are built right into the way that work is structured. One is *technical control*, or control that arises from work's technical organization. A prime example is the assembly line, which compels workers to perform their tasks in a certain way at a certain pace. On a car assembly line, for instance, workers who install the axles must do so quickly and correctly before the car is passed along for wheel installation. Although technical control is usually associated with blue-collar jobs, office automation has introduced it into the white-collar workplace as well. The output of employees who work at computers, for example, can be precisely monitored by management, and these employees can be pressured to work faster, just as factory workers can be pressured to tighten more bolts or solder more connections per hour. A more prevalent form of control in the office workplace is *bureaucratic control*. Here control is exerted by a hierarchical system that assigns rewards according to a job's level. Employees work harder to obtain special privileges like their own letterhead stationery, a reserved parking spot, access to the executive dining room, and so on. We will look again at the issue of control when we focus on technology in the workplace.

Changing Patterns of Work

In recent decades the composition of our civilian labor force has changed dramatically. While the proportion of American men who currently hold a job or are actively looking for one has actually fallen somewhat since 1960 (from 83 percent to 75 percent) due largely to more men staying in school longer and retiring at a younger age, the proportion of women in the labor force has grown sharply during the same time period. This sharp rise of women in the workforce has been caused by a major shift from women as full-time homemakers to women as paid employees. In 1960, only a little over a third of American women (38 percent) were employed outside the home, whereas now 58 percent are working. Today even women with children under six years old have as high a labor force participation rate as other women do (U.S. Bureau of the Census, 1995b). This striking change in social structure has significant implications for marriage, family, the birth rate, and other aspects of social life (see Chapters 11 and 12).

During this century, the first sharp rise in the proportion of women in the American workforce occurred during World War II, when women were needed to keep the economy running while men were fighting overseas. After the war, most women were pushed out of their wartime jobs or persuaded to leave them. Then, in the 1960s and 1970s, a new, more permanent trend emerged. More and more women were encouraged to find paid employment due to a number of social changes: an increase in the divorce rate, the development of reliable contraception, the revival of the feminist movement, and the need for a second family income to counter the effects of inflation. The increase in women workers went hand in hand with another major shift in labor patterns: a dramatic rise in the number of service-oriented jobs which, although white-collar, are relatively low-paying. Since such occupations have traditionally been held by women, the creation of more of them provided increased employment opportunities for women (Shank and Getz, 1986).

Accompanying the increase in service occupations has been a sharp drop in agricultural work and a decline in manufacturing jobs. The decline in farm work has been due primarily to mechanization in agriculture, which has increased the amount of land each farmer can cultivate. Manufacturing jobs have also declined because of technological innovations, such as computers and industrial robots. Other causes have to do with changes in the global economy, such as a shift in manufacturing production to other countries where labor costs are cheaper. As a result of these changes, a great many American factory workers have found themselves laid off. Many have had to accept jobs at a fraction of their former pay, and others have not been able to find work at all in their ailing local economies.

Major declines in agricultural and manufacturing jobs are likely to continue into the twenty-first century in the United States. Figure 15.3 shows some other occupations that will be on the decline through the year 2005, as well as some of the winners in the occupational sweepstakes (Bureau of Labor Statistics, 1995). The biggest gains are projected for workers who help care for people in their homes, especially home health-care workers. Such gains reflect the gradual aging of our population as the baby boomers grow older and approach retirement age and people in general live longer. Other big winners among American occupations will be some high-tech jobs, such as computer engineer and systems analyst. Such jobs will be among the best paid of those that are on the rise. The many service jobs that will also be increasing (from home care aid to manicurist) will usually be paid much more poorly.

Labor Markets

The social structure involved in the buying and selling of human services and skills is called a **labor market** (Reskin and Roos, 1990). Opportunities in a particular labor market are determined by the skill level of workers, by the number of jobs of that kind available, and by the number of people competing for them. For instance, as computers came into widespread use in the second half of the twentieth century, the number of positions for computer programmers grew enormously. Because the skill level required to fill them was relatively high, these jobs were quite well paid. In the twenty-first century, however, the market for programmers is expected to decline as more and more programming tasks become automated (Gabriel, 1995). Many people trained as programmers will find it harder to locate work, and those who do may be paid less because of increased competition for the few remaining positions. Some programmers may have to accept much lower-paying alternative employment because no jobs are available in their chosen occupation. An out-of-work programmer, for instance, might have to take a job delivering pizzas.

The difference between secure, well-paying jobs and jobs that are insecure and poorly compensated reflects the distinction between two broad labor markets in modern capitalist economies: the primary and the secondary (Sabel, 1982). The **primary labor market** is that in which workers are employed by stable, successful, usually relatively large firms. These workers have health-care and retirement benefits, relatively good incomes, and some job security. Most workers who are advantaged in terms of education, experience, and socioeconomic background find employment in the primary labor market.

The **secondary labor market** is smaller and much less stable than the primary labor market. Workers in the secondary market are employed in domestic service, in fast-food restaurants, and in small businesses like florists, caterers, and liquor stores, many of which do not survive very long. Jobs in the secondary labor market are often part-time or seasonal. Wages are low and layoffs are frequent, especially during recessions. Health insurance and other benefits are rarely provided. Most jobs in the secondary labor market offer no chance for career advancement and seldom teach skills that could lead to better positions.

With corporate downsizing and restructuring, many employees who thought they were in stable, primary labor–market jobs are finding that their security is vanishing. Layoffs are common at big corporations like AT&T and IBM, where jobs used to be almost guaranteed for a lifetime. But at least such workers get benefits while they are on the job and unemployment and severance pay when they lose jobs, unlike workers in the secondary labor market. Many workers in this market struggle to make ends meet even when they are employed full-time. For example, a single parent with one child who earns the minimum federal wage of $4.25 an hour and works forty hours a week with no vacations does not earn enough money to stay above the poverty line of $10,030 annually (Quigley, 1995).

The need to raise the minimum wage has been hotly debated in our society. On the one hand are

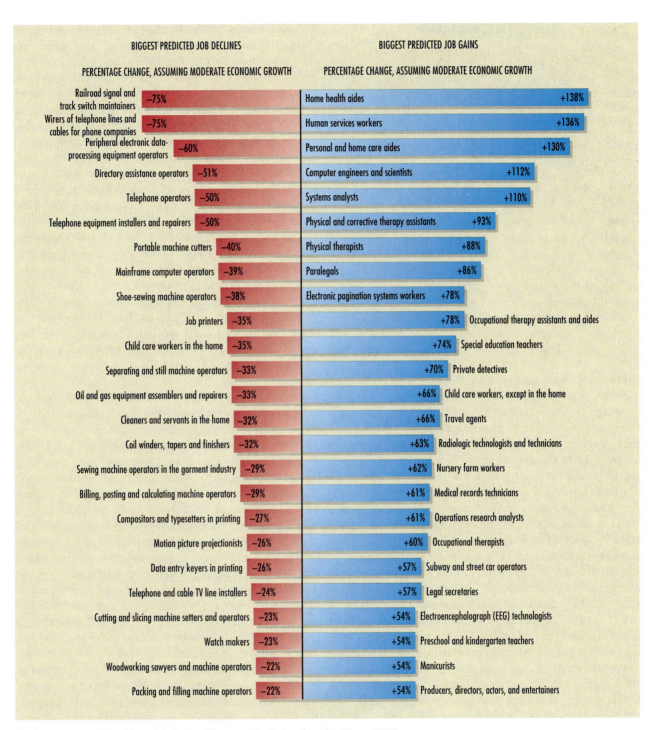

FIGURE 15.3 / Predicted Job Declines and Gains by the Year 2005

Job losses and gains reflect broad technological and social patterns. Automated equipment developed during the twentieth century will eliminate many kinds of jobs in the twenty-first. Similarly, population trends that began in the middle of the twentieth century will increase the need for people who can assist aging baby boomers in the twenty-first.

Source: *New York Times,* September 3, 1995, p. F9.

TABLE 15.1

Value of the Minimum Wage since the 1960s

The value of the minimum wage has dropped greatly over the past 30 years. In the 1960s a full-time minimum-wage income could support a family of three above the poverty level, but by the 1990s if offered a family this size only a little over three-quarters of what it needed to be out of poverty.

Period	1992 Dollars	Percent of Poverty Line, Family of Three
1960s	$5.65	104.7%
1970s	5.54	102.6
1980s	4.52	83.9
1992	4.25	78.8

Source: James K. Glassman, "Raising Minimum Wage Is Not the Answer," The Washington Post, April 4, 1995, p. 23.

those who argue that people who work full-time in a country as affluent as ours should be able to earn a living above the poverty level. They point out that the financial position of minimum-wage workers has been steadily declining as inflation takes its toll (see Table 15.1). In the 1960s and 1970s a minimum-wage earner could even support a family of three slightly above the poverty level. Today, in contrast, a full-time minimum-wage income is about $4,000 short of what it takes for a family of three to stay out of poverty. However, others contend that raising the minimum wage would have an undesirable side effect. It would force employers in the secondary labor market to lay off American workers and produce more of their goods in countries where labor costs are cheaper. The validity of this argument is questionable, however. Many of the lowest-paid jobs in our society cannot be readily carried out in other nations. Dishes in an American diner cannot be washed by workers in Mexico, nor can clothes be shipped to China for dry cleaning. A higher minimum wage is not usually a threat to employment but rather a way of ensuring what President Franklin Roosevelt called "a fair day's pay for a fair day's work."

There are also large numbers of workers in the U.S. secondary labor market who toil for wages substantially *below* the federal minimum. This is because their employers are either exempt from minimum-wage laws (usually because of their small size) or

choose simply to disregard government-set standards (Schiller, 1994). Workers in the garment-making sweatshops of New York, San Francisco, and L.A. are good examples. This largely immigrant workforce is typically paid by the piece (so many cents to put in a zipper, so many cents to sew up a seam), and piecework rates are set so low that many of the slower (often elderly or inexperienced) workers earn less than $1 an hour (Lii, 1995; Udesky, 1994). Even the fastest seldom come close to the minimum wage. Yet the labor is grueling. Workers are required to spend sixty hours or more a week bent over their machines, sewing as fast as they can (a thirty-inch inseam might be finished in only three seconds). Twelve-hour workdays seven days a week are not uncommon in this industry. Many of the workrooms are poorly ventilated, so workers are forced to cover their noses and mouths with bandanas to keep from inhaling the lint that hangs in the air. In winter the shops are inadequately heated; in summer they become suffocatingly hot. Children often work alongside a parent, snipping threads, fastening buttons, or attaching labels that read "Crafted with Pride in America." No one gets overtime pay, vacations, or insurance benefits. The coffee break so standard in the corporate world is unheard of here. Time is crucial when contractors are paying only $1.80 for each finished blouse (Headden, 1993).

These low wages cannot be justified by low profit margins for the manufacturer or the retailer. The same blouse that costs only $1.80 to make would usually be sold by the name-brand manufacturer to a store for $16, which in turn would sell it to consumers for $32. A dress that sweatshop labor turns out for $6 is typically bought by the retailer for $50 and resold for $100. Apparently, the profit margins in this business are quite adequate for those at the top of the pyramid. What, then, explains the exploitive wages paid to those who actually make the clothes?

The answer lies in the structure of the manufacturing process. Name-brand clothing manufacturers like Esprit, Guess, and Levi Strauss have few if any employees whose jobs are to sew garments. Instead, they farm out the job of assembling their products to sewing subcontractors. In the United States there are an estimated 50,000 such subcontractors, all vying for the same work. This fierce competition sets the stage for driving contract prices down to rock-bottom levels. The only way that subcontractors can stay in business is to offer their workers a piece rate that matches the low contract price paid to them.

Sweatshops—small manufacturers that employ mostly immigrant workers at subminimum wages in unsafe working conditions—have made a comeback in most major cities. Min Hua Fashions Inc. (shown here) was cited for blocking fire exits and payroll irregularities. If shut down, however, such small factories can easily relocate and reopen under other names.

And because in urban areas there is a ready supply of immigrant workers willing to labor for whatever they can get, the subcontractors are able to keep their sewing machines humming for wages that most native-born Americans would scoff at (Foo, 1994).

Government agencies do not have the manpower to investigate all the violations of state and federal labor laws that occur in urban sweatshops. As a result, most of these violations go unprosecuted. It will take dramatically stepped-up enforcement of existing labor laws to improve the lot of workers in this lowest segment of the secondary labor market.

Pay Inequalities

As our discussion of sub-minimum-wage jobs implies, pay for less-skilled workers in our society has been declining. Over the past fifteen years, some less-skilled workers have suffered drops in real income (what their paychecks will actually buy) as high as 14 percent (Borjas, 1995). This loss of earning power is due to a number of factors. One is the decline of labor unions as the production of durable goods has increasingly moved overseas. Another is the fact that lower-cost imports tend to depress the wages of the remaining American workers who make competing products. Couple this with a sizable influx of unskilled immigrants who are thankful just to get a job regardless of the pay, and the stage is set for a significant drop in what people at the bottom of the labor market earn (Borjas, 1995; Brauer and Hickok, 1995).

Although more highly skilled American workers are maintaining their earning power better than less-skilled workers are, many are simply holding their own against inflation, and some are not even doing that. Yet the American economy continues to grow and produce more wealth. Who is getting all the money associated with this expansion?

Some of the biggest winners have been the CEOs (chief executive officers) of large corporations. Together, the top-earning twenty-five CEOs of American-based firms earned nearly $1.5 billion over the last five years, roughly two-thirds of this coming from lucrative stock options (Hardy, 1995). Walt Disney Company chairman, Michael Eisner, alone earned $235 million during this time. Although such gargantuan pay packages as Eisner's are still rare enough to make headlines, they point to a general trend in American business. Pay scales for CEOs are rising at a rapid rate, even while those for most other

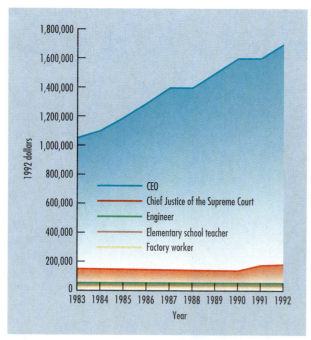

FIGURE 15.4 / Comparison of Median Pay Packages for U.S. CEOs and Other Kinds of American Workers, 1983–1992

The pay gap between CEOs and other kinds of workers in the United States was already enormous in the early 1980s. Even a Supreme Court justice did not come close to earning what the head of a large corporation earned. Ten years later, this huge pay differential had widened even further. In fact, it had nearly doubled.

people have remained stagnant. Figure 15.4 compares the median pay package for American CEOs with those for factory workers, elementary school teachers, engineers, and Supreme Court justices. As you can see, the pay gap between CEOs and these other occupations nearly doubled in a ten-year period (Blair, 1994). Today, what the average American corporate CEO earns annually is fast approaching the $2 million mark. This is probably three to four times more than a CEO in Japan makes, and 120 times more than a U.S. factory worker earns.

One of the reasons for the staggering earnings of CEOs in the United States is that our companies are increasingly bidding against each other for top executives, causing the stakes to spiral. And because of the value that Americans place on competition and individual achievement, we are probably more accepting of great inequalities in pay than people in many other societies are (Inglehart, 1990). In fact, in

many areas of economic life we have created what economists Robert Frank and Philip Cook (1995) call a "winner-take-all" system. By this they mean a system in which the vast majority of rewards go to a few "top" people. These people do not really earn all of their income through their productive contributions alone. Their pay is too great. As Frank and Cook put it: "It is one thing to say that people who work 10 percent harder or have 10 percent more talent should receive 10 percent more pay. But it is quite another to say that such small differences should cause pay to differ by 10,000 percent or more" (p. 17).

Winner-take-all systems of this magnitude tend to encourage waste because such huge pay packages are not really needed to keep the top performers at work. These systems also breed resentment on the part of lesser-paid people who feel that the gap in earnings is growing out of control. In the United States, for instance, mega-compensation payments to CEOs are coming at a time when the average person is feeling less financially secure due to the "streamlining" of organizations and "downsizing" of staffs that sometimes involve layoffs of thousands of workers. CEOs can still earn huge incomes for running these reduced-size firms because most of their income is based on the value of the company's stock, which tends to rise when a firm is restructured. "Thus, rising pay packages for CEOs and worsening job security for many ordinary working people are often driven by the same phenomenon: relentless pressure from financial markets to drive stock prices up" (Blair, 1994).

The Problem of Unemployment

In capitalist economies, some amount of unemployment is considered "normal." This is because, with free enterprise, there are always certain firms and industries that are on the rise while others are falling out of favor. As a result, the available jobs do not always match the skills of the available workers. This discrepancy produces *structural unemployment*, so called because it is tied to the structure of an economic system as it undergoes market changes. Technological change usually causes some structural unemployment. For instance, when the automobile was invented, there was a steady drop in the demand for goods and services related to horse-drawn vehicles, and eventually these products virtually disappeared from the market. In the process, many workers (from blacksmiths, to wagonmakers, to producers of buggy whips) were forced out of work. Unless these people acquired new skills or were willing to work for lower wages in unskilled occupations, they could remain without a job for a substantial period of time. Structural unemployment also occurs when firms lose out in competition with other firms because they are either inefficiently run or produce inferior products. If these firms go out of business, their employees lose their jobs and may have trouble finding new work if other firms in their area do not need their skills. Then, too, corporate mergers and other kinds of business reorganization can make some employees redundant and cause them to be laid off.

In addition to structural unemployment, the periodic downturns in capitalist economies create another kind of job layoffs, called *cyclical unemployment*. Cyclical unemployment can rapidly spiral upward if measures are not taken to check it. When supply outstrips demand, businesses cut back on employees, and the resulting drop in income and spending can trigger more job layoffs, causing a recession to set in.

Temporary joblessness is very common in our own capitalist economy, although the incidence of it varies considerably among regions of the country. Overall, an estimated two out of three Americans will lose a job at some time in their lives (Kates, Greiff, and Hagen, 1990). One out of five Americans was unemployed at some point during the recession year of 1991 (Pomice, et al., 1992). Many of these people found new jobs quickly, but some suffered long periods of anxiety, economic deprivation, personal humiliation, and a devastated sense of self-worth.

Government statistics seldom reveal the true magnitude of unemployment at any given time, because the official unemployment rate is determined by counting only those who are actively seeking a full-time job. It does not include those who are looking for part-time employment, nor those who have grown so discouraged that they have virtually given up trying to find a job. For instance, during the economic downturn in 1991, at least 1 million unemployed Americans had stopped looking for work. Still more had been pushed into early retirement. There were also many young people who delayed entering the labor force because they knew that opportunities were limited. Only when these people are added to the 8.6 million who were actively seeking work do we get a true picture of the extent of unemployment. In fact, we might also count the 5.9 million American workers who held part-time jobs in that year but would have preferred full-time ones.

Unemployment happens disproportionately to the poor, who are least able to weather financial crises.

A highly skilled aircraft machinist, Robert Muse was a victim of corporate downsizing. So was one of his brothers, and a third expects his job to be eliminated any day. Muse earns half what he did before he lost his job. He still gazes longingly at planes passing overhead, but doubts he will ever be able to say, "I helped build that plane" again.

During periods of recession, the rate of unemployment for young, lower-class high school dropouts is an alarming 25 percent or even higher (Kasarda and Appold, 1990). But unemployment also strikes the middle class and even the wealthy. For instance, in the wave of corporate mergers during the 1980s, many senior executives lost their jobs. Similarly, when the computer industry took a downturn in the late 1980s and early 1990s, highly paid engineers and other computer specialists suddenly found themselves out of work, with few prospects of finding new jobs very quickly. In the 1990s, downsizing and restructuring became common as corporations sought to increase profits at the expense of jobs.

How well people cope with unemployment depends largely on the social and institutional support available to them. This includes the support of family and friends, who can help the unemployed person maintain a sense of competence and self-worth. It also includes financial support, such as severance pay and unemployment benefits, as well as support from agencies that offer counseling and job-hunting assistance. When many such supports exist, prolonged unemployment is more bearable.

Professionalization

Professionalization has transformed many occupations. The field of medicine has been one of the pioneers in this change, as we discussed in Chapter 14. Professionalization has also accompanied the general growth of large, formal organizations as the chief employers in modern societies. The basic pattern has been for large workplaces to reinforce the distinction between professionals (including managers) who make decisions about the overall direction of work and ordinary workers who carry out the instructions or plans of others (see Chapter 3). Professionals are not all well off, but with regard to income, security, and autonomy in their work, they are generally at the opposite end of the spectrum from minimum-wage workers and people in the secondary labor market.

Professions can be defined as categories of jobs in which entrance is restricted to those who possess highly specialized knowledge and skills acquired from a relatively long period of formal education. Because of this ability to limit new entrants, professional status is an exercise of power on the part of an occupational group (Abbott, 1993). Evaluation of the members of a profession is performed by other members (not by "outsiders"), and the members are largely self-organized in their work. The oldest and most respected professions are law and medicine. Religious ministry, in some other countries and historical periods the most elite profession, is less prestigious in the United States today, partly because we have no state church and no government certification of clergy.

With their numbers restricted by educational credentials, professionals often command good incomes. Some professionals are self-employed, working alone or in partnerships. Instead of being supervised by a boss, they are governed by professional codes of ethics and the desire for a good reputation. The majority of professionals, however, work for large organizations. While privileged when compared with most other workers, corporate professionals are still subject to some degree of bureaucratic control (Freidson, 1985; Powell, 1985). In general, though, professionals resist interference by others in the regulation of their work. Doctors, for instance, hold that only another doctor can judge the quality of a physician's services. This attempted exercise of power is sometimes contested, as when a patient sues a doctor for malpractice, in effect asking the courts to evaluate that doctor's work (Abbott, 1988).

In recent years, people in a number of traditionally nonprofessional occupations have sought to organize themselves as professionals. Some have succeeded fairly well (dentists, accountants), while others have been less successful (nurses, social workers). Predominantly female occupations have had a harder time winning recognition as professions. Because professionals typically enjoy high prestige, high pay, and high autonomy, there is an incentive for occupational groups to try to achieve professional status. As this occurs, more credentials are needed to enter these fields. An oversupply of members, which occurs when credential requirements are not very stringent, tends to weaken a claim to professional status (Freidson, 1985).

Productivity and Automation

Productivity refers to the amount of labor, land, machinery, or other factor of production that is required to produce a given amount of output. For example, an acre of land might yield five tons of soybeans or ten tons, depending on a farmer's skill, the amount of fertilizer used, the quality of the land, and so on. Sociologists' main concern is the productivity of labor: how much human work is needed to produce a given amount of goods. Better tools and technology, better work organization (a more efficient division of labor, for example), and greater effort are all ways of increasing the productivity of labor.

One of the most important social and economic trends since the Industrial Revolution has been rapid and continuing increases in labor productivity. Rising productivity has been the basis for the generally high standard of living in the United States. During the 1950s and 1960s the productivity of American labor grew at an annual rate of nearly 3 percent, enough to double in only thirty years. If this rate of increase were sustained, each new generation of Americans would produce twice as much as the last, with an accompanying rise in earnings (Public Agenda Foundation, 1990). The problem is that this rapid growth in productivity has *not* been sustained. After the Arab oil embargo of 1973, the annual rate of increase in American labor's productivity took a dive from which it has never recovered. It now hovers at 1 percent per year or less. Many believe that boosting labor productivity is the only way to cure our country's economic ills and restore the United States to the preeminent position it enjoyed for much of this century.

The ways in which higher labor productivity has traditionally been accomplished are not without negative effects. The introduction of new laborsaving machinery and the reorganization of the workplace around it—a process known as **automation**—sometimes makes work less satisfying, especially when it reduces people's sense of control over their own labor and output. Thus, workers may initially welcome the challenge of mastering and putting to efficient use a new technological tool, such as computerized equipment, but then find themselves excluded from programming it and even from controlling the on/off switch. The result can be damaged self-esteem and a gnawing sense of alienation (Howard, 1985).

A feeling of alienation and lack of control is not restricted to lower-paid workers. Even highly educated, well-paid specialists are subjected to new forms of control in high-technology companies. For example, Robert Howard (1985) has examined the development of corporate campuses in Silicon Valley, where in times of prosperity highly skilled computer workers have been treated to free company gyms, health-food bars, and counseling services. Although such benefits are very attractive on the surface, they are also an exercise of power on the part of management, designed to promote loyalty and motivation among workers by enmeshing them in a system that dominates much of their lives. At the same time, management may try to manipulate the emotions of workers to further increase their output. Howard tells of workers who were expected not just to do their jobs well but to smile constantly to show how much they liked their work.

This kind of pervasive psychological control could become an increasing part of the modern workplace (Hochschild, 1983). Hochschild calls this vision of the future the "brave new workplace" after the title of Aldous Huxley's book *Brave New World*. That novel describes a nightmarish twenty-fifth-century society in which governmental control over people is so complete that possibilities for individuality and creativity are lost, but various high-technology pleasures are provided to keep everyone superficially happy. Long before the twenty-fifth century, we face the challenge of figuring out how to increase efficiency and productivity without surrendering individuality and the satisfaction of being creative.

SUMMARY

1. The economy is a social institution that accomplishes the production and distribution of goods and services. Capitalism is the most widespread and important form of economic organization today. In a pure capitalist system the means of production are all privately owned, workers and consumers make economic choices in accordance with their own self-interest, producers are governed by the profit motive, competition exists in virtually all markets, and the owners of businesses repeatedly invest for the purpose of capital accumulation.

2. Modern capitalism operates on a global scale unimagined by its founders. Capitalist corporations today do not simply buy and sell abroad; they also produce there. High-volume standardized production is now largely being done in countries where wages are low, while more costly skills are being purchased in whatever parts of the world these talents can be found.

3. Government is deeply involved in modern capitalist systems. In the United States this trend has been dramatic since the Great Depression. The influential economist John Maynard Keynes suggested that government spending programs are needed to control economic swings from unemployment to inflation. The welfare state that resulted has been challenged in recent years.

4. Another economic arrangement is socialism, which arose in response to some of the abuses of nineteenth-century capitalism. socialism involves public ownership and control of at least some of the means of production. In the former Soviet Union, extensive public ownership was combined with extensive centralized planning regarding economic decisions. Such centralized planning is enormously complex and gives rise to many problems.

5. Many of America's large corporations are multinational, with operations in many different countries. Multinational corporations influence both the economic and political life of countries in which they operate. The stockholders of such large corporations are too diffuse to exert much control over policy, so decisions affecting both the corporations and the host countries are largely in the hands of corporate managers.

6. Although large corporations dominate business in the United States, small businesses also play an important role because they employ a sizable number of people and create many new jobs. For a variety of reasons, recent immigrants to the United States are especially attracted to owning a small business. In part because they are often underfinanced and run by inexperienced people, small businesses have a high mortality rate.

7. Work is rewarded not only by pay but by the sense of identity it gives to people. Today, white-collar workers are more prevalent than blue-collar workers and seem to be more satisfied as well, particularly those in professional and technical occupations for which substantial training is required. All people employed by someone else are subject to control, or the coordination of their work effort. Blue-collar workers are controlled by the technical requirements of the production line, while white-collar workers are controlled by the promise of nonmonetary rewards built into a bureaucratic system.

8. Two current work trends in America are an increasing proportion of women in the paid labor force and a decline in farm and factory work coupled with an increase in service occupations, including many low-paying ones. Many women (and minorities) work in the secondary labor market, where jobs are part-time or seasonal and offer few career opportunities. The better-paying and more secure primary labor market is reserved for those with academic degrees and other job credentials. Because these credentials have risen in recent years, unskilled workers who cannot find jobs in the shrinking farm and factory sectors are often forced into the secondary labor market. At the high end of the primary labor market are the professions, such as law and medicine, which offer the best pay, most prestige, and most autonomy. Unemployment is most common in the secondary labor market, but in the 1990s it has begun to affect increasing numbers of highly skilled workers in the primary labor market as well.

9. The productivity of labor (or output per labor-hour) has been increased by automation, which involves the introduction of machinery and reorganization of the workplace around it. However, automation often has reduced job satisfaction by making jobs less interesting.

REVIEW QUESTIONS

1. What are the four basic features of capitalism?

2. Explain the origins of capitalism and socialism, with particular attention to social developments during the eras in which they arose.

3. List some of the positive and negative aspects of corporate life in the United States.

4. Why must any comprehensive approach to understanding corporations and modern capitalism take a global perspective?

5. Identify several factors that affect satisfaction with work.

6. How has work in the United States changed over the last century?

CRITICAL THINKING QUESTIONS

1. Some economists argue that capitalism may not survive in the Western world. Others argue that capitalism's dominance demonstrates its survivability regardless of social changes. Present your own views and your reasons for holding them.

2. Do you think Marx would have had more or less impact had he written today rather than 150 years ago? How do you think he would have responded to the social and economic changes of the past few years in the former Soviet Union and in Eastern Europe?

3. How deeply should the government be involved in economic life? Who would suffer if the government reduced performance of any of its roles: as enabler, assister, regulator, or consumer?

4. Develop a speech to a group of senior business students about improving corporate life in the United States. Include specific strategies and provide a rationale for each.

5. Develop the essentials of a program to improve work in the United States. Be specific about what you mean by "improve" and about your strategies. Who would have the power to make your plan work? To block it? Which groups of workers would benefit most? Which, if any, would be left out?

GLOSSARY

Automation The use of machinery to replace human workers and the reorganization of the workplace around it.

Capital Wealth that is invested in the production of more wealth—for example, factories, which are investments in the manufacture of goods.

Capitalism An economic system based on private ownership of the means of production; self-interest and the profit motive as the major economic incentives; competition in the markets for labor, raw materials, and products; and repeated investment for the purpose of capital accumulation.

Communism In Marx's theory, the stage of a truly classless society in which totalitarian control by the state would no longer be needed.

Corporation An organization created by law that has an ongoing existence, powers, and liabilities independent from those of its owners, managers, and employees.

Economic system The social institution that accomplishes the goal of producing and distributing goods and services within a society.

Interlocking directorships Networks of people who serve on the boards of directors of two or more corporations.

Labor market The social structure involved in buying and selling human services and skills. Opportunities in a labor market are determined by the number of jobs available and the number of people competing for them.

Multinational corporation A very large and usually diversified corporation that has operations and subsidiaries in many countries.

Primary labor market The labor market in which workers are employed by stable, successful, usually large firms that offer job security, health-care and retirement benefits, and relatively good pay.

Productivity The amount of output that a given input of labor or other resource can create.

Professions Categories of jobs in which entrance is restricted to those who possess highly specialized knowledge and skills acquired through a relatively long period of formal education.

Secondary labor market A small, relatively unstable sector of the labor market, one in which jobs are generally insecure, low-paying, and dead-end.

Socialism An attempt to replace the individualistic competition of capitalism by some form of social cooperation, placing the needs of society as a whole ahead of the benefits of a wealthy class. The most common means suggested for achieving socialism is ownership or control of the means of production by society as a whole or by communities of workers.

CHAPTER 16

The State and Politics

On April 19, 1995, just after 9 a.m., a blue-orange fireball burst from a parked rental van and rolled through the glass doors of the Alfred P. Murrah Federal Building in Oklahoma City, collapsing all nine floors of the front of the building and killing 169 people, including nineteen small children in the building's day-care center.

As news of the Oklahoma City bombing spread, most Americans, including many government officials, assumed it was the work of Islamic extremists—a replay of the 1993 terrorist attack on New York City's World Trade Center. For many Americans, New York City is an alien place where anything can happen, but Oklahoma City lies in the nation's heartland, a supposed haven of normalcy. If Oklahoma City could be attacked, was any American city or town safe? Outrage turned to shock as the nation learned the bombing was the work not of foreign terrorists but of American citizens associated with the growing patriot/militia movement. How could Americans who considered themselves patriots blow up a U.S. government building, killing innocent fellow citizens?

Unnoticed and unreported by the media, the patriot/militia movement grew rapidly in the early 1990s. This growth can be traced in part to changes in social structure. The movement attracted primarily white, working-class men—in Arizona and Montana, where the mining, timber, and grazing industries were in decline; in Michigan and New Hampshire, where mill towns had shut down when manufacturing was moved to Mexico and other Third World countries; and in California, where the aerospace industry vanished as the cold war ended (Cooper, 1995). People in these areas felt abandoned by a government preoccupied with international trade agreements, environmental regulations, and endangered species, as well as urban minorities, gay rights, and women's issues.

The patriot/militia movement developed an ideology that appealed to people who saw themselves as "real Americans" (and "real men"), with the federal government as their enemy. To such people the global communist threat of the cold-war years had been replaced by the threat of globalism itself; the federal government, in league with the UN, was ready to surrender to a "New World Order," and the expansion of federal regulations—especially concerning gun control—was part of a conspiracy to rob Americans of their freedom to defend themselves from tyranny. To these self-styled "patriots," no less than the future of the American way of life was at stake. Instead of hunting and fishing on weekends, these men dressed in camouflage to attend secret paramilitary training camps and prepare for doomsday.

The action of the Oklahoma City bombers was partly a response to government actions that fueled these fears. The deaths of a white supremacist's wife and son in a confrontation with the agents of the FBI and Bureau of Alcohol, Tobacco, and Firearms (ATF) in 1992 gave the movement its first martyrs. This was followed, a year later, by the siege of the Branch Davidians' compound in Waco, Texas, which ended with the deaths of seventy-eight cult members, including more than a dozen children. "Waco," said one cult survivor, "is a wake-up call for people in the sense that they saw their government at work against citizens, perhaps for the first time" (*Time*, May 1, 1995, p. 47). The final straw was the passage of the Brady Bill in 1994, which regulated the sale of firearms, and the ban on assault weapons. The patriot/militia people equated guns with independence, and gun control with unilateral disarmament and surrender.

This conspiratorial, apocalyptic view of U.S. politics was fed by fantastic rumors of unmarked black helicopters hovering over ranches, the preparation of concentration camps for government resisters, foreign police training on U.S. soil, microchips secretly implanted in ex-soldiers' buttocks, and even a map printed on boxes of Kix cereal.

These beliefs may sound "crazy," but the actions and ideology of the patriot/militia movement are grounded in American culture. Opposition to strong government is a recurrent theme in our national history. Most Americans have believed, with Thomas Jefferson, that the government that governs least gov-

erns best (in Lipset, 1995). April 19—the date of the Oklahoma City bombing—was not only the second anniversary of the fire at Waco but also the date of the Battle of Lexington, the beginning of the Revolutionary War. The right of citizens to bear arms, guaranteed in the Second Amendment to the Constitution, derives from the revolutionary era and the belief that citizen militias were "necessary to the security of a free State." Local militias have long since been replaced by the National Guard (though not in the eyes of the new "patriots"), but antigovernment sentiments run deep. The 1960s movement against the War in Vietnam likewise cast the federal government as "public enemy number one" (Applebome, 1995b).

The patriot/militia movement is only the latest chapter in what the historian Richard Hofstadter called "the paranoid style in American politics" (in Applebome, 1995b). Conspiracy theories are part of our political culture. At various times various groups have blamed the Masons, Catholics, Jews, international bankers, Mormons, and even the Bavarian Illuminati for America's problems. In the early 1950s, Senator Joseph McCarthy galvanized the country with his campaign to rid the nation of "Communist infiltrators," a campaign that cost thousands of Americans their jobs and reputations. Moreover, since the Civil War, advances for black Americans have routinely provoked backlashes from white Americans; and explicitly or implicitly, the patriot/militia movement endorses the racist and anti-Semitic views of such groups as the Ku Klux Klan, White Citizen Councils, and the neo-Nazi Aryan Nation.

While harking back to earlier times, in some ways the patriot/militia movement is distinctly modern. Faxes, videotapes, and Internet sites like "Cyberhate" enable supporters to broadcast or receive information quickly, cheaply, and often anonymously (Janofsky, 1995). A small industry has developed around do-it-yourself bomb manuals, home videos and desktop publications, and paramilitary gear. Using modern communications technology to bypass traditional forms of organization, patriot/militias are a network of "leaderless cells" that are difficult to infiltrate or to connect to a given action. Were the men accused of planting the bomb at Oklahoma City members of one particular group? No one knows. Radio and TV talk shows tend to attract like-minded audiences. Listeners may interpret the host's opinion as fact and the views of a few dozen regular

A Preparedness Expo in Dallas, Texas, attracts patriot/militia members and survivalists dedicated to protecting themselves from what they see as unconstitutional government infringement on citizens' rights, especially the right to bear arms.

callers as "public opinion." An audience differs from an actual organization or community in that participation does not necessarily include reality checks or entail responsibilities.

The Oklahoma City bombing was not intended as an act of violence against the individuals who were killed but rather as a *political* act, presumably designed to remind the nation of Waco (which the bombers saw as an act of government terrorism), to weaken confidence in the government's ability to ensure public safety, and to disturb the balance of power in the United States, however briefly. In a sense, the bombing achieved its goal. Patriot/militia spokesmen were quick to denounce the bombing and equally quick to assert that the attack was part of a government plot to discredit *them*. However, before the bombing, the media had dismissed patriot/militias as "crazies" and "weirdos," a radical fringe. Oklahoma City called attention to the alienation brewing in the nation's heartland and to the emergence of an antigovernment subculture. It also put the patriot/militia on the political map.

We begin this chapter by looking at different types of power and different views of the structure of power in the United States today. In the second section we trace the rise of modern states, analyze the cultural phenomenon of nationalism, and then look at today's welfare state. In the third section we focus on social action, emphasizing the structural and cultural factors that influence participation in American democracy and the transition to democracy in other countries.

THE CONTEST FOR POWER

Politics is the process by which people gain, use, and lose power. Almost all social relationships contain an element of politics. Parents seek to maintain power over their children; husbands and wives exercise power over each other; teachers wield power over their students; and business executives have power over their employees. This breadth is part of what makes *power* a key sociological concept. In this chapter, however, our focus is on politics in a narrower sense, that is, on politics as it relates to specialized institutions of power, especially those related to government.

When we speak of politics as the pursuit of power we are usually referring to **power** in the sense of the ability to exert control over other people's behavior or experience, even when they resist (Weber, 1922/1968). Politics also involves the pursuit of increased power for everyone—the increased collective capacity to get things done (to manufacture products, for example, or to build skyscrapers) through social organization (Parsons, 1960; Rueschemeyer, 1986). Thus, the government exercises power not just when it uses police or soldiers to force people to perform some action but also when it prints money to make it easier for people to conduct business.

Legitimacy and Authority

Legitimacy is an important issue in the study of power. It refers to the extent to which power is recognized as valid and justified, not just by those who wield it but also by those who are subject to it. For instance, the power of Congress to pass legislation is widely considered legitimate, but the power of an armed robber to take money from a bank is not. Sociologists often refer to legitimate power as **authority**. Authority is a matter of right, and ideally it should not need to be backed up by coercive power, or force. Power is illegitimate when it is solely a matter of coercion.

Most political systems rest on the exercise of both authority and coercion. In the United States, for instance, some force is used in support of authority, as when police give out tickets for speeding or ATF agents enter private property to seize illegal weapons. Even governments that use much more force than ours usually have at least *some* legitimacy, or consent from the governed. Power based exclusively on coercion tends to be unstable both because it is inefficient and because it relies on fear rather than allegiance. Eventually such a regime is likely to encounter rebellion and be overthrown. The government of the former USSR, for example, fell when it lost legitimacy in the eyes of the people, who no longer believed in communist ideology and the government's claim to be pursuing the interests of the people (as distinct from the interest of the leaders themselves). Some members of the patriot/militia movement compare the U.S. government to the Soviet government, claiming the U.S. government uses coercion to collect taxes, require that children be enrolled in school (rather than taught at home by their parents), force racial integration and women's equality, and otherwise intrude on people's private lives.

How do sociologists determine whether a government is legitimate? Some look for the absence of widespread, direct public opposition: As long as peo-

ple are not openly rebelling, they must consider their regime at least moderately legitimate (Lipset, 1981). However, people may lose faith in the government but not actively revolt because they see no hope of change or fear the consequences. A stronger view calls only positively supported government legitimate (Habermas, 1975). Some say that a political system is legitimate only if the people in it have the power to make changes they desire (Arendt, 1965; Honig, 1995). Others argue that legitimacy requires power to be exercised in the people's best interest (Connolly, 1984).

Americans often assume that democracy is the only kind of political system that people voluntarily support, but this is not so. In some settings, people have been happy to live under kings. Benevolent dictatorships may have widespread support—and therefore considerable legitimacy—in countries that have experienced harsh colonial rule or internal chaos. People may favor strong government over a chance to participate in it themselves, so long as the government can deliver peace and relative prosperity. In such cases, relatively little force is needed to gain the people's compliance.

Max Weber identified three forms of legitimate power, or authority: traditional, charismatic, and legal/rational. Historically, **traditional authority** has been the most common. It stems from beliefs and practices passed down from generation to generation and usually consists of inherited positions based on kinship and descent, such as king, chief, or even father. People accept traditional authority because they have always done so. In some societies, traditional authority is considered sacred, and political leaders are also religious leaders. Responsibility for maintaining a sacred order can set limits to the free exercise of traditional authority.

Charismatic authority derives from the belief that leaders have exceptional personal qualities that deserve respect and devotion. There is no objective way to determine whether leaders actually have such gifts; by definition, charisma is in the eye of the beholder. Charismatic authority is unstable because it is closely tied to the individual personality of the leader; successors are not easily found. Examples of charismatic leaders in recent history are Mahatma Gandhi, who led the nonviolent struggle for independence in India, and Martin Luther King, Jr. and Malcolm X, black leaders in the United States.

Legal/rational authority derives from a system of explicit laws that define legitimate uses of power. Power is vested in offices or positions, not in their

Martin Luther King, Jr. held no public office, but his courage and vision made him a charismatic source of power and direction for the civil rights movement.

temporary occupants. It is also limited to "official business"; it cannot be extended beyond the law. For example, the president of the United States cannot order American couples to limit themselves to two children, because the president's legal/rational authority under the Constitution does not extend into this sphere of people's lives. Legal/rational authority permits officeholders to exercise power only within specified limits. They act within the context of a "rational" system defined by rules and regulations.

Leadership is often conceptualized as grounded in only one type of authority. In practice, however, two or three types may be combined. Nelson Mandela, for example, has legal/rational authority because he was elected president of his country; the traditional authority that goes with this political office; and to many South Africans, charismatic authority as well.

The Social Structure of Power

Power is not distributed equally or randomly among people; it has a hierarchical social structure. By the very nature of power, some people have more than others, although some systems distribute power more equitably than others do. There are three basic sociological views on the structure of power in modern, capitalist societies like the United States. Marxists argue that the most important forms of power are controlled by the capitalist class. Power-elite theorists

agree that a relatively small group wields far more than its share of power but think there are routes to membership in this elite besides ownership of economic capital. Pluralists hold that there are multiple bases for power and that different groups compete with and balance one another.

Marxism and Class Structure

Karl Marx was one of the first to draw attention to economic roots of power. He argued that those who own the means of production tend to control the rest of society through their domination of the economy. In an agricultural society, land is the most important means of production, so those who control land have the most power. In the Middle Ages in Europe, this meant that feudal lords were the ruling class. In order to exercise their power, however, they required support by others. They needed a military apparatus, which was centered on knights in armor. These knights gained a good deal of power themselves through their role as protectors of the feudal lords. Equally important was the Catholic church, whose support gave feudal lords legitimacy and authority. In addition, priests and monks provided many services—including doing much of the writing for kings and lords, who were often illiterate. Moreover, the church came to control a good deal of property of its own and thus was in a position to challenge the feudal lords on occasion.

With the rise of modern capitalist industry, Marxists argue, power passed gradually from feudal lords to industrialists, or the "bourgeoisie." The captains of industry did not run the government directly. Most government officials came from the old aristocracy and were trained in law, diplomacy, or other fields. According to the Marxist analysis, however, they were able to exercise their official power only because they served the interests of capitalist elites. When American workers started to form unions, for example, the government took the side of big business against the workers. Because the bourgeoisie controls the means of production in a capitalist society, it directs not only economic activity but also the institutions that shape the moral and intellectual life of the country, including law, government, art, literature, science, and philosophy.

In analyzing American society's power structure, Marxists note the extent to which giant corporations dominate government and other power relations

The rise of industrial capitalism created a new class of workers, who were brought together in factories and cities where conditions were often squalid. They were pressed to learn new kinds of work and were subjected to stricter discipline and greater pressure to produce than earlier craft workers had been. At the same time, factory owners lacked the established legitimacy of older, aristocratic elites. All these factors combined to produce a widespread struggle between owners and workers over economic power. Strikes were among the most important weapons that workers could employ. Early capitalists often used violence or state power to repress strikes. Here, the Massachusetts militia guards a plant entrance from striking workers in Lawrence in 1912.

(Wright, 1986). For example, the federal government saved the giant Lockheed and Chrysler Corporations from bankruptcy with loan guarantees. Tax cuts during the Reagan and Bush presidencies benefited corporations and the rich, not the middle-class or the poor, and in pursuing the North American Trade Agreement (NAFTA) the Clinton administration sided with business against labor.

Marx held that, over time, workers would recognize that they were being exploited, join together, overthrow the capitalist elite, and establish a classless society. Contemporary Marxists argue that advanced capitalist societies have avoided revolution by "buying off" workers with an abundance of consumed goods, making them slaves to credit cards as well as their paychecks.

Power Elites

Many sociologists who agree that power in contemporary society is very unequally distributed have questioned Marx's strong focus on economic struc-

ture as the primary source of power and his predictions about the coming of a classless society. They have stressed other explanations of inequality and focused on the power of more narrow and more flexible elites than the capitalist class.

Two Italians, Vilfredo Pareto (1848–1923) and Gaetano Mosca (1858–1941), argued early on that inequalities of power are inherent in any social order. They considered a classless society to be an impossibility. According to Pareto and Mosca, the main reason for inequality of power is that talent is unequally distributed. In any society, they suggested, some lawyers are inevitably more clever than others, some royal mistresses more influential, some thieves more successful. Pareto and Mosca held rather than complete equality, the most desirable social organization was one open to the "circulation of elites," in which there was a possibility for all people of talent to rise to the top.

Writing in the first decades of the twentieth century, the German social scientist Robert Michels also argued that inequality was inevitable. In all organizations, Michels said, power tends to end up in the hands of a small group of leaders. As organizations grow larger and more complex, this tendency toward **oligarchy** (rule by a few) becomes stronger (Mayhew, 1978; Michels, 1915/1949). Leaders chosen for their special talents in administration and public relations gradually take command. In time, these leaders develop a vested interest in maintaining their positions. The ruling clique becomes more conservative, seeks compromise with its enemies, avoids risks, and erects barriers to challenges by opponents—all measures designed to protect its position and advance its fortunes. Michels's proposition that large-scale organization always leads to rule by a small minority has become known as the **iron law of oligarchy.**

The American sociologist C. Wright Mills (1959) showed how elites became entrenched and closed. The **power elite** that he identified in the United States consists of a coalition of military leaders, government officials, and business executives; this coalition effectively runs America. According to Mills, this small group makes most major policy decisions, especially those related to war and peace. While the power elite generally supports and is supported by the broad capitalist class, it is a smaller, more elite group. Sometimes, to retain power, it works out compromises that are not immediately in the interests of capitalists (as when the U.S. government legalized labor unions, for example).

Several social scientists have collected evidence on the American power elite (Domhoff, 1978, 1983, 1993; Useem, 1984). About one-half of 1 percent of the U.S. population controls up to 25 percent of the country's wealth and holds a disproportionate number of high-level positions in government and business. Members of "the governing class" attend the same schools, belong to the same clubs and civic associations, and intermarry, producing a fairly tightly knit inner circle. This system is less structurally fixed than the Marxist view of a ruling class based solely on capitalist economic relations, but it is not open and democratic, either.

Mills argued that the different branches of the power elite—in the economy, the government, and the military—are interlocking. Throughout the cold war, Congress approved billions of dollars in military appropriations each year; as recently as 1991, the government spent $82 billion on weapons (Sterngold, 1996). The military consumes about 20 percent of the federal budget. Why do we spend so much on the military? In part for national defense; in

part because military contracts create jobs and support communities; and in part because military suppliers are important campaign contributors and often provide jobs to former government officials. Even today, with the military procurement budget falling (to $55 billion in 1995), the government continues to support military industries—for example, by allowing mergers that raise questions about antitrust violations. All three sectors—economic, political, and military—have a vested interest in what Mills called "military capitalism."

Pluralism and Competing Interests

While acknowledging that elites are more powerful than the unorganized masses, sociologists who take a pluralist view do not believe that a single ruling clique dominates America. Rather, **pluralism** is the view that argues that social power is dispersed among a variety of competing interest groups—the oil industry and the coal industry, car manufacturers and environmentalists, union and business associations, hunters' lobbies and wildlife foundations, the navy and the air force, General Motors and Ford. All these groups control resources and influence policy decisions with varying degrees of success, but no one group is in command. In most cases each can do little more than stop programs that threaten its interests (Dahl, 1961, 1989; Keller, 1963; McLennan, 1995). Thus, society's problem may not be too little pluralism but rather too much of it. With competing groups constantly erecting barriers to programs they do not like, major social and economic problems become impossible to solve (Thurow, 1980). Either decision making becomes deadlocked or legislation is filled with so many compromises that it is ineffectual.

The existence of competing interests does not foreclose the possibility of elites. For instance, the sociologist Arnold Rose (1967) concluded that foreign affairs are dominated by a small group of people who resemble Mills's power elite, but the growth of the federal government and the emergence of special interest groups (such as environmentalists, women's lobbies, and retired people) have weakened the power of big business. In Rose's view, there are many power structures in America, not just one, and nationwide decisions are made through a process of bargaining (the pluralist view). However, the power structures themselves (political parties, government agencies, legislatures, businesses, and so on) tend to be dominated by oligarchies (the power-elite perspective). The power structure of American society, in short, consists of a complex plurality of elites.

THE STATE

A distinctive feature of modern societies is the existence of complex institutions and organizations specialized for exercising authority. These include courts, police departments, legislatures, regulatory agencies, executive offices (the presidency, governorships), and the military. Taken together, these specialized political institutions and organizations form the **state**. The state has a monopoly over the legitimate use of force within a given territory. People who try to use force outside the authority of the state are considered criminals, terrorists, or revolutionaries.

Note that the concept of the state is not the same as the concept of government. While the state is all the specialized organizations and institutions in which power over a given geographic region is concentrated, a government is a body of elected and/or nonelected officials who direct the state at any given time. Thus, people can be loyal to their state even while discontent with the current government.

The Rise of Modern States

Through most of human history, states as we know them did not exist. Tribes or other small groups formed the basic social units, and kinship was the foundation of the social order. Power was concentrated in people, usually elders or heads of families, not in organizations. Personal power and official power were one.

The state came into being largely through ever-greater distinctions between officials as private persons and officials in their public capacities. This gradual process began with the emergence of tribal chieftains, then kings. Eventually, the office of king came to be understood as something separate from the person who held it (Gluckman, 1965; Kantorowicz, 1957; Mann, 1993). The expression "The King is dead; long live the king!" captures this idea. Although one king has died, the position of king remains to be filled by another individual.

Between the sixteenth and nineteenth centuries the states of Europe grew in size and strength. Two ma-

jor forces were behind this growth: the expansion and consolidation of political territories and the growth of international trade. These in turn were linked to other historical trends: the uniting of principalities through inheritance and royal marriage; improvements in transportation; wars of conquest; and the colonization of the Americas, Africa, and Asia. To maintain control over large, often far-flung regions, rulers had to impose taxes, build roads, and assemble large armies. At the same time, merchants were demanding that their goods be protected from pirates at sea and bandits on land. Rulers had to see that treaties were negotiated, roads and seas were policed, and domestic peace was ensured (Anderson, 1974; Hall, 1985; Mann, 1993).

To accomplish these diverse tasks, the rulers of European states developed new governmental institutions, which operated on two basic principles: (1) the strict separation of public duties from private lives and personal connections and (2) formal rules to govern official behavior. Officeholders were not to profit, for example, from privileged information obtained in their public roles. A new class of "public servants" came to staff what we now call bureaucracies (Weber, 1922/1968). A **bureaucracy** is an organizational structure characterized by specialization and division of labor, a hierarchy of offices, explicit rules and regulations, impersonality in decision making, and rewards and promotions based on merit (see Chapter 3). Bureaucracies continue to be central to the operation of every modern state.

In some countries—particularly communist ones—the state bureaucracy controls industry and economic life in addition to performing its political functions. In Marxist regimes, major industries are nationalized (run by the government for the benefit of the people). In capitalist countries, the state plays a role in economics, but private bureaucracies, in the form of large corporations, dominate the economy (Harbeson, 1994; World Bank, 1995a). Bureaucracy has also spread throughout the less developed countries of the Third World (Thomas and Meyer, 1984). Although personal relationships continue to play a large role in distributing power in many Third World countries, the ideology of a state free from personal rule—one of the principles of a bureaucracy—is widespread. Even in countries in which changes of regime are common, each successive coup is likely to be justified in terms of the corruption of the previous rulers. What corruption means in this context is largely a

Great kings like France's Louis XIV, "the Sun King," were fawned over by their courtiers, venerated by their subjects, and given great power; but they did not have the capacity to affect the lives of ordinary people that modern states, with their more impersonal bureaucracies, have developed.

failure to conform to the notion of a state in which the public and private realms are kept separate.

Nations and Nationalism

The rise of the modern state and state bureaucracies is associated with the emergence of nations and nationalism (Anderson, 1991; Gellner, 1983). **Nation** refers to the cultural bonds that give a sense of shared identity to a group of people who occupy or aspire to occupy the same geographic territory. Whereas the state is a social structure, a nation is a cultural phenomenon; the two may or may not coincide.

People have always lived in groups defined largely by a common language and common beliefs—in short, by a common culture. The idea of "people-hood" is an ancient one. However, the fact that a group saw themselves as "one people" did not necessarily mean that they claimed exclusive rights to a particular territory or that they were self-governing. Many different peoples lived together in the Holy Land, which was ruled first by the Egyptians, then by the Babylonians, and in the time of Christ, by the

Roman Empire. In recent times the Middle East has been the scene of ongoing political and military struggle for territory and "self-determination" by people who see themselves as distinct nations.

Nationalism—the belief that people who share a common cultural identity should have political autonomy—is a distinctly modern way of organizing the relationship between power and culture (Calhoun, 1995; Gellner, 1983; Greenfeld, 1992). Consider France, a nation most people think of as highly unified and steeped in tradition. In reality, most people in France did not speak French or think of themselves as "French" until the 1850s (Weber, 1976). For centuries, Burgundy, Brittany, Languedoc, and Provence each had its own provincial ruler, local traditions, and language or dialect. Gradually, as political boundaries were solidified, transportation was improved, and government became more centralized, local differences began to decline (though not disappear). Institutions such as public schools promoted national identity. France had become a nation-state. Even now the clashes in values often erupt between, say, the Béarnaise in the hills of southwestern France and the Parisians. But however much French people may differ from one another, they are certain that being French is quite different from being German or English.

As this brief history of France shows, nationality is not "given" but is socially constructed (Calhoun, 1994a; Przeworski, 1995). Nationalists use myths of a common ancestry, of struggles against oppression and acts of heroism, and of great cultural achievements in the past to construct an identity—and to press claims for statehood. National identities are no more real or natural than communism or Catholicism, identities that are in part the result of historical and social circumstances and personal choice.

Nationalism accentuates the differences between countries while promoting cultural uniformity and conformity within countries. To some degree, people are expected to put their national identity ahead of other identities (for example, as women, workers, or members of a minority religion). Especially during wars, nations emphasize the similarities among fellow citizens and their differences from the enemy (Alexander and Smith, 1993). Nationalism even penetrates such seemingly private matters as childbearing (Watkins, 1992). In the eighteenth century, fertility patterns varied from locality to locality. In the nineteenth and twentieth centuries, as national identities grew stronger, differences between nations became greater while fertility patterns within nations became increasingly uniform.

In places where state boundaries have been imposed from the outside rather than developed through a long historical process of unification, nationalism may undermine the state. In Africa and the Middle East, for example, Europeans carved up colonial territories without regard for tribal boundaries and local identities (Wolf, 1982). This has been a source of much later conflict as, for example, between the Tutsi and Hutus. Their genocidal clashes in the 1990s reflected among other things the fact that each group was divided between the neighboring countries of Rwanda and Burundi. The collapse of communism in the Soviet Union and Eastern Europe revealed that communist states governed many very different peoples. Russians, Ukrainians, Georgians, and others claimed to be separate nations after the breakup of the USSR.

Separatist movements (such as Croatian or Ukrainian nationalism) and unification movements (such as "pan-Slavism") are opposite sides of the same coin. At the same time that countries on the eastern fringes of Europe are dividing into smaller nations, France, Germany, Spain, and most other European countries have joined together to create the European Union. The movement to unify Europe draws on the new views that emphasize the cultural connections and common historical experiences that distinguish Europe from the rest of the world (rather than the cultural factors and historical experiences that distinguish France from Britain or the Netherlands). The goal is to unite Europe through political, economic, and educational collaboration—in effect, to create a "united states of Europe." Europeans no longer need passports to go from one country to another, and there are plans to create a common currency.

The movement for unity is under challenge from national movements and claims for regional autonomy within Europe. Many Scots, for example, would like Scotland to be a separate nation within the European Union, rather than part of Great Britain. In some cases, nationalist movements have been resolved peacefully, as in the post-communist division of Czechoslovakia into the Czech and Slovak Republics. Elsewhere, nationalism has led to violent conflict—most notably, among the Serbs, Bosnians, Croats, and other groups in former Yugoslavia (see the Global Issues/Local Consequences box).

A second challenge to European unity comes from immigrants from outside Europe. Indians, Pakistanis, and Jamaicans move to Britain; Algerians and West Africans to France; Indonesians to the Netherlands. Germany is home to Poles, Spaniards, Turks, and others from Europe's poorer nations. Whether poor, illiterate laborers or highly trained, well-paid professionals who work in international relations or for global corporations, the new arrivals are not entirely welcome. In Germany, for example, gangs have attacked immigrant housing complexes, in what some see as a revival of Nazism.

All modern states are struggling to maintain a steady course in global markets, to exercise some control over multinational corporations, and to cope with large-scale migration and internal "tribalism" (Calhoun, 1994a). The position and power of nation-states in the global political arena are in flux. Nationalism provides a foothold in shifting sands, an identity and sense of common purpose. It can be a force for unity and cooperation as well as for division and conflict.

The Modern Welfare State

In the United States and in other relatively rich, industrialized, democratic countries—Canada, New Zealand, Australia, and most of Western Europe—the role of the state has expanded dramatically since the early nineteenth century. At first limited to such tasks as expanding transportation and communication systems, the state became increasingly involved in education, health care, housing, social security, and working conditions. A state that takes responsibility for the welfare of its people in such areas is called a **welfare state.**

The emergence of welfare states is a major sociological and political phenomenon of the twentieth century (Flora and Heidenheimer, 1981; Przeworski, 1985). As the sociologist Theda Skocpol (1992) has shown, the American pattern was unique. In Europe, social benefits were initiated around the turn of the century by politicians and bureaucratic officials in the central government, primarily to maintain a strong workforce. Public benefits were channeled to families via the male breadwinner. As part of this process, the working class was politicized and labor parties became regular features of Western European democracies. In the United States, social programs were initiated primarily by female professionals and women's groups working outside the political system. Excluded from the public sphere and denied the vote (until 1920), American women portrayed themselves as "society's housekeepers" and sought to expand the domestic sphere to the community as a whole. Not only did women play a major role in designing and implementing the first welfare policies, women and their children were also the prime beneficiaries of pensions and protective regulations in the workplace. While universal suffrage for men, winner-take-all elections, and local party patronage systems organized along ethnic lines, all diffused the development of a labor movement in the United States, welfare policies nevertheless progressed. The fact that they were presented as programs for widows and children was crucial, for who would be so callous as to speak out against motherhood?

In the United States, the welfare state expanded dramatically with President Franklin Roosevelt's New Deal. This set of wide-ranging government programs was launched in the 1930s to deal with the economic problems and personal hardships of the Great Depression. Other countries began expanding the roles of their state governments at about the same time. The most influential theorist supporting an expanded role for government was the English economist John Maynard Keynes. As we discussed in Chapter 15, Keynesian theory encouraged enormous growth in government social programs for the poor and unemployed, in the peacetime military (including defense research), and in the government workforce, all of which meant a tremendous increase in the size of the state bureaucracy.

The modern welfare state provides many **collective goods and services,** things that individuals cannot readily buy because they are too expensive and cannot be easily divided into "shares." Examples are national defense, clean air and water, public transportation, and the services provided by regulatory government agencies such as the Food and Drug Administration and the Civil Rights Commission. In addition, the modern welfare state is deeply involved in managing the economy. Through its monetary and fiscal policies it attempts to dampen the cyclical swings in unemployment and inflation that occur under capitalism.

Some sociologists argue that governments took on these new roles to counteract problems inherent in capitalism—in effect, "to save capitalism from itself" (O'Connor, 1973; Offe, 1984, 1985). A capitalist system necessarily creates hardships for those who lose out in economic competition. Hardship may prompt disadvantaged people to question the system's legitimacy. To maintain the existing power structure, the government spends money on welfare programs. If these programs become too costly, however, middle-class taxpayers may resist them. Thus, a delicate balance is required to keep the welfare state functioning.

In recent years criticism of big government has spread. Ronald Reagan was elected president twice on a platform that included a promise to reduce the size of the federal government's regulatory and social programs. Although the Reagan administration cut a number of programs that regulated big business, it did not reduce the overall size—and cost—of government.

Government spending continued to grow largely because of "entitlement programs," which guarantee benefits to specific groups, such as veterans, the elderly, and the poor. These programs—including Medicare, Medicaid, VA services, and Social Security—have become more and more expensive

The War in Bosnia

The brutal war in former Yugoslavia involves local ethnic conflicts, local claims to territory, local struggles for power. Yet this civil war is the product of global forces. Inescapably, Europe, the United States, Russia, and the UN, representing the world community, have been drawn in. To understand this global involvement requires background.

The nation known as Yugoslavia sat at the crossroads of Europe and Asia, West and East. For centuries the region had been traded among superpowers, including the Greeks, the Byzantines, the Ottoman Turks, the Austro-Hungarian empire, the Nazis, and most recently, the communists. The peoples of former Yugoslavia share common Slavic roots—*Yugoslavia* means "pan-Slavic"—but have long been divided into distinct ethnic groups: Serbs, most of whom are Eastern Orthodox; Croats, mostly Roman Catholics; Bosnian Muslims (Slavs converted to Islam when the area was occupied by Ottoman Turks in the fifteenth century, declared a "nationality" under communism); Macedonians; Albanians; and other smaller groups.

The nation of Yugoslavia was created in part to prevent incursions by outside powers and in part to deal with rivalries among these ethnic groups. From World War II until 1990, Yugoslavia was a federation of six republics, each with its own Communist party, held together by the authoritarian leadership of Marshal Joseph Tito. Each republic was named for its dominant ethnic group, but the boundaries were drawn so that each republic also included members of other ethnic groups, to prevent the development of separatist movements. Under Tito's iron rule, nationalist rivalries were held in check. To a large degree, this policy worked: Despite memories of atrocities in World War II, intermarriage rates between Croats and Serbs living in Croatia were as high as one in three in the 1980s (Mansfield and Snyder, 1995).

When Tito died in 1980, however, no single leader emerged to replace him. Yugoslavs created a national council composed of representatives of the major ethnic groups, who would alternate being president for one year at a time. In fact, the council devoted more time to competing for territory and resources than to maintaining Yugoslav unity. In particular, the head of the Serbian communist party—Slobodan Milosevic—began talking about a "greater Serbia." Based in the old Yugoslav capital of Belgrade, Milosevic controlled the federal government and, equally important, the Yugoslav Army.

In 1989–1990, in the wake of the anticommunist revolutions that swept Eastern Europe, Yugoslavia began to unravel. The republics of Slovenia and Croatia declared their independence in June 1991. Fighting broke out between these republics and the Yugoslav (predominantly Serbian) Army, but the fighting gradually subsided. Then, in October of that year, Bosnia-Herzegovina declared its independence. Of all the Yugoslav republics, Bosnia had been the most diverse (or multicultural), a region where Bosnians, Serbs, and Croats, Christians and Muslims, lived as neighbors. The Bosnian capital of Sarajevo was one of the most cosmopolitan cities in the region. But when Bosnia de-

and now account for the largest share of federal government spending. The Clinton administration came to office proposing changes in the welfare system to encourage more people to work, as well as reorganization of the health-care system to reduce the cost of Medicare, Medicaid, and other programs. However, fighting between Democrats and Republicans, as well as lobbying by special interest groups, blocked reforms. In 1994, a Republican majority was elected to Congress and launched a renewed attack on government spending. As of this writing, the primary outcome of the so-called Republican Revolution has been gridlock, including federal government shutdowns because Republicans and Democrats could not agree on the federal budget.

A key issue is the expansion of "rights" into "entitlements" (Elshtain, 1995). At the time the Constitution was written, "rights" referred primarily to freedom from tyranny, meaning immunity from government interference. In this definition, rights entailed responsibility: People took care of "their own." Over time, however, "rights" became entitlements: the right to a (college) education, the right to Social Security after retirement, the right to be culturally "different." But entitlements require big government, taxation, regulation, and so forth.

Most Americans oppose high taxes and high levels of government spending; however, while most people favor cuts in general, they want cuts to be made in programs that benefit *other* people. Powerful

clared independence, the Serbs sent in troops to en-force their claims to parts of Bosnia inhabited predom-inantly by Serbs as part of "Greater Serbia," slaughter-ing or evicting Bosnian Muslims who lived in those areas. Likewise, Croatian forces invaded territories they believed rightfully belonged to Croatia.

In the four years of the Bosnian war, tens of thou-sands were killed and millions became refugees. While there were atrocities on all sides, the main victims of "ethnic cleansing" were Bosnian Muslims, who were murdered and tossed into mass graves, sent to deten-tion camps from which few returned, evicted from their homeland, and in the case of women, systematically raped and defiled in their own and their families' eyes.

The common explanation of these horrors is that, in the absence of authoritarian rule, old ethnic hatreds boiled over, tearing Yugoslavia to pieces. An equally plausible explanation is that the failure to replace Tito's regime and maintain an effective central government caused cultural groups to mobilize and seek autonomy (Przeworski, 1995). Furthermore, political leaders (many of them former communists) who sought to maintain or to expand their power deliberately fanned nationalist fires to achieve political aims. In other words, ethnic conflicts were not the cause of the war in Bosnia but rather a means to political ends.

Why did other countries become involved? One rea-son is humanitarian—the world should not sit back and passively allow genocide (as happened during the Holocaust in Nazi Germany). The same humanitarian concerns came into play in Somalia, Rwanda, Ireland,

and Haiti. The main relief in such situations often comes from NGOs (nongovernment organizations, such as "Doctors Without Borders"). Another, equally impor-tant reason other countries become involved in such conflicts is that local wars have widespread conse-quences. The war in former Yugoslavia threatened European unity, because the Germans had been allies with the Croats and the French with the Serbs. Islamic fundamentalists have gained political strength in for-mer European colonies in North Africa, and many of the new immigrants to Europe are Muslim—a fact that may have reduced sympathy for Bosnian Muslims. Moreover, local conflicts are no longer confined to spe-cific countries or regions. As the United States learned most dramatically in the bombing of the World Trade Center, terrorism—the most powerful "weapon of the weak"—does not respect national borders. Every coun-try is vulnerable; hence, every country has a stake in world peace. This "truism" has taken on new meaning in the post-cold war era.

As of this writing, the United States has sent troops into Bosnia to enforce a peace treaty hammered out at a military base near Dayton, Ohio. But this effort, like those in Somalia and Haiti, is tentative and exploratory. So far, neither the United States, nor the European Union, nor the UN has developed a comprehensive policy or effective strategy for achieving peace and sta-bility in the new world order. The war in Bosnia will not be the last conflict of its kind.

---

groups support most major programs and threaten elected officials with defeat if their favorite programs are cut. For example, the American Association of Retired Persons (AARP) does not oppose cuts to ed-ucation, but it strongly opposes cuts to Medicaid and Social Security; the American Medical Association does not take a position on cuts in school budgets but objects to cuts in medical research. Behind this pattern is the fact that most Americans have accepted the basic idea of the welfare state, and it is now part of our national culture to expect government to pro-vide a wide range of services. While people may ob-ject to specific entitlement programs, they feel enti-tled to a high—and relatively expensive—level of government services.

DEMOCRACY

The idea of democracy, or government by the people, is very old, dating back to ancient Greece. The word itself comes from the Greek: *demos,* meaning "the people," and *kratos,* meaning "authority." In a **de-mocratic state,** authority is rooted in the consent of the people, that is, in the belief that people have the right to run or at least to choose their government. Democracies impose clear, legally established limits to what elected officials can do. All participants in the system must obey the rules regarding such prin-ciples as open elections, one person/one vote, and acceptance of majority decisions while respecting a minority's right to dissent. The law guarantees extensive civil liberties, including the freedom to associate with whomever one chooses, freedom of speech and the press, and freedom from unreasonable search and seizure. A democracy does not claim exclusive, unquestioning loyalty from its people; in fact, if those in power overstep their authority, the people have a right—even a duty—to vote them out of office.

The opposite of democracy is **totalitarianism,** in which the government attempts to control every aspect of the lives and even the thoughts of its citizens. No opposing view is tolerated in a totalitarian system. Cultural institutions from schools to art are used to reinforce the official ideology. The press is an arm of the government; television, books, movies, magazines, and even private mail must be approved by government censors; and the government attempts to control communication and the flow of information both within the country and with the outside world (though new technologies make this increasingly difficult). Power is concentrated in the hands of one ruling party that is permanently identified with the state. The ruling elite selects its own successors. Government officials and bureaucracies are responsible to the party and its leaders, not to the people. Legislatures (if they exist) have no policy-making powers but function merely to "rubber-stamp" decisions that have already been made. Power may be exercised in capricious and arbitrary ways. Citizens may be arrested at any time; allowed no contact with their family or a lawyer; imprisoned without trial; beaten and tortured; or made to "disappear." People may be rewarded for spying on their friends, neighbors, or even family members, creating widespread insecurity and distrust.

Although we are accustomed to thinking of states as being either democratic or totalitarian, in reality there are no perfect democracies and no completely totalitarian states. For instance, for much of American history, blacks, women, and Native Americans were denied the right to vote, meaning that our political system was not purely democratic. Even today, some citizens (the very rich, the heads of major corporations and other influential organizations) have a much stronger voice in the political system than others do. By the same token, most totalitarian regimes do not completely disregard the rights and wishes of the people. For instance, the Chinese totalitarian state holds elections, and citizens are given many chances to participate in local affairs—as long as they stick to the party line. Most totalitarian rulers realize that "there are certain bound to their power beyond which they cannot expect compliance" (Moore, 1978, p. 18). Leaders who consistently overstep those bounds— for example by seeking to increase their personal wealth and power at the expense of society—are usually challenged and eventually overthrown.

Participation in American Democracy

More than any other political system, democracy depends on the participation of ordinary citizens in the political process. In a **direct democracy,** citizens run

No state is purely democratic or purely totalitarian. Under China's constitution, the National People's Congress (NPC) is the "supreme organ of government," though it rarely challenges decisions made by the Communist Party's Central Committee. This 1994 session of the NPC was convened to debate economic reform.

their own government, gathering at town halls (or the equivalent) to vote directly on the issues. Most high school student governments are direct democracies. In a large, modern society such as the United States, the size of the population makes it impossible for everyone to gather together to make government decisions. Moreover, many issues are extremely complex and not everyone has the ability or time to study them carefully. Our government is basically a **representative democracy,** in which elections provide all adult citizens with the opportunity to choose representatives to make laws and provide public leadership on their behalf.

Although mainly a representative democracy, our system still has mechanisms for direct participation. Most states allow citizens to put a referendum on the ballot for public vote by gathering a specified number of signatures from registered voters or other eligible citizens. (The law does not provide for national referendums, however.) Referendums allow people to vote directly on specific issues and have been used to ban cigarette smoking from public places, to lower property taxes, to oppose nuclear power facilities, and (most recently) to ban affirmative action. Supporters stress that referendums are an opportunity for people to speak directly, rather than through elected representatives. Critics point to the potential for big-money advertisers to influence public opinion, though many referendums have been grassroots initiatives. Most attract relatively few voters, however, probably because voters lack adequate information (Cronin, 1989).

Some political leaders and social scientists point to the Internet and electronic communications generally as providing a new mechanism for direct democracy, circumventing elected representatives, party platforms, and network control of the news. A few people—such as Texas businessman and former presidential candidate H. Ross Perot—have called for the creation of "electronic town halls" that would allow people to use their home computers to vote on issues, maybe even to pass laws. Critics argue that "electronic democracy" would be unstable—people would vote on specific issues without reference to the bigger picture, that is, how different practices and policies are functionally integrated. Furthermore, "electronic democracy" would favor enthusiasts over people with neither the time for constant participation nor the money for high-tech equipment (see Splichal, Calabrese, and Sparks, 1994).

Americans participate in self-government in other ways as well: by going to official hearings and voicing their opinions, by writing to their representatives, by joining organizations that lobby legislators or one side or another of a public issue, and by becoming active in social movements and other organizations that try to shape public opinion and/or get the government involved in an issue (see Chapter 20). However, the most common forms of political participation are voting and running for office. While these are individual actions, they are also socially structured and organized.

Voting

American representative democracy is based on mass participation through periodic elections. Ideally, the principle of one person/one vote offsets inequalities of social class, sex, and race, but relatively few Americans vote regularly. In fact, most Americans seem apathetic when it comes to organized politics. Thus, if the United States has a government "by the people," it is only by *some* of the people (Teixeira, 1988). Whereas in Western Europe 80 to 90 percent of voters regularly turn out for national elections, only 55 percent of Americans eligible to vote did so in the 1992 presidential election (see Figure 16.1). Fewer

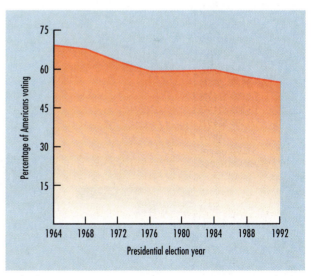

FIGURE 16.1 / Percentage of Americans Voting in Presidential Elections

In late-nineteenth-century America, more than 80 percent of eligible voters routinely turned out for national elections. Voter turnout dropped to 73 percent in the presidential election of 1900 and 59 percent in 1912, and it has not reached 70 percent since then (Brinkley, 1993).

Source: U.S. Bureau of the Census, *Current Population Reports.*

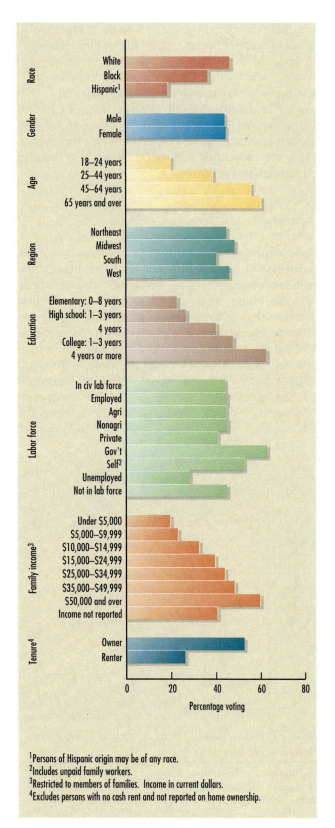

[1] Persons of Hispanic origin may be of any race.
[2] Includes unpaid family workers.
[3] Restricted to members of families. Income in current dollars.
[4] Excludes persons with no cash rent and not reported on home ownership.

FIGURE 16.2 / Characteristics of the Voting-Age Population Reporting Having Registered or Voted, Election of 1994

Analysis of data like these allows parties and candidates to target those segments of the population most likely to vote—for example, Americans age sixty-five and older.

Source: Census Bureau Homepage, http://www. census. gov, November 1994.

than 45 percent voted in the 1994 congressional elections, which means that many winners did not even receive the votes of a quarter of the people they represent. Of Western democracies, only Switzerland has lower voter turnouts.

Why do so many Americans abdicate their right to vote? One reason may be distrust of political leaders and political institutions in general. Confidence in the government has decreased dramatically, beginning with the protest years of the 1960s. Polls (summarized in Lipset, 1995) show that the percentage of Americans who have "a great deal" of confidence in the executive branch of government dropped from 41 percent in 1966 to 12 percent in 1994; the proportion who agree that "the government is pretty much run by a few big interests looking out for themselves [rather than] for the benefit of all the people" grew from 29 percent in 1964 to 80 percent in 1992; 66 percent of those polled in 1994 felt that "most elected officials don't care what people like me think" and that "government is almost always wasteful and inefficient," up from 33 percent in the 1960s. Perhaps nonvoters feel that one candidate is as dishonest as another and that government bureaucracies are too entrenched to be reformed.

Although many Americans see the government as corrupt and inefficient, most still believe in our political system (Lipset, 1995). Most Americans are happy with their personal lives and future prospects; believe they live in the best country in the world; and subscribe to the American Dream: "If you work hard, you can be anything you want to be." Complacency (not cynicism) may lead people to let others take care of politics while they pursue their private lives (Hirschman, 1982; Harwood Group, 1991).

Who *does* vote in U.S. elections? Older, married, working people who attend church regularly are the most likely to vote, as are highly educated, high-income Americans (Crotty, 1991). Young, unemployed, poor Americans with less education are least likely to vote (see Figure 16.2). Young people tend to be geographically mobile and so more often fail to meet voter registration requirements; in addition, once people start voting, they tend to continue. People who do not speak English as their first language, have not been in this country for very long, or have limited educations may find voting procedures (and issues) confusing.

Another factor is political efficacy, or the feeling that one's vote counts (Dennis, 1991). Political efficacy, in turn, is enhanced by group consciousness (such as racial identification); association with an interest group (whether a union, a professional association, or a social movement such as the "right-to-life" or environmental movements); and communication with a network of people who share common standards, common concerns, and a common sense of purpose. Childhood socialization—whether one's parents voted regularly, one's teachers encouraged active interest in elections, and so on—also influences who votes and who does not. People may think about voting as their civic duty—or not think about voting at all.

Political Parties

Traditionally, political parties have been the main channel for structuring political action and mobilizing voters. A political party is an organization designed for gaining and holding legitimate political power. Parties perform several crucial functions in large, complex political systems. Ideally, they link citizens with their government, transmitting public opinion to policymakers and mobilizing grassroots support for policy decisions. They also serve as a link between different branches and levels of government (executive and legislative, federal and state) and between governmental and nongovernmental power structures. Parties play a major role in recruiting candidates for elective office. Ideally, parties help people to understand the connections between different issues, to make compromises with each other, and to develop an overall program or platform on which to base policy.

Americans are accustomed to thinking in terms of two major political parties; other countries have five or more parties, and some have only one. The main reason for these national differences lies in the structure of a country's electoral system. In the United States, officials are elected by a *simple-plurality sys-*

tem: The candidate who gets the most votes wins, and everyone else loses. In *proportional-vote systems,* such as Italy's, a party receives the same proportion of representatives as the proportion of votes it gets in the election. If a minority party receives only 10 percent of the votes, it still gets 10 percent of the seats in the legislature. This system not only ensures that minority views will be heard but also encourages parties to form coalitions on issues where the majority does not have the votes to win.

The simple-plurality system has the dysfunctional effect of discouraging clear representation of divergent views and interests. To succeed, the Democratic and Republican parties must appeal to a broad cross section of the American people, either by taking bland positions that will offend no one or by appealing to some basic emotion, such as fear. This system discourages the major parties from developing distinct ideological identities or taking strong positions on the issues.

The U.S. system of checks and balances also weakens political parties (Lipset, 1995). In a parliamentary system, such as that of Britain or Canada, the head of state is not elected directly. Rather, the party that wins a majority of seats in the legislature choose the prime minister. As the head of the majority party, he or she can act quickly and decisively. In our system, the president is chosen in one election* and members of the Senate and House of Representatives are chosen in separate elections and for different terms. Even if the president and the majorities in both bodies of Congress belong to the same party, there is no guarantee that representatives (who represent different regions, states, and constituencies) will pass the legislation the president proposes. The result is compromise, which may dilute executive policies and programs or lead to "gridlock" (failure to act).

Nevertheless, for most of this century the Republican and Democratic parties dominated

---

*The president and vice president are not elected directly by the people, however, but by the electoral college. Each state is entitled to a number of electors equal to the number of senators and representatives that state sends to Congress. To be elected, a presidential candidate must win a majority in the electoral college. Because some states have many more electoral votes than others, a vote means more in some states than in others. This procedure has given the nation ten "minority" presidents—who received a majority in the electoral college but not a majority of the popular vote—including Abraham Lincoln, Harry Truman, John Kennedy, Richard Nixon, and Bill Clinton.

American politics. Candidates for political office were chosen at caucuses and conventions "of the party faithful interested in securing patronage, rewards, jobs, and contracts from elected officials" (Lipset, 1995, p. 10). In broad terms, Republicans represented business, and Democrats represented working people and liberals. The South and big cities were solidly Democratic; the Midwest, staunchly Republican. People tended to vote the party line (Democratic *or* Republican nominees, with few "crossovers"). Party affiliation also reflected social characteristics. Older, established people with advanced education, high incomes, and prestigious occupations (managers and professionals) overwhelmingly voted Republican; young people and those with less education, lower incomes, and blue-collar jobs voted Democratic. African-Americans nearly always voted for Democrats, as did most Jews and Catholics; white Protestants favored Republicans.

Since the 1960s, however, parties have become weaker and less important in American politics, for a number of reasons. First, political reforms have undercut the patronage system that allowed "bosses," like Chicago's Mayor Daley, to create party "machines" that reliably delivered votes in exchange for favors. Primaries play a greater role than party caucuses in nominations today; polls have replaced wheeling and dealing in smoke-filled back rooms in deciding the front-runner; and party conventions are more like pep rallies than electoral bodies that choose a candidate in late-night, cliff-hanger balloting.

Second, the mass media, particularly television, have taken over some of the campaign functions traditionally performed by parties. One such function is informing voters about candidates (Salmore and Salmore, 1985). The nightly news now brings candidates' messages right into voters' living rooms. TV news programs function as political talent scouts, speculating about various people's suitability to hold office even before they announce their candidacies. TV ads, often in the form of accusations and counteraccusations, can be more important than the news (and indeed, sometimes make news). In the past, presidential hopefuls worked their way up through party ranks; campaigns depended on local party members ringing doorbells, distributing buttons and pamphlets, and phoning voters. Today, candidates with no political experience but plenty of money (such as Ross Perot or Steve Forbes) can bypass political parties and appeal directly to voters through TV commercials.

Media-oriented campaigns have decreased the importance of party organizations on the one hand and increased the importance of fund-raising on the other. Hiring campaign managers, media consultants, pollsters, speechwriters, and advertising agencies for two campaigns (the primary and the general election) is enormously expensive. Furthermore, technological advances enable candidates to run more personalized campaigns, aided by computerized direct-mail targeted at specific groups.

As a result of these changes, elections tend to be less party-oriented and more candidate-centered (Dahl, 1993; Price, 1986; Salmore and Salmore, 1985). The impact of special interest groups (such as AARP and the NRA) and specific issues (such as the environment and abortion) have also increased (Lipset, 1995). Socioeconomic indicators have become less reliable as predictors of how people will vote. In 1994, for example, 40 percent of labor union votes went to Republicans (Barone, 1995).

To some extent, both the political center and the yardstick that arranged voters in a straight line with liberals on the left and conservatives on the right have disappeared. The proportion of voters who identify themselves as "independent" has increased, as have the proportions who change parties or vote across party lines. Analyzing the results of a nationwide survey, pollsters Celinda Lake and Ed Goeas concluded that American voters are divided along new dimensions (Figure 16.3). In their view, "culture is now more important in shaping voters' attitudes than race, geography, gender or political ideology" (in Barone, 1995, p. 18). In short, American politics has become increasingly fragmented (Dahl, 1993).

Given the volatility of American voters and the absence of stable coalitions, there is much talk of a third party. In the 1992 presidential election, Ross Perot received the highest percentage of popular votes (19 percent) of any third-party candidate in U.S. history except Theodore Roosevelt in 1912. As the 1996 election approached, one out of five respondents in a national poll said they preferred Perot to either incumbent President Clinton or Republican front-runner Robert Dole (Lipset, 1995). The Green Party, the New Party, and the Liberal Party have scored victories at the local level in New York and elsewhere (Cantor, 1995; Sifry, 1995). But a third-party vote is often simply a protest. Our winner-take-all system works against third parties. On election day, supporters of third-party candidates may decide that voting for the candidate will be a wasted vote (because the can-

Liberal Activists (20 percent of voters)

Positions: Pro-choice, tolerant about race and sexual orientation, opposed to increased military spending, against big-business, strongly Democratic.
Characteristics: Relatively young, well-educated, the least religious, and urban (including high proportions of working or single mothers and African Americans).
Distrust: Religious right, talk radio, gun owners, large corporations.

Conservative Activists (15 percent of voters)

Positions: Pro-family, pro-free market, pro-Christian right, strongly Republican.
Characteristics: Relatively young, highest-income males, almost half college graduates, often married with children, gun owners, traditionally religious, live in suburbs and small towns.
Distrust: News media, welfare recipients, lawyers, prime-time TV, labor unions, feminists.

Ethnic Conservatives (16 percent of voters)

Positions: Favor government intervention in economy, strongly religious, pro-labor and pro-New Deal in the past, now "lapsed Democrats."
Characteristics: Older and lower income than average, few college graduates, ethnically diverse (with the highest percentages African-American, Catholic, and Southern Baptist), live in America's heartland.
Distrust: Gays, gun owners, prime-time TV, talk radio.

Stewards (15 percent of voters)

Positions: Strongly pro-management, and anti-union, religiously lukewarm, very often ancestrally Republican, strongly pro-gun control, positive toward most institutions.
Characteristics: Affluent, attended or graduated from college, married with no children at home, often retired, live in comfortable suburbs.
Distrust: Welfare recipients, labor unions, the National Rifle Association (NRA).

Populist Traditionalists (15 percent of voters)

Positions: Protectionist, actively religious, anti-gun control, anti-state.
Characteristics: Describe self as working-class, young and married, few college graduates and many union members and gun owners, middle income, live in outlying suburbs and small towns.
Distrust: Gays, welfare recipients, news media, large corporations.

Agnostics (12 percent of voters)

Positions: Tolerant culturally, cautiously conservative on economics, averse to conflict, favorable to both corporations and unions, with few negative feelings toward any group.
Characteristics: Baby boomers approaching age fifty and older, mostly secular, with high education levels and slightly above-average incomes, solidly middle class.
Distrust: Prime-time TV, talk radio, NRA.

Dowagers (7 percent of voters)

Positions: Watch TV news often but uncertain about whether different groups are friendly or hostile, likely to be negative to minorities.
Characteristics: Mostly elderly women, describe self as middle class but have low incomes and low education levels, live in small towns in Midwest and Florida.
Distrust: Lawyers, the NRA, feminists, immigrants, gays.

FIGURE 16.3 / New Divisions in American Politics

Analyzing voter attitudes, pollsters Celinda Lake and Ed Goeas identified seven distinct clusters of voters. Only two of the seven lean heavily toward one party or the other; rather they line up with different groups on different issues.

Source: Michael Barone, 1995, "The New America," *U.S. News and World Report.* (vol. 119, 2), p. 18.

Republican presidential candidate Steve Forbes stops at a local pub for a friendly chat with patrons—accompanied, as all candidates are today, by dozens of TV cameras and microphones.

didate will not get elected) and may help elect the Democratic or Republican candidate they dislike most. On the positive side, third parties (and independent voters) raise issues that the major parties must address to avoid losing dissatisfied voters.

Interest-Group Politics

When political parties are weak, interest groups tend to gain members and power. **Interest groups** are organizations created to influence political decisions that concern their members. They range from business associations (National Association of Manufacturers) to labor unions (the powerful AFL-CIO), agricultural groups (the National Milk Producers Association), professional associations (the American Medical Association, the American Bar Association), civil rights and similar advocacy groups (the National Association for the Advancement of Colored People, or NAACP; the National Organization for Women, or NOW), political groups (Americans for Democratic Action, the Christian Coalition), and single-issue groups (the Environmental Defense Fund).

Special interest groups have been part of the American political scene from the nation's beginning (Schlesinger, 1979). Lobbies were never more powerful than in the years following the Civil War. Likewise single-issue movements—antiabortion groups, anti-gun-control groups, antinuclear groups, environmentalists—are not a modern innovation. In the past, groups operating outside the party system have pressured the government to act on issues ranging from the abolition of slavery to the free coinage of silver, the restriction of immigration, and prohibition. What *is* relatively new in American politics is the prominence of formal organizations with large advertising budgets and lobbying staffs and well-developed fund-raising programs, dedicated to representing particular interests on a permanent basis. Over the last twenty years, the number of lobbyists in Washington has doubled, reaching about 7,000 (Lipset, 1995).

The campaign finance reform laws passed by Congress in the mid-1970s sought to limit the impact of big-money interests on elections and to encourage grassroots participation. Under the new laws, an individual or a group can donate no more than $1,000 to a candidate in presidential and congressional races. This measure was intended to prevent wealthy donors (including corporations, labor unions, and professional organizations) from demanding favors from the candidates that they helped to elect. However, a loophole allows political parties to underwrite candidates with unlimited amounts of "soft money," or money collected by the party itself.

The campaign finance reform laws encouraged the formation of **political action committees (PACs).** A PAC is created by an interest group to further its political goals partly through financial support of candidates for political office. Because PACs represent many individual donors, they are allowed to contribute up to $5,000 to a candidate for each campaign (primary, runoff, election). PACs are also permitted to spend an unlimited amount of "soft money" (donations to the party). An interest group can establish a PAC and solicit donations from its thousands of members and supporters. Likewise, a corporation can solicit contributions from its many employees. United Parcel Services's PAC gave $1.4 million to Democrats and $1.1 million to Republicans during the 1994 midterm elections. With the rising cost of political campaigns, PACs have grown in numbers and importance.

One of the oldest and most successful interest groups is the century-old National Rifle Association (NRA), which claims 2 million members. In the 1994 election, the NRA targeted districts of Democrats who had voted for the Brady bill (a gun-control measure named after President Reagan's press secretary who was severely wounded when an attempt was made to assassinate the President) and the ban on assault weapons, starting with the primaries. All told, the NRA gave $1 million directly to candidates; spent nearly $1.5 on advertising (about half of this on commercials attacking their opponents); donated $280,500 to the Republican National committee; and spent another $200,000 on phone banks and mailings to its members (Babson and St. John, 1994). The campaign worked. Of the twenty-four races the NRA targeted, their candidates won nineteen; a majority of the new House of Representatives (224 members) were "A-rated" by the NRA (Isikoff et al., 1994). One

of the most feared lobbies in Washington is the American Association of Retired Persons (AARP), whose membership skyrocketed from 400,000 in 1960 to 33 million in 1993, making it the second largest private organization in the world (after the Catholic church) (Putnam, 1995). Over age fifty and relatively affluent, AARP members belong to one of the highest voting segments of the population.

By far the most powerful and generous PACs are funded by business interests (Figure 16.4). Of the 4,618 PACs registered with the Federal Election Commission, nearly two-thirds represent corporations, cooperatives, and trade organizations. In the 1993–1994 election cycle, such PAC groups accounted for $128.7 of the $189.4 million spent by PACs (Salant and Cloud, 1995). These PACs usually adopt a safe strategy, backing incumbents (especially those on important committees) who have the best chance of winning and the most power in Congress. For years business PACs walked a fine

THE 10 MOST
GENEROUS INTEREST GROUPS
(in terms of PAC donations to congressional candidates over the past decade)

Interest Group	10-Year Contributions
1 Banking & Finance	$56,096,840
2 Energy	50,494,379
3 Agribusiness	48,901,280
4 Transportation Unions	45,928,239
5 Insurance	42,120,605
6 Real Estate	40,692,087
7 Media	37,994,112
8 Gov't Employee Unions	37,443,503
9 Doctors, Dentists, Nurses	36,831,744
10 Transportation Firms	30,148,453

Source: Common Cause

FIGURE 16.4 / The Ten Most Generous Interest Groups in Terms of PAC Contributions to Congressional Candidates over the Past Decades

Because of the high cost of political campaigns, organized interest groups influence who can afford to run for office and who cannot. Business and professional associations—and unions—are leaders of the pack.

Source: Common Cause in *Time*, August 14, 1995, p. 20.

line between Democrats, who controlled Congress, and Republicans, who were ideologically closer to business (and controlled the White House under Presidents Reagan and Bush). Most business PACs divided their contributions more or less evenly between candidates from the two parties.

When Republicans won a majority of seats in Congress in 1994, however, this quickly changed. The House of Republicans' "Contract with America"—which proposed cutting taxes, rolling back government regulations, and putting a cap on damages citizens could collect from corporations (including medical malpractice)—was a probusiness agenda. Before the 1994 election, the American Banker's Association, AT&T, and the American Society of Anesthesiologists, for example, divided their contributions roughly 60–40 in favor of Democrats; after the elections, 87 percent, 80 percent, and 92 percent of their contributions, respectively, went to Republicans (Salant and Cloud, 1995). The close links to big business and the rich generated opposition among other Republicans—notably in the form of Pat Buchanan's campaign for the presidency.

Critics argue that PACs violate the intention of campaign reform laws by providing a new means for big-money interests to influence the government. Some critics contend that votes on political issues have now become commodities to be bought and sold. "Politics themselves become defined by the market ethos," Nicholas O'Shaughnessy (1990) writes. "Issues are peddled, sold, and discarded as new ones come into fashion." Common sense says that PACs would not continue giving if they did not get a return on their money. Direct bribes are risky business for the giver as well as for the receiver, but there is nothing illegal about providing legislators with information, drafting bills or speeches, or having silent understandings. As a result, it is difficult to connect a specific donation to a particular vote or other political act. Nevertheless, big donors clearly have easier access to elected officials. At its annual fund-raising dinner in January 1996, the Republican National Committee collected more than $16 million—a record for a single event (Fritsch, 1996). The inducement was an open invitation to speak with important House and Senate committee members, personal meetings with House Speaker Newt Gingrich and Senate Majority Leader Bob Dole, and (for donations of $250,000) a private breakfast with the Republican presidential nominee. Most ordinary citizens could not afford this ride on the Republican bandwagon.

Through donations made directly to candidates, PACs have reshaped the political landscape. As the major source of campaign funds, PACs have contributed to the decline of political parties. As special interest groups focusing on short-term goals and narrow agendas, they also contribute to single-issue politics and government "gridlock." For example, the Clinton administration's plans for health-care reform stalled in large part because so many different groups used their clout to protect their own interests that they canceled each other out. PACs are more likely to back white, male professionals and business leaders who run for office than female and minority candidates. Finally, the power and influence of PACs raises questions about who really governs America and may discourage individuals from participating in politics.

On the positive side, interest groups invite people to become active, raise new issues, gather information, and alert legislators to public concerns. Furthermore, various PACs operate as checks on one another, creating numerous crosscurrents in American politics. Without this overlapping of interest and affiliations, a country might become polarized into rigid, hostile groups (Lipset, 1963).

Citizenship and Civil Society

Democratic political systems do not depend just on formal political institutions and activities such as parties, elections, congresses, and courts. They also depend on freedom of activity and patterns of social organization in everyday life (Calhoun, 1994a; Tester, 1992). Democracy requires a **civil society**—a realm of free activity and association that is neither organized by the state nor driven by market forces (Selgiman, 1992). Families, neighborhood groups, lodges, clubs, churches, unions, charities, community-service groups, professional associations, scientific and literary societies, party precincts, and the like are the foundation of a civil society, and by extension, democracy.

When Alexis de Tocqueville visited America in the 1830s he was impressed how "Americans of all ages, all stations in life, and all types of disposition are forever forming associations" (in Putnam, 1995). In his classic work *Democracy in America*, de Tocqueville held that voluntary associations are an integral part of a democratic society, providing a buffer between citizens and the government, encouraging independence, communication, community participation, political leadership and skills, and limited government. Echoing de Tocqueville, Robert Putnam (1995) holds that "civic engagement" enhances social networks, generalized norms of reciprocity, and social trust. Putnam writes, "Researchers in such fields as education, urban poverty, unemployment, the control of crime and drug abuse, and even health have discovered that successful outcomes are more likely in civically engaged communities" (1995, p. 66). Civic engagement helps to translate the "I" into the "we," and incentives for opportunism into a commitment to the public good.

The problem, according to Putnam, is that participation in public life is declining. Church attendance in America is still relatively high (compared to other Western countries), but membership in other voluntary associations—from labor unions to PTAs, the Elks and Shriners, the League of Women Voters, and even the Boy Scouts—has fallen off sharply. Putnam gives the suprising example of bowling: Between 1980 and 1993, the number of American bowlers increased by 10 percent but *league* bowling decreased by 40 percent. (This is not a trivial example: About 80 million Americans bowled at least once in 1993, a third more than voted in the 1994 elections!) The rise of solo bowling has hurt bowling-alley owners: League bowlers consume three times as much pizza and beer as solo bowlers, and proprietors make money off of pizza and beer, not the shoes and the balls. But the real loss lies in social interaction, in the banter about sports, families, work, and politics that takes place among league members. For Putnam, bowling alone—like widespread distrust of government and low voter turnouts—is a symptom of civic *dis*engagement.

Putnam considers the argument that new organizations—such as the Sierra Club, NOW, and AARP, whose memberships are growing—have replaced the old. However, participation in these organizations is usually limited to writing an annual check and perhaps reading a newsletter. Like Red Sox fans or Honda owners, members root for the same team and share some of the same interests, but they do not go to meetings, interact with one another, or even recognize one another should they meet. Rather these are "tertiary associations," based on relationships mediated by electronic communications technology or formal organizations (see Chapter 3). "From the point of view of social connectedness, the Environmental Defense Fund and a bowling league are just not in the same category" (Putnam, 1995).

The sociologist Robert Wuthnow (1994a) found that two in five Americans say that they belong to a small group "that meets regularly and provides support or caring." Such groups range from book-reading clubs to Alcoholics Anonymous and, no doubt, play an important role in many individuals' lives. But unlike traditional civic groups, support groups do not require commitment (members are free to attend meetings or not, speak or not, remain connected or not). Rather than promoting social connections, they "provide occasions for individuals to focus on themselves in the presence of others" (Wuthnow, 1994).

A number of factors have contributed to the decline of civic engagement and social connectedness, including women's movement into the labor force (working women have less time to devote to community organizations); geographic mobility (when people move they need time to put down roots); changes in family patterns (fewer married, middle-class parents, the backbone of civil organizations); and changes in scale (the replacement of familiar corner groceries with impersonal supermarkets and, now, anonymous electronic at-home shopping). But Putnam holds that the greatest change is the "privatization" of leisure. To a large degree, television has replaced socializing with family and neighbors; VCRs have supplanted movie theaters; and where families once gathered around the radio, Walkmans isolate individuals in their own private bubbles of sound. To simplify somewhat, Americans have gained unprecedented individual choice at the cost of sociability and civic engagement.

Transitions to Democracy

In the past two decades, the ideal of democracy has spread around the globe (Hanley, 1995). In just the last ten years, the number of countries claiming democratic—or at least democratizing—governments has almost doubled, from about sixty to 115. The wave of democracy began with the collapse of military dictatorships in Spain and Portugal in the mid-1970s; rolled to Latin America, where one "generalissimo" after another was ousted in the 1980s;

crashed the communist regimes in the former USSR and Eastern Europe at the end of that decade; and pulled some African countries (most notably South Africa) in its wake in the early 1990s. Yet despite dramatic change, it is too soon to declare democracy a "winner."

Americans tend to equate democracy with free elections; once people gain the right to vote, we assume, everything else will fall into place. However, democracy requires more than free (and fair) elections. Among other essential ingredients are the establishment of rule of law; legal guarantees of civil liberties; competition among political parties; and a rational-legal bureaucracy responsible to elected officials (Bunce, 1995). Ideally, these features reinforce each other in a functionally integrated system.

Democracy requires that citizens be able to exchange ideas with one another, not just one-to-one but in public debate (Habermas, 1989). They must have freedom from censorship and from reprisals for expressing unpopular views. Citizens also need places for open discussion, whether at town meetings in a rural school's gymnasium or in the formal auditoriums of state capitals, or just over coffee at a café. When the Solidarity movement was trying to bring democracy to communist Poland in the 1980s, Catholic churches were often the only places where public meetings were safe from disruption by government forces. In addition, the free exchange of ideas requires a communication system through which people throughout a country can both learn about current issues and make their own opinions and experiences known. Because the Soviet Union's communist government wanted to stifle free public discourse, it banned citizens from owning copy machines and even limited the availability of telephones. It encouraged only those communications technologies (like TV and newspapers) that the government could control and use to speak to the people without enabling them to communicate with one another.

Another important foundation for democracy is some dispersion of economic resources. If the gulf between a wealthy elite and a mass of poor people is too wide, they may have too few interest in common for democracy to succeed. The existence of a large middle class is a structural support for democracy. In contrast to those who are very poor, middle-class people are more likely to have a vested interest in their political system. They are also likely to feel free to express their views, even when they oppose elites.

The fact that high productivity in the wealthier capitalist countries tends to create a strong middle class is one reason capitalism is often linked with democracy (Berger, 1987; Schumpeter, 1942). On a cultural level, capitalism emphasizes individual economic choice, which can serve as a model of individual freedom in the political realm.

Finally, people need to know how a democratic system works and have some experience in organizing themselves to pursue and protect their collective interests. The typical totalitarian communist regime had *none* of these democratic features; hence, the transition has been (and will likely continue to be) rocky.

Latin America and Eastern Europe

To highlight the problems, Valerie Bunce (1995) contrasts the transitions to democracy in Latin America to those in Eastern Europe (including the former Soviet Union). Most Latin American countries had histories of alternation between authoritarian and democratic rule. Even when military juntas were in power, "the memory of democratic politics" and the knowledge among elites "of what democracy is, what it requires, and what undermines it" remained alive (Bunce, 1995, p. 88). Eastern Europe had no such democratic tradition, no "feel" for democracy. The military governments in Latin America were political dictatorships. Leaders used their positions for personal gain and skimmed profits off local enterprise (and foreign investments) but left capitalist economies essentially intact. As long as there was no threat to their power, they did not interfere with religion or other aspects of cultural life. In Eastern Europe, communist governments exercised a monopoly over economics, politics, and social life. The government owned and operated industry and agriculture; dictated where people could live and work; and banned religion, native languages, and most cultural activities. Finally, statehood was not an issue in Latin America; national boundaries had been decided long ago. Throughout Eastern Europe, democratic movements were linked to national liberation movements: twenty-two of the twenty-seven states that made up the former Soviet Union and Eastern Europe are *new* states. The transitions to democracy in Latin America were largely a matter of changing regimes, restoring civil rights, and reforming existing institutions. In contrast, Eastern Europe is starting from scratch. "Everything that defines a social system—national identity, social structure, and the state and its relationship to citizens, the economy, and the international system—is a subject for intense negotiation in the post communist world" (Bunce, 1995, p. 92).

The relationship between nationalism and democracy is very complex. Under communism, virtually all other sources of identity and common cause—religion, occupation, scientific societies, literary movements, and other potential interest groups—were suppressed or coopted for propaganda purposes (Bunce, 1995; Calhoun, 1994a). When communism collapsed, nationalism was the one available identity through which people could express their aspirations. In some cases elites may manipulate nationalism to create a sense of unity between themselves and the masses, diverting attention from other sources of division (Yugoslavia is one example). In its extreme forms, nationalism, like fundamentalist religion or communism, claims a monopoly over legitimate identities: "You're either one of us or you're not, and nothing else matters." Extreme nationalists not only repress other people but also deny freedom of expression and association among their own people.

The current situation in Russia and other Eastern European countries is chaotic at best. Former party officials, industrial planners, and weakened military officers compete with populist demagogues, ultranationalists, free-market entrepreneurs, and newly mobilized ethnic groups, seemingly unable to build stable coalitions (Mansfield and Snyder, 1995). Unemployment is high, coal miners and hospital workers go months without pay, inflation is spiraling, the gap between a few wealthy entrepreneurs (some tied to organized crime) and the poor is widening, and violent crime is rampant. In half a dozen countries, "reformed communists" have been returned to power in free elections. One reason is that people are nostalgic for the old days and believe that only communists can restore law and order. Another is that communists are better organized than any other group. Communists lost their monopoly over politics during the revolutions of 1989–1991, but party members and party networks did not simply vanish (Bunce, 1995). Under whatever name or names, they are still part of the political scene. But the election of communists does not mean a return to

totalitarian rule. Before 1989, the Communist party was "the only game in town." Joining the party was the one way young, ambitious, would-be leaders—including those who sought reform—could get ahead and have some impact. Now middle-aged, these men and women have the organization and skills to lead, but not the power (or the desire, in most cases) to turn back the clock.

South Africa

The democratic revolution in South Africa was, if anything, more surprising than the collapse of communism in Eastern Europe. In the mid-1980s, there were basically two South Africas, separated by apartheid. "White" South Africa was a prosperous, modern, Western-style democracy; "black" South Africa was an impoverished, backward police state whose population enjoyed none of the civil rights or economic opportunities available to white South Africans (see Chapter 8). International pressures played a key role in the transformation of South Africa. Economic sanctions—disinvestment, trade restrictions, and a ban on long-term credit—were taking a toll. South Africa could not "make it" alone in a global economy. Moreover, South Africa was ostracized culturally as well, excluded from world sporting, scientific, and academic circles. "Whites knew all too well that [full] democracy was the price of admission to the Western world" (Giliomee, 1995). F.W. de Klerk, leader of the ruling Nationalist party (NP), convinced his constituents that they had to choose between a declining standard of living and increasing internal violence on the one hand, and negotiation on the other. In a referendum, white South Africans chose negotiation.

De Klerk's first move toward reconciliation was to free Nelson Mandela and lift the ban on the African National Congress (ANC) and other black political groups. His goal at this time was to liberalize the existing system (granting civil rights), not to create a democracy. For its part, the ANC was essentially an African liberation movement. Like independence movements from Ghana to Zimbabwe, the ANC sought to overthrow the "colonial" Afrikaner government, reclaim stolen land, nationalize industry, and establish a unified, one-party government. With the collapse of communism, however, the ANC lost its main source of funds (the USSR); moreover, the

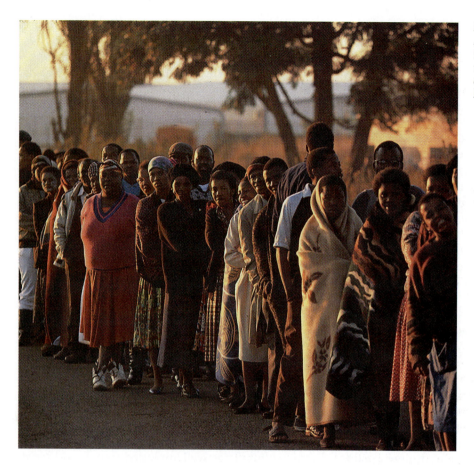

In Kathelong Township, South Africa, voters line up before dawn to cast their ballots in the first multiracial elections in that country's more than 300-year history.

idea of a controlled, socialist economy had been discredited.

The two sides had reached checkmate (Giliomee, 1995). On its own, the ANC had no hope of overthrowing the existing South African government; by itself, the NP government had no hope of regaining the legitimacy it had lost in the world community. Even after the fall of apartheid, each depends (sometimes grudgingly) on the other. This is an example of the pluralist account of competing interests described above. The NP has the support of South Africans with advanced skills and capital, the top levels of the government bureaucracy and the security forces, and both local and international investors. The ANC has the support of a majority of the labor force, a majority of the population, and the international public. Each is dependent on the other. "Together they can govern the country; at loggerheads they can make the country ungovernable" (Giliomee, 1995).

Unlike in Eastern Europe, the transition to democracy in South Africa was the result of the combined actions of the government in power and the opposition. Each side had a clear constituency and distinct agenda.* Both sides opted for continuity, using existing democratic institutions to extend civil rights to disenfranchised blacks and "coloureds" and leaving existing capitalist economic institutions intact, at least for now. In the first free elections in South Africa's more than 300-year history, in April 1994, the ANC won 62 percent of the seats in Parliament and control of the cabinet. More than 90 percent of whites and blacks "voted their color" (for the party associ-

---

*There were, of course, divisions among Afrikaner and English, pro- and antiapartheid whites, as well as between the ANC, the Zulu-based Incatha Party, and others. But the broad outlines of the conflict were clear.

ated with whites or Africans). If this trend continues, South Africa is likely to become a one-party dominant state (Giliomee, 1995). Meanwhile, the government must contend with the grinding poverty that entraps most of its black citizens.

The transition to democracy is one of the leading issues in the contemporary world. As these examples suggest, this transition is never easy, and it takes different routes and produces various outcomes. The political systems in Eastern Europe or South Africa may not be democracy as we know it, but despite ongoing problems these countries have slid back into totalitarianism.

WAR: POLITICS BY ANOTHER NAME

Politics is not always pursued by peaceful means. Because it involves the struggle over power, politics always holds the potential for violence. We looked at one example—the Oklahoma City bombing—at the beginning of this chapter. A much larger pattern of political violence is **war,** the use of military means—such as organized armies and weapons—to resolve a dispute between societies or between factions within a society. War is distinguished from a police action and other forms of organized, governmental violence by its larger scale of mobilization and its greater length. Wars have shaped the boundaries, political systems, and social organization of most of the world's countries. Trying simultaneously to avoid war and to maintain readiness for war are among the priorities of nearly all governments.

In the modern world, war usually arises only when more peaceful means of engaging in political conflict and power struggles have broken down. War between modern states depends on citizen support, and citizens are unlikely to undertake violent mass conflict if they believe that other means of achieving their goals are available. They must accept that their government's or leaders' decision to wage war is legitimate. They must also identify with their state (or their side, in a civil war) and share the perception that another country or people is threatening their way of life. When they do not, modern war is difficult to wage (as the U.S. experience in Vietnam shows).

As a way for societies to resolve conflicts and assert rights, war is an ancient invention. Gwynn Dyer has written:

War is an institution as old, as complicated, and as pervasive as religion or property, and to understand why the unchanging things about it have not changed—why every state in the world constantly prepares for war, no matter what its propaganda says—we have to go back to the beginning of civilization. (1985, p. 3)

In early human societies, which were composed of kin groups or tribes, war was largely a ritual activity in which warriors confronted one another in episodic skirmishes. These conflicts were unusually contained, and few people were killed. There was simply no basis for larger-scale, all-out armed aggression, for there were few stable territorial boundaries and not much tangible property over which to fight (M. Mann, 1986). Small early wars were fought to settle disputes over debts and injuries and were usually aimed at restoring a balance that had been upset. War was a means of maintaining functional integration within societies and among societies in a region, not an occasion for one society to try to take over another.

Modern Warfare

Modern warfare began with the development of rich and settled agricultural societies and fortified cities (Giddens, 1985). Such societies had governments, boundaries, and enough wealth to tempt other peoples. These three conditions were necessary for the emergence of warfare as a rational, strategic institution—that is, as a means of getting something of value from the other side (Dyer, 1985).

Of all ancient wars, the three Punic wars between Rome and Carthage (264–146 B.C.) came the closest to total war between modern superpowers. At the height of the conflict, nearly a third of Rome's male citizens were serving in the army (a figure seldom matched in modern wars) and 10 percent of Rome's adult men were killed (Hopkins, 1978). When Rome finally defeated Carthage, the city was completely demolished; salt was ground into the earth so that the very soil could not support life. Carthaginian captives were sold into slavery, and no one lived on the site of the city for over 100 years. Thus, even though the technology of this era was primitive, it was possible to achieve a devastation not much different (except perhaps for the numbers of civilian casualties) from that which a nuclear bomb would have caused (Dyer, 1985). What kept such total destruction from being common was not so much the level of technology as social organization: If the goal of warfare was to extend an empire or demand payment of tribute, it made no sense to destroy the enemy's country.

The rise of modern states, with their centralized power structures, tighter control over their territories, and growing national integration paved the way for a new kind of social organization: citizen armies. Ancient wars were fought by professional soldiers and mercenaries, paid to defend or expand a ruler's territory; modern wars are fought by bodies of citizen soldiers, to defend their nation and way of life. The first great example was the mass mobilization of the French in 1793, which turned some 770,000 Frenchmen into soldiers in a matter of months (Dyer, 1985). Because citizen soldiers were motivated not just by money but also by a desire to defend their state, they did not need to be as tightly controlled as mercenaries did. As a result, they could be deployed in new ways. For instance, small groups of citizen soldiers could carry out raids on larger armies that occupied their lands, using their superior knowledge of the terrain, as well as the support of friendly civilians. This pattern of fighting, known as *guerrilla warfare,* is characteristic of many wars today (*guerrilla* in Spanish means "little war"). Guerrilla warfare works best against a foreign invader, when repeated raids make it increasingly costly for the foreign army to remain. (This was essentially the problem U.S. forces faced in Vietnam.)

The Industrial Revolution further transformed warfare, encouraging, for example, the development of new weapons technologies. Starting with the invention of the rifle at the end of the eighteenth century and continuing with the development of machine guns, missiles, and bombs, military technology has become more lethal and the distance between killer and killed much greater. In addition, the development of improved methods of transportation has made deployment of troops and supplies easier. Armies no longer have to live off the land they fight in. They can now bring their own provisions with them, even to remote regions of the world, in inhospitable weather conditions.

Although technology has made war "easier" and more "efficient," it has also made it more expensive.

Modern armies depend on costly weapons and great quantities of materials, which are rapidly used up in battle. The high cost of modern warfare makes any major war partly a matter of domestic production. It is no coincidence that both world wars were won by the side with superior industrial capacity (McNeill, 1982). The victors outproduced the losers and ultimately outlasted the losers' resources. When two sides are badly mismatched in their productive capacities, the superior side may simply overwhelm the enemy.

The 1990–91 war in the Persian Gulf illustrated the importance of industrial and technological power: The United States relied heavily on its superior air force to overwhelm Iraq's large army. This war also showed the importance of social organization in military struggles. The United States and its allies had to mobilize tens of thousands of soldiers and to airlift troops, weapons and other equipment, food and shelter to a distant location. When the United States attacked Iraq, it targeted communications and transport facilities, seeking to disrupt not only the functional integration of Iraq's military but also its industrial production and civilian army. The goal was both to deprive Iraq's army of supplies and to demoralize Iraq's citizens, in the hope they might overthrow dictator Saddam Hussein.

Since the collapse of the Soviet Union, the threat of large-scale conventional war has been sharply reduced. The threat of nuclear war now stems less from East–West tensions than from the fact that nuclear weapons may fall into the hands of terrorists or dictators of small and otherwise not very powerful states. The United States and other countries face a dilemma. On the one hand, they need to remain prepared for conventional war; on the other hand, they need to develop the capacity to deal with terrorism and small-scale guerrilla wars. The war in Bosnia exemplifies this (see the Global Issues/Local Consequences box earlier in this chapter). The NATO troops stationed in Bosnia to enforce peace are equipped with high-tech weapons designed primarily for conventional warfare; but the major threat to peace (and to the troops) are recurrent guerrilla and sniper attacks. Terrorism depends on its ability to disrupt routine social life. Large-scale, high-technology military action depends on social organization in both the military and in civilian social life. Both are likely to remain dangerous alternatives to conventional politics in coming years.

SUMMARY

1. Politics is the process by which people gain, use, and lose power. One type of power is the ability to exert control over others even when they resist. Another is the increased collective capacity to get things done through social organization.

2. Legitimacy is the extent to which power is recognized as valid and justified, not just by those who wield it but also by those who are subject to it. Legitimate power is known as authority. Weber distinguished three types of authority: traditional authority deriving from beliefs and practices passed down from generation to generation, charismatic authority deriving from exceptional personal qualities, and legal/rational authority deriving from law. In contrast to authority, illegitimate power is exercised without social approval and tends to involve force. Most political systems rest on the exercise of both authority and force.

3. There are different views of how power is distributed in societies. Marxists believe that in capitalist societies power is lodged in the hands of the owners of the means of production, who dominate and manipulate the workers in pursuit of their own class interests. Marxists also contend that this power distribution is inherently unstable because it generates class conflict that can lead to revolution. Power-elite theorists agree that power is monopolized by a relative few, but they maintain that this pattern is inevitable and unlikely to change. In contrast, pluralists see power as more broadly dispersed. They believe that the distribution of power is constantly shifting, as groups compete with one another for influence and as alliances are formed and broken.

4. The state is the sum of the institutions that specialize in wielding power and authority. These include the courts, police, legislatures, executive offices, the military, regulatory agencies, and other official bodies. Throughout most of history, states did not exist. States arose as rulers sought to expand their territories and commercial interests. The modern state is based upon a distinct separation of private and public lives. It also involves bureaucracy, a formal, rule-governed hierarchical organization of public servants.

5. A nation is a cultural construct that provides a shared identity to people who occupy, or seek to occupy, a geographic territory. Nationalism—the belief that people who share a common cultural identity should be self-governing—is a modern development. A source of both unity and diversity, to some extent nationalism has replaced political ideologies in contemporary struggles for power.

6. A welfare state is one that has expanded its social and governmental programs to take more responsibility for the well-being of its citizens. It not only provides assistance to the poor, elderly, and ill but also attempts to stabilize the economy and to protect citizens by regulating private enterprise. Recent attempts to cut back the welfare state (and reduce government spending) have collided with entitlements, or benefits that citizens view as rights.

7. In a democratic state, authority derives from the consent of the people. Modern states are not direct democracies but rather are representative democracies whose citizens elect public officials to represent their wishes and interests. The opposite of democracy is totalitarianism, in which government attempts to totally control citizens, the state is identified with one party, opposition to this regime is considered treason, and power is exercised arbitrarily.

8. Mass participation is the cornerstone of a democracy, represented by, however, only 55 percent of the American electorate votes. Various social factors such as age, income, and education influence who does and does not vote.

9. U.S. public officials are elected through a simple-plurality system in which the candidate with the most (electoral) votes wins. This system reinforces the American two-party structure. In some other Western nations, a proportional-vote system prevails: A party receives the same proportion of representatives as votes. Political reforms, the mass media, the high cost of campaigns, and disaffection with both Democrats and Republicans have all contributed to making American politics less party-oriented and more candidate-centered.

10. Interest groups and political action committees (PACs) seem to be gaining influence, especially as campaigns grow more expensive and technology allows candidates to reach voters and supporters directly, without a party's help.

11. Democracy depends not only on formal political institutions but also on a civil society—that is, on patterns of association that are neither organized by the government nor driven by market forces. But changes in social structure (such as women working) and new technologies have contributed to a decrease in civic engagement in the United States.

12. As more people in the world seek self-government, the transition to democracy has become a major issue. Whereas some countries have a history of on-and-off democracy, depending on the current regime, others must start from scratch. Many countries lack the institutions (a free press, independent judiciary, political parties) and cultural experience that are the foundation of democracy.

13. Since ancient times, societies have used large-scale organized violence—war—to resolve conflicts and assert their rights. Modern warfare arose with the development of settled agricultural societies and fortified cities and has along the way been transformed by technology, particularly since the start of the Industrial Revolution. Trying to avoid war and yet maintain a readiness for it are among the priorities of most governments.

REVIEW QUESTIONS

1. Define *politics, legitimacy,* and *authority* and give an example of each.

2. What are three sociological views on the structure of power in industrial capitalist societies?

3. What is the difference between a nation and a state?

4. Summarize the research on voter turnout and party preference presented in the chapter.

5. How is waging war today different from waging war fifty or 150 years ago?

CRITICAL THINKING QUESTIONS

1. When people feel that the government is not functioning very well, they often put the blame on "politics." How is this use of the term different from the sociological use?

2. How much traditional authority, charismatic authority, and legal/rational authority does the current president of the United States have?

3. "Democracy is clearly the best way to run a govern-

ment." Do you agree or disagree with this statement? Explain your answer.

4. Develop a plan, including policy or legal changes if necessary, to help increase the participation of citizens in American democracy.

5. Present an argument for increasing the number of political parties in the United States.

GLOSSARY

Authority   Power viewed as legitimate and exercised with the social approval of most individuals in a group or society.

Bureaucracy   Formal, rule-governed hierarchical organization of public servants.

Charismatic authority   A type of authority identified by Weber that derives from public recognition of exceptional personal qualities.

Civil society   Those aspects of free association that are neither controlled by the government nor driven by market forces.

Collective goods   Goods including services not easily bought and sold by individuals and so provided to citizens by the modern welfare state.

Democratic state   A state based on rule by the people or their elected representatives.

Direct democracy   Government run directly by its citizens, who gather to vote on issues.

Interest groups   Organizations created to influence political decisions that directly concern their members.

Iron law of oligarchy   According to Robert Michels, the chain of events that leads to the concentration of power in the hands of a few.

Legal/rational authority   A type of authority identified by Weber that derives from explicit laws defining the legitimate uses of power. It is vested in positions, not in individuals.

Legitimacy   The extent to which power is recognized as valid and justified by people in a social relationship and by society at large.

Nation   A group united by shared cultural bonds who usually share a state.

Nationalism   The belief that a people with a distinct culture (that is, a nation) should have their own state. Pride in one's nation is linked with this belief.

Oligarchy   Rule by a few, a narrow elite.

Pluralism   The view that a political power structure is composed of a variety of competing elites and interest groups.

Political action committees (PACs)   Organizations designed to further an interest group's political goals partly through financial support of candidates for political office.

Political party   An organization designed for gaining and holding legitimate political power.

Politics   The social process by which people gain, use, and lose power.

Power   Either (a) the ability to control people's behavior or experience even when they resist or (b) the capacity to accomplish some end.

Power elite   A coalition of military leaders, government officials, and business executives united by common interests and social background. In C. Wright Mills's view, such a coalition rules America.

Representative democracy A democratic system in which the people are not *directly* involved in making political choices, but rather elect public officials to represent their wishes and interests.

State An abstract entity composed of the political institutions and other organizations that are specialized for exercising authority within a given territory (may include welfare administration, public schools, and the like).

Totalitarianism A political system in which no opposing opinion or party is tolerated and in which the government controls many aspects of citizens' lives.

Traditional authority A type of authority identified by Weber that stems from traditional beliefs and practices passed down from generation to generation.

War The use of military means to resolve a dispute between societies or between factions within a society.

Welfare state A state that takes responsibility for the warfare of its people in such areas as health care, education, housing, social security, and working conditions.

CHAPTER 17

Global Integration and Global Inequality

"The rich get richer and the poor get poorer." Ordinarily we apply this bit of folk wisdom to individuals and families (the usual focus of research in social stratification; see Chapter 9). However, the concepts of rich and poor also apply to different communities within a country and to entire countries. Thus in New York City, midtown Manhattan is richer than the South Bronx; the state of California is richer than Arkansas; and the United States is far richer than, say, Mali or Sudan. This does not mean that there are no poor people in Manhattan, California, or the United States as a whole, or that there are no prosperous or even wealthy individuals in Mali and Sudan. But the average wealth of individuals is less in poor places, and less wealth is available for such public purposes as building schools, hospitals, and roads. Moreover, the wealth and power of European, North American, and other industrialized nations (especially Japan) have grown ("the rich get richer"), while many poor, underdeveloped countries have suffered one economic, environmental, or political crisis after another, undercutting any progress they manage to make ("the poor get poorer"). Indeed, the gap between the rich and poor countries is increasing: In 1970, the income of the richest fifth of the world's people was 30 times that of the poorest fifth; by 1989 it was 60 times more. As a result, 80 percent of the "global pie" goes to the richest fifth, while the poorest fifth are left with crumbs (1.4 percent) (U.N. Human Development Programme [U.N.D.P.], 1993).

Mali and Manhattan illustrate how uneven levels of development are in the world today. The glass and steel skyscrapers of midtown Manhattan are monuments to the rapid growth of corporate America, especially since World War II. The shops lining Fifth Avenue offer the best of everything, from toys at F.A.O. Schwarz to diamonds at Tiffany's. Apartments in midtown Manhattan sell for $1 million or more; hotel rooms rent for $300 a night and up; lunch for two at one of the better restaurants might run $100. Tourists flock to Manhattan to visit its museums and theaters and to gaze at its shop windows. Despite its problems—crime, homelessness, overcrowding—Manhattan is one of the world's centers of wealth: the Big Apple.

The nation of Mali, in West Africa, is a study in contrast. With a gross national product (GNP) of only $270 per person, it is one of the poorest countries in the world (World Bank, 1995c). The average secretary in midtown Manhattan earns more in a year than the average Malian earns in a lifetime. Life expectancy in Mali is forty-six years (compared to seventy-six in the United States); one in two children dies before the age of five years. There is only one physician for every 21,180 people (compared with one per 470 in the United States). Since 1970, Mali has been hit by two major droughts and widespread famine. More than 68 percent of adults are illiterate, and less than 20 percent of children are enrolled in school. The few young people who complete secondary school are unlikely to find jobs at home and are forced to migrate to the Ivory Coast or France, either seasonally or permanently, where they usually work in menial jobs.

Mali's current poverty contrasts with its rich history as the cradle of West African civilization (Imperato, 1989). In 1200 B.C., Mali was the cultural and technological equal of Rome. Three great empires—Ghana, Mali, and Songhay—with ministers, bureaucrats, scribes, and court musicians, thrived within its traditional borders. Strategically located on the trade routes from North Africa across the Sahara to the Guinea Coast, all three were trade empires, or "market empires" (Harrison, 1984). Their wealth derived primarily from the exchange of gold, ivory, and slaves from the south for horses, salt, beads, and cloth from the north. The kings of Ghana lived in a separate royal city, where they entertained traders from all over North Africa; the Keita dynasty of Mali ruled for more than four centuries. In the fifteenth century their fabled city of Timbuktoo was a center of Islamic scholarship as well as trans-African commerce. Being wealthy and powerful at one stage of world history, however, is no guarantee of future wealth and power.

Globalization—the flow not only of money and products, but also information (through satellite broadcasts and the Internet), greenhouse gases, and refugees across borders—is a fact of contemporary life. So is global inequality. To explain this situation, sociologists must look beyond the histories of individual nation-states, such as Mali and the United States. More than ever, nation-states are part of a *functionally integrated* global system, so that what happens in one country or region affects others. AIDS is a tragic example. Originating in remote parts of Africa, AIDS spread around the globe (in part because of transportation systems that make global travel relatively easy and common). No country is immune; however, how well a country deals with the AIDS epidemic depends on how developed its health, educational, and communications facilities are, as well as cultural factors. Such are the consequences of global inequality.

This chapter focuses primarily on the structure of global inequality, how the actions of colonial powers contributed to this structure, why independence did not lead to economic growth and political stability in many former colonies, and what strategies might help or hinder development in the future.

GLOBAL INEQUALITY: AN OVERVIEW

Each year, the World Bank collects data on "development indicators" for countries with populations of a million or more; it then ranks them in terms of per capita GNP* and groups them into low-, middle-, and high-income economies. A selection of countries from each category appears in Table 17.1. Most scientists who study global issues rely on this data, but like all measures, the World Bank rating system has limitations (Sklair, 1995).

Income-based rankings are not necessarily a measure of development. Some high-income countries—especially desert kingdoms with large oil reserves—are relatively underdeveloped. Measures of per capita GNP do not include goods and services produced outside the wage-labor market, especially women's work. In poor countries, most people grow their own food, and women bear primary responsibility for planting, harvesting, processing, and cooking—vital economic activity that is ignored in national accountings. Natural resources—not only

*GNP is a measure of a country's total economic activity, including income earned by residents through foreign investments and minus income earned by foreign investors in the domestic market.

TABLE 17.1

Levels of Development and Structural Characteristics: Basic Indicators (Selected Countries)

| | Population (Millions) Mid-1993 | Area (Thousands of Square Kilometers) | GNP PER CAPITA | | Life Expectancy at Birth (Years) 1993 | ADULT ILLITERACY (PERCENT) | |
			Dollars 1993	Average Annual Growth Rate (Percent) 1980–1993		Female 1990	Total 1990
Low-income economies	**3,092.7**	**39,093**	**380**	**3.7**	**62**	**53**	**41**
Viet Nam	71.3	332	170	..	66	16	12
Kenya	25.3	580	270	0.3	58	42	31
Mali	10.1	1,240	270	−1.0	46	76	68
Nicaragua	4.1	130	340	−5.7	67	..	..
Egypt, Arab Rep.	56.4	1,001	660	2.8	64	66	52
Middle-income economies	**1,596.3**	**62,452**	**2,480**	**0.2**	**68**	**..**	**17**
Indonesia	187.2	1,905	740	4.2	63	32	23
Bolivia	7.1	1,099	760	−0.7	60	29	23
Tunisia	8.7	164	1,720	1.2	68	44	35
Turkey	59.6	779	2,970	2.4	67	29	19
Mexico	90.0	1,958	3,610	−0.5	71	15	13
Korea, Rep.	44.1	99	7,660	8.2	71	7	*
High-income economies	**812.4**	**32,145**	**23.090**	**2.2**	**77**	**..**	**..**
Singapore	2.8	1	19,850	6.1	75	*	*
United States	257.8	9,809	24,740	1.7	76	*	*
Norway	4.3	324	25,970	2.12	77	*	*
Japan	124.5	378	31,490	3.4	80	*	*

*According to UNESCO, illiteracy less than 5 percent. (Note that .. means data not available.)

Source: World Bank, World Development Report 1995 (Oxford University Press, New York, 1995), pp. 162–163.

oil and minerals but also farmland, forests, and clean water—influence whether a country is rich or poor. "Natural wealth" can be a mixed blessing. A recent study found that countries that export natural resources are less likely to invest in industry, technology, and the knowledge and skills needed to compete in the world market (Passell, 1995a). Import/export patterns are critical. In general, rich countries import raw materials and export manufactured goods and capital; in contrast, poor countries export raw materials (and cheap labor), import manufactured goods (and often food), and depend on foreign investors and loans. As a result, poor countries are more vulnerable to fluctuations in world demand and world prices. They also receive a smaller return on their investment. For example, in 1992 it cost $5.60 to produce a pair of Nikes in Indonesia, shoes that sold for $45 to $85 a pair in the United States (Brecher and Costello, 1994).

The World Bank's social indicators include measures of education, the availability of health care, and life expectancy, but other measures of the quality of life receive little attention. One such measure is the status of women. Gender inequality is global in scope. In varying degrees, women the world over work longer hours, earn less than men (if they are paid at all), and are less likely to be professionals, managers, or administrators—much less hold political office. In too many places women still have unequal access to education and health care, face legal

Produced cheaply in less developed countries, sports shoes acquire status and high price tags through advertising. In 1992, the entire annual payroll for Nike's Indonesian factories was less than the reported $20 million Michael Jordan was paid to promote Nike.

discrimination, and are stalked by violence (from genital mutilation, to domestic violence, to war, which increasingly results in civilian casualties—mainly women and children) (U.N.D.P., 1995).

A second omission is the distribution of income *within* countries. If white South Africa were a sepa-

rate country, it would rank near the top of world economies; black South Africa, in contrast, would rank near the bottom. In terms of the UN's Human Development Index, whites in the United States would rank number 1 in the world, blacks would rank 27 (next to Luxembourg), and Hispanics would rank 32 (next to Uruguay) (U.N.D.P., 1995). National ranking obscures internal inequalities.

To correct some of these problems, the World Bank is developing new scales (Passell, 1995b). Traditional measures of the wealth of nations are based on financial capital (money available for investment) and physical capital (factories, refineries, electric plants, means of transportation, and other tangible "things" used to produce wealth). The World Bank plans to add measures of "natural capital" (including fuel and mineral deposits, fertile land, protected wilderness, and clean water, as well as an estimate of environmental degradation) and of "human and social capital" (including knowledge and skills, health, and social organization). These new measures will not simply add more information but in many cases change country rankings. For example, by old standards, which look only at current transactions, not enduring resources, Norway increased its physical capital by 10 percent a year in the late 1980s—an impressive rate of growth. However, most of this growth was offset by depletion of Norway's oil and gas reserves. By the new standards, which take account of such losses, Norway's wealth has increased only slightly. Portugal, usually considered a poor relative of Europe, has abundant farmland (natural capital) plus relatively high rates of school enrollment and health standards (human and social capital). Ranked 106 of 132 based on current measures, Portugal would move up to 41 by the new standards.

But another problem remains. Using nation-states as the basic unit of analysis in studying global issues is itself misleading (Sklair, 1995). Nation-states are not the only social actors on the global stage. First, the top 100 economies in the world include 47 corporations, each of which is wealthier than 130 countries. Alliances blur the boundaries between corporations. In the auto industry, for example, Ford owns 25 percent of Mazda; General Motors and Toyota are involved in a joint venture; General Motors owns part of a Fiat subsidiary in the United States, and Fiat, part of a Ford subsidiary; Nissan produces a Volkswagen in Japan. Increasingly, large corporations are shedding their national identities and loyalties (see Barnet and Cavanagh, 1994a; B. Harrison, 1994). Second, independent, international financial institutions—especially the General Agreement on Trade and Tariffs (GATT), the International Money Fund (IMF), and the World Bank—have the power to shape a nation's development by granting loans for some projects but not for others. Third, regional organizations—the European Union (EU); the North American Free Trade Agreement (NAFTA), linking Canada, the United States, and Mexico; the Group of Seven (G-7) industrialized nations; the Association of Southeast Asian Nations (ASEAN); and others—function almost as another layer of government (Brecher and Costello, 1994). Partly as a result of the growth of global corporations, global institutions, and regional groups, the amount of control a country's government can exercise over that country's fortunes has declined. This is particularly true in poorer countries.

THE LEGACY OF COLONIALISM AND IMPERIALISM

The less developed nations of the world are not a homogeneous group in terms of politics, economics, culture, or other common criteria. Many are one-party states or dictatorships, but some are democracies and some are constitutional monarchies. Thailand's royal family, the Chakri, is as old as the Windsors of Great Britain. Most underdeveloped countries are poor, but some have amassed great wealth, notably the oil-producing Arab nations. Some, such as Taiwan and Korea, have industrialized rapidly in recent decades and produce high-tech goods that rival those manufactured in the United States, Europe, and Japan. Nevertheless, these countries have certain characteristics in common.

One common theme is a history of domination by Western powers (Worsley, 1984). History is full of examples of large powers invading, conquering, and annexing smaller ones. Western colonialism, which began in the late fifteenth century and continued into this century, was unique in at least three respects (Harrison, 1984; Magdoff, 1982).

First, whereas earlier empires, in both the West and the East, were the result of political ambitions and the desire for power, Western colonization usually was driven by the profit motive and the individual pursuit of wealth. For example, the *conquista-*

dores were not members of royal armies, sent out to acquire the Americas for Spain and Portugal; rather, they were entrepreneurs who signed contracts with their kings and queens, used their own or their friends' wealth to buy and equip ships, hired mercenaries, and expected a share of the booty as a return on their investment. The first British and Dutch outposts in Asia and Africa were trading posts, not forts, and were the result of private enterprise, not government initiative. Only when merchants were threatened by "uncooperative" local leaders, by pirates, or by rival trading companies did the state reluctantly step in. For the most part, "the flag followed trade, rather than vice versa" (Harrison, 1984, p. 43). In some places (notably China and Japan), outright conquest never occurred; rather, Europeans used threats of invasion or brief demonstrations of military prowess to make favorable trade agreements. The exception to this pattern was Africa, which was not subjugated until the 1800s. By then so many European nations had entered the race for territory that political considerations took priority.

Second, earlier empires built on existing social and economic structures. The conquerors may have carried off slaves and treasure, but they usually left local modes of production intact, content to skim a tribute off the top. At first, European conquerors followed the traditional route of plunder—for example, carting off the gold and silver artifacts of the decimated Inca and Aztec empires. But the rise of capitalism and spread of industrialization in Europe created new demands: Factories needed raw materials, and growing urban populations needed food. To meet these demands, Europeans began to restructure the traditional economies of their colonies. Large tracts of land were bought or simply seized for plantations, and egalitarian systems of communal landholding were replaced with private property. New, commercial crops (sugar, coffee, cotton, rubber) were introduced. Slaves were abducted from Africa and "coolie" laborers imported from Asia. In addition, colonial settler societies were established in North America, Australia, and New Zealand. As the volume of their machine-made goods increased, Europeans needed new and bigger markets. Again they turned to the colonies. In some places they intentionally destroyed local industry (for example, India's textile industry) to create demand for their own manufactured goods (British cloth). In settler colonies such as the United States, local peoples were either moved onto reservations or killed off to make room for an expanding population of European farmers. Traditional rulers and systems of authority were also destroyed and replaced by Western governors and administrators, who sometimes worked with local collaborators and puppets, established Western laws and courts, and used the police and armies to enforce them. By 1914, European colonial powers directly or indirectly controlled almost 85 percent of the earth (Magdoff, 1982).

A third unique aspect of Western colonialism was "cultural imperialism" (Harrison, 1984). Earlier conquerors had usually settled into their new territories, intermarried with local peoples, and adopted many of their customs. European colonials were different, however. Some were more racist than others, but virtually all were ethnocentric (see Chapter 4). They viewed their religion, their language, and their manners and morals as innately superior to those of non-Europeans and thus made little or no effort to assimilate. Through missionary (and later, government) schools, small native elites were indoctrinated with the ways of Western culture. Others were indoctrinated by exclusion—that is, by countless daily experiences designed to make them ashamed of their own race and culture. The only route to upward social mobility in European colonies was through acceptance and imitation of white ways. To be Western in appearance and attitude meant to be modern, a goal toward which much of the world aspired (including the elites of countries that had not been colonized, such as Japan).

After World War I, European powers began to loosen their grip. Ownership of colonies was reshuffled and boundaries redrawn to suit the needs of the victors. The Communist Revolution in Russia illustrated an alternative to the capitalist/colonial system, inspiring nationalist leaders in the colonies as well as labor leaders and intellectuals in Europe and the United States. Further, the United States and Japan began to rival Great Britain and Europe as naval, industrial, and quasi-colonial powers. Japan invaded Manchuria and in 1937 began a campaign to conquer all of China. Although the United States never officially owned colonies, it established "protectorates" in Guam, Puerto Rico, the Panama Canal Zone, and Alaska and Hawaii. American imperialism (dominance and exploitation without extensive settlement) took the form of military intervention and economic infiltration, especially in Latin America and to a lesser degree the oil-producing Arab world.

After World War II, the United States emerged as the undisputed economic leader of the West. The Soviet Union consolidated its hegemony over Eastern Europe, establishing a political bloc and a largely self-contained trade network. After its own Communist Revolution in 1949, China chose an independent route, closing its borders, rejecting economic aid even from the Soviet Union (after the middle 1950s), and relying on its own resources. One former European colony after another fought for and won independence, beginning with India in 1947.

Political independence did not automatically mean economic independence, however. U.S. policy toward nationalist movements and newly independent countries depended in large part on whether they sought to remain in the world capitalist system. (Likewise, Soviet policy depended on whether the emerging nations wanted to join that country's sphere of influence.) U.S. aid to developing nations was usually geared toward making the world safe—and profitable—for multinational corporations. Advertising and marketing, reinforced by Western-style entertainment, paved the way for Western goods, from jeans and Coca-Cola to tractors and tanks. (See the Global Issues/Local Consequences box.)

In short, Western colonialism and imperialism created a global economy that was almost impossible for new nations to avoid. Once self-sufficient societies were transformed into appendages of European powers, into suppliers of raw materials and agricultural products and consumers of manufactured goods. A global division of labor was established that, with some modifications, persists today.

If independence failed to bring wealth to former colonies, neither did it bring political stability. Few are "nations" as defined in Chapter 16: one people with a common history and culture. This is particularly evident in Africa. The boundaries of today's African nations were drawn by colonial powers with little regard for the distribution of people and resources. Some countries are torn by civil war because traditional enemies were thrown together into a single nation. In colonizing Sudan, for example, the British not only joined two geographically and culturally dissimilar peoples but also widened the gap between them by encouraging Christian missionaries in the south to oppose the spread of Islam from the north. Other African countries are perpetually at odds with their neighbors either because they must compete for scarce resources or because artificial bor-

GLOBAL ISSUES/LOCAL CONSEQUENCES

Fallout from the Cold War

One of the best pieces of international news in recent decades was the end of the cold war coinciding with the collapse of the USSR. Since August 6, 1945, the world had lived with the fear of nuclear disaster. That was the date when the United States dropped the first atomic bomb on Hiroshima, Japan. For the following four decades the conflict that worried people most was between the great communist powers (especially the Soviet Union and the People's Republic of China) and the capitalist powers (especially the United States and its European allies). The end to this conflict was a cause for celebration.

But old conflicts have continuing consequences. For more than four decades, the communist countries and their allies had been amassing arsenals of nuclear weapons. So had the capitalist democracies. The end of the cold war brought an end—apparently—to the threat that these weapons would be used in a new world war, a global conflict that could easily have spelled the end of human life. But the same good news also opened the door to some bad news—that nuclear arms might go on the open market to the highest bidder. The end of the global cold war brought a new level of arms to local hot wars. Ironically, in fact, during the cold war the United States and the USSR had both tried to keep local wars from getting out of hand. Both sides had armed client states, but both had also restrained them. After 1989, the arms were still there but the restraint was reduced. The Persian Gulf War of 1990–1991 was but one of several local wars that followed.

Between 1970 and the end of the cold war, $168 billion worth of conventional (non-nuclear) weapons were transferred to the Middle East, $65 billion to Africa, $61 billion to the Far East, $50 billion to South Asia, and $44 billion to Latin America (Commission on Global Governance, 1995). As a result, the world is "armed to the teeth." During the cold war, an estimated 50 million people died in wars fought mainly in the less developed countries, often with cheap, small-caliber, mass-produced weapons provided by the two superpowers and their allies (Keegan, 1993). Arms provided by the superpowers also contributed to the persistence of military dictatorships in many less developed countries, especially in Africa. In heavily armed poor countries, wars of liberation led to oppression, not freedom, and increasing poverty, not prosperity.

The end of the cold war did not end the arms race or the spread of nuclear weapons. To the contrary, a new, potentially more dangerous arms race is taking shape (Commission on Global Governance, 1995). Estimates are that 150 kilos of weapons-grade plutonium—enough to make about fifty bombs as deadly as the one dropped on Hiroshima—are for sale to the highest bidder on the European black market (Crozier, 1994). Former Soviet nuclear scientists are available for hire. More countries (such as North Korea and Iraq) are attempting to build nuclear arsenals. More instruments of mass destruction, including biological and chemical weapons, are involved. And the arms market has expanded to include drug syndicates, organized crime, and terrorist groups.

During the cold war the arms trade was rationalized on political grounds; today it is driven by profits. As part of the logic of the cold war, both the United States and the USSR built massive military–industrial complexes that employed millions of people. Neither Russia nor the United States can afford to dismantle these operations now. Soviet-produced cars, televisions, appliances, and the like were notoriously shoddy; Russia (and other former Soviet republics) cannot compete with other developed countries on the global market for consumer goods. Thus, virtually the only high-tech products Russia has to sell are arms (Khripunov, 1994). Indeed, many see weapons export as the key to reviving the failing Russian economy. Not surprisingly, Russia is aggressively marketing arms, seeking new buyers in new regions, selling state-of-the-art technology it used to keep for itself, and even arranging barter deals (such as the sale of 18 MiG-29s to Malaysia, paid partly in palm oil). Russia is not alone. Despite the collapse of the Soviet Union and despite heated debate over cutting the federal budget, U.S. military spending has remained at cold war levels. The United States accounts for almost half of global arms exports, primarily to developing countries (Commission on Global Governance, 1995). The often-overlooked sale of light weapons is a major part of the legal (and illegal) arms trade: Automatic rifles fuel drug wars on the streets of U.S. cities, as well as civil wars in Afghanistan, Sudan, former Yugoslavia, and elsewhere (Karp, 1994).

Ending local wars may prove much harder than ending the cold war. After all, local wars have innumerable distinct local causes. Outside intervention in such local wars has not met with much success so far (Keegan, 1993). It is ironic, though, that the end to the world's biggest source of military risk—the cold war—should bring the spread of high-risk weapons into areas with so many local conflicts.

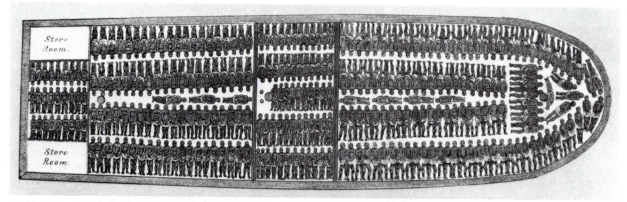

Slaves from Africa were first imported into Central and South America as a labor force after the native populations were killed, fled, or died from the diseases introduced by European conquerors. This diagram of an efficient way to load a slave ship shows the "rationality" of a system in which humans are, in fact, dehumanized.

ders divided a single tribe or cultural group into two. Some countries are landlocked, like Mali, because colonial authorities wanted to separate the interior from the coast. With many different factions vying for power, plus shortages of the expertise and capital needed to run modern economies, African governments tend to be weak. The allure of urban, semi-Western lifestyles further undermines the vestiges of traditional social organization and authority.

EXPLAINING DEVELOPMENT AND UNDERDEVELOPMENT

As is evident from a map of development such as that in Figure 17.1, most poor countries are in the tropics, where droughts and relentless heat alternate with monsoons and floods. The tropics provide an ideal environment for all manner of insects, fungi, microbes, and diseases that are hostile to humans. This is why countries in the southern hemisphere have been slow to develop—or is it? Nonsense, says the sociologist Peter Worsley (1984). The great civilizations of the ancient world—Egypt, Mesopotamia, the Indus Valley, and the Mayan and Chinese empires, as well as the kingdoms of Mali—all lay on or near the equator; when Europeans first traveled to these places, they often found civilizations far more advanced than their own.

Their underdevelopment today is not a natural condition, but an unnatural one, a social state which is the product of history; not a passive condition, but the consequence of conscious action; not something that just happened, governed by the logic of an impersonal system, but something that was done to people by other people. (Worsley, 1984, p. 3)

If actions created global inequality, what actions might help less developed countries catch up? What actions or structures block development?

Modernization Theory: Culture and Functional Integration

In the 1950s, the dominant view among sociologists and economists was **modernization theory**—the belief that most poor countries would eventually experience industrial revolutions like those that had occurred in England and the United States, and the only questions were when and how. Attention focused on identifying the social and cultural conditions that would be required for them to "take off" economically (Rostow, 1952, 1990). Poor countries, it was thought, were missing crucial prerequisites for development. They lacked the *cultural* traits—self-discipline, emphasis on savings, and devotion to hard work—that Weber attributed to the Protestant Reformation and the rise of capitalism in Europe and

North America (see Chapters 1 and 15). Poor countries also lacked functional integration, including the complex division of labor and the capacity for strong organizations that Émile Durkheim thought developed with organic solidarity (see Chapter 1). Above all, they lacked the technological and material means of production and the capitalist relations to which Karl Marx drew attention.

In an update of modernization theory, W. W. Rostow (1990) described five stages of economic growth:

Stage I: *The traditional society.* In such societies, production and technology are essentially prescientific. People tend to be fatalistic, believing that their grandchildren will have about the same options that they had.

Stage II: *The preconditions for take-off.* The most important precondition, in Rostow's view, is that people come to believe that economic progress is not only possible but necessary, whether for national dignity, individual happiness, or general welfare. In Western Europe in the seventeenth and eighteenth centuries, the emergence of Newtonian science—the belief that it is possible to understand the physical world through scientific methods and to predict and manipulate the physical environment to human advantage—was the turning point. (In non-Western societies, this view was imposed from the outside, disrupting but not replacing traditional beliefs and practices.) Equally important is the emergence of a new breed of entrepreneurs, whether in government or the private sector, who are able to mobilize capital and willing to take risks for a profit. Investments increase, especially in transportation, communications, and exportable raw materials; trade expands; banks and other institutions for managing capital are set up; and modern manufacturing plants begin to appear.

Stage III: *Take-off.* Industries expand rapidly and with them the demand for factory workers and support services. Cities grow. Agriculture is commercialized, which not only frees people for industrial work but produces the huge quantity of food required by a growing class of factory workers.

Stage IV: *The drive for maturity.* Growth is more or less steady; the country finds its niche in the global economy; and there may be a shift from heavy industry (such as steelmaking) to high-technology goods (such as electronics and chemicals).

Stage V: *The age of high mass consumption.* There is a shift from the production of durables to consumer goods. Per capita income has risen to the point where much of the population can afford more than the basics of food, clothing, and shelter. More people live in or near cities and work in offices or in skilled factory jobs. In addition to meeting consumer demand, a society may devote more resources to social welfare and security. The United States and Western Europe are in this stage now, as is Japan to a lesser degree.

Perhaps the most important contribution of modernization theory is its emphasis on culture, on the ideas and attitudes that promote savings, investment, and economic innovation (see Eisenstadt, 1973; Inkeles, 1983). Another strength is its emphasis on functional integration. Modernization theory holds that many different elements of a society must be working together for development to occur. Some countries neglected agricultural development in their rush to industrialize, with disastrous consequences. Other countries devoted too few resources to the physical infrastructure (roads, railroads, telephones, and the repair services that go with them).

In the 1950s and 1960s, policies toward poor countries were based on modernization theory (as well as political considerations). The general hypothesis was that the route out of poverty was Western-style economic and social development. Aid to poor countries was designed to help them leapfrog into the modern world, by building dams and roads, supplying tractors and fertilizers to increase agricultural output, and the like, and by building schools and providing scholarships to Western universities, especially for doctors and engineers. Underlying this aid was the assumption that all countries would (or should) follow in the footsteps of Great Britain and the United States.

Modernization theorists can point to a number of successes. Clearly, the "Little Tigers" of Asia—South Korea, Taiwan, Hong Kong, and Singapore—have taken off. India, Thailand, and Malaysia are not far behind. But the expected modernization failed to occur as hoped—and planned—in most of the world's poor countries. One explanation for this failure is dependency theory.

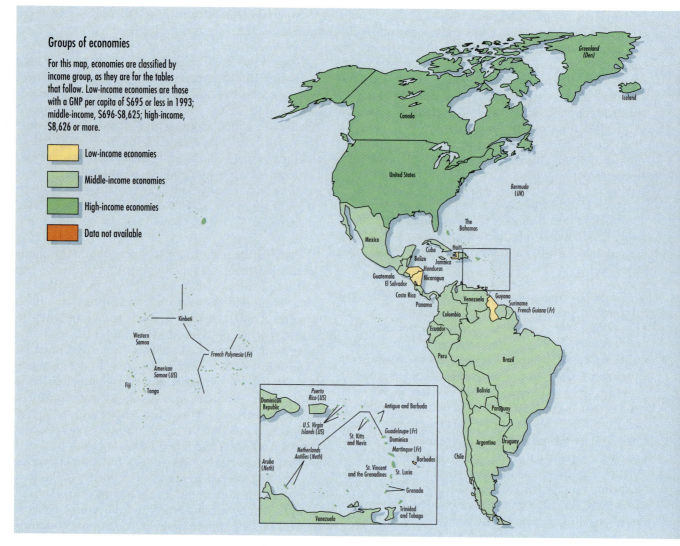

FIGURE 17.1 / A World Map of Development

The world's high-income countries lie in the northern and western hemispheres (except for the European settler countries, Australia and New Zealand, and Japan). However, the "geographical theory" of development is an extreme oversimplification. (Note that Portugal, discussed in the text, is the only "middle-income" country in Western Europe.)

Source: World Bank, *World Development Report 1995* (Oxford University Press, New York, 1995).

Dependency Theory: The Role of Power

Modernization theory tended to gloss over the role that the actions of colonial (and imperial) powers played in creating—and maintaining—global inequality. André Gunder Frank (1967, 1980), an American who spent much of his career in Latin America, was among the first to address the issue in unequal power. According to his **dependency theory,** the main reason Third World countries have failed to "take off" is that they are dependent on the already developed nations. According to this view, in buying raw materials from poor countries, building factories in their cities, hiring their citizens, sup-

porting their governments, and even providing them aid, rich nations do more harm than good.

Dependency theory applies more to the stunted growth of Latin America than to the nonexistent growth of Africa or the successful development of parts of Asia. Chile, Brazil, and Argentina, for example, all have substantial natural resources—excep-

tional resources in the case of Brazil. All three of these countries were relatively well off at the beginning of the twentieth century; indeed, Argentina was one of the ten richest countries in the world (Waisman, 1987). Moreover, all have received substantial investments from the United States and other developed countries. But all have lost economic

According to modernization theory, the road to development requires investment in large-scale projects such as highways, dams, power plants, and commercialized agriculture. For decades, loans and foreign aid to developing countries were based on this model. As a result, local needs and small-scale "cottage" industries were ignored. In some cases, the country prospered but the people did not.

ground in relation to more developed societies. None has developed a strong, modern industrial sector with a secure, capitalist middle class. And all have been politically unstable and ruled by authoritarian military governments.

One problem is that the political leaders of these (and other) **underdeveloped** countries have not been fully autonomous but instead have been dominated by their rich "allies." Their leaders might have been dictators in their own countries, but in their relations with patron countries and organizations they were dictated to. The United States and other industrial nations were selective in their assistance, giving the most aid to countries they considered friendly. Partly for economic reasons, the United States supported repressive dictators, such as Anastasio Somoza in Nicaragua and Ferdinand Marcos in the Philippines. Likewise, corporations invested only in countries they perceived as hospitable. This meant that government leaders had to be at least as attentive to the foreigners who gave them aid or did business in their country as they were to the needs and wishes of their own people. To a greater or lesser degree, they became agents of the world economy whose main role was to keep their country's workforce in line. Their power depended on allegiance to the rich countries that provided aid, as well as on cooperation with the global corporations. As a result, democracy often was put on hold.

For similar reasons, dependent development tended to slow or prevent the emergence of a strong, autonomous middle class, a precondition for development and for democracy (see Chapter 16). Typically, members of local business elites became dependent on their (often corrupt) government. For example, the government might grant a businessman a license to be the sole importer of automobiles (in exchange for a bribe or share of his profits). The importer could then reap high profits without investing much in his own country. Others became middlemen or agents for foreign-owned corporations. Instead of starting their own businesses to compete with foreign companies, they worked for those companies, selling their products or managing their plants. This dependent middle class did not create new local jobs or new domestic enterprises. Moreover, they imitated the lifestyles of foreign elites, buying imported goods and thus depriving their countries of potential investment money. The best-educated and most ambitious citizens often moved to New York, London, or other Western cities.

Even foreign aid, which obviously helps in some ways, can be a problem when countries depend on it too long. Foreign technology can throw the local economy off balance by making it dependent on foreign supplies and expertise. A new shoe factory built with American aid, for example, provides some new jobs but at the same time puts local shoemakers out of work. If the equipment in the factory breaks down, the owners have to pay for new American parts with scarce American dollars. Often no one in the country receiving aid is familiar with the machinery, so that foreign technicians have to be brought in. An additional problem is that foreign assistance often came in the form of loans. When development did not occur as planned, the receiving countries had trouble making their loan payments. The governments of richer countries often encouraged banks to lend the receiving countries still more money; the result was the current international loan crisis.

Peter Evans's classic analysis of Brazil (1979) is a case study of dependent development. In the early 1970s Brazil was widely hailed as an economic miracle, a country that had developed from little more than a huge coffee plantation into a world-class industrial state. Certain urban elites benefited from this rapid industrialization, as did rural landlords who sold produce like coffee and bananas to the United States. Most of Brazil's population did not share in this success, however. Brazil's rapid but uneven growth depended largely on partnerships the government formed with multinational corporations. In order to attract and keep foreign investment, a country has to be hospitable and dependable. Authoritarian governments are in a position to provide what multinational corporations are looking for.

What multinationals are looking for, first and foremost, is political stability. A government has to demonstrate that it is in control and will not be seriously threatened by radical political movements, militant nationalists who oppose foreign business, or powerful labor movements. The military government that came to power in Brazil in the early 1960s was able to deliver this assurance. Multinationals also need an inexpensive and docile supply of labor, which the Brazilian government ensured by systematically preventing the formation of unions. A third thing multinationals require is a developed infrastructure (transportation, communications, energy, access to raw materials). The Brazilian government met this requirement by gradually taking control of these sectors of the economy. Finally, multinationals need favorable terms that enable them to profit from their investment. The Brazilian government offered tax credits, low export fees, and minimal regulation. Brazil's economy grew steadily, but as one former president commented, "Brazil is doing well, but the people are not."

One of the costs of doing business with multinationals, and of dependent development generally, is that profits flow out of the country rather than being invested in local businesses. To attract foreign companies, wages are kept artificially low, so that most workers do not benefit from development. As a result, the gap between political and business elites and ordinary people widens, setting the stage for social unrest. Typically, the government's response is to crack down on dissenters. More repressive government leads to more unrest, in a vicious cycle. The only true winners in this situation are the global corporations, at least temporarily.

Dependency theory shows how reliance on aid and investment from rich nations (especially the United States) limited and distorted development, particularly in Latin America, which had the natural resources to make investment profitable. Support from wealthy nations benefited local elites at the expense of balanced development that would have benefited the population as a whole. Dependency theory shows how inequality is perpetuated, but how did these inequalities originate?

World Systems Theory: Global Social Structure

A third perspective on uneven development is **world systems theory.** Whereas dependency theory emphasizes power and the relations between global corporations and local elites, world systems theory emphasizes the structure of global inequality. As defined by the American sociologist Immanuel Wallerstein (1974, 1984, 1988), the modern, capitalist world system is the web of production and consumption relations that has linked poor and rich countries since the rise of capitalism. It is a global social system with a structure and logic of its own. Its main feature is that it is capitalist, and thus driven by competitive pressures, which give international trade its structure. Those countries with high levels of accumulated capital always have an edge over those with less. Rich countries have advanced technology, skilled labor forces, and other advantages. The deck is stacked against poorer countries, which cannot compete with wealthy countries in high-technology fields. The poor countries' only tactic is to keep wages as low as possible, but there are so many poor countries with cheap labor that this approach really does not offer much of an advantage.

Throughout the modern era, a system of unequal trade has moved resources from underdeveloped to developed countries. Colonialism was one factor in this process, but even ordinary trade is structured so that more rewards go to producers of industrial or high-technology goods than to those who mine or farm. Poor countries are still in the position of trying to catch up with richer, more advanced countries that had almost two centuries to develop. They cannot take the path England or the United States followed because England and the United States already block that path. The rich countries continue to reap advantages from having industrialized first.

The world system has produced a global division of labor that has three levels: the core, the periphery, and the semiperiphery. The **core nations** are the world's powerful industrial economies, which now include the United States, most of Western Europe, and Japan. The core nations provide the management and much of the essential machinery for the production of the world's goods, and they provide the home bases for global corporations. They also reap most of the profits.

Peripheral nations are countries on the edges of the world system—not because they are traditional or because they are in a transitional stage, but because they are the sellers of low-priced raw materials. Most are predominantly agricultural, depend to some degree on foreign aid, and participate in the world system only on terms set by the core nations. Many are not able to enter large-scale international trade at all, having nothing valuable to sell to the world markets. Countries like Chad, Botswana, Peru, and Guatemala are in this category. Most have experienced very little economic growth in recent years, and some have slipped backward.

Between the core and the periphery are the **semiperipheral nations,** countries that are moving up or down in the system. They are actively involved in the world system but are limited in their ability to influence it. The newly industrialized countries of Asia developed out of this group. Turkey, Mexico, and Malaysia, all of which have improved their global position in recent years, are part of the semiperiphery. A formerly powerful core country can slide down into the semiperiphery if it fails to stay competitive in the world market. Some would argue that this is happening in Great Britain today, although it may yet recover, especially as part of a more integrated Europe. Some critics (Rostow, 1990) object that the semiperiphery is a catchall category, designed to cover nations that do not fit neatly into either of the other two groups. Wallerstein (1974, 1979) counters that semiperipheral countries play a vital role in the world system, acting as a buffer between the poor countries of the periphery, which might rise up in revolt, and the rich nations of the core, which prefer the status quo. In effect, the semiperiphery is the middle class in the world system.

A country's opportunities for development, according to Wallerstein, depend largely on where it fits into the world system of capitalist trade. By and large, the core nations are able to set the terms of this trade. They control the world's currency system, shipping, communications, and markets. Further, they are in a position to trade high-priced machines and technology for raw materials, agricultural products, and low-priced goods that require little technology or skill to manufacture. The latter sell for lower prices, provide jobs for fewer people in the countries where they are produced, and are highly vulnerable to oversupply and market crashes. One problem is that too many peripheral countries are trying to produce the same sorts of goods, like sugar and rubber.

The main strategy for self-improvement by a semiperipheral country is to keep its wages very low and its rate of investment—especially domestic investment—very high (as Japan has done). The result may be policies that enrich the political and business elites of the countries but keep their masses relatively poor (as in Mexico and Korea). The payoff for the workers in such countries is deferred to the distant future. This strategy may work temporarily in countries that are endowed with high-priced natural resources (oil in Mexico's case) or in countries like Korea that have skilled workforces, a sound infrastructure, and (often) strong authoritarian governments. It does not work well when countries are torn by deep ethnic tensions produced by colonial boundaries, as in Africa.

Whereas modernization theory sees different countries as more or less developed but all moving on essentially the same path at a rate determined in part by cultural differences, world systems theory reveals the global structures that put different countries on different paths. World systems theory also helps explain why dependency theory fits Latin America best and why Asia and Africa have diverged from that model. First, countries like Argentina, Chile, and Brazil were never part of the core, even when they were relatively wealthy by world standards. They never called the shots in the world economy; their currencies were not used in international trade; and they could not dictate terms of trade to the United States or other rich countries. When there was a coup in one of these countries, world stock markets did not crash as they probably would have if a political revolution had occurred in the United States or Japan. Yet because these Latin American countries offered minerals and agriculture for export, they came to be fairly well integrated into the world system: They produce goods that are in demand on the world market (although not always at high prices); they are in-

volved with global corporations, albeit in minor roles; and they are important markets for goods produced by advanced industrial economies.

By contrast, most African nations are on the periphery, barely part of the world system. Global corporations see little reason to do business in Africa; when they do, it is usually limited to selling a few popular goods (such as Coke and Pepsi) or purchasing minerals or small amounts of agricultural products (such as coffee). Many African countries are especially vulnerable to outside influences because they have only one major export. Thus, when the world price of copper plunged in the 1970s, Zambia, dependent on copper exports, was left destitute.

Asian countries provide the main examples of the progression from peripheral to semiperipheral to core countries. Japan led the way. Japan had a strong government and a high level of cultural homogeneity (unlike Latin America and Africa) because it was not created or carved up by European colonial powers. Government support of corporations—a tradition of placing the interests of the family, group, or nation ahead of those of the individual—and accumulated wealth gave Japan a head start. Other Asian countries have followed Japan's lead (see below on Korea).

Downtown Tokyo glitters with the affluence of success in the global economy. According to world systems theory, Japan was able to move from the semi-periphery to the core of the global economy because it had the wealth and social structure to invest in coordinated development, and to put development first (for example, by keeping wages low and prices high).

The obstacles facing the poorest countries, those underdeveloped countries still on the periphery, are much greater.

AGRICULTURE: THE BASE

One of the main differences between countries at different levels of development is what proportion of the population works in agriculture and how productive that agriculture is. The world's less developed countries remain overwhelmingly agricultural, but their farmers and herders produce only a little more than they need for their own subsistence—if that. As a result, many largely agricultural countries are not able to feed their growing populations (see Chapter 18). Making agriculture more productive is one of the prerequisites for moving into the middle or upper levels of the world economy.

Americans are sentimental about this country's agricultural past, but fewer than 2 percent of

Americans are farmers today. By contrast, in most of the world's poor countries farming is by far the most common occupation—and is hardly bucolic. Most farmers are chronically poor; often they lack not only adequate food, clothing, and shelter but also such basic necessities as a pure water supply, sanitation, health care, education, and public transport (see Table 17.2). The farmers of less developed countries fall into two main groups, peasants and landless laborers.

Peasants

Peasants are small farmers who, working with family labor and simple technology, grow crops and raise livestock primarily for their own consumption (Shanin, 1990). Economically, socially, and culturally, peasants are tied to the land. They may or may not own the ground they till. In some cases the land is held by the tribe or community and parceled out to families according to need; in others it belongs to a landlord, who is owed a certain percentage of the

TABLE 17.2
Rural Poverty in Less Developed Countries

Region and Country	Rural Population as % of Total (1992)	PEOPLE IN POVERTY, % (1990)		ACCESS TO SERVICES, % (RURAL) (1988–1993)		
		Urban	Rural	Health	Safe Water	Sanitation
Sub-Saharan Africa						
Ivory Coast	58	...	...	11	51	62
Ghana	65	59	54	45	35	32
Kenya	75	...	...	40	43	35
Asia						
India	74	38	49	80	78	12
Indonesia	67	20	16	...	43	36
Malaysia	49	8	23	...	66	...
Philippines	49	40	54	74	79	62
Thailand	81	7	29	90	72	72
Latin America						
Honduras	58	74	80	56	51	57
Mexico	26	23	43	60	66	17
Panama	48	36	52	64	66	68
Peru	29	52	72	...	18	25
Venezuela	28	30	42	...	89	70

Source: U.N. Development Programme, Human Development Report 1995 (Oxford University Press, New York, 1995), table 6, pp. 166–167; table 12, pp. 178–179.

produce as rent; in still others it belongs to the state. The family household is the center of peasant life, providing for most of its members' needs. The peasant family is also embedded in a community that tends to be highly traditional and conformist. The individual's status in the community depends on his or her family's position.

In some ways, today's peasants resemble the traditional family farmers of the United States. Two main differences are that peasants usually reside in a village, rather than isolated houses, and that they own or control tiny plots of land rather than larger spreads. Indeed, many American farm families are descended from European peasants—German, Swedish, Irish—who immigrated to America in search of more land. Peasants become modern farmers when they begin to commercialize, producing crops and livestock for the marketplace first and home consumption second, and when they specialize—for example, by raising dairy cattle or growing oranges to sell and buying whatever else they need with their earnings.

Peasants are not necessarily poor. Given enough land and labor, plus good weather, they may produce a substantial surplus to sell or trade. However, most peasants live close to the edge. As an English visitor to prerevolutionary China put it, "There are districts in which the position of the rural population is that of a man standing permanently up to the neck in water, so that even a ripple is sufficient to drown him" (Tawney, in Scott, 1976, p. 1). This description still applies in many places, and it helps to explain important aspects of peasant culture. Most peasants remember times when food was so scarce that the young and the weak died, while others were reduced to eating their last livestock, or seeds for next year's crop, or food they ordinarily fed to animals. Many people are living under such conditions today. Constant uncertainty encourages what James Scott (1976) called a "subsistence ethic." On the one hand, peasants feel that everyone in the community is entitled to a minimal living, so rich peasants are expected to give to poor ones, communal land and communal work act to redistribute risks and rewards, and favors must be reciprocated. On the other hand, peasants tend to be suspicious of outsiders and innovations, clinging to methods and practices that have worked for them in the past. This can be the source of resistance to the changes that might bring economic development, like new farm techniques or population control.

The household of sixty-year-old Moumouni Ouedraogo, in a northern corner of the African nation of Burkina Faso (formerly Upper Volta), illustrates some of the problems peasants face today (Harrison, 1984). First, they often have too little land, water, fertilizer, and other resources to produce even a minimal living. When Moumouni was a child, his father's compound included twelve people; today it has thirty-four members, not counting five young men working in the Ivory Coast. Other families in the village have also expanded. But while the village population has grown, its traditional lands—hemmed in by other villages on every side—have not, so bigger families must get by with less land.

Second, peasants often farm by relatively primitive techniques. Moumouni's people traditionally practiced slash-and-burn agriculture, a method well suited to thin tropical soils. The farmer clears a patch of brush, allows the brush to dry, then sets it on fire. The ash fertilizes the soil; the tree stumps, which are left in place, help to prevent soil erosion; and crops are planted around them, using hoes and digging sticks. After two or three years, the soil is exhausted and the farmer clears another plot. The old garden is allowed to return to forest, a process that takes about fifteen years, after which it can be farmed again. This system works well for a sparse population with abundant land, but not for a growing population with limited land, as in Burkina Faso and much of Africa. Why don't Moumouni and his neighbors use more modern techniques? Even in fat years, Moumouni does not sell extra grain, but rather stores it for the inevitable lean years. Thus, he and his neighbors are hesitant to innovate. They have little margin for risk-taking, and little cash for extra supplies.

A third problem is ecological damage. Moumouni lives in the Sahel, the dry region that stretches across a dozen countries just south of the Sahara. Throughout this region overcultivation and overdrilling for water have taken their toll. Around Moumouni's village there is no ground cover—not even weeds—to soften the impact of the rain, which washes away precious topsoil, leaving hard, infertile red clay to bake in the sun. The possibility of revitalizing this moonscape seems remote. Burkina Faso is one of the places where the Sahara is slowly moving southward, forcing people and animals to migrate south and start the cycle of environmental degradation and desertification over again (see Chapter 19). Yet Moumouni is better off than some.

Landless Laborers

Paul Harrison (1984) describes a tea plantation he visited in Sri Lanka. From the air the plantation looked lush and green; on the ground, however, conditions were grim. Hundreds of Tamil tea workers lived in rows of barracks built by the British in the nineteenth century. Whole families were crowded into dank, windowless, ten-foot-square cells, sleeping on sacks spread on the cement floor. A man might earn sixty cents a day hoeing, weeding, and pruning (when there was work); his wife might make forty-five cents a day picking tea leaves. The government provided free education and health care and subsidized food prices. Even so, the tea workers could afford little beyond food.

The Tamil tea workers are part of an army of **landless laborers**—peasants who have lost the rights to land, children of landless peasants, or, in much of Latin America, Indians who formerly lived by hunting and gathering. For the most part they work as hired hands on plantations and other large farms. Because they do not own or have rights to land of their own, they always lack autonomy. This is the social-structural constant in their situation around the world. Their living conditions, however, are variable. In some cases the landowner provides decent housing, living wages, health care, schools for children, and the like, but in others the laborers are subjected to near-slave conditions. In some cases they are steadily employed, but in others they are only seasonally employed or work as day laborers.

Many landless laborers from Latin America and the Caribbean come to the United States as migrant workers. A few come illegally, but more are legal "guest workers," under contract to middlemen who supply large farms with cheap labor as needed. (Guest workers in the United States are not legally entitled to the minimum wage paid Americans.) Likewise, France employs landless laborers from Morocco and Algeria; Germany employs Turks; oil-producing Arab states hire Egyptians, Palestinians, and others; and Great Britain depends on workers from all over the Commonwealth (especially India, the West Indies, Pakistan, and Bangladesh). Often living conditions are deplorable, pay is low, and the availability of work is uncertain. But there are always workers. The steady flow of landless laborers from poor to rich countries, or from small village ar-

eas to big cities in their homelands, testifies to the degree and scope of rural poverty.

Leaving the land and joining the ranks of the landless laborers is rarely voluntary. "It means going into exile, leaving your home village, leaving the supportive network of the extended family, leaving the complex culture of status and ceremony in which you hoped to one day play your part. It is a last resort, when all else has failed" (Harrison, 1984, p. 140). People may be forced off the land for a number of reasons, including population growth; inheritance systems, which may favor older sons or divide the land into plots too small to provide a living; wars, which create refugees who are forced to accept whatever work they can get; and pestilences and droughts, which may bankrupt peasants and allow rich landowners to move in and buy (or take) their land, and then possibly hire them.

Often, landlessness is an outgrowth of colonialism. In Latin America, for example, *conquistadores* and their descendants took the best land, forcing Indians onto land too meager to farm, and thus eventually compelling them to labor on the new landlord's estate. When Indians fled or died from starvation rations and diseases from Europe for which they had no immunity, colonists imported slaves from Africa. In the nineteenth century, when slavery and indentured servitude were outlawed, the landlords introduced peonage—granting workers loans to buy food, clothes, and other necessities at inflated prices, while ensuring that they never earned enough to pay off the accumulating debt. Further, under a system that victims call "the yoke," laborers were (and in some places still are) required to provide landlords with several weeks of free labor each year. Most large landowners in Latin America today are descended from Spanish and Portuguese colonists, while those who work the land tend to be descended from local Indians and African slaves.

European colonists were not the only villains in this sad history. To escape racism in the United States, freed slaves founded a new country in Africa, Liberia. In doing so, they appropriated land from the indigenous populations (sometimes with U.S. military backing) and joined with multinational corporations to exploit the newly landless laborers. Liberia's Firestone rubber plantations were among the largest in the world until the price of rubber collapsed, leaving thousands unemployed. In 1980 indigenous Liberians staged a revolution against the "Americo-

Three phases in the process of commercialization are illustrated here. Top left: *Commercialization drives people off the land, creating landless migrant workers like these men advertising their skills in Mexico City.* Top right: *This plantation in Brazil produces coffee mainly for export and is probably owned by an international corporation.* Bottom: *This Brazilian factory packages cashews for export. These images suggest the dependency and loss of meaningful social existence that accompany the social-structural changes brought about by commercialization.*

Liberians" descended from the ex-slaves. Civil war continues to plague Liberia.

The shift from a peasant-based agricultural economy to market-driven "agribusiness" has numerous social consequences. The yield from a large mechanized and irrigated farm usually is much higher than that from hundreds of small plots, worked by hand and watered by rain. But the people who used to work the land often cannot afford to buy food produced by modern methods. Moreover, much of the food is not intended for local consumption but rather for sale on the international market.

Commercialization—the shift from village-based food production to the production of cash crops on private property—undermines self-sufficiency at both the individual and the national levels. It also increases vulnerability. Many less developed countries depend on the export of primary commodities (fuel, minerals, metals, and agricultural goods). The prices that commodities command on the global market fluctuate widely, making it difficult for developing countries to budget and plan (see Figure 17.2). Many of the less developed countries use more acres to produce fruits, vegetables, and cotton for sale to the

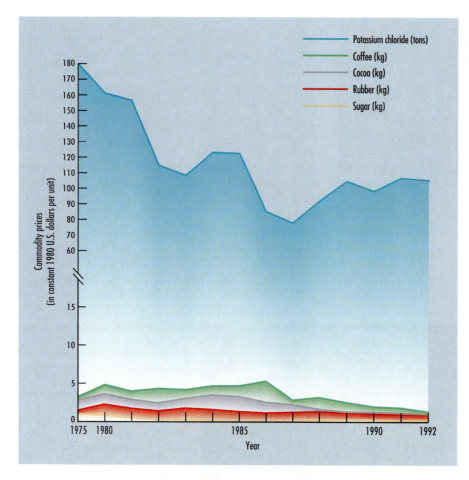

FIGURE 17.2 / World Price Fluctuations for Five Commodities

World prices for raw materials rise and fall unpredictably, making planning difficult for less developed countries that depend on these exports.

Source: World Resources Institute, *World Resources* (Oxford University Press, New York, 1994).

highly industrialized countries than to grow food for their own people. While the rich countries import luxuries (coffee, sugar, bananas), the poor agricultural countries are forced to import staples (wheat, corn, rice). Dependency on food imports and aid has increased in recent years.

Private property and commercialization tend to lead to economic polarization, widening the gap between the rich and the poor. Thus in Latin America there are the *latifundia* (huge estates) and the *minifundio* (tiny holdings, often on steep hillsides and other marginal land)—the wealthy landowners and the landless laborers or marginal peasants—and very little in between. The gap between the wealthy and everyone else is probably more extreme in Latin America than elsewhere, but it exists in Asia and Africa as well. Land reform—redistribution of large holdings to small peasants and landless laborers—is often a top priority for revolutionaries. In El Salvador, where a tiny elite controls most of the countryside,

land reform was the major issue in a twenty-year civil war. The Sandinistas, who threw Anastasio Somoza out of power in Nicaragua in 1979, were backed by landless laborers who sought land redistribution and reorganization of the ownership of the country's coffee plantations.

However, population growth tends to undercut potential gains from land reform. As populations expand, more and more land must be opened to cultivation and/or grazing, often with disastrous ecological consequences (see Chapter 18). In Brazil, the government offered landless laborers free or subsidized farms in the Amazon rain forest. However, tropical soils do not support intensive agriculture, so more and more acres of forest must be cut down each year—causing ecological problems that may affect the entire world. In much of Africa, deforestation and soil erosion are turning vast areas into deserts (as in Burkina Faso, described earlier in this chapter). Repeated famines in Africa have killed millions of people, as a single year of drought forces farmers to eat the seed grain they would have planted the next year, or the rain that follows the drought washes away the scarce fertile soil. Floods and other "natural disasters" in these places often result from agricultural development that alters the environment in unpredictable ways. Nine out of ten disaster deaths occur in the less developed countries (Sen, 1990).

INDUSTRIALIZATION AND URBANIZATION

The "great transformation"—industrialization, urbanization, and the emergence of modern societies as we know them—actually began in the countryside. Over a period of centuries, agricultural productivity in Europe expanded. Farmers opened more land to cultivation, for example by draining swamps; developed more advanced techniques, such as crop rotation, which meant land could be cultivated continuously (without fallow or "resting" periods); and improved the quality of crops and livestock through selective breeding. The result was a surplus of agri-

cultural products—and of agricultural laborers. One way rural families made up the slack was through "cottage industries." Entrepreneurs provided poor families with the raw materials to spin yarn, weave cloth, and sew garments in their own homes with their own spinning wheels and looms.

In the mid- to late eighteenth centuries, a series of inventions—beginning with the flying shuttle and culminating with the first true steam engine—transformed England's textile industry (Lenski, Lenski, and Nolan, 1991). New machines, powered by steam, vastly increased the amount of fabric workers could produce in a day. The heavy, expensive new machines and the engines to run them required entrepreneurs to make large investments and to construct buildings to hold the massive equipment. Thus the factory system was born. Factories and mill towns sprang up almost overnight in Lancaster, Yorkshire, and other places. Still an agrarian society in the mid-eighteenth century, England had become the world's first industrial society by the mid-nineteenth century.

England was also the first predominantly urban society. As increased agricultural productivity and population growth outstripped the demand for agri-

This modern day chemical and power plant in Espenhain, Germany (formerly East Germany) is reminiscent of the factories of nineteenth-century England, with their chimneys spouting industrial pollution. While industrialization creates jobs and goods, it has also led to world-wide degradation of the environment.

cultural workers, people migrated to towns and cities to seek work in factories. Not all displaced farmers found jobs; unemployment was a problem (as it has been ever since). Nor was factory work "pleasant": light and ventilation were poor, the machines were hazardous, the hours were long, and the wages were low. But people survived. Increased agricultural productivity made it possible to feed a growing population of non-farm workers, and manufacturing (and, increasingly, office work) made it possible for the new urban population to earn a living—and, over time, greatly improve their standard of living.

Clearly, new technology played a key role in the growth of manufacturing; however, the main driving force behind industrialization was trade. From the beginning of recorded history (and probably before), people have exchanged goods. Until relatively recent times most trade was local, and most families produced the food and other goods they needed for themselves. Only in the nineteenth century did trade become a primary activity. As the great social theorist Karl Polanyi put it in his classic study *The Great Transformation*, ". . . previously to our time no economy has ever existed that, even in principle, was controlled by markets" (1944, p. 43). In a "pre-market" (or premodern) economy, trade occurs face-to-face, takes the form of barter, is governed by traditions, and provides luxuries or extras. To be controlled by markets means that principles like supply and demand and activities like producing, shipping, buying, and selling become central features of social life. Markets are one of the defining features of modern societies. They link together large numbers of people who will never know each other or have any face-to-face dealings with each other. The patterns of functional integration that markets help to establish are not always fair or friendly, but they are basic to the very existence of large-scale, modern societies (Calhoun, 1992).

Societies based on large-scale markets grew rapidly from the nineteenth century on and in varying degrees have spread throughout the world. Markets have extended the boundaries of nation-states and helped to integrate the entire world in a global social and economic system. The steam-driven weaving machines of nineteenth-century England have given way to assembly-line production, new sources of energy, and computer-assisted design and manufacturing. At whatever level of technology, modern industry depends on the production of goods that can be sold widely, producing wealth for capitalists and wages for workers.

Today's less developed societies face challenges similar to those European societies faced in the nineteenth century. Industrial production—the manufacture of physical goods—is a key to creating wealth. Growing urban populations need food, housing, and jobs. They need roads to link manufacturing centers to ports, communication systems to coordinate business activities, and so on.

In other ways, though, conditions for development on the brink of the twenty-first century are different. Building an infrastructure (or technological framework) for the global market requires not just roads and ports, but expensive airports and communications satellites. Rich and technologically advanced societies are sources of aid and investment, but they are also formidable competitors. Moreover, just as new agricultural technologies reduced the need for farmers in Western Europe and (later) the United States, so today new technologies are reducing the need for industrial workers.

The result is a world in which some countries gradually "take off" into industrial and even post-industrial spheres, while other countries lack basic industry—especially to produce goods that can compete successfully in global markets. Even in countries that are growing rapidly, like Korea and Taiwan, development has exacted a cost. In their race to catch up and compete in global markets, wages have been kept low and consumption held down so that profits can be invested in further development. But their situation is better than that of other countries, like Mali, that are not developing at all. While Mali can boast a rich cultural history and international stars like singer Salif Keita, books about Mali's architecture are printed in France and Keita's CDs are manufactured in the United States.

Markets, Inequality, and Growth

Households the world over have the same basic economic goals: to meet their basic needs, improve their standard of living, minimize risk and uncertainty, and expand opportunities for their children. As things stand, opportunities to achieve these goals vary widely.

Figure 17.3 illustrates wage differences (adjusted for purchasing power) for five occupations, within

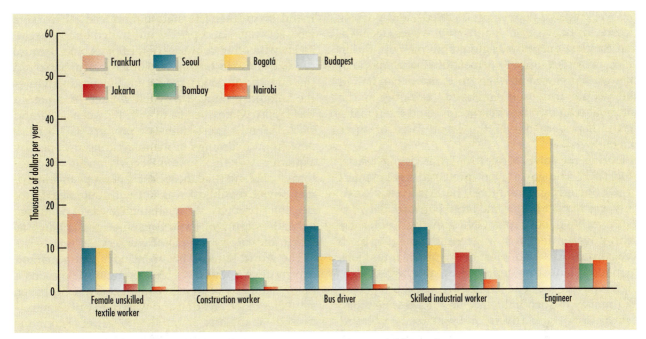

FIGURE 17.3 / *The International Wage Structure: Variations within and between Countries*

How much people earn depends not only on what they do and how much skill and training their occupation requires but also on whether they live in a high-, middle-, or low-income country.

Source: World Bank, *World Development Report 1995* (Oxford University Press, New York, 1995).

countries and across occupations. An engineer in Frankfurt, Germany, earns three times as much as an unskilled female textile worker in the same city, and fifty-six times as much as a textile worker in Nairobi, Kenya. Why? Wage differences across occupations reflect productivity, as well as supply and demand (World Bank, 1995c). The market value or "payoff" from a year spent designing a textile machine is significantly higher than the cloth produced by a worker operating that machine for a year. Moreover, the supply of highly skilled engineers is much smaller than the supply of unskilled machine operators. But why does a bus driver in Seoul, Korea, earn three times as much as a bus driver in Bombay, India? The reason is not that driving a bus in Seoul requires more skill than the same job in Bombay. To explain wage differences within occupations we must look at *economy-wide* productivity. People in Seoul are willing and able to pay more for a bus ride than are people in Bombay, many of whom cannot afford public transportation. In addition, there are more job op-

portunities (in relation to population) in Seoul than in Bombay, which means bus companies must pay drivers enough to entice them to drive a bus rather than do something else for a living.

To illustrate the importance of market economies—and the very unequal rates of growth in different countries—we can compare Ghana, Malaysia, and Poland. Ghana, in sub-Saharan Africa, was poorly integrated into global markets at the beginning of the 1960s. Like a number of former colonies, Ghana leaned toward socialism as a way of improving the domestic economy, rather than catering to the needs of international capitalist markets. The government exercised control over the domestic market, for example by setting prices for food staples and regulating the mining and timber industries. But state control of the economy and nationalization can be an invitation to corruption and domination by a small elite, as well as to inefficiency. After two decades of economic decline, a major reform program led to modest recovery, which continues today. Meanwhile, the working-age population doubled—and poverty deepened. Between 1960 and 1990, wages declined, and they are only now beginning to pick up. But in 1989, as in 1960, only 14 percent of Ghana's population was employed at wage labor; more than half of the people were self-employed, working in the informal economy, described below, and the remainder either were not in the labor force or were unemployed.

During the same period, Malaysia, in East Asia, "took off." The government protected public enterprises (including agriculture), but Malaysia's economy was market-driven and faced outward. Between 1960 and 1990, per capita GNP grew by 4 percent a year, poverty declined, wage employment tripled, and earnings doubled. Most new workers found jobs in modern industries and services, and high-skilled, higher-paying jobs opened up. Because more people had money to spend, the incomes of street vendors, hairdressers, truck drivers, and other self-employed workers also grew.

Poland's economy grew as rapidly as Malaysia's from 1959 to 1970, but for different reasons. Part of the former communist sphere in Eastern Europe, Poland's economy was a planned economy. The government moved thousands of farmers to cities and factory jobs and pushed almost as many women into the labor force. Thus industrialization was planned and orchestrated without regard to supply and de-

mand or profits. The state guaranteed all workers jobs, set wages and prices, and traded almost exclusively with other countries in the Soviet bloc. Because the size of the industrial workforce increased, so did the amount of goods produced. But productivity—the amount produced by each worker—did not. In the 1980s, wages began to fall. Between 1980 and 1992, Poland's gross domestic product (GDP) fell 9 percent and earnings in manufacturing dropped by a quarter. After the communist government was overthrown, Poland (like most Eastern European and former Soviet republics) was left with outdated factories, inferior physical capital, high levels of pollution, an undersupply of basic consumer goods (such as soap), and an oversupply of workers.

The World Bank (1995c) concludes that a market-driven development strategy brought Malaysians a rising standard of living, while government-driven strategies of job creation and wage and price controls caused Ghanaians and Poles to suffer. Economic growth not only boosts household income but also changes the employment status of workers. The proportion of self-employed agricultural and service workers declines, while the proportion of salaried workers in modern industries and services grows. This transformation paves the way for further growth by increasing opportunities for specialization, pooling risk, and creating greater income security. The search for profits encourages businesses—from fam-

A Western Digital Corporation assembly plant in Jaya, Malaysia. Like the other "Little Tigers" of Southeast Asia, Malaysia has pursued an outward-facing development strategy, courting foreign investors and providing them with skilled, disciplined workers as a way to establish a foothold in the global economy.

ily farms to large corporations—to invest in new equipment, technology, and training workers. Likewise, households increase their human capital through better health and nutrition and more schooling. The government's role is to invest in public goods, such as education and rural roads; to protect property rights; and "above all, [to] enable businesses and households to invest in themselves" (World Bank, 1995c, p. 19). In the World Bank's view, opportunities exist for countries to move from low-income to middle-income and even high-income status—if governments, businesses, and households adopt a market strategy. Global markets do not work to the equal benefit of everyone, however (see the Sociology and Public Debates box).

The World Bank data suggest that economic growth can even be adequate to compensate for rapid population growth. Between 1960 and 1990 the population of Malaysia grew faster than that in Ghana, without stopping development, while the population of Poland grew hardly at all. From a regional perspective, the growth rate of working-age populations (people who need jobs and have children to feed) is much the same worldwide, yet economic growth (measured by GDP) has been highly unequal (as shown in Figure 17.4). When economic growth

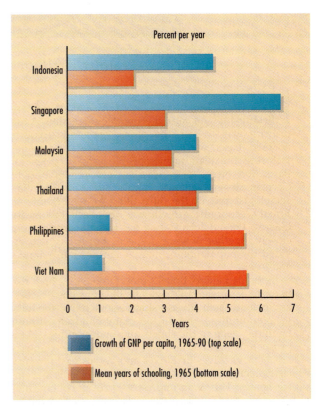

FIGURE 17.5 / Education and Development

High initial levels of schooling have not guaranteed development, even in Southeast Asia.

Source: World Bank, *World Development Report 1995* (Oxford University Press, New York, 1995).

lags behind population growth, as in Africa and in Asia not long ago, development is suppressed. But when economic growth outstrips population growth, as in Asia today, GDP and household incomes rise.

Education is necessary for development, but not sufficient (World Bank, 1995c) (see Figure 17.5). Between 1960 and 1990, worldwide enrollment in school, at all levels, increased fivefold; the proportion of literate adults in low- and middle-income countries rose from one-third to more than one-half. Why, then, has economic growth proved so elusive in many places? Education does not "pay off," for an individual or a country, unless there is a market for new skills. The Philippines, for example, has long had a higher rate of adult literacy and educational attainment than other countries in Southeast Asia, but development lagged behind education. As a result, many educated Filipinos took their skills abroad. In some places, governments have spent more on ed-

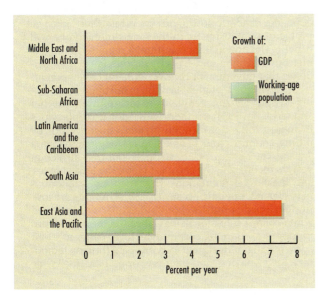

FIGURE 17.4 / Population Growth and Development

Growth in working-age population has been similar across regions, but GDP growth has not.

Source: World Bank, *World Development Report 1995* (Oxford University Press, New York, 1995).

"Global Village or Global Pillage?"

In the 1990s, Brazil emerged from years of military dictatorship and related economic stagnation. A top priority was to join the global economy. Exports boomed, based on both natural resources and manufacturing. Brazilian businesspeople jumped on jets for Paris and New York; Brazilian consumers bought German cars and Japanese stereos. But as one Brazilian sociologist put it, the only thing as remarkable as Brazil's economic growth was its social inequality (Soares, 1996). Globalization has knit the world more closely together in some respects, but it has also divided the population of many countries into winners and losers.

In Rio de Janeiro, Brazil's most famous city, high rise luxury apartment buildings line the gorgeous beaches, and behind them *favelas*—slums—stretch into the hills. Whole families—and all too many children without families—sleep in the streets and under bridges. Yet a prosperous middle class (not to mention the country's aristocracy) drives its BMWs and Volvos past the *favelas,* deeper into the hills, to spend the weekends in country homes. This is an impressively cosmopolitan middle class, reading the latest French theory and Indian literature, employed by or trading with multinational corporations, often educated partly abroad, and keeping up with trends during foreign holidays. Listening to Caetano Velso, a singer treated almost like a national treasure, some may worry romantically about globalization's effects on national culture, but all in all, the middle class is satisfied with the country's international involvements. And the masses are nervous.

> Is globalization an opportunity or a threat? Are we becoming a global village or witnessing the "pillage of the planet and its people"?

The same could be said for dozens of countries around the world, give or take some scenic geography and different levels of local cultural creativity. Globalization is clearly one of the perceived threats that drives some Russians to vote communist (or right-wing nationalist). It is part of the anxiety that fuels resurgent and violent Hindu nationalism. And this is not just a Third World story: globalization is one of the forces behind Patrick Buchanan's popularity in the recent Republican primaries in the United States. NAFTA, the North American Free Trade Agreement that links the economies of Canada, the United States, and Mexico, may spell profits for corporate leaders, but it spells competition for workers worried about their jobs.

THE DEBATE

Is globalization an opportunity or a threat? Are we becoming a global village or witnessing the "pillage of the planet and its people" (Brecher and Costello, 1994, p. 33)? On one side of the debate are those who see a free global market as the key to the economic future. As David Rockefeller of Chase Manhattan Bank put this two decades ago, "Broad human interests are being served best in economic terms where free market forces are able to transcend national boundaries" (*International Finance*, May 19, 1975; cited in Brecher and Costello, 1994, p. 15). In a competitive global market, countries will specialize in the products they make best (such as wine in Italy, sugar in Jamaica). Improved efficiency leads to lower prices. While there may be problems of adjustment, in the long run everyone will benefit. The downfall of communist regimes in the former Soviet Union and Eastern Europe is cited as evidence that government controls impede development.

Critics argue that globalization is hurting—not helping—countries and people (see, for example, Brecher and Costello, 1994). In their view, global corporations increase profits not through greater efficiency but by pitting countries and people against one another in a "race to the bottom." Undeveloped countries attract investors by offering the cheapest labor, the lowest taxes, and the fewest regulations; their national economies may expand, but only because living standards are low. In developed countries, both blue-collar workers and white-collar professionals have been laid off in record numbers as part of corporate "disinvestment" and "downsizing." Most new jobs are part-time or temporary, lower-paying, and offer few or no benefits. While some people have prospered under corporate globalization, "the majority of people in most parts of the world . . . have endured rising unemployment, falling real incomes, mass layoffs, cutbacks in public services, deteriorating working conditions, elimination of small farms and businesses, accelerating destruction of the environment, and loss of democratic control over their governments and societies" (Brecher and Costello, 1994, p. 4).

ANALYSIS

Globalization is not completely new. It has been proceeding throughout the modern capitalist era (Robertson, 1992). Global integration is already dramatic; there is no longer much possibility for any of the world's major countries to withdraw from the global economy; all are interconnected by networks of trade. Beyond this, multinational corporations operate with little respect for borders and with enterprises that employ people from dozens of different countries and sell their products even more widely. Globalization will continue, but this does not mean that there is only one form it can take. It is currently taking place in ways that place most of the power in the hands of the managers of multinational capitalist corporations, along with state elites in various countries. While state elites have the capacity to rein in corporate profit seeking (for example, by imposing pollution control standards) in developed countries they are often desperate for investment and/or so weak that this is not an effective option. At present, there is very little regulation on an international scale.

The issue is one of structure: the modern world system is organized so that political power lies mainly with the governments of states. It is within states that democracy can bring opportunities for ordinary people to participate in political decision-making. But the economy is coming more and more to be structured on an international scale, through institutions that are not within the control of any one country. An ostensibly American corporation can do business anywhere and is minimally regulated by the U.S. government in what it does overseas. U.S. environmental laws do not apply to the destruction of the Amazonian rainforest in Brazil.

Brazil can try to limit damage, but it faces an extremely tough choice: protecting the environment can limit economic opportunities—and in a democracy this can mean the government will be turned out. If Brazil—or any other country—puts too many limits on what businesses can do, they can take their investments elsewhere. Capital—the wealth behind business—can flow rapidly across national borders. Aided by computerization and global telecommunications, in fact, international capital flows now reach $1 trillion a day. In the United States, we experience aspects of this with "disinvestment," as when companies move their operations from Ohio or Michigan to Malaysia or Mexico, leaving unemployed workers and economic crises behind. Moving production processes abroad has been one important factor in the loss of more than 43 million American jobs since 1979. Of course at the same time, producing for international markets has brought many new jobs to the United States, though these do not always go to the same people. When countries compete for new investment, they gain in economic growth, but often give up power to shape its course, protect the environment and make sure working conditions are safe. Indonesia has gained jobs not just from the United States but from somewhat richer Asian countries such as Japan and Korea (where wage rates and regulations cut into corporate profits). Reebok and Nike both produce shoes there, for example. But Indonesia's minimum wage is so low—$1.30 a day—that almost 90 percent of women working full time are malnourished (*Boston Globe*, July 10, 1994). Forced to work as many as twelve hours a day, the women are housed in barracks, which they can only leave on Sundays—with a letter of permission from management. Indonesia's "corporate friendly" environment is maintained by a repressive government that delivers harsh prison sentences to union organizers and uses the army to combat strikes.

The global economy is functionally integrated. This does not mean it works to everyone's advantage, but it does mean that anything major that happens in one place or sector is connected to what happens elsewhere. Recession in North America can increase unemployment in Asia—because it cuts demand for products made by Asian workers. When fiber optic cables replace traditional copper ones in Los Angeles, the price

"Global Village or Global Pillage?" *(continued)*

of copper—produced mainly in Africa—plummets. Functional integration creates pitfalls to countries that would follow the example of others in developing their economies. For example, countries that want to develop economically have often been advised to sell minerals like copper or bauxite and agricultural goods like sugar or coffee. International export does bring in needed money, which is crucial to maintaining functional institutions locally. But, if the World Bank and other agencies are giving similar advice to many countries, or if these "primary products" are all they have to sell, this is likely to result in a glut on the market and a collapse in the prices of these basic commodities (Passell, 1995a; see Figure 17-2). The worst thing that ever happened to Cuba may not have been communism or the U.S. boycott of Cuban goods but the collapse in the price of sugar on the world market.

Culture is also shaped and challenged by global economic integration. People everywhere want to have a better standard of living for themselves or at least their children. But this does not mean that they want to see the production and distribution of culture turned into a multinational corporate project that displaces local traditions and distinctive national cultures. Most people want to preserve their own cultural identities while also getting richer. But the existing patterns of global integration make this hard. Globalization also means that media like American TV reach the whole world—encouraging desires for Western fashions (like short skirts that may offend traditional moral norms), processed foods (that are more expensive and less nutritious than locally produced meals), cigarettes, and so on. Ironically, thus, reactions against Westernization like the growth of Islamic fundamentalism are produced by the way global integration affects culture, not just by traditional cultures on their own. They are one form of global resistance to the existing structure of power and benefits in the global economy (Brecher and Costello, 1994, Ch 5).

Mentioning resistance brings up action. Obviously the global economy doesn't just happen. There are corporate executives making investment decisions and dealing with problems of labor unrest, bankers deciding whether to give loans to developing countries, government officials determining who gets aid and on what terms. Equally, people throughout the world take

action when they choose jobs, decide how much to invest in their children's educations, and vote for political leaders (where they have that option). But people also take actions of other kinds. In Chiapas, Mexico, rural rebels took up arms against the federal government partly because of the way the government was handling Mexico's integration into the global economy. Mexico was selling billions of dollars of oil and other goods, but most of the benefits were going to an entrenched, wealthy elite. That elite was seeking to integrate Mexico's economy more closely with that of the United States through the North American Free Trade Agreement (NAFTA) and the rebels saw the opening of markets as "the death certificate for the indigenous people of Mexico" (Marcos, 1994). In the United States at the same time, many workers feared that their jobs would be lost to Mexico.

Protesters sometimes hope to stop the processes of global economic integration altogether. There is little evidence that this can be done. But the directions and forms of integration can be shaped by collective action. A worldwide boycott of Nestle products in the 1980s, for example, eventually led the Swiss manufacturer to stop marketing commercial infant formula to Third World countries where it was an expensive and inferior substitute for mother's milk. Sociological analysis suggests that it is misleading to form the debate in terms of such extreme oppositions as either "free trade" or "protectionism," "globalization" or "isolationism" (Brecher and Costello, 1994). The key, rather, is to recognize that globalization is a deeply rooted long-term trend that cannot be ended without overturning the whole structure of modern economies (Calhoun, 1992). At the same time, globalization can take many forms, and citizens do have the potential to choose these forms, not just accept specific economic arrangements as though they were inevitable. Globalization combined with strong social movements (including unions) may encourage more equal—or at least broad—distribution of benefits (Rueschemeyer, Stephens, and Stephens, 1992). Without such citizen activism, globalization is more likely to foster the kind of radical inequality that besets contemporary Brazil.

ucational bureaucracies and school construction than on qualified teachers and school supplies. The number of schools and enrollments may have increased, but the quality of schooling did not. Elsewhere, governments invested more in higher education than in primary and secondary schooling. Increasing the number of doctors may be beneficial, but raising basic knowledge of health and nutrition is more so. In the more successful developing countries, education and the demand for labor have developed hand in hand.

Looking at countries or regions obscures another form of inequality in the global economy: that between men and women. One reason for gender inequality (as noted earlier) is that unpaid "women's work" is not counted—that is, it is not included in calculations of GNP and other comparative measures, nor is it valued as highly as the work men do. Whereas rates of male enrollment in school and participation in the labor force are much the same the world over, rates for women are highly variable. For example, 80 percent of Romanian women ages twenty to twenty-four work for wages, compared to a little over 40 percent of Brazilian women and less than 20 percent of Pakistani women (World Bank, 1995c). Gender inequality reflects different cultural traditions, as well as government policy.

The UN Human Development Report concludes that "no society treats its women as well as its men" (U.N.D.P., 1995, p. 75). As shown in Table 17.3, gender equality varies widely from society to society but does not depend on a country's income level. In terms of gender equality, China is ten ranks above Saudi Arabia, though its per capita income is only a fifth of Saudi Arabia's. Thailand outranks Spain, though its per capita income is less than half of Spain's. Poland is fifty ranks ahead of Syria, though their per capita incomes are the same. Scandinavia (Sweden, Norway, Finland, and Denmark) ranks highest, largely because of conscious government policy to promote gender equality. Afghanistan, Sierra Leone, Mali, Niger, and Burkina Faso are at the bottom. Women in these countries face the double disadvantage of limited opportunities generally, compounded by gender inequality. A number of developing countries rank quite high on gender equality, including Barbados, the Bahamas, Uruguay, and Thailand. Ideally, future development programs will take into account the (unpaid) work women do and make opportunities available to all working-age adults.

The Informal Sector

In many less developed countries more and more people are leaving the countryside, pushed by population growth, declining opportunities for agricultural workers, and environmental degradation and pulled by the hope of a better life.

The result has been an explosion in the size of cities in low-income countries, some of which are larger than the major cities of the industrial world. The rate of growth is also unprecedented. Estimates are that the total urban population of poor countries will grow by 2 billion, or 160,000 people per day, during the 1990s (Kasarda and Crenshaw, 1991). This is more than twice the growth rate of European and American cities at a comparable stage in their development. Even the most sophisticated traveler may be overwhelmed by the size and density of the population of Third World cities. Paul Harrison describes arriving in Calcutta during a hot, damp, evening rush hour:

> It is the nearest human thing to an ant heap, a dense sea of people washing over roads hopelessly jammed as taxis swerve round handpulled rickshaws, buses run into handcarts, pony stagecoaches and private cars and even flocks of goats fight it out for the limited space. (1984, pp. 165–166)

One result of mass migration from the country to the city is **hyperurbanization,** that is, a rate of urban growth that outstrips industrial and other forms of economic growth, leading to widespread unemployment and overburdened public services. No economy, no matter how rich, could absorb the huge, steady stream of job seekers that is flowing into these cities. No city could build houses, hospitals, and schools, pave roads and provide buses, dig sewers and lay water pipes and electric cables fast enough to keep up with this human tide. These Third World cities and nations are not rich. Except where immigration is controlled (as in some oil-producing Arab states), urban planning and budgets are overwhelmed. How do people survive? The informal economy.

A quarter to two-thirds of workers in less developed countries do not hold regular, salaried jobs. They survive through the **informal sector** of the economy (Portes and Castells, 1989). This term refers to the economic activity that takes place outside of regular employer–employee relations and government

TABLE 17.3

Gender Development,* by Selected Countries

GDI rank	Gender-related development index (GDI)	Share of earned income (%)*		Life expectancy (years) 1992		Adult literacy rate (%) 1990		Total school enrollment rate (%)		HDI rank minus GDI rank
		Female	Male	Female	Male	Female	Male	Female	Male	
Sweden	0.919	41.6	58.4	81.1	75.4	99.0	99.0	79.3	76.7	8
Finland	0.918	40.6	59.4	79.6	71.7	99.0	99.0	100.0	90.6	3
Norway	0.911	37.8	62.2	80.3	73.6	99.0	99.0	88.6	86.4	3
Denmark	0.904	39.8	60.2	78.2	72.5	99.0	99.0	85.6	82.3	10
USA	0.901	34.6	65.4	79.3	72.5	99.0	99.0	98.1	91.9	−3
Japan	0.896	33.5	66.5	82.5	76.4	99.0	99.0	76.3	78.4	−5
Canada	0.891	29.3	70.7	80.7	74.2	99.0	99.0	100.0	100.0	−8
Barbados	0.878	39.4	60.6	77.9	72.9	96.3	97.8	73.1	74.8	10
New Zealand	0.868	30.9	69.1	78.6	72.5	99.0	99.0	85.6	83.5	3
Poland	0.838	39.3	60.7	75.7	66.7	99.0	99.0	76.4	74.4	21
Hungary	0.836	39.1	60.9	73.8	64.5	99.0	99.0	66.9	66.1	19
Bahamas	0.828	28.3	71.7	77.9	68.7	97.7	98.4	76.8	71.8	−4
Uruguay	0.802	26.2	73.8	75.7	69.3	97.3	96.5	81.9	71.8	−5
Thailand	0.798	34.6	65.4	71.8	66.3	91.4	95.8	52.8	53.1	15
Spain	0.795	18.6	81.4	80.5	74.6	98.0	98.0	88.7	83.0	−26
Brazil	0.709	22.9	77.1	68.7	64.0	81.3	82.2	69.7	71.1	−1
China	0.578	31.2	68.8	70.4	66.7	70.0	88.2	51.8	58.0	7
Syrian Arab Rep.	0.571	11.3	88.7	69.2	65.2	51.6	83.6	61.5	71.4	−9
Saudi Arabia	0.514	5.3	94.7	71.4	68.4	46.3	69.9	49.3	55.0	−20
Ghana	0.460	32.7	67.3	57.8	54.2	49.0	72.9	39.0	50.6	1
Pakistan	0.360	10.1	89.9	62.6	60.6	22.3	47.8	16.3	32.6	−12
Burkina Faso	0.214	38.5	61.5	49.0	45.8	8.0	27.2	14.1	23.1	−1
Niger	0.196	39.6	60.4	48.1	44.9	5.8	19.3	10.2	18.0	3
Mali	0.195	11.8	88.2	47.6	44.4	19.6	35.2	11.1	18.9	0
Sierra Leone	0.195	26.2	73.8	40.6	37.5	15.9	42.2	22.0	33.5	0
Afghanistan	0.169	7.1	92.9	44.0	43.0	12.7	44.1	9.6	18.7	−4

*The Human Development Index (HDI) is an attempt to measure whether people lead long and healthy lives, are educated and knowledgeable, and enjoy a decent standard of living. An index of 1.0 would indicate that people in a country are achieving their full potential (none do, though some come close). The Gender-related Development Index (GDI) is the same measure, adjusted for gender inequality.

Source: U. N. Development Programme, Human Development Report 1992 (Oxford University Press, New York, 1992), table 3.1, pp. 76–77.

scrutiny and taxation. The cornerstones of the informal economy are bartering and cash deals. If you paint your brother's house and he gives you his old car in return, you are bartering and have entered the informal sector. Similarly, if you pay your car mechanic cash so that he does not have to report it on his income tax return and he gives you a lower rate, you are operating in the informal sector.

An informal sector exists in the United States and other industrial nations, but it is a relatively small part of the economy, located on the fringes. In less developed countries, however, the informal sector is central. The informal sector provides migrants from the rural areas to capital cities with goods, services, and income they could not obtain otherwise. The formal sector is out of bounds for most of the poor. They cannot afford to buy its products or use its accommodations, nor are they qualified for its jobs. The main advantage of the informal sector is that it does not require significant amounts of capital or formal schooling (see Figure 17.6 for other differences). Virtually anyone can set up shop. The formal and informal sectors are not totally separate. Street vendors and small, back-alley workshops provide goods and services for global corporations and their employees (Sklair, 1995).

One aspect of the informal sector is the *black market,* the illegal trade in stolen, untaxed, or other illegally distributed goods, drugs and other contraband, and foreign currency. The informal sector also includes restaurants and bars, barbershops and beauty shops, tailors, scribes (to help the illiterate), photographers, impromptu "factories," and all manner of repair shops, often set up in temporary quarters to serve the residents of shantytowns and slums. These activities are part of the informal sector not because they are illegal but because they are not licensed, inspected, or taxed. Shoeshiners, who need no permanent address and only a tiny investment, usually are part of the informal sector. So are many self-appointed tour guides, taxi and rickshaw drivers who operate without formal registration, domestic servants, and street vendors. The informal sector specializes in recycling used or discarded products—manufacturing sandals from old rubber tires, pots

and pans from used tin cans, and the like. Because they improvise in this way and because they dodge government regulations and fees, informal entrepreneurs can offer goods and services at prices the poor can afford; but neither their customers nor their employees (if any) receive the protection of government health standards and work safety rules. While some individuals grow rich through the informal sector, many more merely scrape by or work only sporadically.

SUCCESS STORIES: THE NEWLY INDUSTRIALIZED ASIAN COUNTRIES

In the years following colonial independence, a single goal dominated the thinking and behavior of developing nations, development agencies, and already developed countries alike. "Development, all but a few radical spirits agreed, involved following the yellow brick road painted by Western societies toward an Oz of industrialization and consumerism" (Harrison, 1983, p. 23). Yet one, two, three, and even (in Latin America) fifteen decades later, the gap between rich and poor nations is as wide as ever. Neither massive inputs of aid nor forced modernization has led to the gains expected a generation ago. The situation is not all bleak, however. Some nations have made rapid economic progress and are on the brink of graduating into the ranks of rich industrialized nations. This has not come about as easily as modernization theory predicted. It has happened more—especially in Asia—than dependency theorists expected. But as world systems theory showed, the path to development calls for a highly disciplined, often authoritarian model of social action, with high costs.

The case of South Korea illustrates one path to economic development. Occupied by the Japanese even before World War II, torn by the Korean war (1950–1953), which divided the country in half and cut off the industrial centers in the North, the Republic of Korea faced a future that looked dim. In the 1950s South Korea depended heavily on U.S. aid and imports but, after a military coup in 1961, embarked on an ambitious program of economic expansion (Griffin, 1989; Haggard, 1990). Korea focused on industrial development rather than agriculture or mining because manufacturing offered the best possibility of long-term advancement in the world system. The first factories used pirated designs to pro-

Informal

- Ease of entry
- Reliance on local resources
- Family ownership of enterprises
- Small-scale
- Labor-intensive and innovative, ad hoc technology
- Skills acquired outside the formal school system
- Unregulated and competitive markets

Formal

- Difficult to enter
- Dependence on imports
- Corporate ownership
- Large-scale
- Capital-intensive, imported technology
- Skills often acquired abroad
- Markets protected by tariffs, import, and exchange licenses

FIGURE 17.6 / Characteristics of the Formal and Informal Sectors of the Economy

Source: Peter Worsley, *The Three Worlds* (University of Chicago Press, Chicago, 1984), p. 210.

A street barber in Varanasi, India. The informal economy—improvised shops and services requiring little investment or formal training—provides a living for large segments of the populations of less developed countries.

duce parts for the international market. But Koreans soon began to produce finished goods for export, targeting industries where they could underprice core countries, such as consumer electronics, steelmaking, and shipbuilding. They deliberately diversified to avoid becoming dependent on a single export. And instead of importing technology, machinery, and products from core countries, Koreans learned how to manufacture for their own consumption. Foreign investment was tightly controlled. In most cases, only joint ventures in which Koreans were part owners were permitted, and plans included the systematic replacement of foreign technicians and managers with Koreans.

From the beginning, expansion was guided and directed by the government. One of the military government's first acts was to repossess privately owned shares in commercial banks and open two state-run financial institutions. An Economic Planning Board oversaw planning and budgeting and used loans, tax policy, and price controls to reward companies that complied with government plans and to penalize those that did not. The emphasis was on goods for the world market, and an Export Development Committee was involved in every stage of the process, from technical and design assistance to quality control, marketing, arranging visits by foreign buyers, and even packaging.

Korea's business community, like Taiwan's and to some extent Japan's, is dominated by a small number of family-owned businesses and closely held firms. This entrepreneurial elite is something like a European aristocracy, growing in part by mergers and by marrying their sons and daughters to one another. Both social ties and formal business associations serve to limit unnecessary domestic competition and in some cases to pool resources for international competition. These business families are extremely wealthy by any standard, but the distribution of income among Korea's factory workers and farmers is more equitable than in many other Third World countries. A series of land reforms created a peasant agricultural system based on owner-operated farms; Korea does not have the masses of landless agricultural laborers found elsewhere. And although factory wages are low, so is unemployment. Korea's factories are labor-intensive, employing people rather than machines where possible. In addition, the government has invested heavily in "human capital," especially through public health care and education, including a competitive university system that emphasizes science and technology. In short, Korea's success has not been a matter of luck, but one of planning. Korea is a decidedly capitalistic country, with a high level of private ownership, but its rise as an industrial power was planned and coordinated by the government, in collaboration with a more or less unified, entrepreneurial elite. In purely economic terms, the results have been spectacular. Between 1961 and 1972, Korea's total exports increased by forty times, and manufactured exports, 170 times.

The social cost of this "violent rush to modernization," however, has been an extremely repressive political regime (Wariavwalla, 1988, p. 258). In the early stages of development, authoritarian government was largely tolerated as the population sought to recover from the war and rebuild its economic foundation. However, as Korea's wealth increased while that of the average Korean did not, demonstrations against the government became more common. In response, the Korean government moved from a policy of "restricted democracy" to a state of martial law: Opposition political leaders were exiled, jailed,

and sent to work camps; peasant associations and labor unions were outlawed; and student uprisings were violently suppressed. Yet the demonstrations continue, as workers seek higher wages and better working conditions and students seek the freedoms and the voice in government that they see in other relatively rich countries. The very success of Korea's "dictatorship of development," which transformed a traditional society into an industrial one, may prove its undoing.

With the cold war over, issues of trade, money, and energy are likely to overtake security on the world's political agenda. Korea and other newly industrialized countries (especially Taiwan, Singapore, and Hong Kong) will become increasingly important, perhaps in some cases even core countries. Whether underdeveloped, peripheral countries can improve their situations, and what impact further development will have on the environment, are basic questions for the future of the whole world. In the time it takes to read this paragraph, 100 children will be born—six in industrial countries and ninety-four in developing countries. As the World Bank (1991) puts it, "No matter what the outlook in the industrial economies, the world's long-term prosperity and security—by sheer force of numbers—depend on development" (p. 157).

SUMMARY

1. Data collected each year by the World Bank provide a measure of levels of development—and the degrees of inequality—among nation-states. New proposals would go beyond income rankings to include nonwage labor (especially women's work), the distribution of income within countries, and measures of natural and of human and social capital, as well as to recognize the role of global corporations, financial institutions, and regional treaties in today's world.

2. One common thread among less developed nations is the legacy of colonialism. European colonialism (and American imperialism) was guided by the profit motive and the need for raw materials and open markets. To this end, European colonials usually replaced local leaders, reorganized local modes of production, imposed European cultural standards on local peoples, and redrew boundaries to suit their own interests. The result was a global division of labor and system of social stratification that has persisted long after former colonies achieved their political independence.

3. Sociologists have proposed three explanations of the continuing poverty in many countries: modernization theory, dependency theory, and world systems theory.

4. Modernization theory holds that development depends on certain prerequisites, especially positive cultural attitudes toward progress and willingness to invest in infrastructure.

5. Dependency theory traces the underdevelopment of poor countries to reliance on foreign governments and corporations; often such reliance benefits a small elite at the cost of long-term development of the nation itself (and thus at the cost of the majority of the population). Dependency tends to delay the emergence of democratic political institutions and social welfare programs.

6. World systems theory holds that the rise of capitalism produced a global division of labor, in which core nations are the owners and managers of the most important technology and industries, semiperipheral nations provide the middlemen and smaller factories, and peripheral countries have been left behind, except as providers of raw materials (including cheap labor).

7. In a world of high technology, poor countries are still predominantly agricultural. Most of their populations are either peasants, who use simple technology to eke a subsistence living from small plots of land, or landless laborers who have been forced off their traditional lands and now work for meager wages, often under deplorable conditions. Overpopulation and the commercialization of agriculture have undermined food self-sufficiency and caused serious environmental deterioration in many places.

8. The emergence of modern, industrial societies (beginning with England) depended on increases in agricultural productivity, technological innovations, the development of factories, and urbanization, but the defining feature of modern, industrial societies is the emergence of market economies, in which trade, wage labor, and the principles of supply and demand replace self-sufficiency.

9. Global inequality reflects the degree to which different nations and regions have developed market economies. Competition with already-developed nations and government attempts to control or circumvent market forces have impeded development in former colonies as well as in ex-communist nations.

10. Forced into the global economy on unequal terms, as exporters of natural resources and agricultural products, burdened by hyperurbanization, many less developed countries remain on the periphery of the global marketplace. Most of their citizens subsist on the informal sector, providing improvised goods and services outside the market/money economy, with no government protections, income security, or future—for themselves or their children.

11. The most hopeful signs for the future come from newly industrialized countries. South Korea, for example, has achieved rapid progress by investing heavily in industrialization geared toward the global market, limiting foreign involvement in local industry, reforming land ownership to maintain agricultural self-sufficiency, providing citizens health care and education (especially in science and technology), and maintaining strict control over business and finance—but all at the cost of a highly repressive government.

REVIEW QUESTIONS

1. Describe some of the ways conditions of life are different in the world's richest and poorest countries.

2. How did colonialism and imperialism shape the current pattern of global inequality?

3. Distinguish among modernization, dependency, and world system theories.

4. What are the major problems faced by Third World peasants?

5. What are the advantages and disadvantages of the informal sector of the economy?

6. What factors helped South Korea achieve its successful economic development?

CRITICAL THINKING QUESTIONS

1. Do you think that increasing globalization is increasing or decreasing the economic gaps between rich and poor countries? Why?

2. Do you favor modernization theory, dependency theory, or world systems theory as a basis for understanding global inequality today? Give reasons for your choice.

3. Do you think that foreign aid from the world's richer countries is a good way to help the world's poorer countries? Do you regard it as an obligation for rich countries?

4. What policies do you think would best help Third World peasants improve their situations?

5. How do the circumstances of Third World peasants and landless laborers affect citizens of the United States and other rich countries?

6. Do you think it would be easier to reduce the inequality between rich and poor countries or that between men and women? What are the biggest obstacles in each case?

GLOSSARY

Core nations   In world systems theory, the rich industrial countries that provide most of the management, financing, and machinery for global production.

Dependency theory   The view that the underdevelopment of less developed countries is due in large part to reliance on industrially advanced nations and global corporations, which have a vested interest in maintaining a stable climate for investment, regardless of the local, social, and political costs.

Hyperurbanization   A rate of urban growth that outstrips industrial and other forms of economic growth, leading to widespread unemployment and overburdened public services.

Informal sector   Economic activity that takes place outside of regular employer–employee relations and outside of regular government scrutiny and taxation.

Landless laborers   Peasants who have lost the rights to land; children of landless peasants; or peoples who formerly lived by hunting and gathering but now must work as hired hands.

Modernization theory   The view that economic development depends on cultural attitudes (and perhaps foreign aid) that promote investment in industrial enterprise and related support systems.

Peasants   Small farmers who, with family labor and simple technology, grow crops and raise livestock primarily for their own use.

Peripheral nations   In world systems theory, countries on the fringes of the global capitalist economy; the role of such countries is largely limited to providing raw materials and purchasing minor consumer goods.

Semiperipheral nations   In world systems theory, countries that actively participate in the global capitalist economy but have only limited influence on the terms and conditions of trade.

Underdevelopment   The absence of modern economic growth that characterizes less developed countries by comparison with the developed nations.

World systems theory   Immanuel Wallerstein's theory that a nation's development is determined by its place in a world system that is defined by capitalist trade and divides the world into three categories: core, peripheral, and semiperipheral nations.

CHAPTER 18

Population and the Environment

Imagine this: 1,190,431,000 (1.19 billion). That's the population of the People's Republic of China (Reddy, 1994, p. 194)—a fifth of all the world's people. With a territory only slightly larger than that of the United States (and with much less farmland), China must support a population more than four times as large.

China's population has been large for centuries, but the current huge numbers are primarily the result of government-directed modernization, which brought more food, better medical care, and improved sanitation to a land where mass epidemics and famines had been common. In the years following the Communist Revolution of 1949, birth rates stayed high and death rates fell. The most dramatic change was in child mortality: Between 1950 and 1975, the death rate for children under the age of five dropped from 266 per 1,000 live births to eighty-three *(World Resources, 1990–91)*. China's health-care system was a model for developing countries. Rather than investing scarce resources in expensive technology, the government concentrated on preventive care, especially large-scale projects to improve sanitation and inoculate children. Today a baby born in Shanghai has a better chance of surviving infancy than a child born in New York City, and life expectancy there is 75.5 years, compared with seventy-three years for whites and seventy years for nonwhites in New York City (Kristof and WuDunn, 1994).

That's the good news. The bad news is that China's population is growing at a rate that threatens to destroy the country's chances of improving or even maintaining its current standard of living. Even though China's economy is booming, just providing food and other necessities for everyone consumes most of its economic gains. Despite a record harvest in 1990, there was less to eat per person than five years earlier because there were more people (Oka,

1991). At current growth rates, China's population will increase by about 150 million in the 1990s, and all these new people will need housing and jobs in the first quarter of the twenty-first century.

Even if China had the resources to create millions upon millions of new houses and jobs, the impact on the environment would be staggering. Already what novelist Pearl Buck called "the good earth" of China is turning bad (Harrison, 1992; Smil, 1984, 1989). The area around Beijing used to be heavily wooded. Today the trees are gone, cut down for firewood by the growing population. At night a fine layer of dust, blown in from the naked hills, settles on the streets, only to be whisked into the air by the next day's traffic and mixed with the fumes from the soft coal now used for heating and cooking as well as industry. Beijing residents suffer constant respiratory problems. Deforestation is a problem throughout China, causing shortages of fuel, lumber, and paper and contributing to soil erosion and air pollution. China's Yellow River (the Huang He) gets its name from mud that runs off adjacent farmland, leaving cracks in the earth as deep as a man is tall. Because of erosion, overplanting, and housing construction, China loses more than a million acres of farmland a year (Smil, 1989). Long stretches of the Yangtze River are not only muddy but dead: Human and industrial pollution from cities along its course have killed all the fish. And industrialization is spreading from cities to small towns and suburbs, providing new jobs and products but also fouling country air and local waterways.

The pressures on China's resources could be worse, however, if vigorous efforts had not been made to check China's mushrooming population. During the nearly thirty years that revolutionary leader Mao Zedong was in power, China's population growth was largely ignored. Mao subscribed to Marx's view that so-called population problems were really symptoms of poor economic development or the unfair distribution of goods. The underlying problem, he thought, was not too many mouths, but too little food; not too many workers, but too few jobs. This was one-sided. After Mao died in 1976, China's new leaders began to pay close attention to social research showing that population growth was the root of other problems (Smil, 1990). In 1979, after an unsuccessful campaign to encourage smaller families through education, the Chinese government launched a new policy of allowing only two children per couple, in the hopes of stabilizing the population at 1.2 billion by 2001 (Moffett, 1994). By the early 1980s, the gov-

ernment realized that this was not a drastic enough action and lowered the limit to one child per family. Had the government *not* imposed strict controls, the country's population would be 240 million more than it is today—an increase equal to the entire population of the United States (Kristof and WuDunn, 1994; WuDunn, 1991a).

Under the one-child policy, a couple who plan to conceive a baby must obtain official permission in the form of a small red certificate. Otherwise, they are expected to use contraceptives or undergo sterilization, available from the state at no cost. To enforce this policy, the government has instituted a variety of incentives and penalties (Smil, 1990). Couples who have only one child receive a monthly stipend until the child is fourteen, special consideration for scarce housing, easier access to good schools, free medical care, and extra pension benefits. The pressure to conform is powerful. After one child, a woman may be required to undergo regular examinations to ensure that she has not conceived again. If she has, party officials, neighbors, and respected elders will visit her home to persuade her to have an abortion. Couples who resist this pressure and have additional children may be taxed, fined, denied land, or evicted from their homes.

Nonetheless, couples resist. Perhaps the most important reason is the desire to have at least one son to carry on the family line; a daughter becomes part of her husband's family and thus does not count as an heir. The tradition of *duo zi duo fu* (more sons, more happiness) is particularly strong in the countryside. Also encouraging rural families to resist the one-child policy are the agrarian reforms that have been instituted in China (Greenhalgh, 1990). To increase food production, the government gave peasants the opportunity to sell much of what they grew on the open market. Newly prosperous farmers were willing and able to pay stiff fines (or bribes) for additional children who could work on the family farm, and local officials were willing to look the other way. The plan was successful in increasing food production, but millions of "illegal" babies were born.

To combat violations of the one-child policy, the Chinese government, in 1983, decreed mandatory intrauterine birth-control devices (IUDs) for women who already had one child and sterilization or abortion for all couples with two or more children. Soon reports of forced abortions late in pregnancy, involuntary sterilization, and even female infanticide began to surface in the world press. How many of these actually occurred is not known, but about 10 million abortions are performed each year (Oka, 1991). Female babies are the most vulnerable. Chinese law now prohibits doctors from telling prospective parents the sex of the fetus after prenatal tests, but many will do so for a price. Females may be aborted, drowned at birth, given up for adoption, provided less food than male babies, or not taken to a doctor during a medical crisis. If the baby girl dies, her parents are legally free to try for a boy. Using data from China's 1990 census on the male-to-female ratio, demographers calculate that some 30 million females are "missing" in China (and millions more elsewhere in Asia and the Middle East). The Chinese government claims that the low proportion of females is the result of couples' not registering girls at birth so that they can obtain permission to try for a son (Kristof and WuDunn, 1994). Under international pressure the government relaxed the rules in the late 1980s, but since 1992 the use of force in birth-control programs has apparently increased (Hartmann, 1995; Kristof, 1993).

The success of China's population-control efforts depends upon the goal used in assessing them. The growth of population has certainly been slowed. The average number of live births per woman dropped from nearly 6 in the 1970s to just 2.1 in the 1990s (UN Population Fund, 1993). China alone accounts for most of the world's fertility reduction during the 1980s. But the larger goal—a stabilized population—is far from sight. Because so many children were born between 1965 and 1975 (and survived), nearly a quarter of China's population is now at or approaching childbearing age. Even if couples limit themselves to one child, the population will continue to grow at the rate of about 15 million people a year well into the twenty-first century. This is the equivalent of adding a population the size of the Netherlands every year (Smil, 1989), and it may exceed the limit of what either the economy or the environment can bear.

China's population dilemma dramatically illustrates that population data are an important way of telling a society's story. The sheer number of people **(population size)** is only part of this story. A society's **population structure**—the age, sex, education, income, occupation, marital status, race, and religion of its members—has important implications for the nature of social relationships. Traditionally, the Chinese have venerated old age in part because it was so rarely achieved. However, their population is now aging rapidly. The proportion of Chinese over age sixty-four is projected to grow from 5 percent in 1982 to 25 percent in 2050 (World Bank, 1995b). This

In France and several other northern European countries, fertility is at or below the replacement level. The governments of these nations encourage people to have children through billboards like the one above, which says: "There is more to life than sex . . . . France needs children."

changing age ratio could lead to radical change in Chinese social, economic, political, and cultural systems. At the family level, each child without siblings will have to care for two aging parents. At the national level, smaller generations of workers will have to produce goods and services for increasing numbers of retirees (a problem China shares with the United States and other developed nations). Culturally, old age may be transformed from a privilege into a problem (WuDunn, 1991b).

Likewise, **population distribution**—people's location in world regions, countries, provinces, states, cities, neighborhoods, and blocks—has far-reaching consequences. For instance, the combination of population growth and agrarian reform in China in the 1980s freed tens of millions of rural Chinese from farmwork (Smil, 1989). Some found jobs in small local factories, but at least 90 million flocked to China's already overcrowded cities (Tien, 1991). Their impact was overwhelming. Beijing's 10 million permanent residents were joined by a floating population of a million or more shoppers, peddlers, and job seekers. The city of Guangzhou had to ask for state help to cope with a deluge of 2.5 million migrants seeking jobs and shelter. Each day Shanghai's Nanjing Road is flooded with 1.5 million shoppers. Basic urban services are overloaded. In most Chinese cities the water supply is sporadic at best; air quality is poor even compared with that of Tokyo or Los Angeles; and despite a strong tradition of recycling, garbage removal has become an almost impossible task.

Population size, distribution, and concentration take on added significance for a nation's resources and environment. With a mere one-fifteenth of the world's farmland, China must feed almost a fourth of the world's people. So far it has succeeded, but only by using intensive agricultural techniques, including high levels of chemical fertilizers and pesticides. Intensive agriculture may lead to short-term gains but long-term losses, as fields are exhausted, toxic chemicals accumulate in the soil and water, and more people are forced off the land into cities.

The study of population and environment, and the interaction between the two, has moved to the forefront of the social sciences. Public-policy makers, business leaders, and ordinary citizens cannot afford to ignore the impact of human population on the global environment. Of course, population is not the only factor shaping the condition of the world's environment—the burning of fossil fuels, the use of various technologies like chlorofluorocarbons, and the choice of ways to dispose of waste all matter too. But the effect of population is basic, which is why we look at population and environment together. We begin this chapter by looking at how sociologists identify and assess changes in the size, structure, and distribution of populations. The scientific study of how births, deaths, and migration affect these aspects of populations is called **demography.** Next we consider current and future trends in the world's population, such as the general trend toward lower fertility rates with economic development and a rise in the status of women. In the third section we use the issue of food supplies to illustrate the connection between population and environment. Finally, in the last section, we look at why the planet is endangered and what can be done to halt or reverse the damage.

Each of our five key sociological concepts will be discussed in our exploration of population and environment. Because demography is among the most basic of sociological approaches to social structure, this chapter accordingly emphasizes structural dimensions of populations. But population also has a close functional relationship to other aspects of collective life such as markets (shaped by numbers of people), transport and migration (shaped by their spatial distribution), and health care and retirement (shaped by their age distribution). Population structure is also influenced by culture—factors such as

norms concerning when women should marry and/or begin childbearing. And as we saw in the case of China's one-child family policy, governments and activists may use political power in attempts to shape population and change the basic patterns of social action—starting from sex, protected or otherwise—that give rise to it.

POPULATION DYNAMICS

China is unique in its rapid success in curbing population growth; nowhere else in the world have government policies brought about such dramatic changes in so short a time (World Bank, 1995b). More often, shifts in the structure and dimensions of a population occur gradually and are barely perceptible. They are not events but rather trends that can be appreciated only in hindsight or through careful statistical analysis. This is the work of demography, which helps sociologists not only to understand the past but also to predict trends and describe the problems that may lie ahead.

The most important source of demographic data is a **census,** a periodic count of an entire population rather than a sample survey (see Chapter 2). Commonly, a census also describes the regional composition and distribution of people according to their age, family status, ethnic origins, skills, employment, incomes, and other characteristics. A census provides the basis for doing economic analyses, setting the boundaries of electoral districts, and determining the need for family planning. The 1990 census of China was the largest ever taken. Even tallying the much smaller U.S. population is a major operation.

The U.S. Census

Article I of the U.S. Constitution requires that the population of the United States be counted every ten years. The 1990 census was a $2.5 billion undertaking, temporarily employing some 200,000 "enumerators," or census takers. Preparation is already under way for the census to be taken in the year 2000. Much rides on the results. Seats in the House of Representatives are based on census figures, which means that states (and political parties) may gain or lose power depending on the results. Every year some $40 billion in federal funds is distributed among states, counties, and cities on the basis of census figures. A minor miscount (one or two missing blocks or large apartment buildings) could cost a local program thousands of dollars. Governors and mayors, school boards and community services, political pollsters and news organizations, corporations and advertisers—all employ census data for planning, marketing, and forecasting consumer or client demand.

Here is how the U.S. census works. In May the Census Bureau mails forms to every address on its master list. This list is based on the bureau's own records, supplemented by commercial mailing lists and triple-checked by postal workers, bureau employees, and local officials. In 1990, the list included some 106 million residences. Not everyone on this list responds, however. In 1990, the return rate was a disappointing 64 percent. In April, census workers set out to visit each of the 37 million residences from which they did not get a reply (*Science*, May 10, 1990). In most cases, they are able to interview the residents directly, but in others they are forced to rely on secondhand data from neighbors, postal workers, or building superintendents. For the 1990 census, data on more than 7 million households were based on such hearsay (*New York Times*, February 23, 1991, p. A10). The 1990 census also included "S night" (*S* stands for *street* and *shelter*), on which census workers attempted to interview and count the homeless, and "T night" (*T* is for *transients*), on which they tacked census questionnaires on the doors of 70,000 hotel and motel rooms. Information from all these questionnaires is fed into computers programmed to cross-check for such errors as double filing and to spot implausible data, such as individuals over the age of one hundred thirty (Gleik, 1990).

Inevitably, the census is controversial. Actually counting every man, woman, and child in the population is impossible, and both people and computers make mistakes. Most observers agree that the census undercounts the poor, the young, minorities, immigrants, and males, all of whom tend to be mobile and wary of government officials asking questions. This in turn hurts both the cities and states where these groups are concentrated and the Democrats, for whom they tend to vote. When New York and fourteen other cities sued for a recount after the 1990 census, the Commerce Department (which oversees the census) agreed to check its results by a postcensus sampling. This survey suggested that the census may have missed 4 million to 6 million people, but other studies indicated the opposite (*New York Times*, October 17, 1990; April 19, 1991). Although a margin of error between 4 million and 6 million is not insignificant, it actually suggests a high level of accuracy for such a large survey. A count of 250 million, plus or minus 4 million, is accurate within 2 percent—a fairly narrow "confidence interval." What concerns researchers most is that those not counted may be concentrated among certain categories of people.

Regardless of its limitations, census data offer the most detailed and accurate picture available of the country's people. Even if the census is flawed, it reveals patterns and trends that might otherwise be overlooked (see Figure 18.1). Because it can change the way we see ourselves as a nation, the census is itself a historic event.

Assessing Population Change

Change in the overall numbers of a population is caused by a combination of three variables: fertility (births), mortality (deaths), and migration (movement into or out of an area). Demographers focus on all three of these factors in assessing why particular populations shrink or grow.

Fertility

The crude birth rate is the number of births per 1,000 people during a given year. In 1947, at the beginning of the baby boom, the crude birth rate in the United States was about twenty-seven per 1,000. In 1975, by contrast, it was down to 14.6 per 1,000. Though useful for some purposes, the crude birth rate is not a reliable basis for long-term projections or analysis. For this we need the **total fertility rate** (often referred to simply as TFR, or *fertility*). This is the average number of births a woman will have in her lifetime.

The total fertility rate in the United States hit a peak of 3.77 in 1957 and then dropped to 1.77 in the bicentennial year of 1976. This "baby bust" was largely the result of delayed childbearing: Many baby boomers postponed starting families from their twenties to their thirties. When they began having babies in the mid-1980s, the fertility rate climbed to just short of 2.1 in 1990, then declined slightly again (*Statistical Abstract of the United States*, annual). Demographers refer to a fertility level of 2.1 as the **replacement rate,** or the rate at which a population will remain stable (in the absence of immigration). In other words, given the loss of some children to diseases and accidents, it takes about 2.1 births for each

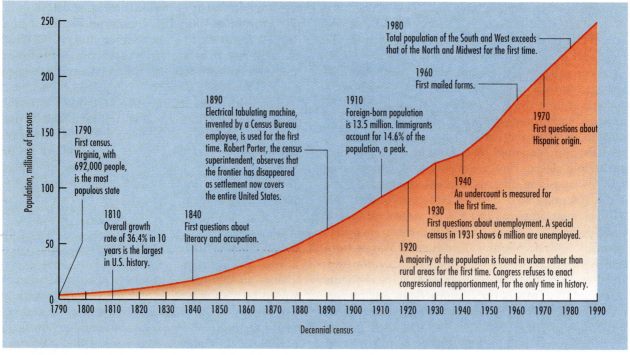

FIGURE 18.1 / Resident Population of the United States at Each Census, 1790–1990

In the 200-year history of the United States there have been twenty-one censuses, or efforts to count all the inhabitants of our country. These censuses have revealed important trends, such as the shift from rural to urban living, the changing ethnic composition of our people, and the sizable migrations from the North to the West and the South.

Sources: *New York Times*, April 1, 1990, p. 27; U.S. Bureau of the Census, *Statistical Abstract of the United States, 1982–1983*, Washington, D.C., table 1.

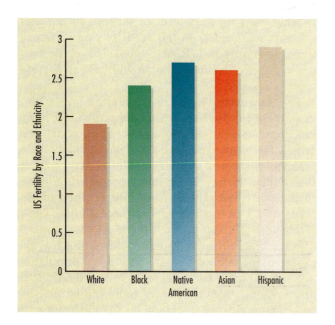

FIGURE 18.2 / U.S. Fertility by Race and Ethnicity

In the U.S. population overall, the total fertility rate, or average number of births per woman, is just below the replacement level of 2.1. This is the level needed to keep the population stable in the absence of immigration. However, the fertility rate among different ethnic groups varies significantly, from a low of 1.9 among white Americans to a high of 2.9 among Hispanics. This relatively high Hispanic fertility rate, coupled with continuing Hispanic immigration, explains why Hispanics are expected to surpass African-Americans soon as the country's largest ethnic minority.

Source: U.S. Bureau of the Census, *Statistical Abstract of the United States*, 1994, Washington, D.C., p. 78.

set of parents to "replace" themselves without adding to the population. Overall, the U.S. fertility rate is just below this level, but the fertility rates of groups within the population vary a great deal (see Figure 18.2). Compared to the rates of other high-income countries, the U.S. fertility rate is relatively high. The average for the world's rich countries is 1.7. Will the United States move in this direction? There is likely to be a decline in the crude birth rate as the social structure of our population changes when the baby boom generation moves beyond childbearing age, but fertility rates depend in part on social action: What size families will the next generation's potential parents decide to have?

Overall, the trend in the United States has been toward smaller families. At the turn of the century, most Americans preferred a family of three or more children. Nowadays a two-child family is the most commonly expressed ideal. This cultural change has had a predictable effect on fertility patterns. Except for the baby boom and the recent "baby boomlet," birth and fertility rates in the United States have been declining more or less steadily, as we described in Chapter 11 (see also Cherlin, 1995). The pattern of the decline has varied according to socioeconomic status. Birth rates dropped first in upper- and middle-class families and later in poorer families. Also, the white birth rate began declining earlier than did that of African-Americans. The overall black birth rate is now declining, but socioeconomic stratification is at work here, too: Middle-class black families have fewer children than middle-class whites, but poor blacks have more children than poor whites. Moreover, as Figure 18.2 shows, Hispanic and Asian birth rates still are much higher than white or black rates. Even so, the total U.S. fertility rate today is just below the replacement level. This is one reason the average age of the U.S. population is rising. There are not enough new babies to counteract the effects of the huge baby boom generation now in middle age and growing older.

Figure 18.3 shows fertility rates around the world. Fertility in developed countries, such as the United States, is relatively low compared with that of the

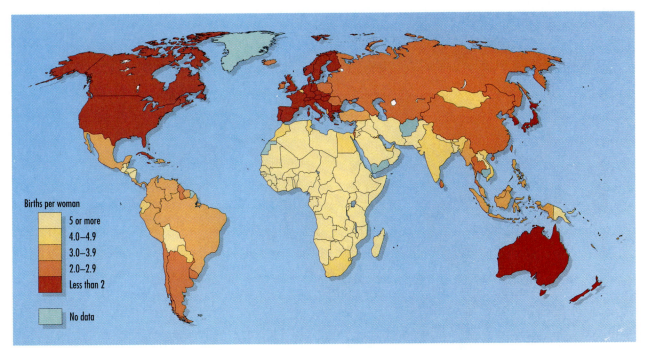

Births per woman

- 5 or more
- 4.0–4.9
- 3.0–3.9
- 2.0–2.9
- Less than 2

- No data

FIGURE 18.3 / World Fertility Rates

There are very large differences in fertility rates around the world. The United States, Canada, Western Europe, and Australia have total fertility rates at or below the replacement level of 2.1, so their populations are roughly holding steady, or growing relatively slowly due to immigration. In contrast, countries in Africa and the Middle East have fertility rates of 4 to 5 or more, enough to cause rapid growth in population, even with death rates that exceed those of developed nations.

Source: *The World Bank Atlas 1990* (World Bank, Washington, D.C., 1990), pp. 22–23.

rest of the world (especially the least developed countries). This is a point we will return to later.

Mortality

The crude death rate is the number of deaths per 1,000 people during a given year. In 1994, there were just over 2.1 million deaths in the United States, for a rate of nine deaths per 1,000 (U.S. Department of Health and Human Services, 1995a, p. 1). The *number* of people who die is not particularly revealing, however, because everyone dies sooner or later. More important are *age-adjusted mortality rates.*

The **infant mortality rate** is the number of deaths among infants under one year of age per 1,000 live births in a given year. It is widely used as a measure of the economic and social development and quality of life in a country. In 1993, there were 8.6 infant deaths per 1,000 live births in the United States, the lowest rate ever recorded in this country. Even so, this rate is higher than in most other developed nations. Japan has the lowest infant mortality rate in

the world (4 per 1,000 live births), followed by Sweden and Finland (5), and Taiwan and Switzerland (6) (World Bank, 1995b). Infant death rates in this country are much higher among blacks (15.1) than among whites (7.3); and infant mortality rates are even higher in our country's poorest neighborhoods, both rural and inner-city. Figure 18.4 shows infant mortality rates around the world.

Life span, the maximum number of years human beings can live, has not changed much over the centuries. Eighty years is still a full life, as it was in biblical times, and twenty years past one hundred is still the maximum. What has changed is the number of people actually living to very old ages. This increase is producing a rise in **life expectancy,** the number of years of life remaining, on average, for an individual of a given age. Data on life expectancies are used, for example, by insurance companies in calculating what level of premiums they should charge people of different ages. The life expectancy of people born in industrialized countries today averages about seventy-five years. In the less developed world, the life

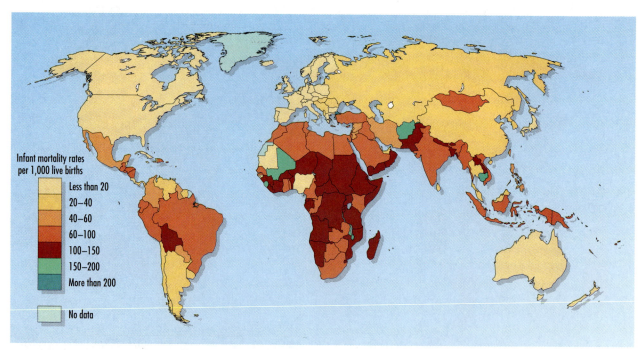

Infant mortality rates
per 1,000 live births

- Less than 20
- 20–40
- 40–60
- 60–100
- 100–150
- 150–200
- More than 200

- No data

FIGURE 18.4 / World Infant Mortality Rates

Although the United States has a higher infant mortality rate than many other developed nations, the incidence of death among American babies is much lower than in the Third World. Throughout much of Africa, the Middle East, India, and East Asia, the death of a baby is a fairly common occurrence, striking about 10 percent of all the children born.

Source: United Nations Population Fund, 1995. *Concise Report on the World Population Situation in 1995*, New York.

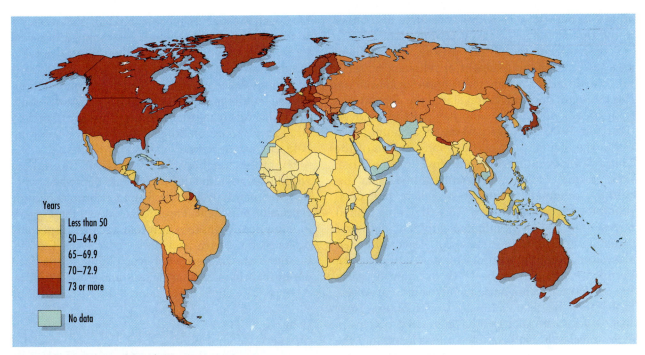

FIGURE 18.5 / World Life Expectancy

Not surprisingly, given their higher rates of infant mortality and their generally poorer nutrition and health care, people in Third World countries have significantly shorter life expectancies than people in highly developed nations do. Whereas in the United States, Canada, Western Europe, Australia, and Japan people expect to live at least into their seventies, there are a dozen or so countries in Africa where life expectancy is less than age fifty.

Source: *The World Bank Atlas 1990* (World Bank, Washington, D.C., 1990), pp. 20–21.

expectancy is only sixty-two years. White females can anticipate living the longest, almost eighty years; nonwhite women can expect to live slightly more than seventy-five years. Men have shorter life expectancies than do women: White males can expect to live seventy-two years and nonwhite males about sixty-five years. Figure 18.5 shows the differences in life expectancy at birth for various regions of the world. Life expectancy is still significantly shorter in developing countries but is increasing rapidly.

One of the reasons for increased life expectancy in the United States is the decline in deaths caused by infectious diseases, which means that more infants and children survive into adulthood. Accidents remain a major killer of young adults, but the rate of fatal accidents is also declining. Increasingly, Americans are dying of diseases and conditions that strike *later* in life, especially heart disease, cancer, and strokes. The main reason that cancer rates have risen in this country, ironically, is that Americans are living longer (see Chapter 14).

Of all the demographic variables, changes in mortality have had the strongest impact on the demographic history of the human population. Fertility rates have remained constant and even declined in the Third World, but death rates have plummeted in most countries. Today's global population explosion results more from successful death control than from lack of birth control (Harrison, 1992; Hauchler and Kennedy, 1994).

Migration

The movement of people from one place to another is measured by **migration** rates. The **net migration rate** is the difference between the number of people who leave and those who arrive each year, per 1,000 people. **Emigration** is migration *outward* from a population; **immigration** is migration *into* a population. These terms are usually used to refer to international migration. But **internal migration**—movement within a country, such as from one state to another in the United States—is also very important.

People migrate for various reasons, among them natural disasters, government or religious persecution, the desire for adventure or improvement in life chances, and, once migration starts, the desire to be with friends and family who have already moved (Petersen, 1975). All these reasons have brought people to the United States. The potato famine of the 1840s—a natural disaster—started a wave of Irish immigration. Violent anti-Semitism in Russia (including organized expulsions called pogroms) prompted many Russian Jews to settle in the United States in the late nineteenth and early twentieth centuries. The desire for economic betterment attracted 6 million immigrants from Southern and Eastern Europe by 1910. From the 1970s through the early 1990s, political events caused many Southeast Asians to flee their homelands for the United States. Their economic success, along with continued problems in their homelands, has prompted others to attempt the same migration, although it has become more difficult as the United States has raised its barriers against immigration.

Immigration has always been a major source of growth and diversity for the United States, as well as of intergroup tension and other problems (Waldinger, 1996). Since 1820 more than 50 million people have come to live in the United States, including some 3 million slaves who came from Africa against their will. Immigrants accounted for at least a third of this country's population growth in the 1980s and early 1990s. High birth rates among immigrants were partly responsible for the baby "boomlet" of the late 1980s. Immigrants have also influenced the distribution of population: Whereas native-born Americans have been moving from the North and East to the South and West, many immigrants have settled in older industrial cities, providing "new blood" to these urban economies (Suro, 1990). One of the major impacts of immigration is change in the ethnic composition of the U.S. population. Both Asian and Hispanic populations are growing rapidly. Indeed, sometime in the early twenty-first century, the Hispanic population will probably overtake the African-American population as the largest minority group in the United States.

Recently, immigration has brought similar changes to Europe, to the dismay of many nationalists (Brubaker, 1992; Enzenberger, 1994). While the United States is a society of relatively recent settlers and continuous immigration, European countries have seen themselves more as senders than receivers of immigrants. This situation has changed in recent years, often breeding anger and resentment toward the new arrivals. For many Europeans, it has come as a shock to see television news of Germans storming the buildings where Southeast Asian refugees are housed, French youth attacking mosques built by Arab immigrants, or British "skinheads" beating up Pakistani immigrants.

Migration has been a major factor throughout world history. In the turbulent years of the late twentieth century, however, *forced* migration has become especially prevalent. Figure 18.6 shows the exploding number of refugees in recent decades, especially in Asia and Africa and most recently in Europe. Refugees are created whenever people are pushed out of their home countries by some crisis. Wars, re-

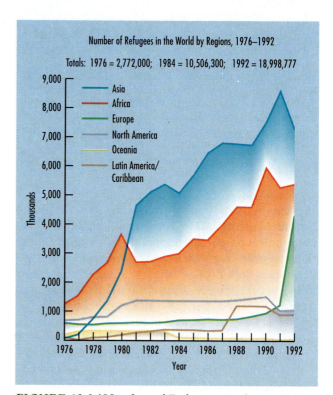

FIGURE 18.6 / Number of Refugees in the World by Regions, 1976–1992

Between 1976 and 1992 the total number of refugees in the world increased nearly sevenfold—from about 2.7 million to almost 19 million. National and international organizations are unequipped to handle this huge explosion of displaced people in search of a new home.

Source: Ingomar Hauchler and Paul M. Kennedy, *Global Trends: The World Almanac of Development and Peace* (Continuum, New York, 1994), p. 123 (based on U.N. High Commission for Refugees, annual statistics).

pressive dictatorships, genocidal ethnic clashes, and environmental catastrophes all produce refugees. In the mid-1990s, for example, genocide and ethnic conflict between Hutu and Tutsi populations in the central African countries of Burundi and Rwanda repeatedly drove millions of refugees into neighboring countries like Zaire. Refugees suffer tremendous hardships, often living in makeshift camps in countries that are already poor and have few resources, such as health care and food, for their own citizens. Receiving refugees can be a huge burden on an underdeveloped country, yet most have borne this burden with generosity. The United Nations High Commission for Refugees helps to coordinate assistance and eventual repatriation efforts. While most refugees move into neighboring countries, a few (usually the more educated) are able to move longer distances. Among the developed countries, the United States, Canada, Australia, and the Scandinavian countries have traditionally set relatively generous limits on the numbers of refugees they will accept.

Age Structure

The impact of the birth, death, and migration rates can be seen in a population's **age structure**, the pattern that emerges when people in a society are grouped by age (see Chapter 10). The population pyramids shown in Figure 18.7 are graphic representations of age structure. In societies where birth rates are high but death rates are also high, age structure takes the form of a triangle. The pattern in which many children are born, but few reach old age, is typical of developing countries. In contrast, with lower birth rates and fewer people dying young, the age structure of developed countries is more rectangular, narrowing only near the top. Because birth and death rates have both declined, the numbers of people in each age group are roughly equal.

A large increase in births, deaths, or migration will also change the shape of a society's age structure. The baby boom of 1946–1964 created uniquely large *birth cohorts*, which (as we saw in Chapter 10) are people born in the same year, or in a small number of consecutive years. This huge bulge in the U.S. population is composed mainly of people now in their late thirties and forties, as Figure 18.8 shows. After the year 2000, the baby boomers will begin turning

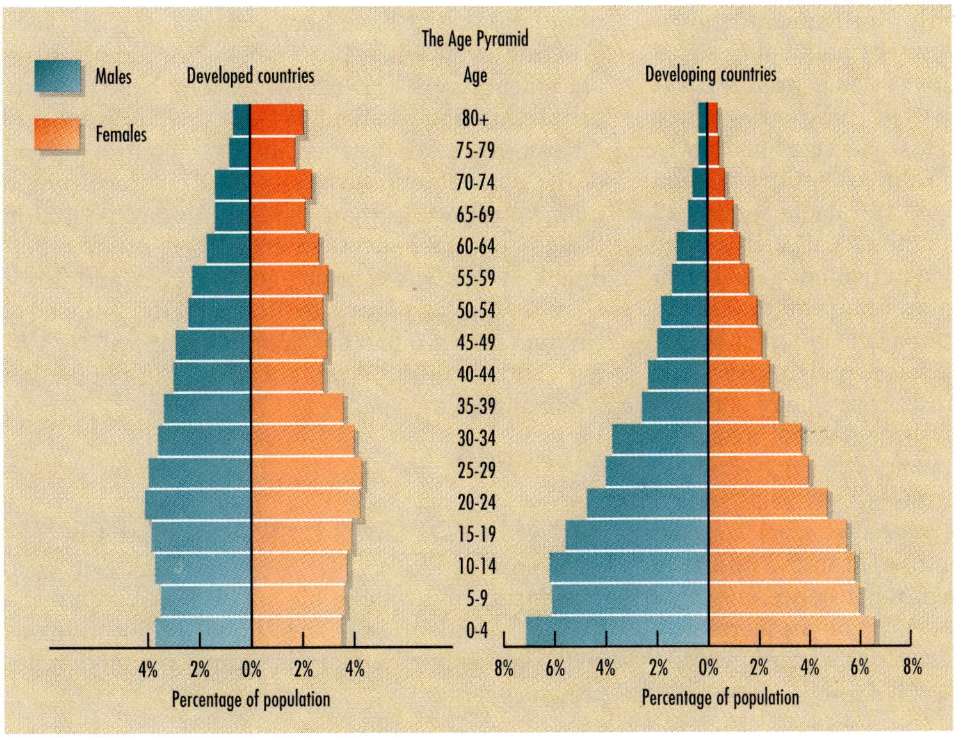

FIGURE 18.7 / Typical Population Structures of Developed and Developing Nations

The age structures of developed and developing nations are quite different due to the differences in their birth and death rates. In a developed country like ours, where both the fertility and mortality rates are low, the number of people in each age group is relatively equal except at the end of the life course, when people reach their seventies, eighties, and nineties. In developing nations, in contrast, the age structure forms a true pyramid. Many babies are born, giving the pyramid a large base, but death takes a sizable toll throughout the life course, increasingly reducing the number of people at each consecutive age level. By old age there are very few people left.

The Age Pyramid

Males / Females

Developed countries — Developing countries

Age: 80+, 75-79, 70-74, 65-69, 60-64, 55-59, 50-54, 45-49, 40-44, 35-39, 30-34, 25-29, 20-24, 15-19, 10-14, 5-9, 0-4

Percentage of population

Source: Ingomar Hauchler and Paul M. Kennedy, *Global Trends: The World Almanac of Development and Peace* (Continuum, New York, 1994), p. 114 (based on United Nations data).

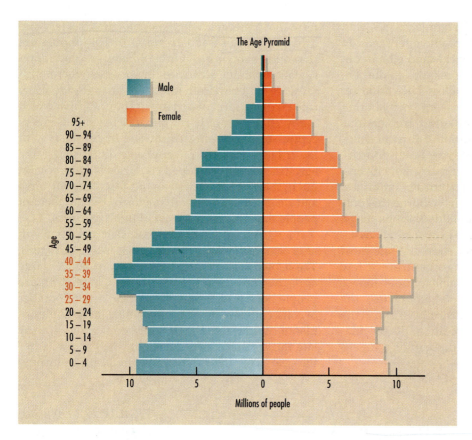

FIGURE 18.8 / The Age Structure of the United States, 1989

The baby boomers born between 1946 and 1964 make a clear bulge in the U.S. population structure. In the last years of the twentieth century, as shown in this figure, baby boomers are swelling the ranks of the middle-aged. In the next century, as the boomers grow old, they will cause the top of the age structure chart to expand.

Source: Carl Haub, "World and United States Population Prospects," *Population and Environment: A Journal of Interdisciplinary Studies* 12, no. 3 (1991), p. 304.

sixty and retiring. At the peak of the baby boom generation's retirement years (about 2020), there may be as many as 58 million elderly Americans. A similar bulge has been created in Israel's population structure by the mass immigration of Jews from the former Soviet Union in recent years. In contrast, mass emigration or war may create a shortage of adults in their productive years. For example, the Soviet Union lost 20 million people in World War II and another 15 million to Stalin's purges; all those deaths left a huge dent in the country's population pyramid. The recent wars between Iraq and Iran, and Iraq and the United States, have nearly wiped out a generation of young men in both these Middle Eastern countries. This loss will affect everything from their national economies and political strategies to marriage chances for their young women.

Knowing the age structure of a society helps policymakers and social planners predict what sorts of goods and services may be needed in the future. A large proportion of children, for instance, means a growing demand for schools, while an increasing number of elderly people may strain pension plans and health services.

Age structure also affects population growth rates. As Paul Ehrlich and Anne Ehrlich (1990) point out, populations that have been growing rapidly keep growing even when birth rates slow down to replacement levels. This is because they have so many people entering or about to enter their prime reproductive years. For instance, in 1989, about 40 percent of the population of less developed nations were in their youth. More than a billion young people in these countries had yet to enter their prime reproductive years between the ages of fifteen and thirty. Even if there is a sharp reduction in the number of children each woman has, more women will be having children in the years ahead, so the population will continue to expand.

WORLD POPULATION PRESSURES

The impact of demographic forces does not stop at a nation's boundaries. It has global implications as well, especially now that the human population has grown so large.

When agriculture was invented, about 10,000 years ago, probably no more than 5 million people were on the entire earth—about as many as currently live in the San Francisco Bay Area. In the time of Christ, a mere 2,000 years ago, the entire human population was no larger than that of the United States today. Until just a few hundred years ago the pattern of human population growth was one of dramatic ups and downs, as populations swelled in good times, only to be cut back by famines, wars, and disease. In the fourteenth century, for example, the European population was decimated by the plague. But then a long period of continuous population growth began in the late seventeenth century. By the mid-1800s, the world population had reached 1 billion (Wilford, 1981), and by 1930, 2 billion. The third billion was added by 1960, and the fourth by 1975. The 5 billion mark was passed in 1987 (see Figure 18.9). Even though the world's population is growing more slowly today than it was in the 1960s and 1970s, 275 new humans are born each minute, 16,482 an hour, 395,579 a day, 144 million a year. Unless massive famine, epidemics, or nuclear holocaust intervenes, the world's population is predicted to reach 6 billion before the year 2000 and 8.1 billion by 2025 (World Bank, 1994).

Another significant pattern shaping the impact of the world population is its distribution. The developed countries' share of world population has been dropping steadily since 1950, when it was about one-third. Of the 3.2 billion people projected to increase the human race over the next thirty-five years, 3 billion—95 percent—will be born in the less developed countries of the southern hemisphere, compared to fewer than 200 million in the developed countries of the northern hemisphere (Keyfitz, 1989; UN Population Fund, 1993). The good news is that while population is still growing rapidly, the rate of in-

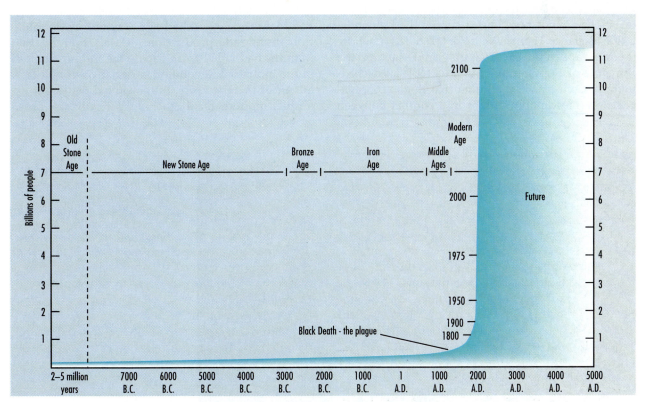

FIGURE 18.9 / World Population Growth from 8000 B.C. to the Present

The human population got off to a slow start, but it is now growing very rapidly. At current rates, another billion people are added to the world population every twelve to thirteen years. In contrast, it took about ten *thousand* years for the five million people alive when agriculture was invented to produce a billion descendents.

Source: *World Population Data Sheet*, Population Reference Bureau, Inc., Washington, D.C.

crease is no longer going up; family planning efforts are having some success (Brown, Lenssen and Kane, 1995). If current growth rates are maintained in Sweden, it will take another 350 years for its population to double. At the other extreme, India's population is expected to double within twenty years, at which point India will be even more populous than China. Thus, the world population is becoming more polarized, with fewer people (relatively speaking) in the rich areas of the world and more people concentrated in those regions that are the least able to provide for them. In 2025, four out of five people on earth will be living in the less developed countries, or Third World.

Malthus Versus Marx

How large can world population ultimately become, and, more particularly, how many human beings can the planet feed and the environment sustain? These questions are not new. They haunted the influential English scholar Thomas Malthus (1766–1834), whose theories appeared in 1798 in "An Essay on the Principle of Population." Malthus took an exceedingly pessimistic view, arguing that human populations are inescapably caught in a conflict between their "need for food" and the "passion between the sexes." Population, he maintained, increases geometrically (2, 4, 8, 16, . . . , thus doubling and redoubling), while food supplies increase only arithmetically (2, 3, 4, 5, . . .). No population can continue to grow indefinitely, because people will increase their numbers to the limit of subsistence. Whenever advances in food production improve people's standard of living, thought Malthus, the population inevitably catches up and literally eats away the higher living standard. The only way to stave off doom was to teach people to restrain their natural sexual urges—to marry later and have fewer children (Malthus did not approve of birth control or abortion). If this was not done, population growth would continue until checked by drastic means: starvation, pestilence, or war.

One of the foremost critics of Malthus was Karl Marx (1867/1976). Malthus had placed the blame for overpopulation and poverty on the individual members of society who succumbed to their sexual urges. For Marx, however, the issue was not overpopulation but underproduction. Marx thought that Malthus had failed to anticipate the full possibilities of the Industrial Revolution, especially technological advances in agriculture. In the United States, for example, modern farm machinery, fertilizers, pesti-

A typical street scene in India. Population growth rates have dropped in the developed countries of the northern hemisphere and slowed in the less developed countries of the southern hemisphere. Even so, India's population is expected to double in the next 20 years.

cides, irrigation, hybrid plants, and genetically selected animals have contributed to a more rapid growth in the nation's agricultural output than in its population (though U.S. agricultural surpluses have not ended hunger and starvation in other parts of the world). In fact, for the past fifty years the U.S. government has sponsored programs designed to cut back agricultural production: Farmers receive subsidies to let fields lie fallow. Marx believed that the system of capitalism had the capacity to produce food and other necessities for an indefinitely expanding population. It was only capitalism's unequal distribution of social wealth that made it seem that there had to be a natural limit on population. Moreover, in Marx's view, the system of property relations in capitalism skewed production away from meeting the needs of poor people and toward increasing the accumulation of capital. Capitalists further benefited from the fact that a surplus population created competition for jobs, thus driving down wages and maximizing profits. Marx's solution to the problem of overpopulation was socialism. Thus, whereas Malthus focused on individual actions and sought the answer to population problems in moral restraint, Marx focused on the economic structure of society and sought the solution in a new social order.

Mao Zedong was following Marx's lead when he decreed that China did not need population control, only economic expansion. However, as we saw earlier in this chapter, Mao's successors in the Chinese government disagreed. They believed that if population growth was not slowed drastically, all the benefits of economic improvement would go toward providing basic subsistence for the larger population instead of raising the standard of living. Hence, they imposed the limit of one child per family.

Marx may have been too optimistic about our ability to provide for large populations, but Malthus was too pessimistic. Despite many crises, the world's population (and that of most individual countries) has continued to grow and be fed enough to survive. Marx was right in believing that technological and social factors—not just natural limits—determine how many people the earth can support. Neither Marx nor Malthus, however, anticipated the most basic contribution that modern demography has made to this ongoing debate: the observation that economic development not only increases the food supply and lowers death rates (thus allowing for a larger population) but over the long term generally leads to choices of smaller families and thus to reductions in the rate of population growth. This process is known as the *demographic transition*.

The Demographic Transition

The idea of a **demographic transition** is a generalization from the historical experience of Western Europe (Teitelbaum, 1975). As Europe industrialized during the nineteenth century, fertility rates fell. Demographers theorized that such declining fertility rates could always be expected as a consequence of industrialization. This left two questions open, however. First, what specific characteristics of industrialization caused the European decline in fertility rates? And second, must other countries follow the same path? As we will see in the next section, in response to both these questions, more recent research has improved on the basic idea of a demographic transition. The basic model is still important, however, for even if it does not specify the underlying causes of fertility changes, it does indicate the pattern of stages in which population first increases and then levels off in response to decreasing mortality and fertility rates.

The model of the demographic transition consists of four stages that characterize the population dynamics of societies undergoing industrialization (see Figure 18.10). In the first, or preindustrial, stage, both the birth rate and the death rate are high, so the population is relatively stable. In stage, 2, the birth rate stays high while the death rate declines as nutrition, health, and sanitation improve. In particular, the infant mortality rate drops, and more babies survive and in due course become parents themselves. Hence, this stage has the potential for explosive population growth. In stage 3, the birth rate also drops as families realize they do not need so many children to provide for their old age and as new economic opportunities develop, especially for women. In stage 4, both the birth rate and the death rate are low and in balance again.

Few countries today are still in stage 1, with high birth and death rates, although parts of rural Africa come fairly close. For example, the death rate per 1,000 people in East Africa is fifteen and the birth rate forty-eight—approximately twice the rates for either Asia or Latin America (Hauchler and Kennedy, 1994). A similar situation existed in China in the years before the Communist Revolution. In contrast, India, Nigeria, Brazil, and most other developing countries

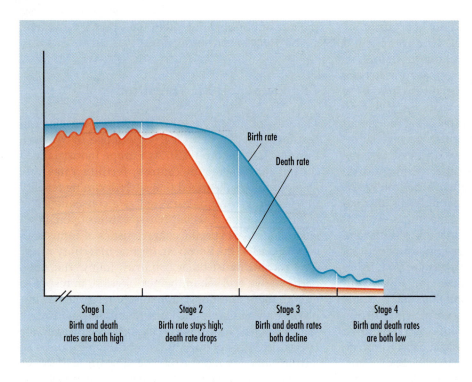

FIGURE 18.10 / The Four Stages of the Demographic Transition in Industrializing Nations

During the demographic transition, the technological improvements that accompany industrialization first bring about a marked decline in the death rate. Since the birth rate is still high, population is now set to grow rapidly. But then a decline in fertility occurs, as smaller families are increasingly viewed as more appropriate to the changing economy. The end result (stage 4) is both a low death rate and a low birth rate.

are in stage 2 of the demographic transition, with continuing high birth rates but decreased death rates. This is a stage of high population growth. China, where birth control is becoming widespread, is an example of stage 3. Europe, North America, and Japan are in the fourth and (apparently) final phase, with a low but fluctuating birth rate and a low, steady death rate. Indeed, the number of births has fallen below the number of deaths in some industrialized countries, such as Germany.

The demographic transition should not be seen as a fixed sequence that all industrializing countries inevitably experience. Under some conditions, cultural, political, and other factors have altered fertility and mortality patterns more profoundly than economic development. Right now, for example, in the former communist countries of Eastern Europe, fertility rates are falling much faster than death rates—which may actually be rising. In the midst of great economic uncertainty, people are deciding not to have children. Between 1989 and 1991, Russia's birth rate fell by between 15 and 20 percent, and Romania's fell by 30 percent (*New York Times*, December 31, 1991). At the same time, the quality of health care and nutrition has suffered with communism's collapse.

Stage 2 of the demographic transition brings acute problems in many developing nations. The death rate has dropped precipitously in India, for example, primarily because of the introduction of vaccines and other imported technology (improvements in nutrition and sanitation, crucial to lowering the death rate elsewhere, have been relatively slow there). The words of an elderly man in Calcutta capture the suddenness of this change:

> When I was a boy, they took away forty or fifty bodies after a cholera epidemic. It happened every five or ten years. Now they come and vaccinate our children. I have lived here almost seventy years. The biggest change in my time has been health. We've learned to keep from dying. (Quoted in Thomlinson, 1976, p. 29)

Changes in health care, nutrition, sanitation, and so forth that took place over a century or two in the Western world have been compressed into just a few decades in the Third World. However, the high value that many people place on large families has not changed as rapidly as the technologies that have lowered death rates.

Lowering Fertility Rates

Many groups and organizations today are working to hurry the demographic transition along by encouraging population planning worldwide. Such groups include private charities and nonprofit organizations like the Population Council, as well as the United Nations Population Fund, which helps developing countries conduct censuses, provide family-planning programs, and offer maternal and child health support. Within most developing countries, governments set population policies and charge ministries of health or other agencies with carrying them out. Most of these policies are based on the awareness that high population levels and continued rapid population growth cause social, economic, and environmental problems.

When lower rates of population growth become national policy, however, private and public values are likely to clash. From the perspective of the individual parent, having a large family is likely to make sense. In agricultural societies, for example, children typically produce more than they cost. From the perspective of society as a whole and over the long term, though, population growth is "the master lock on the national poverty trap" (Harrison, 1984, p. 250), not to mention a threat to the global environment and world peace (Harrison, 1992, p. 274). Paul Harrison draws an analogy between the Third World's desire for many children and the First World's love affair with cars:

Every household wants [at least one] car to increase its freedom and mobility, but when too many people have one they get stuck in traffic jams, motorways are pushed through their neighborhoods, public transport . . . declines so that eventually people take far longer to get to work than their grandfathers did on the trams. Because everyone strives for individual freedom and mobility, eventually their freedom and mobility are restricted more than ever before. So it is with children. People have large families in a bid to escape poverty, yet their poverty is increased because everyone else is following the same strategy. (1984, pp. 226–227)

Since rapid population growth can be an enemy of development, policymakers seek ways to lower fertility rates. One effective strategy is to make contraception readily available. While it is possible to limit births without modern birth-control devices, it is difficult. Even where such devices are available, they are not always used. Family-planning programs have had to be creative and persistent.

Thailand, for example, has used a combination of community involvement and economic incentives to break down taboos against birth control. Carnivals, village fairs, and even weddings feature such birth-control games as condom "balloon-blowing" con-

In traditional cultures, women who want to practice birth control may fear repercussions from their husbands and families. At this family planning clinic in Dakalai, Egypt, most women choose IUDs.

tests. Vasectomy marathons are held on Labor Day and the King's birthday, with teams of doctors and nurses competing to perform the highest number. Registered family planners, who promote birth control in their home communities, may be rewarded with discounts on the rental of buffalo to plow their fields, on the purchase of fertilizer and seed, and on transport of their goods to market. More than 16,000 villages have their own family-planning centers. About 60 percent of Thai couples practice birth control, and total fertility dropped from 6.1 in 1965–1970 to 2.1 in 1994 (Reddy, 1994; World Bank, 1990). Not all programs are so successful. For example, Kenya initiated family-planning programs in 1967 but with less effective organization and less government support. Kenya still has one of the highest fertility rates and fastest-growing populations in the world (*Euromonitor*, 1992).

Cultural Influences on Fertility Rates

Overall, in 1965, Third World women averaged more than six children each; by 1991, this fertility rate had fallen to 3.9 children. China accounts for much of the improvement, but not all. The UN Population Fund estimates that more than 55 percent of Third World women were using some form of contraception by 1994 (Sadik, 1994). The most important influence on a nation's fertility rate is how many children people want to have, and this preference is shaped by cultural attitudes as well as economic opportunities (Harrison, 1992). Love of children is a universal reason for having them, but culturally specific reasons also play a part. For example, the tradition of *machismo* encourages men in Latin countries to prove their virility by fathering as many children as they can. Even more basically, cultural values and traditional economic incentives combine to make large families attractive.

In much of the Third World, the family functions something like a private corporation (Harrison, 1984). The head of the family, usually a man, is responsible for the fortunes of all its members (or stockholders). His success depends not on the accumulation of capital in the modern sense but rather on the accumulation of people. Family members, including children, are either the mainstay or the whole of his workforce. Children begin performing chores as soon as they are able and by about age thirteen are full-

fledged workers. In the countryside, they work in fields or tend animals; in the city, they may be sent out to peddle small goods or to beg. The head of a large family is likely to wield considerable power and influence in his community. He commands an "army" of kin and through marriages forms alliances with other families, all of whom can be called on in time of need or during feuds over land, water rights, or debts. Equally important, a large family provides extra insurance against old age in countries that do not provide old-age assistance programs. The more children a couple have, the better off they will be in old age.

In particular, families commonly want sons. The reason is not simply that sons often carry on the family name (as we noted in considering China). In general, men earn more than women do, so sons add more to the family coffers before they marry and are better able to support their parents in old age. Furthermore, in Asia sons traditionally receive dowries (money or goods from the bride's family) when they marry. The more sons a couple have, the more they stand to gain (conversely, the more daughters, the more they lose). In countries where death in infancy or childhood is still common, one son is not enough, because he might not survive. According to a Chinese proverb, "One son is no son, two sons are an undependable son, and only three sons can be counted as a real son"; Iranians say, "The first two sons are for the crows" (Harrison, 1984, p. 220). So men envy fathers with several strong sons and women envy the mothers who bore them, because these families often enjoy extra wealth, power, and status.

Changing this cultural outlook is not easy, even when medical advances and better nutrition enable more children to live into adulthood. For many decades, prevailing wisdom held that the key to population control was economic development. According to this view, a country must reach a certain level of modernization (in such areas as industrialization, urbanization, and education) before people will realize the economic advantage of small families. Supporters of this argument (which is central to the supposedly "natural" workings of the demographic transition) point to the rapid fall in birth rates experienced by such newly industrialized countries as Singapore and Korea. However, the pattern is not uniform. Fertility has also declined in countries that have not experienced such major economic gains (Sri Lanka and Costa Rica, for example), and it has remained high in countries that have made substantial economic progress (Brazil and Mexico) (Ehrlich and Ehrlich, 1990).

Contraception and the Status of Women

Opposition to birth control is often a reflection of sexual politics, specifically men's fear that if women control their own fertility, fathers will lose control over their daughters and husbands over their wives (Hartmann, 1995; Harrison, 1992). Women in such settings who want no more babies may be afraid to practice birth control because they fear their husbands will beat them if they find out. Or they may believe that using birth-control devices is sinful because it is against religious teachings. These fears suggest that family planning will be accepted only when and where the status of women improves. Indeed, as Betsy Hartmann (1995) has argued, rapid population growth is not an independent cause but rather a *symptom* of problems in economic and social development that center on the status of women.

In most Third World countries, women (and children) are "the poorest of the poor." In many places women cannot inherit land or other property from their fathers or husbands, nor are they permitted to acquire property on their own. Although they supply most of the agricultural labor, they have no rights to the land or to any profits. Agricultural development programs may be run by and restricted to men on the grounds that admitting women would violate cultural norms. Industrialization often reduces the market for the handicrafts women traditionally produce, and factory jobs may be unattainable because women lack the educational credentials to compete with men. Although Latin American and Caribbean girls are catching up to boys educationally, African and Asian girls are far less likely to attend school than their brothers are. Three-quarters of the women aged twenty-five and older in these regions are illiterate (*United Nations*, 1991). The net result of all these handicaps is that for many Third World women, marrying and bearing children (preferably sons) is the only way they can achieve security and status. Typically, women marry young and have numerous pregnancies, often losing several children in infancy.

A growing body of research shows that the more education women receive, the fewer children they are likely to bear. One study of women in Kenya analyzed the impact on a woman's total fertility of her age at first marriage, level of education, place of residence (rural versus urban), marital status, religion,

People's desire to have children is profoundly influenced by cultural beliefs and economic realities. In much of the Third World, the family functions as a basic economic unit whose success depends on the contributions of children as well as adults.

contraceptive use, and work status (Agyei and Mbamanyo, 1989). The researchers found that of all these factors, education had the most impact. Women with secondary or higher education had an average of 3.12 fewer children than did women with no formal education. The second most important factor in reducing fertility was age at first marriage. The two often go together: Women who have equal access to education are likely to postpone marriage longer than those who do not.

Education and equal rights for women are perhaps the two key prerequisites for lowering fertility (Sadik, 1994). Education provides women with both the know-how and the motivation to limit the size of their families. Educated women are more likely to obtain salaried jobs and so to delay marriage and childbearing. Paid employment not only makes women less dependent on their fathers and husbands but also provides an alternative status to motherhood. Educated women are more likely to know about birth-control services and to be able to use contraceptives properly. Furthermore, schooling presents both sexes with ideas about alternative futures and helps to reduce suspicion of social change, making contraception less frightening.

SUSTAINING THE WORLD'S POPULATION: THE EXAMPLE OF FOOD SUPPLY

The future of humanity and the future of the environment are tightly intertwined. Human beings have colonized some two-thirds of the world's land, and most of the rest is either inaccessible or unproductive mountaintops, ice caps, tundra, or desert (Ehrlich, 1991). Technological advances are sometimes described as "freeing" humanity from dependency on nature, but this global takeover has made humankind dependent on the physical environment in new ways—and in the process has threatened that very environment. Already we are straining the earth's capacities to the limit.

High levels of population are not the only way in which we put stress on the earth's **ecology**, the pattern of relationships among biological organisms (including humans) and between organisms and their environments. Consumers in the world's rich countries put far more than their share of strain on the earth by demanding abundant energy and foods (like

beef), whose production uses up enormous natural resources, and by producing enormous amounts of waste (much of it hazardous). In other words, the earth is challenged not just by its numbers of people but by how they live. A small number of car-driving, beef-eating, waste-producing Americans pumping water long distances and using air-conditioning so they can live comfortably in desert areas like Arizona may do more ecological damage than ten times as many poor people in the Third World.

Nonetheless, large populations are a source of environmental problems and a strain on resources. Even at a low level of technology, a swelling population is likely to strip land of its forests, largely for fuel, and it is also likely to overtax water supplies and to foul them with its waste. Perhaps the best example of the tension between population growth and resource allocation has to do with the food supply. Historically, famines were frequent, but generally local. Transport and storage systems were not good enough to overcome local effects of climate and pests. Improving transport and storage has helped to distribute food supplies throughout the world. This has allowed for better famine relief, but it has also made the potential for famine a global problem. Even more important, the growth of world food markets means that farmers are less likely to produce for local consumption. Everyone depends on the markets, and crises become larger-scale.

About 1 billion of the earth's 5 billion people have more than enough to eat (Ehrlich and Ehrlich, 1990). Approximately a third of the world's grain is fed to livestock so that the well-to-do, most of whom live in the rich countries of the First World, are supplied with meat, eggs, and dairy products. Perhaps 3 billion more people get enough to eat, though their diets are primarily vegetarian. That leaves nearly a billion people who are chronically hungry, and as many as 400 million who are so undernourished that their health is threatened or their growth is stunted. Severe hunger is concentrated in the Third World, especially Latin America and Africa, where the environment is severely overtaxed and economic development is limited. Here populations are vulnerable to recurrent crises of terrible proportions. The almost continuous famine in the Sahel, the area just south of the Sahara, is virtually the Malthusian nightmare come true. Overpopulation led to excess grazing, cultivation, and water pumping; combined with civil war, it resulted ultimately in mass starvation. Famine is not constant, but frequent. In the last major episode dur-

Population growth, overgrazing, and deforestation (where wood is the only fuel)—aggravated by civil wars—have led to seemingly endless cycles of famine in the Sahel, the region between the Sahara Desert to the north and the savannahs farther to the south.

ing the 1980s, one out of every five children born in this region—5 million infants—died each year from hunger-related causes (Independent Commission on International Humanitarian Issues, 1985).

If all the food produced in the world were distributed equally (and if Westerners ate less meat and milk products), there might be enough to feed everyone on earth today. However, there would not be enough left over to accommodate the 95 million additional people who join the population each year. Lester Brown, an agricultural economist and president of the Worldwatch Institute, estimates that 28 million more tons of grain must be harvested each year just to keep pace with population growth in the 1990s (Brown et al., 1990). In Brown's estimation, such expanded food production is unlikely. In fact, compared with 1984, the 1994 total world grain harvest was *down* 10 percent (Brown, Lenssen, and Kane, 1995).

From 1950 to about 1984, worldwide grain production increased steadily (though distribution was uneven). The main reason was the so-called **Green Revolution**—the invention of new strains of cereal crops such as corn, wheat, and rice that doubled or tripled the yield per acre. When they were introduced in the 1950s, in countries such as India and Pakistan, these high-yielding grains were hailed as the solution to world hunger. The Green Revolution did produce spectacular short-term gains, but at the price of long-term damage to the environment.

Green Revolution crops depend on intensive agriculture, using high levels of irrigation, fertilizers, and pesticides. This combination takes a toll on the environment. One problem is soil erosion. Every year farmers lose about 24 billions tons of topsoil worldwide (Brown et al., 1990; Brown, Lenssen and Kane, 1995). In addition, much land is exhausted by intensive farming. As a result, more acres must be taken out of cultivation each year. Not enough new fields can be added to replace them, because the amount of land suitable for farming is dwindling. Chemical fertilizers do not replace the soil that is washed away, nor do they substitute for the natural fertility of soil (Ehrlich and Ehrlich, 1990). Rather, they temporarily mask the effects of erosion and the loss of certain soil nutrients. When these fertilizers are washed into rivers and streams, they contribute to pollution by promoting the growth of algae, which consume oxygen and lead to the death of fish. To irrigate high-yield crops, farmers must drill wells ever deeper into the water table, withdrawing more water than nature can replenish. Any successful irrigation is temporary, because it often causes salt buildup or waterlogging, again rendering the land unusable. In short, the Green Revolution is reaching the point of diminishing returns.

Grain production has only held steady during the 1990s, while population has grown about 1.8 percent a year (Brown, Lenssen, and Kane, 1995). The result is that the world is using up its grain reserves and increasingly suffering shortages. Even without considering such influences on agricultural output as pollution and global warming, feeding the world in the 1990s and beyond will be a problem. World grain production may continue to increase, but the amount of food per person will decline (see Figure 18.11). Few researchers anticipate a technological solution that will solve the problem by simply increasing the food supply, without limiting population. Most current research in biotechnology (especially genetic engineering) is aimed at reducing the input or cost of agricultural production, not increasing the output. In the final analysis, the solution is a social one. Writes the French agronomist René Dumont, "The future of the world hinges above all on whether or not we can curb, and then stop, the world's terrifying population explosion" (1990, p. 37).

Besides straining the world's food-producing capacities, rapid population growth means increased

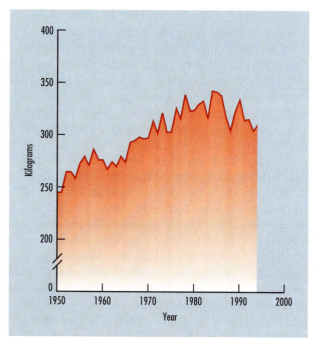

FIGURE 18.11 / World Grain Production per Person, 1950–1994

Although world grain production per person increased overall between 1950 and the mid-1980s due to the Green Revolution, it has since started a general downturn, which is not expected to end soon. Global population is simply growing at too fast a pace for grain production to keep up.

Source: Lester R. Brown, Nicholas Lenssen, and Hal Kane, *Vital Signs, 1995: The Trends That Are Shaping Our Future* (W.W. Norton, New York, 1995), p. 27 (based on USDA data).

pressure to exploit limited, often irreplaceable, natural resources and increased pollution of the air and water that sustain all life. Without careful management and international cooperation, the planet itself is endangered.

THE ENDANGERED PLANET

The first Earth Day, in April 1970, was a national event organized by groups of activists whom many Americans regarded as alarmists and kooks. Today, Earth Day is celebrated each year by people of all ages and walks of life in 140 countries. Three out of four Americans describe themselves as "environmentalists." Even many corporate executives have stopped arguing that saving the environment will eliminate jobs and have begun competing to show how "green" they are (Wald, 1990). The bald eagle, once threatened by DDT, is about to be moved off the endangered species list; the Cuyahoga River no longer bursts into flames as it winds through Cleveland; the tailpipes of new cars emit 75 to 95 percent fewer toxic gases than old models did.

Unfortunately, the good news about the environment is offset by bad. The increasing number of cars means that despite tighter regulations on auto emissions, almost half of Americans live in communities that violate federal clean air standards. The fish that have returned to the Cuyahoga River have so many poisons in their flesh that they are inedible. Worldwide, some 500 million acres of forest (an area equal to that of the United States east of the Mississippi River) were cut down between 1970 and 1990; deserts are spreading on every continent; aquifers (underground water reservoirs formed during the last Ice Age) are being drained; and the air quality in dozens of cities often is so poor that it is dangerous for children to play outdoors. Moreover, new problems which no one had heard of on the first Earth Day have surfaced, including the greenhouse effect, holes in the ozone layer, and acid rain.

In this section we will look at the social causes and consequences of *resource depletion* and *pollution*. While it is useful for the sake of discussion to separate these two types of assault on the environment, in reality they are intertwined. Both are results of capitalist economic development. As the sociologist James O'Connor points out, "The natural wealth of the world is depleted and turned into garbage, often dangerous garbage, through global capital accumulation. And the unwanted by-products—pollution—have the effect of depleting [or] exhausting resources" (1989, p. 11). For example, oil is extracted from the earth (depleting resources) and transported to industrial centers, where it is used as fuel (causing pollution) or turned into virtually undecomposable products such as plastics (causing further pollution).

This system has also accelerated the division between rich and poor countries. The Third World provides most of the raw materials for capitalist growth and so suffers greater resource depletion, while industrial nations generate more than their share of pollution. The First World also "exports" pollution to the Third World, not only in the form of dangerous airborne and waterborne chemicals but also as cars, factories, soda cans, and in some cases, products and production methods that have been deemed unsafe and banned in the home countries.

Resource Depletion

Human beings have always exploited nature, in the sense of breathing the air, eating plants and animals, drinking fresh water, and using skins and tree branches for clothing and shelter. But all these natural resources are renewable, and for most of human existence the population was small and widely scattered. "[H]uman groups therefore consumed [natural resources] no faster than natural processes produced them" (Ehrlich and Ehrlich, 1990, p. 49). Only in recent times did this balance begin to tip. One reason was that humans began to use *nonrenewable resources*—first metals and then fossil fuels (oil, coal, natural gas, and peat) which took millions of years to form and cannot be replaced. The second reason was population growth, which, combined with increasing demand for goods, has led to the consumption of renewable resources (such as trees and water) faster than they can be replenished, often along with damage to the earth.

Consumption of Fossil Fuels

The fossil fuel we burn today took roughly a million years to develop (Gibbons, Blair, and Gwin, 1989). Oil provides about 40 percent of the world's energy, coal about 30 percent, and natural gas about 20 percent. Nuclear and hydroelectric plants and, in the Third World, wood and organic wastes such as ani-

mal dung provide most of the rest. Consumption of these resources is not distributed evenly. With less than a quarter of the world's population, industrialized nations consume more than three-quarters of the world's commercially available energy (Hauchler and Kennedy, 1994). The United States accounts for the largest share by far: One American uses as much energy as two Japanese or Germans, five Mexicans, thirty-five Indians or Indonesians, and fifty-six Nigerians (Durning, 1990). The root of Americans' dependence on oil is the automobile. Two out of three barrels of oil used in the United States go into the tanks of cars and other light vehicles. Worldwide, the number of vehicles on the road—half a billion—is growing even faster than the population (*Euromonitor,* 1992). Most cars and drivers are in industrialized nations, but the Third World (especially Asia and South America) is catching up. Although Third World nations use far less oil than First World countries do, their citizens spend a larger proportion of their incomes on fuel and are the hardest hit when the flow of oil and gas is interrupted.

Dependence on fossil fuels is problematic for several reasons. One is location. About two-thirds of the world's proven oil reserves are in the Persian Gulf area. The same is true for natural gas. As Iraq's invasion of Kuwait in 1990 demonstrated, the Middle East is politically unstable, which makes the global supply of oil unpredictable. A second problem with the current energy system is pollution. Fossil fuels are the major source of both local smog and such world problems as acid rain and global warming (discussed below). Unfortunately, coal, the one fossil fuel available in large quantities on every continent, is also the dirtiest. "Coal extracts a heavy human and ecological toll," writes Nicholas Lenssen, "particularly when burned without adequate pollution control equipment" (1995, p. 50). Mining it scars the land, and burning it produces two or three times as much air pollution as the combustion of other fuels. Coal also causes acid rain that destroys crops, forests, and buildings.

People around the world have rebelled against their governments' proposed solutions to energy problems. Some of the first demonstrations against the central government in the Soviet Union were sparked by environmental issues, even before the accident at the nuclear reactor in Chernobyl in April 1986. Because people fear nuclear accidents, radioactive wastes, regular exposure to low levels of radiation (as can occur when people work in nuclear power plants or live near them), and the use of energy technology for the secret production of nuclear bombs (as in Iraq), worldwide construction of nuclear plants has almost stopped. Citizens of Germany have voted down nuclear expansion in their country. Plans to build hydroelectric plants in India have also been met with massive public protests. Coal-powered, as well as nuclear, energy plants have been blocked by voters in the United States. Citizens may not know exactly what kind of energy they want, but are passionate about what they do *not* want. As a result, U.S. energy policies and practices have shifted from one extreme to another.

For decades, Americans took the availability of cheap energy—and the desirability of huge, gas-guzzling cars—for granted. Then, in the early 1970s, the Organization of Petroleum Exporting Countries (OPEC) imposed an embargo on the sale of oil to the United States. The price of gas skyrocketed, and the federal government and many state governments set up a number of programs to encourage conservation: Energy prices were deregulated, minimum efficiency standards were set for cars and appliances, tax credits were offered for better home insulation, and funds were made available for research and development of renewable sources of energy. Between 1973 and 1986, energy efficiency in the United States increased by about 30 percent, oil imports fell from 9 billion barrels a day to 5 billion, and the nation's annual fuel bill decreased by $150 billion (Flavin, 1991). New technologies were developed, such as the photo-voltaic cell, which converts sunlight directly into electricity (and which probably powers your pocket calculator). Research funding increased for solar, geo-thermal, and other non-fuel-consuming energy technologies. Old technologies, such as windmills and wind turbines, were revived. Then, in 1985–1986, when world petroleum prices fell, oil imports and consumption began to creep upward again, and today are back near their peak (Brown, Lenssen, and Kane, 1995). Many pollution control regulations were relaxed and conservation programs allowed to lapse, on the grounds that they hurt the economy. Nonetheless, experimentation with renewable energy sources continues. Indeed, global wind-power-generating capacity grew by 22 percent in 1994 alone, though the industry remained in the doldrums in the United States (Flavin, 1995).

This brief history of energy use in the United States shows, first, that people can be motivated to change their energy habits. Further, the technology for more efficient sources of energy already exists. During the war in the Persian Gulf, for example, solar panels in Jordan, Israel, and Cyprus continued to operate, undisturbed by the threat of disrupted oil supplies. Some 6,000 villages in India rely on photovoltaic cells for electricity (Flavin and Lenssen, 1991). "Superinsulated," airtight homes in Sweden use 90 percent less energy than the average American home (*World Resources, 1990–1991*, 1990). Some homes in California get 40 percent of their electricity from wind turbines (Flavin, 1991). Electronic communications could greatly reduce the energy spent on business travel (Ehrlich and Ehrlich, 1990). None of these technologies alone will replace fossil fuels, but in combination they could help to reduce dependence on more dangerous and less dependable energy sources.

Deforestation

Forests are the lungs of the earth: They absorb carbon dioxide from the atmosphere and exhale oxygen. They also store energy from the sun, bind topsoil to the land, and aid in climate control by capturing and releasing water. In addition, they provide a habitat for innumerable species of plants and animals, serving as a global storehouse of genetic diversity. Ancient forests are not a renewable resource in the sense that they can be replaced simply by replanting and waiting; they represent special ecosystems that developed over hundreds of years and may never be regenerated. Tropical forests that cover just 12 percent of the earth's land surface provide the habitat for between 50 and 90 percent of the world's species (Acharya, 1995). But about 42 million acres of forest are currently being lost each year—compared with 27 million acres per year in 1980 (Hauchler and Kennedy, 1994).

Deforestation is not a new phenomenon; it dates back to the beginnings of agriculture. The ancient Greek philosophers warned of the dangers of over-cultivation and overgrazing, especially by goats. They were right: Today Greece is almost a desert, its forests gone and its soil poor and thin (Ehrlich and Ehrlich, 1990). But the great destruction came with population explosion, larger-scale agriculture, and industry in the nineteenth and twentieth centuries. Between 1850 and 1980, more than 15 percent of all the world's forests—over 220 billion acres—was destroyed. Only about 5 percent of the virgin forests that European settlers found in what is now the

The tropical rain forest is being destroyed because of population pressure, commercial development for the global timber market, and the need for additional arable land.

United States remains; most forests were cut down to make way for cattle and crops. Concern is growing that the tropical rain forests of the Southern Hemisphere will suffer the same fate, with severe consequences both for local inhabitants and for the world as a whole.

Some 140 square miles of rain forest are cut down every day (Jagger, 1991). There are two main reasons for this deforestation. One is population pressure: Many people in Third World nations use wood for cooking, heating, and lighting, as well as for houses and furniture. The more people, the more trees they cut down. New trees do not spring up to replace the old ones, especially in the tropics. Rather, the deforested land reverts to grass or scrubland, or in some cases desert. So people have to travel farther every day to find wood, and the process of environmental degradation spreads.

The second main reason for rain-forest depletion is commercial development for the global market. Foreign investors or local entrepreneurs strip large areas of rain forest to obtain export lumber and minerals or to make way for ranches and plantations. Examining data on thirty-six countries, the environmental scholar Thomas Rudel (1989) concluded that the main reason for high rates of deforestation in the Third World is population growth. However, in countries with large rain forests, political and economic factors also play a role. Thus the cattle farms in the Amazon produce cheap meat for sale in fast-food chains in the United States, while wood from the forests of Papua New Guinea, Thailand, Malaysia, Colombia, and Cameroon is ground up to make cardboard for packaging electronic equipment in Japan (Ehrlich and Ehrlich, 1990).

Brazil illustrates both patterns, population pressure and commercial development. In the Amazon, Brazil has both the largest remaining tropical forest and the highest rate of deforestation in the world (Goldemberg, 1989; World Resources Institute, 1991). Under a program begun in the 1960s, the Brazilian government opened this area for development by building the Trans-Amazonia Highway and other roads and by offering plots of land at giveaway prices, tax credits, and even a year's wages to people who would settle there (Harrison, 1984). The program was designed both to tap the resources of the Amazon and to solve the problem of overpopulation in northeastern and southern Brazil, where commercial agriculture had left many peasants landless. However, the development was carried out with little attention to the ecology of the Amazon basin or its traditional inhabitants. The one requirement was that settlers "improve" or clear their land, usually by cutting and burning off trees. In the Amazonian state of Rondônia, the infusion of settlers led to a drop in total forest cover from 97 percent in 1980 to 76 percent in 1990, and this pace of forest destruction continues (Acharya, 1995). Settlers sought to farm, but as often as not the land would not support conventional farming for more than a few years. Most of the energy in rain forests is stored in the trees, not the soil; once they are cut down, the soil's nutrient value deteriorates rapidly. This is why traditional inhabitants practice slash-and-burn agriculture, in which small fields are rotated frequently, allowing the forest to grow back in the unplanted areas. Some settlers made a living by clearing land, selling it to large-scale commercial ranchers, and moving on.

In the late 1980s, the invasion and destruction of the Amazon rain forest began to capture world attention. Under international pressure, the Brazilian government suspended tax credits for developers and joined other nations in an Amazon Pact, dedicated to conservation, sustainable use of the area's natural resources, and protection of indigenous peoples. At the same time, however, negotiations began with Japan for funds to build a highway connecting the Amazon forest with the Pacific seaport of Lima, Peru, to facilitate the export of hardwoods. And large landowners in Brazil still receive tax credits for clearing land to graze cattle (World Bank, 1990); their actions are economically rational (Hecht, 1993).

With some justification, the Brazilian government argues that the United States and other industrialized nations, whose citizens use fifteen times more energy than Brazilians, have no right to demand that Brazil become a leader in conservation. Since deforestation helped to "buy" the development of today's rich countries, perhaps we must pay if we want the citizens of poorer countries to restrict their development to save forests. The future of the Amazon and other tropical forests will require international effort, perhaps in the form of an international protection fund or arrangements with Third World nations to forgive part of their foreign debt in exchange for preservation of natural areas (see the Global Issues/Local Consequences box).

Pollution

Snow in Mexico City? That is what residents of the northern suburb of Ecatepec call the fine white dust that blankets their houses and streets every morning. The cloud of chemical dust produced by a nearby caustic-soda plant kills trees and shrubs, burns resi-

dents' eyes and throats, and is probably responsible for their frequent skin rashes and respiratory diseases. This toxic snow is only one symptom of the growing environmental crisis in Mexico City. Air pollution causes or contributes to 90 percent of respiratory illnesses and infections (Harrison, 1992, p. 176).

In the past forty years the population of the Mexico City metropolitan area has grown from 5 million to 16 million, making it one of the largest metropolitan areas on earth and one of the most polluted. Nearly 3 million vehicles and tens of thousands of poorly regulated factories, some of which burn tires or sawdust soaked in fuel oil, pour an estimated 4.35 million tons of pollutants into the atmosphere each year. In the city's vast squatter settlements, latrines and sewers are rare; the dust carries dried fecal matter and such infectious microorganisms as salmonella and streptococcus. The banks of the Rio de los Remedios are lined with trash, and the river itself is a stream of black sludge. Oil from industrial discharge shimmers on the surface, while untreated sewage decaying below the surface sends up bubbles of gas. The U.S. government pays its diplomatic staff a 10 percent hardship bonus for having to breathe Mexico City's air, rents them houses outside the city, and advises women not to have babies while on duty there (*New York Times,* May 12, 1991). Mexico City may be a worst-case pollution scenario, but it captures the impact of uncontrolled population growth, urbanization, and industrialization on the environment—and serves as a warning.

The production of waste is a natural part of life. Waste becomes **pollution** when so much is produced that it overloads natural recycling processes, or when human beings produce materials (such as plastics and radioactive dust) that cannot be broken down by natural processes. Pollution is made into a crisis by two social factors: (1) new technologies with new waste products and (2) levels of population density (the number of people per square mile) unprecedented in world history.

Air Pollution

Air pollution first became a problem during the Industrial Revolution. By the beginning of the twentieth century, many cities in Europe and North America were blanketed with smoke, soot, and ash—the by-products of industrialization. In 1952, a "black fog" covered London, killing 4,000 people and mak-

GLOBAL ISSUES/LOCAL CONSEQUENCES

At Home in the Rain Forest

When environmentalists talk about the impact of destroying rain forests, they usually focus on the effect on global climate or the loss of biological and genetic diversity. To many thousands of people, however, losing the forest means losing their homes.

Tu'O, from the Malaysian island of Borneo, is a hunter-gatherer turned environmental activist. "To us the forest is everything," he says. "It is like our supermarket and also our bank" (quoted in Ryan, 1991, p. 8). Tu'O's people, the Penan, have lived in the Sarawak forest for as long as they can remember, collecting, hunting, fishing, and growing crops in small clearings. In the last decade, commercial loggers have invaded the region, displacing local people, polluting rivers, eroding hillsides, and leaving ruined forest in their wake. With some companies operating twenty-four hours a day, nearly 2,200 acres of forest are lost daily (Carothers, 1990; Ryan, 1991). The Asian region is the world's largest and fastest growing source of timber. Most of the wood is sold internationally for lumber. The Penan and their neighbors, the Kelabit, are fighting back. Thousands have participated in roadblocks, and hundreds have been arrested. The Malaysian courts rejected the first arrests, but a new law makes interfering with logging a state crime.

Resisters to development of the Amazon region in Brazil have fared better than the Penan in some ways, but worse in others. After much controversy and many deaths, a reserve the size of Missouri was set aside for the Amazon's Yanomamo Indians in 1991. Brazilian labor leader Chico Mendes helped to organize another group, Amazonian rubber tappers, into a national political force. The rubber tappers, who make a living by bleeding natural latex from trees and gathering Brazil nuts (neither of which depletes the resource base), were being squeezed out by ranchers. Under Mendes's leadership the union won four protected areas from the Brazilian government and convinced the Inter-American Development Bank to place environmental restrictions on future loans to Brazil. Mendes paid for his achievements with his life: He was assassinated in December 1988. Amnesty International (1989) estimates that as many as 1,000 union leaders, rubber tappers, peasants, and Indians were killed in the fight over the Amazon during the 1980s.

The activities of the Penan in Sarawak and the Yanomamo and rubber tappers of the Amazon illustrate that deforestation is not simply an environmental issue but also an issue of social justice (*World Resources, 1990–91*, 1990). The global ecological crisis—a product in part of certain countries' affluent lifestyles and energy- and resource-intensive forms of social organization—threatens the local habitats and ecologically benign lifestyles of hundreds of thousands of indigenous people. As Polly Ghazi writes:

In June, 1992, participants in the Earth Summit in Rio de Janeiro [attended by heads of state from around the world] agreed to protect the tropical rain forests, which house nearly half the world's living organisms. A public relations offensive by the international timber lobby helped create a public perception in the West that the future of the Amazon and its peoples was secure. The reality could hardly be more different. . . . There are signs that many of the country's 180 indigenous tribes are close to cultural and physical extinction. (1994, p. 46)

Clearly, global social and economic actions can have far-reaching local consequences.

---

ing tens of thousands sick (French, 1990). At mid-century, air pollution was mainly a local problem, but since then its impact has become global. For example, use of certain industrial products such as chlorofluorocarbons (CFCs, used in spray cans, refrigerators, and air conditioners) has caused the partial destruction of the earth's ozone layer, leading to global warming.

Efforts to control air pollution have brought progress in some cases. The production of CFCs has plummeted (Ryan, 1995). The concentrations of such common pollutants as sulfur dioxide, which comes largely from burning coal and contributes to respiratory diseases and acid rain, have declined in twenty of the thirty-three cities that participate in the United Nations' Global Environmental Monitoring System (GEMS). By restricting automobile emissions and requiring power plants to install cleaning devices, Sweden, Austria, Switzerland, and Germany have cut pollution rates by almost two-thirds.

For every success story, however, there are failures and setbacks. The former communist countries were among the world's worst polluters, driven by the imperative to produce industrial goods at all costs (see

Population growth must be viewed in the context of the environmental, social, and other problems of Third World cities. This photograph of Mexico City shows air pollution so severe that it is health-threatening— a dramatic example of urban growth that has outstripped the social infrastructure's ability to prevent or control it.

Chapter 16). In Eastern Europe, the former Soviet Union, and much of the developing world, there are still no emission controls on industry or vehicles. In the beautiful ancient city of Krakow, Poland, damage to historical buildings is so severe that people speak of the stone as "melting." In fourteen of the cities GEMS monitors in China, sulfur dioxide levels are rising and now stand three to five times as high as in North America. In the developing world, the need for economic growth often leads governments to ignore environmental problems.

In addition to these local pollution problems, many modern practices and technologies are contributing to a more general destruction of the earth's atmosphere. The atmosphere functions like a blanket to trap warmth from the sun and keep rivers and oceans from freezing, and to shield the earth from harmful ultraviolet rays. In recent years, pollution from human activities has begun to threaten both functions. The **greenhouse effect** refers to the way atmospheric gases, like the roof of a greenhouse, trap heat. The most common "greenhouse gases" are water vapor, carbon dioxide, methane, nitrous oxide, and ozone. Life on earth depends on the maintenance of a certain concentration of greenhouse gases in the atmosphere. With too few, the earth would be as frozen as Mars, and with too many, as hot as Venus. The concentration of these gases, which has been growing since the beginning of the Industrial Revolution, has accelerated rapidly in recent decades. The main rea-

sons are the burning of fossil fuels and the cutting and burning of forests (live trees collect and store carbon, and burning trees releases it). The current scientific consensus is that if this trend continues, it will probably cause a dangerous level of global warming (Roodman, 1995). This increase in average temperatures might cause the polar ice caps to melt and the oceans to rise, flooding many cities; droughts in the major breadbaskets of the world, such as the American Midwest; mass migrations and extinctions of plant and animal species; and changes in the distribution of disease-bearing organisms. No one knows exactly how severe global warming might be, but there is clear cause for concern. Although developed nations are prime contributors to the greenhouse effect, developing nations also make a contribution, which increases as their populations grow (see Figure 18.12).

Acid rain, the result of air pollutants trapped in water vapors, falls on every continent, changing the chemistry of lakes and rivers to the point that fish can no longer survive and damaging crops and trees. In Northern Europe, 125 million acres of forest have been affected. Acid rain illustrates that pollution does not respect political boundaries: Often the sources of pollution are far from the effects. Coal burned in eastern Europe affects the West; coal burned in New England affects Canada; coal burned in Tennessee affects North Carolina, where acid rain has begun to kill trees on the Smoky Mountains.

Water Pollution

Water pollution from human activity dates back to antiquity, but the scope and severity of the problem are increasing. There are three basic sources of pollution of the earth's fresh water (World Resources Institute, 1991). One is domestic waste, which has become a critical problem in Third World cities like Mexico's capital. Untreated sewage dumped into waterways not only carries health-threatening bacteria but also depletes the water of oxygen that is essential to aquatic life. A second source of freshwater pollution is industrial waste, a problem in all cities and, increasingly, in industrialized suburbs. A third source is land use. When land is cleared for agriculture, erosion becomes more common and pesticides and fertilizers leach into both groundwater and waterways. Dense human habitation—cities—is even more destructive of fresh water than is agriculture.

Water pollution combines with depletion of water reserves to threaten a critical shortage of clean drinking water. Already, many people in the world lack access to safe drinking water, and most of the lakes and rivers in the world (including most of those in the United States) are polluted to some degree. In Mexico City, the enormous population draws deeper into the groundwater supply every year, using far more water than arrives in the form of rain. As a result, Mexico City is sinking—going down about ten feet during the 1980s alone. As the depletion of water supplies proceeds, remaining groundwater grows ever saltier and must be treated before it can be drunk—or even used for some industrial purposes (G. Gardner, 1995).

People in the world's richer countries tend to behave as if water is so plentiful that it's almost free, but in many developing countries people now pay a significant percentage of their disposable incomes for drinking water (Harrison, 1992, pp. 195–201). Others must walk as much as two hours a day to haul it. This is a clear example of a more general sociological phenomenon: As supplies of natural resources dwindle and pollution spreads, access to the resources that once seemed equally given to all humankind comes to depend more on ability to pay. Those who can afford it move from central cities to suburbs for clean air. Cities like Los Angeles buy water from hundreds of miles away, often pricing it out of the reach of farmers nearer the source. Oil and gas are already out of the reach of most Third World consumers.

There is little doubt that human activity, particularly during the last century, has endangered the planet. The question is whether human activity can save it. Successful efforts will depend not just on direct environmental conservation and cleanup but on limiting or reducing the pressure large human populations place on the natural environment.

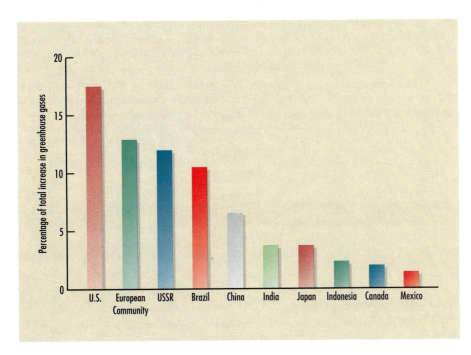

FIGURE 18.12 / The Ten Countries with the Most Greenhouse-Gas Emissions, 1987

When it comes to contributing the emissions that cause the greenhouse effect and global warming, the big four in the world are the United States, the European Economic Community nations, the countries of the former Soviet Union, and Brazil. For an industrialized country with such a high level of economic output, Japan does quite well at restricting its share of these atmospheric pollutants.

Source: *World Resources, 1990–91* (World Resources Institute, Washington, D.C., 1991), p. 3.

SUMMARY

1. Demography is the study of how births, deaths, and migration affect the composition, size, and distribution of populations. Sociologists use demographic information to describe social structure, to evaluate the cumulative impact of individual decisions, and to predict future trends.

2. China is the world's most populous country, with nearly a fifth of the world's people. Through the use of rigidly enforced family-planning policies, it has also become one of the most successful Third World examples of population control, accounting for most of the world's reduction in fertility during the 1980s.

3. The main source of population data is the census, a periodic counting of the population and a collection of information about it. A full census of the U.S. population is conducted every ten years. The census attempts to reach every person in the country but may underestimate the numbers of poor, males, minorities, and immigrants especially.

4. Population growth depends on the relationship among three demographic variables: fertility (the number of births an average woman will have in her lifetime), mortality (usually expressed as the number of deaths in a given age group), and migration. In the twentieth century, fertility rates in the United States have dropped steadily (except for the post-World War II baby boom), while mortality rates have also dropped, and life expectancy has increased. Declining death rates have contributed to the growth of our population, but the main source of U.S. population growth has been immigration. The impact of birth, death, and immigration rates can also be seen in our population's age structure.

5. Until fairly recently the world's human population grew slowly, in fits and starts. Beginning in about 1850, the population began to spiral upward. Barring mass epidemics, famine, or nuclear holocaust, it will reach 8.5 billion in 2025, and four out of five people will live in the Third World.

6. Thomas Malthus was the first scholar to analyze population growth and to worry about its consequences for humankind. He felt that increases in the food supply could never keep pace with population growth. The only way to halt population growth, in his opinion, was voluntary abstinence from sexual relations. Otherwise, population growth would be checked drastically by war, pestilence, or starvation.

7. Karl Marx took exception to Malthusian doctrine, believing that the problem was not one of overpopulation but of underproduction and the inequitable distribution of the world's wealth. Whereas Malthus saw the solution in moral restraint, Marx saw it in socialism.

8. The basic model of population change in the West over the past two centuries is known as the demographic transition. In stage 1, high birth and death rates keep population size stable. In stage 2, the death rate begins to decline as public hygiene and sanitation improve and better food supplies become available. Population grows rapidly. In stage 3, the birth rate drops, too. Finally, in stage 4, as in the industrialized nations today, the birth and death rates are low and in balance again.

9. Demographers are cautious about applying the model of the demographic transition to the developing world. In much of the Third World, death rates have dropped precipitously in a very short time because of imported technology. However, birth rates are high and are likely to remain so as long as large families provide advantages to individuals. A number of studies show that the surest way to reduce fertility is to raise the status of women.

10. Already the Malthusian nightmare is a reality for millions of people. As population growth puts a strain on available resources, hunger, starvation, environmental deterioration, underemployment, and civil unrest become increasingly common.

11. Awareness of human threats to the environment has grown, but not enough to halt or significantly slow the depletion of natural resources and pollution. Resource depletion is most obvious in the use of nonrenewable fossil fuels (especially by American drivers) and in the destruction of forests (often the tropical forests of the southern hemisphere).

12. Pollution is most obvious in Third World cities. Scientists now realize that pollution is not merely a local problem but has global consequences, especially the greenhouse effect and global warming, destruction of the ozone layer, and acid rain. Reversing such trends will require a reordering of priorities on a global scale.

REVIEW QUESTIONS

1. How is population structure different from population distribution? (Illustrate your definitions with examples.)

2. How does the U.S. census work?

3. Discuss the role of the three central variables in demographic analysis: fertility, mortality, and migration.

4. What is the demographic transition?

5. What factors speed up or hold back efforts to reduce fertility?

6. How do resource depletion and pollution endanger the planet?

7. How do population growth and concentration lead to environmental problems?

CRITICAL THINKING QUESTIONS

1. Think of a city or town that you know well. How would you describe its population structure?

2. Malthus and Marx disagreed over the question of whether the world's population could grow indefinitely or would necessarily be blocked by natural limits. What factors did both of them overlook? If they had stressed the key sociological concept of culture, how would their thinking have been helped?

3. What factors could prevent the demographic transition from proceeding through all its potential stages to the point where lowered fertility rates match lowered death rates?

4. China has lowered its fertility rate considerably, which has contributed to economic growth and higher incomes. It relied heavily on government coercion to do so. Do you think this is always necessary? Why or why not? What are some alternative approaches?

5. Resource depletion and pollution are two major factors endangering the earth. To what extent do you think new technologies can cope with each? To what extent are social changes necessary? What kind?

6. This chapter describes a number of conservation measures that might contribute to a sustainable world. Do you think these measures alone will accomplish the goal? Are there others that would help? What are some strategies that might make more people comply with conservation measures?

GLOSSARY

Age structure   The way in which members of a population are distributed into different age categories.

Census   A periodic counting of a population, in which age, sex, occupation, and other facts are also recorded.

Demographic transition   A three-stage process in which a population shifts from a high birth rate and a high death rate, to a high birth rate but a low death rate and hence rapid population growth, to a low birth rate, a low death rate, and a more or less stable population.

Demography   The scientific study of how births, deaths, and migration affect the composition, size, and distribution of populations.

Ecology   The pattern of relationships among biological organisms (including humans) and between organisms and their environments.

Emigration   The movement of people *out* of a population or area.

Greenhouse effect   A collection of gases emitted into the earth's atmosphere that traps heat and may lead to global warming.

Green Revolution   The creation of new strains of wheat, rice, and other grains that doubled and tripled the yields per acre in the late 1950s.

Immigration   The movement of people *into* a population or area.

Infant mortality rate   The number of deaths among infants under one year of age per 1,000 live births in a given year.

Internal migration   Movement from one location to another *within* a country.

Life expectancy   The average number of years of life remaining for an individual of a given age.

Life span   The maximum number of years of human life.

Migration   Movement into or out of a population or locality.

Net migration rate   The difference between the number of people who leave and those who enter any population or country each year, per 1,000 people.

Pollution   Damage to the environment caused by waste levels that overload natural recycling systems or by synthetic materials that cannot be broken down by natural processes.

Population distribution   The proportions of people in different locations, such as world regions, countries, provinces, states, cities, or neighborhoods.

Population size   The sheer number of people in a population.

Population structure   The pattern that results from the age, sex, education, income, occupation, marital status, race, and religion of members of a population.

Replacement rate   The fertility rate at which a population will remain stable (in the absence of immigration).

Total fertility rate (TFR)   The average number of births a woman will have in her lifetime.

CHAPTER 19

Communities and Urbanization

Diagonal, Iowa, is the kind of place most Americans picture when they think about small towns (Hundley, 1989). Main Street climbs three blocks, past a collection of storefronts, to the top of a gentle hill. From there the surrounding countryside spreads out toward the horizon like a patchwork quilt in amber, green, and brown. The heart of Diagonal is the high school gymnasium, which holds about 1,000 spectators. On winter nights, when the basketball team is playing, the gym is packed to the rafters, even though the entire population of Diagonal is only 362. In 1938, the tiny school won the state championship, overpowering big-city schools in a season that seemed like a Hollywood movie script. That championship season has become part of local legend, passed from generation to generation.

The legend lives on: Fifty years later the high school is still producing winning basketball teams, despite an enrollment of just forty-two students. Almost every boy in the school turns out for the team, and hopes for each season usually run high. Except for basketball nights, teenagers find Diagonal deadly dull; but the adults, many born and raised in the town, can't imagine a better life. Says one who returned after a spell in Philadelphia:

> People don't get lost. It's a sense of things being small enough that you can have an impact. A school play or a band recital is a major community activity in a small town. People are involved. They aren't home flipping the remote control in front of the TV set. When you walk down the street or go into a grocery store, people are glad to see you. It's totally different from when I used to go into a supermarket in Philadelphia. (Quoted in Hundley, 1989, p. 21)

New York City is 2,000 miles away from Diagonal, but considering the New York lifestyle, the distance seems more like 200,000. On Manhattan's Upper West Side, Columbus Avenue is a center of conspicuous consumption. Young urban professionals stroll through its stores on weekends, buying $500 sports jackets and $200 slacks, perfect for sitting in a fashionable café, sipping Perrier at $5 a glass. On a typical Sunday thousands of people are part of this Yuppie scene. Some come from the suburbs and some from other sections of New York City, but a great many are Upper West Siders. They all live in the same small area (five blocks wide by about twenty-seven blocks long), yet while browsing through a new shop, dining in a restaurant, or drinking at a bar, they usually do not know *any* of the people around them. The Upper West Side is decidedly a "community" of strangers. Each resident is acquainted with only a tiny fraction of its population of 100,000.

In almost every way, Diagonal and the Upper West Side of Manhattan appear to be opposites. In Diagonal everyone knows everyone else personally; people are involved in a continual round of community-centered activities (the few who do not participate are thought aloof and antisocial); and everyone's activities are subject to close scrutiny. Gossip keeps most Diagonal residents from stepping very far out of line. Of course, sexual transgressions, public drunkenness, and teenage vandalism occasionally take place, but serious crime is rare. On the Upper West Side most people know only a few of the people who live in their apartment building; everyone has his or her own circle of friends; and community-based activities are rare (perhaps just an occasional block party). Neighborliness is often considered nosiness. Anonymity is the norm, and widely different lifestyles are tolerated or simply ignored. At the same time, crime is common: Most Upper West Siders either have been the victims of a mugging or robbery or know someone who has been.

Is New York, then, *nothing* at all like Diagonal? Not entirely. As we discuss more fully later in this chapter, traditional communities—and sometimes whole new kinds of communities—can thrive in even the most urbanized settings. Thus, New York is also home to the close-knit Orthodox Jewish community of Brooklyn and an impressively organized gay community centered in Greenwich Village. The tendency of people to form communities depends on more than just the density of their population.

This chapter takes a sociological look at community life in cities, suburbs, and small towns in the indus-

trialized world. (See Chapter 20 for a look at community life in the less developed world.) The organization of these communities is functionally integrated with that of the larger societies of which they are part. They are joined economically—for example, to places that sell them goods and buy what they produce—and politically, to a government that regulates life throughout the country. In fact, functional integration on a global scale now links American communities to others throughout the world. As a result, our cities and towns are gradually being transformed by global changes in technology and trade. Communities are also units of social structure. They are among the building blocks that make up the organization of whole countries, and at the same time they are internally structured by differences in wealth and ethnicity (recall the introduction to Chapter 8 on stratification). Urbanization, the process by which small towns grow into cities, is a transformation of social structure in response to changing patterns of functional integration. These two key concepts—social structure and functional integration—are the ones that we will refer to most often as we explore both communities and urbanization.

Of course, urbanization also affects culture. Communities have their own local cultural traditions, as we saw when looking at Diagonal and the Upper West Side. These can be threatened by structural transformations like urbanization or the relocation of jobs as cities grow older and start to decline. Such structural transformations are not entirely "natural" processes; they result from social action and the use of power. Individuals decide whether to move to big cities, stay put in small towns, or return to small communities. Their decisions, however, are shaped by the power of those in charge of corporations to close factories and offices in or near older cities in order to build new facilities in rural areas where costs are lower. The shape of a city like Los Angeles is the result of active decisions by powerful individuals and groups who tore up older streetcar systems and literally paved the way for commuting by car. Different sorts of communities are also the contexts for different kinds of social action—from charity to crime. Thus, the role of both police and churches is shaped by whether they exist in large, relatively impersonal urban areas or in small towns where most people know one another.

We begin this chapter by examining whether urbanization—the growth of big cities—has destroyed community or has simply given new form to the kinds of close, enduring relationships found in small towns like Diagonal. Then we consider the historical process of urbanization: where and when cities first appeared and why and how they developed. Next we look more closely at the contemporary urban environment and evaluate several theories that attempt to explain its spatial organization. We conclude by examining current trends in rural, urban, and suburban communities.

THE EFFECTS OF URBANIZATION ON COMMUNITY

Urbanization is the process whereby large numbers of people leave the countryside and small towns to settle in cities and surrounding metropolitan areas. Thus, urbanization involves migration from sparsely populated regions to densely populated ones. The scope of this migration has been enormous in the twentieth century. In 1900, 86.4 percent of the world's population lived in rural areas, and only 13.6 percent lived in cities. Today, nearly half of the world's people are city dwellers, and by 2025, the United Nations estimates that 60 percent of the world's people will live in urban areas (Population Reference Bureau, 1995; Wilken, 1995). Densely populated urban regions have become a dominant feature of the modern landscape.

Sociologists have disagreed sharply on the consequences of urbanization. Some emphasize the positive. They view cities as the high point of human civilization: as places where people of different backgrounds can mingle and exchange ideas and outlooks, places that encourage innovations in business, science, technology, and the arts. Other sociologists contend that the problems of city life outweigh the benefits. Cities, they say, are polluted, crime-ridden, hectic environments that promote stress and mental illness.

This debate centers on whether urbanization has meant a loss of community. By *community*, sociologists mean more than a particular place inhabited by people. The term also describes a certain depth and quality of relationships. People who form a **community** have common values and interests, relatively dense and enduring ties, engage in frequent face-to-face interactions, feel close to one another, and tend to think of themselves as part of a group (they have a sense of "we-ness").

What effect has urbanization had on community? Sociologists suggest three different answers (Hunter, 1978). One view is that large, densely populated urban areas like the Upper West Side have destroyed all possibility of community. A second view holds that a sense of community similar to that of Diagonal can persist within the neighborhoods of even the biggest, most populated cities: New York, Chicago, and Boston have enclaves where relationships are in some ways like those in small towns. A third view argues that urbanization has given rise to a new kind of community, one that does not depend on people's living near one another. In the following sections we will explore the evidence for each of these perspectives.

The Disintegration of Community

The idea that urbanization destroys community has deep roots in sociology. As early as 1887 the German sociologist Ferdinand Tönnies contrasted the social relations in a community (which he called *Gemeinschaft*) to those in a society or "association" (which he called *Gesellschaft*). Tönnies viewed old and settled small towns as the model for *Gemeinschaft*. In a *Gemeinschaft*, each person is embedded in a close-knit network of relatives and friends. Members of the community have a common ancestry and common values, aspirations, and traditions, as well as many common roles. Shared histories, common activities, and frequent face-to-face relations help to create strong social and emotional bonds. In a *Gemeinschaft*, status tends to be ascribed at birth. The squire's son does not become a tenant farmer, and the tenant farmer's son does not marry a daughter of the gentry. People tend to remain what they were born to be. Geographic mobility is also limited. Most individuals live and die in the same small area. As a result, people think of their identity in terms of their place within the community.

Urban, industrial society, according to Tönnies, is dramatically different. It is a *Gesellschaft* because people are linked together through formal organizations and markets, rather than informal relations and a sense of belonging. Big and rapidly growing cities epitomize *Gesellschaft*. Their large and close-packed populations guarantee that many of the people who encounter each other in the course of a typical day will be strangers, and their interactions will be impersonal. Relationships tend to be very superficial, even with neighbors. Often neighbors come from very different backgrounds, so they may not share ancestry, values, norms, or attitudes. They are also not likely to have the same work roles, since work in urban society is highly specialized. All these differences create social distance. Those ties which urban dwellers do have tend to be fragmented. Friends may live across town, coworkers miles away, and relatives on the other side of the country. In small towns, in contrast, because of their much smaller structure, neighbors are more apt to be coworkers, to attend the same church, and to participate in the same leisure activities, thus drawing them into a single, tightly knit community (Calhoun, 1980). Urbanites are also much more mobile than are residents of traditional small towns. In our own highly urbanized country, one out of every ten people moves each year. Urbanites move socially as well, leaving old friends behind as they make new ones.

Tönnies saw urbanization, the shift from *Gemeinschaft* to *Gesellschaft*, as one of the defining trends of the modern era. He regretted this development, for he thought it meant a loss of community. Other European sociologists also stressed the impersonality of urban life, though some saw more good points in the balance. In a classic essay, "The Metropolis and Mental Life" (1902–1903/1950), another influential German sociologist, Georg Simmel, also looked at interaction patterns in urban areas. He focused partly on the effects of the noisy, crowded, hectic backdrop on urbanites' everyday dealings with one another. According to Simmel, such constant stimulation encourages people to develop a blasé attitude toward what is going on around them. This attitude enables them to screen out much of what they see and hear, thus shielding them from emotional exhaustion or what we today call *psychic overload* (Milgram, 1970). The result is that city dwellers seem to be cold and heartless, indifferent to the feelings and actions of others. This protective shell contrasts sharply with the mutual concern and caring typical of people in very small towns. On the other hand, Simmel thought that urban life was much more conducive to the development of individuality, partly because its social structure allows anonymity and a wide variety of personal relationships.

In the United States, Louis Wirth (1938) echoed the ideas of both Tönnies and Simmel. Wirth was a member of the University of Chicago's department of sociology, which did a great deal to develop the field of urban sociology. On the basis of his studies of Chicago during the 1920s and 1930s, Wirth argued that city populations have three main structural characteristics: large size, high density (crowding), and

The word "community" describes a kind of social bond that exists among people as well as their physical settlement. Traditionally, many Native American tribes were nomadic hunters and gatherers. After their defeat by the U.S. military in the nineteenth century, they were forced to settle permanently on isolated, often barren reservations. Their culture destroyed, for many decades the community of Native Americans was in steep decline.

great heterogeneity (many differences among people). Each of these characteristics, according to Wirth, tends to discourage close personal relationships. For instance, a large population makes it impossible for everyone to know everyone else. Because the Upper West Side of Manhattan has 100,000 residents and is part of a city of over 7 million and a metropolitan region of nearly 20 million, most social encounters are necessarily with strangers. This does not mean that New Yorkers have fewer friends than people elsewhere or care less about them, but those friends make up a smaller proportion of the people with whom they interact each day. Similarly, crowding can encourage impersonal and aloof social encounters because it tends to give rise to friction and irritation, as people find it hard to obtain space and privacy. Wirth agreed with Simmel that the closer the physical contact that people must have with strangers, the more distant their social relations will be. Finally, a heterogeneous population can undermine close personal ties as well. When neighbors do not share values, norms, and attitudes, they tend to lose the sense of "we-ness" characteristic of community.

Wirth linked the impersonal nature of city life to the spread of serious social problems. When people feel isolated and cut off from emotional support, they are more vulnerable to mental breakdowns, depression, and suicide. Similarly, an indifferent attitude toward others can permit increased rates of crime, delinquency, and corruption. Urban residents are more likely to prey upon each other because they think of their neighbors as anonymous faces, not as individuals. Moreover, deviance in cities is difficult to control because people do not keep an eye on one another and condemn wrongdoers, as small-town residents often do. Instead, city dwellers try to maintain social order through formal mechanisms of control: the law, the police, the courts. These are seldom as effective as the informal social pressures that operate in villages and towns.

Empirical evidence suggests that Wirth may have overstated his case in claiming that urban life breeds serious social problems. After reviewing a number of studies, Harvey Choldin (1978) concluded that population density is not the primary cause of crime and juvenile delinquency. Rather, these social problems are based on a variety of social-structural factors, such as the racial mix of a population or the distribution of wealth and jobs, which vary considerably from one city to another.

The Persistence of Community

Other sociologists have questioned the notion that traditional community ties cannot survive in large, modern cities. In their view, many urban neighborhoods are similar to small towns in both social structure and interaction patterns. Herbert Gans was one of the first sociologists to collect evidence for this view. In 1957, he rented an apartment in Boston's West End so that he could observe life there firsthand. At the time, the West End of Boston was a low-income, working-class district of about 7,000 people living in three- and five-story tenement buildings. Most of the residents were second- and third-generation Italian-Americans, although enclaves of Poles, Jews, Greeks, Ukrainians, and other nationalities could be found there, too. Government officials considered the West End a decaying slum and planned to demolish it.

Gans found that the area's social structure made it far from the depersonalized, alienating kind of place that Wirth had described. In fact, he discovered that the West End was a community with the same close, enduring ties and networks of mutual support thought to exist only in very small towns. When Gans wrote a book about West End residents, he aptly titled it *The Urban Villagers* (1962).

Gans believed that what made the West End an urban village was interpersonal relationships. Obviously, all 7,000 West End residents were not intimately acquainted; but they did know and routinely talked with the neighbors on their own blocks. A very active social life took place in the hallways of apartment buildings, in shops, on stoops, and on the streets. Neighbors would greet one another, stop to chat, and catch up on gossip. In this way West Enders learned about other members of their own ethnic groups, even about people they had never met. They might hear that a friend's second cousin three blocks away had just given birth to twins, or that the father-in-law of another friend's niece had lost his job. Through such intimate personal information, West Enders felt connected to hundreds of others around them. They knew one another's joys and sorrows, strengths and weaknesses, triumphs and failures. By no means a collection of strangers, they enjoyed the close social ties characteristic of a true community, even though they lived in the midst of a modern city.

The most intensive social interactions among West Enders took place among their small peer groups made up of relatives and close friends who got to-gether several times a week in someone's home. The men would congregate in the living room, the women around the kitchen table. For hours on end they would talk, joke, laugh, swap stories, report the lat-est gossip, and simply enjoy being part of the group. For the Italian West Enders on whom Gans focused, group life was all-important. Peer groups started to form in early childhood and continued into adoles-cence and adulthood. They provided companion-ship, emotional support, and even outlets for ex-pressing individuality; West Enders felt lost without them.

The West End of Boston is not unique. The sociol-ogist Gerald Suttles (1968) found similar patterns in Chicago. The Near West Side of Chicago was clearly divided into ethnic neighborhoods—Italian, Mexican, black, Puerto Rican—each a village unto it-self. Like Boston's West Enders, Near West Siders were well acquainted with neighbors from their own ethnic groups. To walk along their block was not to pass through a sea of strangers, but to greet people they had known all their lives—people who shared their culture.

Local businesses, catering to the dominant ethnic group in the neighborhood, helped to create a small-town atmosphere. An Italian-owned grocery store, a black-owned barbershop, a Mexican-owned café all were places where people of these ethnic back-grounds could find the products and services they preferred. At the same time, these establishments be-came centers of neighborhood social life. People would stop by to banter and gossip, discuss their problems, and air their views. Very often people came and went without purchasing anything. Economic transactions were considered secondary to the real business of social give-and-take. If someone was a little short of cash, credit would be extended with no embarrassment or fuss. (These social patterns are very similar to those in small towns like Diagonal, where residents often visit the shops of Main Street just to see and chat with friends.) Such patterns bear little relationship to the stereotyped view of cold and highly depersonalized life in a large city. More re-cently, Mitchell Dunier (1992) has shown that similar social bonds and gathering places link residents of even the poorest and most economically troubled of Chicago's neighborhoods.

Gans, Suttles, and like-minded researchers argue that community may persist *despite* urbanization. They point out that even in the largest cities, the res-idents of a neighborhood may develop a shared sense of belonging, intimacy, and caring. Often these urban villagers are immigrants from small rural towns in Europe or South America, or the children or grand-children of such immigrants. They are maintaining the kind of community ties that their families have always thought of as natural and right.

The Transformation of Community

Close-knit ethnic neighborhoods are not the only places where community survives in big cities. Other sociologists have proposed that the high concentra-tion of people in urban settings gives rise to a dis-tinctive social structure, which in turn fosters new forms of community attachment, not necessarily based on common origins or residential proximity. According to this view, city dwellers often form so-cial networks (see Chapter 3) that transcend neigh-borhood boundaries and even city lines (Webber, 1966). These networks are based on shared interests, occupations, and activities. Thus, feminists from dif-ferent parts of a city might meet regularly to share their views and undertake joint projects, or people who love classical music might form an amateur chamber orchestra and play together once a week. Rural villagers are not conducive to these kinds of interest-based networks, for their populations are not large and diverse enough to support them. Only the city, with its huge concentration of people, allows such urban subcultures to form. Ironically, then, pop-ulation size and density (the very traits that Wirth thought alienated people from one another) enable new kinds of social ties to develop and help perpet-uate community.

The sociologist Claude Fischer (1982) tested this theory by interviewing more than 1,000 men and women who lived in places that varied greatly in their degree of urbanism. He found that urbanism did encourage people to find friends in a wider geo-graphic area, and the physical distance between friends did not weaken the personal bonds they formed. Friends who lived in widely separated sec-tions of a city were just as likely to feel close to one another as friends who lived next door. Urbanism, in other words, did not destroy community. Rather, ur-banism transformed community by broadening the geographic boundaries within which community was built up. Fischer also found that living in an urban area changed the composition of people's social net-

An urban oasis. New York City encourages neighborhood associations to plant gardens in vacant, often trash-strewn, city-owned lots. Urban gardens not only provide beauty and calm, but also bring neighbors together.

works. Relationships tended to be based less on kinship and membership in the same church, and more on shared work roles and shared involvement in secular associations (clubs, interest groups, and civic organizations).

But if community survives in cities, why do we get the sense that urbanites are remote and uncaring? The answer, according to Fischer, is that city dwellers differ from rural residents in their general distrust of strangers. One reason for this distrust is a greater fear of crime and other forms of victimization. In public, urbanites don a protective shell of aloofness, as Simmel described. In their private lives, however, they have close and caring relationships just as people in villages and small towns do.

Thus, all the views of urban life that we have described may be correct to some extent at the same time. The sense of community in cities may be simultaneously disintegrating, persisting, and changing. Depending on which particular urban districts we look at, and the context of the situation, we can find empirical support for each of these three theories. The task for sociologists is to identify the specific conditions under which urbanization destroys, sustains, or creates community ties. (See the Sociology and Public Debates box.) We will return to this task later in this chapter.

CHANGING PATTERNS OF URBAN LIFE: A TALE OF THREE CITIES

A **city** is a relatively large, densely populated, and permanent settlement of people who are socially diverse and who do not directly produce their own food. In general, cities dominate the surrounding countryside and smaller towns. This characterization applies to cities through the ages, from ancient Thebes in Egypt and Athens in Greece to modern-day New York, Tokyo, and Paris.

At the dawn of human culture, people lived in small bands, hunting, fishing, and foraging for their food. In most places, wild foods were not plentiful enough to support more than a small number of people, so humans were forced to be nomadic. They would settle in a place for only a short time, moving on when the food supply ran short.

Why did people begin to live in villages, towns, and cities? What led to these new forms of social organization? To answer these questions, we must look back 10,000 years, to the era when people first began to domesticate plants and animals. Probably in areas where food supplies were scarce, people began weeding and watering stands of edible plants, adding organic matter to fertilize the soil, and saving the seeds from the strongest, most desirable plants to sow the

Community Development or Community Loss?

Through the first half of the twentieth century, the midwestern city of Indianapolis had a thriving African-American community, with industry, a nationally important jazz scene, and a sense of collective identity. Spatially compact, partly because of forced segregation, this community centered on Indiana Boulevard, just east of and across the river from downtown. It was internally diverse and included its own public institutions, such as churches and theaters, and its own commercial establishments; also, it had both more prosperous and more depressed sections. Like other such communities in several American cities, the Eastside community in Indianapolis declined as a result of changes in urban ecology and political economy and was ultimately destroyed in the name of community development. Well-intentioned social actions by those who sought to eliminate poverty-stricken areas from Indianapolis also eliminated what was left of a once-strong community. Was this good?

> They sought to make Indianapolis as a whole a "better" community, but they did not consider the value of Eastside as a community in and of itself.

THE DEBATE

Like many African-American communities, the Eastside of Indianapolis was hit hard by the Great Depression of the 1930s. After World War II, economic recovery was only partial, and the cohesiveness of the community was undermined both by new opportunities for individual mobility that drew many talented young people away and by the penetration of large-scale business organizations replacing local establishments. The community nonetheless survived, maintained in significant part by a close-knit web of interpersonal relationships and mutual support, and also by a shared knowledge of important local traditions. But to outsiders and to some of Indianapolis's black elite, this cohesive Eastside community appeared "depressed" and was a "public problem."

During the 1960s and 1970s, concerned citizens began to call for "community development" efforts to improve the economy and make Indianapolis more attractive. The Eastside community was destroyed as part of these efforts. In its place, a large, predominantly white branch of the state university system was built, complete with hotel and convention facilities. Next door, there is open space, but little residential development.

Earlier efforts to improve the lot of impoverished African-Americans had presumed that they would stay more or less where they were. Public housing was thus constructed in the midst of the existing Eastside community. In this context, the public-housing projects became relatively socially stable. But the new thinking did not see maintenance of the community as a value in and of itself, and instead sought to disperse what had been the concentration of African-Americans in a traditionally black community and to bring in new economic resources by removing "eyesores" and building new buildings for new uses. The public-housing projects, among the country's oldest, were razed to make way for university student housing. Thousands of people were forced to move.

Developers championing revitalization were aided by well-intentioned philanthropists and urban plan-

next spring. At the same time, they began protecting herds of small wild animals such as goats and sheep from predators and moving them to more plentiful pastures during the dry months of summer and supplementing their diets during the harshest periods of winter. These innovations, coupled with a few simple techniques for storing grain and meat, enabled people to settle in small, semipermanent villages. These villages, which consisted of only 200 to 400 people, were the basic form of human social organization for the next several thousand years (Childe, 1952).

Then, sometime between 6000 and 5000 B.C., in the basins of the Nile, Tigris-Euphrates, and Indus river valleys, settlements emerged more than ten times the size of any earlier ones. Housing between 7,000 and 20,000 people, these first true cities developed largely because innovations in agriculture and transportation enabled people to take advantage of the valleys' exceptionally fertile soils. The domestication of new, higher-yield grains and the development of the ox-drawn plow, metalworking, and irrigation made possible large surpluses of food. These surpluses permitted some of the population to become full-time

ners. They sought to make Indianapolis as a whole a "better" community, but they did not consider the value of Eastside as a community in and of itself. This approach did not give much weight to the distinctive culture that had developed and been passed on in the Eastside community. It dispersed African-Americans from what had been a real, centered community into a mix of suburbs and more impoverished urban districts.

The older Eastside community had also been a base for social action, including public participation. It had housed a wide variety of voluntary associations and public institutions: major and vital churches, the Indianapolis *Leader,* the Flanner Guild, the Twentieth Century Literary Society (and many others), the Woman's Improvement Club of Indianapolis, and the Afro-American Council. The African-American community was prominent enough to lure national organizations like the Knights of Pythias and the Anti-Lynching League to hold meetings there (Ferguson, 1988; Specht, 1989).

Eastside was also a center of employment and business development. Most famously, it was the base for Madame C. J. Walker, the first African-American woman to become a millionaire entrepreneur. "Madame," as she was almost universally called, employed 3,000 people in the manufacture of cosmetics and hair products, with a payroll of about $200,000 by 1917 (Doyle, 1989). Beyond party politics and business, the Eastside community had been a center of artistic and cultural activity. It was still an important jazz center as recently as the 1950s, and community leaders like Madame Walker built theaters and sponsored performers. Eastside had remained a community not just because of jobs, but because of a sense of cultural continuity.

But with the destruction of the neighborhood, this is lost. Most black children in Indianapolis today have no knowledge that J. J. Johnson, Freddie Hubbard, and other jazz greats were born there. Johnson has in fact moved back, but in four years he has not played publicly in Indianapolis, complaining that there is simply not the audience that exists, say, in Chicago. Madame C. J. Walker is celebrated in African-American history classes, but in her old neighborhood, if she is remembered at all, it is often for the theater named after her that now stands alone as a historical monument with no community around it. The solidarity and continuity of the Indianapolis African-American community has been sharply reduced.

ANALYSIS
Community provides the social structure that enables people to participate in economic and political life. When it is lost, they lose clout. This social structure also sustains culture. Without the base of strong communities, African-Americans are in danger of losing touch with their own traditions. Communities prosper or decline as a result of large impersonal forces of functional integration, such as the changing demand for different economic products and the shift from manual work to high-technology manufacturing and service and office jobs. What happens to communities is also a matter of power, because their fate is shaped by the decisions of corporations and urban elites who choose where and how to invest resources. In this way, communities are partly a product of social action. The actions of community members are very important too. Without effort by members to sustain their community, that community may be lost. This is what happened on the Eastside of Indianapolis.

artisans, merchants, teachers, soldiers, and priests, rather than farmers. Specialization of labor, in turn, required that people live close to others on whose skills they depended. Densely populated areas became necessities, and cities began to increase in size and number (Davis, 1955).

Yet the emergence of cities cannot be explained solely in terms of a more complex division of labor. For cities to grow and flourish, a centralized system of power was needed, both to coordinate the new diversity of social and economic activities and to settle conflicts between groups with competing interests

(Sjoberg, 1960). Not accidentally, then, the development of the first true cities coincided with the emergence of powerful governments, administrators, lawmakers, and judges. This was the basis of Rome, Beijing, Istanbul, and Cairo, all of which were capitals of great empires.

During the Middle Ages (from the fall of Rome in the fifth century A.D. until about 1350), urban development in Europe came to a standstill (though cities did grow and flourish in India, China, the Middle East, and elsewhere). With the coming of the Renaissance, European cities began to grow again, not only in size but also in political, technological, and artistic achievements. Fairly typical of cities during this period was Venice, which is located in northeast Italy on the Adriatic Sea.

The Preindustrial City: Venice in Its Golden Age

Venice was built on a cluster of small islands nestled close together in a large lagoon and linked by an intricate network of 177 canals, which still serve as roads to move people and goods throughout the city. By 1492 (ten centuries after its founding) Venice boasted an estimated 190,000 inhabitants, all crowded into a very small space (Davis, 1955).

Even if Venice had not been built on islands, it would still have remained geographically small by today's standards because transportation was limited to horse- and ox-drawn wagons, small boats, or foot. In order for residents to get fairly quickly from one point to another, a preindustrial city could be no more than a few miles across. Before the nineteenth century, the cities of the world were mostly small, concentrated settlements dotting a vast and otherwise rural landscape. Urban sprawl, in other words, is mainly a modern-day phenomenon.

Preindustrial cities were also limited in population. Only so many people could be packed within their borders, because of the problems of supply. For example, food for Venice first had to be carried by wagon to the water's edge, then conveyed by barge to the islands and by gondola through the city. Because this system was so slow, food had to originate in the countryside very near to Venice, and farmers there produced only a limited amount, so the population of Venice could not grow very large.

Without modern technology, the dense population of a preindustrial city tended to be a breeding ground for disease. Rotting garbage and raw sewage were dumped into the canals of Venice, causing foul odors to permeate the city. In 1438, a Spanish visitor to Venice described how residents tried to camouflage the stench by burning sweet-smelling spices in the streets (Chambers, 1970). Spices could do nothing to halt the spread of bacterial and viral infections, however, and epidemics were common.

Venice was dark and dangerous at night. The city's narrow alleys and shadowy canals were the scenes of many murders and other acts of violence, some the result of personal conflicts, others politically motivated. A special police force, the *signori di notte* ("lords of the night"), patrolled the city after dark. Anyone found carrying a sharp knife was automatically fined and imprisoned for two weeks. Even so, Venice's crime rate remained quite high (Chambers, 1970).

Life in preindustrial Venice nevertheless had its attractions. Venice was a beautiful city, an architectural masterpiece. Magnificent churches, piazzas, and houses, many built during the fifteenth and sixteenth centuries, graced (and still grace) the major canals.

Cities like Venice, whose wealthy merchants were patrons of the arts and learning, played a key role in the Renaissance. A city of magnificent churches and palaces, filled with artistic treasures, seemingly floating on the water, Venice still hosts many festivals devoted to contemporary painting, film, drama, and music. Tourism has replaced trade in the city's economy.

Wealthy Venetians were the patrons of many great painters, and the city's glassware and textiles were coveted throughout Europe (Davis, 1973). Like other preindustrial cities, Venice was a center for the arts, handicrafts, the sciences, and learning.

Although life in preindustrial Venice was generally harmonious, the population was sharply divided by social class. A huge gap in wealth existed between the *tabarro* (ordinary citizens) and the *toga* (aristocrats). Aristocratic families lived in great palaces that had large, richly furnished rooms with glass windows; ate lavish meals with silver utensils; and slept on beds with real mattresses (Davis, 1973). A common laborer would have had to work for a year to earn the price of an aristocrat's cloak. There were even legal restrictions on what members of each class could wear. Still, the commoners of Venice were better off than the commoners in most other European cities. The employment rate in preindustrial Venice usually remained high. Although the city had its beggars, they were not as numerous nor as destitute as their counterparts in Rome, Paris, or London. The relative well-being of the common worker is one reason that intense class conflict never erupted in Venice. Another reason was the absolute power of the ruling class. Secret "inquisitors of state" identified those disloyal to the existing regime, keeping most Venetians in line (Rowdon, 1970).

Industrialization and Urbanization: Nineteenth-Century Boston

The next explosion in urban growth was linked to industrialization. We tend to think of the Industrial Revolution only in terms of transforming the production of things like iron and steel, textiles and clothing. However, the Industrial Revolution also affected farming. The introduction of new agricultural equipment (tractors, cultivators, harvesters, milking machines) reduced the need for farm labor while greatly increasing yields. Mass-produced and mass-applied pesticides, herbicides, fertilizers, and feeds had the same effects, as did new, mechanized methods of irrigation. The result was a tremendous leap in the number of people a single farmer could supply. Whereas in 1820 one American farmer fed only four people (including himself), by 1900 one American farmer fed seven people. Over the next eighty years even more impressive gains were made. Such massive food production has made it possible to support huge urban settlements.

Just as industrialization made urban growth possible, so urban growth made industrialization possible. The two processes were interdependent. Workers no longer needed on farms flocked to cities, where they supplied the labor force needed to run the growing number of factories. In the Boston area, early industrialists built factories in small towns to tap surplus farm labor (mainly women and children). Boston itself focused on trade and a few elite crafts. By the 1840s, however, the new steamships were delivering waves of immigrants (many of whom were displaced farmers, desperate for work) to Boston's harbor. To employ this cheap labor pool, industrialists began locating factories in Boston itself. Thus, immigrants played a central role in the industrialization and urbanization of the United States (Warner, 1962).

Boston and other growing cities could support a huge industrial labor force for several reasons. One reason, already mentioned, was the great increase in agricultural productivity. Another was the development of railroad systems, which tremendously improved the speed and efficiency of transportation. Trains could deliver large amounts of food to downtown Boston, much more than could be hauled in with horses, carts, and wagons. The invention of refrigerated freight cars and warehouses further improved this system, making it possible to feed huge concentrations of city dwellers. At the same time, new building materials, such as steel and reinforced concrete, plus the invention of the elevator, enabled architects to design much taller buildings in their efforts to accommodate the increasingly dense population. Finally, improvements in public hygiene (indoor plumbing, municipal sewer systems, citywide garbage collection) cut the mortality rate caused by contagious diseases.

Nineteenth-century Boston differed from preindustrial cities in other ways as well. One way was physical layout. While fifteenth-century Venice was a city of narrow, crooked alleys and canals, nineteenth-century Boston was increasingly developed in a gridlike pattern, with rows of parallel streets intersecting other rows at right angles. The square blocks of land thus formed were divided into uniform lots, each with a relatively narrow frontage on the street. This grid arrangement became the norm for neighborhoods of all kinds, from the tightly spaced three- and five-story tenements of the West End to the spacious one-family houses of the outlying suburbs.

Suburbs themselves were another new feature of industrial urbanization. In nineteenth-century Boston and other cities of that era, suburbs tended to spring up along expanding trolley lines (trolleys were first horse-drawn and then later electrically powered). From an aerial view, Boston began to look like a giant bicycle wheel: The crowded industrial district lay at the center, and suburbs extended out along the fixed-rail spokes. Later, manufacturing plants also started to migrate from the city's central hub to the suburbs, where land was less expensive (Warner, 1962). The factories remained close to train depots, however, for they depended on the railroads to deliver raw materials and ship finished products.

The development of nineteenth-century suburbs intensified the residential segregation of social classes. Because of the small size of preindustrial cities, the rich and the poor never lived very far apart. On the canals of preindustrial Venice, for example, the crowded houses of working-class people sat side by side with the palaces of aristocratic families. Nineteenth-century Boston, in contrast, was developing into a divided city. By 1900, mainly lower-income families lived in the central core, within walking distance of the large factories in which they worked. Most middle- and upper-income families had moved to the suburbs, where the surroundings were less noisy, hectic, and dirty. Still, the distance between rich and poor was not very great. In the 1880s and 1890s, the distance from Boston City Hall to the farthest outlying suburb was only about six miles. Beyond the outermost ring of commuter housing lay great stretches of farms and undeveloped woodland.

The Modern Metropolis: Los Angeles Today

This picture of nineteenth-century Boston bears little resemblance to the huge, contemporary **metropolis,** which is a major city with surrounding municipalities caught up in its economic and social orbit (Herbers, 1983). While Boston has grown into a metropolis, the most striking American example of a metropolis is Los Angeles.

Urban experts describe Los Angeles as a metropolitan "galaxy" with numerous "constellations" (Lockwood and Leinberger, 1988). In sharp contrast to the pattern of older industrial cities in the East, Los Angeles's settlement pattern is relatively low in density. The single-family house is the most common living place; high-rise apartment buildings are relatively rare. Housing sub-divisions, retail shopping districts, entertainment centers, and industrial parks stretch for miles. The Bureau of the Census calls a metropolis like this one a **Consolidated Metropolitan Statistical Area (CMSA).** Each CMSA is an interlinked cluster of one or more cities and their surrounding suburbs that together have a population of over 1 million people. There are twenty-one CMSAs in the United States. Greater Los Angeles, with its 15 million inhabitants, is the second largest in population size after the one centered around New York.

Los Angeles is also huge in physical area. Greater Los Angeles covers nearly 4,100 square miles, an area about *forty times* larger than greater Boston at the turn of the century. Rather than being dominated by a single downtown district, Los Angeles consists of some eighteen diverse urban centers, all fluidly linked by an enormous system of freeways. And Los Angeles is only part of a closely linked metropolitan system that stretches throughout Southern California.

Perhaps the single most important reason Los Angeles is so spread out is the automobile. Californians were among the first to embrace Henry Ford's Model T. With the coming of the private automobile, people were much less restricted as to where they could live and still be able to commute to work. No longer did they have to build houses near trolley or train lines. They could settle in any area *between* these fixed transportation routes or even in districts beyond them. The same freedom applied to businesses deciding where to locate plants. With trucks delivering raw materials and transporting finished products, a factory could now be far removed from railroad facilities. Relatively inexpensive roads were all that were needed to link one place with any other. In the 1920s, Los Angeles residents voted down a proposal for a system of subways and elevated trains in favor of expanding the street system and building the first "parkway."

In part, this reflected the value Californians placed on the personal freedom that the automobile brought. But it was also the result of campaigns by individuals and companies that stood to profit or gain power from the new way of organizing a city without much public transport and with a heavy reliance on cars. General Motors, Standard Oil, and Firestone Tire & Rubber pushed hard for the new automobile system, which brought them profits because Los Angeles residents came to depend heavily on automobiles, gas, and tires (Davis, 1992; Smith, 1988). Real estate developers who had bought land in outlying areas needed only two things to make huge profits: roads and a water supply. Here we can see social structure being shaped by the actions of the powerful. The new road system gave freedom to relatively well-off people but made it harder for poor and working-class people who could not afford cars to get around.

While at the turn of the century, what we now call Los Angeles was a collection of several dozen towns, linked by the Red Trolley network, by the 1930s it was already beginning to be the first modern metropolis linked primarily by automobiles. The average Los Angeleno today drives 117 miles a week (Clifford, 1989). As Figure 19.1 shows, about three-quarters of Southern Californians, Los Angelenos included, have two or more cars.

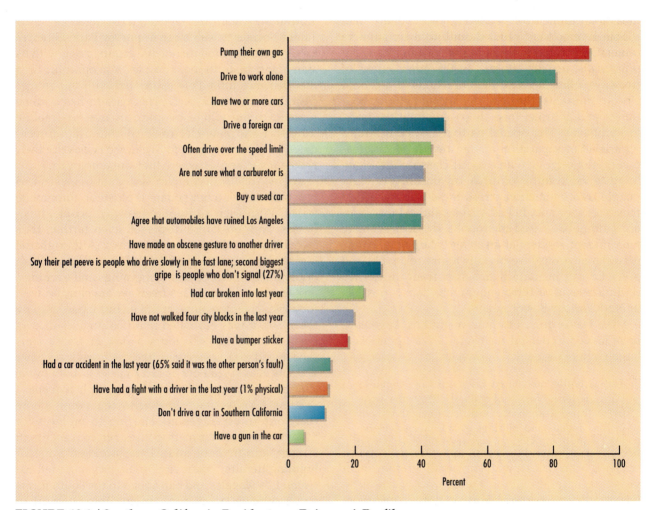

FIGURE 19.1 / Southern California Residents as Drivers: A Profile

This chart reveals many interesting characteristics of Southern California drivers. One is their widespread tendency to drive to work alone. Even though many Southern Californians commute 100 miles a day by car, nearly 80 percent of them do not carpool. A major reason is probably that places of employment are quite widely distributed across the Southern California region, so neighbors are seldom going to work near one another. Notice, too, how Southern Californians tend to live up to their national image as high-speed, rather impatient drivers. Well over two-fifths admit to driving above the speed limit, over a third confess to having made an obscene gesture to another motorist, and more than a quarter list as a pet peeve people who drive slowly in the fast lane.

Sources: Frank Clifford, "A Driving Passion for Cars Fuels California Style," *Los Angeles Times,* October 1, 1989, and Frank Clifford, "We Curse the Traffic, But Won't Give Up Our Cars," *Los Angeles Times,* October 4, 1989.

Extensive car travel and sprawling development make life in a modern metropolis like Los Angeles very different from that in an early industrial city like Boston. While nineteenth-century Bostonians considered ten miles a substantial roundtrip commute, many modern-day residents of Los Angeles travel 100 miles to and from work. Moreover, unlike their nineteenth-century counterparts, relatively few Los Angelenos commute to the central city. The majority have jobs in outlying areas, making daily commuting an immense crisscrossing of the entire metropolitan area. Most retail shops and entertainment centers are located in the suburbs. Vast indoor shopping malls, usually situated at the intersections of freeways, offer many of the attractions of a central city—restaurants, theaters, department stores, boutiques, and gourmet food shops—without the parking problems. This spatial pattern also allows for a high level of separation among people of different races, ethnic groups, and social classes. The older, more crowded forms of urban organization brought people into interaction across these lines (whether they liked it or not). In Los Angeles and in most modern automobile-based metropolises, however, there are different residential areas and shopping centers for different groups—especially for the relatively well off, who can insulate themselves from those they find distasteful or threatening more than is possible in New York or Boston.

Mike Davis describes how many Los Angelenos have moved to defend their middle- or upper-class, largely white residential enclaves.

> The carefully manicured lawns of Los Angeles's Westside sprout forests of ominous little signs warning: "Armed Response!" Even richer neighborhoods in the canyons and hillsides isolate themselves behind walls guarded by gun-toting private police and state-of-the-art electronic surveillance. (Davis, 1992, p. 223)

Davis calls this pattern "Fortress LA." Clusters of houses are built within walls and behind gates. Streets connect to the larger grid of urban routes only at points monitored by guards. Fear of crime—based in part on the extremes of inequality that exist in cities like Los Angeles—leads citizens to cut themselves off from each other.

Already in the early twentieth century the pioneering urban sociologist Robert Park and his colleagues (1925, p. 40) described cities as comprising

"a mosaic of little worlds that touch but do not interpenetrate." Contemporary metropolises have increasingly developed into collections of ethnic, lifestyle, and social-class enclaves. An **urban enclave** is a residentially compact and socially homogenous community within a larger and more diverse metropolis. There are enclaves of Cubans in Miami's "Little Havana," of Hasidic Jews in Brooklyn, of gays and lesbians in San Francisco's Castro District, of upper-crust elites in Boston's Beacon Hill, and of Taiwanese-Americans in greater Los Angeles's "Little Taipei" located in suburban Monterey Park. Often, in modern cities, "each distinctive group, along with its stores and institutions, occupies a geographic area that becomes intimately associated with the group" (Abrahamson, 1995, p. 1). This pattern has become more extreme where people can use automobile transport and new electronic communication technologies to enable them to live in the enclave of their choice regardless of where they are employed.

In Los Angeles, a complex system of freeways was constructed to accommodate the rise of automobile travel. With each additional freeway, people, businesses, and jobs were dispersed even farther, thus creating a need for more freeways. Although the highway system is huge, it is still overloaded. Rush hours often last three hours, mornings and evenings, and even on "good" days freeways are clogged with motorists creeping along at fifteen miles per hour. By the 1980s, it was estimated that Los Angeles drivers wasted some 100,000 hours a day in traffic jams (Lockwood and Leinberger, 1988). Although no other U.S. city is as spread out as Los Angeles is, both traffic jams and urban sprawl are widespread phenomena.

Some CMSAs have grown to the point where their outermost edges are starting to merge with those of neighboring metropolises. Such a vast urban stretch, hundreds of miles long, is called a **megalopolis** (literally, "great city"). The urban sprawl between Los Angeles and San Diego to the south forms a megalopolis. At its northern end this huge urban region may soon start to merge with the southernmost tip of the San Francisco metropolis. On the East Coast, a megalopolis extends from Kittery, Maine through Boston, New York City, Philadelphia, Baltimore, and Washington to Quantico, Virginia. More than 40 million people, a fifth of the nation's population, live in this sprawling 500-mile belt (sometimes called "BosWash"). Other growing megalopolises are Palm Beach-Miami, Dallas-Fort Worth,

Pittsburgh-Youngstown-Canton-Akron-Cleveland, and Milwaukee-Chicago-Detroit.

HOW CITIES GROW

No city ever develops at random. Affluent housing does not spring up in the middle of decaying slums, nor do smoke-belching factories suddenly get built next to elegant office towers. The shape of a city, in other words, is not haphazard. It is the product of social, economic, political, and geographic forces. In this section we consider two influential sociological perspectives on how cities grow: the urban-ecology approach and the political-economy view. We focus our attention on the growth of American cities, postponing our discussion of fast-growing Third World cities until Chapter 20.

Urban Ecology

Ecology is a subfield of biology that studies how living organisms interact with their physical environments and with one another to affect the development of their communities. In the early and mid-twentieth century, a number of sociologists began to borrow ecological concepts and apply them to the social interaction of human beings. Based at the University of Chicago, Louis Wirth, Robert Park, and Ernest Burgess developed **urban ecology,** the study of how the social uses of urban space result from an interaction between diverse groups of people and their physical and geographic environments. The urban ecology perspective has produced three major models of urban area development.

Three Models of Urban Ecology

In the 1840s, when walking through Manchester, England, the world's first industrial city, Karl Marx's collaborator Friedrich Engels (1844/1975) noticed that the air was most polluted in the industrial center. Around this center, there were rings of residential development. To avoid the air pollution, the richest people bought property at the furthest edge of the urban area. In turn-of-the-century Chicago, early American sociologists noticed the same pattern and developed it into a more formal theory.

The Chicago sociologists argued that as the size of an urban population increases, people begin to compete for space (Park, Burgess, and McKenzie, 1925). This competition tends to produce six **concentric zones** of development, each serving a different function (see Figure 19.2a). The first zone, at the center of the city, is the business district, made up of stores and offices. The second zone, which surrounds the first, is in a state of transition and is characterized by residential instability, low rents, high crime rates, and various forms of vice. Businesses and light manufacturing are beginning to move into it. Beyond the zone in transition lie four residential zones. The first is inhabited by the working class; the second and third are occupied by the middle and upper classes; and the fourth is a zone of wealthy commuter suburbs outside the city limits. A concentric-zone model best describes a city like Chicago, which developed very rapidly after the Industrial Revolution, before the introduction of the automobile.

A second model of urban development (Hoyt, 1943) emphasized the importance of transportation routes—railroad lines, highways, rivers, and canals—as a structural basis for the growth of cities. Hoyt's **sector model** also featured an outward movement of population, but in the form of pie-shaped sectors surrounding a central business district (see Figure 19.2b). According to Hoyt, the various zones of urban land use tend to be distributed along major transportation routes radiating out from the downtown area. As activity of a certain type expands, it tends to do so within its particular sector, extending outward toward the edge of the metropolis. One example is the development of the Boston suburbs along trolley lines. Another is the recent development of California's Silicon Valley, where computer firms have settled along freeways running south out of Oakland and San Francisco.

Both the concentric-zone and the sector models assume that cities expand outward from a single business district in the city center, as was commonly true of industrial cities. This pattern does not hold for all urban areas, however. To describe those that have followed a different pattern, such as Los Angeles, Chauncy Harris and Edward Ullman (1945) proposed the **multiple-nuclei model.** In this model, cities develop a series of separate centers, called *nuclei,* each with its own specialized functions (see Figure 19.2c). Four basic factors encourage this pattern of functional specialization:

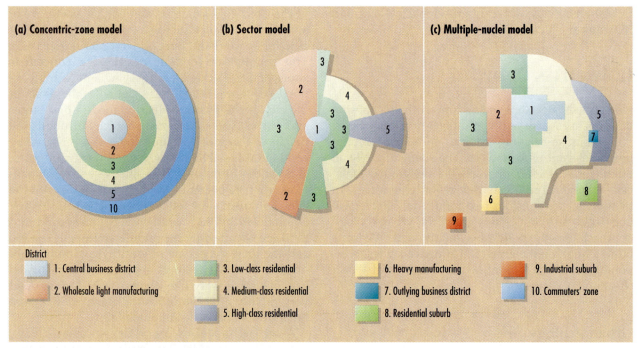

FIGURE 19.2 / Three Models of Urban Land Use

Concentric rings, pie-shaped sectors, or clusters of nuclei—all are models of urban area development proposed by proponents of the urban-ecology perspective. These three models have in common a view of urban development as driven largely by patterns of functional integration. Each separate zone, sector, or nuclei that develops in a city is seen as serving a purpose which tends to mesh with and complement the roles served by its neighbors.

Source: Chauncy D. Harris and Edward Ullman, "The Nature of Cities," in Paul K. Hatt and A. J. Reiss, Jr. (eds.), *Cities and Society* (Free Press, Peoria, Ill., 1957).

■ First, certain activities require specialized facilities. Heavy manufacturing, for example, requires nearness to highways or railroad lines, just as international importing requires nearness to a port.

■ Second, certain activities (such as retail trade) benefit when those involved in it are clustered close together (clusters of retail stores increase the pool of shoppers in an area).

■ Third, certain dissimilar activities can harm each other when located close together. Warehousing, for example, with its high demand for truck traffic, discourages pedestrian shopping, and vice versa.

■ Fourth, certain activities (such as wholesaling, which requires a great deal of space) are economically inefficient to locate in high-rent districts.

These four factors together give rise to various specialized districts within a city. The city grows as the specialized districts expand and increase in number.

Ecological Processes and Neighborhood Change

To understand why patterns of urban land use change as a city's population grows, consider the dramatic transformation of New York City's Harlem neighborhood. Today Harlem is one of America's best-known urban slums, but it was not always so. In fact, in the late nineteenth century it was among the most fashionable residential districts of the city. Harlem's transformation began around the turn of the twentieth century, when it was at its peak of affluence (Osofsky, 1982).

In the late 1890s the city government announced that construction would soon begin on a new subway line extending from midtown Manhattan into Harlem. The news set off a wave of speculation in Harlem real estate. People were convinced that property values, which were already high, would double and triple when the subway link was completed. Developers began to build apartments on every piece of vacant land. Because of Harlem's reputation as the home of the genteel and wealthy, most of the new buildings offered elegant accommodations, designed to reap high rents for developers. The apartments were large and richly detailed, with spacious living and dining rooms, maids' quarters, butler's pantries, dumbwaiters, and elevators. The building boom soon led to a glut of new housing at highly inflated prices. Many units were completed years before the new subway began to operate. Even after the subway line was opened, the massive influx of wealthy new residents that had been expected never materialized. Buildings stood partly or even entirely vacant, and rents began to drop precipitously. Developers stood to lose their investments.

One group in the city was in desperate need of more and better housing: the large and rapidly growing black population. Taking advantage of the plummeting rents in Harlem, black realtors began trying to place their clients there. At first only a few black families settled in Harlem, all of them in the newly developed west section. Many white apartment owners tried to prevent more from coming by signing agreements among themselves that they would not rent to blacks. These efforts proved ineffective, however, because the whites could not create a unified front. Some were willing to cut their losses by opening their buildings to blacks. Others engaged in panic selling (disposing of their property to whomever would buy it at whatever price they could get). The result was a steady movement of blacks into west Harlem and from there into other parts of the district. By World War I, Harlem was predominantly black.

For a time, Harlem was the most luxurious black community in American history. Middle-class black families, whose counterparts still suffered from segregation and substandard housing in much of the country, occupied elegant apartments intended for the rich. Art, music, and other forms of creativity flourished in what became known as the "Harlem Renaissance." The problem was that the steady stream of blacks wanting to move to Harlem pushed rents higher than most black people could afford. Some families were forced to take in boarders, and many smaller buildings were converted into rooming houses. Conditions became increasingly overcrowded:

With its core of office buildings and commercial establishments, circled by poor and working-class residential neighborhoods, and fed by highways leading to affluent suburbs, Atlanta illustrates the concentric model of urban development.

People were packed together to the point of "indecency." Some landlords, after opening houses to Negro tenants, lost interest in caring for their property and permitted it to run down—halls were left dark and dirty, broken pipes were permitted to rot, steam heat was cut off as heating apparatus wore out, dumbwaiters broke down and were boarded up, homes became vermin-infested. (Osofsky, 1982, p. 192)

By the 1920s, Harlem had become one of the worst slums in the country.

Park, Burgess, and McKenzie (1925) introduced the **invasion/succession model** to explain neighborhood change like that which occurred in Harlem. The concepts of invasion and succession are borrowed from plant and animal ecology. *Invasion* refers to the appearance in an environment of a new species which unsettles an existing ecological balance; *succession* refers to the process of change by which a new mix of different species eventually develops a new equilibrium. In Harlem, the invasion/succession process began with the new subway line that encouraged a dramatic expansion in housing construction and the arrival of new families. When these turned out to include residents racially different from those already there, competition and conflict resulted. Many whites left; more blacks arrived. Harlem might have become a stable middle-class black community except for the racism in the rest of American society which encouraged more and more people to try to squeeze into this once attractive community. This created competition among black residents, as well as between blacks and whites. Additional problems, such as neglect by white landlords, further led to a collapse in the quality of life and eventually in real estate values. As values declined, landlords provided even fewer services, causing middle-class blacks to leave, especially after civil rights reforms of the 1960s made it easier for them to find attractive housing elsewhere. The new ecology of Harlem was dominated by the presence of those with fewer resources and fewer options.

What happened in Harlem did not take place in isolation. Harlem's rise and fall (and indeed, the current revitalization of some parts of Harlem by a new influx of middle class, mostly black residents) were shaped by the pattern of population growth in New York and the cost of housing in other neighborhoods. Within such a context, there is a predictable **neighborhood life-cycle** (Hoover and Vernon, 1959), a pattern of rise and fall and perhaps rise again. A neighborhood may begin its life cycle undergoing extensive *development*, just as Harlem did in the late nineteenth century. Then a period of *transition* may occur in which major social forces change (the overbuilding in Harlem, for example, followed by plummeting land values and the movement of black people into the district). A *downgrading* of the area may follow, as occurred in Harlem when landlords let their properties run down. Eventually, stores and houses may be so decayed that a *thinning out* of population occurs. The final stage may be urban *renewal* and a new wave of development. City neighborhoods do not necessarily pass through all these stages. Sometimes a neighborhood will become stable at a certain point, but this stability is always based on the neighborhood's relationship to the rest of the urban context, as well as on what is occurring within the neighborhood. The life-cycle perspective, and the ecological perspective in general, can be applied not only to neighborhoods and cities but to the organization of whole regions and their relationship to national and international economic change.

The Political Economy of Urban Space

Urban ecologists see the development of urban areas as a more or less natural process of adaptation in which neighborhoods, cities, and regions respond to changes in their environments. While conflict is common in particular settings, ecologists see the overall process as driven largely by patterns of functional integration. Other sociologists, taking a **political-economy view,** emphasize power and social action more than functional adaptation (Gottdiener and Feagin, 1988; Smith, 1988). They see the changing shapes of cities as reflecting deliberate decisions that have been made by powerful groups and coalitions in order to direct urban growth to their own advantage. These powerful groups control the major economic and political institutions of the city: its corporations, banks, financial markets, real estate and construction industries, local government, and government programs. Their decisions, in turn, are based on the logic of the capitalist economy: maximizing profits and minimizing costs. According to the political-economy view, "Changing urban development patterns are best understood as the long-term outcomes of actions taken by economic and political *actors* operating within a complex and changing matrix of global and national economic and political *forces*" (Smith and Feagin, 1987, p. 17).

The Rise of the Corporate City

Across America and much of the economically developed world, old, industrial cities have largely been replaced by modern corporate cities, in which the center city is dominated by corporate headquarters and the firms that serve them (banks, law firms, advertising agencies, and the like). Old factories and warehouses are converted into housing and shops. New factories and warehouses are now located in the suburbs. According to urban ecologists, the emergence of corporate cities was largely the result of structural factors such as innovations in transportation and communications, especially the advent of cars, trucks, and highways. The political-economy view, however, looks to different causes. David Gordon (1984) argues that while technological innovations *enabled* the corporate city to emerge, they were not the fundamental impetus for it. Rather, the corporate city was the product of capitalist profit making carried out by huge, wealthy corporations with immense control over worldwide markets.

One change that these corporations deliberately brought about was the relocation of production plants from the downtown district to the periphery of the city, or even beyond city limits. The major motivation for this shift was a need to control labor unions and reduce worker–management conflict. In the early twentieth century, capitalists were increasingly faced with picketing, strikes, and even sabotage of their operations. The clustering of factories in central cities made the problem worse, for workers in different plants could compare conditions and demand changes from exploitative employers. One solution was to move to the suburbs, where employees would be more isolated from incidents of labor unrest. So corporations moved out in ever-increasing numbers. This exodus of production from the central cities was made possible by the wave of corporate mergers and rapid corporate growth that occurred between 1898 and 1903. Many corporations became large enough and sufficiently well-financed to afford the investment in new facilities. The move to the suburbs fit the growing size and wealth of American business.

The proliferation of downtown corporate headquarters lodged in towering skyscrapers also fit the character of twentieth-century capitalism. By the 1920s, many American corporations had acquired control over vast markets. "They were now large enough to separate administrative functions from the production process, leaving plant managers to oversee the factories while corporate managers supervised the far-flung empire" (Gordon, 1984, p. 43). As anyone knows who has ever stood at the foot of a huge corporate tower, this feature of the modern

In modern cities like Houston, the gleaming skyscrapers of corporate headquarters and the banks, law firms, and advertising agencies that serve them have replaced the factories and warehouses at the center of older, industrial cities.

city is the very symbol of enormous, highly centralized economic power. However, changing forms of capitalism also bring changing symbols. For every giant central-city corporate office tower built today, there are several corporate "campuses" dispersed through megalopolises and even outside them. Global capitalism, aided by new technologies, makes centralization less of a benefit (Harvey, 1989).

The City as a Growth Machine

While some sociologists with a political-economy perspective have tried to explain the spatial organization of capitalist cities, others have looked at the forces that fuel the general process of urban expansion. According to sociologists Harvey Molotch and John Logan, "The city is, for those who count, a growth machine" (Logan and Molotch, 1987; Molotch and Logan 1976, p. 310). By this they mean that the city is a giant device that helps make it possible for business and commerce to expand, for the labor force to increase, and for land resources to be put to more intensive and widespread use. This device is not produced simply by natural processes but rather is created and run by the social action of powerful elites and corporations. Growth, rather than the welfare and quality of life of residents, is the primary purpose of the elites who shape capitalist cities. The reason is simple. Growth is a source of greater wealth and power for those who own the city's resources. Through growth, an acre of land that once sold for a few hundred dollars becomes worth millions. Through growth, urban landowning elites multiply their profits many times over. The Global Issues/Local Consequences box explores the impact of the international economy on growth in one particular American city.

Logan and Molotch see the American city as an aggregate of land-based interests: a coalition of individuals, groups, and organizations that stand to gain or lose financially from the way the city's land resources are developed. The objective is more intensive use of land, which means greater profits. Many of the property owners in New York's Harlem, for instance, broke up large apartments into one-room flats in order to maximize their profits. By the 1920s, space in Harlem that would normally have earned only $40 a month was earning $100 or $125 because of intensified use. Some landlords even rented out space in basements and coal bins to get the most they could

from their landholdings (Osofsky, 1982). This example shows how powerful coalitions of interests can promote growth regardless of other considerations (such as the availability of services and the impact on the urban environment).

Local government is eager to assist urban growth, because elected officials are often deeply involved with the city's land interests. Many are large landowners themselves, or they are bankers, realtors, and investment brokers whose success and income depend on a growing community. These officeholders try to maintain a favorable "growth climate," which means sizable tax breaks for developers and investors, harmonious labor relations to attract new industry, and a police force that gives high priority to protecting private property. A political-economic analysis suggests that growth is not good for the whole community, as those in power contend. Urban growth can bring many distressing problems such as air and water pollution, traffic congestion, and residential overcrowding. It can also increase what people must pay for public utilities, police and fire protection, and other city services. And growth does not necessarily create jobs for residents, as proponents usually claim. Most of the jobs created in the corporate city are either in the high-wage information sector (which attract highly educated workers from around the country and so do not necessarily increase employment for residents) or in the low-wage service sector (restaurants, laundries, residential construction, and the like, which offer little job security and few benefits) (Smith and Feagin, 1987). Urban growth, in other words, bestows the greatest benefits on those who own the resources used in the process—namely, the community's economic elite.

CURRENT TRENDS IN AMERICAN COMMUNITIES

Cities are a defining feature of the modern era. For most of this century, the trend in the United States has been toward increasing urbanization. Yet every day we read about the exodus from cities, cities cutting back on services, cities going bankrupt. Is the era of cities drawing to a close? Is small-town America due for a revival, or is such a revival an unrealistic dream? Here we look at current trends and future prospects for all three types of American settlements: small towns, big cities, and suburbs.

Urban Growth and the World Economy

The city is a growth machine on a worldwide scale. Within the context of a worldwide capitalist economy, the fortunes of particular communities are tied to international patterns of trade and production. Sociologist Joe Feagin has studied this process for many years. One key example comes from Houston, Texas, the global center of the petrochemical and oil industries.

Houston began as a boomtown and has grown phenomenally for over a century. Population there increased at least 29 percent in every decade from 1850 to 1980, and in one decade (the 1920s) it more than doubled. Whereas in 1890 Houston ranked only 112th in population among all U.S. cities, today it ranks fourth, after New York, Los Angeles, and Chicago (U.S. Bureau of the Census, 1995b). This dramatic growth has been accomplished partly by a huge migration of people to Houston and partly by the city's annexation of surrounding land. Houston covered only nine square miles in 1900 (the year before oil was first discovered ninety miles to the east). By 1980, it had annexed an additional 550 square miles (Feagin, 1988).

This impressive rate of growth has been due not just to the push of local land-based interests but also to the pull of the worldwide demand for oil and oil products. Over the years, Houston has become a global center for the export of oil technology and equipment, as well as for oil refining and the manufacture of oil-based chemicals. Thirty-four of America's top thirty-five oil companies have major research, production, or administrative facilities in Houston, and 400 other major oil and gas companies have operations there. In all, about 25 percent of America's oil-refining output and 50 percent of its petrochemical production take place in Houston (Feagin, 1988; Hill and Feagin, 1987). Houston thus occupies a vital niche in the global capitalist system.

Because of this niche, Houston's fate is tied more to global economic trends (especially the price of crude oil) than it is to national ones. When the price of crude oil rises rapidly, Houston is a boomtown. In 1973–1974, for example, when oil prices soared, there was a surge in oil exploration and drilling that stimulated Houston's economy even though the rest of the United States was in an economic recession. While cities like nearby Dallas at the time suffered a 6 percent drop in manufacturing employment, Houston enjoyed an 18 percent *increase* because it manufactures mainly for the world oil market (Hill and Feagin, 1987). In contrast, when the price of oil falls (as it did in the 1980s), Houston sinks into serious recession even if other parts of the country are prospering.

This boom-or-bust cycle in Houston during the last two decades illustrates how sensitive the city's development is to changes in the global economy. Because Houston is a major component of a worldwide capitalist market system, its fortunes ebb and flow with decisions made in the boardrooms of multinational corporations. These changing fortunes, in turn, affect the daily lives of Houston's citizens. Whether it is easy or hard to find a job there, what kinds of jobs are scarce or plentiful, how much money is being channeled into urban development, and whether local taxes must be raised to compensate for falling corporate profits are all matters that are intimately connected to Houston's niche in the world capitalist system.

The growth or decline of other cities throughout the modern world is likewise tied to trends in the global capitalist economy and to the niches occupied by these cities within that worldwide economic order. For instance, many Third World cities have now become centers for the modern capitalist assembly line. As a result of this trend, employment in these cities has increased significantly, giving jobs to thousands of people. At the same time, however, this global trend has contributed to the decline of local industries and trade, neglect of rural areas, overcrowding in the major centers of production and export, and stagnation in Third World cities not selected for large-scale capitalist investment. Similar issues shape the future of cities in Eastern Europe as they enter the capitalist world market with its competitive pressures and opportunities for elites to benefit from turning cities into growth machines.

The Crisis of Rural America

"$1,000 Reward!" shouts a poster seen all over Jefferson, Iowa, a rural county seat eighty miles north of Des Moines. The text under the headline promises this bounty not to someone who catches a bandit but to anyone who helps to attract an employer who will provide at least fifteen jobs (*New York Times*, September 11, 1990, p. A20). By the 1990s, hundreds of small rural towns like Jefferson were threatened with extinction. No one knows how many small towns have already been wiped off the map in recent decades. The Census Bureau calculates that 200 vanish each decade, but many experts believe the actual number is much higher (*New York Times*, January 3, 1990, p. A16). As small towns continue to disappear, a way of life and a form of community is dying with them.

In 1950, about 36 percent of Americans lived in small towns and rural areas; by 1990, only 25 percent did (see Figure 19.3). The depopulation of rural America is due in large part to advances in technology, starting with the tractor. In the 1950s and 1960s, the size of farms increased while the number of farmers decreased. A brief agricultural boom in the 1970s led many farmers to mortgage their land to purchase new and expensive equipment. When the demand for U.S. farm products on the world market and commodity prices within the United States fell in the 1980s, many of these mortgages were foreclosed and former farmers were forced to look elsewhere for work. Iowa—the heart of the Midwestern farm belt—lost more than 5 percent of its population in the 1980s alone. Young people (especially those with higher education) are most likely to move away, often leaving their parents behind. As a result, rural America is aging: The average age in Greene County, Iowa, is over fifty (*New York Times*, September 11, 1990, p. A20).

The quality of life in rural America is also declining (Hundley, 1989). Contrary to stereotypes, only a small proportion of rural Americans (less than 2 percent) make their living from farming; even in farm families, at least one spouse usually works off the farm. Because many small towns depend on a single employer, their economies are fragile. Moreover, with more people than jobs, employers are able to pay only the minimum wage. The poverty rate for young people in rural areas more than doubled in the 1980s (to more than 35 percent), and the unemployment rate is twice the national average (Duncan, 1991).

Town after town has seen its Main Street close down. In the 1980s, small towns in Iowa lost 41 percent of their gas stations, 27 percent of their grocery stores, and 37 percent of their variety stores. Part of the reason is simply that there are fewer customers, and part is that local stores face stiff competition from national chains like Wal-Mart and Kmart, which offer a big-city array of goods at bargain prices.

Health care in rural America is deteriorating. Of the 300 hospitals that closed in the 1980s, more than half were in small towns. The country doctor is also disappearing. Many small towns have only a part-time physician who serves several communities, and some have no doctor at all. Twelve of eighteen counties in southern Illinois do not have a single obstetrician. The reason is not only that small towns have too few patients to support a doctor but also that Medicare reimburses rural doctors 20 to 50 percent less than city doctors for the same procedure, on the grounds that their overhead is less. With $50,000 to $100,000 in medical school debts, even those new doctors who would like to establish small-town practices cannot afford to do so.

Small-town schools are also in trouble. With dwindling numbers of students, the cost of educating a single student often becomes prohibitive, and many small districts have been forced to merge. In 1945, Missouri had 8,607 school districts; today the state has only 545. In the 1980s alone, enrollment in

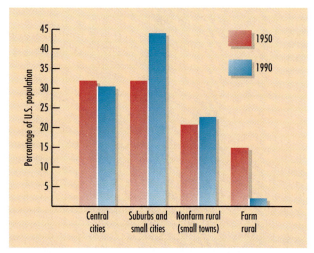

FIGURE 19.3 / Rural Exodus, Metropolitan Sprawl: Changes in U.S. Residential Patterns, 1950–1990

Although the percentage of Americans who live in center cities and the percentage who live in small towns have not changed much in the forty years from 1950 to 1990, the percentage of those on farms and the percentage in suburbs have changed significantly. Farm families are fast becoming an endangered species in this country (less than 3 percent of our population is on farms), while suburbanites are now by far more common than any other type of resident (about 45 percent of Americans live in suburbs).

Sources: U.S. Bureau of the Census, Washington, D.C., and Department of Agriculture, Washington, D.C.

Across the country, Main Street— once the heart of rural America—is closing down, as small towns fade into history.

Missouri schools dropped by 20 percent. In consolidated districts, students may be forced to travel fifty miles back and forth to school each day. Athletic and other school events used to be the high points of small-town life. "When you lose your school," says the principal of tiny Diagonal High in neighboring Iowa, "you lose your town" (quoted in Hundley, 1989, p. 13).

The crisis in rural America is taking its toll on residents. A study of Iowa farmers found that one in three suffered symptoms of depression (Belyea and Lobao, 1990). A University of Minnesota study of rural adolescents found that they are far more prone to depression and suicidal thoughts than are their urban counterparts (in Hundley, 1989).

Not all small, rural towns are in decline, of course. A few have succeeded in attracting big industry, such as the multibillion-dollar plant General Motors built in Spring Hill, Tennessee (former population 1,100). Some small towns have attracted large numbers of retirees; others have become weekend spots for restless urbanites; and still others have grown into suburbs of suburbs. Rural development can be a mixed blessing, though. Some residents may prosper, but traditional community ties may be torn in the process (Brown, Greersten, and Krannich, 1989; Summers and Branch, 1984). Moreover, these success stories are the exception to the rule. At the moment, the prognosis for America's small towns is not good.

The Restructuring of America's Cities

In the early 1980s, U.S. cities seemed on the verge of a revival. **Gentrification**—the conversion of working-class or run-down areas of a city into middle- and upper-middle-class neighborhoods—was hailed as the wave of the future. City after city launched massive urban renewal projects. Blocks of abandoned and dilapidated buildings were razed, and office complexes, luxury condominiums, and recreation centers (with hotels, restaurants, theaters, and attractions like aquariums) were constructed in their place. This optimism, however, turned out to be premature (Beauregard, 1993; Kasinitz, 1988).

Today's cities are a study in contrasts: between affluence and poverty, chaos and creativity, optimism and fear. For example, one section of downtown Los Angeles boasts sixty major corporate headquarters, a dozen banks with assets of more than $1 billion, five of the eight biggest international accounting firms, a battalion of corporate law firms, condominiums selling for $11 million—*and* the highest concentration of homeless people in the nation (Soja, 1989).

From Industry to Information

The most profound change in American cities is a functional one: their transformation from centers for the production and distribution of goods to centers of administration, finance, and information processing (Beauregard, 1993; Castells, 1989; Kasarda, 1989). Gone are the "smokestack" (heavy manufacturing) industries built up in the nineteenth and early twentieth centuries. Los Angeles once had the second-largest automobile assembly complex in the country; today, only one factory remains (Soja, 1989). Gone, too, are the skilled, unionized, better-paying blue-collar jobs that used to be the backbone of urban economies. Center cities have also lost large numbers of sales and clerical jobs to suburbs and smaller cities.

To some extent, manufacturing jobs have been replaced by white-collar, managerial, and professional jobs in such knowledge-intensive fields as finance, law, accounting, and advertising (see Chapter 18). Because these jobs generally require at least a college degree, which many urban residents lack, they are filled by suburban commuters. Minorities have been hardest hit by the changes in urban jobs and educational requirements. In particular, blacks with high school educations or less may be trapped in urban ghettoes, unable to find work in the city and unable to move or commute to jobs in the suburbs (Wacquant, 1993). Lack of opportunity, in turn, contributes to high rates of school dropouts, crime, drug use, and the swell of social problems plaguing cities today.

The number of low-skill and low-wage service and light-manufacturing jobs in cities has also increased. For example, in the 1970s the garment industry in Los Angeles grew by almost 60 percent, creating an estimated 125,000 new jobs (Soja, 1989). In many ways, though, the new garment factories resemble the sweatshops of the nineteenth century. Violations of minimum-wage laws, mandatory overtime, unsafe working conditions, and child labor are widespread. Perhaps 80 percent of garment workers are undocumented aliens (and thus unable to protest exploitation), and 90 percent are women.

Temporary and part-time jobs in cities have also increased. A growing number of self-employed urban residents work as free-lance consultants out of their homes, "telecommuting" to their jobs via computer modems and fax machines and moving in and out of the labor force. While such work may pay well, it is not steady, and self-employed people do not enjoy such benefits as health insurance, sick leave, pension plans, and paid vacations.

In short, the occupational structure of cities has changed. Employment has increased at the top and the bottom of the occupational hierarchy, but the middle is shrinking. A few displaced blue-collar laborers work their way up into white-collar jobs, but many more slide downward into marginal jobs—a process that has been called the "Kmarting" of the labor force. Some working- and lower-middle-class residents have fled the city, and others have fallen out of the working class. As a result, cities have become more polarized, with a small number of highly affluent residents, a large number of residents who are just scraping by, and fewer middle-class residents in between.

The Global City

In addition, the ethnic composition of some U.S. cities has changed. In the past two decades, for example, almost 2 million people from Third World countries (mostly in Asia and Latin America) have immigrated to Los Angeles (Rieff, 1991; Waldinger 1996). In one of the largest immigrations on record, almost 400,000 people have moved there from El Salvador since 1980. Today Los Angeles has the largest Mexican, Korean, Vietnamese, and Philippine populations outside those countries, as well as substantial Chinese and Japanese populations. The numbers of some Pacific Island peoples have actually begun to exceed the populations in their homelands. Anglos (whites of European ancestry) are now a minority in Los Angeles, making it a truly "global" city in terms of its ethnic makeup. It is estimated that by the year 2010 only 40 percent of Los Angeles's population will be Anglo, another 40 percent will be Hispanic, 10 percent will be non-Hispanic black, and 10 percent will be Asian (Lockwood and Leinberger, 1988). This is why Los Angeles has been called the "capital of the Third World" (Rieff, 1991). A similar ethnic mosaic has developed in New York City, where blacks, Hispanics, and Asians together already outnumber whites (*New York Times*, February 21, 1991).

Third World immigration into American cities can be economically beneficial, as it has been in Los Angeles (Waldinger, 1996). A combination of First World management and plentiful Third World labor has helped that city's economy to thrive. Third World immigrants, accustomed to very low wages, are of-

In terms of its population, its economy, and its culture, Los Angeles is a global city. A magnet to foreign investors as well as immigrants from Asia and Latin America, Los Angeles exports Hollywood films and American culture to almost every country on earth.

ten willing to work for subsistence incomes in the United States. This cheap labor has enabled certain manufacturing industries (such as garment making and furniture manufacturing) to remain alive in Los Angeles. Sometimes, however, the working conditions are substandard. One UCLA professor who was given a tour of small factories in a certain industrial area of the city (on the condition that he would be led to each location blindfolded) found many sweatshop settings staffed largely by illegal immigrants. In one shop that made wheels on which car tires are mounted, dozens of Hispanics and Asians, protected only by bandannas tied over their mouths and noses, labored in air that was filled with metal particles (Lockwood and Leinberger, 1988). Few American citizens would tolerate this kind of working environment.

The "globalization" of a city's population is often accompanied by a surge in foreign investments. This has occurred in Los Angeles, where investments by Asian corporations and entrepreneurs are especially common. Asian investors gravitate to Los Angeles partly because they feel at home with the growing network of Asian businesspeople and workers there. Whatever other causes are at work, the mushrooming foreign investment and trade are helping to make Los Angeles one of the world's leading international business centers.

Los Angeles and similar urban centers in rich countries are not the only "global cities." Today major

cities around the world are linked by communications media, migration, and economic ties. Third World cities like Calcutta and Cairo share with Los Angeles the characteristics of centers in an increasingly global network of social relations.

Cities in Decline: The Case of Camden

Not all of L.A.'s citizens have shared in that city's prosperity, nor have all U.S. cities followed its pattern of development. A prime example of an American city that has not adapted well to changing times is Camden, New Jersey, now in chronic decline.

First settled in 1688, Camden grew slowly but steadily in the eighteenth and early nineteenth centuries. Located across the Delaware River from Philadelphia, Camden provided ferry service for New Jersey farmers. With the coming of steam power in the 1830s, Camden rapidly expanded into a rail, shipping, and industrial center. Campbell's opened its first food-processing plant there in the 1860s; New York Shipbuilding Co. opened its renowned boatyards there in the 1890s; and RCA Victor chose Camden as the site of its first recording studio around the turn of the century. By 1920, Camden was a thriving metropolis, its population growing toward a peak of 3 million-plus in 1950.

Today, writes Daniel Lazare (1991), "Camden is less a city than a shell." With a mere 10,000 jobs, nearly one-third of its 87,000 residents live in poverty. Camden is the poorest city in New Jersey and the fifth poorest in the United States. Per capita income is less than a third of what people earn in the neighboring suburb of Cherry Hill. Roughly two out of three buildings in Camden's once prosperous business district were leveled for urban renewal programs that never materialized. Camden has no supermarkets, no movie theaters, no local newspaper, and a shabby shopping district. Camden's distinguishing features include "two prisons, a thriving prostitution and drug trade, and a murder rate well above New York's" (Lazare, 1991, p. 267). In 1995, Camden's citizens suffered a record sixty homicides (*New York Times*, March 7, 1996, p. B6).

Lazare cites three main factors that contributed to Camden's demise, which he characterizes as "death by suburbanization" (p. 268). The first and most significant factor was "motorization." Whereas in Europe automobiles remained an elite mode of transportation until years after World War II, cars have long been seen as a necessity in the United States. By 1929, one in five New Jersey residents owned a car—almost ten times as many as in France or the United Kingdom. As a result, there was little incentive to invest in cities but considerable incentive to move to the suburbs.

The second factor, according to Lazare, was federal support. The growth of suburbs has been financed by the tax dollars that built the nationwide highway system, provided low-cost mortgages to veterans, and gave tax breaks to home owners. Suburbanites thus benefit from a hidden government subsidy—one large enough to build or rebuild mass transit systems in every major city. Lazare calculates that if motorists were required to pay the full cost of driving, the price of gasoline would rise by between $4 and $6 per gallon—and the popularity of suburbs would swiftly decline.

The third factor in the death of Camden was a 1917 New Jersey law that allows neighborhoods to secede from the city that spawned them and incorporate as separate municipalities, thereby evading city taxes. This "home rule" act formalized New Jersey's longstanding hostility toward urban giants (especially Philadelphia and New York). "Suburbanites sought to bottle up the cities with their immigrants, racial minorities, political strife . . . and heavy industry" (Lazare, 1991, p. 269). Surrounded by hostile suburbs, one New Jersey city after another found itself too small and too poor to attract residents and businesses or to maintain city services and structures.

Thus, Newark, Jersey City, Paterson, and other urban centers have problems like those of Camden, though some are struggling to maintain or revive community.

Lazare sees Camden and similar cities essentially as "good machinery gone to rust." He argues that the decline of cities is not inevitable. In most of the world, cities remain vital centers of culture and commerce. In Lazare's view, the decisions to invest in private homes and cars, rather than in public housing and transportation, and to abandon cities rather than work to make them "safe, attractive, and livable" are peculiarly American. The result is peculiarly American too: declining cities with urban cores that become "bubbling caudrons" of racial, ethnic, and urban crisis (Feagin, 1995).

Suburbs: Where American Communities Are Growing

While the populations of many big cities and most rural areas have declined, the suburbs have continued to grow. Suburbs are fast becoming the "normal" American community, the place most of us call home. As the name implies, suburbs are spin-offs of metropolitan centers, to which most (but not all) remain economically tied. The major attractions of the suburb include the opportunity to own a single-family home; a degree of protection from the problems of the city (such as drugs and crime); greater opportunity to control schools and other local institutions; the possibility of living in a community of people of similar race, religion, class, and culture; and the convenience of having easy access to stores, schools, and so on.

According to the 1990 census, suburbs themselves are changing. In the last decade, twenty-nine communities passed the 100,000 population mark, the unofficial dividing line between a town and a city. Of these, twenty-two were on the edges of a metropolis. They are not freestanding cities in the classic sense, but they are not "bedroom communities" either—that is, they do not simply send commuters onto freeways each morning to jobs in a center city. Rather, these suburbs are increasingly being knit together to create a new form of community: the suburban city. The change is clearly visible from an airplane. A decade or two back, metropolitan areas took the form of a cluster of office buildings (the center or core city), surrounded by a region of housing. Today they consist of the core city plus clumps of office buildings at highway interchanges (suburban cities)

Americans dream of a home of their own in a neighborhood with people of similar ethnic and socioeconomic backgrounds, and similar tastes. And so suburbs continue to grow. Here, a new development in Mission Viejo, California, pushes into the foothills of surrounding mountains.

stretching well into the surrounding countryside. More and more of these center and suburban cities are growing together into megalopolises.

An example is the Dallas–Fort Worth megalopolis, or "Metroplex," a constellation of the two core cities and five suburban cities with populations of 100,000 or more. In the 1980s alone, the population of this area increased by almost a third, reaching 3.8 million. Once a classic commuter suburb, Plano, Texas, now includes a complex of telecommunication-manufacturing plants; a huge office park with the world's largest data-processing centers, the national headquarters of four major corporations, plus the beginnings of J.C. Penney's new corporate "campus"; and two fiber-optic communications stations that keep Plano plugged into the global economy. Plano also boasts its own chamber music ensemble, a wide variety of ethnic restaurants, and quaint antique and crafts shops in stores where cotton farmers used to buy supplies. At rush hour, the traffic into Plano is as heavy as the traffic out toward Dallas or Fort Worth. Conspicuously absent from Plano are the immigrant and minority populations that fill low-wage jobs in center cities. More than 87 percent of the students in Plano's public schools are white, whereas the 1990 census showed that a majority of the population of Dallas was either black or Hispanic (*New York Times*, February 23, 1991, pp. A1, 10).

One effect of the emergence of suburban cities is that the socioeconomic gap is widening between cen-

ter cities and suburbs and between whites and minorities. The location of corporate headquarters and related services in suburban cities, attracting the middle class, has further reduced both the tax base and the labor market in center cities. Another effect of suburban cities is the "invasion" of small towns by suburbanites and the construction of housing complexes on what used to be farmland. Increasingly, the lifestyle distinctions among city, suburb, and rural community are becoming blurred. Suburban cities have developed not only in the Sunbelt states of Texas, California, and Arizona but also around some old Eastern cities, notably Boston and Stamford, Connecticut, outside New York.

Summarizing recent changes, the demographer William H. Frey (1990) writes:

> If . . . the past two decades have taught us anything, it is that regional and metropolitan population growth in the United States has become much more volatile and responsive both to local and worldwide forces. . . . Improvements in communication and production technologies, the diffusion of urban amenities throughout the country, and the rise of a global economy have created new distribution dynamics. . . . As a result, the fortunes of metropolitan areas and smaller communities increasingly will be determined by corporate decisions, people's residential preferences and, perhaps most importantly of all, how effectively areas can adapt to rapidly changing economic conditions. (1990, p. 39)

SUMMARY

1. In the twentieth century the world has become highly urbanized, with people leaving the countryside and small towns to settle in cities and surrounding metropolitan areas. Today almost half of the world's population lives in cities.

2. Sociologists disagree on the consequences of urbanization for community life. Some argue that it inevitably brings a loss of community, that is, a loss of the common values and the close, enduring ties characteristic of small towns. Others contend that community persists within urban neighborhoods. They say that cities have enclaves in which relationships are similar to those in small towns. Still others argue that urbanization has produced a different kind of community, one that does not depend on people's living near one another. Research suggests that each of these views has validity, but each tends to apply under different circumstances.

3. Cities have undergone great changes since they first arose. Preindustrial cities were necessarily small because ground transportation was limited to horse, wagon, and foot. In this confined space, aristocrats and commoners lived in close proximity. Preindustrial cities were also foul-smelling and dirty and were prone to outbreaks of infectious diseases.

4. The explosive urban growth that gave rise to the modern city was made possible by the Industrial Revolution and the greatly improved agricultural technology it brought. Farmers could now grow enough food to support very large, densely populated cities. Displaced farm workers migrated to these cities, where they provided the labor to run the factories that dominated the downtown area. Beyond the central city, residential suburbs developed along rail and trolley lines. These suburbs housed mainly middle- and upper-income families. Low-income families remained in the cities near their places of work.

5. Suburbs expanded with the development of the sprawling metropolis, traversed by an intricate network of highways. In the metropolis, manufacturing has also moved out to the suburbs, as has much of retail trade and entertainment. The downtown area, now the home of financial institutions and corporate headquarters, is surrounded by the traditional low-income residential districts.

6. According to the urban-ecology approach, cities are integrated wholes, each part serving functions that complement and support those being served by other parts. Urban ecologists have proposed several models to explain the development of a city's spatial organization. They include the concentric-zone model, the sector model, and the multiple-nuclei model. Urban ecologists have also described the processes involved in neighborhood change. Change often begins with invasion by a new group of residents, which then leads to a shift in the population's composition and a new use for that area.

7. The political-economy perspective stresses the importance of powerful groups in directing urban growth to their own advantage. These groups often form a coalition of land-based interests, including landlords, real estate developers, bankers, and financial investors. Powerful corporations did much to encourage the rise of the modern metropolis. Corporations sometimes moved their manufacturing operations to the suburbs largely to avoid labor unrest in the central cities. In other cases, corporate interests turned cities into "growth machines" that promoted capitalist profits and expansion rather than trying to meet the needs of local citizens. At one extreme, many U.S. cities have become "global cities"—links in an international chain of capitalist production and exchange, often forged by patterns of migration and investment.

8. Current trends in U.S. communities include the decline of small towns (as a result of economic forces and depopulation), the restructuring of cities, the seemingly permanent decline of some industrial cities, and the growth of suburbs (including the urbanization of suburbs and the suburbanization of rural areas). Increasingly, the distinctions among city, suburb, and rural areas are becoming blurred and regions are becoming urbanized megalopolises.

REVIEW QUESTIONS

1. Describe three views of the effects that urbanization has on community.

2. How can knowledge of the development of early cities help us to understand communities and urbanization today?

3. Summarize the three models of urban development described in this chapter.

4. How do urban neighborhoods change as the result of invasion/succession processes and neighborhood life-cycles?

5. How does the political-economy approach help us to understand urban development and urban life?

6. Contrast life in rural, suburban, and urban communities.

CRITICAL THINKING QUESTIONS

1. Using examples from the community (or communities) in which you have lived, which approach most accurately describes the effects of urbanization on community: disintegration, persistence, or transformation?

2. How well do Tönnies's notions of *Gemeinschaft* and *Gesellschaft* help account for the nature of contemporary social life?

3. Each of the models or patterns of urban development described in this chapter has consequences—both good and bad—for individuals who have to live in the communities concerned. Identify and evaluate as many of these consequences as you can.

4. In your view, is the rise and fall of neighborhoods primarily a natural process based on shifting patterns of functional integration or primarily a power struggle? What about urban growth?

5. To what extent do you think the capitalist economic processes (as described by the political-economy perspective) explain trends in both urban development and urban life?

6. What kind of communities do you think will be most common fifty years from now? What will life be like in America's largest cities?

GLOSSARY

City A relatively large, densely populated, and permanent settlement of people who are socially diverse and who do not produce their own food.

Community A population knit together by common values and interests, relatively dense and enduring ties, frequent face-to-face interactions, and a sense of being close to one another.

Concentric zones Ernest Burgess's model of urban land use in which cities develop a central business district that is surrounded by several concentric rings, each dominated by a different set of economic and social activities.

Consolidated Metropolitan Statistical Area (CMSA) An interlinked cluster of one or more cities and their surrounding suburbs that together have a population of more than 1 million people.

Gemeinschaft The German term for a community used by Ferdinand Tönnies to describe smaller, more stable, traditional settlements in which people tend to remain from birth and form strong social and emotional bonds.

Gentrification The conversion of working-class or run-down areas of a city into middle- and upper-middle-class neighborhoods.

Gesellschaft The German term for a society or association used by Ferdinand Tönnies to describe settlements characterized by large populations, social and geographic mobility, and relatively impersonal relations in which most people are strangers to one another.

Invasion/succession model A model of neighborhood change that focuses on invasion by a new kind of resident, followed by competition for available land and ultimately by the emergence of a new use for the area.

Megalopolis Two or more neighboring metropolises that have sprawled so much in geographic area that their outermost edges merge and they form an integrated complex.

Metropolis A major city with surrounding municipalities caught up in its economic and social orbit.

Multiple-nuclei model Chauncy Harris and Edward Ullman's model of urban land use in which cities develop as a series of separate centers, called nuclei, each with its own specialized functions.

Neighborhood life-cycles The way in which the rise and fall of neighborhood fortunes fits into a predictable pattern within a larger series of invasion/succession episodes. The

complete cycle includes stages of development, transition, downgrading, thinning out, and renewal.

Political-economy view A sociological view of cities that sees them as the product of decisions made by powerful groups acting on largely economic self-interest and advancing capital accumulation.

Sector model Homer Hoyt's model of urban land use in which cities develop a series of pie-shaped sectors surrounding a central business district. The sectors tend to be distributed along major transportation routes radiating out from the downtown area, and each is devoted to a distinct purpose.

Urban ecology A sociological approach to studying cities that examines how the social uses of urban land are the results of interactions between various groups of people and their physical/geographic environments.

Urban enclave A residentially compact and socially homogeneous community within a larger and more diverse metropolis.

Urbanization The process whereby large numbers of people leave the countryside and small towns in order to settle in cities and surrounding metropolitan areas.

CHAPTER 20

Social Movements
and Collective Action

On April 29, 1992, a jury in Ventura County, California, acquitted four Los Angeles police officers on charges of using excessive force in the arrest of black motorist Rodney C. King.* The trial featured a videotape, made by a witness in an apartment across the street, of the officers kicking and clubbing King as he rolled on the ground. Black leaders had long charged the Los Angeles Police Department with systematic brutality toward African-American people. The 81-second videotape, shown over and over again on national television, seemed to offer proof of these charges. King was hit not once or twice, but fifty-six times. Yet the jurors, none of whom was black, found three of the officers innocent and could not reach a decision on the fourth. (Charges had been dismissed against seventeen other police officers who had observed but not participated in the beating.) On the steps outside the courtroom, Councilwoman Patricia Moore called the verdict "a modern-day lynching." Another observer predicted, "This is a time bomb. It's going to blow up" (*Newsweek*, May 11, 1992, p. 33). The observer was right.

The first hint of unrest came over the police radio band between 4:30 and 5:00 p.m. A group of "gang-bangers" had gone into Tom's Liquor Store, on the corner of Florence and Normandie Streets in the South-Central district of Los Angeles, helped themselves to bottles of liquor, and started out the door without paying. When the son of the store's Korean owner tried to block them, he was hit over the head with a beer bottle. Police arriving at the scene found a crowd of black youths hurling cans and bottles at passing motorists. When officers attempted an

---

*Except where noted, descriptions of the King trial and the violence that followed are drawn from coverage in the *Los Angeles Times*, April 30–May 11, 1992.

565

arrest, the crowd turned on them. At 5:45 the field commander ordered the outnumbered police to withdraw. They retreated to their cars and reassembled at a bus depot, where they waited several hours for further instructions.

More than a thousand South-Central residents had gathered at the First African Methodist Episcopalian church to sing gospel music and listen to black leaders denounce the injustice but plead for calm. Outside, groups of youths were blocking traffic, attacking drivers, and torching their cars when they fled. At about 6:45, white truck driver Reginald Denny stopped at a red light. Several men surrounded the truck, dragged Denny from the cab, beat and kicked him, robbed him, and left him lying in a pool of blood. News helicopters whirled overhead, feeding live coverage to horrified television audiences. There was no sign of police, but four black residents later braved rocks and bottles to drive Denny to a hospital.

Across town another crowd had gathered outside police headquarters, demanding the resignation of Police Chief Daryl Gates. In effect, the police there were under siege, unable to move in or out. For a time this multiethnic crowd was vocal but nonviolent; later some of its members fanned out, smashing doors and windows and lighting fires as they went. By 10:00 p.m., four emergency calls a minute were pouring in to the fire department, but snipers and bands of angry youths, coupled with a lack of police escorts, prevented firefighters from handling more than a few. In one case firefighters had to barricade themselves inside the home of a nearby Latino family, awaiting police rescue. The smoke from out-of-control fires was so thick that Los Angeles International Airport was able to keep only one runway open.

For reasons that were never made clear, city officials were slow to react to the growing violence. Full police mobilization was not ordered until 7:30 p.m.; by then many officers had trouble getting to their posts. A 8:55 p.m. Mayor Tom Bradley declared a state of emergency, imposed a curfew, and asked California Governor Pete Wilson to send in the National Guard. But guardsmen were not deployed to the streets until mid-afternoon Thursday. On Friday President George Bush ordered 4,500 military troops and 1,000 federal law enforcement officers into Los Angeles.

On Thursday, carloads of youths armed with baseball bats, crowbars, and guns roamed the city. Normal activities ground to a halt: Buses and trains stopped running; schools closed; banks, businesses, and even some post offices shut their doors. Looters emerged from stores with their arms full of stolen merchandise, clowning for TV cameras and calling out, "Everything is free." Some arrived by car, filled their trunks, went home, and came back for another load. Anything that could be moved—from cigarettes to personal computers, couches, and even a cash machine—was carted away. Typically, after a store was emptied, it was set afire. Hopelessly outnumbered, the police could only watch. In self-defense African-American store owners taped "black-owned" signs on their doors, while Korean shopkeepers, who were singled out as targets by rioters (Morrison and Lowry, 1994), cleared their shelves or tried to guard their stores.

The violence and looting spread through Hollywood toward Beverly Hills and wealthy, mostly white West Los Angeles. Violence erupted in other cities as well, from San Francisco and Las Vegas to Atlanta, Tampa, and even Toronto, Canada. Not until Friday evening did the Los Angeles police, backed by guardsmen and federal troops, begin to restore order. By then, sixty people were dead, some 2,400 were injured, and more than 15,000 had been arrested. Nearly 5,200 buildings had been destroyed or severely damaged by arson and vandalism, many of them businesses, at an estimated cost of $1 billion and 40,000 jobs.

Immediately after these disturbances were over, the media verdict was clear: This was the worst urban riot in recent U.S. history. Comparisons were made to the ghetto riots of the 1960s, usually in terms of property damage and body count. Since 1992, however, sociologists who have studied the events have noted that they had a number of distinctive features. They were not, for example, simple black-versus-white upheavals, even though they were triggered by anger at the acquittal of white policemen for beating a black man. In fact, more than half of those arrested were Hispanic (Petersilia and Abrahamse, 1994), and the targets of choice were not elements of the white power structure but rather Korean-owned retail stores (Morrison and Lowry, 1994). Furthermore, interpretations of "what the riots were about"—or even whether they should be called riots, rather than "rebellions"—differed in different racial communities. Ronald Jacobs (1996), a sociologist who compared coverage of the April 1992 events and their aftermath in the mainstream *Los Angeles Times* and

A scene of looting during the L.A. riot of 1992, in which some crowd members participated while others stood and watched. The incident that touched off the riot was the acquittal of white policemen who had beaten a black man, but the riot itself was "multiracial."

the black-owned *Los Angeles Sentinel,* found that two very different narratives emerged. In the *Times,* the police beating of Rodney King was seen as shocking deviation in which individual officers were out of control and irrational. The *Sentinel,* by contrast, saw the policemen's actions as part of a familiar pattern of abuse of black men by white law enforcement officials (Jacobs, 1996).

However they are interpreted, the events in Los Angeles illustrate what sociologists call **collective action,** socially organized and self-conscious but relatively nonroutine responses to events, efforts to pursue shared interests, or attempts to realize ideals. **Collective behavior**, by contrast, is less consciously and rationally organized but socially shared activity. Participants usually involving large numbers of people (Marx and McAdam, 1995) may not even know one another, yet share behavior that differs, often strikingly, from the habitual patterns of everyday life (G. B. Rose, 1982). A clothing fashion that sweeps the country, a bizarre rumor that spreads from city to city, a sudden mass hysteria or panic, a riot or other unusual form of mob action are all incidents of collective behavior. In some cases collective

behavior and collective action are more or less isolated events that subside as suddenly as they erupt. In other cases they may be part of a **social movement,** which is "a conscious, collective, organized attempt to bring about or resist large-scale change in the social order by noninstitutionalized means" (J. Wilson, 1973, p. 8).

The collective actions involved in the disturbances in Los Angeles were brought about by a number of factors. The social structure of the South-Central neighborhood—especially the availability of a large number of poor young minority men who were neither employed nor in school—was crucial. The media coverage of the Rodney King case and the repeated playing of the videotape of his beating on TV involved residents emotionally in the outcome of the case, confirming the ideas common in minority culture that police regularly abuse them (Tierney, 1994). Failures in functional integration in the larger society, which left Korean and Hispanic immigrants competing with blacks for low-level jobs just as the Los Angeles area was deindustrializing, meant widespread unemployment, poverty, and frustration. To some extent, the disturbances represent an attempt by the poor in South-Central Los Angeles to redress the extreme imbalance of power inherent in their social position. Collective action is a special type of social action, thus understanding it also calls for consideration of the other four key concepts.

CROWDS AND COLLECTIVE ACTION

A **crowd** is a temporary collection of people who gather around some person or event and who are conscious of and influenced by one another. Crowds differ from other social groups primarily in that they are short-lived, are only loosely structured, and use conventional spaces or buildings for unconventional purposes (Snow, Zurcher, and Peters, 1981).

Types of Crowds

In his classic essay "Collective Behavior" (1939/1951), the sociologist Herbert Blumer described four kinds of crowds: *casual, conventional, expressive,* and *acting.* A **casual crowd** forms spontaneously when something attracts the attention of passersby. For instance, when a number of people walking along a city street stop to view a window washer high overhead, they form a casual crowd. The members of such a crowd, writes Blumer, "come and go, giving but temporary attention to the object which has awakened [their] interest . . . and entering into only feeble association with one another" (p. 178).

Passengers on a plane, shoppers in a store, or the audience at a concert illustrate what Blumer called a **conventional crowd.** Members of a conventional crowd gather for a specific purpose and behave according to established norms. For example, although booing is expected of the crowd at a football game, it is considered inappropriate for the crowd at a classical music concert. Relatively little interaction occurs in a conventional crowd. People are pursuing a common goal, but they tend to do so as individuals. Exchanges among such people are usually highly routinized and impersonal.

People at rock festivals, revival meetings, and Mardi Gras celebrations present examples of **expressive crowds.** The emotionally charged members of an expressive crowd get carried away by their enthusiasm and intense feelings, behaving in ways they would consider unacceptable in other settings. Expressing their feelings becomes their primary aim. The legendary Woodstock Music and Art Fair, held

in New York's Catskill Mountains in August 1969, provides an example of such a crowd. An impressive array of rock stars drew more than 300,000 young people to the farm where the festival was held. The mood of the crowd became increasingly joyous, and today the event is remembered perhaps more for this experience and expression of good feeling than for the concert itself.

The emotional tone of an acting crowd is different from that of an expressive crowd. An **acting crowd** is an excited, volatile collection of people who focus on a controversial event that provokes their indignation, anger, and desire to act. Examples of acting crowds might be gang members who beat up a youth from another neighborhood who strays onto their turf and fans at a soccer match who go on a rampage when a referee makes a questionable call. Unlike members of an expressive crowd, who see release of their feelings as an end in itself, members of an acting crowd seek redress of a perceived wrong. When a large acting crowd engages in violence or threatens to do so, it is often referred to as a **mob** (Hoult, 1969). Because the social effects of crowd action can be far-reaching, we will examine it in some detail.

Crowd Action

For centuries, mass uprisings and destructive riots have been the nightmare of people in power. Crowd action was common in eighteenth- and nineteenth-century Europe (Rudé, 1964). In town and country, throngs of armed men and women took over markets and warehouses, demanding the rollback of prices and sometimes seizing goods. In England, angry bands of craftspeople burned factories and destroyed the machines that threatened their livelihood. On July 14, 1789, Parisians stormed the ancient Bastille prison in the most famous confrontation of the French Revolution.

Violent crowds have also figured importantly in American history. The nineteenth century was marked by farmers' revolts, miners' rebellions, bloody battles between unions and police, lynchings, and urban riots. The 1863 Civil War draft riot in New York City, which raged for four days and left 1,000 dead, was probably the worst riot in this country's history. Crowd action has also turned violent in the twentieth century. In the 1960s especially, one black ghetto after another exploded; the nation as a whole seemed threatened. The recent violence in Los

The storming of the Bastille (an old prison and arsenal in Paris) was a key moment in the French Revolution, but it was only one action in a long, socially organized process. As in all revolutions, different groups played a part, each using its special resources to compete for power and influence. Underlying structural conditions, such as inequality between social classes and the government's financial crisis, helped to make the French Revolution happen.

Angeles frightened the whole country and led people to demand answers to questions like these: Why do riots break out? Why do crowds engage in actions that most people ordinarily condemn? Were rioters just emotionally upset, or were they consciously choosing their actions, perhaps as a kind of rebellion?

The Social Psychology of Crowds

Until recently, mobs were seen as little more than unchained beasts, spurred by powerful, violent urges and with no sense of reason. What people did in crowds was seen not as the collective *action* of rational humans, but as collective *behavior* that was the result of regression to primitive levels of psychology. A chief proponent of this psychological perspective was the Frenchman Gustave Le Bon. Le Bon (1841–1931) was an aristocrat in an era when the masses of common people were challenging the hereditary ruling class. As far as Le Bon was concerned, the old social system, with its privileges and security for elites like himself, was being threatened by emotionally volatile mobs. Le Bon regarded mobs as purely irrational and destructive, capable of tearing apart the social order.

He developed a deep distrust of all political dissent, whether it was in support of parliamentary democracy or socialism. "The age we are about to enter," wrote Le Bon, "will be in truth the era of crowds." He meant this as a dire warning.

In his book *The Psychology of Crowds* (1895/1960), Le Bon argued that involvement in a crowd puts individuals "in possession of a collective mind" that makes them think, feel, and act quite differently than they would if each person were alone. Contemporary psychologists refer to this as *deindividuation:* Members of mobs become anonymous to themselves and others, and inhibitions are lost in the thrill of being part of something larger than oneself (Wallace and Zamichow, 1992, p. A25). Crowds, Le Bon maintained, gain control over people much as hypnotists do. Individuals in crowds become highly suggestible; they "will undertake . . . acts with irresistible impetuosity." Waves of emotion sweep through crowds, "infecting" one person after another. This phenomenon is known as **social contagion:** the rapid spread of a mood or behavior from one individual to another. As Le Bon saw it, the thin veneer of civilization falls away, allowing primitive motivations and antisocial impulses to rise to the surface.

In the 1950s, the sociologist Herbert Blumer (1939/1951) refined Le Bon's ideas. He traced the social contagion to an "exciting event" (such as the verdict in the King case) that creates unrest in a group of people. The people begin milling about, "as if seeking to find or avoid something, but without knowing what it is they are trying to find or avoid" (p. 173). As they search for clues, excited behavior or rhetoric catches their attention. Instead of judging these actions, as they ordinarily would, they respond impulsively and model their own behavior after them. This reaction reinforces the original actors, making them still more excited (what Blumer called the *circular reaction*). As excitement builds, people become more inclined to act on their mounting feelings of agitation. Often the result is *mass hysteria.*

Mass hysteria can be seen not only in mobs and crowds but also in fads and crazes. In one famous case, Seattle newspapers in the spring of 1954 carried the first of several stories about damage to automobile windshields in a town eighty miles to the north of the city. The windshields had small pit marks and bubbles in them, and tiny, metallic-looking particles were sometimes found embedded in the glass. The cause of this curious damage was unknown, but police suspected vandals. On the evening of April 14,

the mysterious destructive agent appeared to hit Seattle itself. During the next two days, nearly 250 people called the Seattle police, reporting windshield damage to more than 3,000 cars. By far the most frequently rumored explanation for the epidemic was radioactive fallout from H-bomb tests in the north Pacific. As this rumor swept Seattle, frightened residents desperately tried to devise ways of protecting their windshields. On the evening of April 15, the mayor of Seattle appealed to the governor and to the president for emergency help. Then, as quickly as it had arisen, the mass hysteria died down. Later, a team of experts determined that the windshields had always been pitted. People simply had not noticed them before because drivers customarily look *through* their windshields, not *at* them. Their own fear had made them imagine a threat that did not exist (Medalia and Larson, 1958).

Communication: Rumors and the Mass Media

For any type of collective action to take place, people must have some means of communicating their fears or frenzy to one another. Rumors play a prominent role in mob action. A **rumor** is an unverified story that circulates from person to person and is accepted as fact, although its original source may be vague or unknown. Rumors proliferate in tense and ambiguous situations, when people are unable to learn the facts or when, for one reason or another, they distrust the information they receive (Rosnow and Fine, 1976). Rumors reflect people's desire to find meaning in events, and thus represent a form of group problem solving. In Seattle, residents thought the pits in their windshields were caused by radioactive fallout from H-bomb tests. Although this interpretation turned out to be wrong, it did temporarily solve their problem of finding some explanation of the mysterious damage they believed they saw.

Most rumors are born, live, and die within a relatively short period. After studying the transmission of rumors in the laboratory and in the field, the psychologists Gordon W. Allport and Leo Postman (1947) discovered a basic pattern. A person hears a story that seems interesting and repeats it—or what is remembered of it—to a friend. Gradually, the original story is reduced to a few essential details that are easy to tell. Allport and Postman call this process *leveling:* "As a rumor travels, it tends to grow shorter, more concise, more easily grasped and told. In successive versions, fewer words are used and fewer details are mentioned" (p. 75). People also tend to alter details to make the story more coherent and more in keeping with their preconceptions. In the early stages of the 1992 disturbance in Los Angeles, rumors that police had donned riot gear apparently inflamed the crowd, encouraging them to arm themselves with stones, bottles, clubs, or whatever was handy. In fact, only one police officer had put on a helmet. But the rumor of police preparations for attack conformed to widespread beliefs about police brutality, confirming the crowd's expectations. The next day, rumors that carloads of African-American youth were "invading" affluent white suburbs caused panic and sent residents to supermarkets to stock up for the expected siege.

The mass media also play an important role in crowd action today. In the Los Angeles incident, television was both a catalyst and a target. As noted earlier, throughout the trial of the police officers, TV networks had replayed the video of the King beating. The fact that it was a "home movie," rather than a glossy professional report, added to people's sense of its truthfulness. When people see an event on television, they tend to believe that they saw it firsthand, for themselves—and to disbelieve people who interpret the images differently.

The verdict in the King case was broadcast live, followed by shouts of disbelief among customers at an African-American barbershop on one station and outraged statements by public officials (including Mayor Bradley) on others. When the mood on the street turned ugly, news stations competed for the most sensational footage. In watching the news on TV, people tend to forget that reporting is selective, with editors deciding which events are newsworthy and which are not (Gans, 1979; Gitlin, 1985). As is often the case, shots of violence were selected over shots of calm. One TV station superimposed images of street violence over choir music from the church gathering. Another actually reported the news *before* it happened: The reporter commented that he hadn't seen "any fires *yet*" (*Newsweek*, May 11, 1992, p. 43). Simply by being there, reporters created news—namely, assaults on themselves and their equipment. Television reporters also broadcast the message that the police were not responding to the violence and looting. In effect, the cameras showed potential participants where the action was. In the words of one commentator, "Helicopter one-upmanship on

Wednesday night led to a two-hour invitation, delivered by an airborne minicam, to riot" (Hewitt, 1992, p. M1). At the very least, television reinforced the feeling that law and order had broken down. Moreover, without media coverage it seems unlikely that the violence would have spread to other cities.

Emergent Norms and Social Relationships

Few contemporary sociologists dispute the observation that emotions and behavior sometimes spread through crowds, whether via rumors or the mass media, as if they were contagious. However, most contemporary sociologists believe that Le Bon and Blumer underestimated the organization of crowds and their capacity for rational behavior. It is simplistic, they argue, to view people in crowds as impulsive, unpredictable creatures who can no longer control their own behavior. Ralph Turner and Lewis Killian (1972), for example, question the implicit assumption that social conformity no longer operates in a crowd. According to their **emergent-norm theory**, people develop new social norms as they interact in situations that lack firm guidelines for coping. These norms then exert a powerful influence on their behavior.

The new norms evolve through a gradual process of social exploration and testing. One or more people may suggest a course of action (shouting obscenities or hurling bottles, for example). Other suggestions follow. The crowd begins to define the situation, to develop a justification for acts that would in other circumstances seem questionable. In this way new norms may emerge that condone violence and destruction but still impose some limits on crowd behavior. For example, all the motorists assaulted during the Los Angeles violence were Caucasian, Hispanic, or Asian; none were black, though many more African-Americans were accidentally injured or killed by gunfire. Similarly, Asian (mostly Korean) businesses were singled out for looting because of special resentment against their owners as outsiders and successful immigrants who were perceived as taking opportunities away from African-Americans.

The emergence of new norms, Turner and Killian argue, does not mean that members of a crowd come to think and feel as one. Although it may appear to outsiders that a crowd is a unanimous whole, some participants may just be going along to avoid disapproval and ridicule. Thus, unlike Le Bon and Blumer,

Turner and Killian believe that crowd unanimity is little more than an illusion. The illusion is created by the fact that crowd members tend to demand at least surface conformity to the new norms that have evolved.

Extending Turner and Killian's ideas, other sociologists have argued that new social relationships also emerge in crowds (Weller and Quarentelli, 1973). Consider lynching, a fairly common form of crowd violence in the early American West and, until recent decades, in the South as well. A lynch mob dispenses with conventional norms of trial by jury, rule of law, and execution only by the state, replacing them with the norms of a vigilante trial and punishment by mob consensus. But new social relationships develop, too. Participants, improvising a division of labor, informally designate such roles as prosecutor, witnesses, jury members, and executioners. Crowds, in short, are neither normless nor totally lacking in social organization. Both norms and social relationships always emerge in them, making them much more structured than they seem at first glance.

Crowd Action as Rational Decision Making

Contrary to the common view of "crowd madness" and "irrational rioting," rational-choice theories have shown that people do not always "lose their heads" (their rationality) simply because they are part of a crowd (Berk, 1974). They continue to weigh the costs and benefits of possible courses of action. The costs associated with rioting are the risk of personal injury and the likelihood of being arrested. In a crowd that greatly outnumbers police, these risks are relatively small. Moreover, the benefits of mob action may outweigh the risks for people who are disadvantaged and have many pent-up frustrations. These benefits may be either tangible, such as looted merchandise, or intangible, such as social recognition and emotional release. In any case, Berk argues, people in mobs calculate that violence will pay off in their particular situation.

Not all sociologists agree that crowd action is this calculated. But riots clearly do gain attention. In the aftermath of the riot in the Watts section of Los Angeles in 1965, Martin Luther King, Jr., toured the ruins. He was approached by a group of young men claiming victory. "How can you say you won when 34 Negroes are dead, your community is destroyed and whites are using the riots as an excuse for inac-

tion?" King asked. The youths replied, "We won because we made them pay attention to us" (quoted in *Los Angeles Times,* May 2, 1992, p. A2). And so it was in 1992. President Bush ordered the Justice Department to press federal civil rights charges against the officers who beat Rodney King only *after* the riot. Before the riot, neither the president nor Congress had paid serious attention to the problems of inner cities. Program after program had been cut back or canceled. After the riot, politicians scrambled to be associated with urban initiatives. Within a week of the violence, President Bush had pledged $600 million for restoration, Congress had introduced emergency legislation for $300 million in small-business loans, and California Governor Pete Wilson had proposed $20 million in state funds for job training. Many community leaders—and sociologists—hold that these measures do not address the underlying causes of the riot. Nonetheless, whether the violence is called a riot or a rebellion, it did call public attention to the desperate situation of South-Central Los Angeles.

USING THE KEY CONCEPTS TO ANALYZE THE LOS ANGELES "RIOT"

Everyday explanations of the Los Angeles violence focus on the verdict in the Rodney King case. Certainly the trial touched off the riot or rebellion. It was what the sociologist Neil Smelser (1963) called a **precipitating event,** an incident that confirms people's suspicions and fears—in this case, about how the criminal justice system is biased against African-Americans. But injustices occur every day; riots and rebellions do not. Our five key concepts can help explain the underlying causes and significance of the events in Los Angeles.

Crowd Action as Social Action

The behavior of a crowd is social action by definition, because crowd members' actions are in response to, or coordinated with, or oriented toward, one another. As we noted earlier, people sometimes try to explain crowd action by the characteristics of the people who participate. This was certainly true of the Los Angeles events. One popular explanation was a kind of "riffraff theory." It held that only criminal types participate in riots, and that a hard core of agitators incites violence despite the strong disapproval of area residents. Thus, many outsiders blamed the violence on criminals and opportunists, especially gang members (Merina and Mitchell, 1992). However, eyewitnesses reported that a broad spectrum of citizens—young and old, African-American and Hispanic, Asian and Caucasian—joined the action. "You had 7- and 8-year-olds all the way up to 60-year-olds," said one South-Central resident. "You had everyday citizens. . . . I thought about participating myself" (p. A12). While some people in the crowds saw themselves as making a political statement or avenging past insults, others seized the opportunity to acquire goods they could not afford, and still others felt compelled to steal before the stores were stripped bare and they would not be able to feed and care for their families. (Along with televisions, sneakers, and guns, disposable diapers were among the most popular items seized by looters.)

This mixture of motives is common to many crowd actions. It was also the case in the ghetto riots of 1967, as the National Advisory Commission on Civil Disorders (1968), appointed by President Lyndon Johnson, pointed out. In Detroit, for instance, the commission found that nearly 40 percent of ghetto residents either participated in the crowd action or were bystanders to it. This hardly represents a deviant minority. The Detroit "rioters," moreover, were on average better-educated, better-informed, and more involved in the community than were the nonrioters. And most of the rioters were employed, although many thought their jobs were beneath them.

Even a riot has a kind of social organization. In Los Angeles, groups of young men—not simply thousands of isolated individuals—were drawn into collective action. For some, this meant deciding to burn down a store. For others, it meant organizing to try to protect their homes. In South-Central Los Angeles, crowds gathered at specific places, not randomly throughout the area. In particular, they gathered wherever the police were congregated—partly to taunt them—and wherever the media were present. In these crowds, some young men performed while larger groups served as their audience: The young men shouted insults at police, ran out in front of the crowd to throw a rock or bottle, and threatened any white or Asian passersby. These actions can be understood only in terms of the relationship between the individuals who performed them and the audiences who watched and sometimes shouted their approval. However, all these kinds of crowd action depended not just on the other people around but on the patterns of social organization by which people were both motivated to join the crowd and organized within it. For example, people in the crowds were often with small groups of friends; this helped to reduce their fear. Larger, more structural factors were also involved.

Structural Conduciveness

Smelser (1963) coined the term **structural conduciveness** to describe aspects of social structure that facilitate collective action. Perhaps the most important structural issue behind the Los Angeles upheaval—and smaller crowd actions that took place around the country—was the deterioration of inner cities in recent decades. Ghetto residents were left in a state of economic isolation. At least one member of most inner-city families was unemployed, and young men were particularly likely to be without jobs. With more than half a million people, South-Central Los Angeles had only thirty-five supermarkets and fewer than twenty bank branches (*Los Angeles Times*, May 1, 1992). Many residents had to either take two bus rides to shop for food or patronize higher-priced neighborhood grocery stores. For those who had jobs, cashing a paycheck meant waiting in long lines or paying high fees at check-cashing stores. About one in four South-Central residents was poor, almost twice the rate for urban whites. Yet the poor watched the same TV shows, with their tantalizing portrayals of goods and lifestyles they could not afford, that the middle class did. Such economic frustration is one of the structural preconditions for crowd action.

Significantly, the main targets of the 1992 crowds were not the police, as in earlier riots, but retail stores, factories, and other enterprises. Much of the rioters' wrath was aimed specifically at shops owned by Korean-Americans (Freer, 1994). Immigrants, with only small amounts of capital to invest, often fill the need for goods and services in inner-city neighborhoods. They succeed in part by working long hours themselves and hiring family members; but as a result, they are less likely to hire local residents and more likely to be cut off socially from the neighborhoods they serve (Abelmann and Lie, 1995; Morrison and Lowry, 1994). Their success, however modest, also invites the envy of local residents. "They just charge high prices and take our money," said one looter of Korean businesses. "Now we are taking

The absence of stores in South Central Los Angeles created an opportunity for Korean immigrants, whose success with family-owned and family-operated businesses in turn created resentment among residents. Korean-American stores were prime targets during the 1992 riot.

some back" (quoted in *Los Angeles Times*, May 1, 1992, p. A24). Relations between African-American residents and Asian store owners in South-Central were particularly tense because a Korean storekeeper had recently been given probation for shooting to death a fifteen-year-old girl she suspected of shoplifting (Tierney, 1994).

The fact that poor African-Americans are crowded together in inner cities also facilitates crowd action. Residents live in close proximity to one another, and substandard housing encourages many to spend a great deal of time outdoors. In addition, many are unemployed or employed at irregular hours. As a result, the streets are normally filled with people. If an incident enraged, say, Irish-Americans, who are dispersed all over the Los Angeles suburbs, mobilization for immediate crowd action would be difficult. But when something happens in South-Central, crowds gather rapidly. News of the verdict in the King case, broadcast live on radio and TV, spread like wildfire. So did news that a riot was under way.

Functional *Dis*-Integration

Under optimal conditions, the different elements of a social system work together, each contributing to the smooth functioning of the whole. When this functional integration breaks down, collective action is more likely.

To a large degree, American society has passed inner cities by. Businesses have moved their factories to the countryside or even to Third World nations and their retail outlets and offices to the suburbs. The middle class, both black and white, has largely abandoned the city as well. As a result, big-city mayors and political machines no longer play a pivotal role in politics. Beltways enable commuters to avoid even driving through urban neighborhoods. In a way, today's inner cities are like yesterday's rural backwaters: They are literally *dis*-integrated, cut off from the mainstream of economic, political, and social life.

The Los Angeles riot provided an example of disintegration at the local political level. Los Angeles is the only major city in the United States in which the mayor cannot hire and fire the chief of police. Rather, the chief reports to a police commission. To remove a chief, the police commission must file formal charges with the civil service commission, a procedure that can take months. Moreover, the city council can override the police commission. In short, there is no clear chain of command. Mayor Bradley had tried to force Chief Gates to resign after the Rodney King beating, but without success. At the time of the riot, the two men apparently had not spoken to each other for almost a year. Mayor Bradley did not have the authority to order police into neighborhoods where the riot was gathering force, and Chief Gates decided to avoid confrontation. When the mayor asked Governor Wilson to send in the National Guard, on the first night of rioting, it was the governor who had to arrange a conference call to convince Chief Gates and his deputy to agree. The second day of the riot, guardsmen sat in armories awaiting orders; again, the governor had to step in to demand action. Thus, divisions within local government prevented a quick police response, which might have prevented a full-scale riot or at least cut it short.

Cultural Clashes

Most Americans, including President Bush, were surprised by the not-guilty verdicts in the Rodney King case. Polls found that a majority of white as well as black Americans thought that the verdicts were wrong and that the federal government should bring charges (*Newsweek*, May 11, 1992). This surface agreement obscured the legacy of racism in American culture, and the long-term, continuing separation between black and white Americans. A white person watching the videotape of King's beating might feel sickened: "How can they do that to that poor guy?" An African-American would probably feel threatened as well: "That poor guy could be me!" To a degree that most white Americans cannot imagine, most African-Americans (especially males) live in fear of police brutality, not to mention insults from white cab drivers, store clerks, headwaiters, and others. The verdict in the King case seemed to confirm that however innocent they might be and however badly they have been treated by authorities, African-Americans are presumed to be guilty by white authorities. At the same time, many white Americans live in fear of black crime and violence. "For blacks the acquittal, and for whites the aftermath, tended to confirm each race's worst fears and suspicions about the other" (*Time*, May 11, 1992, p. 20).

Blacks and whites also tended to differ in their explanations of the events in Los Angeles (Lauter and Fluwood, 1992). Many African-Americans saw the basic problem as racial oppression, the product of a system that routinely neglects and often brutalizes blacks. Many white Americans saw the primary problem as social pathology, due in part to individual ir-

responsibility and irreverence for basic family and community values. These differences helped produce the contrasting labels among blacks ("rebellion") and whites ("riot").

The division between black and white Americans was not the only cultural gap that surfaced in Los Angeles, however. As we have noted, much of the violence was directed against Korean-Americans. Ghetto residents saw Asian shopkeepers not only as exploitative but also as arrogant and exclusive (Koppel, 1992). In a meeting held to bring the two groups together, African-Americans complained that Koreans typically put change on the counter rather than in the customer's hand, which they perceived as an act of disdain. Koreans explained that in their culture it is insulting to physically touch a nonrelative, particularly a woman. Koreans expect customers to ask for what they want; African-Americans like to browse. Under conditions of economic conflict and inequality, violations of such minor cultural norms can lead to major hostility.

Koreans, too, are a minority community in Los Angeles, and although many are more prosperous than their black and Latino neighbors, they also suffer from discrimination. Many have sought to recreate a homelike community, and the riots shattered their feeling that they had constructed a safe haven in an alien culture (Abelmann and Lie, 1995). They also had grievances against the police, who failed to protect their property from looting and destruction. As one said,

> The greatest shock for me was the Hispanic looting of Koreatown—you know it was the Hispanics who did most of it. It was shocking—they were the very same people that I live with, drive by, walk by, talk to, the very same ones who were looting the stores. And here they were, a baby carriage full of looted goods in one arm and a baby in the other—it freaked me out. (Quoted in Abelmann and Lie, 1995, p. 41)

Other cultural groups were drawn into the conflict. Japanese- and Chinese-Americans admitted worrying that they would be mistaken for Korean-Americans and also feeling guilty about wanting to dissociate themselves from other Asians (Woo, 1992). Hispanics occupied an ambiguous role in the upheaval, sometimes becoming the victims of mob violence and other times joining the mob. White Anglo-Americans joined the crowd outside police headquarters the night the riot erupted, and sometimes participated in the looting on subsequent days. Los Angeles had often been cited as a "world city," a model of the changing ethnic mix in the United States. The events of 1992 showed just how volatile that mixture could be.

Power and Powerlessness

Riots are an assertion of power by the powerless—the last resort of people who cannot make themselves heard through conventional political and economic channels. They nearly always pit the poor against the rich. To the upper classes, riots may look like senseless, self-destructive, emotional outbursts. To participants, however, such collective action may be a form of collective bargaining (Piven and Cloward, 1979; Thompson, 1971). By creating or threatening to create civil disorder, rioters prod government into action. That action may be repressive, but very poor people may feel they have little to lose. The dangers they face may seem well worth the feeling of being in control for once, however briefly. Shortly after midnight on the first night of the Los Angeles disturbance, Police Chief Gates announced that the city was calming down. But a rioter told reporters, "It ain't over till *we* say it's over"—and he, not Gates, proved to be right (Koppel, 1992).

In the urban riots that swept the United States in the 1960s, violence was confined almost entirely to the African-American ghetto. White-owned stores may have been destroyed, but white neighborhoods were not threatened. In Los Angeles in 1992, violence did spill over ghetto borders and involve other ethnic groups. The number of rioters who left downtown for the beaches, the hills, and the malls was small, and the damage relatively slight; but the danger seemed real to well-to-do whites who were used to feeling protected by the power their wealth bestowed and who were not accustomed to seeing poor blacks try to exert power directly. "There was a siege mentality out here—a sense of the have-nots coming after the haves," said the owner of a suburban bookstore (quoted in *Los Angeles Times*, May 7, 1992, p. J1). Suddenly, affluent Angelenos who had been watching the riots from a safe distance, on TV, smelled smoke. Although few stores outside South-Central were looted and few homes burned, the psychological barrier—the feeling of suburban invulnerability—was breached.

SOCIAL MOVEMENTS

Social movements are special cases of collective action. Riots, panics, fads, and other types of collective action are generally short-lived and, though sometimes calculated, typically heedless and emotional. In contrast, social movements are sustained and deliberate efforts to bring about or resist social change. Although they may attract crowds, most social movements include formal organizations with hierarchical structures and formal ties to one another (Marx and McAdam, 1995). They differ from more institutionalized efforts to influence social patterns in their willingness to use unconventional tactics. Social movements frequently employ mass marches and rallies, sit-ins, boycotts, and sometimes even violence, sabotage, and other illegal acts (especially when agents of social control try to suppress them) to make their grievances known.

Because they challenge existing patterns of functional integration, social movements nearly always face a variety of obstacles. Some people may actively oppose them, while others remain indifferent. Social movements succeed only when they are able to wield significant power. Revolutions do this by attempting to seize control of the government or state and use its power to bring about social change. Other social movements, such as the women's movement, focus on altering the culture—on changing people's attitudes, beliefs, and values, and thereby their behavior.

Explaining Social Movements

Let's turn now to the reasons that social movement arises—to what makes people engage in unconventional, often risky, collective action in order to bring about or resist change.

Social and Economic Deprivation

Social movements may arise from social and economic deprivation. When discontent with existing social arrangements becomes deep and broad enough, people join together and fight back. Karl Marx held that the basic causes of revolutions and other social movements were structural. The owners of the means of production in a society are driven to increase their privileges by exploiting the laboring

The social movements of the 1960s were based on the hopes and frustrations of certain groups, such as African-Americans; but they also brought very different groups together. Top left: Bob Dylan jams with Student Nonviolent Coordinating Committee (SNCC) workers. Top right: Vietnam war veterans lead an antiwar demonstration. Bottom: National Guardsmen rough up a photographer at a black civil-rights demonstration.

masses. Over time this exploitative economic structure leads to widespread poverty and deprivation, which in turn sparks revolution. The French Revolution, for instance, was preceded by a sharp increase in the price of bread (the highest price in seventy years) as a result of poor harvests in 1787 and 1788. Workers in the cities and even rural residents faced severe hunger. In 1789 they rebelled.

As we discussed in Chapter 1, Marx contended that in capitalist societies, the ever-increasing use of machinery and factory production would condemn workers to more and more menial tasks, thus continually depressing their wages and feeding their sense of alienation. The economic cycle of boom and bust that characterizes capitalist societies would aggravate the misery of the working class. Eventually, workers would find their exploitation intolerable and would organize to overthrow their oppressors.

Not all sociologists agree with the view that progressive impoverishment puts people in a revolutionary frame of mind. The French observer Alexis de Tocqueville (1856) emphasized the role of culture in revolutions and social movements. People's actual conditions may not get very much worse (indeed, they may improve); but new cultural beliefs and ideas may cause them to view their situation as intolerable. Thus the notion of continual progress, faith that democracy could solve all sorts of social problems, and belief in the value of individualism—all new to the eighteenth century—were destabilizing. When the downtrodden begin to believe that a better life is possible, they react by reaching for it. "Evils which are patiently endured when they seem inevitable," wrote Tocqueville, "become intolerable once the idea of escape from them is suggested" (p. 214). Sociologists call this gap between people's expectations and their actual conditions **relative deprivation** (Gurr, 1970).

Relative deprivation occurs under a variety of circumstances. Tocqueville identified one condition, that of *rising expectations*. It was a sense of rising expectations, some sociologists say, that bred the black protest movement and the ghetto outbreaks of the 1960s (Abeles, 1976; Geschwender, 1964). The economic prosperity of the 1950s and the early gains of the civil rights movement led African-Americans to believe that their circumstances would soon improve substantially. The new civil rights legislation and President Lyndon Johnson's War on Poverty program, however, delivered little. The Johnson administration's promise of a Great Society faded as the United States became increasingly preoccupied with the war in Vietnam. To raise people's expectations of a feast and then deliver crumbs is to create a socially explosive situation. The 1992 L.A. rebellion was shaped by disappointment and frustration with the setbacks of the 1980s, after the advances of the civil rights movement.

The sociologist James Davies (1962, 1974) has described this pattern as a "J-curve" because a graph of a sudden, sharp reversal in a pattern of long-term improvement can look like an upside-down "J" (see Figure 20.1). Davies bases his analysis on the observation of such events as Dorr's Rebellion in Rhode Island in 1842, the Pullman strike of 1894, the Russian Revolution of 1917, and the Egyptian Revolution of 1953. Davies concludes that revolutionary movements are most likely to spring up when a prolonged period of economic and social improvement is followed by a drastic reversal in people's fortunes. The first period presumably creates an expectation that things will steadily get better; the second period stimulates a terrible fear that all past progress will suddenly be irretrievably lost. Davies believes that the actual conditions prevailing in the period of reversal are less important than the psychological state they foster. Revolutions flare up when the gap between what people expect and what they actually receive suddenly widens.

Resource Mobilization

Most contemporary sociologists see deprivation alone as an insufficient explanation for the rise of a social movement (McAdam, McCarthy, and Zald, 1988; Tilly, 1978). They contend that discontent is always widespread; yet full-fledged social movements are relatively infrequent. The reason, they argue, is that discontent must be coupled with the ability to mobilize resources on behalf of a group's collective interests. Without sufficient resources and the organization to use those resources effectively, even the most aggrieved people cannot launch a social movement.

The resources that can be mobilized in support of a social movement consist of tangible assets and human skills (Freeman, 1979; McCarthy and Zald, 1977). Among the primary tangible assets are money (which can purchase many other assets), channels of mass communication (leaflets, newspapers, radio, and television) to publicize the movement's goals, and space to house its headquarters. Human skills include lead-

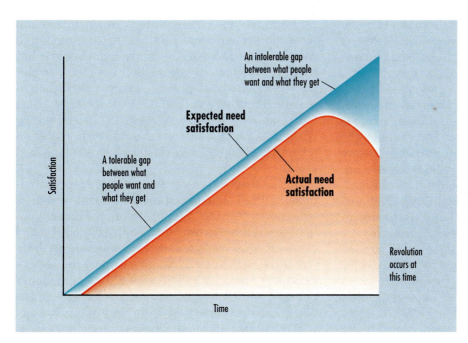

An intolerable gap between what people want and what they get

Expected need satisfaction

A tolerable gap between what people want and what they get

Actual need satisfaction

Satisfaction

Time

Revolution occurs at this time

FIGURE 20.1 / Davies's J-Curve Theory of Revolution

In Davies's view, revolutions are most likely to occur when a period of economic and social progress is succeeded by sharp reversals, fueling fears that all gains will be lost.

Source: Adapted from James C. Davies, "Toward a Theory of Revolution," *American Sociological Review* 27 (February 1962), fig. 1, p. 6.

ership, organizational talent, personal prestige (which is helpful in attracting followers and in gaining social acceptance), and intimate knowledge of the people or institutions the movement hopes to change. Also crucial are the time to devote to movement activities and a commitment to the cause (that is, a willingness to endure risk and inconvenience so that the movement's goals can be achieved). Support may come from people who are not directly involved but are sympathetic with the cause as well as from inside.

The ability to mobilize resources also depends on favorable opportunities in the social environment (Tilly, 1978; Zald and McCarthy, 1987). It was not an accident that the prosperous 1950s and 1960s gave birth to a number of social movements, including the civil rights, women's, and environmental movements, which we will analyze below. During times of prosperity people generally are more receptive to calls to improve the conditions of underprivileged groups and more willing to give time, money, and other resources to causes than they are when they are struggling to keep their own heads above water.

Still another factor conducive to resource mobilization is what Doug McAdam (1982) calls *cognitive liberation*. Cognitive (or mental) liberation occurs when members of an aggrieved group come to view their situation both as unjust and as potentially changeable through collective action. People must come to see their troubles as the result of social injustice, not personal failure; identify with others in the same situation; and put combined interests ahead of personal gain. Cognitive liberation depends on both a favorable opportunity structure (which holds out hope that change is possible) and organization (which allows insurgents to share their views). The result of all these factors is collective action.

Whether or not collective action is successful is another matter. Usually, a social movement owes much of its success to effective leadership. Sociologists have identified several types of leaders, ranging from the "agitator" or "prophet," whose skills at articulating some demand compel public attention, to the "administrator," who puts together the nuts and bolts of an organized campaign (Wilson, 1973). Sometimes a single leader exerts several kinds of leadership simultaneously. Martin Luther King, Jr., and Betty Friedan were both influential prophets who voiced the concerns of blacks and women, respectively. In addition, both functioned as administrators. King was spokesperson for the Southern Christian Leadership Conference and Friedan for the National Organization for Women. Such versatile leaders tend to be the exception. More often, a movement develops a division of labor among several leaders who have different kinds of skills.

The sociologists John McCarthy and Mayer Zald (1973, 1977; Zald and McCarthy, 1987) have proposed that many modern-day social movements are largely the creation of outside or professional leadership. A groundswell of discontent among aggrieved individuals is not necessary to generate a social movement. Skilled leaders can take weak and ill-defined discontent and broaden its base. For this reason, grassroots support for some social movements actually comes *after* the movement is under way. For example, the movement to provide federally funded health care for the elderly in the United States did not derive initially from an outcry among senior citizens. Instead, the movement's principal organization, the National Council for Senior Citizens for Health Care through Social Security (NCSC), was staffed primarily by young and middle-aged professionals and funded by the AFL-CIO. Organizers staged rallies across the country and encouraged mass petitioning. Later, when the movement encountered opposition from the American Medical Association, the NCSC began to use its resources to mobilize a large membership base among the elderly. Thus, active support from the aggrieved group was sought only after the movement was in full swing. Far from involving a popular outcry of discontent, this social movement was professionally planned and directed by outsiders (Rose, 1967).

Social Revolution as Structural Change

Many of the movements studied by sociologists seek only moderate reforms—like the improvement of access to public transportation and buildings sought by the movement for the rights of handicapped people. Other movements seek more basic change, and these can result in revolutions. The sociologist Theda Skocpol defines **social revolutions** as "rapid, basic transformations of a society's state and class structures . . . accompanied and in part carried through by class-based revolts from below" (1979, p. 4). The simultaneous occurrence of class upheaval and sociopolitical transformation distinguishes a social revolution from a rebellion (which does not result in any structural change), from political revolution (which involves no change in social structure), and from such revolutionary processes as industrialization (which involve no change in political structure).

Skocpol explains social revolution by combining aspects of Marxist and resource-mobilization theories. She finds that although underlying class conflict is fundamental to revolution, it is also necessary to consider how the class members are organized and what their resources are. Rather than attempting to create a general theory for all revolutions, she has tried to construct an explanation for social revolutions in three agrarian states: France at the time of the overthrow of Louis XVI (1789), Russia at the time Czar Nicholas II was deposed (1917), and China when the Qing dynasty was ousted (1911) and again when the communist government was established (1949).

On the basis of her careful study of these revolutions, Skocpol highlights three factors that tend to be ignored in other theories of revolution. First, revolutions are rarely started intentionally though leaders can later seize control; they generally emerge from structural crises, such as government budgetary deficits or wars. Both the cost and the unpopularity of World War I contributed to the Russian Revolution of 1917, for example. Second, revolutions are not purely products of internal forces. International relations and developments (particularly long-drawn-out wars and military defeats) contribute to the emergence of crises and revolutions by undermining old political regimes. Third, states have an existence of their own and are not necessarily dependent on the interests and structure of the dominant class. Revolutions are against states, not directly against ruling classes.

Skocpol's account of revolution places major emphasis on social structure, on the basic conditions that make states vulnerable. Jack Goldstone (1991) has extended this line of argument, showing how rapid population growth helps to produce government crises by creating more job seekers, inflation in food prices, and other demands on government treasuries. All weaken the support structures for the state.

Interests and Identities: Social Movements New and Old

The idea of social movement originated with the labor and working-class movements of nineteenth-century Europe. Many observers—including Karl Marx but also a variety of less radical thinkers—saw labor movements as the crucial source of progress and social change in modern societies. Debates over the appropriate role of working people in modern societies were often referred to as "the social question" because they addressed the question of what kind of society industrialization and related changes were producing. Was it one in which there would always, inevitably, be a great deal of inequality and poverty, or could these social ills be cured? In this context, the term *social movement* connoted both the forward movement of society in gradually addressing such problems and achieving progress, and the activities of workers and their sympathizers who sought to push progress along.

The labor movement and the social democratic and socialist movements that joined forces with it in much of Europe did bring dramatic changes. It is largely because of the labor and "social" movements that free public education, health care, and unemployment benefits were introduced in much of Europe. In addition, these movements brought their members higher wages, better working hours, and guarantees against unfair dismissal. But we can now see that these were not the only social movements afoot. There were many different forces for change, and change did not move all in one direction. There were also nationalist and religious movements, and eventually women's movements, gay rights movements, free love movements, antiabortion movements, animal rights movements, and even conservative movements.

What all these movements have in common is the desire to affect the course of social change. Whether they seek to speed up change or alter its direction or stop it, all modern movements reflect an understanding of the world as one in which human beings' destinies are at least to some extent open to being shaped by human action, not dictated entirely by God or fate. As the sociologist Zygmunt Baumann has put it, moderns think of the world as being like a garden: not a natural growth of plants but a place where human cultivation and shaping can pursue perfection (Baumann, 1991). Revolutions reflect this mentality and are attempts to bring great changes very rapidly. However, many other kinds of movements may produce even greater changes by slowly altering whole cultures and patterns of social action and social structure. This has been true, for example, of both the women's movement and the labor movement.

We have seen the role of several different factors, from culture to structure, in explaining how social movements take place. In understanding what movements pursue, we also have to look at multiple factors. Most movements pursue *interests* of their participants. Interests are often economic, like higher wages for workers—or working women—but they

may also be political: for example, working-class men and all women had to organize movements to win the right to vote in Europe and the United States in the nineteenth and early twentieth centuries.

Movements are also commonly about *identity*. Identity issues shape movements in two ways. First, in order for any group of people to determine what their common interests are, they need to establish what identity they have in common. Should they think of themselves as workers, for example, or only in terms of their specific occupations, like shoemaker and steelworker? Will black and white workers join together because they share the identity worker, or will they be separated by their racial identities? In most of American history, the latter has been the case. Since a shared identity is an important condition of common struggle, racial divisions have undermined labor movements. Second, identity is itself one of the possible objects of struggle. In many movements participants seek recognition that their shared identity is legitimate and deserving of respect from other members of society (Taylor, 1995). This is true today of movements like that of gay men and lesbians. The gay movement does pursue its members' interests, of course, such as nondiscrimination and equal rights. These interests, however, are crucially linked to acceptance of gay identities. The gay movement does not focus mainly on economic issues but on the question of whether a gay identity is to be seen as legitimate in American (or global) culture.

Some theorists have pointed out that issues of identity seem to play a much larger role in today's social movements (including the environmental movement, the women's movement, the movement of gay men and lesbians, and the rise of the religious right) than they did in the labor movement and other earlier social movements. This has led them to describe those movements in which identity issues are more central than instrumental interests as "new social movements" (Cohen and Arato, 1992; Melucci, 1989; Touraine, 1981, 1988). Other theorists have pointed out that identity issues were important to earlier movements as well, arguing that we can see identity and interests as important in different balances in all social movements (Calhoun, 1993; Tucker, 1991).

Social movements that focus considerably on identity have some distinctive characteristics. They are likely to stress defense more than offense, for example, as the environmental movement seeks to defend ecology against technology and exploitation, or the new religious right seeks to defend traditional values against forces that erode them. They are likely to bring political action to bear on aspects of personal life—like family and sexual relations—because these are basic to people's identities. It is also possible for people to participate in several different social movements at the same time—to be active in both religious and environmental causes, for example, or in both women's and gay movements. In this, theorists of the new social movements suggest, today's movements are different from the traditional labor or socialist movements which tried to provide one all-encompassing solution to the problems of working-class people.

We look next at two important American social movements in which both interests and identities were (and are) important. The civil rights movement and the women's movement have both profoundly shaped the course of social change in contemporary America. In important ways both of them continue as active social movements. Though participants in each define progress in different ways, there is widespread agreement that much still needs to be done to improve the material conditions (interests) of African-Americans and American women of all ethnicities. At the same time, both blacks and women seek a level of respect that has often been denied them. And last but not least, identity is an issue in both movements because blacks and women have more than just those single identities. The identities overlap and sometimes compete. Thus the Million Man March organized by Nation of Islam Minister Louis Farrakhan in 1995, for example, focused on the identity of black men and drew criticism from some black women. Indeed, there have been general questions about whether the mainly male black nationalist movement speaks adequately to the concerns of black women, and also about whether the mainly white women's movement took seriously enough the specific needs of black women (Collins, 1991; hooks, 1989).

The Civil Rights Movement

The 1992 riot in Los Angeles might be seen as an echo or aftershock of the civil rights movement of the 1950s and 1960s. One of the most sweeping and effective crusades in modern U.S. history, the civil rights movement continues today to address the problems, advance the interests, and affirm the identity of African-Americans.

The civil rights movement began in the South in the 1950s, as a grassroots protest against the so-called Jim Crow laws that enforced racial segregation and excused racial terrorism. African-Americans had never accepted white domination, even under slavery, but they had seldom confronted the existing power structure directly. Why did a movement take shape in the 1950s? One reason had to do with relative deprivation. In World War II, black and white soldiers fought together against a common enemy, the Nazi regime of Adolf Hitler, whose racist policies were universally condemned. In the army and in Europe, they had been treated as full citizens. Yet many black veterans returned to Southern communities where they were forbidden to vote, or even to drink water from a public fountain. Laws and customs that had once seemed inevitable became intolerable (Morris, 1984).

A second reason was rising expectations. In its 1954 decision in *Brown* v. *Board of Education*, the U.S. Supreme Court had rejected the separate-but-equal doctrine, declaring segregated schools "inherently unequal." By implication, any form of segregation was unconstitutional. But black hopes for integration soon crashed against organized, sometimes violent, white opposition. Southern governors declared they would ignore the Court's order; white citizens' councils were formed to keep blacks "in their place" by any means necessary; and neither Republican President Eisenhower nor the Democratic Congress was offering wholehearted support (Morris, 1984).

A third factor was structural opportunity (Evans and Boyte, 1992; Tilly, 1978, 1986). The mechanization of agriculture in the 1950s had pushed sharecroppers off farms into Southern cities (as well as to the North). No longer so dispersed, black communities had achieved the "critical mass" necessary for effective collective action.

The precipitating event in the civil rights movement was the 1956 arrest of Rosa Parks, a black seamstress and former secretary of the Alabama chapter of the National Association for the Advancement of Colored People (NAACP), for refusing to give up her seat on a public bus to a white passenger. Within a week, the local black community founded the Montgomery Improvement Association, elected as president the young minister Martin Luther King, Jr., and organized a boycott of city buses. Planned to last one day, the boycott continued for a year and became the model for the civil rights movement as a whole. Note that the goal of the boycott was not only to help end discrimination but also to advance the notion that blacks were full-fledged citizens who deserved the same treatment as whites. Thus, like the civil rights movement as a whole, the boycott was about both promoting blacks' interests and affirming their identity.

As head of the Southern Christian Leadership Conference (SCLC), King led the movement from Montgomery on to Selma and then Birmingham, Alabama. King was an advocate of nonviolent confrontation. Lacking conventional political power, he argued, black people could use civil disobedience, economic boycotts, and public shame to pressure white legislatures to grant them their rights. In the spring of 1960 the movement was joined by students from predominantly black colleges across the South, who began holding sit-ins at restaurants and other public accommodations under the auspices of the Student Nonviolent Coordinating Committee (SNCC). Soon "black America was on the march" (Newman, et al., 1978, p. 19). In 1960 alone, some 50,000 people (most African-American) participated in demonstrations in a hundred cities. The demonstrators were threatened; attacked with police dogs, fire hoses, and electric cattle prods; jailed; fired from their jobs; evicted from their homes; and driven from their churches by firebombs. But the demonstrations continued. White sympathy for the protesters grew—as much from revulsion at the brutal attacks and mass jailings as from agreement with the movement's goals. In 1963, an estimated 250,000 demonstrators, including many whites, marched on Washington, D.C., to hear King deliver his famous "I have a dream" speech. Finally, in 1964 President Johnson convinced Congress that the finest monument to the assassinated John F. Kennedy would be passage of a Civil Rights Act. The movement was by no means over, but a milestone in American history had been passed.

Although King was its acknowledged leader, and organizations like SCLC, SNCC, CORE (Congress of Racial Equality, founded in 1940), and the NAACP (founded in 1909) were important, the drive for civil rights was a true grassroots movement, composed of dozens of local protest groups with their own organizations, leaders, and strategies. The most important way local people were mobilized was through black churches (Morris, 1984). Religion was the one institution in which white Southerners permitted blacks any organizational freedom during the Jim Crow years. The black churches were what sociologists call *free spaces*, where people can think, talk, and socialize among themselves and can discover their true identities and aspirations, away from the

At the 1963 March on Washington, more than 250,000 black and white Americans heard Martin Luther King, Jr. deliver his most famous speech, "I have a dream . . . ."

scrutiny and control of those who hold power over other aspects of their lives (Evans and Boyte, 1992). Churches provided Southern blacks with experience in owning and directing an organization of their own; with leaders—ministers—who were largely independent of white society; with communications networks; and with the cultural traditions of gospel music and oratory for expressing shared hopes and fears.

The civil rights movement also had outside support. The mass media helped to mobilize white sympathy in the North. Images of police turning fire hoses and attack dogs on unresisting black men, women, and children—whether seen on television or the pages of *Life* magazine—awakened the nation's conscience. In the early days of the movement, a number of the students who risked their lives to demonstrate in the South were Northern whites; their characteristics are discussed in the Research Methods box. The Supreme Court stood squarely behind black civil rights during this period. So did some members of the government. Thus John Kennedy, while still a presidential candidate, helped to win Martin Luther King's release from jail, and, as we have noted, Lyndon Johnson used his power to push civil rights legislation through Congress. The mainstays of the movement, however, were poor, rural, often elderly and poorly educated Southern blacks who gave shelter and support to young activists (Newman et al., 1978).

By the late 1960s, the civil rights movement seemed to be losing momentum. Even before King was assassinated in 1968, there were disputes over leadership and the direction the movement should be taking. Often the arguments followed generational lines. Younger blacks tended to be more militant than their elders, to focus on the problems of the urban poor in Northern cities, to question the effectiveness of nonviolent action, to call for separatism (rather than integration), to identify with Africa and the Third World, and to talk of revolution (Newman et al., 1978). After the 1963 march on Washington, the news media, too, began to lose interest in peaceful protest and to search for more dramatic stories. When Stokely Carmichael, a young member of SNCC, called for "Black Power," the media seized the phrase as signifying a change of heart in the movement. Although African-Americans interpreted the slogan in different ways (ranging from an assertion of black pride, to a call for greater participation in electoral

politics, to endorsement of militancy), many whites were convinced that Black Power could mean only one thing: violence against them.

As if to confirm the change, a riot erupted in the largely black Watts section of Los Angeles in the summer of 1965, leaving thirty-four dead. Riots broke out across the country in the summers of 1966 and 1967, when sixty-seven cities were affected, and again in 1968, following the assassination of Dr. King (National Advisory Commission on Civil Disorders, 1968). The riots inflamed white fears, but they also worried many black leaders, who saw them as destroying black communities. This is a common problem with social movements. To attract public attention and demonstrate the importance of the cause, a movement needs to grow; but it may outgrow the organizational capacities of the original leaders and take directions they never intended. New recruits often lack the discipline and dedication of original members.

Partly in response to the riots and partly as the result of the long years of peaceful agitation by the civil rights movement, the government of the United States began to increase its efforts to overcome racial inequality. In addition to enforcing laws against segregation and discrimination, the government began to make—and to require other organizations to make—positive efforts to ensure integration and equal opportunity. One reason the growth of the civil rights movement slowed after the late 1960s was that the government appeared to be taking on many of the movement's goals.

The civil rights movement of the 1950s and 1960s did not end unequal treatment of African-Americans, but it was a special chapter in U.S. history. Its impact reached beyond black communities, influencing society as a whole. In many ways, the civil rights movement changed the shape of politics in the United States. The concept of nonviolent confrontation in the form of marches, sit-ins, and other demonstrations to achieve goals not attainable through conventional channels has become part of the political culture. In more concrete terms, the civil rights movement was the model and often the training ground for leaders of other social movements, including the student and antiwar movements of the 1960s, the modern women's movement, the migrant farmworkers' movement, the pan-Indian movement, the gay rights movement, and most recently the environmental movement.

Studying Active Participants in a Social Movement

In the early 1960s, many students sympathized with the goals of the civil rights movement, but only a much smaller number became active participants in the movement. Who were the activists, and what impact did their movement activities have on their later lives? One sociologist interested in the causes and consequences of civil rights activism used an interesting combination of research techniques—the study of historical documents plus a program of follow-up interviews—to explore this question.

Doug McAdam (1986, 1989) studied participants in the Freedom Summer of 1964. This project drew hundreds of Northern college students, most of whom were white, to Mississippi to help staff freedom schools, register black voters, and dramatize the continuing violation of African-Americans' civil rights in the South. It is difficult to imagine a more dangerous or demanding example of social activism. The students literally put their lives on the line: Just days after the project began, three volunteers—Michael Schwerner, James Chaney, and Andrew Goodman—were kidnapped and murdered by a group of hard-core segregationists. Other volunteers suffered beatings, bombings, and arrests, and all shared the grinding poverty and constant stress of the black families who housed them.

To participate in Freedom Summer, volunteers were required to fill out a lengthy application. Fortunately for McAdam's research purposes, these forms were stored in archives. (Records created for a nonsociological purpose often become important data for later sociological research.) Using these records, he was able to compare the 720 participants with the 239 students who had been accepted but later withdrew. He found very little difference in attitudes between the two groups: All were strongly committed to the goals of the civil rights movement. Nor did he find significant differences in their educational, employment, or marital status, all of which might have influenced their availability for active participation.

The main differences were, first, that participants were more likely than withdrawers to belong to several political organizations. They were joiners, not simply observers. Second, participants were more likely to list other volunteers and activists as people they would want to be kept informed of their summer activities. Thus, they were already linked to activist networks and perhaps more subject to social pressure to honor their applications (and less pressure to put their personal safety first). Finally, participants had more prior experience in high-risk/high-cost activities (such as listening to speakers or giving money). McAdam concludes that although beliefs and attitudes were important, the deciding factors were structural—namely, the participants' preexisting organizational and interpersonal ties to the civil rights movement.

To study the consequences of activism, McAdam conducted follow-up interviews of more than 200 participants and 100 withdrawers twenty years later (McAdam, 1989), a step that required a good deal of initial detective work to locate his interview subjects. McAdam found that for many participants, Freedom Summer marked the beginning of an "activist career." When white involvement in the civil rights movement became problematic, many redirected their energies into the student, antiwar, and women's movements. More than a third had worked as paid activists at some point. And nearly half reported that they were still active in some social movement. Compared with withdrawers, participants had lower incomes and were less likely to be currently married—suggesting to McAdam that they tended to value political over personal goals. Activists emerged from Freedom Summer even more committed than before, and with even stronger ties to activist networks. "For many," McAdam (1989) writes, "New Left politics became the organizing principle of their lives, personal as well as political" (p. 758). These interesting conclusions illustrate the usefulness of combining research techniques—interviews and analysis of historical documents—to answer sociological questions.

The Women's Movement

Organized political protest by women has a long history in the United States. In the early twentieth century a strong women's movement arose to demand the right to vote. Following this victory, feminist protest waned as women entered a period that has been called the *barren years* (Klein, 1984). Even then, some activism remained, keeping women's issues alive until social forces set the stage for renewed grassroots support (Rupp and Taylor, 1987).

One of those social forces was the publication in 1963 of Betty Friedan's book *The Feminine Mystique.* This book was so influential that many scholars equate its publication with the birth of the modern women's, or feminist, movement. In it, Friedan spoke to millions of American women about "the problem that has no name." Trained from childhood to relinquish self-reliance, careers, and personal autonomy and to dedicate their lives to the full-time care of home and children, many women felt dependent, isolated, and unfulfilled. Friedan helped them to identify the causes of these feelings. She also brought to public attention the private grievances of women who worked outside the home and were trapped in dead-end, low-paying, unchallenging jobs. Thus, women across the country became aware of a shared discontent and the possibility that together they might improve their lives. It was the start of their **cognitive liberation**, their sense that things did not have to stay as they were (McAdam, 1989).

A number of factors besides Friedan's book triggered the drive for equal rights for women. One was the black civil rights movement, which stimulated increased awareness of injustice and oppression in a number of groups. Interestingly, women's experiences in the civil rights, student, and antiwar movements served as important catalysts. In these movements, women were often relegated to routine jobs such as typing, answering phones, and making coffee. They were forced to confront the contradiction of working for equal rights for others without enjoying equal rights themselves. In so doing, they began to define a new identity for themselves.

A social movement requires not just a sense of shared injustice but also the mobilization of resources. This mobilization is, in turn, facilitated by organization. Especially important were the commissions to investigate the status of women that were established in each of the fifty states in 1963. The sociologist Jo Freeman (1973) argues that the women's movement of the 1960s would not have materialized without the communications network that these commissions provided. They brought together large numbers of knowledgeable and politically active women and gave them channels for discussing common problems and planning collective solutions. Thus, although the position of women in the 1960s was the same as it had been for decades, something critical had changed. "What changed," writes Freeman (1973), "was the organizational situation. It was not until a communications network developed between like-minded people beyond local boundaries that the movement could emerge and develop past the point of occasional, spontaneous uprising" (p. 804).

The resurgent women's movement worked at two levels (Boles, 1991; Stoper, 1991). The first was an effort to advance women's *interests* by securing equality of official rights between men and women. Most activists who focused on women's rights emphasized moderate reforms, especially the opportunity for women to enter the workforce on an equal footing with men. At the same time, a number of other activists sought deeper changes in women's identity and in the way women fit into society. These radical feminists emphasized the need for more profound changes in American cultural institutions, especially the family. These changes, activists suggested, would have to go beyond the recognition of equal public rights for men and women. As a popular slogan put it, "The personal is political." In other words, power differences that shaped people's personal relations needed to be made the object of public attention and political activism.

The women's movement mobilized for action through both large formal organizations and small, more informal groups. By far the most important organization was the National Organization for Women (NOW). NOW was founded in June 1966 when a small group of women attending the Third National Conference of Commissions on the Status of Women met in Betty Friedan's hotel room. They were concerned that the work of the commissions was not going far enough or fast enough. With Friedan as president, NOW began to attract women in the professions, labor, government, and the communications industry. NOW received a major boost in 1969 when the national media began to carry news stories on women's liberation.

Through its national board and 800 or more local chapters, NOW has used lawsuits, lobbying, demonstrations, boycotts, and other methods to press for such goals as educational reform; nonstereotyped portrayal of women in the media; repeal of laws outlawing abortion; lesbian rights; enhanced roles for women in religion, politics, and sports; and passage of the Equal Rights Amendment (ERA). A number of other organizations of professional women have been formed, such as WEAL (Women's Equity Action League), which focuses on legal questions, and the NWPC (National Women's Political Caucus), which works to get women elected to public office.

While usually supporting the work of organizations like NOW, many feminists also sought to develop a grassroots movement with many independent local groups. Some of these activists were concerned about keeping NOW from working only on "safe" issues like equal access to higher education and making sure that it would represent the needs of lesbians, battered wives, and others who were usually ignored by the media and the political mainstream. Many radical feminists also rejected hierarchical, highly structured organizations, believing that they inevitably stifled those at the bottom. Instead, they created egalitarian groups, which sought not only to increase opportunities for women but also to change the structure of human relationships and roles. Many of the groups emphasized consciousness-raising: Through sharing their ideas and experiences, members attempted to identify their previously unconscious attitudes and behaviors in dealing with both males and females. This new awareness, they hoped, would help to change their attitudes and behaviors, fostering a more egalitarian society. Many local activists branched out into educational and service projects, establishing women's centers, abortion-counseling clinics, shelters for rape victims and battered wives, feminist bookstores and publications, and day-care facilities.

By the 1970s the women's movement had made substantial progress in expanding female career opportunities. Barriers and inequalities still remained, but women were entering fields once considered the domain of men, and their salaries were rising. The entry of many women into full-time professional jobs, however, raised a new issue: namely, how to manage both career commitments and family roles. Women activists responded to this problem by pressing for affordable day care, paid maternity and parental leaves, more flexible work hours, and job sharing between husband and wife.

A countermovement to passage of the ERA posed a major obstacle to the progress of the women's movement in the 1970s. A **countermovement** is a social movement that forms to resist a movement already under way. The leaders of the antifeminist countermovement blamed the women's movement for a variety of social changes (from no-fault divorce laws to legal abortion) that they saw as threats to family stability. To them, the ERA represented the final assault on the traditional roles of wife and mother. To block its ratification, they formed countermovement groups, such as Humanitarians Opposed to Degrading Our Girls (HOTDOG) in Utah, Protect Our Women (POW) in Wisconsin, and Women Who Want to Be Women (WWWW) in Texas (Marshall, 1985). Leading the countermovement at the national level was Phyllis Schlafly, who organized several thousand women in a campaign called Stop-ERA.

Although most of these countermovement groups remained much smaller than NOW and other leading feminist organizations, they were very damaging to the women's movement. In particular, they gave legitimacy to antifeminist men by allowing them to point out that many women were antifeminist too. The antifeminist countermovement was heavily supported by money from conservative political groups, which tried to portray all feminists as extremely radical and "antifamily." Although this charge was not true, it led many women's rights activists to shy away from the label *feminist.* All these efforts proved at least partially successful. The strong initial momentum in favor of the ERA slowed dramatically after 1973 and came to a halt by 1977. Between 1977 and the deadline for ratification, in 1982, not a single additional state voted to ratify the amendment.

The battle lines between the women's movement and the antifeminist countermovement became closely drawn. On one side were mostly younger, better-educated, professionally employed women who want to extend the gains of the 1960s and 1970s. On the other side were primarily older, less educated women, who were often full-time homemakers with strong religious beliefs (Luker, 1984). With the ERA defeated, these antifeminists set new goals, such as making abortion illegal again and banning affirmative-action programs for women. Members of NOW and other women's movement organizations were forced to spend much of their time, energy, and money defending against these attacks (Chavez, 1987).

Put on the defensive, the women's movement did not disappear. Indeed, it helped to redefine politics in America (Butler and Scott, 1992). The ongoing debate helped to put new issues on the national political agenda, including women's health care, day care, domestic violence, sexual assault, reproductive rights, and the plight of displaced homemakers. (See the Sociology and Public Debates box.)

At the national level, the women's movement has become institutionalized (Boles, 1991). Women's rights organizations such as NOW rely in large part on paid leaders and professional staffs (Staggenborg, 1988). Many of their members are "conscience constituents," who contribute money and may occasionally participate in protests, such as marches, but are

The Antiabortion Movement and Attacks on Women's Clinics

The issue of abortion has a long history in the United States. Abortion was legal until it attracted the attention of moral reformers in the late nineteenth and early twentieth centuries. Abortion was then banned, although illegal abortions continued on, often in "back alley" settings, in conditions that damaged the health of women and caused the death of some. In the late 1950s and especially in the 1960s, a campaign began to legalize abortion once again. This movement was related to the effort to provide safe and reliable means of contraception to women who sought it (McKeegan, 1992), which in turn reflected the more liberal sexual attitudes of the 1960s.

> On one side are those who believe in a woman's right under certain conditions to choose abortion . . . , and on the other are those who argue that even a fertilized egg is a person.

THE DEBATE

The effort to legalize abortion reached a climax in 1969 when a class-action lawsuit was brought on behalf of a woman legally prevented from obtaining an abortion. The woman assumed the pseudonym "Jane Roe" to protect her privacy, and the case, which was decided by the Supreme Court in 1974, is known today as *Roe v. Wade*. This decision legalized abortion on the grounds that women have a private right to choose what happens to their bodies, and it has been a focal point of controversy ever since. On one side are those who believe in a woman's right under certain conditions to choose abortion when she and her doctor agree that it is necessary, and on the other are those who argue that even a fertilized egg is a person, and that since abortion results in the death of this "person," it is a form of killing and should be illegal. Having failed in their attempts to ban abortion outright, some of those on the antiabortion side have sought to prevent abortions by violent means.

ANALYSIS

Opposition to the *Roe v. Wade* decision arose at a time of great social upheaval in the United States. The riots of the 1960s were followed by a sense of worsening social pathology—rising rates of street crime, out-of-wedlock births, drug abuse, divorce. At the same time, women were beginning to demand a wider role in the world of work outside the home. To many people, especially members of conservative religions, these changes seemed to threaten the nation's moral and social order (McKeegan, 1992). Some political conservatives, who shared a sense of alarm about these social changes, wished strongly to attract a large body of followers who would unseat the politicians that they believed were responsible for the nation's ills. Seizing on abortion as a profoundly emotional issue that could unite disparate groups, particularly drawing in many people who had once supported the Democratic party (urban ethnic Catholics and southern conservative Protestants), some conservative strategists began to promote abortion as a crucial political rallying point. Implicit in their appeal was a rejection of the advances of the women's movement, which was in favor of legalized abortion but advocated many other issues as well, such as equal pay for equal work, paid parental leaves, and so on. The antiabortion movement grew large and influential throughout the 1970s and 1980s. In the 1990s, however, it began to fragment as some members began to advocate not just conventional political activities and peaceful protest but varying degrees of confrontation and violence. (Interestingly, this pattern occurs in various movements; it was characteristic of both the civil rights movement and the protests against the Vietnam war.)

Although there had been many incidents of arson and other violence against abortion clinics in the 1980s, the year 1993 was something of a turning point. In August of that year, a woman named Shelley Shannon shot and wounded Dr. George Tiller in Wichita, Kansas. With this act, violence against clinics and the doctors who practiced in them escalated dramatically. In 1994 alone, there were four murders (two of doctors), eight attempted murders, three bombings, five cases of arson, forty-two acts of vandalism, seven cases of assault and battery, fifty-nine death threats, three burglaries, twenty-two incidents of stalking, fourteen bomb threats, twenty-five clinic blockades, and several hundred cases of hate mail and phone calls (Clark, 1995). In one case, an ex-minister named Paul Hill shot and killed Dr. John Britton of Pensacola, Florida, and his unarmed escort. In an even more notorious case, a hairdresser named John Salvi was charged with killing two women who worked as receptionists at clinics in Massachusetts. Although much of America was horrified by these acts, they were greeted with praise by some antiabortion activists. One Mississippi activist was quoted as saying, "It wouldn't bother me if every abortionist in the country today fell dead from a bullet" (Frantz, 1995). It has even been argued in some antiabortion publications that the killing of doctors and others who provide abortion services is "justifiable homicide" as it saves the lives of the "unborn" (Van Biema, 1994).

The wave of violence, added to a long-standing campaign of opposition—involving such things as harassing phone calls to a doctor's home, protests at doctors' children's schools, and other activities—has led many doctors to stop providing abortions. Therefore, even though it is legal to obtain an abortion, it now may be very hard to find a doctor to provide one. It has been estimated that 84 percent of U.S. counties have no known abortion provider, with the shortage most acute in rural areas. Perhaps because of this, the number of abortions performed annually has been declining slightly (Rubin, 1995).

The antiabortion movement is a classic countermovement—it formed to resist the women's movement's demand for reproductive rights. More generally, however, it can be seen as a movement to resist the broader demands of the women's movement. The antiabortion movement became influential just as the functionally integrated pattern of women's roles broke down in the late 1960s and early 1970s. With more women completing higher education and entering the workforce, some questioned whether women were not abandoning their "proper" roles as wives and mothers to do so. Many women who did not work outside the home felt devalued and criticized by the women's movement and were particularly likely to join the antiabortion movement as a way of expressing their feelings about motherhood (Luker, 1984). At the same time, other critics saw abortion as symbolizing a laxer set of moral values, including toleration of premarital sex. So both the women's movement and the antiabortion movement were closely linked to cultural values.

The two movements also reflected social structure. The women's movement arose among middle-class women, and its activists were often highly educated professionals. The antiabortion movement, by contrast, has attracted much of its following from the working class. The emergence of the women's movement was also related to a basic structural change in the family: Families had become smaller once they were no longer basic units of production (industrialization had made families units of consumption rather than production). Therefore, as families fulfilled fewer social functions women had less work to do at home and they began to be able to work at paid jobs away from home.

The antiabortion movement also changed social structure by bringing together social groups that had long been suspicious of each other, principally Catholics and conservative Protestants. Catholicism was the religion of immigrants (Italians, Irish, Polish, Hispanics), and conservative Protestantism was largely the religion of rural and working-class Americans whose ancestors had come from England and northern Europe. The antiabortion movement also built some bridges between white conservatives and black Americans, many of whom were also conservatively religious and opposed abortion.

The antiabortion movement, like all social movements, was organized for purposes of social action; merely being in the movement is a form of social action, and a variety of activities are also social actions: blockading clinics, confronting patients and clinic employees, and so on. One reason these actions have become more aggressive and violent is that social movements often need more and more extreme tactics to attract public attention and keep participants motivated.

Finally, all social movements are to some degree about power; they seek to shape the course of social change. The antiabortion movement seeks to stop women from having abortions. To do this it attempts to exercise its power to persuade politicians, voters, and the general public that abortion is wrong. When these methods fail, some members of the movement try to exert power by blockade, intimidation, or violence.

Betty Friedan, a leader of the modern women's movement and one of the founders of the National Organization for Women (NOW), continues to speak out for women's rights, the unfinished social revolution.

not true activists (Zald and McCarthy, 1987). Moreover, the tactics these groups use are often the same as those used by mainstream pressure groups—lobbying and forming electoral alliances. Women's groups are facing the same problems faced by other "mature" movements, namely, complacency, an aging core of activists, and low visibility.

Examining whether the women's movement is fading into the past, Virginia Sapiro (1991) has focused on culture, on changes in attitudes and beliefs over the life of the contemporary women's movement. She finds that the daughters of the generation that launched the movement—young women now entering their twenties and starting families—are "liberated" in some ways but not others. The great majority (more than nine in ten) support equality in the workplace, but a substantial minority (about one in four) believe families suffer when women work. A majority of young women feel that men do not take women seriously in the workplace, despite many gains. Among those who are married, most say they take more responsibility for housework and child care than their husbands do, but most also say their husband is doing his fair share. Many accept the cultural myth that women who are raped (especially by

an acquaintance) or beaten by their husband somehow "asked for" the violent abuse.

Thus, in some ways, less has changed than one might expect. Sapiro does not conclude, however, that the women's movement's days are numbered. Most people surveyed say that while the movement has achieved some goals, much remains to be done and "the United States continues to need a strong women's movement to push for changes that benefit women" (Dionne, in Sapiro, 1991, p. 21). Noting that the women's movement has accomplished significant change in many spheres of American life, Leslie Wolfe and Jennifer Tucker (1995) nevertheless observe that

> . . . the majority of women in the United States have remained in low-income, low-status jobs with few benefits, little respect, and less security. Increasingly, women and their children have been falling into deeper levels of poverty, even homelessness, and violence against women is pervasive. While issues of violence, economic justice, and opportunity are not new ones for feminist organizations, the movement's success in the future will be measured by how well it changes the lives of women who are the most oppressed, despised, and disadvantaged. (p. 456)

Despite reverses such as the defeat of the Equal Rights Amendment and loss of members and resources in the 1980s, the women's movement and its message continue to survive and exert a powerful influence, sometimes within other social movements (Whittier, 1995). Partially started in the United States, the women's movement continues to record gains internationally.

SUMMARY

1. Collective action is a special form of social action, in which people depart from everyday routines, responding to events, things, or ideas in unconventional ways. A social movement is a sustained, coordinated effort by relatively large numbers of people to change or resist change in the social order.

2. Collective action often begins with a crowd, or a temporary collection of people drawn together by some common experience. Crowds may be casual, conventional, expressive, or acting. A mob is an acting crowd that has become violent.

3. Theories of crowd action have focused on group psychology (especially social contagion); the spread of rumors and, in modern times, the impact of the media; the emergence of new norms and relationships under ambiguous circumstances; and rational calculation.

4. Conventional wisdom usually traces an event like the Los Angeles riot of 1992 to a specific incident or series of incidents (the precipitating event). Sociology shows that a number of conditions also must be met for crowd action to take place.

5. The first condition is "structural conduciveness," meaning that elements of the social structure promote or at least allow crowd action. An example would be large numbers of people in close contact with one another and with time on their hands.

6. Second, crowd action often reflects functional *dis*-integration. The crowd may be composed of people who are not well integrated into the mainstream of society, and/or the crowd may take violent actions because social controls are not functioning adequately.

7. Third, crowd action may reflect the buildup of cultural misunderstandings, especially under conditions where groups are in economic competition.

8. Fourth, crowd action often is a "last-ditch effort" by people who feel they lack power and see no other way of making their grievances known.

9. Social movements are sustained efforts by large numbers of people to bring about or resist social change through noninstitutionalized means. Most social movements press for cultural change. In revolutions, the movement attempts to seize control of the government.

10. The idea of a social movement originated in the labor movements of nineteenth-century Europe. These movements brought dramatic changes, among them free public education, health care, unemployment benefits, and better wages and working conditions. Labor movements continue, but the range of social movements has become extremely broad. Movements address all manner of contemporary social issues, and the idea that it is possible to change society by means of such social action has become one of the defining features of the modern era.

11. All social movements aim at affecting the course of social change. Movements typically combine a focus on advancing the interests of their members with concern for creating a common identity among participants and/or gaining public legitimacy and acceptance for members' shared identity.

12. Two social movements that have had enormous impact on American society are the civil rights and the women's movements. Each illustrates the importance of organization, opportunity, communication, and "conscience constituents" to social movements.

REVIEW QUESTIONS

1. What is the difference between crowd action and a social movement? Give an example of each.

2. Define the four types of crowds—casual, conventional, expressive, and acting—and give examples of each.

3. Why do social movements arise?

4. How does Theda Skocpol's explanation of social revolutions differ from Marxist and resource-mobilization theories?

5. Summarize the explanations for the rise of the civil rights movement, emphasizing the role of concepts and theories discussed in the chapter.

6. Summarize the explanations for the rise of the modern women's movement, emphasizing the role of concepts and theories discussed in the chapter.

7. Describe the way in which concerns for advancing members' interests and legitimating their identities combine in contemporary social movements.

CRITICAL THINKING QUESTIONS

1. In a democracy where citizens have the right to vote, do they also need the right to participate in crowd actions, social movements, and other collective actions? Why or why not?

2. Identify a social problem that you regard as important. Is any social movement trying to solve that problem? Do you agree with its approach? What could be done to encourage more effective corrective action?

3. Use the concepts presented in the chapter (including the five key concepts) to analyze a social movement or social revolution that you have studied in a history, political science, or some other course, or a collective action in which you have personally participated.

4. The chapter discusses the civil rights movement and the women's movement in some detail. Select one of these social movements and make projections about what will happen to it in the next ten to twenty years, basing your analysis on what you have learned in this and other chapters.

5. What factors keep social movements from having the results their initiators and leaders hope for or expect?

GLOSSARY

Acting crowd Herbert Blumer's term for an excited, volatile collection of people who are focused on a controversial event that provokes their indignation, anger, and desire to act.

Casual crowd Herbert Blumer's term for a spontaneous gathering whose members give temporary attention to an object or event and then go their separate ways.

Cognitive liberation The change in attitude from accepting existing conditions as fate to believing that they can be changed, which is a crucial condition of social movement activism.

Collective action Socially organized and self-concious but relatively non-routine responses to events, efforts to pursue shared interests, or attempts to realize ideals, usually involving large numbers of people.

Collective behavior Often irrational but still socially organized responses to external stimuli that produce shared activity among many people.

Conventional crowd Herbert Blumer's term for people who gather for a specific purpose and behave according to established norms.

Countermovement A social movement that forms to resist a movement already under way.

Crowd A temporary collection of people who are gathered around some person or event and are conscious of and influenced by one another.

Emergent-norm theory The principle that crowds develop new norms in order to define an ambiguous situation.

Expressive crowd Herbert Blumer's term for a crowd whose members express feelings and behave in ways they would not consider acceptable in other settings.

Mob A large crowd whose members are emotionally aroused and are engaged in, or threaten to engage in, violent action.

Precipitating event An incident that sparks collective action by confirming people's suspicions and fears.

Relative deprivation The gap between people's expectations and their actual conditions.

Rumor An unverified story that circulates from person to person and is accepted as fact, although its original source may be vague or unknown.

Social contagion The relatively rapid and unintentional spread of a mood or behavior from one individual to another.

Social movement A deliberate, organized effort to change or resist large-scale change through noninstitutionalized means.

Social revolution According to Theda Skocpol's definition, a rapid and basic transformation of a society's state and class structures.

Structural conduciveness Neal Smelser's term to describe aspects of social structure that facilitate collective action.

REFERENCES

The number in brackets at the end of each entry is the number of the chapter in which the work is cited.

AAUW Educational Foundation. 1992. *How Schools Shortchange Girls: The AAUW Report.* Washington, DC: The American Association of University Women Educational Foundation and National Educational Association. **[5]**

Abadinsky, Howard. 1981. *Organized Crime.* Boston: Allyn and Bacon. **[6]**

Abbott, Andrew. 1988. *The System of Professions: An Essay on the Division of Expert Labor.* Chicago: University of Chicago Press. **[15]**

Abbott, Andrew. 1993. The sociology of work and occupations. *Annual Review of Sociology,* 19:187–209. **[15]**

Abeles, Ronald P. 1976. Relative deprivation, rising expectations, and black militancy. *Journal of Social Issues,* 32:119–137. **[20]**

Abelmann, Nancy, and John Lie. 1995. *Blue Dreams: Korean Americans and the Los Angeles Riots.* Cambridge, MA: Harvard University Press. **[20]**

Abrahamian, V. 1985. Structural causes of the Iranian revolution. In J. Goldstone, Ed., *Revolutions* (pp. 119–127). San Diego: Harcourt Brace Jovanovich. **[13]**

Abrahamson, Mark. 1995. *Urban Enclaves: Identity and Place in America.* New York: St. Martins Press. **[19]**

Abu-Lughod, J. 1969. *The City Is Dead—Long Live the City: Some Thoughts on Urbanity.* Research Monograph No. 12. Berkeley: Center for Planning and Development. **[3]**

Acharya, Anjali. 1995. Tropical forests vanishing. In L.R. Brown, N. Lenssen, and H. Kane, *Vital Signs, 1995* (pp. 116–117). New York: Norton. **[18]**

Acs, Gregory, and Sheldon Danziger. 1993. Educational attainment, industrial structure, and male earnings through the 1980s. *Journal of Human Resources,* 28 (3, summer). **[12]**

Adler, William M. 1995. *Land of Opportunity: One Family's Quest for the American Dream in the Age of Crack.* New York: Atlantic Monthly Press. **[6]**

Aganbegyan, Abel. 1988. *The Economic Challenge of Perestroika.* Bloomington: Indiana University Press. **[15]**

Agnew, Robert. 1990. The origins of delinquent events: An examination of offender accounts. *Journal of Research in Crime and Delinquency,* 27 (3, August):267–294. **[6]**

Agyei, William K.A., and Joseph Mbamanyo. 1989. Determinants of cumulative fertility in Kenya. *Journal of Biosocial Science,* 21 (3, April):135–144. **[18]**

Akers, Ronald L. 1985. *Deviant Behavior: A Social Learning Approach,* 3d ed. Belmont, CA: Wadsworth. **[6]**

Aldous, Joan. 1995. New views of grandparents in intergenerational context. *Journal of Family Issues,* 16 (1, January):104–122. **[11]**

Aldrich, Howard, and Ellen R. Auster. 1986. Even dwarfs started small: Liabilities of age and size and their strategic implications. *Research in Organizational Behavior,* 8:165–198. **[15]**

Alexander, Jeffrey, Ed. 1988. *Durkheimian Sociology.* New York: Columbia University Press. **[1]**

Alexander, Jeffrey C. 1995. *Fin de Siécle Social Theory: Relativism, Reduction, and the Problem of Reason.* London and New York: Verso. **[3]**

Alexander, Jeffrey C., and Philip Smith. 1994. The discourse of American civil society: A new proposal for cultural studies. *Berliner Journal für Soziologie.* 4:2:157–177.

Allport, Gordon W., and Leo Postman. 1947. *The Psychology of Rumor.* New York: Holt. **[20]**

Almaguer, Tomás. 1994. *Racial Fault Lines: The Historical Origins of White Supremacy in California.* Berkeley: University of California. **[8]**

American Bar Association (ABA), Commission of Women in the Professions. 1988. *Report to the House of Delegates.* Chicago: ABA. **[9]**

American Enterprise. 1995. America, land of the faithful. (Nov.–Dec.):96–104.

American Journal of Public Health. 1995. Infant mortality in the United States: Trends, differentials, and projections, 1950–2010. 85 (7, July). **[14]**

American Medical Association (AMA). 1993. Mortality trends for selected smoking-related cancers and breast cancer—United States, 1950–1990. *Journal of the American Medical Association,* 270(21):2541. **[14]**

American Psychiatric Association (APA) Task Force on Day Care for Preschool Children. 1993. Day care for early preschool children: Implications for the child and the family. *American Journal of Psychiatry,* 150 (8, August):1281–1287. **[11]**

American Sociological Association. 1989. *Professional Code of Ethics.* Washington, DC: American Sociological Association. **[2]**

Ammerman, Nancy T. 1994. Accounting for Christian fundamentalisms: Social dynamics and rhetorical strategies. In Martin E. Marty and R. Scott Appleby, Eds., *Accounting for Fundamentalisms: The Dynamic Character of Movements,* pp. 149–170. Chicago: University of Chicago Press. **[13]**

Ammerman, Robert T., Martin J. Lubetsky, and Karen F. Drudy. 1991. Maltreatment of handicapped children. In Robert T. Ammerman and Michael Gersen, Eds., *Case Studies in Family Violence* (pp. 209–230). New York: Plenum Press. **[11]**

Amnesty International. 1989. Amnesty International Brazil briefing. Background paper released in September. Washington, DC. **[18]**

Anderson, Benedict. 1991. *Imagined Communities: Reflections on the Origin and Spread of Nationalism,* rev. ed. London and New York: Verso. **[16]**

Anderson, P. 1974. *Lineages of the Absolutist State.* Chicago: University of Chicago Press. **[16]**

Angier, Natalie. 1995. If you're really ancient, you may be better off. *New York Times.* **[10]**

Apple, Michael W. 1979. *Ideology and Curriculum.* London: Routledge & Kegan Paul. **[12]**

Apple, Michael W. 1982. *Education and Power: Reproduction and Contradiction in Education.* London: Routledge & Kegan Paul. **[12]**

Applebome, Peter. 1995a. College segregation persists, study says. *New York Times* (May 18):A16. **[12]**

Applebome, Peter. 1995b. An unlikely legacy of the 60's: The violent right. *New York Times* (May 7):A1, 18. **[16]**

Arendt, Hannah. 1965. *On Revolution.* New York: Viking Press. **[16]**

Arjomand, Said Amir. 1996. Islam and politics. In Craig Calhoun and George Ritzer, Eds. *Perspectives.* New York: McGraw-Hill. **[11]**

Armor, David J. 1989. After busing: Education and choice. *Public Interest,* 95 (Spring):24–37. **[12]**

Armor, David J. 1991. Response to Carr and Zeigler's "White Flight and White Return to Norfolk." *Sociology of Education,* 64 (April):134–139. **[12]**

Arno, Peter S. 1986. The non-profit sector's response to the AIDS epidemic: Community-based services in San Francisco. *American Journal of Public Health,* 76(11):1325–1330. **[14]**

Aronowitz, Stanley. 1992. *The Politics of Identity*. Minneapolis: University of Minnesota Press. **[8]**

Arts, Wil, Piet Hermkens, and Peter Van Wijck. 1995. Anomie, distributive injustice and dissatisfaction with material well-being in eastern Europe: A comparative study. *International Journal of Comparative Sociology*, 36:1–16. **[15]**

Asahi Shimbun. 1994. The boom goes bust in Japan. *World Press Review*, 41 (March):38–40. **[15]**

Aslund, Anders. 1989. *Gorbachev's Struggle for Economic Reform*. Ithaca, NY: Cornell University Press. **[15]**

Astin, Alexander W. 1992. Educational "choice": Its appeal may be illusory. *Sociology of Education*, 65 (4, October):255–262. **[12]**

Astone, Nan Marie, and Sara S. McLanahan. 1991. Family structure, parental practices and high school completion. *American Sociological Review*, 56:309–320. **[12]**

Austin, J.L. 1965. *How to Do Things with Words*, 2d ed. Oxford: Oxford University Press. **[4]**

Babson, Jennifer, and Kelly St. John. 1994. Momentum helps GOP collect record amounts from PACS. *Congressional Quarterly*, 52 (47, December 3):3456–3459. **[16]**

Bainbridge, William Sims, and Rodney Stark. 1980. Scientology: To be perfectly clear. *Sociological Analysis*, 41 (Summer, 2):128–136. **[13]**

Bakanic, Von. 1995. I'm not prejudiced, but…: A deeper look at racial attitudes. *Sociological Inquiry*, 65 (1, February):67–86. **[8]**

Baker, P. 1984. Age differences and age changes in the division of labor by sex: Reanalysis of White and Brinherhoff. *Social Forces*, 62:808–814. **[5]**

Balakrishan, Radhika. 1994. The social context of sex selection and the politics of abortion in India. In G. Sen & R.C. Snow, eds., *Power and Decision: The Social Control of Reproduction*. pp. 207–286. Boston: Harvard University Press. **[1]**

Bandura, Albert. 1986. *Social Foundations of Thought and Action: A Social Cognitive Theory*. Englewood Cliffs, NJ: Prentice-Hall. **[6]**

Bandura, Albert, and Richard H. Walters. 1959. *Adolescent Aggression*. New York: Ronald Press. **[6]**

Bane, Mary Jo, and David T. Ellwood. 1989. One fifth of the nation's children: Why are they poor? *Science*, 245 (September 8):1047–1053. **[7]**

Bank, Barbara J. 1995. Friendships in Australia and the United States: From feminization to a more heroic image. *Gender & Society*, 9 (1, February):79–98. **[3]**

Barber, Benjamin R. 1993. America skips school. *Harper's* (November):39–46. **[12]**

Barnet, Richard J. 1993. The end of jobs. *Harper's*, 287 (1720, September):47–52. **[7]**

Barnet, Richard J., and John Cavanagh. 1994a. *Global Dreams*. New York: Simon & Schuster. **[15, 17]**

Barnet, Richard J., and John Cavanagh. 1994b. Just undo it: Nike's exploited workers. *New York Times* (February 13). **[17]**

Barone, Michael. 1995. The new America: A new U.S. poll shatters old assumptions about American politics. *U.S. News & World Report*, 119 (2, July 10):18 ff. **[16]**

Bartkowski, John P., and Christopher G. Ellison. 1995. Divergent models of childrearing in popular manuals: Conservative Protestants vs. the mainstream experts. *Sociology of Religion*, 56(1):21–34. **[11, 13]**

Bates, Timothy. 1994. Social resources generated by group support networks may not be beneficial to Asian immigrant-owned small businesses. *Social Forces*, 72 (3, March):671–690. **[15]**

Baumann, Zygmunt. 1991. *Modernity and the Holocaust*, rev. ed. Ithaca, NY: Cornell University Press. **[8, 20]**

Baylis, Thomas A. 1994. *The West and Eastern Europe: Economic Statecraft and Political Change*. Westport, CT: Praeger. **[15]**

Bearman, Peter. 1992. AIDS and sociology. In Craig Calhoun and George Ritzer, Eds., *Social Problems*. New York: McGraw-Hill. **[14]**

Beauregard, Robert A. 1993. *Voices of Decline: The Postwar Fate of US Cities*. Cambridge, MA: Blackwell. **[19]**

Becker, Howard S. 1963. *Outsiders: Studies in the Sociology of Deviance*. New York: Free Press. **[6]**

Becker, Howard S. 1984. *Art Worlds*. Berkeley: University of California Press. **[4]**

Becker, Howard S. 1986. *Doing Things Together*. Evanston, IL: Northwestern University Press. **[4]**

Beckford, James A. 1989. *Religion in Advanced Industrial Society*. London: Unwin Hyman. **[13]**

Begley, Sharon. 1995. The baby myth. *Newsweek* (September 4):38–45. **[1]**

Belknap, Penny, and Wilbert M. Leonard. 1991. A conceptual replication and extension of Erving Goffman's study of gender advertisements. *Sex Roles*, 25(3–4):103–118. **[5]**

Bell, Carolyn Shaw. 1994. What is poverty? *Boston Globe* (July 12). **[7]**

Bell, Daniel. 1980. *The Winding Passage: Essays and Sociological Journeys, 1960–1980*. Cambridge, MA: Abt Books. **[4]**

Bellah, Robert N. 1970. *Beyond Belief*. New York: Harper & Row. **[13]**

Bellah, Robert N., and Phillip E. Hammond. 1980. *Varieties of Civil Religion*. New York: Harper & Row. **[13]**

Bellah, Robert N., Richard Madsen, William M. Sullivan, Ann Swidler, and Steven M. Tipton. 1985. *Habits of the Heart: Individualism and Commitment in American Life*. New York: Harper & Row. **[4]**

Belyea, Michael J., and Linda M. Lobao. 1990. Psychosocial consequences of agricultural transformation: The farm crisis and depression. *Rural Sociology*, 55(1):58–75. **[19]**

Benet, Sula. 1976. *How to Live to Be a Hundred*. New York: Dial. **[10]**

Bengtson, Vern L. 1993. Is the "Contract Across Generations" changing? Effects of population aging on obligations and expectations across age groups. In Vern L. Bengtson and W. Andrew Achenbaum, Eds., *The Changing Contract Across Generations*, pp. 3–42. New York: Aldine de Gruyter. **[10]**

Benhabib, Seyla, and Drucilla Cornell, Eds. 1987. *Feminism as Cultural Critique*. Minneapolis: University of Minnesota Press. **[8, 9]**

Benson, S.P. 1986. *Counter Cultures: Saleswomen, Managers, Customers in American Department Stores, 1890–1940*. Urbana, IL: University of Illinois Press. **[3]**

Bentham, Jeremy. 1789/1970. *An Introduction to the Principals of Morals and Legislation*. London: Methuen. **[1]**

BenTsvi-Mayer, Shoshanna, Rachel Hertz-Lazarowitz, and Marilyn P. Safir. 1989. Teachers' selection of boys and girls as prominent pupils. *Sex Roles*, 21(3/4):231–239. **[5]**

Ben-Yehuda, Nachman. 1985. *Deviance and Moral Boundaries: Witchcraft, the Occult, Science Fiction, Deviant Sciences and Scientists*. Chicago: University of Chicago Press. **[6]**

Ben-Yehuda, Nachman. 1990. *The Politics and Morality of Deviance*. Albany: State University of New York Press. **[6]**

Berger, Peter L. 1979. *The Heretical Imperative: Contemporary Possibilities of Religious Affirmation*. Garden City, NY: Doubleday/Anchor. **[13]**

Berger, Peter L. 1987. *50 Propositions about Capitalism*. New York: Basic Books. **[16]**

Berk, A.R. 1974. *Collective Behavior*. New York: Brown. **[20]**

Bernardi, B. 1955. The age-system of the Masai. *Annali Lateranensi*, 18:257–318. **[10]**

Berreman, Gerald. 1972. *Hindus of the Himalayas: Ethnography and Change*. Second ed. Berkeley: University of California Press. **[10]**

Berry, Brewton, and Henry L. Tischler. 1978. *Race and Ethnic Relations*. Boston: Houghton Mifflin. **[8]**

Berube, Maurice R. 1994. *American School Reform: Progressive, Equity, and Excellence Movements, 1883–1993*. Westport, CT: Praeger. **[12]**

Beteille, Andre. 1985. Stratification. In Adam Kuper and Jessica Kuper, Eds., *The Social Science Encyclopedia* (pp. 831–833). London: Routledge. **[7]**

Beutel, Ann M., and Margaret Mooney Marini. 1995. Gender and values. *American Sociological Review*, 60 (3, June):436–448. **[9]**

Biblarz, Timothy J., and Adrian E. Raftery. 1993. The effects of family disruption on social mobility. *American Sociological Review*, 58 (February):97–109. **[11]**

Birch, David A. 1987. *Job Creation in America: How Our Smallest Companies Put the Most People to Work*. New York: Free Press. **[15]**

Blair, Margaret M. 1994. CEO pay: Why such a contentious issue? *Brookings Review* (Winter):22–27. **[15]**

Blau, David M., and Philip K. Robins. 1989. Fertility, employment, and child-care costs. *Demography,* 26 (2, May):287–299. **[11]**

Blau, Peter M. 1964. *Exchange and Power in Social Life.* New York: Wiley. **[3]**

Blau, Peter M., and Otis Dudley Duncan. 1967. *The American Occupational Structure.* New York: Wiley. **[7]**

Blau, Peter M., and Marshall W. Meyer. 1987. *Bureaucracy in Modern Society,* 3rd ed. New York: Random House. **[3]**

Blau, Peter M., and Joseph E. Schwartz. 1983. *Cross-Cutting Social Circles: Testing a Macrostructural Theory of Inter-group Relations.* New York: Academic Press. **[8]**

Blauner, Bob. 1991. Racism, race, and ethnicity: Some reflections on the language of race. Unpublished manuscript cited in Omi and Winant, 1994, p. 187, footnote 56. **[8]**

Bleier, Ruth. 1984. *Science and Gender.* New York: Pergamon Press. **[9]**

Blum, Linda, and Vicki Smith. 1988. Women's mobility in the corporation: A critique of the politics of optimism. *Signs,* 13(3):528–545. **[9]**

Blumenfeld, R. 1965. Mohawks: Roundtrip to the high steel. *Transaction,* 3:19–22. **[8]**

Blumer, Herbert, 1939/1951. Collective behavior. In A.M. Lee, Ed., *New Outline of the Principles of Sociology.* New York: Barnes & Noble. **[20]**

Blumer, Herbert, 1969/1986. *Symbolic Interactionism: Perspective and Method.* Berkeley: University of California Press. **[1, 6]**

Boden, Deirdre. 1994. *The Business of Talk: Organizations in Action.* Cambridge: Polity Press. **[3]**

Boles, Janet K. 1991. Form follows function: The evolution of feminist strategies. *Annals of the American Academy of Political and Social Science,* 515 (May):38–49. **[20]**

Booth, A., and D. Johnson. 1988. Premarital cohabitation and marital success. *Journal of Family Issues,* 9:255–272. **[11]**

Booth, Alan and Lynn White. 1980. Thinking about divorce. *Journal of Marriage and the Family,* 42(3):605–616. **[11]**

Borjas, George J. 1995. The internationalization of the U.S. labor market and the wage structure. *Federal Reserve Bank of New York Economic Review,* 1(1):3–9. **[15]**

Bornschier, Volker, and Thanh-Huyen Ballmer-Cao. 1979. Income inequality: A cross-national study of the relationships between MNC-penetration, dimensions of the power structure and income distribution. *American Sociological Review,* 44 (June):487–506. **[15]**

Bornschier, Volker, and Jean-Pierre Hoby. 1981. Economic policy and multinational corporations in development: The measurable impacts in cross-national perspective. *Social Problems,* 28:363–377. **[15]**

Bourdieu, Pierre. 1984. *Distinction: A Social Critique of the Judgment of Taste.* R. Nice (Trans.). Cambridge, MA: Harvard University Press. **[7, 12]**

Bourdieu, Pierre. 1987. *Choses Dites.* Paris: Edition de Minuit. **[7]**

Bourdieu, Pierre. 1990. *The Logic of Practice.* Stanford, CA: Stanford University Press. **[4]**

Bourdieu, Pierre. 1991a. Genesis and structure of the religious field. *Comparative Social Research,* 13:1–43. **[13]**

Bourdieu, Pierre. 1991b. *Language and Symbolic Power.* Cambridge, MA: Harvard University Press. **[4]**

Bourdieu, Pierre. 1993. *The Field of Cultural Production.* New York: Columbia University Press. **[4, 12]**

Bourdieu, Pierre, Jean-Claude Chamboredon, and Jean-Claude Passeron. 1991. *The Craft of Sociology: Epistemological Preliminaries.* New York: de Gruyter. **[1]**

Bourdieu, Pierre, and Jean-Claude Passeron. 1991. *Reproduction in Education, Culture, and Society* (rev. ed.). Newbury Park, CA: Sage. **[12]**

Bouvier, Leon F., and Carol J. De Vita. 1991. The baby boom—Entering midlife. *Population Bulletin,* 46 (3, November). **[10]**

Bowles, Samuel, and Herbert Gintis. 1976. *Schooling in Capitalist America.* New York: Basic Books. **[12]**

Bradsher, Keith. 1995. America's opportunity gap. *New York Times.* June 4, 1995. p. E4. **[10]**

Brain, R. 1976. *Friends and Lovers.* New York: Basic Books. **[3]**

Brauer, David A. and Susan Hickok. 1995. Explaining the growing inequality in wages across skill levels. *Federal Reserve Bank of New York Economic Review,* 1(1):61–76. **[15]**

Braus, Patricia. 1995. The baby boom at mid-decade. *American Demographics,* 7 (4, April):40–45. **[10]**

Bray, Anna J. 1994. Who are the victims of crime? *Investor's Business Daily,* (January 12):1–2. **[6]**

Bray, Rosemary. 1992. So how did I get here? *New York Times Magazine* (November 8). **[7]**

Brecher, Jeremy, and Tim Costello. 1994. *Global Village or Global Pillage? Economic Reconstruction From the Bottom Up.* Boston: South End Press. **[17]**

Brenner, Harvey M. 1987. Economic instability, unemployment rates, behavioral risks, and mortality rates in Scotland, 1952–1983. *International Journal of Health Services,* 17(3):475–487. **[14]**

Brinkley, Alan. 1993. *The Unfinished Nation: A Concise History of the American People.* New York: McGraw-Hill. **[16]**

Brown, David W. 1995. *When Strangers Cooperate: Using Social Conventions to Govern Ourselves.* New York: Free Press. **[3]**

Brown, J. Larry. 1987. Hunger in the U.S. *Scientific American,* 256(2):37. **[14]**

Brown, Jane D., and Kenneth Campbell. 1986. Race and gender in music videos: The same beat but a different drummer. *Journal of Communication,* 36 (Winter):94–106. **[2]**

Brown, Lester R., et al. 1990. *State of the World,* 1990. New York: Norton. **[18]**

Brown, Lester R., Nicholas Lenssen, and Hal Kane. 1995. *Vital Signs, 1995: The Trends that are Shaping Our Future.* New York: W. W. Norton. **[18]**

Brown, Ralph B., H. Reed Greersten, and Richard S. Krannich. 1989. Community satisfaction and social integration in a boomtown: A longitudinal analysis. *Rural Sociology,* 54(4):568–586. **[19]**

Browne, Irene. 1995. The baby boom and trends in poverty, 1967–1987. *Social Forces,* 73 (3, March):1071–1095. **[10]**

Browner, Carole H., and Nancy Ann Press. 1995. The normalization of prenatal diagnostic screening. In G. Sen & R.C. Snow, Eds., *Power and Decision: The Social Control of Reproduction,* pp. 307–322. Boston: Harvard University Press. **[1]**

Brubaker, Rogers. 1984. *The Limits of Rationality.* London: George, Allen and Unwin. **[1]**

Brubaker, Rogers. 1992. *The Politics of Citizenship.* Cambridge, MA: Harvard University Press. **[18]**

Buchmann, Marlis. 1989. *The Script of Life in Modern Society.* Chicago: University of Chicago Press. **[10]**

Bumpass, Larry L. 1990. What's happening to the family? Interactions between demographic and institutional change. Population Association of America, 1990 Presidential Address. *Demography,* 27 (4, November):483–498. **[11]**

Bumpass, Larry L., Teresa Castro Martin, and James A. Sweet. 1991. The impact of family background and early marital factors in marital disruption. *Journal of Family Issues,* 12 (1, March):22–42. **[11]**

Bumpass, Larry L., and James A. Sweet. 1989a. National estimates of cohabitation: Cohort levels and union stability. *Demography.* 26:615–625. **[11]**

Bumpass, Larry L., and James A. Sweet. 1989b. Children's experience in single-parent families: Implications of cohabitation and marital transitions. *Family Planning Perspectives,* 21 (6, November/December):256–260. **[11]**

Bumpass, Larry L., James A. Sweet, and Andrew Cherlin. 1989. *The Role of Cohabitation in Declining Rates of Marriage.* NSFH Working Paper 5. Madison: University of Wisconsin, Center for Demography and Ecology. **[11]**

Bumpass, Larry L., James A. Sweet, and Teresa Castro Martin. 1990. Changing patterns of remarriage. *Journal of Marriage and the Family,* 52 (August):747–756. **[11]**

Bunce, Valerie. 1995. Comparing east and south. *Journal of Democracy*, 6 (3, July):87–100. [16]

Burawoy, Michael, and János Lukács. 1992. *The Radiant Past: Ideology and Reality in Hungary's Road to Capitalism*. Chicago: University of Chicago Press. [15]

Burke, Thomas P., and Rita S. Jain. 1991. Trends in employer-provided health care benefits. *Monthly Labor Review*, 114(2):24–30. [14]

Burnham, David. 1983. *The Rise of the Computer State*. New York: Random House. [15]

Burns, Alisa, and Ross Homel. 1989. Gender division of tasks by parents and their children. *Psychology of Women Quarterly*, 13:113–125. [5]

Burns, Lawton R. 1990. The transformation of the American hospital: From community institution toward business enterprise. *Comparative Social Research*, 12:77–112. [14]

Burris, Beverly H. 1991. Employed mothers: The impact of class and marital status on the prioritizing of family and work. *Social Science Quarterly*, 72 (1, March):50–66. [11]

Burris, Val. 1983. Who opposed the ERA? An analysis of the social bases of antifeminism. *Social Science Quarterly*, 64:305–317. [20]

Burrow, James G. 1971. *Organized Medicine in the Progressive Era: The Move Toward Monopoly*. Baltimore: Johns Hopkins University Press. [14]

Busby, Linda, and Greg Leichty. 1993. Feminism in Traditional and Nontraditional Women's Magazines," *Journalism Quarterly*, 70(2):247–264. [5]

Buss, David M., et al. 1990. International partner preferences in selecting mates: A study of 37 cultures. *Journal of Cross-Cultural Psychology*, 21 (1, March):5–47. [3]

Butler, Judith. 1990. *Gender Trouble: Feminism and the Subversion of Identity*. New York: Routledge, Chapman & Hall. [9]

Butler, Judith and Joan W. Scott, Eds. 1992. *Feminists Theorize the Political*. New York: Routledge. [20]

Butler, Robert N. 1989. Dispelling ageism. *Annals*, 503 (May):138–147. [10]

Butterfield, Fox. 1995. California's courts clogging under its 'three strikes' law. *New York Times* (March 23):A12, 9. [6]

Calderón José. 1992. "Hispanic" and "Latino": The viability of categories for panethnic unity. *Latin American Perspectives*, 19 (4, Fall):24–37. [8]

Calhoun, Craig. 1980. The authority of ancestors. *Man*, 5(2):304–319. [13, 19]

Calhoun, Craig. 1991. Imagined communities and indirect relationships: Large-scale social integration and the transformation of everyday Life. In P. Bourdieu and J.S. Coleman, Eds., *Social Theory for a Changing Society* (pp. 95–120). Boulder, CO: Westview Press. [3]

Calhoun, Craig. 1992. The infrastructure of modernity: Indirect social relationships, information technology, and social integration. In H. Haferkamp and N.J. Smelser, eds., *Social Change and Modernity*, pp. 205–236. Berkeley: University of California Press. [3, 16, 17]

Calhoun, Craig. 1993. "New social movements" of the early 19th century. *Social Science History*, 17(3):385–427. [20]

Calhoun, Craig. 1994a. Nationalism and civil society: Democracy, diversity and self-determination. In C. Calhoun, Ed., *Social Theory and the Politics of Identity*, pp. 304–335. Cambridge, MA: Blackwell. [16]

Calhoun, Craig, Ed. 1994b. *Social Theory and the Politics of Identity*. Cambridge, MA: Blackwell. [1, 4, 9]

Calhoun, Craig. 1995. *Critical Social Theory*. Cambridge, MA: Blackwell. [1, 4, 8, 16]

Calhoun, Craig, and Henryk Hiller. 1988. Coping with insidious injuries: The case of Johns-Mansville Corporation and asbestos exposure. *Social Problems*, 35(2):162–181. [6, 15]

Callahan, Daniel. 1987. *Setting Limits*. New York: Simon and Schuster. [10]

Campbell, Robert A., and James E. Curtis. 1994. Religious involvement across societies: Analyses for alternative measures in national surveys. *Journal for the Scientific Study of Religion*, 33(3):217–229. [13]

Cancian, Francesca. 1986. The feminization of love. *Signs: Journal of Women and Culture in Society*, 11:692–709. [3]

Cancian, Francesca. 1987. *Love in America: Gender and Self-Development*. New York: Cambridge University Press. [3]

Cantor, Daniel. 1995. New party time. *Progressive* (January 26):26–27. [16]

Capaldi, Deborah M., and Gerald M. Patterson. 1991. Relation of parental transitions to boys' adjustment problems: I: A linear hypothesis. II: Mothers at risk for transitions and unskilled parenting. *Developmental Psychology*, 27:489–504. [6]

Carothers, Andre. 1990. Defenders of the forest. *Greenpeace*, 154, (4 July–August):8–12. [18]

Carroll, Jackson W., and Penny Long Marler. 1995. Culture wars? Insights from ethnographies of two Protestant seminaries. *Sociology of Religion*, 56(1):1–20. [13]

Carter, Stephen. 1991. *Reflections of an Affirmative Action Baby*. New York: Basic Books [8]

Casper, Lynne M., Irwin Garfinkel, and Sara S. McLanahan. 1994. The gender-poverty gap: What we can learn from other countries. *American Sociological Review*, 59 (August):594–605. [9]

Castells, Manuel. 1989. *The Informational City: Information Technology, Economic Restructuring, and the Urban-Regional Process*. New York: Blackwell. [19]

Cater, Douglass, and Stephen Strickland. 1975. *TV Violence and the Child: The Evolution and Fate of the Surgeon General's Report*. New York: Russell Sage Foundation. [5]

Cattan, Peter. 1988. The growing presence of Hispanics in the U.S. work force. *Monthly Labor Review* (August):9–14. [8]

Chafetz, Janet. 1970. *Masculine, Feminine, or Human?* 2d ed. Itasca, IL: Peacock. [9]

Chafetz, Janet. 1984. *Sex and Advantage*. Totowa, NJ: Rowman & Allenheld. [9]

Chambers, D.S. 1970. *The Imperial Age of Venice, 1380–1580*. New York: Harcourt Brace Jovanovich. [19]

Chambliss, William J. 1973. The Saints and Roughnecks. *Society*, 11 (December):24–31. [6]

Charles, Maria. 1992. Cross-national variation in occupational sex segregation. *American Sociological Review*, 57(4, August): 381–404. [9]

Chase-Dunn, Christopher. 1975. The effects of international economic dependence on development and inequality: A cross-national study. *American Sociological Review*, 40 (December):720–738. [15]

Chaves, Mark. 1994. Secularization as declining religious authority. *Social Forces*, 72 (3, March):749–774. [13]

Chavez, Lydia. 1987. Women's movement, its ideals accepted, faces subtler issues. *New York Times* (July 17). [20]

Cherlin, Andrew J. 1995. *Public and Private Families*. New York: McGraw-Hill. [11, 18]

Cherlin, Andrew. 1990. Recent changes in American fertility, marriage, and divorce. *Annals of the American Academy of Political and Social Science*, 510 (July):145–154. [11]

Cherlin, Andrew, and Frank Furstenberg. 1986. *The New Grandparent: A Place in the Family, a Life Apart*. New York: Basic Books. [11]

Cherlin, Andrew J., and Frank F. Furstenberg, Jr. 1994. Stepfamilies in the United States: A reconsideration. *Annual Review of Sociology*, 20:359–381. [11]

Childe, V. Gordon. 1952. *Man Makes Himself*. New York: New American Library. [19]

Chittister, Joan D., and Martin E. Marty. 1983. *Faith & Ferment*. Minneapolis: Augsburg. [13]

Chodorow, Nancy. 1978. *The Reproduction of Mothering: Psychoanalysis and the Sociology of Gender*. Berkeley: University of California Press. [5]

Chodorow, Nancy. 1994. *Femininities, Masculinities, and Sexualities: Freud and Beyond*. Lexington, KY: University of Kentucky Press. [5]

Choldin, Harvey M. 1978. Urban density and pathology. *Annual Review of Sociology*, 4:91–113. [19]

Chryssides, George D. 1991. *The Advent of Sun Myung Moon: The Origins, Beliefs and Practices of the Unification Church*. New York: St. Martin's Press. [13]

Chudacoff, Howard P. 1989. *How Old Are You?* Princeton, NJ: Princeton University Press. **[10]**

Chun, Ki-Taek. 1995. The myth of Asian American success and its educational ramifications. In D.T. Nakanishi and T.Y. Nishida, Eds., *The Asian American Educational Experience: A Sourcebook for Teachers* (Chapter 5). New York: Routledge. **[8]**

Clark, Charles S. 1995. Abortion clinic protests. *C Q Researcher,* 5(13):299–316. **[20]**

Clark, Reginald M. 1983. *Family Life and School Achievement: Why Poor Black Children Succeed or Fail,* Chicago: University of Chicago Press. **[12]**

Clark, Reginald M. 1990. Why disadvantaged students succeed. *Public Welfare,* 48(2):17–23. **[12]**

Clark, Robert L., and Richard Anker. 1993. Cross-national analysis of labor force participation of older men and women. *Economic Development and Cultural Change:* 489–512. **[10]**

Clausen, John A. 1986. *The Life Course: A Sociological Perspective.* Englewood Cliffs, NJ: Prentice-Hall. **[10]**

Clifford, Frank. 1989. California on wheels; a driving passion for lifestyle, car culture. How automobiles shaped southern California. *Los Angeles Times* (October 1). p. A1. **[19]**

Clifford, Frank. 1989. We curse the traffic, but won't give up our cars. *Los Angeles Times* (October 4). **[19]**

Clifford, Mark. 1990. Messianic Mission. *Far Eastern Economic Review,* 150 (44, November):24–31. **[13]**

Clinard, Marshall B., and Peter C. Yeager. 1980. *Corporate Crime.* New York: Free Press. **[6]**

Cohen, Albert K. 1965. The sociology of the deviant act: Anomie theory and beyond. *American Sociological Review,* 30 (February):5–14. **[6]**

Cohen, Albert K. 1966. *Deviance and Control.* Englewood Cliffs, NJ: Prentice Hall. **[6]**

Cohen, Jean, and Andrew Arato. 1992. *Civil Society and Political Theory.* Cambridge, MA: MIT Press. **[20]**

Coleman, James S. 1961. *The Adolescent Society.* New York: Free Press. **[10]**

Coleman, James S. 1966. *Equality of Educational Opportunity.* Washington, DC: U.S. Government Printing Office. **[12]**

Coleman, James S. 1982. *The Asymmetric Society.* New York: Syracuse University Press. **[15]**

Coleman, James S. 1987a. Families and schools. *Educational Researcher,* 16(6):32–38. **[12]**

Coleman, James S. 1990. *Foundations of Social Theory,* Cambridge, MA: Harvard University Press. **[1, 15]**

Coleman, James S., Ed. 1992. *Rational Choice Theory: Advocacy and Critique.* Newbury Park, CA: Sage. **[1]**

Coleman, James S., and T. Hoffer, 1987. *Public and Private High Schools: The Impact of Communities.* New York: Basic Books. **[12]**

Coleman, John A. 1983. The Christian as citizen. *Commonweal,* 110:457–462. **[13]**

Coleman, R.P., and L. Rainwater. 1978. *Social Standing in America: New Dimensions of Class.* New York: Basic Books. **[12]**

Colley, Linda. 1992. *Britons.* New Haven, CT: Yale University Press. **[2]**

Collins, Patricia Hill. 1990. *Black Feminist Thought:* Boston: Northeastern University Press. **[1]**

Collins, Patricia Hill. 1991. *Black Feminist Thought:* New York: Routledge. **[4, 5, 8, 9, 20]**

Collins, Randall. 1979. *The Credential Society.* New York: Academic Press. **[12]**

Commission on Global Governance. 1995. *Our Global Neighbourhood: The Report of the Commission on Global Governance.* Oxford and New York: Oxford University Press. **[17]**

Comte, Auguste. 1875–77. *Systems of Positive Polity.* London: Longmans Green. **[4]**

Congressional Quarterly. 1993. Paying for retirement: Will baby boomers have a rough time when they retire? *CQ Researcher,* 3 (41, November 5):961–984. **[10]**

Conklin, J.E. 1992. *Criminology,* 4th ed. New York: Macmillan. **[6]**

Connolly, William. 1984. The dilemma of legitimacy. In W. Connolly and S. Lukes, Eds., *Legitimacy and the State* (pp. 122–149). New York: New York University Press. **[16]**

Conrad, Peter. 1992. Medicalization and social control. *Annual Review of Sociology,* 18:209–232. **[14]**

Conrad, Peter, and Joseph Schneider. 1980. *Deviance and Medicalization: From Badness to Sickness.* St. Louis: Mosby. **[14]**

Consumer Reports. 1990a. The crisis in health insurance: Health insurance for all? *Consumer Reports,* 55(9):608–617. **[14]**

Consumer Reports. 1990b. The crisis in health insurance: Who loses it? What happens? *Consumer Reports,* 55(8):533–549. **[14]**

Cook, Karen S., and J.M. Whitmeyer. 1992. Two approaches to social structure: Exchange theory and network analysis. *Annual Review of Sociology.* 18:109–127 **[3]**

Cooley, Charles H. 1905/1956. *Social Organization: A Study of the Larger Mind.* Peoria, IL: Free Press. **[3, 5]**

Cooley, Charles H. 1964. *Human Nature and the Social Order.* New York: Schocken. **[5]**

Cooney, Rosemary Santana, and Jiala Li. 1994. Household registration type and compliance with the "one child" policy in China, 1979–1988. *Demography,* 31 (1, February):21–32. **[1]**

Coontz, Stephanie. 1992. *The Way We Never Were: American Families and the Nostalgia Trap.* New York: Basic Books. **[11]**

Cooper, Marc. 1995. Montana's mother of all militias. *Nation,* 260(20):714ff. **[16]**

Corsaro, William A. 1985. *Friendship and Peer Culture in the Early Years.* Norwood, NJ: Ablex. **[2]**

Corsaro, William A. 1992. Interpretive reproduction in children's peer cultures. *Social Psychology Quarterly,* 55(2):160–177. **[5]**

Corsaro, William, and Donna Eder. 1990. Children's peer culture. *Annual Review of Sociology,* 16:197–220. **[5]**

Corsaro, William A., and Francesca Emiliani. 1992. Child care, early education, and children's peer culture in Italy. In Michael E. Lamb, Kathleen J. Sternberg, Carl-Philip Hwang, and Anders G. Broberg, Eds., *Child Care in Context: Cross-Cultural Perspectives* (pp. 81–115). Hillsdale, NY: Erlbaum. **[5]**

Corsaro, William A., and Thomas Rizzo. 1988. *Discussione* and friendship: Socialization processes in the peer culture of Italian nursery school children. *American Sociological Review,* 53:879–894. **[5]**

Corwin, Ronald G., and Marcella R. Dianda. 1993. What can we really expect from large-scale voucher programs? *Phi Delta Kappan,* 75 (1, September):68–74. **[12]**

Costanzo, Mark, and Lawrence T. White. 1994. An overview of the death penalty and capital trials: History, current status, legal procedures, and cost. *Journal of Social Issues.* 50:2 (Summer):1–18. **[6]**

CQ Researcher. 1995. Rethinking affirmative action. 5 (April 28):369–392. **[8]**

Cronin, Thomas E. 1989. *Direct Democracy: The Politics of Initiative, Referendum, and Recall.* Cambridge, MA: Harvard University Press. **[16]**

Crotty, William, Ed. 1991. *Political Participation and American Democracy.* New York: Greenwood-Press. **[16]**

Crozier, Brian. 1993. *Free Agent: The Unseen War.* 1941–91. London: HarperCollins. **[17]**

Crystal, David. 1989. Asian Americans and the myth of the model minority. *Journal of Contemporary Social Work,* 70(7):405–413. **[8]**

Crystal, Stephen, and Dennis Shea. 1990. Cumulative advantage, cumulative disadvantage, and inequality among elderly people. *Gerontologist,* 30:437–443. **[10]**

Cunningham, Kamy. 1993. Barbie doll culture and the American waistland. *Symbolic Interaction.* 16:1 (Spring):79–93. **[5]**

Current Population Reports. 1990a (March). Washington, DC: U.S. Government Printing Office. **[11]**

Current Population Reports. 1990b (July). Series P-60, No. 166. Washington, DC: U.S. Government Printing Office. **[11]**

Current Population Reports. 1990c (December). Washington, DC: U.S. Government Printing Office. **[12]**

Current Population Reports. 1993 (March). Household and Family Characteristics. Series P-23, No. 162. Washington, DC: U.S. Government Printing Office. **[11]**

Current Population Reports. 1995 (February). *Consumer Income.* Series P60–188. Washington, DC: U.S. Government Printing Office. **[7]**

Cushman, John H., Jr. 1995. Rivals criticize welfare plan offered by Dole. *New York Times* (August 7):A1, B6. **[7]**

Dahl, Robert. 1961. *Who Governs?* New Haven, CT: Yale University Press. **[16]**

Dahl, Robert. 1989. *Democracy and Its Critics.* New Haven, CT: Yale University Press. **[16]**

Dahl, Robert. 1993. The ills of the system. *Dissent,* 40 (Fall):447–462. **[16]**

Dalecki, Michael G., and C. Milton Coughenour. 1992. Agrarianism in American Society. *Rural Sociology,* 57(1):48–64. **[4]**

Dan-Cohen, M. 1986. *Rights, Persons and Organizations.* Berkeley: University of California Press. **[15]**

Daniels, Norman. 1995. *Seeking Fair Treatment: From the AIDS Epidemic to National Health Care Reform.* New York: Oxford University Press. **[14]**

Davidson, Osha Gray. 1990. *Broken Heartland: The Rise of America's Rural Ghetto.* New York: Free Press. **[7]**

Davies, Christie. 1989. Goffman's concept of the total institution: Criticisms and revisions. *Human Studies,* 12:77–95. **[5]**

Davies, James. 1962. Toward a theory of revolution. *American Sociological Review,* 27:5–19. **[20]**

Davies, James. 1974. The J-curve and power struggle theories of collective violence. *American Sociological Review,* 39:607–619. **[20]**

Davies, Mark, and Denise B. Kandel. 1981. Parental and peer influence on adolescents' educational plans: Some further evidence. *American Journal of Sociology,* 87:363–387. **[5]**

Davis, F. James. 1993. *Who is Black? One Nation's Definition.* University Park: Pennsylvania State University Press. **[8]**

Davis, Fred. 1992. *Fashion, Culture, and Identity.* Chicago: University of Chicago Press. **[4]**

Davis, John Hagy. 1973. Venice. *Newsweek.* **[19]**

Davis, Karen, and Diane Rowland. 1983. Uninsured and underserved: Inequities in health care in the United States. *Milbank Memorial Fund Quarterly/Health and Society,* 61(2):149–176. **[14]**

Davis, Kingsley. 1955. The origin and growth of urbanization in the world. *American Journal of Sociology,* 60:429–437. **[19]**

Davis, Kingsley, and Wilbert E. Moore. 1945. Some principles of stratification. *American Sociological Review,* 10(April):242–249. **[7]**

Demerath, N. J., III. 1995. Rational paradigms, a-rational religion, and the debate over secularization. *Journal for the Scientific Study of Religion,* 34(1):105–112. **[13]**

Dennis, Jack. 1991. Theories of turnout: An empirical comparison of alienationist and rationalist perspectives. In W. Crotty, Ed., *Political Participation and American Democracy* (pp. 23–65). New York: Greenwood Press. **[16]**

DeNora, Tia. 1996. *Beethoven and the Social Construction of Genius.* Berkeley: University of California Press. **[4]**

DeStefano, Linda, and Diane Colastrano. 1990. Unlike 1975, today most Americans think men have it better. *Gallup Poll Monthly.* February:29. **[9]**

de Tocqueville, Alexis. 1856. The Old Regime and the French Revolution. J. Bonner (Trans.). New York: Harper & Row. **[20]**

Deutchman, Iva E., and Sandra Prince-Embury. 1981. Political ideology of pro- and anti-ERA women. *Women and Politics,* 1:39–55. **[20]**

DeWitt, Paula M. 1992. The second time around. *American Demographics,* 14 (11, November):60–63. **[11]**

DiBlasio, Frederick A., and Brent B. Benda. 1994. A conceptual model of sexually active peer association. *Youth and Society,* 25 (3, March):351–367. **[10]**

Dizard, Jan E., and Howard Gadlin. 1990. *The Minimal Family.* Amherst: University of Massachusetts Press. **[11]**

Domhoff, G. William. 1978. *The Powers That Be.* New York: Random House. **[16]**

Domhoff, G. William. 1983. *Who Rules America Now?* Englewood Cliffs, NJ: Prentice Hall. **[16]**

Domhoff, G. William. 1993. Who rules America? In C. Calhoun and G. Ritzer, Eds., *Introduction to Social Problems.* New York: McGraw-Hill/Primis. **[7, 16]**

Dorius, Guy L., Tim B. Heaton, and Patrick Steffen. 1993. Adolescent life events and their association with the onset of sexual intercourse. *Youth and Society,* 25(1):3–23. **[10]**

Dornbusch, Sanford M. 1989. The sociology of adolescence. *Annual Review of Sociology,* 15:233–259. **[5]**

Dorr, Aimee. 1986. *Television and Children: A Special Medium for a Special Audience.* Beverly Hills, CA: Sage. **[5]**

Douglas, M. 1970. *Purity and Danger.* New York: Penguin. **[13]**

Doyal, Lesley. 1995. *What Makes Women Sick.* Brunswick, NJ: Rutgers University Press. **[14]**

Doyle, James A. 1983. *The Male Experience.* Dubuque, IA: W. C. Brown. **[8]**

Doyle, Kathleen. 1989. Madame C.J. Walker: First black woman millionaire. *American History Illustrated,* 24: 24–25. **[19]**

Du Bois, W.E.B. 1903. *The Souls of Black Folk.* New York: Dover. **[1, 8]**

Du Bois, W.E.B. 1989. *The Souls of Black Folk.* New York: Bantam. **[4]**

Du Bois, W.E.B. 1940. Dusk of dawn: An essay towards an autobiography of a race concept. In David Levering Lewis, *W.E.B. Du Bois: A reader.* New York: Holt. **[1]**

Dumont, Louis. 1977. *From Mandeville to Marx: The Genesis and Triumph of Economic Ideology.* Chicago: University of Chicago Press. **[15]**

Dumont, René. 1990. The coming food crisis. *World Press Review, Le Monde* (January):35–37. **[18]**

Duncan, Cynthia. 1991. Stagnation in the countryside. *Dissent* (Spring):279–281. **[19]**

Duncan, Greg J. 1984. *Years of Poverty, Years of Plenty.* Ann Arbor: Institute for Social Research, University of Michigan. **[7]**

Duncan, Greg, and Ken Moore. 1989. The rising affluence of the elderly. *Annual Review of Sociology,* 15:261–289. **[10]**

Dunier, Mitchell. 1992. *Slim's Table.* Chicago: University of Chicago Press. **[19]**

duPreez, Peter. 1994. *Genocide: The Psychology of Mass Murder.* New York: Marion Boyers. **[8]**

Durkheim, Emile. 1893/1985. *The Division of Labor in Society.* New York: Free Press. **[1, 6, 7, 15]**

Durkheim, Emile. 1895/1982. *Rules of Sociological Method.* New York: Free Press. **[1, 6]**

Durkheim, Emile. 1897/1951. *Suicide: A Study of Sociology.* J.A. Spaulding and G. Simpson (Trans.). New York: Free Press. **[2, 15]**

Durkheim, Emile. 1912/1965. *The Elementary Forms of Religious Life.* J.W. Swain (Trans.). New York: Free Press. **[1, 13]**

Durning, Alan. 1990. How much is "enough"? *WorldWatch,* 3 (6, November/December):12–19. **[18]**

Dweck, C.S., W. Davidson, S. Nelson, and B. Enna. 1978. Sex differences in learned helplessness. *Developmental Psychology,* 14:268–276. **[5]**

Dyer, Gwynn. 1985. *War.* New York: Crown Books. **[16]**

Early, Gerald. 1995. Understanding Afrocentrism. *Civilization* (July/August):31–39. **[8]**

Easterlin, Richard. 1987. *Birth and Fortune: The Impact of Numbers on Personal Welfare,* 2d. Chicago: University of Chicago Press. **[10]**

Easterlin, Richard A., Christine Schaeffer, and Diane J. Macunovich. 1993. Will the baby boomers be less well off than their parents? Income, wealth, and family circumstances over the life cycle in the United States. *Population and Development Review,* 19(3):497–522. **[10]**

Ebaugh, Helen Rose, Ed. 1991. *Vatican II and US Catholicism.* Greenwich, CT: JAI Press. **[13]**

Economic Policy Institute. 1993. *The State of Working America,* Lawrence Mishel and Jared Bernstein for Economic Policy Institute. Armonk, NY: M.E. Sharpe. **[7]**

Economic Report of the President. 1991. Washington, D.C.: Government Printing Office. **[15]**

Edelman, Marian Wright. 1987. *Families in Peril.* Cambridge, MA: Harvard University Press. [11]

Eder, Donna. 1991. The role of teasing in adolescent peer group culture. *Sociological Studies of Childhood Development,* 4:181–197. [5]

Education Digest. 1993. Can Boston University turn Chelsea public schools around? *Education Digest,* 59 (4, December):4–7. [12]

Educational Testing Service. 1995. *College-Bound Seniors National Report: 1994 Profile.* Princeton, NJ: Educational Testing Service. [12]

Edwards, Richard. 1979. *Contested Terrain: The Transformation of the Workplace in the Twentieth Century.* New York: Basic Books. [15]

Ehrenreich, Barbara, and Diedre English. 1989. Blowing the whistle on the "mommy track." *Ms.* (July/August):56, 58. [9]

Ehrlich, Anne H. 1991. People and food. *Population and Environment: A Journal of Interdisciplinary Studies,* 12(3, Spring):221–229. [18]

Ehrlich, Paul R., and Anne H. Ehrlich. 1990. *The Population Explosion.* New York: Simon and Schuster. [18]

Eisenstadt, Schmuel Noah. 1973. *Tradition, Change, and Modernity.* New York: Wiley. [17]

Eisenstadt, Shmuel A. 1990. The Jewish experience with pluralism. *Society,* 28 (1): 21–25. [13]

Ekstrom, Ruth B., Margaret E. Goertz, Judith M. Pollack, and Donald A. Rock. 1986. Who drops out of high school and why? Findings from a national study. *Teachers College Record,* 87(3):356–373. [12]

Elam, Stanley M. 1990. The 22nd annual Gallup poll of the public's attitudes toward the public schools. *Phi Delta Kappan,* 72(1):41–55. [12]

Elam, Stanley M., Lowell C. Rose, and Alec M. Gallup. 1993. The 25th Annual Phi Delta Kappa/Gallup Poll of the Public's Attitudes Toward the Public Schools. [12]

Elder, Glen H., Jr. 1974. *Children of the Great Depression.* Chicago: University of Chicago Press. [10]

Elder, Glen H., Jr. 1978. Approaches to social change and the family. *American Journal of Sociology,* 84 (suppl.):170–199. [10]

Elder, Glen H., Jr. 1987. Families and lives: Some developments in life-course studies. *Journal of Family History,* 12(1–2):170–199. [10]

Elder, Glen H., Jr., John Modell, and Ross D. Parke. 1993. Studying children in a changing world. In G.H. Elder, J. Modell, and R.D. Parke, Eds., *Children in Time and Place: Developmental and Historical Insights* (pp. 3–21). Cambridge, England: Cambridge University Press. [10]

Elkind, David. 1994. *Ties That Stress: The New Family Imbalance.* Cambridge, MA: Harvard University Press. [11]

Ellis, Desmond. 1989. Male abuse of a married or cohabiting female partner: The application of sociological theory to research findings. *Violence and Victims,* 4(4):235–255. [11]

Ellison, Christopher G., and Bruce London. 1992. The social and political participation of black Americans: Compensatory and ethnic community perspectives revisited. *Social Forces,* 70 (3, March):681–701. [8]

Ellsworth, Phoebe C., and Samuel R. Gross. 1994. Hardening of the attitudes: Americans' views of the death penalty. *Journal of Social Issues,* 50(2):19–52. [6]

Elshtain, Jeane Bethke. 1995. *Democracy on Trial.* New York: Basic Books. [16]

Embree, Ainslie T. 1994. The function of the Rashtriya Swayamsevak Sangh: To define the Hindu nation. In Martin E. Marty and R. Scott Appleby, Eds., *Accounting for Fundamentalisms: The Dynamic Character of Movements* (pp. 617–652). Chicago: University of Chicago Press. [13]

Emerging Trends. 1987 (Nov/Dec.). Princeton: Princeton Religious Research Center.

Emerson, Richard M. 1976. Social exchange theory. *Annual Reviews of Sociology.,*2:335–362. [3]

Encyclopedia Britannica. 1994. Fifteenth edition. The Study and Classification of Religions/Systems of Religions and Spiritual Belief. [13]

Engels, Friedrich. 1844/1975. *The Condition of the Working Class in England, 1844.* In *Marx-Engels Collected Works,* Vol. 4 (pp. 297–596). London: Lawrence and Wishart. [19]

England, Paula. 1992. *Comparable Worth: Theories and Evidence.* New York: Aldine de Gruyter. [9]

Ensminger, Margaret E., and Anita L. Slusarcick. 1992. Paths to high school graduation or dropout: A longitudinal study of a first-grade cohort. *Sociology of Education,* 65:95–113. [12]

Enzenberger, Hans Magnus. 1994. *Civil War.* Harmondsworth, England: Penguin. [18]

Epstein, Cynthia Fuchs. 1988. *Deceptive Distinctions: Sex, Gender, and the Social Order.* New Haven, CT: Yale University Press, and New York: Russell Sage Foundation. [9]

Epstein, Gerald. (1990–1991). Mortgaging America. *World Policy Journal,* VIII (1):27–59. [15]

Epstein, J.L. 1986. Parents' reactions to teacher practices of parent involvement. *Elementary School Journal,* 86(3):277–294. [12]

Epstein, J.L. 1987. Parent involvement: What researchers say to administrators. *Education and Urban Society,* 19(2):119–136. [12]

Erikson, Erik. 1950. *Childhood and Society.* New York: Norton. [10]

Erikson, Erik. 1982. *The Life Cycle Completed: A Review.* New York: Norton. [10]

Ermann, M. David, and Richard J. Lundman. 1982. *Corporate Deviance.* New York: Holt, Rinehart and Winston. [6]

Eschbach, Karl. 1995. The enduring and vanishing American Indian: American Indian population growth and intermarriage in 1990. *Ethnic and Racial Studies,* 18 (1, January):89–108. [8]

Espiritu, Yen Le. 1996. Panethnicity. In Craig Calhoun and George Ritzer, Eds. *Perspectives.* New York: McGraw-Hill. [8]

Espiritu, Yen, and Paul Ong. 1994. Class constraints on racial solidarity among Asian Americans. In P. Ong, E. Bonacoch, and L. Cheng, Eds., *The New Asian Immigration in Los Angeles and Global Restructuring* (Chapter 10). Philadelphia: Temple University Press. [8]

Euromonitor. 1992. *The World's Emerging Markets: Business Opportunities in the World's Fastest Growing Regional Economies.* London: Euromonitor. [18]

Evans, Peter. 1979. *Dependent Development: The Alliance of Multinational, State, and Local Capital in Brazil.* Princeton, NJ: Princeton University Press. [17]

Evans, Sara M., and Harry C. Boyte. 1992. *Free Spaces: The Sources of Democratic Change in America.* Chicago: University of Chicago Press. [20]

Evans, Sara M., and Barbara J. Nelson. 1989. Comparable worth: The paradox of technocratic reform. *Feminist Studies.* 15:1. [9]

Evans, Terry. 1988. *A Gender Agenda: A Sociological Study of Teachers, Parents, and Pupils in Their Primary Schools.* Sydney, Australia: Allen & Unwin. [5]

Evans-Pritchard, E.E. 1965. *Theories of Primitive Religion.* London: Oxford University Press. [14]

Evens, Terence, and James Peacock, Eds. 1990. *Transcendence in Society: Case Studies.* Greenwich, CT: JAI Press. [13]

Fahim-Nader, Mahnaz, and William J. Zeile. 1995. Foreign direct investment in the United States. *Survey of Current Business,* May: 57–81. [15]

Fantasia, Rich. 1995. From class consciousness to culture, action, and social organization. *Annual Review of Sociology,* 21:269 ff. [7]

Feagin, Joe R. 1988. *The Free Enterprise City: Houston in Political-Economic Perspective.* New Brunswick, NJ: Rutgers University Press. [19]

Feagin, Joe R. 1995. *The Bubbling Cauldron: Race, Ethnicity, and the Urban Crisis.* Minneapolis: University of Minnesota Press. [19]

Featherman, David L., and Robert Hauser. 1978. *Opportunity and Change.* New York: Academic Press. [7]

Federal Register. 1989. Washington, D.C.: Office of the Federal Register, National Archives and Record Service; distributed by the Superintendent of Documents, U.S. Government Printing Office.

Fenstermaker, Sarah, Candace West, and Don H. Zimmerman. 1991. Gender inequality: New conceptual terrain. In Rae Lesser Blumberg, Ed., *Gender, Family, and Economy: The Triple Overlap.* Newbury Park, CA: Sage. [9]

Ferguson, Earline Rae. 1988. The Women's Improvement Club of Indianapolis: Black women pioneers in tuberculosis work, 1903–1938. *Indiana Magazine of History,* 84:237–61. **[19]**

Ferguson, Thomas, and Joel Rogers. 1986. *Right Turn: The Decline of the Democrats and the Future of American Politics.* New York: Hill and Wang. **[15]**

Fine, Gary Alan. 1987. *With the Boys: Little League Baseball and Preadolescent Culture.* Chicago: University of Chicago Press. **[4]**

Fine, Gary Allen. 1993. The sad demise, mysterious disappearance, and glorious triumph of symbolic interactionism. *Annual Review of Sociology,* 19:61–87. **[3]**

Fine, Gary Alan, and Sherryl Kleinman. 1979. Rethinking subculture: An interactionist analysis. *American Journal of Sociology,* 85(1):1–20. **[4]**

Firestone, Juanita M., and Richard J. Harris. 1994. Sexual harassment in the U.S. military: Individualized and environmental contexts. *Armed Forces and Society,* 21 (Fall):25–43. **[9]**

Fischer, Claude S. 1982. *To Dwell Among Friends: Personal Networks in Town and City.* Chicago: University of Chicago Press. **[19]**

Fisher, Bernice. 1991. Affirming social value: Women without children. In David R. Maines, Ed., *Social Organization and Social Process: Essays in Honor of Anselm Strauss* (pp. 87–104). New York: De Gruyter. **[9]**

FitzGerald, Frances. 1986. *Cities on a Hill: A Journey Through Contemporary American Cultures.* New York: Simon and Schuster. **[10]**

Flannery, Daniel J., David C. Rowe, and Bill L. Gulley. 1993. Impact of pubertal status, timing, and age on adolescent sexual experience and delinquency. *Journal of Adolescent Research,* 8 (1, January):21–40. **[10]**

Flavin, Christopher. 1991. Conquering U.S. oil dependence. *World Watch,* 4 (1, January–February):28–36. **[18]**

Flavin, Christopher. 1995. Wind power soars. In L.R. Brown, N. Lenssen, and H. Kane. *Vital Signs, 1995* (pp. 54–55), New York: Norton. **[18]**

Flavin, Christopher, and Nicholas Lenssen. 1991. Designing a sustainable energy system. In *State of the World,* 1991 (pp. 21–38). New York: Norton. **[18]**

Fligstein, Neil. 1990. *The Transformation of Corporate Control.* Cambridge, MA: Harvard University Press. **[15]**

Fligstein, Neil. 1995. Networks of power or the finance conception of control?: Comment on Palmer, Barber, Zhou, and Soysal. *American Sociological Review,* 60:500–503. **[15]**

Fligstein, Neil, and Brantley, Peter. 1992. Bank control, owner control, or organiztional dynamics: Who controls the large modern corporation? *American Journal of Sociology,* 98(2):280–307. **[15]**

Flora, Peter, and Arnold J. Heidenheimer, Eds. 1981. *The Development of Welfare States in Europe and America.* New Brunswick, NJ: Transaction. **[16]**

Flynn, Clifton P. 1994. Regional differences in attitudes toward corporal punishment. *Journal of Marriage and the Family,* 56 (May):314–324. **[11]**

Foley, Douglas E. 1990. *Learning Capitalist Culture: Deep in the Heat of Tejas.* Philadelphia: University of Pennsylvania Press. **[12]**

Foner, Nancy. 1993. When the contract fails: Care for the elderly in non-industrial cultures. In Vern L. Bengtson and W. Andrew Achenbaum, Eds., *The Changing Contract Across Generations.* New York: Aldine de Gruyter. **[10]**

Foo, Lora Jo. 1994. The vulnerable and exploitable immigrant work-force and the need for strengthening worker protective legisla-tion. *Yale Law Journal,* 103(8):2179–2212. **[15]**

Forer, Lois G. 1994. *A Rage to Punish: The Unintended Consequences of Mandatory Sentencing.* New York/London: Norton. **[6]**

Formisano, Ronald P. 1991. *Boston Against Busing: Race, Class, and Ethnicity in the 1960s and 1970s.* Chapel Hill, NC: University of North Carolina Press. **[12]**

Fortes, Meyer. 1969. *Kinship and the Social Order.* Chicago: Aldine. **[13]**

Fox, Renée C. 1977. The medicalization and demedicalization of American society. *Daedalus* (Winter). **[14]**

Frank, André Gunder. 1967. *Capitalism and Underdevelopment in Latin America.* New York: Monthly Review Press. **[17]**

Frank, André Gunder. 1980. *Crisis in the Third World.* New York: Holmes and Meier. **[17]**

Frank, Ellen J. 1988. Business students' perceptions of women in man-agement. *Sex Roles,* 19(1/2):107–118. **[9]**

Frank, Robert H., and Cook, Philip J. 1995. *The Winner-Take-All Society.* New York: Free Press. **[15]**

Frankel, Arthur J. 1991. The dynamics of day care. *Families in Society,* 72(1):3–10. **[11]**

Franko, L.G. 1989. Global corporate competition: Who's winning, who's losing, and the R&D factor as one reason why. *Strategic Management Journal:* 449–474. **[15]**

Franks, David D., and Viktor Gecas. 1992. Autonomy and conformity in Cooley's self-theory: The looking-glass and beyond. *Symbolic Interaction,* 15(1):49–68. **[5]**

Frantz, Douglas. 1995. The rhetoric of terror. *Time* (March 27):48–51. **[20]**

Fraser, Nancy. 1992. Sex, lies, and the public sphere: Some reflections on the confirmation of Clarence Thomas. *Critical Inquiry,* 18 (Spring):595–612. **[9]**

Freeman, Jo. 1973. The origins of the women's liberation movement. *American Journal of Sociology,* 78:792–811. **[20]**

Freeman, Jo. 1979. Resource mobilization and strategy. In M.N. Zald and J.D. McCarthy, Eds., *The Dynamics of Social Movements.* Cambridge, MA: Winthrop. **[20]**

Freer, Regina. 1994. Black-Korean conflict. In Mark Baldassare, Ed., *The Los Angeles Riots.* Boulder, CO: Westview Press. **[20]**

Freidson, Eliot. 1970. *Professional Dominance: The Social Structure of Medical Care.* New York: Atherton Press. **[14]**

Freidson, Eliot. 1986. *Professional Powers: A Study of the Institutionalization of Formal Knowledge.* Chicago: University of Chicago Press. **[15]**

French, Hilary F. 1990. Clearing the air in WorldWatch Institute. *State of the World, 1990* (pp. 98–118). New York: Norton. **[18]**

Freud, Sigmund. 1920/1953. *Beyond the Pleasure Principle.* In J. Strachey, Ed. and Trans., *The Standard Edition of the Complete Psychological Works of Sigmund Freud,* Vol. 18. London: Hogarth Press. **[5]**

Freud, Sigmund. 1923/1947. *The Ego and the Id.* London: Hogarth Press. **[5]**

Frey, William H. 1990. Metropolitan America: Beyond the transition. *Population Bulletin,* 45(2):3–49. **[19]**

Frey, William H., and Jonathan Tilove. 1995. Immigrants in, native whites out. *New York Times Magazine* (August 20):44–45. **[8]**

Friedman, Jonathan. 1994. *Cultural Identity and Global Process.* London and Thousand Oaks, CA: Sage. **[4]**

Friedman, Samuel R., Don C. Des Jarlais, Jo L. Sotheran, Jonathan Garber, Henry Cohen, and Donald Smith. 1987. AIDS and self-organization among intravenous drug users. *International Journal of the Addictions,* 22(3):201–219. **[14]**

Fries, James F. 1983. The compression of morbidity. *Midbank Memorial Fund Quarterly/Health and Society,* 61(3):397–419. **[14]**

Fritsch, Jane. 1996. A bribe's not a bribe when it's a donation. *New York Times* (January 28):E1, E5. **[16]**

Fruch, Terry, and Paul E. McGhee. 1975. Traditional sex role develop-ment and amount of time spent watching television. *Developmental Psychology,* 11(1):109. **[5]**

Frykenberg, Robert Eric. 1994. Accounting for fundamentalism in South Asia: Ideologies and institutions in historical perspective. In Martin E. Marty and R. Scott Appleby, Eds., *Accounting for Fundamentalisms: The Dynamic Character of Movements,* (pp. 591–616). Chicago: University of Chicago Press. **[13]**

Fucini, Joseph J., and Suzy Fucini. 1990. *Working for the Japanese. Inside Mazda's American Auto Plant.* New York: Free Press. **[5]**

Fukuyama, Francis. 1995. *Trust: The Social Virtues and the Creation of Prosperity.* New York: Free Press. **[15]**

Furnham, Adrian, and Nadine Bitar. 1993. The stereotyped portrayal of men and women in British television. *Sex Roles,* 29(3–4):297–310. **[5]**

Furstenberg, Frank F., Jr. 1994. History and current status of divorce in the United States. *The Future of Children: Children and Divorce,* 4 (1, Spring):29–43. **[11]**

Fuss, Diana. 1989. *Essentially Speaking: Feminism, Nature and Difference.* New York: Routledge. **[9]**

Fyfe, Alec. 1989. *Child Labour.* Cambridge, England: Polity. **[10]**

Gabriel, Trip. 1995. Peering into the murky jobs crystal ball for 2015. *New York Times* (September 3):F9. **[15]**

Gamoran, Adam. 1992. The variable effects of high school tracking. *American Sociological Review.* 57:812–828. **[12]**

Gamoran, Adam, and Martin Nystrand. 1990. Tracking, instruction, and achievement. Paper prepared for the World Congress of Sociology, Madrid Spain. **[12]**

Gans, Herbert J. 1962. *The Urban Villagers,* New York: Free Press. **[19]**

Gans, Herbert J. 1979. *Deciding What's News.* New York: Pantheon. **[20]**

Gans, Herbert J. 1988. *Middle American Individualism: The Future of Liberal Democracy.* New York: Free Press. **[4]**

Garb, Paula. 1984. *From Childhood to Centenarian.* Moscow: Progress. **[10]**

Gardner, Gary. 1995. Water tables falling. In L.R. Brown, N. Lenssen, and H. Kane, *Vital Signs 1995* (pp. 122–123). New York: Norton. **[18]**

Gardner, Howard. 1995. Cracking open the IQ box. In Stephen Fraser, Ed., *The Bell Curve Wars* (pp. 23–35). New York: Basic Books. **[5]**

Gardner, Robert W. 1992. Asian immigration: The view from the United States. *Asian and Pacific Migration Journal,* 1(1):64–99. **[8]**

Garfinkel, Harold. 1967. *Studies in Ethnomethodology.* Englewood Cliffs, NJ: Prentice Hall. **[3, 4]**

Garrett, Laurie. 1994. *The Coming Plague: Newly Emerging Diseases in a World Out of Balance.* New York: Farrar, Straus and Giroux. **[14]**

Garsten, Christina. 1994. *Appleworld: Core and Periphery in Transnational Organizational Culture.* Stockholm University Studies in Social Anthropology. **[3]**

Gay, Peter. 1995. *The Naked Heart.* New York: Norton. **[2]**

Gaylord, Mark S., and John F. Galliher. 1988. *The Criminology of Edwin Sutherland.* New Brunswick, NJ: Transaction. **[6]**

Geertz, Clifford. 1973. *The Interpretation of Culture.* New York: Basic Books. **[4]**

Gellerman, Saul W. 1986. Why good managers make bad ethical choices. *Harvard Business Review* (July–August):85–90. **[6]**

Gelles, Richard J. 1983. Violence in the family. In D.H. Olson and B.C. Miller, Eds., *Family Studies Review Yearbook* (Vol. 1). Beverly Hills, CA: Sage. **[11]**

Gelles, Richard. 1985. Family violence. *Annual Review of Sociology,* 11:347–367. **[11]**

Gelles, Richard. 1995. Family violence. In Craig Calhoun and George Ritzer, Eds. *Introduction to Social Problems.* New York: McGraw-Hill. **[11]**

Gelles, Richard J., and Murray A. Straus. 1988. *Intimate Violence.* New York: Simon and Schuster. **[11]**

Gelles, Richard J., and Murray A. Straus. 1990. *Physical Violence in American Families: Risk Factors and Adaptations to Violence in 8,145 Families.* New Brunswick, NJ: Transaction. **[11]**

Gellner, Ernest. 1972. *Legitimation of Belief.* London: Weidenfeld and Nicholson. **[13]**

Gellner, Ernest. 1983. *Nations and Nationalism.* Oxford, England: Basil Blackwell. **[16]**

Gelman, David. 1990. A much riskier passage. *Newsweek* (Special Issue: The New Teens): 10–16. **[10]**

George, Linda K. 1993. Sociological perspectives on life transitions. *Annual Review of Sociology,* 19:353–373. **[10]**

Geschwender, James A. 1964. Social structure and the Negro revolt: An examination of some hypotheses. *Social Forces,* 43:248–256. **[20]**

Geyer, Georgie Ann. 1995. Criminalization across the globe. *Chicago Tribune* (March 10). **[6]**

Ghazi, Polly. 1994. The continuing fight for Amazonia. *World Press Review* (September):46. **[18]**

Gibbons, John H., Peter D. Blair, and Holly I. Gwin. 1989. Strategies for energy use. *Scientific American* (September): 136–143. **[18]**

Giddens, Anthony. 1984. *The Constitution of Society.* Berkeley: University of California Press. **[1]**

Giddens, Anthony. 1985. *The Nation–State and Violence.* Berkeley: University of California Press. **[16]**

Giddens, Anthony. 1990. *The Consequences of Modernity.* Stanford, CA: Stanford University Press. **[4]**

Giliomee, Herman. 1995. Democratization in South Africa. *Political Science Quarterly,* 1(1, Spring):83–105. **[16]**

Gilligan, Carol. 1982. *In a Different Voice: Psychological Theory and Women's Development.* Cambridge, MA: Harvard University Press. **[5,9]**

Gilligan, Carol. 1987. Moral orientation and moral development. In Eva Feder Kittay and Diana T. Meyers, Eds., *Women and Moral Theory.* Totowa, NJ: Rowman & Littlefield. **[9]**

Gilligan, Carol. 1989. *Mapping the Moral Domain.* Cambridge, MA: Harvard University Press. **[5]**

Gilman, Sander L. 1985. *Difference and Pathology: Stereotypes of Sexuality, Race, and Madness.* Ithaca, NY: Cornell University Press. **[6]**

Gilroy, Paul. 1993. *The Black Atlantic: Modernity and Double Consciousness.* Cambridge, MA: Harvard University Press. **[4]**

Gitlin, Todd. 1985. *Inside Prime Time.* New York: Pantheon. **[20]**

Glassman, James K. Raising minimum wage is not the answer. *Washington Post.* April 4, 1995:23. **[15]**

Glazer, Sarah. 1990. Why schools still have tracking. *Congressional Quarterly's Editorial Research Reports,* 1(48):746–758. **[12,13]**

Gleik, James. 1990. The census: Why we can't count. *New York Times Magazine* (July 15):22. **[18]**

Gluckman, Max, Ed. 1962. *Essays on the Ritual of Social Relations.* Manchester, England: Manchester University Press. **[13]**

Gluckman, Max. 1965. *Politics, Law and Ritual in Tribal Society.* New York: New American Library. **[16]**

Goffman, Erving. 1959. *The Presentation of Self in Everyday Life.* Garden City, NY: Doubleday. **[3]**

Goffman, Erving. 1961. *Asylums.* Chicago: Aldine. **[5]**

Goffman, Erving. 1967. *Interaction Ritual.* New York: Doubleday. **[3]**

Goffman, Erving. 1974. *Frame analysis: An Essay on the Organization of Experience.* Cambridge, MA: Harvard University Press. **[3]**

Golant, Stephen M. and Anthony J. La Greca. 1994. Differences in the housing quality of white, black, and Hispanic U.S. el-derly households. *Journal of Applied Gerontology,* 13(4, December):413–437. **[10]**

Goldemberg, José. 1989. *Amazonia: Facts, Problems and Solutions.* Sao Paulo, Brazil: University of Sao Paulo and Institute for Space Research (INPE). **[18]**

Goldsmith, Jeff. 1984. Death of a paradigm. *Health Affairs,* 3 (3):5–19. **[14]**

Goldstone, Jack. 1991. *Revolutions in the Early Modern World.* Berkeley: University of California Press. **[2,20]**

Golombok, Susan, and Robyn Fivush. 1994. *Gender Development.* Cambridge, MA: Cambridge University Press. **[9]**

Gondolf, Edward W., and Ellen R. Fisher. 1991. Wife battering. In Robert T. Ammerman and Michael Gersen, Eds., *Case Studies in Family Violence* (pp. 273–292). New York: Plenum Press. **[11]**

Goode, William J. 1978. *The Celebration of Heroes: Prestige as a Control System.* Berkeley: University of California Press. **[7]**

Gordon, David M. 1984. Capitalist development and the history of American cities. In W.K. Tabb and L. Sawers, Eds., *Marxism and the Metropolis,* 2d ed., New York: Oxford University Press. **[19]**

Gordon, Milton M. 1978. *Human Nature, Class and Ethnicity.* New York: Oxford University Press. **[8]**

Goring, Charles. 1913. *The English Convict.* London: His Majesty's Stationery Office. **[6]**

Gorman, Christine. 1996. Battling the AIDS virus. *Time.* February 12: 62.

Gottdiener, M., and Joe R. Feagin. 1988. The paradigm shift in urban sociology. *Urban Affairs Quarterly,* 24(2):163–187. **[19]**

Gottfredson, Michael, and Travis Hirschi. 1990. *A General Theory of Crime.* Stanford, CA: Stanford University Press. **[6]**

Gough, Kathleen. 1978. *Dravidian Kinship and Modes of Production.* New Delhi: Indian Council of Social Science Research. **[11]**

Gould, Harold. 1971. Caste and class: A comparative view. *Module,* 11:1–24. **[7]**

Gould, Stephen J. 1984. Similarities between the sexes. Review of *A Critique of Biology and Its Theories on Women,* by Ruth Bleier. *New York Times Book Review* (August 12):7. **[9]**

Gould, Stephen Jay. 1995. Mismeasure by any measure. In Russell Jacoby and Naomi Glauberman, Eds. *The Bell Curve Debate.* New York: Times Books. **[5]**

Gouldner, Alvin W. 1973. The norm of reciprocity. In *For Sociology* (Chapter 8). New York: Basic Books. **[3]**

Gove, Walter, Suzanne Ortega, and Carolyn Briggs Style. 1989. The maturational and role perspectives on aging and self through the adult years. *American Journal of Sociology,* 94:1117–1145. **[10]**

Graham, Ellen. 1995. As baby boomers hit 50, tough times loom ahead. *Providence Journal-Bulletin* (November 1):A1, A7. **[10]**

Gramsci, Antonio. 1971. *Selections from Prison Notebooks.* London: Lawrence and Wishart.**[7]**

Graubard, Stephen R. 1990. Doing badly and feeling confused. *Daedalus,* 19(2):257–279. **[12]**

Greeley, Andrew M. 1972. *The Denominational Society.* Glenview, IL: Scott, Foresman. **[13]**

Greeley, Andrew M. 1989. *Religious Change in America.* Cambridge, MA: Harvard University Press. **[13]**

Greeley, Andrew M. 1990. *The Catholic Myth.* New York: Scribners. **[13]**

Green, Arthur H. 1991. Child neglect. In Robert T. Ammerman and Michael Gersen, Eds., *Case Studies in Family Violence* (pp. 135–152). New York: Plenum Press. **[11]**

Greenfeld, Liah. 1992. *Nationalism: Five Roads to Modernity.* Cambridge, MA: Harvard University Press. **[2,16]**

Greenhalgh, Susan. 1990. Socialism and fertility in China. *Annals of the American Academy of Political and Social Science,* 510(July):73–86. **[18]**

Greenstein, Robert, and Scott Barancik. 1990. *Drifting Apart: New Findings on Growing Income Disparities Between the Rich, the Poor, and the Middle Class.* Washington, DC: Center on Budget and Policy Priorities. **[7]**

Greenwood, Peter W. et al. *Three Strikes and You're Out: Estiamted Benefits and Costs of California's New Mandatory Sentencing Law.* Santa Monica, CA: Rand Corp. **[6]**

Greif, Geoffrey L. 1985. *Single Fathers.* Lexington, MA: Heath. **[11]**

Griffin, Keith. 1989. *Alternative Strategies for Economic Development.* New York: Macmillan and OECD Development Center. **[17]**

Gringlas, Marcy, and Marsha Weinraub. 1995. The more things change . . . Single parenting revisited. *Journal of Family Issues,* 16(1, January):29–52. **[11]**

Gross, Samuel R. 1993. The romance of revenge: Capital punishment in America. *Studies in Law, Politics, and Society.* 13:71–104. **[6]**

Grossberg, Lawrence. 1992. *We Gotta Get Out of this Place: Popular Conservatism and Postmodern Culture.* New York: Routledge. **[7]**

Guillemard, Anne-Marie, and Martin Rein. 1993. Comparative patterns of retirement: Recent trends in developed societies. *Annual Review of Sociology,* 19:469–503. **[10]**

Gumperz, John J., Ed. 1982. *Language and Social Identity.* New York: Cambridge University Press. **[4]**

Gurr, Ted Robert. 1970. *Why Men Rebel.* Princeton, NJ: Princeton University Press. **[20]**

Guterman, Stuart, and Allen Dobson. 1986. Impact of Medicare prospective payment for hospitals. *Health Care Financing Review,* 7(3):97–114. **[14]**

Gutierrez, G. 1973. *A Theory of Liberation.* Maryknoll, NY: Orbis. **[13]**

Gutierrez, G. 1983. *The Power of the Poor in History.* Maryknoll, NY: Orbis. **[13]**

Habermas, Jürgen. 1975. *Legitimation Crisis.* Thomas McCarthy, Trans. Boston: Beacon. **[16]**

Habermas, Jürgen. 1988. *The Theory of Communicative Action,* Vol. 2. Boston: Beacon Press. **[3]**

Habermas, Jürgen. 1989. *The Structural Transformation of the Public Sphere.* Cambridge, MA: MIT Press. **[16]**

Habib, Jack. 1990. Population aging and the economy. In R. Binstock and L. George, Eds., *Aging and the Social Sciences,* 3d ed. San Diego: Academic Press. **[10]**

Hacker, Andrew. 1992. *Two Nations: Black and White, Separate, Hostile, Unequal,* rev. ed. New York: Ballantine **[8]**

Hadaway, C. Kirk, Penny Long Marler, and Mark Chaves. 1993. What the polls don't show: A closer look at U.S. church attendance. *American Sociological Review,* 58 (December): 741–752. **[13]**

Hadden, Jeffrey K. 1993. The rise and fall of American televangelism. *Annals, Annals of the American Academy of Political and Social Sciences,* 527(May): 113–130. **[13]**

Hagan, John. 1990. The gender stratification of income inequality among lawyers. *Social Forces,* 68(3, March):835–855. **[9]**

Hagan, John, and Alberto Palloni. 1990. The social reproduction of a criminal class in working-class London, circa 1950–1980. *American Journal of Sociology,* 96(2, September):265–299. **[6]**

Haggard, Stephan. 1990. *Pathways from the Periphery: The Politics of Growth in the Newly Industrializing Countries.* Itaca, NY: Cornell University Press. **[17]**

Hall, G. Stanley. 1905/1981. *Adolescence: Its Psychology and Its Relations to Physiology, Anthropology, Sociology, Sex, Crime, Religion, and Education* (2 vols.). Norwood, PA: Telegraph Books. **[10]**

Hall, John A. 1985. *Powers and Liberties.* Berkeley: University of California Press. **[16]**

Halle, David. 1993. *Inside Culture: Arts and Class in the American Home.* Chicago: University of Chicago Press. **[4]**

Hamer, Dean H., and Peter Copeland. 1995. The Science of Desire: The Search for the Gay Gene. New York: Simon and Schuster. **[5]**

Hanley, Charles J. 1995. Nations learn democracy requires more than lip service. *The News & Observer* (December 7):23, 27A. **[16]**

Hannerz, Ulf. 1992. *Cultural Complexity.* New York: Columbia University Press. **[4]**

Hanson, Sandra L. 1983. A family life-cycle approach to the socioeconomic attainment of working women. *Journal of Marriage and the Family,* 45(2)323–338. **[10]**

Harasim, Linda M. 1993. Networlds: Networks as social space. In L.M. Harasim, Ed., *Global Networks: Computers and International Communication* (pp. 15–34). Cambridge, MA: MIT Press. **[4]**

Haraway, Donna. 1992. *Simians, Cyborgs, and Women.* New York: Routledge. **[9]**

Harbeson, John, Ed. 1994. *Civil Society and the State in Africa.* Boulder, CO: Lynn Reiner. **[16]**

Hardy, Eric S. 1995. America's highest-paid bosses. *Forbes,* 155(11, May 22):180–183. **[15]**

Hare, A. Paul. 1976. *Handbook for Small Group Research.* Glencoe, IL: Free Press. **[3]**

Harris, Chauncy D., and Edward L. Ullman. 1945. The nature of cities. *Annals of the American Academy of Political and Social Science,* 242(November):7–17. **[19]**

Harris, Chauncy D. and Edward Ullman. 1957. The nature of cities. In Paul K. Hatt and A.J. Reiss, Jr., Eds. *Cities and Society.* Peoria, IL: Free Press. **[19]**

Harris, Kathleen Mullan. 1993. Work and welfare among single mothers in poverty. *American Journal of Sociology,* 99 (2, September):317–352. **[7]**

Harris, Kathleen Mullan. 1996. Single-mother families. In C. Calhoun and G. Ritzer, Eds., *Social Problems.* New York: McGraw-Hill/PRIMUS. **[7,11]**

Harris, Marvin. 1975. *Cows, Pigs, Wars, and Witches: The Riddles of Culture.* New York: Random House. **[4]**

Harrison, Barbara Grizzuti. 1994. Arguing with the Pope. *Harper's,* 288(1727, April):41–56. **[13]**

Harrison, Bennett. 1994. *Lean and Mean: The Changing Landscape of Corporate Power in the Age of Flexibility.* New York: Basic Books. **[17]**

Harrison, Paul, 1983. *The Third World Tomorrow: A Report from the Battlefront in the War Against Poverty,* 2d ed. New York: Pilgrim Press. **[17]**

Harrison, Paul. 1984. *Inside the Third World*, 2d rev. ed. Harmondsworth, England: Penguin. [17,18]

Harrison, Paul. 1992. *The Third Revolution: Environment, Population, and a Sustainable World*. London/New York: I.B. Tauris and Co. and New York: St. Martin's Press. [18]

Hart, Stephen. 1987. Privatization in American religion and society. *Sociological Analysis*, 47(4):319–334. [13]

Hartmann, Betsy. 1995. *Reproductive Rights and Wrongs: The Global Politics of Population Control*. Boston: South End Press [18]

Hartmann, Heidi I. 1987. *Pay Equity: Empirical Inquiries*. Washington, DC: Academy Press. [9]

Harvey, David 1989. *The Condition of Postmodernity: An Enquiry into the Origins of Cultural Change*. New York: Basil Blackwell. [19]

Harwood Group. 1991. *Citizens and Politics: A view from Main Street America*. Dayton, OH: Kettering Foundation. [16]

Hathaway, Dale A. 1993. *Can Workers Have A Voice?: The Politics of Deindustrialization in Pittsburgh*. University Park, PA: Pennsylvania State University Press. [15]

Haub, Carl. 1991. World and United States populations prospects. *Population and Environment: A Journal of Interdisciplinary Studies*. 12:3. [18]

Hauchler, Ingomar, and Paul M. Kennedy, Eds. 1994. *Global Trends: The World Almanac of Development and Peace*. New York: Continuum. [4,18]

Haunschild, Pamela R. 1993. Interorganizational imitation: The impact of interlocks on corporate acquisition activity. *Administrative Science Quarterly*, 38:564–592. [15]

Hauser, Robert M., Archibald O. Haller, David Mechanic, and Taissa S. Hauser, Eds. 1982. *Social Structure and Behavior*. New York: Academic Press. [7]

Hauser, Robert M., Shu-Ling Tsai, and William H. Sewell. 1983. A model of stratification with response error in social and psychological variables. *Sociology of Education*, 56:20–46. [7]

Hawkins, David. 1990. The roots of literacy. *Daedalus*, 19(2):1–14. [12]

Hayward, Mark D., Melissa A. Hardy, and Mei-Chun Liu. 1994. Work after retirement: The experiences of older men in the United States. *Social Science Research*, 23:pp.82–107. [10]

Headden, Susan. 1993. Made in the U.S.A. *U.S. News and World Report*, (November 22):48–55. [15]

Headden Susan. 1995. One nation, one language? [and] Tongue-tied in the schools. *U.S. News & World Report* (September 25):38–42, 44–46. [4]

Hecht, Susanna B. 1993. The logic of livestock and deforestation in Amazonia. *BioScience*, 43:687–699. [18]

Heikes, E. Joel. 1991. When men are in the minority: The case of men in nursing. *Sociological Quarterly*, 32(3):389–401. [9]

Heilman, Samuel C. 1994. Quiescent and active fundamentalisms: The Jewish cases. In Martin E. Marty and R. Scott Appleby, Eds., *Accounting for Fundamentalisms: Social Dynamics and Rhetorical Strategies* (pp. 173–196). Chicago: University of Chicago Press. [13]

Hein, Jeremy. 1994. From migrant to minority: Hmong refugees and the social construction of identity in the United States. *Sociological Inquiry*, 64(3):281–306. [5]

Hellinger, Fred J. 1993. The lifetime cost of treating a person with HIV. *Journal of the American Medical Association*, 270(4):474. [14]

Helson, Ravenna, and Geraldine Moore. 1987. Personality change in women from college to midlife. *Journal of Personality and Social Psychology*, 53:126–186. [10]

Herbers, John. 1983. Large cities and suburbs giving way to the sprawl of small urban areas. *New York Times* (July 8):1. [19]

Herbert, Bob. 1995. Firing their customers. *New York Times* (December 29):A35. [3]

Herdt, Gilbert H. 1984. A comment on cultural attributes and fluidity of bisexuality. *Journal of Homsexuality*, 10(3/4):53–61. [5]

Herman, Edward. 1981. *Corporate Control, Corporate Power*. New York: Cambridge University Press. [15]

Herrnstein, Richard J., and Charles Murray. 1994. *The Bell Curve*. New York: Free Press. [5]

Hess, Beth, and Elizabeth Markson. 1991. *Growing Old in America*, 4th ed. New Brunswick, NJ: Transaction. [10]

Hess, John L. 1990. Confessions of a greedy geezer. *Nation*, 250(April 2):1, 42. [10]

Hewitt, Hugh. 1992. When television throws a riot. *Los Angeles Times* (May 3):M1,M3. [20]

Heyns, Barbara. 1978. *Summer Learning and the Effects of Schooling*. New York: Academic Press. [12]

Hill, Richard Child, and Joe R. Feagin. 1987. Detroit and Houston: Two cities in global perspective. In Michael Peter Smith and Joe R. Feagin, Eds., *The Capitalist City: Global Restructuring and Community Politics*. London: Basil Blackwell. [19]

Himmelstein, Jerome L. 1990. *To the Right: The Transformation of American Conservatism*. Berkeley: University of California Press. [13]

Hirschi, Travis. 1969. *Causes of Delinquency*. Berkeley: University of California Press. [6]

Hirschi, Travis. 1993. Crime. In C. Calhoun and G. Ritzer, Eds., *Social Problems*. New York: McGraw-Hill/Primus. [6]

Hirschi, Travis, and Michael Gottfredson. 1988. Towards a general theory of crime. In W. Buikhuisen and S.A. Mednick, Eds., *Explaining Criminal Behaviors* (pp. 8–26). Leiden: Brill. [6]

Hirschman, Albert O. 1977. *The Passions and the Interests: Political Arguments for Capitalism Before Its Triumph*. Princeton, NJ: Princeton University Press. [15]

Hirschman, Albert, 1982. *Shifting Involvements*. Princeton, NJ: Princeton University Press. [16]

Hochschild, Arlie Russell. 1978. *The Unexpected Community: Portrait of an Old Age Subculture*. Berkeley: University of California Press. [10]

Hochschild, Arlie Russell. 1983. *The Managed Heart: Commercialization of Human Feeling*. Berkeley: University of California Press. [3,15]

Hochschild, Arlie Russell, with Anne Machung. 1989. *The Second Shift: Working Parents and the Revolution at Home*. New York: Viking. [2,9,11]

Hogan, Dennis P., David J. Eggebeen, and Clifford C. Clogg. 1993. The structure of intergenerational exchanges in American families. *American Journal of Sociology*, 98(6, May):1428–1458. [10]

Holden Karen C., and Pamela J. Smock. 1991. The economic costs of marital dissolution: Why do women bear a disproportionate cost? *Annual Review of Sociology*, 17:51–78. [11]

Holmes, Steven A. 1994. The boom in jails is locking up lots of loot. *New York Times* (November 6):E3. [6]

Holstein, William J. 1990. Hands across America: The rise of Mitsubishi. *Business Week* (September 24):102–107. [3]

Holtz-Eakin, Douglas, and Timothy M. Smeeding. 1994. Income, wealth, and intergenerational economic relations of the aged. In Linda G. Martin and Samuel H. Preston, Eds., *Demography of Aging* (pp. 102–145). Washington: National Academy Press. [10]

Homans, George C. 1974. *Social Behavior: Its Elementary Forms*, rev. ed. New York: Harcourt Brace Jovanovich. [3]

Honig, Carlye, Ed. 1995. *Science and Technology Policy*. London: British Library. [16]

hooks, bell. 1989. *Talking Back: Thinking Feminist, Thinking Black*. Boston: South End Press. [20]

hooks, bell. 1993. *Sisters of the Yam: Black Women and Self-Recovery*. Boston: South End Press. [8]

Hoover, E.M., and R. Vernon. 1959. *Anatomy of a Metropolis*. Cambridge, MA: Harvard University Press. [19]

Hopkins, K. 1978. *Conquerors and Slaves: Sociological studies in Roman History*. New York: Cambridge University Press. [16]

Horn, Jack C., and Jeff Meer. 1987. The vintage years. *Psychology Today*, 21(5):76–90. [10]

Hoult, Thomas Ford. 1969. *A Dictionary of Modern Sociology*. Totowa, NJ: Littlefield, Adams. [20]

Hout, Michael, Adrian Raftery, and Eleanor O. Bell. 1993. Making the grade: Educational stratification in the United States. In Yossi Shavat and Hans-Peter Blossfeld, Eds., *Persistent Inequality: Changing Educational Attainment in Thirteen Countries*. Boulder, CO: Westview Press. [12]

Howard, Robert. 1985. *Brave New Workplace*. New York: Viking. **[3,15]**

Hoyt, Homer. 1943. The structure of American cities in the post-war era. *AmericanJournal of Sociology*, 48(January):475–492. **[19]**

Huber, Joan, and Glenna Spitze. 1980. Considering divorce: An expansion of Becker's theory of marital instability. *American Journal of Sociology*, 86(1):75–89. **[11]**

Hundley, T. 1989. Small-town blues. *Chicago Tribune Magazine* (January 29):9–21. **[19]**

Hunter, Albert. 1978. Persistence of local sentiments in mass society. In D. Street et al., Eds., *Handbook of Contemporary Urban Life* (pp. 134–156). San Francisco: Jossey-Bass. **[19]**

Hunter, James Davison. 1990. Fundamentalism in its global contours. In Normal J. Cohen. Ed., *The Fundamentalist Phenomenon: A View From Within; A Response from Without* (pp. 56–71). Grand Rapids, MI: Eerdmans. **[13]**

Hunter, James Davison. 1991. *Culture Wars: The Struggle to Define America*. New York: Basic Books. **[11,13]**

Hyde, Janet S. 1981. How large are cognitive gender differences? *American Psychologist*, 36:892–901. **[9]**

Hyde, Janet S. 1984. How large are gender differences in aggression? A developmental meta-analysis. *Developmental Psychology*, 20:722–736. **[9]**

Ianni, Francis A.J. 1989. *The Search for Structure: A Report on American Youth Today*. New York: Free Press. **[10]**

Idle, Tracey, Eileen Wood, and Serge Desmarais. 1993. Gender role socialization in toy play situations: Mothers and fathers with their sons and daughters. *Sex Roles*, 28(11–12):679–691. **[5]**

Ikels, Charlotte, Jennie Keith, Jeanette Dickerson-Putman, Patricia Draper, Christine Fry, Anthony Glascock, and Henry Harpending. 1992. Perceptions of the adult life course: A cross-cultural analysis. *Ageing and Society*, 12:49–84. **[10]**

Imperato, Pascal James. 1989. *Mali: A Search for Direction*. Boulder, CO: Westview Press. **[17]**

Independent Commission on International Humanitarian Issues. 1985. *Famine: A Manmade Disaster?* New York: Vintage. **[18]**

Ingelhart, Ronald. 1990. *Culture Shift in Advanced Industrial Society*. Princeton, NJ: Princeton University Press. **[15]**

Inkeles, Alex. 1983. *Exploring Individual Modernity*. New York: Columbia University Press. **[17]**

Inkeles, Alex. 1991. Transitions to democracy. *Society*. 28:4 (192):67–72. **[14]**

Isikoff, Michael, Rick Thomas, Daniel Glick, Patricia King, and Paul O'Donnel. 1994. Of tobacco, torts and tusks. *Newsweek*, 124(22, November 28):30–31. **[16]**

Ivins, Molly. 1990. Good ol debs. *Ms.*, 18(August):22. **[10]**

Jackall, Robert. 1988. *Moral Mazes: The World of Corporate Managers*. New York: Oxford University Press. **[15]**

Jacklin, Carol N., Eleanor E. Maccoby, Charles H. Doering, and David R. King. 1984. Neonatal sex-steroid hormones and muscular strength of boys and girls in the first three years. *Developmental Psychobiology*, 20(3, May):459–472. **[9]**

Jackson, Philip W. 1968. *Life in Classrooms*. New York: Holt, Rinehart and Winston. **[12]**

Jacobs, Ronald N. 1996. Civil society and crisis: Culture, discourse, and the Rodney King beating. *American Journal of Sociology*. **[20]**

Jacobsen, Joyce P. 1994. Sex segregation at work: Trends and predictions. *Social Science Journal*, 31(2):153–169. **[9]**

Jacoby, Russell, and Naomi Glauberman, Eds. 1995. *The Bell curve debate*. New York: Times Books. **[5]**

Jagger, Bianca. 1991. Save the rain forest in Nicaragua. *New York Times* (November 12):A25. **[18]**

Janis, Irving L. 1982. *Groupthink: Psychological Studies of Policy Decisions and Fiascoes*. Boston: Houghton Mifflin. **[3]**

Janis, Irving L. 1989. *Crucial Decisions*. New York: Free Press. **[3]**

Jankowski, Martin Sañchez. 1991. *Islands in the Street*. Berkeley: University of California Press. **[6]**

Janofsky, Michael. 1995. Panel focuses on Internet as tool for terror. *New York Times* (May 12). **[16]**

Jencks, Christopher. 1972. *Inequality: A Reassessment of the Effect of Family and Schooling in America*. New York: Basic Books. **[12]**

Jencks, Christopher. 1994. *The Homeless*. Cambridge, MA: Harvard University Press. **[7]**

Johnson, Benton. 1963. On church and sect. *American Sociological Review*, 28:539–549. **[13]**

Johnson, Colleen L., and Lillian E. Troll. 1994. Constraints and facilitators to friendship in late late life. *Gerontologist*, 34(1):79–87. **[3]**

Johnson, Michael P. 1995. Patriarchal terrorism and common couple violence: Two forms of violence against women. *Journal of Marriage and the Family*, 57(May):283–294. **[11]**

Jonas, Andrew E.G. 1992. Corporate takeover and the politics of community: The case of Norton Company in Worcester. *Economic Geography*, 68(4, October):348–373. **[15]**

Jones, Landon Y. 1980. *Great Expectations: America and the Baby Boom Generation*. New York: Coward, McCann & Geoghegan. **[10]**

Jordan, Nick. 1983. You've run a long way, baby. *Psychology Today* (June):79. **[9]**

Jylha, Marja, and Jukka Jokela. 1990. Individual experiences as cultural—A cross-cultural study on loneliness among the elderly. *Ageing and Society*, 10:295–315. **[10]**

Kalmijn, Matthijs. 1994. Assortive mating by cultural and economic occupational status. *American Journal of Sociology*, 100 (2, September):422–452. **[3]**

Kalof, Linda. 1993. Dilemmas of feminity: Gender and the social construction of sexual imagery. *Sociological Quarterly*, 34(4):636–651. **[5]**

Kaminer, Wendy. 1994. Federal offense: Politics of crime control. *Atlantic Monthly*, 273(6, June) **[6]**

Kanter, Rosabeth Moss. 1977. *Men and women of the Corporation*. New York: Basic Books. **[9]**

Kantorowicz, Ernest. 1957. *The King's Two Bodies*. Princeton, NJ: Princeton University Press. **[16]**

Karp, Aaron. 1994. The rise of the black and gray markets. In Robert E. Harkavy and Stephanie G. Newman. *The Arms Trade: Problems and Prospects in the Post-Cold War World*. Thousand Oaks, CA: Sage Publications. **[17]**

Kasarda, John D. 1989. Urban industrial transition and the underclass. *Annals of the American Academy of Political and Social Science*, 501(January):26–47. **[19]**

Kasarda, John D., and Stephen J. Appold. 1990. Comments. In JOhn D. Kasarda, Ed. *Jobs, Earnings, and Employment Growth Policies in the United States*. Boston: Kluwer Academic Publishers. **[15]**

Kasarda, John D., and Edward M. Crenshaw. 1991. Third world urbanization: Dimensions, theories and determinants. *Annual Review of Sociology*, 17:467–501. **[17]**

Kasinitz, Philip. 1988. The gentrification of "Boerum Hill": Neighborhood change and conflicts over definitions. *Qualitative Sociology*, 11(3, Fall):163–182. **[19]**

Kates, Nick K., Barrie S. Greiff, and Duane Q. Hagen. 1990. *The Psychosocial Impact of Job Loss*. Washington, DC: American Psychiatric Press. **[15]**

Kaye, Steven D., Mary Lord, and Pamela Sherrid. 1995. Stop working? Not boomers. *U.S. News and World Report* (June 12):70–76. **[10]**

Keegan, John. 1993. *A History of Warfare*. London: Hutchinson. **[17]**

Keith, Jennie. 1990. Age in social and cultural context. In R. Binstock and L. George, Eds., *Aging and the Social Sciences*, 3d ed. San Diego: Academic Press. **[10]**

Keller, Suzanne. 1963. *Beyond the Ruling Class: Strategic Elites in Modern Society*. New York: Random House. **[16]**

Kepel, Gilles. 1994. *The Revenge of God: The Resurgence of Islam, Christianity and Judaism in the Modern World*. Cambridge, England: Cambridge University Press. **[13]**

Kerbo, Harold R., 1991. *Social Stratification and Inequality*. New York: McGraw-Hill. **[7]**

Kerckhoff, Alan C. 1995. Institutional arrangements and stratification processes in industrial societies. *Annual Review of Sociology,* 21:(323 ff.). **[7]**

Kern, Rosemary Gibson, and Susan R. Windham, with Paula Griswold. 1986. *Medicaid and Other Experiments in State Health Policy.* Washington, DC: American Enterprise Institute for Public Policy Research. **[14]**

Kerr, Peter, 1987. Drug smugglers: New breed of ethnic gangs. *New York Times* (March 21):A1, 31. **[6]**

Kessen, William, Ed. 1975. *Childhood in China.* New Haven, CT: Yale University Press. **[5]**

Kessler, Ronald C., James S. House, and J. Blake Turner. 1987. Unemployment and health in a community sample. *Journal of Health and Social Behavior,* 28(March):51–59. **[14]**

Kett, Joseph F. 1977. *Rites of Passage: Adolescence in America, 1790 to the Present.* New York: Basic Books. **[10]**

Keyfitz, Nathan, 1989. The growing human population. *Scientific American,* 261(3, September):119–126. **[18]**

Khripunov, Igor. 1994. Russia's arms trade in the post-cold war period. *Washington Quarterly.* 17:4 (Autumn):3–19. **[17]**

Kidder, Tracy. 1981. *The Soul of a New Machine.* Boston: Little, Brown. **[3]**

Kimball, M.M. 1986. Television and sex-role attitudes. In T.M. Williams, Ed., *The Impact of Television: A Natural Experiment in Three Communities,* Orlando, FL: Academic Press. **[5]**

Kirsch, Irwin, Ann Jungeblut, Lynn Jenkins, and Andrew Kolstad. 1993. *Adult Literacy in America.* Washington, DC: U.S. Department of Education **[12]**

Klein, Ethel, 1984. *Gender Politics: From Consciousness to Mass Politics.* Cambridge, MA: Harvard University Press. **[20]**

Kleinman, Sherryl, and Martha Copp. 1993. *Emotions in Fieldwork.* Newbury Park, CA: Sage. **[2]**

Klerman, Jacob A., and Arleen Leibowitz. 1990. Child care and women's return to work after childbirth. *American Economic Review,* 80 (2, May):284–288. **[11]**

Klostermaier, Klaus K. 1989. *A Survey of Hinduism.* Albany: State University of New York Press. **[13]**

Kohlberg, L. 1969. Stage and sequence: The cognitive-developmental approach to socialization. In D.A. Goslin, Ed., *Handbook of Socialization Theory and Research.* Chicago: Rand McNally. **[9]**

Kohn, Melvin L. 1959. Social class and parental values. *American Journal of Sociology,* 64(January): 337–351. **[5]**

Kohn, Melvin L. 1976. Occupational structure and alienation. *American Journal of Sociology,* 82(July):111–130. **[5]**

Kohn, Melvin L. 1981. Personality, occupation, and social stratification: A frame of reference. In D.J. Treiman and R.V. Robinson, Eds., *Research in Social Stratification and Mobility: A Research Annual,* Vol. 1(pp. 276–297). Greenwich, CT: JAI Press. **[5]**

Kohn, Melvin L., and Carmi Schooler. 1978. The reciprocal effects of the substantive complexities of work and intellectual flexibility: A longitudinal assessment. *American Journal of Sociology,* 84(July):24–52. **[5]**

Kohn, Melvin L., and Carmi Schooler. 1983. *Work and Personality: An Inquiry into the Impact of Social Stratification.* Norwood, NJ: Ablex. **[5]**

Kohn, Melvin I., Atushi Naoi, Carrie Schoenbach, Carmi Schooler, and Kazimierz M. Slomczynski. 1990. Position in the class structure and psychological functioning in the United States, Japan, and Poland. *American Journal of Sociology,* 95(4, January):964–1008. **[5]**

Kohn, Melvin I., Kazimierz M. Slomczynski, and Carrie Schoenbach. 1986. Social stratification and the transmission of values in the family: A cross-national assessment. *Social Forces,* 1(1):73–102. **[5]**

Kolata, Gina. 1992. New insurance practice. Dividing sick from well. *New York Times* (March 4):A1, A15. **[14]**

Kollmann, Geoffrey, and David Koitz. 1986. How long does it take for new retirees to recover the value of their Social Security taxes? *Congressional Research Service* (January 21), Report no. 86-10 EPW, table 1, p. 11. **[10]**

Kominski, Robert. 1990. *What's it worth? Educational background and economic status: Spring 1987.* Current Population Reports: Household Economic Studies, Series P-70, No. 21. Washington, DC: U.S. Government Printing Office. **[12]**

Kondrachine, Anatoli V., and Peter Trigg. 1995. Malaria: Hope for the future. *World Health,* 48(2, March–April):26–27. **[14]**

Koppel, Ted. 1992. Moment of crisis: Anatomy of a riot. *ABC Nightline Special Investigation* (May). **[20]**

Kosmin, Barry A., and Seymour P. Lachman. 1995. Religious self-identification. In Kenneth B. Bedell, Ed., *Yearbook of American & Canadian Churches 1995* (pp. 20–23). Nashville: Abingdon Press. **[13]**

Kosofsky-Sedgwick, Eve. 1990. *Epistemology of the Closet.* Berkeley: University of California Press. **[5]**

Kovács, János Mátyás, and Márton Tardos, Eds. 1992. *Reform and Transformation in Eastern Europe: Soviet-Type Economics on the Threshold of Change.* London: Routledge. **[15]**

Kozol, Jonathan. 1988. *Rachel and Her Children: Homeless Families in America.* New York: Crown. **[7]**

Krauss, Clifford. 1995. Mystery of New York, the suddenly safer city. *New York Times* (July 23):E1, E4. **[6]**

Kristof, Nicholas D. 1993. In China's crackdown on population growth, force is a big weapon. *International Herald Tribune* (April 28):4. **[18]**

Kristof, Nicholas D. 1995. Japan's schools: Safe, clean, not much fun. *New York Times.* (July 18):A1, A6. **[5]**

Kristof, Nicholas, and Sherryl WuDunn. 1994. *China Wakes: The Struggle for the Soul of a Rising Power.* New York: Times Books. **[18]**

Krosnick, Jon A., and Charles M. Judd. 1982. Transition in social influence at adolescence: Who induces cigarette smoking? *Developmental Psychology,* 18:359–368. **[5]**

Krymkowski, Daniel H., and Tadeusz K. Krauze. 1992. Occupational mobility in the year 2000: Projections for American men and women. *Social Forces,* 71(1, September):145–157. **[10]**

Kuper, Leo, and M.G. Smith. 1969. *Plural Societies.* Chicago: Aldine. **[8]**

Kurian, George Thomas. 1990. *The New Book of World Rankings,* 3d ed. Updated by James Marti. New York: Oxford University Press. **[6]**

Kusum. 1993. The use of pre-natal diagnostic techniques for sex selection: The Indian scene. *Bioethics,* 7(2/3):149–165. **[1]**

Lang, Michael H. 1989. *Homelessness Amid Affluence: Structure and Paradox in the American Political Economy.* New York: Praeger. **[7]**

Laqueur, Thomas. 1990. *Making Sex: Body and Gender from the Greeks to Freud.* Cambridge, MA: Harvard University Press. **[3]**

Larabee, David F. 1992. Power, knowledge, and the rationalization of teaching: A genealogy of the movement to professionalize teaching. *Harvard Educational Review,* 62(2, Summer):123–154. **[12]**

Lareau, Annette. 1989. *Home Advantage: Social Class and Parental Intervention in Elementary Education.* Philadelphia: Falmer Press. **[12]**

Larson, Edward J. 1995. *Sex, Race, and Science: Eugenics in the Deep South.* Baltimore: Johns Hopkins University Press. **[1]**

Larson, Magali Sarfalti. 1977. *The Rise of Professionalism: A Sociological Analysis.* Berkeley: University of California Press. **[14]**

Lasch, Christopher. 1995. *The Revolt of the Elites: And the Betrayal of Democracy.* New York: W. W. Norton. **[4]**

Lash, Scott. 1993. *Postmodernist Sociology.* Newbury Park, CA: Sage. **[4]**

Lasker, Judith N., and Susan Borg. 1994. *In Search of Parenthood: Coping with Infertility and Hi-tech Conception.* Revised and updated. Philadelphia: Temple University Press. **[1]**

Laslett, Barbara, and Johanna Brenner. 1989. Gender and social production: Historical perspectives. *American Sociological Review,* 15:381–404. **[9]**

Laslett, Peter. 1973. *The World We Have Lost,* 2d ed. New York: Scribners. **[1]**

Laumann, Edward O., John H. Gagnon, Robert T. Michael, and Stuart Michaels. 1994. *Sexual Practices in the United States.* Chicago: University of Chicago Press. **[3, 5]**

Lauter, David, and Sam Fluwood, III. 1992. U.S. racial slumber ends in jolt. *Los Angeles Times* (May 3):A1, A8. [20]

Lavelle, Robert, and the Staff of Blackside, Eds. 1995. *America's New War on Poverty: A Reader for Action.* San Francisco: KQED Books. [7]

Lazare, Daniel. 1991. Collapse of a city: Growth and decay of Camden, New Jersey. *Dissent* (Spring):267–275. [19]

Le Bon, Gustave. 1895/1960. *The Crowd: A Study of the Popular Mind.* New York: Viking. [20]

Lee, Benjamin. 1991. Critical internationalism. Working paper of the Center for Psychosocial Studies, Chicago. [8]

Lee, Rensselaer W., III. 1989. *The White Labyrinth: Cocaine and Political Power.* New Brunswick, NJ: Transaction. [6]

Leek, Margaret Guminski, and T. Allan Pearson. 1991. Demographic subgroup contributions to divorce cause constellations. *Journal of Divorce and Remarriage,* 15(1/2):33–49. [11]

Leiss, William, Stephen Kline, and Sut Jhally. 1986. *Social Communication in Advertising: Persons, Products, and Images of Well-Being.* Toronto: Methuen. [4]

Lemert, Edwin M., 1951. *Human Deviance, Social Problems, and Social Control.* New York: McGraw-Hill. [6]

Lenski, Gerhard E. 1966. *Power and Privilege: A Theory of Social Stratification.* New York: McGraw-Hill. [7]

Lenski, Gerhard E., Jean Lenski, and Patrick Nolan. 1991. *Human Societies: An Introduction to Macrosociology.* New York: McGraw-Hill. [7, 9, 17]

Lenssen, Nicholas. 1995. Coal use remains flat. In L.R. Brown, N. Lenssen, and H. Kane, *Vital Signs, 1995* (pp. 50–51). New York: Norton. [18]

Lerman, Lisa G., and Naomi R. Cahn. 1991. Legal issues in violence towards adults. In Robert T. Ammerman and Michael Gersen, Eds. *Case Studies in Family Violence* (pp. 73–85). New York: Plenum Press. [11]

LeVay, Simon. 1991. A difference in hypothalmic structure between heterosexual and homosexual men. *Science,* 253:1034–1037. [5]

Levin, Jack, and William C. Levin. 1980. *Ageism.* Belmont, MA: Wadsworth. [10]

Levine, Daniel H. 1995. On premature reports of the death of liberation theology. *Review of Politics,* 57(1):105–131. [13]

Levinson, Daniel J., et al. 1978. *The Seasons of a Man's Life.* New York: Knopf. [10]

Levinson, Stephen C. 1983. *Pragmatics.* New York: Cambridge University Press. [4]

Levitas, Mitchel. 1990. Homelessness in America. *New York Times Magazine* (June 10):45. [7]

Levitt, Jane. 1986. The corporation of health care. In S. Jonas, Ed., *Health Care Delivery in the United States.* New York: Springer. [14]

Levy, Frank. 1988. *Dollars and Dreams: The Changing American Income Distribution.* New York: W. W. Norton. [12]

Levy, G.D. 1989. Relations among aspects of children's social environments, gender schematization, gender role knowledge, and flexibility. *Sex Roles,* 21:803–823. [5]

Lewin, Miriam P., and Lilli M. Tragos. 1987. Has the feminist movement influenced adolescent sex role attitudes? A reassessment after a quarter century. *Sex Roles,* 16(3/4):125–135. [9]

Lewin, Tamar. 1994. So now we know what Americans do in bed. So? *New York Times* (October 9):E3. [3]

Lewin, Tamar. 1995. Who decides who will die? Even within states, it varies. *New York Times* (February 23):A1, B6. [6]

Lewis, Anne C. 1995. Changing views of parent involvement. *Phi Delta Kappan,* 76(6, February). [12]

Lewis, Catherine C. 1989. Cooperation and control in Japanese nursery schools. In James J. Shields, Jr., Ed., *Japanese Schooling* (pp. 28–44). University Park: Pennsylvania State University Press. [5]

Leyerle, Betty. 1984. *Moving and Shaking American Medicine: The Structure of a Socioeconomic Transformation,* Westport, CT: Greenwood Press. [14]

Lieberson, Stanley. 1961. A societal theory of race relations. *American Sociological Review,* 26:902–910. [8]

Lieberson, Stanley. 1980. *A Piece of the Pie: Black and White Immigrants Since 1880.* Berkeley: University of California Press. [7]

Lienesch, Michael. 1993. *Redeeming America: Piety and Politics in the New Christian Right.* Chapel Hill, NC: University of North Carolina Press. [13]

Light, Donald W. 1986. Corporate medicine for profit. *Scientific American,* 255(6):38–45. [14]

Light, Donald W. 1988. Social control and the American health care system. In H.E. Freeman and S. Levine, Eds., *Handbook of Medical Sociology,* 4th ed. Englewood Cliffs, NJ: Prentice Hall. [14]

Lii, Jane H. 1995. Week in sweatshop reveals grim conspiracy of the poor. *New York Times* (March 12):1, 16. [15]

Lillard, Lee A., and Linda J. Waite. 1995. Til death do us part: Marital disruption and mortality. *American Journal of Sociology,* 100(5, March):1131–1156. [11]

Lincoln, Alan Jay, and Murray A. Straus. 1985. *Crime and the Family.* Springfield, IL: Charles C. Thomas. [11]

Linton, Ralph. 1947. *The Study of Man.* New York: Appleton Century-Crofts. [4]

Lipovetsky, Gilles. 1994. *The Empire of Fashion: Dressing Modern Democracy.* Princeton, NJ: Princeton University Press. [4]

Lipset, Seymour Martin. 1963. *Political Man.* New York: Doubleday/Anchor. [16]

Lipset, Seymour Martin. 1981. *Political Man,* 2d ed. Chicago: University of Chicago Press. [16]

Lipset, Seymour Martin. 1990. *Continental Divide: The Values and Institutions of the United States and Canada.* New York: Routledge. [13]

Lipset, Seymour Martin. 1995. Malaise and resiliency in America. *Journal of Democracy,* 6(3, July):4–18. [16]

Lockwood, Charles, and Christopher B. Leinberger. 1988. Los Angeles comes of age. *Atlantic Monthly,* 261(1, January):31–56. [19]

Logan, Charles H. 1985. Incarceration, Inc.: The Privatization of Prisons. Paper presented at the Society for Study of Social Problems annual meeting, Washington, DC, August 23–26. [6]

Logan, J.R., and H.L. Molotch. 1987. *Urban Fortunes: The Political Economy of Place.* Berkeley: University of California Press. [19]

Longman, Phillip. 1987. *Born to Pay: The New Politics of Aging in America.* Boston: Houghton Mifflin. [10]

Loomis, Laura Spencer, and Alan Booth. 1995. Multigenerational caregiving and well-being: The myth of the beleaguered sandwich generation. *Journal of Family Issues,* 16(2, March):131–148. [11]

Lorber, Judith. 1994. *Paradoxes of Gender.* New Haven, CT: Yale University Press. [9]

Lotspeich, Richard. 1995. Crime in the transition economies. *Europe-Asia Studies,* 47(4, June):555–590. [15]

Lowenthal, Marjorie F., Majda Thurnher, and David Chiriboga. 1975. *Four Stages of Life.* San Francisco: Jossey-Bass. [10]

Luckmann, Thomas. 1967. *The Invisible Religion.* New York: Macmillan. [13]

Luhmann, Niklas. 1986. *Love as Passion.* Cambridge, MA: Harvard University Press. [11]

Luker, Kristin. 1984. *Abortion and the Politics of Motherhood.* Berkeley: University of California Press. [20]

Lyons, Paul. 1994. *Class of '66: Living in Suburban Middle America.* Philadelphia: Temple University Press. [10]

Lyotard, Jean-Francois. 1984. *Postmodernism Explained.* Minneapolis: University of Minnesota Press. [4]

Lystra, Karen. 1989. *Searching the Heart: Women, Men, and Romantic Love in Nineteenth-Century America.* New York: Oxford University Press. [3]

Lytton, Hugh, and David M. Romney. 1991. Parents differential socialization of boys and girls. A meta-analysis. *Psychological Bulletin,* 109(2):267–296. [5]

Maccoby, Eleanor E., and Carol N. Jacklin. 1974. *The Psychology of Sex Differences.* Stanford, CA: Stanford University Press. [9]

Machung, Anne. 1989. Talking career, thinking job: Gender differences in career and family expectations of Berkeley seniors. *Feminist Studies,* 15(1, Spring):35–58. [9]

Macunovich, Diane J., Richard A. Easterlin, Christine M. Schaeffer, and Eileen M. Crimmons. 1995. Echoes of the baby boom and bust: Recent and prospective changes in living alone among elderly widows in the United States. *Demography,* 32(1, February):17–28. **[10]**

Madan, T.N. 1989. Religion in India. *Daedalus,* 118(4, Fall):115–146. **[13]**

Magdoff, Harry. 1982. Imperialism: A historical survey. In Hamza Alavi and Teodor Shanin, Eds., *Introduction to the Sociology of "Developing Societies"* (pp. 11–28). New York: Monthly Review Press. **[17]**

Mahler, Halfdan. 1980. People. *Scientific American,* 243 (September):67–77. **[14]**

Mahler, Halfdan. 1981. The meaning of health for all by the year 2000. *World Health Forum,* 2:5–22. **[14]**

Mahmood, Cynthia Keppley. 1989. Sikh rebellion and the Hindu concept of order. *Asian Survey,* 29(3, March):327–340. **[13]**

Maines, David R., and Monica J. Hardesty. 1987. Temporality and gender: Young adults' career choices and family plans. *Social Forces,* 66:102–120. **[9]**

Makadon, Harvey, George Seage, Kenneth Thorpe, and Harvey Fineberg. 1990. Paying the medical cost of the HIV epidemic: A review of policy options. *Journal of Acquired Immune Deficiency Syndromes,* 3:123–133. **[14]**

Malik, Yogendra K., and Dhirendra K. Vajpeyi. 1989. The rise of Hindu militancy: India's secular democracy at risk. *Asian Survey,* 29(3, March):308–325. **[13]**

Mann, Dale. 1986. Can we help dropouts: Thinking about the undoable. *Teachers College Record,* 87(3):307–323. **[12]**

Mann, Michael. 1986. *The Sources of Social Power Vol. 1: Power from the Beginning to 1760 A.D.* New York: Cambridge University Press. **[16]**

Mann, Michael. 1993. *The Sources of Social Power. Vol. II: The Rise of Classes and Nation-States, 1760–1914.* New York: Cambridge University Press. **[16]**

Manno, Bruno V. 1995. The new school wars: Battles over outcome-based education. *Phi Delta Kappan,* 76(9, May):720–726. **[12]**

Mansfield, Edward D., and Jack Snyder. 1995. Democratization and war. *Foreign Affairs,* 74(3, May/June):79–97. **[16]**

Mansfield, Phyllis Kernoff, et al. 1991. The job climate for women in traditionally male blue-collar occupations. *Sex Roles,* 25(1/2):63–79. **[9]**

Manzo, Kathleen Kennedy. 1994. SAT scores continue recent trends. *Black Issues in Higher Education,* 11(14, September 8). **[12]**

Maranto, Gina. 1995. Delayed childbearing. *Atlantic Monthly,* 275(6, June):55–66. **[1]**

Marcos, Subcomandante. 1994. Statement quoted in *InterAmerican Trade Monitor.* 3:2 (January 10). **[17]**

Marger, Martin N. 1991. *Race and Ethnic Relations: American and Global Perspectives.* Belmont, CA: Wadsworth. **[4]**

Margolis, Richard J. 1990. *Risking Old Age in America.* Boulder, CO: Westview. **[10]**

Marks, Jonathan. 1994. Black, white, other. *Natural History,* (December):32–35. **[8]**

Marks, Stephen R. 1994. Intimacy in the public realm: The case of co-workers. *Social Forces,* 72(3, March):843–858. **[3]**

Markusen, Ann R., and Michael B. Teitz. 1985. The world of small business: Turbulence and survival. In *Small Firms in Regional Economic Development: Britain, Ireland, and the United States,* (pp. 193–218). Cambridge, England: Cambridge University Press. **[15]**

Marmor, Theodore R. 1994. *Understanding Health Care Reform.* New Haven, CT: Yale University Press. **[14]**

Marsden, George M. 1990. Defining American fundamentalism. In Norman J. Cohen, Ed., *The Fundamentalist Phenomenon: A View from Within, a Response from Without* (pp. 22–37). Grand Rapids, MI: Eerdmans. **[13]**

Marshall, Gordon. 1982. *In Search of the Spirit of Capitalism: An Essay on Max Weber's Protestant Ethic Thesis.* New York: Columbia University Press. **[13]**

Marshall, Patrick G. 1990. Setting limits on medical care. *Congressional Quarterly's Editorial Research Reports,* 1(4):666–678. **[14]**

Marshall, Susan E. 1985. Ladies against women: Mobilization dilemmas of anti-feminist movements. *Social Problems,* 32(4):348–362. **[20]**

Martin, Teresa Castro, and Larry L. Bumpass. 1989. Recent trends in marital disruption. *Demography,* 26(February):37–51. **[11]**

Marty, Martin E. 1985. *Pilgrims in Their Own Land.* Second ed. New York: Penguin Books. **[13]**

Marty, Martin E. 1991. Two years that shook the world of religion. *Encyclopedia Britannica, 1991 Book of the Year.* Chicago. **[13]**

Marx, Gary, and Doug McAdam. 1994. *Collective Behavior and Social Movements: Process and Structure.* Englewood Cliffs, NJ: Prentice Hall. **[19]**

Marx, Karl. 1852/1979. The eighteenth brumaire of Louis Bonaparte. In *Collected Works,* Vol. 11 (pp. 99–197). London: Lawrence and Wishart. **[1]**

Marx, Karl. 1867/1976. *Capital,* Vol. 1. B. Fowkes (Trans.). Harmondsworth, England: Penguin. **[1, 7, 15, 18]**

Marx, Karl, and Friedrich Engels. 1848/1976. Manifesto of the Communist Party. In *Collected Works,* Vol. 6. London: Lawrence and Wishart. **[15]**

Marx, Karl, and Friedrich Engels. 1848/1967. *Communist Manifesto.* New York: Pantheon. **[7]**

Masse, Michelle A., and Karen Rosenblum. 1988. Male and female created they them: The depictions of gender in the advertising of traditional women's and men's magazines. *Women's Studies International Forum.* 11(2):127–144. **[5]**

Massey, Douglas S., and Nancy A. Denton. 1992. *American Apartheid: Segregation and the Making of the American Underclass.* Cambridge, MA: Harvard University Press. **[8]**

Massey, Douglas S., and Mitchell L. Eggers. 1990. The ecology of inequality: Minorities and concentration of poverty, 1970–1980. *American Journal of Sociology,* 96(5, March): 1153–1188. **[8]**

Massey, Douglas S., Andrew B. Gross, and Mitchell L. Eggers. 1991. Segregation, the concentration of poverty, and the life chances of individuals. *Social Science Research,* 20:397–420. **[7]**

Mayhew. 1978. **[16]**

McAdam, Doug. 1982. *Political Process and the Development of Black Insurgency.* Chicago: University of Chicago Press. **[20]**

McAdam, Doug. 1986. Recruitment to high-risk activism: The case of freedom summer. *American Journal of Sociology,* 92, 1(July):64–90. **[20]**

McAdam, Doug. 1989. The biographical consequences of activism. *American Sociological Review,* 54(October):744–760. **[20]**

McAdam, Doug, John D. McCarthy, and Mayer N. Zald. 1988. Social Movements. In N.J. Smelser, Ed., *Handbook of Sociology* (pp. 695–738). Beverly Hills, CA: Sage. **[20]**

McCarthy, John, and Mayer Zald. 1973. *The Trend of Social Movements.* Morristown, NJ: General Learning. **[20]**

McCarthy, John D., and Mayer N. Zald. 1977. Resource mobilization and social movements: A partial theory. *American Journal of Sociology,* 82:1212–1214. **[20]**

McCarthy, Paul. 1989. Ageless sex. *Psychology Today,* 23(March):62. **[10]**

McDowall, David, and Alan J. Lizotte. 1993. In C. Calhoun and G. Ritzer, Eds., *Social Problems.* New York: McGraw-Hill/Primus. **[6]**

McGuire, Jacqueline. 1988. Gender stereotypes of parents with two-year-olds and beliefs about gender differences in behavior. *Sex Roles,* 19(3/4):233–240. **[5]**

McKeegan, Michele. 1992. *Abortion Politics: Mutiny in the Ranks of the Right.* New York: Free Press. **[20]**

McLanahan, Sara, and Karen Booth. 1989. Mother-only families: Problems, prospect, and politics. *Journal of Marriage and the Family,* 51(August):557–580. **[11]**

McLennan, Gregor. 1995. *Pluralism.* Minneapolis: University of Minnesota Press. **[16]**

McNeill, William H. 1982. *The Pursuit of Power.* Chicago: University of Chicago Press. **[16]**

Mead, George Herbert. 1934. *Mind, Self and Society.* Chicago: University of Chicago Press. [1, 3, 5, 8]

Mead, Margaret. 1928/1968. *Coming of Age in Samoa.* New York: Morrow. [9]

Mead, Margaret. 1935/1963. *Sex and Temperament in Three Primitive Societies.* New York: Morrow. [9]

Medalia, Nehum Z., and Otto N. Larson. 1958. Diffusion and belief in a collective delusion: The Seattle windshield pitting epidemic. *American Sociological Review,* 23:221–232. [20]

Melucci, Alberto. 1989. *Nomads of the Present.* Philadelphia: Temple University Press. [20]

Mensh, Elaine, and Harry Mensh. 1991. *The IQ Mythology: Class, Race, Gender, and Inequality.* Carbondale, IL: Southern Illinois University Press. [12]

Merina, Victoria, and John Mitchell. 1992. Opportunists, criminals get blame and riots. *Los Angeles Times* (May 1):A1, 12. [20]

Merton, Robert K. 1957. *Social Theory and Social Structures.* New York: Free Press. [8]

Merton, Robert K. 1968a. *Social Theory and Social Structure.* New York: Free Press. [1, 3, 6, 8, 12]

Merton, Robert K. 1968b. Social Problems and social theory. In R. Merton and R. Nisbet, Eds., *Contemporary Social Problems* (p. 447). New York: Harcourt, Brace and World. [8, 12]

Michels, Robert. 1915/1949. *First Lectures in Political Science.* A. de Grazia (Trans.). Minneapolis: University of Minnesota Press. [16]

Mickelson, Roslyn Arlin, and Carol Axtell Ray. 1994. Fear of falling from grace: The middle class, downward mobility, and school desegregation. *Research in Sociology of Education and Socialization,* 10:207–238. [12]

Milgram, Stanley. 1970. The experience of living in cities. *Science* 167(March 13):1461–1468. [19]

Miller, Brent C., and Kristin A. Moore. 1990. Adolescent sexual behavior, pregnancy and parenting. *Journal of Marriage and the Family,* 52:1025–1044. [11]

Miller, E., and A.K. Rice. 1967. *Systems of Organization.* London: Travistock. [3]

Miller, Laura. 1995. Two aspects of Japanese and American co-worker interaction: Giving instructions and creating rapport. *Journal of Applied Behavioral Science,* 31(2, June):141–161. [3]

Miller, Louisa F., and Jeanne E. Moorman. 1989. Married-couple families with children. *Current Population Reports.* Special Studies, Series P-23, No. 162. Washington, DC: U.S. Government Printing Office. [11]

Mills, C. Wright. 1951. *White Collar.* New York: Oxford University Press. [15]

Mills, C. Wright. 1959/1970. *The Sociological Imagination.* New York: Pelican. [1]

Mills, C. Wright. 1959. *The Power Elite.* New York: Oxford University Press. [16]

Minnesota Department of Employee Affairs. 1989. In Sara M. Evans and Barbara J. Nelson. Comparable worth: The paradox of technocratic reform. *Feminist Studies.* 15:1. [9].

Mintz, Beth, and Michael Schwartz. 1981. Interlocking directorates and interest group formation. *American Sociological Review.* 46 (Dec.). [15]

Mintz, Beth, and Michael Schwartz. 1986. Capital flows and the process of financial hegemony. *Theory and Society,* 15(1–2):77–101. [15]

Mirowsky, John, and Catherine E. Ross. 1995. Sex differences in distress: Real or artifact? *American Sociological Review,* 60(June):449–468. [9]

Mishima, Yasuo. 1989. *The Mitsubishi: Its Challenge and Strategy.* Greenwich, CT: JAI Press. [3]

Moen, P. 1989. *Working Parents: Transformations in Gender Roles and Public Policies in Sweden.* Madison: University of Wisconsin Press. [9]

Moffett, George D. 1994. *Critical Masses: The Global Population Challenge.* New York: Viking. [18]

Moller, Lora C., Shelley Hymel, and Kenneth H. Rubin. 1992. Sex typing in play and popularity in middle childhood. *Sex Roles,* 26(7–8):331–353. [5]

Molotch, Harvey, and J.R. Logan. 1976. The city as a growth machine: Toward a political economy of space. *American Journal of Sociology,* 82(2):309–332. [19]

Monaghan, Peter. 1993a. Facing jail, a sociologist raises questions about a scholar's right to protect sources. *Chronicle of Higher Education* (April 7). [2]

Monaghan, Peter, 1993b. Sociologist is jailed for refusing to testify about research subject. *Chronicle of Higher Education* (May 26). [2]

Monaghan, Peter. 1993c. When the source is a suspect. *Science,* 261(July 16). [2]

Moody, Fred. 1995. *I Sing the Body Electric: A Year with Microsoft on the Multimedia Frontier.* New York: Viking. [3]

Moore, Barrington, Jr. 1978. *Injustice: The Social Bases of Obedience and Revolt.* White Plains, NY: Sharpe. [16]

Morgan, Leslie A. 1991. Economic security of older women. In B. Hess and E. Markson, Eds. *Growing Old in America,* 4th ed. New Brunswick, NJ: Transaction. [10]

Morganthau, Tom, and Mary Hager. 1992. Cutting through the gobbledygook. *Newsweek* (February 3):24–25. [14]

Morris, Aldon D. 1984. *The Origins of the Civil Rights Movement: Black Communities Organizing for Change.* New York: Free Press. [8, 20]

Morris, Robert, and Scott Bass. 1988. A new class in America. *Social Policy* (Spring):38–43. [10]

Morrison, Peter A., and Ira S. Lowry. 1994. A riot of color: The demographic setting. In Mark Baldassare, Ed., *The Los Angeles Riots.* Boulder, CO: Westview Press. [20]

Moseley, Christopher, and R. E. Asher. Eds. 1994. *Atlas of the World's Languages.* London: Routledge. [4]

Moskos, Charles. 1990. Army women. *Atlantic Monthly* (August):71–78. [9]

Mueller, Carol, and Thomas Dimieri. 1982. The structure of belief systems among contending ERA activists. *Social Forces,* 60:657–675. [20]

Murdock, George Peter. 1949. *Social Structure.* New York: Macmillan. [11]

Musgrove, Philip. 1987. The economic crisis and its impact on health and health care in Latin America and the Caribbean. *International Journal of Health Services,* 17(3):411–441. [14]

Myers, George C. 1990. Demography of aging. In R. Binstock and L. George, Eds., *Aging and the Social Sciences,* 3d ed. San Diego: Academic Press. [10]

Myrdal, Gunnar. 1944. *An American Dilemma.* New York: Harper & Row. [8]

Nasar, Sylvia. 1995. Older Americans cited in studies of national savings rate slump. *New York Times* (February 21):A1, D12. [10]

National Advisory Commission on Civil Disorders. 1968. *Report of the National Advisory Commission on Civil Disorders (Kerner Commission).* New York: Bantam. [20]

National Center for Health Statistics. 1994. Advance Report of Final Natality Statistics, 1992. *Monthly Vital Statistics Report,* 43(25, October). Hyattsville, MD: Public Health Service. [7]

National Center for Health Statistics. 1995a. Advance Report of Final Divorce Statistics, 1989 and 1990. *Monthly Vital Statistics Report,* 43(9, Supplement, March 22). Hyattsville, MD: Public Health Service. [11]

National Center for Health Statistics. 1995b (June). *Vital and Health Statistics: Births to Unmarried Mothers: United States, 1980–1992.* Series 21, No. 53. U.S. Department of Health and Human Services. [11]

National Educational Association (NEA). 1990. Academic Tracking. Report of the NEA's Executive Subcommittee on Tracking (June). [12]

National Housing Task Force. 1988. *A Decent Place to Live.* Washington, DC: National Housing Task Force. [7]

National Research Council. 1990. *AIDS: The Second Decade.* Washington, DC: National Academy Press. [14]

Natriello, Gary, Aaron M. Pallas, and Edward L. McDill. 1986. Taking stock: Renewing our research agenda on the causes and consequences of dropping out. *Teachers College Review,* 87(3):430–440. **[12]**

Neff, Robert. 1990. Mighty Mitsubishi is on the move. *Business Week* (September 24):98–101. **[3]**

Nelson, Candace, and Marta Tienda. 1985. The structuring of Hispanic ethnicity: Historical and contemporary perspectives. *Ethnic and Racial Studies,* 8(1, January):49–74. **[8]**

Neugarten, Bernice L., and Dail A. Neugarten. 1987. The changing meanings of age. *Psychology Today,* 21(5):29–33. **[10]**

Neustadter, Roger. 1993. Grow up! The devaluation and stigmatization of childhood as a threat to progress in contemporary social thought. *Sociological Focus,* 26(4, October):301–314. **[10]**

Newman, Dorothy K., Nancy J. Amidei, Betty L. Cater, Dawn Day, William J. Kruvant, and Jack S. Russell. 1978. *Protest, Politics, and Prosperity: Black Americans and White Institutions, 1940–1975.* New York: Pantheon. **[20]**

Newman, Graeme. 1976. *Comparative Deviance and Perception: Perception and Law in Six Cultures.* New York: Elsevier. **[6]**

Newman, Katherine S. 1993. *Declining Fortunes: The Withering of the American Dream.* New York: Basic Books. **[7]**

N'galy, Bosenge, and Robert Ryder. 1988. Epidemiology of HIV infection in Africa. *Journal of Acquired Immune Deficiency Syndromes,* 1:551–558. **[14]**

Nisbet, Robert, and Robert G. Perrin. 1977. *The Social Bond,* 2d ed. New York: Knopf. **[1]**

Nisbett, Richard. 1995. Race, IQ, and scientism. In Stephen Fraser, Ed., *The Bell Curve Wars,* (pp. 37–57). New York: Basic Books. **[5]**

Nock, Steven L. 1995. A comparison of marriages and cohabiting relationships. *Journal of Family Issues,* 16(1, January):53–76. **[11]**

Nord, Warren A. 1995. *Religion and American Education: Rethinking a National Dilemma.* Chapel Hill, NC: University of North Carolina Press. **[13]**

Novak, Michael, et al. 1993. *New Consensus on Family and Welfare.* Washington, D.C.: American Institute for Public Policy Research. **[7]**

Oakley, Ann. 1972. *Sex, Gender and Society.* London: Temple Smith. **[9]**

O'Connor, Brian P. 1995. Family and friend relationships among older and younger adults: Interaction motivation, mood, and quality. *International Journal of Aging and Human Development,* 40(1):9–29. **[3]**

O'Connor James. 1973. *The Fiscal Crisis of the State.* New York: St. Martin's Press. **[16]**

O'Connor, James. 1989. Uneven and combined development and ecological crisis: A theoretical introduction. *Race and Class,* 30(3, January–March):1–11. **[18]**

Offe, Claus. 1984. *Contradictions of the Welfare State.* J. Keane, Ed. Cambridge, MA: MIT Press. **[16]**

Offe, Claus. 1985. *Disorganized Capitalism: Contemporary Transformations of Work and Politics.* J. Keane (Trans.). Cambridge, MA: MIT Press. **[16]**

O'Hare, William P., Kenneth M. Pollard, Taynia L. Mann, and Mary M. Kent. 1991. African Americans in the 1990s. *Population Bulletin,* 46(1, July). **[8]**

Oka, Takashi. 1991. The anomalies of China's one-child policy. *Christian Science Monitor* (January 11):18. **[18]**

Okey, Ted N., and Philip A. Cusick. 1995. Dropping out: Another side of the story. *Educational Administration Quarterly,* 31(2):244–267. **[12]**

Okun, Lewis. 1986. *Woman Abuse.* Albany: State University of New York Press. **[11]**

Ole Saitoti, Tepilit, and Carol Beckwith. 1980. *Masai.* New York: Abrams. **[10]**

Oliver, Melvin L., and Thomas M. Shapiro. 1990. Wealth of a nation: A reassessment of asset inequality in America shows at least one third of households are asset-poor. *American Journal of Economics and Sociology,* 49(2, April):129–151. **[7]**

Olson, Laura Katz. 1994. Public policy and privatization: Long-term care in the United States. In Laura Katz Olson, Ed., *The Graying of the World: Who Will Care for the Frail Elderly?* (pp. 25–58). New York: Haworth Press. **[10]**

Olzak, Susan, Suzanne Shanahan, and Elizabeth West. 1994. School desegregation, interracial exposure, and antibusing activity in contemporary urban America. *American Journal of Sociology,* 100(1):196–241. **[12]**

Omi, Michael, and Howard Winant. 1994. *Racial Formation in the United States: From the 1960s to the 1990s,* 2d ed. New York: Routledge. **[8]**

O'Rand, Angela, and Margaret Krecker. 1990. Concepts of the life cycle. *Annual Review of Sociology,* 16:241–262. **[10]**

Orenstein, Peggy. 1994. *Schoolgirls: Young Women, Self-Esteem, and the Confidence Gap.* New York: Doubleday. **[5]**

Orenstein, Peggy. 1995. Looking for a donor to call Dad. *New York Times Magazine* (June 18):28–58 *passim.* **[1]**

Organization for Economic Cooperation and Development (OECD). 1990. *OECD Economic Surveys, USA, 1989/1990.* Paris: OECD. **[15]**

Orwell, George. 1951. *Down and Out in Paris and London.* London: Secker and Warburg. **[3]**

O'Shaughnessy, Nicholas J. 1990. *The Phenomenon of Political Marketing.* New York: St. Martin's Press. **[16]**

Osofsky, Gilbert. 1982. *The Making of a Ghetto.* New York: Harper & Row. **[19]**

Osterman, Paul. 1993. Why don't "they" work? Employment patterns in a high pressure economy. *Social Science Research,* 22:115–130. **[7]**

Ott, E. Marlies. 1989. Effects of the male–female ratio at work: Policewomen and male nurses. *Psychology of Women Quarterly,* 13:41–57. **[9]**

Ouchi, William G. 1981. *Theory Z.* Reading, MA: Addison-Wesley. **[3]**

Pace, Richard. 1993. First-time televiewing in Amazonia: Television acculturation in Gurupá, Brazil. *Ethnology,* 32(2, Spring):187–205. **[4]**

Paludi, Michele A., and Dominic F. Gullo. 1986. The effect of sex labels on adults' knowledge of infant development. *Sex Roles,* 16(1/2):19–30. **[5]**

Pampel, Fred C. 1994. Population, aging, class context, and age inequality in public spending. *American Journal of Sociology,* 100(1, July):153–195. **[10]**

Pampel, Fred C., and Melissa Hardy. 1994. Status maintenance and change during old age. *Social Forces,* 73(1, September): 289–314. **[10]**

Paradiso, Louis V., and Shauvan M. Wall. 1986. Children's perceptions of male and female principals and teachers. *Sex Roles,* 14(1/2):1–7. **[5]**

Parcel, Toby L., and Elizabeth G. Menaghan. 1994. Early parental work, family social capital, and early childhood outcomes. *American Journal of Sociology,* 99(4):972–1009. **[5]**

Park, Robert E., Ernest W. Burgess, and Roderick D. McKenzie, Eds. 1925. *The City,* Chicago: University of Chicago Press. **[8, 19]**

Parkin, Frank. 1976. *Marxism and Class Theory: A Bourgeois Critique.* New York: Columbia University Press. **[7]**

Parsons, Arthur S. 1989. The secular contribution to religious innovation: A case study of the Unification Church. *Sociological Analysis,* 50(3):209–227. **[13]**

Parsons, Talcott. 1959. The social class as a social system. Some of its functions in American society. *Harvard Educational Review,* 29(Fall):297–318. **[5, 12]**

Parsons, Talcott. 1960. *Structure and Process in Modern Societies.* New York: Free Press. **[1, 16]**

Passell, Peter. 1995a. The curse of natural resources: They can keep a country poor. *New York Times* (September 21):C2. **[17]**

Passell, Peter. 1995b. The wealth of nations: A "greener" approach turns the list upside down. *New York Times* (September 28): B-5, B12. **[17]**

Patterson, Orlando. 1994. Ecumenical America: Global culture and the American cosmos. *World Policy Journal,* 11(2, Summer):103–117. **[4]**

Patterson, Orlando. 1995. For whom the Bell curves. In Stephen Fraser, Ed., *The Bell Curve Wars*, (pp. 187–213). New York: Basic Books. **[5]**

Pavetti, LaDonna A. 1992. The Dynamics of Welfare and Work: Exploring the Process by Which Young Women Work Their Way Out of Welfare. Paper presented at the APPAM Annual Research Conference, October, Denver, CO. **[7]**

Pear, Robert. 1991. Hungry children put at 5.5 million. *New York Times* (March 27):A18. **[14]**

Pear, Robert. 1995. HMO's refusing emergency claims, hospitals assert. *New York Times* (July 9):A1. **[14]**

Pebley, Anne R., and David E. Bloom. 1982. Childless Americans. *American Demographics*, 4(January):18–21. **[11]**

Peck, Janice. 1993. *The Gods of Televangelism*. Cresskill, NJ: Hampton Press. **[13]**

Pena, Milagros. 1994. Liberation theology in Peru: An analysis of the role of intellectuals in social movements. *Journal for the Scientific Study of Religion*, 33(1):34–45. **[13]**

Pescosolido, Bernice A., and Robert Mendelsohn. 1986. Social causation or social construction of suicide? An investigation into the social organization of official rates. *American Sociological Review*, 51:80–101. **[2]**

Petersen, William. 1975. *Population*, 3d ed. New York: Macmillan. **[18]**

Petersilia, Joan, and Allan Abrahamse. 1994. A profile of those arrested. In Mark Baldassare, Ed., *The Los Angeles Riots*. Boulder, CO: Westview Press. **[20]**

Peterson, Ruth D., and Lauren J. Krivo. 1993. Racial segregation and black urban homicide. *Social Forces*, 71(4, June):1001–1026. **[6]**

Peterson, V. Spike, and Anne Sisson Runyan. 1993. *Global Gender Issues*. Boulder, CO: Westview Press. **[9]**

Phillips, David P. 1974. The influence of suggestion on suicide: Substantive and theoretical implications of the Werther effect. *American Sociological Review*, 39:340–354. **[2]**

Phillips, David P. 1986. The found experiment: A new technique for assessing the impact of mass media violence on real-world aggressive behavior. In G. Comstock, Ed., *Public Communication and Behavior*, Vol.1. San Diego: Academic Press. **[2]**

Phillips, David P., and Lundie L. Carstensen. 1986. Clustering of teenage suicides after television and news stories about suicide. *New England Journal of Medicine*, 315(September 11):685–689. **[2]**

Phillips, Kevin. 1991. *The Politics of Rich and Poor*. New York: Simon and Schuster. **[7]**

Piaget, Jean. 1926/1955. *The Language and Thought of the Child*. New York: New American Library. **[5]**

Pill, Cynthia J. 1990. Stepfamilies: Redefining the family. *Family Relations*, 36:186–193. **[11]**

Pillemer, Karl A. 1986. Risk factors in elder abuse: Results from a case-control study. In K.A. Pillemer and R.S. Wolf, Eds., *Elder Abuse: Conflict in the Family* (pp. 239–263). Dover, MA: Auburn House. **[11]**

Piller, Charles. 1994. Dreamnet. *Macworld*, (October):96–111. **[4]**

Pinchbeck, Ivy. 1930. *Women and the Industrial Revolution, 1750–1850*. London: Cass. **[9]**

Piscatori, James. 1994. Accounting for Islamic fundamentalisms. In Martin E. Marty and R. Scott Appleby, Eds., *Accounting for Fundamentalisms: The Dynamic Character of Movements* (pp. 361–373). Chicago: University of Chicago Press. **[13]**

Pittman, Karen. 1993. Teenage pregnancy. In Craig Calhoun and G. Ritzer, *Social Problems*. New York: McGraw-Hill. **[11]**

Piven, F.F., and R. Cloward. 1979. *Poor People's Movements*. New York: Vintage. **[20]**

Platt, Anne E. 1994. Why don't we stop tuberculosis? *World Watch* (July/August):31–34. **[14]**

Pletsch, Carl. 1992. *The Young Nietzche and the Idea of Genius*. New York: Free Press. **[4]**

Plotnick, Robert D. 1992. The effects of attitudes on teenage premarital pregnancy and its resolution. *American Sociological Review*, 57(December):800–811. **[11]**

Plotnick, Robert D. 1993. The effect of social policies on teenage pregnancy and childbearing. *Families in Society: The Journal of Contemporary Human Services*, 74(6, June):324–328. **[11]**

Podus, Deborah. 1996. Should churches be tax exempt? (. . . And how do you know a church when you see one?) In C. Calhoun and Ritzer, *Introduction to Social Problems*. New York: McGraw-Hill Primus. **[13]**

Polanyi, Karl. 1944. *The Great Transformation*. Boston: Beacon Press. **[17]**

Pollan, Stephen M., and Mark Levine. 1992. The graying Yuppie: Reality zaps the baby-boomers. *New York*, 25(10, March 9):29–37. **[10]**

Pomice, Diane, et al. *U.S. News and World Report*, January 13, 1992. p. 408. **[15]**

Pope, Liston. 1942. *Millhands and Preachers: A Study of Gastonia*. New Haven, CT: Yale University Press. **[13]**

Poponoe, David. 1990. Family decline in America. In D. Blankenhorn, S. Bayme, J.B. Elshtain, Eds., *Rebuilding the Nest: A New Commitment to the American Family* (Chapter 3, pp. 39–51). Milwaukee: Family Service America. **[11]**

Popowski, Slawomir, Grzegorz Lubczyk, Jerzy Haszczynski, and Barbara Sierszula. 1994. The New Capitalism's capitalists. *World Press Review*, 41(2, February):14–18. **[15]**

Population Bulletin. 1994. Immigration to the United States: Journey to an uncertain destiny. 49(2, September). **[8]**

Population Reference Bureau. 1994. World population data sheet. 1994. Washington, DC: Population Reference Bureau. **[14]**

Population Reference Bureau. 1995. World population data sheet. Washington, DC: Population Reference Bureau. **[18, 19]**

Portes, Alejandro, and Manuel Castells, Eds. 1989. *The Informal Sector*. Baltimore: Johns Hopkins University Press. **[17]**

Portes, Alejandro, and Rubén G. Rumbaut. 1990. *Immigrant America: A Portrait*. Berkeley: University of California Press. **[5]**

Postman, Neil. 1982. *The Disappearance of Childhood*. New York: Delacorte. **[10]**

Powell, Michael J. 1985. Developments in the regulations of lawyers: Competing segments, and market, client, and government controls. *Social Forces*, 64(2):281–305. **[15]**

Power, Thomas G., Hiroko Kobayashi-Winata, and Michelle L. Kelley. 1992. Childbearing patterns in Japan and the United States: A cluster analytic study. *International Journal of Behavioral Development*, 15(2):185–205. **[5]**

Presser, Harriet B. 1994. Employment schedules among dual-earner spouses and the division of household labor by gender. *American Sociological Review*, 59(June):348–364. **[9]**

Preston, Richard. 1994. *The Hot Zone*. New York: Random House. **[14]**

Price, David. 1986. *Bringing Back the Parties*. Washington, DC: Congressional Quarterly. **[16]**

Przeworski, Adam. 1985. *Capitalism and Social Democracy*. New York: Cambridge University Press. **[16]**

Przeworski, Adam. 1995. *Sustainable Democracy*. Cambridge, MA: Cambridge University Press. **[16]**

Public Agenda Foundation. 1990. *Regaining the Competitive Edge: Are We Up to the Job?* Booklet prepared for National Issues Forums Institute. Debuque, IO: Kendall/Hunt Publishing. **[15]**

Purdum, Todd S. 1995. Clinton asks rise in minimum wage. *New York Times*. (February 4):A1, A8. **[7]**

Putnam, Robert D. 1995. Bowling alone: America's declining social capital. *Journal of Democracy*. (January):65–78. **[16]**

Quadagno, Jill. 1986. Aging. In G. Ritzer, Ed., *Social Problems*, 2d ed. New York: Random House. **[10]**

Quigley, William. 1995. The minimum wage and the working poor. *America* (June 3):6–7. **[15]**

Quindlen, Anna. 1991. Women warriors. *New York Times* (February 3):E19. **[9]**

Quinn, Joseph F., and Richard V. Burkhauser. 1994. Retirement and labor force behavior of the elderly. In Linda G. Martin and Samuel H. Preston, Eds., *Demography of Aging*. (pp. 50–101). Washington: National Academy Press. **[10]**

Ragin, Charles. 1987. *Beyond Qualitative and Quantitative Approaches: Methods of Comparative Sociology*. Berkeley: University of California Press. **[2]**

Ramsoy, Natalie R. 1994. Non-marital cohabitation and change in norms: The case of Norway. *Acta Sociologica*, 37:23–37. **[11]**

Rawlins, William K. 1992. *Friendship Matters: Communication, Dialectics, and the Life Course*. New York: Aldine de Gruyter. **[3]**

Reddy, Marlita A., Ed. 1994. *Statistical Abstract of the World*. New York: Gale Research. **[18]**

Reed, Adolph Jr. 1995. Assault on affirmative action. *Progressive* (June):18–20. **[12]**

Reed, John Shelton. 1994. *One South*. Baton Rouge: Louisiana State University Press. **[8]**

Reich, Robert B. 1991. *The Work of Nations: Preparing Ourselves for 21st Century Capitalism*. New York: Knopf. **[15]**

Reich, Robert B. 1996. How to avoid these layoffs? *New York Times* (January 4):A21. **[3]**

Reinventing America. 1992. *Business Week*. Special Issue. **[8]**

Reiter, Laura. 1989. Sexual orientation, sexual identity, and the question of choice. *Clinical Social Work Journal*, 17(2). **[5]**

Relman, Arnold S. 1980. The new medical-industrial complex. *New England Journal of Medicine*, 303:963–970. **[14]**

Remick, Helen, and Ronnie Steinberg. 1984. Technical possibilities and political realities: Concluding remarks. In Helen Remick, Ed., *Comparable Worth and Wage Discrimination*. Philadelphia: Temple University Press. **[9]**

Rendon, Laura L., and Terri B. Mathews. 1989. Success of community college students: Current issues. *Educational and Urban Society*, 21(3):312–327. **[12]**

Repetti, Rena L. 1984. Determinants of children's sex stereotyping: Parental sex-role traits and television viewing. *Personality and Social Psychology Bulletin*, 10:456–468. **[5]**

Report on Minorities in Higher Education. 1988. Hearing before the Committee on Education and Labor, House of Representa-tives, September 13. Serial No. 100-92. Washington, DC: U.S. Government Printing Office. **[8]**

Reskin, Barbara F., and Irene Padavic. 1994. *Women and Men at Work*. Thousand Oaks, CA: Pine Forge Press. **[9]**

Reskin, Barbara F., and Patricia A. Roos. 1990. *Job Queues, Gender Queues: Explaining Women's Inroads into Male Occupations*. Philadelphia: Temple University Press. **[15]**

Resnick, Lauren B., and Katherine J. Nolan. 1995. Who's afraid of the big, bad test? In Diane Ravitch, Ed., *Debating the Future of American Education: Report of a Conference Sponsored by the Brown Center on Educational Policy at the Brookings Institute*. Washington, DC: Institute. **[12]**

Rhoads, Steven. 1993. *Incomparable Worth: Pay Equity Meets the Market*. Cambridge, England: Cambridge University Press. **[9]**

Rhode, Deborah L. 1990. Gender equality and employment policy. In Sara E. Rix, Ed., *The American Woman, 1990–1991: A Status Report* (pp. 170–200), Women's Research & Education Institute, New York: Norton. **[9]**

Rich, Dorothy. 1986. "The Parent Gap in Compensatory Education and How to Bridge It." *Designs for Compensatory Education: Conference Proceedings and Papers*, Washington, DC. June 16–18, p. 24.**[12]**

Riche, Martha Farnsworth. 1990. The boomerang age. *American Demographics*, 12:24–27. **[10]**

Richmond-Abbott, Marie. 1992. *Masculine and Feminine: Gender Roles Over the Life Cycle*. New York: McGraw-Hill. **[5, 9]**

Rick, Katherine, and John Forward. 1992. Acculturation and perceived integrational differences among Hmong youth. *Journal of Cross-Cultural Psychology*, 23(1):85–94. **[5]**

Ridgeway, Celia L., Joseph Berger, and LeRoy Smith. 1985. Nonverbal cues and status: An expectation status approach. *American Journal of Sociology*,90(5):955–978. **[3]**

Rieff, David. 1991. *Los Angeles: Capital of the Third World*. New York: Simon and Schuster. **[19]**

Rieff, David. 1993. A global culture? *World Policy Journal*, 10(4, Winter):73–81. **[4]**

Riley, Matilda W. 1987. On the significance of age in sociology. *American Sociological Review*, 52(February):1–14. **[10]**

Roberts, Sam. 1995. The greening of America's black middle class. *New York Times* (June 18):E1, E4. **[8]**

Robertson, Roland. 1992. *Globalization: Social Theory and Global Culture*. Newbury Park, CA: Sage. **[4]**

Robinson, Ann. 1990. Cooperation or exploitation? The argument against cooperative learning for talented students. *Journal for the Education of the Gifted* (Fall). **[12]**

Roethlisberger, F.J., and William J. Dickson (with H.A. Wright). 1939/1961. *Management and the Worker*. Cambridge, MA: Harvard University Press. **[2, 3]**

Roodman, David Malin. 1995. Global temperature rises again. In L.R. Brown, N. Lenssen, and H. Kane, *Vital Signs 1995* (pp. 64–65). New York: Norton. **[18]**

Rose, Arnold M. 1967. *The Power Structure*. New York: Oxford University Press. **[16, 20]**

Rose, Gerry B. 1982. *Outbreaks*. New York: Free Press. **[20]**

Rosen, B., and T. Jerdee. 1978. Perceived sex differences in managerial-ly relevant characteristics. *Sex Roles*, 4:837–843. **[9]**

Rosenfeld, Anne, and Elizabeth Stark. 1987. The prime of our lives. *Psychology Today* (May):62–72. **[10]**

Rosenfeld, Rachel A., and Kenneth I. Spenner. 1992. Occupational sex segregation and women's early career job shifts. *Work and Occupations*, 19(4, November):424–449. **[9]**

Rosnow, Ralph L., and Gary Alan Fine. 1976. *Rumor and Gossip: The Social Psychology of Hearsay*. New York: Elsevier. **[20]**

Rossi, Peter H. 1989. *Down and Out in America: The Origins of Homelessness*. Chicago: University of Chicago Press. **[7]**

Rostow, Walt Whitman. 1952. *The Process of Economic Growth*. New York: Norton. **[17]**

Rostow, Walt Whitman. 1990. *The Stages of Economic Growth: A Noncommunist Manifesto*, 3d ed. New York: Cambridge University Press. **[17]**

Roth, Guenther, and Wolfgang Schluchter. 1979. *Max Weber's Theory of History*. Berkeley: University of California Press. **[1]**

Rothschild, N. 1984. Small group affiliation as a mediating factor in the cultivation process. In G. Melischek, K.E. Rosengren, and J. Stappers, Eds., *Cultural Indicators: An International Symposium*. Vienna: Osterreichischen Akademie der Wissenschaften. **[5]**

Rougemont, Denis de. 1939/1990. *Amour l'occident. [Love in the Western World]*. Montgomery Belgion (Trans.). New York: Schocken. **[11]**

Rowdon, Maurice. 1970. *The Silver Age of Venice*. New York: Praeger. **[19]**

Roxborough, Ian. 1990. Theories of revolution: The evidence from Latin America. *L.S.E. Quarterly*, 3(2, June):99–121. **[15]**

Rubin, J.Z., F.J. Provenzano, and Z. Luria. 1974. The eye of the behold-er: Parents' views on sex and newborns. *American Journal of Orthopsychiatry*, 44:512–519. **[5]**

Rubin, Lillian, 1976. *Worlds of Pain: Life in the Working-Class Family*. New York: Basic Books. **[5]**.

Rubin, Rita, with Susan Headden. 1995. Physicians under fire. *U.S. News & World Report* (January 16). **[20]**

Rudé, George. 1964. *The Crowd in History: A Study of Popular Disturbances in France and England, 1730–1848*. New York: Wiley. **[20]**

Rudel, Thomas K. 1989. Population, development, and tropical defor-estation: A cross-national study. *Rural Sociology*, 54(3):327–338. **[18]**

Rueschemeyer, Dietrich. 1986. *Power and the Division of Labor*. Stanford, CA: Stanford University Press. **[16]**

Rueschemeyer, Dietrich, Evelyne Huber Stephens, and John D. Stephens. 1992. *Capitalist Development and Democracy*. Chicago: University of Chicago Press. **[17]**

Ruether, Rosemary Radford. 1992. A world on fire with faith. *New York Times Book Review* (January 26):10–11. **[13]**

Ruggles, Patricia. 1990. The poverty line—Too low for the 1990s. *New York Times* (April 26):A31. **[7]**

Ruggles, Steven. 1994a. The origins of African-American family structure. *American Sociological Review*, 59(February):136–151. **[11]**

Ruggles, Steven. 1994b. The transformation of American family structure. *American Historical Review*, 99(1,February):103–128. **[11]**

Rukeyser, William S. 1995. Let's do the hobble: The generation that won't go away. *Atlantic Monthly*, 276(1, July):16–18. **[10]**

Rumbaut, Rubén G. 1991. Passages to America: Perspectives on the new immigration. In Alan Wolfe, Ed., *America at Century's End* (pp. 208–224). Berkeley: University of California Press. **[8]**

Rupp, Leila J., and Verta Taylor. 1987. *Survival in the Doldrums: The American Women's Rights Movement, 1945 to the 1960s*. New York: Oxford University Press. **[20]**

Russell, Charles H. 1989. *Good News About Aging*. New York: Wiley. **[10]**

Russell, Louise B., and Carrie Lynn Manning. 1989. The effect of prospective payment on Medicare expenditures. *New England Journal of Medicine*, 320(7):439–444. **[14]**

Ryan, John C. 1991. Plywood vs. People in Sarawak. *World Watch*, 4(1, January–February):8–9. **[18]**

Ryan, Megan. 1995. CFC production plummeting. In L.R. Brown, N. Lenssen, and H. Kane, *Vital Signs 1995* (pp. 62–63). New York: Norton. **[18]**

Sabel, Charles. 1982. *Work and Politics: The Division of Labor in Industry.* Cambridge, England: Cambridge University Press. **[15]**

Sabini, John P., and Mary Silver. 1980. Destroying the innocent with a clear conscience: A sociopsychology of the holocaust. In J.E. Dinsdale, Ed., *Survivors, Victims, and Perpetrators: Essays in the Nazi Holocaust* (pp. 329–330). Washington, DC: Hemisphere. **[8]**

Sadik, Nafis, Ed. 1994. *Making a Difference: 25 Years of UNFPA Experiences*. New York: United Nations Population Fund. **[18]**

Sahlins, Marshall D. 1958. *Social Stratification in Polynesia*. Seattle: University of Washington Press. **[7]**

Salant, Jonathan D., and David S. Cloud. 1995. To the '94 victors go the fundraising spoils. *Congressional Quarterly Weekly Report*, 53(15, April 15):1055–1060. **[16]**

Salmore, Stephen A., and Barbara G. Salmore. 1985. *Candidates, Parties and Campaigns: Electoral Policies in America*. Washington, DC: Congressional Quarterly Press. **[16]**

Saluter, A.F. 1992. Marital Status and Living Arrangements: March 1992. U.S. Bureau of the Census, *Current Population Reports,* Series P20, No. 468. Washington, DC: U.S. Government Printing Office. **[10]**

Sampson, R.J., and J.H. Laub. 1990. Crime and deviance over the life course: The salience of adult social bonds. *American Sociological Quarterly*, 55(October):609–627. **[6]**

Sandys, Marla, and Edmund F. McGarrell. 1995. Attitudes toward capital punishment: Preference for the penalty or more acceptance. *Journal of Research in Crime and Delinquency*. 32:2 (May): 191–213. **[6]**

Sapiro, Virginia. 1991. Feminism: A generation later. *Annals of the American Academy of Political and Social Science*, 515(May):10–22. **[20]**

Scarr, Sandra, and R.A. Weinberg. 1986. The early childhood enterprise: Care and education of the young. *American Psychology*, 41:1140–1146. **[11]**

Schaefer, Richard T. 1990. *Racial and Ethnic Groups*. Fourth ed. Glenview, IL: Little, Brown and Co. **[8]**

Scheff, Thomas J., and Suzanne M. Retzinger. 1991. *Emotions and Violence: Shame and Rage in Destructive Conflicts*. Lexington, MA: Lexington Books. **[3]**

Schein, Edgar H. 1978. *Career Dynamics: Matching Individual and Organizational Needs*. Reading, MA: Addison-Wesley. **[5]**

Schell, Orville. 1989. *Discos and Democracy: China in the Throes of Reform*. New York: Anchor. **[4]**

Schiller, Bradley, R. 1994. Below-minimum-wage workers: Implications for minimum-wage models. *Quarterly Review of Economics and Finance*, 34(2, Summer):131–143. **[15]**

Schlesinger, Arthur, Jr. 1979. Crisis of the party system. *Wall Street Journal* (May 10):22. **[16]**

Schluchter, Wolfgang. 1979. *The Development of Occidental Rationalism: An Analysis of Max Weber's History*. Tubingen: J.C.B. Mohr. **[1]**

Schmalzbauer, John. 1993. Evangelicals in the new class: Class versus subcultural predictors of ideology. *Journal for the Scientific Study of Religion*, 32(4):330–342. **[13]**

Schudson, Michael. 1984. *Advertising: The Uneasy Persuasion*. New York: Basic Books. **[4]**

Schuman, Howard, and Stanley Presser. 1981. *Questions and Answers in Attitude Surveys*. New York: Academic Press. **[2]**

Schumpeter, Joseph A. 1942. *Capitalism, Socialism, and Democracy*. New York: Harper & Row. **[16]**

Schutz, Alfred. 1967. *The Phenomenology of the Social World*. George Walsh and Frederick Lehnert. Trans. Evanston, IL: Northwestern University Press. **[3]**

Schutz, Alfred, and Thomas Luckman. 1973. *Structures of the Life World*. London: Heinemann Educational Books. **[1]**

Schwartz, Gail Garfield, and William Neikirk. 1983. *The Work Revolution*. New York: Rawson Associates. **[15]**

Schwebel, Andrew I., Mark A. Fine, and Maureen A. Renner. 1991. A study of perceptions of the step-parent role. *Journal of Family Issues*, 12(1, March):43–57. **[11]**

Schwenk, F.N. 1992. Income and expenditures of older widowed, divorced, and never-married women who live alone. *Family Economics Review*, 5(1):2–8. **[10]**

Scott, James C. 1976. *The Moral Economy of the Peasant*. New Haven, CT: Yale University Press. **[17]**

Scott, James C. 1985. *Weapons of the Weak*. New Haven, CT: Yale University Press. **[8]**

Scott, James C. 1987. Resistance without protest and without organization. *Comparative Studies in Society and History*, 29. **[8]**

Scott, Janny, And Victor Zonana. 1990. AIDS conference ends on note of confidence. *Los Angeles Times* (June 25):A1. **[14]**

Scott, Joan W. 1986. Gender: A useful category of historical analysis. *American Historical Review*, 91(5):1053–1075. **[9]**

Scott, Peter Dale, and Jonathan Marshall. 1991. *Cocaine Politics: Drugs, Armies, and the CIA in Central America*. Berkeley: University of California Press. **[6]**

Sculley, John, with John A. Byrne. 1987. *Odyssey: Pepsi to Apple . . . A Journey of Adventure, Ideas, and the Future*. New York: Harper & Row. **[3]**

Secord, Paul F., and Carl W. Backman. 1974. *Social Psychology*, 2d ed. New York: McGraw-Hill. **[3]**

Segers, Mary C., Ed. 1990. *Church Polity and American Politics: Issues in Contemporary American Catholicism*. New York: Garland. **[13]**

Seidman, Steven. 1991. *Romantic Longings: Love in America, 1830–1980*. New York: Routledge. **[5]**

Seidman, Steven. 1994. *Contested Knowledge: Social Theory in the Postmodern Era*. Oxford, England: Blackwell. **[4]**

Seligman, Adam. 1993. *The Ideal of a Civil Society*. New York: Free Press. **[3]**

Sen, Amartya. 1990. *Disasters*. Cambridge, England: Cambridge University Press. **[17]**

Serbin, Lisa A., Kimberly K. Powlishta, and Judith Gulko. 1993. The development of sex typing in middle childhood. *Monographs of the Society for Research in Child Development*, 58(2):v-97. **[5]**

Sewell, William H., and Robert M. Hauser. 1976. Causes and consequences of higher education: Models of the status attainment process. In W.H. Sewell and R.M. Hauser, Eds., *Schooling and Achievement in American Society*. New York: Academic Press. **[7]**

Shanin Teodor. 1990. *Defining Peasants*. Oxford, England: Blackwell. **[17]**

Shank, Susan E., and Patricia M. Getz. 1986. Employment and unemployment: Developments in 1985. *Monthly Labor Review*, 109(2):3–12. **[15]**

Shaw, Clifford R. 1930. *The Jack-Roller*. Chicago: University of Chicago Press. **[6]**

Shaw, Clifford R., and Henry D. McKay. 1969. *Juvenile Delinquency and Urban Areas*. Chicago: University of Chicago Press. [6]

Shaywitz, Bennett A., Sally E. Shaywitz, Kenneth R. Pugh, R. Todd Constable, et al. 1995. Sex Differences in the Functional Organization of the Brain for Language. *Nature*, 373(6515, February):607–609. [9]

Sherman, Barry L., and Joseph R. Dominick. 1986. Violence and sex in music videos: TV and rock and roll. *Journal of Communication*, 36(Winter):79–93. [2]

Sherman, Julia. 1978. *Sex-Related Cognitive Differences*. Springfield, IL: Charles C. Thomas. [9]

Shirley, Edward G. 1995. Is Iran's present Algeria's future? *Foreign Affairs*, 74(3, May/June):28–44. [13]

Shlay, Anne B., and Peter H. Rossi. 1992. Social science research and contemporary studies of homelessness. *Annual Review of Sociology*, 18:129–160. [7]

Shmelev, N., and V. Popov. 1989. *The Turning Point: Revitalizing the Soviet Economy*. M.A. Brady (Trans.). New York: Doubleday. [15]

Shorter, Edward. 1975. *The Making of the Modern Family*. New York: Basic Books. [10]

Siegel, Judith M. 1995. Looking for Mr. Right? Older single women who become mothers. *Journal of Family Issues*, 16(2, March):194–211. [11]

Siegel, Karolynn, Frances Mesagno, Jin-Yi Chen, and Grace Christ. 1989. Factors distinguishing homosexual males practicing risky and safer sex. *Social Science and Medicine*, 28(6):561–569. [14]

Siegel, Larry J., Ed. 1990. *American Justice: Research of the National Institute of Justice*. St. Paul, MN: West Publishing. [6]

Sifry, Micah L. 1995. The third way. *Nation*, 260(25):907–908. [16]

Signorielli, Nancy. 1989. Television and conceptions about sex roles: Maintaining conventionality and the status quo. *Sex Roles*, 21(5/6):341–360. [5]

Signorielli, Nancy. 1991. *A Sourcebook on Children and Television*. New York: Greenwood Press. [5]

Signorielli, Nancy, and Margaret Lears. 1992. Children, television, and conceptions about chores: Attitudes and behaviors. *Sex Roles*, 27(3–4):157–170. [5]

Silverstein, Merril. 1995. Stability and change in temporal distance between the elderly and their children. *Demography*, 32(1, February):29–45. [10]

Silvestri, George T., and John M. Lukasiewicz. 1987. A look at occupational employment trends to the year 2000. *Monthly Labor Review* (September):46–63. [10]

Simmel, Georg. 1902a. Number of members as determining the sociological Form of the group I. *American Journal of Sociology*. 8:2 (July 1–46. [3]

Simmel, Georg. 1902b. Number of members as determining the sociological Form of the group II. *American Journal of Sociology*. 8:2. (Sept.) 158–196. [3]

Simmel, Georg. 1902–1903/1950. *The Sociology of Georg Simmel*. Kurt H. Wolff (Ed. and Trans.). Glencoe, IL: Free Press. [19]

Simmel, Georg. 1950. The metropolis and mental life. In Kurt Wolff, Ed. and Trans., *The Sociology of George Simmel* (pp. 409–424). New York: Free Press. [3]

Simon, Robin W., Donna Eder, and Cathy Evans. 1992. The development of feeling norms underlying romantic love among adolescent females. *Social Psychology Quarterly*, 55(1):29–46. [3]

Simpson, Richard L. 1985. Social control of occupations and work. *Annual Review of Sociology*, 11:415–436. [15]

Sjoberg, Gideon. 1960. *The Preindustrial City: Past and Present*. Peoria, IL: Free Press. [19]

Sklair, Leslie. 1995. *Sociology of the global system*, 2d ed. Baltimore: Johns Hopkins University Press. [17]

Skocpol, Theda. 1979. *States and Social Revolutions: A Comparative Analysis of France, Russia, and China*. New York: Cambridge University Press. [2, 20]

Skocpol, Theda. 1992. *Protecting Soldiers and Mothers: The Political Origins of Social Polity in the United States*. Cambridge, MA: Harvard University Press. [16]

Skolnick, Arlene. 1978. *The Intimate Environment: Exploring Marriage and the Family*, 2d ed. Boston: Little, Brown. [3]

Skolnick, Jerome H., and David H. Bayley. 1986. *The New Blue Line: Police Innovation in Six American Cities*. New York: Free Press. [6]

Slavin, Robert E. 1990. Achievement effects of ability grouping in secondary schools: A best-evidence synthesis. *Review of Educational Research*, 60(3):471–499. [12]

Smelser, Neil J. 1963. *Theory of Collective Behavior*. New York: Free Press. [20]

Smidt, Corwin. 1980. Civil religious orientations among elementary school children. *Sociological Analysis*, 41:24–40. [13]

Smil, Vacal. 1984. *The Bad Earth: Environmental Degradation in China*. Armonk, NY: Sharpe. [18]

Smil, Vacal. 1989. China's environmental morass. *Current History* (September):257–277. [18]

Smil, Vacal. 1990. Feeding China's people. *Current History* (September):257–277. [18]

Smith, Adam. 1776/1976. *The Wealth of Nations*. Chicago: University of Chicago Press. [1, 15]

Smith, Anthony. 1993. *National Identity*. Harmondworth, England: Penguin. [2]

Smith, Christian. 1994. The spirit and democracy: Base communities, Protestantism, and democratization in Latin America. *Sociology of Religion*, 55(2):119–143. [13]

Smith, Dorothy E. 1987. *The Everyday World as Problematic: A Feminist Sociology*. Boston: Northeastern University Press. [9]

Smith, Dorothy E. 1990. *The Conceptual Practices of Power: A Feminist Sociology of Knowledge*. Boston: Northeastern University Press. [9]

Smith, Dorothy. 1992. *The Everyday World as Problematic*. Boston: Northeastern University Press. [1]

Smith, M.G. 1974. Pre-industrial stratification systems. In *Corporations and Society*. London: Duckworth. [7]

Smith, M.G. 1991. Pluralism and social stratification. In Selwyn Ryan, Ed., *Social and Occupational Stratification in Contempo-rary Trinidad and Tobago* (pp. 3–35). St. Augustine, Trinidad: Institute of Social and Economic Research, University of the West Indies. [7]

Smith, Michael Peter. 1988. *City, State and Market: The Political Economy of Urban Society*. New York: Basil Blackwell. [19]

Smith, Michael Peter, and Joe R. Feagin, Eds. 1987. *The Capitalist City: Global Restructuring and Community Politics*. New York: Basil Blackwell. [19]

Smith, Thomas Spence. 1992. *Strong Interaction*. Chicago: University of Chicago Press. [3]

Snipp, C. Matthew. 1992. Sociological perspectives on American Indians. *Annual Review of Sociology*, 18:351–371. [8]

Snow, David A. and Leon Anderson. 1993. *Down on Their Luck: A Study of Homeless Street People*. Berkeley: University of California Press. [7]

Snow, David A., Susan G. Baker, Leon Anderson, and Michael Martin. 1986. The myth of pervasive mental illness among the homeless. *Social Problems*, 33(5):45. [14]

Snow, David A., Louis A. Zurcher, Jr., and Robert Peters. 1981. Victory celebrations as theater: A dramaturgical approach to crowd behavior. *Symbolic Interaction*, 4(1). [20]

Snow, Margaret Ellis, Carol Nagy Jacklin, and Eleanor E. Maccoby. 1983. Sex-of-child differences in father-child interactions at one year of age. *Child Development*, 54:227–232. [5]

Soares, Luiz. 1996. "Introduction" to UNESCO Conference on Multiculturalism, Globalization, and Identity. Rio de Janeiro, April 10–12, 1996. [17]

Soja, Edward W. 1989. *Postmodern Geographies: The Reassertion of Space in Critical Social Theory*. London: Verso. [19]

Soldo, Beth J., and Vicki A. Freedman. 1994. Care of the elderly: Division of labor among the family, market, and state. In Linda G. Martin and Samuel H. Preston, Eds., *Demography of Aging* (pp. 195–216). Washington: National Academy press. [10]

Somers, Margaret R., and Gloria D. Gibson. 1994. Reclaiming the epistemological "other": Narrative and the social construction of identity. In Craig Calhoun, Ed., *Social Theory and the Politics of Identity*. Oxford, England: Blackwell. [5]

Sorensen, Elaine. 1994. *Comparable Worth: Is It a Worthy Policy?* Princeton, NJ: Princeton University Press. [9]

Sorrentino, Constance. 1990. The changing family in international perspective. *Monthly Labor Review* (March):41–58. [9]

Sowell, Thomas. 1995. Ethnicity and IQ. In Stephen Fraser, Ed., *The Bell Curve Wars* (pp. 71–79). New York: Basic Books. [5]

Specht, David. 1989. A church and its neighborhood. *National Civic Review*, 78:456–64. [19]

Spencer, Herbert. 1974. *The Evolution of Society: Selections from Herbert Spencer's "Principles of Sociology."* Robert L. Carniero (Ed.). Chicago: University of Chicago Press. [7]

Spencer, Paul. 1988. *The Maasai of Matapato.* Bloomington: Indiana University Press. [6]

Spicer, Edward H. 1980. American Indians. In S. Thernstrom, Ed., *Harvard Encyclopedia of American Ethnic Groups.* Cambridge, MA: Harvard University Press. [8]

Spitze, Glenna, John R. Logan, Glenn Deane, and Suzanne Zerger. 1994. Adult children's divorce and intergenerational relationships. *Journal of Marriage and the Family*, 56(May):279–293. [11]

Splichal, Slavko, Andrew Calabrese, and Colin Sparks, Eds. 1994. *Information Society and Civil Society: Contemporary Perspectives on the Changing World Order.* West Lafayette, IN: Purdue University Press. [16]

Spragins, Ellyn E. 1995. Simon says, join us! *Newsweek* (June 19):55–58. [14]

Stack, Steven, and Jim Gunlack. 1992. The effect of country music on suicide. *Social Forces*, 7(1, September):211–218. [2]

Staggenborg, Suzanne. 1988. The consequences of professionalization and formalization in the pro-choice movement. *American Sociological Review*, 53(August):35–50. [20]

Stark, Rodney. 1984. The rise of a new world faith. *Review of Religious Research*, 26(1). [13]

Stark, Rodney, and William Sims Bainbridge. 1985. *The Future of Religion: Secularization, Revival and Cult Formation.* Berkeley: University of California Press. [13]

Starr, Paul. 1982. *The Social Transformation of American Medicine.* New York: Basic Books. [15]

Statham, Anne. 1987. The gender model revisited: Differences in the management styles of men and women. *Sex Roles*, 16(7/8):409–429. [9]

Statistical Abstract of the United States. 1994. U.S. Bureau of the Census. Washington, DC: U.S. Government Printing Office. [11, 12, 14]

Statistical Abstract of the United States. 1995. U.S. Bureau of the Census. Washington, DC: U.S. Government Printing Office. [8, 10, 12, 15]

Stearns, Linda Brewster. 1992. How America can best compete in a global economy. In C. Calhoun and G. Ritzer, Eds., *Social Problems.* New York: McGraw-Hill/Primus. [15]

Stearns, Peter, and Mark Knapp. 1993. Men and romantic love: Pinpointing a 20th-century change. *Journal of Social History* (Summer):769–795. [3]

Steinmetz, Suzanne K., and Murray A. Straus, Eds. 1974. *Violence in the Family.* New York: Harper & Row. [11]

Stern-Gillet, Suzanne. 1995. *Aristotle's Philosophy of Friendship.* Albany, NY: State University of New York Press. [3]

Sterngold, James. 1996. A 90's military-industrial complex. *New York Times* (January 21):p. E4. [16]

Steuerle, C. Eugene. 1994. Financing and administering health care. *Society*, 32(1, November–December):69–70. [14]

Stevenson, Harold W. 1995. What Is a Bad Kid? Answers of Adolescents and Their Mothers in Three Cultures. *Journal of Research on Adolescence*, 5(1):71–91. [12]

Stevenson, Harold W. 1992. Learning from Asian schools. *Scientific American* (December):70–76. [12]

Stewart, Edward C., and Milton J. Bennett. 1991. *American Cultural Patterns: A Cross-Cultural Perspective.* Yarmouth, ME: Intercultural Press [4]

Stoesz, David, and Howard Karger. 1991. The corporatisation of the United States welfare state. *Journal of Social Policy*, 20(1):157–171. [14]

Stoper, Emily. 1991. Women's work, women's movement: Taking stock. *Annals of the America Academy of Political and Social Science*, 515(May):151–162. [20]

Straus, Murray A., and Richard J. Gelles. 1986. Societal change and change in family violence from 1975 to 1985 as revealed by two national surveys. *Journal of Marriage and the Family*, 48(August):465–479. [11]

Sue, Stanley, and Sumie Okazaki. 1995. Asian American educational achievements: A phenomenon in search of an explanation. In D.T. Nakanishi and T.Y. Nishida, Eds., *The Asian American Educational Experience: A Sourcebook for Teachers* (Chapter 7). New York: Routledge. [8]

Sullivan, Harry Stack. 1953. *The Interpersonal Theory of Psychiatry.* New York: Norton. [5]

Summers, Gene F., and Kristi Branch. 1984. Economic development and community social change. *Annual Review of Sociology*, 10:141–166. [19]

Suransky, Valerie Polakow. 1982. *The Erosion of Childhood.* Chicago: University of Chicago Press. [10]

Suro, Roberto. 1990. Behind the census numbers, swirling nodes of movement. *New York Times* (September 16):E4. [18]

Sutherland, Edwin. 1949. *White Collar Crime.* New York: Dryden Press. [6]

Suttles, Gerald D. 1968. *The Social Order of the Slum.* Chicago: University of Chicago Press. [19]

Suzuki, Bob H. 1995. Education and socialization of Asian Americans: A revisionist analysis of the "model minority" thesis. In D.T. Nakanishi and T.Y. Nishida, Eds., *The Asian American Educational Experience: A Sourcebook for Teachers* (Chapter 6). New York: Routledge. [8]

Swanson, Guy E. 1974. *The Birth of the Gods.* Ann Arbor: University of Michigan Press. [13]

Swidler, Ann. 1986. Culture in action: Symbols and strategies. *American Sociological Review.* 51:273–286. [4]

Taeuber, Karl. 1990. Desegregation of public school districts. *Phi Delta Kappan*, 72(1):18–40. [12]

Tang, Joyce. 1995. Differences in the process of self-employment among whites, blacks, and Asians: The case of scientists and engineers. *Sociological Perspectives*, 28(2):273–309. [15]

Tannen, Deborah. 1990. *You Just Don't Understand: Women and Men in Conversation.* New York: Morrow. [3]

Tannen, Deborah. 1994. *Gender and Discourse.* New York: Oxford University Press. [1, 3]

Tausky, Curt. 1984. *Work and Society: An Introduction to Industrial Sociology.* Itasca, IL: Peacock. [15]

Tavris, Carol, and Carole Wade. 1984. *The Longest War: Sex Difference in Perspective*, 2d ed. San Diego: Harcourt Brace Jovanovich. [9]

Taylor, Charles. 1985. Legitimation crisis? In *Philosophy and the Sciences of Man.* New York: Cambridge University Press. [1, 16]

Taylor, Charles. 1989. *Sources of the Self.* Cambridge, MA: Harvard University Press. [3]

Taylor, Charles. 1993. *The Ethics of Authenticity.* Cambridge, MA: Harvard University Press. [3]

Taylor, Charles. 1995. *Multiculturalism and the Politics of Recognition*, revised & expanded ed. Princeton, NJ: Princeton University Press. [1, 8, 20]

Taylor, Marylee. 1995. White backlash to workplace affirmative action: Peril or myth? *Social Forces.* 73:4 (June) 1385–1414. [8]

Taylor, Robert Joseph, Linda M. Chatters, M. Belinda Tucker, and Edith Lewis. 1990. Developments in research on black families: A decade review. *Journal of Marriage and the Family*, 52(November):993–1014. [11]

Teitelbaum, Michael S. 1975. Relevance of demographic transition theory for developing countries. *Science*, 188:420–425. [18]

Teixeira, R. 1988. Will the real non-voters please stand up? *Public Opinion* (July–August):41–59. [16]

Telles, Edward E., and Edward Murguia. 1990. Phenotypic discrimination and income differences among Mexican Americans. *Social Science Quarterly,* 71(4, December):682–696. **[8]**

Terkel, Studs. 1972. *Working: People Talk About What They Do All Day and How They Feel About It.* New York: Pantheon. **[15]**

Testa, Mark, and Marilyn Krogh. 1989. The Effect of Employment on Marriage Among Black Males in Inner-City Chicago. Unpublished manuscript, University of Chicago. **[7]**

Thomas, G.M., and J. Meyer. 1984. The expansion of the state. *Annual Review of Sociology,* 10:461–482. **[16]**

Thomas, William I., and Dorothy Swaine Thomas. 1928. *The Child in America.* New York: Knopf. **[1]**

Thomlinson, Ralph. 1976. *Population Dynamics,* 2d ed. New York: Random House. **[18]**

Thompson, E.P. 1968. *The Making of the English Working Class.* Harmondsworth, England: Penguin. **[9, 15]**

Thompson, E.P. 1971. The moral economy of the English crowd in the eighteenth century. *Past and Present,* 50:76–136. **[20]**

Thorne, Barrie. 1993. *Gender Play: Girls and Boys in School.* New Brunswick, NJ: Rutgers University Press. **[5, 9]**

Thornton, Arland. 1989. Cohabitation and marriage in the 1980s. *Demography,* 25:497–508. **[11]**

Thurow, Lester C. 1980. *The Zero-Sum Society: Distribution and Possibilities for Change.* New York: Basic Books. **[16]**

Tien, H. Yuan. 1991. The new census of China. *Population Today* (January):6–8. **[18]**

Tierney, Kathleen, J. 1994. Property damage and violence: A collective behavior analysis. In Mark Baldassare, Ed., *The Los Angeles Riots.* Boulder, CO: Westview Press. **[20]**

Tilly, Charles. 1978. *From Mobilization to Revolution.* Reading, MA: Addison-Wesley. **[20]**

Tilly, Charles. 1986. *The Contentious French.* Cambridge, MA: Belknap Press. **[20]**

Time. 1995. Common cause. The ten most generous interest groups. (August 14) p. 20. **[16]**

Tipton, Steve M. 1982. *Getting Saved from the Sixties: Moral Meaning in Conversion and Cultural Change.* Berkeley: University of California Press. **[13]**

Tobin, Joseph J., David Y.H. Wu, and Dana H. Davidson. 1989. *Preschool in Three Cultures: Japan, China, and the United States.* New Haven, CT: Yale University Press. **[11]**

Tordoroff, Istvan. 1994. *We and Others.* Cambridge, MA: Harvard University Press. **[8]**

Tönnies, Ferdinand, 1887/1963. *Gemeinschaft and Gesellschaft.* C.P. Loomis (Trans.). New York: American Book. **[19]**

Touraine, Alain. 1981. *The Voice and the Eye.* Cambridge, England: Cambridge University Press. **[20]**

Touraine, Alain. 1988. *The Return of the Actor.* Minneapolis: University of Minnesota Press. **[20]**

Traub, James. 1994. Can separate be equal? *Harper's* (June):36–47. **[12]**

Treiman, D.J., and H.I. Hartmann Eds. 1981. *Women, Work, and Wages: Equal Pay for Jobs of Equal Value* (Committee on Occupational Classification and Analysis, National Research Council). Washington, DC: National Academy of Sciences. **[9]**

Troeltsch, Ernst. 1931. *The Social Teaching of the Christian Churches.* New York: Macmillan. **[13]**

Tucker, Kenneth. 1991. What's new about new social movements. *Theory, Culture, and Society.* 8:2 (May):75–98. **[20]**

Turner, Jeffrey S., and Donald B. Helms. 1988. *Marriage and Family.* New York: Harcourt Brace Jovanovich. **[11]**

Turner, Ralph H. 1990. Role change. *Annual Review of Sociology,* 16:87–110. **[3]**

Turner, Ralph H., and Lewis M. Killian. 1972. *Collective Behavior,* 2d ed. Englewood Cliffs, NJ: Prentice Hall. **[20]**

Turner, Victor W. 1970. *The Ritual Process.* Chicago: Aldine. **[13]**

Udesky, Laurie. 1994. Sweatshops behind the labels: The "social responsibility" gap. *Nation,* 258(19, May 16):665–669. **[15]**

Udry, J.R., and John Billy. 1987. Initiation of coitus in early adolescence. *American Sociology Review,* 52:841–855. **[10]**

United Nations. 1991. *The World's Women, 1970–1990: Trends and Statistics.* New York: United Nations. **[9, 18]**

U.N. Commission on Transnational Corporations. 1978. Trans-national corporations in world development: A re-examination. Fourth session. New York (May 15–26). **[15]**

United Nations Development Programme. 1990. *Human Development Report.* New York: Oxford University Press. **[17]**

United Nations Development Programme. 1992. *Human Development Report 1992.* New York: Oxford University Press. **[17]**

United Nations Development Programme. 1993. *Human Development Report 1993.* New York: Oxford University Press. **[17]**

United Nations Development Programme. 1995. *Human Development Report 1995.* New York: Oxford University Press. **[17]**

U.N. Population Fund. 1993. *The State of the World's Population, 1993.* New York: United Nations Family Planning Association. **[18]**

U.N. Population Fund. 1995. *Concise Report on the World Population Situation in 1995.* New York: United Nations. **[18]**

U.S. Bureau of the Census. 1954. *Vital Statistics of the United States,* vol. 1. Washington, DC.: National Vital Statistics Division. **[12]**

U.S. Bureau of the Census. 1976. *Historical Statistics of the United States, Colonial Times to 1970.* Bicentennial Edition, part 1. Washington, DC: U.S. Government Printing Office. **[17]**

U.S. Bureau of the Census. 1983. *Statistical Abstract of the United States, 1982–83.* Washington, DC: U.S. Government Printing Office. **[18]**

U.S. Bureau of the Census. 1987. *Statistical Abstract of the United States.* Washington, DC: U.S. Government Printing Office. **[10]**

U.S. Bureau of the Census. 1990a. *Current Population Reports.* Series P-20. Washington, DC: U.S. Government Printing Office. **[16]**

U.S. Bureau of the Census. 1990b. Money Income of Households, Families, and Persons in the United States: 1990. *Current Population Reports.* Series P-60, No. 174. Washington, DC: U.S. Government Printing Office. **[8]**

U.S. Bureau of the Census. 1990c. *Statistical Abstract of the United States.* Washington, DC: U.S. Government Printing Office. **[10, 15]**

U.S. Bureau of the Census. 1994a. The Hispanic Population in the United States: March 1993. *Current Population Reports.* Series P-20, No. 475. Washington, DC: U.S. Government Printing Office. **[8]**

U.S. Bureau of the Census. 1994b. Health Insurance Coverage—1993. Statistical Brief. Washington, DC: U.S. Department of Commerce. **[14]**

U.S. Bureau of the Census. 1994c. *More Education Means Higher Career Earnings.* Statistical Brief. Washington, DC: U.S. Department of Commerce, Economics and Statistics Administration, Bureau of the Census. **[12]**

U.S. Bureau of the Census. 1994d. *Statistical Abstract of the United States, 1994.* Washington, DC: U.S. Government Printing Office. **[8, 9, 10, 11, 12, 14, 18]**

U.S. Bureau of the Census. 1994e (Nov.). *Census Bureau Homepage.* http://www.census.gov. **[16]**

U.S. Bureau of the Census. 1995a. *Sixty-Five Plus in the United States.* Statistical Brief. Washington, DC: U.S. Department of Commerce. **[9, 10]**

U.S. Bureau of the Census. 1995b. *Statistical Abstract of the United States, 1995.* (115th edition). Washington, DC: U.S. Government Printing Office. **[8, 10, 11, 12, 15]**

U.S. Bureau of Labor Statistics. 1990. *Monthly Labor Review,* 113(3):14–19. **[15]**

U.S. Bureau of Labor Statistics. 1995. *Employment and Earnings.* (January). Washington, D.C.: U.S. Department of Labor. **[9]**

U.S. Congress, House of Representatives, Select Committee on Aging. 1990. *Emptying the Elderly's Pocketbook: Growing Impact of Rising Health Care Costs.* Washington, DC. **[10, 11]**

U.S. Department of Health and Human Services (USDHHS). 1990 (August). *Child Abuse and Neglect: Critical First Steps in Response to a National Emergency.* U.S. Advisory Board on Child Abuse and Neglect, Washington, DC. **[11]**

U.S. Department of Health and Human Services. 1990. *Vital Statistics of the United States.* National Vital Statistics Division. **[12]**

U.S. Department of Health and Human Services (USDHHS). 1995a. *Monthly Vital Statistics Report,* 43(June). **[18]**

U.S. Department of Health and Human Services. 1995b. *Morbidity and Mortality Weekly Report,* 44(15, April 21):289–291. **[2]**

U.S. Department of Justice. 1987. Washington, DC: U.S. Government Printing Office **[6]**

U.S. Department of Justice. 1994 (December). Young male black victims. *Crime Data Brief.* Washington, DC: U.S. Government Printing Office. **[6]**

U.S. Department of Justice. 1994a. *Uniform Crime Reports, 1993.* (December 4). Washington, DC: U.S. Government Printing Office **[6]**

U.S. Department of Justice. 1994b. *Firearms and Crimes of Violence.* Washington, DC: U.S. Government Printing Office **[6]**

U.S. Department of Justice. 1995. *Correctional Populations in the United States.* Washington, DC: U.S. Government Printing Office **[6]**

U.S. Department of Justice. 1995. *Sourcebook of Criminal Justice Statistics, 1994.* Washington, DC: U.S. Government Printing Office. **[8]**

Useem, Michael. 1980. Corporations and the corporate elite. *Annual Review of Sociology,* 6:41–77. **[15]**

Useem, Michael. 1984. *The Inner Circle: Large Corporations and the Rise of Business Political Activity in the U.S. and U.K.* New York: Oxford University Press. **[16]**

Vaillant, George. 1977. *Adaptation to Life.* Boston: Little, Brown. **[10]**

Van Biema, David. 1994. Apologists for murder. *Time* (August 15):39. **[20]**

VandeBerg, Leah R., and Diane Streckfuss. 1992. Prime time television's portrayal of women and the world of work: A demographic profile. *Journal of Broadcasting and Electronic Media,* 36(2):195–208. **[5]**

Van den Berghe, Pierre. 1978. *Race and Racism: A Comparative Perspective,* 2d ed. New York: Wiley. **[8]**

Van Gennep, Arnold. 1908/1961. *Rites of Passage.* M.B. Vizedon and G.L. Caffee (Trans.). Chicago: University of Chicago Press. **[10]**

Varshney, Ashutosh. 1993. Contested meanings: India's national identity, Hindu nationalism, and the politics of anxiety. *Daedalus,* 122(3, Summer):227–261. **[13]**

Viorst, Milton. 1995. Sudan's Islamic experiment. *Foreign Affairs,* 74(3, May/June):45–58. **[13]**

Virk, Indermohan. 1995. Intermarriage as a Test of Asian-American Panethnicity. Unpublished MA thesis. Chapel Hill, NC: University of North Carolina. **[8]**

Wacquant, Löic. 1989. The ghetto, the state, and the new capitalist economy. *Dissent* (Fall):508–520. **[7]**

Wacquant, Löic. 1994. The new urban color line: The state and the fate of the ghetto of postFordist America. In Craig Calhoun, Ed., *Social Theory and the Politics of Identity* (pp. 231–276). Cambridge, England: Blackwell. **[7]**

Wacquant, Löic, and William J. Wilson. 1989. The cost of racial and class exclusion in the inner city. *Annals of the American Academy of Political and Social Science,* 501(January):8–25. **[7]**

Waisman, Carlos. 1987. *Reversal of Development in Argentina.* Princeton, NJ: Princeton University Press. **[17]**

Waite, Linda J., and Lee A. Lillard. 1991. Children and marital disruption. *American Journal of Sociology,* 96(4, January):930–953. **[11]**

Wajcman, Judy. 1994. Delivered into men's hands? The social construction of reproductive technology. In G. Sen and R.C. Snow, Eds., *Power and Decision: The Social Control of Reproduction* (pp. 153–175). Cambridge, MA: Harvard University Press. **[1]**

Wald, Matthew I. 1990. Guarding the environment: A world of challenges. *New York Times* (April 22):A1, A24–A25. **[18]**

Waldinger, Roger. 1996. Immigration. In C. Calhoun and G. Ritzer, Eds., *Perspectives on Social Issues.* New York: McGraw-Hill. **[18]**

Walinksy, Adam. 1995. The crisis of public order. *Atlantic Monthly* (July):39–54. **[6]**

Walker, Karen. 1994. Men, women, and friendship: What they say, what they do. *Gender & Society,* 8(2, June):246–265. **[3]**

Walker, Lenore. 1979. *The Battered Woman.* New York: Harper & Row. **[11]**

Wallace, Amy, and Nora Zamichow. 1992. When right and wrong blur. *Los Angeles Times* (May 2):A2, A25. **[20]**

Wallerstein, Immanuel. 1974. *The Modern World System,* Vol. I. New York: Academic Press. **[17]**

Wallerstein, Immanuel. 1979. *The Capitalist World Economy,* New York: Academic Press. **[17]**

Wallerstein, Immanuel. 1984. *The Modern World System,* Vol. II. New York: Cambridge University Press. **[15, 17]**

Wallerstein, Immanuel. 1988. *The Modern World System,* Vol. III. New York: Cambridge University Press. **[17]**

Wallerstein, Judith S., and Sandra Blakeslee. 1989. *Second Chances: Men, Women, and Children a Decade After Divorce.* New York: Ticknor & Fields. **[11]**

Wallerstein, Judith S., and Joan Berlin Kelly. 1980. *Surviving the Breakup: How Children and Parents Cope with Divorce.* New York: Basic Books. **[11]**

Walsh, Norman J. 1995. Public Schools, Inc.: Baltimore's risky enterprise. *Education and Urban Society,* 27(2, February): 195–205. **[12]**

Ward, Geoffrey C. 1985. *Before the Trumpet: Your Franklin Roosevelt, 1882–1905.* New York: Harper & Row. **[6]**

Wariavwalla, Bharat. 1988. Interdependence and domestic political regimes: The case of the newly industrializing countries. *Alternatives,* 13:253–270. **[17]**

Warner, Michael. 1992. Critical multiculturalism. *Critical Inquiry.* **[8]**

Warner, R. Stephen. 1993. Work in progress toward a new paradigm for the sociological study of religion in the United States. *American Journal of Sociology,* 98:1044–1093. **[13]**

Warner, Sam Bass, Jr. 1962. *Streetcar Suburbs: The Process of Growth in Boston, 1870–1900.* Cambridge, MA: Harvard and MIT Press. **[19]**

Warner, Samuel Bass. 1972. *The Urban Wilderness: A History of the American City.* New York: Harper and Row. **[19]**

Waters, Mary C. 1990. *Ethnic Options: Choosing Identities in America.* Berkeley: University of California Press. **[8]**

Watkins, Susan Cott. 1992. *Provinces into Nations.* Princeton, NJ: Princeton University Press. **[16]**

Webber, Melvin. 1966. Order in diversity: Community without propinquity. In L. Wingo, Ed., *Cities and Space: The Future Use of Urban Land* (pp. 23–54). Baltimore: John Hopkins Press. **[19]**

Weber, Eugen. 1976. *Peasants into Frenchmen: The Modernization of Rural France, 1870–1914.* Stanford, CA: Stanford University Press. **[16]**

Weber, Max. 1904/1958. *The Protestant Ethic and the Spirit of Capitalism.* Talcott Parsons (Trans.). New York: Scribners. **[1, 15]**

Weber, Max. 1922/1968. *Economy and Society.* E. Fischoff et. al. (Trans.). New York: Bedminster Press. **[1, 3, 16]**

Weeks, Julie R. 1993. Women in business: Dramatic work-force change. *Public Perspective,* 5(1, November/December):31–32. **[9]**

Weinberg, Martin S., and Colin J. Williams. 1975. Gay baths and the social organization of impersonal sex. *Social Problems,* 23(2):124–136. **[2]**

Weintraub, Pamela. 1991. The Brain: His and hers. In Evelyn Aston-Jones and Gary A. Olson, Eds., *The Gender Reader* (pp. 12–22). Boston: Allyn and Bacon. **[9]**

Weitzman, Lenore J., and Deborah Eifler. 1972. Sex role socialization in picture books for preschool children. *American Journal of Sociology,* 77(May):1125–1144. **[5]**

Weller, Jack M., and E.L. Quarantelli. 1973. Neglected characteristics of collective behavior. *American Journal of Sociology,* 79(November):665–685. **[20]**

West, Cornel. 1994. *Race Matters.* New York: Vintage. **[8]**

Wheeler, C. Gray. 1993. 30 years beyond "I Have a Dream." *The Gallup Poll Monthly,* 337(October). **[8]**

White, Harrison. 1992. *Identity and Control*. Princeton, NJ: Princeton University Press. **[15]**

White, Lynn K. 1990. Determinants of divorce: A review of research in the eighties. *Journal of Marriage and the Family*, 52(November):904–912. **[11]**

White, Lynn. 1994. Coresidence and leaving home: Young adults and their parents. *Annual Review of Sociology*, 20:81–102. **[11]**

White, Lynn K., and Alan Booth. 1991. Divorce over the life course: The role of marital unhappiness. *Journal of Family Issues*, 12(1, March):5–21. **[11]**

White, Lynn, and John N. Edwards. 1990. Emptying the nest and parental well-being. *American Sociological Review*, 55:235–242. **[10]**

Whittier, Nancy. 1995. *Feminist Generations: The Persistence of the Radical Women's Movement*. Philadelphia: Temple University Press. **[20]**

Wiley, Norbert. 1994. The politics of identity in American history. In C. Calhoun, Ed., *Social Theory and the Politics of Identity* (pp. 131–149). Cambridge, England: Blackwell. **[8]**

Wilford, John Noble. 1981. 9 percent of everyone who ever lived is alive now. *New York Times* (October 6):13, 14. **[18]**

Wilken, Helen. 1995. Urbanization spreading. In. L.R. Brown, N. Lenssen, and H. Kane, *Vital Signs 1995*. New York: Norton. **[19]**

Wilkinson, Richard G. 1990. Income distribution and mortality: A natural experiment. *Sociology of Health and Illness*, 12(4):391–412. **[14]**

Williams, Christine L. 1992. The glass escalator: Hidden advantages for men in the "female" professions. *Social Problems*, 39(3, August):253–267. **[9]**

Williams, Gregory Howard. 1995. *Life on the Color Line: The True Story of a White Boy Who Discovered He Was Black*. New York: Dutton. **[5]**

Williams, J. Allen, Jr., Joetta A. Vernon, Martha C. Williams, and Karen Malecha. 1987. Sex role socialization in picture books: An update. *Social Science Quarterly*, 68(March):148–156. **[5]**

Willis, Frank, and Roger A. Carlson. 1993. Singles ads: Gender, social class, and time. *Sex Roles*, 29(5–6):387–404. **[5]**

Willis, Paul. 1977. *Learning to Labor: How Working Class Kids Get Working Class Jobs*. New York: Columbia University Press, 1977. **[12]**

Willis, Paul. 1990. *Common Culture: Symbolic Work at Play in the Everyday Cultures of the Young*. Boulder, CO: Westview Press. **[5]**

Wilson, Bryan R. 1990. *The Social Dimensions of Sectarianism: Sect and New Religious Movements in Contemporary Society*. Oxford, England: Clarendon Press. **[13]**

Wilson, John. 1973. *Introduction to Social Movements*. New York: Basic Books. **[20]**

Wilson, William J. 1980. *The Declining Significance of Race: Blacks and Changing American Institutions*. New York: Basic Books. **[7]**

Wilson, William. J. 1987. *The Truly Disadvantaged: The Inner City, the Underclass, and Public Policy*. Chicago: University of Chicago Press. **[7]**

Wilson, William J. 1991. Studying inner-city dislocations: The challenge of public agenda research (1990 Presidential Address). *American Sociological Review*, 56(February):1–14. **[7]**

Winkelstein, Warren Jr., et al. 1987. Sexual practices and risks of infection by the human immunodeficiency virus: The San Francisco men's health study. *Journal of the American Medical Association*, 257(January):321–323. **[14]**

Winn, Marie. 1984. *Children Without Childhood*. New York: Penguin. **[10]**

Winn, Marie. 1985. *The Plug-in Drug: Television, Children and the Family*. New York: Penguin. **[5]**

Winnick, Louis. 1990. America's "model minority." *Commentary*, 90(2, August):22–29. **[8]**

Wirth, Louis. 1938. Urbanism as a way of life. *American Journal of Sociology*, 44:1–24. **[19]**

Witelson, Sandra F. 1992. Cognitive neuroanatomy: A new era. *Neurology*, 42(4, April):709–713. **[9]**

Witmer, Judith. 1993. Outcomes based education. In Charles E. Greenawalt, II, Ed., *Educational Innovation: An Agenda to Frame the Future* (pp. 347–375). Lanham, MD: University Press of America. **[12]**

Wittig, Michele Andrisin, and Rosemary Hays Lowe. 1989. Comparable worth theory and policy. *Journal of Social Issues*, 45(4):1–21. **[9]**

Wolf, Eric. 1982. *Europe and the People Without History*. Berkeley: University of California Press. **[16]**

Wolfe, David A. 1985. Child abusive parents: An empirical review and analysis. *Psychological Bulletin*, 97:462–482. **[11]**

Wolfe, Leslie R., and Jennifer Tucker. 1995. Feminism Lives: Building a Multicultural Women's Movement in the United States. In Amrita Basu, Ed., *The Challenge of Local Feminism: Women's Movements in Global Perspective*. Boulder, CO: Westview Press. **[20]**

Wolff, Kurt H., Ed. 1993. *From Karl Manheim*, 2d ed. New Brunswick: Transaction. **[10]**

Wong Bernard P. 1982. *Chinatown: Economic Adaptation and Ethnic Identity of the Chinese*. New York: Holt, Rinehart and Winston. **[8]**

Woo, Elaine. 1992. *Los Angeles Times*, May 5, 1992. p. A1. Fissures of race tear fabric of L.A. **[20]**

Wood, Floris W., Ed. 1990. *An American Profile—Opinions and Behavior, 1972–1989*. Detroit: Gale Research. **[11]**

Woody, Bette. 1989. Black women in the emerging services economy. *Sex Roles*, 21(1/2):45–67. **[9]**

World Bank. 1990. *World Bank Atlas 1990*. Washington, D.C.: World Bank. **[18]**

World Bank. 1990. *World Development Report 1990: Poverty*. New York: Oxford University Press. **[18]**

World Bank. 1991. *World Development Report 1991: The Challenge of Development*. New York: Oxford University Press. **[17]**

World Bank. 1994. *World Population Projections, 1994–95*. Baltimore: Johns Hopkins University Press. **[18]**

World Bank. 1995a. *Bureaucrats in Business*. New York: Oxford University Press. **[16]**

World Bank. 1995b. *Social Indicators of Development: 1995*. Baltimore: Johns Hopkins University Press. **[18]**

World Bank. 1995c. *World Development Report 1995*. New York: Oxford University Press. **[15, 17]**

World Health Organization (WHO). 1992. *Women's Health: Across Age and Frontier*. Geneva: WHO. **[1]**

World Resources Institute. 1991. *World Resources, 1990–91*. Washington, D.C.: World Resources Institute. **[18]**

World Resources Institute. 1994. *World Resources*. Washington, D.C.: World Resources Institute. **[17]**

Worsley, Peter. 1984. *The Three Worlds*. Chicago: University of Chicago Press. **[17]**

Wray, William D. 1984. *Mitsubishi and the N.Y.K. 1870–1914*. Cambridge, MA: Harvard University Press. **[3]**

Wright, Erik Olin. 1986. *Classes*. London: New Left Books. **[16]**

WuDunn, Sheryl. 1991a. China, with ever more to feed, pushes anew for small families. *New York Times* (June 16):A1, A4. **[18]**

WuDunn, Sheryl. 1991b. For China, it's the year of the spoiled child. *New York Times* (February 17):A10. **[18]**

Wuthnow, Robert. 1983. The political rebirth of American evangelicals. In Robert C. Liebman and Robert Wuthnow, Eds., *The New Christian Right: Mobilization and Legitimization* (pp. 167–185). Hawthorne, NY: Aldine. **[13]**

Wuthnow, Robert. 1988. *The Restructuring of American Religion*. Princeton, NJ: Princeton University Press. **[13]**

Wuthnow, Robert. 1990. The social significance of religious television. In Robert Abelman and Stuart M. Hoover, Eds., *Religious Television: Controversies and Conclusions* (pp. 87–98). Norwood, NJ: Ablex. **[13]**

Wuthnow, Robert. 1991. *Acts of Compassion*. Princeton, NJ: Princeton University Press. **[3]**

Wuthnow, Robert. 1994. *Sharing the Journey: Support Groups and America's New Quest for Community*. New York: Free Press. **[16]**

Wuthnow, Robert, and Matthew P. Lawson. 1994. Sources of Christian fundamentalism in the United States. In Martin E. Marty and R. Scott Appleby, Eds., *Accounting for Fundamentalisms: The Dynamic Character of Movements* (pp. 18–56). Chicago: University of Chicago Press. **[13]**

Yee, Doris K., and Jacquelynne S. Eccles. 1988. Parent perceptions and attributions for children's math achievement. *Sex Roles,* 19(5/6):317–333. **[5]**

Yeoman, Barry. 1995. No longer Wellcome. *The Independent.* (September 6):11–13. **[3]**

Yetman, Norman R. 1992. Race and ethnic inequality. In C. Calhoun and G. Ritzer, Eds., *Social Problems.* New York: McGraw-Hill/Primis. **[8]**

Yi, Zeng, Tu Ping, Gu Baochang, Xu Yi, Li Buhua, Li Yongping. 1993. Causes and implications of the recent increase in the reported sex ratio at birth in China. *Population and Development Review,* 19(2, June):283–302. **[1]**

Yoder, Jan D., and Robert C. Nichols. 1980. A life perspective comparison of married and divorced persons. *Journal of Marriage and the Family,* 42(2):413–419. **[11]**

Yoder, Janice D. 1991. Rethinking tokenism: Looking beyond numbers. *Gender & Society,* 5(2, June):178–192. **[9]**

Yuengert, Andrew M. 1995. Testing hypotheses of self-employment. *Journal of Human Resources,* 30(1, Winter):194–204. **[15]**

Zald, Mayer N.M., and John D. McCarthy. 1987. Introduction. In N.M. Zald and J.D. McCarthy, Eds., *Social Movements in an Organizational Society.* New Brunswick, NJ: Transaction. **[20]**

Zamir, Shamoon. 1995. *Dark voices: W.E.B. Du Bois and American Thought, 1888–1903.* Chicago: University of Chicago Press. **[1]**

Zangwill, Israel. 1909. *The Melting Pot.* New York: Jewish Publishing Society of America. **[8]**

Zaslavskaya, Tatyana. 1990. *The Second Socialist Revolution: An Alternative Soviet Strategy.* Bloomington: Indiana University Press. **[15]**

Zelizer, Viviana. 1985. *Pricing the Priceless Child.* New York: Basic Books. **[10]**

Zeman, Ned. 1990. The new rules of courtship. *Newsweek* (Special Issue: The New Teens):25–27. **[10]**

Zimbardo, P.G. 1972. Pathology of Imprisonment. *Transaction/ Society,* 9(April):4–8. **[2]**

Zola, Irving Kenneth. 1972. Medicine as an institution of social control. *Social Review.* 20:4, (Nov.) pp. 487–504. **[14]**

Zukin, Sharon. 1991. *Landscapes of Power: From Detroit to Disney World.* Berkeley: University of California Press. **[7]**

WEBLIOGRAPHY

Sociologists, like other scientists, are always in search of information. What are the latest figures on unemployment or earnings, international migration or birth rates? Sociological research generates new knowledge on these and a host of other topics. Increasingly, the results are stored not just in libraries but on the Internet.

The Internet is the "network of all networks," linking computers through telecommunications around the world. Individual computer users connect to central, more powerful machines that are in turn connected to each other by telephone lines and hard wiring. Each may store a variety of kinds of information that can be accessed from anywhere. As an example, the University of Texas has some of the best computerized collections of information on Latin America anywhere in the world. You don't need to go to Texas to have a look, however; you need only to call up the Texas computer system through the Internet. The Texas Center for Latin American Studies operates a "site" which provides an amazing variety and richness of information.

The part of the Internet that is the easiest to use is the World Wide Web. Here information is organized through a system of linked "home pages." Each home page introduces a purveyor of information and provides a series of doors beyond which may lie a wealth of knowledge. If you call up the home page of a major university, like the University of North Carolina at Chapel Hill, you will find a number of choices. Do you want information on applying to graduate school? On faculty members and their research or community service activities? On specific departments, sports teams, library holdings? Would you like to send a message to the dean or find out the current tuition rate? Each of these is a possibility. An on-screen push-button opens the door to each sort of information; on each successive page there may be more "buttons" leading to more detailed pages of information, or there may be links to other sites with related information. Different university departments, research centers, and special programs maintain their own home pages. Many of these are not just of local interest but offer important information to scientists and other users around the world.

You can use the Internet to explore where you might like to go to graduate school or what sorts of job opportunities exist in different fields. You can use it to get the information you need to write a term paper, or to make your own research findings known to others.

This "Webliography" is a listing of some of the World Wide Web sites that offer the most information about sociology. These include home pages associated with sociology departments at different colleges and universities, with different journals and research centers, and with the American Sociological Association. The Webliography is an introduction, but you should bear in mind that new sites are being added all the time and existing sites are being improved with the addition of new information and new links to other sites. We have developed this Webliography to help you get started. Your textbook, *Sociology*, 7th edition, provides an introduction to the wide range of contemporary sociological research. If you want to know more about a topic discussed in the text, the Web can help you.

In a sense, it doesn't matter where you start. The Internet can be explored by innumerable paths. You can start with one of the sites listed in the Webliography and see what you find. Most sites will not only offer information of their own but will also lead you to other sites. Several sites include links to the United States Census Bureau site, for example, which provides an enormous amount of statistical information from the U.S. government. Some sites include more unusual links—to data on Poland, for example, or to information on law enforcement efforts.

If you want, you can use a "search engine" or "gopher" to explore the Web. This approach requires a computer program (software) that allows you to specify key words and search for all Web sites that mention those words in their home page descriptions. If you use a search engine to search for the word *sociology* you will turn up an overwhelming number of sites—that is why this Webliography is such a useful tool. However, if you are researching a more specific topic—say, gun-control debates—key-word searches can lead you directly to pertinent information—for example, the home pages of both the National Rifle Association (NRA) and the National Association of Chiefs of Police, which will enable you to explore and compare their conflicting views.

When you find a home page or Web site that is especially useful for your purposes, most software programs (like Netscape) will let you mark it with a "bookmark" that makes it easy to find again. If you are interested in socioeconomic conditions in the United States, for example, you will probably want to go back again and again to the Census Bureau, the U.S. Bureau of Labor Statistics, and maybe a few other key agencies. If you are excited about sociological theory, you will not only want to read the American Sociological Association's journal, *Sociological*

Theory, but you will also want to access its home page. There you can check out tables of contents, comment on the articles published in the journal, and "chat" with other sociologists with similar interests. If you write an article yourself, you can find out how to submit it. In addition, you will find links to other sites with information on sociological theory.

Perhaps you want to make connections between topics that others aren't bringing together. You can start your own web page or, better yet, join with others in the Sociology Club or a similar organization at your college or university to offer helpful information and links to useful data sources you have found.

The Internet is not a substitute for a conventional library—at least not yet—but it is an enormously valuable supplement. For many research purposes it is by far the most efficient starting point, and often it is all you will need. But one word of warning: The Internet can be habit forming. It is not only informative—it is a lot of fun.

SELECTED REFERENCE SITES IN SOCIOLOGY FROM THE WORLD WIDE WEB

Due to the temporary nature of some Web sites and their continually changing structure and content, we cannot guarantee that the information listed here will always be available.

Internet Resources

http://www.shu.edu/ ~ brownsam/v1/resource.html
This site includes links to centers for research in sociology, directories of resources available online, electronic journals and newsletters, mailing lists, and organizations.

Sociology

http://refserver.lib.vt.edu/refhtml/subjects/sociology.html
This web site from Virginia Tech includes information on the American Sociological Society, the Canadian Sociology Association, Ethnomethodology, and discussion groups and newsletters.

Sociology Resources

http://www.roanoke.edu/sociology.html
This site includes links to Russian and Eastern European studies and criminal justice information centers.

Bubl Information Server

http://www.bubl.bath.ac.uk/BUBL/Sociology.html
This site includes links to U.S. National Data Archives on child abuse, disaster research center, men's issues, Marxism, and postmodern culture. It also links to Times Higher Education Supplement and the WWW Virtual Library in Sociology.

Humanities Hub

http://www.gu.edu.au/gwis/hub/hub.socio.html
This site includes references to the European Sociological Association, research methods from the American Communication Association, and the Anabaptist Sociology newsletter. Other links offer access to discussion groups on conversation analysis, globalization, and a range of other topics.

Humanities Hub Census Data

http://www.gu.edu.au/gwis/hub/hub.socio.html
This site provides demographics and population study links, along with data from the United States Census Bureau, Eurostat, the Australian government, Norwegian Social Science Data, and South African Data Archive.

American Sociological Association

http://www.asanet.org
This home page for the American Sociological Association includes information on its many journals (*American Sociological Review, Contemporary Sociology, Journal of Health and Social Behavior, Social Psychology Quarterly, Sociological Methodology, Sociological Theory, Sociology of Education,* and *Teaching Sociology*). It also includes membership information, contacts for executive office staff, convention and conference announcements, and links to sites operated by special interest sections of the Association.

Other Sources of Information in Sociology

http://lapop./su.edu/soc.html
This site includes links to the EINet Galaxy Social Science Index, the Society for the Study of Symbolic Interaction, the Universal Codex for Social Sciences, and the Electronic Journal of Sociology.

EINet Galaxy

http://www.einet.net/galaxy/Social-Sciences/Sociology.html
This site covers information on sociology collections, periodicals, discussion groups, and academic organizations.

General Research Sources in Sociology

http://www.socioweb.com/ ~ markbl/socioweb/research.html
This site includes a list of various population studies, software for quantitative research, information gateways, and Web sites operated by various sections of the American Sociological Association.

Society for Applied Sociology

http://www.indiana.edu/ ~ appsoc/
This home page was developed for professionals involved in applying sociological knowledge in a variety of settings; it includes membership benefits, the *Journal of Applied Sociology,* and lists of conferences.

Other Links of Interest

http://www.soc.surrey.ac.uk/Other_links.html

Journals, magazines, libraries, What's New on the Net, and Sites Worth Visiting in Sociology are all listed here.

Selected Sociological Resources on the Web

http://www.lib.umich.edu/libhome/rrs/classes/sociology.html

This site includes reference tools for sociology research such as the Annual Review of Sociology, Women's Studies Resources, Criminology Home-page, and many text and data archives.

Canadian Journal of Sociology

http://gpu.srv.ualberta.ca/ ~ cjscopy/cjs.html

This site covers recent issues, announcements, upcoming events, and resources of the *Canadian Journal of Sociology.*

The Internet Curriculum, Sociology and Psychology

http://darkwing.uoregon.edu/ ~ huayi/SOCPSY.HTML

This site lists gophers of various sources including ones from the University of California, Berkeley, and the University of Michigan; it also includes listserves and news and discussion groups.

Gopher Menu from Berkeley

gopher://infolib.lib.berkeley.edu/11/resdbs/soci

This source provides links to the Berkeley library, Emma Goldman papers, and other highlights.

Gopher Menu, Marvel

gopher://marvel.loc.gov/11/global/socsci/soc

This site includes links to Amnesty International, the Latin American Network, the U.S. Institute for Peace, and other organizations focusing on social issues from human rights and world hunger to population studies.

Sociology World Wide Web Resources

http://www.drake.edu/bgil/www/disc/soc/soc.html

This site covers news groups on sociology including ones on housing, postmodern culture, politics, sociology, and anarchy. Other electronic journals linked include *Mother Jones, The Nation, Bad Subjects, Cultronix,* and *Worker's World.*

Social Science Pages

http://www.uakron.edu/hefe/socsi.html

This site links several university department pages, sociological associations, census and population studies, research engines, and literature review sites.

University of Michigan Documents Center

http://gpu.lib.umich.edu/libhome/Documents.center/stats.html

This complete collection includes census bureau information, food and agriculture reports, world population trends, country reports on economic policy and trade, national debt statistics, World Bank data by topic and country, foreign government data sources, health statistics information from the World Health Organization, and Justice Department Crime Statistics.

Search the Web Sociology

http://www.public.coe.edu/library/Sociology.html

This site includes links to CIA World Fact Book, the Latin America Network Information Center, and a few other interesting sites.

WWW Virtual Library: Sociology

http://www.w3.org/hypertext/DataSources/bySubject/Sociology/overview.hmtl

This is a rich and extensive list of institutions and other Internet resources in sociology, including directories of resources, centers for reserch, organizations, and electronic journals and newsletters.

Penn Library, Sociology

http://www.library.upenn.edu/resources/social/sociology/sociology.html

This site provides indexes of culture and ethnic studies, criminology, population and demographics, and statistical sources.

List Servers, Sociology

http://www.w3.org/hypertext/DataSources/bySubject/Sociology/listserv.html

This site provides a complete collection of mailing lists on sociology topics such as the census, news and analysis, folklore, Marxism, aging, social theory, and storytelling.

University Center for International Studies

http://sunsite.unc.edu/ucis

This site from the University of North Carolina includes updates on world conflicts, international resource guides to cultural studies, demography, and much more.

National Opinion Research Center

http://norcwww/home.html

From the University of Chicago, this new site is a major repository of survey data.

Institute for Research in Social Science

http://www.unc.edu/depts/irss/

This site includes information on social science associations and events, as well as a guide to social science research.

Institute for Social Research

http://www.isr.umich.edu/

From the University of Michigan, this site covers information from its three centers: the Survey Research Center, the

Center for Political Studies, and the Research Center for Group Dynamics.

Sociological Theory
http://www.unc.edu/ ~ theory
Operated by the ASA journal *Sociological Theory*, this site includes information from its editorial board, tables of contents from previous and forthcoming issues, and links to other resources and discussion groups.

Sociological Methodology
http://weber.u.washingto.edu/ ~ socmeth2
This site comes from *Sociological Methodology*, an annual volume on methods of research in the social sciences, sponsored by the American Sociological Association. Information is presented on previous issues, author guidance, the editorial board, software available, and subscriptions.

USEFUL SITES FOR EACH CHAPTER IN THIS TEXTBOOK

Chapter One

Assisted Reproductive Technology
Family Fertility Center
http://www.ihr.com/famfert/index.html

Karl Marx
Letters and Writing of Karl Marx
http://www.idbsu.edu/surveyrc/staff/jaynes/marxism/marx.html

Émile Durkheim
The Durkheim Pages
http://www.lang.uiuc.edu/RelSt/Durkheim/DurkheimHome.html

Max Weber
Electric Library, Max Weber
http://www.elibrary.com

Chapter Two

Suicide Prevention in the Military
Suicide Prevention
http://www.vix.com/men/health/milsui.html

Suicide Prevention
http://wings.buffalo.edu/student-life/center/Depression/suicide.html

Teen Suicide
http://www.psych.med.umich.edu/web/aacap/factsfam/suicide.html

Untreated Depression and Suicide Awareness
http://www.save.org

Chapter Three

Sex in America
http://pathfinder.com/@@wikZbZG35wEAQMuL/twep/Little-Brown/Sex/Sex.html

Mitsubishi Motors
http://www.mitsubishi-motors.co.jp/

Ethnomethodology Newsletter
http://www.comp.loncs.ac.uk/sociology/research/ethnonews/ethnonewsindex.html

Chapter Four

Beethoven
http://www.voyagerco.com/CD/ph/p.beethoven.html

Tiananmen Square
http://www.christusrex.org/www1/sdc/tiananmen.html

Chapter Five

Sigmund Freud
http://www.austria-info.at/personen/freud/index.html

Mass Media
http://www.lib.umich.edu/chouse/inter/556.html

Chapter Six

Canadian Police Chiefs Survey
http://www.kpmg.ca/isi/survey_chiefs95.html

Federal Bureau of Investigation
http://www.fbi.gov/

Janet Reno
http://gopher.usdoj.gov/bios/jreno.html

Strategic Forum for Military Affairs
http://www.ndu.edu/ndu/inss/strforum/z1106.html

Chapter Seven

How the Pie Is Sliced—America's Growing Concentration of Wealth
http://epn.org.prospect/22/22wolf.html

Immigration Resources on the Internet
http://www.wave.net/upg/immigration/resource.html

Welfare and Families
http://epn.org/idea/welfare.html

Chapter Eight

Hispanic Links on the Internet
http://www.clark.net/pub/jgbustam/heritage/othelink.html

Nueva Vista, a Latino Perspective
http://www.epix.net/ ~ syntonic/

Ethnicity, Racism, and the Media
http://www.brad.ac.uk/bradinfo/research/eram.html

The Indian Tribes
http://www.cs.umu.se/ ~ dphln/wildwest/tribes.html

Chapter Nine

Men's Issues Page
http://www.vix.com/pub/men/index.html

Myth of the Feminine Nature
http://www-users.informatik.rwth-aachen.de/ ~ florath/Mixture/Englisch/Weibliche.Natur.html

"Friends" Raping Friends
http://www.cs.utk.edu/ ~bartley/acquaint/acquaintRape.html

Women's Way
http://www.omix.com/womensway

Chapter Ten

Great Depression
http://trinculo.educ.sfu.ca/pgm/depress/greatdepress.html

Baby Boomers
http://www.boomernet.com/boom/

American Demographics
http://www.marketingtools.com/ad_current/ad12toc.htm

Chapter Eleven

The Divorce Page
http://www.primenet.com/ ~ dean/

Advice to Women about Single Motherhood
http://www.parentsplace.com/readroom/smc/advice.html

Chapter Twelve

SATs and College Applications
http://www.kaplan.com/precoll/

What Is a Magnet School?
http://www.misha.net/ ~ desktop/wmagnet.htm

Chapter Thirteen

Mormon Fundamentalism and Violence
http://www.tcd.net/ ~ garn/polygamy.html

Religious Fanaticism and the Labor Movement
http://www.garnet.berkeley.edu:3333/EDINlist/.labor/.labororg/ifw/ifwwe09.htm.html

Chapter Fourteen

Tobacco Marketing to Young People
http://www.boutell.com/infact/youth.html

The Global AIDS Strategy
http://www.gpawww.who.ch/rights/contents.htm

National Health Care Skill Standards
http://www.fw1.org/nhcssp/health.htm

Chapter Fifteen

General Motors Home Pages
http://www.cs.purdue.edu/homes/swlodin/gm/gm.html

Industrial Revolution
http://www.england-info.com/pages/history.html

Chapter Sixteen

Presidential Election 1996
http://www.electionline.com

Nixon and Watergate
http://rnixon.com/

Social Democracy versus Revolutionary Democratic Socialism
http://www.ccme-mac4.bsd.uchicago.edu/DSADocs/Edelstein.html

Global Democracy Network
http://www.gdn.org.proposal.html

Nuclear, Chemical, and Conventional Weapon Systems
http://www.ecel.uwa.edu.au/law/links/fauburn/law-war.htm

Chapter Seventeen

Third World Annual Conference
http://www.ecnet.net/users/gas52r)/3rd_world/call_for_papers.html

World Bank
http://www.worldbank.org/html/extdr/about.html

Indonesia: Environment and Development
http://www.worldbank.org/html/ea3dr/exec.html

Chapter Eighteen

Economy and the Environment
http://www.epa.gov/docs/oppe/eaed/eedhmpg.htm

World Population Clock
http://www.sunsite.unc.edu/lunarbin/worldpop

Census and Demographic Information
http://www.clark.net/pub/lschank/web/census.html

Chapter Nineteen

Michigan Realtors
http://www.science.wayne.edu/ ~ gup/!index_1.htm

Regional Economic Information System
http://www.ciesin.org/datasets/reis/reis-home.html

Report Calls for an End to Urban Sprawl
http://www.rahul.net/gba/beyond.html

Preservation, Mixed Use, and Urban Vitality
http://www.dnai.com/ ~ kvetcher/MixedUse.html

Chapter Twenty

Drum Page, Civil Rights Movement
http://drum.ncat.edu/ ~ carter/civil.html

Feminist Internet Gateway
http://www.feminist.org/gateway/master2.html

National Organization for Women
http://now.org/now/txtindex.html

National Right to Life Committee
http://www.clark.net/nrlc/

Table 9.3 From Harriet B. Presser, "Employment Schedules Among Dual-Earner Spouses and the Division of Household Labor by Gender," *American Sociological Review,* 59, 1994, p. 354. Reprinted by permission of the American Sociological Association and the author.

Figure 10.2 From Erik H. Erikson, *The Life Cycle Completed: A Review,* 1982. Copyright © 1982 by Rikan Enterprises, Ltd. Reprinted by permission of W. W. Norton & Co. Inc.

Figure 10.3 From Daniel J. Levinson, *The Seasons of a Man's Life,* 1978, p. 57. Copyright © 1978 by Daniel J. Levinson. Reprinted by permission of Alfred A. Knopf, Inc.

Pages 328–329 From Douglas E. Foley, *Learning Capitalist Culture: Deep in the Heart of Tejas,* 1990. University of Pennsylvania Press.

Page 337 From Ted N. Okey and Philip A. Cusick, "Dropping Out: Another Side of the Story," *Educational Administration Quarterly,* 31, no. 2, pp. 244–267. Copyright © 1995 by Corwin Press. Reprinted by permission of Corwin Press Inc.

Table 13.1 From Robert A. Campbell and James E. Curtis, "Religions Involvement Across Societies: Analyses for Alternative Measures in National Surveys," *Journal for the Scientific Study of Religion,* 33, no. 3, p. 221. Reprinted by permission of the Society for the Scientific Study of Religion.

Table 13.2 From Lifton Pope, *Millhands and Preachers: A Study of Gastonia,* 1942. Reprinted by permission of Yale University Press.

Table 13.3 From Andrew M. Greeley, *Religious Change in America,* 1989. Reprinted by permission of Harvard University Press.

Figure 15.1 From *World Development Report,* 1995. Reprinted by permission of the World Bank.

Figure 15.2 From Beth Mintz and Michael Schwarz, "Interlocking Directorates and Interest Group Formation," *American Sociological Review,* 46, December, 1981. Reprinted by permission of the American Sociological Association and the authors.

Figure 15.3 From *The New York Times,* September 3, 1995, p. F9. Copyright © 1995 by The New York Times Company. Reprinted by permission.

Figure 15.4 From Margaret M. Blair, "CEO Pay: Why Such a Contentious Issue," *The Brookings Review.* Reprinted by permission of the Brookings Institution.

Table 15.1 From James K. Glassman, "Raising Minimum Wage Is Not the Answer," *The Washington Post,* April 4, 1995, pp. 6–7. Reprinted by permission of the author.

Figure 16.3. From Michael Barone, "The New America: A New U.S. News Poll Shatters Old Assumptions About Politics," *U.S. News & World Report,* 119, July 10, 1995. Copyright 1995 U.S. News & World Report. Reprinted by permission.

Figure 16.4 From Common Cause, published in *Time Magazine,* August 14, 1995. Reprinted by permission of Common Cause.

Figure 17.1 From World Bank, *World Development Report 1995,* pp. 158–9. Reprinted by permission of Oxford University Press.

Figure 17.2 From World Resources Institute, *World Resources 1994–95,* pp. 86ff. Reprinted by permission of World Resources Institute.

Figures 17.3, 17.4, and 17.5 From World Bank, *World Development Report 1995,* pp. 11, 22, and 37. Reprinted by permission of Oxford University Press.

Table 17.1 From World Bank, *World Development Report 1995.* Reprinted by permission of Oxford University Press.

Tables 17.2 and 17.3 From United Nations Development Program, *Human Development Report 1995,* pp. 166–7 and 178–9. Reprinted by permission of Oxford University Press.

Figure 18.3 From World Bank, *World Bank Atlas 1990,* pp. 22–23. Reprinted by permission of World Bank.

Figure 18.5 From *World Bank Atlas 1990,* 1990. Reprinted by permission of the World Bank.

Figure 18.6 From Ingomar Hauchler and Paul M. Kennedy (eds.), "Explosion of Refugee Numbers," *Global Trends: The World Almanac of Development and Peace.* Reprinted by permission of The Continuum Publishing Company.

Figure 18.9 From *World Population Data Sheet.* Reprinted by permission of Population Reference Bureau.

Figure 18.11 From Lester R. Brown, Nicholas Lenssen, and Hal Kane (eds.), *Vital Signs 1995: The Trends That Are Shaping Our Future.* © 1995 by Worldwatch Institute. Reprinted by permission of W. W. Norton & Company, Inc.

Figure 19.1 From Frank Clifford, "Driving Passion for Cars Fuels California Style" and "We Curse the Traffic, But Won't Give Up Our Cars," both from *Los Angeles Times,* 1989. Reprinted by permission of Los Angeles Times.

Figure 19.2 From Chauncey Harris and Edward L. Ullman, "The Nature of Cities," *The Annals of the American Academy of Political and Social Science,* 242, November, 1945. Reprinted in Paul K. Hare and A. J. Reiss, *Cities and Society,* 1957. Reprinted by permission.

PHOTO CREDITS

Chapter 1

2 Ernst Haas/Magnum Photos. 4 J.P. Laffont/Sygma. 6 Allan Tannenbaum/Sygma. 9 George W. Disario/The Stock Market. 13 Momatiuk/Eastcott/Woodfin Camp & Associates. 18 Barnardo Film Library, England. 20 Bettmann. 21 Bettmann. 22 Courtesy of the German Information Center. 23 Courtesy of the University of Chicago, Joseph Regenstein Library. 24 Bettmann.

Chapter 2

30 Dion Ogust/The Image Works. 32 (top left) AP/Wide World Photos. 32 (top right) U.S. Navy. 32 (bottom right) David Powers/Stock, Boston. 32 (bottom left) UPI/ Bettmann Newsphotos. 40 AP/Wide World Photos. 42 Angel Franco/NYT Pictures. 47 (left) Professor Philip G. Zimbardo/Stanford University. 47 (right) Professor Philip G. Zimbardo/Stanford University. 50 (left) Charles Gupton/The Stock Market. 50 (right) Peter Ginter/ Bilderberg/The Stock Market.

Chapter 3

56 Michael Justice/Gamma Liaison. 61 Les Stone/ Sygma. 64 Private Collection. 68 Henryk T. Kaiser/The Picture Cube. 70 Zane Williams/Tony Stone Images. 74 M. Greenlar/The Image Works. 77 Anthony Edgeworth/ The Stock Market. 79 Peter Sibbald/ Sygma. 83 MacDonald Photography/The Picture Cube.

Chapter 4

90 Sygma. 92 (left) Hulton Deutsch/Woodfin Camp & Associates. 92 (right) Archive Photos. 95 Robbie McClaren. 97 (left) Archive Photos. 97 (center) Archive Photos. 97 (right) J. Langevin/Sygma. 101 Mark Peterson/Saba. 107 (left) Jose Azel/Woodfin Camp & Associates. 107 (right) Bill Aron/PhotoEdit. 109 Tom McKitterick/Impact Visuals. 112 Adrian Bradshaw/Saba.

Chapter 5

118 Kerbs/Monkmeyer. 121 L.D. Bohm Studios/Gamma Liaison. 126 Frank Siteman/The Picture Cube. 131 Tom McKitterick/Impact Visuals. 133 E. Crews/The Image Works. 136 Dan Habib/Impact Visuals. 138 David Young-Wolff/PhotoEdit. 140 Karen Kasmauski/Woodfin Camp & Associates.

Chapter 6

144 Thomas Koepker/Magnum Photos. 147 Ellen B. Nelpris/Impact Visuals. 152 Chris Kleponis/Sygma. 153 Ken Lambert/Washington Times/Gamma Liaison. 157 Corbis-Bettmann. 162 Steve Berman/Gamma Liaison. 165 Gus Ruelas/L.A. Daily News/Sygma. 167 Markel/Gamma Liaison. 170 © 1994 Time, Inc.

Chapter 7

176 Mark Peterson/Saba. 178 (left) Oddo & Sinibaldi/The Stock Market. 178 (right) Joseph Rodriguez/Black Star. 182 Lynn Johnson/Material World. 187 Bossu/ Sygma. 192 Owen Franken/Stock, Boston. 197 Harvey Finkle/Impact Visuals. 200 Jamila Mimouni/ Sygma. 201 Michael Newman/PhotoEdit.

Chapter 8

204 Dan Habib/Impact Visuals. 207 Culver Pictures. 211 The Bettmann Archive. 213 Collection Musée de l'Homme. 215 AP/Wide World Photos. 219 Peter Vadnai/The Stock Market. 226 Ralf-Finn Hestoft/ Saba. 227 Steve Liss/Gamma Liaison. 232 Steve Lehman/Saba. 234 Claudio Edinger/Gamma Liaison.

Chapter 9

238 Joel Gordon. 241 John Eastcott/Yva Momatiuk/The Image Works. 243 Shepard Sherbell/Saba. 248 Carrie Boretz/The Image Works. 253 John Feingersh/The Stock Market. 256 Brad Markel/Gamma Liaison. 258 Nathan Nourok/PhotoEdit.

Chapter 10

262 George Disario/The Stock Market. 265 National Archives. 269 Tom & Dee McCarthy/The Stock Market. 273 Rick Reinhard/Impact Visuals. 275 Joel Gordon. 276 Lewis Hine/Bettmann. 279 Chuck Savage/The Stock Market. 281 Mary Kate Denny/ PhotoEdit. 288 Robert Ricci/Gamma Liaison.

Chapter 11

292 Byron/Monkmeyer. 295 Paolo Koch/Photo Researchers. 298 Archive Photos. 300 Eastcott/Momatiuk/Woodfin Camp & Associates. 307 Charlyn Zlotnick/Woodfin Camp & Associates. 309 James Wilson/Woodfin Camp & Associates. 313 © 1995 Time, Inc. 316 Greg Smith/Saba.

Chapter 12

320 Will & Deni McIntyre/Photo Researchers. 324 (top) National Archives/FPG International. 324 (bottom) Jon Feingersh/Stock, Boston. 327 John Giordano/Saba. 330 Paula Lerner/Woodfin Camp & Associates. 332 Elizabeth Crews/The Image Works. 334 Joel Gordon. 340 UPI/ Bettmann. 342 Steve Woit/NYT Pictures. 343 David Young-Wolff/PhotoEdit.

Chapter 13

346 Lindsay Hebberd/Woodfin Camp & Associates. 354 D. Aubert/Sygma. 355 Alain Dejean/Sygma. 363 Kazemi/Rea/Saba. 365 Nickelsberg/Gamma Liaison. 366 Ricki Rosen/Saba. 370 Bob Daemmrich/Stock,

Boston. **371** Tom Zimberoff/Gamma Liaison. **373** Nathan Benn/Woodfin Camp & Associates.

Chapter 14

378 David Toerge/Black Star. **380** Mary Evans Picture Library/Photo Researchers. **381** David Young-Wolff/ PhotoEdit. **385** The Photo Works. **389** Dana Schuerholz/ Impact Visuals. **395** Eugene Richards/Magnum Photos. **396** Will & Deni McIntyre/Photo Researchers. **397** Tom McCarthy/The Picture Cube.

Chapter 15

402 Berenholtz/The Stock Market. **409** J.P. Laffont/ Sygma. **411** UPI/Corbis-Bettmann. **412** Archive Photos. **414** Carolyn Hine/The Picture Cube. **416** Peter Blakely/Saba. **420** Andrew M. Levine/Photo Researchers. **427** Jim Leynse/Saba. **429** Jim Wilson/ NYT Pictures.

Chapter 16

434 Joe McNally/Sygma. **437** Donna Binder/Impact Visuals. **439** Dan Budnik/Woodfin Camp & Associates. **440** Photo Researchers. **443** *(left)* Bettmann. **443** *(right)* Perry Alan Werner/The Image Bank. **448** Forrest Anderson/Gamma Liaison. **454** Porter Gifford/Gamma Liaison. **460** Haviv/Saba.

Chapter 17

466 J.P. Laffont/Sygma. **470** Ben Van Hook/Duomo. **474** Bettmann. **478** Randall Hyman/Stock, Boston. **481** Brian Lovell/The Picture Cube. **485** *(top left)* Stephanie Maze/Woodfin Camp & Associates. **485** *(top right)* Dmitri Kessel/The Stock Market. **485** *(bottom)* Paula Lerner/ Woodfin Camp & Associates. **487** Thomas Hoepker/ Magnum Photos. **490** Shepard Sherbell/Saba. B.P. Wolff/Magnum Photos.

Chapter 18

502 Larry Boyd/Impact Visuals. **505** Ilhami/SIPA. **516** D. Wells/The Image Works. **519** Donna DeCesare/Impact Visuals. **521** Michele Burgess/The Stock Market. **523** Robert Caputo/Stock, Boston. **527** David R. Austen/ Stock, Boston. **531** Wesley Bocxe/Photo Researchers.

Chapter 19

534 Rhoda Sidney/PhotoEdit. **538** Weiner/Gamma Liaison. **541** Renato Rotolo/Gamma Liaison. **544** Michael Newman/PhotoEdit. **551** Alan Schein/The Stock Market. **553** Greg Smith/Saba. **557** Dean Abramson/Stock, Boston. **559** David Young-Wolff/ PhotoEdit. **561** Vince Streano/The Stock Market.

Chapter 20

564 Carolina Kroon/Impact Visuals. **567** John Barr/ Gamma Liaison. **569** ARCHIV/Photo Researchers. **574** Lester Sloan/Woodfin Camp & Associates. **577** *(top left)* Danny Lyon/Magnum Photos. **577** *(top right)* Professor Douglas Harber, University South Florida, Tampa. **577** *(bottom)* Danny Lyon/Magnum Photos. **583** Archive Photos. **590** F. Lee Corkran/Sygma.

GLOSSARY INDEX